THE LIFE SPAN

Human Development for Helping Professionals

SECOND EDITION

Patricia C. Broderick
West Chester University

Pamela Blewitt
Villanova University

PEARSON

Merrill
Prentice Hall

Upper Saddle River, New Jersey
Columbus, Ohio

Library of Congress Cataloging in Publication Data

Broderick, Patricia C.
    The life span : human development for helping professionals / Patricia C. Broderick,
Pamela Blewitt.—2nd ed.
        p. cm.
    Includes bibliographical references and index.
    ISBN 0-13-170684-5
        1. Developmental psychology. I. Blewitt, Pamela. II. Title.

BF713.B755 2006
155–dc22   2005045889

Vice President and Executive Publisher: Jeffery W. Johnston
Publisher: Kevin M. Davis
Development Editor: Autumn Crisp Benson
Editorial Assistant: Sarah N. Kenoyer
Production Editor: Mary Harlan
Production Coordinator: GGS Book Services, Atlantic Highlands
Design Coordinator: Diane C. Lorenzo
Photo Coordinator: Valerie Schultz
Text Design and Illustrations: GGS Book Services, Atlantic Highlands
Cover Design: Jason Moore
Cover Image: SuperStock
Production Manager: Laura Messerly
Director of Marketing: Ann Castel Davis
Marketing Manager: Autumn Purdy
Marketing Coordinator: Brian Mounts

This book was set in Berkeley by GGS Book Services, Atlantic Highlands. It was printed and bound by Courier Kendallville, Inc. The cover was printed by The Lehigh Press, Inc.

Photo Credits: Bill Anderson/Photo Researchers, Inc.: p. 76; Scott T. Baxter/Getty Images, Inc.–Photodisc: pp. 260, 408; Bill Burlingham/ Prentice Hall School Division: p. 318; Robert Clark/Aurora & Quanta Productions, Inc.: p. 420; Elizabeth Crews/The Image Works: p. 117; Scott Cunningham/Merrill: pp. 136, 190, 294, 324, 379, 442; Mary Kate Denny/PhotoEdit: p. 467; Laimute E. Druskis/PH College: p. 167; © Laura Dwight/Corbis: p. 159; John Paul Endress/Silver Burdett Ginn: p. 179; Britt J. Erlanson-Messens/Getty Images, Inc.–Image Bank: p. 446; ExxonMobil Corporation: p. 344; Myrleen Ferguson/ PhotoEdit: p. 265; Leroy Francis/Photo Researchers, Inc.: p. 36; Tony Freeman/PhotoEdit: p. 58; G.D.T./Getty Images, Inc.– Image Bank: p. 328; William Hamilton/Johns Hopkins University/Mary Ainsworth: p. 122; Michal Heron/PH College: pp. 388, 477; Richard Hutchings/PhotoEdit: p. 198; Infantest Corporation: p. 80; Steven W. Jones/Getty Images, Inc.–Taxi: p. 297; Frank La Bua/PH College: p. 149; Anthony Magnacca/Merrill: pp. 193, 430; Steve Mason/Getty Images, Inc.–Photodisc: p. 493; Will & Deni McIntyre/Photo Researchers, Inc.: p. 354; Ryan McVay/Getty Images, Inc.–Photodisc: p. 271; Doug Menuez/Getty Images, Inc.–Photodisc: pp. 45, 351, 444; Michael Newman/PhotoEdit: p. 5; Christine Pemberton/Omni–Photo Communications, Inc.: p. 488; Mark Richards/PhotoEdit: p. 112; Pearson Learning Photo Studio: p. 385; Prentice Hall School Division: p. 303; Barbara Schwartz/Merrill: pp. 164, 214; Rhoda Sidney/PH College: p. 427; Skjold Photographs/PH College: p. 376; Teri Leigh Stratford/PH College: pp. 100, 125; SW Productions/Getty Images, Inc.–Photodisc: pp. 155, 234, 282; Anne Vega/Merrill: pp. 23, 91, 218, 251; David Young-Wolff/PhotoEdit: p. 452; Shirley Zeiberg/PH College: pp. 228, 315.

Pearson Education Ltd.   Pearson Education Australia Pty. Limited
Pearson Education Singapore Pte. Ltd.   Pearson Education North Asia Ltd.
Pearson Education Canada, Ltd.   Pearson Educación de Mexico, S.A. de C.V.
Pearson Education—Japan   Pearson Education Malaysia Pte. Ltd.

10 9 8 7 6 5 4
ISBN: 0-13-170684-5

This book is dedicated to those who devote their professional lives to helping others.

THE SECOND EDITION

The first developmental textbook written specifically for helping professionals, *The Life Span: Human Development for Helping Professionals* is now in its second edition. This revision offers a number of improvements and additions, including

- New **Applications** section in each chapter with greatly expanded coverage of counseling-related practices based on developmental science.
- A new chapter covering issues related to well-being, coping, resilience, spirituality, and faith development in adulthood.
- More detailed coverage of developmental research that has practical applications.
- Further detail on developmental psychopathology throughout the text.

This text provides a rigorous grounding in developmental science to graduate students (or advanced undergraduates) in the helping professions. It also offers many opportunities to see how science can inform the practice of counseling. They begin to understand how both normal and abnormal behavior emerge from developmental processes and how to view clients' problems and needs as part of an adaptive system.

THE CONCEPTUAL FRAMEWORK OF THIS BOOK

The study of human development over the life span reveals the fascinating story of human beings and how they change over time. The story is both universal and uniquely personal, because it speaks to us about ourselves and the people who are important in our lives. Besides being intrinsically interesting, knowledge about development has obvious relevance for professionals engaged in counseling, social work, and other helping fields. We believe that in order to understand our clients and the nature of their problems, we must see clients in context. One important context is clients' developmental history. As helping professionals, we must take into account the threads of continuity and change in people's lives that bring them to their present point in development. This text provides the background and the tools to enable professionals to view their clients from a developmental perspective.

This text also reflects the contemporary view that life span development is a process deeply embedded within and inseparable from the context of family, social network, and culture. People do not progress through life in isolation; rather their developmental course influences and is influenced by other people and systems. Some of these forces are related to the cultural differences that exist in a world of increasing diversity. We recognize the importance of these factors in understanding human development and emphasize cultural and systemic influences on human growth and change throughout the book.

Knowledge about development increases every day, making it exceptionally difficult to summarize this dynamic field. Presumably, every author of a book of this nature needs to make some choices about what to include. This particular text is configured to emphasize selected theories and research that have useful applications for helping professionals. The main purpose of this book is to provide students in the helping professions with information that can be translated into professional "best practice" applications.

Throughout this text, we also emphasize the role of clinicians as reflective practitioners. Reflective practice involves "active, persistent, and careful consideration of any belief or supposed form of knowledge in light of the grounds that support it and the further conclusions to which it leads" (Dewey, 1933/1998, p. 9). Our primary vehicle for accomplishing this goal is twofold: (1) encouraging the reader to reflect on personal experience and assumptions about development, and (2) communicating the value of research-based knowledge as a means of understanding human development. Our particular orientation intentionally emphasizes the significance of developmental research to the work of the professional helper. We attempt to integrate various lines of developmental research into a useful whole that has practical value for helpers in applied settings. This book bears witness to the enormous amount of work done by developmental researchers, particularly in the last several decades. Without their groundbreaking efforts, clinicians' own work to improve people's lives would be greatly impoverished. It has been a challenge and an honor to record their contributions in this book.

COVERAGE AND ORGANIZATION

The opening chapters establish the theme of the text and introduce broad issues in development. Chapter 1 begins with an examination of the role of developmental knowledge in reflective practice. Students are introduced to theoretical models and issues that appear and reappear throughout the text. They are encouraged to reflect on their own theoretical assumptions about development and on the impact those assumptions could have in clinical practice. Boxed features introduce students to Developmental Psychopathology and Prevention Science, emphasizing their embeddedness in developmental science.

Chapter 2 takes a close look at the role of genetics in behavioral development, describing basic hereditary mechanisms by which any genetic influences must operate and examining alternative scientific strategies for assessing the contribution of genetics to behavior. Aspects of prenatal development and the multiple influences on prenatal development are also considered. The remaining chapters follow a chronological sequence, covering a full range of critical topics in physical, cognitive, social, and emotional development.

In Chapters 3 through 5, the infancy and preschool periods are the focus. Among the topics covered are early brain development and many aspects of early cognitive growth, such as the development of representational thought and memory, children's early "theory of mind" or naïve psychology, the early understanding of symbols and of language, and more. Coverage of early social development includes the emergence of emotions, emotion regulation, attachment processes, early self-development, temperament, and the role of parental disciplinary style in the growth of self-regulation.

Chapters 6, 7, and 8 examine important developments in middle childhood and in the transition to adolescence, including the growth of logical thinking, the expanding capacity to process and remember information, perspective-taking skills and friendship development, influences on the developing self-concept, developments in moral thinking, influences on the emergence of prosocial and antisocial behavior, sex-role development, and peer relationships.

Adolescence is the subject of Chapters 9 and 10, covering pubertal change, advances in logical and metacognitive skill, identity development, and the influences of peers, parents, school, and culture on adolescent behavior. Chapters 11 and 12 describe the young adult period, or what has been called "emerging adulthood," and includes a close look at the way thinking changes as adulthood looms and at the progress of work and career and of intimate relationships.

Chapters 13, 14, and 15 describe developmental processes in middle and late adulthood. Chapter 13 focuses on changes in physical, cognitive, and social functioning during the middle adult years. The new Chapter 14 considers the question that all middle adults face: What constitutes a well-lived life, and how do normally functioning adults cope with the enormous demands, progress, and setbacks that adult life brings? Finally, Chapter 15 reviews the challenges and developmental processes involved in late adulthood and end-of-life experiences. These chapters examine the many kinds of change that adults experience and the maintenance of well-being in the face of loss. Among the key developmental tasks discussed are marriage and its discontents, the experience of child rearing, spirituality, coping and health, the role of wisdom, stereotypes about aging, facing death and bereavement, and many more.

FEATURES AND HIGHLIGHTS

- **Depth of coverage:** Because the book is designed for graduate students, most topics, especially those that have special relevance to helping professionals, are covered in greater depth than in a typical life span text. The expanded coverage of research in specific areas will enhance students' understanding of the scientific basis for applications.
- **Applications:** Blending empirically supported information about treatments with the issues covered in each chapter, these revised sections offer more extensive discussion about how developmental science can inform practice. Expanded applications sections include topics such as touch therapy with low birthweight infants, promoting social competence of peer rejected children, using attachment theory in family counseling, mindfulness-based practices, and many more.
- **NEW chapter on adulthood:** The new chapter incorporates many important developments from research on adulthood, such as well-being, faith development, positive psychology, emotion regulation, stress and coping, topics that are pertinent to helping professionals but are not always included in standard developmental texts.
- **Boxed features:** In many chapters, boxes highlight special topics and provide opportunities for in-depth coverage of research. These may be the biographies of influential theorists or detailed examinations of issues such as children's credibility as eyewitnesses, the criminal culpability of juveniles, identity processes in multi-racial individuals, counseling needs of boys, leadership development in women and men, cross-cultural differences in funeral rituals, and many others.
- **Emphases on Developmental Psychopathology and Prevention Science:** The first chapter is revised to incorporate more information from developmental psychopathology, showing linkages between normal and abnormal pathways of development. Topics related to prevention are covered throughout the text.
- **Culture and gender:** In every chapter, cross-cultural and cross-gender issues are discussed wherever relevant developmental research is available.
- **Case studies and case study discussion questions:** Case studies and questions at the end of each chapter are another set of pedagogical tools for helping students think about the clinical implications of the developmental facts and theories they have learned.
- **Journal questions:** Journal questions at the end of each chapter help students reflect on the issues they have read about, encouraging them to consider the relevance of those issues in their own development.
- **Key terms:** Throughout the text, new or technical terms are printed in *bold italics* and defined. At the end of each chapter, a list of these key terms is provided as a study tool.
- **Chapter summaries:** Every chapter ends with a summary of the major topics covered in that chapter, providing yet another study tool for students and a planning tool for instructors.
- **NEW Glossary:** A glossary at the end of the text provides students with a handy reference for key terms.
- **Appendix:** An appendix help students understand how developmental processes are studied scientifically and how scientifically established information can be useful in practice.
- **Writing style:** The writing style is conversational in tone and is aimed at making even complex material accessible. To avoid sexist language use and yet still have the luxury of using the singular pronouns "she" and "he," we use the feminine pronoun in odd-numbered chapters and the masculine pronoun in even-numbered chapters.

SUPPLEMENTAL MATERIALS

- **NEW Instructor's Manual with PowerPoint Transparencies:** New to this edition, a separate Instructor's Manual now accompanies this text. For each chapter this manual contains a chapter outline, teaching suggestions, suggested student activities, resources, and transparencies.
- **NEW Companion Website:** The Companion Website at **www.prenhall.com/broderick** contains a chapter overview, multiple choice and essay questions with suggested responses,

and web links for every chapter. In addition, instructors can manage their courses online with Syllabus Manager™.

- **Expanded Test Bank:** An expanded test bank for instructors accompanies the text. For each chapter, the test bank includes 36 potential test questions, both multiple-choice and essay style. Multiple-choice questions assess both comprehension of basic content knowledge and ability to apply knowledge to problem solving.

ACKNOWLEDGMENTS

We want to express our deep appreciation to Kevin Davis, our editor, who was present at the birth of this book and who continues to nurture its development. We especially want to thank Autumn Benson for her diligence, support and good humor throughout this project. We have also worked closely with Kelly Keeler, whose expertise, efficiency and patience have contributed greatly to the quality of this text. Thanks go as well to Mary Harlan and Val Schultz, whom we very much appreciate. Finally, our deepest gratitude goes to our families for their love and constancy.

We also wish to thank the following reviewers: Dee A. Barclift, Jacksonville State University; Eugenie Joan Looby, Mississippi State University; Bonnie C. Nicholson, University of Southern Mississippi; Fred E. Stickle, Western Kentucky University; and Deborah J. Youngman, Boston University.

Brief Contents

Contents

Note: Every effort has been made to provide accurate and current Internet information in this book. However, the Internet and information posted on it are constantly changing, so it's inevitable that some of the Internet addresses listed in the textbook will change.

CHAPTER 1

Organizing Themes in Development

What importance do difficulties in getting along with others have for a 6-year-old youngster? Is she just "passing through a stage"? How much freedom should be given to adolescents? What implications do social problems with friends and coworkers suggest for a 22-year-old male? How significant is it for a married couple to experience increased conflicts following the births of their children? Does divorce cause lasting emotional damage to the children involved in a family breakup? What kind of day care experience is best for young children? Do we normally lose many intellectual abilities as we age? What factors enable a person to overcome early unfavorable circumstances and become a successful, healthy adult?

These intriguing questions represent a sampling of the kinds of topics that form the core of the developmentalist's study. Life span development, the study of human behavioral change from conception to death, is not a remote or esoteric body of knowledge. Rather, it has much to offer the helping professional both personally and professionally. The study of development allows helpers to understand more completely clients' concerns that are rooted in shared human experience. It provides a knowledge base built upon research and serves as a useful tool for decision making. It encourages a way of thinking about client problems from a developmental perspective. Studying development also facilitates counselors' personal growth by providing a foundation for reflecting on their own lives.

The field of counseling has been intimately tied to that of human development from its historical beginnings (Whiteley, 1984). The preamble from the code of ethics of the American Counseling Association states that its members are "dedicated to the enhancement of human development throughout the lifespan." Steenbarger (1991) noted that the field is unique because it builds upon developmental metatheory for its basic tenets and assumptions. Mosher (1995) further emphasized the connection by stating that helping professionals' reliance on developmental literature can be attributed to the fact that the facilitation of human growth and development is the primary purpose of therapeutic practice.

REFLECTION AND ACTION

Despite strong support for a comprehensive academic grounding in scientific developmental knowledge for the helping professional (Van Hesteren & Ivey, 1990), there has been a somewhat uneasy alliance between practitioners, such as mental health professionals, and those with a more empirical bent, such as behavioral scientists. The clinical fields have depended on research from developmental psychology to inform their practice. Yet in the past, overreliance on traditional experimental methodologies sometimes resulted in researchers' neglect of important issues that could not be studied using these rigorous methods (Hetherington, 1998). Consequently, there was a tendency for clinicians to perceive some behavioral science literature as irrelevant to real-world concerns (Turner, 1986). Clearly, the gap between science and practice is not unique to the mental health professions. Medicine, education, and law have all struggled with the problems involved in preparing students to grapple with the complex demands of the workplace. Contemporary debate on this issue has led to the development of serious alternative paradigms for the training of practitioners.

One of the most promising of these alternatives for counselors is the concept of reflective practice, which is receiving considerable interest and attention. The idea of "reflectivity" derives from Dewey's (1933/1998) view of education, which emphasized careful consideration of one's beliefs and forms of knowledge as a precursor to practice. Donald Schon (1987), a modern pioneer in the field of reflective practice, describes the problem this way:

> In the varied topography of professional practice, there is a high, hard ground overlooking a swamp. On the high ground, manageable problems lend themselves to solution through the application of research-based theory and technique. In the swampy lowland, messy confusing problems defy technical solutions. The irony of this situation is that the problems of the high ground tend to be relatively unimportant to individuals or society at large, however great their technical interest may be, while in the swamp lie the problems of greatest human concern. (p. 3)

The Gap Between Science and Practice

Traditionally, the modern, university-based educational process has been driven by the belief that problems can be solved best by applying objective, technical, or scientific information amassed from laboratory investigations. Implicit in this assumption is that human nature operates according to universal principles that, if known and understood, will enable us to predict behavior. For example, if I understand the principles of conditioning and reinforcement, I can apply a contingency contract to modify my client's inappropriate behavior. Postmodern critics have pointed out the many difficulties associated with this approach. Sometimes a "problem" behavior is related to, or maintained by, neurological, systemic, or cultural conditions. Sometimes the very existence of a problem may be a cultural construction. Unless a problem is viewed within its larger context, a problem-solving strategy may prove ineffective.

Most of the situations helpers face are confusing, complex, ill-defined, and often unresponsive to the application of a specific set of scientific principles. Thus, the training of helping professionals often involves a "dual curriculum." The first is more formal and may be presented as a conglomeration of research-based facts, whereas the second, often learned in a practicum or field placement, covers the curriculum of "what is really done" when working with clients. The antidote to this dichotomous pedagogy, Schon (1987) and his followers suggest, is reflective practice. This is a creative method of thinking about practice in which the helper masters the knowledge and skills base pertinent to the profession but is encouraged to go beyond rote technical applications to generate new kinds of understanding and strategies of action. Rather than relying solely on objective technical applications to determine ways of operating in a given situation, the reflective practitioner constructs solutions to problems by engaging in personal hypothesis generating and hypothesis testing.

How can one use the knowledge of developmental science in a meaningful and reflective way? What place does it have in the process of reflective construction? Consideration of another important line of research, namely, that of characteristics of expert problem solvers, will help us answer this question. Research studies on expert–novice differences in many areas such as teaching, science, and athletics all support the contention that experts have a great store of knowledge and skill in a particular area. Expertise is domain specific. When compared to novices in any given field, experts possess well-organized and integrated stores of information that they draw upon, almost automatically, when faced with novel challenges. Because this knowledge is well practiced, truly a "working body" of information, retrieval is relatively easy (Anderson, 1993). Progress in problem solving is closely self-monitored. Problems are analyzed and broken down into smaller units, which can be handled more efficiently.

If we apply this information to the reflective practice model, we can see some connections. One core condition of reflective practice is that practitioners use theory as a "partial lens through which to consider a problem" (Nelson & Neufelt, 1998). Practitioners also use another partial lens: their professional and other life experience. In reflective practice, theory-driven hypotheses about client and system problems are generated and tested for goodness of fit. A rich supply of problem-solving strategies depends upon a deep understanding and thorough grounding in fundamental knowledge germane to the field. Notice that there is a sequence to reflective practice. Schon (1987), for example, argues against putting the cart before the horse. He states that true reflectivity depends upon the ability to "recognize and apply standard rules, facts and operations; then to reason from general rules to problematic cases in ways characteristic of the profession; and only then to develop and test new forms of understanding and action where familiar categories and ways of thinking fail" (p. 40). In other words, background knowledge is important, but it is most useful in a dynamic interaction with contextual applications (Hoshman & Polkinghorne, 1992). A working knowledge of human development supplies the clinician with a firm base from which to proceed.

Given the relevance of background knowledge to expertise in helping and to reflective practice, we hope we have made a sufficiently convincing case for the study of developmental science. However, it is obvious that students approaching this study are not "blank slates." You already have many ideas and theories about the ways that people grow and change. These implicit theories have been constructed over time, partly from personal experience, observation, and your own cultural "take" on situations. Dweck and her colleagues have demonstrated that reliably different interpretations of situations can be predicted based upon individual differences in people's implicit beliefs about certain human attributes, such as intelligence or personality (see Levy, Stoessner, & Dweck, 1998). Take the case of intelligence. If you happen to hold the implicit belief that a person's intellectual capacity can change and improve over time, you might be more inclined to take a skill-building approach to some presenting problem involving knowledge or ability. However, if you espouse the belief that a person's intelligence is fixed and not amenable to incremental improvement, possibly because of genetic inheritance, you might be more likely to encourage a client to cope with and adjust to cognitive limitations. For helping professionals, the implicit theoretical lens that shapes their worldview can have important implications for their clients.

We are often reluctant to give up our personal theories even in the face of evidence that these theories are incorrect (Gardner, 1991; Kuhn, 1991). The best antidote to misapplication of our personal views is self-monitoring: being aware of what our theories are and recognizing that they are only one of a set of possibilities. (See Chapter 11 for a more extensive discussion of this issue.) Before we discuss some specific beliefs about the nature of development, take a few minutes to consider what you think about the questions posed in Box 1.1.

THE BIG PICTURE: MODELS AND METAPHORS

Now that you have examined some of your own developmental assumptions, let's consider some of the broad models of development that a counselor may bring to bear on client problems. Later, we will examine how these models may differentially affect the counseling process. Like counselors, researchers in developmental psychology bring to their studies theoretical assumptions and beliefs that direct their research and influence how they interpret their findings. Every theorist develops a theory that is consistent with her own cultural background and experience. No one operates in a vacuum. Throughout this text, you will be introduced to many theories of development. Some are broad and sweeping in their coverage of whole areas of development, such as Freud's theory of personality development (see Chapters 7 and 8) or Piaget's theory of cognitive development (see Chapters 3, 6, and 9); some are narrower in scope, focusing on a particular issue, such as Bowlby's attachment theory (see Chapters 4 and 12). Some theories that are very useful for counselors' understanding of human behavior, such as Rogers's person-centered theory or Adler's individual psychology, are not included here because they are not technically theories of development. Only those theories that describe systematic, age-related changes in behavior or functioning are considered.

It is useful to begin by describing three classes into which many developmental theories can be grouped: stage models, incremental models, and multidimensional models. You may find that your own assumptions fit with one of these classifications more than with the others.

Stage Models

Imagine a girl when she is 4 months old and then again when she is 4 years old. If your sense is that these two versions of the same child are fundamentally different in kind, with different intellectual capacities, different emotional structure, or different ways of perceiving others, you

Box 1.1 | *Questionnaire*

Examine Your Beliefs About Development

Rate yourself using the forced-choice format for each of the following items.

1. Physical characteristics such as eye color, height, and weight are primarily inherited.

   ❏ Strongly Disagree   ❏ Moderately Disagree   ❏ Moderately Agree   ❏ Strongly Agree

2. Intelligence is primarily inherited.

   ❏ Strongly Disagree   ❏ Moderately Disagree   ❏ Moderately Agree   ❏ Strongly Agree

3. Personality is primarily inherited.

   ❏ Strongly Disagree   ❏ Moderately Disagree   ❏ Moderately Agree   ❏ Strongly Agree

4. Events in the first 3 years of life have permanent effects on a person's psychological development.

   ❏ Strongly Disagree   ❏ Moderately Disagree   ❏ Moderately Agree   ❏ Strongly Agree

5. People's personalities do not change very much over their lifetimes.

   ❏ Strongly Disagree   ❏ Moderately Disagree   ❏ Moderately Agree   ❏ Strongly Agree

6. People all go through the same stages in their lives.

   ❏ Strongly Disagree   ❏ Moderately Disagree   ❏ Moderately Agree   ❏ Strongly Agree

7. Parents have a somewhat limited impact on their children's development.

   ❏ Strongly Disagree   ❏ Moderately Disagree   ❏ Moderately Agree   ❏ Strongly Agree

8. The cultural context in which the individual lives has a primary effect upon the psychological development of that person.

   ❏ Strongly Disagree   ❏ Moderately Disagree   ❏ Moderately Agree   ❏ Strongly Agree

9. Common sense is a better guide to child rearing than is scientific knowledge.

   ❏ Strongly Disagree   ❏ Moderately Disagree   ❏ Moderately Agree   ❏ Strongly Agree

may be a stage theorist. A **stage** is a period of time, perhaps several years, during which a person's activities (at least in one broad domain) have certain characteristics in common. For example, we could say that in language development, the 4-month-old girl is in a preverbal stage: Among other things, her communications share in common the fact that they do not include talking. As a person moves to a different stage, the common characteristics of behavior change. In other words, a person's activities have similar qualities within stages but different qualities across stages. Also, after long periods of stability, qualitative shifts in behavior seem to happen relatively quickly. For example, the change from not talking to talking seems abrupt. It tends to happen between 12 and 18 months of age, and once it starts, language use seems to advance very rapidly. A 4-year-old is someone who communicates primarily by talking; she is clearly in a verbal stage.

Helping professionals need to understand the needs of clients of different ages.

The preverbal to verbal example illustrates two features of stage theories. First, they posit important qualitative differences in behavior or mental processes from one stage to another. Second, they imply periods of relative stability (within stages) and periods of rapid change (between stages). Development is metaphorically like a staircase. Each stage shift lifts a person to a new plateau for some period of time, and then there is another steep rise to another plateau.

One person might progress through a stage more quickly or slowly than another, but the sequence of stages is usually seen as invariant, even in different cultures. What determines the fixed order of stages? In some theories, the normal maturing of the body is said to underlie the order (see Freud's theory in the next section). For example, a theorist could argue that maturation of the brain is the basis for movement from the preverbal to the verbal stage. In other theories, the accomplishments of one stage are seen as necessary or foundational for the emergence of the more advanced stages. A later stage might organize and integrate the activities and skills of the previous stage into broader, more complex patterns, a process called hierarchical integration (see Piaget's theory later in this chapter). In still other theories, movement from stage to stage is driven by many different factors (Erikson's theory is also discussed later in the chapter).

Another quality of some stage theories is that the "common characteristics" of a person's activities at one stage can be defined as much by their contrast with other stages as by their own particular qualities. For example, the preverbal stage can be defined as the stage before talking begins.

Sigmund Freud's theory of personality development was among the first to include a description of stages (e.g., Freud, 1905/1989, 1949/1969). Freud's theory no longer takes center stage in the interpretations favored by most counselors or by developmental researchers. First, there is little evidence for the specific proposals in Freud's theory. Second, his theory has been criticized for incorporating the gender biases of early 20th-century Austrian culture. Yet, some of Freud's broad insights are routinely accepted and incorporated into other theories, such as his emphasis on the importance of family relationships in development, his notion that some behavior is unconsciously motivated, and his view that internal conflicts can play a primary role in social functioning. Several more current and popular theories, like Erik Erikson's, were originally framed either as extensions of or specifically to contrast with Freud's ideas. For these reasons, it is important to understand Freud's theory. Also, his ideas have permeated popular culture, and they influence many of our assumptions about people's behavior. If we are to make our own implicit assumptions about development explicit, we must understand where they originated and how well the theories that spawned them stand up in the light of scientific investigation.

FREUD'S PERSONALITY THEORY

Sigmund Freud's theory both describes the complex functioning of the adult personality and offers an explanation of the processes and progress of its development throughout childhood. As with many stage theories, to understand any given stage it helps to understand Freud's view of the fully developed adult.

Id, Ego, and Superego. According to Freud, the adult personality functions as if there were actually three personalities, or aspects of personality, all potentially in conflict with one another. The first, the id, is the biological self, the source of all psychic energy. Babies are born with an id; the other two aspects of personality develop later. The id blindly pursues the fulfillment of physical needs or "instincts," such as the hunger drive and the sex drive. It is irrational, driven by the pleasure principle, that is, by the pursuit of gratification. Its function is to keep the individual, and the species, alive, although Freud also proposed that there are inborn aggressive, destructive instincts served by the id.

The ego begins to develop as cognitive and physical skills emerge. In Freud's view, some psychic energy is invested in these skills, and a rational, realistic self begins to take shape. The id still presses for fulfillment of bodily needs, but the rational ego seeks to meet these needs in sensible ways that take into account all aspects of a situation. For example, if you were hungry, and you saw a child with an ice cream cone, your id might press you to grab the cone away from the child—an instance of blind, immediate pleasure seeking. Of course, stealing ice cream from a child might satisfy your hunger quickly, but it could have negative consequences if someone else saw you do it or if the child reported you to authorities. Unlike your id, your ego would operate on the reality principle, garnering your understanding of the world and of behavioral consequences to devise a more sensible and self-protective approach, such as waiting until you arrive at the ice cream store yourself and paying for an ice cream cone.

The superego is the last of the three aspects of personality to emerge. Psychic energy is invested in this "internalized parent" during the preschool period as children begin to feel guilty if they behave in ways that are inconsistent with parental restrictions. With the superego in place, the ego must now take account not only of instinctual pressures from the id, and of external realities, but also of the superego's constraints. It must meet the needs of the id without upsetting the superego to avoid the unpleasant anxiety of guilt. In this view, when you choose against stealing a child's ice cream cone to meet your immediate hunger, your ego is taking account not only of the realistic problems of getting caught but also of the unpleasant feelings that would be generated by the superego.

The Psychosexual Stages. In Freud's view, the complexities of the relationships and conflicts that arise among the id, the ego, and the superego are the result of the individual's experiences during five developmental stages (and especially during the first three). Freud called these psychosexual stages because he believed that changes in the id and its energy levels initiated each new stage. The term *sexual* here applies to all biological instincts or drives and their satisfaction, and it can be broadly defined as "sensual."

The first psychosexual stage, called the oral stage, corresponds to the first year of life, when Freud believed that a disproportionate amount of id energy is invested in drives satisfied through the mouth. Eating, drinking, and even nonnutritive sucking might provide more pleasure in this phase of life than at any other. The baby's experiences with feeding and the degree to which oral pleasure is promoted or prevented by parenting practices could influence how much energy is invested in these activities in the future. For example, suppose that a mother in the early twentieth century believed the parenting advice of "experts" who claimed that nonnutritive sucking is bad for babies. To prevent her baby from sucking her thumb, the mother might tie the baby's hands to the sides of the crib at night—a practice recommended by the same experts! Freudian theory would predict that such extreme denial of oral pleasure could cause an oral fixation: The girl might grow up to need oral pleasures more than most adults, perhaps leading to overeating, to being especially talkative, or to being a chain smoker. The grown woman might also exhibit this fixation in more subtle ways, maintaining behaviors or feelings in adulthood that are particularly characteristic of babies, such as crying easily or experiencing overwhelming feelings of helplessness. According to Freud, fixations at any stage could be the result of either denial of a child's needs, as in this example, or overindulgence of those needs. Specific defense mechanisms, such as "reaction formation" or "repression," can also be associated with the conflicts that arise at a particular stage.

The second psychosexual stage, called the anal stage, is said to begin in the second year of life, caused by a shift in the energy of the id, a shift that is presumably the result of normal biological changes. Now the anal area of the body is the focus of greatest pleasure, and as control over the anal sphincter develops, the child especially enjoys both holding on and letting go. In this stage, Freud hypothesized that parenting practices, especially either overcontrolling or overindulgent practices associated with toilet training, could have long-lasting effects on personality development. Popular use of the term anal personality is a reference to some of Freud's predictions about the effects of an anal fixation, which can include being withholding (of material or emotional resources) and being compulsively cautious about keeping things clean and in order. Freud also suggested that an anal fixation might lead an adult to be overly messy and disorganized, a person who "lets go" too easily.

Freud proposed that in the third stage, the phallic stage, id energy shifts again, this time to be focused primarily in the genital region. Freud's theory has been criticized for its male-dominated focus, which is illustrated by this stage name. From age 3 to about 5, children's special pleasure comes from fondling the genitals. Vague sexual urges embroil children in complex emotional and motivational conundrums that include wanting to be physically closer to the opposite-sex parent and fearing the fallout from competing with the same-sex parent (the Oedipus and Electra complexes described in Chapter 8). It is during this stage that children begin to feel the full force of parental discipline. Feelings of guilt emerge, and the superego develops. The child's resolution of the difficult emotional turmoil of the phallic stage establishes how she will later cope with postpubertal sexual needs and depends, as always, on how parents deal with the child at this stage. For example, excessively strong, punitive action when children are caught masturbating or when children compete jealously for the preferred parent's affections could produce excessively strong internalized prohibitions against sexual behavior or against asserting oneself in adulthood. Conversely, seductive, indulgent behavior on the part of the parent might lead to self-centered vanity or flirtatiousness.

Freud called his final two stages the latency stage and the genital stage. Latency begins at about age 5, when the turmoil of the phallic period recedes and the id's energy is not especially linked to any particular pleasure or body part. The child's nascent personality continues to evolve following the patterns laid down in the first three stages but with the potential conflicts among the three aspects of personality largely latent and unexpressed. Turmoil emerges anew at puberty, the beginning of the genital stage, when the changes of puberty mean that id energy is especially invested in adult sexual impulses, and the child seeks ways of meeting these powerful new needs. The psychosexual stages are summarized in Table 1.1.

Freud's Theory as a Stage Model. The psychosexual stages have many of the characteristics of a stage model. First, the child is qualitatively different across stages, primarily as a function of shifting motivational qualities or "id energy." For example, the 2-year-old is obsessed with anal functioning, the 4-year-old with sexual feelings. Second, the stages are fairly long, and the periods of transition relatively rapid. For example, the anal stage lasts for about 2 years, the phallic stage for about 3 years, but the transition between them appears to occur quickly. Third, because of maturational (that is, biological) changes in the id, the stages occur in invariant sequence regardless of the child's family circumstances or cultural background. Finally, the stages are defined in part by the contrasts among them. The latency stage in particular is defined primarily in not being characterized by the passions of the earlier three.

Notice, however, that despite these clearcut stages with different motivations and different sets of possible outcomes for personality development, there are similarities across stages, which is typical of other stage theories as well. For example, Freud saw parenting experiences as critical for personality development in each stage. (He also argued that parenting effects are, at each stage,

TABLE 1.1   Freud's Psychosexual Stages of Development

Stage	Approximate Age	Description
Oral	Birth to 1 year	Mouth is the source of greatest pleasure. Too much or too little oral satisfaction can cause an "oral fixation," leading to traits that actively (smoking) or symbolically (overdependency) are oral or infantile.
Anal	1 to 3 years	Anal area is the source of greatest pleasure. Harsh or overly indulgent toilet training can cause an "anal fixation," leading to later adult traits that recall this stage, such as being greedy or messy.
Phallic	3 to 5 or 6 years	Genitalia are the source of greatest pleasure. Sexual desire directed toward the opposite-sex parent makes the same-sex parent a rival. Fear of angering the same-sex parent is resolved by identifying with that parent, which explains how children acquire both sex-type behaviors and moral values. If a child has trouble resolving the emotional upheaval of this stage through identification, sex role development may be deviant or moral character may be weak.
Latency	6 years to puberty	Relatively quiescent period of personality development. Sexual desires are repressed after the turmoil of the last stage. Energy is directed into work and play. There is continued consolidation of traits laid down in the first three stages.
Genital	Puberty through adulthood	At puberty, adult sexual needs become the most important motivators of behavior. The individual seeks to fulfill needs and expend energy in socially acceptable activities, such as work, and through marriage with a partner who will substitute for the early object of desire, the opposite-sex parent.

limited by the inborn biological qualities of a particular child's id.) The point is that the qualitative discontinuities that stage theories emphasize in human development are usually combined with functional similarities across stages in the processes by which development is said to proceed.

Let's consider more briefly two other important stage theories to illustrate this point.

ERIKSON'S PERSONALITY THEORY

Erik Erikson was a student of Freud's who later proposed his own theory of personality development (e.g., Erikson, 1950/1963). Like many "neo-Freudians," Erikson deemphasized the id as the driving force behind all behavior, and he emphasized the more rational processes of the ego. His theory is focused on explaining the psychosocial aspects of behavior: attitudes and feelings toward the self and toward others. Erikson described eight psychosocial stages. The first five correspond to the age periods laid out in Freud's psychosexual stages, but the last three are adult life stages, reflecting Erikson's view that personal identity and interpersonal attitudes are continually evolving from birth to death.

The "Eight Stages of Man." In each stage, the individual faces a different "crisis" or developmental task (see Chapter 9 for a detailed discussion of Erikson's concept of crisis). The crisis is initiated, on one hand, by changing characteristics of the person—biological maturation or decline, cognitive changes, advancing (or deteriorating) motor skills—and, on the other hand, by corresponding changes in others' attitudes, behaviors, and expectations. As in all stage theories, people qualitatively change from stage to stage, and so do the crises or tasks that they confront. In the first stage, infants must resolve the crisis of trust versus mistrust. Infants, in their relative helplessness, are "incorporative." They "take in" what is offered, including not only nourishment but stimulation, information, affection, and attention. If infants' needs for such input are met by responsive caregivers, babies begin to trust others, to feel valued and valuable, and to view the world as a safe place. If caregivers are not consistently responsive, infants will fail to establish basic trust or to feel valuable, carrying mistrust with them into the next stage of development, when the 1- to 3-year-old toddler faces the crisis of autonomy versus shame and doubt. Mistrust in others and self will make it more difficult to successfully achieve a sense of autonomy.

The new stage is initiated by the child's maturing muscular control and emerging cognitive and language skills. Unlike helpless infants, toddlers can learn not only to control their elimination but

TABLE 1.2   Erikson's Psychosocial Stages of Development

Stage or Psychosocial "Crisis"	Approximate Age	Significant Events	Positive Outcome or Virtue Developed	Negative Outcome
Trust vs. Mistrust	Birth to 1 year	Child develops a sense that the world is a safe and reliable place because of sensitive caregiving.	Hope	Fear & mistrust of others
Autonomy vs. Shame & Doubt	1 to 3 years	Child develops a sense of independence tied to use of new mental and motor skills.	Willpower	Self-doubt
Initiative vs. Guilt	3 to 5 or 6 years	Child tries to behave in ways that involve more "grown-up" responsibility and experiment with grown-up roles.	Purpose	Guilt over thought & action
Industry vs. Inferiority	6 to 12 years	Child needs to learn important academic skills and compare favorably with peers in school.	Competence	Lack of competence
Identify vs. Role Confusion	12 to 20 years	Adolescent must move toward adulthood by making choices about values, vocational goals, etc.	Fidelity	Inability to establish sense of self
Intimacy vs. Isolation	Young adulthood	Adult becomes willing to share identity with other and to commit to affiliations and partnerships.	Love	Fear of intimacy, distantiation
Generativity vs. Stagnation	Middle adulthood	Adult wishes to make a contribution to the next generation, to produce, mentor, create something of lasting value, as in the rearing of children or community services or expert work.	Care	Self-absorption
Ego integrity vs. Despair	Late adulthood	Adult comes to terms with life's successes, failures, and missed opportunities and realizes the dignity of own life.	Wisdom	Regret

also to feed and dress themselves, to express their desires with some precision, and to move around the environment without help. The new capacities bring a strong need to practice and perfect the skills that make children feel in control of their own destinies. Caregivers must be sensitive to the child's need for independence and yet must exercise enough control to keep the child safe and to help the child learn self-control. Failure to strike the right balance may rob children of feelings of autonomy—a sense that "I can do it myself"—and can promote instead either shame or self-doubt.

These first two stages illustrate features of all of Erikson's stages (see Table 1.2 for a description of all eight stages). First, others' sensitivity and responsiveness to the individual's needs create a context for positive psychosocial development. Second, attitudes toward self and toward others emerge together. For example, developing trust in others also means valuing (or trusting) the self. Third, every psychosocial crisis or task involves finding the right balance between positive and negative feelings, with the positive outweighing the negative. Finally, the successful resolution of a crisis at one stage helps smooth the way for successful resolutions of future crises. Unsuccessful resolution at an earlier stage may stall progress and make maladaptive behavior more likely.

Erikson's personality theory is often more appealing to helping professionals than Freud's theory. Erikson's emphasis on the psychosocial aspects of personality focuses attention on precisely the issues that counselors feel they are most often called on to address: feelings and attitudes about self and about others. Also, Erikson assumed that the child or adult is an active, self-organizing individual who needs only the right social context to move in a positive direction. Further, Erikson was himself an optimistic therapist who believed that poorly resolved crises could be resolved more adequately in later stages if the right conditions prevailed. Erikson was sensitive to cultural differences in behavioral development. Finally, developmental researchers frequently find Eriksonian interpretations of behavior useful. Studies of attachment, self-concept, self-esteem, and adolescent identity, among other topics addressed in subsequent chapters, have produced results compatible with some of Erikson's ideas. (See Chapter 4, Box 4.3, for a biographical sketch of Erikson.)

PIAGET'S COGNITIVE DEVELOPMENT THEORY

Jean Piaget's influential cognitive development theory outlines stages in the development of cognition, especially logical thinking (e.g., Inhelder & Piaget, 1955/1958, 1964; Piaget, 1952, 1954). He assumed that normal adults are capable of thinking logically about both concrete and abstract contents but that this capacity evolves in four stages through childhood. Briefly, the first sensorimotor stage, lasting for about 2 years, is characterized by an absence of representational thought. Although babies are busy taking in the sensory world, organizing it on the basis of inborn reflexes or patterns, and then responding to their sensations, Piaget believed that they cannot yet symbolically represent their experiences, and so they cannot really reflect on them. This means that young infants do not form mental images or store memories symbolically, and they do not plan their behavior or intentionally act. These capacities emerge between 18 and 24 months, launching the next stage.

Piaget's second, third, and fourth stages roughly correspond to the preschool, elementary school, and the adolescent-adult years. These stages are named for the kinds of thinking that Piaget believed possible for these age groups. He characterized the preschooler as a thinking person in the preoperational stage, with *preoperational* meaning "unable to think logically." Piaget believed that the deficiencies in preschoolers' thinking account for problems they have understanding both the world and other people. For example, 3-year-old Tommy can play some simple board games, like "Candy Land," proficiently, but he fails to understand that you might want to win when you play him. He focuses his attention on his own goals—that he wants to win—and cannot at the same time think about or make sense of a different goal: yours!

By about age 7, thinking has advanced in complexity, and children enter the concrete operational stage. *Operational* means "logical." Children's thinking now seems more rational, more like adults'. Children begin to understand and use logical processes, such as addition and subtraction, but they are still limited in some respects. In particular, they find it difficult to think logically about material that is not somehow anchored in the concrete, real world. For example, they can understand that "2 + 6 = 8," because the logical relationships among numbers can be illustrated with concrete things in the real world. But if we ask children of elementary school age to understand the relationships among more abstract concepts, such as the xs and ys of algebra, they usually falter. When the material they must think about is this abstract, elementary school children seem flummoxed, apparently because they need concrete reference points to make sense of a situation.

By age 11 or 12, children are more successful at logically organizing abstract material, and they have entered Piaget's formal operational stage. New cognitive horizons open up as a result. Adolescents become capable of logically planning their futures (the world of the possible, not the real), for example, or of imagining ideal (abstract) political or economic systems. See Table 1.3 for a summary of Piaget's stages.

Piaget's theory is another classic stage model. First, cognitive abilities are qualitatively similar within stages. If we know how a child approaches one kind of task, we should be able to predict her approaches to other kinds of tasks as well. Piaget acknowledged that children might be advanced in one cognitive domain or lag behind in another. For example, an adolescent might show more abstract reasoning about math than about interpersonal matters. These within-stage variations he called decalages. But generally, Piaget expected that a child's thinking would be organized in similar ways across most domains. Second, each stage is fairly long, and is at least partly defined by contrast to other stages. For example, the preoperational stage is a time when children can think, unlike babies at the previous stage, but their thinking is not yet logical, as it will be in subsequent stages. Third, even though progress through the stages could move more

TABLE 1.3 Piaget's Cognitive Stages of Development

Stage	Approximate Age	Description
Sensorimotor	Birth to 2 years	Through 6 substages, the source of infants' organized actions gradually shifts. At first, all organized behavior is reflexive—automatically triggered by particular stimuli. By the end of this stage, behavior is guided more by representational thought.
Preoperational thought	2 to 6 or 7 years	Early representational thought tends to be slow. Thought is "centered," usually focused on one salient piece of information, or aspect of an event, at a time. As a result, thinking is usually not yet logical.
Concrete operational thought	7 to 11 or 12 years	Thinking has gradually become more rapid and efficient, allowing children to now "decenter," or think about more than one thing at a time. This also allows them to discover logical relationships between/among pieces of information. Their logical thinking is best about information that can be demonstrated in the concrete world.
Formal operational thought	12 years though adulthood	Logical thinking extends now to "formal" or abstract material. Young adolescents can think logically about hypothetical situations, for example.

or less quickly depending on many individual and contextual factors, the stages unfold in an invariant sequence, regardless of context or culture, with the simpler patterns of physical or mental activity at one stage becoming integrated into more complex organizational systems at the next stage (hierarchical integration). Finally, despite the qualitative differences across stages, there are functional similarities or continuities from stage to stage in the ways in which children's cognitive development proceeds. At each stage, developmental progress depends on children assimilating experiences (that is, shaping experiences to fit) with their current ways of understanding, and at the same time, accommodating (that is, adjusting) their old ways of understanding, at least a little, to what is new in an experience.

Piaget's ideas about cognitive development were first translated into English in the 1960s, and they swept American developmental researchers off their feet. His theory filled the need for an explanation that acknowledged complex qualitative changes in children's abilities over time, and it launched an era of unprecedented research on all aspects of children's intellectual functioning that continues today. Although some of the specifics of Piaget's theory have been challenged by research findings, many researchers, educators, and helping professionals still find the broad outlines of this theory very useful for organizing their thinking about the kinds of understandings that children of different ages can bring to a problem or social situation.

Incremental Models

Unlike stage theories, some models characterize development as incremental, metaphorically resembling not a staircase but a steadily rising mountainside. Again, picture a 4-month-old girl, and the same girl when she is 4 years old. If you tend to "see" her evolving in small steps from a smiling, attentive infant (at least occasionally!) to a smiling, eager toddler, to a smiling, mischievous preschooler, always noting in your observations threads of sameness as well as differences, your own theoretical assumptions about development may be more compatible with one of these incremental models. Like stage models, they can be very different in the types and breadth of behaviors they attempt to explain. They also differ in the kinds of processes they assume to underlie psychological change, such as the kinds of processes involved in learning. But they all agree that developmental change is not marked by major, sweeping reorganizations that affect many behaviors at once, as in stage theories. Rather, change is steady and specific to particular behaviors or mental activities. Social learning theory and most information processing theories are among the many incremental models available to explain development.

LEARNING THEORIES

Learning theories, in what is called the behaviorist tradition, have a distinguished history in American psychology, having been the most widely accepted class of theories for a significant part of the 20th century. These theories trace their philosophical roots from ancient Greece and the writings of Aristotle through John Locke and the British empiricists of the 17th and 18th centuries. In this philosophical tradition, knowledge and skill are thought to accumulate as the result of each person's individual experiences. The environment gradually leaves its imprint on one's behavior and mind, a mind that in infancy is like a blank slate. Locke described several simple processes—association, repetition, imitation, reward, and punishment—by which the environment can have an impact. Many of the processes Locke described have been incorporated and articulated in modern learning theories.

Some learning theories explain behavioral change as a function of chains of specific environmental events, such as those that occur in classical and operant conditioning. In these processes, change in behavior takes place because environmental events are paired with certain behaviors. For example, suppose a child initially approaches a dog with curiosity and interest, but the dog barks loudly, causing the child to automatically startle and pull back. The next time the dog appears, the child may automatically startle and pull back, even though the dog is quiet. Just the sight of the dog now triggers the same response as loud barking; the child has learned a new response because the formerly neutral event (sight of dog) has been paired with an event (loud barking) that automatically causes a startle. Perhaps the startle reaction is also accompanied by feelings of fear. If so, the child has learned to fear this dog, and will likely generalize that fear to other, similar dogs. When a neutral event or stimulus is associated with a stimulus that causes an automatic response, the neutral stimulus can become a conditioned stimulus, meaning that it can cause the person to make the same automatic response in the future. This is classical conditioning.

Operant conditioning is different. First, a person just happens to perform some behavior. The behavior is an operant, an accidental or random action. Immediately after the operant occurs, there is a "reinforcing event," or reinforcement, something that is experienced by the person as pleasurable or rewarding. For example, suppose that a young child happens to babble "da" just as a dog appears in the child's line of sight, and the child's mother excitedly claps and kisses the child. (She has mistakenly assumed that the child has tried to say "dog.") The mother's reaction serves as a reinforcement for the child, who will repeat the "da" sound the next time a dog comes into view. In operant conditioning, the child learns to produce a formerly random behavior or operant (e.g., "da") in response to a cue (e.g., the appearance of a dog) because the behavior was previously reinforced in that situation.

Social learning theories, which have focused specifically on how children acquire personality characteristics and social skills, consider conditioning processes part of the story, but they also emphasize "observational learning," or modeling. In this kind of learning, one person (the learner) observes another (the model) performing some behavior, and just from close observation, learns to do it too. The observer may or may not imitate the modeled behavior, immediately or in the future, depending on many factors, such as whether the observer expects a reward for the behavior, whether the model is perceived as nurturing or competent, and even whether the observer believes that the performance will meet the observer's own performance standards. Current versions of social learning theory emphasize many similar cognitive, self-regulated determiners of performance and suggest that they too are often learned from models (e.g., Bandura, 1974, 1999).

Whatever the learning processes that are emphasized in a particular learning theory, the story of development is one in which behaviors or beliefs or feelings change in response to specific experiences, one experience at a time. Broader changes can occur by generalization. If new events are experienced that are very similar to events in the original learning context, the learned behaviors may be extended to these new events. For example, the child who learns to say "da" when a particular dog appears may do the same when other dogs appear, or even in the presence of other four-legged animals. Or a child who observes a model sharing candy with a friend may later share toys with a sibling. But these extensions of learned activities are narrow in scope compared to the sweeping changes hypothesized by stage theorists. Overall, development is the product of many independent changes in many different behaviors or mental processes.

INFORMATION PROCESSING THEORIES

Not all information processing theories can be strictly classified as incremental theories, but many can. Like learning theories, these do not hypothesize broad stages, but emphasize incremental changes in narrow domains of behavior or thought. These theories tend to liken human cognitive functioning to computer processing of information. The mind works on information—attending to it, holding it in a temporary store or "working memory," putting it into long-term storage, using strategies to organize it or to draw conclusions from it, and so on. How the information is processed depends on general characteristics of the human computer, such as how much information can be accessed, or made available for our attention, at one time. These characteristics can change to some degree over time. For example, children's attentional capacity increases gradually with age. Yet most changes with age are quite specific to particular domains of knowledge, such as changes in the way that certain kinds of problems are solved.

Furthermore, the individual changes in processing that occur in different knowledge domains are not stagelike; they do not extend beyond the particular situation or problem space in which they occur. For example, Siegler and his colleagues (e.g., Crowley & Siegler, 1993; Siegler, 1996; Siegler & Shrager, 1984) describe changes in the ways that children do arithmetic, read, solve problems of various kinds, and perform many other tasks and skills. Siegler analyzes very particular changes in the kinds of strategies that children use when they attempt these tasks. Although there can be similarities across tasks in the ways that strategies change (e.g., they become more automatic with practice, they generalize to similar problems, etc.), usually the specific strategies used in one kind of task fail to apply to another, and changes are not coordinated across tasks. To illustrate, a kindergartner trying to solve an addition problem might use the strategy of "counting from one": "[T]his typically involves putting up fingers on one hand to represent the first addend, putting up fingers on the other hand to represent the second addend, and then counting the raised fingers on both hands" (Siegler, 1998, p. 93). This strategy is characteristic of early addition efforts, but would play no role in tasks such as reading or spelling. Overall, then, cognitive development in this kind of model is like social development in social learning theories: It results from the accrual of independent changes in many different domains of thought and skill.

Multidimensional or Systems Models

Modern theorists have become more and more ambitious in their efforts to explain and describe the enormous complexity of interrelated causal processes in development. In this third class of models, theorists consider development to be the result of the relationships among many causal components. These multidimensional or systems models generally apply to all domains of development from the cognitive to the social. They suggest that there are layers, or levels, of interacting causes for behavioral change: physical/molecular, biological, psychological, social, and cultural. What happens at one level both causes and is caused by what happens at other levels. That is, the relationships among causes are reciprocal. For example, increased testosterone levels at puberty (biological change) might help influence a boy to pursue an aggressive sport, like wrestling. If his success at wrestling gives him more status among his male friends (social change), his experience of increased social dominance may reciprocally influence his biological functioning. Specifically, it may lead to additional increases in his testosterone levels (Cacioppo & Berntson, 1992).

These models also describe many kinds of change: qualitative, transforming changes, both great (stagelike) and small (such as strategy changes within a particular problem-solving domain), as well as continuous, incremental variations that can even be reversible, such as learning and then forgetting new information (e.g., Overton, 1998). Theories with the characteristics described in this section can be called "multidimensional" or "systems" models (e.g., Thelen & Smith, 1998), but writers use many other names as well, calling them transactional models (Sameroff and Chandler, 1975), relational models (Lerner, 1998), bioecological models (Bronfenbrenner & Ceci, 1994), epigenetic models (Gottlieb, 1992), and so on.

Think again about a girl who is 4 months old, and then later 4 years old. Do you perceive so many changes that she is transformed into a different sort of creature, and yet, at the same time, do you see enduring qualities that characterize her at both ages? Does your sense of the forces that have changed her include influences such as her family, community, and culture? Do you also recognize that she has played a significant role in her own change and in modifying those other forces? If so, your implicit assumptions about development may be more consistent with multidimensional models than with either stage or continuity theories alone.

Multidimensional models can be described metaphorically as a vine growing through a thick forest (Kagan, 1994). In doing so, the vine is propelled by its own inner processes, but its path, even its form, is in part created by the forest it inhabits. There is continuous growth, but there are changes in structure too—in its form and direction—as the vine wends its way through the forest. Finally, its presence in the forest changes the forest itself, affecting the growth of the trees and other plants, which reciprocally influence the growth of the vine. Some examples of multidimensional models will help flesh out the typical characteristics of these theories.

BRONFENBRENNER'S BIOECOLOGICAL MODEL

In Bronfenbrenner's bioecological model, Bronfenbrenner and his colleagues (e.g., Bronfenbrenner & Ceci, 1994; Bronfenbrenner & Morris, 1998) described all developments—including personality and cognitive change—as a function of proximal processes. These are reciprocal interactions between an "active, evolving biopsychological human organism and the persons, objects and symbols in its immediate external environment" (Bronfenbrenner & Morris, 1998, p. 996). In other words, proximal processes refer to a person's immediate interactions with people or with the physical environment or with informational sources (such as books or movies). These proximal processes are modified by more distal processes. Some of these are within the organism—such as genes. Others are outside the immediate environment—such as features of the educational system or of the broader culture. Proximal processes are truly interactive: The organism influences and is influenced by the immediate environment.

The quality and effectiveness of the immediate environment—its responsiveness to the individual's particular needs and characteristics and the opportunities it provides—depend on the larger context. For example, parental monitoring of children's homework benefits children's academic performance. But monitoring is more effective if parents are knowledgeable about the child's work. A parent who insists that his child do her algebra homework may have less effect if the parent cannot be a resource who guides and explains the work. Thus, the parent's own educational background affects the usefulness of the monitoring (Bronfenbrenner & Ceci, 1994).

An individual's characteristics also influence the effectiveness of the environment. For example, motivations affect the impact of learning opportunities in a given context. A man interested in gambling may learn to reason in very complex ways about horses and their relative probability of winning at the track, but he may not display such complex reasoning in other contexts (Ceci & Liker, 1986). Other important individual qualities include demand characteristics, behavioral tendencies that often either encourage or discourage certain kinds of reactions from others. A child who is shy and inhibited, a trait that appears to have some biological roots (Kagan, 1998), may often fail to elicit attention from others, and may receive less support when she needs it, than a child who is open and outgoing (Bell & Chapman, 1986; see also Chapters 4 and 5).

Changes in the organism can be emergent, stagelike qualitative changes, such as a shift from preoperational to concrete operational thought, or they can be more continuous, graded changes, such as shifts in academic interest or involvement in athletics. Both kinds of change are the result of proximal processes, influenced by more distal internal and external causes. Once changes occur, the individual brings new resources to these proximal processes. For example, when a child begins to demonstrate concrete operational thought, she will be given different tasks to do at home or at school than before, and she will learn things from those experiences that she would not have learned earlier.

In earlier versions of his theory, Bronfenbrenner characterized in detail the many levels of environment that influence a person's development (see Figure 1.1). He referred to the immediate environment, where proximal processes are played out, as the microsystem. Babies interact primarily with family members, but as children get older, other microsystems, such as the school, the neighborhood, or a local playground and its inhabitants, become part of their lives. Relations among these microsystems—referred to as the mesosystem—modify each of them.

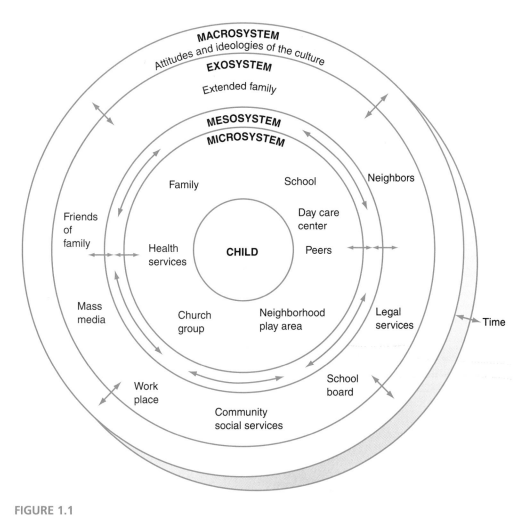

FIGURE 1.1

Bronfenbrenner's Bioecological Model

Source: Early Childhood Development: A Multicultural Perspective, 3rd ed., by Jeffrey Trawick-Smith, © 2003. Reprinted by permission of Pearson Education, Inc., Upper Saddle River, NJ.

For example, a child's interactions with teachers affect interactions with parents. The next level of the environment, the **exosystem**, includes settings that children may not directly interact with but that influence the child nonetheless. For example, a teacher's family life will influence the teacher and thereby the child. Or a child's socioeconomic status influences where her family lives, affecting the school the child will attend, and thus affecting the kinds of experiences the child has with teachers. Finally, there is the **macrosystem**, including the customs and character of the larger culture that help shape the microsystems. For example, cultural attitudes and laws regarding the education of exceptional students influence the operation of a school and therefore a child's interactions with teachers.

The environment, then, is like "a set of nested structures, each inside the next, like a set of Russian dolls" (Bronfenbrenner, 1979). In newer versions of his theory, Bronfenbrenner gives equal attention to the nested internal levels of the organism. As we have seen, a person brings to proximal processes a set of dispositions, resources (preexisting abilities, experiences, knowledge, and skills), and demand characteristics. These, in turn, are influenced by biological and physical levels of functioning that include the genes. Bronfenbrenner now also emphasizes, as other multidimensional theorists do, the bidirectional effects of each level on the adjacent levels. For example, proximal psychological processes playing out in the immediate context are both influenced by, and influencing, physiological processes (Bronfenbrenner & Morris, 1998; Ceci, Rosenblum, de Bruyn, & Lee, 1997). Finally, these interactions continue across time.

Box 1.2 | *Developmental Psychopathology*

The new discipline of developmental psychopathology offers clinicians a unique perspective because its focus is on the shared boundary of three important fields for helpers: abnormal, clinical, and developmental psychology. To appreciate its unique contribution, it is important to understand how it differs from these other disciplines, which have traditionally provided the foundation for much of therapeutic practice. In contrast to abnormal psychology's focus on the characteristic features of clinical disorders, developmental psychopathologists investigate the origins of disordered behaviors that may appear at any time throughout the life span. Unlike researchers in clinical psychology, researchers in this discipline do not emphasize treatment techniques or diagnostic assessments per se. Nor do they focus exclusively on the traditional areas of interest to developmentalists. Instead, researchers search for the linkages between normal development and the factors that cause that development to go awry. They ask questions about why certain individuals fail to meet developmental expectations, how they adapt to those circumstances, and what purposes their particular patterns of adaptation serve. Developmental psychopathologists search for the roots of disordered behavior with the assumption that these problems might be better prevented and better treated if they were better understood developmentally.

One might say that this field attempts to apply the power of advances in genetics, biochemistry, physiology, social and cultural studies, and cognitive and affective development to the problems human beings face at any point in their lifetimes. The Institute of Medicine (IOM) included developmental psychopathology as one of four core areas of research at the forefront of prevention and intervention (1994). At the center of this approach is the assumption that the course of human development follows a lawful coherence. The pattern of a person's adaptation shows continuity even if her specific behavioral traits do not. For example, a maltreated child might deal with a stressful social situation by sucking her thumb, avoiding eye contact with other people, or even crying. That same individual as an adult may adapt or cope with social stress by avoiding social situations, taking a low-threat job, or drinking before a social engagement. The specific behaviors change, but the underlying pattern of avoidant coping does not. Another key principle of this approach is that a "problem" behavior makes sense when we consider its adaptive function. The disturbed or dysfunctional behavior works at least at some level. It is one way, albeit an unhealthy one, to solve a problem that a person faces. Sometimes, as in the case of infants, it may be the only way available.

Developmental psychopathologists believe that studying individuals at the extremes of disordered behavior can enlighten us about the processes that have operated to produce those outcomes. As some stage theorists argue, development can be viewed as a series of progressively higher order integrations of functioning in various areas (social, cognitive, moral, etc.). As individuals generally become more capable of higher levels of functioning, more complex levels of psychopathology can also develop. Much like the qualitative shifts described by Piaget that transform thinking into new forms, psychopathology can also be transformed as people move through life.

The field of developmental psychopathology emphasizes the diversity that is possible in human development, incorporating some key principles from multidimensional or systems theories. The principle of multifinality holds that individual pathways of development may result in a wide range of possible outcomes. For example, children exhibiting conduct-disordered behavior in the elementary school years may as adults display a number of disorders including antisocial personality, depression, substance abuse, and so on. A complementary principle of equifinality specifies that many early developmental pathways can produce similar outcomes. For example, Sroufe (1989) has demonstrated two pathways, one primarily biological and one primarily related to parenting style, that lead to attention deficit hyperactivity disorder (ADHD). Using these ideas from general systems theory allows for the study of multiple subgroups and multiple pathways to disorders. Most important, it allows for a more realistic look at the problems people face (Cicchetti & Toth, 1994).

Several key implications for clinicians present themselves. First, interventions and treatments need to be developmentally appropriate to be effective. Treatment approaches for children should not be based upon adult models of psychopathology. Second, periods throughout the life span marked by disequilibrium or disorganization with resultant reorganization may be considered points at which individuals might be most receptive to change. Developmental psychopathologists suggest that at these "sensitive" periods, interventions may be most effective because the individual can incorporate treatment into new levels of cognitive, emotional, and behavioral organization. Thus, the issue of timing of interventions is one of great interest to this field. In addition, the wide variety of possible pathways and outcomes involved in the development of psychopathology is an argument for the use of multiple means of intervention and treatment. However, interventions should be carefully considered and based upon a thoughtful assessment of a person's developmental level and her quality of adaptation, as well as the availability of external supports. Because this field is relatively new, much more research is needed to establish these principles with greater certainty. However, this discipline's ideas and research findings hold out great promise for helpers. We discuss this approach more in subsequent chapters.

MULTIDIMENSIONAL MODELS OF DEVELOPMENTAL RISK AND OUTCOME

Multidimensional models like Bronfenbrenner's bioecological theory are useful characterizations of the vast web of influences on developmental outcomes for both children and adults. They are particularly helpful for understanding what differentiates "healthy" from "pathological" development. A critical aspect of these models is their emphasis on the complexity of interacting causes: "Single factors can be potent in destroying systems . . . a gunshot can destroy a child. But single factors cannot *create* a child or any other living system" (Sameroff, 2000, p. 37). Similarly, "it is not a single factor that causes . . . difficulties, but an accumulation of adversity that reduces developmental competence" (Sameroff, Gutman, & Peck, 2003, p. 365). Multidimensional views relating normal and abnormal development specify that every individual is an active organism, is influenced in its functioning by multiple levels of internal processes, and is continuously adapting to the contexts in which it functions. Development in every case, regardless of outcomes, is the result of the interplay of the constitution of the individual *and* her experiences across time. Both her constitutional characteristics and her experiences are multilayered at all times.

Two fields that overlap with developmental science, *developmental psychopathology* (see Box 1.2) and *prevention science* (see Box 1.3), have turned to multidimensional theories to explain their findings and to inform the planning of interventions. In these related fields, there is a growing consensus that both normal and pathological behavior is the result of each individual's adaptive strivings. Problematic social, emotional, and behavioral patterns, such as conduct disorder and depression, can be understood as the result of the same proximal processes that produce healthy patterns: as the individual transacts with the environment, she attempts to meet her needs and to adjust to environmental inputs and demands. She brings both strengths and vulnerabilities to these transactions. The environment contributes both stressors and supports, and both the individual and the environment are somewhat altered by each transaction. The strengths, vulnerabilities, stressors, and supports are factors that impact the overall developmental trajectory of the individual. Intervention planning, either to treat disorders or to prevent them, requires identifying these factors, often construed as risk and protective factors, and understanding the complex ways in which they interact (see Box 1.3). Among the individual factors that may matter are various genetic and other biological contributors, temperamental characteristics, cognitive capacities, social skills, attitudes, beliefs, and so on; among the environmental factors are socioeconomic status; safety of the neighborhood; quality of the schools; family history and culture; parental nurturing and monitoring; peer attitudes; friendships; marital and community supports; cultural dynamics, including racial and ethnic processes; and so on. Because so many interacting factors are involved, there is no such thing as perfect prediction of who will have healthy outcomes, who will not, when problems may arise, and when they might recede. Identifying the factors that contribute to an individual's transactions with the environment can increase the probability of successful prediction. For any individual, the more risk factors and the fewer protective factors, the more likely it is that an intervention will be needed (see Cicchetti, Toth, & Maughan, 2000; Lewis, 1997, 2000; Sroufe, 1996, 1997).

LIFE SPAN DEVELOPMENTAL THEORY

In **life span developmental theories**, the same developmental processes that produce the transformation of infants into children, and children into adults, are thought to continue throughout adulthood until death. Developmental change is part of what it means to be alive. Adaptation continues from conception to death, with proximal interactions between the organism and the immediate context modified by more distal processes both within the individual and in the environment. Life span theorists like Paul Baltes (e.g., 1987; Baltes, Lindenberger, & Staudinger, 1998) refer to the interacting web of influences on development as the "architecture" of biological and cultural supports. Baltes proposes that successful adaptation is benefited more by biological supports in childhood than in adulthood. Cultural supports are important in childhood, but if not optimal, most children have biological supports (we could think of them as a complex of biological protective factors) that have evolved to optimize development in most environments. For adults, successful adaptation is more heavily dependent on cultural supports or protective factors. "The older individuals are, the more they are in need of culture-based resources (material, social, economic, psychological) to generate and maintain high levels of functioning" (Baltes et al., 1998, p. 1038). We will have more to say about life span developmental theories in Chapter 13.

Box 1.3 | *Prevention Science*

There is a clear connection between developmental knowledge and prevention. Indeed, it is hard to imagine a more compelling reason for studying human growth and development than to be able to use this knowledge to prevent problems from occurring. Thinking developmentally about prevention automatically leads a helper to consider why problems occur, the nature of the forces acting on individuals that lead to certain endpoints, the strengths and weaknesses that are part of personal histories, and the functions addressed by individuals' maladaptive behaviors.

Primary prevention has been a part of community efforts to improve health and human functioning for over a century in this country (Spaulding & Balch, 1983), and counselors, in particular, have been in the business of prevention for a long time (Wrenn, 1962). However, the science of preventing mental health problems has only recently been taken seriously. Documented increases in the numbers and kinds of problems affecting children and adolescents over the last several decades (Dryfoos, 1997), combined with advances in our knowledge of effective intervention techniques, have breathed new life into prevention efforts.

The relatively new and evolving discipline of prevention science, a multidisciplinary mix of human development, psychopathology, epidemiology, education, and criminology, offers us useful guidelines for understanding what constitutes effective prevention. Coie and his associates (Coie et al., 1993) state that the primary objective of this new field is to "trace the links between generic risk factors and specific clinical disorders and to moderate the pervasive effects of risk factors. If generic risks can be identified and altered in a population, this can have a positive effect on a range of mental health problems, as well as job productivity, and can reduce the need for many health, social, and correctional services" (p. 1014).

The current enthusiasm for the promise of prevention is epitomized by the national interdepartmental initiative Safe Schools/Healthy Students (SS/HS), developed by the Departments of Education, Health and Human Services, and Justice to fund the implementation and testing of effective programs.

In general, prevention scientists study the origins and early sequences of disorders, such as conduct disorder, depression, or drug abuse. They work on detecting early warning signs of disorders and on developing the most effective ways to disrupt a downward spiral. Their contribution to this effort is not purely theoretical, but rather the result of carefully controlled, well-designed intervention trial studies. The beauty of this discipline is that it has the potential to provide a coherent approach to prevention and intervention that is focused, effective, and developmentally appropriate. For the working counselor who is concerned about best practice, it can provide a sound empirical foundation for intervention strategies. By its very nature as a comprehensive model, it encourages interdisciplinary collaboration in empirically tested programs that address problems at multiple levels.

Within the constellation of disciplines that make up prevention science, developmental psychopathology holds a preeminent place (Institute of Medicine, 1994). This is so because any approach used to prevent the development of problems must obviously be informed by knowledge about how problems arise or remit (see Box 1.2). A major contribution from developmental psychopathology to prevention science is its focus on risk and protective factors. Good prevention is designed to reduce risk while enhancing those factors that serve protective functions. As we have noted, prevention researchers are engaged in determining the nature of the complicated interplay between risk and resilience.

What might a counselor need to know about effective prevention and the science that supports it? We have attempted to address that question in question-and-answer format. Because the scope of this chapter precludes more comprehensive coverage of this topic, the interested reader is referred to several excellent reviews (see the series titled *Issues in Children's and Families' Lives*, Volumes 1–9, Sage Publications).

Q & A About Prevention

How Is Prevention Defined?

Historically, clinicians interested in community-based mental health programs differentiated between primary, secondary, and tertiary prevention. Primary prevention is an attempt to forestall the development of problems by promoting health and wellness in the general population through group-oriented interventions. Requiring mandatory vaccinations for children or providing developmental guidance activities in schools might constitute primary prevention activities. Secondary prevention is an attempt to reduce the incidence of disorders among those who are at high risk or to provide treatment to forestall the development of more serious psychopathology in cases that are already established. Programs developed to identify students at risk for dropping out of school and to provide them with remedial programs might be examples of secondary-level prevention. In this case, a selected sample, rather than the general population, receives services. Tertiary prevention is directed toward rehabilitating persons with established disorders.

Because of the need to distinguish between the concepts of tertiary prevention and treatment, another way of categorizing types of prevention was suggested by the IOM report (1994): universal, selective, and indicated. These three levels of prevention are clearly distinguished from treatment, which in this model is similar to tertiary prevention. Universal prevention is directed to the general population. Selective prevention targets individuals at some epidemiological risk, such as low-birth-weight babies. Indicated prevention addresses individuals who show subclinical symptoms of disorders, such as children whose behavioral problems are not yet serious enough to warrant a diagnosis of conduct disorder.

What Are Risk and Protective Factors?

Risk factors are those things that compromise healthy development, whereas protective factors are those things that moderate the negative effects of risk. Generic risk and protective factors may be internal to the individual, may be part of the individual's developmental history, or may reside in the individual's environment. Examples of risk factors include, but are not limited to, sensory or organic disabilities, low levels of intelligence, academic failure, family conflict, poverty, emotional undercontrol, and peer rejection. Protective factors include positive temperamental characteristics, intelligence, parental support and monitoring, good schools and community environments, and positive relationships with competent adults.

Risk and protective factors seem to have both cumulative and interactive effects on development. Negative outcomes are affected by a combination of elements: the number of risk factors present in a person's life, the severity of each, the duration of their effects, and the dearth of protective factors that lessen their ill effects. The presence of several risk factors exponentially increases the probability of a disorder. A good example of this phenomenon was reported by Zagar and his associates in their study of what puts adolescent boys at risk of committing murder (Zagar, Arbit, Sylvies, & Busch, 1991). The probability of murdering someone was doubled for boys with the following four risk factors: history of criminal violence in the family, history of being abused, gang membership, and abuse of illegal substances. The chances of committing murder were three times as great if these additional risk factors were present as well: prior arrest, possession and use of a weapon, neurological problems affecting cognition and affect, and school difficulties, including truancy.

You may recognize that many of these risks seem to fit together. As Garbarino (1999) points out, many children at risk "fall victim to the unfortunate synchronicity between the demons inhabiting their own internal world and the corrupting influences of modern American culture" (p. 23). So not only do risks gain power as they accumulate, but they also operate in clusters that serve as "correlated constraints" (Cairns & Cairns, 1994). In other words, they reinforce each other by their redundancy and work together to shape the developmental trajectory. As a result, although altering one or just a few risk factors *can* have a positive impact on behavior and outcomes, sometimes such limited changes have little effect because the other related risks maintain the status quo.

Certain risks, as well as certain protections, become more important at different points in development. For example, the protection offered by prosocial peers and the risks associated with exposure to deviant ones are particularly powerful as children approach adolescence but less so in early childhood (Bolger & Patterson, 2003). On the other hand, some protections, such as authoritative parenting, retain their power thoughout childhood and adolescence (see Chapters 5 and Chapter 10). Some risk factors are common to many disorders. Deficits in perspective taking or problems with peer relationships may be related to the development of conduct disorder or depression.

How Do Risk and Protective Factors Operate to Produce Developmental Outcomes?

Risk and protective factors are conceptualized as independent, not just opposite ends of a risk-protection continuum. In other words, it is possible to have many risk factors as well as many protective factors operating in a person's life. Researchers are interested in protective factors because they are so closely intertwined with the concept of resilience, that quality that permits developmental success for some individuals despite grave setbacks or early adversity. For example, Hauser (1999), reporting on a retrospective analysis of young adults who had experienced severe trauma in adolescence, found that the ones who made the best adjustment had the highest levels of protection despite their early risks. Those who fared less well in adulthood had less support and greater risk.

It is still unclear how risk and protective factors actually work together, although researchers have hypothesized that protective factors can work in two ways. They can improve life-course outcomes *directly* by their presence so that regardless of whether or not a child is exposed to one or more risks, she will experience some benefit from such a factor. Or, they can operate more *indirectly* by moderating the effects of early vulnerabilities. Gutman, Sameroff, and Eccles (2002) looked at how academic performance by African American adolescents was affected by risk factors that had been identified in other studies, like maternal depression, low family income, father absence, low parent education, and so on. Participants in their sample ranged from low risk (zero to one or two risk factors) to high risk (seven or more risk factors). They also looked at possible protective factors, like parents' positive involvement with their children and supportive peers. They found that some factors, like parental school involvement, benefited children directly. For all adolescents, regardless of whether they were exposed to any risks, parental school involvement was associated with better academic performance. But other factors did have more moderating, interactive (indirect) effects. Peer support for academics really made a positive difference for the academic achievement (especially in math) of high-risk adolescents, but it was not especially important for low-risk kids. More research is needed to identify and explain these relationships with greater precision.

Does Prevention Really Work?

Based upon a rapidly growing body of research findings, the answer is yes. Prevention scientists have provided evidence that well-designed and well-implemented preventive programs can reduce the incidence of problem behaviors such as aggressiveness, violence, and drug abuse as well as increase positive outcomes, such as academic achievement and social competence. We include examples of such programs in later chapters.

What Kinds of Prevention Efforts Work Best?

There is an increasing consensus among researchers, practitioners, and policy makers about criteria for successful prevention efforts. First, good prevention is based on developmentally appropriate, empirically valid approaches. Ideally, programs should show evidence that the positive effects have been maintained over a period of time before being implemented widely. Obviously, this implies the need for high-quality program evaluation research as well.

Second, successful programs take a multidimensional approach to problem prevention, enhancing protective factors while reducing risks (Weissberg, Kumpfer, & Seligman, 2003; Reynolds & Suh-Ruu, 2003). They therefore include components directed to many levels of the system. In other words, clinicians, teachers, parents, health care providers, community leaders, policy makers, and others need to work together to get the job done. The challenge of combining forces given the spectrum of political, cultural, economic, and social diversity that exists in society is formidable indeed. But it can be done. Programs such as Midwestern Prevention Project, or MPP (Johnson et al., 1990; Pentz et al., 1990) have used school-based, parent, and community efforts to reduce substance abuse in young adolescents. This ambitious project combined in-school social skills training exercises, homework assignments to be completed with parents, community intervention such as TV and radio messages, and community policy changes as part of a comprehensive approach. Results after several years of evaluation indicated lower prevalence of substance use for students exposed to the program. (See Chapter 10.)

Third, good programs are sensitive to cultural differences in the application of strategies and in their delivery of messages. Fourth, they focus more on general problem-solving skills rather than on providing didactic information to students, and they are interactive in nature. Fifth, programs are greatly strengthened by the use of peer-oriented strategies, especially for substance abuse prevention (Tobler, 1992). Finally, programs that operate over several years and that are sensitive to the developmental transitions that students experience are more successful than briefer programs.

The failure of prevention programs has been widely attributed to the fact that programs are not fully implemented in accordance with the empirical model or are shortened before they have a chance to work. Commonly observed institutional problems such as lack of funding for services, inadequate training for service providers, lack of effective leadership, and failure to cooperate with "outsiders" who represent various levels or components of the system plague prevention efforts (Gottfredson, Fink, Skroban, Gottfredson, & Weissberg, 1997). Ideally, good prevention should be faithfully executed, be targeted to multiple levels of functioning, have cross-generational linkages, and be kept in place for a sufficient length of time to ease developmental transitions. "To be effective, lifelines that are extended must be kept in place long enough to become opportunities for a lifetime" (Cairns & Cairns, 1994, p. 273).

APPLYING MODELS AND METAPHORS

We have described three major theoretical approaches to development. Favoring one of these paradigms can influence the way counselors assess and interpret client concerns. Let's consider how various theoretical orientations to development might apply to a counseling situation:

Juliana is a 26-year-old Latina female who was raised in an intact, middle-class family. Her father was a teacher and her mother a housewife who occasionally worked in a neighborhood preschool as a teacher's aide. Juliana was the second child in the family, which included an older brother and a younger sister. She attended parochial schools from kindergarten through 12th grade, where she worked very hard to achieve average and sometimes above-average grades. During her early years in school, Juliana had reading difficulties and received remedial instruction. At home, her parents stressed the value of education and kept a close watch on the children. The children were well behaved, respectful, and devoted to the family. Most of their spare time was spent with their close relatives, who lived nearby. Despite Juliana's interest in dating during high school, her parents did not permit her to spend time with boyfriends. They told her that she needed to concentrate on her schoolwork so that she could be a nurse when she grew up. After graduation, Juliana entered a small local college and enrolled in a program designed to prepare her for a career in nursing. She lived at home and commuted to school on a daily basis. Life proceeded as it had for most of her high school years. Her course work, however, became increasingly more difficult for her. She also felt isolated from most of her classmates, many of whom were working and living on their own. She tried to participate in some of the college's social events, but without much satisfaction or success. To pass her science courses, Juliana had to spend most of her time studying. By the middle of her academic program, it was clear that she was in danger of failing. She felt frustrated and angry. At this point, she became romantically involved with Bill, a young White man who worked at the college. She dropped out of school and moved in with him, hoping their relationship would lead to marriage. Her family was shocked and upset with her decision and put pressure on her to come home. Eventually, the relationship with Bill ended, and Juliana, unwilling to return home, moved in with a group of young students who were looking for someone to share the rent. She found a low-wage job, changed her style of dress to look more like the younger students, and quickly became involved in a series of other romantic relationships. Juliana grew increasingly despondent about her inability to maintain a relationship that would lead to marriage and a family. In addition, she felt some distress about not completing her college degree. She enrolled in a night-school program at a local community college to retake her science courses. Once again, she experienced confusion, problems fitting in, and academic difficulty. She went to the college counseling center to ask for help.

Take a minute to think about how you would respond to Juliana. Do any of your views about development enter into your appraisal of her situation? If you tend to be a stage theorist, you might consider Juliana's problems to be based on Erikson's crisis of intimacy in early adulthood (see Table 1.1). She does seem to have difficulties with intimacy, and she is just at the age when these issues are supposed to become central to psychosocial development. But a rigid assumption of age–stage correspondence could prevent you from considering other possibilities, such as an unresolved identity crisis.

If you tend to be an incremental theorist, perhaps favoring social learning explanations, you might perceive Juliana's situation quite differently. You may see Juliana as having problems in her intimate relationships that are similar to her difficulties with school. In both domains she is apparently "delayed," perhaps because she has had insufficient opportunities to learn social and academic skills or perhaps because she has been reinforced for behaviors that are ineffective in more challenging contexts. Although this may be a useful way of construing Juliana's dilemma, any stage issues contributing to her distress may be missed. Also, there could be factors in her social environment, such as cultural expectations, that might not be considered.

If you take a more multidimensional approach, you will try to remain alert to multiple influences, both proximal and distal, on Juliana's development. The roles of her biological status, her individual capabilities, her stage of development, her earlier experiences, her family, and her culture will all be considered as possible influences and points of intervention. One disadvantage could be that the complexity of the interacting factors is so great that you may find it difficult to sort out the most effective place to begin. Another disadvantage is that macrosystem influences, such as cultural expectations about appropriate roles for women, may be quite resistant to intervention. However, one of the advantages of a multidimensional view is that it *does* highlight many possible avenues of intervention, and if you can identify one or a few that are amenable to change, you may have a positive influence on Juliana's future.

Counselors with different developmental assumptions are likely to choose different approaches and strategies in their work with Juliana. In a sense, any set of theoretical biases is like a set of blinders. It will focus your attention on some aspects of the situation and reduce the visibility of other aspects. Knowing your own biases can help you avoid the pitfalls of overreliance on one way of viewing development.

MAJOR ISSUES IN DEVELOPMENT

A number of core issues are addressed in the models we have described, often by framing them as "either-or" possibilities. Which is more important in causing developmental change, nature (heredity) or nurture (environment)? Are some developments restricted to certain "critical periods" in the life cycle, or is any developmental change possible at any time given the appropriate opportunities? Are there important continuities across the life span, or is everything in flux? Are there universal developmental trajectories, processes, and changes that are the same in all cultures and historical periods, or is development more specific to place and time? Is developmental change qualitative or quantitative? Do people actively influence the course and nature of their own development, or are they passive products of other forces?

As with most things, close examination of any of these issues reveals that taking an extreme position does not fit the available data. Human development is best described by a synthesis of the extremes. The best answer to all of the questions just posed appears to be, "Both!"

Nature *and* Nurture

How did you respond to the first three items of the questionnaire in Box 1.1? Did you say that physical traits are primarily inherited? Did you say that intelligence or personality is inherited? Your opinions on these matters are likely to be influenced by your cultural background. For example, Americans have traditionally seen intelligence as mostly hereditary, but Japanese tend to disregard the notion of "native ability" and to consider intellectual achievements as a function of opportunity and hard work (Stevenson, Chen, & Lee, 1993). Alternatively, Americans usually view personality and social adjustment as a result of environmental experiences, especially parents' nurturance and socialization practices, but Japanese usually see these qualities as mostly unalterable, native traits.

Developmental researchers acknowledge that both nature and nurture influence most traits, but they tend to focus their investigations on one or the other. For example, work in the **behavior genetics** tradition (see Chapter 2) was originally motivated by the assumption that many psychological traits are dependent on the genes one inherits. Behavior geneticists also asked whether the environment influences the outcome of genetic inheritance, but a strong focus on genetic causes nonetheless informed their work.

At the opposite extreme, researchers concerned with socialization processes, such as those working in the social learning theory tradition, have assumed that heredity affects some aspects of behavior as well as our responsiveness to some features of the environment, but they focus their research primarily on the impact of the environment on learning and behavioral change.

Most research traditions focus on one kind of cause of behavior, either hereditary or environmental, partly because a research enterprise that examines multiple causes at the same time tends to be a massive undertaking. So, based on personal interest, theoretical bias, and practical limitations, developmental researchers often systematically investigate one kind of cause, setting aside examination of other causes of behavior. Interestingly, what these limited research approaches have accomplished is to establish impressive bodies of evidence, *both* for the importance of genes *and* for the importance of the environment!

What theorists and researchers face now is the difficult task of specifying how the two sets of causes work together: Do they have separate effects that "add up," for example, or do they qualitatively modify each other, creating together, in unique combinations, unique outcomes? Modern multidimensional theories generally make the latter assumption. They are responding to the growing body of evidence that heredity and environment are interdependent: The same genes operate differently in different environments, and the same environments are experienced differently by individuals with different genetic characteristics. Developmental outcomes are always a function of interplay between genes and environment, and the operation of one cannot even be described adequately without reference to the other.

A pair of examples, one from animal and one from human research, should help illustrate the complexity of the interdependence. A species of parasitic wasp lays its eggs in other "host" insects, either a fly or a butterfly. The genetic endowment of the eggs is the same regardless of where the eggs are laid, but the environments in which the eggs are developing are clearly different. Some physical traits of the offspring wasps are different depending on the environment. For example, if the offspring mature in the butterfly, they grow wings; but if they mature in the fly, they do not grow wings (Gottlieb, 1992). The same genes lead to different outcomes, depending on the characteristics of the context in which they operate. Now, consider an example from human research. Identical twins, who share exactly the same heredity, are generally quite similar in height whether raised together or apart, indicating that height is an inherited trait. Yet, in some cultures, heights have changed greatly from one generation to the next—too quickly for genetic changes to be significant. To illustrate, Angoff (1988) found that the average height of young men in Japan had increased by three and a half inches in the three decades following World War II. Only environmental variation, such as improved nutrition, could be responsible for such rapid height changes in a population, an illustration of the same genes (or gene pool in this case) producing different effects in different contexts. We will have much more to say about this topic in Chapter 2.

Critical Periods *and* Plasticity

The issue here is whether some developments, such as first language learning, must take place within a certain time frame, called a critical period, or whether the organism is able to develop or learn any new skill at any time with the right opportunities. There is little doubt that there are some behavioral developments that usually take place within a particular period. Language acquisition is in many ways nearly complete by the age of 5 or 6, for example. But is it possible to acquire a language at another point in the life cycle if this usual time is somehow "missed"? Pinker (1994) reviewed several findings that led him to conclude that although language can be learned at other times, it is never learned as well or as effortlessly as it would have been in the critical period from about 1 to 5 years. One interesting example from Pinker's review concerns the learning of sign language by deaf individuals. American Sign Language (ASL) is a "real" symbolic language, with a complex grammar. Often, however, American deaf children are not given the opportunity to learn ASL in their early years, sometimes because of a belief that deaf children should learn to read lips and speak English (the "oralist" tradition). As a result, many deaf children simply do not learn any language. When these individuals are introduced to ASL in late childhood or adolescence, they often fail to acquire the same degree of facility with the grammar that children who learn ASL as preschoolers achieve.

If findings like these mean that a critical period has been missed, what could be the cause of such time-dependent learning? It is usually assumed that the end of a critical period is due to brain changes that make learning more difficult after the change. An alternative explanation is that the environmental conditions that are likely to exist during the critical period are especially favorable. As with the other issues discussed in this section, the explanation is likely to be complex. Sensitivity to new learning opportunities probably does vary across the life span as a function of changes in the nervous system. But how effectively an individual can learn new skills may be just as much a function of the availability and nature of the opportunities presented, which may need to be different depending on the developmental period in which the opportunities

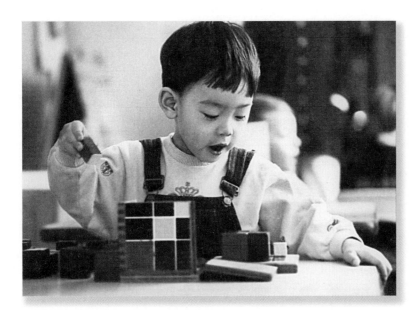

Enriched and stimulating environments provide long-term benefits for children's functioning.

occur. For example, total immersion in a language may be just the right arrangement for a pre-schooler who knows no other communicative system. Older learners, even deaf children or adults who have learned no formal language early in life, may always filter a new language through previously established symbol systems, however informal or idiosyncratic their symbol systems may be. If so, for an older child or adult, total immersion may be less effective than a learning environment that can make correspondences between the new language and the old one. In later chapters, we will examine this issue as it relates to several developments, such as the emergence of sexual identity (Chapter 8) and the formation of bonds between mothers and infants (Chapter 4). In each case, the evidence indicates that some features of a critical period exist alongside continuing plasticity.

Continuity *and* Discontinuity

This question actually presents itself in two different ways. First, there is the issue of whether characteristics that emerge early in life, perhaps even at birth, sometimes persist, relatively unchanged, throughout life. For example, does a shy, inhibited child usually become a shy, inhibited adult? If so, it would appear that some qualities, once established, are intractable, unaffected by the flux of experience in an individual's life. However, if trait persistence does exist, it could actually be a product of dynamic interactions (the proximal processes described by Bronfenbrenner) that have the effect of maintaining a trait that could change. Suppose, for example, that a shy, inhibited youngster is protected by parents from any risk taking, or from having to be sociable, with explanations such as "She's too shy to say 'Hello.'" The child may then miss opportunities to develop social skills and strategies that could help her to become more sociable and less inhibited. Multidimensional models predict that traits can exhibit both continuity and discontinuity, depending on the multiple, interacting forces in play.

A second manifestation of this issue concerns whether early events or experiences can have more or less permanent, continuous effects on an individual's development. These could be normal, expected events, such as parents providing warm responsive care in infancy, or they could be unexpected, "off-time," or nonnormative events such as loss of a job or the untimely death of a parent. In either case, the question is whether or not salient experiences of relatively short duration can have long-term impacts. Freud's stage theory is centered on the notion that early events do have continuous effects. For example, Freud considered an oral fixation in adulthood to be the long-term effect of unsatisfactory or inappropriate oral experiences in the first year of life, which permanently modify the balance of id energies. Multidimensional models, however, usually suggest that early events have long-term effects only if the initial fallout is continuously maintained by proximal processes (e.g., Sameroff, 1989). Suppose an infant's mother suffers from depression immediately postpartum. Many depressed mothers provide their babies with less stimulation, less responsive care, and less affection, on average, than nondepressed mothers (e.g., Fleming, Ruble, Flett, & Schaul, 1988). These are characteristics of infant care that, over time, could have negative consequences for a baby's cognitive performance, emotional and behavioral regulation, and neurological responses to stress (e.g., Brennan, Hammen, Andersen, Bor, Najman, & Williams, 2000; Dawson, Hessl, & Frey, 1994; National Institute of Child Health and Human Development [NICHD], Early Child Care Research Network, 1999). But suppose that the mother's depression lifts shortly after giving birth. As long as the mother's caregiving improves after her depression ends, there are not likely to be long-term effects on the infant (Seifer, 2003).

Universality *and* Specificity

Are there developmental progressions that are universal, having the same qualities across ethnic, racial, or socioeconomic status groups, between genders, and from one historical period to another? Or does development depend entirely on the specific group or time within which it occurs? Let's begin by defining some terms that will appear throughout this text. First, people in the same **ethnic group** are characterized by a shared **culture**: traditions, attitudes, values, and beliefs handed down from one generation to the next (Sternberg, 2004). Second, a **racial group** is more difficult to define and indeed may defy definition. In the past, racial groups, like Blacks, Whites, and Asians, have been considered genetically different, identifiable by variations in hair, skin color, bone structure, or other physiological markers. But apparent differences among racial groups are not greater than the range of differences within groups, and genetic indicators of race have not been found (Blamshad & Olson, 2003). Racial groupings may be no more than a social construction, founded on shifting and superficial characteristics. Third, a socioeconomic status (SES) group is based on social standing or power, and is defined by characteristics of the adults in a household, including educational background, income, and occupational type.

Many developmental theories posit basic similarities in development across different groups and historical periods. Stage models, in particular, specify invariant sequences in personality or cognitive outcomes that are thought to apply to everyone, regardless of culture or group. None of these theories denies that cultural context might affect outcomes. In Erikson's psychosocial stage theory, for example, all adolescents confront the task of formulating an adult identity. But the nature of that identity will certainly differ across groups, and how complex and arduous a struggle the adolescent might face in forming an identity could vary dramatically depending on her culture. Erikson studied development in two Native American groups, the Sioux in South Dakota and the Yurok on the Pacific coast, as well as in the mainstream white culture, and he found different struggles and different outcomes in each (Erikson, 1950/1963).

But there could be more fundamental cross-cultural differences in development. Some sociocultural theories, which trace their roots to the work of Lev Vygotsky (e.g., 1934, 1978; see also Chapter 3), argue that cognitive developments may be qualitatively different in different cultures (e.g., Rogoff, 1998, 2003; Sternberg, 2004). For example, in Western cultures, classifying objects by functional associations (birds with nests) is a trademark of preschoolers' sorting behavior. Hierarchically organized taxonomic classification (e.g., collies and dachsunds grouped as kinds of dogs, dogs and birds grouped as animals) is more typical of elementary-school-age children, and Piaget regarded taxonomic sorting to be an indicator of the logical thinking that emerges in middle childhood. But even adults of the African Kpelle tribe do not sort objects taxonomically. They use functionally based schemes, perhaps because these are more meaningful in their everyday lives, and they would probably consider such schemes more sophisticated than a taxonomic one (Cole, 1998).

Despite the differences that exist across cultural groups, nearly all theories assume that developmental *processes* are the same for all human beings, and cross-cultural research tends to bear this out. Sternberg (2004) studied Kenyan children's intelligence. He found that the content of children's knowledge was quite different from that of North American children. For example, Kenyan children often have limited vocabularies, but they may have very extensive knowledge of natural herbal medicines, which is important in a society where 95% of children have parasitic illnesses. Even though knowledge of vocabulary is a key measure of intelligence in North American children, it seems to have no relationship to intelligence in Kenyan children, for whom breadth of knowledge about herbal medicines is a better indicator. Despite the cultural specificity of children's knowledge, however, Sternberg finds that "the processes of intelligence are not different. (Kenyan) children must still recognize the existence of an illness, define what it is, devise a strategy to combat it, and so forth" (p. 330), problem solving approaches that are not culturally specific.

Cross-cultural findings like Sternberg's demonstrate that development has *both* universal and culture-specific characteristics. A great deal of developmental research has been done only on White, middle-class, North American children. But developmental scientists have begun establishing a multicultural knowledge base; they are now acutely aware of the need to discover how developmental processes play out among other groups both within and outside North America. Throughout this text, we will describe work that has a multicultural focus when it is available.

Qualitative *and* Quantitative Change

What is development? Clearly, it involves change. But does any kind of change qualify, or is there something unique about developmental change? Many stage theories emphasize *qualitative* or "transformational" change—like the emergence of a tree from a seed—as the essence of development. At each new stage, new forms or organizational systems emerge that are both different from and more complex than the ones at previous stages. Increasing complexity suggests that development has "directionality": There is a kind of unfolding or emergence of behavioral organization that can be construed as either moving away from earlier, simpler forms or moving toward some higher or more desirable state (e.g., Overton, 1998; Valsiner & Connelly, 2003).

But many changes that occur during the life span are *quantitative* or "incremental." An example might be adding a new word to your vocabulary or making an adjustment in your understanding of an old word. These changes could include some alteration of an existing behavior or concept, but they do not seem to involve any kind of substantial or wide-ranging reorganizations. They do increase the efficiency or breadth of an individual's activities. This kind of change is sometimes referred to as "growth." As we have seen, learning theories and some information processing theories focus on incremental change. This kind of change is sometimes reversible, as when previously learned words are forgotten. Yet incremental theorists, like stage theorists, seem to consider "change for the better" as a key feature of development. Life span developmental theorists refer to the increases and decreases that occur over time as "gains" and "losses" and argue that both processes occur at all phases of the life span, but they judge "development" to be something more than a sum of gains and losses. It requires moving forward in some way, such as finding ways to compensate for losses. For most developmental theorists then, "development is a process of change with direction" (Valsiner and Connelly, 2003, p. ix).

Modern multidimensional theorists recognize and incorporate both qualitative and quantitative change into their descriptions of development. In essence, the "organism in context" is a dynamic system of interacting forces. The scientific study of other kinds of dynamic systems—like weather systems or chemical interactions—has helped illuminate how change may work in human development. Sudden, dramatic, and extensive qualitative shifts in the organization of dynamic systems can be the outgrowth of many small, incremental changes. If the organism in context works the same way, then quantitative change and qualitative change may be two sides of the same coin in human development (van Geert, 2003).

Activity *and* Passivity

Another question that has been the focus of theorizing by developmentalists concerns whether human development is intrinsically an active or a passive process. Is the course of a person's development primarily shaped by external forces over which the individual has limited control? Or are human beings active "masters of their fate," defining, selecting, and shaping their lives' trajectories? If you espouse the first, or passive, view, you might construe individuals to be highly malleable and receptive to outside intervention, sometimes described as a mechanistic view of the human being. Implicit in this paradigm is the notion that development can ultimately, at least in principle, be reduced to a chainlike sequence of events. Alter a link on the chain, and you can have some effect on the person's subsequent development. Early behavioral approaches to teaching, learning, and counseling held this view of the organism.

The alternative, active, view characterizes organismic theories of development (e.g., Piaget, 1970; Werner, 1948/1973), which depict human beings as active initiators of their own development. In other words, psychological determinants of growth and transformation reside within individuals, who are actively involved in constructing their worlds. If you espouse this perspective, you might believe that human beings are not as amenable to change from outside forces and are not easily coerced by external agents. Teachers and counselors working from this perspective might focus less on directive approaches and more on facilitating personal expression and meaning making, as traditional humanistic approaches to education and therapy have done. From this perspective, people are more than the sum total of their environmental inputs; they need to be "discovered instead of shaped" (Hamer & Copeland, 1998).

To illustrate the opposing sides of this dialectic, consider the example of a 1-month-old infant. For many years, infants were viewed as passive organisms who were "socialized" by parents or other caretakers (Gewirtz & Boyd, 1977). Parents were cautioned by child-rearing experts to establish strict schedules for feeding, napping, and so on, to mold the baby's behavior to acceptable standards. Then, evidence began to emerge that infants have a strong effect on their caregivers (Bell, 1971; Tronick, Als, & Brazelton, 1980). Can the newborn actually be controlling the parent rather than the other way around? Just recall how quickly an adult caregiver responds to a newborn baby's cry! This new perspective changed experts' advice and led them to advise parents to "take their cue" from what the baby seemed to need or want.

It would be incorrect to assume that contemporary developmentalists take either extreme position. They see both the organism *and* the environment as playing active parts in an individual's development, forming a dynamic system. The emphasis is on the *bidirectionality* of influences, with the organism and the environment changing one another. For example, modern multidimensional theories describe developing individuals as self-organizing, filtering incoming information through their own existing mental constructs and influencing the environment's inputs with their actions and reactions. A similar position is taken in the writings of educational and clinical constructivists (Guterman, 1994; Mahoney, 1993, 1995). Constructivism, although not a single, unified theory, is rooted in older psychological theories such as Piaget's. The key assumption in all constructivist approaches is that individuals are not just passive receptors of information who acquire knowledge via external stimulation or manipulation. Nor does knowledge or ability simply emerge from within, as though preformed. Instead, people actively construct their knowledge by interpreting information *in light of* prior learning, by actively restructuring prior knowledge, or by co-constructing knowledge in interactions with others (Moshman, 1982). Social constructivism, a variation of cognitive constructivism, emphasizes that knowledge is constructed within the context of social relationships with others and stresses the influence of such variables as gender, class, and culture on the development of beliefs (Lyddon, 1990).

Consider the example of a class of students taking a multiple-choice exam. Frequently, students' answers will differ not because they have failed to study the material but because they interpret the questions in idiosyncratic ways. They have actively built their knowledge of course content on the foundations of earlier understandings that may or may not have been consonant with the meanings of the test maker. Similarly, many interpersonal conflicts that provide the raw material for therapy are often the result of idiosyncratic "meaning making" by each of the parties involved. This phenomenon, constructivists tell us, describes the human condition. Recent developments in therapy such as the use of narratives and therapeutic metaphors capitalize on this constructivist process. By questioning, offering interpretations, and explaining, a therapist can alter the client's frame of reference, help change meaning, and encourage revision of previously held beliefs (see Haley, 1976).

APPLICATIONS

In this chapter, we have discussed the importance of the study of development and introduced you to some of the worldviews and issues central to the field. The value of developmental knowledge to practitioners of the helping professions cannot be underestimated, as is underscored by a consensus growing out of a number of different theoretical orientations. Some of these include the emerging field of applied developmental science, which has begun to synthesize and apply the findings of developmental psychology to the solution of real-world problems (Fisher & Lerner, 1994). As you have read, the field of developmental psychopathology, another new and influential subspecialty, has applied a developmental focus to the study of abnormal behavior and dysfunction. Clinically oriented writers have also applied specific developmental theories such as Piaget's theory of cognitive development (Ivey, 1986), Freud's psychosexual stage theory (Garcia, 1995), and Kohlberg's moral development theory (Hayes, 1994) to the counseling process. Ivey and Ivey (1998, 1999) remind counselors of the developmental underpinnings of their profession and advocate for

a contextualized perspective on client functioning, similar to the multidimensional approaches we have described in this chapter. Finally, Noam (1992, 1998), who also takes a developmental and constructivist approach to the study of disorders, has developed a therapeutic approach called clinical-developmental psychology, which blends developmental knowledge with clinical practice.

These developmental approaches to counseling and therapy, for the most part, have encouraged clinicians to take into account the developmental features of client functioning as a critical part of assessing and treating problems. These approaches share a number of commonalities: a sensitivity to the fact that persons grow and change over time and that their capacities and concerns also shift over the life course; an appreciation for the knowledge that scientific studies of developmental change can provide for clinicians; and a commitment to the application of this knowledge to improving the lives of individuals, families, and society as a whole. Instead of asking clinicians to choose a therapeutic approach from a set of treatment modalities, each with its own bounded theoretical tradition, Noam (1998) argues for a developmental viewpoint in training programs, which can help new clinicians organize the vast amount of information they need to master. "Developmental psychology and developmental psychopathology need to become 'basic sciences' for the mental health field" (Rolf, Masten, Cicchetti, Neuchterlein, & Weintraub, 1990). Use of developmental knowledge as a kind of metatheory helps counselors integrate the problems presented by the "person-in-situation" and can help reduce the confusion often felt by helpers exposed to a heterogeneous array of treatments for isolated problems.

Many writers have called for a rethinking of diagnostic taxonomies as well to make them more developmentally and culturally sensitive (Ivey & Ivey, 1998). Because good treatment begins with an in-depth understanding of issues, current diagnostic systems need to move beyond superficial descriptions of symptoms. Instead of providing just a "book of names," Jensen and Hoagwood (1997) argue that diagnostic classification systems need to include a comprehensive understanding of the way people grow and adapt, for better or for worse, to their changing circumstances. One system, proposed by Sadler and Hulgus (1994), would incorporate three levels of symptom assessment into treatment planning. Examples of these three levels include syndromes related to personal history (such as early parental deprivation), syndromes related to interpersonal environments (such as victimization or divorce), and syndromes related to extrapersonal environments (such as job loss or systemic discrimination). What these approaches share is the desire to shift the prevailing theoretical paradigm from a model of pathology "within the individual" to a more integrative model that incorporates critical developmental principles such as the importance of contextual features.

Noam suggests that, in this age of short-term treatments, the goal is often to "jump start" those normal developmental processes that can promote healthy functioning. What is needed is a developmental template that the helper can use to facilitate this process. For example, if part of the client's difficulty involves relatively immature thinking about the self in relationship with others, knowledge of the typical sequence of social-cognitive development may be useful in assessing the problem. Strategies can be tried that encourage the growth of perspective-taking skills along the lines of typical development. Not only is this approach useful in addressing immediate difficulties, but it also has the secondary benefit of anticipating what clients will need at later points in their growth.

Knowledge of developmental science helps clinicians in other ways as well. The helper must be able to distinguish normal developmental perturbations from real deviations in development to intervene wisely. A prime example of this occurs in adolescence, which Freud described as a period of "normal psychopathology." Understanding some of the issues typical of this time of life can inform a clinician's guidance, advocacy, and support. Moreover, using a developmental focus can allow the helper to consider ways to support developmental transitions (Lerner, 1996) to later life stages by taking steps to promote a caring network.

Some Rules of Thumb

In this chapter, we have introduced you to some of the classic paradigms and issues in the field of human development and have specified ways in which knowledge of development is fundamental to practitioners. We now suggest a few general guidelines for the application of developmental research to the work of the helping professional.

1. Keep abreast of new and reliable developments in the field. It is important to sort out the worthwhile information in this ever expanding field of study to help clients more effectively. Tavris (1998) makes the point that helpers who are unaware of current developmental knowledge may even be practicing unethically. She recounts the story of one mother who consulted a therapist because of her young daughter's extraordinary shyness. Rather than recognizing the child as temperamentally inhibited (see Chapter 4), the therapist diagnosed the little girl as suffering from "repressed rage syndrome" due to the mother's work outside the home. Ignorance of the developmental roots of various other behavioral symptoms may cause clinicians to misidentify problems and apply ineffective, and potentially harmful, solutions.

2. Interpret stage sequences as guidelines for development. It helps to bear in mind that the various theoretical models or metaphors for developmental growth that we have presented should not be applied rigidly. Steenbarger (1991) cautions against thinking about developmental progress as movement through a fixed set of stages that are the same for all people. Obviously, this view can be excessively rigid and can lead to interpretations of problems in which the complexities of person–environment interactions go unrecognized. Nonetheless, radical constructivist views that abandon all sense of developmental stage progressions may prove unwieldy for the helper who needs to construct a developmental map of the client. What is the answer? As usual, an informed middle ground may be the best alternative. Stages of psychosocial development are not entirely dependent upon chronological age and maturational attainments. However, are not independent of these achievements, either. The skilled clinician must consider a number of possibilities at the same time and, like the reflective thinker described earlier, work to find the best fit.

3. Take a multidimensional view of developmental processes. With respect to the traditional dilemmas in development, it is most consistent with current research that helpers refrain from taking an either–or position in favor of a both–and stance. Above all, awareness of the interacting contributions of genetics and environment can allow helpers to take a more reasoned and accurate view of problems. The current trend toward "over-biologizing" (Tavris, 1998) many kinds of physical and psychological conditions can lead people to the false belief that our genes control our behavior. In fact, they may produce tendencies for people to respond to environments in certain ways.

4. Keep in mind the scientific meaning of *theory*. The term *theory* is often used differently in science than it is in everyday language. In science, a theory frequently represents a synthesis of hypotheses that have been tested and supported by careful research, such as the theory of relativity or evolution. In everyday use, a theory can mean one's personal opinion, such as one's opinion about the best way to educate or counsel children or one's guess about what causes marriages to fail. Scientific theories are not immutable; they can evolve or be disproved with the accumulation of evidence. Although evaluating theories in light of evidence is by no means the only way we learn about life, this approach offers many strengths that set it apart from everyday speculation. Consequently, skilled clinicians should keep themselves well informed about current research findings, but they must also avoid overgeneralizing from single studies.

5. Be selective about your sources of information. Clinicians should be cautious about the sources of information they accept. As with any scientific endeavor, knowledge builds relatively slowly and is buttressed by repeated observations of similar results. A simplistic approach to developmental issues typically will miss the mark by ignoring the complexities of interacting factors, including contextual and historical influences. Additionally, the kinds of direct causal connections between experiences and outcomes that would make prediction much easier for therapists and consultants are, unfortunately, almost impossible to obtain.

6. Be committed to ongoing education in the field. Finally, if we are to pursue the best possible outcomes for our clients, we need to be committed to advancing our professional knowledge. We will try in this book to present the best available information that applies to helpers; however, it is important to be aware that the field of developmental science is itself continually developing. Helpers and others need to keep an open mind and continually work to accommodate new information as they practice reflection in action.

SUMMARY

Reflection and Action

1. The fields of counseling and human development have long been linked. Counselors are dedicated to the enhancement of human development, and researchers in human development provide counselors with theories and data that can contribute to therapeutic practice. In the approach to counseling called reflective practice, developmental research and theory are among the resources counselors use to generate hypotheses about appropriate problem solutions, which the counselor will then test and revise in practice. The more extensive and well organized the counselor's knowledge of basic developmental issues, the more able the counselor will be to retrieve developmental information that is useful to problem solving.

The Big Picture: Models and Metaphors

2. Theories of human development fall into three broad classes: stage models, incremental models, and multidimensional models. In stage models, a person's activities share some common characteristics during the period called a stage. These common characteristics change qualitatively as the person moves from one stage to another. Thus, the period within a stage is a time of relative stability, which ends in a period of rapid change (stage shift), which leads to another relatively stable time. Stages occur in a fixed sequence, though different individuals may progress through the stages at different rates.

3. In Freud's theory of psychosexual stages, personality develops in childhood through five periods: the oral, the anal, the phallic, the latency, and, finally, the genital stages. A child moves from one stage to another as the biological self, or id, changes. In each stage, the child's experiences of need fulfillment, such as the satisfaction of oral needs in the first stage, play a critical role in the formation and further development of the other aspects of personality—the ego and the superego. Although there is little evidence to support Freud's developmental theory, it has influenced other theories, and Freud's ideas are so widely known that they are a part of our culture.

4. In Erikson's eight psychosocial stages of development, personal identity and interpersonal attitudes are expanded and reworked throughout the life span. At each stage, changes in the individual's needs or abilities or changes in societal expectations create new challenges or crises. As each crisis is faced, a new aspect of self-concept emerges, along with feelings or attitudes toward others. If others are sensitive and responsive to the individual's needs during a given stage, positive feelings will result. If the individual's needs are not adequately met, predominantly negative feelings toward self or others may be the consequence. Erikson's emphasis on explaining the development of feelings about self and other has been appealing to counselors, and many of his ideas are compatible with findings from developmental research on issues such as attachment formation and the development of self-esteem.

5. Piaget's cognitive developmental theory describes changes in children's logical thinking skills through four stages. Infants in the sensorimotor stage do not yet have the capacity for representational thought. Children in the stage of preoperational thought, from 2 to 7, can think, but their thinking is not yet logical. In the concrete operational stage, 7- to 11-year-olds think logically, but they

do so most effectively if what they are thinking about can be directly related to the concrete, real world. By the formal operational stage, however, the young adolescent begins to be able to think logically about abstract contents. Although many details of Piaget's theory are no longer considered correct, his general characterizations of children's abilities at different ages are widely seen as useful descriptions.

6. Incremental models of development come in many different forms, but they all characterize behavioral change as a gradual, step-by-step process. Learning theories, for example, emphasize that behavior changes as children learn responses through the processes of classical and operant conditioning. Social learning theories stress one more learning process: modeling, or observational learning. All learning theories portray any change in behavior as a result of specific experiences, affecting specific behaviors. Development results from many independent changes in many different behaviors or mental processes.

7. Among incremental models are many information processing theories. As the mind attends to, analyzes, and stores information, there are gradual changes in the amount of information stored, in the availability of strategies to process information or solve problems, in the links established between or among pieces of information, and perhaps in the size of one's attentional capacity. Most of these changes are limited to whatever kind of information is being processed, so that, for example, acquiring a new strategy for adding or subtracting numbers does not affect the strategies a child might use in reading. Thus, development involves the accrual of small changes within specific domains of knowledge rather than broad, sweeping changes that affect many domains at once.

8. Multidimensional models are broad in scope, explaining both cognitive and social developments. Changes in behavior are the result of causes both within the organism and in the environment. These causes mutually influence one another as well as behavior. In Bronfenbrenner's bioecological model, all developments are seen as the result of proximal processes—reciprocal interactions between an active organism and its immediate environment. More distal processes modify proximal processes and include aspects of the organism, such as genetic functioning, and aspects of the environment, such as family structure or cultural institutions. Proximal processes, such as a child's particular interactions with peers or adults, also influence distal processes, such as the child's internal physiological functioning or the dynamic structure of the child's family.

9. Two related fields, developmental psychopathology and prevention science, specify that both normal and pathological behavior are the result of each individual's adaptive strivings. Using multidimensional theoretical approaches, these fields explain outcomes as the result of proximal processes. Both organismic (e.g., genes) and environmental (e.g., socioeconomic status) influences

contribute to these processes and may be either protective or risk factors. The more risk factors and the fewer protective factors, the more likely an individual will need some therapeutic intervention.

Applying Models and Metaphors

10. In counseling practice, applying a particular developmental model to the assessment of a client's needs can help a counselor organize what the counselor knows about a client and to gain insight into how to intervene. But our theories also provide a set of blinders, focusing our attention on some aspects of a situation and reducing the visibility of other aspects. Maintaining an awareness of our own theoretical biases can help us avoid the problems of a narrowed perspective.

Major Issues in Development

11. Among the core issues that developmental theorists often address is whether nature (genes) or nurture (environment) is more important in development. Although specific theories often focus attention on the importance of just one type of cause, research has established that for most behavioral developments, genetic and environmental processes interact, mutually affecting each other and the behavior in question. Modern multidimensional theories take into account the complexity of this interdependency.

12. Another core issue addresses the question of whether some behaviors can develop only at certain crucial times in the life span (critical periods) or whether behaviors can change at any time (plasticity). Some have argued, for example, that learning language is best accomplished in the preschool years. If critical periods exist, a further question (which may have different answers depending on the behavior) concerns whether developmental changes in the brain could be the source of time-limited opportunities for learning or whether favorable environmental conditions are simply more likely to exist in some developmental periods than in others.

13. A third core issue, whether there is continuity or discontinuity in development, has two manifestations. First, we can ask whether early characteristics, once established, can persist unchanged throughout life or whether the flux of experience eventually causes changes in all characteristics. Second, we can ask whether or not early experiences may have continuous or relatively permanent, long-term effects on a person's development, regardless of later experiences. Different theories offer different answers to these questions. Modern multidimensional theories take the position that continuity of either type is likely only if ongoing proximal processes support that continuity. For example, the death of a mother in the preschool years might continuously influence a child's

development if no one in the child's immediate environment takes over the mother's role or if there are constant reminders in the child's experience of her loss.

14. A fourth core issue is whether some aspects of development (e.g., cognitive stages) are universal or whether all developments are specific to the individual's cultural context. Although there can be substantial differences in development across different ethnic, racial, gender, and socioeconomic groups, nearly all theorists agree that there are some developmental processes that are universal.

15. A fifth core issue concerns the nature of developmental change. Some theories emphasize qualitative changes that are transformational, whereas others focus more on quantitative or incremental changes. Whichever kind of change is emphasized, development is usually seen as "change with direction," a kind of advancement.

16. A final core issue concerns the degree to which the developing person is an active agent in his or her own developmental processes. On one side of the activity versus passivity debate, theorists argue that human beings help shape their own lives. Individuals are to some important extent self-organizing, actively participating in the construction of their own knowledge and experience. On the other side of the debate, theorists suggest that experience is the primary determiner of knowledge, behavior, and developmental change. Modern theorists tend to accept the notion of an active organism, but do not discount the importance of experience in the construction of behavior and knowledge.

CASE STUDY

Charles, a 5-year-old Black youngster, lives with his mother Valerie and his maternal grandparents in a high-rise apartment in an urban area. Valerie's mother works regularly as a member of a small housecleaning business. Valerie's father is unemployed because of an injury. Valerie was 16 when she gave birth to her son. At that time, she was a sophomore at the local public school but had never been very interested in schoolwork and was a marginal student academically. Valerie did enjoy participating in some of the extracurricular activities, such as the chorus and the musical productions, provided by her public school. Her teachers felt that she was quite talented in these areas. When she became pregnant, she dropped out of high school and all related activities to take care of her infant son. Charles's father Howard was uninvolved in the pregnancy and has had virtually no contact with his son for the past 5 years. Recently, Valerie learned that Howard has been convicted of burglary and is awaiting sentencing. She does not want her son to have any contact with his father.

After learning that she was pregnant, Valerie concealed the news from her family for several months, fearing their disapproval. Her parents are very religious and hold strong views against premarital sex. Consequently, Valerie did not receive any prenatal medical care until she was 5 months pregnant. Charles was born 3 weeks premature and weighed only 4 pounds, 2 ounces. He had to remain in the hospital for 4 weeks after birth because of his immature respiratory system. Fortunately, Charles's health improved, and he has had only the typical childhood illnesses since that time.

Valerie has three older siblings who no longer live at home. One of her brothers does live nearby and regularly visits the family. Valerie's unemployed father serves as a babysitter for Charles during the day. The family looked for a nursery school for Charles in their neighborhood, but they were unable to find one that they could afford. Consequently, Charles remains inside the apartment during the day with TV and toys to occupy his time. His grandfather is concerned about his safety and does not allow him to play outside very often. Occasionally, his grandfather will take Charles to a neighborhood playground where he can interact with other children his age.

Valerie has worked sporadically for the last 2 years, mostly as a cashier for a local grocery store. She comes home feeling tired and likes to have some time to go out or to talk with her friends on the telephone after work. At 5 years old, Charles is now a very active child who is often hard to handle. Most of the time Valerie ignores his misbehavior because she is preoccupied with getting herself ready for work or is engaged in other activities. When she does ask Charles to do something and he refuses, she gets irritated and screams at him. Charles's grandparents are more patient with him, but they, too, are frustrated by his noncompliance. They worry that he will be a problem when he goes to school next year, because he does not seem to be able to sit still and listen for any length of time.

Charles's grandfather is a deacon in their church, and religion figures very prominently in the life of the family. They all attend church services regularly, and Valerie sings in the choir. She enjoys this opportunity to express her musical talents in the company of people her own age. Although Valerie has dated occasionally since Charles's birth, she has had no serious relationships. Primarily because of her parents' encouragement, she is contemplating enrolling in a local night school program to complete her high school education.

Discussion Questions

1. Consider Charles's development with regard to the following issues or concepts: contributions of nature; contributions of nurture; proximal processes; distal processes.

2. Can you predict outcomes? Consider issues of continuity and change.

3. What are the strengths and weaknesses of each of the family members?

4. What environmental modifications would be helpful to promote healthy developmental outcomes? Be specific about each family member.

JOURNAL QUESTIONS

1. The long-standing debate on the value of empirically based knowledge versus applied knowledge can be applied to a course such as this. Empirically based knowledge is often explanatory, providing explanations that answer the question "Why does this happen?" Applied knowledge provides solutions and answers the question "What should I do about this?" As a professional counselor, and as an educated person, what are your views on this debate?

2. What do you hope to gain from this course? What are your specific learning goals?

KEY TERMS

life span development
reflective practice
stage
hierarchical integration
id
pleasure principle
ego
reality principle
super ego
Freud's psychosexual stages
oral stage
oral fixation
anal stage
anal personality
anal fixation
phallic stage
latency stage
genital stage
Erikson's psychosocial stages
trust versus mistrust
autonomy versus shame
    and doubt

Piaget's cognitive
    development theory
sensorimotor stage
preoperational stage
concrete operational stage
formal operational stage
decalages
incremental models
behaviorist tradition
classical conditioning
operant conditioning
conditioned stimulus
operant
reinforcement
social learning theories
modeling
generalization
information processing
    theories
multidimensional models
systems models
transactional models

relational models
epigenetic models
Bronfenbrenner's
    bioecological model
proximal processes
distal processes
demand characteristics
microsystem
mesosystem
exosystem
macrosystem
developmental
    psychopathology
principle of equifinality
primary prevention
secondary prevention
tertiary prevention
universal prevention
selective prevention
indicated prevention
risk factors
protective factors

resilience
prevention science
life/span developmental
    psychology
behavior genetics
critical period
ethnic group
culture
racial group
socio economic (SES) group
sociocultural theories
mechanistic view
organismic theories
self-organizing
constructivism
social constructivism
applied developmental
    science
clinical-developmental
    psychology
principle of multifinality

Now go to our Companion Website to assess your understanding of chapter content with Multiple Choice Questions, apply comprehension in Essay Questions, and broaden your knowledge of development with related Web Links.

CHAPTER 2

Heredity, Environment, and the Beginnings of Human Life

THE NATURE–NURTURE ILLUSION

Look at the image in Figure 2.1. Do you see a young woman's face or a saxophone? If the figure that you focus on is the woman, the other parts of the image fade into the background or become the "ground." If you change your focus, the saxophone will become the "figure" and the rest background. It is virtually impossible to maintain both perspectives simultaneously.

Images like this one have been used by Gestalt psychologists to illustrate a perceptual phenomenon known as figure-ground, but we introduce it here because it provides a useful model for understanding the nature–nurture debate. No one would dispute that both heredity and environment influence human development, but when we focus on information about one of these contributors, the other seems to fade into the background. Evidence from both sides is compelling, and the clinician may be persuaded to attend to one side of the argument to the exclusion of the other. The challenge is to guard against taking such a one-sided perspective, which allows for consideration of only half of the story. More and more, helping professionals are called upon to help their clients and the public in general to understand the complex interplay of heredity and environment in physical and behavioral outcomes (Dick & Rose, 2002). In this

FIGURE 2.1

Shepard Illusion

Source: Illustration "Sara Nader" from *Mind Sights* by Roger Shepard, © 1990 by Roger Shepard. Reprinted by permission of Henry Holt and Company, L.L.C.

chapter, we will review the major contemporary approaches to the nature–nurture debate. We begin with an overview of genetic mechanisms, then we examine the role of genetics in behavior and the nature of gene–environment interactions. Finally, we consider clinical applications.

MECHANISMS OF GENETIC INFLUENCE: HOW DO GENES WORK?

Is television watching inherited? Do genes cause young teens to take up smoking or to abuse other drugs or to shoplift? If you follow science reporting in the popular press, or even dip into a scientific journal on human development, you are likely to find articles that seem to link heredity to human behaviors of every description. The genetics of behavior is a "hot" issue in science today. But to understand the real implications of research reports on heredity for science or practice, it is important to have basic knowledge of hereditary mechanisms and what they can and cannot do. In this section, we will provide an overview of the biological structures and processes that contribute to intergenerational inheritance. Then we will examine the most current approaches to investigating the relationship between genes and behavior.

Biological Inheritance

CHROMOSOMES AND DNA

Whether it comes from the inside of your mouth or from the cartilage in your thumb bone, each cell in your body has a nucleus, and inside that nucleus are 46 tiny structures called chromosomes. Chromosomes are the source of biological inheritance. They come in pairs—23 of them. Twenty-two of these pairs are matched and are called autosomes. In autosome pairs, the two chromosomes look and function alike. In the 23rd pair, the chromosomes are alike in females but not in males and are called the sex chromosomes.

During certain stages in the life cycle of a cell, the chromosomes are easily visible under a microscope. Figure 2.2 is an example of a male and female karyotype, a display of the actual chromosomes from human body cells, photographed under a microscope and laid out in matching pairs. Notice the 23rd pair is matched in the female example but not in the male example.

Chromosomes are strands of a complex organic substance called deoxyribonucleic acid or DNA, which is constructed from four simple molecules or bases, adenine, thymine, guanine, and cytosine. Genes make up only about 3% of chromosomal DNA. The function of the remaining 97%, called intergenic DNA, is not well understood. DNA has the remarkable property of self-replication, which means that chromosomes can reproduce themselves. In this complex chemical process, the

FIGURE 2.2

Human Karyotypes

Female Karyotype

Male Karyotype

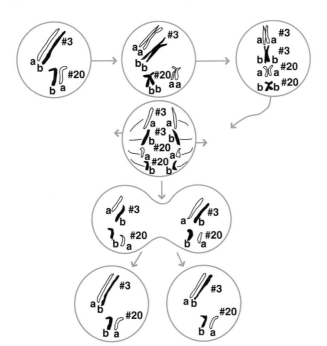

FIGURE 2.3

Cell Dividing by Mitosis (Only 2 of the 23 pairs of chromosomes— pairs #3 and #20— are depicted for illustration.)

helical strands of DNA separate, and each becomes a template for a new DNA molecule. At first the duplicate chromosomes remain joined at one location, called the centromere. In the karyotypes shown in Figure 2.2, the chromosomes were photographed after they had duplicated, but they remained joined at the centromere. When a cell begins to divide, the chromosomes line up in the middle of the nucleus, as if there were an invisible axis running through the center of the cell. (See Figure 2.3.) The duplicates then pull apart along that axis and migrate to opposite ends of the original cell. Two new cells now form, each of which contains one full set of 46 chromosomes. This kind of cell division, called mitosis, produces two new cells identical to the original cell. Nearly all body cells undergo mitosis, making growth possible.

INTERGENERATIONAL TRANSMISSION OF CHROMOSOMES

Where do the chromosomes in a human body come from in the first place? They are passed on at conception. One member of each chromosome pair comes from the mother and one member comes from the father. This intergenerational transport begins in special cells, called germ cells, located only in the ovaries of females and in the testes of males. Germ cells undergo a special kind of cell division, called meiosis. Meiosis begins like mitosis, with the duplication of chromosomes. When germ cells prepare to divide, each duplicated chromosome matches up with the other chromosome in its pair. (See Figure 2.4.) So, for example, the chromosomes in pair number 12 line up together. When the cell begins to divide, the duplicate chromosomes do not pull apart at the centromere—they remain attached. One chromosome in each pair migrates to one side of the cell; the other member of the pair migrates to the other side. When two new cells are formed, each one contains only 23 chromosomes, one member of each pair. Each of the 23 is duplicated, but the duplicates remain attached until each of these new cells begins to divide again. Now the duplicated chromosomes line up, single file, in the middle of the cell, just as they would for mitosis, and as the cell divides, the duplicates pull apart. The important outcome of this multistage process is that the four new cells that are formed each will contain only 23 chromosomes, one member of each pair.

What happens to these four new cells now depends on whether they were produced in an ovary or a testis. In an ovary, three of the new cells disintegrate, and the fourth becomes an ovum or egg. In males, all four new cells form tails and become sperm. Thus, all ova and sperm contain only 23 chromosomes each. When an ovum is released into a woman's fallopian tube, if a sperm fertilizes the ovum, the two cells merge to form one cell with one nucleus. This fertilized ovum is called a zygote, and its nucleus contains 46 chromosomes, 23 pairs. The mother and

FIGURE 2.4

Cell Dividing by Meiosis (Only 2 of the 23 pairs of chromosomes—pairs #3 and #20—are depicted for illustration.)

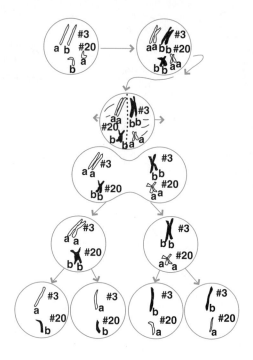

the father of this newly conceived human each contributed one member of each of the chromosome pairs.

Once formed, the zygote immediately begins to divide by mitosis. Soon there are two cells, which quickly divide to produce four new cells, and so on. The cell divisions continue in quick succession, and before long there is a cluster of cells, each one containing a duplicate set of the original 46 chromosomes, half inherited from the mother and half from the father. As the cluster forms, the growing organism migrates down the mother's fallopian tube, into the uterus, and may succeed in **implanting** itself, that is, becoming attached to the uterine lining. The progress of intrauterine growth and development is summarized in Figure 2.5.

How Genes Influence Traits

GENES AND THEIR FUNCTIONS

Now that you know how chromosomes are passed on from generation to generation, let's consider how they function. Chromosomes, as we have said, are strands of DNA. **Genes** are functional units or sections of DNA. Altogether, in one individual's 46 chromosomes, there are approximately 20,000 to 25,000 genes (International Human Genome Sequencing Consortium, 2004). For each member of a pair of chromosomes, the number and location of genes are the same. Thus, genes come in matched pairs also.

The moment of conception: Sperm and ovum unite to create a new organism.

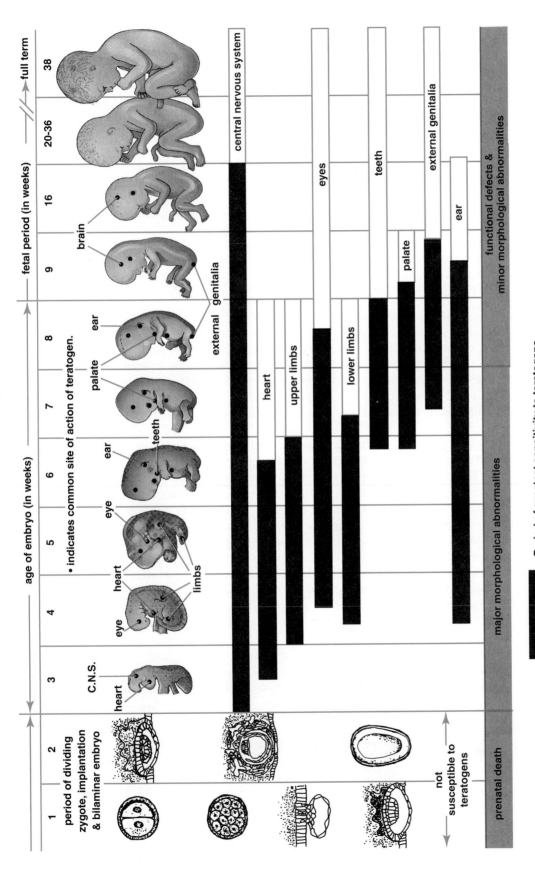

FIGURE 2.5

Fetal Development

Source: From *Before We Are Born: Basic Embryology and Birth Defects,* 3rd ed. (p. 118), by K. L. Moore and T. V. N. Persaud, 1984, Philadelphia: Saunders. Reprinted with permission from Elsevier.

Genes provide a blueprint or code to the cell for how to produce proteins and enzymes. Each set of four bases in a gene—adenine, guanine, thymine, and cytosine—codes for an amino acid; the gene provides the codes for the full sequence of amino acids in a protein. Proteins are the building blocks of the body; for example, melanin, the pigment that affects the color of your eyes, is a protein. Enzymes are protein-like substances that facilitate chemical reactions, such as those involved in metabolizing food; for example, lactase is an enzyme necessary for digesting milk.

In a process called transcription, the intertwined strands of DNA separate, and one of the strands acts as a template for the synthesis of a new, single strand of messenger ribonucleic acid or mRNA. The sequence of bases in a gene are replicated in the mRNA, and then the RNA guides the cell's construction of a protein.

The body is built from proteins, and the proteins are built following the code provided by genes. However, most genes do not function full time. Also, genes may be turned "on" in some cells and not in others. When a gene is on, transcription occurs and the cell manufactures the coded product. How and when a gene's code will be transcribed and used by the cell is determined by regulator genes, also called "noncoded genes," which appear to be located on the long stretches of intergenic DNA. But what regulates the regulators? A critical factor is the environment, both within the cell and surrounding the cell. In later sections of this chapter, we will examine the role of the environment more closely. For now, let's continue to examine genetic factors.

GENE ALLELES AND THEIR RELATIONSHIPS

What significance is there to having matched pairs of genes, one from each parent? One important effect is that it increases hereditary diversity. The genes at matching locations on a pair of chromosomes often are identical, coding for exactly the same protein, but they can also be slightly different forms of the same gene, providing somewhat different messages to the cell. These slightly different varieties of genes at the same location or locus on the chromosome are called alleles. For eye color, for example, an individual (call him Tom) might inherit from one parent an allele that would usually produce brown eyes but inherit an allele for blue eyes from the other parent. (Both alleles provide the cell with a blueprint for melanin production, but the brown eye allele dictates that it be produced in larger quantities.) These two alleles represent Tom's genotype for eye color. But his actual, expressed eye color, or phenotype, is brown.

This example illustrates two characteristics of our genetic endowment. First, two alleles of the same gene can have a dominant-recessive relationship, with the first being expressed and the second being suppressed. Second, as a result, not all of a person's genes actually influence the body or behavior. Tom, for example, is a carrier of the unexpressed trait because recessive genes can "surface" in the phenotype of an individual's offspring. If a child receives two recessive alleles, one from each parent, the child will have the recessive trait. For instance, in Table 2.1 a mother and a father both have curly hair. Each of the parents has one dominant gene allele for curly hair and one recessive allele for straight hair. On the average, three out of four children born to these parents will inherit at least one curly hair allele. Even if they also inherit a straight hair allele, they will have curly hair. But one child out of four, on average, will inherit two

TABLE 2.1 Intergenerational Transmission of Recessive Traits (by parents who are carriers)				
		Mother	**Father**	
	Genotype:	Cc	Cc	
	Phenotype:	Curly Hair	Curly Hair	
	Child₁	**Child₂**	**Child₃**	**Child₄**
Genotype:	CC	Cc	Cc	cc
Phenotype:	Curly Hair	Curly Hair	Curly Hair	Straight Hair*

*On average, one child in four will have the recessive trait if both parents are carriers.

Note: *C* stands for the dominant curly hair allele: *c* stands for the recessive straight hair allele.

TABLE 2.2　Dominant and Recessive Traits Linked to Single Pairs of Genes	
Dominant Trait	**Recessive Trait**
Curly hair	Straight hair
Dark hair	Blonde or red hair
Dimpled cheeks	No dimples
Immunity to poison ivy	Susceptibility to poison ivy
Thick lips	Thin lips
Roman nose	Straight nose
Farsightedness	Normal vision
Type A blood	Type O blood
Type B blood	Type O blood

straight hair alleles, one from each parent. Without a curly hair allele to suppress the effects of the straight hair allele, such a child will have straight hair, probably much to the surprise of the parents, who were unaware that they were carriers of the straight hair trait! Table 2.2 lists several traits that seem to be heavily influenced by a single gene location where alleles of the gene usually have a dominant-recessive relationship, so that to get the recessive trait, a person must inherit two recessive alleles.

Two different alleles will not necessarily have a dominant-recessive relationship. Sometimes alleles exhibit codominance, producing a blended or additive outcome. For example, Type A blood is the result of one gene allele; Type B blood is the result of a different allele. If a child inherits a Type A allele from one parent and a Type B allele from the other parent, the outcome will be a blend—Type AB blood.

Some traits, such as eye color, the curliness of hair, and blood type are heavily influenced by gene alleles at a single gene location. But most traits are affected by the products of many different gene pairs. Often these pairs are located on different chromosomes. Such polygenic trait determination makes the prediction of traits from one generation to another very difficult and suggests that any one pair of gene alleles has only a modest influence on phenotypic outcomes. Height, skin color, and a host of other physical traits are polygenic, and most genetic influences on intelligence, personality, psychopathology, and behavior appear to be of this kind as well. The effects of gene alleles on traits are complicated by many factors. For example, one recently discovered phenomenon is genomic imprinting (Reik & Walter, 2001). In this process, a gene allele is "imprinted" in the sperm or the ovum, meaning that the allele is deactivated. How this deactivation takes place is not fully understood, but it is clear that imprinted gene alleles do not influence the phenotype of the offspring. Some gene alleles are imprinted in ova, but not in sperm, and so can only be expressed if inherited from the father. Others are imprinted in sperm but not in ova, and so can only be expressed if inherited from the mother. Imprinting occurs at a relatively small number of gene locations, but it certainly complicates the process of genetic expression.

The Inheritance of Sex

So far, we have seen that pairs of genes, single pairs or multiple pairs, located on chromosomes, are the source of hereditary influences for most traits. But the hereditary explanation for an individual's sex, whether male or female, is linked to the entire 23rd pair of chromosomes: the sex chromosomes. In females, this is a matched pair of elongated chromosomes called X chromosomes. But in males, this pair is mismatched; one is an X chromosome, and the other is a shorter Y chromosome. Because females have only X chromosomes, when they produce eggs each ovum contains an X chromosome as its representative of the 23rd pair. But because males have an X and a Y chromosome, half of the sperm they produce contain an X chromosome, and the other half contain a Y chromosome. At the time of conception, if a sperm containing an X chromosome fertilizes the ovum, the resulting child will be female: She will have an X chromosome from each parent. However, if a sperm containing a Y chromosome fertilizes the ovum, the child will be male, with an X chromosome from his mother and a Y chromosome from his father. (See Figure 2.6.) Given that the biological determiner of a child's sex is the sperm that wins the race to the egg, it is

FIGURE 2.6

Sex Chromosome Transmission

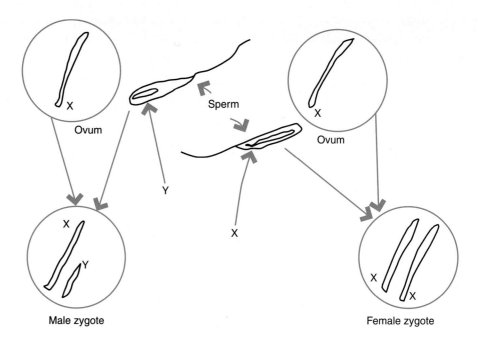

ironic that in many cultures of the world, women are held responsible for the sex of their offspring. In some patriarchal societies, sons are more highly valued than daughters. In the past, women have been punished, divorced, or even put to death for failing to produce a son.

The development of female characteristics is the natural or default process in human fetal development. Development of male characteristics typically depends on the presence of a gene located on the Y chromosome. This gene leads to the development of testes, which produce male hormones called androgens, primarily testosterone. When androgens are released in adequate quantities and at appropriate time intervals, other male reproductive organs develop and some aspects of brain development appear to be affected. As Ward (1992) described the process, "if these hormones are not present in adequate amounts or over the correct temporal intervals, the natural tendency to retain female characteristics prevails" (p. 158), which is what happens in individuals with two X chromosomes.

Given that sperm containing X chromosomes and sperm containing Y chromosomes are produced in equal numbers, it seems reasonable to expect that male and female zygotes would be conceived with equal frequency. However, male conceptions far outnumber female conceptions, with some estimates of the ratio (e.g., Shettles, 1961; Zaslow & Hayes, 1986) being as high as 140 to 100! Yet, male births only slightly outnumber female births because males are less likely to survive the prenatal period than females. More males than females are spontaneously aborted early in pregnancy, often before a woman knows that she is pregnant, and more are miscarried later in pregnancy. As you will see in the next section, the vulnerability of males is at least partly a function of their susceptibility to hereditary diseases, and that vulnerability continues into childhood.

Hereditary Diseases

Some disorders, such as sickle-cell anemia, Huntington's chorea, muscular dystrophy, and Down syndrome, are passed on through hereditary mechanisms from parents to children, even when the parents do not have the disorders themselves. Problems can arise as a function of normal hereditary processes or because something goes haywire in the production of ova or sperm. Here are some examples.

DISORDERS INFLUENCED BY RECESSIVE, DEFECTIVE ALLELES

In sickle-cell anemia, the red blood cells are abnormally shaped, more like a half moon than the usual, round shape. The abnormal cells are not as efficient as normal cells in carrying oxygen to the tissues; victims of this disorder have breathing problems and a host of other difficulties that

TABLE 2.3　Some Disorders Caused by Recessive Gene Alleles

Disorder	Description
Cystic fibrosis	Inadequate mucus production; breathing & digestive problems; early death.
Phenylketonuria (PKU)	Metabolism of phenylalanines in food is insufficient; gradually compromises the nervous system, causing mental retardation.
Sickle-cell anemia	Blood cells have an unusual "sickle" shape; causes heart and kidney problems.
Tay-Sachs disease	Enzyme disease; causes degeneration of the nervous system and death in the first few years of life.
Thalassemia	Blood cells abnormal; low energy, paleness, poor resistance to infection.
Hemophilia*	Blood-clotting factor not produced; vulnerable to death by bleeding.
Duchenne's muscular dystrophy*`	Wasting of muscles produces gradual weakness, eventual death.

`*Disorders that are X linked and are therefore expressed primarily or exclusively in males.

typically lead to organ malfunctions and, usually, to death by adolescence. A recessive gene allele causes the malformed blood cells. If one normal gene allele is present, it will be dominant, and the individual will not have sickle-cell anemia. Many hereditary disorders are caused by such recessive, defective alleles, and it is estimated that most people are carriers of three to five such alleles. Yet, most of these illnesses are rare because to get them an individual has to be unlucky enough to have both parents be carriers of the same defective allele and then to be the one in four (on average) offspring to get the recessive alleles from both parents (refer again to Figure 2.5, explaining the inheritance of recessive traits). Table 2.3 lists some examples of these illnesses.

Some recessive, defective genes are more common in certain ethnic or geographic groups than in others. The sickle-cell anemia gene, for example, is more common among people of African descent. For some of these disorders, tests are available that can identify carriers. Prospective parents who have family members with the disorder or who come from groups with a higher than average incidence of the disorder may choose to be tested to help them determine the probable risk for their own offspring. Genetic counselors help screen candidates for such testing, as well as provide information and support to prospective parents, helping them to understand and cope with the choices that confront them—choices about testing, childbearing, and parenting (Shiloh, 1996).

DISORDERS INFLUENCED BY DOMINANT, DEFECTIVE ALLELES

Some genetic disorders are caused by dominant gene alleles, so that only one defective gene need be present. There are no carriers of such disorders—anyone who has the defective gene will have the problem it causes because a dominant gene allele is always expressed in the phenotype. Suppose that such an illness causes an early death, before puberty. Then, the defective, dominant gene that causes the illness will die with the victim because no offspring are produced. When these alleles occur in some future generation, it must be through mutation, a change in the chemical structure of an existing gene. Sometimes mutations occur spontaneously, and sometimes they are due to environmental influences, like exposure to radiation or toxic chemicals (Strachan & Read, 2000). For example, progeria is a fatal disorder that causes rapid aging, so that by late childhood its victims are dying of "old age." Progeria sufferers do not survive long enough to reproduce. When the disease occurs, it is caused by a genetic mutation, so that while it is precipitated by a genetic defect, it does not run in families.

Some disorders caused by dominant, defective alleles do not kill their victims in childhood, and thus can be passed on from one generation to another. When one parent has the disease, each child has a 50% chance of inheriting the dominant, defective gene from that parent. Some of these disorders are quite mild in their effects, such as farsightedness. Others unleash lethal effects late in life. Among the most famous is Huntington's chorea, which causes the nervous system to deteriorate, usually beginning between 30 and 40 years of age. Symptoms include uncontrolled movements and increasingly disordered psychological functioning, eventually ending in death. In recent years the gene responsible for Huntington's chorea has been identified, and a test is now available that will allow early detection, before symptoms appear. Unfortunately, there is no cure, and the offspring of victims face a difficult set of dilemmas, including whether or not to have the test and, if they choose to do so and find they have the gene, how to plan for the future. Again, genetic counselors may play a critical role in this process (Morell, 1993; Shiloh, 1996).

DISORDERS OF POLYGENIC ORIGIN

As with most normal characteristics, many inherited disorders seem to be related to multiple pairs of genes, such that some combination of defective alleles at several chromosomal sites predispose the victim to the illness. Like all polygenic traits, these disorders run in families, but they cannot be predicted with the precision of disorders caused by genes at a single chromosomal location. Most forms of muscular dystrophy are polygenically determined. Polygenic influences have also been implicated in diabetes, clubfoot, some forms of Alzheimer's disease, and multiple sclerosis, to name just a few. As we noted earlier, genetic effects on behavioral traits are usually polygenic. This appears to be true for many mental illnesses and behavioral disorders as well, such as alcoholism, criminality, schizophrenia, and clinical depression (e.g., Charney, Nestler, & Bunney, 1999; DeAngelis, 1997; Heath et al., 1997; Plomin, Owen, & McGuffin, 1994).

DISORDERS CAUSED BY CHROMOSOMAL ABNORMALITIES

Occasionally, a zygote will form containing too many chromosomes, or too few. Such zygotes often do not survive. When they do, the individuals usually have multiple physical or mental problems. Among the most well known of these disorders is Down syndrome (also called Trisomy 21), caused by an extra copy of chromosome number 21. Children with Down syndrome experience some degree of mental retardation, although educational interventions can have a big impact on the severity of intellectual impairment. In addition, they are likely to have several distinctive characteristics, such as a flattening of facial features, poor muscle tone, and heart problems. The causes of chromosomal abnormalities are not well understood. Either the mother or the father could be the source, and ordinarily, the older the parent, the more likely that an ovum or sperm will contain a chromosomal abnormality. Oddly enough, however, with Down syndrome, the increased risk with parental age holds only for mothers. Older fathers are at less risk than younger fathers to produce sperm carrying an extra chromosome number 21 (Merewood, 1991)!

SEX-LINKED DISORDERS

Males are more susceptible to some genetic disorders than females, which helps account for males being less viable both before and after birth. The problem for males is the mismatched sex chromosomes. The smaller Y chromosome does not carry all of the genes that the longer X chromosome does. There are a slew of X-linked recessive disorders, such as hemophilia, baldness, color blindness, night blindness, Duchenne's muscular dystrophy, and so on, and males are much more likely to suffer from these disorders than are females. To understand why, consider color blindness. Normal color vision is influenced by a gene on the X chromosome that is ordinarily dominant over any defective allele. Thus, even if a girl (who has two X chromosomes) has on one X chromosome a defective allele that could cause color blindness, she will not be color-blind as long as she has a normal color-vision allele on her other X chromosome. If she happens to inherit defective alleles from both parents, then she will be color-blind. In other words, for females only, color blindness, and all of the other X-linked recessive disorders, function like all inherited diseases caused by recessive, defective gene alleles. For males, the process is different. If a boy inherits a defective gene allele for color vision on the X chromosome, which comes from his mother, he will be color-blind because his Y chromosome, inherited from his father, bears no matching gene. This is true for all the X-linked recessive diseases. The result is that females tend to be carriers, and males are more likely to be victims.

As with the genetic transmission of normal traits, genetic transmission of disorders is complicated and can involve a wide range of processes. One unusual mechanism that has only recently been identified involves the expansion, across generations, of what are called trinucleotide repeats (e.g., Brown & Brown, 2004). These are repeated sequences of three bases that are part of the code in many normal gene alleles. For example, some genes have several sequences of CGG (cytosine-guanine-guanine) in a row. The number of trinucleotide repeats will sometimes spontaneously increase, constituting one type of gene mutation. Too large a number of trinucleotide repeats can cause a gene to function improperly or not at all. Fragile X syndrome, a disorder that is a leading cause of mild to moderate mental retardation, appears to result from exactly this kind of mutation. CGG repeats that are part of the fragile X syndrome gene expand to a point that the gene becomes nonfunctional and fails to trigger the production of an important protein (Pandley, Phadke, & Mittal, 2004). Because the gene is located on the X chromosome, the symptoms are usually more severe in males than in females. Females are likely to have a normal gene allele on their other X chromosome that helps to mitigate the effects of the defective allele, whereas males have no corresponding gene on their Y chromosome.

The expansion of trinucleotide repeats across generations can have other effects on inherited diseases as well. For example, the gene allele that causes Huntington's chorea has a series of CAG (cytosine-adenine-guanine) repeats. Across generations, the number of repeats tends to increase, causing the onset of the disease to occur earlier in successive generations (Brown & Brown, 2004).

EXPLAINING BEHAVIOR: FOCUS ON GENETICS

Having examined some of the mechanisms of genetic influence on physical traits, we are ready to tackle the questions of whether and how genetics can influence behavior and its development. Could it be true that complex, culturally dependent activities, such as television watching, are hereditary, as one recent scientific article implied (Plomin, Corley, DeFries, & Fulker, 1990)? If, as we have seen, genes code for protein and enzyme production, the influence of genetics on behavior must be indirect. Genes impact the development and functioning of the nervous system, its structures, and its chemical processes. The nervous system, interacting with other body systems and with the environment, generates behavior.

It's easy to be confused by popular-press reports of genetic advances. Newspaper headlines routinely broadcast "discoveries" of new links between genes and behavior. But what do we really know? To figure this out, it helps to understand that there are two main scientific approaches to this question: molecular genetics and behavior genetics.

Molecular Genetics

The study of what genes do and how their products influence the body and behavior is called molecular genetics. Molecular geneticists study the cascade of biochemical changes that occur in the transmission and translation of DNA information to cells, a process called gene expression. This science is rapidly progressing, but in reality, little is yet known about the impact of specific genes on complex behavioral characteristics, like motor coordination or social inhibition. The Human Genome Project, a massive effort in molecular genetics that involved thousands of scientists around the world for 13 years (ending in 2003), successfully mapped the sequence of chemical bases comprising all human chromosomes. An international consortium has continued this work and has identified the locations of most of the 20,000 to 25,000 genes on human chromosomes. It is hoped that now rapid progress can be made in discovering each gene's functions (Human Genome Program, U.S. Department of Energy, 2003; International Human Genome Sequencing Consortium, 2004; Plomin, DeFries, Craig, & McGuffin, 2003).

One thing we have learned from molecular genetics to date is that complex human behaviors or behavioral tendencies are not often likely to be traced to the impact of a single gene or pair of gene alleles. As we have already noted, most influences on behavior appear to be polygenic. Take intellectual functioning, for example. A number of genes, if they are defective, can influence the development of mental retardation. In many cases, the defective genes seem to result in an important cell product being missing. For example, in the disorder called phenylketonuria (PKU), children are missing an important enzyme. Without the enzyme, an amino acid in food, called phenylalanine, cannot be metabolized. Unless the victim's diet is severely restricted, phenylalanine soon accumulates in the body and causes mental retardation (Strickberger, 1985). Thus, a single missing cell product disrupts intellectual functioning. But no single cell product is responsible for intelligence; rather, normal functioning is the result of the combined impact of a large number of genes and their products (e.g., Helmuth, 2001; Wahlsten, 2003).

Behavior Genetics

Molecular genetics addresses questions such as where are genes located, how do they turn on and off, what is their structure, how do they function, what are their products, and what do those products do to influence physical and behavioral traits. But we can ask a different question about heredity: *If a behavior or characteristic varies from one person to another, how much of the difference is due to genetic influences?* This question is the domain of behavior genetics (Plomin et al., 1994; Plomin & Rutter, 1998).

Most of the available research on genetics and behavior comes from the behavior genetics tradition. Behavior geneticists are the scientists who have implicated heredity in such complex activities as television watching, work attitudes, cigarette smoking, and criminality. Their research tools are not microscopes and petri dishes, but the tools that all behavioral scientists use to measure individual differences in behavior: interviews, questionnaires, standardized tests, and observational techniques. They apply these measures to special populations of people, such as twins and adoptees. Their goal is to identify behavioral variations that run in families and to figure out how much of the similarity among family members is due to shared nature (genes) as opposed to shared nurture (environment).

Behavior genetics relies on the assumption that with the right methods, the influence of genes can be separated from the influence of environment and that the contribution of each can be measured. In a twin study, for example, scores on a behavioral trait are obtained both for identical twins (monozygotic) and for fraternal twins (dizygotic). Identical twins come from a single zygote and have exactly the same genes. Fraternal twins develop from two separate zygotes, and, like any two siblings, on the average they share about 50% of their genes. The underlying assumption in a twin study is that the environment is as similar for fraternal twins as it is for identical twins. Thus, if identical twins are more alike on a trait than fraternal twins, the greater similarity must be due to their shared genes. Some twin studies have been done with twins who have been raised apart, in many cases separated in infancy and raised by different families. In these special circumstances, the environments of twins may be quite different, but again the assumption is that the similarities or differences in environments will be about the same, on average, both for identical and for fraternal twins. Therefore, if identical twins are more alike than fraternal twins on some trait, genes are responsible. From such studies, researchers produce heritability estimates for a given trait, like intelligence. *Heritability* does not mean the same thing as inherited. It refers specifically to the degree to which differences among individuals on a trait may be the result of their having different genes. For many behavioral traits, like intelligence and some personality characteristics, such as introversion or extroversion and empathic concern, heritability estimates are around 50%, meaning that when people are different, about half of the variation is due to genetic differences. It does not mean that genes contribute half of an individual's intelligence or personality.

Adoption studies capitalize on the fact that adoptees share genes (50%), but not environments, with a biological parent and that they share environments, but not genes, with adoptive parents or siblings. If adoptees are more like their biological parents than their adoptive parents or siblings on some trait, it is assumed that heritability of the trait is the only explanation.

Twin and adoption studies have produced evidence of genetic contributions to behavioral traits from intelligence to gender atypical behavior to, yes, television viewing (e.g., Knafo, Iervolino, & Plomin, 2005; Plomin et al., 1990). Such studies have also provided evidence for differences in the heritability of behavioral characteristics that, on the surface, seem quite similar. For example, some antisocial behaviors appear to be more heritable than others. When antisocial behavior is accompanied by other problems, including early-onset hyperactivity and poor peer relationships, heredity seems to play a larger role than it does for other antisocial behavior that does not include these additional factors. Also, some kinds of crime, such as petty theft, appear to be more heritable than others, such as violent crime (Rutter, 1997; Silberg, et al., 1996).

When behavior geneticists estimate the proportion of trait variation that is affected by genes, they also produce estimates of the influence of the environment, both nonshared and shared environment (e.g., Hetherington, Reiss, & Plomin, 1994; Rutter, 1997). The degree to which identical twins tend to differ on some trait is considered a measure of the role of nonshared environment, that is, different environmental input. Because identical twins have exactly the same genes, when they differ on a characteristic, such as propensity for violent behavior, then their differences must be due to experiences that were not the same for both. Perhaps their parents treated them differently, or they became members of different crowds in high school. Alternatively, similarities between twins that go beyond estimates of genetic influence can be attributed to shared environment, that is, to having similar experiences. For example, behavior geneticists estimate a moderate effect of shared environment, like growing up in the same household, on children's intelligence.

Genetic Influences on Environments

Behavior geneticists have made the interesting observation that some environmental influences on behavior are themselves affected by a person's genes. There are three kinds of effects that genes can have on the environments that a developing individual experiences: passive, evocative, and active (Scarr & McCartney, 1983). First, passive effects are due to children and their parents sharing genes. Parents' genes affect the kind of environment that they create for their children. For example, suppose that parents have genes that contribute to musical talent. Because of their own musical interest and skill, such parents are likely to provide their children with exposure to music, opportunities for music education, and experiences with music that help to cultivate their children's own musical proclivities. When the genes of a parent lead to environmental experiences that are compatible with a child's own hereditary tendencies, the child's genes are a passive source of environmental influence.

Evocative gene influences on environment are important when an individual's genes affect his behavior, which in turn affects the reactions of others. Recently, for example, researchers have reported that adoptive children whose biological parents have a history of antisocial behavior frequently have adoptive parents who use negative, hostile forms of control with their adopted child. Apparently, children who are at genetic risk for the development of antisocial behavior may act in ways that tend to evoke negative parental behaviors, which in turn, researchers have found, tend to increase the antisocial behavior of the children (O'Connor, Deater-Deckard, Fulker, Rutter, & Plomin, 1998).

Active gene influences could be in play when people choose their own environments, companions, and activities. As children get older and are less constrained by their parents' choices, behavior geneticists argue that niche picking increases: People choose environments that are compatible with their interests (Scarr, 1992; Scarr & McCartney, 1983). These environments then provide support for and probably strengthen those interests. For example, a musically talented adolescent may choose friends with the same interests, and the social environment they create together encourages each member's continuing pursuit of music (see Rose, 2002). Another example is provided by long-term studies of antisocial children. As adults they tend to put themselves into high-risk environments, often by partnering with or marrying individuals who engage in criminal and addictive behavior. These companions and the environments they create then support the likelihood of continuing antisocial behavior (Champion, Goodall, & Rutter, 1995; Plomin, et al., 2003; Quinton, Pickles, Maughan, & Rutter, 1993). The description of passive, evocative, and active genetic effects on environments is consistent with the notion that children and adults play a role in shaping their own experiences. Recall from Chapter 1 that modern developmental theories, especially multidimensional models of development, posit that there are layers, or levels, of interacting causes of behavior. What happens at one level both causes and is

Niche picking: As children get older, they choose environments and companions that are compatible with their interests.

caused by what happens at other levels. There is little disagreement among modern developmental scientists about the bidirectional character of effects. What is often disputed, however, is the degree to which the individual's influence on his or her own environment can be traced specifically to the mediating effects of genes. Behavior geneticists have sometimes described the role of genes as if they had a direct line to behavior and, through behavior, to the environment. But many interacting causal layers of functioning exist between the physical/molecular level at which genes operate and the level of the social environment. Can behavior geneticists actually specify the impact of genes, per se, on behavior and the environment? At the present, we have clear evidence that genes are important, and we even have some information about which ones are important. What has yet to be deciphered is how specific genes express themselves behaviorally. In the next section, we will examine the relationships between genes and environment, with a critical eye to the contribution of the behavior genetics approach.

SHIFTING FOCUS TO THE COACTION OF GENES AND ENVIRONMENT

Behavior geneticists have made us aware that genes really do matter for the expression of behavior, but critics have argued that the approaches traditionally employed by behavioral genetics researchers can be misleading. There are two major sources of concern. First, studies of twins and adoptees seem to underestimate some environmental influences on behavior, overemphasizing heredity. Second, the assumption that genes and environment "add up" to produce behavioral outcomes appears to be a dramatic oversimplification of their joint effects.

Unexpected Sources of Environmental Effects

Behavior geneticists rely heavily on intensive study of twins and adoptees, and in both cases, researchers' assumptions may lead to underestimation of environmental effects on behavior. Let's first consider the problem of sorting out genetic versus environmental causes of behavior in twin studies. Many findings in this area come from studying identical twins separated in infancy and reunited in adulthood. A variety of behavioral characteristics are highly correlated in these monozygotic twin pairs, more highly correlated than in dizygotic or fraternal twins. Variations in traits such as extraversion, leadership, alienation, religious conviction, and so on appear to be strongly influenced by genes. Researchers assume that similarities between monozygotic twins raised apart can be attributed to the genes they share, but there may be confounding environmental effects even for the twins who are separated at birth. First, twins share a prenatal environment. In animal studies, many features of the uterine environment, such as temperature, gravity, chemical composition (Yoshinaga & Mori, 1989), location (Crews, 1994), and stress and nutrition (Morgane, et al., 1993) have been shown to make important contributions to later development.

Second, even after birth, many "separated" twins have spent some of their lives together. For participants in the large Minnesota Twin Study (Bouchard, Lykken, McGue, Segal, & Tellegen, 1990), for example, the average age at the time of separation was 5 months, the average age at reunion was 30 years, and the average age at testing was more than 10 years after reunion! Both before and after separation, then, there was plenty of time for shared environments to have had some influence on observed behavioral similarities.

When researchers compare identical to fraternal twins they usually assume that the environments of the two kinds of twins are equally similar or dissimilar. But identical twins may often have more similar experiences than fraternal twins. Some (though not all) monozygotic twins develop in the same placenta, for example; dizygotic twins do not. Identical twins are more likely to be dressed alike and may be treated alike in many other ways as well, so that behavioral similarities not found in fraternal twins could be the result of either shared genes *or* shared environment (Wahlsten, 2003).

When behavior geneticists study adoptees, they assume that adopted children share environment only with their adoptive families, not with their biological families. So, if the children are more like their biological mothers than their adoptive mothers or siblings, that similarity is attributed to shared genetics. However, we are learning that during prenatal development many environmental features affecting the mother are also experienced in some fashion by the fetus, so that either heredity or shared environment could contribute to a child's similarity to his biological mother. Shared environmental influences on prenatal development, like maternal stess and nutrition, are described later in this chapter, and in Box 2.1 we examine the impact of maternal sensory experiences on the developing fetus.

The Case for Coaction

Behavior genetics is based on an additive model: phenotype = genes + environment. Yet, as you will see, the contributions of genes and environment do not just add up. Rather, they interact in complex ways. In some environments, genes play a major role in affecting behaviors; in other environments, the same genes have less influence on outcomes (Gottlieb, 1992, 2003).

In the early 1970s, researchers who studied prenatal development began investigating the importance of environmental or exogenous experience in initiating and channeling developments (e.g., Gottlieb, 1970). Their approach reflected a significant shift from a unidirectional model (genes direct prenatal development) to a reciprocal view (gene activity affects and is affected by other levels of the system). It is now generally accepted among molecular biologists that genes do not by themselves produce finished products such as nerve cells, blue eyes, or behavioral patterns such as obsessive-compulsive disorder. In fact, Johnson (1998) reported that the use of the term *innate* has been dropped from use or even banned in some scientific writings of geneticists and ethologists. This is so because of the widespread recognition that the term is inaccurate. Nothing exists in the natural world that is purely genetic, with the exception of the genes themselves. As Gottlieb notes, "genes in themselves cannot cause development any more than stimulation in itself can cause development" (2003, p. 9).

Recall that when a gene is on, transcription of its code causes protein production in a cell. Proteins affect behavior indirectly by serving as the body's building blocks. They influence the structure of the brain, and they make up substances like hormones that affect both the brain and other internal organs, neurotransmitters that relay messages between neurons (see Chapter 4), and enzymes that synthesize or erase neurotransmitters. These substances do not, in and of themselves, directly cause particular behavioral manifestations. But they do contribute to behavioral tendencies or predispositions to react in certain ways.

| Box 2.1 | *Sensory Experience in the Prenatal Environment Helps Channel Later Food Preferences* |

In the final months of pregnancy, many of a mother's sensory experiences—for example, what she tastes and smells—are shared by her fetus. Research with pregnant women and young babies has established that these shared experiences can have effects on an infant's preferences, perhaps channeling later developments as well.

The developing fetus floats in amniotic fluid, a watery substance contained by a membrane called the amniotic sac. Amniotic fluid buffers the baby from bumps and helps maintain a constant temperature. Amniotic fluid is breathed and swallowed by the fetus after its respiratory and digestive systems begin to function.

Could the foods that mothers eat alter the taste and smell of the amniotic fluid? To answer this question, researchers have taken advantage of the fact that many women undergo a medical procedure called amniocentesis during their pregnancies, in which a small amount of amniotic fluid is extracted from the uterus with a special syringe.[1] Mennella, Johnson, and Beauchamp (1995) asked women undergoing routine amniocentesis if they would also participate in a study of fetal sensory experience. Mothers in one group ingested capsules of "essence of garlic" about 45 minutes before amniocentesis. Another group ingested capsules with an odorless liquid. Small samples of the amniotic fluid of all of the women were given to judges to "sniff." The judges described the odor as more like garlic in the samples from the women who ingested garlic, demonstrating that what mothers eat affects the smell of the amniotic fluid.

Could the tastes and smells of fetal experience affect babies' food preferences later? Mennella, Jagnow, and Beauchamp (2001) asked one group of women to drink carrot juice for 3 weeks during the last trimester of their pregnancy. A comparison group of women drank equivalent amounts of water during the same period. About 4 weeks after their babies had begun eating baby cereal, but before they had been given other solid foods (at about 5 to 6 months for most of the babies), the mothers were asked to feed their babies cereal mixed with carrot juice. Videotapes of the babies' behavior confirmed that the ones whose mothers drank carrot juice during their pregnancies reacted more positively to the carrot-flavored cereal than babies who had not had that prenatal exposure. Mennella et al. propose that prenatal odor and flavor experiences, mediated by the amniotic fluid that surrounds the developing fetus, may actually contribute to children's acceptance of, and preference for, the cuisine of their culture later in life. Their work is certainly a striking demonstration of the fact that a mother and baby share important experiences even before a baby's birth.

1. Amniocentesis is often recommended for older mothers whose offspring are at higher than average risk of experiencing some chromosomal abnormalities, like Down syndrome. Fetal cells from the fluid can be cultured and analyzed for chromosomal abnormalities, and DNA analyses can be done to identify some genetic defects in the fetus as well. The results may be used by genetic counselors to help expectant parents decide whether to continue a pregnancy or to begin planning for the needs of a special child. Other medical procedures, like chorionic villa sampling (CVS), are also now available for similar purposes. In CVS, a sample of the placenta is analyzed for chromosomal and DNA characteristics.

Gene transcription appears to be under the control of regulator genes, segments of DNA located near the coded genes. But how do regulator genes know when to turn on the coded genes? The action of the regulator genes is influenced by the environment of the cell, which in turn is affected by factors outside the cell. For example, circulating hormones, produced in the brain or elsewhere in the body, can affect regulator genes. The production of hormones themselves can be influenced by environmental conditions such as nutrition, stress, light, and so forth. Thus, genes and environment operate from the very beginning in an intricate pattern of coaction. "The activity of the genes can be affected through the cytoplasm of the cell by events originating at any other level in the system, including the external environment" (Gottlieb, 2003, p. 7).

One manifestation of coaction is that the same complement of genes produces different outcomes in different environments. You can see this process at the cellular level. Each cell of an organism has the same chromosomes and genes and therefore has the same developmental potential. But cells differentiate during fetal development, becoming structurally and functionally quite different, depending on their surrounding environments. For example, cells located in the anterior portion of an embryo develop into parts of the head, whereas cells located in the embryo's lateral portion develop into parts of the back, and so on. Something in the cell's chemical environment, perhaps influenced by some other level of the developing system, interacts with genetic material to direct the cell's developmental outcome.

Let's consider another example from the higher, postnatal level of brain development of rat pups that are exposed to enriched environmental stimulation after birth. When compared to pups with the same genetic makeup that are reared in social isolation, the enriched pups have more differentiated neuronal connections and show greater amounts of protein synthesis in their brains (Renner & Rosenzweig, 1987). At even higher levels of development, those involving whole behavioral systems, the genetic–environmental coaction principle also holds true. For example, Cierpal and McCarty (1987) discovered that pups of a particular rat strain with the genetic potential to become hypertensive will not develop hypertension unless reared by hypertensive mothers! Interestingly, genetically nonhypertensive rats will not develop hypertension if reared by hypertensive mothers. The expression of hypertension appears to depend upon some combination of the context created by the hypertensive mother and qualities of the hypertensive pup. Despite the fact that hypertensive rat pups have the genetic programming for hypertension, its functional expression is not inevitable and depends upon the environment.

Perhaps you are thinking that these results from animal studies do not apply to humans. However, biologists claim that there is no evidence at the molecular level to suggest that human prenatal development proceeds very differently from that of other animal species (Wahlsten & Gottlieb, 1997). In addition, the overwhelming majority of genes recognized as important for healthy human brain functioning are shared with many other vertebrate species. Furthermore, evidence is also accumulating from human infancy research to support the principle of coaction. In Boxes 2.2 and 2.3, we see coaction at work in human development. Striking findings with

---

Box 2.2 | *Genetic Influence on Intelligence: Now You See It, Now You Don't*

Standardized tests of intelligence, or IQ (intelligence) tests, provide a rough measure of an individual's learning and problem-solving skills. There has been a long-standing and sometimes bitter debate among scientists about whether IQ test scores are more heavily influenced by inherited capacities (nature), or by socialization practices and educational experience (nurture) (see Chapter 1). Behavior geneticists, using twin and adoption studies, have produced a range of heritability estimates that tend to average about 50%, interpreted to mean that about 50% of the variation among people on IQ scores can be attributed to heredity. But recent research has demonstrated that heritability estimates depend heavily on the socioeconomic status (SES) of the people being studied. Most previous studies have worked with middle-class samples. But in the newer work, people from impoverished backgrounds have been included, and the results are an object lesson in coaction.

Eric Turkheimer and his colleagues used data from the National Collaborative Perinatal Project to study the effects of heredity on IQ (Turkeheimer, Haley, Waldron, D'Onofrio, & Gottesman, 2003). Mothers from urban centers across the United States were enrolled during their pregnancies and the sample included a high proportion of racial minorities and impoverished families. Children were assessed at various times from birth through 7 years, when they were given a standardized intelligence test, the Wechsler Intelligence Scale for Children (WISC). At the 7-year-old assessment, there were 114 monozygotic twin pairs and 205 dizygotic twin pairs. Twenty-five percent of the families had incomes below the poverty line. The researchers estimated

the contribution of heredity, shared environment, and non-shared environment to IQ scores, but they computed these estimates taking SES into account. The amount of variance—or difference among IQ scores—that was attributed to genetic influence turned out to be dramatically different depending on the SES of the families. In the most affluent families, genes were estimated to contribute about 60% of the variance in IQ scores. But in the poorest families, the contribution of genes to IQ differences was close to zero!

Estimates of heritability have to be evaluated with caution. But these major differences in heritability estimates lead to one very clear conclusion: The environments in which genes operate substantially affect the impact that genes can have on outcomes. SES is an indicator of many environmental factors. As you will see throughout this text, compared to their more advantaged peers children in impoverished environments experience less adequate nutrition and health care, poorer air and water quality, more daily stress, more family turmoil, more violence and family separation, more authoritarian parenting, poorer quality day care and schools, and a greatly reduced range of opportunities to learn and to practice a wide variety of skills (Evans, 2004). The study by Turkheimer et al. (2003) suggests that in such impoverished environments genetic differences among individuals have little impact on their IQs. In more enriched environments, genetic differences are a more powerful source of interindividual differences in intellectual skill. As Turkheimer et al. conclude, "the developmental forces at work in poor environments are qualitatively different from those at work in adequate ones" (p. 628).

| Box 2.3 | *The Environment's Influence on Violent Behavioral Outcomes: Now You See It, Now You Don't* |

We can all cite examples of how differently people "turn out" despite their experience of the same difficult circumstances. For example, we read a report of unthinkable abuse visited upon a whole family of children by their parents. Later, one of the children also becomes an abusive husband and parent. His siblings may show other emotional or behavioral effects of the maltreatment, but they have no inclination to abuse their families or others. Research on parental abuse corroborates our informal observations: Experiencing early maltreatment increases the chances that a child will grow up to be a violent adult, but not all children who suffer from abuse will later victimize others (Bolger & Patterson, 2003).

Recent work in molecular genetics demonstrates that sometimes the differences in human outcomes that we see may have to do with genetic variation: The same environmental factors can have different effects on people who have different genotypes. Molecular geneticists have begun to identify some of the genes that affect the structure and function of the nervous system, including some genes that impact the production of hormones, neurotransmitters, and the enzymes that metabolize neurotransmitters. In some cases, genes come in different forms or alleles that geneticists can also identify through DNA testing techniques.

Among the genes that have been identified is the monoamine oxidase A (MAOA) gene. This X-linked gene occurs on the X chromosome but not on the Y chromosome and encodes the MAOA enzyme, which metabolizes a number of important neurotransmitters in the brain, like serotonin, norephinephrine, and dopamine. Its effect is to inactivate these neurotransmitters, a normal process in neurological functioning. In mice, if the MAOA gene is deleted, aggressive behavior increases. One very rare defective allele of this MAOA gene in humans is also linked to aggressive behavior. This defective gene results in no MAOA production at all. Males in one Dutch family with this allele were found to be more prone to violent, antisocial behavior than others in the

family who had a normal MAOA allele (Brunner, Nelen, Breakefield, Ropers, & van Oost, 1993). However, normal variations of the MAOA gene, some of which result in less MAOA production than others, do not seem to be related to aggressive behavior in humans.

Avshalom Caspi and his colleagues (2002) followed a trail of behavioral and genetic findings that led them to the following hypothesis: Variations in MAOA production caused by normal variations in the MAOA gene may have no effects on aggression in *normal* (nonabusive) environments, but some of these genetic variations might make children susceptible to the negative effects of early *abusive* environments. Specifically, they predicted that abused children who produce lesser amounts of MAOA enzyme would be more likely to become aggressive, antisocial adults than abused children who produce more MAOA enzyme.

Working with a large representative sample of New Zealand residents who had been followed from birth through age 26 in the Dunedin Multidisciplinary Health and Development Study, Caspi et al. (2002) analyzed each person's genotype and looked at four indicators of antisocial, aggressive behavior, such as diagnosis of conduct disorder during adolescence and convictions for violent crimes in adulthood. The variations in MAOA enzyme production were not associated with differences in aggressive behavior in the nonabused members of the sample; but MAOA enzyme production was correlated with violent behavior in those males who had experienced early maltreatment. Just as predicted, those abused males who produced less MAOA enzyme became more violent adults than those who produced more MAOA.

Again, we see the impact of gene–environment coaction. In this case, the same severe environmental characteristics have different effects depending on variations in heredity. Normal variations in the MAOA gene contribute substantially to different outcomes for children raised in abusive environments.

regard to human intelligence illustrate the impact of environment on gene action in humans (Box 2.2). We also see that variations in genotype can moderate the effects of an abusive environment on children's later antisocial behavior (Box 2.3).

The Epigenetic Model: A Multidimensional Perspective

The principle of coaction is the centerpiece of the epigenetic model, which is a type of multidimensional or systems theory of the nature–nurture relationship (see Chapter 1). The epigenetic model assumes that development is the result of interacting genetic and environmental elements, that these interactions are complex, and that they occur at multiple levels of functioning.

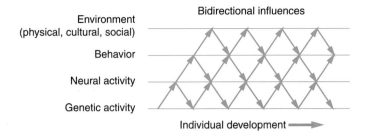

FIGURE 2.7

Gottlieb's Epigenetic Model of Gene/Environment Coaction (from Gottlieb, 1992).

Source: "Figure 14.3, p. 186", from *Individual Development and Evolution: The Genesis of Novel Behavior* by Gilbert Gottlieb, copyright © 1991 by Oxford University Press, Inc. Used by permission of Oxford University Press, Inc.

Ongoing developmental changes have effects that are bidirectional, with influences on both the environment and the biological system (Gordon & Lemons, 1997). Figure 2.7 illustrates many of the features of the epigenetic model as described by Gottlieb (1992). You can see that in this approach, genes, through their products, can affect an individual's neural activity; neural activity affects the individual's behavior; and behavior influences the external environment and the experiences that an individual is likely to have. Simultaneously, environmental influences channel or constrain behavior, which can alter neural activity and change genetic activity. Each level in this system can influence each of the other levels. The complexity of the multiple levels of interaction is somewhat mindboggling, but as Gottlieb (2003) points out, if anything this model represents a simplification of the many influences on any individual's behavior. "It is known, for example, that external environmental factors such as social interactions, changing day length, and so on can cause hormones to be secreted . . . and the hormones in turn result in the activation of DNA transcription inside the nucleus of the cell (i.e. 'turning genes on')" (p. 7).

Gottlieb (1991) provides an example of complex coaction in the development of acoustical recognition in animals. He demonstrated that animals need to be exposed to certain behaviors of their own species to develop normally. Typically, wood ducklings and mallard ducklings show a preference for the maternal calls of their own species. Across species, maternal calls differ in several critical acoustic dimensions. However, the ducklings' own vocalizations share some of the acoustic features of their own mothers' calls. Gottlieb hypothesized that the early experience of the newly hatched duckling, that is, hearing its own and its siblings' calls, helps establish the duckling's preference for maternal vocalizations. In other words, if ducklings were raised in incubators and were prevented from hearing either their own or their siblings' calls, they would be as likely to respond to the social signals of other species as those of their own species. This is exactly what happened in the experiment. When ducklings were prevented from hearing their own species-specific calls, they did not show their selective response and were likely to respond to the maternal calls of other species. (This is a little like toddlers responding in a similar way to any adult who calls their names.) For ducklings, early exposure to the calls of their own species inoculates them against the possibility of extraspecific responsivity.

The development of species-specific acoustic responsivity is an example of canalization, a kind of developmental outcome that is not really learning but a limiting or channeling of behavior over the course of ontogenesis. Once established, the behavior is unlikely to change, so there is a decrease in plasticity over time. In this elegant experiment, Gottlieb (1991) demonstrated that canalization does not represent just the unfolding of a genetically determined capacity. Rather, environmental experience plays an important role in the development of this particular kind of behavior. Gottlieb proposed that "canalization can take place not only at the genetic level, but at all levels of the developing system, including the developing organism's usually occurring experiences" (p. 5).

In humans, similar processes appear to be at work. Reiss and Neiderhiser (2000), summarizing evidence from their studies of adolescent social relationships, suggest that for some children, qualities, such as irritability, that appear to have a heritable component evoke negative reactions from other members of their social worlds. In response, the social environment for these youngsters becomes hostile, further supporting the expression of genetically influenced tendencies toward irritability. These authors propose that heritable tendencies can be modified by environmental circumstances that do not support their expression. Speaking about adolescents, they hypothesize that

> most, but not all, parents, peers, teachers, and best friends react adversely to a difficult child. The "off-diagonal" responders—the ones who do not respond to provocations—may hold the key to the powerful suppression achieved by positive social environments on adverse genetic influences. Those environments that do not respond adversely may interrupt a fundamental mechanism of socially mediated gene expression as effectively, and more selectively and safely, than pharmacological agents that are currently used to block the transcription of DNA into RNA (p. 365).

As we noted earlier, the behavior genetics approach to studying the role of genetics in behavior has been criticized for its dependence on a simple additive model, seemingly ignoring the complex, ever-present coaction of heredity and environment. But modern behavior genetics research is marked by a more integrative approach to genetic and environmental influences. Heritability estimates are recognized to be only rough indicators of potential genetic involvement in outcomes, and they are seen as variable, depending on environmental circumstances (Dick & Rose, 2002).

Behavior genetics began with the goal of demonstrating to a sometimes doubting clinical and scientific community that genes influence behaviors of many kinds. With this goal clearly reached, recent work pays equal attention to genetics and social and environmental factors, as demonstrated by increased efforts to understand the contribution of genotype-environment interaction on behavior (see Reiss, Neiderhiser, Hetherington, & Plomin, 2000). *Genotype-environment interaction* refers to the way genes express themselves, for good or for ill, within particular environmental circumstances, and sounds much like coaction.

An interesting and complex picture of genetic influences on behavior is emerging from these newer investigations. For example, genes appear to exert their influence on behavior at all stages of the life span. Some influence behavior early in life, whereas others, such as genetic influences on maternal attachment or antisocial behavior, appear to become important in adolescence or adulthood (see Lyons et al., 1995). Contrary to what many people think, genetic influences on certain behaviors can be stronger at later points in the life course than at earlier points. Consider intelligence, for example. Genetic influences increase rather than decrease as children approach adolescence (Plomin, Fulker, Corley, & DeFries, 1997). Most important, many recent studies by behavior geneticists have been designed to investigate just how closely tied gene action is to environmental influences, as we see in the work of Turkheimer in Box 2.2.

Despite the fact that an oversimplified view of the nature–nurture controversy is still remarkably tenacious, either-or dualism is truly out-of-date. To ask which of the two, nature or nurture, is more important is a little like asking which element is more important in salt, sodium or chlorine. Clearly, the interplay of genes and environment must be considered in any comprehensive theory of development. In the next section, we begin a description of developmental change from conception onward, a process that at every stage is a function of bidirectional and complexly interacting genetic and environmental influences.

HEALTHY PRENATAL DEVELOPMENT

The amazing story of human prenatal development is one of orderly and continuous progress from a single fertilized cell to a highly differentiated organism with many interconnected and efficiently functioning systems. The principle of coaction operates at every level of this developmental drama—with genes and environment in constant communication. Typically the 9-month gestational period is divided into three parts, which reflect the kind of development taking place at each specific period of time. The period of the ovum spans the first 3 weeks of pregnancy, from the time of fertilization through implantation into the uterine lining to the development of the neural tube, the rudimentary beginnings of the central nervous system. The period of the embryo lasts from the fourth week through the eighth week of gestation. During this time, most of the body's organ systems and structures are forming. Nature has determined that this progression move in a "head-to-tail" (called cephalo-caudal) as well as "near-to-far" (called proximo-distal) direction. Thus, the head forms before the legs, and the most vital inner organs form before the extremities. The period of the fetus, lasting from the ninth week until birth, characterizes a time of rapid growth and further differentiation. The reproductive system forms, gains in body weight occur, and the brain and nervous system continue to develop. Refer again to Figure 2.5 for more information.

Genetic Interventions

What can be done to promote a healthy start? From the helper's point of view, there is much that can be done, even before the baby is born. Interventions can address either of the major players, genes or environment. Recent advances in genetic research promise revolutionary treatments based upon the detection of genes or disease-causing mutations within the genes that are involved in inherited disorders, birth defects, or other medical conditions. It is hoped that the genetic map that was the crowning achievement of the Human Genome Project will eventually provide a guide for identifying where specific disease genes are located so that interventions can be applied.

What are the benefits that can come from this kind of information? First, we will be able to diagnose more reliably those conditions that are presently inferred from clinical evaluations. It is possible to detect the genetic markers for disorders in advance of the presence of the symptoms both in the person with the disease and in the person who is a carrier of the disease. Understanding the genetic contribution to disease is also a first step in the possible development of vaccines. Recently, researchers investigating diabetes discovered that a certain gene in mice (called GAD) influences the production of a protein (called glutamate acid decarboxylase) that, when circulating in the body, triggers an immune system response that kills cells involved in insulin production (Yoon et al., 1999). This knowledge may, in time, result in the production of a vaccine that could desensitize the body to the presence of the GAD gene and protect the insulin-producing cells. These innovative treatments hold more promise for physical rather than for behavioral disorders, given the extraordinary complexity of the polygenic influences associated with the latter.

In addition to diagnosis, screening, and the development of vaccines, researchers are currently using genetic research to develop methods that would replace or correct defective genes. This kind of gene therapy, although still very experimental, holds out the hope for a cure for genetically caused diseases. Two possible approaches are under investigation: somatic cell therapy, which involves insertion of healthy genes into appropriate tissue, and germline gene therapy, which involves altering the sperm or egg cells to pass on healthy genes to future generations (e.g., Gelehrter & Collins, 1990; Smith 2002, 2003).

Most of these methods, however, are still in the experimental stage and are prohibitively expensive. Clinical trials have met with more failures than successes at this point. Because this field is so new, very little is known about the possible side effects of genetic manipulations. Interventions such as these also raise many serious ethical questions about the appropriateness of treatment and who should be able to get it. Certainly these are questions that helpers will be asked to help their clients deal with as genetic treatment options become more commonplace in the future. At this time, however, let us consider the kinds of cost-effective, environmental approaches that have been well established to help the most people. What can be done to promote healthy practices during the prenatal period? To answer this question, it is important to understand the mechanisms through which development can go awry.

Environmental Influences on Prenatal Development

Teratogens

Many agents and circumstances can cause harm to the developing fetus. Public health efforts have made great strides in alerting the general population to the risks faced by the developing fetus during pregnancy. Despite what appears to be a relatively recent concern, it is interesting to note that even the ancient Greeks, like Hippocrates who wrote 2,500 years ago, recognized that ingestion of certain drugs particularly during the early stages of pregnancy could weaken the fetus and cause it to be misshapen. Those substances or agents, which produce fetal deformities when taken or absorbed by the mother during pregnancy, are called teratogens. The fetus is surrounded by a placenta, an organ that develops with the fetus and exchanges blood products

TABLE 2.4   Selected Teratogens

Legal and Illegal Drugs	Effects on Fetus	Safe Dosage	References
Alcohol	Great variability in outcome. May include: distinct facial structure, cardiac, skeletal, & urogenital abnormalities; dental abnormalities, growth deficiencies, metacognitive deficits, attentional problems, social perception problems, language deficits, & other learning problems.	No safe dosage during pregnancy	Stressiguth, A. P., Aase, J. M., Clarren, S. K., Randels, S. P., LaDue, R. A., & Smith, D. F. (1991). Fetal alcohol syndrome in adolescents and adults. *Journal of the American Medical Association, 265*, 1961–1967.
Tobacco	Low birth weight due to constricted blood flow and reduced nutrition; prematurity; respiratory problems, cleft palate; learning problems, hyperactivity.	No safe dosage during pregnancy	Floyd, R. L., Rimer, B. K., Giovino, G. A., Mullen, P. D., & Sullivan, S. E. (1993). A review of smoking in pregnancy: Effects on pregnancy outcomes and cessation efforts. *Annual Review of Public Health, 14*, 379–411.
Cocaine	Prematurity or stillbirth, low birth weight; drug withdrawal after birth including irritability, restlessness, tremors; medically and psychologically fragile; higher rates of later learning problems and ADHD.	No safe dosage during pregnancy	Bateman, D., Ng, S., Hansen, C., & Heagarty, M. (1993). The effects of interuterine cocaine exposure in newborns. *American Journal of Public Health, 83*, 190–194.
Marijuana	Less well studied: some data to link its use to neurological effects; low birth weight, learning problems, etc.	No safe dosage during pregnancy	Dahl, R. E., Scher, M. S., Williamson, D. E., Robles, N., & Day, N. (1995). A longitudinal study of prenatal marijuana use: Effects on sleep and arousal at age 3 years. *Archives of Pediatric and Adolescent Medicine, 149*, 145–150.
Infections			
AIDS	Transmitted through contact with maternal blood via the placenta or at delivery. Causes damage to immune system, facial abnormalities, growth problems, brain disorders, developmental delays; usually fatal.		Nozyce, M., Hittelman, J., Muenz, L., Durako, S. J., Fisher, M., & Willoughby, A. (1994). Effect of perinatally acquired human immunodeficiency virus infection on neurodevelopment during the first two years of life. *Pediatrics, 94*, 883–891.
Environmental Hazards			
Lead	Prematurity, low birth weight, brain damage, mental retardation, physical deformities.		Dye-White, E. (1986). Environmental hazards in the work setting. Their effect on women of childbearing age. *American Association of Occupational Health and Nursing Journal, 43*, 76–78.
PCBs (Polychlorinated biphenyls)	Low birth weight, cognitive impairments.		Jacobson, J. L., Jacobson, S. W., Padgett, R. J., Brumitt, G. A., & Billings, R. L. (1992). Effects of prenatal PCB exposure or cognitive processing efficiency and sustained attention. *Dev. Psych., 28*, 297–306.

with the baby through the umbilical cord. The placenta allows nutrients from the mother's blood to pass into the baby's blood and allows waste to be removed by the mother's blood, but otherwise it keeps the two circulatory systems separate. Teratogens can cross the placental barrier. They include some drugs and other chemicals, certain disease organisms, and radioactivity. The name comes from the Greek and literally means "monstrosity making." The list of known teratogens is quite lengthy, so we have presented in Table 2.4 a summary of the main characteristics of a few of the most well-researched agents. A few principles are helpful to understand in guiding your thinking about the operation of these causes of birth defects. Generally, the potential for harm is impossible to determine with absolute precision. Rather, what happens to the developing organism depends upon several conditions (Wilson, 1973).

The first principle is that the kind of damage done is related to the stage of development during which the mother is exposed to the teratogen. If, for example, exposure to some harmful substance occurs during the fourth or fifth week of gestation when the major organ systems are being laid down, the result may be major structural malformation. If the mother is exposed to the same teratogen during the last month of her pregnancy, possible neurobehavioral rather than gross structural deficits may occur. Rubella, or German measles, contracted during the first trimester of pregnancy can produce blindness, deafness, heart defects, and mental retardation. However, if the infection occurs during the second trimester, less severe problems involving vision and hearing may result. It is important to note that although prenatal development can be divided into trimesters or periods (e.g., ovum, embryo, fetus) for convenience sake, development is orderly and continuous throughout gestation. "At any time in the total span of development, these ongoing processes can be subtly deflected, severely perturbed, or abruptly halted, resulting in death or abnormal development" (Stratton, Howe, & Battaglia, 1996, p. 37).

A second principle is that not all developing organisms will be susceptible to teratogenic effects. Both the mother's and the baby's genes play a role in sensitivity or resistance to a teratogen. A teratogen that is harmful to one individual may produce different outcomes or no outcome in another individual. These differences appear to be related to specific characteristics such as metabolism rates or variations in placental structure. Streissguth and Dehaene (1993) report that monozygotic (identical) twins, who are alike genetically, show more similar patterns of alcohol-related birth defects than dizygotic (fraternal) twins, who share only about one half of their genes. These data suggest that genes play a role in moderating the influence of alcohol on the developing fetus. Other researchers (e.g., Sonderegger, 1992) have found that male fetuses are more susceptible than female fetuses to the effects of teratogens.

A third principle is that adverse outcomes also depend upon dosage amount. Larger amounts of a teratogenic agent over longer periods of time generally have more potent effects than smaller doses over shorter periods. For example, babies who are exposed to alcohol prenatally may be born with fetal alcohol syndrome (FAS), which is identifiable in its victims by virtue of their unique facial configuration (small head, widely spaced eyes, flattened nose, and so on). In addition to the facial characteristics, children with FAS may also suffer from mental retardation and behavior problems. Children exposed to smaller amounts of alcohol prenatally do not necessarily have to meet the diagnostic criteria of FAS to exhibit deficits. Such children are said to exhibit fetal alcohol effects (FAE). Recent research has identified significant learning impairments in children who had been prenatally exposed to alcohol but who did not have the physical features or growth deficiencies of FAS children. The researchers concluded that the absence of physical symptoms or structural malformations does not rule out serious cognitive limitations from prenatal alcohol exposure (Mattson, Riley, Gramling, Delis, & Jones, 1998).

The possible toxic effects of a teratogen such as alcohol can be construed to range along a continuum from no observable effect to one that is lethal to the embryo or fetus. If the amount of alcohol ingested by the mother exceeds that of the no observable effect level, the fetus will experience some functional impairment (lowest observable adverse effect level) but may sustain structural malformations only as dosage is increased. This hypothetical dose–response relationship presumes that the effects of alcohol ingestion on the fetus are always more potent than they are on the mother. In other words, the fetus may have crossed the toxic threshold even if the mother experiences few or very mild alcohol-related effects (Stratton et al., 1996). Consequently, as the Surgeon General has warned, there is no safe level of alcohol consumption during pregnancy.

A final principle regarding the effects of teratogens is that their negative effects can be amplified if the fetus or infant is exposed to more than one risk factor. For example, mothers who take cocaine typically use other drugs such as alcohol, marijuana, tobacco, and heroin and have poorer nutrition. They may also experience more poverty and stress during and after pregnancy than other women. Drug effects are therefore confounded by, and can be amplified by, the effects of the maternal lifestyle, and the results of these interacting risk factors are not yet well understood (Lester, Freier, & LaGasse, 1995). Generally, babies born to cocaine-abusing mothers are at increased risk for poor developmental outcomes. Bendersky and Lewis (1998) found that infants exposed to cocaine use prenatally showed less enjoyment during playful interactions with their mothers and had more difficulty calming themselves after they sustained a period of maternal nonresponsiveness. The result was still significant when other variables (such as abuse of other drugs, bad environmental conditions) were controlled. This evidence points to cocaine's negative impact on regulation of arousal, which can have an impact on the child's social interactions. Needless to say, the presence of other deleterious factors, such as nonresponsive parenting, can only exacerbate the situation. Thus, babies who were prenatally exposed to cocaine benefit from a stabilizing environment, and their postnatal risks are reduced.

NUTRITION

Teratogens are problematic because they add something to the ordinary fetal environment, intruding on the developing system and driving it off course. But what happens when contextual factors that belong in the ordinary fetal environment are missing or in short supply? A rapidly growing body of evidence reveals that when food sources are short on protein or essential vitamins and minerals during prenatal and early postnatal development, an infant's physical, socio-emotional, and intellectual development can be compromised (Eysenck & Schoenthaler, 1997). For example, Rush, Stein, and Susser (1980) provided nutritional supplements to pregnant women whose socioeconomic circumstances indicated that they were likely to experience inadequate diets. At age 1, the babies whose mothers received a protein supplement during pregnancy performed better on measures of play behavior and perceptual habituation (which is correlated with later intelligence) than those whose mothers received a high-calorie liquid or no supplement at all (Rush et al., 1980).

Are there longer term behavioral consequences of prenatal nutrition? Some research does reveal enduring effects. For example, in a study of Guatemalan village populations, pregnant women and later their children received either daily protein supplements or supplements consisting of a low-calorie drink (a placebo). Children who had received protein supplements both pre- and postnatally were generally larger than those who received the placebo, and there were cognitive and behavioral effects as well. Follow-ups of the children at age 4 indicated that differences in social and cognitive functioning could be traced to the amount or kind of supplement they had received. But the longer term follow-ups were perhaps the most interesting: The children who received the protein supplements both prenatally and for 2 years postnatally continued to show benefits in adolescence, long after the supplements had been discontinued, performing better on a variety of cognitive measures, such as reading achievement, vocabulary comprehension, and number skills, with children in the lowest socioeconomic groups benefiting most. Thus, some advantages of good early nutrition seem to be long range (Barrett, Radke-Yarrow, & Klein, 1983; Pollitt, Gorman, Engle, Martorell, & Rivera, 1993; Townsend, Klein, Irwin, Owens, Yarbrough, & Engle, 1982).

It is not surprising that prenatal nutrition has such effects, given what we have learned about the effects of postnatal nutrition on children's functioning. We have known for decades that children who suffer severe protein and calorie shortages at any age may develop kwashiorkor, characterized by stunted growth, a protuberant belly, and extreme apathy (Williams, 1933). Therapeutic diets can eliminate the apathy of kwashiorkor, but cognitive impairments are likely to persist (e.g., Yatkin & McClaren, 1970). Some research indicates that much less severe nutritional deficits may have impacts on children's cognitive functioning. An intriguing study of changes in the food supplied to New York City schools provides a strong illustration (Schoenthaler, Doraz, & Wakefield, 1986). In a three-stage process, from 1978 to 1983, many food additives and foods high in sugar (sucrose) were eliminated from school meals, so that children's consumption of "empty calories" was reduced, and, presumably, their intake of foods with a higher nutrient-to-calorie ratio increased. With each stage of this process, average achievement test scores increased in New York City schools, with improvements occurring primarily among the children who were performing worst academically.

Findings such as these suggest that children whose prenatal and postnatal environments are short on protein and other essential nutrients may not achieve the levels of behavioral functioning that they could have with adequate diets. But the long-range impact of early diet, like the effects of teratogens, depends in part on the presence or absence of other risk factors. Recall that in the Guatemala study, children for whom protein supplements made the most difference were from the poorest homes. Although these children may have been the most nutritionally deprived, most of the other participants in this study experienced protein-poor diets as well. Other aspects of being poor apparently made the dietary inadequacies more problematic. Poor children, for example, are likely to have limited access to education and health care; they may have more than average exposure to unsanitary conditions and infectious agents; they may be more subject to unresponsive care or even abuse than other children, and so on. When children are not exposed to multiple risk factors, long-range effects of prenatal or postnatal malnutrition are less apparent. For example, studies of economically advantaged children subjected to early malnutrition due to illness or to the privations of war have not found long-term cognitive or behavioral deficits (Hart, 1993; Pollit et al., 1996; Stein, Susser, Saenger, & Marolla, 1975). Apparently, social, educational, and medical advantages help moderate the effects of early food deprivation. As we saw in Chapter 1, any single developmental risk factor, either biological or environmental, often has its effects lessened by other more benign influences. It is in combination that risk factors do the most harm. One heartening consequence is that when we intervene to reduce one risk factor, such as malnutrition, we may actually modify the impact of other negative influences on development as well.

STRESS

Stress seems to be the affliction of our modern age, and coping with stress has become a cottage industry. It is routine to hear experts tell us that we should avoid stress. Buoyed by research on the relationship of stress and health, employers commonly sponsor "stress-management" seminars. Stores are full of stress-relieving vitamins and relaxation-enhancing gadgets. If stress has an important part to play in the health of an adult, what is its impact on the well-being of the unborn child? To answer that question, we need to look at what we know about the effects of stress on the body in general.

Stress is an unavoidable part of life, and despite its negative connotation, it is not all bad. The happy anticipation of a new baby is for many couples a form of positive stress, or eustress as defined by Selye (1980). This can be contrasted to distress, which refers to the kinds of frustrations, conflicts, pressures, and negative events that people experience in their lives either intermittently or chronically. The body has a characteristic way of handling these stressors, which involves three stages: the alarm phase, during which the activity of the sympathetic nervous system and adrenal glands increases in preparation for flight or fight; the resistance phase, during which the body is moderately aroused, the parasympathetic system takes over, and the body continues to resist the effects of the stressor; and finally, the exhaustion phase, which occurs if the struggle persists to the point that the body's resources are depleted. Depression, illness, or even death can occur after severe, prolonged stress.

The actual physical response of the body to stress involves what is called the hypothalamic-pituitary-adrenal (HPA) axis, which works something like this. When a person experiences or anticipates stress, the amygdala, or one part of the brain that controls emotions, detects the danger and immediately informs the hypothalamus, a small centrally located region in the midbrain (see Chapter 3 for information on brain structure). Next, the hypothalamus communicates the danger message to the pituitary gland, which is positioned directly below it. The message is read by the pituitary as a sign to release adrenocorticotropic hormone, or ACTH, into the bloodstream. ACTH makes its way to the adrenal glands, situated atop the kidneys, which receive the message to release epinephrine, norepinephrine, and cortisol. Some of these so-called stress hormones (particularly cortisol) then travel back to the brain and bind to receptors on the amygdala and the hippocampus.

Children whose prenatal or postnatal environments are nutritionally deficient may suffer long-term cognitive deficits.

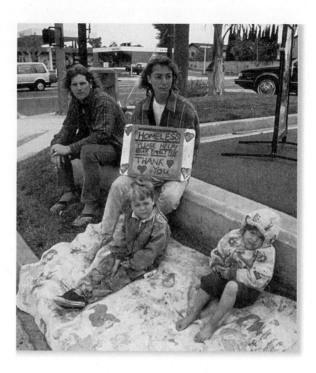

So far, so good. Hormones such as epinephrine and norepinephrine prepare the body to resist the stressor by sending a burst of energy to those parts of the body necessary for fighting or fleeing (e.g., heart, lungs) while diverting energy from less necessary systems (e.g., digestion, reproduction). Cortisol acts to increase blood glucose levels and to suppress the immune response. Under normal conditions, the returning cortisol tells the hippocampus to alert the HPA axis to slow down its attack because all is well. The problems start when stress is prolonged and a communication gap develops between the hippocampus's messages to "cease and desist" and the amygdala's "fire away" message. Ultimately, the hippocampus becomes unable to shut down the stress response effectively, and the individual's stress-response system may become chronically activated, putting a great deal of wear and tear on the body. The capability of the immune system to fight infection and ward off disease is compromised. Growth hormone is suppressed. Long-term negative effects on cardiovascular and nervous system functioning result. Some studies have found damaged or shrunken nerve cells in the hippocampus of humans and animals exposed to traumatic or social stressors. For example, McEwen and Sapolsky (1995) reported that the hippocampi of veterans with posttraumatic stress disorder (PTSD) were 25% smaller than those of a control group, causing those veterans significant problems in memory formation and retrieval despite the fact that they had otherwise normal brains. It is not yet clear whether such effects are due to an excess of cortisol, pumped in from the agitated adrenals, or to a highly sensitized cortisol-response system, but it is clear from studies such as these that a negative relationship exists between excessive stress and memory functions.

All of this leads us back to our discussion of early fetal development. The increased levels of stress hormones secreted by the pregnant mother under stress can cross the placental barrier and eventually affect the developing child in a number of ways. First, these hormones will contribute to the shaping of the infant's own neuroendocrine system, which will greatly influence responsivity to stimulation, activity rhythms, and ability to modulate and regulate behavior. The relationships between maternal stress and neonatal hyperactivity and irritability have been well documented (Levine, 1969). Second, heightened levels of maternal epinephrine decrease blood flow to the uterus and, ultimately, to the placenta. Consequently, oxygen flow to the fetus is reduced (Nathanielz, 1992). Third, evidence from animal studies suggests that sexual orientation may be altered by severe maternal stress during pregnancy. The timing of the stress and the release of stress hormones interfere with fetal testosterone production and affect the sexual orientation of male offspring (Ward, 1992). Finally, as we have seen, hormones influence the expression of the genes and work in coaction with them to direct development. The impact of the stress hormones on the developing brain can be lasting and profound, as in the case of damage to the cells of the hippocampus. The stress experienced by mothers can actually alter the environment in which their unborn children develop and can lead the children to be hyperreactive to stress later on (Lederman, 1996). Some studies relate maternal stress during pregnancy with children's increased risk of psychopathology. O'Connor, Heron, Golding, Glover, and the ALSPAC Study Team (2003) followed a large sample of mother–child dyads from late pregnancy through the children's 7th birthday. Mothers' reports of stress and anxiety during pregnancy predicted children's behavioral problems both at 4 years and again at 7 years old, even when controlling for other risk factors like mothers' postpartum depression. Although the precise relationship between prenatal exposure to stress and later psychopathology is still being investigated, many researchers agree that early exposure can produce lasting biological changes (Benes, 1994; Chrousos & Gold, 1999). We should remember, however, that postnatal environmental factors, such as positive child-rearing experiences, can modify the effects of early deleterious exposure (Meyer, Chrousos, & Gold, 2001).

APPLICATIONS

In this chapter we have summarized information that is important for understanding how human life begins and develops. Those time-honored players, nature and nurture, take center stage as the story unfolds. What is the point of this theoretical debate for someone in the helping professions? It is far from an "ivory-tower" issue, as we have noted before. A bias in either of the possible directions, toward nature or nurture, can powerfully affect attitudes and expectations about behavior. These attitudes and expectations will be communicated directly or indirectly to clients, parents, and others who come to us for help. For example, a tendency to view genetics as the powerful "quarterback" (Scarr & McCartney, 1983) of the nature–nurture team may tip the balance in favor of reliance on oversimplified genetic explanations for academic, social, or emotional difficulties. It may predispose the helper to minimize environmental influences and to suggest medical or psychopharmacological remedies as the routine way of handling problems. It could discourage a helper (and the helper's clients) from working on a problem because the problem is framed as virtually impossible to change, a belief that is clearly unsupported by the evidence we have presented. One of the author's students told her about a fifth-grade youngster she was counseling in the schools. This young girl had made repeated visits to the counselor (as well as to the principal!) for a number of behavioral missteps during the school year. Sarah (not her real name) usually got into trouble for acting out, talking during class, and so on, and understandably exasperated her well-meaning teacher. Attempting to explain her side of the story to the counselor, Sarah blurted out, "What they don't understand, Mrs. Johnson, is that people like you were born to follow the rules and I was not. It's all *genetic*!" Imagine how powerfully this explanation has permeated our culture if even grade school students use it to make attributions for causality.

A bias in the other direction, toward nurture, could predispose a helper to hold unrealistically high expectations for what can be changed. It may encourage a comparably simplistic, molecular approach to problem solving in situations that are complicated and multilayered. Also, it could promote a kind of intolerance for diverse expressions of human behavior and personality by attempting to change behavior deemed inappropriate. In some ways, the emphasis on nurture may place too much responsibility on the individual, or perhaps on parents of children, to produce outcomes that may not be possible given the niche-picking tendencies of their offspring. Seligman (1993) has described the collision between helpers' cherished beliefs in self-improvement and advances in biological psychiatry. Just peruse the self-help section of your local bookstore, and you will be bombarded with texts that promise recipes for changing everything from weight to shyness to unruly children. The proliferation of quick-fix advice found in books, magazines, TV, and radio feeds the notion that physical, behavioral, emotional, intellectual, and social change is a combination of the "right" strategy and some good, old-fashioned willpower. Seligman cautions that an ideology that holds that all human problems are the result of poor environmental conditions is "seriously incomplete" (p. 7).

Genetic Counseling

Counselors frequently help clients with issues that directly or indirectly involve inherited medical conditions. These problems can affect individuals and their families at any time during the life span, from preconception to later life. For example, a client might struggle with the decision to seek testing for an inherited disorder before having children or another might wrestle with the decision to be tested for breast cancer because of a close relative's diagnosis. Often these issues require that helping professionals refer to or collaborate with genetic counselors who have expertise in this area (Bodenhorn & Lawson, 2003).

With recent progress in our understanding of the human genome, the specialty area of genetic counseling has come into its own. This profession is situated at the juncture of genetics and counseling, requiring extensive knowledge in human genetics and training in counseling skills and techniques. Often employed in medical settings, genetic counselors help people with or at risk of genetic disorders understand and manage their conditions. The field has established science-based professional guidelines to assist practitioners in decision making and to ensure ethical practice based on the most currently available knowledge of diagnostic procedures and treatments (Bennett, Pettersen, Niendorf, & Anderson, 2003b).

Some objectives of genetic counseling are psychoeducational. People who are considering genetic testing for a disorder need to understand the implications of testing, the extent of the information that can be ascertained, and all the ramifications of the answers on their lives. This calls for a balanced blend of expert knowledge and support as described by Bennett and colleagues:

> The traditional dogma that genetic counseling must be nondirective is being challenged in favor of a psychosocial approach that emphasizes shared deliberation and decision making between the counselor and the client. The genetic counseling intervention is designed to reduce the client's anxiety, enhance the client's sense of control and mastery over life circumstances, increase the client's understanding of the genetic disease and options for testing and disease management, and provide the individual and the family with the tools required to adjust to potential outcomes. (Bennett, Hampel, Mandel, and Marks, 2003a, p. 1275)

Typically, the process begins with constructing a pedigree or graphic depiction of inheritance patterns, based on family medical records and careful psychosocial and developmental history (Bennett et al., 2003a). Counselors then help clients determine risks and educate them about possible choices of action. If genetic testing is performed, counselors help clients manage the psychological and material consequences of the diagnostic results. Depending upon the outcome of testing, some common counseling issues that may surface in this process include anger, anxiety, denial, guilt, rationalization, grief, and shattered hopes. Another component of the counseling process can include helping clients plan for medical management of disorders.

Healthy Baby Guidelines

As you have read in this chapter, certain practices really do promote healthy prenatal development and others put the fetus's well-being at substantial risk.

1. One of the most well-established recommendations offered to pregnant women is to eat a healthy diet that includes a variety of foods. To prevent the risk of brain and spinal birth defects, foods high in folic acid should be eaten regularly and supplemented by a multivitamin.

2. Because alcohol is such a powerful teratogen, its consumption during pregnancy should be completely eliminated. Drugs, both legal and illegal, and cigarettes should be avoided as well because of their potential to damage the fetus. The spouses or partners of pregnant women should also avoid dangerous substances, both to provide support for their partners and to reduce the availability of the substance in the home. If a woman must take prescription medication for preexisting conditions such as epilepsy, bipolar disorder, cancer, or thyroid dysfunction, she should inform her physician, if possible, when she is considering a pregnancy and certainly if she suspects she is pregnant. No over-the-counter medication should be taken without the advice of a physician. Even the innocuous aspirin tablet, if taken in excess during the last trimester, can prolong labor and cause excessive bleeding. Herbal supplements should be taken only with the approval of a health care provider. Exposure to toxic chemicals like lead, solvents, mercury, paint, paint thinners, and so on should be avoided.

3. Stress, particularly if chronic and serious, can be detrimental to a healthy pregnancy. Every effort should be made to provide social support and to reduce ongoing interpersonal conflict during this time. Fathers and extended family members are likely support-system candidates. When they are not available, the helper must use creative means to provide for contacts (support groups, church members, agency contacts, etc.) who will lend a listening ear and a helping hand to mothers-to-be experiencing the emotional upheaval of pregnancy.

4. Good medical care is one of the most important elements in a healthy pregnancy and delivery. Research has shown that it is significantly associated with fewer birth complications and lower rates of infant mortality (Kotch, Blakely, Brown, & Wong, 1992). Pregnant women should see their health care provider early in the pregnancy and frequently thereafter.

Helping the Most Vulnerable: Preterm and Low-Birth-Weight (LBW) Babies

For some populations, primarily women who live in poverty, who abuse drugs and alcohol, who are unmarried or teenagers, or who live in highly stressful circumstances, the stakes are higher during pregnancy. Poverty, teratogens, insufficient prenatal care, and inadequate health insurance are all associated with the risk of delivering an infant preterm (less than 37 weeks gestation) or of low birth weight (less than 5 pounds, 8 ounces). From 2000 to 2001, approximately 16% of infants in the United States were born with disorders related to prematurity and LBW, the leading cause of death for neonates—from birth through 28 days (Anderson & Smith, 2003). Preterm and LBW infants who survive are much more likely to suffer from a number of chronic medical problems such as respiratory infections; delays in achievement of developmental milestones; behavioral problems; feeding problems; and low IQ and related academic consequences, such as grade retention, dropping out of high school, and increased need for special education services for learning disabilities and ADHD (Conley & Bennett, 2002; Wallace & McCarton, 1997). The price of prevention seems eminently reasonable, given the huge burden associated with preterm and LBW births both in human and economic terms.

The Healing Touch

Touch has long been recognized as one of the primary forms of human communication, bonding, and healing (Hertenstein, 2002), and it appears to be the infant's best developed sense at birth (Reisman, 1987). Field and her associates have applied the power of touch to enhance the development of preterm and LBW infants by developing a standard infant massage therapy protocol. Outcome studies of this intervention demonstrate that massage is effective for increasing weight gain (Field et al., 1986; Scafidi, Field, & Schanberg, 1993); social responsiveness (Field, Scafidi, & Schanberg, 1987); bone growth and development (Moyer-Mileur, Brubstetter, McNaught, Gill, & Chan, 2000); and for decreasing cortisol levels, crying, and sleep disturbances (Acolet et al., 1993). Improvements in weight gain and reductions in stress after massage therapy have also been found for infants exposed to cocaine and HIV (Field, Hernandez-Reif, & Freedman, 2004; Wheedon et al., 1993).

Because it has been demonstrated that touch can be excessively arousing and disorganizing to extremely fragile infants who have great difficulty regulating tactile stimulation (Als, 1986), infant massage therapy is indicated for preterm and LBW infants who are considered medically stable and who need to gain weight. It is important that professionals consider the infant's medical condition and vulnerabilities so as to adjust the therapeutic regimen accordingly. More research is needed in this area to clarify just how treatments should be individualized for the most vulnerable infants.

What Is Massage Therapy?

The massage therapy protocol used in research and practice involves three standardized segments of massage, each lasting 5 minutes. Stroking of the infant's body using moderate pressure from the top of the head to the feet in a systematic way comprises the first and third segments. During the middle segment, the infant's limbs are gently flexed and extended. The beneficial outcomes obtained in research studies have resulted from a fairly brief course of therapy—three sessions per day for 5 to 10 days—offering a potentially cost-effective way to improve health and shorten hospitalizations for these babies. Mothers suffering from postpartum depression who were trained to use massage therapy for one 15-minute period two times a week for 6 weeks were able to reduce infant crying and improve their infants' sleep. The mothers also reported less depression themselves (Raver, 1997). Based on these findings, it appears that massage can be a useful skill to teach parents and grandparents because it helps reduce stress both for the one who gives and the one who receives.

Beyond Massage Therapy

As we have noted, prevention efforts that are comprehensive in their scope are most successful. For women in at-risk groups (with diabetes, chronic hypertension, or who have experienced preterm labor), the health of their infants might be further enhanced by a combination of services and continuity of care. In an experimental study that investigated the effectiveness of such a program, Brooten and associates (2001) were able to reduce the rate of infant mortality, preterm deliveries, and infant rehospitalizations for high-risk women by providing prenatal medical care, education, and counseling (partly in the women's homes), frequent telephone contact and daily telephone availability, and postpartum visits by nurse specialists. The rate of infant mortality was over four times as high ($n = 9$) in the control group of 88 mothers when compared to the rate ($n = 2$) in the treatment group of 85 mothers. This result suggests that consistency of care and ongoing relationships with caregivers offer clinicians a good chance of supporting a healthy start for infants at high risk of prematurity and LBW. Similar principles have been applied to programs for pregnant teenagers, who often face multiple risks as well. Teen pregnancy represents a particular challenge to the helper because the normal tasks of adolescent development (see Chapters 9, 10, and 11) are overlaid on the issues of pregnancy and parenthood. Whereas rates of teenage births have stabilized or have declined slightly in recent years (National Campaign to Prevent Teen Pregnancy, 1999), the numbers are still unacceptably high. Studies have demonstrated that children of teenage mothers are likely to face a grim future that includes poverty, academic failure, high rates of family violence, unemployment, contact with the criminal justice system, and the likelihood of becoming teenage parents themselves. Pregnant teens experience more health problems, have higher rates of birth complications due to poor prenatal care, and tend to drop out of school, risking under- or unemployment in the future (Furstenberg, Brooks-Gunn, & Chase-Lansdale, 1989; Hayes, 1987).

For a multifaceted and cyclical problem such as this, interventions need to be embedded in the social and cultural system of the teenager, and most effective programs address concerns of parenthood and adolescent development together. Although evidence is somewhat scanty, the best approaches appear to involve coordination of school and clinic services. In other words, programs that target multiple issues, providing support and information on birth control, pregnancy, and child care, academic and vocational education, and the social and emotional concerns of the teenager hold out the promise of greater success than do programs that address single issues alone (Cowen et al., 1996). Programs for pregnant teens should also provide coordinated services for the new moth-ers, their babies, and the grandmothers who often play a central role in the caretaking functions. To break the repetitive cycle of early pregnancy, children of teenage mothers should be the target of preventive efforts as they approach adolescence themselves (Chase-Lansdale & Brooks-Gunn, 1994).

SUMMARY

The Nature–Nurture Illusion

1. Both heredity and environment influence human development, but when we focus our attention on one of these causes the other seems to fade into the background. It is an especially important challenge for the helper to avoid taking a one-sided perspective.

Mechanisms of Genetic Influence: How Do Genes Work?

2. Understanding how genetic processes work is important if we hope to evaluate claims about the role heredity plays in development. Each human has 23 pairs of chromosomes in each of his body cells. Chromosomes are composed of deoxyribonucleic acid (DNA). Chromosomes divide during normal cell division (mitosis), and each new cell then contains a duplicate set of the original 46 chromosomes.

3. Specialized germ cells in ovaries and testes can undergo meiosis, a multistage cell division. The resulting cells, ova (eggs) in females and sperm in males, contain only one member of each chromosome pair, or 23 chromosomes altogether. When a sperm fertilizes an ovum, the resulting zygote contains 46 chromosomes. Thus, mother's ovum and father's sperm each contribute one member of every chromosome pair to their offspring.

4. Genes are the functional units of DNA. Genes provide cells with a kind of blueprint for the production of proteins, which are the building blocks of the body, and enzymes, which facilitate chemical reactions. The transcription of genes can be turned on and off by other genes (regulator genes), which are affected by the environment of the cell. Genes, like chromosomes, come in matched pairs, one from the mother, one from the father. Matching genes can have slightly different forms, called alleles, presenting cells with slightly different blueprints to follow. Different alleles of the same gene can have a dominant-recessive relationship such that one has a larger influence on the phenotype. In this situation, a person is a carrier of an unexpressed trait, which can be passed on to the next generation. Sometimes two different alleles have a codominance relationship and together produce a blended trait.

5. Most frequently, our traits are affected by many pairs of genes at many chromosomal sites. Such polygenic influences probably characterize most behavioral traits, such as intelligence and personality.

6. Whether one is male or female is affected by a whole pair of chromosomes: the XX pair in females and the XY pair in males. Mothers pass on one of their X chromosomes to their offspring, but fathers can pass along either an X or a Y, determining the sex of a child.

7. Hereditary diseases can occur either as a function of defective genes or because an ovum or a sperm contains the wrong number of chromosomes. Some disorders are caused by a single pair of genes. In this case, defective gene alleles can be recessive, so that a victim must have two of them to have the disorder, or a defective allele can be dominant, causing the disorder in anyone who has one of the defective genes. Many hereditary diseases, including many mental illnesses and behavioral disorders, are polygenic. Finally, some hereditary disorders result when a zygote forms containing too many chromosomes or too few. Often, the age of the parent at conception has some effect on the likelihood of such a problem. The genetic counselor can help parents and prospective parents who may be at risk of passing on hereditary diseases. The counselor's role includes helping clients to understand the benefits and risks of screening procedures and to understand and cope with the choices that confront them about testing, childbearing, and parenting.

8. Sex-linked disorders are more likely to affect males than females. They are caused by defective, recessive alleles on the X chromosome at a site that is unmatched by the smaller Y chromosome. For these diseases, a female must have two defective alleles to be a victim, but a male need only have one defective allele on his X chromosome.

Explaining Behavior: Focus on Genetics

9. There are two scientific approaches to understanding the role of genetics in behavior. Molecular genetics addresses questions such as where are genes located and what is the specific function and product of each gene. Behavior genetics determines heritability, how much of the variability between people on some trait can be attributed to differences in their genes. Behavior geneticists also

estimate the degree of environmental influence on behaviors. They assess the degree to which both non-shared environments (dissimilar experiences) and shared environments (similar experiences) affect behavioral outcomes. Behavior geneticists rely heavily on studies of twins and of adoptees to estimate the contributions of heredity to behavior.

10. Some behavior geneticists have described ways in which genes can influence the environments we experience. Passive genetic effects occur when the genes of a parent affect the environment the parent provides for a child. Evocative genetic effects occur when a person's genes influence his behavior, which in turn affects how others react. When genes influence an individual's choice of environments, companions, or activities, the gene effects are called active.

Shifting Focus to the Coaction of Genes and Environment

11. Two methodological criticisms have been leveled at the behavior genetics approach. First, it may sometimes underestimate environmental effects in twin and adoption studies. For example, some similarities attributed to shared genes may actually be a function of shared environment, such as shared uterine environment. Second, calculations are based on the assumption that phenotype is the sum of genetic and environmental influences. But this assumption violates the observation that genes behave differently in different environments and that the same environment has different effects in combination with different genes.

12. Some biologists argue that environment always reciprocally interacts with gene activity in an intricate pattern called coaction. Coaction can be seen in the development of cells and at each level of functioning, from the molecular to the behavioral.

13. Current epigenetic models take into account the complexity of gene–environment interactions and provide an alternative to behavior genetics. In these systems approaches, ongoing developmental changes are seen as influencing both the environment and the biological system. Both genetics and environment can canalize behavior, guiding it in certain directions and determining which new pathways for development become available.

Healthy Prenatal Development

14. During normal prenatal development, the first 3 weeks is the period of the ovum, when implantation occurs and the neural tube forms. The period of the embryo, from the 4th through the 8th weeks, is when most organ systems form, with development moving in cephalocaudal and proximo-distal directions. From 9 weeks until birth is the period of the fetus, when the reproductive system forms and all other systems continue to mature.

15. Counseling interventions to promote healthy development can be targeted at either genetic or environmental influences. Most interventions targeted at changing or influencing gene function are experimental, but as they become available, counselors will help clients evaluate the ethics and feasibility of these options for themselves and their offspring.

16. Counselors can affect environmental influences on prenatal development more effectively than we can affect genetic influences. Helping parents understand teratogens and their influences on fetal development is important. These environmental agents, including many disease organisms and drugs, can have varying effects on the developing fetus, depending on when they are introduced, the mother's and baby's genes, and the amount of exposure or dosage the fetus experiences. For example, the effects of prenatal exposure to alcohol can range from subtle learning and behavior problems to fetal alcohol syndrome, which includes physical abnormalities, mental retardation, and behavioral problems. The number of risk factors to which a child is exposed, both prenatally and postnatally, can also influence how severe the long-term effects of teratogens will be.

17. It is also important for parents and parents-to-be to understand the significance of prenatal nutrition. A number of studies demonstrate that adequate protein, vitamins, and minerals in the prenatal and immediate postnatal diet can have long-term benefits for children's social and cognitive development. These findings suggest that inadequate prenatal nutrition has negative effects on cognitive and behavioral functioning, just as inadequate postnatal nutrition does. But like other risk factors, poor pre- or postnatal nutrition is more problematic the more risks a child experiences. Children who have experienced early food deprivation but who otherwise are socially, educationally, and medically advantaged show no long-term effects of poor pre- or postnatal nutrition.

18. The environment can be a source of prolonged stress for a pregnant woman, another factor that can have effects on the developing fetus. Stress experienced by the mother activates a complex set of responses involving parts of her brain and the endocrine glands—the hypothalamic-pituitary-adrenal (HPA) axis. Part of the reaction includes a process for returning to normal, but continued exposure to stress sometimes interferes with the brain's ability to shut down the stress response. There can be long-term negative effects for the fetus as well as for the mother. Hormones involved in the stress reaction cross the placenta from mother to fetus and can affect the infant's own developing neuroendocrine system, increasing neonatal hyperactivity and irritability.

CASE STUDY

Jennifer and Jianshe Li have been married for 10 years. Jennifer is a White, 37-year-old woman who is an associate in a law firm in a medium-sized, midwestern city. Her husband, Jianshe, a 36-year-old Chinese American man, is a software developer employed by a large locally based company. The couple met while they were in graduate school and married shortly thereafter. They have no children. They own a home in one of the newly developed suburban areas just outside the city. Jennifer was adopted as an infant and maintains close ties with her adoptive parents. She is their only child. There has been no contact between Jennifer and her biological parents, and she has never attempted to learn their names or find out where they live. Jianshe's parents, two brothers, and one sister live on the West Coast, and all the family members try to get together for visits several times a year. Jennifer and Jianshe are active in a few local community organizations. They enjoy the company of many friends and often spend what leisure time they have hiking and camping.

The Lis have been unsuccessful in conceiving a child even though they have tried for the past 4 years. Both husband and wife have undergone testing. Jennifer has had infertility treatment for the past 3 years but without success. The treatments have been lengthy, expensive, and emotionally stressful. Approximately a year ago, Jennifer began to experience some mild symptoms of dizziness and dimmed vision. At first, she disregarded the symptoms, attributing them to overwork. However, they persisted for several weeks, and she consulted her physician. He thought that they might be a side effect of the medication she had been taking to increase fertility. Jennifer's treatment protocol was changed, and shortly afterward, much to the couple's delight, Jennifer became pregnant.

Unfortunately, the symptoms she had experienced earlier began to worsen, and she noticed some mild tremors in her arms and legs as well. Jennifer's physician referred her to a specialist, who tentatively diagnosed a progressive disease of the central nervous system that has a suspected genetic link and is marked by an unpredictable course. The Lis were devastated by the news. They were very concerned about the risks of the pregnancy to Jennifer's health. They also worried about the possible transmission of the disease to the new baby whom they had wanted for such a long time. In great distress, they sought counseling to help them deal with some of these concerns.

Discussion Questions

1. As a counselor, what are some of the issues you would need to be prepared to discuss with this couple? What information or training do you think you would need to deal effectively with this family?
2. List the possible problems faced by this couple as well as the supports available to them. What are the options available to Jennifer and Jianshe?
3. As a genetic counselor, how would you help them in the decision-making process?

JOURNAL QUESTIONS

1. Consider one feature of your own development (a trait, talent, behavior). Discuss the development of this feature using the idea of nature–nurture coaction. How has this particular feature of your personality influenced other people?
2. Interview your mother or father, if possible, about your prenatal developmental period. What can you learn about this important period of your development?
3. How has increased knowledge about prenatal development changed the behaviors of pregnant women? Are there any beliefs specific to your particular cultural background that shaped the way your mother viewed her pregnancy or acted during her pregnancy? Ask a member of a different culture about the ways that culture views pregnancy.

KEY TERMS

chromosomes	intergenic DNA	sperm	melanin
autosomes	centromere	zygote	lactase
sex chromosomes	mitosis	implanting	transcription
karyotype	germ cells	genes	messenger ribonucleic acid
deoxyribonucleic acid	meiosis	proteins	(mRNA)
(DNA)	ovum	enzymes	regulator genes

alleles
genotype
phenotype
dominant-recessive
carrier
codominance
polygenic
genomic imprinting
X chromosome
Y chromosome
androgens
testosterone
sickle-cell anemia
genetic counselors
mutation
progeria
Huntington's chorea
Down syndrome (Trisomy 21)

X-linked recessive disorders
trinucleotide repeats
fragile X syndrome
molecular genetics
gene expression
Human Genome Project
phenylketonuria (PKU)
behavior genetics
identical, or monozygotic, twins
fraternal, or dizygotic, twins
heritability
nonshared environment
shared environment
passive gene effects
evocative gene effects
active gene effects
niche picking
amniotic fluid

amniotic sac
amniocentesis
chorionic villa sampling (CVS)
coaction
epigenetic model
canalization
genotype-environment interaction
period of the ovum
neural tube
period of the embryo
cephalo-caudal
proximo-distal
period of the fetus
somatic cell therapy
germline gene therapy
teratogens
placenta

fetal alcohol syndrome (FAS)
fetal alcohol effects (FAE)
no observable effect level
lowest observable adverse effect level
kwashiorkor
eustress
distress
alarm phase
resistance phase
exhaustion phase
hypothalamic-pituitary-adrenal (HPA) axis
adrenocorticotropic hormone (ACTH)
epinephrine
norepinephrine
cortisol
low birth weight (LBW)

Now go to our Companion Website to assess your understanding of chapter content with Multiple Choice Questions, apply comprehension in Essay Questions, and broaden your knowledge of development with related Web Links.

3

Neural and Cognitive Development in the Early Years

Is there any value for helping professionals in learning the details of infant and preschool development? Of course, some clinicians work primarily with infants, preschoolers, and their parents, and the benefits to them are clear. But what about helpers for whom the majority of clients will be older children, adolescents, and adults? As you have already seen, developments at these later ages cannot be divorced from earlier events. Skills, abilities, and tendencies that develop in the early years of life establish trajectories that influence the progress and direction of later developments. To put it simply, who a person will become is at least partially channeled even before birth. Pre- and postnatal brain development are particularly important elements of developmental knowledge.

Consider this analogy: Any discussion of specific counseling techniques would be incomplete without first understanding the fundamental principles of the counseling theory from which they are derived. It is difficult to imagine that helpers could be expected to develop, for example, a cognitive-behavioral treatment plan for depressed adolescents without first understanding how cognitive-behavioral therapy is supposed to work. Imagine, as well, a helper who is expected to embark on a therapeutic relationship with a young adult client without ever hearing about the concept of empathy. These counselors might muddle through, but how effective would they be?

Although this analogy may be a stretch, trying to understand how people develop without understanding how their brains work is similar. You might not miss the obvious physical and behavioral changes your clients exhibit, but part of the mystery behind them would elude you. The new millennium began following a decade of intensive brain research, aided by new technologies. It is important to understand how far scientists have come in unraveling the complexities of this most mysterious part of human beings. Helpers of all theoretical bents stand to understand better how their clients think and feel and learn if they give some attention to the workings of this marvelous internal organ, the brain. In this chapter, we describe prenatal brain development. We then go on to look at the emergence of perceptual, motor, and cognitive skills in early childhood. In the next two chapters, we will consider parallel developments in the social and emotional life of the young child.

THE BRAIN

Early Prenatal Brain Development

When you were just a 2-week-old embryo, your very existence still unknown to your parents, cells from the embryo's upper surface (see Chapter 2) began to form a sheet that rearranged itself by turning inward and curling into a neural tube. This phenomenon, called neurulation, signaled the beginning of your central nervous system's development. Once formed, this structure was covered over by another sheet of cells, to become your skin, and was moved inside you so

25 Days 35 Days 40 Days 50 Days 100 Days

Four Months Six Months Seven Months

Eight Months Nine Months

FIGURE 3.1

Stages of Brain Development

The developing human brain viewed from the side in a succession of embryonic and fetal stages. The small figures beneath the first five embryonic stages are in proper relative proportion to the last five figures.

Source: Cowan, W. M. The development of the brain. In Llinas, R. R. (Ed.) *The workings of the brain* (p. 41). *Scientific American* (Sept. 1979) p. 166. Illustration by Tom Prentiss. Reproduced by permission of the illustrator.

that the rest of your body could develop around it. Around the 25th day of your gestational life, your neural tube began to take on a pronounced curved shape. At the top of your "C-shaped" embryonic self, three distinct bulges appeared, which eventually became your hindbrain, midbrain, and forebrain. (See Figure 3.1.)

Within the primitive neural tube, important events were occurring. Cells from the interior surface of the neural tube reproduced to form neurons, or nerve cells, that would become the building blocks of your brain. From about the 40th day, or 5th week, of gestation, your neurons began to increase at a staggering rate—one quarter of a million per minute for 9 months—to create the 100 billion neurons that make up a baby's brain at birth. At least half would be destroyed later either because they were unnecessary or were not used. We will have more to say about this loss of neurons later.

Your neurons began to migrate outward from their place of birth rather like filaments extending from the neural tube to various sites in your still incomplete brain. Supporting cells called glia, stretching from the inside of the neural tube to its outside, provided a type of scaffolding for your neurons, guiding them as they ventured out on their way to their final destinations. Those neurons that developed first migrated only a short distance from your neural tube and were destined to become the hindbrain. Those that developed later traveled a little farther and ultimately formed the midbrain. Those that developed last migrated the farthest to populate the cerebral cortex of the forebrain. This development always progressed from the inside out, so that cells traveling the farthest had to migrate through several other already formed layers to reach their proper location. To build the six layers of your cortex, a neuron with genetically influenced knowledge of its ultimate address had to move through the bottom layers that had been already built up before it could get to the outside layer. (See Box 3.1 and Figures 3.2 and 3.3.)

Scientists have discovered that neurons sometimes need to find their destinations (for example, on the part of the cortex specialized for vision) before that part of the cortex develops. It's a little like traveling in outer space. Or as Davis (1997) has suggested, "It's a bit like an arrow reaching the space where the bull's-eye will be before anyone has even set up the target"

Box 3.1 | *The Major Structures of the Brain*

The human brain is composed of three main parts, forebrain, midbrain, and hindbrain, which reflect the evolutionary history of this amazing organ. The oldest part, or hindbrain, evolved more than 500 million years ago and "carries our evolution inside us" (Ornstein & Thompson, 1984). This particular part of the brain has been called the reptilian brain because it is the most primitive and even looks like a reptile's brain. Refer to Figure 3.2 for a depiction of the brain structures described here.

The main parts of the hindbrain, the medulla, the pons, the cerebellum, and the reticular formation, regulate autonomic functions that are outside our conscious control. The medulla contains nuclei that regulate functions that are basic for survival, such as heart rate, blood pressure, and respiration. Damage to this area of the brain can be fatal. The pons, situated above the medulla, is involved in the regulation of the sleep–wake cycle. Individuals with sleep disturbances can sometimes have abnormal activity in this area. The medulla and the pons are also especially sensitive to an overdose of drugs or alcohol. Drug effects on these structures can cause suffocation and death. The pons transmits nerve impulses to the cerebellum, a structure that looks like a smaller version of the brain itself. The cerebellum is involved in the planning, coordination, and smoothness of complex motor activities such as hitting a tennis ball or dancing.

With the brainstem (medulla, pons, and midbrain) is a bundle of neural tissue called the reticular formation. This structure acts together with specific nuclei to form the reticular activating system, that part of the brain that alerts the higher structures to "pay attention" to incoming stimuli. This system also filters out the extraneous stimuli that we perceive at any point in time. For example, it is possible for workers who share an office to tune out the speech, music, or general background hum going on around them when they are involved in important telephone conversations. However, they can easily "perk up" and attend if a coworker calls their name.

The midbrain, the next highest structure on the evolutionary scale, consists of several small structures (superior colliculi, inferior colliculi, and substantia nigra) that are involved in vision, hearing, and consciousness. The midbrain is also a part of the reticular activating system. These parts of the brain receive sensory input from the eyes and ears and are instrumental in controlling eye movement.

The forebrain is, by far, the dominant part of the brain and is the part that most clearly differentiates us as human. Its most recognizable aspect is the cerebrum, which comprises two thirds of the total mass. A crevice, or fissure, divides the cerebrum into two halves, like the halves of a walnut. Information is transferred between the two halves by a network of fibers comprising the corpus callosum. These halves are referred to as the left and right hemispheres. Research on hemispheric specialization pioneered by Sperry

(1964) demonstrated that the left hemisphere controls functioning of the right side of the body and vice versa. Language functions such as vocabulary knowledge and speech are usually localized in the left hemisphere, and visual–spatial skills are localized on the right. Recently, this research was introduced to lay readers through a rash of popular books about left brain–right brain differences. Overall, many of these publications have distorted the facts and oversimplified the findings. Generally the hemispheres work together, sharing information via the corpus callosum and cooperating with each other in the execution of most tasks (Geschwind, 1990). There is no reliable evidence that underlying modes of thinking, personality traits, or cultural differences can be traced to left–right hemispheric lateralization.

Each hemisphere of the cerebral cortex can be further divided into lobes, or areas of functional specialization (see Figure 3.3). The occipital lobe, located at the back of the head, handles visual information. The temporal lobe, found on the sides of each hemisphere, is responsible for auditory processing. At the top of each hemisphere, behind a fissure called the central sulcus, is the parietal lobe. This area is responsible for the processing of somatosensory information such as touch, temperature, and pain. Finally, the frontal lobe, situated at the top front part of each hemisphere, controls voluntary muscle movements and higher level cognitive functions such as planning, goal setting, and decision making. A great deal of the cortex, approximately three quarters, is not so clearly specified for primary involvement in vision, hearing, sensory, or motor functions. This area is called the association area, and its job is to integrate information coming from the various primary cortical areas. It appears to be important for complex cognitive functioning.

Completing the forebrain are the structures of the limbic system (hippocampus, amygdala, and septum), the thalamus, and the hypothalamus. These structures work to produce feelings such as pleasure, pain, anger, sexuality, fear, and affection. Often referred to as the "emotional brain," the limbic system works in concert with other parts of the brain, such as the frontal lobes, to help us think and reason. We will have more to say about the workings of the emotional brain and its ties to several emotional disorders in a later chapter. (See Box 4.1 in Chapter 4.)

The structures of the limbic system have direct connections with neurons from the olfactory bulb, which is responsible for our sense of smell. It has been noted that pheromones, a particular kind of hormonal substance secreted by animals and humans, can trigger particular reactions that affect emotional responsivity below the level of conscious awareness. Although the evidence is still suggestive, there is some support for the belief that humans can sense sexual signals by means of pheromones (Grammer, 1993). Other parts of the limbic system, most notably the hippocampus, are very important in the process of learning and the formation of memory.

The thalamus is a primary way station for handling neural communication, something like "information central." It receives information from the sense of sight, hearing, touch, taste, and the limbic system and sends these messages to their appropriate destinations. For example, the thalamus projects visual information, received via the optic nerve, to the occipital lobe. The hypothalamus is divided into groups of neurons called nuclei, which help sort out the information. Consequently, the thalamus behaves like an efficient switchboard operator in a large company, who takes incoming calls and connects the caller with the proper office. A study by Andreason and colleagues (1994) reveals that the thalamus is much smaller in the brains of schizophrenic patients than in those of normal individuals, suggesting that an unregulated flood of stimulation may be overwhelming and lead to disorganized thinking.

The hypothalamus, situated below the thalamus, is a small but important structure that regulates hunger, thirst, body temperature, and breathing rate. Lesions in areas of the hypothalamus have been found to produce eating abnormalities in animals, including obesity (Leibowitz, Hammer, & Chang, 1981) or starvation (Anand & Brobeck, 1951). It is also important in the regulation of emotional responses. Recall our discussion of the stress response from Chapter 2. The hypothalamus functions as an intermediary, translating the emotional messages received from the cortex and the amygdala into a command to the endocrine system to release stress hormones in preparation for fight or flight. The hypothalamus is involved in the expression of sexual behavior as well. Although results are still inconclusive, LeVay (1991) found that the size of one of the hypothalamic nuclei is twice as large in heterosexual men as in homosexual men. This evidence has been seen as an indicator of a biological basis for sexual orientation. As we can see, the size of the various brain structures as well as the brain's patterns of neural connections and levels of neurotransmitters all play a part in shaping the individual's personality and behavior.

Hindbrain, Midbrain, and Forebrain
This is a picture of the brain from the left side. Beneath the cortex are three parts of the brain: the hindbrain, the midbrain, and the forebrain. The hindbrain controls some basic processes necessary for life. The midbrain is a relay station to the brain. The forebrain is where complex thoughts, motives, and emotions are stored and processed.

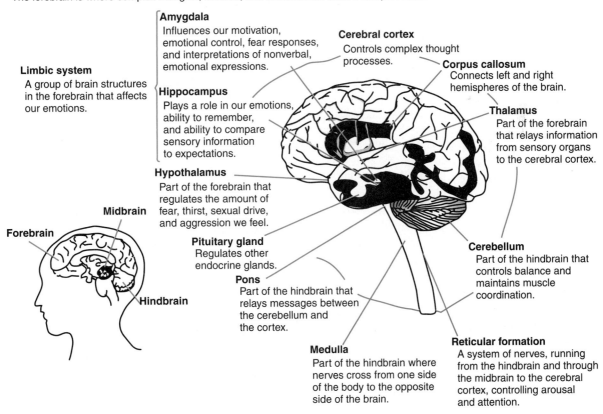

FIGURE 3.2

The Major Structures of the Brain

Source: Psychology by L. Uba and K. Huang. ©1999. Reprinted by permission of Pearson Education, Inc., Upper Saddle River, N.J.

FIGURE 3.3

The Cerebral Cortex

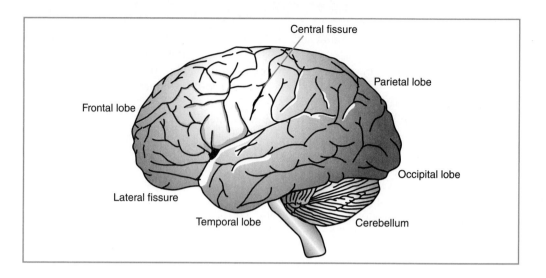

(pp. 54–55). Certain cells behave like signposts, providing the traveling neurons with way stations as they progress on their journey. Neurons may also respond to the presence of certain chemicals that guide their movements in a particular direction.

About the 4th month of your prenatal life, your brain's basic structures were formed. Your neurons migrated in an orderly way and clustered with similar cells into distinct sections or regions in your brain, such as in the cerebral cortex or in the specific nuclei. The term nucleus here refers to a cluster of cells creating a structure, rather than to the kind of nucleus that is found in a single cell. An example is the *caudate nucleus*, part of the *basal ganglia* in the brain's interior. Like-minded neurons that clustered in these areas or structures were destined to handle certain kinds of information. Figure 3.3 presents a picture of the major functional areas of the cerebral cortex.

One important question concerns just how this specialization occurs and what directs it. Do the neurons possess a "protomap" (Rakic, 1988) that tells them where to locate and what to do? Or are the functions of neurons somehow influenced by the environmental input they receive (O'Leary, 1989)? This issue is still controversial and extraordinarily complicated to research. However, most available evidence supports the view that cortical differentiation is primarily influenced by the kinds of environmental inputs the cortex receives. In other words, the geography of the cortex is not rigidly built in but responds to activity and experiences by making changes in its structural organization. This principle was demonstrated by researchers who transplanted part of the visual cortex of an animal to its parietal lobe (O'Leary & Stanfield, 1989). The transplanted neurons began to process somatosensory rather than visual information. Studies such as these have shown that the brain is amazingly malleable and demonstrates great plasticity, particularly during early stages of development. In time, however, most cells become specialized for their activity, and it is harder to reverse their operation.

Structure and Function of Neurons

The neurons in your brain are one of nature's most fantastic accomplishments. Although neurons come in various sizes and shapes, a typical neuron is composed of a cell body with a long extension, or axon, which is like a cable attached to a piece of electronic equipment. The axon itself can be quite long relative to the size of the cell's other structures because it needs to connect or "wire" various parts of the brain, such as the visual thalamus to the visual cortex. At the end of the axon are the axon terminals, which contain tiny sacs of chemical substances called neurotransmitters. Growing out from the cell body are smaller projections, called dendrites, resembling

FIGURE 3.4

Structure of a Neuron

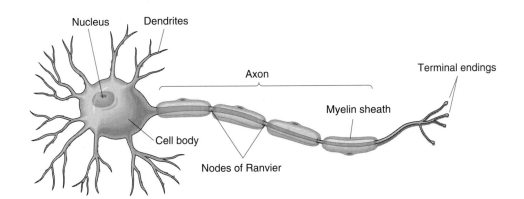

little branches, which send or receive messages or transmissions from other neurons. The unique structure of the neuron equips it to do its job very effectively. (See Figure 3.4.)

So how do brain cells "talk" to each other? Even though we speak of wiring or connecting, each neuron does not actually make physical contact with other neurons but remains separate. Communication is a process of sending and receiving electrochemical messages. Simply put, when a neuron responds to some excitation, or when it "fires," an electrical impulse, or message, travels down the axon to the axon terminals. The sacs in the axon terminals containing neurotransmitters burst and release their contents into the space between the neurons called the **synaptic gap**. About a hundred different neurotransmitters have been identified, and many more are likely to be. Among those that have been widely studied are *serotonin, acetylcholine, glutamate, gamma-amino butyric acid (GABA), norepinephrine*, and *dopamine*. Some of these are more common in specific parts of the brain than in others. They are literally chemical messengers that stimulate the dendrites, cell body, or axon of a neighboring neuron to either fire (excitation) or stop firing (inhibition). For example, glutamate is an excitatory transmitter that's important for transmission in the retina of the eye; GABA is an inhibitory transmitter that is found throughout the brain.

If the message is to fire, the speed of the resulting electrical impulse is increased when glial cells wrap themselves around the axon, thus facilitating conduction. This phenomenon, called **myelination**, begins prenatally for neurons in the sensorimotor areas of the brain but happens later in other areas. The myelination of some areas of the frontal cortex is not complete until adolescence or even later (Michel & Moore, 1995).

Neurons are not "wired together" randomly. Rather, they are joined via their synaptic connections into groups called **circuits**. Circuits are part of larger organizations of neurons, called systems, such as the visual and olfactory systems. Two main types of neurons populate these systems, **projection neurons**, which have axons that extend far away from the cell body, and **interneurons**, which branch out closer to the local area (see Katz & Shatz, 1996). The intricate neural fireworks described earlier are going on all the time in your brain. Perhaps as you read this chapter, you are also listening to music and drinking a cup of coffee. Or you may be distracted by thoughts of a telephone conversation that you had earlier. The neuronal circuitry in your brain is processing all these stimuli, allowing your experiences to be perceived and comprehended.

Later Prenatal Brain Development

To return to your prenatal life story, your neurons began to fire spontaneously around the 4th month of gestation. This happened despite a lack of sensory input. Even though your eyes were not completely formed, the neurons that would later process visual information began firing as though they were preparing for the work they would do in a few months' time. By the end of the second and beginning of the third trimesters, your sense organs had developed sufficiently to respond to perceptual stimulation from outside your mother's womb. Sounds were heard by

15 weeks. Not only did you learn to recognize the sound of your mother's voice, but you also became familiar with the rhythms and patterns of your native language. DeCasper and colleagues conducted an interesting study in which they directed pregnant women to recite a child's nursery rhyme out loud each day from the 33rd to the 37th week of pregnancy (DeCasper, Lecaneut, Busnel, Granier-Deferre, & Maugeais, 1994). During the 38th week, the women were asked to listen to a recording of either the familiar rhyme or an unfamiliar one while their fetuses' heart rates were being measured. The fetal heart rates dropped for the group who heard the familiar rhyme, signifying attention, but did not change for the group who heard the unfamiliar one. This result suggests that the fetus can attend to and discriminate the cadence of the rhyme. Studies such as this one should not be misinterpreted to mean that the fetus can "learn" as the term is commonly used. No one has suggested that the fetus can understand the poem. However, what this and other similar studies do indicate is an early responsivity to experience that begins to shape the contours of the brain by establishing patterns of neural or synaptic connections.

By your 25th week, you could open and close your eyes. You could see light then rather like the way you see things now when you turn toward a bright light with your eyes closed. At this point in development a fetus turns her head toward a light source, providing her visual system with light stimulation that probably promotes further brain development. Sensory experience has been found to be critical for healthy brain development after birth, and vision provides a good example of this principle. The interplay between neurons and visual experience was documented dramatically by Wiesel and Hubel (1965), who, in a series of experiments with kittens for which they won the Nobel Prize, showed that early visual deprivation has permanently deleterious effects. They sewed shut one of each kitten's eyes at birth so that only one eye was exposed to visual input. Several weeks later when the eyes were reopened, the kittens were found to be permanently blinded in the eye that had been deprived of stimulation. No amount of intervention or aggressive treatment could repair the damage. The neurons needed visual stimulation to make the proper connections for sight; in the absence of stimulation, the connections were never made, and blindness resulted. The existence of a critical period for visual development was established. This research prompted surgeons to remove infant cataracts very shortly after birth so that permanent damage to sight could be avoided, instead of waiting several years.

Sensory systems, such as the auditory and visual systems, influence each other so that their eventual development is a function of their interrelationships. The integration of these systems seems to serve the baby well in making sense of her world. So, for example, when a 4-month-old sees an object she also has some sense of how it feels. (See the discussion of intermodal perception later in this chapter.)

The amount of stimulation is also important. A series of studies lends support to the idea that there is an optimal range of sensory input that is necessary for proper development. Too much stimulation or too little can cause disturbances in the sensory systems at birth. Moreover, from birth and perhaps even before, babies partially control how much or how little sensory stimulation they experience. Lewkowicz and Turkewitz (1980, 1981) showed that young infants attend to high- or low-arousing visual and auditory stimuli depending upon their own level of arousal. For example, if they are hungry they pay less attention to highly arousing external stimuli. Scientists continue to examine the interaction between the amount of stimulation, the timing of the stimulation, and the arousal level of the individual, which together influence the way sensory systems develop.

Postnatal Brain Development

After your birth, your neurons continued to reproduce at a rapid pace, finally slowing down around 12 months of age (Huttenlocher, 1994). Except for those pruned or lost, the neurons you formed as an embryo will survive until you die. For many years it was assumed that nerve cells do not reproduce after early infancy. Recent research, however, has documented the duplication of neurons in the hippocampus of adults, thus shedding new light on this issue and raising new questions about typical brain development (Kempermann & Gage, 1999). Nonetheless, it still appears that most brain growth after birth is due not to the creation of more neurons but to the formation of synapses, new connections among neurons. The growth spurt in synapses reflects the vast amount of learning that typically occurred for you and for most babies in the early months of postnatal life. Some areas of your developing brain experienced periods of rapid synaptic growth after birth, such as in the visual and auditory cortices, which increased dramatically between 3 and 4 months. In contrast, the synapses in your prefrontal cortex developed more slowly and reached their maximum density around 12 months. As you will see in the following sections, infants make rapid strides in cognitive development at the end of the 1st year, at about the time when prefrontal synapses have reached their peak density.

The growth of these connections was the product of both internal and external factors. Certain chemical substances within your brain, such as **nerve growth factor**, were absorbed by the neurons and aided in the production of synapses. Your own prenatal actions, such as turning, sucking your thumb, and kicking, as well as the other sensory stimulation you experienced, such as sound, light, and pressure, all contributed to synaptic development. However, as we noted earlier, the major work of **synaptogenesis**, the generation of synapses, took place after birth, when much more sensory stimulation became available.

You arrived in the world with many more neurons than you would ever need. Over the next 12 years or so, through a process known as **neural pruning**, many neurons would die off and many synaptic connections would be selectively discarded. Some of these neurons migrated incorrectly and failed to make the proper connections, rendering them useless. Some of the synaptic connections were never established or were rarely used, so they ultimately disappeared as well. What counts most after birth is not the sheer number of neurons, but the number and strength of the interconnections. Those branching points of contact that remained to constitute your brain would be a unique reflection of your genetics, the conditions of your prenatal period, the nutrition you received, and your postnatal experience and environment. This rich network of connections makes for your thinking, feeling brain, and its structure depends heavily upon what happens to you both before and after your birth.

You may be wondering how to account for the simultaneous processes of synaptogenesis and pruning, which seem to be acting at cross-purposes. What is the point of making new synaptic connections if many will just be culled eventually? Greenough and Black (1992) offer an explanation for the apparent contradiction. They argue that **synaptic overproduction** occurs when it is highly likely that nature will provide the appropriate experience to structure the development of a particular system. For example, many animal species, as well as humans, go through a predictable sequence of activities designed to provide information for the brain to use in the development of vision. These include opening eyes, reaching for and grasping objects, and so on. This type of development depends upon environmental input that is **experience-expectant** because it is experience that is part of the evolutionary history of the organism and that occurs reliably in most situations. Hence, it is "expected." Lack of such experience results in developmental abnormalities, as we saw in the kitten experiments performed by Hubel and Wiesel. The timing of this particular kind of experience for nervous system growth is typically very important; that is, there is a critical period for such experience-expectant development. Nature may provide for an overabundance of synapses because it then can select only those that work best, pruning out the rest. This process may "fine-tune" the quality of a system and could be critical to species survival.

In contrast to overproducing synapses in anticipation of later experience, some synaptic growth occurs as a direct result of exposure to more individualized kinds of environmental events. This type of neural growth is called **experience-dependent**. The quality of the synaptic growth "depends" upon variations in environmental opportunities. Stimulating and complex environments promote such growth in rat pups and other mammals (e.g., Kolb, Gibb, & Robinson, 2003); it seems likely that the same is true for infants and children. Imagine what might be the differences in synaptic development between children raised by parents who speak two different languages in their home and children raised by those who speak only one. Or imagine the synaptic growth of an infant raised in impoverished conditions with very little verbal interaction from adults, and very little chance to explore the environment, as compared to that of an infant reared in an environment rich in adult attention and opportunities for engagement with interesting objects. Experience-dependent processes do not seem to be limited to sensitive periods but can occur throughout the life span. Connections that remain active become stabilized, whereas those that are not used die out. This type of experientially responsive synaptic growth and the concomitant changes in brain structure it induces have been linked to learning and the formation of some kinds of memory.

Sensory and Motor Development

From what you have just read, it should be obvious that babies have a number of emerging competencies at birth, which enable them to begin to interact with the world and with their caregivers. This understanding, however, is of fairly recent origin. Only a few decades ago, newborns were considered almost blind and deaf, virtual "blank slates" waiting for the first environmental imprint. Some of this thinking persists in the often expressed idea that nurture begins after birth or in the lack of appreciation for the temperament differences found among newborns (see Chapter 4). Nonetheless, it is true that the major work of cognitive, emotional, and sensorimotor development will occur over the baby's early years. During the first 12 months of life, the sensory and motor systems that functioned in a rudimentary way prenatally develop greatly and become more smoothly integrated. Table 3.1 provides examples of major milestones in sensory and motor development.

Sometimes, communication between the motor systems and the sensory systems (touch, sight, hearing, balance, and movement) does not develop in a coordinated way. Difficulties such as extreme hypersensitivity or hyposensitivity to sensations such as bright lights, loud sounds, pain, certain textures, or human touch; motor clumsiness; balance problems; fidgeting; and poor eye–hand coordination, to name some of the most common, may be part of a disorder called **sensory integration dysfunction**. Recognition of this problem is becoming more frequent, and interventions, such as those performed by occupational therapists, can be done to ameliorate the symptoms (Greenspan & Weider, 1997). Even in normal children, sensory and cognitive development is somewhat uneven, with certain abilities, such as vision, developing faster than others, such as problem solving. Scientists have begun to link these sequences of sensorimotor and cognitive development to actual brain changes. For example, Fischer (1987) has provided evidence for a convergence between Piaget's stages of sensorimotor development (see the next sections of this chapter) and the sequence of bursts of synaptogenesis that occur over the 1st year of life.

COGNITIVE DEVELOPMENT

If you had to guess, would you say that more intellectual growth occurs in the first few years of life or in the transition from childhood to adulthood? John Flavell, a noted cognitive researcher, has argued that "the brief span from young infancy to young childhood is marked by a momentous transformation of the cognitive system unparalleled by any other period of life" (Flavell, Miller, & Miller, 1993). In this section, we look first at how Jean Piaget described the vast changes that occur in these early years. Then, we examine a few of the many intellectual changes that take place from earliest infancy through the preschool years, with an eye to evaluating how well Piaget's theory accounts for these changes. Finally, we take a look at another major theory of cognitive development, that of Lev S. Vygotsky, whose ideas and findings were compatible with Piaget's in many ways but who added a special emphasis on the importance of culture and social experience to the story of intellectual change in childhood.

Piaget's Constructivist Theory

Debbie, age 10, and Mark, age 4, are overheard discussing their mother's pregnancy. Their parents have read them children's books about how babies are conceived and born, and the topic has been discussed openly in the family. The children have the following conversation:

DEBBIE: Do you know how the baby got there?

MARK: Sure. Mommy got a duck.

DEBBIE: A duck?

TABLE 3.1   Major Milestones in Motor, Visual, and Auditory Development

Age	Motor Development		Visual Development	Auditory Development
	Gross Motor	Fine Motor		
1 Month	Lifts head.	Holds things placed in hands.	Visual acuity: 20/600; scans edges of figures and visual objects.	Alert to sounds; prefers sound of mother's voice.
2 Months			Visual acuity: 20/300; shows preference for faces over objects; discriminates basic colors.	
3 Months			Faces (especially mother's face) perceived as attractive; scans interiors of faces and objects.	Locates where sounds come from.
4 Months	Sits with support; rolls over from front to back.	Visually guided reaching.	Visual acuity: 20/160; smooth tracking of slowly moving objects; development of *stereopsis*, or ability to perceive depth based upon information from both left and right eyes.	
5 Months				
6 Months				Coordination of vision and hearing; turns eyes to nearby sounds smoothly.
7 Months	Sits without support.	Transfers objects from hand to hand; plays with simple toys.	Visual acuity: 20/80.	
8 Months				
9 Months	Crawls.	Pincer grasp.	Interprets others' facial expressions.	
10 Months	Stands holding on; drops and throws things.			
11 Months				
12 Months	Walks holding on.	Scribbles with crayon.	Visual acuity: 20/20.	
12–18 Months	Walks alone.			
18–23 Months		Draws lines; constructs simple tower; drinks from cup using one hand.		
2–3 Years	Runs, jumps, climbs; balance improves; kicks ball forward. Stands on one foot briefly.	Pours milk; dressing and feeding improves; builds towers of 6 blocks; turns pages in book.	Oldest age at which surgical correction of crossed eyes for depth perception can be successful.	
3–4 Years	Walks up stairs alternating feet; walks on tiptoes; throwing improves; buttons clothing; eats with spoon and fork.	Completes simple puzzles; uses art materials, scissors; more careful in execution of art and drawing projects.	Continued integration of visual-motor systems.	
4–5 Years	Ties knots; dresses and undresses easily.	More skillful with scissors.		

Piaget was one of the first theorists to propose that children actively construct their knowledge.

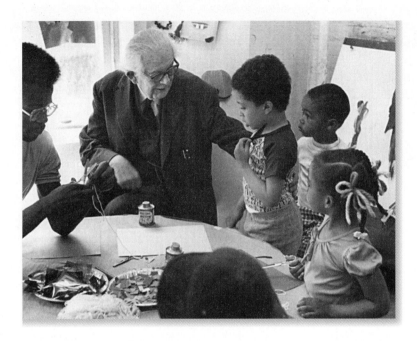

MARK: Yeah, they just get a duck or rabbit and it grows a little more and it turns into a baby.

DEBBIE: A duck will turn into a baby?

MARK: Sure. They give them some food, people food, and they grow into a baby.

DEBBIE: Where did you get that idea?

MARK: I saw it in a book and Mommy and Daddy told me.

DEBBIE: They told you that ducks turn into babies?

MARK: Yeah! (As reported by Cowan, 1978, adapted from Bernstein & Cowan, 1975).

This anecdote illustrates a fundamental feature of learning, knowing, and understanding according to Piaget's theory: that the human mind constructs its knowledge. When infants and children are presented with new stimuli or pieces of information, what is learned or stored is not just a "true" reflection of what comes from the environment. That is, new information is not simply written on a blank slate, as John Locke and other empiricists assumed. Rather, children learn by a process of **adaptation**. First, they interpret new stimulation in ways that fit with what they already know, sometimes distorting it as a result. This aspect of adaptation is called **assimilation**. As the new information is assimilated, the child's existing knowledge may be modified somewhat, providing a better match or fit to what is new. The latter process is called **accommodation**. Assimilation and accommodation are complementary activities involved in every interaction with the environment. To accommodate (learn), children must be able to assimilate. In other words, they cannot learn something that they cannot make some sense out of already. Assimilation often means that new information is distorted or changed so that sense can be made of it! A child's understandings are gradually changed as a result of interactions with the environment, although what a child will learn in any single step is always shaped by what the child already knows, and the new "understanding" may not be a completely accurate reflection of reality. In Mark's case, his parents' explanations, which apparently included comparing human reproduction to ducks laying eggs, far outstripped Mark's knowledge structures, and Mark's assimilation and accommodation of his parents' elaborate explanations produced a charmingly naive linear progression: Ducks turn into people.

Piaget spent a lifetime doing intensive research on the development of knowledge; he wrote dozens of books on his findings and hundreds of articles (see Box 3.2). His own ideas evolved and changed as new work was completed, discussed, and challenged by scientists around the world. Since his death, developmental researchers have followed up on his pioneering work, and, naturally, the field has moved on. Not all of his ideas have been corroborated, but in a remarkable number of areas, his research has been the starting point for more expanded, clarifying work, and his theoretical explanations have informed newer theories.

The idea that knowledge is constructed by the developing child (and adult!) is a Piagetian view that has become an underlying assumption of much of the current research on cognitive development and educational practice (e.g., American Psychological Association's [APA] Board of Educational Affairs, 1995). This constructivist stance takes the child to be an active participant in the learning process, constantly seeking out and trying to make sense of new information. In other words, children are intrinsically motivated to learn—another idea that is widely accepted by modern developmental scientists. Piaget also considered a child's active exploration to be organized and organizing. When children assimilate new information to what they already know they are fitting the new information into an organized way of thinking—some sort of knowledge structure. When they accommodate their knowledge structures to fit what is new in the environment, the organization is changing. (We will have more to say about knowledge structures in later chapters.) The ideas that mental activity is organized and that the organization evolves in response to the environment are further Piagetian notions that seem to be taken for granted by many modern researchers.

Thus, many widely accepted assumptions about cognitive development are derived from Piaget. But some of his fundamental ideas are particularly controversial. Among these is the idea that cognitive development can be characterized by stages (see Chapter 1). Although Piaget saw cognitive change as the result of small, gradual reorganizations of knowledge structures, he described periods of time in which all of a child's mental structures can be expected to have some organizational properties in common. For example, the infancy and preschool periods covered in this chapter were divided by Piaget into two stages, the sensorimotor stage (from birth to about age 2) and the preoperational stage (between ages 2 and 7). Each of these stages was further divided into substages. The notion of stages implies that children's understandings within a stage (or a substage) about many different things will have some general similarities. So, for example, in the early preoperational stage, whether we are examining a child's understanding of number or causality, we should be able to detect some similarities in the ways in which children organize their thinking about these concepts.

Although Piaget did find many such similarities, more recent research, using different kinds of tasks, often finds less support for the notion of overarching stages. In particular, newer work suggests that infants and preschoolers sometimes show signs of understandings that Piaget believed to be possible only for much older children. And children's progress in understanding concepts from different domains of knowledge is not always organized or structured in the same ways at the same time. In fact, an important addition to cognitive developmental work since Piaget is the idea that progress is often domain specific. That is, development can proceed at different rates in different domains. Domains that have been studied in detail include number concepts, morality, biological versus physical realities, and so on. For example, if we want to learn about children's understanding of causality, we may need to look at it within particular domains of knowledge. Children's understanding of physical causality (e.g., how objects move) may progress differently from their understanding of human or animal agency (e.g., how animate organisms move). We should note that Piaget, in his later years, continued to revise his theory. Recent translations of his later work show that he put less emphasis on stages and more on the dynamic quality of repeated assimilation and accommodation in the context of feedback from the environment (e.g., Piaget, 1975/1985).

Nonetheless, most developmental scientists, clinicians, and educators still find Piaget's stage divisions to be useful for many purposes. On the whole, for example, infants' understandings of many different concepts are more similar to one anothers than to those of a 5-year-old. For this reason, in this chapter and in other discussions of cognitive development in this book, we will use Piaget's stage divisions as an aid in describing children's cognitive progress.

Box 3.2 | *Biographical Sketch: Jean Piaget*

Jean Piaget (1896–1980) was remarkably precocious as a child, publishing his first scholarly paper at the age of 10. At 14, after producing a series of scientific reports, he was offered a position as curator of a museum of natural history—an offer promptly withdrawn when his age was discovered! Piaget completed a bachelor's degree by age 18 and a Ph.D. by 22, despite spending a year away from school when he suffered a nervous breakdown (which he later attributed to his study of philosophy). His early education, research, and writing ranged widely from biological science (his first published article reported his observations of an albino sparrow), to mathematics and logic, to experimental psychology, to psychoanalysis, to psychopathology. He even wrote a philosophical novel! He found a way to integrate many of his interests when he was hired by Henri Simon, an early developer of IQ tests, to standardize an English test with French children. Piaget soon lost interest in the task he was assigned—asking children test questions, recording their responses, and specifying whether they were right or wrong for the purposes of quantifying intelligence. But he was intrigued by the qualitative features of children's answers. Even children's wrong answers often seemed to reveal an underlying structure or pattern of thought. While studying psychopathology, Piaget had learned to conduct clinical interviews with mental patients. Now, he began to combine clinical interview techniques with the use of standardized questions in an effort to reveal the nature of children's knowledge and reasoning. After publishing several articles on his findings, Piaget was invited to become the director of studies in the Institute Jean Jacques Rousseau in Geneva, a center for scientific child study and teacher training. At the age of 25, his life's work had begun. Until his death at 84, Piaget wrote prolifically on the development of children's knowledge, reporting an endless stream of studies, and constructing a wide-ranging, coherent theory. His empirical methods combined observations of children's hands-on problem solving with the probing, clinical interview technique that he pioneered in Simon's laboratory. He originated a remarkable array of problem tasks that are easy for adults to solve but not for children, revealing what appeared to be astonishing age changes in our reasoning about the world. As Piaget put it, "Just as the tadpole already breathes, though with different organs from those of the frog, so the child acts like the adult, but employing a mentality whose structure varies according to the stages of its development" (1970, p. 153).

It is rare today to find any subject in cognitive development, from perception to mathematical reasoning to memory to social perspective taking, for which Piaget did not pose key questions and design provocative, ingenious research

tasks. Given the breadth, depth, and complexity of Piaget's work, it is not surprising that others often oversimplify it in their effort to understand. For example, Piaget has been described as a nativist by some, as an empiricist by others. In fact, Piaget was a true inter-actionist. He, like modern systems theorists, viewed development as taking place at the proximal interface between the organism and the environment. Biological and psychological systems affect how the knower acts on the environment, and the environment "feeds" the knower. What the environment provides is absorbed and changed by the organism, but the environment also shapes and changes the organism's knowledge.

Educators have been especially affected by Piaget's work, although again, they have sometimes misinterpreted its implications. Piaget saw schooling as an opportunity to provide children with food for their naturally occurring "mental digestion." He warned teachers, however, that children will either memorize new information by rote or ignore it if it is beyond their current level of understanding. But if information is at least partially comprehensible to them or moderately novel, children will actively and eagerly explore and absorb it. Unfortunately, educators have sometimes misinterpreted Piaget's emphasis on children's active exploration as a recommendation that children simply be provided with lots of interesting and fun "stuff" and then left on their own to learn. Instead, Piaget encouraged educators to plan the presentation of learning opportunities carefully, being especially sensitive to children's current level of functioning in introducing tasks and allowing children to actively explore and discover but recognizing that an orchestrated, if flexible, presentation of tasks aimed at the child's level of understanding can promote development (e.g., 1970).

Interestingly, although Piaget recognized the advantage of teachers' carefully crafting a program of learning opportunities to optimize a child's progress, he was somewhat exasperated by what he referred to as "the American question": "How can we speed up children's development?" He once remarked that kittens have been found to go through some developments in 3 months that take human babies 9 to 12 months to achieve. But "the kitten is not going to go much further. The child has taken longer, but he is capable of going further so it seems to me that the nine months were not for nothing" (as quoted in Elkind, 1968). Respect and appreciation of the human child's cognitive pace is perhaps symptomatic of what made Piaget so successful in uncovering the mysteries of cognitive development in general, an enormous empathy for children.

(*Biographical sources:* Brainerd, 1996; Cowan, 1978; Elkind, 1968, Flavell, 1963.)

Infant Cognition: The Sensorimotor Stage

Infants' cognitive functioning seems more mysterious than that of older children and adults because infants do not talk. We cannot ask them to describe what they can see or how many objects are in front of them or to tell us their solutions to a problem. Most efforts to probe cognition at all other age levels depend on giving verbal instructions, and they usually also require at least some verbal responses from study participants.

How then can we understand what a baby knows, thinks, or even feels? Piaget's research with infants, done primarily with his own three children, focused on detailed analyses of babies' motor interactions with the environment. A newborn's reflexive responses to sensory stimuli— like looking and following when a visual stimulus moves across the visual field, head turning in the direction of a sound, grasping at a touch to the palm, and sucking at a touch to the lips— were examined under many different stimulus conditions. Piaget carefully noted how these sensorimotor patterns functioned and, especially, how they changed with time and experience. From such observations, Piaget inferred what babies might actually understand or be capable of learning.

Today, additional techniques have been added to the infant research repertoire. Among these, for example, is the habituation paradigm, which takes advantage of a baby's tendency to orient to new stimulation and to habituate to repeated or old stimulation. Suppose, for example, that a baby is propped up in an infant seat in a darkened room in front of a large, blank video screen. Suddenly, a picture of a green circle flashes on the screen. The baby is likely to produce an orienting response to this new stimulus. She will look longer at the picture than she had at the blank screen. She will suck more vigorously on the pacifier in her mouth, and her blood pressure and her heart rate are likely to decrease from their previous base rate. If the green circle is repeatedly presented, however, after a time the baby will seem to grow bored with the stimulus. Perhaps it now seems familiar, even "old." We call this response habituation, and it is indicated by shorter looking times, less vigorous sucking, and a return to base rate for heartbeat and blood pressure. With the help of video cameras and computers, all of these subtle response changes can be closely monitored. Now, suppose we flash a new picture on the screen, a picture of a yellow circle. We are looking for a dishabituation response, that is, a renewed orienting response, which we will take to mean that the baby has noticed the difference between the first circle and the second, and her interest is renewed. If the baby is a newborn, we will be disappointed. Newborns show no sign of being able to tell the difference between green and yellow: They do not dishabituate to yellow after becoming habituated to green. But if the baby is 3 months old, she probably will dishabituate to the yellow stimulus, indicating to us that she can discriminate between the two colors. Thus, we have learned that babies cannot perceive differences between green and yellow when they are born but that by 3 months they can do so.

Research using the habituation paradigm has provided us with much of what we know about the infant's perceptual abilities, especially what they can see and hear (described earlier and in Table 3.1). But researchers are also using habituation methods to make inferences about what babies can understand and how they think, as you will see. Modern researchers do not always agree about what inferences to draw from such data (e.g., Haith & Benson, 1998), but their work has certainly stimulated a great deal of interest in looking more closely at infant development, and it has led to several challenges of Piaget's ideas. Let's consider now three interesting and important cognitive developments in infancy, combining data from both older and newer approaches.

UNDERSTANDING OBJECTS

There would be little that you and I would understand about the physical or social world if we did not have a fundamental understanding that there are objects (including human objects, such as ourselves!) with substance and constancy, occupying locations in a spatial field. To become attached to a parent and to begin the process of healthy emotional development, a baby must have some conception of the parent as a permanent, substantive object in her world. (See Chapter 4 for an account of the infant's ability to conceptualize the parent as a separate being.)

What must infants understand to "know" about objects—that is, to have an object concept? First, they need to know that objects have properties that can stimulate all of their senses: vision,

Researchers have learned a great deal about infant cognition and perception using methods that measure habituation or preference.

hearing, taste, smell, and touch. For example, what they feel in their mouths as they suck a pacifier is the same as what they see when Mom or Dad holds the pacifier up in front of them. When can they make such connections? It appears that they have some capacity to do so as early as the 1st month of life. Meltzoff and Borton (1979) gave 1-month-olds an opportunity to suck on either a smooth pacifier or a bumpy one, without letting the infants see the pacifiers. Then, the researchers used a technique known as the preferential looking paradigm to explore whether the babies had learned anything about the visual characteristics of the pacifiers that they had sucked on but had never seen. The babies looked at a split video screen. On one side was a picture of the smooth pacifier, on the other side a picture of the bumpy pacifier. A camera recorded the infants' eye movements. The babies spent more time looking at whichever pacifier they had previously sucked—suggesting that they were capable of recognizing the appearance of the pacifier from their tactile experience of it. Findings like this one indicate that the senses are already somewhat related very early in infancy, perhaps at birth, and that when babies perceive an object in one way, they can construct some notion of the object's other perceptual characteristics. This quality of intersensory integration (also referred to as crossmodal matching or intermodal perception) is not surprising given what we now know about prenatal brain development: that the development of one sensory system is influenced by the development of other systems (see the discussion of the brain, earlier in this chapter). Piaget (1954), without the benefit of today's research methods, assumed that intersensory integration appeared later in infancy, after babies have learned to coordinate their reflexive responses to stimulation. For example, not until about 6 weeks do babies reach up to grasp an object that they are sucking; and not until 4 to 6 months do they smoothly coordinate grasping and looking, allowing easy exploration of objects through visually guided reaching. Surely, these motor coordinations enrich a baby's understanding of objects as "packages" of perceptual characteristics, but such understanding is initiated earlier than Piaget realized.

What else must infants know to have an understanding of objects? Piaget pointed out that adults realize that objects have a separate existence from the perceiver. Think for a moment about something that is out of sight, like the sink in your bathroom. Despite your inability to see the sink at this moment, you realize that it still exists. Your perceptual processes or actions on the object are not necessary to its continuation. This quality of objects is referred to as object permanence: they exist apart from the perceiver.

It can be argued that to understand the permanence of objects, a child must have at least a rudimentary capacity to keep the object in mind when it is not present. To put it another way, the child must have a mental representation of the object, like your mental image of the bathroom sink. The capacity to think about things or events that are not currently stimulating our senses is called representational thought. Thus, if we could find out when a baby understands object permanence, we would not only know something about her object concept, but we would also know that she was capable of representational thought. Piaget invented the hidden object test to assess object permanence. An interesting object, like a small toy, is placed in front of a baby, within her reach. As the baby watches, we cover the object with a cloth, so that it is out of sight. What we want to know is, will the baby search for the object under the cloth, or does the baby act as if the object's disappearance means that the object no longer exists? Studies using the hidden object test, beginning with Piaget's own studies, have consistently found that infants younger than 8 to 12 months fail to search for the object, even though they have the motor skills they need to succeed much earlier (e.g., they engage in visually guided reaching by about 4 months, and they can sit without support by about 6 months). Piaget concluded that understanding object permanence has its rudimentary beginnings late in the 1st year of life and gradually improves thereafter. It may also be that representational thought—the ability to form mental representations, such as images—is a skill that begins to develop only in the late months of the 1st year of life. This representational ability evolves and improves through the 2nd year of life, until, by the end of the sensorimotor period, children not only think about objects but can mentally plan their actions, solve simple problems "all in their heads," remember past experiences, and so on. In other words, they have developed a broad capacity for thinking.

In recent years, studies using procedures such as the habituation paradigm have indicated that babies may have some understanding of object permanence, and therefore, perhaps, some representational thinking skills, much earlier in infancy. In one famous study, Baillargeon (1987) worked with infants only 4 months old, too young to do the hidden object test. Babies sat in front of an apparatus that consisted of a board attached by a hinge to a table top. The board lay flat on the table and gradually swung on its hinge up and away from the watching baby until it was again flat on the table (see Figure 3.5). Babies watched the action of the board repeated until they had habituated. Then the researchers placed a box on the table, so that if the board swung up and away from the baby, it would eventually be stopped by the box, although the baby could no longer see the box at that point. Then, babies saw either what you would expect—the board stopping partway through its descent because of the box being in the way—or an impossible event, with the board continuing to swing smoothly down to the table (because the researchers had sneakily removed the box). Babies looked longer and harder at the impossible event, dishabituating, even though it was more like the event they had previously seen. It seemed as if they were surprised that the box, no longer visible, had failed to stop the board's movement. Because the babies acted as if they believed the box was still there, even though they could not see it, Baillargeon argued that even 4-month-olds understand object permanence, calling into question Piaget's views that object permanence and representational thinking begin to emerge only late in the 1st year of life.

Findings such as Baillargeon's have created lively controversy about just when representational thinking begins and have even raised the possibility that it might be characteristic of

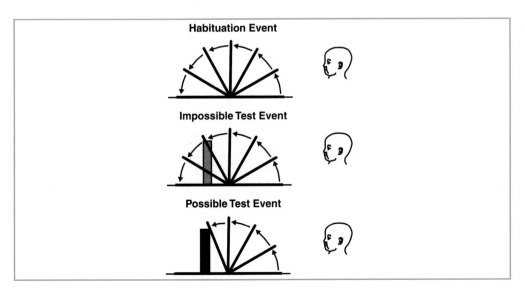

Habituation Event

Impossible Test Event

Possible Test Event

FIGURE 3.5

Baillargeon's Habituation Study of Infant Object Permanence

Source: Baillargeon, R. (1987). Object permanence in 3½-and 4½-month-old infants. *Developmental Psychology, 23,* 656. Copyright © 1987 by the American Psychological Association. Adapted with permission.

human babies from birth (see discussions by Haith & Benson, 1998; Kagan, 2002; Mandler, 2004). Nonetheless, most research supports the general idea that thinking, and conceptual developments that are dependent on thinking, such as object permanence, gradually emerge and improve through the 1st and 2nd years of life and beyond. In the next section, we will see that studies of infant memory and of babies' abilities to plan their actions indicate the same kind of gradual development.

REMEMBERING

New research on infant memory is becoming available at a very rapid rate, stimulated by the availability of methods such as the habituation and preferential looking paradigms and by the special interest of researchers who favor information processing theories of cognitive development (see Chapter 1). Storage of information, duration of storage, retrieval of stored information—these are the centerpieces of cognitive functioning from the point of view of scientists who think about the human cognitive system as akin in some ways to a computer processor. Their special interest has provided us with a much better picture today of what infants can learn and remember than we had even a decade ago. What follows is only a sampling of what we are discovering about infant memory, that is, the ability to learn and to store information.

First, memory is not just one mental function. There are different kinds of memory. Here we will describe two: recognition and recall. Recognition memory is the ability to differentiate between experiences that are new and experiences that we have had before. When you see a face across a room and say to yourself, "I've seen that person before," you are demonstrating recognition. Piaget (1952) guessed from the way babies use their reflexes that at least a primitive form of recognition is possible in earliest infancy. Babies will suck anything that touches their lips, but if they are hungry, they continue to suck only objects that have become associated with nourishment, like nipples. Thus, they show a kind of motor recognition of the nipple through their sucking.

Today's researchers typically use the habituation paradigm to assess infant recognition. When babies habituate to a stimulus that is repeatedly presented, they are showing us that the stimulus is becoming familiar. Because even newborns will habituate to at least some repeatedly presented stimuli, we are now confident that newborns are capable of recognition. Operant conditioning has also demonstrated that recognition skills are present from birth. For example, a 3-day-old infant will learn to suck harder for the reward of hearing its own mother's voice (rather than a stranger's voice), indicating that the baby recognizes the mother's voice (e.g., DeCasper & Fifer, 1980). The newborn's recognition of the mother's voice seems to be a result of opportunities to hear her voice before birth, suggesting that the capacity for recognition is already in place before birth (DeCasper & Prescott, 1984; DeCasper & Spence, 1986).

Recognition improves throughout infancy. In many instances, recognition in the newborn period fades after a few minutes or even seconds, although some studies have found much longer durations (e.g., DeCasper & Spence, 1986). If infants are 3 months old or older when they are exposed to a stimulus, they sometimes recognize it after several months of nonexposure, especially if it is a moving stimulus (e.g., Bahrick & Pickens, 1995).

Not only does the duration of recognition increase with age, but the speed with which babies habituate increases as well. Younger babies need more exposures to a stimulus than older babies before they show signs of recognition. But there are also individual differences among babies of the same age. Interestingly, how quickly babies habituate to a new stimulus is one of the few measures of infant functioning that has been found to correlate with later intelligence test performance. Apparently, recognition speed is an early indicator of the efficiency with which a child may later process information (Bornstein & Sigman, 1986; Fagan, 1990).

In contrast to the early and rapid development of recognition memory, recall seems to emerge later in infancy. Recall is the ability to bring to mind an experience that has happened in the past. It is different from recognition because the to-be-remembered experience is not presently occurring, but must be mentally represented. In other words, thinking that involves mental representation, such as forming mental images, is necessary for recall. One indicator of recall is deferred imitation, in which children observe the actions of another on one occasion, and then imitate those actions sometime later. We should note that babies imitate some *immediate* actions as early as the newborn period. For example, if you stick out your tongue at a newborn, you are likely to see the baby's tongue protrude as well (Meltzoff & Moore, 1977), an action that is often interpreted as a reflexive response to a looming stimulus (e.g., Mandler, 2004). But soon babies will imitate other actions. If you clap your hands at a 4-month-old, she may clap her hands as well (Piaget, 1951). It seems that babies slowly work out the correspondences between their own and other people's body parts, and as they do, they extend their range of imitation. But immediate imitation does not indicate recall. Only if there is a time delay between the observed action and the baby's imitation of it can we say that representations in memory were necessary for the imitation.

Based on observations of his own children's behavior, Piaget believed that deferred imitation begins around the middle of the baby's 2nd year. At 16 months, for example, his daughter Jacqueline watched a visiting boy have a temper tantrum, screaming and stamping his feet in a playpen. The next day, Jacqueline did the same, only she was smiling and her foot stamping was gentle. She was not actually having a temper tantrum, but was imitating her little friend's fascinating performance (Piaget, 1962). More recent research demonstrates that infants from about 9 months of age will recall, and later imitate, actions that they have witnessed. For example, Meltzoff (1988) showed babies an interesting box, then demonstrated that pushing a button on the box would produce a beep. The next day, the babies were given the opportunity to play with the box themselves for the first time. Nine-month-old babies who had watched the button pushing the previous day were much more likely to push the button themselves than were babies who had not previously observed the action. On the whole, available research suggests that deferred imitation can begin late in the 1st year but that it does improve dramatically over the next year, both in duration and in the complexity of what can be recalled. For example, 11-month-old babies will imitate a simple sequence of actions a few minutes after observing them, but 20-month-olds can do so as long as 2 weeks later (Bauer & Mandler, 1989, 1990). Deferred imitation is, of course, what makes observational learning, or modeling, possible. Once children can mentally represent and thus recall the actions of others, they have a cognitive skill that is critical for social learning. A toddler who has watched his big sister painting pictures might on his own open a jar of paint, dip a paintbrush into it, and then sweep the paintbrush across some available surface. His proficiency at each of these actions will be limited, but the sequence will be executed more or less correctly because he recalls his big sister's past actions.

Searching for a hidden object, which begins at about 8 months of age, can be seen as a sign not only that a child believes in the object's permanence but that the child recalls the object. A particularly important sign of such recall is the beginning of separation anxiety. When parents leave a young baby with another caregiver, the baby typically does not seem to miss the absent parents or to mourn their loss while they are gone. When they are out of sight, they seem to be out of mind. But in the second half of the 1st year, at about 8 months for most babies, leaving a child with another caregiver may be more difficult. The baby may continue for some time to watch for the missing parents, to cry or fuss, and to generally act distressed. Bouts of separation anxiety are usually of fairly short duration at first, but tend to increase in length, suggesting that the child's ability to recall the parents is increasing in duration. An 18- to 24-month-old left with a babysitter might show signs of anxiety repeatedly throughout the parents' absence. Of course, many factors contribute to separation anxiety: the familiarity of the alternate caregiver and of the surroundings, the quality of the infant's relationship to the parents, the infant's temperament (see Chapter 4), and so on. But the consistency with which babies around the world begin showing separation distress at about 8 months is attributable to the development of the basic cognitive skills of recall and object permanence (Kagan, Kearsley, & Zelazo, 1978; McBride & DiCero, 1990).

HAVING AND INFERRING INTENTIONS

If we intentionally act, choosing to pick up a fork rather than a spoon, searching through a closet for just the right outfit to wear, or planning a presentation at work, we are thinking about what we do before we do it. Very little conscious effort may be involved in some intentional acts, but at least some thought is required. Like many other cognitive skills, the ability to intend to do something has important consequences not just for intellectual performance but for social interactions as well. A child who can choose whether or not to cry to call for attention, for example, is likely to be treated differently than one who can only reflexively cry in response to discomfort. Obviously, the development of intentional action is related to the development of self-control and decision making, which we will discuss at greater length in future chapters.

Having Intentions. When does intentional action begin? Piaget (1952) assumed that infants' earliest behaviors are entirely unintentional and are typically based on reflexive responses to incoming stimulation and on the need to act, that is, to repetitively exercise one's reflexes. By 4 to 8 months, infants' behaviors have expanded as a result of constant differentiation and integration of the original reflexes, according to Piaget, and now a baby has a large repertoire of behavioral responses to stimuli. If one of these behaviors accidentally produces an interesting event, a child is likely to notice the effect and repeat the action, as if she is hoping to repeat the effect. Piaget called this making interesting sights last. He did not consider it to be intentional behavior, but a precursor of intentional behavior. In fact, it appears to be simple operant conditioning. After a behavior occurs, there is a reinforcing event, and the behavior is likely to be repeated. But there is a twist. Piaget described infants as appearing somewhat reflective, as if they had noticed the connection between their action and the outcome, and they were trying to make it happen again. Rovee-Collier (1990) has reported a similar sequence of events in infants as young as 3 months old. When a mobile hanging over a baby's crib is tied to a baby's foot, the child will soon learn to shake her foot to make the mobile move. At some point, the baby appears to notice the connection, as if she were having an insight, and the baby shakes her foot more vigorously afterward.

From these first inklings of intentional behavior, infants move to more clearly intentional action in that magical time, the last few months of the 1st year. By 8 to 12 months, Piaget reported that babies will engage in means–end behavior: They will divert their attention from a goal, such as grasping a toy, to produce another action that will help achieve the goal. For example, a baby might try to grasp a rattle that is behind a clear Plexiglas screen. When her hand touches the screen, the baby redirects her attention to the screen, perhaps pushing it aside, before focusing again on the rattle. Younger babies simply keep reaching for the rattle and failing. Their behavior seems more controlled by the stimulus of the rattle than by their own plans. Thus, again, it appears that a behavior that requires mental representation, planning, begins in the 8- to 12-month period. Recent studies also indicate that infants may do some fairly complex sizing up of such situations. Willatts (1989) found that 9-month-olds would put aside a barrier and then pull a cloth to get an out-of-reach toy resting on the cloth. But when the toy was not on the cloth, babies tended to simply play with the barrier, as though they realized there was no point in pulling on the cloth.

More sophisticated intentional control of behavior emerges in the 2nd year. Whereas a 10-month-old typically will use only previously practiced actions as means to an end, 12- to 18-month-olds begin to actively invent new variations on their actions to fit the situation, trying out one variation after another. By 24 months, toddlers' control of their mental representations is advanced enough that they will mentally invent new means to an end. Rather than trying this and trying that, sometimes they solve a problem by quietly studying the situation first, and producing a useful means to an end on the first try.

The beginning of intentional behavior by the end of the 1st year is evident in babies' communicative behaviors. When a younger baby repeats an action that has attracted attention in the past, such as patting Mommy's cheek, the child may be doing no more than "making interesting sights last." But by 8 to 12 months, most babies are using some of their behaviors, including some vocalizations, not just to attract attention but as a communicative means to an end. For example, a typical 12-month-old might make a wailing sound while intently looking at her father. When he looks in her direction, she extends her hand in an urgent reach, apparently indicating a toy that she would like retrieved. It is difficult not to interpret such complex means-end behavior as intentional communication (Golinkoff, 1983).

Inferring Others' Intentions. As babies are developing intentions of their own, what do they understand about the intentions of others? Researchers make a distinction between a child's understanding of human agency and of human intention. *Agency* refers to the ability to act without an external trigger. People and animals have agency because they can act without being pushed or "launched" by some other force, whereas objects require launching. *Intention* is an internal mental state, such as a plan or a desire, that is the source of an action. Infants begin to understand agency by the end of the 1st year. Just trying to get other people to do things for her, like the baby described in the last paragraph, suggests that a baby has some sense that others are agents. Understanding that other people have intentions, desires, feelings, and so on, and inferring what those intentions might be, appear to be much more difficult achievements. As you will see in the discussion of the preoperational stage, understanding intentions is part of developing a theory of mind, and it is a complex and long-term process.

Yet, as with other cognitive skills, there appear to be preliminary developments in the understanding of intentions by the end of the 1st year. Using an habituation task, Woodward (1998) has found some apparent awareness of the goal-directedness (intentionality) of human action even in babies as young as 6 months. In her study, babies saw an actor's arm reach for one of two toys that were side-by-side on a platform. Say, for example, that the arm reached for the toy on the left. The sequence was repeated until the babies habituated. Then, the position of the toys was switched, so that the toy that had been on the left was now on the right. The babies now witnessed one of two events. In the first event, the actor reached for the same toy as before, but the actor's arm had to reach in a different direction (to the right in our example) because the toys had been switched. In other words, the actor's goal remained the same—to pick up the same toy. In the second event, the actor reached for a new toy that was now in the original location (on the left in our example). Babies dishabituated more to the second event, as though they were surprised by the change in goal. The change in the direction of movement in the first event did not seem to be experienced as particularly new or important. Rather, it was the change in goal that the babies noticed. The same study done with an inanimate rod "reaching" toward the toys did not produce the same results. The babies seemed to expect goal-directedness from humans, but they did not expect it from an inanimate rod. The results of Woodward's study suggest that although full understanding of human intentions may take a long time, babies appear to have a rudimentary sense that there are significant differences between humans and other objects as early as 6 months.

Preschoolers' Cognition: The Preoperational Stage

By the age of 2, children have moved beyond the limits of sensorimotor activity to become thinkers. Instead of responding to the world primarily by connecting sensation to action, constantly exercising and adapting reflexive patterns of behavior, children can engage the world on the plane of thought. As we have seen, they understand that objects exist apart from their own perceptions and actions; they can call to mind previously experienced events; they can plan and execute complex behaviors, even behaviors they have not tried before; and they know that humans, unlike objects, are agents of action whose behavior is goal-directed. Whereas there are precursors to most or all of these skills even in early infancy, and scientists argue about when the earliest representations actually occur (e.g., Mandler, 2004), the flowering of thinking in the 2nd year of life is indisputable. Among the abilities that toddlers' thinking permits is the use of symbols (Piaget, 1962). *Symbols* are stand-ins for other things. Words are symbols; so are the props used in pretend play when they stand for something else, the way a broom stands for a horse when a child gallops around "riding" the broom. To use and understand such symbols, children must be able to mentally represent the things being symbolized. As babies' representational skills grow, especially over the 2nd year, language skill and pretend play begin to blossom.

In this section, we will highlight some of the cognitive developments of the preschool years that are launched as the infancy period ends. You will find that Piaget, although celebrating the accomplishments of what he called the "preoperational" or prelogical years, also identified many limitations of children's early thought. You will also learn that in recent years developmental scientists have focused heavily on exploring the limitations that Piaget identified. Sometimes, the newer data suggest that preschoolers possess greater skill than Piaget may have realized, and some of the newer findings have helped us to specify step-by-step changes in some of the abilities that Piaget first described.

UNDERSTANDING NUMBERS

Piaget (1952) launched the systematic study of children's number skills by inventing the number conservation task. A set of discrete items, let's say five candies, is laid out in a neatly spaced line. Below the first set is a second set, laid out the same way, with the candies in each row matched one to one. A child is asked if the two rows have the same number or whether one or the other has more candies. Typically, 3- and 4-year-olds recognize that the two rows have the same number of candies. But when the researcher then changes the appearance of the second row by spreading out the candies, preschoolers usually think that the number has changed along with the appearance of the row. Most frequently, they say that the longer row now has more candy. Even if they count the candies and report that each has five, they believe that the longer row has more. Do they really believe that? They seem to: If you ask them which row they would rather have to eat, they will choose the longer row!

Endless debate has swirled around the meaning of preschoolers' failure on this number conservation task. Piaget felt that children were revealing some fundamental characteristics of preoperational thought. Most important, preoperational thought tends to be centered or focused on one salient feature of an experience or event at a time, a characteristic referred to as centration. In a sense, young thinkers can think about only one thing at a time. In the number conservation task, when they look at the rows of candies, preschoolers focus on the differences in length, but they ignore the differences in density. If they noticed both, especially the transformations that occurred in both as the second row was reconfigured, they might recognize that as the length of the row increased, the density of the row decreased, so that the number of candies stayed the same despite the increased length. Because their thought is centered, Piaget argued, preoperational children tend to link observations in serial order, rather than discovering and representing the more complex relationships among them. In the number conservation task, even when children notice both the change in length and the change in density of the second row, they observe these changes serially, and they do not recognize the reciprocal relationship between them. All in all, the contents of preoperational thought tend to be limited to the most salient perceptual characteristics. Young children have trouble recognizing "underlying realities" (Flavell et al., 1993). For example, children fail to realize that the number of candies is conserved even when they are moved around, because they do not take into account all the relevant observations at one time. As a result, young children do not discover the relationships among the facts, and they draw conclusions that to adults are quite illogical.

Piaget argued that as children interact with the world and practice representing the events they observe, their thinking becomes more efficient, and eventually they are able to decenter, that is, to take into account multiple pieces of information simultaneously, a process referred to as decentration. As a result, important relationships among their observations can be discovered and represented, and their thinking becomes more logical and sensible from an adult's point of view. Piaget found that improvements in children's thinking moved forward rapidly in the years from 5 to 7, so that most children were successful on tasks such as number conservation by about age 7.

Newer research on children's understanding of numbers emphasizes how much preschoolers do know about numbers, even though they still fail Piaget's number conservation task. Even newborns appear to discriminate differences between small numbers; they will habituate to displays of two items, but then dishabituate to a display of three items (Antell & Keating, 1983). In exploring the number skills of preschoolers, Gelman and her colleagues (e.g., Gelman & Gallistel, 1978; see also Gelman, 1982; Gelman & Williams, 1998) found that 2- to 3-year-olds have at least implicit understanding of many fundamental counting principles. For example, they know that counting requires the "one-to-one" principle: one number for one item. Such young children sometimes do mistakenly recount items, but they seem to realize that recounting is not really acceptable. Between 3 and 5 years, children can count the same set of items in versatile order, starting once with the item on the left, another time with the item on the right, and so forth. Gelman calls this the "order-irrelevance principle." She has even found that children as young as 3 can sometimes remain focused on number despite changes in the length and density of rows.

In a series of studies using "magic number games," Gelman showed children two plates, each with a row of toy mice, two mice on one plate, three mice on the other. For some children, the rows of mice were of equal length but of unequal density; for other children, the rows of mice were of unequal length but equal density. First, the children were trained to pick the "winner" plate (the one with three mice) by giving them lots of trials and telling them whether they were right or wrong. Once they had learned to pick the correct plate without error, the researcher surreptitiously changed the appearance of the plates. For example, if the rows of mice had been of equal length, they were changed to be of equal density. Children tended to register surprise when the changed plates were revealed, but they still correctly picked the winners. Thus it was clear that they had learned to select the correct plate on the basis of number, not on the basis of length or density differences. It appears that under the right circumstances, young children can pay attention to "underlying realities," although their ability to do so is quite fragile and easily disrupted: The same children who succeeded in the magic number games still failed Piaget's classic number conservation tasks.

Gelman's magic number games are characteristic of many of the tasks that modern researchers have designed to explore the apparent limitations of preschoolers' thinking. They are different from Piaget's tasks in that they provide simple instructions, and they often do not require verbal responses or explanations. They also establish different criteria for granting children some knowledge or skill. Piaget's criteria were conservative. He wanted children to demonstrate that they had complete mastery of a skill or concept, such as the concept of number, so that it could not be disrupted by counter suggestions or by superficial transformation, before he granted that the skill was present. He often required that children be able to give sensible explanations of their right answers before he credited them with true understanding (Haith & Benson, 1998). Modern researchers tend to make minimal demands on children and to grant them the presence of a skill even when children's success can be easily disrupted by increased demands. The data are not in dispute, but the interpretation of the data is. One approach to resolving the dispute is to assume that concepts such as number are understood by children in ever-increasing depth and breadth. Specifying the levels of understanding and the experiences that help children to advance from one level to another is what researchers must aim to discover (Bidell & Fischer, 1997; Blewitt, 1994; Haith & Benson, 1998).

At this time, many of Piaget's characterizations of the limitations of preoperational thought remain useful. As Flavell has argued (e.g., Flavell et al., 1993), for example, preschoolers do seem to make appearance-based conclusions, and they often miss the deeper significance of events. Also, their thinking often does seem especially affected by singular, salient dimensions of a situation. However, most researchers recognize that such limitations aptly describe young children's abilities sometimes, but not always. Specifying the conditions that govern these limitations is more and more a focus of research.

UNDERSTANDING THE MIND

Piaget (1926; Piaget & Inhelder, 1956) pioneered the investigation of children's understanding of other people's mental processes by studying perspective-taking skills in preschoolers. In his "three mountains task," a three-dimensional model of three mountains was shown to children from several different angles. Children then had to select a picture of how the scene looked to them, as well as a picture of how it looked to another observer on a different side of the display. Until about age 7, children tended to select the same picture both times, suggesting that they believed that other observers shared their perspective. Piaget believed children's poor perspective-taking skills reflected preoperational egocentrism. Because preschoolers can think about only one thing at a time, they are centered on their own perspective and have no awareness of the possibility of a different perspective.

Egocentrism is often evident in young children's encounters with others. A young girl may suggest that Daddy would like a dollhouse for his birthday; she assumes that he wants what she wants. When parents eagerly ask for information about what happened in nursery school, their son fails to respond, as if he cannot fathom what it is the parents do not know; if he knows what happened today, surely they do too. During a telephone conversation, when her grandmother asks a toddler what she's going to wear to her birthday party, the child responds "This!" and points to the dress she is wearing, as if her grandmother can see what she can see. These are all typical examples of a failure to take another person's perspective.

Today, researchers see such behaviors as reflecting aspects of a child's theory of mind or "naive psychology," that is, the child's understanding of psychological processes. Such understanding is ultimately critical for developing satisfactory relationships with others. We have already seen that in the 1st year of infancy children begin to have a sense that humans are agents of action and that others' (and perhaps their own) behaviors can be goal directed. Among the earliest signs that children have some notion of the existence of mental states is their use of "mental" words. Words for emotions or desires, such as *need, feel,* and *want,* tend to occur as early as age 2, and words such as *think, forget,* and *remember* that describe cognitive functions are often used by age 3 (Huttenlocher & Smiley, 1990; Ruffman, Slade, & Crowe, 2002). What concepts underlie these words we do not really know. It is likely that they are not the same as an adult's, but clearly the young preschooler is beginning to assign some meaning to these words.

Thus, in the early preschool years, children have a sense that they and others have mental states, such as thoughts, desires, feelings, and plans. Piaget's perspective-taking work focused on what children infer those states to be, and he found that preschoolers usually assume that others' mental states match their own. Newer work has expanded the focus of research to address questions such as what do children understand about how people acquire information, when do they understand that mental states may or may not match reality, and do children correctly impute to others some mental states before other mental states. There is some dispute about the answers to these questions (see Flavell & Miller, 1998), but available findings do indicate that children very gradually build such understandings. Two- and 3-year-olds often seem oblivious to what others know and how they know it, although they show some signs of making progress on these issues. For example, as early as age 2, a child can understand that if she is looking at a picture of a cat and you are standing opposite her, looking at the back of the picture, you will not be able to see the cat. In other words, the child can figure out that you see or do not see something under these conditions. However, suppose we place the picture of the cat on a table, face up, so that the child can see it right-side-up and you see it upside-down. At age 2, the child cannot understand that you have a different perspective on the cat, and she assumes that you also see it right-side-up. By age 3, in this simple situation, the child will be able to attribute a different visual perspective to you. She still will not be able to compute any kind of complex perspective difference, such as Piaget's three mountains task requires, but she can understand that someone else might see the same picture differently from herself (e.g., Masangkay et al., 1974).

Understanding that people know different things is more difficult for the young child. Until 4 or 5 years, most children attribute the same knowledge to others that they have themselves, as research using false belief tasks illustrates. In such tasks, one person has correct knowledge of a situation, but another person (or the same person at another time) has incorrect knowledge, or a "false belief." Suppose a child is aware that a box of candy has been removed from its original location and is now hidden in a cabinet. The child is asked where a second person, let's call him Sam, will look for the candy. Even though the child knows Sam was not present for the hiding, the child does not attribute a false belief to Sam but assumes that Sam will search in the appropriate hiding place, as if Sam must know what the child knows (e.g., Wimmer & Perner, 1983; see also Wellman, 1990; Wellman, Cross, & Watson, 2001). In fact, until age 4 or 5 children have trouble realizing that they themselves have not always known what they know now (Gopnik & Astington, 1988). If they open a candy box expecting to find candy and are surprised to find something else instead, say pencils, they will later say that they knew before they opened the box that the pencils were there.

The trouble young children have figuring out what other people know, or need to know, is reflected in their attempts to communicate and can be responsible for both the charm and sometimes the spectacular failure of their efforts. Here are some samples from children's attempts to describe their favorite recipes (Martel, 1974):

"SKABBETTI": First you decide what it will be tonight—sausages or meatballs. When your father tells you which one, then you cook. (p. 1)

"POPCORN": Put the popcorn seeds in the popcorn bowl and plug it in the plug hole—and get the toaster out of the way. . . . If your brother takes the lid off, popcorn go zinging all over the kitchen . . . POW! POW! POW! (p. 45)

"BANILLA CAKE": 1 cake stuff; 2 eggs (But on "Sesame Street" they put 8 eggs in a cake. I always watch "Love American Style" after "Sesame Street"); a drop of milk; 7 of those little silver baseballs for on the top. Put every single thing you have into a mother-size pan—a little one wouldn't do. . . . Put it in the oven department of the stove. Make it as hot as a coffee pot. Pretty soon it will come popping right out! Eat it when the news comes on. (p. 34)

Most research on children's theory of mind indicates that, on one hand, preschoolers are less egocentric than Piaget inferred based on his very complex perspective-taking task, but that on the other hand, he was on target in assuming that taking another's perspective and understanding the limits of one's own perspective are difficult, and sometimes impossible, tasks for young children. The implications for children's social development are far reaching. For example, when toddlers want to grab a dog's tail or to chase a ball into the street, they do not understand that the adults who restrain them want something different. Disciplinary action by others is frustrating to a 2-year-old, because she does not get what she wants of course, but also because she does not understand that other people's desires are different from her own. Three-year-olds do better understanding that others may not share their own desires or preferences. They might accept, for example, that their parents like coffee even though they themselves do not. But when two people have different beliefs, even 3- and 4-year-olds are often mystified (Flavell, Mumme, Green, & Flavell, 1992). For example, 3-year-olds found it difficult to comprehend that a girl in a story could think a toothbrush was hers when another child thought it was his!

Finally, when children's own emotions are strongly involved, taking another's perspective seems especially difficult. Apparently the salience of one's own perspective, especially in an emotionally charged situation, can undermine the child's fragile understanding of the differences between her own mental state and that of another person. For example, one 6-year-old girl, who in many situations was quite capable of understanding that others have different feelings and motives than she, was furious whenever she lost a board game or any other competition, calling her competitor "mean." Her own desire to win was so overwhelmingly salient that she assumed that it was shared by others, and that any interference with her success was simply mean-spiritedness!

How do young children overcome their problems with perspective taking and build a more realistic theory of mind? Piaget credited two processes: first, the gradual improvement in a child's ability to hold in mind multiple ideas at the same time (decentering), and second, the continual give and take of social interaction in which a child repeatedly confronts feedback from other people indicating that others do not always share the child's feelings, desires, or knowledge. Children find it difficult to assimilate such feedback, but gradually they accommodate their views of others until they can conceive of independent mental states. Modern theorists have proposed several other explanations, but many, like Piaget, consider experience in social interaction to be a key factor (see Flavell & Miller, 1998; for changes in perspective-taking skill in older children, see Chapter 6).

UNDERSTANDING SYMBOLIC ARTIFACTS

When and how do children make sense of the many symbols that humans use to communicate? A symbol, remember, stands for something other than itself. In the next section we will look at the development of language, or linguistic symbols, which are quite arbitrary (e.g., the word *elephant* bears no resemblance to the real thing that it symbolizes), but first let's consider more analogical symbols, such as pictures or maps or scale models, which DeLoache (1999; DeLoache, Miller, & Pierrovutsakos, 1998) calls **symbolic artifacts**. Because these kinds of symbols are often similar to the things they represent, one might think that children would find them easier to interpret than words, but in fact the reverse may be true. DeLoache suggests that young children have difficulty with symbolic artifacts because of their dual nature: They are both concrete objects themselves and symbols for other things. To understand a symbolic artifact, a child must mentally represent the same thing in two ways at once, and as we have already seen, young children often have difficulty holding more than one idea in mind simultaneously. Perhaps as a result, children often understand less about things such as pictures or models than adults may think. For example, research on children's understanding of pictures indicates that if a picture is realistic, like a photograph, 9-month-olds attempt to pick up the object in the picture. Eighteen-month-olds are indifferent to whether a picture is right-side-up or upside-down, and even 2-year-olds often cannot pick which picture represents a real object. Beilin (1999) found that even older preschoolers sometimes attribute the qualities of the object that is depicted to the picture itself, thinking, for example, that a photograph of an ice cream cone will be cold.

Young preschoolers have similar trouble with television (e.g., Troseth & DeLoache, 1996). When children younger than 2½ watch a doll being hidden in a room on a video screen, the children will not be able to figure out where the doll is when they search for it in the real room. These children are able to respond directly to what they see on the screen. For example, they can follow the action and imitate what the actors do. However, they have trouble understanding that what they are watching symbolizes something that is happening somewhere else, other than on the screen. Curiously, children's performance improves if the edges of the video screen are covered and children believe that they are witnessing a scene through a window into a room. Then, even a 2-year-old will be able to find a doll hidden in a room after watching the hiding "through the window"! In this situation, the child does not have to perceive the screen events as symbolic of something happening elsewhere.

Children have even more trouble with scale models. DeLoache (1987) showed children a scale model of a room. She hid a miniature doll in the scale model and explained to the children that a full-size model of the doll was hidden in the full-size room. Typically, not until age 3 could children use what they knew about the location of the miniature doll in the model to help them find the full-size doll in the real room. Even though 2-year-olds recognized the similarity between the rooms, they could not use one as a symbol for the other. This point was vividly revealed when researchers convinced 2-year-olds that the scale model was actually the larger room in a shrunken state (DeLoache, Miller, & Rosengren, 1997). In this situation the children did not see the scale model as a symbol of the large room. After witnessing the hiding of the miniature doll in the "shrunken" room, the children were then further duped into thinking that the scale model had been reenlarged into its full size. Now they had no trouble locating the "enlarged" hidden doll!

DeLoache (1999) points out that recognizing the problems that children can have understanding symbolic artifacts has important practical implications. For example, anatomically accurate dolls are often used to question children about their experiences when sexual abuse is suspected. Such dolls are scale models of humans, and our assumption that the symbolic use of the doll is understandable to young preschoolers is highly questionable.

UNDERSTANDING LANGUAGE

Language development is a remarkable achievement of almost all young children, made even more notable by the fact that many aspects of language learning are nearly complete by the end of the preoperational stage. Volumes can, and have, been written summarizing the research on language acquisition. Here we will provide only a sampling of what is entailed when preschoolers master language.

Phonology. First, when children learn language they are learning its phonology, that is, the sound system of the language. Every language uses only a subset of the sounds that humans can use for language. Babies are beginning to learn something about what sounds are important for their language even before they are born. For example, soon after birth young infants show a preference for listening to voices speaking the native language of their mothers, apparently because they have heard their mothers while in the womb (Locke, 1993). One group of researchers found that by 6 months babies exposed to just one language show signs of sharpening their ability to discriminate distinctions that are important in that language, but have begun to lose the ability to perceive distinctions that are unimportant. Japanese babies, for example, start to lose the ability to distinguish *l* sounds from *r* sounds by this time (Kuhl, Williams, Lacerda, Stevens, & Lindblom, 1992). Babies begin babbling at about 6 months, repeating consonant-vowel-consonant sequences such as *bababa* or *doodoodoo*. At first these babblings

As childrens' language ability advances, their social interaction becomes more complex.

include most possible language sounds, but by 9 months they are limited to the sounds permissible in the baby's native language.

Thus, phonological development begins before birth, and there are measurable advances long before babies begin to talk. Yet the full sound system may not be mastered for many years. Most adults find it difficult to understand the speech of a 2-year-old, although doting parents, tuned in to the toddler's phonological errors, can usually translate. The problem often is that 2-year-olds have not learned how, where, or when to use some of the sound distinctions that are important for their native tongue. For example, in English, we take advantage of voicing, using our vocal chords to make some consonant sounds but not others. The difference between the *d* sound and the *t* sound is only that the *d* is voiced and the *t* is not. A toddler may not yet have caught the importance of this distinction, and when she means to say *toy* she may say *doy*. Children master most sound distinctions like these by age 3, but may continue to struggle with other aspects of phonology, such as making the *th* sound in the right places, for much longer. By age 3, most children can make themselves understood to familiar listeners. If a child's speech is still difficult for nonfamily members to follow by age 4, evaluation by a speech pathologist may be advisable. See Table 3.2 for other milestones to watch for in children's communicative development.

Semantics. Second, when children learn language they are learning which words and word parts express what meanings. This is referred to as the semantic system of a language. Progress in producing words begins by the end of the 1st year, as already noted, and moves slowly for a time. In the first 6 months of word use, many words are produced only in limited contexts, as though tied to particular cues. For example, a child might say *daw* only when she sees the family's cocker spaniel, and then only if the dog barks.

At about the time that children can produce about 50 words, they typically go into a new phase of vocabulary learning called the vocabulary spurt: Suddenly, at about 18 to 24 months, toddlers begin learning words very rapidly, expanding their productive vocabulary from 50 to about 500 words in just a few months. Their comprehension vocabulary appears to be even larger. It seems as if the child has had a sudden insight into the fact that anything can be labeled and thus communicated through words. Some have suggested that the vocabulary spurt marks the end of the sensorimotor period and is made possible by a fully functioning representational capacity; words are now truly being used as symbols for concepts and ideas, rather than being triggered by contextual cues. By age 5, the typical child may understand 15,000 words, so that an average of 9 or 10 words have been added every day for 3 years! The rapidity with which young children add new words to functional vocabulary after only one or two exposures is described as fast mapping.

TABLE 3.2 From Birth to Five: Typical Changes in Communicative/Interactive Skills

Age	Skill
Newborn to 1 month	Reflexively signals needs through cries, facial expressions
1 to 3 months	Coos, grunts, makes some other vocal sounds Quiets or smiles when spoken to
3 to 5 months	Smiles and shows interest in favorite people Makes wider range of vocal sounds (e.g., vowel sounds, squeals)
6 to 7 months	Babbles (consonant-vowel-consonant repetitions)
9 to 12 months	Shows, gives objects Reaches or points to indicate desired object Engages in simple interactive games, routines (e.g., peek-a-boo, patty-cake) Responds to simple requests (e.g., "Look at Daddy.") Produces one or two words (e.g., *bye-bye, mama*) Deaf child produces one or two signs Produces first meaningful gestures (e.g., nodding to mean "Yes," waving "Bye-bye")
13 to 18 months	Increases expressive vocabulary slowly, acquiring up to 50 words for familiar actions, events, and objects (e.g., *bottle, allgone, no, kiss, shoe*) Engages in simple pretend play, using self-directed acts (e.g., eating, washing, phone to ear)
18 to 24 months	Increases expressive vocabulary rapidly (3 or more words per day) Uses short (2-word) sentences, using content words (e.g., "Baby ball?" "Allgone Daddy.") Engages in pretend play involving some coordination with partners (e.g., exchanges parent–baby roles with adult)
2 to 3 years	Speaks clearly enough to be understood by family members Requests labels for objects Uses sentences of 3 or more words; uses some function words (e.g., prepositions, articles, word endings) Overuses some grammatical rules—overregularization (e.g., "I *goed* to the store.") Takes turns in conversation
3 to 4 years	Speaks clearly enough to be understood by nonfamily members Uses some complex sentences (e.g., "I think I saw the truck.") Pretends in complex, reciprocal interactions with others, engages in interactive planning for play
4 to 5 years	Produces most speech sounds correctly (continued exceptions might be *l, s, r, v, z, ch, sh, th*) Tells stories that stick to the topic, have some structure (beginning, middle, end) Coordinates conversation with multiple partners

Sources: Adapted from American Speech-Language-Hearing Association (ASHA), 1997–2004; Bloom, 1998; Brazelton & Greenspan, 2000; Brown, 1973; Fenson et al., 1994.

Using words as symbols may be a bit simpler in one respect than the use of artifactual symbols, in that words are not things themselves: They function only to represent meanings. Using them correctly probably does not require representing them in two ways at once, as children must do with artifactual symbols. Rather, a word may at first be perceived by children as more like a part of the concept to which it refers. Understanding that words are arbitrary symbols seems to be much more difficult for children than using them to make meaning. Although toddlers and preschoolers rapidly acquire vocabulary, even at age 5 children may still fail to realize that labels are arbitrary and conventionally determined. For example, if we propose to change around our words and call things by different names, like calling a dog a *cat* and vice versa, a 5-year-old is likely to object that it cannot be done. The child seems to feel that the word, in a sense, "belongs" to the thing it symbolizes and cannot be shifted (Homer, Brockmeier, Kamawar, & Olson, 2001).

Syntax.　Third, learning language requires learning to produce sentences that make sense. The aspect of language that specifies how to link words into meaningful sentences is called the **syntactic system** or **grammar**. Words must be ordered in a sentence in just the right way to communicate what we mean to someone else. Linguists have found that proper ordering of words and word parts (such as prefixes and suffixes in English) is governed by a complex set of rules.

One of the most baffling things about children's language acquisition is that they learn these rules with little difficulty, despite the fact that no one teaches them.

Beginning with two-word strings at about the time of the vocabulary spurt, children quickly progress, until by age 5 they can produce most sentence structures. To give you a sense of how complex the rules are that children implicitly know, consider the following "tag questions":

That boy kicked the dog, didn't he?
The ceiling leaks all the time, doesn't it?
You and I are getting along well, aren't we?

Making the right question tag at the end of the sentence requires knowledge of several rules, including how to add an auxiliary (such as *did* or *does*) to a verb and how to negate a verb, for starters. To make proper tag questions requires so many rules that children are slow to learn this particular sentence form (Brown & Hanlon, 1970). Nonetheless, most children can produce tag questions effortlessly by age 5.

Pragmatics. Finally, children must learn the pragmatics of language use, that is, how to use language effectively to communicate. Knowing how to put together a proper sentence, or knowing the labels for things, is not enough. One must be able to craft a narrative, a story or event description, that conveys the full sense of an experience or gets at the point of an event while taking into account what the listener needs to hear to understand. Different listeners have different needs—say a little sister versus a grandfather—and there are different conventions of address that are acceptable in different situations. All of these kinds of language-use issues must be learned in addition to the mechanics of language. Preschoolers begin to construct narratives, usually with the help of others, by about 2 or 3 years old. Initially, their narratives are sketchy and largely uninformative. A child telling about an all-day trip to the zoo, for example, might mention only that "we went" and indicate one salient experience: "We saw a lion." A listener counting on the narrative to learn where, when, and what is likely to be quite disappointed. Some aspects of developing pragmatic skill are dependent on cognitive developments in perspective taking, which helps account for the inadequacy of children's early narratives (Cameron & Wang, 1999; Uccelli, Hemphill, Pan, & Snow, 1999).

Pragmatic skill also requires making appropriate adjustments in speech depending on the listener. Most children gradually learn code switching, shifting from using, say, slang with friends to using more polite forms with teachers. They also learn, eventually, to distinguish between what people really mean and the literal meaning of their words. Everyday expressions such as "What do ya' know" or "That's cool" are not to be taken literally in most social exchanges. And many such expressions require similar idiomatic responses. For example, today a greeting like "What's happening?" is usually followed by "Nothing much!"

How Language Is Learned. Language consists of so many complex systems, and it is learned so early, that it is difficult to explain how children manage the task. Some psycholinguists have proposed that language is learned by special genetically programmed procedures that are unique to language learning (e.g., Chomsky, 1968; Pinker, 1994). Others contend that the general analytic capacity of the human brain is such that even complex language rules can be worked out without any innate knowledge or special language acquisition procedures (e.g., Karmiloff-Smith, 1992, 2000). Regardless of which view is correct, experience with one's native language must be critically important. Recognizing the importance of experience raises two questions: First, how much exposure to language is necessary, and second, are there particular language experiences that can facilitate the process of learning?

Researchers have only scratched the surface in addressing these questions. Two domains in which both the quantity and the quality of experience have been linked to quality of learning are semantic development in the learning of vocabulary, and pragmatic development in the production of narratives.

Although most 5-year-olds know enough vocabulary to communicate about everyday things, there are large individual differences among children in the size of their vocabularies. In recent years, it has become clear that vocabulary size is a key predictor of later literacy and success in school. Even if children with relatively small vocabularies are reading at grade level by the end of second grade, they are likely to fall behind in reading starting in third grade when reading comprehension begins to depend more and more on the breadth of a child's vocabulary (Senechal & LeFevre, 2002). It has also become clear that children's vocabulary is related to home and preschool environment (e.g., Cunningham, Stanovich, & West, 1994; Senechal & LeFevre, 2002; Weizman & Snow, 2001).

The amount and kind of language experience children have with adults, in parent–child conversations and in joint book reading, are linked with children's vocabulary. In one study, researchers made monthly visits for over 2 years to the homes of children whose families were either poor and on welfare, lower middle class (mostly in blue-color occupations), or upper middle class with at least one professional parent (Hart & Risley, 1992, 1995). All of the parents were actively involved with their children, playing with them, expressing affection, providing them with toys, and so on. But there were marked differences in how much the three groups of parents talked to their children right from the start. (Children were about 9 months old at the beginning of the study.) In a 100-hour week, a toddler in a professional family might hear 215,000 words on the average; in a lower-middle-class family children heard about 125,000 words; and in the poorest homes about 62,000. All of the children learned to talk on schedule, but the differences in parental input were correlated with children's vocabulary measures by age 3; children who heard the most language performed best. The content of parents' conversations with their youngsters also differed. Those who spoke with their children most tended to ask more questions and elaborated more on topics of conversation. Parents who spoke with their children the least tended to utter more prohibitions. Even when the researchers looked within a single socioeconomic group, so that social class was not a factor, children whose parents talked with them more had the most advanced vocabularies. From this and many other studies, it appears that, regardless of social class, the quantity and quality of parent–child conversation can be a significant factor in vocabulary expansion.

Children's narrative skills may also be tied to the kinds of language opportunities that parents and other caregivers provide. Consider how different the narrative skills of two 5-year-olds in the same classroom proved to be. Both children were retelling a story they were told about a boy's trip to a grocery store. Both children were clearly familiar with all of the details of the story, having successfully acted it out with dolls and other props.

FIRST CHILD: John went to the grocery store. He got a cake for his grandmother's birthday party. And he paid the clerk and ran home.

SECOND CHILD: He got cake and he ran home. (Feagans & Farran, 1981, p. 723)

Several studies have found that narrative skill differences like these are connected to the way that mothers converse with their children. If they use an elaborative style, engaging in lengthy discussions about children's past experiences, providing lots of details, asking questions and encouraging children to provide details as well, their children's narratives tend to be more adequate and informative (e.g., Reese & Fivush, 1993). An interesting twist is that mothers who engage their children in this kind of high-quality narrative practice also have children who remember past events in their own lives better (e.g., Boland, Haden, & Ornstein, 2003; Haden, Ornstein, Eckerman, & Didow, 2001). In one study, after 3-year-olds visited a museum with their mothers they could remember *only* what they had actually talked with their mothers about during the trip (Tessler & Nelson, 1994). Discussing an event with preschoolers either before, during, or after it actually happens benefits children's later memory of it (McGuigan & Salmon, 2004). Katherine Nelson (1993b, 1996) has proposed that narrative practice is a key ingredient in the development of autobiographical memories. We are all familiar with the phenomenon of infantile amnesia, the difficulty we have remembering events in our lives earlier than about our 3rd or 4th year. There are probably many factors that contribute, but perhaps one is that our early experiences occur before we have much mastery of language. Nelson argues that it is the mastery of narrative language that is particularly important. When we tell our own life experiences in conversation with others, we also learn to encode stories in language form, a form that is well suited for later recall. In a way, talking out loud about our experiences teaches us not just how to tell stories but how to remember them as well. As you will see in the next section, Nelson's view of how autobiographical memory develops is consistent with the ideas of a highly influential psychologist and educator, Lev Vygotsky, who was a contemporary of Piaget and who emphasized the importance of social experience in many aspects of cognitive development.

Vygotsky's Sociocultural Theory

As we have seen, it would be virtually impossible to consider the topic of cognitive development in children without considering Piaget's contributions. His ideas have been so widely adopted that they provide the foundation for many of our beliefs about child development, and they inform our notions of developmentally appropriate practice in profound ways. As Elkind (1968) noted, he is the "giant in the nursery." However, another theorist also lays claim to widespread influence in the area of cognitive development and has attracted much contemporary attention. His name was Lev S. Vygotsky. (See Box 3.3.) Frequently, Vygotsky's ideas are presented as a counterpoint to those of Piaget, as if the two theorists were in opposing camps. Whereas Vygotsky did criticize some of Piaget's ideas, the criticisms need to be understood in context. Both men understood that the advancement of scientific thinking depended upon the kind of dialectic that a mutual critique of ideas provides. Even though Piaget himself was slow to respond to Vygotsky's criticisms, he applauded the work of the young Russian scholar and actually came to agree with him in certain areas, such as the usefulness of egocentric speech (van der Veer, 1996; see below). The celebrated differences between the two more often than not reflect Vygotsky's differing emphases rather than any outright rejection of major Piagetian constructs. Readers need to be careful not to misinterpret the philosophy of either theorist by oversimplifying their ideas or by construing their positions as concrete "either-or" sets of beliefs. Let's examine some of the ideas for which Vygotsky is best known and consider how these two theorists compare.

Vygotsky, as did Piaget, found the question of how thinking develops in human beings an intriguing one. However, he did not identify a progression of stages that the individual child traverses on her way to logical, abstract thought. Nor did he emphasize the importance of the individual's construction of knowledge in the cognitive developmental process. Instead, he focused on themes that provide a different perspective on development. Vygotsky is arguably best known for his emphasis on the critical role that the culture or society into which one is born plays in the transmission of knowledge. Hence, his theory is called "sociocultural." He also stressed that human thinking was mediated by the tools humans use (Wertsch, 1991).

It seems quite understandable that he would take this point of view, embedded as he was in his own cultural context. Vygotsky was a Marxist who had been powerfully influenced by the writings of Marx and Engels. He was accustomed to the concept of a dialectic, that logical advancement comes from mutual examination of ideas, generating point and counterpoint and, ultimately, perhaps a more adequate synthesis of ideas. He was grounded in the idea that society could be improved by the collective efforts of its members. Marxist philosophy also emphasized human mastery of the physical world by using and producing tools (Marx & Engels, 1846/1972). Vygotsky took this concept and applied it to psychological development, reasoning that cognitive growth also resulted from continuous expansion in the use and scope of tools. Tools, or signs as Vygotsky came to refer to them, meant anything that people used to help them think and learn, such as numbering or writing systems. The most important tool for Vygotsky was language.

Let's consider the simple example of a vocabulary word, *television*. Vygotsky pointed out that the child does not independently construct a definition for such a word but rather learns the meaning that her culture has ascribed to it. Understanding this shared meaning enables the child to use the "tool" to communicate. But the word can be used not only in its literal sense. It can be transformed to create a new tool or sign, like "telemarketing," which incorporates part of the original idea but is qualitatively different. Such new signs are the products of cultural and historical mediation. That is, the signs are shaped and developed by others. Vygotsky claimed that a child's use of such tools or signs actually transforms thinking and shapes it into new kinds of thought. The idea of mediated learning, so central to Vygotsky's theory, is reminiscent of Piaget's concepts of assimilation and accommodation (van Geert, 1998), although Piaget tended to emphasize the development of thinking within the child, whereas Vygotsky's focus was squarely

Box 3.3 | *Biographical Sketch: Lev S. Vygotsky*

Lev Semenovich Vygotsky was born in 1896 in the small Russian village of Orscha in the province of Belorussia. His parents were both well-educated, middle class individuals of Jewish descent. Vygotsky's father, a manager for a local bank, actively supported educational causes such as the development of the local public library. Vygotsky's experience with the Russian school system began when he reached junior high school age. Prior to this time, his parents had paid for him to be educated by a private tutor.

Vygotsky was clearly an extraordinary student from a very early age. Like Piaget, he began to write while he was still a young man: His essay on *Hamlet* was written when he was 18 and was later published. He loved to study and had wide academic interests, which included the philosophy of history, literature, art, and poetry. When he entered the University of Moscow in 1913, he was a student in the medical school. During his first semester there, he decided to transfer to the law school. As if this were not challenging enough, Vygotsky simultaneously enrolled in Shaniavsky University to study history and philosophy with some of Russia's most brilliant professors of that time.

Upon graduation from Moscow University in 1917, be secured a position teaching literature in a secondary school in the province of Gomel, where his parents lived. He worked in this capacity from 1918 to early 1924, when he left the school to join the faculty of a nearby teachers' college. He also worked to complete the requirements for his doctoral degree, which was granted from Moscow University in 1925.

One of Vygotsky's responsibilities at the college was to give lectures in the area of psychology. While presenting a lecture to professionals at the Second Psychoneurological Congress in Leningrad in early 1924, he attracted the attention of a young man named Alexander Luria. Luria was the academic secretary at the Moscow Institute of Psychology and would go on to become quite famous in the area of neuropsychology. Luria was so impressed with Vygotsky that he prevailed upon his director to hire him. Toward the end of 1924, Vygotsky moved with his wife to Moscow to take this appointment.

During his career at the Institute, he studied the development of human mental functioning. Many of his ideas were not available to scientists and educators in the West until quite recently because of the general ban on dissemination of information as well as problems involved in translation. Since the release of his ideas, Vygotsky has enjoyed great popularity in the West, particularly with those involved in education. During his lifetime, Vygotsky carried out many experiments on children using qualitative methods similar to those used by Piaget. His thinking was influenced by Piaget, and he actively tried to initiate a dialogue with him about certain points of disagreement. A full-fledged dialogue never developed, possibly because of the barriers of language and ideology. However, Piaget was aware of Vygotsky's ideas. In 1962, Piaget stated that he respected Vygotsky's position and noted their areas of agreement.

While at the Institute, Vygotsky wrote prodigiously and traveled extensively to oversee work in clinics with children and adults suffering from neurological disorders. Throughout much of his adult life, Vygotsky himself was in poor health. Toward the end of his life, colleagues such as Luria helped him conduct research projects because Vygotsky was too weak to leave Moscow. His promising life was cut short in 1934, when he succumbed to an attack of tuberculosis. In Vygotsky, we have another example of a truly great mind whose ideas have inspired the work of many students of cognitive development.

on the "child-in-context." In his view, because children acquire and use tools that are the products of others' thinking, "the mind is no longer to be located entirely inside the head" (Cole & Wertsch, 1996, p. 253) but is part of a collective experience. We have already learned that multidimensional models of development, such as Bronfenbrenner's bioecological model, recognize the powerful influence of the individual's environment on her development. Vygotsky went a step further. He believed that the individual could never really be separated from her environment or culture.

Another theme in Vygotsky's work is that progress or improvement in thinking is both possible and desirable. The press toward more advanced levels of thinking not only pulls the individual forward but improves the society as well. Vygotsky placed great importance on the transmission of formal knowledge because he believed that learning culturally defined concepts, which he referred to as scientific concepts, presented the learner with an internal organizational system for ideas and allowed the learner to utilize the ideas more efficiently (Vygotsky, 1934). But how do these cognitive advances occur? Vygotsky believed that more advanced thinkers or more capable members of a culture provide novice learners with scaffolding that enables the novices to reach higher levels of thinking. Scaffolding serves as a temporary prop until the child has mastered a task. Interestingly, Vygotsky did not apply his ideas to specific kinds of educational practice despite the obvious parallels to teaching and the widespread popularity of his ideas among educators (van der Veer & Valsiner, 1994). He did discuss education in the broad sense of the term and highlighted the important role of society in providing the tools that form the basis for thinking.

In educational circles, the concept of scaffolding has been interpreted as learning that occurs when a more cognitively advanced individual (a teacher or peer) guides a learner with prompts, cues, and other supports to reach a point where the learner can manifest in actuality what had previously only been her potential. The notion that children have a zone of proximal development is one of Vygotsky's most influential ideas. It describes the situation in which a learner is able to grasp a concept or perform some skill only with support or scaffolding from someone else. She would not yet be capable of the task on her own, but she can do it with assistance. Obviously, this does not mean simply telling a child an answer to a question! It means, instead, that a parent or teacher assesses the child's thinking, provides judicious support and appropriate cognitive tools, and in so doing, propels the child's development forward. Let's consider an application of this concept presented by Tharp and Gallimore (1988):

> A 6-year-old child has lost a toy and asks her father for help. The father asks where she last saw the toy: The child says, "I can't remember." He asks a series of questions: "Did you have it in your room? Outside? Next door?" To each question, the child answers, "No." When he says, "In the car?" she says, "I think so" and goes to retrieve the toy. (p. 14)

In this case, the father scaffolded the child's thinking and, in the process, helped her develop a way of remembering where her toy was. It should be noted that neither father nor daughter knew the answer to the question, "Where is the toy?" However, by encouraging the child to consider the right questions, her father was able to help his daughter to remember. The joint effort was possible because both shared certain kinds of information, such as knowledge of which toy was missing and what the layout of the house was. And both focused attention on a common goal, finding the toy. This process has been called intersubjectivity. From a Vygotskian point of view, the scaffolding occurred in the intermental space between parent and child.

Current research on young children's language learning, memory development, problem solving, planning, and understanding of cultural artifacts, including the symbolic artifacts described earlier in this chapter, support Vygotsky's notion of the importance of scaffolding. Parents and other adults often guide children's processing of new information in everyday social interactions, and doing so clearly supports their cognitive progress (e.g., Gauvain, 2001). See Box 3.4 for an example.

Vygotsky's ideas have had a major impact on education in large measure because of their applicability to the teaching–learning process. Piaget was also sensitive to the role of outside influence on the developing learner. The frequent characterizations of Piaget as concerned only with individual cognitive development and of Vygotsky as concerned only with social influences on learning are both inaccurate. Piaget noted that the relationships between the individual and her social environment are essential to cognitive development (Piaget, 1977), as we have seen in his view of the development of perspective taking. Piaget's view of the role of teachers in cognitive development is also similar to Vygotsky's (see Box 3.2). For his part, Vygotsky posited two kinds of developmental lines that accounted for cognitive development, one that was "sociohistorical" or cultural, and one that was "natural," coming from within the infant, much like Piaget's stage of sensorimotor development (Vygotsky, 1931/1981). Despite differences in their emphases, both Piaget and Vygotsky can be described as concerned with the interpenetration of the individual mind and society in the formation of thought.

One difference between Piaget's and Vygotsky's ideas concerns the role of egocentric speech in cognitive development. Although Piaget originally stated that the egocentric speech of the child (talking aloud to the self, with no apparent communicative function) serves no useful purpose and simply disappears with the growth of more mature language use, Vygotsky had a different idea. To him and his colleague, Alexander Luria, egocentric speech serves an eminently

Box 3.4 | *Vygotsky's Legacy: Studying the Role of Scaffolding in Parent–Child Interaction*

When parents read storybooks to young children, they often point to the illustrations to reinforce understanding of the text. Yet, as we have seen, children can have difficulty interpreting symbolic artifacts, like pictures, accurately. Illustrators use some pictorial conventions that are especially confusing to young children. One 2-year-old was distressed, for example, when a picture showed only part of a person; she wondered why the person had no feet (Crago & Crago, 1983).

Are parents sensitive to the difficulties that pictures can create for their youngsters? If they are, then a Vygotskian approach to cognitive development would suggest that many parents will scaffold children's understanding not only of the text of a storybook, but also of its illustrations. Further, children whose parents provide such scaffolding should advance more rapidly in their understanding of pictures than other children.

Szechter and Liben (2004) asked parents of 3- to 5-year-olds to look at a picture book with their children, the way they might do it at home. The book, titled *Zoom*, has no text, and shows the same scene repeatedly but with a broader view in each successive picture, as though a camera were zooming out farther and farther with each shot (Banyai, 1995). For example, in one picture you can see only the comb on a rooster's head. In the next picture, you see the top half of the rooster, including his whole head. In the next picture, a wider angle shot depicts two children from behind, looking through a window at the rooster. The next picture provides a broader view of the children, who are actually standing on a bench, looking out the window at the rooster, as seen from behind through an open door, and so on.

The researchers videotaped the parent–child interactions with two cameras, one focused on the storybook pages, the other on the participants. Parents' remarks as they looked through the book were later coded with the help of split-screen recordings. Some parents made many "spatial graphic" comments, giving their children information about spatial relationships within or between pictures. These parents were scaffolding their children's understanding of the pictorial technique of zooming. One strategy parents used was to repeatedly point out the same object, often the rooster, in each successive picture, flipping back and forth between pages to demonstrate the sameness of the object as well as the different views. This exchange between a mother and her 5-year-old son demonstrates:

PARENT: [Can you find the rooster on this page? (flips to previous page, then back)

PARENT: Not quite huh? You can see the boy and girl. . . . We're getting farther away from the rooster, huh?

PARENT: (later page) Ohh. Where did we start? Do you remember? Where's the rooster?] (*Source:* Szechter & Liben, 2004, p. 875.)

Another spatial graphic strategy was to provide a physical demonstration of the zooming effect. For example, the mother of a 3-year-old made this comment:

PARENT: [". . . It's just that we're looking at him really, *really* close. Just like if I went like this (parent moves very close, pressing her face against child's). There's Steven. And then (parent leans far back away from him), "Oh look! There's all of Steven!"] (*Source:* Szechter & Liben, 2004, p. 876.)

Only about 20% of parents failed to provide spatial graphic scaffolding. Their comments tended to focus on each page as a separate entity, perhaps labeling or asking questions about content, but never highlighting connections between pages that might help the child interpret the zooming technique. One mother with her 5-year-old daughter proceeded as follows:

PARENT: [. . . What's that (points to page)?

CHILD: I don't know.

PARENT: Don't know?

CHILD: What is it?

PARENT: (Turns to next page) What is it?

CHILD: A hen!

PARENT: A rooster you silly.

CHILD: I can't tell them apart.

PARENT: Oh. See the crown—comb—up here (traces comb with her fingers)? Roosters have big combs!

CHILD: Oh.

PARENT: (Turns page) Now what do you see?

CHILD: A rooster on a farm.

PARENT: Right. Little kids looking at it.] (*Source:* Szechter & Liben, 2004, p. 877.)

After the storybook sessions, children were tested for spatial graphic understanding. For example, in a "scene-ordering" task, children had to arrange six photographs of a water fountain taken from successive distances. The quantity and quality of parents' spatial graphic strategies during the book reading task were strongly related to children's spatial graphic performance. Studies examining whether children experience longer term benefits from such parental strategies have not yet been reported, but clearly in the immediate situation parents' scaffolding enhanced children's ability to interpret the pictorial conventions that illustrators use. This study is part of a growing research literature that focuses on how everyday interactions, like parent–child book reading, enculturate children and impact their understanding of the world.

useful purpose in human development (Vygotsky & Luria, 1930). It was construed as the precursor to problem solving, planning ability, and self-control. From this perspective, egocentric or private speech eventually becomes internalized or transformed into inner speech, the kind of internal dialogue that facilitates thinking. If you happen to be someone who talks to yourself as you think something through, you are probably in very good company.

Vygotsky identified three stages in the movement of private speech to inner speech. First, the child of about 3 years of age engages in running commentaries about his actions, intentions, objects of interest, and the like whether anyone is nearby to listen or not. Very often, young children manifest a kind of "parallel" conversation, playing side by side without really interacting. Children also talk themselves through problems such as "Where is my toy?" Despite the fact that they may pose the statement as a question, they act as though they do not really expect anyone to answer it. Vygotsky believed that this speech was actually directing their thoughts and keeping them focused on the task at hand.

As children reach about 6 years of age, this private speech becomes more subdued and idiosyncratic, often capturing only the general sense of the idea. Children may subvocalize the dialogue or only move their lips. Finally, around the age of 8, children truly internalize the dialogue, and it is no longer audible. Vygotsky claimed that egocentric speech "went underground" and became inner speech, which was maintained for its self-regulatory properties. Research has demonstrated that the use of private speech enhances children's attention and involvement when faced with a difficult task (Berk & Spuhl, 1995). Also, as we have seen, internalized narrative speech is thought to play a role in the development of autobiographical memory (Nelson, 1993b, 1996). Meichenbaum and Goodman (1971), using Vygotsky's analysis of the benefits of inner speech, pioneered the use of self-talk, or the enhancement of inner speech, to facilitate impulse control in children. Many schools of therapy, particularly cognitive-behavioral approaches, owe a debt to Vygotsky for his elucidation of the inner speech concept.

APPLICATIONS

Some special skills are required of those counselors who work with young children and their families. As Shirk points out, "The process of child psychotherapy is embedded in and, at times, constrained by the process of development" (1988, p. 12). Children are not simply clients with limited vocabulary knowledge. Development brings about a series of qualitative reorganizations of competencies in cognitive, affective, behavioral, and social areas that need to be understood and respected if counseling is to be effective. Young children generally attend to things in their environment that grab their attention (centration) and react to salient perceptible features of the environment while ignoring its other more subtle aspects (concreteness). Counselors who take a "child's-eye view" are more successful in avoiding the unmodified application of adult therapy models to their work with young children. Perhaps the most important initial task for adult professionals, then, is to recognize their own cognitive egocentrism in the many ways it might present itself, from overreliance on verbal explanations, to unfounded assumptions about young children's understanding of cause and effect, to other age-inappropriate expectations.

Also critically important to the work of child psychotherapy is the need to focus on developmental processes as mediators of presenting problems. Very often, the shape of a symptom will change depending upon the cognitive and emotional resources available to the child. For example, sadness or depression in an adolescent subsequent to a family breakup may take the form of crying, ruminating, or writing long, self-absorbed diary entries. For a preschooler who lacks such verbal and introspective capacities, reaction to the same problem might be displayed in regressive behavior (wetting the bed, having tantrums) or pronounced social difficulties (biting, hitting). Ability to profit from therapeutic techniques also depends upon what the child can understand. Whereas a mature adolescent may be intrigued by the notion of the "unconscious," a younger child lacks the understanding of mental states needed to comprehend such a concept.

Young children's egocentrism often makes it impossible for them to consider other points of view, including those of their parents, siblings, and teachers. A helper may encounter parents who punish a 15-month-old for not being toilet trained. A preschool teacher might express concern that a 3-year-old is selfish because she won't share a special toy with her playmates. In these cases, the adults fail to recognize the nature of the young child's thinking, and they attribute to the child abilities that she has not yet mastered. Sometimes these cognitive biases also indicate deep frustration, high stress levels, or limited empathy on the part of the adults. In some cases, support and understanding should be made available to the caretaker, and measures should be taken to protect the child from a potentially neglectful or abusive situation.

Helping professionals, like parents, adjust the environment, including their own speech, to scaffold children's understanding.

Sharing the Wealth: Providing Knowledge About Child Development to Caregivers

Giving information about child development to parents and caretakers, such as information about the normal fears of childhood, can also reduce adults' misinterpretations of child behavior. For example, most normal children exhibit mild to moderately intense fears over the course of childhood (Murphy, 1985). In general, the younger the child, the more their fears result from what they *see* rather than from what they *hear* (Hayes & Birnbaum, 1980). Because preoperational children do not necessarily distinguish playing from real life and because their understanding of the world is rather limited anyway, they tend to perceive what they see as reality. Therefore, younger children are more often frightened by fearful images, by ghosts, monsters, imaginary creatures, the dark, and being alone than are older, school-aged children whose fears are more often associated with some real situation like school or personal safety. A sixth grader's intense test anxiety that is provoked by hearing about a particular teacher's reputation for giving impossible exams would be lost on a 3-year-old.

Before any clinical intervention is needed, counselors should ask about the intensity and duration of the fears, because fears tend to wax and wane over childhood. Another very important question concerns the amount of distress the child is experiencing and the degree to which the fear is preventing the child from engaging in other activities that are important for her development. Clinical intervention for severe, persistent fears and phobias of young children can involve a number of approaches, including systematic desensitization procedures, cognitive behavioral techniques, modeling, and operant conditioning (Burns, Hoagwood, & Mrazek, 1999). For more commonplace fears, adults should resist trying to explain to young children how their fears are

irrational. Research indicates that "telling yourself it's not real" is a largely ineffective intervention for young children (Cantor & Wilson, 1988). Concrete measures, such as crafting comforting rituals like bedtime routines, asking children to engage in an activity like holding onto a favorite stuffed animal or doll, and decreasing the exposure to frightening images on TV and in movies are far more helpful.

Play Therapy: Helping the Youngest Clients

Most therapies for young children emphasize play for good reason (see Axline, 1947; Landreth, 2002a; O'Connor & Braverman, 1997). Because language skills are still under construction, children reveal themselves more clearly in play than in words. For example, the ability to express complicated feelings, like love and anger toward a parent, is not available to young children, but such feelings may be acted out in play. Suppose 3½-year-old Charlotte takes a doll from the doll house and uses it to hit the baby doll lying in a bassinet. The counselor's comments "She's hitting her baby sister. I wonder if the big girl is mad?" links the act to a verbal label and gives her the option of putting feelings into words. The counselor's goal may be to understand the child's concerns, to support the child in expressing them, to help the child learn more adaptive ways to behave and express feelings, and to educate parents to better understand their child's needs. Play therapists generally advocate a nondirective, nonintrusive counseling approach with young children. This means not talking too much or being controlling. Therapists need to be patient when working with children who, by virtue of their developmental level, are less goal directed than adults. The temperament of the child and the nature of the presenting problem might signal the need for different amounts of structure, perhaps more structure for a defiant child than for an anxious one. Landreth (2002b) suggests, however, that limits be imposed only when it becomes necessary for prevention of self- or other-directed destructive behavior. At that point, therapists should acknowledge the wish or need the child is trying to express, communicate the limit, and provide an alternative outlet that is more acceptable.

Some thoughtfully chosen toys can increase the attractiveness of the play therapist's office. In general, creative toys, such as dolls, puppets, and art supplies, are preferable to highly structured games for this age group. Remember that the counselor's office can be a scary place for young children. Therefore, attempts to child-size some of its elements (chairs, tables, etc.) can help make it less threatening. For very young children, parents should stay in the room to minimize separation anxiety (see Chapter 4).

1. *Be attentive and get out of the way.*   A major part of therapeutic work with young children is to assess the nature of their concerns. For that task, good observation skills are needed. Notice what the child does and does not do; what she says and doesn't say; what she looks at and how she approaches and interacts with objects in the space. How does she interact with you and what feelings does she elicit in you? Whether in the assessment or treatment phases, it is important to give children the space and time they need to express themselves while the observant counselor tunes into the multiple dimensions of child behavior. As a rule of thumb, remember that the young child's development is occurring simultaneously on many fronts and may reflect unevenness or decalage. Therefore, pay attention to each of the following areas: physical development and motor skills, cognitive and language (both receptive and expressive) development, relatedness to caregivers, primary affects and overall mood, and exploration and use of the environment (Greenspan, 1981).

2. *Maintain cooperation over time.*   Young children have short attention spans and they are easily distracted by interesting stimuli in the external environment as well as internal stimuli like hunger, boredom, fear, and fatigue. The sensitive clinician is careful to note these changes, perhaps waiting a bit to see how the child copes with stress or distraction, and then changing the environment. Maintaining flexibility is an important skill in engaging the child. An abrupt shift in attention or activity, such as when a child refuses to continue playing with toys that seemed to engage her previously, might signify a self-protective move away from an area of concern (Greenspan, 1981). Enjoyable gamelike techniques that sustain cooperation and attention can be useful in counseling very young children (see Hall, Kaduson, & Schaefer, 2002 for a description of techniques).

3. *Watch your language.*   Keep your language as simple and concrete as possible. Avoid complicated sentence structure. If you need to give directions, they should be simple and short. Try not to give multistep sets of directions, such as "First put your coat over there and then we'll sit at the table for a while and then I'm going to ask you to color a picture."

Because children of this age are still constructing their understanding of cause-and-effect relationships, helpers should not assume that preschoolers can easily grasp the connection between actions and consequences except at a very simple level. Saying to a youngster "Since you hit Jimmy at day care yesterday, you won't be able to go to the playground tomorrow" will probably be ineffective if it is intended to teach the child about the consequences of her acts. Young children's sense of time is not well developed, and their memory for event sequences is rather poor. Tying tomorrow's consequences to yesterday's behavior is really asking a child to construct or detect an underlying organization or logical connection. The child has a better chance of remembering and understanding the sequence if misbehavior is linked to immediate consequences.

Very often, children from bilingual families may be more proficient in a language other than English, a challenge to an English-speaking counselor. Obviously, all steps must be taken to ensure accuracy of communication and to reduce the chances for misinterpretations. Any interpreters that participate in counseling should be knowledgeable about the therapeutic process (Vasquez & Javier, 1991).

4. *Don't be afraid.*   Sometimes in our eagerness to make clients feel good, we unconsciously ignore or gloss over the problems or conflicts they are experiencing. This may be even more true when our clients are children. Greenspan (1981) encourages counselors to take seriously the concerns of children. When the counselor notices and comments on an area of difficulty for the child, he notes that "children are often greatly relieved to know that finally they have met someone who is not frightened by what frightens them" (p. 112).

5. *Don't jump to conclusions.*   Do a complete developmental interview with the parents or guardians. Knowing about early developmental milestones, prenatal and birth history, illnesses, family dynamics, cultural background, and parenting practices enriches the understanding of the child and complements what is observed in the counseling office. Behavior is multiply determined and can be the expression of multiple needs and concerns. In some respect, the child therapist is like a detective, trying to sort out from the clues provided by the child's behavior the most important issues. Parental interviews not only involve the parent in the process but add immeasurably to the clinician's assessment picture. Parental interviews are an important element of any assessment, regardless of the age of the child, because assessment should always be based upon multiple pieces of information (Sattler & Ryan, 1998). For older children and adolescents, academic and social history should be included in the interview.

Lessons from Piaget and Vygotsky

One of the most useful guidelines for helpers from Piaget's work is the idea that learning results from the dynamic interaction between assimilative and accommodative processes. Because much, if not all, of what transpires in any counseling and therapy comes under the broad rubric of learning, these ideas can be readily translated into applications for therapeutic work with children and even adults. Piaget's ideas suggest that the helper should find ways to relate new information or insight to a client's current knowledge structures. In other words, if new knowledge, ideas, or information is too discrepant or if the individual lacks the context or experience to understand it, the new information will be ignored or discounted. On the other hand, if the new information is too similar to what the individual already knows, it will be assimilated into existing knowledge structures without any learning or cognitive change at all. To maximize learning, the counselor needs to understand how clients are thinking and what meanings they have already made. Interventions or examples that build on previous knowledge allow the client the best chance of incorporating the new information into useful working knowledge.

With young children, learning new things takes time. From studies of brain development we have seen that initial connections are somewhat fragile. The new connections involved in learning need to be reinforced regularly for them to be firmly established. Adults are sometimes dismayed by the number of times children need to hear an idea or message repeated before they can understand it. Yet, this is the essence of cognitive development. Mature thinking is constructed bit by bit, each part building on the previous one and helping to shape the next.

One of the particularly interesting legacies of Vygotskian theory for practice is his emphasis on culture in cognitive development. In this view, our ideas, including our ideas about children's development, are conditioned and shaped by our culture. It should be stressed, however, that culture is not monolithic. Within any kind of cultural group, be it ethnic, socioeconomic, gender-based, religious, or the culture of our family homes, individual differences still flourish. Indeed individuals may be more similar in beliefs, values, and practices to members of another cultural group than they are to those with whom they share a similar cultural heritage (Greenfield & Suzuki, 1998). It has been frequently stated, for example, that Eurocentric cultures place more importance on the value of individualism than do Asian cultures, which hold more communitarian ideals. Certain assumptions, such as these about individualism and collectivism, need to be refined, clarified, and carefully evaluated to avoid dualistic overgeneralizations. Recent analyses of cultural differences in orientations to individualism and collectivism found that Latinos/Latinas, African Americans, and European Americans do not differ significantly in their levels of individualism, as defined in these studies, nor are European Americans less collectivist in orientation than Japanese and Koreans (see Oyserman, Coon, & Kemmelmeier, 2002).

Nonetheless, members of distinct cultural groups can differ systematically in certain beliefs and values (Greenfield, 1994). Therefore, when the cultural orientation of a family is different from that of the helper, professionals need to recognize and appreciate that different developmental goals can and do exist. For example, Japanese parents generally place great value on the interdependence of family members and their mutual responsibilities toward each other. This value is expressed concretely in the sleeping arrangements parents make for their infants. In the United States, infants generally sleep in a room separated from their parents (Morelli, Rogoff, Oppenheim, & Goldsmith, 1992).

Co-sleeping is the most frequently used sleeping arrangement for children in many non-Western cultures worldwide (Konner & Worthman, 1980). Unless this and other practices, such as co-bathing and care of young children by siblings, are understood contextually, the risk of misinterpreting them as harmful is a real one. Clinicians need to be able to separate culturally different child-rearing practices from those that are truly abusive or neglectful.

Whereas each cultural practice has its own costs and benefits, understanding the cultural underpinnings of different child-rearing approaches can provide us with helpful information that can reduce our own culture-bound ways of thinking. To use the sleeping example, researchers have reported that childhood problems such as sudden infant death syndrome (SIDS), sleep disturbances, and thumb-sucking are all reduced in cultures that practice co-sleeping (Greenfield & Suzuki, 1998). Co-sleeping has also been shown to enhance the quality of infants' sleep and the time infants spend breastfeeding (McKenna, Mosko & Richards, 1997). Recently, some warnings have been issued about co-sleeping, highlighting the potential danger to infants of falling out of beds or being asphyxiated unintentionally (Drago & Dannenberg, 1999). Many have challenged this blanket condemnation of co-sleeping, arguing that, when safety precautions are taken, this practice has many beneficial effects as previously noted. Some studies show that the risk of infant death appears to be associated with other variables and not co-sleeping per se, such as smoking by the co-sleeping parent (Scragg, Mitchell, Taylor, Ford, Thompson et al., 1993), excessive alcohol consumption by the parent, and co-sleeping with very young infants on a restricted space like a sofa or couch (Blair, Fleming, Smith, Platt, Young et al., 1999).

Knowledge about the outcomes of cultural variations in practice may allow helpers to consider a fuller range of options for child care and to make sensible recommendations. Our communication with parents will be more helpful and compassionate if we understand, as Vygotsky pointed out, that our own ideas and values are mediated by the culture in which we live. (See Table 3.3.)

TABLE 3.3 Contrasting Cultural Models of Parent–Child Relations

	Developmental Goals	
	Independence	**Interdependence**
Developmental trajectory	From dependent to independent self	From asocial to socially responsible self
Children's relations to parents	Personal choice concerning relationship to parents	Obligations to parents
Communication	Verbal emphasis	Nonverbal emphasis (empathy, observation, participation)
	Autonomous self-expression by child	Child comprehension, mother speaks for child
	Frequent parental questions to child	Frequent parental directives to child
	Frequent praise	Infrequent praise
	Child negotiation	Harmony, respect, obedience
Parenting style	Authoritative: controlling, demanding, warm, rational	Rigorous and responsible teaching, high involvement, physical closeness
Parents helping children	A matter of personal choice except under extreme need	A moral obligation under all circumstances

Source: Greenfield, P. M., & Suzuki, L. K. Cultural human development. In W. Damon et al. *Handbook of Child Psychology vol. 4* (5th ed., pp. 1059–1109). Copyright © 1998. This material is used by permission of John Wiley & Sons, Inc.

SUMMARY

The Brain

1. The embryo begins to form a neural tube at about 2 weeks of gestation. By the 5th week, neurons are being produced at a remarkable rate, such that by birth there are 100 billion of them. Until about 4 months of gestation much of brain development involves neuron migration. The first neurons produced at the interior surface of the neural tube migrate the shortest distance and form the hindbrain. Later developing neurons travel farther to form the midbrain, and the last neurons to be produced travel farthest and form the forebrain or cerebrum and its cortex. Neurons in different parts of the brain later specialize for certain functions. Specialization is at least partially influenced by the context or environment of the cell. Neurons from one part of the cortex will respecialize if transplanted to another part of the cortex.

2. A neuron has one long extension called an axon, and may have many shorter extensions called dendrites. Electrical impulses begin when dendrites or cell bodies pick up a message from another cell. The impulse then passes through the axon to the axon terminals, where chemicals called neurotransmitters are released into the gap—or synapse—between neurons. The neurotransmitters carry the message to the next cell, causing it to fire or to stop firing. Myelination, formation of an insulating substance around axons, promotes efficient conduction of electrical impulses. Myelination occurs prenatally and throughout childhood and adolescence. Neurons begin firing spontaneously at about 4 months of gestation. Before birth, sensory neurons are beginning to be functional. A fetus will turn toward a light source by 25 weeks of gestation, and she can begin to recognize some aspects of sounds, like her mother's voice, in the later weeks of pregnancy. Availability of appropriate stimulation appears to be critical in the late prenatal and early postnatal period for normal sensory functioning to develop. There is an optimal range of stimulation—too much as well as too little may be problematic. Different sensory systems influence one another's development.

3. Rapid neuron reproduction continues after birth until the end of the 1st year. Although some neurons can reproduce even in adulthood, most nerve cell reproduction seems to end in infancy. The formation of synapses is ongoing throughout childhood and adolescence, and perhaps even into adulthood, and seems to be linked to cognitive advances. Many more synapses are formed than will be needed, and brain development postnatally involves synapse formation and neural pruning. Experience-expectant synapses are formed in anticipation of typical experiences. Experience shapes the pruning process—synapses that are used remain, and those that are not may be discarded. Experience-dependent synapses are formed as a result of exposure to certain kinds of experience and may be pruned if they do not remain active.

4. Sensory and motor systems are laid down at a rudimentary level in human prenatal development but become integrated in complex ways in the first 2 years of life, partly as a function of experience. Some degree of sensory integration dysfunction may occur in some children. Hyper- and hyposensitivity to some kinds of stimulation, motor clumsiness, and poor eye–hand coordination are among the resulting difficulties.

Cognitive Development

5. In Piaget's theory, the mind constructs knowledge through adaptation. First, children interpret new information coming in from the environment in ways that fit what they already know or can do, called assimilation. They also show accommodation, with existing knowledge somewhat changed to create a better fit to what is new. Thus, children's understandings change only a little at a time, and the child may distort completely new information as she tries to assimilate it to her current knowledge structures. Piaget saw children as active learners, intrinsically motivated to seek out and understand new information. He believed that at any age their knowledge is organized or structured and that its organization changes over time as adaptation occurs. According to Piaget, for some periods of time, called stages, a child's mental structures can be expected to have organizational properties in common. That is, within stages there are similarities in the ways children organize their thinking across a variety of concepts.

6. Modern research indicates that cognitive development is often domain specific, so that understandings in different domains of knowledge are not always organized in similar ways. The idea that children's cognitive development progresses in stages may not be strictly accurate. Yet, Piaget's stage divisions are broadly useful for organizing our thinking about children, their understandings, and their limitations at different ages.

7. Piaget studied infants' cognition in the sensorimotor stage (ages 0 to 2) by making inferences from babies' motor interactions with the environment. Today, researchers have available some additional tools, such as the habituation and preferential looking paradigms. Modern research techniques produce findings that challenge some of Piaget's ideas about infants.

8. The object concept requires knowing first, that objects can stimulate multiple senses and second, that objects are permanent. Piaget assumed that infants develop the first understanding at about 2 to 4 months, as they coordinate their reflexive motor responses to stimulation. The second understanding requires representational thought, and Piaget assumed it began between 8 and 12 months, when babies will search for a hidden object. Newer research, however, indicates earlier understandings of both aspects of the object concept. Intersensory integration is apparently possible in the first weeks of life, so that very young babies in some sense know that objects can be the source of many different forms of sensation. With use of the habituation paradigm, some early signs of object permanence have been observed in 4-month-olds.

9. Despite these findings, most memory research indicates that representational thought in infants begins in earnest in the last part of the 1st year. Recognition ability, which requires only that a stimulus can be identified as familiar, is present by birth. However, the earliest indicator of recall, which requires representational thought, occurs at about 8 or 9 months. Two indicators of recall are deferred imitation and separation anxiety.

10. Intentional or planful action has precursors in early infancy, such as making interesting sights last, but means–end behavior, which seems to require some degree of representational thought, begins in the last part of the 1st year, when babies' communicative behaviors also begin to appear intentional. In the last few months of the 1st year, infants also begin to attribute to others agency, the ability to act without an external trigger. Understanding that other people have intentions, part of a theory of mind, seems to require a long developmental process beginning in the second half of the 1st year.

11. By age 2, children are in Piaget's stage of preoperational (meaning prelogical) thought. In his studies of preschoolers' skills, including understanding of numbers and of perspective taking, Piaget identified what he believed to be important limitations on early representational thought, limitations that are overcome by the end of this stage. Preoperational thought is centered, focused on one salient experience or event at a time. Because they cannot keep in mind all the relevant facts in a situation at one time, young children have trouble identifying the logical relationships among such facts, as indicated by children's early failure at number conservation. Since Piaget's work, researchers have developed simpler tasks and have been able to specify some of the early skills that children do have. Regarding number understanding, for example, Gelman found that young children's counting skills include adherence to the one-to-one principle and to the order-irrelevance principle, and that in very simple situations they can even recognize that a number stays the same when objects are rearranged.

12. Piaget pioneered the study of children's theory of mind with his perspective-taking tasks. Preschoolers find perspective taking difficult and usually assume that others have the same perspective that they do. Piaget argued that young children are egocentric, centered on their own perspective and therefore unaware of the possibility of another perspective. Newer work supports this idea, but identifies a gradual progression of perspective-taking skill in early childhood. Even 2-year-olds realize that others do not always see what they can see. By age 3, children can sometimes attribute a different visual perspective on the same object to another viewer. Between

ages 4 and 5, children begin to realize that others some-times know different things, as illustrated by their ability to recognize, in false belief tasks, that another person may be misinformed even when the child is not. These understandings are fragile, and when a situation is emotionally charged, even older children often fall back on the assumption that another's perspective must be like their own. In addition to growth in the ability to hold in mind multiple pieces of information, advances in perspective taking are generally seen as an outgrowth of experience with social interaction.

13. Preschool children can use and understand symbols, but research with symbolic artifacts indicates that their symbolic skills progress gradually. For example, before age 3 they cannot treat a video presentation or a toy model as both the concrete objects that they are and as symbols for other things.

14. Young children seem to have less difficulty understanding the use of words as symbols, perhaps because words are not objects in themselves—they are used only to represent other things. At first, children seem to construe words as one property of the concepts to which they refer. Language acquisition is a complex process that requires learning several systems.

15. Children begin to learn the phonology of their native language even before birth. By 6 months, babies have begun to lose the ability to discriminate sounds that are not important in their native language, and by 9 months their babbling is limited to only the sounds of their native language. Learning how, when, and where to use those sounds can take several years.

16. The semantic system includes the words and word parts that carry meaning. First words appear by the end of the 1st year, and a vocabulary spurt begins by 18 to 24 months. For many years, children learn new words at a rapid pace, fast mapping 9 or 10 new words a day.

17. Learning the syntactic system of a language requires learning the rules for creating meaningful sentences.

Children begin to produce two-word utterances about the time of the vocabulary spurt, and can produce most sentence structures by the time they are 5.

18. Pragmatics involves using language effectively to communicate: learning to construct well-organized, clear narratives, code switching, and learning to distinguish actual meaning from literal meaning.

19. Because of the complexity of language learning, some theorists argue that aspects of language learning must be innate. But all theorists recognize that language experience has to affect the language learning process in some ways. Two that have been identified are the importance of language experience to vocabulary acquisition and to the development of narrative skill. How much language is addressed to children in conversation and book reading is important for vocabulary growth. The kinds of narrative exchanges young children have with adults affect their narrative skill as well.

20. Vygotsky's theory of cognitive development is focused on the role of culture and society in children's intellectual growth. One theme is that often novice learners grasp a concept or perform a skill only when others provide scaffolding. When understanding or performance requires scaffolding, it is said to be in the child's zone of proximal development.

21. Vygotsky especially emphasized language as a tool through which others convey formal knowledge, or scientific concepts. Language mediates learning in children and is one of the primary means by which culture and society help children's thinking to advance. Preschool children eventually come to use language as a way to mediate their own thinking. The private speech of 3-year-olds eventually becomes the inner speech of 8-year-olds. Internalization of speech is linked to attentional control, autobiographical memory, and impulse control.

CASE STUDY

Shady Grove Preschool is located in an old suburban neighborhood adjacent to a large metropolitan area. It serves infants, toddlers, and preschoolers from families with diverse cultural and ethnic backgrounds who have lower- to upper-middle-class income levels. The director of the facility, Mrs. Anthony, has decided to implement a new component, monthly group discussion sessions for parents. She has employed a counselor to facilitate the discussions and to field questions about child development from the parents who come to the sessions.

At the first meeting, the participants, primarily a group of mothers, begin with introductions and questions of a general nature. "How do I know when my toddler is ready for toilet training?" "How can I get my 6-month-old to sleep through the night?" Then the discussion becomes more animated. One mother, Mrs. Winger, a white woman, starts to raise concerns about the educational program at the school. Her son, Brad, who is 4½, is a precocious child who enjoys learning. "I can't understand why they don't teach the children how to use computers in this school," she says. "These children need to get a head start on technological education because they will be competing with so many other students in schools for good colleges and, eventually, good jobs. We need to give them every advantage that we can."

Mrs. Winger is quick to add that she does not believe the children should be stressed. However, she clearly feels the days when children spend their time in preschool playing in a sandbox, drawing, and building with blocks should be over.

She mentions that she has been reading some new information in parenting magazines about children's brain development, and she cautions the group against letting opportunities for the children's brain development pass them by.

Mrs. Ramirez, a Latina, has a different concern. Her daughter Tina is 2½, and her 8-month-old son Nicky is in the infant program. "Tina is so jealous of her baby brother," says Mrs. Ramirez, "that she can't stand when I pay attention to him. She whines and cries when I play with him, even if I let her watch TV when I'm doing it. She won't let him touch anything that is hers. Her father gets very upset with her behavior, too. We've talked to her about being a big girl and about sharing with her brother. We can't believe that she is so selfish." After a pause she notes, sadly, "My sister's children are the same ages and they seem to get along much better. We're too embarrassed to take her to family gatherings now, because she doesn't know how to behave and only draws attention to herself. My parents insist that we are spoiling her."

Discussion Questions

1. What are the underlying assumptions about child development in Mrs. Winger's comments? What is your assessment of her concerns based upon what you know? How would you respond to her concerns?

2. Consider Mrs. Ramirez's statements. What are her beliefs about child development? How would you go about helping her resolve her problem? How have her assumptions about development affected her family relationships?

3. If you were the counselor in this situation, how would you plan a series of parent discussion sessions? What topics would you consider most important to cover? How could you present this information?

4. What is your position on accelerating development? Do you think that children can learn more than they are typically expected to? Should they be encouraged to do so?

JOURNAL QUESTIONS

1. *Culture* is a broad concept. Identify an idea, belief, or value that you learned as a child that came from the culture of your family, one that came from the culture of your community or neighborhood, one that came from your broader cultural or ethnic background, and one that came from your religious culture.

2. Discuss why it might be easier to talk to people of your own culture(s) from the perspective of Vygotsky's notion of intersubjectivity. Give an example from your experience.

KEY TERMS

neural tube
neurulation
neurons
glia
hindbrain
midbrain
cerebral cortex
forebrain
medulla
pons
cerebellum
reticular formation
autonomic functions
brainstem
reticular activating system
superior colliculi
inferior colliculi
substantia nigra
cerebrum
corpus callosum
hemispheric
   specialization
occipital lobe

temporal lobe
central sulcus
parietal lobe
frontal lobe
association area
limbic system
hippocampus
amygdala
septum
thalamus
hypothalamus
endocrine system
nucleus
plasticity
axon
axon terminals
neurotransmitters
dendrites
synaptic gap
myelination
circuits
projection neurons
interneurons

critical period
synapses
nerve growth factor
synaptogenesis
neural pruning
synaptic overproduction
experience-expectant
experience-dependent
sensory integration
   dysfunction
adaptation
assimilation
accommodation
sensorimotor stage
preoperational stage
domain specific
habituation paradigm
orienting response
habituation
dishabituation
object concept
preferential looking
   paradigm

intersensory integration or
   intermodal perception
object permanence
representational thought
hidden object test
recognition
recall
deferred imitation
observational learning or
   modeling
separation anxiety
making interesting sights last
means–end behavior
agency
intention
theory of mind
symbols
number conservation task
centration
decentration
preoperational egocentrism
false belief tasks
symbolic artifacts

phonology
babbling
voicing
semantic system or
    semantics
vocabulary spurt
fast mapping

syntactic system or grammar
pragmatics
narrative
code switching
elaborative style
infantile amnesia
tools or signs

mediation
mediated learning
scientific concepts
scaffolding
zone of proximal
    development
developmental lines

egocentric or private speech
inner speech
sudden infant death
    syndrome (SIDS)

Now go to our Companion Website to assess your understanding of chapter content with Multiple Choice Questions, apply comprehension in Essay Questions, and broaden your knowledge of development with related Web Links.

CHAPTER 4

Emotional Development in the Early Years

In the course of their daily work, most clinicians encounter an array of human problems. Despite their different presenting features, all concerns—a young child's difficulty adjusting to school, a teenager's uncertainty about the future, a couple's recurring arguments about money, a widower's difficulty living alone—have a common aspect: They all, to a greater or lesser degree, involve human emotion. You probably could identify the emotional responses that would most likely be manifested by the hypothetical individuals in the previous examples. The child might feel lonely; the teenager, anxious; the couple, angry; and the older person, sad. Depending upon your particular theoretical orientation, you could probably suggest ways to help each individual. Yet, simply identifying the emotions and proposing techniques, as good a starting point as that may be, reveals nothing about the person's emotional development, nor does it provide you any insight as to whether your techniques might work. Are these clients' reactions appropriate or even adaptive in light of their situations? How concerned should you be about their symptoms? What were the precursors that led to their particular level of emotional adjustment or maladjustment? What coping styles have they developed over time and how useful are they? Unless we understand the process of emotional development in its normative context, we may view our clients' emotions only clinically, as if we were looking at their snapshots, detached from context and earlier experience. Their problems might be seen as manifestations of individual differences (for example, depressed versus anxious) rather than as reflections of their development, and their diagnoses might imply only possession of a set of clinical criteria. Overall, our understanding of clients would be impoverished.

The study of emotional development is a critical link to a better understanding of emotional problems whenever they appear during the life span. Sroufe (1996) states that "emotional development is the foundation for the study of individual adaptation and psychopathology. Pursuing these fields without being fully grounded in emotional development is analogous to trying to do research in genetics without being grounded in biology" (p. xii). Perhaps being an interpreter of emotional messages and a forger of affective change in a therapeutic context (Strupp, 1988) is also impossible without a fundamental working knowledge of emotional development. In this chapter, we review the beginnings of emotional development, the processes involved in early bonding, and the implications of these events for later well-being.

THEORIES OF EMOTIONS: THE STATE OF THE ART

Before we can address the topic of emotional development, we need to concern ourselves briefly with the question of what emotions are. This fundamental dilemma has occupied the time, attention, and brainpower of many gifted writers in the fields of philosophy, psychology and psychiatry, biology, and the neurosciences. However, there are still many unanswered questions and some major controversies in this area. For example, theorists disagree about whether emotions are best defined as physiological states, action tendencies, subjectively perceived experiences, or some combination of the above. A clear, comprehensive, universally accepted theory of the nature of emotions, the way emotions develop, the function of emotionally related brain structures, and the role of emotions in psychotherapy and mental health (Greenberg & Safran, 1989) has not yet been fully constructed.

One central question is whether there is a biological or evolutionary reason for emotions in humans. The consensus on this issue is that there is. Emotions are built into our nature for their survival value (Ortony & Turner, 1992). Less agreement is found on what constitutes the set of basic human emotions. Most researchers agree that babies possess an emotional repertoire; however, opinions differ on the number, nature, and names of the emotions babies display. This is partly because different researchers emphasize different aspects of the question. Some writers have focused on the physical, particularly facial, manifestations of emotions (Ekman & Oster, 1979; Izard, 1991), others on the neurological underpinnings (Damasio, 1994; Panksepp, 1982), whereas still others have centered their attention on the emergence of changes in kinds of emotional expression over the first few years of life (Sroufe, 1996). Despite these differences, studies of emotional development are beginning to converge with brain science to enrich our understanding of this vitally important aspect of human nature.

Functions of Emotions

Emotions exist to serve many purposes for human beings. It would be hard to disagree that they provide us with a trusty arsenal of survival skills. The fear response that alerts us to a dangerous situation signals us to fight back or escape to protect ourselves. The urge to engage in sexual relations propagates the species. The disgust we experience when we encounter decaying material protects us from exposure to potentially toxic bacteria. The affection elicited by a baby's smiling face promotes the caregiving needed to ensure his continued survival. Emotional responses have ancient, evolutionary significance.

Examples of the role emotions play in survival demonstrate how powerful emotions are as motivators of behavior. The force of conscience provides another clear example of the motivational properties of emotion. Conscience is like a thermostat that is ordinarily set at the "feel good" level. If we do something we consider morally or ethically wrong, our emotional temperature changes and we may experience shame or guilt. These feelings prod us to make restitution or to change our errant ways so that we can regain the "feel good" setting.

Emotions also serve as a major means of communication. An infant's distressed facial expression and piercing cry after receiving an inoculation serve as preemptory commands to the caretaker: "Help me! I'm in pain." When counselors speak of nonverbal communication, an essential component is always the emotional message conveyed through the face, posture, and gestures (Ekman & Friesen, 1969). The view of emotion-as-communication underscores the basic social significance of the emotions and captures an essential quality of the attachment relationship, to be discussed later in this chapter. Emotions are the stepping-stones that infants use to develop reciprocity with caregivers, ultimately leading to the capacity for emotion management.

The role of emotions in cognitive functions has received notice as well. Contrary to that age-old warning to keep your feelings out of your logical decision making, Damasio (1994) has provided compelling evidence that the absence of emotion clearly impairs rather than enhances cognition. Damasio observed patients with damage to the frontal lobe region and noted that they shared a syndrome that he called the Phineas Gage matrix. This syndrome consists of cognitive dysfunctions such as poor planning, inadequate decision making, inability to take another's perspective, and problems in sustaining employment. These cognitive limitations go hand in hand with emotional problems such as shallow affect, lack of an enriched emotional life, lack of passion and initiative, and a diminished sense of pleasure and pain. Far from enabling us to be more "rational," the absence of emotion in our intellectual functioning leaves us sadly lacking in resourcefulness.

Last, but certainly not least, emotions have a role to play in overall mental health and wellness. Research originally done by Salovey and Mayer (1990) and popularized by Coleman (1995) has emphasized the importance of so-called emotional intelligence (or emotional IQ), defined as the ability to perceive emotions, to identify and understand their meaning, to integrate them with other kinds of cognition, and to manage them. Despite recent claims found in the popular press that people with high emotional IQs have strong advantages in life over those not so well endowed, the scientific research in this area is in its infancy and cannot support such claims at the present time (Mayer & Cobb, 2000; Pfeiffer, 2001). Nonetheless, available data indicate a modest yet reliable correlation between emotional intelligence and certain positive life outcomes. Counselors very often deal with problems in emotional recognition and management. These can range from emotional underexpression, as in the case of affectively constricted or autistic individuals, to overexpression or poor regulation, as in the case of individuals who are chronically angry or anxious. The key to well-being is a healthy balance between emotional awareness, emotional acceptance, and emotional expression. So where does it all start? Let's begin our developmental story with a review of the evidence for innate emotional states.

Basic Emotions: Do They Exist?

Charles Darwin, writing in 1872, viewed certain emotions as innate and universal among humans and primates, rather like primitive instincts. He believed that facial expressions communicated the underlying emotions and that these emotions were present because they were necessary for survival. Modern evidence supporting the position that emotions are inborn and universal comes from three main sources: cross-cultural research, investigations of infant and child facial expressions, and physiological studies.

There is consistent evidence (Ekman, 1994; Ekman & Friesen, 1971) that people across a wide variety of cultures, including societies without exposure to Western ideas, fundamentally agree on what constitute expressions of basic emotions such as fear, sadness, happiness, anger, and surprise. Some disagreement currently surrounds the distinction between the emotions of contempt and disgust. The standard methodology used in cross-cultural research involves asking participants from different cultures to view pictures of facial expressions and then to identify the emotions depicted in the photographs. In reviewing studies conducted during the past 50 years, Ekman (1992) concluded that certain facial expressions are interpreted as the same emotions regardless of cultural context. From American cities to the highlands of New Guinea, both industrialized and nonindustrialized peoples derive the same meanings from certain characteristic facial expressions.

Drawing on this Darwinian tradition, Izard (1992), to help determine basic emotions, focused his attention on babies and their ways of communicating emotional messages. He reasoned that infants have little time to learn social conventions and therefore will exhibit only those emotional responses that are inborn. Izard developed coding schemes that enable researchers and clinicians to identify different emotions based upon the position of the facial musculature (Izard, 1979; Izard, Dougherty, & Hembree, 1983). Generally, research done with infants and children using these coding approaches has also supported the existence of basic emotions. Infants display predictable facial expressions in certain circumstances, implying, according to Izard, the underlying presence of a comparable feeling. For example, when an infant is presented with a new and interesting picture, he will show the facial response of interest. When interacting pleasantly with a beloved caretaker, the infant's face conveys happiness or joy.

A third line of evidence for the biological basis of emotions comes from brain research. As mentioned in Box 4.1 (pp. 115–116), specific brain systems or circuits, governing the expression of certain emotional states, appear to be prewired but responsive to experience. Although there is diversity in the language used to describe them and some disagreement on the number of circuits, at this point researchers generally agree about the neural executive systems that mediate fear, expectancy, panic, and rage or anger (Gray, 1990; Panksepp, 1992). These subcortical circuits register the feeling components of experience. They have reciprocal associations with cortical areas that involve higher order thinking and decision making. They can also come under the control of conditioning processes. Several writers have hypothesized that chemical substances such as drugs and alcohol become addictive because they have rewarding emotional effects, creating high levels of euphoria or an "emotional high" (DuPont, 1997). Cues associated with these substances may come to elicit physiological responses even in the absence of the original substance.

Theories and Sequence of Emotional Development

So infants do have some basic emotional systems in place at birth. Witness a group of crying newborns in a hospital nursery for evidence of this! However, the range of their emotional expression increases dramatically over the first 2 years of life. At birth or close to it, infants display distress (crying), contentment (smiling), disgust (avoiding bitter tastes or unpleasant odors), and interest (staring at faces and objects) (Izard & Malatesta, 1987). Anger, surprise, fear, and sadness begin to emerge from 2 months to approximately 6 months of age. So-called social emotions, such as pride, shame, embarrassment, and guilt, depend upon self-recognition and higher levels of cognitive functioning (Lewis & Brooks-Gunn, 1979). These social emotions, which emerge during the last half of the 2nd year of life, will be discussed in Chapter 5. Not all researchers agree about the particulars of early emotional development. Disagreements center on which emotions emerge first and on what early emotional expressions mean. The central ideas of two of the main researchers in this field, Izard and Sroufe, will be reviewed next.

IZARD'S DIFFERENTIAL EMOTIONS THEORY

Izard (1991) concluded that infant expressive behaviors are components of basic emotions. In other words, babies' faces are mirrors of the felt emotions within them. Izard's theory, called differential emotions theory, construes emotions to be the direct product of the underlying neural processes related to each of the emotional expressions. For example, a sad expression implies the operation of the neural circuitry associated with sadness. If a baby looks sad, he is sad. In Izard's view, emotions are based on evolution rather than learning and do not require cognitive components, such as appraisal or intent, to exist. Emotions emerge in infancy and early childhood in a form that is comparable to the emotions experienced by adults. In Izard's theory, socialization or learning plays a role in emotional expression, mainly to expand or facilitate the individual's capacity to regulate the innate forms of emotions.

SROUFE'S DEVELOPMENTAL POSITION

In contrast, Sroufe (1996) takes the position that emotions are not fully formed at birth but that they develop from undifferentiated responses into more differentiated ones and finally into an integrated emotional repertoire. This principle is called orthogenetic: As behavior becomes differentiated or elaborated, it also becomes hierarchically organized or controlled by higher levels of functioning. Early infant emotional expressions are considered precursors or forerunners of more mature emotions. Emotions start in this fashion, Sroufe reasons, because infants lack the cognitive ability needed to ascribe meaning to emotional experiences. An example of this notion is that the generalized distress of the early infant period can be reliably differentiated into either fear or anger roughly at 6 months, only after the infant can recognize a threat. At this later time, the infant's facial expressions can be interpreted more reliably as communicating anger or fear.

EARLY CAREGIVER–INFANT INTERACTIONS AND EMOTIONAL DEVELOPMENT

As we have already seen, it is hard to argue with the idea that emotions provide for human beings' continued survival. Given our long period of dependence, human infants, for obvious reasons, cannot do much to ensure survival on their own. To grow and thrive, babies depend upon the nurturance of adult caregivers who can "read" their emotional expressions and attend to their physical and emotional needs. As it turns out, babies are masters in the art of eliciting the care and attention they need from adults. Among the tools of their art are their physical characteristics, which entice adults to care for them. Characteristics such as small body size, large eyes, and large head size relative to the total body size have been called releasers because they appeal to the nurturant proclivities of caregivers (Fullard & Reiling, 1976). Just think of the people you know who cannot pass an infant without smiling and gazing at the baby, perhaps even engaging in a bit of "baby talk" for good measure.

Caregivers' emotional messages influence babies' willingness to crawl over the edge of the visual cliff.

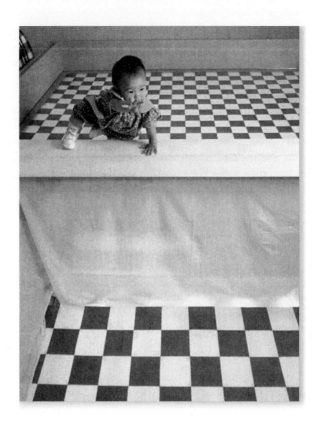

Infant behaviors also serve the function of eliciting care as well as positive attention. Crying and clinging typically bring or keep caregivers close by. Infants have been shown to display more "greeting" or communicative responses to people than to objects and appear more contented and relaxed when they see people (Brazelton, Koslowski, & Main, 1974). With the onset of the social smile around 5 weeks of age, babies lavish many more smiles on their primary caregivers than on others. Mothers, most often the primary caretakers, and their infants engage in increasingly longer mutual gaze interactions. By the age of 3 months, actual turn taking can be observed. The mother's responses and movements are in synchrony with those of her infant (Condon & Sander, 1974).

All these behaviors facilitate the creation of a social and communicative bond between infant and caregiver, ensuring that needs as basic as food, shelter, and safety are met. They also are important for the development of the infant's emotional health. Recall our earlier discussion of experience-expectant and experience-dependent brain development (see Chapter 3). The newborn's development is only partially laid down at birth and depends upon certain types of environmental input to continue normally. Like all other aspects of brain development, the development of emotions depends upon the interaction of genetics and environment. The specific, facilitative environmental circumstances needed for healthy emotional development to occur include supportive, responsive caregiving. As we will see later in the chapter, the attachments that result between infants and caregivers allow feelings of security and trust to flourish in infants. Responsive caregiving also helps infants develop emotion regulation.

Emotion Regulation

Emotion regulation is one of the cornerstones of emotional well-being and positive adjustment throughout the life span. How do we learn to manage the power of our emotions? The emotions of the newborn are poorly regulated. Emotional states can range from contentment to intense distress within minutes. Typically, adult caregivers serve the critical function of helping to manage the newborn's affect or to modulate affective expression while scaffolding the infant's own developing self-regulation. Sensitive adults adjust their management efforts to the needs and abilities of the infant. For example, in a study of infants' emotional reactions to inoculations, mothers used primarily touch to soothe 2-month-olds, holding and rocking them, but used more vocalizing and distracting efforts when their infants were 6 months old, apparently appreciating their infants' changing abilities to respond to visual and auditory stimuli. The infants also showed a typical developmental pattern: The intensity and duration of their crying declined with age, reflecting their own growing capacity to regulate their emotional reactions (Jahromi, Putnam, & Stifter, 2004).

With older infants, the caretaker's emotional expressions can teach the child how to make sense of the world when dealing with emotionally charged situations. Experiments by Campos and his colleagues demonstrate that 10-month-old infants who are able to crawl over a "visual cliff" (a glass-covered surface that looks like a sharp "drop-off") actively seek out their mothers' responses before proceeding to crawl over the cliff (Campos, Barrett, Lamb, Goldsmith, & Sternberg, 1983). Infants whose mothers respond with fearful facial or vocal expressions do not advance, whereas those whose mothers respond with smiles or encouragement proceed to cross the surface without fear. Interestingly, infants use the emotional information provided by caregivers to help them interpret situations that are ambiguous to them.

However, a baby is not totally dependent upon his caregivers to manage emotional experiences. Nature also provides some inborn coping strategies, both other-directed and self-directed, that help a baby begin to regulate his emotions. Imagine, for example, an infant who gazes, smiles, and coos at his mother and receives smiles, attention, and verbalizations in return. The infant's emotional state is likely to remain positive, opening the way for further social engagement. Now imagine the infant who smiles at his mother but gets no response. The infant's needs (to establish contact, maintain security and proximity, experience positive emotions, and control distress) are frustrated. Such frustration usually leads to a negative emotional state and allows us to observe how infants respond to frustration. The dynamics of social engagement and frustration, distress, and coping are stunningly apparent in a research technique called the "still-face" paradigm (Tronick et al., 1980). The infant, usually around 3 months of age, is placed in an infant seat directly in front of his mother. The mother is instructed to interact in a normally pleasant and playful way with her child. The mother responds to her infant's emotional displays, and a synchronous "dance" between her and her child develops. Then the mother is instructed to change her behavior, either by remaining completely nonresponsive or by acting in an emotionally withdrawn fashion. When the infant observes this change, he initially responds with other-directed coping behaviors, using facial expressions, movements, and verbalizations that seem designed to get his mother to resume the previous interactive style. The baby's distress heightens if the mother still fails to engage, and the infant will usually resort to self-directed coping behaviors that seem designed for self-comfort. Babies look away or may even self-stimulate by rocking, sucking, and so on. Interestingly, this effect is observed if the mother is unresponsive for only a few seconds. The baby's negative mood persists even when the mother resumes contact. Babies look at their mothers less for several minutes after this experience (Tronick, 1989).

It is important to note that normal mother–infant interactions are not all positive. Tronick has reported that only about 30% of the face-to-face interactions during the 1st year of life are positive in the sense that the baby is calm and alert and able to be responsive to the mother in interactions that are mutually coordinated. Coordinated sequences involve frequent shifts from positive emotional states to negative emotional states and then back to positive states. It takes the sensitivity of the patient caregiver to gently prod the baby toward longer periods of positive affect, resulting in fewer and briefer periods of negative emotion. The key, as we shall see, seems to be the ability to move the derailed interaction back onto a positive track. Under normal circumstances, the caregiver–baby interaction gets repaired because of efforts of the caregiver. This positive movement or interactive repair allows the infant to come to depend upon his caregiver for help as well as to shape his own sense of effectiveness as a social agent. Ultimately, the infant's other-directed coping strategies, which he learns are effective in the context of sensitive caregiving, enhance communication and promote engagement with the external environment. Essentially, the effect of this reciprocal process is to help babies learn to be content most of the time. Note that the caregiver provides the experience-dependent environment in which the baby's coping strategies play out. Once again, the interplay of native and environmental factors is required for a successful outcome.

Infants of Depressed Mothers

Infants of depressed mothers are a group at particular risk because this synchrony is chronically interrupted. Depressed caretakers typically show less positive affect than nondepressed caretakers. They look away from their babies more often and display more anger, intrusiveness, and poorly timed responses. In short, they thwart their babies' efforts to establish predictable contact, leading to more negative emotional periods for the infant and increased levels of self-directed coping (see Hammen, 2003). A baby needs help regulating his emotions and learning the predictability that characterizes well-coordinated interactions. Unfortunately, the depressed caregiver is unable to provide the kind of help that is needed. For infants of depressed mothers, interactions frequently go unrepaired, and the infant resorts to a style of affective coping marked by escaping and turning away. Both future social relationships and cognitive development can be negatively affected.

Physiological studies have documented differences in the brain activity of infants of depressed and nondepressed mothers (e.g., Dawson et al., 1999; Field et al., 1995). For example, Field and her colleagues (1995) reported asymmetrical electrical activity in the right frontal area of 3- to 4-month-old infants of depressed mothers. This pattern of heightened right frontal activation and lowered left frontal activation is consistent with the patterns observed in extremely fearful and inhibited children and in chronically depressed adults, suggesting the experience of more negative than positive emotions. The authors point out that this physiological marker may be a useful indicator of infants who are at risk of emotional problems and who might profit from early intervention. In addition, infants of depressed mothers showed elevated heart rates and cortisol levels, both symptomatic of stress (Field, 1989).

Does all this mean that depressed mothers *pass on* their depression? As with other questions, experts take somewhat different stands. Field and colleagues (1988) hold the view that a mother's depression does predispose her child to more depressed affect. Their position is supported by findings that infants' depressed behaviors generalize to other nondepressed adults, indicating a style of relating characterized by negative affect. Some infants of depressed mothers may become sensitive to others' emotional states by virtue of their experience, making them more socially adept and skilled at obtaining social support. Nonetheless, it is fair to say that infants exposed to chronically depressed or nonresponsive caregivers are at risk for increased interactive failure. These caregivers need treatment aimed at reducing their depression and teaching effective parenting skills.

Neurobiology of Early Social Bonding

One exciting new area of research focuses on the underlying neurophysiology associated with the formation and expression of emotional relationships (see Box 4.1). We know from research on adults that the brain's right hemisphere is specialized for recognizing and interpreting nonverbal communication (Borod, Koff, & Buck, 1986). Although research support is still tentative at this point, the right hemisphere appears to be more mature than the left hemisphere in infancy (Tucker, 1986). Thus, nature may have equipped the infant with a sensitive period for the development of social attachments based upon the brain's developmental trajectory. Tucker reasons that the more rapid development of the left hemisphere in the 2nd year of life is manifested outwardly by the toddler's achievements in motor and language skills. Tucker also interprets the toddler's increasing autonomy as a shift away from the right-hemisphere-mediated attention to emotional and social contexts that characterize the 1st year of life. We need to be careful, however, not to think exclusively in terms of hemispheric specialization. As we have seen, cortical brain functions interact with subcortical structures in an integrated way.

Schore (1994), for example, cites the importance of the right hemisphere in his discussion of the biological roots of emotional development, but he emphasizes the relationship between cortical and subcortical regions. He reports evidence from animal and some human studies that identifies the right orbitofrontal region, located in the internal region of the right frontal lobe, as the primary brain region involved in social bonding. This area is enlarged in humans and has dense connections to the brain's emotional centers, the limbic system, hypothalamus, and brain stem. He posits that the development and reorganization of this brain area over the first 2 years

Box 4.1 | *The Emotional Brain*

Are you a person who is used to going to bed early at night and who is typically more alert and energetic early in the morning? If so, you may have occasionally had the difficult experience of trying to keep yourself awake late at night to study for a test. Or perhaps you are a right-handed person who once had your writing hand in a cast and needed to maneuver with your left hand. In either of these cases, you would have been "fighting" your body's natural inclinations, either to sleep according to its accustomed cycles or to write using a preferred hand. It's not easy. Moreover, it's more time consuming and labor intensive than it would be otherwise. Some current writers in the neurosciences make the same point when talking about the brain. If we do not understand and accept how our brains work, they claim, we may be operating at cross-purposes. That is, we may be fighting against our biology when we employ clinical and educational strategies that do not make sense from the perspective of *brain-behavior relationships*. Even though it seems fair to say that most clinicians are interested more in people than in the science of brain function, it is also fair to say that we stand to profit immensely from some understanding of what science has to offer in this area.

Probably this is of greatest importance to clinicians in the area of emotions. For what human problem or concern does not, in some way, touch on our feelings? Because our brains process emotions, it is worth our time to try to understand the biology involved. What areas of the brain are responsible for handling emotional messages? What causes emotions to get out of control? What is the relationship between thinking and emotion? Recently, researchers have addressed these questions and have provided some intriguing, although admittedly incomplete answers. Allowing brain science to inform our psychological theories of emotion will guide us to choose theories that are compatible with biological processes and that will be more effective therapeutically. Furthermore, knowledge of the brain can open up possibilities for new understanding about how emotions operate (LeDoux, 1995). Let us examine some of this new information about the emotional brain so that we can make better informed decisions as reflective practitioners.

Historically, the study of emotion has not received the kind of attention from researchers that, for example, learning or memory has been given (Neisser, 1967). Perhaps this happened because researchers had difficulty defining emotions. Perhaps researchers had a bias against "soft, subjective" topics in favor of those considered more objective and, therefore, more appropriate to science. The somewhat artificial split between "cognition" and "emotion" resulted in the common perception that information processing involved only higher order thinking capacities separate from emotion. This perception existed despite the fact that higher

order cognitive processing is *just one kind* of information processing that the brain is able to accomplish. In any case, the study of emotions, so central to human experience and so critical to helpers, was largely left out of the cognitive revolution that started around the middle of the 20th century. In the words of LeDoux (1996), cognitive scientists seemed to view people as "souls on ice" (p. 22). Clinicians were further distanced from an appreciation of the emotional brain because traditional academic training separated students of social science and of science into different tracks, thus leaving students with clinical interests ill-prepared in the biological sciences (deCatanzaro, 1999).

This is not to say that there has been little interest in emotions. Early theorists such as William James, Carl Lange, Walter Cannon, Philip Bard, and others provided theories of emotions that held sway for many years. These theorists tended to disagree about the directionality of emotional responses and the primacy of body or brain. James believed that environmental events lead to bodily changes and behaviors, which people then interpret as particular emotions. Cannon and Bard argued that external stimuli had to be detected and evaluated by the rational brain before conscious feelings and bodily changes could be produced (see deCatanzaro, 1999, for a review of classic theories). From the biological camp, the most influential ideas came from James Papez (1937), who identified the structures of the limbic circuit, and Robert MacLean (1952, 1970), who proposed that the limbic system was the *visceral brain*, or the site of emotions. MacLean, building on the earlier work of Papez, concluded that the brain had evolved over millions of years to its present tripartite, or "three-brains-in-one," state. His *triune brain* included the (1) reptilian, (2) paleomammalian, or limbic, and (3) mammalian brains, each with its own particular structures and functions. All three were thought to exist in humans and in other advanced animal species. Lower level mammals had both paleomammalian and reptilian brains, whereas lower level species had only the latter.

According to MacLean's theory, each brain was distinct, represented successfully higher levels of cortical functioning, and arrived on the scene at a different time in history. The limbic brain was composed of evolutionarily "old" cortex or brain matter that was present in species that were phylogenetically older than humans. The functions served by this system—fight, flight, feeding, mating, and so on—were necessary for the survival of the species. Many early studies of anatomy supported the ties between limbic structures and emotional responses, so that the limbic system as the processor and repository of emotions was dogma for many years.

Beginning in the 1970s, however, researchers began to uncover evidence that poked holes in MacLean's theory. First, it was shown that species that are very primitive (and old in the evolutionary sense) have brain structures that function as the cerebral cortex does in more advanced species (Northcutt & Kaas, 1995). This cast doubt on the evolution of a triune brain. Furthermore, some parts of the limbic system do not deal with emotions at all, whereas parts of the cerebral cortex do. Rather than consider the limbic system as the all-purpose emotional power plant, researchers such as LeDoux (1996) claim that there are several discrete emotional systems or circuits in the brain designed to take care of different problems that have faced humans and animals over the course of evolution. For example, the brain system that helps us deal with fearful situations appears to be distinct from the one that enables us to feel pleasure. Therefore, if we want to understand the emotions (and the disorders linked to them), we probably need to consider these systems as separate but interacting. We also need to consider the relationships of these emotional systems, or modules, to the higher cortical areas.

LeDoux's ideas have been supported by evidence for several different emotional "circuits," seven to be precise, identified by scientists such as Panksepp (1982, 1992). These circuits operate semiautomatically when triggered, producing the emotional responses of seeking, rage, fear, lust, nurturance, sorrow, and play.

We can find some specific answers to the question of how the brain processes emotion by considering LeDoux's illuminating work on the fear circuit. Conventional wisdom used to be that the cerebral cortex receives sensory input first before conveying such input to the limbic structures for an emotional "reading" (Schacter & Singer, 1962). Thus, the cortex was perceived as the broker of all brain activity. It had a hand in all the action, able to exert its rational control over all thinking and feeling. Much to the surprise of many researchers, LeDoux identified a neural "back alley" through which information about a fearful stimulus travels directly from the sensory systems through the thalamus to the amygdala, bypassing the cortex altogether. Information traveling via this "low road" pathway leads to quicker, more powerful, and longer lasting, but also less rational, responses than information processed first via the cortex.

Let us consider what this means. Given this state of biological affairs, it is possible for people to experience an emotional response, such as fear, and to start to react in typical flight-or-fight ways before the more rational cortex has even registered the event. Emotions such as fear are present in humans for some adaptive purpose; they have helped us survive. LeDoux's findings suggest that we have a *biological preparedness* to respond emotionally to at least some harmful stimuli. It is far easier to learn to fear snakes, for example, than it is to fear shrubbery!

Imagine that one sunny summer afternoon you are swimming alone in the ocean, off the coast of your beach resort. Out of the corner of your eye, you spot a gray triangular shape rising above the water not too far away. Your body responds in characteristically defensive ways. Your hair stands on end, your stomach tightens, your heart races, and so on. The threat is transmitted to your brain's emotional centers almost instantaneously so that your body can ready itself against the danger. Now, suppose the putative shark fin turns out to be only a piece of debris. Upon closer observation, your cortex distinguishes the difference and allows you to adjust your response to one that is more appropriate. Your initial emotional reaction is only a split second ahead of your rational response. Nature has apparently given us an early warning emotional system to provide us with a survival advantage. It is the cortex's job to decide whether the response is warranted or not. Thus, high-road and low-road processing, involving both reason and emotion, work in concert.

The glitch is that low-road emotional processing could be responsible for persistent emotional responses that we don't understand. This can happen through *conditioning*, or the pairing of emotional responses to stimuli that were once neutral. LeDoux believes that phobias, panic, posttraumatic stress disorder, and anxiety all arise from the operation of the brain's fear system. As helpers know, these problems and reactions can persist despite the absence of real threat. Another tricky part is that these fears do not extinguish by themselves; probably active new learning or extinction training is needed for their control. They appear to lay in wait until, under stressful conditions, they rear their ugly heads again and affect our responses.

Because emotional memories seem to be indelibly fixed in the neural circuits, the best chance we have to change things therapeutically is to help the more rational cortex gain control over emotional centers through new learning. LeDoux states that therapy rewires the brain pathways to facilitate a kind of emotional control but never completely erases the amygdala's memory. Thus, the therapeutic process is fairly daunting from a biological perspective. He notes:

> It is well known that the connections from the cortical areas to the amygdala are far weaker than the connections from the amygdala to the cortex. This may explain why it is so easy for emotional information to invade our conscious thoughts, but so hard for us to gain conscious control over our emotions. (1996, p. 265)

LeDoux suggests that psychotherapy may be a long process "because of this asymmetry in connections between the cortex and the amygdala" (p. 265).

of life are critically dependent upon the caregiver's rhythmic, sensitive responses, which help regulate the infant's uneven hormonal, autonomic, and behavioral states.

Working at the neurochemical level, Panksepp and his colleagues have hypothesized that the brain's opiate system plays a special role in the formation of social attachments (Panksepp, Herman, Conner, Bishop, & Scott, 1978). Studying puppies and other animal species, these researchers have found that low doses of opiates can effectively reduce the specific kinds of distress caused by social separation, although they are ineffective with other kinds of pain. These researchers reason that normal social interaction and the formation of affective social bonds activate the brain's own opiate system. Externally delivered opiates apparently mimic the normal operation of the brain's internal opiate system. In essence, narcotics may function like a social relationship. These authors speculate that problems as diverse as drug addiction and autism are human responses to the perception of social isolation and may be related at the neurological level to the brain's opiate system.

ATTACHMENT: EARLY SOCIAL RELATIONSHIPS

Human infants are emotionally and behaviorally equipped to elicit responsive care and stimulation from adults. Adults, in turn, are prepared by nature to stimulate and nurture infants. The social interactions that result help an infant to expand his emotional repertoire, and they support the development of his capacity for emotion regulation. But early interpersonal interactions may have a much broader impact on the infant's development. Theorists such as John Bowlby (1969/1982, 1973, 1980) and Erik Erikson (1950/1963) have proposed that the relationships that an infant has with one or a few caregivers during the 1st year of life provide him with a working model of himself and of others. (See Box 4.2, pp. 118–119 and Box 4.3, p. 120.) These emerging models play an important role in determining how secure and optimistic a child will later feel about venturing forth to explore the broader world. Thus, early relationships are said to lay the groundwork for future interactions with others, for the child's self-concept, and even for his outlook on life.

For Erikson, the characteristics of early caregiving enable a child to form his first feelings about others. When care is timely, sensitive to the infant's needs, and consistently available, he begins to establish basic trust, seeing others as dependable and trustworthy. As his rudimentary view of others takes shape, it influences how he begins to see himself. If others can be trusted to provide for his needs, then his needs must be important and he must be a worthy recipient of care. Feeling trust and feeling worthy emerge together, two sides of the same coin. These early

Around 8 months of age most babies will show separation anxiety accompanied by wariness of strangers.

Box 4.2 | *Two Biographical Sketches: John Bowlby and Mary D. Salter Ainsworth*

In the 1950s, 7-year-old Marianne was hospitalized for a tonsillectomy. The small-town hospital where the surgery was performed had very strict policies governing visitors to its child patients: 1 hour in the afternoon, maximum of two visitors. Marianne's experiences with doctors had generally been positive up until then. In addition, her mother was a nurse, so Marianne was warmly disposed to women dressed in white from head to foot and smelling wonderfully clean, and she was, blessedly, old enough to understand what was happening to her. The first afternoon and evening, preoperatively, were a pleasant adventure, and Marianne was able to sleep without distress despite the separation from her family. But the next day, after the early morning surgery, the pain struck, and Marianne wanted her mother's cool hand and soothing voice. The hours until her mother's first visit were endless, and the end of the visit was agony. The release into her parents' care the next afternoon was a respite from hell.

Through the middle 1900s, restricted visitation to child hospital patients was standard policy, based on concerns about infection and about disruptions to medical routines. Today, parents not only are allowed complete access to their children in most hospitals but are encouraged to stay with their children continuously and to be part of the healing and helping process. Many hospitals provide cots and even rooms for showering and changing to encourage parental involvement. It was John Bowlby's groundbreaking theorizing and research on the sometimes devastating emotional costs of mother–child separations, especially during hospitalizations, that initiated a major shift in thinking about the relative benefits of separating children from their families.

John Bowlby (1907–1990) and Mary D. Salter Ainsworth (1913–1999) were jointly responsible for a revolution in the way that parent–child relationships are perceived by researchers and clinicians. Bowlby began his professional life in England as a psychoanalyst who worked with children. In the 1930s, Bowlby's clinical work was supervised by Melanie Klein, who invented psychoanalytic play therapy. Bowlby was inclined to look for a relationship between his young patients' behavior and the kind of parenting they were receiving, but Klein discouraged his family-oriented approach, arguing that the child's "object" relations (interpersonal beliefs and behaviors) were a function of fantasy, not experience in relationships. Bowlby, however, was convinced that early relationships play a large role in personality and behavioral development. He discovered in the work of ethologists, biologists who do careful observations of animal behavior in natural environments, that animals such as ducks and geese are inclined to become devoted followers of whatever they first see moving—usually their mothers, but sometimes a different animal, such as a human researcher.

Such bonding, when it works "the way nature intended," promotes the survival of ducklings and goslings by keeping them close to a protective adult.

Eventually, Bowlby integrated ideas from ethology, from systems theory, from cognitive development (including the work of Piaget), and from psychoanalysis into attachment theory, arguing that some human infant behaviors, for example clinging and sucking, help keep the mother close, whereas others, for example smiling, naturally elicit maternal caregiving. Such behaviors initiate the development of an attachment system that promotes the infant's survival and creates a feeling of security. That system changes and consolidates over time as the child's skills develop. Early clinging and sucking are later replaced by other attachment behaviors, such as protesting when mother leaves or joyfully greeting her when she returns, but the system's evolutionary function remains the same. The attachment system is enhanced and developed by the responses of the environment (i.e., of the caregiver) and helps the child develop a working model of the self (e.g., I am valuable, worthy of care) and of others (e.g., others are reliable and caring).

Bowlby's theoretical work was enhanced and enriched by research into the importance of early relationships on children's behavior. For example, he and his colleagues studied the effects of hospitalization and institutionalization on 15- to 30-month-olds using the careful, detailed observational style of ethology. They documented a series of stages of distress and withdrawal that helped create the impetus for change in hospital visitation policies described earlier (see also Box 4.5). But the research that captured the attention of both the scientific and the clinical community was Ainsworth's studies of mothers and babies in their own homes.

Ainsworth, who earned a Ph.D. in psychology at the University of Toronto, submerged her own career to follow her husband to London. There she answered Bowlby's newspaper ad seeking researchers. His views of the importance of early relationships were consistent with many of her own ideas, and Ainsworth became an eager student and associate. When her husband's career took her to Uganda, she launched a study of local mothers caring for their unweaned infants. She became convinced from her observations that Bowlby was right: Babies actively help create an attachment system that protects them and provides a foundation for later developments. She also believed that the 28 Ganda babies she studied were forming attachments of different qualities, and she looked for relationships between the infants' attachment quality and the mothers' sensitivity and responsiveness.

When her husband moved again, this time to Baltimore, Ainsworth took a position at Johns Hopkins University. Eventually, she launched a more detailed and intensive study of 26 mother–infant dyads. After 18 home visits over the course of each baby's 1st year, she invented the "strange situation test" to assess the infants' feelings of security when they were 1 year old. That test is now the preeminent means for assessing attachment quality and has been used in dozens of studies since, by researchers around the world eager to test the tenets of attachment theory and to explore the precursors and consequences of an infant's first attachments. Ainsworth's careful research both enhanced the credibility of Bowlby's views and demonstrated that interpersonal relationships, not just individual behaviors, could be meaningfully investigated using scientific techniques.

(*Source:* Karen, 1998.)

attitudes toward others and toward the self create a sense of hope or optimism that experiences beyond the caregiving relationship will also be positive and are therefore worth pursuing.

Bowlby described the infant's connection with the primary caregiver (usually the mother) as his first attachment relationship. Bowlby's theory of how it changes and what it means for the child's psychosocial life is called **attachment theory**. In Bowlby's description, infant and caregiver participate in an attachment system that has evolved to serve the purpose of keeping the infant safe and assuring his survival. As we have already noted, both the infant and the adult bring to the system a set of biologically prepared behaviors. These behaviors change as the infant's repertoire of abilities changes, partly as a function of interactions with others. Early in infancy, as we have seen, infant cries and clinging bring a caregiver. Later, instead of clinging, the toddler may keep an eye on one particular adult, often the mother, keeping track of her whereabouts in case of need. Instead of crying, the toddler may call to the caregiver or communicate by reaching or pointing. When the baby does cry, the caregiver may respond differently to different cries, assessing the level and kind of need from variations in the sound, apparently recognizing that crying can serve multiple purposes for the older baby (see Thompson & Leger, 1999). Thus, the system broadens to include and accommodate the infant's more advanced physical and cognitive abilities, but it still serves the purpose of making the child secure.

In the context of this attachment system, an affectional bond develops between infant and caregiver. Bowlby argued that as a result of cognitive and emotional developments in the infancy period, the baby's connection to the caregiver emerges in stages, with a full-fledged attachment likely by about 7 or 8 months. Schaffer and Emerson (1964) followed the development of a group of infants through their first 18 months and found a sequence of attachment stages consistent with those Bowlby has described. In the first 2 months, infants signal their needs, producing behaviors such as clinging, smiling, and crying. Although we now know that even newborns have some ability to recognize their mothers' voices (e.g., DeCasper & Fifer, 1980), they show little sign of discriminating among potential caregivers or of having a social preference, so that babies cannot yet be seen as attached to anyone. Next, between about 2 and 7 or 8 months, infants gradually show stronger and stronger preferences for particular caregivers, as when a baby smiles more brightly or is more readily soothed by Mom or Dad than by Grandma or Uncle Bill. Usually by 8 months, babies behave in ways that signal a strong preference for one caregiver, most often the mother. The chief indicator of attachment is that an infant will protest being separated from the mother and will greet her happily when she returns. Along with this **separation anxiety** (see Chapter 3 for a full description) may come **stranger anxiety**: an increased tendency to be wary of strangers and to seek the comfort and protection of the primary caregiver when a stranger is present. Note that infants can recognize familiar faces and voices much earlier than 7 or 8 months, and they may show some wariness with strangers, but a more intense reaction is common once other indicators of the first attachment emerge. Finally, Schaffer and Emerson observed that soon after babies show signs of their first emotional attachment, many of them are forming other attachments as well, with their fathers, with regular babysitters, with older siblings, and with other family members. By 18 months, most of the babies in their study were attached to more than one person.

Attachment is a system, not a particular set of behaviors. The system serves three purposes: It maintains proximity between infant and caregiver, nurturing the emotional bond (called **proximity maintenance**); It provides the potential for ongoing protection (called **secure base**); and It creates a haven for the infant when distressed (called **safe haven**). Behaviors as diverse as

Box 4.3 | *A Biographical Sketch: Erik H. Erikson*

The parents of a 4-year-old boy named Peter brought him to Erik Erikson for treatment of a frightening problem that appeared to be emotionally based. Peter retained his feces for up to a week at a time, and his colon had become enlarged. As he learned more about Peter, Erikson came to see his problem as a reaction to the way others had dealt with normal, stage-appropriate behavior. Before the problem began, Peter had entered what Erikson described as the developmental stage of initiative versus guilt, when it is common for children to intrude themselves on others in a rather aggressive way—such as trying to take over the conversation at the dinner table or, as in Peter's case, being physically aggressive and bossy with adults (see Table 1.2 in Chapter 1). Peter's aggressive style was tolerated amiably by his nanny, but his mother was disturbed by it and by the nanny's tolerance, so she fired the nanny. Peter's anal retention problem started soon afterward. Eventually, Erikson helped Peter to see that his problem was related to his distress at losing his beloved nanny. Peter, Erikson felt, was identifying with the nanny, who had told Peter that she was going to have a baby of her own, and he was trying to hold on to her by retaining his feces.

Erikson's work with Peter reflects the Freudian roots of his perspective. He saw Peter's 4-year-old aggressiveness with his nanny as having sexual overtones, a normal process for a child in Freud's phallic stage. When Peter's aggressiveness led to the painful loss of the beloved nanny, he regressed to using behaviors more typical of the anal stage: holding on to his feces. But Erikson's interpretation also reveals his innovative, psychosocial perspective, which went well beyond his Freudian training. Preschoolers need to express their bold new sense of initiative. Adults can be accepting of this need, even as they impose some constraints so that children will learn to behave in socially acceptable ways. In the process, children will learn to curb their own behavior, controlled by their own feelings of guilt. But when constraints are imposed in an abrupt, disapproving, unsupportive way, or when they are excessive, children's appropriate exuberance can be stifled, leading a child to be overly restrained and guilty about normal behavior. Just as in infancy, when children must form basic trust, the warmth,

sensitivity, and understanding of responsive adults is an important ingredient in the development of positive feelings about self or others.

Erik H. Erikson (1902–1994) was the son of Danish parents; his mother was Jewish, his father, Prostestant. His parents separated before he was born, and he was raised in Germany by his mother and stepfather. His undistinguished youth seems an unlikely beginning for a great developmental theorist. He was something of a misfit as a young boy. His ethnicity as a Jew coupled with his Gentile appearance caused him to experience social rejection from both his Jewish and his Gentile peers. As a young man, Erik, born Erik Homberger, changed his surname to Erikson—a clear attempt to construct his own identity. He was not much of a student, and after high school, uncertain of his goals or interests, he wandered through Europe rather than attend college. He studied art for a while, wandered again, and eventually accepted an offer to teach children at a school where Anna Freud, daughter of Sigmund, was a cofounder. Thus began his life's work as a child clinician. He studied psychoanalysis with Anna Freud, and when he and his wife, Joan, fled Europe in 1933 with the rise of Hitler, he became the first child analyst in Boston. In his career as a therapist and developmental theorist, he held faculty appointments at Yale, in the University of California system, and finally at Harvard, despite the fact that he had earned no degrees beyond high school. In his scholarly work he not only contributed to research and theory on normal personality development, including the formerly uncharted area of adult life stages, but he also pioneered exploration into cross-cultural variations in development, observing the life experiences of Sioux Indians in South Dakota and of Yurok Indians in California. Although Erikson extended his work to include adult developmental issues, he seems to have had a special concern for the vulnerability of children. In his writing on child rearing, he urged parents to recognize that the most fundamental requirement of good parenting is to provide a sense of security, to give children the benefit of calm, reliable care, starting in earliest infancy.

(*Sources:* Coles, 1970; Crain, 1992.)

smiling and crying all serve attachment functions, and as already noted, the particular behaviors serving these functions can change over time and circumstance. When helpers reflect on problems faced by children and families, attachment theory indicates that the proper unit of analysis is at the level of relationships. That is, a behavior (e.g., crying or clinging) must be interpreted within its social context to understand its significance.

Let's consider the notion of safe haven more specifically, for it is here that attachments serve the important function of stress management. Think back, for a moment, to the earlier discussion of emotion regulation. The infant has limited ability to regulate his episodes of physiological distress. Threats such as hunger, pain, fatigue, loneliness, or overstimulation can produce periods of dysregulation or heightened arousal. Some infants are more easily aroused than others because of individual differences in autonomic reactivity. For all infants, and especially for these more sensitive and vulnerable ones, the stressfulness of physical or emotional discomfort activates the attachment system. By crying, clinging, or showing distress in some other way, the infant signals his need for his caregiver to step in to help manage stress. Distress, triggered from within the infant or from without, activates the attachment system. The helpless infant needs a caregiver to deactivate his escalating discomfort. With time, sensitive caregiving episodes become associated with relief and love for the caregiver. The caregiver scaffolds the child's own developing capacity to regulate his emotions and helps build the tolerance necessary for healthy emotional control.

Bowlby, like Erikson, assumed that the quality of care that an infant receives will affect the nature and the eventual impact of his attachments. With responsive, sensitive care, infants come to see their primary attachment figure as a source of security, a secure base from which to explore the world (Ainsworth, Blehar, Waters, & Wall, 1978). They correspondingly feel confidence in themselves and in their ability to negotiate that world. The infant learns that his signals of distress are heard by others—that they are adaptive in helping him get needs for care and attention met. He also learns that the very expression of these needs is legitimate in that others take them seriously.

More broadly, the nature or quality of the infant's first attachments affects his expectations and behaviors in other relationships, "providing implicit decision rules for relating to others that may, for better or worse, help to confirm and perpetuate intuitive expectations about oneself" (Thompson, 1998, p. 36). In sum, early experience with a primary caregiver helps the child form his first representations of the self, of others, and of relationships. Bowlby referred to these representations as **working models**—prototypes of social functioning that affect the child's expectations and behaviors in future relationships.

Bowlby's attachment theory prompted developmental researchers to explore babies' earliest relationships, seeking a better understanding of how the first attachments develop and how important they really are for psychosocial development. In the following sections, we take a look at what this research has revealed and what it might mean for the helping professions.

Attachment Quality

Using a measurement technique called the **strange situation test**, Mary Ainsworth and her colleagues found that infants form different kinds of attachments to their primary caregivers (Ainsworth et al., 1978). For the test, 12-month-olds and their mothers were brought to a room (the strange situation) where the child experienced a series of eight 3-minute episodes, each one introducing changes in the social situation, some of which were likely to be stressful to an infant. The stress component was important, given that attachment theory assumes that infants cannot handle stress on their own. At first the mother and baby were left alone in the room; in subsequent episodes, the mother and a stranger (one of the researchers) entered and left the room in various combinations. The baby's reactions to all of these events were carefully recorded, particularly his tendency to explore the room and the toys and his reactions to his mother and the stranger. The researchers paid special attention to the baby's response to his mother when she returned after an absence.

Ainsworth and her colleagues identified three patterns of infant response, now considered indicative of three different kinds of infant attachment to an adult caregiver. In subsequent research a fourth category of attachment has been identified (Main & Soloman, 1990). It is important to note that all of these patterns do represent attachments, as all babies seem to have needs for proximity maintenance, a secure base, and safe haven. The style of the attachment, however, varies. The following paragraphs describe all four types of attachment patterns.

Researchers use the strange situation task to investigate the nature of infants' attachments to caregivers and the ways that infants cope with the stress of separation.

SECURELY ATTACHED

Most babies are found to be securely attached (originally described as the "B" category). They show distress on separation from the mother, often crying and trying to go after her, but they greet her happily on her return, usually reaching up to be held, sometimes molding their bodies to the mother as they seek comfort. Once reassured by her presence and her gestures, they tend to go off and explore the room. Ainsworth argued that babies in this category can use mother as a secure base from which to explore the world; perhaps they are showing the beginnings of optimism or hope, as Erikson suggested. They may also have learned to tolerate more separation because they have confidence in the mother's availability if they need her. Sixty-five percent of the 1-year-olds in the Ainsworth et al. (1978) study showed this response pattern, and in most subsequent research the majority of babies fit this description (Thompson, 1998).

ANXIOUS AMBIVALENT—INSECURELY ATTACHED

Babies in this and the remaining two categories are considered to be attached, in that they show signs of having a special pattern of behavior vis-à-vis their mothers, but their attachments seem insecure, often laced with high levels of anxiety, as though the infant cannot quite achieve a sense of security and ease even when mother is available. Anxious ambivalent babies (originally called "C" babies, comprising about 10% of many samples) often seem stressed even in the initial episode (e.g., sometimes failing to explore at all), and they are quite distressed when separated from their mothers. It is their reunion behavior, however, that distinguishes them as insecurely attached. They may act angry, alternately approaching and resisting the mother, or they may respond listlessly to her efforts to comfort. They seem preoccupied with their mothers and rarely return to exploration after a separation.

AVOIDANT—INSECURELY ATTACHED

Avoidant babies, about 20% of most samples, typically fail to cry when separated from their mothers. They actively avoid or ignore her when she returns, sometimes combining proximity seeking and moving away, but mostly turning away. In contrast to babies in other categories, these children often appear unemotional during the episodes of separation and reunion. However, Spangler and Grossmann (1993) found that their heart rates are elevated as much as other babies' during separations from their mothers. Unlike other infants, when they are attending to toys instead of mother as they typically do, avoidant babies do not show the heart rate drop that normally accompanies concentration and interest. Mary Main has suggested that, in response to the stress of the strange situation test, avoidant babies may direct their attention to toys as a way of defending themselves against anxiety, whereas other babies direct their attention to Mother for that purpose (Main, 1996; Spangler & Grossmann, 1993).

DISORGANIZED-DISORIENTED—INSECURELY ATTACHED

The category disorganized-disoriented (referred to as "D" babies) was first described by Main and Soloman (1990), who examined strange situation videotapes from several studies, focusing on babies who had previously been difficult to classify. These infants produced contradictory behaviors, showing both an inclination to approach the mother when stressed and a tendency to avoid her when she approached! Their resulting array of behaviors could be quite unusual: rocking on hands and knees with face averted after an abortive approach (toward mother); freezing all movement, arms in air, with a trancelike expression; moving away from the parent to lean head on wall when frightened; and rising to greet the parent then falling prone (Main, 1996, p. 239).

Maternal Care and Attachment Quality: Linking Mother's Sensitivity to Infant Security

Where do attachment types or styles originate? As we have indicated, attachment theory suggests that caregiving during the baby's 1st year is the key, and Ainsworth's early study strongly supported that claim (Ainsworth et al., 1978). All 26 babies and mothers in her study had been observed in their homes at regular intervals from the time of birth. The middle-class mothers were their infants' primary caregivers, and they did not work outside the home. Yet, they did not all provide the same quality of care. Infants who became securely attached had mothers who responded promptly and consistently to crying during the 1st year, who handled the infant with sensitivity, who held the baby tenderly and often, and whose face-to-face interactions were responsive to the baby's signals. In other words, they showed many of the features that both Bowlby and Erikson proposed to be important for infant care to create security or trust.

Babies who became insecurely attached had mothers who seemed insensitive to their infants in one way or another. The mothers of ambivalent babies were affectionate but were often awkward in holding. They were inconsistent in their responsiveness to crying. In face-to-face interactions, they often failed to respond to their babies' signals. For example, in a game of peek-a-boo, an infant might begin to seem overstimulated and turn away his gaze. A responsive mother would be likely to wait until the baby reengaged before saying or doing anything, whereas an unresponsive mother might try to force the reengagement by vocalizing or jiggling the baby.

The mothers of avoidant babies seemed to actively avoid holding their babies. They were more often rejecting and angry, and they showed less warmth and affection than other mothers. Babies in the disorganized-disoriented category of attachment were not identified in Ainsworth's study. Main (e.g., 1996; Main & Hesse, 1990) has proposed that the mothers of these infants have subjected their children to neglect or maltreatment, so that they are themselves frightening to their babies. For this reason, when such a baby is stressed in the strange situation procedure, he "suffer[s] a collapse of behavioral strategy" (Main, 1996, p. 239). He does not feel safe approaching his mother, but he also cannot use the avoidant baby's strategy of shifting attention away from the mother, because the mother must be watched. Some recent studies have found that maltreated children typically do show the disorganized attachment pattern (e.g., Cicchetti, Toth, & Lynch, 1995), and that babies of depressed mothers are also at risk of falling into this category (Lyons-Ruth, Connell, Grunebaum, & Botein, 1990; Lyons-Ruth, Repacholi, McLeod, & Silva, 1991), although Main's interpretation of the underlying dynamics needs further corroboration.

Ainsworth's initial research linking mother care to infant security was striking in the strength of the correlations she reported. Her work excited the research community and attracted the attention of clinicians, especially those interested in developmental psychopathology (see Box 1.1 in Chapter 1). More recent studies have sometimes replicated her finding of a strong connection between mother care and infant–mother attachment, but not always. De Wolf and van IJzendoorn (1997) examined more than 60 studies done since Ainsworth and colleagues' (1978) pioneering work, all of which measured the quality of maternal care and of infant attachment security. The average correlation was significant but much more moderate than initially thought. De Wolf and van IJzendoorn concluded that "maternal sensitivity is an important condition of attachment security" but that other influences must also be important.

Beyond Maternal Caregiving: Other Influences on Relationship Quality

Many attachment theorists and researchers now take a multidimensional approach to attachment, seeking to understand how factors in addition to early caregiving might impact on the attachment system that Bowlby described. Among the influences that appear to interact with caregiving to predict attachment outcomes are infant characteristics such as temperament, cultural context, family variables such as socioeconomic status, and so on.

INFANT TEMPERAMENT

A visit to a newborn nursery provides convincing demonstrations that different babies have different emotional and behavioral characteristics, or temperaments, from the time they are born. Consider Ahmed and Joseph, born at the same hospital on the same day. Ahmed has been sleeping in fairly long stretches, averaging 3 hours, with about 40 minutes of wakefulness between naps. When he is awake, he is often quiet, although like any newborn he cries when he's hungry or uncomfortable. When the nurses pick him up he calms quickly, and his breastfeeding mother says he sucks on the nipple peacefully, with moderate force. Joseph sleeps more irregularly; at 1 day old he has had two sleep periods of about 3 hours each, and many others that have ranged from 10 to 30 minutes. When he awakens, he cries lustily and is not easy to soothe. He also seems to be in constant motion, and his mother finds him squirmy and erratic in his breastfeeding attempts.

Different researchers have identified somewhat different infant traits, but they often include fearfulness or reactivity (the infant's proneness to cry or pull away from new stimuli), irritability or negative emotionality (the infant's tendency to react with fussiness to negative or frustrating events), activity level (the intensity and quantity of movement), positive affect (smiling and laughing, especially to social stimuli), attention-persistence (duration of orienting or looking), and rhythmicity (predictability of sleep, feeding, elimination, and so on). (See reviews by Kagan, 1998, and by Rothbart & Bates, 1998, for the many ways of conceptualizing such traits.)

The cataloging of infant temperament traits raises a number of intriguing questions. Are these traits stable over time, predicting personality characteristics of older children and adults? Where do temperament traits come from? How is infant temperament related to parents' caregiving? (This question has several component parts: Do infant traits affect the sensitivity and responsiveness of parents' caregiving? Can caregiving affect temperament? Are babies with different temperamental traits affected differently by sensitive versus insensitive caregiving?) Finally, does temperament play a role in the development of attachment security?

Lively debate has raged around each of these questions. We will save the first question, whether infant temperament is continuous with later personality characteristics, for later chapters. For now, we will focus on characterizing infant temperament, identifying its relationship to parental caregiving, and understanding its role in attachment security.

Where Do Temperament Traits Come From? They are often assumed to be biologically based reactivity patterns. Researchers have found that some temperamental characteristics among infants are correlated with physiological differences. The most famous attempts to connect temperament to biology are studies done by Jerome Kagan and his colleagues on children who as infants are "high reactive" or "low reactive" (e.g., Kagan 1997, 1998; Kagan, Arcus, Snidman, & Rimm, 1995; Kagan et al., 1994). High reactive 4-month-olds produce frequent vigorous limb activity, have high levels of muscle tension, and react irritably (e.g., crying) to sensory stimulation, such as new smells or sounds. Low reactive infants, of course, score unusually low on these kinds of measures. Early reactivity is related to later measures of behavioral inhibition, or shyness. For example, by 7 to 9 months, when stranger anxiety tends to peak, high reactive

Infants who show behavioral inhibition often become shy children requiring sensitive handling by adults.

infants often show more extreme avoidance or distress than most other infants. These infants also tend to have relatively high heart rates before birth and in some contexts after birth. Kagan has proposed that the behavioral and physiological characteristics of high reactive infants may indicate a lower than average threshold of excitability in parts of the limbic system of the brain—the amygdala and many of its associated structures.

Most infant temperament characteristics have not been examined as intensively as high reactivity. It is not clear whether physiological correlates exist for other traits, but researchers such as Kagan suggest babies may be born with a push from nature to react to environmental conditions in somewhat different ways.

How Is Infant Temperament Related to Parents' Caregiving? In the landmark New York Longitudinal Study, psychiatrists Alexander Thomas and Stella Chess (1977) found that they could categorize 3-month-olds in their large sample into four "temperament types" (using a set of 9 temperament traits; see Table 4.1). **Difficult babies** (about 10%), compared to the others, were more fearful, more irritable, and more active, displayed less positive affect, were more irregular, and so on—a mix of traits that made them difficult and challenging to parent. Joseph, in the above example, might fit this category. **Easy babies** (about 40%) were more placid, less active, more positive, and more regular in their rhythms than most, and thus easier to care for. Ahmed seems to fit this description. **Slow-to-warm-up babies** (about 15%) were like easy babies in many ways, but they were like difficult babies in their fearfulness, showing more wariness in new situations than most other babies. The last category (about 35%) were more variable in their traits and did not fit well into any of the more extreme groups.

Over the course of many years, Thomas and Chess (1977) tracked the personalities and adjustment of the babies they had first observed at 3 months. Fortunately, they also followed the parents' experience with their children, and they found that on the whole, parents too could be categorized. Some were generally accepting of the particular characteristics of their infants. They either happened to have a baby whose emotional and behavioral reactions were consistent with their own propensities and expectations, or they responsively adjusted their caregiving to match the infants' qualities. In either case, these parents provided care that was a "good fit" for their babies. Other parents were jarred by having a baby that did not match their expectations, something that was most likely to happen with a difficult or slow-to-warm-up infant. These parents often felt stymied and angry, sometimes blaming themselves and their poor caregiving skills for

TABLE 4.1   The New York Longitudinal Study: Behavioral Traits Assessed in Infancy and Their Characteristic Levels in Babies with Easy and Difficult Temperaments

Trait	Description	Level of Trait in Two Temperament Styles
1. Activity level	Frequency and speed of movement	*Easy:* Low *Difficult:* High
2. Rhythmicity	Biological regularity, as in sleep-wake cycles and frequency of hunger	*Easy:* High regularity *Difficult:* Low regularity
3. Approach/withdrawal	Child's immediate reaction to new experience: acceptance or rejection	*Easy:* Approaches, acceptance *Difficult:* Withdraws, rejection
4. Adaptability	When child does withdraw, does adaptation take a short, moderate, or long time?	*Easy:* Short period of adaptation *Difficult:* Long period of adaptation
5. Threshold	Minimum strength of stimulus required for child to attend or react	*Easy:* High *Difficult:* Low
6. Intensity	Energy the child expends in expressing mood	*Easy:* Low *Difficult:* High
7. Mood	Predominance of positive vs. neutral or negative mood expression	*Easy:* More positive *Difficult:* More negative
8. Distractibility	Ease with which child's attention is drawn away from an ongoing activity by a new stimulus	*Easy:* Low *Difficult:* High
9. Attention span and persistence	Length of uninterrupted attention to a single activity, and spontaneous return to a task after interruption	*Easy:* Long *Difficult:* Short

Sources: Chess, S., & Hassibi, M. (1978). *Principles and practice of child psychiatry.* New York: Plenum: Chess, S., & Thomas, A. (1987). *Origins and evolution of behavior.* Cambridge, MA: Harvard University Press.

their infants' irritability and resistance. They felt disappointed, discouraged, and guilty when the baby did not fit their expectations or did not adjust to their demands. Not surprisingly, parents of babies with easy temperaments were more likely to be able to create a good fit between their caregiving and the child's characteristics, although some parents did not. For example, parents who were active, feisty people might find a placid, inactive baby hard to tolerate.

In time, some of the children showed signs of socioemotional problems. The majority of these had displayed a difficult temperament in infancy. In fact, 70% of the difficult babies eventually had some adjustment problems, ranging from learning difficulties to stealing to phobias. What differentiated the 70% with later problems from the 30% who seemed well adjusted, however, was the "goodness of fit" that the parents were able to achieve between their caregiving and the child's needs. If the parents were consistent and patient, difficult babies often became less irritable and more adaptable in time, and they were less likely to have adjustment problems as they got older.

Easy babies were not often represented in the group with later adjustment problems. Even when their parents had trouble accepting their characteristics, they usually were able to cope effectively. But when they did have later problems, caregiving seemed to be a critical ingredient—there was usually a poor fit between parental demands and the child's temperament.

The picture that emerges from the Thomas and Chess study is complex. First, it suggests that infant temperament may show some persistence into childhood and beyond. Second, it provides some indication that infant temperament affects caregiving. For example, infant temperament can make it easier or harder for a parent to be a responsive, sensitive caregiver. Third, it indicates that caregiving can change or at least moderate temperamental qualities. A parent's care influences the impact of early temperament on later adjustment. A child with difficult temperamental traits appears to be at risk for later adjustment problems, but the right caregiving can make that child much less vulnerable. Finally, it suggests that some children, especially those with easy temperaments, can tolerate a wider range of caregiving responsiveness without developing emotional or behavioral problems later. It is also important to note that parenting quality is only one of many factors that influence children's socioemotional development. Examples of others are peer networks and the quality of schooling. Some factors, such as socioeconomic status, have direct effects on the parents and their levels of stress, indirectly influencing their parenting quality.

Does Temperament Play a Role in the Development of Attachment Relationships? Thomas and Chess did not look at children's attachment security, but the goodness of fit model suggests that temperament and caregiving should similarly interact in determining the quality of a child's attachment relationships. This has proved to be a particularly contentious issue both for researchers and clinicians. Some have argued strongly that what appears to be attachment security or insecurity could be nothing but a manifestation of infant temperament (see Karen, 1998). For example, in the strange situation test, easy babies who experience no stress in new situations might look avoidant; difficult, irritable infants might look ambivalent. Some attachment findings, but not all, are consistent with this general idea. For example, Stevenson-Hinde and Marshall (1999) found that insecurely attached infants are likely to be at the extremes of behavioral inhibition, with avoidant babies low on behavioral inhibition and ambivalent babies high on behavioral inhibition.

Others have argued that what appear to be biologically based temperamental differences among infants could be nothing but a reflection of the sensitivity of care the infant has experienced. For example, mothers who are inconsistent and unresponsive to infant cues may create babies who find social interactions stressful and frustrating. Soon their infants begin to look more irritable and negative than other babies (see Karen, 1998).

Neither of these extreme views accounts for the full complement of research findings, however. A multidimensional view, such as Thomas and Chess's goodness of fit model, seems to best explain the available evidence: Temperament and sensitivity of care (both also influenced by other variables) interact at several levels to produce attachment security.

Three studies from this rapidly growing literature illustrate the kinds of interactions there may be. In the first study, 9-month-olds' "proneness to distress," defined as a baby's tendency to exhibit negative emotions (e.g., crying, fussing), was inversely related to mothers' warmth, support, and positive emotional tone (Mangelsdorf, Gunnar, Kestenbaum, Lang, & Andreas, 1990). More supportive, emotionally positive mothers tended to have babies who were more placid— less prone to distress. Less supportive, more depressive mothers had fussier babies. These data do not tell us who influenced whom, but they make clear that by 9 months the behavior of the mother and of the infant are coordinated. It is very likely that infant fussiness and mother's emotional tone have influenced one another. At 13 months, the babies' strange situation test performance was related both to their proneness to distress and to their mothers' personalities. Babies who were high on proneness to distress and whose mothers had "constrained" personalities (rigid, fearful of risk taking) were most likely to be insecurely attached. Babies low on proneness to distress were more likely to be securely attached, even when their mothers had "constrained" personalities. Goodness of fit seems to be key here. As the researchers argue,

> The prone-to-distress infant most likely taxes the caregiver more, requiring that the caregiver has better emotional supports and a personality better suited for taking care of a demanding child. In addition, the prone-to-distress infant may also be more vulnerable to nonoptimal care. (Mangelsdorf et al., 1990, p. 821)

A second study suggests that maternal caregiving predicts whether infants will be securely or insecurely attached. However, infant temperament predicts the type of insecure attachment that develops and even the tone of the secure attachment. Kochanska (1998) measured infants' fearfulness (comparable to Kagan's behavioral inhibition) and mothers' responsiveness when the babies were 8 to 10 months and when they were 13 to 15 months. Attachment security in the strange situation was assessed at the later time as well. Maternal responsiveness was linked to whether babies would be securely or insecurely attached. But for insecurely attached infants, fearfulness predicted the type of insecurity. More fearful infants tended to be ambivalent; less fearful babies were more often avoidant. Even the tone of secure attachment behavior was related to the babies' fearfulness, with more fearful babies more highly aroused in the separation and reunion episodes.

Finally, a third study is important because it goes beyond suggesting that caregiving affects infants' attachment security, which is all that correlational research can do. Van den Boom (1994) was able to demonstrate that caregiving actually plays a causal role in attachment security, especially with children at the more difficult temperamental extreme. In a large sample of low-income families, van den Boom identified a group of 100 1- to 2-week-olds who were assessed as highly "irritable." The author assigned half of the infants to a treatment condition in which their mothers were trained to be sensitive and responsive. The remaining infant–mother pairs simply had to fend for themselves. The mothers in both groups tended to be frustrated by their fussy babies, and, without intervention, their caregiving was often insensitive and unresponsive. By 12 months, 72% of the infants whose mothers had received no training were insecurely attached. But after being given caregiving support and training, the mothers in the intervention group treated their babies more sensitively and were more responsive to their needs. Sixty-eight percent of their infants were securely attached by 12 months! This study demonstrates experimentally that sensitive caregiving does make a difference in security of attachment.

CLASS AND CULTURE

Van den Boom's (1994) study also underscores the need to look beyond both the infant and the caregiver to understand infant attachments. About 72% of the babies in her nonintervention group developed insecure attachments to their mothers, as compared to about 30% of infants in most other studies. Part of the difference, of course, is probably due to the difficult temperaments of the babies in van den Boom's sample, but social class probably also contributed to the poor outcomes. Indeed, van den Boom selected lower class dyads because previous research indicated that greater numbers of insecure attachments (presumably linked to poor quality care) are found in lower economic groups (NICHD, 1997; see Thompson, 1998). It hardly seems likely that poorer families love their children less. But the caregiving environment can be impacted by the stresses confronting families who have inadequate, or barely adequate, education, housing, and income (McLoyd, 1990). Vaughn, Egeland, Sroufe, and Waters (1979) measured attachment security both at 12 months and at 18 months in 100 babies from lower income families. Ten of the babies who were securely attached at first had become insecurely attached by 18 months. The mothers of those babies were more likely than other mothers to report significant increases in their life stresses during the intervening 6 months. Apparently, the attachment relationship can be vulnerable to events that may distract, depress, or preoccupy the mother or otherwise upset family life. This dynamic does not operate only in low-income families. Studies that have investigated the relationship between job stress and parenting have found that work hassles are linked to greater parental irritability, more emotional withdrawal, and less attention focused on children in play sessions. (See Perry-Jenkins, Repetti, & Crouter, 2000.)

The broader culture is also a factor in understanding how attachment relationships evolve. The distribution of attachment patterns varies from one country to another, and even from one subculture to another in the United States. For example, some studies of Japanese and Israeli infants have found fewer avoidant attachments and more ambivalent attachments than in the United States (e.g., Sagi et al., 1995; Takahashi, 1986, 1990), whereas studies of German samples (e.g., Grossmann, Grossmann, Huber, & Wartner, 1981) find more avoidant infants, sometimes more than in the securely attached category! These differences are yet to be adequately explained. They may partly reflect how stressful the strange situation test is for infants with differing amounts of separation experience. For example, Japanese infants rarely are parted from their mothers, whereas German infants are strongly encouraged to be independent.

Although some theorists argue that attachment theory describes only the development of relationship quality in Western cultures (Rothbaum, Weisz, Pott, Miyake, & Morelli, 2000), several researchers have corroborated the relationship between maternal sensitivity and attachment security across cultures (e.g., Posada, Carbonell, Aolzate, & Plata, 2004; Valenzuela, 1997; Vereijken, Riksen-Walraven, & Kondo-Ikemura, 1997; see van IJzendoorn & Sagi, 1999, for a review), even though the specifics of what constitutes sensitive care may vary somewhat from culture to culture (see Kondo-Ikemura, 2001; Posada et al., 2004).

Cross-cultural differences in attachment patterns do underscore the fact, however, that cultural context must contribute in some meaningful way to the kinds of attachments that are likely to develop. If different degrees of dependency are valued (or devalued) in different ways in different cultures, perhaps the working models of self and other that Bowlby believes are spawned from attachment relationships have different meanings and consequences in different cultures as well. For example, an ambivalent attachment pattern in Japan may be more adaptive and have more positive impact on a child's future development than it would in North America.

Variations in Attachment Relationships

MOTHERS AND FATHERS

Infants form attachments to familiar caregivers. Mother is usually the primary caregiver, and so infant–mother attachments tend to be the first to form. But we have already noted that soon babies become attached to their fathers, their babysitters, and other significant caregivers in their lives. The existence of multiple attachments raises several questions: Is attachment quality uniform across caregivers? In other words, once attached to the primary caregiver, do babies extend the same kind of attachment to others? Or does each relationship produce its own attachment pattern? Fox, Kimmerly, and Schafer (1991) compared attachment quality for mothers and fathers in 11 studies and found substantial similarities. If an infant was securely attached to one parent, he was unlikely to be insecurely attached to the other parent, although many exceptions were found. There are several ways to explain this tendency toward consistency. First, we might be seeing the impact of an infant's forming a working model of self and other from his primary attachment relationship and then extending that model to other attachments, as Bowlby described. Or, second, each early attachment may develop as a function of the attachment figure's caregiving sensitivity. If so, then mothers and fathers must often be similar in their handling of their infants. Belsky and Volling (1987) did find that both mothers and fathers tend to be highly involved and responsive (or not), so this remains a possible explanation. However, it should be noted that Belsky, Gilstrap, and Rovine (1984) found on the average that mothers were more positive and more responsive than fathers. There are also some studies that indicate discordance (inconsistency) between infants' maternal attachments and their attachments to nonfamily caregivers (e.g., Goossens & van IJzendoorn, 1990; Sagi et al., 1985), which could mean that quality of caregiving in each relationship is what is important, rather than that infants are generalizing from their primary attachment figure to others. (See Box 4.4.)

| **Box 4.4** | *Infant Day Care: Is There an Attachment Risk?* |

John Bowlby (e.g., 1973) brought attention to the damage that could be done to young children's relationships if they were separated from attachment figures for long periods of time. For example, when hospitalized children are denied regular access to their mothers, their emotional distress is intense and it progresses through a worrisome series of stages, beginning with typical separation protest such as crying and searching for the lost parent followed by "despair," which is marked by listlessness, loss of appetite, and reduced emotional vitality. Finally, after many days or weeks, the child seems to become detached, treating the mother with indifference when she visits, or attending only to the "treats" that mother brings (e.g., Robertson & Robertson, 1989).

Extrapolating from the effects of long-term separations, Bowlby also expressed concern about shorter term separations, such as the daily breaks in maternal care that babies experience when their mothers are employed and leave their children with relatives or nonfamilial caregivers for many hours a day. Given that attachment quality is significantly related to sensitive, responsive caregiving, could regular interruptions of that caregiving impede the development of

secure attachments? When there is a change in child care arrangements—when beloved nannies or day care teachers leave—does the disruption of the child's attachment to that caregiver also disrupt the child's sense of security? Bowlby felt that although there might not be definitive answers to these questions, the potential risks associated with forming insecure attachments were great enough that parents should be encouraged to avoid regular substitute care for children under age 3.

Research over the last several decades has begun to address the questions that Bowlby raised, and a sense of the scope and nature of the risks in infant day care is beginning to emerge. The following points capture the primary conclusions that can be drawn thus far about the relationship between substitute care and infant-mother attachments. The following discussion summarizes the status of findings on the relationship between substitute care and infant-mother attachments at this time. This summary is drawn from several reviews and analyses of multiple data sets (Belsky & Rovine, 1988; Clarke-Steward, 1989; Lamb & Sternberg, 1990; Scarr, 1998; Thompson, 1998). It also includes data from several recent and ongoing large-scale studies. One study sponsored by the National Institute of Child Health and Human Development (e.g., NICHD, 1997; 2003a; 2003b) included more than 1100 U.S. babies in a longitudinal investigation. Another study included many thousands of Israeli mother-infant pairs in the babies' first few months and continued to follow 758 pairs longitudinally (e.g., Sagi, Koren-Karie, Gini, Ziv, & Joels, 2002).

It appears that the majority of infants who experience nonparental care on a regular basis still form secure attachments to their parents; there is little disagreement among studies or their authors on this point. There is, nonetheless, an increase in the risk of insecure attachments for infants in day care as compared to infants in full-time home care.

Many studies suggest that this risk of insecure attachment is associated with substitute child care that is of poor quality or involves many hours per week or that involves more than one substitute care arrangement or that changes frequently. Boys are more likely to experience attachment problems than girls when these risk factors are present.

In the NICHD study, the increased risk of insecure attachments for infants in day care existed only when these infants were also exposed to low levels of maternal sensitivity and responsiveness, referred to as "the dual risk" effect. In other words, when mothers were providing insensitive care themselves, infants in day care were even more likely than infants in full-time home care to develop insecure attachments. When mothers were sensitive and responsive to their infants, substitute care did not interfere with the formation of a secure infant-mother attachment. However, in other studies, like the Sagi et al (2002) study of Israeli infants, poor quality center care alone was a predictor of increased mother-infant attachment problems, even when maternal care was sensitive and responsive.

Overall, mothers and babies can, and usually do, form secure attachments, even if mothers work outside the home during the 1st year, as long as mother provides her infant with quality care when she is with the baby, and as long as the substitute care is also of high quality. Substitute care becomes a significant risk to mother-infant attachment when the quality of alternative care arrangements is not adequate. The "dual risk" of insensitive maternal care combined with less than high quality substitute care is particularly problematic.

Fortunately, employed mothers are about as likely as unemployed mothers to provide sensitive care to their babies, despite the stresses of balancing family responsibilities and work (e.g., Schubert, Bradley-Johnson, & Nuttal, 1980). Some research even indicates that employed mothers might be more positive in their caregiving (e.g., Crockenberg & Litman, 1991). However, at least one study suggests that very early return to work (before the baby is 12 weeks old) might put a mother at risk of being a less sensitive care-giver than she might otherwise have been (Clark, Hyde, Essex, and Klein, 1997). Mothers who returned to work at 6 weeks postpartum were less sensitive to their 4-month-old babies than mothers who returned to work at 12 weeks, especially if the mothers were exposed to other risk factors, such as depressive symptoms or a baby with a difficult temperament. Very early return to work may make it somewhat more difficult for a mother to learn to read her baby's cues (Brazelton, 1986). It may just be harder to feel effective and competent as a caregiver when a mother begins work in her infant's first weeks because the baby has not yet become very socially responsive. Sensitive caregiving appears to be easier when mothers feel competent (Donovan, Leavitt, & Walsh, 1990; Teti & Gelfand, 1991).

On the whole, mothers' use of substitute caregivers does not put the mother–infant attachment relationship in jeopardy. But clearly, parents are well advised to proceed cautiously in making decisions about alternative care arrangements for their infants. Substitute care is a risk factor when it combines with poor maternal care, and other risk factors, such as poor-quality day care, make the danger greater.

Parents should also recognize that attachment risk is not the only issue of concern for infants in alternative care arrangements. Development of social and cognitive skills is also related to the quality, quantity, and timing of substitute care. Recent analyses of the NICHD data make clear, for example, that although quality of maternal caregiving in the infancy period is a stronger predictor of children's later cognitive competence than measures of substitute care, amount and kind of substitute care still matter. If mothers were employed full time (30 hours per week or more) by the time their babies were 9 months old, their children were not scoring as well on general cognitive tests at 3 years old as children whose mothers returned to the workforce later or for fewer hours per week. *These results were moderated by quality of child care:* The more sensitive the mother was, the better the home care environment, and the better the alternative care environment, the less likely it was that early maternal employment would have negative effects (Brooks-Gunn, Han, & Waldfogel, 2002).

In addition, the more time young children spend in nonmaternal care, especially center-based care, the more aggressive and oppositional they tend to be by kindergarten age, although the effects are small (Belsky, 2001; NICHD, 2003a). Also, Gunnar and colleagues have found that children in center-based child care show increases in stress levels in the course of a day as indicated by elevations in cortisol (a hormone produced in response to stress; see Chapter 2), especially if they have difficult or fearful temperaments (see Gunnar & Cheatham, 2003, for a review). What is striking is that when the same children have been tested at home with their families, their cortisol levels have either remained stable or declined in the course of a day. Cortisol increases in the child care setting have been found in about 35% of infants studied and in about 70 to 80% of older children. Toddlers (about 1 to 3 years), especially younger toddlers, show the steepest rise, suggesting that child care may be especially stressful for this age group (Dettling, Gunnar, Donzella, 1999; Watamura, Donzella, Alwin, & Gunnar, 2003).

Children's experience of stress in child care programs is linked, not surprisingly, to the quality of the program. In one study of family based child care, for example, stress-related increases in cortisol were diminished or eliminated for preschoolers who were in high-quality programs where caregivers gave them focused attention and stimulation (Dettling, Parker, Lane, Sebanc, & Gunnar, 2000). It is obviously critical for parents to understand what constitutes quality in substitute care and to be able to weigh the risks and benefits of different care arrangements. In the Applications section of this chapter, we discuss considerations for helping parents make good infant care decisions.

STABILITY AND CHANGE

Not only do infants sometimes form different kinds of attachments to different caregivers but they also may change their attachment status across time with the same caregiver. Secure attachments are less likely to change than insecure attachments (Thompson, 1998), although it appears that the insecure attachments of maltreated infants may be highly stable (Schneider-Rosen, Braunwald, Carlson, & Cicchetti, 1985). As we have seen, children from lower socioeconomic groups are more likely to shift from secure to insecure, or vice versa, than children from higher income groups. Changes in family stressors, presumably causing changes in caregiving quality, are usually associated with these shifts.

That the security of infants' attachments can change raises yet another question: When does attachment security stabilize, or does it? The shifts we are describing have usually been observed in the 2nd year of a child's life. Might later changes in caregiving quality lead to similar changes, or are there limits to when a child's security can be renegotiated? One reasonable working hypothesis is that children's attachment security can change after the infancy-toddler period if caregiving quality changes substantially, but that the longer a particular attachment status is in place, the more entrenched it is likely to become and the more it will influence other relationships, especially as children begin to mentally represent constructs of self and other, assign meanings to their experiences, and relate present events to past ones.

Research with children whose early attachments are seriously distorted or even nonexistent—what is now called reactive attachment disorder—suggests that attachment security may be established, or refurbished, in later childhood. Children with this disorder have been seriously deprived of opportunities to interact with a responsive attachment figure in their early years. For example, prior to the collapse of the Soviet government in Romania in 1990, large numbers of Romanian children were being warehoused in orphanages that were notably inadequate. Caregivers were few, and they frequently changed. Infants and toddlers received almost no attention, so they had little opportunity to form attachments. Americans began adopting these children after their plight was publicized, providing researchers an opportunity to assess their attachment prognosis—that is, their ability to form secure attachments in the postinfancy period. Because these children had almost no opportunity to interact with adults in infancy, attachment theory would argue that they had formed distorted and impoverished working models of themselves, of others, and of relationships from their early experiences.

Chisholm (1998) followed Romanian adoptees in the United States for 3 years. Despite their lack of early attachments, most were able to form secure attachments with their adoptive parents, although the rate of insecure attachments was higher than in a sample of American children being raised by their own parents. An unusual pattern of failure to form any bond at all was identified among some children, who showed "indiscriminate friendliness," marked by a willingness to go with any stranger and failure to check back with a parent in an anxiety-provoking situation. In a study of Romanian adoptees in Britain, this pattern of "disinhibited attachment disturbance" characterized only 16% of children who were adopted by 18 months of age, but a full 33% of children adopted between 24 and 42 months of age (Rutter, O'Connor, & the English and Romanian Adoptees [ERA] Study Team, 2004). Overall, such findings suggest that initial attachments can be, and often are, formed after the infancy period, but the process is more difficult with time and may not be successful in some cases.

The Importance of Early Attachments

Secure early attachments are said to pave the way for later psychosocial developments. Erikson and Bowlby portrayed the trusting, secure infant as one who is fortified with positive attitudes toward self and others. He enters new relationships with an expectation that his needs will be respected and with a willingness to respect the needs of others. His security helps him face new challenges; he trusts in the future.

Neither Erikson nor Bowlby saw the positive outlook of the secure child as immutable. Whereas secure children play a role in making their positive expectations come true by their choice of partners and through their own responses to others (Sroufe, 1996), they are not all powerful. If later experiences, especially with caregivers, violate their expectations, their burgeoning ideas about self and others could be modified, incorporating more negative expectations. In sum, early attachment is said to launch processes that can have long-term consequences; but the quality of care that the child continues to receive can either strengthen or redirect those processes.

Does early attachment quality predict later psychosocial functioning? Sroufe, Egeland, and their colleagues followed a large sample of Minneapolis children, beginning with two assessments of attachment status in the strange situation at 12 and 18 months (e.g., Vaughn et al., 1979). Children whose attachment status was stable from the first to the second assessment were later evaluated on a variety of interpersonal and cognitive dimensions, and differences were found between the insecurely and securely attached children on many measures. For example, when the children were 4 years old, 40 of them participated in a summer nursery school program at the University of Minnesota (Sroufe, Fox, & Pancake, 1983). Teachers, who knew nothing about the earlier attachment ratings, ranked the children each day on characteristics related to autonomy, such as attention seeking, extreme reliance on the teacher, involvement with teachers at the expense of peers, and so on. The children who had been securely attached as toddlers were more often seen by teachers as direct and appropriate in their dependency behaviors, seeking help when they realistically needed it but functioning independently in other situations. Insecurely attached children were more likely to act helpless, to act out for attention, or in some cases to passively avoid seeking help when they genuinely needed it.

In assessments at later ages, the children in the Minneapolis project showed other continuities as well. In a summer camp at age 10, for example, securely attached children tended to be more self-confident, to have more friends, to have better social skills, and so on. Many studies, though not all, have found similar continuities (see Thompson, 1998, for a review of these findings).

If infant–mother attachments predict later developments, what about infant–father attachments? When infants are securely attached to both parents they seem to have the best outcomes; if they are securely attached to one parent, but not the other, their outcomes are better than if they are insecurely attached to both (e.g., Belsky, Garduque, & Hrncir, 1984; Main, Kaplan, & Cassidy, 1985; Suess, Grossmann, & Sroufe, 1992). Thus, a secure attachment relationship with a second parent adds a protective factor, perhaps helping to safeguard a child from the negative influence of an insecure attachment. Several investigators have also suggested that because fathers and mothers tend to interact differently with their infants, the attachment relationship with each parent may affect different aspects of the child's psychosocial development. For example, in American families, mothers spend more time with infants in quiet, ritualized routines such as peek-a-boo games, where synchrony of eye contact, vocalizations, and facial expressions are key factors. Fathers tend to engage in more energetic, stimulating games (such as whirling the baby through the air); they are more unpredictable and exciting (MacDonald & Parke, 1986; Pecheux & Labrell, 1994). Of course, though there tend to be differences in the types of interactions infants have with each parent, there is much overlap, especially when fathers are highly involved in infant care. Whether infant attachments to mothers versus fathers affect different aspects of later social functioning is yet to be determined. One study is suggestive, however. Pecheux and Labrell (1994) found that 18-month-olds were more playful and more inclined to smile with a stranger if their fathers were present when the new person approached than if their mothers were present.

Overall, there is little doubt that infant attachment relationships are predictive of some later behaviors. What is presently uncertain is, how important are early attachments in producing such outcome differences? More specifically, does the early attachment actually have long-term effects, or could the more recent and current caregiving environment be responsible for the apparent continuities? In the Minneapolis study, for example, some children who had been securely attached as infants were having behavior problems by age 4. The quality of parenting during the preschool period helped account for this change. Mothers of these children were less supportive when engaging their children in educational tasks at age 3. They provided less encouragement and were less effective teachers than mothers whose children did not develop later behavior problems. Also, children who had been insecurely attached as infants but who were well adjusted at 4 years tended to have mothers who were supportive and effective in their interactions with their preschoolers (Erickson, Sroufe, & Egeland, 1985). It seems that the role of early attachments in later development can be diminished, and perhaps even eliminated, when parental acceptance, support, and responsiveness changes substantially, either rising to the challenges of the child's new developmental stage or failing to do so (see also Easterbrooks & Goldberg, 1990; Youngblade & Belsky, 1992). The importance of ongoing quality parenting for children's socioemotional development will be taken up again in Chapter 5.

What, then, is the value of getting a "good start" with a secure infant attachment? It may be that the primary influence of infant attachments is their tendency to perpetuate themselves. Once a relationship pattern between parent and child is established, it tends to be repeated; when it is, the older child's behavior is consistent with predictions from the early attachment. In his first relationships, a baby may well form an incipient "working model" of what to expect from interactions. That model affects his behavior and expectations in the future, but the model is in progress and will be reworked in the context of new interactions, just as Erikson and Bowlby proposed. (See Box 4.5.)

Box 4.5 | *Attachment Security and Children's Cognitive Development*

Infants who receive sensitive, responsive care tend to form secure attachments to their caregivers. Securely attached youngsters begin to see themselves as worthy and lovable, and to see others as caring and reliable. These beliefs or concepts about self and others are part of a child's working model of relationships according to Bowlby's attachment theory. A working model is said to do two things. First, it influences the child's processing of information in social situations, for example, affecting whether a child might construe an event as positively or negatively valenced. Second, it biases a child to react in certain ways, for example, contributing to the child's willingness to cooperate with an adult. Together, the filtering of information and the biasing of responses help the child to have experiences that are consistent with the working model and that tend to reinforce or maintain it. Because of the working model, attachment theory predicts that the security of a child's attachments influences the child's cognitive functioning in social contexts, affecting what he learns and remembers.

Suppose that Csonger, a 3-year-old, watches a puppet show in which a puppet child has both a happy experience (receiving a birthday present) and an unhappy one (spilling his juice). In addition, the puppets in the show interact directly with Csonger in both positive and negative ways. At one point the mother puppet asks him to pick up the puppet child's birthday present and then thanks Csonger with a great deal of warmth. Another time the puppet child criticizes Csonger for wearing an "ugly vest." If he has a secure attachment history, Csonger's working model might influence him to remember the more positive aspects of this event better than the more negative ones, or perhaps to recall events as more positive than they were. But if Csonger is insecurely attached he should be more likely to remember the negative events or perhaps to misremember positive events as negative.

Belsky, Spritz, and Crnic (1996) brought 12-month-olds into their lab and measured the security of the babies' attachments to their mothers in the strange situation test.

Two years later, the children were invited back to watch a series of puppet shows, like the one that Csonger saw. The researchers tested the 3-year-olds' delayed recognition of the shows' events using pairs of detailed drawings, accompanied by verbal descriptions, that either accurately or inaccurately depicted the emotional content of the events. In one picture, for example, the puppet child was receiving its birthday present with a happy expression on its face (accurate depiction). The other picture in the pair showed the same event, but the puppet's expression was sad (inaccurate depiction). Securely attached children were more likely to select the accurate depiction for positive events than for negative events, but insecurely attached children selected the accurate depiction for the negative events more often than they did for the positive events. Interestingly, this was true even though all the children seemed to be at least somewhat more attentive to the negative than to the positive events while they were happening. It seems that some kind of cognitive filter affected their later recollection of the emotional tone of the events. The researchers were careful to statistically equate children in the secure and insecure attachment groups for overall verbal intelligence and for temperament characteristics, so the differences in their memories for emotional content did seem to be a function of their attachment status per se.

Working models of attachment should not only affect how information is processed, they should also influence how children respond to interpersonal events. This, in turn, could affect what children learn from interactions and how well they learn it. We saw in Chapter 3 that children's memory for events is better if their parents engage them in conversations about shared experiences using an elaborative style, that is, asking lots of questions and providing details when needed. Mothers' use of an elaborative style is linked to the security of attachment: More securely attached dyads are more likely to engage in these elaborative reminiscences (Fivush & Vesudeva, 2002; Laible, 2004; Reese, 2002).

Thompson and his colleagues speculated that not only are securely attached children more likely than insecurely attached children to be engaged in elaborative reminiscences with their parents, but they are also more likely to learn effectively from such conversations: "[A] parent's elaborative narrative style may have a different influence in the context of a conflicted or insecure parent-child relationship than in a warm or secure relationship . . . because relational quality is likely to influence the content and style of what the parent says and how the child responds to it" (Thompson, Laible, & Ontai, 2003, p. 151).

In two studies, Thompson's research team examined whether attachment security influences how effective parent–child conversations are for helping young children understand the emotional content of events. First, they compared securely attached to insecurely attached preschoolers to see how well they understood the emotions of others (Laible & Thompson, 1998). The children's current attachment status was measured using a "Q-sort" technique (Waters & Deane, 1985). In this procedure, a parent is carefully trained to sort a set of statements about his or her child according to how true the statements are of the child. Security status measured this way can be very consistent with the results of the strange situation test with infants, and it is widely used to assess the security of attachments in older children. Children's emotional understanding was measured in two tasks. In one, puppets acted out short stories, and children were asked to attach a felt face to a puppet's head at the end of each story to show how the puppet felt (sad, happy, angry, or fearful). In the other measure, children were observed and interviewed in their child care or preschool settings. When a peer was involved in an emotionally arousing event, children were asked to explain how the peer felt and why. (Five to 10 interviews were conducted with each participant.) As expected, the participants' attachment security and their emotional understanding were highly correlated: More secure children had a better understanding of emotions, especially negative emotions.

In a second study, Ontai and Thompson (2002) used many of the same methods to test children both when they were 3 years old and again when they were 5. In this study, the researchers also evaluated parents' conversational style as they engaged their 3-year-olds in discussions of emotionally charged events. If parents used an elaborative style to talk about emotional content when the children were 3 years old, by age 5 their children understood emotions better than if parents did not use an elaborative style. But the effectiveness of the parents' conversation, as Thompson had predicted, depended on the security of the child's attachment: Securely attached children whose parents used an elaborative style understood emotions better at age 5, but insecurely attached children were less likely to benefit from their parents' elaborative conversations. Clearly, Bowlby's notion that attachment security engenders a working model that influences both a child's information processing and his responsiveness in social situations is gaining empirical support.

Working Models of Attachment

As we have just seen, what may be most important about infant attachments is that they influence the internal working model of relationships that children begin to construct. Researchers studying adult romantic relationships describe the concept of the internal working model of attachment as providing a template for adult social relationships. Investigators have recently begun to study the nature and development of these models, or representations. We will examine some of this work in later chapters, as we discuss the development of self-concept and relationship capacity beyond the infancy period, but one aspect of this research bears directly on the formation of infant attachments, and we will touch on this work here.

Main and her colleagues (Main et al., 1985) evaluated mothers' and fathers' models of attachment using a structured interview procedure called the Adult Attachment Inventory (AAI) (see Chapter 12 for a full discussion). Parents described their memories of the parenting they had received and their beliefs about whether that parenting influenced their own personalities. The "security" of their attachment representations (categorized using a procedure devised by Main & Goldwyn, 1985–1994) was related to the quality of attachment they had established with their own infants.

"Secure-autonomous" parents valued relationships and believed that their own personalities were influenced by them. They could talk openly and objectively about their early experiences, good or bad. Their ideas were coherent and showed signs of previous reflection. Not all of these adults recalled their early experiences as positive; some had even been abused. But by whatever means, these adults had apparently come to terms with their early experiences and had faith in the power of relationships. These parents tended to have secure attachments with their own infants.

"Insecure" parents showed several patterns. In one, attachment relationships were not readily recalled, not valued, and not seen as influential. Infants tended to have avoidant attachments with parents who showed this "dismissive" pattern. Another group of parents ("preoccupied-entangled") were preoccupied with their own parents, often still struggling to please, and they seemed confused, angry, or especially passive. Their infants' attachments to them were typically ambivalent. Finally, an "unresolved-disorganized" pattern characterized parents who made irrational and inconsistent comments, especially when discussing traumatic experiences. For example, they might talk about a dead parent as if he were alive. Infants whose parents showed this pattern tended to be disorganized-disoriented in the strange situation test.

A substantial correspondence between parents' and infants' attachment classifications has been found in other studies as well (see van IJzendoorn, 1995). As Main (1996) points out, this correspondence could be affected by many factors, including similarities in temperament between parent and infant. But the match in parent-infant security measures may indicate that parents' working models of attachment can influence their infant caregiving, thereby affecting their babies' attachment security. Perhaps, for example, parents whose concepts of relationship are more coherent, or who have come to terms with past relationships, are more likely to behave consistently and sensitively with their infants, fostering a secure attachment.

Parenting Practices Versus Relationship Quality in Infant Development

It should be clear from this overview of theory and research on infant attachments that focusing attention on relationship quality in infant–caregiver interactions has proven to be a highly productive enterprise. As Mary Ainsworth noted in her earliest observations of mother–infant dyads, the specifics of parenting practices may not be very important in the long run. For example, breastfeeding versus bottle feeding does not seem to be critical for later emotional adjustment. Rather, it is the relationship context within which such practices occur that is significant. Some parenting practices may be more conducive to, or consistent with, responsive caregiving. Breastfeeding, for example, requires that a mother hold her baby close during feeding, providing the "contact comfort" infants find soothing. When babies are bottle fed, they can be held and

Helping professionals have an important role to play in communicating with parents about their children's development.

soothed just as effectively, but it is also possible to "prop" a bottle or to hold a baby away from the caregiver's body when feeding, thus failing to provide contact comfort. So, both breast and bottle feeding can be practiced in a way that provides close, comforting interactions, but breastfeeding is more conducive to such interactions.

It should also be noted that although both breastfeeding and bottle feeding can be done sensitively and responsively, breastfeeding has substantial advantages for healthy physical and cognitive development that bottle feeding does not (American Academy of Pediatrics, 1997; Rogan & Gladen, 1993). In comparison to baby formulas, breast milk is more digestible and more adequately balanced for infant nutrition. It contains antibodies that the mother carries, and it is sterile, a particularly important benefit in countries with water that may contain disease organisms. Breast milk even carries growth hormones and other substances that may affect long-term development. The World Health Organization now recommends exclusive breastfeeding for the first 6 months and breastfeeding with solid food supplements through the 2nd year (United Nations International Children's Emergency Fund [UNICEF], 1995).

Ainsworth's observations of a Ugandan baby and his mother (as described in Karen, 1998) help illustrate, however, that feeding by breast is not the critical factor in the formation of secure attachments. Muhamidi's mother kept him close most of the time, as is the custom in Ugandan families. She slept with him and breastfed him on demand. Yet by 8 months, Muhamidi seemed insecure. Not yet having invented the strange situation test, Ainsworth depended on a variety of observations to make this classification, most notably that over time he seemed to lose his vitality, to become sadder and duller. Unlike other babies whose mothers used similar infant care practices, he did not tolerate his mother's absence even when left with an older sibling. Muhamidi's mother seemed anxious and overtaxed by the demands of her large family, and Ainsworth observed that despite her nearly constant availability, the mother's caregiving responses were somewhat brusque and did not necessarily match Muhamidi's needs. For example, on one visit, she responded to Muhamidi's crying by putting him "immediately to breast, without stopping to wipe his nose, which was streaming, or to wipe his face, which was muddy" (Ainsworth, 1967, p. 144).

A student of social and personality development in the mid-1900s would probably have read extensive discussions about the relative importance of particular child-rearing practices such as breastfeeding versus bottle feeding. The current trend, spawned by attachment theory, is to emphasize the overall quality of infant–caregiver relationships instead. This approach seems to be bringing us much closer to an understanding of the role of infancy in later socioemotional development.

APPLICATIONS

What are we to make of this information on attachment? No one has demonstrated that relatively infrequent incidents of caretaker unavailability will harm a child for life, nor are chronic interactive failures the single pathway to a depressive future. *However, it would be incorrect to assume that early interactive patterns have no influence at all on later emotional and social development.* As Tronick (1989) observed:

> The pathways leading to the varieties of normalcy and psychopathology derive from the divergent experiences infants have with success, reparation of failure, and the transformation of negative emotions to positive emotions. Typically, there is no single traumatic juncture or special moment separating these pathways, only the slowly accumulating interactive and affective experiences with different people and events in different contexts that shape the regulatory processes and representations of the infant over time. (p. 117)

If we conceptualize the infant as constructing a framework for interacting with the world, using both the tools provided by nature and the materials available in daily experience, it is difficult to imagine that this early experience-dependent affective learning would not be important for later emotion regulation and social relationships. Outcomes, however, are rarely the result of only one early relationship. Although mothers are most often primary caretakers, fathers, siblings, grandparents and others are also significant. It is important to resist the assumption that all the responsibility for social and emotional development rests solely on the mother's shoulders. Future outcomes also involve co-occurring and later occurring experiences that build on and reshape prior configurations.

Van IJzendoorn and Bakermans-Kranenburg (1997) provide a promising model that describes how this may work. They propose a modification on the model of intergenerational transmission of attachment: that is, from parents' own early attachment experiences to their parenting behavior to their infant's attachment classification. As we have seen, the available research does not support such strict determinism. In fact, Bowlby (1988) and traditional object relations theorists (Klein, 1921/1945; Mahler, Pine, & Bergman, 1975; Winnicott, 1965) have held that therapists (or intimate partners and friends) can realign or reconstruct an originally problematic early relationship by becoming another "secure base" (see Chapter 12).

Van IJzendoorn and Bakermans-Kranenburg's multidimensional model of intergenerational transmission reflects the effects of context and later experience on the attachment classification of the infant. A parent's own early attachment experiences are modified (for good or for ill) by later attachment relationships with others, which together determine the parent's attachment representation or mental model of close relationships. So one's memories of past experiences are never totally pure but are reconstructed, at least in part, on the basis of current attachments. These authors conclude that parents operate more on their current belief systems about the past than on what actually may have happened. The parent's mental model of attachment is further influenced by the present social context. A supportive spouse, for example, might ameliorate the effects of earlier negative experiences. A difficult divorce might complicate earlier positive attachment representations. These factors combine to influence actual parenting behavior. These behaviors are further modified by the temperament of the child. Having an extremely fussy or irritable baby may increase the amount of time spent in poorly coordinated communication sequences and may ultimately affect the baby's emotion regulation and the quality of attachment. So attachment classification can be remarkably stable through adolescence provided that the environment is also relatively stable. As we have indicated, disruptive experiences in the child's or adolescent's life—such as loss of a parent, divorce, economic hardship, abuse, serious illness of the child or the parent, to name a few—can result in discontinuity of attachment (Van IJzendoorn & Bakermans-Kranenburg, 1997). An implication we can draw from this is the recognition of the importance of prevention and early intervention. Addressing problematic parent–infant relationships as early as possible can redirect developmental pathways into healthy directions. Providing continuing supports for good parent–child relationships can sustain them over time.

Infant Mental Health

If the primary caregiver's own mental representations as well as current life experiences are so important to attachment quality, how can we help parents with troubled attachment histories do better for their own children? What can be done for less troubled but stressed-out families to support security of attachment? The field of infant mental health (Zeanah & Zeanah, 2001) offers us some suggestions in this area. A major assumption of this approach is that intervention must take into account the needs of the parent as well as the child. Therapies that support the parent can reap rewards for the children and are more effective than those that focus on the child alone (Blackman, 2002). Thus, counselors should consider the dyad or the family as the target of intervention because the goal is to repair or improve a *relationship*, not just one member's behavior. Some components of effective programs include the following key elements:

1. *Provide a voice for the baby.* The therapist is the one who needs to sensitively and carefully articulate the baby's "point of view." One way is to provide parents with basic knowledge about child development. We believe that this knowledge should not just be descriptive of ages and stages, but should also emphasize the needs of infants, particularly in the affective area. Sometimes

parents feel that babies will be spoiled if they are picked up and held or that they should be spanked for some perceived misbehavior. Parents may view their babies as "not listening" to them or as disrespectful. Or they may believe that infants need lots of exposure to groups of children to develop good social skills, a developmental goal that is inappropriate at this age.

These misperceptions and flawed attributions are often the basis for insensitive caregiving. Therefore, the mother of an angry toddler who does not want to share his toy can be helped to understand that the child is not selfish but is asserting his will and acting as most normal toddlers do. The mother of a difficult infant might benefit from an understanding of the concept of temperament. With the counselor's support, she can be given ways to understand her baby's communication and respond to it sensitively. Her baby's fussiness might signal his feeling overstimulated, or his clinging behavior might mean that he needs more "lap-time" from her. Tomlin and Viehweg (2003) suggest that clinicians take a nonjudgmental, coaching approach when "speaking for the baby" (p. 621). The counselor might ask, for example, "I wonder why Devon is fussing so much. Do you think she might want to be held for a while?"

Recognizing the baby's bids for attention will be useful only if the parent also recognizes that these needs are normal and, if sufficiently met, will foster emotional security in the long run. These shifts in knowledge and attitude, as well as new skills, can bolster parent confidence in their ability to be good parents.

2. *Provide support for the parent.* Active listening skills, well known to counselors, could be used to communicate a nonjudgmental and supportive attitude toward parents. Parents have reasons for the ways they behave toward their children. Sometimes their parenting reflects their own painful history of emotional neglect or abuse. As we have seen, they can operate according to inaccurate assumptions about child development. Often they are preoccupied and may not be paying attention due to stress, depression, illness, or overwork. Allowing parents to talk about their own struggles and attachment histories gives voice to underlying emotions and helps them make connections between their own histories and their relationships to their children.

3. *Learn some new skills.* Clinicians can help parents let their children be their teachers. A technique developed by Greenspan (Greenspan & Weider, 1999), called "floor time," is a good example. This approach is designed to improve parents' observational skills, to assist them in sharing experiences and meanings with a child, to teach them to communicate in a respectful give and take with the child taking the lead, and to ultimately teach recognition of emotions. Parents literally get down on the floor for approximately 30 minutes and tune into the child's world. The goal is to let the child take the lead

rather than allow parents to dominate or turn the session into a "teachable moment." The tasks vary depending upon the age of the child. Parents of infants are helped to recognize their babies' signals and temperamental styles. They are asked to notice, for example, when the baby smiles, what kind of touch the baby likes or dislikes, when the child makes eye contact, and to respond fully to his bids for attention. At about 4 months of age, babies show more interest in the outside world. Parents are helped to notice what the baby is attending to, such as a kitten sleeping nearby, and to enjoy the sight together. Parents of older, more mobile infants, about 8 months and beyond, can learn to join in their child's play or movement while not trying to control the activity. Essentially, the parent is taught to notice the child's intention, mirror and expand on the child's activity, and respond to the child's words and gestures.

Clinicians can also teach games or routines that practice turn-taking and sharing. Even something as simple as passing a toy back and forth, "Now it's Brandon's turn," teaches the basics of social interaction. Also important are family routines or rituals, such as bedtime and mealtime patterns. Counselors can help busy parents identify routines that work for them and encourage parents to adopt simple ones. Predictable routines provide security for children and opportunities for parents and children to relate to each other in a calm, attentive, and loving way.

Clinicians should be heartened by the fact that recent research has confirmed the power of attachment interventions to improve security (Bakermans-Kranenburg, van IJzendoorn, & Juffer, 2003). In general, the most effective interventions are relatively brief (fewer than 16 sessions) and are focused on the kinds of behavioral training already described. Results suggest that these interventions increase parental sensitivity which, in turn, has a positive impact on security of attachment.

The Day Care Dilemma

Counselors may also be called upon to help parents make important decisions about caretaking arrangements for their infants. As we have seen in Box 4.5, the child care issue is complicated. Although researchers have made great progress in clarifying some pros and cons of child care, there are questions that await further investigation. Addressing these questions is a pressing issue because so many infants and toddlers in this country are cared for in some form of nonmaternal arrangement. In the NICHD longitudinal studies, 72% of the infants in the sample experienced regular, nonparental child care during their first 12 months. Most of these babies entered day care before they were 4 months old. Many parents have few choices available to them as they struggle to care for families and maintain jobs. The high cost of infant and toddler care, the limited availability of caregiving options in some areas, the pressures of the workplace on dual-career couples, and the poor quality of too many facilities increase the stresses on families with young children. It is impossible to draw easy solutions to this problem. However, researchers in general no longer accept the argument that all nonmaternal child care initiated in the 1st year of life is risk-free. What follows are a few important factors to consider in helping parents decide about infant care.

1. *Consider the combination of age of entry and the amount of time spent in day care.*   Although there are no absolutes, there appears to be a dose–response relationship between early (before 4 months), more extensive (full or almost full time), and cumulative (across many years) care that is associated with greater noncompliance, aggression, and neediness at school age (Belsky, 2001; NICHD, 2003b). Multiple child care settings over the early childhood years seem to exacerbate the risk.

2. *Consider the quality of the day care providers.*   Infants and toddlers need the experience of felt security that comes from sensitive caregiving. Do the caregivers respond quickly and sensitively to the needs of the children? Are they warm, affectionate, and patient or do they ignore the children or become easily irritated by their needs? Do they hold the children and provide physical comfort? Are they educated in child development so that their expectations for children are reasonable and age appropriate? Do they tend to remain in the facility or is there rapid staff changeover?

3. *Consider the quality of the center.*   Unfortunately, reports indicate that the quality of 85 to 90% of out-of-home child care in the United States is less than high quality (Cost, Quality and Child Care Study Team, 1995; NICHD, 2000). Before making decisions about care, parents should consider the stability and child-caregiver ratios in the facility. Is the staff stable or is there a frequent turnover of employees? Stability of caregivers, perhaps even allowing caregivers to remain with a group of babies over several years (Greenspan, 2003), is important for children in the construction of attachments. Is the caregiver-child ratio small enough to ensure enough attention and promote nurturant interactions? The optimal ratio is *up to* 3 infants to 1 adult (American Academy of Pediatrics, American Public Health Association, and National Resources Center for Health and Safety in Child Care, 2002). Greenspan (2003) suggests only two babies per caregiver. In the large scale Israeli study mentioned earlier, the infant-adult ratio was the major factor in determining security of attachment between infants in center care and those cared for by home-based providers (Sagi et al., 2002).

4. *Consider the uniqueness of the child.*   Not every child responds to child care in the same way. Both temperament and gender appear to be related to differential outcomes. Greenspan (2003) notes that children with underreactive or overreactive sensory system thresholds (sensitivity to sounds, touch, movement, etc.) may find the experience of group care more challenging than other children. Overreactive, difficult-to-soothe children may have trouble modulating arousal and regulating emotions in a context that is noisy, possibly crowded, and filled with children whose needs compete with their own. Underreactive children risk becoming more disengaged without adults to scaffold nurturant interactions. The higher risk of insecure attachment due to low quality care is greater for boys than for girls as we have seen, and increases in internalizing behavior, which sometimes result from long hours in care, are regularly found more often for boys than for girls (Tout, deHann, Campbell, & Gunnar, 1998; Howes & Olenick, 1986). Out-of-home care insofar as it involves coping with the demands of a group situation is somewhat stressful for all young children, let alone those with temperamental sensitivities (Watamura et al., 2003). Therefore Crockenberg (2003) concludes that "professionals have an obligation to inform parents and child care providers that males and reactive children who lack adequate regulatory abilities may be adversely affected when they spend long hours in certain types of nonparental care. To do less is to deny parents information that may help them make better decisions for the family as a whole" (2003, p. 1036).

5. *Consider the family.*   Parental sensitivity is of the utmost importance to the baby's well-being. Parent training or counseling, as we have discussed, can benefit the baby by increasing caregiver sensitivity. The NICHD studies stress the importance of the "dual risk" interaction between low-quality day care and maternal insensitivity. In some cases, high-quality out-of-home care can have a positive impact on children's cognitive and social development, particularly when families are stressed or when caregivers are insensitive. Yet it is also possible that exposure to low-quality care on a regular basis may stress infants to the point that they challenge their primary caregivers' capacity for sensitive care, thus giving rise to insecure attachments (Cassidy & Berlin, 1994). Counselors should take the approach of strengthening protective factors (by facilitating secure bonds) while reducing risks as much as possible.

6. *Consider advocating for child care.*   Various governmental policies related to taxes, subsidies, welfare, and so on can be shaped to help families better provide for their young children. Employers can offer more flexible schedules and alternative work assignments that allow parents more time to care for children, especially during the critical 1st year. Professional day care providers should be afforded adequate wages, education, supervision, and respect for the important contribution they make to our children's future.

Summing Up

Attachment theory provides many useful ideas for clinicians as they assess the socioemotional needs of parents and children. First, the concept of attachment as a constellation of behaviors in a goal-corrected partnership is particularly significant in helping us understand problems and motivations for behavior. This perspective emphasizes the fundamentally social nature of human development. It reminds us that all human growth and human problems occur in some relational context. Second, attachment theory provides clinicians with a new way to view behavior that might, at first glance, seem puzzling. Because the principal goal of attachment is to maintain proximity, either physical or psychological, seemingly contradictory behaviors can be interpreted as means to this end. Even avoidant behaviors, for example, can help maintain some distant relationship while minimizing psychological threat to the self. As Greenberg and Speltz (1988) have pointed out, noncompliant child behaviors can be interpreted as bids for more attention (or closer attachment).

Presumably, all behaviors are functional in that they help individuals adapt to present circumstances. Their adaptiveness may be more or less well suited to any given situation or context. For the infant who needs to reduce the risk of rejection, avoidant behaviors or withdrawal may be an effective method for adapting to negative circumstances. However, this pattern of withdrawal from close relationships, particularly when under stress, can be counterproductive in the context of close adult relationships. Even though the behavior is not suited to the new context, it certainly can be understood.

Finally, attachment theory comes as close as any psychological theory to blending developmental and clinical orientations. It highlights the truth that not only do we grow from relationships but that we suffer from them too. Noam and Fischer (1996) make the excellent observation that, inasmuch as we are all dependent upon one another, we have all experienced injuries in relationships and are beset by specific interpersonal vulnerabilities as a result of our attachment histories. They believe that developmentalists need to incorporate into their work the "periods of regression and fragmentation" that characterize development and that coexist with capacities for integration and growth. Noam and Fischer add that clinicians "need to, and have begun to, account for the adaptive nature of psychopathology, including attempts to solve complex problems, through the detour of symptom formation. Traditional medical models of mental health need to be supplanted by truly developmental, interpersonal accounts that allow for dynamic interweaving of problems and strengths" (Noam & Fischer, 1996, p. xxx).

SUMMARY

Theories of Emotions: The State of the Art

1. Although theorists do not all agree about how to define or characterize basic emotions, they do agree that emotions have survival value. Emotions are powerful motivators of behavior, and spontaneous emotional expressions help us to communicate with one another. For infants, this communicative function helps initiate reciprocal interaction with a caregiver. Emotions enhance cognitive functioning such as planning and social perspective taking, and they play a role in mental health and wellness. More positive life outcomes are associated with higher levels of emotional intelligence.

2. The biological basis of basic emotions has been demonstrated in three lines of research. First, across cultures people agree about what expressions signal fear, sadness, happiness, anger, and surprise. Second, young infants' facial expressions appear to display basic emotions. Third, researchers have identified some specific brain systems or circuits governing the expression of some emotions.

3. Izard's differential emotions theory argues that infant emotional expressions are innate, a product of evolution. Learning only facilitates an individual's capacity to regulate emotions. In Sroufe's more orthogenetic theory, early emotional expressions are precursors of more mature emotions, and the later emotions depend on cognitive developments. Emotions are differentiated over time and come under the control of higher levels of functioning.

Early Caregiver–Infant Interactions and Emotional Development

4. Human infants depend on caregivers for survival. Caregivers must read an infant's signals and meet his physical and emotional needs. Infant physical characteristics, such as large head and large eyes, and infant behaviors, such as crying and smiling, are releasers of adult caregiving. The caregiving relationship fosters feelings of security in infants and helps infants regulate their emotions.

5. Infants have some inborn strategies for coping with emotional arousal. When mothers are asked to be unresponsive to children's cues, in the still-face paradigm, young babies at first initiate other-directed coping behaviors, actions designed to reengage the caregiver. If these don't work, babies initiate self-directed coping behaviors, such as looking away and self-stimulating. When caregiver–infant interactions go off-track, caregivers often respond positively to infants' other-directed coping behaviors, and they initiate interactive repair procedures. Gradually the infant comes to depend upon

his caregiver for help in emotional control and begins to experience himself as an effective social agent.

6. Depressed mothers are less responsive than nondepressed mothers to infants' other-directed coping behaviors, and their infants more often turn to self-directed coping behaviors. Chronic experiences like this may affect brain development and influence future social relationships.

7. Several lines of research suggest connections between brain development and the importance of social interaction for infant emotional development. First, the brain's right hemisphere, which is specialized for interpreting nonverbal communication in adults, appears to be more mature in early infancy than the left hemisphere. Second, the right orbitofrontal region, located in the interior of the right frontal lobe, may be the primary brain region involved in social bonding, and a caregiver's rhythmic, sensitive responses may influence the development of this region in infancy. Finally, social interaction and social bonding may activate the brain's internal opiate system, helping to explain why caregiver responsiveness is so effective in regulating infants' distress.

Attachment: Early Social Relationships

8. Theorists such as Bowlby and Erikson have proposed that the infant's first relationships with caregivers provide him with working models of the self, of others, and of relationships. Erikson argued that consistent, sensitive care helps the infant establish basic trust in others and feelings of worthiness, both of which contribute to optimism about future relationships. In Bowlby's attachment theory, biologically prepared behaviors bring infant and mother into a close relationship, or attachment system, that emerges in stages such that by 7 or 8 months the infant has a strong affectional bond to the primary caregiver, which leads to both separation anxiety and stranger anxiety. The attachment system serves the purpose of proximity maintenance and provides a secure base and safe haven.

9. Using the strange situation test to measure the quality of infant–mother attachments, Ainsworth and her colleagues identified three different types of attachment quality. Securely attached infants explore a new situation when mother is present, are distressed if she leaves, and are comforted and happy when she returns. They appear to use their mothers as a secure base. Anxious ambivalent babies are insecurely attached. They are most clearly different from other babies in their response to their mothers' return from an absence. They may alternately approach and resist the mother, or may respond listlessly to her, rather than taking ready comfort. Avoidant babies are also insecurely attached. They actually avoid or ignore their mothers when they return after an absence, although their heart rates reveal that they are stressed in her absence. Main and others have identified a fourth attachment category, another insecurely attached group called disorganized-disoriented. These babies react to their mothers in contradictory ways, engaging in an odd array of behaviors.

10. Maternal caregiving in the 1st year of life is correlated with infants' attachment quality at 12 months. The mothers of securely attached babies provide consistent, sensitive care to their infants. Mothers of insecurely attached babies are more likely to be insensitive in one way or another, and the mothers of disorganized-disoriented babies can be abusive. Across many different studies, the correlation between mother care and infant attachment quality is moderate, indicating that other influences must also be important.

11. Infant temperament may be one influence on attachment quality. Babies have different emotional and behavioral characteristics. Such traits make up infant temperament, and for at least one of these traits, reactivity, physiological correlates have been identified, such as high heart rates before birth. Some babies have difficult temperaments: They are highly reactive and irritable and have a number of other traits that make them more difficult than average babies to care for. Easy babies have a combination of traits that make them easy to care for. A longitudinal study by Thomas and Chess included babies with different temperaments and indicates that temperament can persist beyond infancy and that it can affect caregiving, making it easier or harder for a parent to be responsive and sensitive. But this study also found that parents who adjust to their infants' temperament, creating goodness of fit between their caregiving and the needs of a particular infant, can moderate their child's temperament and influence the impact of early temperament on later adjustment.

12. Temperament and caregiving seem to interact to affect security of attachment. For example, some caregivers may react to the frustrations of caring for a difficult baby by becoming less sensitive and responsive to their baby's needs. Their unresponsive caregiving may then contribute to an insecure attachment.

13. Across social classes and across cultures, there are differences in the proportion of infants who are categorized as securely or insecurely attached. Larger numbers of insecure infant attachments are found in lower income families. It appears that increases in life stress are related to less responsive care and to increases in insecure attachments. Across cultures, the connection between sensitive caregiving and security of attachment has been corroborated.

14. Attachment quality can change over time if caregiving quality changes. It is also possible for children with reactive attachment disorder, who have been deprived of adequate adult care as infants, to later form secure attachments. Early attachment launches processes that can have long-term consequences; but the quality of care

a child continues to receive can either strengthen or redirect those processes.

15. Early attachment quality has been found to predict later psychosocial functioning, including dependency, self-confidence, and social skills. Moreover, if children have secure attachments with both parents, their later functioning is more positive than if they have a secure attachment with only one parent. However, it is unclear whether the early attachment quality is the cause of later psychosocial adjustment or whether the ongoing quality of the parents' caregiving is the key predictor. The primary influence of early infant attachments may be their tendency to perpetuate themselves. Once a pattern is established between parent and child, it tends to be repeated. However, it can be changed, and if it is, the child's working model of relationships, of self, and of others can also change.

16. Methods for assessing attachment security in adults have been devised, such as the Adult Attachment Inventory (AAI). In some studies, parents' own attachment quality has been predictive of the quality of attachment they establish with their infants.

17. The specifics of infant care—such as bottle feeding versus breastfeeding—may be less important to child outcomes than the sensitivity of caregiving. Focusing on the quality of infant–caregiver relations, rather than the specifics of parenting practices, seems to provide a better understanding of later socioemotional development.

CASE STUDY

Angela is a White 17-year-old girl who is also the mother of a baby named Adam, now 11 months of age. Both Angela and her baby live with Angela's mother, Sarah, in a small rented house in a semirural community in the Midwest. Sarah, a single mother herself, works as a food server in a local restaurant. Sarah has another child, David, who is 13. Angela's father abandoned the family when she was 7 years old. Wayne, Angela's boyfriend and Adam's father, has also become estranged primarily because Sarah refuses to allow him in her house. She is angry that Angela became pregnant and views Wayne as incapable of, and uninterested in, taking on his share of the responsibility.

During her pregnancy, Angela continued to attend classes at her high school. She dropped out, however, when she was 7 months pregnant. She had grown increasingly depressed about the prospect of caring for an infant, and she found dealing with schoolwork and her pregnancy overwhelming. Following Adam's birth, Angela tried hard to be a good mother to her son. She took on most of the caretaking responsibilities by herself, which gave her some measure of satisfaction. However, she also felt deeply ambivalent. Above all, she resented the restrictions that the baby placed on her life. Adam's frequent crying for no apparent reason was particularly frustrating. According to Angela, Adam cried even when he was not hungry or wet. Sometimes she handled Adam roughly, when he wouldn't quiet down after a feeding or around bedtime. At other times, Angela was upset that Adam didn't seem to smile enough at her when she wanted to play with him. Sometimes, Adam paid no attention to her when she wanted interaction. At these times, she would raise her voice and hold his face in her hands to make him look at her. She was beginning to feel that she was not a very good mother to her son after all.

Sarah and Angela's already strained relationship grew more hostile as Adam approached his first birthday. Angela felt that her mother wasn't interested in helping her. Angela always idealized her father and believed that it was her mother's frequent outbursts of anger that led to her father's leaving home.

For her part, Sarah believed that her daughter wasn't doing enough to help herself. Angela chose not to go back to school, even though she could have access to school-based child care services. All through Angela's high school years, Sarah had expected her daughter to find a steady job after graduation and to contribute to the family financially. Instead, Sarah found herself in the role of financial provider for another child. She was very angry and hurt that Angela didn't seem to appreciate all she had done for her over the years. Whenever the mother and daughter had an argument, Angela would say that she felt her mother never really cared about her. What was even worse for Sarah was that Angela had begun seeing Wayne again, without her mother's permission. She made it clear to Angela that she and the baby would need to move out if she ever got pregnant again.

Discussion Questions

1. Comment on the quality of the attachment relationship between Angela and Adam and between Sarah and Angela. Do you think that Adam is at risk for developmental problems? Discuss.

2. Using the model of intergenerational transmission of attachment presented in this chapter, discuss the transmission sequence as it applies in this case.

3. What kinds of interventions could you suggest to help the members of this family?

JOURNAL QUESTIONS

1. Present five adjectives that describe your early childhood relationship to each parent.
   a. Why did you choose these adjectives?
   b. To which parent did you feel the closest?
   c. What did you do as a child when you were upset, hurt, or ill?
   d. What do you remember about any separation that you experienced as a child?
2. How would your parents describe your temperament as a young child? In what ways is it the same now and in what ways is it different?

KEY TERMS

Phineas Gage matrix
emotional intelligence
differential emotions
   theory
orthogenetic principle
releasers
still-face paradigm
other-directed coping
   behaviors
self-directed coping
   behaviors

interactive repair
basic trust
ethologists
attachment theory
separation anxiety
stranger anxiety
proximity maintenance
secure base
safe haven
working models
strange situation test

securely attached
anxious ambivalent
avoidant babies
disorganized-disoriented
temperaments
fearfulness or reactivity
irritability or negative
   emotionality
activity level
positive affect
attention-persistence

rhythmicity
behavioral inhibition
difficult babies
easy babies
slow-to-warm-up babies
goodness of fit model
reactive attachment
   disorder
Adult Attachment Inventory
   (AAI)

Now go to our Companion Website to assess your understanding of chapter content with Multiple Choice Questions, apply comprehension in Essay Questions, and broaden your knowledge of development with related Web Links.

CHAPTER 5

The Emerging Self and Socialization in the Early Years

"Mirror, mirror on the wall, who is the real me, after all?" Philosophers, poets, wicked stepmothers, and regular human beings have pondered versions of this question since the time of the ancient Greeks advised, "Know thyself." The search for self embodies within it many of the profound questions at the heart of the human condition: What is the nature of human consciousness? Are we the same or different across situations? How do people come to understand and accept who they are? Modern cultures, as we have noted, are not the first to express interest in these matters. Nonetheless, critics have raised concerns that the level of attention directed toward the self has increased in recent decades. Note the amount of press devoted to the ideas of self-concept, self-esteem, self-enhancement, and self-actualization, and you might agree that we have become downright self-centered!

Those of us in the helping professions are no exception to this trend. Even a cursory review of the professional literature in counseling reveals an intense interest in topics related to the self. Therapeutic approaches that emphasize self-development are very common. Educational institutions struggle to incorporate self-development into their more traditional academic objectives. Popular magazines are saturated with advice about self-concept and self-esteem. All together, the pieces add up to a crazy quilt: part folklore, part research, part anecdote, and part good intention. Our task in this chapter is to unscramble some of this information and present the self in its developmental context.

Helpers need to understand the research findings in this critically important area lest they assume that all of our popular, contemporary notions about self-development are valid. For example, the postmodern focus on individualism might convey the idea that the self is truly independent and autonomous when, in fact, it is largely a product of social interaction. Bowlby (e.g., 1969/1982) suggested that working models of the self develop in concert with working models of attachment figures. Erikson (1950/1963) developed the idea that when others respond sensitively to their needs, children develop concepts of themselves as valuable. Cultural groups differ in their emphasis on an autonomous self. So self-development, despite our Western predilection for thinking of the self as independent, occurs in interaction with others and is influenced by culture and context. In this chapter, we will describe the earliest roots of self-development from a western scientific perspective and emphasize the importance of parenting to this process. As we will see, the role of caretakers is of major significance in the development of many of the processes related to the self.

THE SELF-SYSTEM: TRADITIONAL CONCEPTIONS

The self and its development are complicated, abstract topics. Writers still grapple with the question of what constitutes a self. In their search for answers, theorists and researchers need to account for the fact that selves are multifaceted and possess elements of both stability and change. If you have ever said that you are not the same person that you were some time ago, you can understand this point. Recently, writers have begun to use the term *self-system* to replace "self," because the latter seems too unidimensional (see Damon & Hart, 1988). The **self-system** includes aspects related to the self, such as self-concept, self-regulation, and self-esteem.

We will begin our look at the nature of the self-system with a brief description of the classic work of James, Cooley, and Mead. William James (1890) made a distinction between the "I" and the "Me," a distinction that is still used productively in contemporary research about the self. That part of the self called "I" refers to the **self-as-subject**, as active agent, or as the knower. It is that part of the self that experiences a sense of subjective self-awareness. The part called "Me" is that part of the self that is the object of self or others' observations, or in other words, the part that is known. One might think of the **"Me"** part of the self as the **self-concept**.

Implicit in James's traditional construction of selfhood is the idea that the self is multidimensional. Freud (1956) once wrote that a person could be construed as a whole "cast of characters." Interestingly, this view of the multiplicity of selves was rejected by a number of influential writers in the first half of the 20th century. Gergen (1971) described the emphasis placed on the importance of maintaining a unified, coherent self by important therapists and scholars such as Horney (1950), Jung (1928), Maslow (1954), and Rogers (1951). Considerable recent evidence, however, has not supported the view of the unified self but has demonstrated that individuals vary across situations, that they may possess conflicting self-ideas that speak with different voices at different times, and that the self-concept differentiates with maturity. A basic feature of the self, then, is that it incorporates both the private and the more public sides of our nature, accommodating our ability to keep our own counsel and still be known to others by virtue of our interactions with them.

Recently, writers have developed alternative ways of categorizing the classic "I–Me" distinction. Among these are Lewis's (1994) subjective and objective self-awareness, Case's (1991) implicit and explicit self, and Neisser's (1993) ecological and remembered self. All the newer contrasts share the original distinction between the self as knower and the self as known. Furthermore, there is consensus between classic and contemporary theorists that the "I" self emerges first.

What specifically does the "I" comprise? James proposed that this is the side of the self that experiences continuity over time. Even though we all grow and change, we know we embody core elements of the same "self" throughout our lifetime. The "I" also recognizes the distinctiveness of the self as a person compared to other persons. You know where you end and the person sitting next to you begins. Finally, the "I" reflects agency or is that part of the self that engages in self-directed activity, self-control, and contemplation of the "Me." With time, these elements will be explored and further consolidated in the adolescent search for identity.

The "Me" includes all those attributes that are used to define the self and that make up the self-concept. In James's typology, these are the "material self," the "social self," and the "spiritual self," ranked in that order of importance from lowest to highest. The material self encompasses a person's physical characteristics and material possessions. The social self includes her social standing, her reputation, and those personal characteristics that were recognized by others, such as gregariousness or stubbornness. The spiritual self, viewed by James as the most precious, incorporates her qualities of character, beliefs, and personal values.

Self-concept, as defined here, is distinct from **self-esteem**. The former is a description of personal attributes. The latter is one's evaluation of these attributes, or the positive or negative valence associated with those attributes. *Valence* refers to the affective value of a characteristic, either good, bad, or neutral. James believed that self-esteem is more than just the measure of accomplishments. Rather, he believed that it depends upon the number of successes we enjoy relative to our aspirations, or, in his terminology, pretensions. Pretensions are goals that we choose to meet for ourselves because of their personal importance. For example, if it is highly important to you to be popular and socially active, the lack of a date for an important New Year's Eve party can be a real blow to your self-esteem. However, if you really care more about earning enough money to become rich at an early age, you might consider working overtime on New Year's Eve to be highly congruent with your aspirations. Your dateless condition is less damaging to your self-esteem. Failures or even successes in areas that are relatively unimportant to us may be discounted and will have less effect on self-esteem.

If James provided ideas about the structure of the self that resonate with contemporary theorizing, Charles Cooley (1902) introduced a developmental perspective that describes how interactions with others help construct the self-system. Using his now-famous metaphor of the "looking-glass self," Cooley described the process of self-development as one that originates from observing the reflected appraisals of others, primarily attachment figures. Cooley hypothesized that this process consists of three steps. As we interact with others, we first imagine how we must appear to the other person on a certain dimension, such as intelligence. Then, we interpret or imagine how that other person evaluates us on that certain dimension. Finally, we experience some emotional response to that perceived evaluation. The resulting interpretation and its affective valence constitute a building block for constructing self-knowledge. So it is that our self-representations are shaped and given affective valences by the significant people in our life.

Let's consider a simplified example of a young child's display of affection for a parent. A 4-year-old girl approaches her father to give him a hug. The father, preoccupied with a pressing business matter, looks annoyed by the interruption. He gives her a quick hug and returns to his work. If this type of sequence is repeated on a regular basis across various situations, the child may come to develop a "self-idea" that she is bothersome and not important enough to interrupt her father's work. She may begin to construct a vague impression of herself as unappealing or possibly too emotionally expressive or dependent. Because the child perceives her father's response as impatient and irritated, her interpretation of the event includes a self-appraisal—presumably that she is irritating—that is incorporated into her self-system. The youngster comes to regard herself in certain ways by looking at the mirror of her parent's view of her, warped as that mirror might be. The emotional valence associated with this aspect of the child's self-image is negative. This self-representation may serve as a standard for her behavior in social interactions (e.g., in her willingness to express her need for attention and affection from others) and inform her sense of right and wrong.

Now imagine this same little girl in another family. She interrupts her father to give him a hug, and he beams, expressing evident satisfaction in his daughter's affectionate nature. This child's self-concept is likely to include a positively valenced sense of being emotionally expressive. The same child and the same behavior could lead to different social responses in different families, setting the child's developing sense of self, relationships, and morality on a different pathway. Thus early attachment and parenting interactions have been viewed as instrumental in the development of individual differences in self-concept (Sroufe, 1996).

Although the development of the self is obviously influenced by many factors and is extraordinarily complex, Cooley believed that it was largely the product of social influences. Recent researchers have investigated the possibility that the sequence Cooley proposed can also operate in reverse order, namely that a positive appraisal of oneself can generate positive interpretations of others' appraisals.

George Herbert Mead (1934) expanded on Cooley's work, enlarging the scope of influence to include the role of language and society in shaping the self-system. He held that the self-idea, or self-concept, becomes internalized or "generalized" through repeated interactions with others of the same cultural group. The individual adopts the perspective of others who share the same societal perspective, producing a kind of ecological self (Neisser, 1993). An example of this phenomenon is provided by Markus and Kitayama (1991), who found cultural differences in preferred ways of viewing the self. In their study, Japanese were more likely to describe themselves by emphasizing their affiliations, such as family membership, whereas Americans used self-descriptors that emphasized their individuality. Children not only adopt descriptive information about the self from their cultural milieu, they also incorporate those standards, rules, and goals that their family and their culture have determined to be appropriate ways of behaving and thinking (Stipek, Recchia, & McClintic, 1992). Note the parallels between Mead's approach and Vygotsky's (see Chapter 3).

These classic formulations of the self as multidimensional, as influenced by the reflected appraisals of significant others, and as shaped by the cultural milieu, provide a foundation for current thinking about the self-system. You may have noticed that conceptions of self and of morality overlap in these models. Damon and Hart (1992) have noted:

> Children cannot know themselves without some sense of the other. Nor can they forge their self-identities without an awareness of their own values. Moreover, at all developmental periods, social

activities derive from—and in turn shape—judgments about the self, other, and morality. In these and many other ways, self-understanding, social interaction, and morality are intertwined in a developing psychological system that grows and changes throughout the life span. (p. 421)

Self-understanding is one of the key building blocks of personality, social, and moral development. How does this mysterious self begin? In the next section, we will review the earliest stages of developing self-awareness.

THE EARLY DEVELOPMENT OF THE SELF-SYSTEM

The Beginnings of the "I" and the "Me"

Settling on a time that marks the beginning of the self is a difficult task because various aspects of the self emerge at different rates and may be identified differently depending upon one's theoretical viewpoint. A child's ability to describe herself as "smart" or "funny" will not be apparent until several years after birth. Does this mean there is no sense of self until the time when she can recognize and articulate her personal characteristics? Most contemporary developmentalists would disagree with this idea. In general, the development of self is viewed as a gradually unfolding process, beginning at birth and lasting throughout life. Even adults continue to grow and change, thus experiencing self-development. However, the adult sense of self is far more differentiated than that of the infant, or even that of the articulate preschooler. What are the competencies of the infant that make self-development possible? How do these competencies interact with the social relationships that ultimately give birth to the self as a manifestation of personal consciousness?

PRECURSORS OF SELF-AWARENESS IN INFANCY—THE "PRE-SELF"

We might say that the newborn's capacities for rudimentary information processing and social bonding provide the building material out of which the self is born. For example, one early competency is the infant's capacity for imitation. As we saw in Chapter 3, babies can imitate the facial gestures of adults a few days after birth (Meltzoff, 1990). When a baby imitates an adult opening and closing his mouth, she is detecting, at least at a behavioral level, similarity between herself and the adult model. Meltzoff argues that such early imitative skills are precursors of the older child's ability to draw parallels between her own and another person's mind or feelings.

As we saw in Chapter 4, from birth through the first half year of life, the infant is primarily engaged in the business of regulating physiological and emotional states, largely in the context of infant–caregiver interactions. Young infants have limited power to regulate a caregiver's responses, and so it is primarily the caregiver's responsibility to scaffold interactions, providing the sensitive care that allows for the establishment of routines. Meltzoff (1990) argues that from the regularity and reliability of caregiver–infant interactions babies extract notions of "self-invariance" and "other invariance," which precede self-awareness. We might say that the infant comes to possess a pre-self, composed of early inklings of the permanence of her body, its separateness from others, and the rhythms of interpersonal connections.

Gradually, over the second half year, the infant assumes more control in signaling the caregiver to provide for her needs. The regularity with which the caregiver is available and sensitive or unavailable and insensitive is stored in memory in what Stern (1985) calls representations of interactions (or RIGs). These are "procedural" representations, preverbal, unconscious, and a kind of sensorimotor memory. They are patterns generalized from the repetitive nature of caregiver–infant interactions.

When the infant's attempts to exert some control over caregiver contingencies are successful, she is thought to experience a budding sense of mastery or self-efficacy (Bandura, 1990). She takes pleasure in expressing the agentic "I." Imagine the lesson learned by an infant who, when she coos and babbles, regularly attracts the smiles and responsive vocalizations of her caregivers. This baby's world, in some small way, begins to come under her control. She might encode the message, "When I am upset or need attention, my parent responds and takes care of me." Again, the infant does not represent these ideas linguistically, but rather encodes these kinds of organized sequences as procedural models or patterns of the self-in-relationship. Affective responses, such as feelings of love and relief, also become associated with these memories. The infant's self-system is under construction.

As the infant approaches the end of the 1st year, other cognitive and affective developments point to an increasing sense of self as separate from the caretaker. We saw in Chapter 4 that by about 8 to 10 months infants display separation anxiety, signaling the formation of an attachment to the primary caregiver. For example, they might show distress even at an impending separation from an attachment figure, perhaps by looking anxiously at the door when the babysitter arrives. Many babies cry and cling to a departing caregiver. These behaviors serve to maintain proximity, and they demonstrate the infant's recognition that the caregiver is separate from herself.

Attachment theorists like Bowlby assume that the attachment between infant and caregiver gives rise to a sense of security and optimism in an infant, what Erikson described as a burgeoning trust in others and an early sense of self-worth. From this perspective, when the 1-year-old begins to use the caregiver as a secure base from which to explore the environment, we are seeing the emergence of a kind of preliminary sense of self-worth. Once again, the infant's self-development evolves from her experience in relationships.

We also saw in the last chapter that late in the 1st year, caregivers' facial expressions influence infants' reactions to situations, such as their willingness to cross a visual cliff (Campos et al., 1983; Klinnert, 1984). Social referencing—the baby's adjustment of reactions depending on feedback provided by a caregiver—also implies recognition of the separateness of the other. This phenomenon is thought to be a source of information for the self-system, providing the baby with a context in which she begins to differentiate experience of the self from experience of the other and from the combined experience of the "we" (Emde & Buchsbaum, 1990). Social referencing demonstrates how transactional the self-development process really is. The child uses the caregiver's emotions to discern meaning in events and to intuit information about the self.

Campos, Campos, and Barrett (1989) have suggested that when caregivers communicate consistent emotional signals about environmental events, certain pervasive emotional dispositions are created. These processes can have far-reaching effects: "Can I trust other people? Is it safe to take risks?" These emotional dispositions constitute a part of the "value system" of a family or a culture. Furthermore, these authors note that emotional signaling by caregivers may affect the process of emotion regulation and emotional self-knowledge well beyond infancy. For example, a child growing up in an emotional climate marked by parental anger and blame might "read" and internalize the parents' emotional messages as shame and guilt, concluding that she is shameful (Zahn-Waxler & Kochanska, 1990).

THE EMERGENCE OF SELF-AWARENESS AND SELF-CONCEPT

Certain cognitive advances in the 2nd year seem to play important roles in the development of the self-system. For example, the toddler's capacity for establishing joint reference with another supports the early development of a theory of mind. Imagine that the father of a 15-month-old girl tries to get the toddler to look at a kitten that has just walked into the room. The father points to the kitten, looks at the child, smiles broadly and says, "cat." This sequence is repeated until the child, following the direction of her father's gaze, spies the cat and looks back at him with a big grin. She and her father are sharing the same point of reference. Jointly attending to the pet, in this case, may encourage a beginning understanding of "mind," of private experience that is sometimes shared. The toddler's sense of herself as a separate person is enhanced. Note, as well, that the affective part of the experience can also be shared. The toddler and her caregiver both delight in the kitten's appearance.

A benchmark event occurs in self-development roughly around the age of 18 months, perhaps supported by an emerging capacity for mental representation (see Chapter 3). Up to this time, human infants do not show self-recognition when they view themselves in a mirror. Self-recognition is typically manifested by the observer's display of self-directed behavior upon

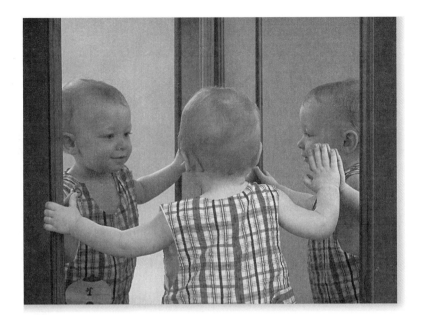

This toddler recognizes that the image in the mirror is her own reflection, a milestone in self-recognition.

viewing her reflection. Reasoning that self-directed behavior signals the presence of objective self-awareness, Lewis and his colleagues used a mirror recognition technique to study infants and children (e.g., Lewis & Michalson, 1983). The researchers placed the children in front of a mirror after marking their faces with a spot of rouge. Toddlers over about 15 months old showed mark-directed behavior, such as touching their faces, averting their gaze, and then turning back to look again. No children younger than 15 months had this reaction, and all children in the 24-month-old group displayed it. Children over 15 months were also able to distinguish their own images from those of age mates on videotapes. Such consistent age-related findings suggest that self-recognition is universally acquired late in the 2nd year of life.

The timing of self-recognition is highly reliable. For children whose development is delayed, as in the case of children with Down syndrome, self-recognition occurs whenever they achieve a developmental level of approximately 2 years (Kopp & Wyer, 1994). Comparison studies of maltreated and nonmaltreated children show no differences in the timing of self-recognition (Schneider-Rosen & Cicchetti, 1984, 1991). These studies also suggest that self-evaluation, or self-esteem, begins to emerge along with self-recognition. Maltreated children show considerably more negative or neutral affect when seeing their faces in the mirror than do nonmaltreated children, who display more positive affect.

Self-recognition is a clear signal that a child has begun to formulate a conscious concept of self. Roughly after the child's second birthday, an increase in language skills makes possible further elaboration of the self-concept or "Me-self." Children begin to describe themselves as "a boy" or "a girl" or as "big" or "little," and they begin to use appropriate personal pronouns to refer to themselves. These achievements mark a watershed in the development of the self-concept, and caregivers make important contributions by virtue of the labels they apply to children. Parental statements such as "You are a big girl" can now be stored in a child's semantic memory as part of her self-knowledge (e.g., Nelson, 1993a). Caregivers' descriptions can be neutral and objective (such as the child's name or personal pronoun) or evaluative and subjective (such as "pretty" or "good"), and these appear not to be differentiated by young children according to their objectivity or subjectivity. Stipek, Gralinski, and Kopp (1990) reported that toddlers appear to believe both objective and subjective claims about themselves, apparently because the claims come from an authoritative source. In other words, young children cannot discount the negative part of the parental evaluation "bad girl" as due to parental bias or temporary bad mood. A study by Beeghly and Cicchetti (1994) found that when self-description begins, maltreated children use fewer words to describe their feelings than do nonmaltreated children, despite comparable performance on measures of receptive language ability. The authors conclude that these results, together with the less-positive affective responses maltreated children display on the self-recognition task, are early indicators of poor self-esteem and of the influence of caregivers' words and deeds on children's earliest self-evaluations.

As toddlers become preschoolers, their self-concepts become more and more differentiated and complex. For example, as early as 3 years of age, children can correctly identify their race, ethnicity, and skin color (Katz & Zalk, 1974). In general, children from minority groups tend to develop racial awareness faster than do nonminorities. A study by Feinman and Entwhistle (1976) demonstrated that young African American children outperform other children in their ability to discriminate colors of faces, suggesting the early influence of race on perception. Ramsey and Myers (1990) also found that race is one of the primary dimensions children refer to when describing people.

Unfortunately, many early studies of preschool children found evidence for a pro-White bias among children from minority groups (see Banks, 1976; Beuf, 1977; Spencer, 1982). Typically, these studies involved questioning young children about their preferences for, and identification with, dolls that represent their own ethnic or racial group and that represent the majority culture. Overall, young children tended to perceive a White doll as possessing more positive attributes, and some researchers have interpreted these findings to be early predictors of identity formation problems or misidentification among minority group children. However, more recent studies of African American children have found that a pro-White bias may coexist with high levels of personal self-esteem (Powell, 1985). Spencer and Markstrom-Adams (1990), after reviewing this body of work, conclude that these dissonant results reflect the child's cognitive awareness of social stereotypes, but not necessarily a self-esteem deficit. In other words, young children from minority groups may be somewhat more attuned to society's valuing of White culture without necessarily devaluing themselves or their cultural heritage.

Consistent with their level of cognitive development, preschoolers generally describe themselves in concrete, physical terms, such as "little" or "strong," whereas older children and adolescents employ more abstract words. As children mature, they become more skilled at identifying various aspects of themselves. For example, a 7-year-old might describe herself as helpful, a good soccer player, and smart in reading but not in math. As we shall see in a later chapter, the self-concept continues to become more differentiated with age.

In summary, the self-system begins to develop in earliest infancy. There are many precursors to a conscious concept of self in the 1st year, a kind of procedural knowledge of the self in action and interaction, or "pre-self." But awareness of self as a distinct entity begins with self-recognition in the 2nd year and is followed by explicit self-description in the 3rd year. Self-evaluation or self-esteem is evident as soon as toddlers show signs of self-recognition. See Table 5.1 for a summary of the early phases of self-development.

Throughout infancy and beyond, the self-system is a joint construction of child, caregiver, and cultural and family milieu. We have described some ways in which caregiver–infant interactions seem to contribute to the development of the self. Later in this chapter, we will discuss in greater detail how parenting in the toddler and preschool years contributes to child outcomes, including the development of the self-system.

TABLE 5.1	Phases of Self-Development	
Age	**Developing Aspects of Self**	**Manifestations**
0–6 months	Pre-Self	Beginnings of "self-invariance" and "other invariance" embedded in infant–caregiver interactions
6–12 months	Intentional or Agentic Self or "I"	Intentional signaling of caregiver; social referencing; shared referents; beginning self-efficacy; using caregiver as secure base (beginning self-worth and trust)
12–24 months	Objective Self or "Me"	Self-recognition; early self-control; early self-esteem (feelings of autonomy)
24–60 months	Self-Monitoring Self	Self-description; self-conscious emotions; self-regulation

Roots of Self-Control and Self-Regulation

Up to now, we have described the emerging "I" and "Me." Now we turn our attention to another important dimension of the developing self-system, self-control or behavior regulation and self-regulation. Self-control refers to two things: first, the child's ability to stop herself from performing a proscribed act, as when a toddler can pull her hand back from the cookie jar after being told "No cookies before dinner"; and second, her ability to make herself perform an act that she may not feel much like doing, such as giving Aunt Matilda a required kiss on the cheek. According to Kopp (1982), self-regulation is a more advanced and flexible version of self-control:

> the ability to comply with a request, to initiate and cease activities according to situational demands, to modulate the intensity, frequency, and duration of verbal and motor acts in social and educational settings, to postpone acting upon a desired object or goal, and to generate socially approved behavior in the absence of external monitors. (pp. 199–200)

Counselors regularly deal with problems involving self-regulation in one form or another. The preschooler who throws tantrums in school, the rebellious adolescent who runs away from home, the young adult who repeatedly loses jobs because she fails to show up on time, all may be examples of difficulties in this area. Many other factors contribute to such adjustment problems; however, they all reflect some lack of compliance with specific requests or rules.

Obviously, achieving self-regulation is a rather formidable task for a mischievous toddler or even for a sophisticated high schooler! Even though this may sound like the accomplishment that many parents of tempestuous 2-year-olds long for, it is not realistic to expect a child to be able to master her behavior and emotions in every circumstance. The movement from dyadic emotion regulation to self-regulation of behavior and emotion, permitting harmonious interchange with the social environment, is a painstaking and long-term process.

The Importance of Emotion Regulation

It is absolutely essential to recognize that emotion regulation underlies any ability to control behaviors. In fact, the earliest developmental task of infancy is to establish physiological balance, or control over fluctuating levels of arousal. The affective tension that the infant experiences when her homeostatic "set point" has been altered through hunger, pain, or too much stimulation motivates her to return to a more balanced state. Unable to manage this on her own, the infant signals the caregiver, whose soothing attentions function as critical ingredients in the development of the affect-regulation system. When the toddler or preschooler experiences periods of high arousal or distress, the sensitive caregiver steps in once again to help the child regain some affective control or to shore up the boundaries of the self. As we have emphasized in Chapter 4, good caregiving in infancy and beyond involves scaffolding the child's developing ability to regulate both emotional and behavioral expression.

The Early Progress of Behavior Regulation

How does behavior regulation come into being? It depends on two major cognitive and emotional advances that emerge in tandem with objective self-awareness or self-recognition: first, representational thought, and second, emotional response to wrongdoing.

Recall from our discussion of Piagetian theory that children around 18 months of age can use a symbol to stand in for an object. Toddlers hear, understand, and store structures such as "Don't jump on the furniture," which might be a manifestation of a broader value that property should not be damaged, or "Share your candy with your sister," a version of "Do unto others." This cognitive machinery allows children to construct internalized representations of standards for everyday behavior (Kopp & Wyer, 1994). These standards or rules might differ somewhat according to the child's family and culture, but every cultural group maintains them and provides sanctions for their violation (Lewis, 1993).

Along with the basic capacity for mental representation, many other cognitive skills contribute to the learning of standards: ability to focus attention, comprehension of caregiver requests, procedural knowledge of rules, and generalization of rules across situations. As these abilities are sharpened in the 2nd year, toddlers begin the process of internalizing rules and prohibitions (Emde, Biringen, Clyman, & Oppenheim, 1991). Obviously, an infant cannot comply with social conventions precisely because she has no comprehension of them. A baby may be prevented from engaging in some activity by external parental displays of control, as when a mother whisks her adventurous 10-month-old away from the edge of a swimming pool. But a 2-year-old who has the requisite level of cognitive maturity to understand and remember some rules, as well as the motivation to comply, begins to show signs of inhibiting her own behavior in such situations.

The growth of emotions often linked to violations of standards for everyday behavior appears to begin late in the 2nd year. Called the self-conscious emotions, shame, embarrassment, guilt, and pride take their place in the child's emotional repertoire after objective self-awareness, or self-recognition, has been attained (Lewis & Michalson, 1983). These emotions are different from the emotions of infancy because they require the ability to consider the self as separate from others and as the subject of others' judgments. Between the ages of 2 and 3, young children often display emotional responses to their wrongdoing and mistakes, suggesting that they have begun to evaluate themselves in ways that they expect to be evaluated by others (Kagan, 1981). At 18 months, a child might take notice of her rule violation but without any discernable emotional response. Consider, for example, the toddler who spills milk on the floor. She may say "Uh oh!" and giggle or point to the spill without much concern. Later, rule breaking becomes associated with some negative affect. This same youngster at 3 may experience a sense of embarrassment, evaluate herself as "bad," and try to hide the evidence.

The capacity for emotional response to wrongdoing is an important milestone, long considered to be the beginning of conscience development (Sears, Maccoby, & Levin, 1957). Although not yet a reflection of full-fledged conscience, the child's emotional responses to rule violations are linked to what she perceives her parents' reactions might be, and these perceptions shape her developing sense of morality (Emde, Johnson, & Easterbrooks, 1987).

EARLY SOCIALIZATION: PARENTING AND THE DEVELOPMENT OF THE SELF-SYSTEM

Theorists from Cooley (1902) to Bowlby (e.g., 1969/1982) and Erikson (1950/1963) have assumed that many parts of the self-system grow out of our social interactions. As we saw in the last chapter, the available data do suggest that our earliest relationships create a trajectory for the development of self-concept and self-esteem. For example, when babies are securely attached to their mothers, they tend to be appropriately independent as 4-year-olds and to be self-confident and socially skilled as 10-year-olds (e.g., Sroufe et al., 1983; see Thompson, 1998, for a review).

We know that early caregiving quality can make an important contribution to the quality of babies' attachments. Infants are likely to become securely attached to caregivers who respond promptly and consistently to crying, who react appropriately to babies' facial expressions, eye contact and other signals, who handle their infants sensitively, and who hold them often during the 1st year, providing the contact comfort that helps infants modulate their emotions. Such caregiving requires patience and a child-centered approach that can be difficult for any parent sometimes, but is especially challenging if the baby has a difficult temperament (irritable, active, difficult to soothe, and so on) or other special needs or if the parent is stressed or depressed. But the effort and self-sacrifice required for parents to create a "good fit," as Thomas and Chess (1977) described it, between their caregiving and a baby's needs does appear to contribute to attachment quality and to the direction that self-knowledge and self-evaluation will take. This process continues after infancy, as the description of self-development in the last section indicates. In this section, we will take a close look at parent–child relationships in the toddler and preschool years. We will focus especially on the characteristics of parenting that may be most conducive to helping young children to develop positive self-esteem and adaptive self-regulatory mechanisms.

As the infant becomes a toddler, gaining cognitive, communicative, and motor skills, there are new challenges for parents trying to be sensitive and responsive, to create a good fit between their care and the child's needs. First, caregivers are faced with the need to grant some autonomy to the child. As toddlers become capable of doing more on their own, they are motivated to practice and expand their growing competencies. The strong dependency that characterizes young babies is gradually replaced by a capacity and need for independent action. Erikson theorized that toddlers' emerging feelings of worth are benefited when they can use their growing skills to function at least somewhat autonomously, whether it is by feeding themselves or by buttoning their own buttons, or more subtly, by saying "NO!"—that is, refusing to do what someone else requires (see Table 1.1 in Chapter 1). Thus, although the earliest feelings of worth grow out of an infant's trust in others to meet all her needs, those feelings of worth grow in the toddler years when the child begins to experience self-sufficiency, or autonomy, a sense that "I can do it myself."

Second, also because the child's behavioral and cognitive skills are growing, the caregiver must begin to socialize the child, limiting some behaviors and demanding others, so that the child will be safe ("No, you cannot climb on the counter") and so that she will learn the standards of her culture and behave in ways that are conventionally acceptable ("You must wear clothes"). Socialization pressure requires discipline, when parents limit or demand behavior by exerting or requiring control. Parents generally impose more discipline on the child as they perceive her to be more and more capable of self-control. When parents tell a child to do, or not to do, something, they are depending on the child's ability to initiate or to stop her own actions. As we saw earlier, the only way to make an infant do, or not do, something is to rely on physically moving or restraining the child. Parents do a lot of that with infants, but they rely more and more on controlling by request or command during early childhood, as the requisite abilities (such as representational and comprehension skills) grow.

Thus, caregiver–child relationships are reorganized in the postinfancy period, with the additions of children's autonomy seeking, on one hand, and parents' imposition of discipline, on the other hand. What are the important features of this more complex relationship between parent and child? What role does the parent–child relationship play in the child's developing self-system? Let's begin by examining what research indicates are the most important dimensions or features of a parent's behavior in this relationship.

The Dimensions of Parenting Style

Studies of parenting after infancy have a long history and have produced many complicated findings. Remarkably, researchers from very different theoretical traditions have repeatedly identified two major dimensions or aspects of parents' behavior that seem to characterize the quality of parenting. These can be thought of as the primary contributors to what is called parenting style (for reviews see Baumrind, 1989, 1993; Darling & Steinberg, 1993; Maccoby & Martin, 1983; Parke & Buriel, 1998).

THE WARMTH DIMENSION—PARENTAL RESPONSIVENESS

In the postinfancy period, parents continue to create an emotional climate for their children. Contributing to a positive climate is parental responsiveness: listening to the child, being involved and interested in the child's activities, accepting the child, making positive attributions toward the child, being "tuned in" and supportive (e.g., Baumrind, 1989). In essence, high levels of warmth with toddlers and older children are comparable to high levels of responsive, sensitive care with infants. But some of the child's needs have changed. With toddlers, as we have seen, autonomy needs begin to be important, and responsive parents accept these needs, acquiescing when possible to their children's reasonable demands for autonomy (Baumrind, 1993). So, when 25-month-old Amanda begins to insist that she can dress herself, her mother tries to accommodate her by setting aside extra time for the morning dressing ritual. She also ignores the inconvenience and the sometimes strange-looking outcomes and gives Amanda positive messages about the process: "You're getting to be such a big girl to put on your own clothes!" Her attitude is child centered, sidelining parental needs (for time, convenience, and coordinated outfits) to meet Amanda's developmental needs.

Some parents create a more negative emotional climate. Their behavior is often parent centered: they show little responsiveness to their children's concerns and are unlikely to do things just to meet those concerns. They may even make hostile attributions when children's needs are out of line with their own. When 20-month-old Jessie wants to feed herself her morning cereal, for example, at first her mother ignores her, and when Jessie insists, her mother attends to her demands by making negative attributions, such as "You'll just make a mess" and "Why do you always make things so hard in the morning?" When Jessie accidentally spills the milk, her mother responds in frustration, "I told you that you couldn't do it yourself!"

We have seen that sensitive, responsive mother care in infancy promotes secure attachments. Likewise, mothers' warmth and responsiveness with their toddlers help maintain secure attachments and increase the likelihood that toddlers will be cooperative when mothers place demands on them (e.g., Emde et al., 1991; Lay, Waters, & Parke, 1989; NICHD, 1998). In one study, for example, toddlers' compliance with their mothers was observed in toy cleanup tasks and in a situation where mothers designated some attractive toys as "off limits." The most enthusiastically compliant toddlers were those who were securely attached to their mothers (according to a separate assessment), and whose mothers maintained a warm, positive emotional climate throughout the sessions (Kochanska, 1995; Kochanska, Aksan, & Koenig, 1995).

THE CONTROL DIMENSION—PARENTAL DEMANDINGNESS

The second major dimension of parenting style is parental demandingness or control. If parental responsiveness means that parents sometimes acquiesce to their children's demands, parental demandingness leads parents to impose discipline. Demanding parents require their children to curb some of their behaviors and insist that they perform other behaviors that are suitable to their level of maturity (sometimes called maturity demands). Demanding parents impose standards and rules and enforce them. Interestingly, this dimension of parenting can be either child centered or parent centered. If the parent's concern is the development of self-control necessary for children to feel secure, to behave in ways that gain social acceptance, and to become skillful at social give and take, then discipline has a child focus. If the parents' concerns—for example, for quiet, or convenience, or orderliness, and so on—are primary, then discipline has a parent focus. Of course, parents' disciplinary motives may sometimes combine both kinds of concerns, and the same parents may shift their focus depending on the given situation. For example, Hastings and Grusec (1998) found that parents expressed more parent-centered concerns (such as wanting to be in control) when disciplining their children in public, but more child-centered concerns (such as teaching a child not to give up easily) in private interactions.

Four Parenting Styles

We can describe four basic parenting styles, or constellations of parenting characteristics, as shown in Table 5.2, by combining and crossing the positive and negative poles of parental responsiveness and demandingness (Maccoby & Martin, 1983). As you will see, these styles are often predictive of child characteristics (e.g., Baumrind, 1989, 1993).

THE AUTHORITATIVE STYLE

Parents with an authoritative style are both highly responsive and highly demanding. So, they create a positive emotional climate for their children, promoting autonomy and supporting assertiveness and individuality. At the same time these parents accept responsibility for socializing their children by expecting mature behavior and setting and enforcing clear standards. Other qualities also tend to be part of this constellation: These parents are often openly affectionate;

TABLE 5.2 Parenting Dimensions and Parenting Styles		
	Parental Warmth	
	Accepting, Responsive, Child-Centered	**Rejecting, Unresponsive, Parent-Centered**
Parental Demandingness:		
Demanding, Controlling	*Authoritative Style*	*Authoritarian Style*
Undemanding, Not Controlling	*Permissive Style*	*Neglecting-Uninvolved Style*

Source: Maccoby, E. E., & Martin, J. A. Socialization in the context of the family. In P. H. Mussin &
E. M. Hetherington, *Handbook of child psychology* vol. 4 (4th ed., pp. 1–101). Copyright © 1983.
This material is adapted by permission of John Wiley & Sons, Inc.

they encourage two-way communication with their children (that is, they genuinely listen and pay attention as well as talking themselves). Their communications about expectations and standards are usually clear and come with explanations that go beyond "You do it because I said so" to statements that help children make sense of their parents' demands.

THE AUTHORITARIAN STYLE

Authoritarian parents are low on responsiveness, but highly demanding. Thus they do not create a positive emotional climate nor encourage children's individualistic strivings or assertiveness, but they do tend to exercise considerable control, making maturity demands and requiring conformity to rules. In addition, other qualities tend to be characteristic of authoritarian parents. First, authoritarian parents usually communicate less effectively with their children than authoritative parents; their communications are more one-sided ("I say what will happen; you listen"); they express less affection; and their control tends to be more restrictive, meaning that they tend to restrict their children's emotional expressiveness and other self-assertive behaviors. They also are more likely to exercise control by using power assertion (see the section on parenting practices below) and are less likely to provide explanations that go beyond "Because I said so."

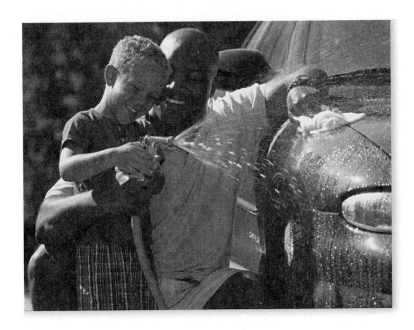

Parents who create a positive emotional climate promote autonomy and elicit cooperation from their children.

THE PERMISSIVE STYLE

Permissive parents are moderately to highly responsive to their children, but low on demandingness. Thus, they exercise less control than other parents, putting fewer maturity demands on their children, especially with regard to expressions of anger and aggressive behavior. They are more nurturing and affectionate than authoritarian parents, but usually not as nurturant as authoritative parents.

THE NEGLECTING–UNINVOLVED STYLE

Some parents are both low on responsiveness and low on demandingness, so that they actually invest little time or attention in a child and are largely parent centered in their concerns. Like permissive parents, neglecting–uninvolved parents seem to neglect their responsibility to socialize the child, but they also express less affection and are not likely to be responsive to their children's needs, perhaps even expressing hostility or making negative attributions to their children. When they do impose limits on their children, they tend to use power assertive techniques and little explanation.

Parenting Style and Child Outcomes

Through the long history of research on parenting, small but significant correlations have been found between parenting style, on one hand, and children's typical behaviors, on the other. Briefly, authoritative parenting has been associated with many positive outcomes in young children: adaptability, competence and achievement, good social skills and peer acceptance, and low levels of antisocial or aggressive behavior. Of particular interest to us in this chapter, authoritative parenting seems to promote positive self-development, especially high self-esteem and the capacity for self-regulation.

The children of authoritarian parents are more likely to be irritable and conflicted, showing signs of both anxiety and anger. They are conforming (self-controlled) with authority figures, but are not socially skillful and are susceptible to being bullied (e.g., Ladd & Ladd, 1998). They tend to have low self-esteem, and although they exhibit self-control with authorities, they may lack self-regulation when not being observed, so that they are unlikely to get caught.

Permissive parents are more likely to have children who exhibit uncontrolled, impulsive behavior and low levels of self-reliance. They are low on cognitive competence and social agency, and high on aggression, especially in family interactions. In some studies they have had high self-esteem, apparently when parents exhibit high levels of warmth, but many studies suggest that warmth combined with demandingness is more certain to be associated with self-esteem (see Maccoby & Martin, 1983).

Finally, the children of neglecting/uninvolved parents are likely to be impulsive, to show high levels of both externalizing problems (e.g., aggressiveness) and internalizing problems (e.g., depression), and to have low self-esteem.

Be cautious in interpreting these relationships between parenting style and child outcomes. The strength of the associations is modest, cueing us that many factors interact with parenting and modify its effects. Researchers have begun to identify a multiplicity of interacting factors, which we will discuss in a later section of this chapter. (See Collins, Maccoby, Steinberg, Hetherington, and Bornstein, 2000, for further discussion.)

Parenting Practices: Methods of Control

Thus far, we have looked at parenting style—parents' combined responsiveness and demandingness—as a source of children's behavior and self-development. Another aspect of parenting concerns the method of control parents choose when they attempt to exercise control. Researchers have identified three categories of control method: power assertion, love withdrawal, and induction. Power assertion can involve physical punishment or the threat of physical punishment,

Box 5.1 | *Effective Ways to Use Time-Out*

In many Dennis the Menace cartoons, Dennis sits in a pint-sized chair, hugging his teddy bear, facing into a corner, banished for some infraction. Dennis's parents use time-out as a disciplinary procedure: During a short span of time, Dennis is required to discontinue his involvement in ongoing activities to quietly sit somewhere apart. The technique involves mild power assertion and is suitable for use with toddlers and preschoolers. There is no pain involved, but time-out gets the attention of young children. Requiring a child to sit in a corner is one approach, but you can choose any place that separates the child from the action, while keeping her in a safe place that is within calling distance. Do not choose a spot where the child might be overwhelmed by feelings of isolation. The purpose of time-out is to eliminate the rewards of misbehavior, not to frighten a child. Indeed, it will work even if the "place apart" is in the midst of things. For example, in one day care center, the time-out chair is in the middle of a busy classroom so that the teachers can keep an eye on the offender. For the children, just being confined to the chair is sufficiently aversive to be effective.

Hamilton (1993) offers a number of pointers for using time-out effectively. To start, it helps to choose just two or three target behaviors that need to be changed. Reserve time-out for behaviors that are important to control because of safety, such as climbing on the kitchen counter, or because they are antisocial and hurtful, such as hitting or biting. Explain to the child which behaviors will lead to time-out, why they are unacceptable, and what alternative behaviors would be acceptable. It works best if children know the rules in advance so that what will lead to time-out is clear. (Don't forget to provide some positive attention for those more acceptable behaviors.) Don't use time-out for behaviors that have not been previously identified as inappropriate, and when the time-out is over, follow up with a reminder of your reasons for restricting this behavior. Remember, mild power assertion combined with induction can be very effective. Although Dennis the Menace is allowed to have a teddy bear in time-out, it is more consistent to eliminate access to toys, television, and attention from others.

Don't expect everything to go smoothly right from the start. At first a child may refuse to stay in time-out, or she may repeat the offending behavior just to test your resolve. If the child won't stay in time-out, make it very brief—a minute or so—and hold the child in place, turning your face away to create the condition of no attention. Then make eye contact and praise the child for staying in time-out. Stick it out—it will pay off. Time-out needs only to be long enough to get the point across. The younger the child, the less time is appropriate. One rule of thumb is 1 or 2 minutes for each year of age, so that the maximum time-out for a 2-year-old would be 4 minutes. Longer times are likely to become so aversive that they could defeat the purpose of simply getting the child's attention and creating an opportunity for her to think over her behavior.

Time-out, like most effective discipline, requires putting aside what you are doing to attend to the misbehavior when it happens. It can be inconvenient, but *immediacy* is important to help young children make the right connection between their behavior and its consequences. Similarly, *consistency* is essential. When a parent's responses are unreliable, it is difficult for a child to learn what the rules are. Just how consistent can a parent be? There are going to be times when you simply cannot follow up on a misbehavior. But most times you can, if you make it a priority and if you are careful to use time-out for just a few important behaviors. Suppose, for example, that you are teaching your 4-year-old, Jenny, not to hit her baby brother. In the middle of your grocery shopping, sure enough Jenny hauls off and whacks him. Immediately, tell Jenny what's wrong with this picture: "Jenny, you know that hitting is not okay. It hurts and it makes people cry, and we don't hit in our family, ever! You have to go to time-out for that." Pick up the baby, grab Jenny's hand, leave the cart, and head for the car. In the car, put Jenny in the back seat and sit in the front with the baby. Say clearly, "You are in time-out," and face forward for the designated time. At the end, explain the rule again, tell Jenny that time-out is over, and head back to the shopping cart. In other words, if at all possible, improvise. (No car? Stand silently on the sidewalk for the time-out period.) There are bound to be situations that make immediate and full follow-through impossible. You could have been in the middle of checking out your groceries, for example. But if your usual response is swift and sure, your efforts will pay off.

ranging from mild (e.g., a calm whack on a diapered bottom), to harsh (e.g., screaming in rage; a beating); or it can involve withdrawal of privileges, from mild forms (such as time-out procedures with toddlers, see Box 5.1), to severe denial (e.g., withholding meals). Power assertion is usually effective for the immediate control of behavior: Children often show self-control when they feel threatened. But there can be unwanted side effects: Harsh or severe power assertion has been linked to high levels of anger and anxiety in children, and children whose parents use harsh, punitive practices tend to be more aggressive than other children (e.g., Baumrind, 2001; Strassberg, Pettit, Gregory, & Bates, 1994; Straus & Gelles, 1990; Straus, Sugarman, & Giles-Sims, 1997; Straus & Yodanis, 1996).

If a child is accustomed to power assertive control, what happens when the threat is removed (e.g., Mom or Dad is not present or unlikely to find out)? Does the child engage in self-regulation? In other words, will she regulate her own behavior because she is committed to an internalized set of standards? There are conflicting data on this issue. On the whole, power assertion does not seem to be particularly effective in promoting self-regulation. Interestingly, milder forms of power assertion are more effective than harsher forms. But the picture is complex and cannot be fully understood without considering other factors, such as child temperament, culture, and overall parenting style. We will return to this issue later.

Love withdrawal—such as a parent's withdrawing attention or affection, expressing disappointment or disillusionment with a child, turning away from a child, cutting off verbal or emotional contact, or enforcing separations—is rarely used alone by parents, but when it is used, it seems to generate high anxiety and is more effective in eliciting immediate compliance than any other method. As with power assertion, there is little evidence that the compliance that love withdrawal generates is anything but short term (Maccoby & Martin, 1983).

Induction refers to parents' use of explanation: giving reasons for rules ("If everybody touched the paintings they would soon be very dirty from fingerprints") and appealing to children's desires to be grown-up ("Big girls don't take toys away from babies"). "Other-oriented" explanations seem to be especially powerful in promoting empathy ("When you hit people, it hurts them and makes them sad"). Using induction seems to be the most effective way to promote the internalization of rules, so that children regulate their own behavior by the standards they have learned regardless of whether authorities are present and whether immediate consequences are likely. For example, Laible and Thompson (2002) observed mothers with their 30-month-olds in contexts where conflicts were likely to arise, such as a cleanup task and a "frustration task" where children had only a too-difficult puzzle to play with while their mothers were busy and while other more interesting toys were off-limits. The more mothers used inductive control strategies, like justification ("We can't touch those toys because they might break"), and the less they used more punitive or aggravating control strategies, like threats, teasing, and harsh commands, the more likely their children were to exercise self-control in a resistance to temptation task 6 months later.

Many studies have found that the same parents may use one practice on some occasions and another in other situations, and sometimes parents use multiple practices in the same disciplinary episode (e.g., Hastings & Grusec, 1998; Kuczynski, 1984). But most parents favor using one type of practice more than the others, and when they do, their primary practice is somewhat predictive of certain child outcomes. But, much as we found with rearing practices in infancy, such as breast versus bottle feeding, particular practices may be less important than the overall quality of the parent–child relationship. For toddlers and older children, the meaning that the child attributes to parents' practices is likely to be important and appears to be tied to the emotional climate established by parenting style (Darling & Steinberg, 1993). In particular, when parents are warm and responsive, their children are more likely to comply with parental demands (e.g., NICHD, 1998).

Parenting style, then, affects how effective a parenting practice will be with a child (Darling & Steinberg, 1993). As it happens, certain practices tend to be combined with certain parenting styles. Authoritative parents, for example, are often characterized by extensive use of induction, regardless of what other practices they might sometimes use. As we have seen, the children of authoritative parents are likely to show higher levels of competence, self-esteem, and self-regulation than children exposed to other parenting styles. But what might happen if parents who show most of the qualities of an authoritative style—especially high responsiveness and high demandingness—were to use primarily power assertion to enforce their demands? In the next section, we will consider how parenting style interacts with practice for different children and in different cultural contexts, focusing on what we are learning about how these factors interact in the early phases of self-development, during the toddler and early preschool years. We will revisit these issues in later chapters when we describe self-regulatory and moral development in older children and adolescents.

Moderators of Parenting and Parenting Effectiveness

Authoritative parents seem to get the best results from their children, but are their behaviors really having any influence? Both developmentalists (e.g., Scarr, 1993) and popular writers (e.g., Harris, 1998) have asked whether we are wrong to assume that correlations between parenting and child outcomes imply that parenting style and practice are actually causing children's behavior. Several other possibilities exist. First, the shared biological inheritance of parents and children might account for both the parental and the child characteristics measured in these studies (Scarr, 1993, 1997). For example, the same genetic endowment that makes parents affectionate and responsive might produce children who are cooperative and good-natured. Second, children's predispositions and temperaments may actually cause parents' behaviors rather than vice versa. For example, perhaps children who are "naturally" sunny and compliant could elicit authoritative parenting, but hostile, negative children might elicit more authoritarian or neglectful parenting behaviors.

Overall, although controversy persists on these issues, most researchers and clinicians take a multidimensional approach to the question of direction of effects in children's social development (e.g., Bell & Chapman, 1986; Collins et al., 2000; Kochanska, 1993; Lytton, 1990). That means that multiple causes are thought to be interacting, mutually modifying one another. As in Bronfenbrenner's bioecological model, proximal processes—reciprocal interactions between the child and the people and things that surround the child—as well as distal processes, such as genes and culture, are all playing a role (e.g., Bronfenbrenner & Ceci, 1994; see also Chapter 1). In this section, we will consider two important factors in the multidimensional mix: the child's temperament and the broader cultural environment.

THE CHILD'S TEMPERAMENT, PARENTING, AND CHILD OUTCOMES

Recall that in infancy, both parents and infants contribute to the quality of the caregiving relationship. It is harder for mothers to be sensitive and responsive to a baby with a difficult temperament, for example. But when mothers are highly responsive during infancy, the good fit they create between their caregiving and the baby's needs supports the development of a secure attachment even for babies with difficult temperaments. When mothers are not able to create a good fit, the type of insecure attachment that emerges often seems to be at least partly influenced by the baby's temperament (e.g., Kochanska, 1998).

With toddlers and preschoolers, temperament and other child characteristics continue to contribute to the quality of the parent–child relationship. Children's typical behaviors can affect both parenting style and the particular disciplinary practices that parents are most likely to use.

Time out when well-implemented is an effective disciplinary strategy with young children.

Bell and Chapman (1986) reviewed 14 studies that demonstrated the influence of children on parents. Many of these studies were at least partly experimental, with adults (usually parents) reacting to, or interacting with, children who were not their own, in situations created by the researchers. The studies examined adults' responses to children's dependence versus independence behaviors, their tendencies to be aggressive or to withdraw, and their responsiveness to adults (e.g., tendencies to smile, chat, imitate, and so on). For example, in one of these studies, Marcus (1975, 1976) showed parents videotapes of a child actor solving a puzzle. The child in the film behaved either dependently (e.g., seeking help, like, "Would this piece go better here or here?") or independently. The adults' reactions were more directive with the dependent than with the independent child. Stevens-Long (1973) examined parents' reactions to unrelated children's aggressive, uncooperative behavior or to anxious, withdrawn behavior. The adults were more likely to command or ignore the more aggressive children, but to verbally help or reward the more depressive children. Bell and Harper (1977) found that adults used more power assertive behaviors with socially unresponsive girls and more inductive behaviors with girls who were highly responsive. All of these studies demonstrate that adults' reactions are moderated by the characteristics or behaviors of the particular child with whom they are interacting.

Studies such as these, along with research on parents with their own children, have begun to paint a picture of a multilayered, complex interactive system between parent and child. The child's characteristics are likely to affect the parent's behavior, and the parent's style and practices affect the child's behavior. But other factors modify parents' and childrens' effects on each other. The degree to which the child affects the parent's practices and beliefs depends in part on the parent's initial attitudes toward children and child rearing, as well as the parent's emotional state and ability to manage stress. For example, parents who have child-centered rather than adult-centered concerns are able to be more supportive and responsive to their youngsters. Parents' emotional states influence how child centered they are likely to be. Depressive mothers report fewer child-oriented positive emotions and concerns than nondepressive mothers (Dix, Gershoff, Maunier, & Miller, 2004). Similarly, as we saw in the last chapter, parents' own relationship histories and their working models of attachment are likely to influence how they respond to their children and how well they adapt to their children's characteristics. How parenting affects the child depends in part on the child's temperament, abilities, and vulnerabilities! The following study of aggressiveness in toddlers provides a good illustration of some of these interactive complexities.

CHILD TEMPERAMENT, PARENTS' NEGATIVITY, AND TODDLERS' AGGRESSIVENESS

In a study by Rubin, Hastings, Chen, Stewart & McNichol (1998), 2-year-olds who frequently expressed negative emotion, especially anger, and low levels of behavioral and emotional self-control were considered to show "emotion dysregulation," one feature of a difficult temperament in toddlers. These children were not wary when a stranger approached them with new and unusual toys, and they showed strong frustration and distress when they were unable to get a toy out of a container or when asked to wait briefly before drawing with a new set of crayons. Other studies have found a connection between difficult temperaments in young children and aggressive, disruptive behavior (e.g., Zahn-Waxler, Iannotti, Cummings, & Denham, 1990; see also Lytton, 1990), but the correlations are low, suggesting that other factors are also important. In this study, the researchers found that the link between difficult temperament and aggressive behavior depended on parents' reactions to their children's temperaments. Those boys who showed emotion dysregulation, and who also had mothers who responded with negative control (such as being physically intrusive) and with hostile emotion (such as frowning, criticizing, yelling), were the children who were at high risk to be aggressive with peers. When mothers showed high levels of warmth (positive tone, praise, verbal affection, and so on), boys with difficult temperaments were not likely to be aggressive. Note that mothers' negative control and hostile emotion failed to predict aggressive behavior in children who did not have difficult temperaments, or in girls, so that both child characteristics and mothers' behaviors played important roles in children's aggressive behavior.

THE CULTURAL CONTEXT, PARENTING, AND CHILD OUTCOMES

Just as children's characteristics can affect parenting and outcomes, cultural factors, such as the race, ethnicity, and socioeconomic class of the family, can moderate parenting practices and may even alter their effects. In particular, the constellations of parenting behaviors that "go together" seem to be somewhat different across cultures. For example, European American parents who are warm and responsive also tend to use gentle parenting practices—offering suggestions, making polite requests, distracting a child, using induction, and so on. But Harwood, Schoelmerich, Schulze, and Gonzalez (1999) found another pattern of associations between parents' warmth and parenting practices in Puerto Rican American mothers as they interacted with their 12- to 15-month-olds. They found no differences between the two ethnic groups on maternal warmth: Both European American and Puerto Rican American mothers tended to be affectionate and committed to providing a supportive emotional climate for their toddlers. But the Puerto Rican mothers were more directive and more likely to issue commands. Consistent with other research on European Americans, the Anglo mothers were more likely to let their toddlers try to do things for themselves and were more likely to make suggestions than to issue commands. These differences in mothers' behavior were consistent with their long-term goals. Puerto Rican mothers were more concerned about "sociocentric" outcomes, focusing more on wanting children to recognize their obligations and their connectedness to others. In this study, Anglo mothers were perceived as emphasizing "individualization" as a long-term socialization goal, valuing assertiveness and self-reliance. Clearly, to the extent that parenting goals differ across cultural groups, parenting practices are likely to differ as well.

As we have noted, disciplinary practices that involve physical punishments have been associated with externalizing, aggressive child outcomes. Actual physical abuse (inflicting bodily injury by beating, kicking, punching, scalding, and so on) is consistently associated with problematic child outcomes like conduct disorders and depression (see Baumrind, 1997; Deater-Deckard & Dodge, 1997). But even the use of more normative physical punishments, like hitting, spanking, and paddling, is linked to aggression and other types of misbehavior in children. For example, in a large study of mother-child pairs, Straus and his colleagues (1997) asked mothers how often they had spanked their child in the last week when the children were between ages 6 and 9. The

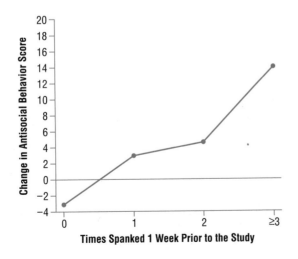

FIGURE 5.1

Change in antisocial behavior from 1988 to 1990 for children aged 6 to 9 years as a function of spanking.

Source: Strauss, M., Sugarman, D. B., & Giles-Sims, J. (1997). Spanking by parents and subsequent antisocial behavior of children. *Archives of Pediatric Medicine, 151*, 761–767. Reprinted by permission of the American Medical Association.

Box 5.2 | *Popular Views of Parenting: What Should We Believe?*

Child-rearing "experts" abound in today's society, each touting his or her own set of certainties about how to raise good or happy or successful kids. Popular beliefs about effective parenting have varied from one historical era to another, and, like today, even within each era there has been wide divergence among the kinds of advice that parents could confront. Consider these two wildly different suggestions. The first is from an *Infant Care* bulletin published by the U.S. Department of Labor in 1914, a tract heavily influenced by animal studies of associationism. It seems insensitive to the emotional needs of both the child and the parent, emphasizing routine over all else.

> A properly trained baby is not allowed to learn bad habits. It is a regrettable fact that the few minutes of play that the father has when he gets home at night, which is often almost the only time he has with the child, may result in nervous disturbance of the baby and upset his regular habits . . . much of the play that is indulged in is more or less harmful. (As quoted in Lomax, Kagan, & Rosenkrantz, 1978, p. 130)

In contrast, the second example, from a *Parents Magazine* article in 1950, is based on a misinterpretation of Freudian ideas and seems remarkably overindulgent of children's emotional excesses, with no regard for control. As described in Lomax et al.:

> mothers were told that they must learn to face and accept all types of emotional outbursts on the part of their children, so that the children would not become fearful of their own feelings. . . . "we should feel suspicious of ourselves when we react strongly to something as absurdly simple, for example, as a child calling us names." (p. 66)

Ironically, as Lomax et al. note, Freud actually expected that parents *would* set limits on their children's antisocial behaviors.

Today, some self-styled "experts" advocate a "return" to authoritarian parenting from earliest childhood, reacting to what they perceive as overly permissive trends (Bolotin, 1999). These "traditionalists" encourage parents not to be child centered. John Rosemond, for example, exhorts parents to make their marriage the focus of attention. Children, he argues, acquire self-esteem from successfully facing hardship and frustration. Give them a lot of responsibility for household chores, and punish all disobedience with unpleasant, memorable consequences. He has expressed disdain for parents who place a high priority on having a "warm and fuzzy" relationship with their children (Rosemond, 1991). Gary and Anne Marie Ezzo, a former pastor and his wife, advocate "biblical principles" for families, among which they include: expecting immediate obedience to first-time directions or commands; feeding babies on a schedule and expecting them to sleep through the night when they are 8 weeks old; potty training by 18 to 24 months, with children accountable for their own cleanup of toilet "accidents" by 30 months; and the use of corporal punishment, starting with hand swatting or squeezing in infancy and moving to spanking with something that creates "a sting" by 18 months (Ezzo & Buckman, 1995, 1999). What is especially notable in the advice of these and other "traditionalists" is their lack of concern for what researchers describe as the "warmth factor" (see text): parental responsiveness to children's needs, high levels of expressed affection, and willingness to listen and explain. Their emphasis is clearly on the "control factor" alone: take care of the child's need for discipline and all else will follow. They also ignore data indicating that mild power assertion is often more effective than severe forms and that the children of parents who use physical punishment tend to be physically aggressive themselves.

What is a parent to do, and how can a counselor help guide inexperienced or dissatisfied parents as they struggle to sort through the confusing array of advice? The most valuable guidance a counselor can offer is advice informed by research. From research reviewed in this and other chapters on social development, it is clear that parents have an abiding influence on their children's development, although outcomes are the product of many interacting factors, including temperament differences among children and family and cultural context. It is also clear that *both* parental warmth *and* control are important. Awareness of such information can help parents evaluate the suggestions they encounter. For example, is it true, as Rosemond argues, that self-esteem is a product of accomplishments that include overcoming hardship? It sounds sensible, but the data indicate that the picture is much more complex. Parents' responsiveness and sensitivity to children's individual and developmental needs are core elements of successful parenting. Making children do things that are too difficult for them is insensitive—in such a case, hardship seems unlikely to lead to anything but frustration and a sense of defeat or abandonment for the child. Rigid age formulas are therefore a risky business. For example, many 2-year-olds may be ready to potty train quickly, but some are not. Many 8-week-olds probably cannot sleep through the night, because they get too hungry or because their neurological systems are too immature to maintain such a routine.

But when parental demands are embedded in a context of warmth, so that they are appropriately keyed to the child's emerging skills, and when children feel safe expressing their own feelings and concerns, high levels of demandingness do indeed seem to be associated with feelings of competence and self-confidence. Authoritative, not authoritarian, parenting has the best track record.

researchers measured children's antisocial behavior then and over the course of the next two years. As you can see in Figure 5.1, more frequent spanking at the first assessment predicted increases in the children's antisocial behavior over the next two years. This was true regardless of the family's social class, ethnicity, the child's gender, or maternal warmth.

Other researchers have found, however, that the effects of spanking and other normative forms of corporal punishment vary somewhat in different cultures. In European-American samples, there is a linear relationship between amount and harshness of physical discipline and children's aggressive behavior. The more severe the punishment, the more aggressive children are likely to be. For African American children, this relationship has been found in some studies (e.g., Nix et al., 1999), but a number of researchers either have reported no association between harsh punishment and aggressiveness in children (e.g., Baumrind, 1993; Deater-Deckard, Dodge, Bates, & Pettit, 1996), or they have found that harsh punishment is related to less aggressive outcomes (Lansford, Deater-Deckard, Dodge, Bates, & Pettit, 2004). This kind of reversal has been reported for some Mexican American groups as well (Hill, Bush, & Roosa, 2003).

Although the findings are inconclusive at the present time, some explanations for inconsistency across ethnic groups have been submitted. It may be that the meanings children attach to the discipline their parents use makes a difference. So, for example, some children might interpret their parents' high levels of control and use of physical discipline as an expression of caring and protectiveness. Harsh discipline may be seen by both adults and children in some cultural groups as an indicator of parental concern and involvement (e.g., Deater-Deckard & Dodge, 1997; Hill et al., 2003; McLoyd & Smith, 2002).

Thus, the way that these practices affect children may depend in part on how clearly they are connected to parents' positive feelings for, and concerns about, their children (Darling & Steinberg, 1993; Dix, 1991). McLoyd and Smith (2002) looked at outcomes across a 6-year period in nearly 2,000 American children. For all children, African American, European American, and Hispanic, amount of spanking in the home predicted the level of children's problem behavior over time. But mothers' emotional support of their children moderated this link in all three groups. Thus, physical punishment was clearly a risk factor for children. However, when mothers were warm, positive, and supportive the risk was reduced, and at the highest level of maternal warmth spanking was not associated with behavior problems. In other words, when physical punishment was part of a more authoritative parenting style, its consequences were moderated by the protective factor of parental warmth. But as part of an authoritarian style, physical punishment was a strong predictor of conduct problems (see also Baumrind, 1997).

It may be that when we find racial or cultural groups in which harsh discipline is not consistently associated with negative outcomes, it is because physical punishment is more often used by parents who show high levels of warmth and positive regard for their children. Under such circumstances, the negative impact of such discipline appears to be reduced.

Two points are important to keep in mind, however. First, parents who physically punish their children are modeling the use of aggression to solve problems. They need to consider whether this practice reflects a moral principle that they want their children to learn. Children can be expected to perceive physical aggression as an acceptable means to the attainment of at least some ends. So, on the whole, using physical punishment increases the risk that children will use aggressive behavior to achieve their goals (Gershoff, 2002). Second, power assertion of any type can be effective for short-term control of children's behavior, but appears to have little influence on the goals that parents want most to achieve with discipline—the development of self-regulation and morality. Considering these two facts, parents may be well advised to avoid the use of corporal punishment.

CONSCIENCE: THE BEGINNINGS OF A MORAL SELF

You can see that research on parenting supports the many theories of self-development that emphasize the importance of social interactive experiences in the development of the self-system. Parenting style especially has been found to correlate with children's self-esteem—how worthy and competent children feel—and it appears to be linked to self-confidence in social interaction.

Children whose parents are child centered, responsive, and warm tend to show high levels of self-esteem, and they are likely to be skillful in social interaction, as evidenced by peer acceptance and teacher ratings of social competence. These findings suggest that Erikson (1950/1963) may have been on the right track when he argued that after initial feelings of worth are laid down in late infancy, these feelings will be reworked by the child as she changes. For example, as toddlers become more capable of self-sufficiency, they acquire needs, such as autonomy and control needs, that sensitive, responsive caregivers accommodate. If a toddler's needs are met in a positive, affirming way, the child will go beyond having global feelings of worth and will acquire more differentiated feelings of competency.

Parenting appears to contribute to other aspects of the developing self-system as well. In particular, parenting style and practice are related to children's self-regulation, including the child's ability to "generate socially approved behavior in the absence of external monitors" (Kopp, 1982, p. 200). This last ability is assumed to be a function of **internalization**, the process by which children adopt adults' standards and rules as their own. Internalization, in turn, is associated with the development of **conscience**, feelings of discomfort or distress when the violation of a rule is contemplated or carried out. Internalization and conscience formation are both aspects of the broader topic of moral development and will be discussed again in later chapters as we look at the course of moral development in older children, adolescents, and adults.

At this point, let's take a closer look at the complex connections among early parenting, the beginnings of self-regulation, and the associated processes of internalization and conscience formation. We have already noted that children can begin to learn self-control when they can understand and remember adults' behavioral commands—when statements such as "No cookies before dinner" have meaning for them—certainly during their 2nd year. At about age 2, children often begin to show signs of emotional distress if a standard is violated (e.g., Cole, Barrett, & Zahn-Waxler, 1992; Hoffman, 1970; Stipek et al., 1990) and soon after they can show strong reactions if they are tempted to break a prohibition (Emde & Buchsbaum, 1990). At the same time, toddlers begin to offer comfort to others in distress (e.g., Zahn-Waxler & Radke-Yarrow, 1982).

Two aspects of parenting seem to promote these processes (Kochanska, 1995). First, parents' warmth and responsiveness facilitate compliance (self-control) and promote the development of

Social interactive experiences contribute to children's developing self-systems.

concern for others (Maccoby & Martin, 1983). Sensitive, responsive parents seem to establish a cooperative, mutually responsive relationship with their toddlers—an ongoing secure attachment—and toddlers tend to be eager to maintain such relationships. Second, children's anxiety or emotional arousal seems to play a role in their willingness to comply and in the internalization of standards. Hoffman (1983) proposed that a parent's discipline causes a child to feel anxious arousal. He proposed that mild arousal helps the child pay attention but is not really upsetting. When a child is aroused enough to take notice, but not to be especially fearful, she is likely to notice, to try to understand, and to remember the parent's "socialization message." She may attribute her own compliance with the rule to her acceptance of it, which is a step toward internalization of the rule. But if the child experiences intense arousal during a disciplinary episode, she may pay more attention to concerns other than the socialization message. She might notice, and later remember, how scared she is, for example, of her parent's loud and angry voice, and then attribute her compliance to these factors rather than to the standard or rule that could have been learned. Hoffman's ideas help explain why mild power assertion is more effective for long-term internalization of rules than harsh power assertion. His views are also consistent with findings that induction—parents' use of explanation and reasoning—is helpful for internalization. Children are more likely to remember and accept rules they can understand.

If anxious arousal is an important ingredient in how children respond to their parents' discipline, individual differences among children in how easily their anxiety is aroused should also be important (Kochanska, 1993). In other words, temperament differences among toddlers should influence the early development of conscience. For fearful children, gentle discipline that deemphasizes power and emphasizes requests and reasoning should be sufficiently arousing to produce optimal effects. But what about children who are not easily aroused—who seem almost fearless? Do they need harsh discipline to be sufficiently aroused to pay attention? To find out, Kochanska (1995) studied 2-year-olds' committed compliance, that is, their eager and enthusiastic willingness to go along with their mothers' requests. Committed compliance in 2-year-olds is predictive of measures of internalization and conscience in the later preschool period (Kochanska, Aksan et al., 1995). Kochanska found that toddlers' fearfulness is indeed an important ingredient in the effectiveness of mothers' discipline. Highly fearful children, as expected, showed the most committed compliance if their mothers used gentle discipline. Harsh discipline was not as effective. However, neither gentle nor harsh discipline was more effective in promoting compliance for the most fearless toddlers! For them, only the security of their attachment to their mothers made a difference. Securely attached, fearless toddlers tended to show committed compliance, but insecurely attached, fearless toddlers were much less likely to do so. We can begin to see why correlations between parenting behaviors and child outcomes tend to be moderate. Parenting clearly is important, but it works somewhat differently with different children.

To clarify Kochanska's findings, imagine a 2-year-old, Joel, who tends to be more fearful than the other children in his play group. For example, he holds back and ducks his head when a supervising adult offers him a turn to ride the new "race car" at the neighborhood playground, even though many of the other children are clamoring for a turn. When Joel's mother encourages him gently to participate in a cleanup session, explaining how much help it would be, he is quite cooperative. She tells an observer that she never "yells" at him because he gets so upset that it is counterproductive. José's mother, on the other hand, says that her son seems unfazed by yelling. José does not seem to be afraid of anything. He can't wait for his turn to ride the new race car, and the fact that the supervising adult is a stranger is of no concern to him. Fortunately, José and his mother seem to share a warm relationship, and José, too, cooperates enthusiastically when his mother asks him to help with the cleanup. Andrew, another toddler in the play group, seems a lot like José in his fearlessness. He is panting to ride the race car and to try all the toys in the playground, and he marches right up to the supervising adult, asking for help. But there seems to be very little warmth between him and his mother, and when she asks him to help out with cleanup, he ignores her. Even when she gives him a shove and speaks sharply to him, he only halfheartedly moves to pick up a toy and abandons the cleanup effort almost immediately.

In sum, parenting influences the development of the self-system in early childhood. Which aspects of parenting will be influential depends in part on the particular child. For the development of self-regulation, the quality of attachment, grounded in warm, responsive caregiving, may be all-important for some children. For others, particular parenting practices (methods of control) also play an important role.

APPLICATIONS

Because the stages of infancy and early childhood have long been viewed as important ones for later socioemotional development, it is worthwhile to attempt to link theories of early attachment, self-development, and parenting into a framework that provides a working knowledge for counselors. Crittendon's (1994, 1997) insightful theoretical formulation is a good starting point because it knits together these three topics and attempts to explain the effects of sensitive and insensitive parenting on children as they get older.

Building a Self Through the Attachment Relationship

In Crittendon's view, attachment classifications are linked to operant conditioning processes. Securely attached infants and toddlers receive predictable, soothing care when their physiological needs, fear, aggression, excitement, or anxiety threaten to overwhelm their capacity for homeostatic regulation. These children learn that expressions of their positive as well as their negative feelings (anxiety, distress, and anger) are acceptable because they will be tolerated by a caregiver who accepts and helps them. In other words, they are positively reinforced for expressing both positive and negative feelings. Let's consider an example that might apply to adult students. Imagine a time when you were close to despair because of all the work you had to do. You had a number of responsibilities to complete at your job, you had family obligations to attend to, and your professors were being unreasonably demanding about their assignments! On top of everything, you felt tired and on the verge of getting your annual cold. Your level of crankiness increased significantly, suggesting that you were starting to lose some emotional control. Now imagine that some loving person in your life approached you, and instead of telling you to "grow up," was able to see through the irritability to the anxieties underneath. This person offered to help shoulder some of your burdens. Emotionally you experienced what amounts to a sigh of relief. You were able to function much better with the support, and your sense of yourself as a valuable and loved person increased greatly. In this supportive context, you would probably be even more receptive to constructive suggestions about how you might schedule your time to improve your situation.

Although this example is not a strict analogy to early experience, young children have special needs for caregiver support to help them regulate their emotions and internalize positively valenced self-understanding. Crittendon believes

that secure reciprocity with a caregiver allows the child to be open to both cognitive and affective experiences, gradually building procedural models of the self as competent to communicate with the caretaker, able to manage affect with the caretaker's reliable help, and able to accept and express both positive and negative parts of the self. Essentially, the positive message the secure child encodes is that she is a valuable and loved person even when she's not being particularly grown up. Crittendon believes that these repeated dyadic patterns of attachment are encoded as procedural memories that serve as precursors to the mature self.

The Emotionally Constricted Self

In contrast, insecure-avoidant infants who learn that displays of distress elicit rejection, punishment, or withdrawal become conditioned to inhibition of affect. These infants are, in fact, punished for their emotional displays, so these children come to actively avoid or block out perceptions that arouse their feelings because of the aversive consequences. Crittendon and DiLalla (1988) have reported that even very young children who have been severely abused actively block out information about their own feelings and demonstrate false affect—that is, affect that is superficially positive and incongruent with true feelings. Consistent with the general assumption of attachment theory, this pattern of avoidance is adaptive for an early nonresponsive caregiving environment but may have significantly negative consequences for later functioning. A highly defended or "false self" (Kernberg, 1976; Miller, 1981; Winnicott, 1965) may result from the inhibition of affect because the child distorts or mistrusts the evidence of her feelings. This situation effectively reduces the information that the young child can access in constructing the self. The message the child encodes is that feeling anger or distress is unacceptable and should be avoided because the expression of these feelings distances the caregiver, emotionally if not physically. The child views the self as able to communicate with caregivers only if her own emotional needs are kept in check. Positive aspects of the self may be expressed, but negative aspects, such as emotional neediness, need to be repressed.

Avoidant children who have learned that emotional expression can be dangerous take on the responsibility of their own emotion regulation without seeking caregiver help. They function defensively to keep the caregiver "close but not too close" (Crittendon, 1994, p. 95). To cope with this style of parenting, they learn a style of relating that involves repressing emotions that might anger or distance their more authoritarian caregivers. Negative affect (feelings of distress, sadness, anger) is not well integrated into the self-system, and a false self develops that is biased in favor of its "good" parts and against its more shameful ones. These avoidant or defended children may appear self-reliant to their parents, who may not be very responsive to their children's feelings anyway. In extreme circumstances, these children may demonstrate what Bowlby called compulsive caregiving. This is the pattern of taking emotional care of a caregiver. A pattern of compulsive self-sufficiency represents an opposite yet equally unhealthy result. These children are at risk because they appear so self-possessed. A closer look reveals their self-evaluations to be based on others' negative appraisals, including shaming for their expressions of dependency or needs for closeness. Parents of these children can be helped to develop the nurturant side of authoritative parenting by using some of the attachment-related approaches described in Chapters 3 and 4.

The Emotionally Volatile Self

Insecure-anxious infants learn that their displays of distress elicit unpredictable results, sometimes positive and sometimes negative. They essentially lack a method of communicating with the caregiver that works reliably, possibly because of inconsistent or sometimes neglectful parenting. Consequently, they experience the "anxiety of unresolvable arousal in which desire for the attachment figure, distress at her absence, and aggression toward her are all felt concurrently" (Crittendon, 1994, p. 93). Their model of themselves becomes one of incompetence with respect to communicating with a caregiver. Ultimately these children learn they can trust neither their affect nor their cognitions. However, they may learn that escalation of affect often works best in getting their caregivers' attention. These children might develop highly coercive strategies (aggressiveness or tantrums) and very coy behaviors (disarming manipulation) to maintain proximity. The self incorporates messages that reflect its ineffectiveness in communicating its needs to caregivers. Their aggressive behavior threatens the caregiver ("You must listen to me!"), whereas their coy behavior disarms ("Please don't get angry at me"). This pattern has been hypothesized to represent the child's attempts to cope with an unpredictable and inconsistent parental environment. Parents of these children might describe them as "out of control."

Not all noncompliant child behavior problems are due to early insecure attachments, however. Children may discover, as they become more independent and more verbal, that coercion works well in getting them what they want. Patterson (1982; see also Reid, Patterson, & Snyder, 2002), who studied the development of defiance in children, maintains that an intermittent (or inconsistent) schedule of reinforcement sustains the coercive child's behavior problems. A pattern of negative reinforcement, when the cessation of a stimulus increases the frequency of some behavioral response, follows the child's display of intense negativity or misbehavior. For example, a parent might tell her 4-year-old to go upstairs because it is time to go to bed. The little boy, detesting this interruption of his play time, begins to whine. The parent repeats her command several more times only to be met by continued resistance. The parent's patience begins to thin and she escalates into threats, which, according to Patterson's research, are usually not carried out. Instead, the parent appeases the child out of guilt or exasperation. The parent gives up and the child's noncompliance is reinforced. This pattern strengthens the child's coercive interaction style, which with time and repetition can become the predominant mode of communication. Ironically, Patterson believes that coercive children do not really want parents to give in. Instead, they crave the predictability that derives from knowing what their limits are and the security of knowing that parents will enforce them. Coercive children, however, need help developing a communication style that expresses their needs more directly so that caregivers will understand and respond appropriately. If left unchecked, child noncompliance can be a significant risk factor for later maladaptive outcomes, such as peer rejection and aggression. In such situations, some parent training is generally a very good idea.

Why Train Parents?

Parent training (PT; Patterson, Chamberlain, & Reid, 1982), or parent management training (PMT; Brestan & Eyberg, 1998), has the distinction of being one of a relative handful of therapies deemed efficacious for children (Kazdin, 2003). Studies have shown that PT is more effective in reducing noncompliance and promoting prosocial behavior, especially for children ages 4 through 8, than alternatives such as family therapy, relationship therapy, or play therapy (Feldman & Kazdin, 1995). The term *efficacious* is applied to therapies that have demonstrated empirical support. This is very good news, given the protective power of authoritative parenting to reduce risks for many concurrent or later disorders and its ability to greatly improve positive outcomes for children (Steinberg & Avenevoli, 2000). Authoritative parenting enhances security of attachment and provides children with a positive context in which to learn socialization skills. Difficulties with child behavior and discipline are frequently reported referral problems for parents. Even if these problems are a rather more intense version of normal developmental strains and even if they never materialize into more significant problems, the burdens on families who are trying to cope with them can be great. Parent training can substantially strengthen the limit-setting side of authoritativeness, improve the quality of life in the home, and reduce stress for parents who must grapple with children's noncompliance.

In some cases, an added parent management component can make a good therapeutic program even better. For example, in the case of treatments for ADHD (attention deficit hyperactivity disorder), a multimodal treatment that included medication and behavioral (including parent management) treatment demonstrated an advantage over medication alone for children with comorbid conditions (anxiety or conduct problems), for children with more highly educated mothers, for members of minority groups, and for families who learned to improve their discipline techniques via this training (as cited in Arnold et al., 2004). The principles involved in parent management training have also been effectively adapted to classroom management for teachers.

Parent training is successful, no doubt, because it has a strong theoretical rationale. It draws on a set of well-established principles from operant conditioning and social learning theory that can be used in individual counseling, group counseling, psychoeducation, and consultation. The empirically supported benefits that accrue to PT, however, have been documented in outcome studies that involve sustained work with a parent or couple over the course of several sessions. Moore and Patterson (2003) note that a typical course of treatment takes an average of 20 hours of professional time. Whereas benefits of well-delivered programs can be great, they are most effective for families with young children. Given the developmental needs of older children and adolescents, training for their parents should take into consideration adolescents' need for some measure of personal control and autonomy by incorporating skills in decision making and negotiation into the counseling.

How Does Parent Training Work?

Effective parent training programs incorporate a few essential elements (Kazdin, 1991; Moore & Patterson, 2003).

1. These programs are directed toward parents or guardians; children are not directly involved in treatment. An exception to this is treatment with adolescents, which typically does require the adolescent's participation.
2. Parents are taught to observe and define their children's noncompliance in behavioral terms. They are instructed to note their own part in interaction cycles that reward and sustain noncompliance. The most problematic behaviors and their prosocial opposites are identified.
3. Basic principles of learning theory, such as reinforcement, shaping, mild punishment, generalization, and so on, are taught to parents, used to illustrate the nature of parent–child interactions, and applied in contingent

ways to achieve the goals of treatment. These principles provide the basis for therapeutic change.

4. Parents (with the counselor's help) put these ideas to the test at home. Target behaviors that parents wish to modify are identified, skills are practiced in sessions using role-play, modeling, therapist feedback, and discussion. These techniques are then employed in the home, and the results of the new behavior management strategies are recorded, reviewed, and further developed during subsequent sessions.

Parent management approaches depend upon the careful application of behavioral principles. Therefore, the therapist who uses this modality needs to understand behavioral terms correctly, must be precise about selecting and defining target behaviors, and must be able to identify contingencies that increase or decrease behavior. One method involves asking parents to identify two to four of the child's behaviors that are most problematic. This is often supplemented by the use of more formal observational assessment tools. Moore and Patterson (2003) report that a typical initial concern can be defined as "minding" versus "not minding." Once the parents are helped to notice the context wherein the "not-minding" occurs, principles like positive reinforcement (using tangible objects or the very powerful attention of parents), mild punishments (like time-out or restriction of privileges), and shaping (rewarding closer and closer approximations of "minding" with social praise) can be incorporated into some contingency management system. Contingency management involves presenting and withdrawing reinforcers and punishments in a systematic and consistent way to effect behavioral change. The linchpin of these approaches is the mindful use of positive reinforcement, a particularly potent response from parents when it comes in the form of warm encouragement, acceptance, and attention. A correct understanding of concepts like negative reinforcement, which is central to understanding the coercion cycle (Patterson, 1982) and which is distinct from the concept of punishment, is particularly important as well. Daily documentation of progress can be a useful part of the program, helping parents become more consistent in their use of techniques.

Forewarned Is Forearmed

Higher rates of noncompliance appear to occur at certain times throughout the day (7:30 a.m., 11:30 a.m., 5:30 p.m., and 8:30 p.m; Goodenough, 1931, as cited in Moore and Patterson, 2003). Consider this scene in the Arnold family. Mom, whose shift at work ends at 5:00 p.m., has just returned from the babysitter's house with her 6-year-old twins. Both children are hungry and tired from a long day at school. Yvonne needs help with a homework project; Kenney

has a Cub Scout meeting at 6:30 and needs to find some items for the pack's activity. As their mother struggles to put together a meal, the children become more intense in their demands for her attention. Pretty soon, they are fighting with each other. She yells at them to stop, but this only makes matters worse. Yvonne ends up in tears and Kenney runs to his room. No one feels like eating dinner.

What makes scenes like this one so recognizable to so many people? The rates of noncompliance rise when several factors intersect: changes in biological states, a spike in demands for compliance, and simultaneous transitions that are occurring for all members of the system (parents and children). Because these are predictable, the use of contingency management skills, especially positive encouragement, and establishment of consistent routines can help parents navigate these flash points more successfully.

The Flexible Work of Parenting

It would be incorrect to assume that the quality of the early attachment relationship will automatically be transformed into a complementary pattern of parent–child relationships in early childhood. That is, it is not necessarily the case that every securely attached baby becomes a securely attached preschooler, and so forth. But, as our discussion of parenting style in the toddler and preschool years illustrates, the elements of sensitive parenting that characterize the infancy period are not much different from those that are right for preschoolers. The specific parenting behaviors might change, but the underlying requirement to be psychologically available and sensitive to the child's developmental needs and capabilities remains the same. For the most part, messages about the self-in-relationship that the child has internalized become the foundation for more mature interactions. Cicchetti and Toth (1994) believe that the negative adolescent and adult self-views that undergird many psychological disorders stem from insults to the self experienced during childhood. Consequently, clinicians need to apply primary prevention strategies to strengthen early parent–child relationships.

As children get older, they should be provided with experiences that allow for the growth of mastery, autonomy, and self-efficacy. Parent education and discussion groups can be helpful forums for parents in which to gain support for their strengths and to learn about the developmental needs of toddlers and preschoolers. Parents sometimes construe insensitive parenting to mean actions that are mean or rejecting. But intrusive interference, such as picking up the child to give her a hug when she is absorbed in an activity, or arbitrarily restricting a child's mobility, may also be insensitive to the child's needs if done repeatedly. Of particular relevance to self-concept development is educating parents about the implications of their language when conversing with their children. Insulting or insensitive remarks, particularly those intended to shame the child, should be avoided lest they become part of the young child's self-concept.

The growth of a healthy self-system depends upon an environment that provides the child with love and limits appropriate to her developmental level. When the proximal environment is distorted, as is the environment of defended and coercive children, youngsters will make adaptations. However, their adaptations will come with a cost to the development of a child's true self. Fostering the growth of the authentic self in infancy and early childhood sets the child on a developmental pathway that will support healthy functioning at every stage thereafter.

SUMMARY

The Self-System: Traditional Conceptions

1. Some traditional theorists viewed the self-system as multidimensional. William James, for example, distinguished between the self-as-subject, as active agent or "I", and the self-concept, the object of our own observations and evaluations, or the "Me." The "I" is continuously experienced, is distinguished from others, and is an agent of action. The "Me" consists of personal attributes, the material (or physical), social, and spiritual characteristics of self. Self-esteem, the evaluation of one's attributes, can be good, bad, or neutral. The valence assigned to one's own attributes depends on the number of successes we enjoy relative to our aspirations.

2. James Cooley introduced a developmental perspective into theorizing about the self. Self-representations are constructed from our interactions with others, especially caregivers. We build a looking-glass self that reflects our view of how others see us.

3. George Herbert Mead added that language and society contribute to shaping the self-system. There are culturally determined differences in people's preferred ways of viewing themselves. For example, Japanese emphasize affiliations in their self-descriptions, whereas Americans emphasize more individualistic qualities.

The Early Development of the Self-System

4. The pre-self that develops in infancy begins with early inklings of one's body permanence and separateness from others that are derived from the regularity and reliability of infant–caregiver interactions. Procedural representations of interactions are established and may promote a budding sense of mastery by the second half of the 1st year, if babies' behavior controls caregiving responses. A sense of self as self-in-relationship begins to emerge. By the end of the 1st year, separation distress signals the baby's deepening understanding that the other is separate. Additional indicators include the baby's tendency to explore more readily in the presence of a familiar caregiver. If the caregiver provides a secure base, the baby in a sense has the self-worth or confidence to explore. Social referencing also implies recognition of separateness. All of these indicators of a growing sense of the self as separate emerge from and depend on the baby's relationship to others.

5. Toddlers in the second year engage in joint reference, suggesting the earliest inkling that some separate experiences are shared—the first sign of a sense of mind. Self-recognition is demonstrated as early as 15 months in tests of mirror recognition. It is a strong indicator that children are forming a self-concept, or a "Me." After the second birthday, children begin to use self-descriptive words. Self-evaluation or self-esteem advances with self-recognition, with abused children showing signs of poorer self-esteem than nonmaltreated children from the beginnings of mirror recognition. Gradually, more differentiated self-descriptions emerge, with preschoolers describing more concrete characteristics, such as "little," and older children beginning to refer to more abstract, less obvious qualities, such as "funny."

6. Self-control and self-regulation are dependent on the development of the emotion regulation that begins in infancy. The attentions of a caregiver when an infant is aroused (e.g., hungry) help the baby return to a more comfortable emotional state. The interaction process gives a baby outside assistance with affective control. The caregiving relationship is the context in which the infant's own capacity for emotion regulation develops.

7. Behavior regulation begins in the 2nd year when toddlers achieve objective self-recognition. The simultaneous emergence of symbolic or representational thought and other cognitive skills allow the child to begin learning and storing rules or standards of conduct. By late in the 2nd year, self-conscious emotions emerge, such as embarrassment or guilt, emotions that require awareness of self and of others' judgments. Between 2 and 3, children show some such emotions when they realize they have broken a rule or made a mistake. Once these capacities are in place, self-regulation can begin. How its

development proceeds depends on many factors, especially socialization processes.

Early Socialization: Parenting and the Development of the Self-System

8. As the infant becomes a toddler, her needs shift from total dependency to growing independence, and the parent–child relationship reorganizes such that sensitive responsive caregiving begins to include efforts to socialize the child—to shape or control the child's autonomous action, so that she remains safe and behaves in culturally appropriate ways.

9. Two dimensions of parenting style, parents' approach to caring for and disciplining their children, are important. First is warmth or parental responsiveness, which includes affection, acceptance, involvement and interest, and so on. Second is control or parental demandingness, the degree to which parents impose and enforce standards of conduct.

10. Four parenting styles can be described, crossing the positive and negative poles of the two dimensions. Authoritative parents are high on warmth and on demandingness. Authoritarian parents are low on warmth but high on demandingness. Permissive parents are high or moderate on warmth but low on demandingness, and neglecting or uninvolved parents are low on both dimensions. Authoritative parenting is associated with the most positive outcomes in child development, including adaptability, competence, good social relations, low levels of antisocial behavior, high self-esteem, and good self-regulation. The correlations between parenting styles and outcomes are significant but moderate, indicating that such outcomes are also influenced by other factors, not just parenting style.

11. Parents use a variety of methods of control. Power assertion, which involves either physical punishment or withdrawal of privileges, tends to be effective for immediate control of behavior, but may not have longer term benefits, and harsher forms can have some negative side effects, such as increased aggressiveness in children. Love withdrawal generates high anxiety and elicits immediate compliance, but seems to have few effects on long-term self-regulation. Induction, providing explanations and emphasizing benefits to the child and to others, seems most effective for promoting internalization of rules and longer term self-regulation.

12. Are parenting practices actually having an effect, or are there other reasons why parenting is correlated with child outcomes? For example, could it be that the correlation is the result of shared inheritance of traits between parents and children? Data support a multidimensional approach. Parenting, genetics, child temperament, and other factors all contribute to child outcomes.

13. Parenting practices are partly the result of child characteristics, such as temperament traits. For example, adults are more directive with dependent than with independent children. Also, the effectiveness of different parenting practices is partly a function of a child's temperament. For example, toddler boys with difficult temperaments respond with high levels of aggressiveness when parents use physically intrusive control methods, whereas boys with easy temperaments do not.

14. The broader cultural context seems to have an influence on parenting practices and may have an impact on their effectiveness. For example, Puerto Rican American mothers emphasize sociocentric goals with their young children, whereas European American mothers focus more on individualization. Some parenting practices may have different meaning, and therefore different outcomes, depending on ethnicity and culture. For example, some evidence suggests that physical punishment is less clearly associated with increased child aggressiveness in African American children than it is in European American children.

Conscience: The Beginnings of a Moral Self

15. Parenting affects the developing self-system in many ways. Children's self-esteem is related to their parents' warmth and responsiveness. Children's self-regulation is associated with parenting style and practice. A child's ability to monitor her own behavior even in the absence of authority figures is considered a function of internalization, that is, the degree to which she has adopted standards and rules as her own. Internalization is associated with conscience, feeling distress when one violates a rule.

16. Children are more cooperative and compliant when they share a warm, responsive relationship with a parent. Their compliance can also be related to anxious arousal. Hoffman argued that mild arousal can help children pay attention to a rule, but doesn't make them so anxious that they pay attention only to how afraid they are. This is consistent with the finding that mild power assertion practices are more likely to lead to children's internalization of rules and long-term compliance than strong or severe power assertion practices. Further, Hoffman's ideas help explain why children who have fearful temperaments respond best to gentle discipline, but children who are fearless are unfazed by either gentle or harsh disciplinary practices. The most important determiner of compliance for fearless children is the warmth of their relationship to the parent.

CASE STUDY

Terry and Bill, married for 5 years, are a Black couple who live in a small suburban community. Terry graduated from high school and worked as a receptionist before her marriage to Bill, a telephone company manager. Because both of them believed that mothers should stay at home with young children, Terry quit her job when she had her first child, who is now an intense and active 4-year-old daughter named Dawn. Both parents were very attentive to their daughter and enjoyed caring for and playing with her when she was a baby. As Dawn got older, she became more active and assertive. When Dawn fussed, resisted, or showed frustration, Terry was patient and affectionate with her. She was able to coax Dawn out of her bad temper by making up little games that Dawn enjoyed. Both Terry and Bill liked Dawn's spirited personality. Because her parents wanted her to have access to playmates, Dawn attended a church-related program for toddlers and preschoolers three mornings a week.

When Dawn was 3 years old, Terry gave birth to the couple's second child, a son named Darren. Soon after the baby's birth, the family learned that Darren had a congenital heart problem that would require ongoing medical treatment and a specific regimen of care at home. Darren was an irritable baby. He fussed for long periods and was very difficult for Terry to soothe. Because of Darren's need for medical care and the limitations of Bill's medical insurance, the couple soon found themselves in financial difficulty. Bill began to take on overtime work at the phone company to subsidize some of the bills and was away from the home several nights a week and part of each weekend.

Terry found the care of two demanding young children and the worries about money to be increasingly more stressful. She was always tired and seemed to have less patience with her family. When she once had the leisure time to read to Dawn, to take her for walks, and to help her master tasks that proved frustrating, Terry now had to shift her attention to the care of her medically fragile infant. Because Dawn looked so grown-up compared to the vulnerable newborn, Terry began to perceive her daughter as able to do many things for herself. When Dawn demonstrated her neediness by clinging or whining, Terry became abrupt and demanded that Dawn stop. Many battles revolved around Terry's new rule that Dawn have a nap or "quiet time" each afternoon so that mother and baby could get some rest.

One day, Dawn's preschool teacher, Mrs. Adams, asked to speak with Terry. Mrs. Adams noted that Dawn's behavior was becoming a problem in the morning preschool sessions. Dawn had begun throwing toys when she became upset and often refused to cooperate in group activities. Terry was greatly embarrassed to hear about her daughter's misbehavior. Dawn was the only Black child in the small class, and her mother wondered if this was part of the problem. When Terry got home, she put her tearful, clinging daughter in her room for time-out for being bad at school. She loved Dawn, but she could not tolerate this kind of behavior, especially when Darren needed so much of her time. She began to wonder if she and Bill had spoiled their daughter. Terry feared that Dawn would have problems when it came time for her to enter kindergarten if they didn't take a strong stand with her now.

Discussion Questions

1. Explain Dawn's behavior from an attachment point of view. How would you describe Dawn's attachment history?
2. Describe Terry's parenting style. Has the style changed? What suggestions would you make to Terry and Bill about handling this problem?
3. What are some of the contextual influences on Dawn's behavior?

JOURNAL QUESTIONS

1. How would you describe your parents' parenting style?
2. What kinds of discipline were used in your family? What would you advise other parents about disciplining their children?
3. What do you believe is the relationship between your early self-development and your later self-esteem?

KEY TERMS

self-system	pre-self	self-control or behavior	discipline
"I-self" or self-as-subject	representations of	regulation	warmth dimension (parental
"Me-self" or self-concept	interactions (RIGs)	self-regulation	responsiveness)
self-esteem	social referencing	self-conscious emotions	child centered
"looking-glass self"	self-recognition	socialize	parent centered

control dimension (parental
   demandingness)
maturity demands
parenting styles
authoritative style
authoritarian style
permissive style

neglecting–uninvolved
   style
externalizing problems
internalizing problems
method of control
power assertion
love withdrawal

induction
time-out
internalization
conscience
anxious arousal
committed compliance
compulsive caregiving

compulsive self-sufficiency
negative reinforcement
ADHD (attention deficit
   hyperactivity disorder)
contingency management
   system

Now go to our Companion Website to assess your understanding of chapter content with Multiple Choice Questions, apply comprehension in Essay Questions, and broaden your knowledge of development with related Web Links.

CHAPTER 6

Realms of Cognition in Middle Childhood

In the preceding chapters, we have described some of the major developmental tasks and achievements of infancy and the preschool years. The pace of developmental progress is quite remarkable during those periods, and much of the foundation for later achievements is laid down. Consider, for example, the qualitative difference between the skills of a newborn and those of his 6-year-old sibling. Development has been so rapid during this first 6 years that it is not uncommon for parents with a newborn second child to view their older child as having grown up, almost overnight, because of physical size, motor skills, and verbal ability. However, children in middle childhood, the years spanning the elementary school period, are still far from grown up. Their growth takes on new forms in this stage, metamorphosing into ever more highly differentiated patterns of cognitive, emotional, and social functioning.

For children at the start of the middle years, school and its peer group structure represent a new frontier. The movement into the school years ushers in a whole new set of developmental challenges for children. Youngsters at this age must spend longer periods away from home and adjust to more rigorous schedules. They must learn to control their behavior, monitor their attention, and acquire more formal and more complicated academic competencies than had been formerly attained. They must make friends and learn to navigate the schoolyard, with its greater demands for athletic prowess, social skill, and cooperative negotiation of conflicts. They must also learn the rules of the group and when to abide by them. They must learn what it means to be male or female, not to mention what it means to be themselves. So many challenges await them.

However, children at elementary school age are also more adept at almost every task when compared to their preschool-aged siblings. Observing the eagerness and energy young children exhibit in the early school years makes it easy to understand the capacity for industry that Erikson described (see Chapter 1). For most children, the challenges of school and peer group will be mastered gradually, and in many different ways. Armed with foundational skills in language, mobility, understanding of self and others, and self-control, the youngster is now poised to assume membership in a larger social network.

Clearly, the years of elementary school, as the years to follow, are marked by ups and downs. These normal fluctuations create opportunities for helpers to provide support or guidance for children, their families, and their teachers. What are the cognitive, emotional, and social needs of children at this stage? What approaches are most helpful given children's developmental level? In the next two chapters, we will attempt to provide you with information that will be useful when working with children at this point in their development. Your understanding of cognitive development, the focus of this chapter, will enable you to understand children's ways of construing the world, helping you appreciate their academic needs as well as the intellectual bases for their friendships, gender roles, moral understanding, and conflicts.

PHYSICAL AND BRAIN-RELATED CHANGES

During the first 2 years of a child's life, physical growth is very rapid. As the child moves closer to the school years, growth slows down a bit, becoming steadier and more even. However, not all youngsters grow and mature at the same rate. A look at a typical second-grade classroom will make this point obvious. Children come in all shapes and sizes, and these differences are relevant to what children think about themselves and how they are perceived and accepted by other members of their social network.

Motor development improves greatly over the preschool to school years. Elementary school children make great strides in motor coordination. At 6, most children can ride a bike, skate, climb trees, and jump rope with ease. The development of gross motor coordination is followed by refinements in fine motor development. By 8 or 9, most children have mastered the fine motor coordination needed to write, draw, and use tools. Eye–hand coordination also improves, as demonstrated by legions of youngsters on the T-ball or softball fields.

Changes in the brain underlie these achievements and the cognitive advances that we will describe later in this chapter (e.g., Janowsky & Carper, 1996). Improvements in coordination are benefited by maturing of the corpus callosum, which provides a network of connecting fibers between the right and the left hemispheres, and by the maturing of the cerebellum, which plays a large role in motor learning (Diamond, 2000). The part of the brain that is involved in alertness and consciousness, called the reticular formation, myelinates throughout childhood and into adolescence. This ongoing process coupled with increased synaptogenesis in the frontal lobe area results in increases in attention, concentration, and planning abilities. Roughly by age 7 or 8, frontal lobe maturation has also contributed to children's increasing ability to inhibit inappropriate responses and block out extraneous stimuli, although this process continues through and beyond adolescence (Diamond, 2000; Siegler, 1998). It is hard to imagine a child successfully negotiating the years of formal schooling without the capacity to sustain attention and to show increased control over thinking and behavior. Certain association areas of the cortex that are involved in cross-modal processing of information are not myelinated until around age 8. These areas are instrumental in the development of higher order thinking skills. Later in childhood and continuing into adolescence, changes in the frontal cortex are correlated with improvements in memory for verbal material (Sowell, Delis, Stiles, & Jernigan, 2001).

Changes in the brain's development and functioning also influence the acquisition of basic academic skills. Recent advances in technology have provided new information about how the brain works and what may go wrong when children can't learn. For example, in the area of mathematics, we know that adults generally perform calculations by relying heavily upon previous rote learning and retrieval of number facts from verbal memory, a left-hemisphere function. Children, on the other hand, rely more heavily on concept formation, strategy use, and reasoning, utilizing right-hemisphere capacities. Once the number facts and basic arithmetic procedures have been learned, they become "automatic" and are carried out by left-hemisphere systems. In essence, arithmetic procedures that begin as novel, conceptual, and visual-spatial for the child eventually become routine for the adult (Rourke & Conway, 1997). This developmental trajectory can result in mathematical learning problems for children whose right-hemisphere functions are immature or compromised.

Studies of reading using brain imaging technology have illustrated the neural circuitry at work in the reading process. Roberts and Kraft (1987) demonstrated that among younger students (6- to 8-year-olds), reading activity is primarily centered in the left hemisphere. For older students, (10- to 12-year-olds), reading activity is more evenly distributed between left and right hemispheres, demonstrating the effects of brain maturation, practice, and more strategic, planned approaches to reading.

Increased knowledge about brain development and functioning has contributed to our understanding not only of the normal cognitive achievements and limitations we will describe in this chapter but also of the specific learning difficulties some children experience in the school years. In general, clinicians need to remember that there is a significant amount of unevenness in brain development among all children at this age (Berninger & Hart, 1992). Even for normal children, relatively poor performance in isolated skills, such as problems with letter or number recognition or letter reversals in writing, is quite common. Despite the cognitive achievements of school age children, brain maturation is far from complete. Myelination continues, particularly in the frontal lobes, until at least the early 20s (Sowell, Thompson, & Toga, 2004).

COGNITIVE DEVELOPMENT

When children leave behind the preschool years, they begin to seem much more "savvy" to adults. They can be given fairly complex responsibilities ("Take out the dog before you go to school, and don't forget to lock the door after you leave"). They can participate in discussions of local or world events, and they often appreciate humor that would have been lost on them earlier. The cognitive developments that underlie these new capacities have been described and studied from several different theoretical traditions. We will first present Piaget's characterization of cognitive change in middle childhood.

Piaget's Stage of Concrete Operations

Since the days of Christopher Columbus, we have been teaching children that the earth is round. Of course, it looks flat, especially if you live somewhere in the midwestern United States, such as Minnesota. How do children reconcile what they are told with what they perceive? When Vosniadou and Brewer (1992) asked Minnesota school children in Grades 1 through 5 about this apparent contradiction, they got some surprising answers. Figure 6.1 illustrates a few of them. Some children said the earth was a flat disc—like a coin. Some thought it was a ball that has a flat surface within it and a domed sky overhead. Others saw the earth as spherical but with a flattened side where people live. The researchers found that the older the child, the more likely he

FIGURE 6.1

Children's Images of a Round Earth

Source: From Mental models of the earth: A study of conceptual change in childhood by S. Vosniadou and N. F. Brewer in *Cognitive Psychology*, Volume 24, p. 549, copyright 1992, Elsevier Science (USA), reproduced by permission of the publisher.

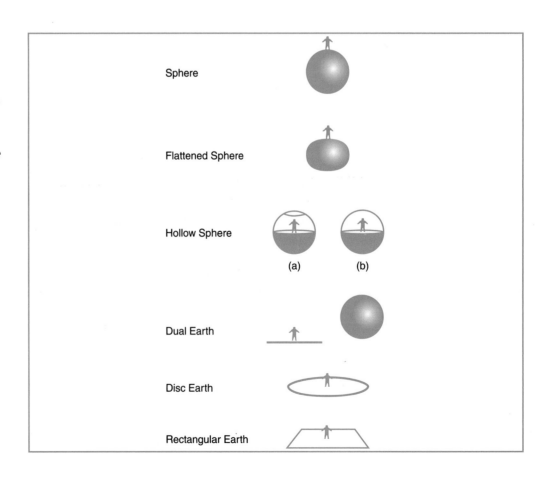

was to represent the earth as the sphere that scientists believe it to be. But even in fifth grade, 40% of the children still had some other idea of what it meant for the earth to be round.

The inventive solutions of the Minnesota kids in the round earth study remind us of what Jean Piaget considered the fundamental characteristics of learning and cognitive change. As we saw in Chapter 3, he stressed that knowledge is not just stamped in by experience or teaching; it is constructed. Children assimilate new information, meaning that they change it, interpreting it in ways that fit in with what they already know or with the way their thinking is structured; they also accommodate their existing knowledge structures, adjusting them somewhat. If new information is presented in ways that do not match children's current understandings, their resulting understanding probably will not be completely consistent with reality or with the information that adults mean to convey. Gradually, as new experiences are assimilated and accommodated, better approximations of reality are achieved.

You'll recall that despite the gradual construction process that Piaget described, in which knowledge structures are continually changing, he considered there to be stages of thought development, so that within a relatively broad period of time, children's thinking about many different things has some similar organizational properties. We have already discussed some of the characteristics that Piaget attributed to the sensorimotor (0 to 2 years) and preoperational (2 to 6 or 7 years) stages (see Chapter 3). In this chapter, we will be considering his view of children's thinking in the **concrete operational stage**, the period spanning the elementary school years from about age 6 to 12.

To understand how Piaget described the thinking of young school-aged children, recall the limitations of the younger, preoperational thinker. Generally, preschoolers focus on one salient dimension of a situation at a time, and so they often miss the important relationships among aspects of a situation. Logical thinking is difficult to characterize, but it certainly includes the ability to recognize and take into account all of the relevant information in a problem situation and then to identify how those pieces of relevant information are related to each other. Consider the following simple problem in deductive logic: "All glippies are annoying. George is a glippy. Is George annoying?" To answer correctly, you must take into account a number of pieces of information—that there are glippies, that they are annoying, that there is an individual named George, and that George is a glippy. The important relationship you are then in a position to identify is between George and the glippies: he's one of them. From there you can infer that George is, indeed, annoying.

As we saw in Chapter 3, in very simple situations, even preschoolers can sometimes take into account more than one piece of information at a time. For example, sometimes they can solve very simple deductive inference problems (e.g., Blewitt, 1989; Smith, 1979). But more often, their thinking is centered, making it seem quite illogical. Remember the number conservation problems that Piaget invented? Let's consider another kind of conservation problem, in which children must infer that an object remains the same weight even if you change its shape. Imagine two balls of clay of identical size and shape. If we put them on a balance scale, we find their weight to be equal. Now, suppose we roll one ball into the shape of a snake so that it is long and thin. Despite its different appearance we have not adjusted its weight, so it will still be equivalent in weight to the other ball of clay. Preschoolers typically predict, however, that the weight will now be different—they often say it will be lighter than before because it's so skinny, or they might say it will be heavier because it's longer. They focus on one salient dimension and predict weight differences between the ball and the snake based on that dimension. But if they took into account both length and width, they might recognize that the changes in the two dimensions have compensated for each other, and so the weight is the same as before, even though it is differently distributed.

When children are in the concrete operational stage, they usually answer conservation questions correctly. They may look at the snake and say "it looks lighter than before" but they can logically conclude that it remains the same weight as the ball. Piaget argued that their logic is dependent on being able to see and understand the relationship between length and width changes—that one perfectly compensates for the other. Because they can decenter (think about more than one dimension of the situation at once), they can discover the relationships among those dimensions.

The compensatory relationship between the length and width of the clay snake is a kind of reversible relationship. In essence, one change reverses the effects of the other change. Piaget thought that being able to recognize reversible relationships is especially important for solving many kinds of logical problems, allowing children a deeper understanding of the world around them. For example, before he achieves concrete operations, a young child might learn the following two number facts: "2 + 1 = 3" and "3 − 1 = 2." But only when he recognizes reversible relationships is he likely to realize that the second fact is the inverse of the first and therefore that they are logically connected. If the first fact is true, then the second fact must be true. To put it differently, knowing the first fact allows the child to deduce the second one if he can think reversibly. When children's thinking becomes efficient enough to decenter, and thus to identify reversible relationships, children can begin to draw logical conclusions in many situations. This is the hallmark of the concrete operational child.

Piaget also identified limits to concrete operations. School-aged children seem to be most capable when the problems they are solving relate to concrete contents, and they seem to expect their solutions to map onto the real world in a straightforward way. But when a problem is disconnected from familiar, realistic content, these children have a difficult time identifying the relevant aspects of the problem and finding how those aspects are related to each other. In a classic example, Osherson and Markman (1975) asked children to say whether certain statements were true, false, or "can't tell." The experimenter made statements such as "The (poker) chip in my hand is either green or it's not green." Sometimes the poker chip was visible; other times the chip was hidden in the experimenter's fist. If the chip were hidden, children in the elementary school years would usually say "can't tell," asking to see the chip to judge the statements. But the statement's truth was not determined by the actual color of the chip; it was determined by the linguistic elements in the sentence and the relationships between them (e.g., "either/or"). No check with the concrete world was necessary or even helpful. A chip, any chip, is either green or it's not. In other words, the abstract, formal properties of the statement, not concrete objects, were the contents of importance. Concrete operational children find it difficult to think logically about abstract contents, and they seek out concrete or realistic equivalents to think about in order to solve a problem.

Children's tendency to "hug the ground of empirical reality" (Flavell et al., 1993, p. 139) is especially obvious when they need to think logically about their own thinking. Suppose for a moment that you are a child who believes that you're more likely to hit a home run playing baseball if you wear your lucky socks. To test this theory scientifically, you would need to weigh the evidence, pro and con. But before you could do this effectively, you would need to recognize that your belief about your lucky socks is really an assumption or a theory, only one of many possible theories. As such, it could be wrong. Because you already believe your theory, it will seem like a fact to you. You would need to apply careful logical thinking to your own thought processes, first to distinguish your belief from true facts or observations and then to see the relationship between your theory and those facts. However, if you are 8 or 9 years old, you have trouble thinking logically about anything abstract, and theories (or thoughts) are certainly abstract. So, logically evaluating any of your own beliefs or theories is not likely to be easy for you.

What we are describing is a form of egocentrism that emerges in middle childhood. The term egocentrism refers to some failure to recognize your own subjectivity. You fail to see things realistically because you are, in a sense, trapped in your own perspective. Preschool children often exhibit what Piaget called preoperational egocentrism (see Chapter 3): They have trouble recognizing that their own mental experiences are private and may not be shared by others. By about 5 years, children's theory of mind includes knowing that people can have mental experiences that are not all the same from one person to another. So, their preoperational egocentrism recedes, and their ability to take another person's perspective begins to improve. (As you will see later in this chapter, perspective-taking skills increase in complexity and subtlety throughout childhood and adolescence.) But in middle childhood, difficulty thinking logically about abstract contents makes elementary-school-aged children vulnerable to another form of egocentrism: failure to distinguish between their own assumptions or theories and objective fact (see Elkind, 1981; Looft, 1972).

As a result, researchers have found that although elementary-school-aged children can think scientifically sometimes, identifying simple theories and checking them against evidence, they make a muddle of it if they already believe a certain theory (e.g., Kuhn, 1989; Schauble, 1991). It is easy to understand why elementary school children might have difficulty believing that the earth is really round, because they can't observe it. Children get better at evaluating their own theories as they move into adolescence and become capable of what Piaget called formal operational thought—logical thought about abstract contents. As you will see in Chapter 9, adolescents often extend their logical thought processes to many kinds of highly abstract contents, including their own thinking (although even adolescents and adults find this kind of abstract thinking a challenge and may fall into the same egocentric traps as concrete thinkers).

Even though middle childhood has its cognitive limitations, Piaget was onto something in identifying it as a time when children can be expected to think logically. In every culture in the world, adults seem to recognize that somewhere between ages 5 and 7 children become more sensible, reliable problem solvers. In societies with formal schooling, kids are sent to school to work at serious tasks that will prepare them to take their place in the community of adults. In societies without formal schooling, children are given real work to do by age 6 or 7, tasks that are essential to the community (such as watching the younger children, planting, or shepherding).

Piaget's description of the concrete operational child as a logical thinker about concrete contents has proved a useful one, and it seems to capture the typical cognitive characteristics of middle childhood quite well. However, as we saw in Chapter 3, newer work makes it clear that there are at best fuzzy boundaries between the stages Piaget proposed. How advanced a child's thinking will be and what kinds of content a child can think logically about depend on many factors. One important factor is the amount of prior experience a child has had with the domain of knowledge (or particular subject matter) that he is thinking about. If a child has a lot of knowledge about a particular domain, say dinosaurs or chess, his ability to think logically about problems within that domain may be more advanced than in other content areas (e.g., Chi, Hutchinson, & Robin, 1989). Of course, the child may appear more logical simply because he has seen other problems of the same sort more often and can remember effective solutions, so his better problem solving may have less to do with more advanced thinking than with memory for past experiences (see the section in this chapter on memory development; e.g., Anderson, 1980). But it also seems to be the case that a child or adult with a lot of domain knowledge is better at identifying the important features of a problem within that domain and at identifying the relationships among those important features (Flavell et al., 1993). Thus, logical thinking may be at least somewhat domain specific (that is, applicable to a particular area of knowledge) rather than strictly domain general and determined by one's stage of development, as Piaget's theory implies. For a kid who loves experimenting with chemistry sets, reasoning about chemistry may advance more quickly than for a child whose passion is music.

These children's interest in and experience with their hobby may help them think more logically about problems in this domain.

In the next sections, we will consider some other ways of characterizing children's cognitive abilities in the middle years, especially the information processing approach. We will examine what we have learned about some abilities, combining research from the Piagetian, information processing, and other research traditions.

An Alternative Perspective: The Information Processing Approach

Many interesting studies of middle childhood cognition—especially memory and problem solving—have been done by researchers in the information processing tradition. Information processing theories compare cognitive functioning to a computer's processing of information (see Chapter 1). The structural organization of the cognitive system is thought to be the same throughout development. A typical example of the kinds of structural components through which information is thought to "flow" during cognitive processing is presented in Figure 6.2. In this view, there are no qualitative, stagelike changes that characterize most of a child's thinking or processing. There are some changes with time, however, mostly in the amount and efficiency with which information can be processed. With increasing age, children can work with more information at once, and the strategies that children use to organize, understand, or remember information may also change. However, children apply different processing strategies to different specific contents, such as math, reading, and spatial concepts, so that strategies are not usually considered to be the result of broad cognitive skills that are applied across different domains. Instead, strategies appear to be largely domain specific.

Information processing researchers focus heavily on what children do with information of particular kinds: what they pay attention to, how they encode it, what and how much information they store, what other information they link it with, how they retrieve it. In other words, information processing theories are focused on the mechanics of thinking. Thus, whereas a Piagetian researcher might try to demonstrate that one cognitive achievement, perhaps in math, is related to another, perhaps in social perspective taking, to illustrate the global effects of some underlying stage characteristic, an information processing researcher typically tries to track the specific information handling that underlies a child's increasing mastery of a single domain.

The influence of both Piagetian and information processing approaches has fueled a rapid increase in our understanding of cognitive development, and it is not surprising that some theorists have attempted to marry the best components of both approaches. Typically known as **neoPiagetians**, these theorists explain Piaget's stages, or revise the stages, using many information processing concepts (Case, 1985, 1992; Fischer, 1980; Halford, 1993; and others). For example, Case (1985) specifies four stages comparable to Piaget's, but explains the transition from one to another partly in terms of increases in the capacity of **working memory**, the part of the cognitive machinery that holds information we are actively thinking about at the moment (see Figure 6.2, and below).

Let's now take a look at some of what we have learned about elementary school children's cognitive abilities.

Cognitive Achievements: Memory and Attention

Imagine a child who has just had his annual medical examination. With his parent's consent, an interviewer asks a set of questions to explore what he remembers about the experience. Some are open-ended questions, such as "Can you tell me what happened when you went to the doctor?" Others are specific yes–no questions, such as "Did she look in your nose?" A subset of the yes–no questions are strange or silly, such as "Did the doctor cut your hair?"

As you might expect, elementary-school-aged children usually answer such questions more accurately than preschoolers do. If you wait for several weeks and then ask about the doctor's exam again, a 3-year-old will forget more of what he could originally remember than a 7-year-old will. In one study, by 12 weeks after the checkup, 3-year-olds' responses to the silly questions were at chance levels of accuracy (meaning that they were saying "yes" to about half of the silly questions), but 7-year-olds averaged about 90% accuracy, despite the delay. The older children's answers had also remained relatively consistent over time, so that if they answered "yes" to a question right after the exam they tended to do so on repeated tests at later times (Gordon, Ornstein, Clubb, Nida, & Baker-Ward, 1991, as cited in Ceci & Bruck, 1998).

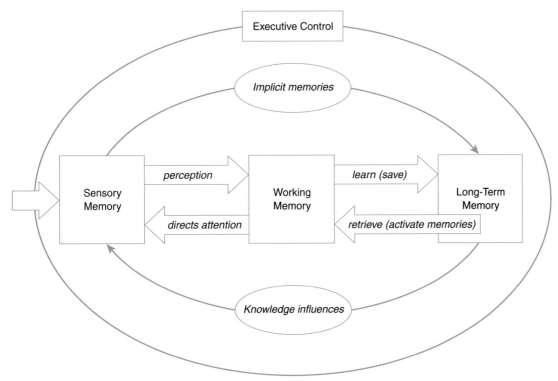

FIGURE 6.2

The Information Processing System

Source: From Anita Woolfolk *Education Psychology*, 9e, Active Learning Edition. Published by Allyn and Bacon, Boston, MA. Copyright © 2005 by Pearson Education. Reprinted by permission of the publisher.

Almost all aspects of memory seem to improve with age, at least up through young adulthood. As you will see, developmental changes in memory are affected by many characteristics of cognitive functioning and development. In this section, we will consider several contributors to memory improvement in the school years and beyond. But before we do, let's briefly define some of the terminology that is commonly used in discussions of memory. Many of these terms were first introduced by information processing theorists, and some are included in the information processing flow model depicted in Figure 6.2.

MEMORY TERMINOLOGY

First, we can describe memory as consisting of different memory stores. Sensory memory refers to a brief retention of sensory experience. For about one third of a second, when we first see a scene, we store most of the sensory information that has come in, almost as though our eyes have taken a snapshot of the whole scene. A similar phenomenon occurs with hearing. Interestingly, sensory memory does not seem to change much with age. Not much research has been done on sensory memory in very young children, but studies comparing 5-year-olds with adults indicate that children's sensory memory is just as good as adults' (e.g., Morrison, Holmes, & Haith, 1974). Working memory, also called "short-term store," is usually described as the thinking part of our cognitive system. Here we execute problem-solving strategies, make inferences, and transfer information into long-term memory, the almost unlimited store of knowledge. The information we pay attention to in working memory comes from our immediate sensory experience and from long-term memory. For example, suppose you are watching a movie about an African adventure, and an array of color and movement suddenly fills the screen. Your working memory combines the sensory data coming from the screen with information drawn from long-term memory to create a meaningful interpretation: It's a charging zebra. Or suppose your supervisor reminds you that your counseling approach to a client's new problem is similar to one that was not very successful in the past. Your thinking about the strategy (in working memory) includes elements of the supervisor's input with stored memories of prior interactions.

Unlike long-term memory, working memory is thought to have a limited capacity. We can pay attention to, and think about, a limited number of meaningful units of information at one time, and material is lost from working memory in 15 to 30 seconds unless we engage in rehearsal (i.e., unless we actually keep working with it, making an effort to pay attention, such as repeating it to ourselves). Generally, it seems that for sensory information to get into long-term memory, it must be attended to in working memory. For example, you may hear the music playing as the zebra on the screen charges, but unless you pay attention to it, you are not likely to remember it later. Or if you're mulling over another problem while your supervisor gives you feedback, you will be unlikely to profit from the comments. So, learning seems to require real work or effort. If you find you have to go back and reread a section of this chapter to commit it to memory, you are making the kind of mental effort that characterizes working memory and accounts for successful learning.

Learning, or acquiring knowledge, involves the storage of information. Retrieval is what we usually mean by remembering, that is, getting information out of storage so we can use it. In Chapter 3, we talked about two kinds of remembering or retrieval: recognition and recall. Recognition happens when the information to be remembered is immediately available to your senses. For example, you see your least favorite teacher from high school crossing the street in front of you, and you realize that you're experiencing someone who is familiar. Your sensory image elicits information about the teacher stored in long-term memory. We saw in Chapter 3 that some ability for recognition seems to be present from birth, and generally young children's recognition skills are very good, especially for visual-spatial information, such as memory for pictures. (Try playing the visual memory game "Concentration" with a 4-year-old. You might not win!) Recognition of verbally presented information shows more long-term developmental improvement (Schneider & Bjorklund, 1998).

Recall is more work. The to-be-remembered information is not present, and you must somehow draw it out of long-term memory and re-present it to yourself, as when you must answer an essay question on an exam. Or, as we described in the opening of this section, a researcher asks a child to remember what he experienced when he went to the doctor. When a child has problems with recall, it could be because he did not attend to the information in the first place, because he did not store the information in long-term memory despite having paid attention to it, or because the child does not have adequate strategies for finding the stored information. Clearly, recall is a multifaceted process.

One feature of human memory is that we can store different kinds of information or knowledge. Knowledge about facts and events, called declarative knowledge, is of two kinds. The first kind is semantic, which includes factual information ("the earth is round"), rules ("red lights mean stop"), and concepts ("an elephant is a large, gray animal"). The second kind is episodic, which refers to our knowledge of the events that we have experienced. When researchers ask children to recall their visit to a doctor's office or when your supervisor asks you to describe a counseling session, they are asking about episodic knowledge. Episodic knowledge is organized around time and space—what happened in what order, where, and when. After we've had several experiences with one kind of event, such as being examined by a doctor, we begin to form a schematic representation of the typical features of the event and the order in which they happen. This is called a script.

In addition to declarative knowledge, we have nondeclarative knowledge, knowledge that we cannot adequately put into words and that may not even enter our awareness. For example, you may know how to shift the gears in a standard transmission vehicle, but you might have a difficult time explaining how to do it. Many physical skills are based on this kind of unconscious, nondeclarative knowledge, which we usually call procedural. You may remember that we have used the term procedural knowledge to describe what infants "know" about how to do things or what to expect from interpersonal interactions (see Chapter 5). Early working models of attachment are probably a kind of procedural knowledge. Much of what infants and toddlers know seems to be nondeclarative rather than declarative.

Now that we have a vocabulary of memory terms, let's take a look at how memory seems to work in middle childhood, and specifically at what improves with age.

WHAT IMPROVES WITH DEVELOPMENT?

With age, working memory seems to expand. Like Piaget, most observers, regardless of theoretical orientation, have noted that older children usually pay attention to more pieces of information at one time than younger children. Digit span tests provide the standard demonstration of this change in working memory capacity. You may recognize them as a typical part of most intelligence tests. A series of digits are presented to the test participant, who must immediately say the numbers back in the same order. A child of 2 years can usually produce about a two-digit string; by the time he is 7, he will probably be able to remember a five-digit string. Adults, on average, can remember about a seven-digit string (hence, the standard telephone number; Dempster, 1981). But what actually accounts for these increases in memory capacity? There could literally be, somehow, more "room" in the older child's working memory. But many other cognitive changes seem to contribute and may actually be more important. We will consider several of these.

Processing Speed. The first cognitive change that contributes to memory improvement is that children can process information more quickly as they get older. Processing speed, such as how quickly children can make a simple response (e.g., pushing a button) to a stimulus (e.g., the onset of a light on a computer screen), increases from early to middle childhood and it continues to improve until about age 15 (e.g, Kail, 1991; Luna, Garver, Urgan, Lazar, & Sweeney, 2004). Piaget attributed the decentering skill of school-aged children (their ability to pay attention to more than one thing at a time) to the speeding up of mental activities with practice, and modern research does support the idea that practice can accelerate information processing. In addition, speed of processing can increase with physical maturation—that is, simply as a function of age (Kail, 1991). The upshot is that as children get older, they can do more with more information at one time.

Breadth and Depth of Knowledge. The second cognitive change that affects memory improvement is that as children get older their knowledge about many things increases: they expand their knowledge base. Consider the study of children's recall of a medical examination mentioned earlier. One reason that a 7-year-old might have recalled information more accurately than a 3-year-old is that the older child probably knew more about medical exams. By 7, a child has formulated a script of the typical medical exam. When an interviewer asks questions about a particular exam, even many weeks after it happened, the 7-year-old may not actually remember whether the doctor cut his hair, for example, but he knows that doctors don't do that sort of thing in medical exams, and so he answers correctly. In general, older children know more about most events, and so they are more likely than younger children to be able to reconstruct accurately what probably happened in any given situation.

It should be noted that prior knowledge can also lead to false memories. For example, in a number of studies, children have been shown videos or pictures of people playing roles such as that of a doctor or a nurse. Sometimes the gender of the adult is consistent with traditional expectations—such as a man playing the role of doctor—and sometimes the person's gender and occupation are not traditionally consistent: such as a man playing the role of nurse (e.g., see Bigler & Liben, 1992). Children's preexisting beliefs about gender and work roles—that is, their gender stereotypes—influence what they will later remember about what they saw. In one particularly interesting study, Signorella and Liben (1984) found that elementary school children with strong gender stereotypes were more likely than children with less stereotyped beliefs to misremember who had played what role in the pictures they had seen when gender and occupation were not traditionally matched. So, for example, if they had seen a woman doctor, the children with strong stereotypes would be likely to remember that it was a man they had seen instead, or that the woman had been a nurse. (See Box 6.1 for other examples of how false memories can be induced.)

In addition to prior knowledge affecting your ability to reconstruct what you've experienced, the more you know about a particular subject, or domain of knowledge, the more easily you can learn new information in that domain and the better you will remember it later. If knowledge in most domains expands with age, then learning and retrieval of information in most

| Box 6.1 | *Children's Eyewitness Testimony* |

The following is an experience reported by Bill, a 4-year-old:

> My brother Colin was trying to get Blowtorch (an action figure) from me, and I wouldn't let him take it from me, so he pushed me into the woodpile where the mousetrap was. And then my finger got caught in it. And then we went to the hospital, and my mommy, daddy, and Colin (older brother) drove me there, to the hospital in our van, because it was far away. And the doctor put a bandage on this finger (indicating). (Ceci, Loftus, Leichtman, & Bruck, 1994, quoted in Ceci & Bruck, 1998, p. 749)

Bill appeared to have a clear memory of this scary event, and he was confident even about details such as where his father was at the time of the accident. But the experience Bill could describe so convincingly never happened! It was a false memory, induced by a researcher who had read brief descriptions of a set of pictures to Bill each week for 9 weeks. The description for one of the pictures had said, "Got finger caught in a mousetrap and had to go to the hospital to get the trap off." The researcher then said, "Think real hard and tell me if this ever happened to you. Do you remember going to the hospital with a mousetrap on your finger?" In the first session, Bill said he had not had such an experience. By the tenth session, as you have seen, he seemed convinced that he had.

Preschoolers can have some difficulty with reality monitoring, distinguishing fantasies from realities. Young children *can* tell the difference between what is real and what is not and between what it feels like to only imagine something versus to actually experience it (e.g., Flavell, Flavell, & Green, 1987), but they have more difficulty with these distinctions than older children or adults (e.g., Foley, Harris, & Hermann, 1994; Parker, 1995). In particular, if they imagine an event, they are somewhat prone to say later that it actually happened. One charming and usually harmless example occurs when a child becomes devoted to an imaginary friend. But a young child's problems with reality monitoring can make him more susceptible to suggestion than older children or adults, a serious concern when children serve as eyewitnesses. Some interviewers and therapists in child sexual abuse cases, for example, use a professional technique called guided imagery as an aid to memory. A child might be asked to pretend that an event occurred, then create a mental picture of the event and its details (Ceci & Bruck, 1998; Gilstrap, 2004). Unfortunately, if an adult encourages a child to construct a fantasy about what *might* have happened, the child may eventually come to believe that it *did* happen, even if it did not.

In considering whether children should serve as eyewitnesses, the key issue is, how valid can children's reports be expected to be? In the late 1600s, children's testimony at the witch trials in Salem, Massachusetts, led to the execution of 20 defendants. Young girls testified convincingly that they had seen defendants doing fantastic things, like flying on broomsticks. Some of the testimony was later recanted, and the whole episode created such a negative view of children's testimony that for three centuries child witnesses were not often seen in American court proceedings. Only in the 1980s did many states end restrictions on children serving as witnesses (see Ceci & Bruck, 1998).

Modern memory research has helped increase the acceptance of children's testimony in America. Many studies indicate that what children remember *can* be accurate, although the number of details a child will recall and with what accuracy improves with age (see text). But at any age, a witness's memory for observed events could be incomplete or distorted or simply wrong, sometimes as a result of exposure to suggestion. And the younger the child, the more susceptible he is likely to be to suggestion (e.g., Ceci, Bruck, & Battin, 2000).

We have seen that preschoolers' difficulties with reality monitoring can be a source of suggestibility, and there are several other sources as well, many of which children might encounter in the course of being interviewed by parents, police, social workers, therapists, and other court officials. When interviewers are biased, they may guide children's testimony, planting suggestions without realizing that they are doing so. So, for example, if an interviewer is already convinced that a child has been abused, she may encourage a child's admission of abuse by asking leading questions, such as "Where did he kiss you?" instead of "What did he do?" The interviewer might also ask the same question repeatedly if the child's initial answers are not consistent with the interviewer's belief. Studies of interview transcripts indicate that even the most well meaning and concerned interviewers, including parents, use many such tactics to try to get at what they believe, or fear, is the truth (Ceci & Bruck, 1998). Unfortunately, they may be planting suggestions that can lead the child to reconstruct his memory of an event.

A study by Pettit, Fegan, and Howie (1990) is just one of many that illustrates how effective such suggestions can be with young children. Two actors visited a preschool classroom. They pretended to be park rangers and talked to the children about helping a bird find a nest for her eggs. In the middle of the discussion, one "ranger" knocked a cake off the top of a piano "by accident." The cake was smashed, and there was silence for a few moments in the classroom, creating a rather distinctive event. Two weeks later, each of the children in the class was interviewed about the incident. Before the children were questioned, the researchers gave some of the interviewers an accurate account of what had happened. Others were provided with false information, and a third group was given no information at all. An interviewer's instructions were to find out what had happened from each child, but without asking leading questions. Despite the instructions, the interviewers did ask leading questions—30% of the time—and half of these were misleading. Naturally, the interviewers who had false beliefs about the event asked the most misleading questions. And the children were often misled, agreeing with 41% of the misinformation suggested to them. Apparently, interviewers biased by false beliefs can unwittingly maneuver children into providing false information.

Elementary-school-aged children are clearly less suggestible than preschoolers (Ceci, Bruck, & Battin, 2000). For example, their reality monitoring is more adequate, and they are less affected by leading questions. But even older children and adults are not immune to suggestion (e.g., Ackil & Zaragoza, 1995; Loftus, 1979). Fortunately, witnesses of all ages can provide more accurate information if they are interviewed under conditions designed to minimize suggestion. A sweeping review of research on children's eyewitness testimony by Ceci and Bruck (1998) reveals a number of characteristics that may reduce the influence of suggestion in interviews. Of course, interviewers should avoid leading questions, as we have seen, and they should keep both the repetition of questions and of interviews to a minimum. The interviewer's tone should also be neutral, rather than urgent, aggressive, or accusatory. For example, an accusatory tone may be set by statements such as "Are you afraid to tell? You'll feel better once you've told." In one study, when interviewers made such comments, even children who previously indicated no recall of an event sometimes agreed with questions that incorrectly suggested abuse (see Goodman & Clarke-Stewart, 1991).

Interviewers should not use inducements such as telling children they can help their friends by making disclosures. In one criminal investigation, for example, investigators said things to children such as "Boy, I'd hate having to tell your friends that you didn't want to help them" and "All the other friends I talked to told me everything that happened. . . . You don't want to be left out do you?"(quoted in Ceci & Bruck, 1998, p. 745). Such pressure might have the effect of encouraging children to produce responses even when they do not recall the events in question. Another interview strategy to be avoided involves stereotype induction, that is, slanting the interviewee's view of an individual. Sometimes interviewers will encourage children to make revelations by indicating that the alleged perpetrator is a bad person or does bad things. But in studies where this strategy was implemented, young children were found to produce incorrect, negative recollections of such an individual's behavior more often than children who were not exposed to the induction (e.g., Leichtman & Ceci, 1995; Lepore & Sesco, 1994).

As Ceci and Bruck (1998) emphasize, interviewers are motivated by concern about the welfare of the child, "no interviewer sets out with the intention of tainting a child's memory" (p. 730). But even with the best of intentions, an interviewer can elicit questionable testimony. An understanding of the ways in which memory is constructed and reconstructed can help investigators to make eyewitness testimony, especially in children, more trustworthy.

domains should get better with age. But age is not what is most important—knowledge is. Suppose, for example, that we show an 8-year-old child a chess board with chess pieces arranged as if in the middle of a chess game. Later, we ask the child to reconstruct the placement of all the pieces on an empty board—that is, to recall the layout of the pieces. If the child happens to be an "expert" chess player—someone who plays in competitions and is highly knowledgeable about the game—his performance on this recall task will be much better than that of an average adult "novice," who knows how to play but who does not have extensive knowledge of the game. In other words, when children are more expert than adults in a domain of knowledge, they can remember more new information from that domain than adults can (e.g., Chi, 1978; Chi & Koeske, 1983). We will see later that other domains of knowledge, such as knowledge about others' perspectives and feelings, improve at this age and enhance social relationships.

Many studies suggest that as we amass knowledge of a subject, new information in that domain is understood more quickly and more completely. Some researchers describe the formation of a rich web of well-organized connections among the pieces of information in long-term store. For example, a counselor's concept of "therapy" might be part of a detailed web of stored information such as the one presented in Figure 6.3. We fit new information into this web, allowing us to retrieve it later through many routes and making it more accessible than if there were fewer connections. The processing speed for new information increases, and the depth of understanding is greater. All aspects of memory seem to be positively affected. Of course, ordinarily, the older you are, the more knowledgeable you are, and so the better you are at remembering, particularly in your area of expertise.

One advantage of a rich web of knowledge is that it allows chunking of information in working memory. Chunking is a process whereby we link several pieces of information together into a single meaningful unit. For example, suppose you were given the following series of numbers in a digit span test: 149217761929. You might notice that you could divide the series into

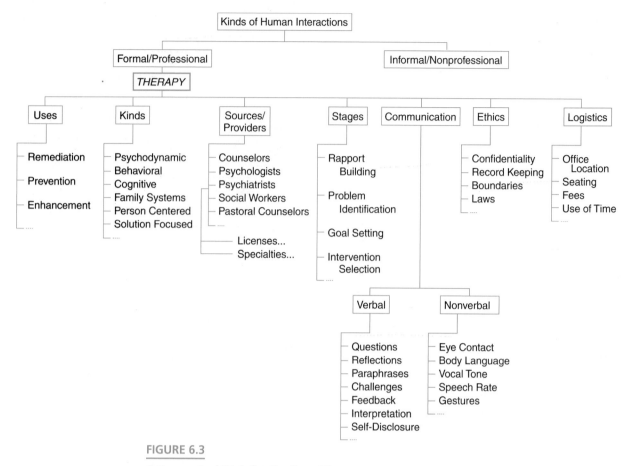

FIGURE 6.3

A Conceptual Web for the Term *Therapy*

three chunks that represent famous dates in American history: 1492, 1776, and 1929. If so, you would be able to remember all the digits because you converted them to just three pieces of information, which would not exceed your working memory capacity. The more extensive the webs of information in your long-term memory, the more likely you are to find ways to chunk information meaningfully in working memory. When expert chess players look at a chess board set up as if in the middle of a chess game, they see meaningfully related chunks consisting of four or five chess pieces each, allowing them to, in effect, rehearse the positions of 20 to 25 individual pieces without exceeding their working memory capacity. Novices see only individual pieces, allowing them to rehearse the positions of only about 5 to 7 pieces (Chase & Simon, 1973).

Logical Thinking Skills. A third cognitive change that contributes to memory improvement with age is advanced logical thinking. If older children can think more logically than younger children, they may have a better understanding of at least some of their experiences, and understanding better helps them to remember more about the experience later. Piaget's own research on memory improvement with age focused heavily on the contribution of logical development (see Piaget & Inhelder, 1973). In a typical study, he showed children from ages 3 to 7 an array of sticks, arranged in serial order by size. One week later, children were asked to draw what they had seen as a test of their recall. They were also given an opportunity to put a series of sticks in order according to size. This seriation task is a lot like the conservation of number task: It looks simple, but children are not usually completely successful at it until about age 7. In other words, it seems to require the logical thinking of the concrete operational stage. What Piaget found was that if children did not have the logical thinking skills needed to seriate sticks themselves, they typically could not remember the serial pattern they had been shown a week earlier; but children who could seriate the sticks (mostly 6- and 7-year-olds) showed better memory for the serial pattern. Remarkably, though, when the children's memory was tested again at least 6 months later, many of the younger children were now more accurate in their memory drawings than they had been originally, depicting some aspects of the serial order. These findings have often been replicated, indicating that children's memory for some experiences can actually improve over time! How could this happen?

The key here seems to be that memory is often reconstructive. That is, when we recall an experience, we integrate "what we currently experience, what we already know, and what we infer" (Kuhn, 2000a, p. 22). We have already seen that older children may use what they know about doctor's examinations in general to reconstruct a particular doctor's examination, thus recalling it more accurately than a younger child. It also appears that if a child's logical understanding of an event improves from the time he first experiences it to the time his memory is tested, he may reconstruct it more accurately than he could have earlier. As the children in Piaget's study got older, they could understand seriation better, and so when they "remembered" the original stick array, they often inferred that the sticks had been arranged according to size.

Language Skills. A fourth cognitive change that can benefit memory with age is greater facility with language, especially improvements in narrative skill, the ability to tell a coherent story. Clearly, one way in which we mentally represent information is in words. As children's vocabularies grow and their skill in describing events develops, their ability to store information about experiences in coherent verbal form also improves (e.g., Tessler & Nelson, 1994). As we saw in Chapter 3, recent research suggests that this aspect of memory improvement is enhanced by narrative interactions with adults. When by asking questions and by constructing narratives together about shared events, parents encourage their children to talk out loud about their experiences, children are better storytellers and show better memory for autobiographical events. On the whole, language skills such as these improve with age and experience, and so older children's memory for events can generally be expected to be better than younger children's (e.g., Nelson, 1993b, 1996).

Memory Strategies. A fifth cognitive change that can facilitate memory improvement with age is learning to use memory strategies. Strategies are "potentially conscious activities a person may voluntarily carry out" to remember something (Flavell et al., 1993, p. 235). Imagine that we asked you to remember all the names of the children in your class when you were in the fifth grade. After you finished groaning, you would probably take a strategic approach to this retrieval task—that is, your retrieval would follow some plan. Maybe you would try to remember all the girls and then all the boys; or maybe all your good friends and then all your enemies; or maybe all the popular kids, then the less popular ones; or maybe you would start with the tallest kids and work your way to the shortest. Generally, adults do approach memory tasks strategically, and when they do, they remember more than if their approach is haphazard. There are a host of strategies that we can call on, both for encoding new material that we expect to have to remember later and for retrieving information that is already stored. People who are really good at remembering names and phone numbers and other details of experience are generally well practiced at applying strategies.

But what about children? Preschoolers are usually considered nonstrategic in their memory efforts. An interesting example is provided by a study of 3- to 8-year-olds who were shown rows of boxes that contained either toy animals or household objects. Boxes with animals had a picture of a cage on top; boxes with household objects had a picture of a house. Children were asked to remember either the locations of the animals or the household objects. The researchers carefully observed the children's actions during a study period, and found that the younger children tended to open all the boxes, whereas the oldest children were more strategic, opening only the boxes with the items that they would have to remember later (animals or objects). In other words, older children selectively attended to the locations that they had to learn about. Younger children did not seem able to use selective attention to help them with the memory task (see Miller, 1994).

Selectively attending to one thing and not to another is very difficult for preschoolers, and so it is not a skill that 3- or 4-year-olds are likely to deploy to aid memory. But sometimes preschoolers seem to use other skills in ways that we might call "prestrategic." When they know that they will be asked to remember something later, sometimes they do things differently than they might otherwise. For example, 4-year-olds were given a set of toys to play with. Some children were told that later they would be asked to remember what some of the toys were. These children tended to play with the toys less and to name them more than children who were not given such instructions (Baker-Ward, Ornstein, & Holden, 1984). So, in other words, they seemed to act in ways that would help them remember.

Systematic use of strategies is much more likely in middle childhood. If you give a group of third graders the job of learning the names of all the states and their capitals, you will probably see them using rehearsal—repeating the names over and over. There are a variety of more complex strategies, but children usually do not use them spontaneously until the late elementary school years or even adolescence. For example, to help with the task of learning the states and their capitals, a child could use an organization strategy: sorting the items to be learned on some meaningful basis, such as grouping the names by region. Or he might use an elaboration strategy—finding or creating some kind of meaningful link between items. To help remember that Baton Rouge is the capital of Louisiana, he might make up a sentence like "Louise saw a bat," or he might create a mental picture, visualizing a girl named Louise with a bat on her head. At about 9 or 10, children will use organization strategies spontaneously and to good effect; not until adolescence are they likely to use elaboration without prompting. Strategies that are particularly useful for learning textual material, such as underlining and summarizing main ideas or key points, also emerge late, during adolescence (see Schneider & Bjorklund, 1998).

Developmental progress in children's use of memory strategies is a bumpy affair. On one hand, children might at first use a strategy quite sporadically, often showing a production deficiency, meaning that they might fail to use it even in situations where it is ordinarily helpful. On the other hand, sometimes children use a strategy, but it does not seem to boost memory; then they are said to have a utilization deficiency. Although strategies usually do aid memory performance, when a child first uses a strategy spontaneously, it may be so much work that it takes up a lot of time and attention, minimizing its effectiveness for improving memory. Yet children still may use the strategy. As Siegler (1998) has argued, it's as though children intuitively understand the "law of practice"—that practice improves efficiency in the long run—even if there is no immediate profit!

We have been describing the development of children's spontaneous use of memory strategies, but it should be noted that effective use of strategies can be taught. Children whose parents or teachers instruct them on how to use a strategy are likely to use it on the tasks where they were taught to do so (e.g., Kurtz, Carr, Borkowski, Schneider, & Rellinger, 1990). However, they typically do not generalize the use of a strategy to new situations.

Metacognitive Skills. The discussion of memory strategies leads us to a sixth, and final, cognitive change that seems to affect memory. It is the development of metacognition, "cognition about cognition" (Flavell et al., 1993), or thinking about our own mental processes and their effects. Preschoolers have some awareness of mental processes. Four- to 5-year-olds have a theory of mind that includes understanding that their own thoughts, beliefs, and desires often differ from those of other people, as we have noted. They also have some beginning skills at judging what they know. For example, if we show a 4- or 5-year-old a classmate's picture, even if the child cannot spontaneously recall the classmate's name, he will be able to accurately judge whether he would know the name if he heard it (e.g., Cultice, Somerville, & Wellman, 1983). This kind of self-monitoring and understanding of what you can and cannot accomplish cognitively, and how to accomplish it, improves dramatically across the elementary school years. In a classic study, Kreutzer, Leonard, and Flavell (1975) found that fifth graders understood that remembering the gist of a story is easier than remembering it word for word; only half of kindergartners understood this point. Kindergartners understood some things about memory, such as the value of writing things down if you want to remember them, but not until fifth grade did children realize that there are differences in memory ability from one person to another or from one situation to another. Many researchers have found that whereas preschoolers are usually overly optimistic about how much they are likely to remember about some material, such as a list of words, older children's estimates are usually much more realistic. This kind of self-knowledge continues to improve past middle childhood, as adolescents produce increasingly accurate depictions of what strategies and approaches are likely to enhance memory in given situations (Schneider & Pressley, 1997). Many theorists have argued that metacognitive awareness at least partially accounts for the increasingly effective use of strategies that develops through middle childhood into adolescence.

One aspect of memory improvement is learning to monitor your own memory and to allocate study time. This is one metacognitive skill that shows little development through elementary school, at least with challenging material. For example, most studies find that elementary-school-aged children don't often spontaneously use self-testing when they study. Interestingly, one of the better ways to help children in this age range use memory strategies more effectively is to train them to explicitly monitor what they have learned through techniques such as self-testing (e.g., Paris, Newman, & McVey, 1982). In other words, teaching children to keep track of what they have learned seems to be an important element in teaching them how to learn.

So metacognitive development involves improvement in three kinds of knowledge: declarative, or knowledge about facts, rules, or oneself as a learner; procedural, or knowledge about how to apply rules and strategies effectively; and conditional, or knowledge of when to apply the rules or strategies (Schraw & Moshman, 1995). Consider 10-year-old Amelia, who, having missed a day of school, calls a classmate to get her homework assignments. She knows that she must repeat the page numbers or write them down to remember them. She also knows how to organize her homework for each of the various assignments, for example, by showing all computations when solving math problems. She might even understand that she should do her science homework first because it takes the most time, and she may be able to judge when she has studied her spelling words sufficiently. Metacognition is the cornerstone of many clinical and educational practices that are collectively known as self-instruction or self-monitoring (Meichenbaum, 1986) and a major part of cognitive therapies for children and youth (Kendall, 1993). The general goal of such practices is to effect some behavior change (such as control of impulsivity or improvement in test-taking skills) by attending to, regulating, and sometimes changing cognitions.

This review of memory improvement through middle childhood has, of necessity, touched on many aspects of cognitive development, including advances in processing speed, growth of knowledge, development of logical thinking and language skills, growth of selective attention and other strategic skills, and metacognitive developments. It is clear that "to study memories is to study much of . . . cognition and cognitive development" (Kuhn, 2000a, p. 22). But memory is more than the product of the cognitive system. It is also influenced by affective and social developments. To illustrate the role of affective characteristics, consider the point that was made about the importance of domain knowledge in how well children learn new information in that domain. Indeed, a child will remember new information better than an adult if the child is an expert in that knowledge domain and the adult is not. But how does a child become an expert in some subject, such as chess, or dinosaurs, or baseball? Although it helps to be a competent learner, exceptional intelligence does not appear to be the determining factor. What is critical is the child's motivation. Expertise comes from long-lasting attention and practice, not typically from genius (e.g., Means & Voss, 1985; Schneider, 1993).

To illustrate the role of social factors in memory, consider that adult interactions with children seem to figure critically into the development of memory skill. As we have seen, teaching children strategies for learning new material improves children's memory performance. Encouraging children to narrate their experiences helps them develop better autobiographical memories. In other words, scaffolding by adults, in the Vygotskian sense (see Chapter 3), contributes substantially to memory development.

Cognitive Achievements: Number and Math Skills

In the early preschool years, the typical child has several number skills. For example, he can count, he knows there is a one-to-one relationship between number word and item when he counts, and he understands that the order in which items are counted is irrelevant (e.g., Gelman,

Children spontaneously develop strategies for solving problems, including math problems.

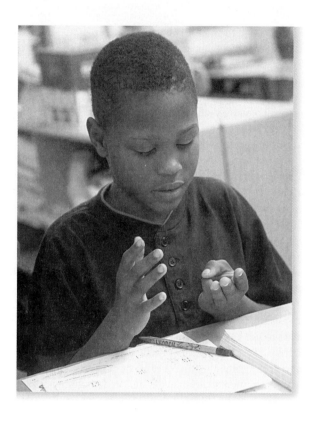

1982; see also Chapter 3). By late preschool, he has informal arithmetic skills such as adding and subtracting small numbers by using counting strategies, like the counting all strategy. For example, given two red blocks and three green ones, he will probably count all the blocks to find out the sum. As children in elementary school are introduced to more formal arithmetic, with its written numbers and standard, step-wise processes (or algorithms) for computation and recording, they continue to use their informal strategies. They also devise more and more strategies, some invented, some derived from what they are taught (e.g., Siegler, 1987). For example, given a simple addition problem such as 3 + 4, they might use a strategy called counting on, starting with the first number and counting four more numbers from there. Soon, this strategy is likely to be modified so that the child usually "counts on" from the larger number. As children are exposed repeatedly to addition and subtraction facts, they begin to use a retrieval strategy, pulling the answer from memory.

Some researchers in the information processing tradition have closely followed young school children's progress in discovering and utilizing these strategies. They have found interesting trends that seem to occur across cultures. First, most children use most of the strategies, sometimes using one, sometimes another. Second, children often use a particular strategy on problems where it is especially effective, and more efficient strategies gradually become more predominant. Third, however, even older school children sometimes use less efficient strategies (Ginsburg, Klein, & Starkey, 1998; Siegler, 1998). Thus, it appears that cognitive development moves gradually toward greater efficiency but that less efficient strategies are not entirely abandoned. "Bumpy" progress in strategy use seems to characterize the development of many skills, as we have seen already in memory development. As in memory development, the shift toward using more adequate math strategies, more often, seems to depend partly on metacognitive development—the child's growing understanding of his own strategies and his increasing awareness of how effective those strategies are (Kuhn, 2000b).

When children assimilate the rules they are taught to their own limited understanding of mathematics, they sometimes invent strategies that produce errors. In the information processing tradition, flawed strategies are referred to as "bugs." An example would be a boy who does not yet truly understand the base 10 system, but who thinks that one should always subtract the smaller from the larger number. When he is given the problem

$$\begin{array}{r} 21 \\ -\ 5 \\ \hline \end{array}$$

he subtracts the 1 from the 5 and comes up with 24 (Ginsburg, 1989).

In the Piagetian tradition, some research specifically explores developmental changes in what children understand about what they are taught about mathematics. Children's progress in understanding the base 10 system provides a good illustration of the extent to which their mathematical knowledge is constructed (e.g., Kamii, 1986; Kamii, 1990). If we ask a first grader to count a set of 13 blocks and then write down the answer, he will probably be able to comply. But if we circle the "3" and then ask, "Does this part of your 13 have anything to do with how many blocks there are?" a first grader might say, "No." He thinks that only the whole number 13 tells about the number of blocks.

When he's in second grade, he might say that the "3" represents a certain three chips; when in third grade, he may talk about ones and tens, but is likely to say that the "1" in 13 represents one single item, not ten. By fourth and fifth grades, about half of children recognize that the "1" represents a 10 (example from Kamii, 1990). Thus, although a child typically hears about the base 10 system from first grade onward, he seems to assimilate it to concepts that are not correct and only gradually constructs its true meaning. Findings such as these on children's understanding of math concepts are a reminder of an important tenet of Piaget's view of education: Teaching children facts or algorithms is not sufficient for developing the kind of understanding they will need to truly advance in a subject, as was the case in the round earth study. Teachers need also to probe children's comprehension, asking questions such as "Does the '3' have anything to do with how many blocks there are?" Such questions both aid teachers in evaluating what kinds of supports a child might need to understand better and may help children begin to recognize inconsistencies in the meanings they have constructed. This kind of probing can also help teachers establish adequate placements for their students. Care should also be taken in choosing curricular materials and in structuring assessments of students' learning. Without practice and elaboration, advanced or accelerated programs of study may outstrip the abilities of many children and lead them to shallow or rote memorization of facts instead of deep conceptual understanding. Knowledge of facts without conceptual understanding is associated with slower, less accurate problem solving even in the early stages of math learning (Canobi, Reeve, & Pattison, 1998).

Although the development of math concepts seems to follow a similar progression in most children across cultures, research in the Vygotskian tradition (see Chapter 3) indicates that social context can moderate the speed of mathematical development and the kinds of strategies that emerge. First, the kinds of practical problems that children face in living seem to affect the kinds of informal strategies they invent, as well as their understanding of mathematical principles. For example, some poor urban children in Brazil sell candy on the streets to make a living. Saxe (1991) compared the math skills of candy sellers to children who did not sell candy. The sellers had little formal schooling, but some of the nonsellers were receiving a formal education. Age affected the math skills that the children exhibited, but so did their experience selling candy. For example, 5- to 7-year-olds typically could not add or subtract currency, whether they were sellers or nonsellers. But by 11 or 12 years many of the sellers had invented strategies that allowed them to count up large numbers of bills, usually by organizing them into sets. One 11-year-old, for example, "began with a 10,000-unit bill. Then he added three 1,000-unit bills; and, finally the remaining 200- and 100-unit bills, to reach the correct total of 17,300" (quoted from Ginsburg et al., 1998, p. 423). Nonsellers typically did not have such strategies. Nonsellers with formal education also had more trouble with some advanced math concepts, such as proportions, than sellers did. Relations expressed in proportions are more abstract than the simple adding, subtracting, multiplying, and dividing of numbers, and children generally seem to do better with them as they approach adolescence (Piaget's stage of formal operations). This was generally true of the children in Saxe's study as well, but the sellers seemed to apply their abstract thinking to the proportion problems that arose from their selling activities sooner than the nonsellers were able to do so.

A second way in which social context is important to math development is that opportunities in early childhood to manipulate countable materials, to learn counting words, to work with shapes, and to verbally interact with adults about numbers seem to be contextual experiences that affect early informal mathematical development, which in turn affects how well children will learn formal mathematics when they reach school age. A number of studies have found that the parents of children from lower socioeconomic groups, especially the very poor, provide fewer and less complex number activities, especially activities that encourage talking and reasoning about numbers, than middle-class parents (e.g., Klein & Starkey, 1995; Saxe, Guberman, & Gearhart, 1987). Such activities might include counting fingers or coins, finding television channels, or spontaneous number games such as practicing number recognition in an elevator: A parent tells the child the number of their floor, and the child pushes the button with the right number. More complex number activities that tend to show the greatest social class differences include demonstrating money equivalences, such as between five pennies and a nickel, and doing addition and subtraction with fingers or coins. Not surprisingly, with less experience of such activities, poor children tend to lag behind middle-class children in their basic, informal mathematical abilities even though they typically acquire some basic skills, such as some counting, and the ability to represent quantities by holding up appropriate numbers of fingers (e.g., Jordan, Huttenlocher, & Levine, 1994).

A third influence of social context comes from the kind of mathematical language that children are taught. In English, the base 10 structure of the numerical system is not as clearly laid out in number words as it is in some other languages, especially Asian languages such as Chinese, Korean, and Japanese. In these languages, there are fewer arbitrary number words to learn, and after 10, number names clearly specify the number of tens. For example, the equivalent of 11 would be "one-one," of 12 would be "one-two," and so on. The equivalent of 21 would be "two-one." Several studies indicate that number names are learned earlier by preschool children learning Asian languages compared to American children learning English (e.g., Miller & Stigler, 1987), and that the regular system of Asian languages may facilitate understanding of the base 10 system in elementary school (Fuson & Kwon, 1992).

Clearly, studies of mathematical development inspired by several different theoretical traditions are beginning to paint a picture of how children learn mathematics. In their review of the research, Ginsburg and colleagues (1998) draw a number of conclusions, including that mathematical development begins in infancy and that an informal mathematics is constructed before middle childhood, "guided by biology, physical environment, and culture" (p. 427). How children understand the formal mathematical system taught in school depends on their cognitive level, the informal mathematics that they bring with them, and a range of social supports. And, as Ginsburg et al. put it, "understanding is connecting . . . not simply correct calculation or correct verbal statements, [but] . . . a complex web of connections among different aspects of mathematical knowledge" (p. 428). Children assimilate what they are taught in school to their existing knowledge, using the thinking abilities that they currently have. Thus they actively construct that web of connections.

Cognitive Achievements: Problem-Solving Progress

Dozens of times a day children are faced with problem-solving tasks, from the mundane to the more esoteric: Should I wear my heavy coat or a lightweight jacket; what's the fastest way to walk to Ailani's new house; should I tell my parents about the argument I had with my teacher; how should I organize my science report; what are the important facts to remember in this social studies unit? Development of problem-solving skills involves several kinds of change with age, many of which we have described already: First, children devise and use an increasing range of strategies as they get older; second, they usually have more resources, such as domain knowledge and logical thinking skills, to allot to a task with age; third, they tend to plan better as they get older, aided by better attentional control, growing metacognitive knowledge, and increases in working memory capacity. These and other typical cognitive changes are influenced or modified by social transactions—in the family, in the classroom, and in other familiar contexts. In this section, we will focus primarily on the influence of one kind of social transaction on learning and problem solving in elementary school children: peer interaction. Specifically, we will examine the benefits and liabilities of cooperative learning environments, that is, classroom or other organizations that encourage children to work in pairs or in groups to solve academic problems and to improve their understanding of concepts or skills.

Before we consider how children working together make progress toward a problem solution, let's take a look at how problem solving proceeds when children work with an adult. First, when a parent or teacher guides a child through a problem, researchers have found that the adult usually works to maintain the child's interest and to keep the child focused on the goal of the task. Second, the adult's behavior tends to be contingent on the child's performance in several ways. In particular, an adult usually keeps track of what the child can and cannot do and then tends to tailor instruction or suggestion to the child's "region of sensitivity"—one step beyond the level where the child is currently performing. Wood, Bruner, and Ross (1976) called this kind of adult behavior scaffolding, and research in the Vygotskian tradition has demonstrated that when an adult provides such scaffolding, children perform at a higher level than they would if they were solving problems by themselves. You will recall that Vygotsky (1978) called this region of improved performance with adult help the zone of proximal development (see Chapter 3). Third, an adult is likely to engage a child in a discussion of possible strategies, encouraging the child both to consider why and how steps should be taken and to make decisions. As Piagetian educators have argued (e.g., Kamii, 1990), when adults ask challenging questions and elicit children's active involvement in discussion and planning, children's learning and performance is enhanced (e.g., Gauvain, 1992; Lacasa & Villuendas, 1990; McLane, 1987; Rogoff & Gauvain, 1986). Finally, as children's performance advances, adults do less themselves, encouraging children to do more of the problem solving.

Adult tutoring in the style we just described helps children learn more effectively than they would on their own. What are the characteristics of children's efforts to learn collaboratively with peers, and how effective are such efforts likely to be? A number of factors linked to age are important. On the whole, the younger the child, the less likely a collaborative arrangement will be as effective as working with an adult or more effective than working alone. Preschoolers and young elementary school children have limited ability to control their own attention and to stay on task. When they work with peers, not surprisingly, the partners have difficulty coordinating their attention (Azmitia, 1996). Further, an important determiner of effective collaborative problem solving is the opportunity to communicate your ideas and to discuss the ideas of your collaborator. Yet, the limited language skills of younger children make good communication difficult when not supported by an adult facilitator. Finally, young children do not often behave contingently in a collaborative setting. Perhaps limited by their immature perspective-taking skills (see the next section of this chapter), they fail either to evaluate the needs of their partner or to adjust their behaviors to those needs. So, for example, if one partner is more expert than another, the more expert partner may simply tell the other what to do without explaining his reasons or asking helpful questions (e.g., Ellis & Rogoff, 1986). Or one partner may do all of the actual reasoning and problem solving while the other does the "manual labor," such as drawing the pictures or typing the paper (e.g., Hawkins, 1987, as cited in Rogoff, 1998). In addition, even when one partner knows more than another, the less skilled partner may be less willing to accept his peer's claims than he would an adult's.

Peer collaboration seems to be most effective—more effective than children working alone—when decision making is shared, with all partners actively involved in discussion, planning, negotiating, and attempting solutions (e.g., Azmitia & Hesser, 1993; Duran & Gauvain, 1993; Gauvain & Rogoff, 1989; Light, Littleton, Messer, & Joiner, 1994). Researchers have found that several factors foster such active participation. Encouraging children to talk over what they do seems to help (e.g., Teasley, 1995). Also, when children feel more comfortable with their partners, they talk more even if one partner is more expert. So, for example, partners are more active if they are of a similar age (Duran & Gauvain, 1993) or if one is the older sibling of the other (e.g., Azmitia & Hesser, 1993). In addition, when adults provide feedback along the way on the effectiveness of children's solutions, peer collaborations work better than when no feedback is given (Ellis, Klahr, & Siegler, 1993). Adult feedback probably helps keep the discussion on course. For example, if one partner, who happens to be wrong, is more persuasive or domineering than the others, feedback can help to balance his influence and keep the discussion going. Alternatively, when one partner's arguments are correct, his peers may be more willing to give him credence if adult feedback is available. Without feedback, the most advanced partner is likely to make no progress, and, at best, his initial level of expertise will serve as the cap for the group (Siegler, 1998).

Overall, it appears that children need support in learning to collaborate effectively. Just telling children to work together is not good enough. Adults who want to encourage cooperative learning need to take into account many factors in providing support: children's age, their roles in their social groups, their personal relationships, their motivation levels, and their relative expertise (Rogoff, 1998). Fortunately, some research indicates that when children have practice collaborating they tend to get better at it, especially when adults provide suggestions, establish rules, and monitor progress (e.g., Socha & Socha, 1994; see Rogoff, 1998). Similarly, if children are encouraged to discuss how well their group is working and what improvements could be made, their collaborations tend to improve (Yager, Johnson, Johnson, & Snider, 1986). In essence, cooperative learning among peers requires active scaffolding by an adult.

It should be noted that cooperative learning is more easily facilitated in some climates than in others. In cultures where group goals in schools are emphasized over individual needs, as in Japan, children's experiences in and out of school are more likely to prepare them for collaborative learning than in schools where individual accomplishment tends to be more important (Hatano, 1994). For example, Toma (1991a, 1991b, as cited in Rogoff, 1998) observed that a common feature in Japanese classrooms is training in how to address one's classmates in a discussion. A list of phrasings—what to say and how to say it—is often posted on a classroom wall. One such list suggested that children express agreement by saying, "I agree with (name's) opinion. This is because" . . . To help children request clarification, the list proposed saying, "Did you mean to say . . ." Most of us, not only children, could probably benefit from such a list!

SOCIAL COGNITION

Just as children's knowledge about the physical world and about logical-mathematical concepts becomes more sophisticated with time, so does their understanding of the social world. This latter domain, generally referred to as social cognition, has been of great interest to developmentalists for many years. Although the field of social cognition is broad and encompasses many aspects of cognition, it focuses primarily on the ways people think about other people and how they reason about social relationships.

Much of what you have already learned has provided the foundation for, and can be subsumed within, social cognition. As you will recall from earlier chapters, infants and toddlers learn a great deal about social relationships within the context of the attachments they form. The discriminations infants make between objects and people, their diligent attention to caregivers, their capacity for imitation and social referencing, and their early attempts at communication presage knowledge about people and human psychology. Toddlers try to change the behaviors of others, empathize with others' distress, and use emotion words indicating that they have explicit knowledge of others' mental states (Zahn-Waxler, Radke-Yarrow, Wagner, & Chapman, 1992). These skills suggest that infants and young children are in the process of learning about social interactions almost from birth.

Studies of the young child's theory of mind focus on aspects of social cognition, addressing questions such as "When does the child come to understand that the other has a mind?" and "How does the child use information about mental states to understand people and social relationships?" We have already seen that by their fifth birthday most children realize that others often have different thoughts and beliefs from their own. For example, they now succeed on false belief tasks in which they must anticipate that a person who has not had the opportunity to see an object moved from its original hiding place to a new location might have a false belief about the object's whereabouts (e.g., Wimmer & Perner, 1983; see also Chapter 3). Success on false belief tasks has been related to reciprocal communication with peers (Slomkowski & Dunn, 1996) and to the ability to communicate about internal mental states with friends (Hughes & Dunn, 1998). Researchers are thus finding links between early cognitive social understanding and children's social relationships. Social cognitive research with school-aged children typically deals with the quality of children's understanding of the nature of other peoples' thoughts, feelings, and desires. Studies have examined theories of children's friendships, methods of conflict resolution, and the developing understanding of social rules and interactions that are central facets of both.

No one has to convince a counselor that the dynamics of social relationships are important ones to understand. Although not every social relationship can be considered a friendship, it can be argued that the special relationships we have with friends teach us about human relationships in general. During the middle years, friendships take on enormous importance for children. Indeed, for school-aged children being reared in difficult circumstances, having a good friend serves as a protective factor, moderating some environmental risks. For example, in the Virginia Longitudinal Study of Child Maltreatment (see Bolger & Patterson, 2003), 107 children who were abused or neglected were identified through state social service records from a larger sample of 1,920 public school children. Most of the maltreated children were at risk in other ways as well. For example, 92% had low enough family incomes that they qualified for federal food subsidies of some kind. During the course of the study children were asked whether they had a best friend, and their friend choices were compared to verify that they were reciprocated. Among the measures collected over time were assessments of the children's self-esteem. Using the Self-Perception Profile (Harter, 1985), children rated their own competence in a variety of domains. As you might expect, maltreated children perceived themselves as less competent than children who had no history of abuse or neglect. But maltreated children with a reciprocal friend showed substantial gains in self-esteem from Grade 3 to Grade 5, gains that were maintained through Grade 7, and on average they were doing about as well on self esteem as other children. Unfortunately, maltreated children who did not have a best friend showed declines in self esteem across the years of middle childhood.

Any child's difficulties in making and keeping friends can consume much of a counselor's time because of the far-reaching consequences of poor peer relationships and inadequate conflict resolution skills on emotional well-being, academic achievement, and behavior. What is important for counselors to understand is that the skills of friendship are not just behavioral but are heavily dependent upon cognitive development. Similarly, problems in social relations may be heavily influenced by limitations in social cognitive skills. In this section, we will introduce some major theoretical approaches to friendship development that have a basis in cognitive developmental theory. In Chapter 7, the research on larger peer group interaction and peer group status will be reviewed.

Perspective Taking and Social Relationships

The idea that satisfactory social relationships are important in the overall picture of adjustment enjoys unanimous support from developmentalists of every theoretical persuasion. Social relationships are necessary for the child to gain experience in learning about others' points of view (Piaget, 1932/1965). They contribute to the child's sense of security and connectedness (Berndt, 1982), and foster the development of the self-concept (Mead, 1934). These three benefits are not as separate as they may seem but are, instead, three highly interconnected outcomes of positive social contact.

Recall for a moment what has been presented in earlier chapters about the development of the self. Self-concept has been defined by symbolic interactionist thinkers such as Mead as the individual's perception of himself that develops from the collective accumulation of social experiences. It is as if the individual proceeds through life viewing himself in the "looking glass" of other people's eyes. But remember as well that this process is not simply a passive reception of information. Rather, it involves the complicated consideration of the perspectives of other people. Mead believed that to define oneself, a person needs to put himself, metaphorically, in another person's shoes and then consider his own actions in the light of that alternative perspective. This uniquely human operation, which lies at the heart of self-recognition and self-knowledge, has been called **perspective taking**, and no relationship survives for very long without it.

The cognitively complex skill of perspective taking develops gradually as children mature, much in the same way that other cognitive abilities change and improve. You have already read that very young children are considered egocentric insofar as they are embedded in their own perspective. In Piaget's view, the ability to decenter, meaning in this case the ability to recognize and hold in mind more than one perspective, is enhanced by repeated interactions with others. When children decenter, they understand that others have minds that are different from theirs and that minds may be coordinated in the service of mutual understanding and problem solving. Implicit in this level of awareness is the cognitive ability to engage in relationships marked by intimacy and mutuality and to solve problems in ways that consider the interests of all parties.

How does such an immensely desirable skill as perspective taking develop and improve? Some of the earliest ideas on the subject stem from Piaget's writing. He believed that about the time children enter elementary school in industrialized cultures, they are forced to consider other children's viewpoints to survive the normal give and take of the classroom community structure. Before then, children may have been able to rely on parents' or other family members' willingness to meet their egocentric needs and to understand their egocentric communication. Peers are typically less willing and able to do so. The child in elementary school, or even before, is forced to clarify his thoughts and adopt better communication skills in order to be accepted by peers. The major and minor conflicts that accompany this process are viewed as essential to a developing awareness of perspectives other than one's own (Flavell, 1963; Piaget, 1928).

This achievement does not mean, however, that children are now free of egocentrism altogether, as we saw earlier in this chapter. Every developmental stage has its own form of this quintessentially human weakness. Even adults are not exempt because specific forms of egocentric thinking appear to be a normal byproduct of cognitive advances.

> The transition from one form of egocentrism to another takes place in a dialectical fashion in such a manner that the cognitive structures that free a child from a lower form of egocentrism are the same structures that entangle him in a higher egocentric form. (Looft, 1972, p. 77)

In fact, Looft, paraphrasing Piaget, describes egocentrism as the "central problem in the history of human affairs" (p. 73). Despite the fact that seeing the world and relationships egocentrically is an inevitable part of the human condition, maturity reduces this tendency to some degree. Friendships play a particularly significant role in this process.

Perspective Taking and Friendship Development

In one of the early theories of friendship development, Sullivan (1953) reiterated the Piagetian perspective that children need interpersonal contact in order to reduce egocentrism and promote altruism. Although very young children, in the "childhood era" according to Sullivan, primarily depend upon parents for reflected appraisals of themselves, children's dependence upon play-mates becomes more important as they enter the "juvenile period" around age 4. However socialized some interactive behaviors (such as sharing, conformity, and expressions of sympathy) may appear at this age, these behaviors are not yet truly altruistic but are demonstrated for the ego-centric purpose of gaining acceptance or building popularity in the larger peer group. A major transformation occurs around age 8, when children enter the stage Sullivan called "preadoles-cence." During this period, children's needs for increased interpersonal intimacy are met through the establishment of an intense, focused interest in same-sex age-mates or "chums." These rela-tionships teach preadolescents that the needs and perspectives of other persons must be consid-ered as carefully as their own. Seeing one's preadolescent self reflected back in the context of a chumship permits the validation of one's thoughts, feelings, and beliefs as well as a more realistic appraisal of oneself. Thus, the egocentrism of the juvenile period diminishes as the child learns to see the world through the eyes of a friend. Because the transition through early adolescence is not without its stresses and strains, attachment to a close friend or chum can function as a secure base, permitting the young person to navigate the many changes inherent in the adolescent tran-sition without feeling totally isolated. Let's try to understand more about the primary cognitive ingredient needed for successful friendship development, perspective taking.

Many writers have documented children's maturing ability to take the perspective of their friends and to communicate this understanding in increasingly more sophisticated ways (Flavell, Botkin, Fry, Wright, & Jarvis, 1968). Possibly the most elegantly developed theory linking perspective taking with actual friendship development has been provided by Robert Selman (1980). Building on a Piagetian framework, Selman identified five stages in the development of perspective taking, beginning at preschool age and continuing though adolescence. Each level of perspective-taking skill is linked to a different level of friendship or shared experience, as well as to a differ-ent level of conflict resolution. Table 6.1 depicts the tight interconnections among one's ability to understand others (perspective taking), one's needs for intimacy in relationship (friendship), one's skill in balancing personal needs without sacrificing the relationship (autonomy), and one's ability to solve conflicts (conflict resolution).

Think for a moment about your own close friendships. Regardless of how overtly agreeable or conflictual these relationships may be, there is always a tension between "what is good for me versus what is good for us" (Barr, 1997, p. 32). No friendship is immune to this underlying dynamic, which surfaces from time to time over the course of the relationship. To sustain friend-ships, friends must be able to coordinate both individuals' needs and resolve the inevitable conflicts that arise in ways that are mutually agreeable. Any imbalance, such as too much coercion from one partner and too little assertiveness from the other, can undermine the friend-ship in the long run. In other words, ineffective management of the dysynchrony between the needs of the individual and the needs of the pair puts the friendship at risk. Healthy friendships

TABLE 6.1   Selman's Stages of Friendship and Levels of Perspective-Taking Skills

Stage	Approximate Ages	Forms of Shared Experience	Social Perspective Taking	Interpersonal Negotiation Strategies
0	3 to 6 years	Unreflective imitation or enmeshment	Undifferentiated/Egocentric	Physical force; impulsive fight or flight
1	5 to 9 years	Unreflective sharing of expressive enthusiasm	Differentiated/Subjective	One-way, unilateral power; orders or obedience
2	8 to 12 years	Reflective sharing of similar perceptions or experiences	Reciprocal/Self-Reflective	Cooperative exchange; reciprocity; persuasion or deference
3	10 to 15 years	Empathic sharing of beliefs and values	Mutual/Third-Person	Mutual compromise
4	Late teen/adulthood	Interdependent sharing of vulnerabilities and self	Intimate/In-Depth/Societal (generalized other)	Collaborative integration of relationship dynamics (commitment)

Source: Adapted with permission from Robert L. Selman, Caroline L. Watts, and Lynn Hickey Schultz, *Fostering friendship: Pair therapy for treatment and prevention* (New York: Aldine de Gruyter). Copyright © 1997 by Walter de Gruyter, Inc., New York.

Although disagreements can be painful, they can help children learn to take another's perspective.

are marked by mutual give and take, allowing both partners to feel affirmed, understood, and respected.

If all this seems too good to be true, let us hasten to say that friendships, even in adulthood, are true "works in progress" that require mutual coordination of perspectives and ongoing balancing of needs. Imagine how short-lived a friendship would be if you typically perceived your friend's momentary insensitivity or inability to participate in some shared activity as a personal insult directed toward you. Your understanding that he might be overextended and thus under stress can help you take a more empathic perspective, despite your own disappointment. Children find this harder to do because they are essentially practicing their perspective taking and other friendship skills. Hurts, betrayals, and conflicts will almost inevitably accompany their friendship development as they struggle to learn to compromise, compete, and cooperate in a civil way. Without this sometimes painful experience, however, children may not learn the intimacy and autonomy strategies they need to reap the benefits of satisfying friendships throughout their lifetimes. Counselors who are knowledgeable about the nature of friendship development are in a unique position to facilitate children's progress in this area.

Selman's Stages of Friendship Development

Selman (1980) provides a stagewise description of the development of children's friendship skills. As with other stage theories, the age ranges are just rough approximations. What is most important is the sequence and nature of the developmental change. Stage 0, or the "Undifferentiated/Egocentrism" stage, is typically manifested in preschool children before about age 5, when perspective-taking capacity is quite limited. Youngsters at Stage 0 have little appreciation for the thoughts and feelings of either themselves or others. Friendship is defined in very concrete terms, without understanding of the other person's psychology. For example, a preschool child might define a friend as someone who lives next to you, who gives you gifts, who shares toys with you, or who likes you. Young children typically establish friendships with children who are like themselves in concrete ways, such as age, gender, race, and ethnicity (see Rubin & Coplan, 1992). Conflicts between friends are not perceived as disagreements that occur between two parties with two different and legitimate points of view but are viewed as struggles to get one's own way. Lacking much ability to consider another's perspective, children typically resort to "flight" ("Go away!") or "fight" ("I'll get you!") strategies to resolve conflicts as they seek to preserve their interests.

In Stage 1, the "Differentiated/Subjective" stage, children from about 5 to about 9 come to understand that others have viewpoints that are different from their own, but they are generally not able to coordinate these perspectives simultaneously. In other words, they can't maintain their own perspective and that of someone else at the same time. So even though they understand that their peers have different points of view, they still may act as though their own perspective or that of an "authority" is correct. They are able to understand, for example, that they can be the subject of another's thoughts, but they generally do not have the capacity to judge how their behavior is being evaluated by that other person. Dyami, for instance, might understand that his friend Kono has a viewpoint or a perspective on him, but Dyami has little insight into what Kono's view of him is really like. We might say that interpersonal perspective at this age is unilateral or one-way. Yet during this period children do become better able to infer the thoughts and feelings of others, especially when they are encouraged to reflect on them. The child's understanding of physical experience, however, is another thing altogether. In the behavioral realm, two-way reciprocity ("You hit me and I hit you back") is readily understood.

On the psychological level, friendship is still largely a one-way proposition. The child at Stage 1 may understand his own psychological perspective but may fail to do the same for his friend. In other words, friendships may be defined by the behavioral and psychological rewards they provide for the individual child and not in terms of the mutual satisfaction afforded both members of the dyad. Eight-year-old Pavla might describe a friend as someone who helps her with her homework, doesn't fight with her, and doesn't walk away from her when she's upset. Notice the mix of behavioral (homework help) and psychological (social support) characteristics that are directed toward the benefit of one person. Conflicts are also viewed as one-way propositions. The responsibility to resolve a conflict is in the hands of the person who was perceived to have initiated it. There is little understanding of problem solving by mutual consensus.

At Stage 2, the "Reciprocal/Self-reflective" stage, older children master a critical developmental task. Between late childhood and early adolescence (about 8 to 12), they become more cognizant of the perspectives of others and learn to put themselves in another's place as a way of evaluating intentions and actions. Children can now actually assume the psychological position of another and reflect on their own behavior and motivation as perceived by someone else. Eleven-year-old Keisha, who doesn't really want to go swimming at her friend Amber's house because she'd prefer to spend the afternoon watching TV, might agree to go anyway. Keisha, seeing Amber as a person who is rather easily hurt, reasons that if she declined the invitation, Amber might think that Keisha didn't like her or that she didn't want to be her friend. This more sophisticated level of perspective-taking ability reflects two-way reciprocity ("I think; you think").

At this stage, children can grasp more highly differentiated patterns of motivations and emotions and make finer discriminations between thoughts and feelings. They can conceive of the fact that people, including themselves, can experience conflicting motives and feelings and can feel one thing but act in a completely different way. In our earlier example, Keisha wants to spend some time alone but she also wants to preserve her friendship with Amber. She may simultaneously feel liking and impatience toward her friend. She may decide to go swimming and cover up her true feelings of disinterest in the activity. Conflict resolution between children at this stage reflects the growing awareness that both parties must give a little to reach a solution.

At Stage 3, the "Mutual/Third-person" stage, adolescents of about 10 to 15 learn to view each other's perspectives simultaneously and mutually. Rather than simply viewing each other's perspective in a back and forth approach ("first me, then you"), adolescents can mentally step back to take the perspective of a "third-party observer" even as they themselves remain a member of the pair. What this allows is a more detached view of the proceedings, somewhat like the way a disinterested spectator might construe a social interaction. Egocentrism is further reduced insofar as the adolescent can view the interchange between himself and his friend and reflect on it from the outside looking in.

Friendship at this stage is characterized by mutual support and shared intimacy and not seen just as a means of obtaining what either party desires as an individual. Consequently, conflict resolution strategies are marked by more attention to the mutuality of the relationship. There is an awareness that problems do not always reside within one of the participants but that they are the responsibility of both parties to address. Harmonious resolution of the conflicts that are inevitable in relationships is perceived to strengthen both parties' commitment to that relationship. Adolescents at this stage are more capable of understanding that a friendship could break down because "it just didn't work out between us" rather than because "she wasn't nice to me."

Finally, at Stage 4, the "Intimate/In-depth/Societal" stage, older adolescents and adults learn to adopt the perspective of the larger society. Perspective-taking ability becomes more abstract and complex. Now the individual can assume the perspective of people beyond the limits of the dyad, namely that of a larger social group. This achievement makes possible the understanding of cultural and other group differences and the increasing appreciation of relativity—that no one person's or one group's perspective is necessarily the only correct one regardless of how deeply valued it might be. Relationships are marked by the individual's increasing ability to balance his needs for intimacy and autonomy while still preserving the friendship. With each new level of perspective-taking skill, understanding of friendship improves, interpersonal values are clarified, and social and conflict resolution skills are refined.

A FRAMEWORK FOR FRIENDSHIP

Perspective taking is an important part of social relatedness, but it is not the only determinant. We should now consider how the understanding of others' perspectives is integrated with other skills and tied to actual success in making and keeping friends. Is there a comprehensive way to look at the nature of friendship competence in children? The following friendship framework, which integrates a number of ingredients, has been proposed by Selman and his associates (Selman, Levitt, & Schultz, 1997a) as one possible comprehensive model. We have chosen to describe this model in some depth because it represents a good example of a theoretical framework that lends itself to clinical applications that are developmentally sensitive. An understanding of the elements of this model can help you assess relative strengths and weaknesses in a child's social relatedness and help you choose relevant interventions.

As always, nature and nurture provide the backdrop for the child's social functioning. For example, one child's predisposition toward shyness or another child's day-to-day experience of parental discord can have some effect on the children's capacities to enter and sustain social relationships with others. In certain situations, the effects of nature or nurture are so pronounced that they make independent contributions to social functioning, as in the case of a child who lacks friends because he lives in an isolated environment. These effects are represented by dotted lines leading directly to friendship outcomes from "Nature" and "Nurture" in Figure 6.4.

What is more typical, however, is that the effects of nature and nurture are integrated with a third area of influence called **psychosocial development**. This has been defined as "the internal psychological processes of interpersonal understanding, skills, and values that comprise an individual's capacity for interpersonal relationships, including friendships" (Selman et al., 1997a, p. 35). **Friendship understanding** refers to a child's changing knowledge of what friendship implies. **Friendship skills** are behavioral skills, such as appropriate assertiveness, good communication, and conflict resolution, that maintain and enhance friendships. **Friendship valuing** describes the emotional attachment or investment that the child makes in a friendship. Each of these three components is influenced and informed by developmental changes in the child's perspective-taking ability. In other words, competence in these three areas will be delimited by a child's cognitive understanding of interpersonal relationships.

To work effectively, clinicians need to appreciate what can be reasonably expected from children at each stage of their development. Teaching appropriate social skills, such as making eye contact and communicating effectively, may be irrelevant for children whose level of friendship understanding is very egocentric or for a child who is not particularly interested in being friendly toward another member of his class. On the other hand, learning how to solve conflicts effectively may be very helpful for a child who is invested in a friendship. All three dimensions need to be considered therapeutically so that interventions can get targeted accurately.

There is one other important element in this model, linking the child's psychosocial competencies to his interpersonal performance (see Figure 6.4). This bridge is the child's **interpersonal orientation**, or the way the child characteristically interacts on a social level. The most mature interpersonal style is characterized by a flexible balance between intimacy and autonomy strivings. Less effective orientations, as identified by Selman, are "other-transforming" and "self-transforming" social interaction styles.

A child with an other-transforming style characteristically tries to dominate or coerce a friend into meeting his needs. He acts to change or transform the other and can be bullying, aggressive, or manipulative. A child with a self-transforming style typically gives in to reduce the level of tension. He changes his own behaviors or feelings to conform. Selman and Schultz (1990) found that very young children or socially immature older children tend to behave in these extreme ways. Such children are both more labile than other children, sometimes moving

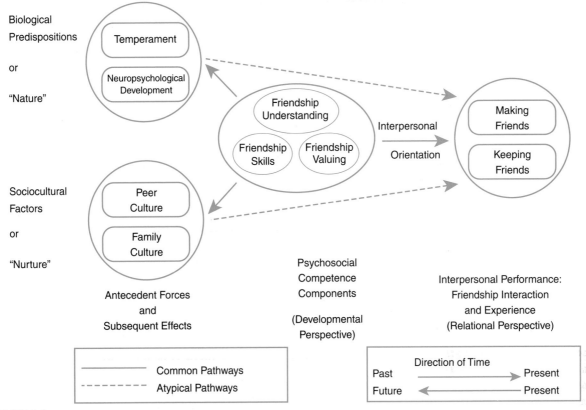

FIGURE 6.4

A Friendship Framework: Spheres of Influence

Source: Reprinted with permission from Robert L. Selman, Caroline L. Watts, and Lynn Hickey Schultz. *Fostering friendship: Pair therapy for treatment and prevention* (New York: Aldine de Gruyter). Copyright © 1997 by Walter de Gruyter, Inc., New York.

from victim to victimizer position depending on the relationship, and more rigid, refusing to compromise their position once established, even at the risk of losing the friendship.

What does it mean for a child to be bossy, impulsive, stubborn, passive, or shy? On its face, each label might prescribe a certain kind of intervention: self-control training for the impulsive child, assertiveness training for the shy one, and so forth. Selman's theoretical model gives us the means to go beyond this level of understanding to unpack the fundamental psychosocial competencies that the child depends upon to engage in any social interaction. From this perspective, the bully and the victim can be functioning at the same developmental level of friendship knowledge, skills, and valuing, only using different personal orientations. Assessment of the fundamental properties that underlie friendship expression can be a helpful means of addressing interpersonal problems.

APPLICATIONS

The middle years of childhood are marked by major advances in reasoning, in memory, and in the comprehension of many domains, including social relationships. From infancy, the child has been navigating the social world, moving from early attachment relationships to the gradually enlarging network of peers in the school setting. There are some fundamental linkages between these early relationships and children's later social interactions. For example, caregivers' encouraging preschool children to take notice of others' perspectives has been related to empathy, good social problem solving, and perspective taking at school age (Dixon & Moore, 1990). Success in relating to others rests upon having a positive internal working model for social responding, having access to peers in settings that promote mutual respect, and knowing how to resolve conflicts, among other things. And, as we have seen in this chapter, cognitive developments contribute importantly to children's social success at this time. Children in the school years need to be successful in the classroom as well as on the playground.

Much progress has been made in understanding the ways children process, store, and retrieve information because of the explosion of research in the area of cognitive psychology. Noting a few general implications may be useful for counselors.

1. Knowledge acquisition is a constructive process, built on the foundation of prior learning and experience. Children benefit from instruction that organizes information, relates it to previously learned material, and stresses its meaningfulness. Too many children, critics have noted, are taught in ways that reflect an emphasis on rote memorization of facts without any fundamental understanding of concepts.

2. Good instructional practice, including psychoeducational training, involves five basic elements: gaining the child's attention and motivation; activating what the child already knows about the material to be taught; presenting the new material in ways that capitalize on multiple sensory modalities (visual, auditory, tactile-kinesthetic); providing adequate, meaningful, and interesting practice to ensure retention; and giving task-specific feedback that scaffolds the child's progress.

3. When adults teach children how to use memory strategies such as chunking, children retain more information. Children can also be encouraged to encode information both visually and verbally to capitalize on the way the mind processes material.

4. Students can also benefit from the use of techniques such as cooperative learning, if teachers or group leaders offer children opportunities to learn how to work effectively together. Encouraging children to talk over their ideas and providing them with techniques for doing so seems to be helpful. Keeping track of their progress and giving them feedback is also important. Cooperative methods should also incorporate some form of individual accountability as well as group recognition for goals achieved (Slavin, 1995).

5. Keep in mind that normal cognitive development is uneven. Theories of development have suffered, to some degree, from their emphasis on stages, because this emphasis leads to perceptions of development in terms of static, monolithic levels. In the real world, children as well as adults are much more variable. Despite the common conception that Piaget emphasized stagewise development, he also recognized that variation in skill exists within stages. Specifically, he found that logical skills were applied to some contents (such as understanding conservation of number) before other contents (such as understanding conservation of weight). This variation he called decalage. This kind of variability in skill level is clearly evident in any classroom. Some may excel in reading and language arts yet find math a chore. Others

may be gifted athletes who have difficulty remembering facts in social studies. Isn't such unevenness characteristic of adults as well? Most people's panorama of abilities reflects a mix of relative strengths and weaknesses.

6. Unevenness in development may be particularly relevant to the area of special education and the concept of disability. Some authors, notably Sternberg and Grigorenko (1999), contend that virtually everyone has a disability in something. The difference is that society determines what constitutes "disability" and identifies a select group as "disabled." Within schools, weaknesses in analytical ability, an important skill for success in most academic subject areas, may be considered particularly problematic. Yet, most contemporary theories of intelligence recognize the fact that intelligence is characterized by many kinds of skills (e.g., Gardner, 1983; Sternberg, 1985). In Sternberg's (1985) theoretical formulation, traditional analytic ability is just one part of the whole picture of intelligence. He includes creative and practical aspects of intelligence in the mix and recommends that teachers provide opportunities for students to manifest these other abilities, as a supplement to more traditional forms of teaching and assessment. For example, developing skits, creating poetry or pictures, designing experiments, establishing classroom government, or running a school store are all activities that tap creative and practical intelligence, which may be areas of relative strength for students with different learning styles.

Assessing and Teaching Metacognitive Skills

Despite typical age-related limitations in children's abilities to reflect on their thinking, metacognitive advances do emerge during this period and open up a range of clinical possibilities. The major elements of metacognition, ability to appraise one's own thinking and ability to regulate one's own thinking, have great relevance for educational and clinical efforts to improve skills like problem-solving and perspective-taking. The role of distorted cognitions in mental health problems is also very well known to clinicians, so understanding children's self-statements can be important in this regard.

As noted above, the first component of metacognition is knowing what one is thinking. Several means of assessing cognition have been used in research, including asking people what they say to themselves while they are currently thinking about some task (called "self-talk"), asking them what they were thinking after they completed the task (called "thought-listing") or, after videotaping an activity and replaying the video, asking them to "dub" the self-talk (called "video-mediated recall"). The purpose of these techniques is to open a window on the thinking process. Lodge, Tripp, and Harte (2000) demonstrated that think-aloud and video-mediated recall, compared to thought-listing, resulted in the most productive record of self-talk among third- and fourth-grade children. A self-talk instruction might be "When you read this short paragraph (or work on this problem), just remember to say out loud all the things that come into your head." The use of self-talk can help the counselor understand how the child understands a particular situation or problem, how he makes attributions about the problem, and how he goes about solving the problem.

The areas of study skills training, academic counseling, or tutoring also depend upon a working knowledge of children's cognition. Counselors can attempt to appraise thinking by informal assessment of memory as described in this chapter. In the case of underachievement, students may be helped to understand the study process though prompts such as: "Do you know that studying every night will help you master the material?" (declarative knowledge); "What do you do when you study for a test?" (procedural knowledge); and "When do you think you should memorize definitions and when should you practice problems?" (conditional knowledge). Once the thoughts are revealed, counselors can clarify misconceptions and help children learn more effective study skills. Table 6.2 presents a sampling of self-monitoring questions.

Another rationale for using self-talk procedures is to help children realize the *existence* of their self-talk, its relationship to their feelings and behaviors, and the ways they can modify it to make it more adaptive. This approach is critical to many cognitive-behavioral treatments for anxiety, depression, anger control, and ADHD (see Kendall, 1991). In this latter case, the content of the self-statements is as relevant as the process of self-instruction. In other words, teaching children (and adults, for that matter) to recognize negative self-statements is a necessary first step before instruction and practice in alternatives.

Meichenbaum and Goodman (1971), who pioneered self-instruction training, began by teaching self-control to impulsive children using guided modeling and self-talk procedures. Their approach included the following steps. The clinician models effective self-talk while doing some task or dealing with some hypothetical scenario. Next, the child is asked to repeat the same process while the clinician provides overt instruction. The child is then asked to redo the activity, first talking out loud by himself and then by subvocalizing

(whispering) the instructions. Finally, the child practices using private (nonvocal) self-talk.

One can imagine a situation wherein therapy involves both learning the steps of self-instruction training and modifying the content of maladaptive cognitions. For example, once self-talk assessment has identified a person's negative self-statements ("I can't do math"), training in self-instruction can strengthen the frequency of positive alternatives ("I didn't do well on this problem because I didn't spend enough time studying"). Researchers report that it is not necessary, and is actually undesirable, for people to expect to have only positive thoughts. The ratio of 2 positive thoughts to 1 negative one appears optimal for healthy adjustment (Schwartz & Garamoni, 1989). Depressed individuals, for example, show an equal 1:1 balance (Kendall, 1991). Therefore, tipping the scales in favor of more positive thoughts appears to be a clinically important goal for adults and children alike.

Focus on the second element of metacognition, self-regulation of thinking—the "how well am I thinking?" part—helps the individual translate knowledge into action. As in self-instructions approaches, this provides the basis for cognitive problem-solving techniques, used to good effect in a variety of clinical and educational settings. Typical problem-solving steps include defining the problem or goal, selecting a plan to solve the problem or meet the goal, monitoring progress toward the goal, and revising goal-directed strategies, if needed.

PATHS to Healthy Development

Therapies designed to teach problem-solving and conflict-resolution skills have figured prominently in the counseling literature for many years and have been widely used with children and adolescents (Shure & Spivak, 1988; Weissberg, Caplan, & Bennetto, 1988). One comprehensive program with demonstrated effectiveness is Promoting Alternative Thinking Strategies (PATHS), a prevention program that includes 131 lessons for children in Grades K through 5 (Greenberg & Kusche, 2002). PATHS is founded on a holistic approach to the development of emotional well-being, and like good prevention programs, reaches out to include multiple levels of the system (peers, parents, and teachers). The primary goals include the promotion of emotional literacy,

---

TABLE 6.2   Sample Self-Monitoring Questions

1. Why am I trying to learn this information? What is the purpose of this exercise or assignment?
2. What do I already know about this subject?
3. Do I already know any strategies that will help me learn this?
4. What is my plan of action?
5. Do I understand the steps I need to take?
6. How should I get help if I need it?
7. How should I correct my mistakes?
8. Am I accomplishing my goals? Am I being successful?
9. How will I know when I've accomplished my goals?

TABLE 6.3   Problem-Solving Unit of the PATHS Curriculum

STOP!

1. Stop and calm down.
2. Identify the problem (collect lots of information).
3. Identify the feelings (your own and other people's).

GO SLOW!

4. Decide on a goal.
5. Think of lots of solutions.
6. Think about the consequences.
7. Choose the best solution (evaluate all of the alternatives).
8. Make a good plan (think about possible obstacles).

GO!

9. Try my plan.
10. Evaluate—How did I do?
11. If you need to, try again.

Source: Greenberg, M. T., Kusche, C., & Mihalic, S. F. (2002). Promoting Alternative Thinking Strategies (PATHS). In D. S. Elliott (Series Ed.), *Blueprint for Violence Prevention, Book Ten* (pp. 29–30). Boulder, Co: Center for the Study and Prevention of Violence, Institute of Behavioral Science, University of Colorado.

self-control, and social problem-solving skills in the context of a positive school environment. The benefits of this program have extended to children from a wide range of ethnic, racial, and social class backgrounds, to children with disabilities, and to children of both genders (Conduct Problems Prevention Research Group [CPPRG], 1999; Greenberg & Kusche, 1998).

The interpersonal cognitive problem-solving portion of this program offers an example of the material we have been discussing in this chapter. This part of the curriculum includes 33 lessons (introduced in Grades 3 or 4) that are presented after the units on emotional recognition, self-control, and communicating with others have been completed. The authors note that problem-solving is not just an isolated cognitive activity but one which flows from a basic understanding of self and others. The lessons in the problem-solving unit have been listed in Table 6.3. To generalize the skills and apply them to everyday life, children are encouraged to write out real problems from their life experience and put them into a "mailbox" on the teacher's desk. These problems are discussed in regular problem-solving meetings. Teachers also build problem-solving practice into other areas, such as academic subjects.

Learning the Skills of Friendship

At the heart of many therapeutic approaches is a fundamental focus on teaching children how to get along with one another, which requires perspective taking. We stress the importance of learning to relate to others in elementary school, but it is clearly not a task just for children. Knowing how to get along with others is essential for people of all ages.

Recent descriptions of emotional intelligence (e.g., Goleman, 1995, 1998) stress the lifelong value of having good "people skills" even in the adult world of work. Some define therapy as the process of building an awareness of how our actions affect other people, the very essence of perspective taking (see Pittman, 1998).

Children in the school years begin this kind of learning in earnest. Because they spend such large amounts of time in school, teachers and peers exert a strong influence on the development of social competence. Counselors often play a role by providing developmental guidance activities, social skills training programs, and other kinds of cognitive, affective, and behavioral interventions.

Selman's (Selman et al., 1997a) friendship framework can be a useful and somewhat unusual guide to developing interventions, because it addresses the fundamental friendship relationship and makes practice applications that are developmentally and theoretically based. His therapeutic technique, called pair therapy, has been applied to both preventive and remedial work with children and adolescents. Although a comprehensive review of this approach is beyond the scope of this text, it is helpful to describe some of its basic ideas.

Children's social skills can be seen as involving both social competence and performance. *Competence* refers to the child's level of perspective-taking ability, and *performance* refers to the child's actual use of skills for getting along with others. Selman's research indicates that adequate competence (perspective taking) is necessary but not sufficient for good performance (social functioning). In other words, children never have high-level social skills without a commensurate level of perspective taking. However, socially unskilled children may either lack interpersonal understanding or possess it without being able to act on it. Pair therapy was designed to help both kinds of poor performers: those with low competence and low performance as well as those with high competence and low performance. This kind of therapeutic approach has been adapted for use in primary prevention efforts in schools that are intended to foster good social relationships among the whole student community. Similar approaches have also been applied at the middle and high school levels in programs to reduce racism and promote intercultural understanding (Schultz, Barr, & Selman, 2000). Table 6.4 presents a comparison of two related interventions, one for therapeutic purposes (pair therapy) and one for prevention (pairing for prevention). In pair therapy, two children with equally ineffective social styles, such as a controlling child and a fearful one, are paired. Both participants meet regularly with a helper whose job it is to encourage both children to be effectively assertive and empathic. The

TABLE 6.4 Pair Therapy and Pairing for Prevention		
	Pair Therapy	**Pairing for Prevention**
Context of treatment	Child Guidance Clinic/Day Treatment/Residential Treatment Program/In-patient Hospitalization (if long-term).	School-Based (during or after school); Community Center/Settlement House/Girls and Boys Clubs.
Clients	Children and adolescents with severe emotional and behavior problems. Range of psychiatric diagnoses, including cognitive and communicative disorders. Very limited peer interactions. Family trauma.	"At-risk" students with conduct and/or academic problems: may have close friends, from low-income, inner-city households; likely exposure to, and/or involvement in societal health/welfare risks. Limited social supports.
General goals	Foster personality and social development. Increase capacity to make and maintain friendships: coordinate social perspectives, communicate more effectively, resolve interpersonal conflicts, manage emotions.	Same goals as therapy but with focus on interpersonal development as vehicle for increasing capacity to make mature decisions with respect to risks. Pairs provides protective factor against risky behaviors.
Theory guiding treatment and evaluation	Primarily Psychological: Orthogenetic and Structural-Developmental Model: Intimacy and Autonomy as functional social management processes organized according to developmental level of perspective coordination.	Primarily Psychosocial Risk-Taking Model: Takes into account sociocultural and biological antecedents, and psychosocial dimensions (knowledge, management, and personal meaning) of risk taking behavior. Incorporates Structural Developmental Model.
Overall treatment plan	Often in conjunction with individual psychotherapy, adjunct therapies (i.e., speech, family), and/or a therapeutic milieu.	May be only special service student receives.
Training level of providers	Supervised clinicians or residential staff, with some understanding of individual psychodynamics.	Supervised Master's level students with some understanding of psychosocial development and the social system within which they are providing service.
Time frame of treatment/research focus	Long-term treatment/longitudinal study of interpersonal development (1–4 years). Process oriented basic research of both the individual and the dyad. Major focus on assessment methods: interviews and observations to assess ego development.	Focus on major transitions (Elementary to Middle School; Middle School to High School) Outcome and Process Oriented research. Focus on both individual assessment and program evaluation. Additional reliance on ethnography.
Evaluation/ Research	In-depth micro and macro level assessment of affective, cognitive, motivational and dynamic dimensions of evolving pair relationship (non-experimental).	Qualitative evaluation of process of change in pair's knowledge, management and personal meaning of risk, and quantitative assessment of risk outcome in treatment group compared to control group (experimental). Additional qualitative and quantitative analysis of participant's view of prevention.

Source: Watts, C. L., Nakkula, M. J., & Barr, D. (1977). Person-in-pairs, pairs-in-program: Pair therapy in different institutional contents in R. L. Selman, C. L. Watts, & L. H. Schultz. (Eds.) *Fostering friendship: Pair therapy for treatment and prevention.* New York: Aldine de Gruyter Copyright © 1997 by Walter de Gruyter, Inc., New York. Reprinted with permission.

therapeutic material is what the children bring to the time they spend together. What they decide to do together, how they decide to do it, where it happens, and so on all become grist for the therapeutic mill. Adult helpers provide a watchful eye and a knowledge of development that facilitates the pair's movement from egocentric, unilateral understanding toward more cooperative modes of interaction. The helper must ensure the physical and emotional safety of both children while allowing for their direct experience of conflict and their increasingly more advanced efforts at resolving it collaboratively. The shy child, for example, must be helped to learn ways to articulate his needs, and the more controlling child must learn to accommodate the other instead of overwhelming him. In general, this approach provides practice in the real-life experience of friendship. The counselor functions to guide the pair toward a more even-handed balance of control and decision-making functions and nurtures them toward experiences of mutual sharing and cooperation. Within this context, children learn the tools of friendship, which include the development of a sense of personal responsibility, motivation to make the friendship work, and the ability to understand firsthand the impact of one's words and actions on another person.

SUMMARY

Physical and Brain-Related Changes

1. Changes in the brain underlie motor developments in middle childhood. First gross motor coordination, then fine motor coordination and eye-hand coordination benefit from continued myelination of the corpus callosum, connecting the left and right cortical hemispheres, and the cerebellum, as well as other brain maturation processes.

2. Brain maturation also contributes to cognitive development. Myelination of the reticular formation and synaptogenesis in the frontal lobe contribute to improved attention, concentration, and planning, and memory. The primary localization of certain intellectual processes, such as math and reading skills, seems to shift during middle childhood, as the brain matures and as skills become more practiced.

Cognitive Development

3. In Piaget's theory, children at the concrete operational stage (6 to 12 years) can decenter, or think about more than one dimension or aspect of a situation at one time. This allows them the possibility of recognizing or constructing the relationships among the dimensions, which is important for logical thinking. Understanding reversible relationships, when one change reverses the effects of another, or one change compensates for the effects of another, is especially important. Recognizing the nature of the relationships among features of an event makes it possible for children to infer underlying realities.

4. At the concrete operational stage, children's thinking is most logical when they are solving problems that relate to real, concrete events. They find it difficult to think logically about abstract contents, like their own thought processes. They are subject to a form of egocentrism, such that they find it difficult to distinguish between their own theories or assumptions and objective fact.

5. Logical thinking can be domain specific to some degree. When children have a great deal of experience with a specific domain of knowledge, they are more likely to think logically about problems in that domain.

6. In the information processing approach, cognition is compared to the functioning of a computer. The organization of the cognitive system stays the same across age, but there are age changes in the amount and efficiency of information flow. With increasing age, children can hold more information in working memory at one time, and they may change the strategies they use to operate on the information. Also, the same child is likely to use different strategies on different contents, so that there are no stage-similar ways of dealing with information across domains. NeoPiagetians are theorists who try to integrate concepts from Piaget's theory and from information processing theory to explain cognitive development.

7. Two kinds of remembering or retrieval are called recognition (realizing that information being experienced now is familiar) and recall (drawing information out of long-term memory and representing it to yourself). Our memories can store declarative knowledge, both semantic (about facts and concepts) and episodic (about events we have experienced). A schematic representation of a frequently experienced event is called a script. We also store nondeclarative knowledge, which is hard to verbalize and is often referred to as procedural, which is "knowing how" rather than "knowing that." Infants' and toddlers' knowledge is largely nondeclarative.

8. Working memory increases in capacity with age, as indicated on digit span tests. This seems related to accelerated information processing, perhaps due to practice, perhaps to maturation, or to both.

9. Children's knowledge base increases with age, and that helps children reconstruct events. They "remember" more accurately because they can infer what must have happened. An expanded knowledge base also helps children learn new information more easily, perhaps because they can fit the new information into a rich web of

well-organized connections. Having an expanded knowledge base also benefits chunking in working memory.

10. Advances in logical thinking can help children improve their memories. The better the child understands the original experience, the more likely he is to reconstruct it accurately.

11. Increasing facility with language helps children store memories for events in coherent verbal form and seems to improve later retrieval of those events.

12. Children also improve in the use of memory strategies with age from preschool through middle school. Rehearsal is an early strategy, with more effective strategies such as organization coming later. Children's progress in strategy use is bumpy. They may exhibit either production deficiencies or utilization deficiencies.

13. Children gradually improve their understanding of their own cognitive processes (metacognition), including memory abilities, as they approach the end of middle childhood, partly accounting for improvements in strategy use with age.

14. Memory is also influenced by affective and social developments, like motivation to learn and the amount of scaffolding available from adults.

15. Preschool children acquire informal mathematical skills, such as adopting simple counting strategies for adding and subtracting small numbers. In elementary school, they continue to invent their own strategies as well as adopting the formal algorithms and strategies they are taught. Gradually, more efficient strategies win out over less efficient strategies, though again development, is bumpy.

16. Children assimilate formal rules to their own concepts, and often misunderstand. Teachers can encourage mathematical development by exploring their students' understanding rather than accepting rote learning of procedures.

17. There are a number of examples of how social and cultural context contributes to some variations in children's acquisition of math concepts.

18. Adults work to keep children focused during problem solving. They respond to a child contingently, tailor instruction to the child's level, ask challenging questions, and elicit the child's active involvement. When children collaborate with other children, the process may be less effective in fostering learning. It works best when all partners are actively involved and when adults provide feedback.

Social Cognition

19. Learning about social interactions, including how to make and keep friends, and acquiring a theory of mind begins in early childhood and is heavily dependent on cognitive developments. For example, children's perspective taking improves as they acquire the ability to think about their own mental experiences and those of another person at the same time.

20. Theorists such as Sullivan and Selman built on Piaget's ideas and linked the gradual improvement in perspective taking with changes in the nature of friendships over age. In Selman's five-stage theory, improvements in perspective taking affect an individual's friendship understanding, influence his friendship valuing, and affect the social and conflict resolution skills (friendship skills) he develops.

21. In Selman's view, a mature interpersonal orientation balances intimacy and autonomy strivings. Less effective orientations may be other-transforming or self-transforming, and are more characteristic of very young children and of socially immature older children. Both a bully and a victim may be functioning at a similar developmental level with regard to perspective-taking skill. Assessing the properties of understanding that underlie relationship skill is a helpful approach to addressing social problems.

CASE STUDY

Alex, the second child of Ernest and Isabel Palacio, a Cuban American couple, is a fourth grader at J. F. Kennedy Elementary School. He has one older sister, Paula, who is in fifth grade, and a younger brother, Thomas, who is 4 years old. Until recently, Alex appeared to be a happy child and a good student in school. Although somewhat reserved, he interacted well with peers, was athletic, and was popular among his classmates.

During the year Alex was in third grade, the Palacios' marriage was seriously affected by Ernest's close relationship with a female coworker. Despite an attempt at counseling, the couple could not resolve their differences. During the

summer before his fourth-grade year, Alex's parents separated. The children continued to live with their mother but maintained a relationship with their father, seeing him every weekend in the apartment he rented nearby.

Both parents tried hard to make this arrangement work for the sake of their children, to whom both were devoted. The fourth-grade school year began fairly smoothly for Alex, who was happy to see his friends again after the summer vacation. His teacher, Mr. Williams, was regarded as tough but usually fair, and Alex seemed to make a good initial adjustment to his class. Ernest continued his employment with an advertising agency and paid for many of the family's living costs. However, the expense of maintaining two residences quickly became burdensome. Isabel, formerly employed as a part-time library aide, needed to find a position that provided a larger income. She began a job as a secretary shortly after the children began school in September.

In December, Isabel fell ill and needed to be hospitalized. Primary care of the children fell to Isabel's mother, the children's grandmother. Ernest took over as much of the caretaking as his work schedule would permit, but he feared that if he took off too much time for family responsibilities, his job would be in jeopardy. Because of these changes in the family, all three children needed to adjust. It became much more difficult for an adult to transport the children after school to music lessons and games, so they had to drop out of some of their activities. As Isabel recuperated, she needed much more rest and general peace and quiet. She could no longer take the children on trips or allow groups of her children's friends to have sleep-overs in her home.

Toward the middle of his fourth-grade year, Alex's grades started to slip, and he began to act up. Alex grew apathetic and sullen in class. His teacher, Mr. Williams, was a relatively young teacher in the school district. His first 2 years of teaching had been spent in the eighth grade of the district middle school. He liked teaching older students and reluctantly accepted the fourth grade position because of his lack of seniority in the system. Mr. Williams, despite his youth, was a fairly traditional teacher. He believed in giving lots of homework and in placing high expectations for performance on his students. He ran a very disciplined classroom that was based on a system of winning and losing points for behavior. Because Alex did not participate actively in classroom exercises or turn in homework, he continually "lost points."

On one particularly difficult day, Alex and one of his friends got into an argument. Alex accused his friend of picking on him and teasing him in the lunchroom. Mr. Williams tried to intervene by taking both boys out into the hallway and listening to each version of the problem. When the disagreement got louder, Mr. Williams told both boys that they would "just have to work it out." He told them he would take away points and was sending them both to the principal's office. Alex became very agitated and said to his teacher "sometimes I feel like throwing my chair at you."

Mr. Williams began to see Alex as a threat and recommended to the principal that the incident be handled as a disciplinary matter. It was the teacher's belief that Alex should be suspended and then referred for special education evaluation by the school psychologist because of his "aggressiveness." He insisted that Alex not be returned to his classroom.

Discussion Questions

1. How would you assess the problem?
2. What are the different perspectives involved in this conflict?
3. What actions would you take and what recommendations would you make as a counselor in this situation?

JOURNAL QUESTIONS

1. If you can remember struggling with some subject or concept in school, describe the impact of this experience on your sense of competence and industry. If you were counseling a student in this situation, what advice would you have for his parent? His teachers?
2. Describe what your friendships were like in elementary school. Did you have a "best friend"? What characteristics did he or she possess?
3. Compare and contrast how you solved conflicts as a child in grade school and how you solve them now. How would you assess your level of perspective taking?
4. Using the "Friendship Framework" presented in this chapter, reflect upon each element in light of one particular relationship that you have experienced or are experiencing. (For example, what is your primary interpersonal orientation, other- or self-transforming?)

KEY TERMS

concrete operational stage	sensory memory	semantic memory	guided imagery
reversible relationship	long-term memory	episodic memory	stereotype induction
egocentrism	rehearsal	script	chunking
formal operational thought	storage	nondeclarative knowledge	narrative skill
domain of knowledge	retrieval	procedural knowledge	memory strategies
domain specific	recognition	digit span tests	selective attention
neoPiagetians	recall	knowledge base	organization strategy
working memory	declarative knowledge	reality monitoring	elaboration strategy

production deficiency
utilization deficiency
metacognition
self-instruction
self-monitoring
counting all strategy

counting on strategy
retrieval strategy
cooperative learning
   environments
social cognition
perspective taking

psychosocial development
friendship understanding
friendship skills
friendship valuing
interpersonal orientation
other-transforming

self-transforming
pair therapy
social competence and
   performance

Now go to our Companion Website to assess your understanding of chapter content with Multiple Choice Questions, apply comprehension in Essay Questions, and broaden your knowledge of development with related Web Links.

CHAPTER 7

Self and Moral Development: Middle Childhood Through Early Adolescence

Honesty, dependability, kindness, fairness, respect, self-control, truthfulness, and diligence. Rare is the adult who would not agree that any one of these traits is desirable for children to attain. The advantage is very basic: Behaving in accordance with these values makes the world a better place for everyone. Certainly, individuals or groups might disagree on the particulars, such as what "being fair" may mean in a given situation. But it is truly difficult to imagine any sizable group of parents, teachers, or clinicians who would promote the opposite values: meanness, laziness, dishonesty, irresponsibility, or disrespect, to name a few.

Not too long ago in this country, there was considerable agreement that inculcating these values, virtues, or behavioral habits was perhaps the most important responsibility that adults have relative to their children. The public schools had as their express purpose the creation of good citizens—people who, for the most part, valued and practiced these virtues. Consider the advice educator Charles Davis presented in 1852 in a lecture to parents and teachers on their duties toward children:

> Education is the system of training which develops in their right direction and in their proper proportions our physical, intellectual, and moral natures. . . . The moral nature of the pupils will be, with the teacher, a subject of earnest and constant solicitude. What are the first things to be done? To establish his [the teacher's] authority over his school—to ensure the obedience of his scholars—to win their confidence—to gain their respect, and to call into exercise their warmest affections. (pp. 6—8)

Hiram Orcutt, writing in a famous manual to parents in 1874, advises thus:

> The child must establish a character of integrity and to be trained to habits of honesty, benevolence and industry or he will be lost to himself and to society. . . . We may not expect benevolence to spring up spontaneously in the heart of the child. . . . Without knowledge and experience, the child cannot appreciate the rights and wants of others, nor his own duty in regard to them. (pp. 72–73)

If this seems a bit quaint and outdated to you, consider the fact that even today there is evidence for broad consensus among parents in this country about what they consider is fundamental for children to achieve their life goals. When David R. Shaffer and his students asked young parents what they considered to be the most important aspect of a child's social development, most placed morality at the top of their lists (Shaffer, 2000). They apparently felt that acquiring a moral sense and living by its dictates were critical for self-development and central to successful adult functioning.

Perhaps this consensus is being shaped by our experience of the culture we share at the beginning of this new millennium. We are benumbed by the repetitious refrain that comes from all manner of media reporting on a world marred by violence, aggressiveness, hopelessness, underachievement, and declining civility.

What is happening to the healthy moral and self-development we wish for our children? As you might have already guessed, the problem is complex and most certainly has many influential antecedents. Whatever answers researchers have made available, however, have profound significance for practice, given counselors' investment in their clients' healthy social and emotional development. In this chapter and the next, we will introduce the topics that are fundamental to understanding social and emotional development in middle and late childhood and provide some guidelines and suggestions for interventions. We pick up the discussion with the topic of the self.

SELF-CONCEPT

The Development of Self-Concept

Imagine that you live across the street from an empty lot. One day, you notice that workers have placed piles of building materials, bricks, lumber, and bags of concrete on the property. After some time, the frame of a large, boxlike house takes the place of the piles of materials. From your vantage point, you can see the empty beginnings of where rooms will be. With more time, the internal structure becomes clear. Walls are assembled; doors and stairways connect the parts. Each section of the new house—living, dining, bedroom, and storage areas—has multiple divisions that provide useful space dedicated to some purpose. The disparate piles have been transformed into a coherent structure, and the once simple structure has become increasingly complex. Finishing touches are made, and ongoing renovations will undoubtedly accompany the life of the home.

This image is offered to provide a rough approximation of how the self-concept might develop from early childhood through adolescence and adulthood. It is important to recognize that self-concept or self-knowledge is very much like any other kind of knowledge, for the self is a cognitive construction. Therefore, knowledge of the self will be constrained by the child's general level of cognitive development and will most likely progress unevenly. As Harter (1999) has pointed out in her description of general cognitive-developmental stages, "decalage is accepted as the rule, rather than the exception; therefore, it is expected that the particular level of development at which one is functioning will vary across different domains of knowledge" (p. 30) as we noted in Chapter 6.

In addition, remember that the self-concept is multidimensional, like a house with various rooms (see Chapter 5). In many homes, rooms are added on after the initial construction. In contrast to this somewhat static analogy, the self-system is dynamic and changes throughout development. Generally, the child's self-concept proceeds from a rather undifferentiated state or simple structure to a much more organized and coherent structure in adulthood through a process of stagelike changes. Let us consider some of the developments in self-knowledge that occur as children mature.

The preschool child's rendering of herself is something like the lot filled with building materials. Self-descriptors such as "big," "girl," and "nice" are separate, uncoordinated elements in the child's self-portrait because she is cognitively unable to integrate these elements into an organized whole. We know from our discussion of cognitive development (see Chapter 3) that young children's ability to hold in mind several ideas at the same time and to integrate these in some meaningful way is quite underdeveloped. Furthermore, preschool youngsters find accommodating opposing characteristics, such as being "nice" and "mean" (Fischer, Hand, Watson, Van Parys, & Tucker, 1984), or opposing emotional states, such as "happy" and "sad" (Harris, 1983), to be especially difficult. Nor do young children make much use of perspective taking at this age, as we saw in Chapter 6. In failing to do so, they show limited ability to use the behaviors or perspectives of others as guides for evaluating their own conduct or performance. Stated in other words, they do not use information gleaned from observing others as a way of assessing their competencies. Consequently, the young child's self-evaluations may not conform to reality but may be overly positive. Four-year-old Jamar might insist he has won the round of miniature golf despite hitting the ball outside the lane every time!

Gradually, the early-elementary-school-aged youngster begins to organize the characteristics of the "Me-self" into sets of categories that display some coherence. For example, the child might relate being good at drawing, at coloring, and at cutting as an indication that she is good at art. However, the child still does not accommodate sets of characteristics with opposing features (e.g., nice versus mean; Fischer et al., 1984). Given her tendency to perceive personal qualities as good and to discount the subtlety of coexisting negative attributes, the child's thinking about herself may still have an all-or-nothing quality that is often unrealistically positive. There is little discrepancy between the "real" and the "ideal" selves. Gradual improvements in perspective-taking ability, however, allow the child to begin to evaluate her own behavior according to others' standards. The child's anticipation of another person's reaction, be it as a reward or a punishment, becomes internalized (Harter, 1998). As others' rules or standards become internalized, they become adopted as self-regulatory guidelines and form the basis for the looking-glass self.

Between middle childhood and early adolescence, the individual becomes capable of integrating opposing characteristics and begins to form more abstract trait-like concepts to describe herself. Self-assessments, such as "being smart," are bolstered by feedback from a wide variety of outside influences across many kinds of situations, and these assessments become more resistant to modification. Self-esteem tends to decline a bit during middle childhood and early adolescence because children recognize, often for the first time, how they fall short in comparison to others. Struggles to integrate abstract representations of the self characterize the period of adolescence as the young person works on defining a unique identity.

The Structure of Self-Concept

Although we continue to use the term *self-concept*, it is not a unidimensional construct, as we noted in Chapter 5. One's overall sense of self is a composite of several related, but not necessarily overlapping, elements that are evaluated by the individual to determine self-esteem, our feelings about ourselves. Although technically separate constructs, self-concept and self-esteem are closely intertwined. Shavelson, Hubner, and Stanton (1976) proposed a highly influential theoretical view of the self that has received recent research confirmation (Byrne & Shavelson, 1996; Marsh, 1990). In this model (see Figure 7.1), children's general self-concept can be divided into two main domains: academic and nonacademic self-concepts. **Academic self-concept** is further divided into specific school subject areas such as math, science, English, and social studies. More recently, developmentalists have proposed the addition of other components such as artistic self-concept (Marsh & Roche, 1996; Vispoel, 1995).

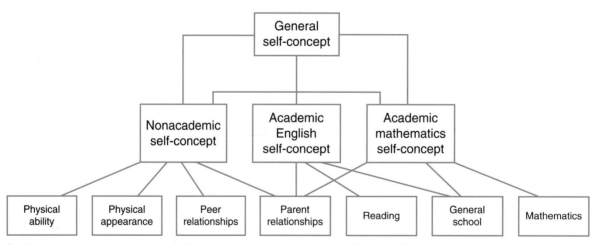

Students have many separate but sometimes related concepts of themselves. The overall sense of self appears to be divided into separate, but slightly related, self-concepts.

FIGURE 7.1

Structure of Self-Concept

Source: From "Self-Concept: Its Multifaceted, Hierarchical Structure," by H. W. Marsh and R. J. Shavelson, 1985, *Educational Psychologist, 20,* p. 114. Copyright © 1985 Lawrence Erlbaum Associates, Inc. Adapted with permission of the publisher and the authors.

The **nonacademic self-concept** is divided into social, emotional, and physical self-concepts. The last domain is further subdivided into physical ability and physical appearance. Other contemporary theories of the self (Harter, 1993; L'Ecuyer, 1992; Markus, 1977; Marsh & Hattie, 1996) also emphasize multidimensional and hierarchically arranged self-structures. Despite this general consensus, however, many researchers have retained the notion of global self-esteem within their frameworks. This appears to reflect the view that a global sense of self coexists with and shapes self-appraisals in specific domains.

By grade school, children can articulate their own assessments of their specific competencies as well as a generalized overall perception of themselves (Harter & Pike, 1984). Using her measures with individuals of different ages, Harter (1985, 1988b) has found that different domains of self-concept emerge at different points in the life span (see Table 7.1). The number of dimensions of the self that can be appraised, however, increases dramatically from early childhood through adolescence and adulthood. In middle childhood, the dimensions of importance include academic or scholastic competence, athletic competence, physical appearance, peer acceptance, and behavioral conduct.

Is any one domain more important than the others to a child's overall sense of self-esteem? Evidence from many studies reported by Harter (1990) clearly documents the powerful association between physical appearance and overall self-esteem (typical correlations are between .70 and .80) for older children, adolescents, college-aged students, and adults. The strength of this association holds up for special student populations such as learning disabled and academically talented groups as well. This somewhat disconcerting reality may be due to the fact that physical attractiveness is such an omnipresent, recognizable aspect of the self. It is also true that more attractive individuals receive more positive attention from others (Maccoby & Martin, 1983), receive more affection in infancy (Langlois, Ritter, Casey, & Savin, 1995), have more good qualities ascribed to them (Dion, Berscheid, & Walster, 1972), and are generally more successful in

TABLE 7.1	Domains of Self-Concept across the Life Span				
Early Childhood	Middle to Late Childhood	Adolescence	College Years	Early Through Middle Adulthood	Late Adulthood
Cognitive competence	Scholastic competence	Scholastic competence	Scholastic competence Intellectual ability Creativity	Intelligence	Cognitive abilities
		Job competence	Job competence	Job competence	Job competence
Physical competence	Athletic competence	Athletic competence	Athletic competence	Athletic competence	
Physical appearance	Physical appearance	Physical appearance	Physical appearance	Physical appearance	Physical appearance
Peer acceptance	Peer acceptance	Peer acceptance Close friendship Romantic relationships	Peer acceptance Close friendship Romantic relationships Relationships with parents	Sociability Close friendship Intimate relationships	Relationships with friends Family relationships
Behavioral conduct	Behavioral conduct	Conduct/morality	Morality Sense of humor	Morality Sense of humor Nurturance Household management	Morality Nurturance Personal, household management
				Adequacy as a provider	Adequacy as a provider Leisure activities Health status Life satisfaction Reminiscence
	Global self-worth	Global self-worth	Global self-worth	Global self-worth	Global self-worth

Source: From *The construction of the self: A developmental perspective*, by S. Harter 1990, New York: Guilford Press.

life (Hatfield & Sprecher, 1986). Thus, physically attractive individuals may be getting a consistently larger number of positive reflected appraisals with which to construct the self than their less attractive counterparts.

It also appears that cultural emphasis on rigid and often unobtainable standards of beauty, particularly for females, contributes to observed differences in self-esteem for males and females, which we will discuss in a later section of this chapter. Beginning around early adolescence, girls report more dissatisfaction with their appearance and their bodies than do boys of the same age (Allgood-Merten, Lewinsohn, & Hops, 1990).

Influences on the Development of Self-Concept

We have already presented the earliest influences on the developing self of the infant, toddler, and preschooler (see Chapter 5). What can we add to the story of self-concept development that applies to older children? Are the same processes at work? What can we say about the nature of self-esteem, that evaluative dimension which colors our self-appraisals? As you might suspect, the traditional positions of James (1890) and Cooley (1902) have much to offer contemporary researchers looking for explanations. Recall that William James believed that self-esteem was dependent upon the ratio of our successes to our aspirations. Harter (1990) found support for James's position. Children's, as well as adolescents' and adults', global self-esteem is heavily dependent upon competence in areas of personal importance. Individuals of all ages are more able to discount weak performance if it occurs in unimportant areas. For example, if it is very important to Ashley (and to her peers and parents) to be athletically competitive, relatively weak performance in this area is likely to lower her overall self-regard. On the other hand, if Sharon's goal is to be a stellar student, a weak athletic showing is likely to have less punishing consequences to her global sense of self.

In general, Harter found that the greater the discrepancy between adequacy in some domain and importance of that domain, the greater the negative impact on self-esteem. This helps explain why some students who display low levels of competence in certain domains may still have high self-esteem overall. Evidence suggests, however, that this reality is not well understood and may even contradict conventional wisdom. Consider a survey of teachers, school administrators, and school counselors in which approximately 60% of the respondents believed poor academic performance was the major cause of low self-esteem among students (Scott, Murray, Mertens, & Dustin, 1996). This belief fails to acknowledge the diversity of attributes that are

As children grow, social comparison processes contribute to the construction of the self-concept.

important to children (e.g., social relationships) as well as the fact that academic success may not be highly valued by everyone. Interestingly, in the same study, 69% of counselors compared to 35% of administrators believed that the self-esteem of underachieving students could be improved by more unconditional validation, a strategy we will examine more thoroughly later in the chapter.

Overall self-esteem seems to depend, at least in part, on a complicated, idiosyncratic calculation of perceived pluses and minuses factored against personally significant competencies. Large discrepancies, such as discrepancies between real and ideal selves as children reach adolescence, are associated with depression and anxiety (Higgins, 1991; Markus & Nurius, 1986). However, even low levels of competency in areas deemed of little personal value may not negatively alter one's general feelings about the self. High levels of competency in personally desirable behaviors, even if they are socially unacceptable (e.g., fighting, delinquent activities), may enhance self-esteem for some youth (Brynner, O'Malley, & Bachman, 1981; Cairns & Cairns, 1994).

How do children appraise their competencies in the first place? For a child at school age and beyond, there are obviously some concrete standards of performance, such as getting good grades or being selected for a sports team, that can be used to infer competency. Cooley also emphasized the importance of social influences on appraisals of competence. In other words, he believed that self-perceptions can be based on the internalization of approval or disapproval of others in the social network. But the role of the social network involves more than just providing an accumulation of comments or responses from others that become part of the self-concept. The self-system assimilates and accommodates evaluative data from internal ("How am I doing in reading compared to math?") and external ("How does my reading performance compare with that of my classmates?") sources in ways that involve comparison (Marsh, 1994).

The process, called social comparison (Festinger, 1954), means that people observe the performance of others and use it as a basis for evaluating their own abilities and accomplishments. When they do this and how they do it vary somewhat depending upon context and level of global self-esteem. Social comparison processes are particularly active in situations that are novel or ambiguous or when more objective standards of performance are unavailable. It is fairly obvious that classrooms provide a wealth of material for this ongoing process. Generally, children tend to make comparisons with other children who resemble them in some important ways (Suls & Miller, 1977). Most people are motivated to maintain moderately positive beliefs about themselves, called the self-enhancing bias (Taylor & Brown, 1988), which is considered a good thing in most cases.

The processes involved in social comparison work somewhat differently for individuals who are lower in self-esteem. When self-esteem is low, children may prefer situations that are rich in positive reinforcement. For example, Smith and Smoll (1990) reported that children with lower levels of self-esteem responded most favorably to coaches and instructors who were highly encouraging and least favorably to those who were least supportive. Children with high or moderate levels of self-esteem showed less variation in their responsiveness to adult reinforcement styles. Researchers (Pyszczynski, Greenberg, & LaPrelle, 1985) have also noted that children will make "downward" social comparisons by comparing themselves to less competent or less successful peers when their own self-esteem is at stake. Such comparisons protect the child from negative self-evaluations. Children and adults with lower levels of self-esteem are more susceptible to the kinds of external cues that carry evaluative messages and are more reactive to social feedback (Campbell, 1990). They are reluctant to call attention to themselves and are more cautious and self-protective. Possibly they feel they have more to lose if they experience negative evaluations from others. This contrasts with individuals with high self-esteem, who demonstrate more self-enhancement strategies and are more likely to call attention to themselves (Campbell & Lavallee, 1993).

Are children's self-perceptions congruent with the appraisals of others? In other words, do the reflected appraisals of others account for some of the substance of the child's self-structure? A study of third- and sixth-grade children carried out by Cole, Maxwell, and Martin (1997) found that the relationships between self-appraisals and others' appraisals were stronger for older students than they were for younger students. The authors hypothesized that older students were more motivated to engage in social comparison processes and more actively used the comparisons as a way of measuring their own performance. As children mature, they appear to put more stock in how peers see them. Can it be that we are what our friends believe we are? The importance of peers' appraisals in shaping self-concept, particularly as children approach adolescence, seems intuitively reasonable. Despite peers' important contribution to self-concept, however, this study also reported that the appraisals of parents and teachers contributed independently to the process.

What message can we draw from research in the tradition of James and Cooley? Harter (1993) concludes that the two theorists' positions operate in an additive way to explain the variation in self-esteem found in older children and adolescents. In other words, both competence and support contribute to the final product. The higher the level of competence in important domains and the greater the level of social support, the higher the level of self-esteem is overall.

Gender, Racial, and Ethnic Differences

GENDER

Much recent attention has been paid to the apparent decrease in self-esteem experienced by females around the time of their entrance to middle school. This phenomenon has been called the "loss of voice" by Gilligan and her colleagues (Brown & Gilligan, 1992), who purport that a girl experiences a gradual silencing of an authentic, imperious, and often willful self in order to identify with certain culturally prescribed roles of women as self-sacrificial and pleasing to others. Speaking one's mind, at least for women in certain contexts, can be threatening to the relationships that are such an important part of their lives. These authors argue that suppressing one's voice becomes the only possible way of maintaining important connections to others. In time, they conclude, women become disassociated from their true selves and may lose touch with their own opinions and feelings. Comparably negative claims of gender bias or silencing have been directed toward schools for "shortchanging" girls by giving them less attention than boys and for attributing their academic failure to lack of ability rather than to lack of effort (Ornstein, 1994; Sadker & Sadker, 1991). Popular accounts of these reports have contributed to the notion that the self-esteem of girls plunges precipitously around the early adolescent period, whereas that of boys remains robust (Daley, 1991).

What actually happens to girls' level of "voice" and to their views of themselves in late childhood and early adolescence? Are gender differences in self-regard real and universal? First, let's consider studies of girls' versus boys' level of voice. Harter and colleagues (Harter, Waters, Whitesell, and Kastelic, 1998) assessed level of voice by asking 9th to 11th graders to rate how able they feel to "express their opinions," "share what they are really thinking," and so on. They also asked the teens about whether others—parents, teachers, male classmates, female classmates, and close friends—listen to their opinions, respect their ideas, and show interest in their views. Finally, the researchers measured "relational self-worth" with different groups of people, asking respondents to say whether they liked or didn't like themselves the way they are around different people in their lives, such as parents or friends. The results support Gilligan's ideas about the importance of voice for self-esteem, but they do not support her notion that girls are more subject to "voice suppression" than boys, at least among today's children. Levels of voice were the same for both girls and boys with teachers, parents, and male classmates. But with female classmates and close friends, girls reported a stronger level of voice than boys did! For neither gender did level of voice decline with age, and for both genders, level of voice varied dramatically depending on whether the adolescent felt support for self-expression. For both girls and boys, feelings of self-worth varied with level of voice: In social contexts where kids felt like they could express themselves freely, they felt more self-worth.

Now, what about the claim that girls' overall self-worth declines in late childhood and early adolescence? One group of researchers looked carefully at the data from two large studies of global self-esteem, which included a combined total of 155,121 participants (Kling, Hyde, Showers, & Buswell, 1999). Results from this analysis provided evidence for a small but consistent gender effect, with males showing higher self-esteem. The level of difference is relatively small, however, compared to gender differences in aggressive behavior (Hyde, 1984) and activity level (Eaton & Enns, 1986). The authors concluded that the idea that girls' self esteem plunges dramatically at adolescence relative to boys' is overstated. Recent studies even indicate that gender gaps in self-esteem for specific competency areas favor girls in some domains (e.g., language arts) and boys in other domains (e.g., sports), usually appear in early elementary school, and do not increase in magnitude at adolescence (e.g., Jacobs, Lanza, Osgood, Eccles, & Wigfield, 2002).

The small but stable gender difference in global self-esteem should be taken seriously, but Kling and her colleagues caution that inflating the significance of the self-esteem slide may create a self-fulfilling prophecy. Adults who believe that girls have lower self-esteem than boys may convey this impression to girls in subtle but powerful ways. Girls may internalize this message and alter their self-appraisals accordingly. In addition, championing the self-esteem deficits of girls may lead some to conclude that boys do not have self-esteem problems. Clearly, there are gender role strains for boys as well. For example, they are more likely than girls to feel social pressure to conform to gender stereotypes (Yunger, Carver, & Perry, 2004). Boys who are not athletically inclined can suffer greatly in social status and self-esteem relative to their peers (Kilmartin, 1994). In Chapter 8, we will examine other facets of the link between gender and self-evaluation.

RACE AND ETHNICITY

For many years it was assumed that the self-esteem of minority group children would be lower than that of White children because of their minority status in North American culture. This interpretation was based on Cooley's idea of reflected appraisals and social comparison processes. Members of oppressed groups, for example, would be more likely than members of non-oppressed groups to internalize the discriminatory appraisals of others in constructing their sense of self (Cartwright, 1950). Similarly, social comparisons would be more negative when oppressed minorities held themselves to the standards of the majority culture (Gerth & Mills, 1953). Classic doll studies, in which investigators asked children to state their preference for dolls or pictures representing different racial groups, supported these interpretations (Clark, 1982). Preference for white dolls over black or brown ones was reported for all children, including those from African American (Spenser, 1970) and Native American groups (Aboud, 1977). These findings were interpreted to mean that children from oppressed minorities suffered from low self-esteem, due to the negative status accorded their racial background and their internalization of pejorative attitudes.

Current research has challenged these interpretations by demonstrating a slight but relatively consistent self-esteem advantage for Black Americans, the minority group most extensively studied, over White Americans. Several explanations have been proposed to account for this phenomenon. Crocker and Major (1989) posit that, to maintain their self-esteem, members of historically marginalized groups engage in three complementary processes. They attribute negative feedback directed toward themselves to the prejudice that exists in society. They make social comparisons to members of their own group rather than to members of the advantaged majority. Finally, they tend to enhance the importance of self-concept domains in which members of their group excel, while discounting the importance of domains in which their members do not excel.

Gray-Little and Hafdahl (2000) have attempted to summarize the existing data on this subject and have concluded that Blacks and other minority groups demonstrate a higher level of ethnocentrism than do Whites. In other words, racial identification is a more salient component of self-concept for members of these groups (see also Chapter 9). African Americans, in particular, benefit from this emphasis on their desirable distinctiveness within the larger society (Judd, Park, Ryan, Bauer, & Kraus, 1995). In fact, studies have found that strong racial or ethnic identity correlates positively with level of global self-esteem (Goodstein & Ponterotto, 1997; Phinney, 1990).

It is important to realize, however, that these results cannot be generalized to members of all minority groups, nor even to all members within a single minority. Gray-Little and Hafdahl (2000) make the important point that race is a complex construct, confounded with socio-economic status, culture, gender, and other important variables. Using race as a dividing criterion to compare groups is appealing because it seems so simple, but it may mask great within-group variability.

Strong ethnic or racial identity appears to enhance self-esteem for children and adolescents who are part of a minority group.

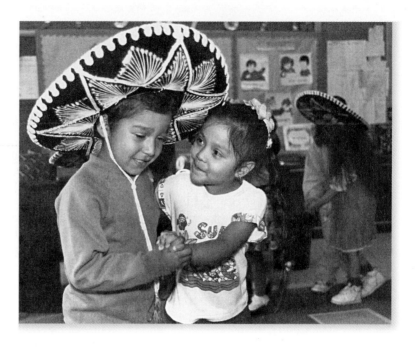

THE MORAL SELF

One important ingredient in self-development is the acquisition of values. Colby and Damon (1992) found that adults who lead exemplary lives tend to have very clear beliefs about what is right, and they consider those beliefs to be a central feature of their own identities. Their self-esteem hinges on acting in responsible ways, consistent with their beliefs. Even for children in the middle years, behavioral conduct is an important self-concept domain that is linked to global self-esteem. Generally, moral beliefs are increasingly central to self-definition as children get older, influencing them to act in responsible ways, but as Damon points out,

> the development of the self can take many paths, and persons vary widely in the extent to which they look to their commitments and convictions in defining their personal identities. . . . For some . . . morality may always remain peripheral to who they think they are. (Damon, 1995, p. 141)

In this section, we will examine some theories and research on how the moral self develops and why for some it is more compelling than for others.

Let's begin by specifying what we mean by a moral sense, or morality. First, it is a capacity to make judgments about what is right versus what is wrong, and second, it is preferring to act in ways that are judged to be "right." In other words, morality involves both an "evaluative orientation" toward actions and events (Damon, 1988) and a sense of obligation or commitment to behave in ways that are consistent with what is right. Early on, this sense of obligation is partly influenced by rewards or punishments from parents, teachers, and other adults. Gradually, a slate of standards and principles—a conscience—is internalized (see discussion of self-regulation in Chapters 4 and 5) and becomes the primary guide to action, so that a moral adult could even behave in ways that are disapproved by others if she judged the behavior to be right.

It is also important to recognize that moral development and religious experience are not the same thing. Religions do, of course, address issues of morality, and they prescribe standards of conduct. But moral development is part of normal self-development in all individuals, regardless of whether or not they are practitioners of a religious faith or whether or not they receive formal religious training.

As we noted in the introduction to this chapter, it is not surprising that parents regard the development of morality as a critical concern. Even though there are cultural and historical variations in the specifics of what is construed as moral, the meaning of morality generally includes some social interactive principles or propensities that are necessary to the successful functioning of all societies and of individuals within society (see Damon, 1988; Turiel, 1998). First, concern for others is important, as well as a willingness to act on that concern by sharing, forgiving, and other acts of benevolence. Second, a sense of justice and fairness, including a willingness to take into account the rights and needs of all parties, is part of a moral sense. Third, trustworthiness, defined primarily as honesty in dealings with others, is critical to most discussions of morality. Finally, self-control is essential. To live by standards requires a capacity and willingness to inhibit one's own selfish or aggressive impulses under some circumstances, that is, to avoid misbehavior. This is one aspect of self-control. Also, to be a useful member of society, or even to fully develop one's talents or abilities, requires effort and persistence regardless of discomfort or difficulty. This is a second aspect of self-control—a willingness to do things that are not much fun, such as work and practicing skills, even when play is more enticing. For example, there may be no exciting way to learn multiplication tables. Hard work and self-control are necessary to achieve long-term goals at any point in the life span. Research on the development of morality has largely focused on this set of fundamentals: concern for others, justice, trustworthiness or honesty, and self-control.

Elements of Morality

Morality requires a complex interweaving of three elements—emotions, cognitions, and behaviors—that do not always work together in perfect harmony. Consider the following true-life experience. Several decades ago, in a blue-collar city neighborhood, 10-year-old Carmen headed for a local grocery store to buy some items for her mother. Her family never saw her alive again. But some other folks later did see her. They were motorists, driving at high speeds on an inner city expressway, heading home in the evening rush hour. They remembered seeing a girl who looked like Carmen, running naked along the edge of the expressway with a man following her. Apparently, she had escaped from his car when he parked along the side of the road. But none of the motorists stopped, and the man caught the girl. Her raped and beaten body was later found in a remote location.

In the days and weeks following Carmen's disappearance, first one motorist and then another either phoned police anonymously or came forward openly to describe what she or he had seen, although none had reported the incident when it happened. The city's inhabitants were horrified both by the crime and by the failure of the witnesses to help or to come forward immediately, but none were more distressed than the witnesses themselves. Their moral emotions—empathy and sympathy for the girl and her family, shame and guilt at their own failure to come to the girl's aid—were experienced by many as overwhelming. These feelings in many cases were triggered from the beginning, when they first saw the naked child. Why did their behavior not match their feelings? Many witnesses reported confusion and disbelief when they passed the strange scene, and though they felt concern for the girl and guilt at their own inaction, they reasoned that there must be a sensible explanation, one that would make them feel foolish if they made the extraordinary effort to stop. Others indicated that it was impossible to process the events—so unexpected and atypical of their ordinary experience—in the split-second of decision making, and they had only "put it all together" when they heard about Carmen's disappearance on the news. Others thought that someone else would take care of it—after all, hundreds of motorists were passing the same spot—or that the risks of helping were too great.

Most adults believe that their behavior is usually consistent with their beliefs or feelings. But the witnesses to Carmen's plight illustrate that even adults with strong moral feelings do not always think clearly about moral issues or behave in ways that are consistent with their moral sense. Some of the earliest research on children's moral development indicated that children are particularly prone to such inconsistencies. Hartshorne and May (1928–1930) observed 10,000 children between the ages of 8 and 16 in a wide variety of situations where they had opportunities to lie, cheat, or steal. For example, children could raise their scores on a test by sneaking a look at an answer key, cheat on a test of strength, pilfer some change, or tell lies that would place them in a good light. In every situation, the researchers had devised techniques to surreptitiously detect cheating, lying, or stealing. They found that children's knowledge of moral standards did not coordinate with how likely they were to cheat or to help others to cheat. They also found that children's honesty varied from one situation to another. Some children cheated in academic tasks, for example, but not on tests of athletic skill. Hartshorne and May concluded that moral conduct is usually determined by the particular situation and is not coordinated with moral reasoning or training. However, more recent research, with more adequate measures of children's emotions and cognitions, indicates that emotions, cognitions, and actions do tend to become more synchronized with age and that their interrelations are influenced by many factors, including training.

Before we consider these many factors, let's take a brief look at some classic theories of moral development with which you may be familiar, theories that emphasize either emotions or cognitions as the most important source of moral behavior. How do these theories fare in light of modern research?

Some Classic Theories of Moral Development

FREUD'S PSYCHOANALYTIC THEORY

In Freud's (1935/1960) psychoanalytic theory of moral development, the behavior of very young children is driven by the inborn impulses of the id, which are completely self-serving desires for sustenance and release, such as hunger or the need to defecate. The superego, which emerges in the preschool period, is the source of moral emotions, such as pride in good behavior and shame or guilt about bad behavior, and once a child has a superego, it is these emotions that impel moral functioning, like an internalized system of rewards and punishments. Freud argued that the superego develops when a complex set of id-driven motives and emotions come into conflict with parental authority. Specifically, beginning at about age 3, vague sexual desire for the opposite-sex parent puts the young child in competition with the same-sex parent, who is much more powerful than the child and thus a frightening competitor. The child's solution to this no-win situation is to identify with the same-sex parent. Identification with the (imagined) aggressor is a solution for two reasons. First, by trying to be like the angry parent, a child wins the parent's approval and affection. Second, by pretending to be the parent, the child attains some vicarious satisfaction of her or his sexual longing for the other parent. The critical element of this situation for moral development is the identification process itself. Identification includes both imitation of the parent's behaviors and, most important, internalization of the parent's standards and values, creating the child's superego.

As we will see in the next chapter, the identification process described by Freud is an explanation of both moral development and sex role development in young children. Unfortunately, research fails to support its predictions. With regard to moral development, attributing moral emotions to the emergence of the superego, sometime between ages 3 and 5, is not consistent with findings that many toddlers show signs of empathy and shame as early as 18 to 24 months, beginning when they demonstrate self-recognition while looking in a mirror (e.g., Lewis & Michalson, 1983; see also Chapter 5). By age 3, sympathy, pride, and guilt appear to be part of the emotional repertoire as well (e.g. Stipek et al., 1992; see also Chapter 4). In addition, even toddlers perform prosocial actions based on empathy, and sometimes they seem eager to comply with a parent's rules, even if the parent is not around. Such early signs of conscience development undermine the psychoanalytic view that early behavior is driven only by selfish impulses (e.g., Kochanska, Casey, & Fukumoto, 1995; Kochanska, Tjebkes, & Forman, 1998; Turiel, 1998). Finally, and perhaps most important, Freud argued that children develop a conscience because they identify with a parent whom they fear. Yet, as we saw in Chapter 5, parents who intimidate their children are least successful in fostering the development of conscience. Rather, warmth, affection, and support are more likely to be characteristic of parents whose children exhibit signs of mature conscience formation—self-control in the absence of authority figures (e.g., Kochanska & Murray, 2000). We should note that psychoanalysts since Freud have increasingly explained conscience formation as linked to the bond between child and parent, that is, more as a function of the strength of attachment and the need to keep the parent close than as a function of fear (e.g., Emde et al., 1991).

THE COGNITIVE THEORIES OF PIAGET AND KOHLBERG

Whereas Freud focused on the impetus that emotions provide to moral behavior, cognitive theorists have emphasized the importance of changes in logical thinking as a source of moral development. To understand how children think about rules and standards of conduct, Piaget

(1932/1965) presented children with moral dilemmas and asked them to both judge the behavior of the protagonists and explain what should be done. He also played marbles with children and asked them to describe and explain the rules of the game. Piaget proposed that preschoolers are premoral in the sense that they seem unconcerned about established rules or standards, making up their own as they go along in a game of marbles, for example, and having little regard even for their own rules. At about age 5, Piaget described children's morality as heteronomous. They regard rules as immutable, existing outside the self, and requiring strict adherence. So, 5-year-old Jasmine might argue that a rule should never be broken, even if some greater good might prevail or even if all the participants in a game agree to the change. When her older sister crosses the street without waiting for a "walk" signal, rushing to help a neighborhood toddler who has wandered into the street, Jasmine might insist that her sister should have waited for the signal no matter what. She might also judge that a boy who broke 15 cups trying to help his mother get ready for a party deserves more punishment than one who broke one cup while actually misbehaving. In heteronomous morality, the letter of the law must be followed, and failure to do so requires punishment. In fact, Jasmine might believe in immanent justice, expecting that misbehavior will eventually be punished, even if no one knows about it, as though some higher authority is always watching.

Piaget argued that heteronomy is based on the child's experiences in relationships with parents and other authority figures, where rules seem to come from above and must be obeyed. But in middle childhood, both experience with the give and take of peer relationships and advances in perspective-taking skill help children to see the rules of behavior differently. As children and adolescents have more experience in egalitarian relationships with their peers, their moral thinking becomes more autonomous, meaning that they begin to understand that rules are based on social agreements and can be changed. Advancements in perspective-taking skills, which also are benefited by interactions with peers, help young people understand that rules and standards are not just a function of authoritarian dictates but that they promote fair play and cooperation, serving to establish justice. They can also be set aside for some greater good or changed through negotiation. So, by about 9 or 10, Jasmine could support her sister's violation of their parents' rule about not crossing the street, recognizing the greater importance of protecting a younger child. Also, she would probably be more consistently well behaved than she was earlier, because, in Piaget's view, she has a better understanding of the value of rules and standards for social interaction.

Kohlberg (e.g., 1976, 1984) further investigated children's moral reasoning from late childhood into the adolescent and early adult years. His theory goes beyond Piaget's, offering a fine-grained analysis of changes in the older child's, adolescent's, and adult's reasoning about moral issues (see Table 7.2 for a comparison of ages and stages in Piaget's and Kohlberg's theories). Unlike Piaget's dilemmas, which focused on everyday challenges familiar in the lives of children, Kohlberg's stories were outside ordinary experience and raised broad philosophical issues. Perhaps the most famous of these is the story of Heinz, whose wife is very ill and will die without a certain medicine, which Heinz cannot afford. The druggist who makes the product refuses to sell it, though Heinz offers all the money he has managed to raise—about half of the retail cost—which would more than cover the druggist's expenses. The druggist argues that he discovered the drug and plans to make money from it. In desperation, Heinz breaks into the druggist's establishment and steals the medicine.

Kohlberg was not interested in whether participants judged Heinz's behavior to be right or wrong, assuming that reasonable people might disagree. He focused instead on the reasons they gave for their judgments. He found there to be three levels of moral reasoning, each characterized by two stages. At the first level, elementary school children usually show preconventional morality, roughly corresponding to Piaget's heteronomous level, in which what is right is what avoids punishment, what conforms to the dictates of authority, or what serves one's personal interests. Then, young adolescents move to conventional morality, more consistent with Piaget's autonomous level, in which what is right depends on others' approval or on the need to maintain social order. Finally, by adulthood, some people move to postconventional morality, in which right is defined by universal principles or by standards of justice, not by the particular rule in question (see Table 7.2 for further elaboration of the stages within each level).

Although individuals at different levels of moral reasoning might come to the same conclusion about what is "right," their explanations reveal that they come to their decisions by different

TABLE 7.2   Piaget's and Kohlberg's Stages of Moral Development

Approximate Ages	Piaget's Stages	Kohlberg's Stages
Preschool	*Premoral Period* Child is unconcerned about rules; makes up her own rules.	
		Preconventional Level
5 to 8 or 9 years	*Heteronomous Morality* Child is a *moral realist*: Rules are determined by authorities; are unalterable, moral absolutes; must be obeyed. Violations always punished.	*Stage 1: Punishment and obedience orientation* Child obeys to avoid punishment and because authority is assumed to be superior or right. Rules are interpreted literally; no judgment is involved.
8 or 9 to 11 or 12 years	*Autonomous Morality* Social rules are arbitrary, and promote cooperation, equality, and reciprocity; therefore, they serve justice. They can be changed by agreement or violated for a higher purpose.	*Stage 2: Concrete, individualistic orientation* Child follows rules to serve own interests. Others' interests may also need to be served, so follow the principle of fair exchange, e.g., "You scratch my back, I scratch yours."
		Conventional Level
13 to 16 years		*Stage 3: Social-relational perspective* Shared feelings and needs are more important than self-interest. Helpfulness, generosity, and forgiveness are idealized.
Late adolescents/ young adults		*Stage 4: Member-of-society perspective* The social order is most important now. Behaviors that contribute to functioning of social system are most valued, e.g., obeying laws, hard work.
		Postconventional Level
Some adults		*Stage 5: Prior rights and social contract* The social contract now is most valued. Specific laws are not most valued, but the process that they serve is, e.g., democratic principles, individual rights.
Some adults		*Stage 6: Universal ethical principles* Certain abstract moral principles are valued over anything else, e.g., above specific laws. Social order is also highly valued, unless it violates highest moral principles. (Theoretical; Kohlberg's subjects did not achieve this stage.)

Sources: Damon (1983, 1988); Kohlberg (1981); Piaget (1932/1965). *The moral child: Nurturing children's natural moral growth.* New York: Free Press; Kohlberg, L. (1984). *Essays on moral development: The psychology of moral development.* San Francisco: Harper & Row; Piaget, J. (1932/1965). *The moral judgment of the child.* New York: Free Press.

routes. Compare the "pro-stealing" decisions of Jay and Jesse when given the "Heinz" dilemma to resolve. Jay, a preconventional thinker, bases his choice on personal need:

Heinz should take the drug, because the druggist won't really suffer, and Heinz needs to save his wife.

Jesse, a conventional thinker, bases her decision on the importance of others' agreement or approval:

Heinz should take the drug, because nobody would blame him for wanting to keep his wife alive. They might blame him if he didn't.

There is some research support for the general trends in moral reasoning suggested in the work of Piaget and of Kohlberg. Consistent with Piaget's view, for example, when young children judge moral culpability they usually pay more attention to consequences (e.g., the number of cups broken by a child who is helping his mother prepare for a party), whereas older children pay more attention to intentions (e.g., whether the child was helping or misbehaving). Consistent with Kohlberg's view, young people around the world progress through the levels of moral reasoning—preconventional, conventional, and postconventional—in the same, invariant order (e.g., Boom, Brugman, & van der Heijden, 2001; Colby & Kohlberg, 1987; Colby, Kohlberg, Gibbs, & Lieberman, 1983), although even many adults do not progress beyond the conventional level of reasoning. Perhaps most important, the role of perspective taking and peer interactions in the growth of moral reasoning skills, emphasized both by Piaget and by Kohlberg, has been supported. For example, advances in perspective-taking skills such as those described in Chapter 5 generally precede, although they do not guarantee, advances in moral reasoning (e.g., Tomlinson-Keasey & Keasey, 1974; Walker, 1980). Also, when children discuss moral issues with their peers they are more likely to think carefully about the ideas and to advance in their reasoning than when they discuss those issues with adults (e.g., Kruger, 1992; Kruger & Tomasello, 1986). Perhaps challenges from a peer may seem less threatening and create less defensiveness than challenges from adults (Walker & Taylor, 1991). See Box 7.1 for a look at the influence that Kohlberg's theory in particular has had on moral education.

Box 7.1 | *Morality as an Educational Goal*

In 1917, W. J. Hutchins published the *Children's Code of Morals for Elementary Schools*, emphasizing "ten laws of right living": self-control, good health, kindness, sportsmanship, self-reliance, duty, reliability, truth, good workmanship, and teamwork. Hutchins's code was a widely used educational resource, supporting a character education movement that spanned the first three decades of the 1900s. This was a time of enormous change in the United States, marked by technological advances, population shifts that included immigration surges, and social and moral upheavals. Educators expressed concern about family breakups, increased political corruption and crime, media cynicism, and the decline of religion. Modern movie portrayals of speakeasies, crime syndicates, and loose morals in the "Roaring Twenties" probably capture some of the issues that Americans feared were having a detrimental influence on the youth of the day. Educators implemented character education by suffusing daily school activities with lessons in right living and by initiating student clubs where moral behavior could be practiced (see Leming, 1977; McClellan, 1992).

As we saw in our discussion of moral development (this chapter), a massive study by Hartshorne and May, published in the late 1920s, led those researchers to conclude that moral training had little impact on children's moral behavior. These rather disconcerting results may have dampened educator's fervor for organized programs of character education. However, some features of these programs continue even today to be typical of most schools in the United States, such as student clubs and activity groups and "conduct" grades on report cards.

In the mid-1960s, there was a new surge of educational interest in what was now deemed "moral education," fueled by theory and research on moral reasoning and by renewed social interest. Several approaches to moral education became available to teachers, but the two most influential were Kohlberg's (1966) own prescription for translating his cognitive developmental model of moral reasoning into educational practice and a "values clarification approach" to moral education by Raths, Harmin, and Simon (1966). Although the latter approach provided a more detailed formula for teachers and students to follow and was probably more widely used, both approaches focused on encouraging students to examine their own thinking about morality and to come to their own conclusions. Teachers were to act as facilitators, but they were not to impose any code or value system on students. Kohlberg's approach heavily emphasized peer discussions of moral dilemmas as a technique; "values clarification" provided a valuing process for students to follow as they critically examined the values they had learned thus far.

Many criticisms were leveled at these and other similar approaches to moral education. There is some limited evidence that peer discussions, skillfully facilitated by teachers, can help children and adolescents advance beyond their current level of moral reasoning (using Kohlbergian measures, e.g., Berkowitz & Gibbs, 1983). But teachers found the facilitation of such discussions difficult, and they worried about some of their efforts ending in children rationalizing unacceptable behavior (Leming, 1986, 1997).

Support for the "moral education" movement had waned by the 1980s. But a new surge of interest in character education has emerged in the last decade or so, fueled again by social concern with what appear to be declining morals. Parents and community leaders are looking to schools to develop systematic approaches to character development, hoping to counter rising crime and violence, increasing conduct problems in the schools, and apparently widespread malaise and disaffection even among our most affluent and privileged young people (see text, this chapter and Chapter 10). Like the character education programs of the early 1900s, newer programs focus on what their authors regard as widely accepted, even universal, standards of conduct. They often have two integrated goals: helping children understand why these standards are important and encouraging behavior consistent with these standards. Clearly, the current programs are more prescriptive than those developed in the 1960s and 1970s, but they are usually aimed at general standards that most people would agree are important (Glanzer, 1998).

Schools often develop their own character education plans, but there are many packaged programs available to teachers. Some of the latter have been the subject of systematic outcome research; many have not. Let's consider briefly one program that incorporates some of the values targeted by most other programs and that uses a broad range of teaching strategies (from Leming, 1997).

Titled the "Child Development Project" (Developmental Studies Center, 1996), this program has the advantage of having been the focus of several evaluation studies. Designed for kindergarten through sixth grade, the program has as one goal to integrate ethical development with all aspects of social and intellectual development. To establish four core values (fairness, concern and respect for others, helpfulness, and responsibility), teachers use five techniques: focusing children's attention on prosocial examples of conduct; applying cooperative learning techniques; using examples from literature as well as real-life incidents to encourage a focus on others' needs and rights; involving children in helping activities; encouraging self-control and moral reasoning by using an authoritative disciplinary style. There's more: The program is implemented schoolwide and includes a home program as well. A number of studies have compared children in the Child Development Project to a comparison group, using interview, questionnaire, and behavioral data. Leming (1997) summarizes the results as follows:

> statistically significant program effects have been detected for the following variables: a) self-esteem, b) sensitivity and consideration of others' needs, c) spontaneous prosocial behavior, d) interpersonal harmoniousness, e) preference for democratic values, and f) conflict resolution skills (p. 18)

(See Leming, 1997, for a comparison of 10 programs, including this one.)

It appears that character education that has clear goals and specifies sound techniques for implementing those goals can be effective in encouraging some aspects of moral thinking, feeling, and behavior. Critics have raised concerns about at least some programs, worrying that children may be indoctrinated, drilled in specific behaviors rather than being encouraged to engage "in deep, critical reflection about certain ways of being" (Kohn, 1997). Indeed, if character education is based on drill and coercion, teachers can be expected to be no more effective in fostering the internalization of values than parents who use authoritarian techniques. But many character educators recognize such dangers. They encourage schools to include reasoning, emotions, and behavior in their notion of "character." They also foster the notion that character education must begin with the character of the school itself, which should be a caring community that shows respect toward all individuals and provides adult models of character (Character Education Partnership, 1995; see Lickona, 1998). Supporters also argue that many values are indeed shared across diverse religious, ethnic, geographic, and political communities and that if educators are careful to focus on these, character education makes sense (e.g., Benninga & Wynne, 1988; Damon, 1988, 1996; Etzioni, 1998; Glanzer, 1998; Lickona, 1998).

LIMITATIONS OF CLASSIC COGNITIVE THEORIES

Despite the support that these cognitive approaches to explaining moral development have received, their usefulness is limited in several ways. First, young children have a greater capacity for moral reasoning than Piaget's theory indicates. For example, although young children judge people's actions by their physical consequences (such as how many cups are broken) more than older children do, still they are capable of focusing on the intentions behind behavior if those intentions are made salient (e.g., Nelson, 1980; Siegel & Peterson, 1998; Zelazo, Helwig, & Lau, 1996). In one study, even preschoolers could tell the difference between intentional lying and unintentional mistakes, and they judged real liars more harshly than bunglers (Siegel & Peterson, 1998).

Another important challenge to Piaget's theory is the finding that young children do not necessarily treat all rules and standards as equally important just because they are specified by parents or other authority figures. Moral philosophers point out that some standards, called **moral rules**, address fundamental moral issues of justice, welfare, and rights, such as rules about stealing, hurting others, or sharing. Other standards, called **conventional rules**, are more arbitrary and variable from one culture to another and are a function of social agreement, such as rules about appropriate dress, forms of address, and table manners. Finally, there are areas of functioning that individuals or families might have standards about—such as choices of friends or recreational activities or participation in family life—which are not governed by formal social rules in Western societies. We'll call these **personal rules** (see Turiel, 1998). Piaget assumed that young children treat all rules as "handed down from above," that is, as determined by authority figures. But researchers have found that even by age 3, children are more likely to judge violations of moral rules as more serious than violations of conventional rules (e.g., Smetana & Braeges, 1990). By ages 4 or 5 they believe that such moral rules should be obeyed despite what authority figures might say (e.g., Crane & Tisak, 1995; Smetana, Schlagman, & Adams, 1993; Tisak, 1993). For example, at 5, Jasmine believed it would be wrong to steal even if there were no laws against it and even if a friend's mother said it was okay. As children get older, they make clearer and clearer distinctions between moral and conventional rules, so that by age 9 or 10 children accurately categorize even unfamiliar rules (Davidson, Turiel, & Black, 1983). Turiel (1978) reexamined data from Hartshorne and May's (1928–1930) classic study of children's honesty and found that the participants were much more likely to cheat in academic tasks than they were to steal when given an easy opportunity. He argued that children probably saw the academic tasks as governed by conventional rules whereas stealing more clearly violates a moral rule.

By adolescence, children assume that their parents have a right to regulate and enforce moral behavior; they usually accept parents' regulation of conventional behavior as well, although there is more conflict with their parents in this domain than in the moral arena. Finally, with regard to personal issues such as appearance, spending, and friendship choices, adolescents balk at parental regulation, often arguing that parents have no legitimate authority in this domain (Smetana, 1988; Smetana & Asquith, 1994). Interestingly, Arnett (1999) has recently argued that parents may push for their right to control personal behavior more as a function of how they judge that behavior (e.g., in some instances they may see it as crossing over into the moral domain) than because they are reluctant to grant their children personal freedom. So, in other words, parents and adolescents may differ in how they categorize rules and regulations. We will address this issue again in Chapter 10.

Like Piaget's theory, Kohlberg's view seems to have some important limitations. When moral issues beyond the legalistic ones studied by Kohlberg are examined, both adults' and children's reasoning seems to include factors not described by Kohlberg. Gilligan (e.g., 1977, 1982) has argued that moral development follows different trajectories for males and females. She views Kohlberg's legalistic moral dilemmas and his approach to scoring people's reasoning as biased toward representing a more typically masculine approach to morality. Her concern is that Kohlberg's theory and the research it inspires tends to disregard the "different voice" women use in their approach to moral decision making. Males, she argues, are more likely to use a justice focus (sometimes called the **morality of justice**) while females are more likely to use a caring focus (**morality of caring**).

In her own research on moral reasoning, Gilligan (1977; Gilligan & Attanucci, 1988) included more practical dilemmas that are representative of the complex problems real people face, such as struggling with how to deal with an unplanned pregnancy. Although she found no significant differences in moral orientation (care vs. justice) between males and females, she did report some tendency in her data for men to focus on issues of justice and for women to focus on caring issues. However, her major finding has been that both women and men are concerned about both justice and caring and that together these concerns contribute to mature moral reasoning. Perhaps the most valuable contribution of Gilligan's critique of Kohlberg's work is that she raised awareness of the need to study real-life moral problem solving and addressed the role that concerns about caring play in moral judgments. (Gilligan's ideas and related research on gender and moral reasoning are revisited in Chapter 8 in the discussion of gender development and in Chapter 11 in the discussion of relativistic thinking.)

Damon (1988) has studied children's thinking about real-life dilemmas in a child's world and has found that children consider matters of fairness even at ages when Kohlberg's scheme would assume they would not. For example, in studies of sharing and distributive justice, preschoolers and young school-aged children rarely justify acts of sharing on the basis of concern about punishment, as one might expect if they were at Kohlberg's preconventional stage. Rather, they talk about fairness, and if their actions do not quite measure up to what we might consider fair, they at least seem to feel a need to somehow explain why their selfish choices might actually be fair. Consider the following exchange between a 4-year-old and a researcher, when the child is asked if she would share some poker chips with an imaginary friend. The child initially decides to keep seven of nine chips, including all the blue ones and some of the white ones, and gives her friend "Jenny" two white ones:

> You would keep all the blues for yourself? *Yes, because I like blue. And then I'd play with them.* Let's pretend Jenny said, "I like blue." Would you give her any blue? *Never, because I have a blue dress at home.* So you wouldn't give her any blue at all. Is it fair to do it this way? *Ah ha, I've got it. I'd give her two (more) of the white—I'd give her those because she's younger than me, and I get four because I'm four.* (Damon, 1988, pp. 37–38)

Even though the child's reasoning cannot disguise her blatant self-interest, she seems to feel an obligation to share (she gives away some white ones), and she wants to believe that she is being fair. Older elementary school children, still at a preconventional level of reasoning in Kohlberg's scheme, often try to balance a complex set of concerns in deciding what is fair, concerns not captured by Kohlberg's descriptions. As Damon (1988) indicates, children can now also take into account hard work, poverty, talent, and issues of equality when trying to assess the best ways of distributing property or remuneration. Consider the reasoning of an older elementary school child who is asked how children in a hypothetical classroom should distribute their earnings from sales of some of their artwork:

> What if Rebecca made more stuff? Should she get more money? *Oh, about seven more pennies. It depends on what she made—if she made something easy or hard.* What if she made something hard? *About ten cents more.* What about Peter, who made the best stuff? *Well, maybe he should. But since she (Rebecca) made more, she may have some good ones (too), so then maybe he can get around five cents more.* What about Billy, who doesn't get any allowance? *He should only get about three cents more, because—if he got a lot more, he might even have more than anybody adding up their allowance.* What about these others? *No, because they don't have such a big reason.* (Damon, 1988, p. 42)

Children's moral considerations can be far more complex and wide ranging than Kohlberg's scheme conveys.

Another limitation of Kohlberg's work seems to be his assumption that moral reasoning is the prime determiner of children's moral behavior. As we have seen, moral reasoning is only imperfectly coordinated with action. Yet counselors who work with parents and teachers are often most concerned with encouraging children's moral behavior. In the next section, we will examine the many factors that influence children's prosocial or antisocial behavior.

Children's Prosocial Behavior

When a child voluntarily acts in ways that seem intended to benefit someone else, we credit her with prosocial behavior or altruism. Although prosocial behaviors are observed even in toddlers, they tend to increase with age, from preschool to grade school ages and continuing into adolescence (Eisenberg & Fabes, 1998). Altruistic tendencies are different from one child to another, and individual differences tend to be somewhat stable across age. In other words, a child who shows prosocial inclinations as a preschooler is somewhat more likely than other children to produce prosocial behavior in grade school.

Sharing, comforting a friend, helping a neighbor carry her groceries, collecting canned goods for victims of a flood—all are examples of simple prosocial behaviors that we might see from a child. You can probably see that whereas behaviors such as these benefit others, they can be motivated in many ways and could even provide some social reward to the benefactor. Sharing, for example, can help a child maintain a pleasant interaction.

When 15-month-old Nadia went trick-or-treating for the first time, as soon as an indulgent neighbor would put a treat in her bag, Nadia would reach into the bag and offer the neighbor a treat as well. She seemed to be sharing, literally, for the fun of the social exchange. When a child successfully comforts a crying friend she might be trying to regain her playmate's company. Or when she participates in an organized effort to provide relief to flood victims she may be hoping for positive attention from teachers or parents. For developmentalists, labeling an action altruistic or prosocial only specifies that it benefits someone other than the actor, not that unselfish motives are necessarily involved. Let's consider what factors have been found to influence the development of prosocial action in children, with an eye toward understanding how counselors and other adults might be able to promote children's prosocial tendencies.

EMOTIONS AS A SOURCE OF HELPING BEHAVIOR

In many cases, our emotional reactions to others' distress can be an important source of helping behavior, and the emotion of empathy may be the "linchpin" (Hoffman, 1982; Kagan, 1984). Empathy can be thought of as "feeling with" another person—recognizing her emotional condition and experiencing what she is assumed to be feeling. Hoffman (1982) argued that children have a biological predisposition toward empathy, the earliest hint of which may be the contagious crying of some infants—that is, their tendency to cry when they hear other babies crying. Sympathy, an emotion related to empathy, involves "feeling for" another, that is, having concern for the other person, but not necessarily sharing the feelings of the other. Both empathy and sympathy seem to propel some prosocial acts from the time that toddlers begin to clearly differentiate self from other (e.g., Miller, Eisenberg, Fabes, & Shell, 1996; Zahn-Waxler, Cole, Welsh, & Fox, 1995; Zahn-Waxler, Robinson, & Emde, 1992; see also Chapter 5). Note, too, that children's empathic responses are also associated with their tendencies to inhibit antisocial behavior, as we will see in the next section. Toddlers' early helping behavior may be the result of their empathic feelings, but they still have little capacity to take another's point of view. Hoffman, for example, described the charmingly egocentric effort of a 13-month-old who sought out his own mother to comfort a crying toddler, even though the other child's mother was readily available.

Empathy and sympathy are evident in young children; however, their tendency to lead to effective prosocial action increases substantially with age, especially after the preschool years. Children's improving perspective-taking skills are an important ingredient. One reason appears to be that better role-taking ability can help a child understand how another is feeling and thereby increase the child's own empathic response (Roberts & Strayer, 1996). Also, increased understanding of another's emotions and thoughts should help a child assess what kind of prosocial action, if any, is likely to be beneficial.

In late childhood, the scope of empathy expands, probably influenced by increasing abilities to think about abstractions. Whereas younger children can empathize with particular people whom they observe, older children and adolescents can empathize with whole groups of people who are living in unfortunate circumstances, such as all those suffering from a famine, or from the abrogation of their rights, and so on (Hoffman, 1982).

Clearly, as important as prosocial emotions may be for altruistic behavior, other influences interact with those emotions in complex ways. These include not only advances in cognitive abilities such as perspective taking and abstract thinking but also individual temperamental and personality characteristics, parenting practices, and peer experiences. Also, prosocial behavior involves more than helping another in need. Behavior such as Nadia's spontaneous sharing of her Halloween treats often occurs in the absence of any apparent need on the part of the other and therefore seems not to rest on emotions like empathy or sympathy. Let's take a look at some of the other factors that can influence prosocial action.

COGNITIVE CONTRIBUTIONS TO PROSOCIAL BEHAVIOR

Let's first consider how reasoning about other people's needs (called needs-based reasoning) changes with age, and then we will look at its relation to children's prosocial behavior. In needs-based reasoning, one must weigh one's own personal needs against those of others. For example, Eisenberg and her colleagues have posed moral dilemmas to children in which a child's needs are in competition with the needs of another. In one story, a child, on her way to a party, comes upon another child who has fallen and broken her leg. The first child must decide whether to continue on to the party, which is very important to her, or to find the parents of the injured child. (Compare this dilemma, focused on caring and concern, to Kohlberg's problems in social justice, like the story of Heinz and the druggist.) Eisenberg has found that preschoolers tend to be hedonistic—concerned for their own needs. By early elementary school, many children express recognition that another person's need is a good reason for helping—they are **needs oriented**—but they often do not express sympathy, nor do they talk about feeling guilty for not helping. By later elementary school, children begin to express a recognition that helping is what is required or socially approved. At the next stage, in late elementary school or adolescence, expressions of sympathy for others, guilt about inaction, and to some minimal degree, reference to duty, become part of the reasoning process. Finally, some adolescents begin talking of the relationship of helping to one's self-respect and of being consistent with one's values. For these young people, it appears, moral values are becoming a core aspect of their self-concept (e.g., Eisenberg, Lennon, & Roth, 1983).

We have seen in our discussion of the cognitive theories of moral development that moral reasoning is somewhat related to moral behavior. If the kind of moral reasoning that is assessed is similar to the kind of moral behavior, there is a stronger (but still moderate) relationship between reasoning and behavior. This is particularly true of needs-based reasoning and altruistic behavior. In middle childhood and adolescence, more advanced levels of needs-based reasoning tend to be associated with certain kinds of prosocial behavior. Specifically, if the behavior requires some real personal sacrifice, such as volunteering some free time after school, kids whose moral reasoning is more advanced are more likely to participate. Prosocial behaviors that incur little or no cost, such as helping a teacher to pick up the papers she has just dropped, are likely to occur regardless of a child's moral reasoning (e.g., Eisenberg et al., 1987).

Interestingly, moral reasoning, which is likely to be benefited by interaction with peers (Tesson, Lewko, & Bigelow, 1987), tends to be more advanced in popular children with good social skills, at least for boys. Bear and Rys (1994) found that boys who tended to be aggressive and to have poor peer relations were also low in needs-oriented reasoning. One explanation may be that children with poor social skills have fewer opportunities for positive peer interactions, contributing to a lag in the development of their moral-reasoning skills. A number of intervention programs, designed to promote children's moral functioning, including prosocial behavior and self-control, are focused on using peer discussions. For example, Gibbs (1987) describes a technique using small-group discussions aimed at encouraging empathic responding in delinquents. Actual problem incidents are recreated and discussed, and both peers and adults provide feedback to a participant about their own emotional reactions to the incident and to the participant's attitudes and emotions. Many violence-prevention programs incorporate components designed to foster empathy development (see Box 1.2 in Chapter 1).

Another interesting observation is that for younger children whose moral reasoning may be "needs oriented" but at the most primitive level, their tendency to engage in prosocial behavior is

Personality factors, like sociability, are linked to prosocial behavior in children.

especially dependent on their prosocial emotions—empathy and sympathy. With children and adolescents at more advanced levels of prosocial reasoning, reasoning is better matched to prosocial action regardless of how strong their prosocial emotions are (Eisenberg, Zhou, & Koller, 2001; Miller et al., 1996). These findings demonstrate that different children can follow different paths to prosocial conduct, suggesting that counselors and other helpers should be able to gain inroads in moral development via more than one route.

TEMPERAMENT, PERSONALITY, AND PROSOCIAL BEHAVIOR

As we saw earlier, children who are prosocial in one situation are somewhat more likely than other children to be prosocial in other situations. Also, there is some consistency in the tendency to behave altruistically from early childhood through later childhood. These kinds of observations imply that temperamental or personality variables that are relatively stable across place and time might foster an "altruistic personality" (Eisenberg & Fabes, 1998). What might these characteristics be?

First, children's relative sociability or shyness might be an influence. Children who score low on social anxiety (behavioral inhibition or shyness) are a little more likely to help others than children who score high on this trait, especially when no one has requested their help, when assisting another requires initiating a social interaction, or when helping involves a stranger (e.g., Eisenberg, Pasternack, Cameron, & Tryon, 1984; Stanhope, Bell, & Parker-Cohen, 1987; Suda & Fouts, 1980).

Second, as we saw in our discussion of moral reasoning, socially competent children who are popular with peers tend to show greater empathy and prosocial behavior (Adams, 1983; Eisenberg et al., 1996). It is difficult to sort out which is cause and which is effect in this relationship, but it seems likely that social competence and prosocial behavior are mutually causal, with several other intervening influences involved as well. Children who are empathic, for example, may do better at perspective taking, making them more appealing social partners, and may have closer friendships. The opportunities this creates for peer interaction help boost their perspective-taking skills, which in turn benefits their moral reasoning and empathy, and so on.

Another of these feedback loops may underlie a third link between personality and altruism: Older children and adolescents with a positive global self-concept generally tend to be more prosocial than other children (e.g., Larrieu & Mussen, 1986). Feeling competent and secure may help a child both focus her attention on others and believe that her help will be effective. But helping others also is likely to foster feelings of competency and self-worth (Damon, 1988, 1995; Yates & Youniss, 1996).

Assertiveness is a fourth personality variable tied to prosocial behavior. This characteristic helps illustrate that even though there is some tendency for individual children to be prosocial in many situations, there is also a great deal of situation-specific altruism. Assertive children, who will, for example, defend their possessions are likely to be prosocial in situations where no one has asked them to help, probably because offering assistance is, at least in part, an assertive act. Children who are unassertive are usually prosocial when it is requested of them, not when they must take the social initiative themselves. Their prosocial behavior seems to be based more on compliance than that of assertive children. It should be noted also that children whose behavior goes beyond assertiveness to being domineering are actually less likely than other children to behave altruistically, regardless of the situation (see Eisenberg & Fabes, 1998).

Finally, a child's capacity for **effortful control**, which helps the child regulate or modulate her emotional reactions, may be important. *Effortful control* is defined as inhibiting a response that is "dominant" to perform a response that is less compelling (Rothbart & Bates, 1998). Eisenberg and Fabes (1992) hypothesized that empathic emotions, although they can motivate prosocial behavior, can also be counterproductive if they are experienced by a child as overwhelming. If the child cannot moderate such emotions, she might focus attention on her own discomfort, and doing so might reduce the chances of a sympathetic response to someone in need. Valiente and colleagues (2004) tested this hypothesis with 4- to 8-year-olds. Children watched a film about a girl who is burned in a fire and later endures cruel teasing by peers because of her scars. After the film, participants were asked about their "self-focused emotions"—feeling upset, scared, and so on—and about their sympathetic emotions—feeling concern, sorry, sad for others, and so on.

The children were also measured for effortful control. For example, they were asked to put together a puzzle "blind." The wooden shapes were covered by a cloth and children manipulated the pieces under the cloth (although it was possible to cheat by peeking at the pieces). How much time children persisted on puzzle solving without cheating or becoming distracted was the measure of effortful control. The higher children's scores were on effortful control, the better able they seemed to be at controlling their self-focused emotions during the film and the more sympathy they expressed.

PARENTS, PEERS, AND PROSOCIAL BEHAVIOR

In Chapter 5 we began an examination of parenting behaviors and of the development of self-control, compliance, prosocial behavior, and conscience in infants and preschoolers. We observed that these aspects of moral development are, on the whole, most effectively launched when parents are authoritative in their style: on one hand, warm, responsive, and sensitive in their caregiving and, on the other hand, demanding, requiring that children live up to standards and values appropriate to their level of maturity (see Baumrind, 1989, 1993; Maccoby & Martin, 1983). The methods of control that seem to foster internalization of those standards and values in the long run involve mild power assertion, sufficient only to capture the child's attention but not to arouse a lot of anxiety, and induction (explaining why it is important to share, for example). It should be noted that parents who are demanding without warmth and sensitivity (the authoritarian style) may actually interfere with prosocial development. At least for toddlers, this parenting style has been associated with reductions in children's empathic responding (Robinson, Zahn-Waxler, & Emde, 1994). Extremes of negative parenting, resulting in child abuse, seem to suppress prosocial responding to others' distress and promote more negative responding, such as aggression (e.g., Main & George, 1985).

In middle childhood, the same conclusions about what elements of parenting are most effective in promoting prosocial behavior (and inhibiting antisocial behavior) still apply. There are also a number of other specific characteristics of parenting that seem to foster children's altruism. First, when parents have strong prosocial values, their elementary-school-aged children are more likely to be seen by peers as prosocial (Hoffman, 1975). Similarly, adults who show unusual prosocial tendencies, such as "rescuers" of Nazi victims in Europe during World War II, frequently report having had parents who strongly valued caring and helping behaviors (Oliner & Oliner, 1988).

Second, adult modeling of prosocial behavior seems to influence children's altruism. On the whole, models who are perceived by children as competent, models who have long-term, nurturant relationships with children, and models who express happiness after prosocial behavior (rather than receiving tangible rewards for their behavior) tend to foster children's prosocial behavior (see Eisenberg & Fabes, 1998).

Finally, providing children with opportunities for prosocial action seems to help encourage a commitment to altruistic action. Eisenberg and Fabes (1998) call this "the foot in the door effect." For example, Eisenberg, Cialdini, McCreath, and Shell (1987) found that starting in middle childhood, children who are encouraged to donate in one context are more likely to engage in helping behavior later in another context. This was mostly true for children who valued being consistent. It may be that once children begin to form a stable self-concept, they are more likely to value consistency, and that practicing prosocial behavior then fosters further prosocial activities as children seek to maintain a coherent self-concept. But there are probably other benefits to practice in some contexts, such as gaining increased feelings of competence and obtaining social approval (Eisenberg & Fabes, 1998).

Children's Antisocial Behavior

Jason, at 3 years of age, is a high-energy youngster who is active and playful. Most days, he engages in regular bouts of toy grabbing, aggressive play, and fighting. His behavior definitely has an impulsive quality to it: Strike now and think later! Two years later at age 5, Jason is still going strong. He communicates his strong-willed temperament in frequent temper tantrums over household rules. His developing language ability permits him to be more argumentative with parents and peers than he had been earlier. Problems with disobedience occur at home and at school. Jason frequently refuses to go to bed on time, pick up his toys, or take a bath. In an occasional squabble with a preschool classmate, Jason may throw something or hit the other child. His teacher finds him a challenge to her patience and her classroom management skills.

Stop for a moment and reflect on 5-year-old Jason's behavior. How would you evaluate this youngster? Do you consider his behavior normal or problematic? If you perceive a problem, what would you do to help? Now consider him at age 8. He is in the third grade. His aggressive behaviors have persisted. He is not well liked by classmates and has difficulty fitting into the social fabric of the class. His academic performance is marginal. Jason has begun to steal toys and money from his classmates and has been caught vandalizing property belonging to one of his neighbors. How would you assess Jason's problems now? Are you more concerned about him? What would you advise?

PATHWAYS OF ANTISOCIAL BEHAVIOR

The development of antisocial behavior differs in some significant ways from the prosocial pathways we have been describing. Earlier chapters have detailed the kinds of positive support children need to develop well. This chapter adds to that picture by including the importance of healthy self-concept, self-control, and the achievement of competence and character as functions of a moral self in middle childhood. Just as we know a great deal about what is good for children's development, a wealth of recent research has illuminated our understanding of what might lead certain children toward more antisocial outcomes. This knowledge base is, admittedly, incomplete, but it is far from being merely suggestive. In this section, we will describe some of the findings that can lead us to a clearer understanding of the dynamics typically present in the lives of children like Jason.

Antisocial behavior is somewhat difficult to define, although it is usually characterized by the presence of aggression or the intent to harm another person. Recent formulations have recognized that antisocial behavior in adolescents and adults may also include such acts as risky sexual activity, substance abuse, defiance, cheating, lying, and vandalism (Jessor, Donovan, & Costa, 1991). Antisocial behavior can be both overt, such as hitting, and covert, such as cheating. Clinicians may identify youth who behave in antisocial ways as having oppositional-defiant disorder (ODD) or conduct disorder (CD). *Oppositional defiant disorder* describes a clinically significant pattern of oppositional, negative or defiant behaviors (like losing one's temper, arguing, deliberately annoying others, etc.) that persist for a six-month period (American Psychiatric Association, 2000). Because these are common problems among children, diagnosis should only be made when the behavioral pattern clearly exceeds the norm for the child's age group. A diagnosis of *conduct disorder* may be appropriate when the problematic behaviors have lasted for at least 12 months and when multiple kinds of disordered behaviors are manifested. Specific categories of disordered behavior include physical aggression, property destruction, deceitfulness or theft, and major violations of age-appropriate norms such as truancy or running away from home (American Psychiatric Association, 2000).

What sets the child's life course in this direction? One way to conceptualize this is to think of several possible developmental pathways that can eventually lead to antisocial outcomes in adolescence and adulthood. One pathway, which we might think of as the early-starter model (Moffitt, 1993a), has a life-course trajectory that is characterized by the presence of oppositional behavior that begins early, persists and diversifies over time, and becomes increasingly more serious. A second pathway for late starters, whose experience with delinquent activities begins at adolescence, is less likely to result in adult criminality. This pattern, called adolescent-onset antisocial behavior or late-starter model, although serious, seems to be more reflective of a difficult or exaggerated reaction to the adolescent period. Both pathways are more complicated than they seem, and others have identified variations on these two pathways (e.g., Loeber et al., 1993). However, early- and late-starter patterns remain among the best understood. We will expand on these topics in Chapter 10.

What might we predict from Jason's behavior? In general, there is strong evidence for the continuity of antisocial behavior from early childhood through adulthood (Robins, 1978). People diagnosed as having antisocial personality disorder as adults almost always report histories of conduct problems in childhood and adolescence (American Psychiatric Association, 2000). Roughly two thirds of 3-year-olds who display extreme problems with impulsivity and defiance continue to show these behaviors at age 8, and these early problems are related to further difficulties in school (S. B. Campbell, 1987). Children diagnosed with oppositional defiant disorder or conduct disorder in early adolescence have typically shown these problems since childhood (Lahey, Loeber, Quay, Frick, & Grimm, 1992). On the other hand, oppositional behaviors such as those depicted in Jason's case are relatively normal for young children of 4 and 5 (Achenbach & Edelbrock, 1983). Sometimes caregivers fail to appreciate the normal variations that occur in activity level and willfulness. The important thing to remember is that in the less extreme cases these oppositional behaviors tend to recede around age 8. The developmental course that is problematic is one in which these aggressive behaviors are maintained into elementary school, then enlarged and expanded upon in more delinquent ways. Like a storm that gathers strength as it moves along, early antisocial behaviors in certain cases are compounded by related problems in classrooms and peer groups that often trap youngsters in a downward spiral.

Researchers and clinicians are very interested in understanding the early predictors of later violent behavior, given the costs of adolescent delinquency and adult criminality to society as a whole. A recent longitudinal study conducted cross-nationally at six different locations from Canada to New Zealand investigated whether high levels of physical aggression, manifested in the early elementary school years, was a particularly significant early marker for later violent offending (Broidy et al., 2003). The authors found that physical aggression was by far the most potent predictor of violent, and sometimes, nonviolent behavior problems for adolescent boys. The pattern is less well understood for girls at this time. Interestingly, although hyperactivity and oppositional, noncompliant behavior may interact with and aggravate aggression, these variables did not increase the risk of later delinquency in and of themselves. As you might assume, not all physically aggressive children develop serious conduct problems. However, the authors reach a conclusion that has practical significance for counselors who work with children and their families:

> The results of these predictive analyses confirm that when the aim is to prevent physical violence and when resources are limited, children with chronic physical aggression and/or serious conduct problems should be the primary targets of intervention. However, we are not suggesting that practitioners wait until age 12 or 13 for confirmation of a chronic trajectory of physical aggression or serious conduct problems to offer a prevention program. One of the important findings of these analyses is that the chronic cases were generally at their highest levels of disruptive behavior when they entered kindergarten. (p. 236)

INFLUENCES ON THE DEVELOPMENT OF ANTISOCIAL BEHAVIOR

What sets this early trajectory in motion? It appears that there are a number of possible factors that, if present, point to the likelihood of antisocial outcomes. These factors are internal as well as external and operate in synergistic fashion, potentiating each other. If present without benefit of counterbalancing positive influences, the negative factors may be experienced as chronic and cumulative stressors, which place the individual at increasing risk for maladaptive outcomes (Garmezy & Masten, 1994). It is very important to remember, however, that the simple presence of risk factors in a child's life is not straightforwardly deterministic. Although the evidence for continuity of antisocial behavior is strong, there is also evidence for discontinuity, such as when a teacher, coach, or other adult steps in to help a child at a critical juncture or when a family moves out of poverty. Other environmental events, such as effective treatment and prevention programs can also turn a child's life around.

Physiological and Neuropsychological Influences. Certain physiological and neuropsychological characteristics have been identified as markers of risk for aggression and antisocial behavior. Children who had difficult temperaments as babies have been found to have significantly more behavior problems at age 3 than other children (Bates, Maslin, & Frankel, 1985), but only those preschool children with difficult infant temperaments who also had inadequate parenting appear to be at risk for maladaptive behavior in late childhood (e.g., Coon, Carey, Corley, & Fulker, 1992). Some research supports the relation of hormones, specifically testosterone, to heightened aggressiveness, although it is difficult to specify direction of effect. In other words, do hormones lead to aggression or does aggression increase hormone levels? Arguing for an interactionist position, Archer (1994) reported that testosterone levels were positively related to aggression and competitiveness but also that success in competitive activities, such as winning a fight, itself led to increased levels of testosterone. Neuropsychological risk factors, such as deficits in attention accompanied by impulsivity, have been associated with the development of conduct problems as well (Barkley, 1997; Hinshaw, 1987; Lahey, McBurnett, & Loeber, 2000). In general, difficulties with inhibition of behavioral responses that coexist with high activity levels appear to set the stage for conflictual behavior management situations at home and school. In time, the child whose behavior frequently provokes parents, teachers, and peers and who receives a steady diet of negative feedback from them ultimately defines herself as deviant (Coie & Dodge, 1998). Finally, weaknesses in verbal skills and problem-solving abilities, which have been tied to such factors as prenatal teratogens, early deprivation, or heritability, reduce the child's ability to cope with problems verbally, to understand consequences, or to take others' perspectives (Moffitt & Lynam, 1994). Instead, such weaknesses encourage reliance on physical means of conflict resolution.

Environmental Influences. Environmental factors can be divided into those operating at a more distal level (e.g., socioeconomic variables) and those exerting a more proximal influence (e.g., parenting practices). These factors interact with a child's internal characteristics to place some children at greater risk for developing antisocial patterns. As we mentioned earlier, these risks operate cumulatively, incrementally increasing the likelihood of maladaptation.

Distal influences such as poverty, substandard housing, low levels of parental education, teen parenting, large family size, inadequate educational opportunities, exposure to violence, and frequent residential moves exert great stress on family resources and are related to less than optimal conditions for child rearing (e.g., Bolger & Patterson, 2001; Bradley & Corwyn, 2002; Serbin & Karp, 2004). Such conditions increase the likelihood of hostile, harsh parenting, and they heighten the risk of physical abuse, which is clearly related to later aggressive behavior (Cicchetti, 1989).

More proximal influences include the characteristics of the parent–child relationship. Much of the current research on the early antecedents of antisocial behavior focuses on parent–child socialization practices. Patterson's influential model of coercive family interaction describes how children learn to act aggressively (see Figure 7.2). Based upon the concept of negative reinforcement, Patterson and his associates have shown that young children learn to escape aversive consequences (such as turning off the TV) by whining, complaining, having tantrums, and so on, which cause parents to give up their demands for compliance (Snyder & Patterson, 1995). As soon as parents or caregivers cooperate with the child by backing off, the child reinforces the

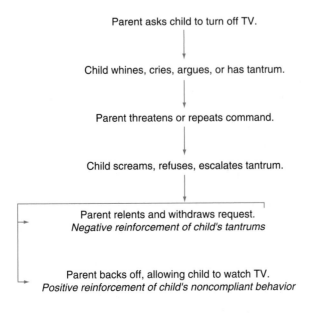

Parent asks child to turn off TV.

Child whines, cries, argues, or has tantrum.

Parent threatens or repeats command.

Child screams, refuses, escalates tantrum.

Parent relents and withdraws request.
Negative reinforcement of child's tantrums

Parent backs off, allowing child to watch TV.
Positive reinforcement of child's noncompliant behavior

FIGURE 7.2

Example of Coercive Parent–Child Interaction

Many aggressive, antisocial children have a hostile attributional bias. They assume negative intentions on the part of others and are often primed to want to "get even."

adults by stopping the unpleasant behavior (whining or crying). Sooner or later, these parents learn that the best way to escape or avoid the unpleasant situation their children create is by giving in to their children's demands. Thus, aggressive children reinforce parental cessation of demands by providing their parents with some short-lived peace and quiet. In such coercive interaction sequences, fairly typical in families of antisocial children, children are trained in the effectiveness of aggressive noncompliance and learn powerful parent-control strategies.

Social-Cognitive Influences. Certain thinking styles also characterize aggressive individuals. Dodge's work adds tremendously to our understanding of the social information-processing of antisocial youth (see Crick & Dodge, 1994, for a review). Idiosyncratic ways of processing social information characterize each step of the model (see Figure 7.3), resulting in the likelihood of aggression. Let's imagine Jason waiting in line for a drink at the school water fountain. Two other youngsters, involved in a clandestine game of tag in the hallway, bump into him and knock his backpack to the floor. How might he respond?

Dodge's model suggests a typical sequence of mental activity for aggressive children. First, the child encodes cues selectively, focusing on situational cues that suggest threatening content. This tendency may develop as a response to harsh discipline, which enhances the hypervigilance needed to protect oneself from ever present threats to personal security (Dodge, Bates, & Petit, 1990). Jason might attend more to the boy's body coming close and bumping him rather than to the smiles on the other boys' faces.

The child next interprets or attributes meaning to the cues. A biased interpretive style, called hostile attributional bias or hostile attribution of intent, characterizes aggressive individuals who tend to perceive threats even in neutral situations (de Castro, Veerman, Koops, Bosche, & Monshouwer, 2002). For example, Jason might conclude that the boys knocked the backpack off intentionally because they dislike him. The next step is to clarify goals. In Jason's emotionally aroused state, the primary goal might be to "get even" with the other boys for the perceived insult. For aggressive children, schemas or mental guides for social interaction may be organized around aggression. In other words, these individuals use aggressive schemas to make sense of or to "figure out" what has transpired socially. Because the situation is likely to be viewed through the lens of perceived hostility and because more socially acceptable responses have not been practiced, the likelihood of aggressive responding is high.

Jason next proceeds to access a behavioral response from his repertoire. Then he evaluates the response and enacts the behavior. Jason, still rather impulsive, is quick to respond in anger.

FIGURE 7.3

Social Information-Processing Model

Source: Crick, N. R. & Dodge, K. A. (1994). A review and reformulation of social information-processing mechanisms in children's social adjustment. *Psychological Bulletin, 115,* 74–101. Copyright © 1994 by the American Psychological Association. Reprinted with permission.

He may start to punch the other boy for the perceived violation. For a child like Jason who is impulsive, who has experienced the benefits of aggression, or who has learned that aggression is a preferred means of problem solving, aggressive responding may become natural. Underdeveloped self-control and weaknesses in verbally expressive means of problem solving add to the tendency to aggress.

Dodge's model emphasizes the role of cognitive processes, such as attention to cues and interpretation of events, in children's antisocial behavior. Other factors, both emotional and cognitive, have been found to be associated with aggressive behavior, and some of these factors work in concert. Emotions such as empathy, sympathy, and guilt seem to be important. In particular, empathy is linked to the inhibition, or control, of aggression (see Miller & Eisenberg, 1988). Presumably, when someone initiates an aggressive act, the ability to empathize with the distress of the target person can help inhibit continued aggression in that situation, and the anticipation of a target's distress may inhibit future episodes of aggressive behavior. A focus on the other, rather than the self, seems to be a key element of self-control in these situations.

As we saw in our discussion of prosocial behavior, empathy is the ability to share the feelings of another, and it becomes more effective as a motivator of behavior as children get older. We also indicated that empathy seems to have both an emotional component that involves feeling with another and a cognitive aspect, understanding of the other, that results from role-taking or perspective-taking skill. Cohen and Strayer (1996) found that both the affective and the cognitive sides of young adolescents' empathic abilities are deficient in young people with conduct disorders, especially in those with strong aggressive tendencies, compared to youngsters without serious behavior problems (see also Chalmers & Townsend, 1990; Chandler, 1973; Feschbach & Feschbach, 1982). As the researchers point out:

it is empathy-related emotionality that is at issue . . . it does not appear that CD [conduct-disordered] youth are unemotional, callous, or indifferent . . . they tended to report higher levels of personal distress than NCD [non-conduct-disordered] youth [when presented with vignettes portraying other people's problems], suggesting the possibility that [they] may be more egocentrically distressed when involved in emotional situations. This self-focused emotion may compete with empathy with another person's emotions and needs. (p. 995)

There may be many reasons why self-focused emotion could overshadow empathic responses. As we have seen, children with low levels of effortful control seem less able than other children to modulate their self-focused emotions when others are distressed. Another factor may be that negative or harsh parenting leaves a child with inadequate opportunities to experience empathy from others, to observe models of empathic behavior, and to discuss or learn from parents' explanations about people's emotional needs and reactions (Cohen & Strayer, 1996). Children who are abused by their parents have been found to show less empathy in response to peer distress than nonabused children. Abused children more often respond to others' problems with fear or anger (Main & George, 1985). We have also seen that children's own characteristics (such as a difficult temperament) may elicit coercive, negative parenting. Parenting that lacks warmth may in turn limit empathic development (e.g., Robinson et al., 1994) and can foster aggressive behavior (e.g., Rubin, Hastings, Chen et al., 1998). Similarly, children whose behavior is aggressive, especially those who are also argumentative and disruptive, often experience peer rejection (Coie, Dodge, & Kupersmidt, 1990), which may further constrain their opportunities to learn adequate perspective-taking skills.

Clearly, many processes influence children's antisocial and aggressive behavior. These processes help explain children who fail to make normal strides in their ability to regulate their own emotional responses, especially anger, and whose concern for self is not adequately balanced by concern for, and understanding of, other people.

APPLICATIONS

A strong sense of self-worth and a sturdy moral compass are elements widely viewed as important for building and participating in a civil society. Some have recently argued that the two have parted ways and that, in Western cultures, the self has been emphasized over morality. Baumeister and Bowden (1994) put it this way: "[T]he modern growth of selfhood has included a love affair with it. Whereas, for centuries, morality and self-interest were regarded as mortal enemies, the modern individual has increasingly linked the self to positive values. Finding oneself, knowing oneself, cultivating oneself, and benefiting oneself are seen not only as moral rights, but even, increasingly, as moral duties" (p. 144). Nowhere is this trend more evident than in the pursuit of self-esteem. As we stated in Chapter 5, self-esteem has been touted as the holy grail of mental health. Low self-esteem has been implicated as a key element in a wide variety of problems manifested by children, adolescents, and adults, including low academic motivation and diminished achievement (Carlson & Lewis, 1993), increasing abuse of drugs and alcohol (Kaplan, 1980), teenage pregnancy (Herold, Goodwin, & Lero, 1979), gang violence (Anderson, 1994), spousal abuse (Gondolf, 1985), hate crimes (Levin & McDevitt, 1993), and even murder (Kirschner, 1992).

Identifying low self-esteem as a correlate of mental health problems does not necessarily provide evidence of a causal relationship, as any student of statistics can point out. However, many preventive and remedial efforts are sometimes structured "as if" low self-esteem caused the problems directly. As a result, interventions are focused on changing affect. The premise is that if children feel better about themselves, they will then do better. Their general mental health will improve, and they will behave in prosocial ways.

Obviously, no one would argue that children should hold negative views of themselves! Abundant research has demonstrated that negative self-views are a feature of depression (Beck, 1963; Peterson, Maier, & Seligman, 1993) and that dwelling on one's negative attributes both prolongs and amplifies the depressive state (Nolen-Hoeksema, Morrow, & Fredrickson, 1993). But it is something different to assume that high self-esteem automatically causes positive outcomes. Dryfoos (1990), in a review of 20 years of research, reports that there is no compelling evidence that high self-esteem is a necessary precursor for competence. In fact, much evidence points in the other direction, namely that competent performance results in feelings of high self-efficacy, and ultimately, self esteem. In recent years the emphasis has clearly shifted toward a "skills-first" approach, that is, toward enhancing competencies that indirectly bolster self-esteem. From this perspective, feeling good becomes a "delicious by-product" of doing well (Seligman, 1995).

How great an effect can counselors have on the promotion of these outcomes in children? Morality and even self-esteem are broad constructs that are difficult to concretize in treatment plans. There is no clinical magic, which when applied, guarantees high self-esteem or morality, for advances in theory have outpaced practice applications in some areas. However, a few key points about the self-system and morality may help counselors make linkages to intervention.

Where Do We Start?

Nothing about the controversy over self-esteem promotion reviewed above should be interpreted as rejecting the importance of a supportive counseling relationship. Research on common factors in psychotherapies (Lambert and Bergin, 1994) points to the importance of empathy, encouragement, respect, and interest, among other things, for therapeutic change. Nonsupportive, nonaffirming counseling is an oxymoron. The point is that self-esteem enhancement may, in some cases, be a dicey primary objective. Crocker and Park (2004) argue convincingly that the pursuit of self-esteem has short-term emotional benefits but a big cost if one fails in the pursuit. Furthermore, autonomy, self-regulation, relatedness, and health can be compromised by the all-out striving to protect self-worth and avoid failure. Therefore, as Harter says, "It may be useful to make a distinction between the goal of our treatment (e.g., enhanced self-esteem or self-worth) and the target of our interventions" (1988a, p. 152). As you have read, many (but not all) children who display oppositional behavior view themselves quite positively (Hughes, Cavell, & Grossman, 1997). For this group, their own estimates of their likeability and popularity do not jibe with teachers' and peers' appraisals. Despite the fact that others find them annoying, they view themselves as popular and likeable. More self-esteem enhancement may be a misguided treatment goal, regardless of whether the child's positive self-image is a true version of how he sees himself or a means of self-protection. This is particularly true for aggressive children who need to learn better ways to manage their feelings and behaviors. Thus, it might be preferable to target the skills and awareness that could lead to increased social self-efficacy.

However, many children, particularly nonaggressive, victimized ones, do suffer from feelings of low self-esteem that often coexist with more clearly defined clinical syndromes like anxiety or depression. The self-esteem of these children might be enhanced as a byproduct of cognitive-behavioral interventions to improve coping skills and reduce anxiety as well as by peer group interventions to promote social development (see Chapter 8). Children are typically uninterested in and unable to comprehend abstract phenomenological insights about themselves, anyway. Helping them to focus on skills like coping with problem situations through greater awareness of their resources seems more effective.

What Do Schemas Have to Do with It?

Self-concept is complex, multidimensional, and strongly influenced by relationship history. So substantive changes in self-perceptions, like changes in other concepts (think of the round earth), do not happen overnight. It takes time and a sufficient number of new experiences to eventually rewrite old cognitive and experiential scripts. Social information processing theories have demonstrated that schemas (including self- and relational schemas) are resistant to change and support consistency in perceptions. This is so, in part, because schemas are economical ways to predict and make sense of the world. They help us filter out a lot of unnecessary information, hone in on the data that have functional significance for us, disregard inconsistent information, and

focus our attention on information that supports (or is consistent with) existing schemas. One can view the hostile attributional bias as a relational scheme that has functional significance for a child with a history of coercive interactions. This scheme is not a distortion of reality for someone whose safety once depended on assuming the imminent presence of threats. Obviously, this kind of social information processing bias may severely hurt a child's peer interaction in the present. Although our theoretical understanding of social information processing far outstrips our present understanding of successful interventions, it may be clinically useful to introduce new ways of interpreting social situations. A typical treatment sequence for many anger management programs includes helping clients to recognize provocative stimuli or events in the environment, to stop long enough to reduce level of reactivity using deep breathing or backward counting, to change distorted thinking by using rational self-statements, and to practice more appropriate social behavior and emotion expression (Kendall, 1991).

The difficulty here is that those strategies that help children generate alternative interpretations, come up with alternative solutions to problems, or increase perspective-taking skills are typically carried out under nonthreatening, nonemotional, intellectualized conditions (called "cold cognitions"; Smith, Haynes, Lazarus, & Pope, 1993). In general, improvements in social-cognitive reasoning following these interventions have not been accompanied by improvements in actual social behavior (Beelman, Pfingsten, & Losel, 1994; Kendall, 1991). As we all know, those cognitive biases that provoke fights or lead to feeling depressed operate below the level of conscious awareness when personally significant and emotionally charged association networks become activated by some event. Bierman (2004) suggests using real conflict situations with real peers, as opposed to hypothetical ones, when working with children to increase the generalizabiliy of treatment effects. Videotaping children in social situations, reviewing the tape with the child and stopping the action to process "online" those cues the child was attending to and how she was interpreting them may be a way to provide more access to "hot cognitions" (Putallaz, 1983).

Self-Concept, Perceived Competence, and the Looking Glass

The teachings of James and Cooley provide important implications for interventions in this area as well. It seems obvious, but still worth emphasizing, that words can and do hurt. Shaming, sarcasm, demeaning, and name calling by adults are incorporated by children and seep into the fabric of their self-concept. These internal voices can resonate in our psyches throughout adulthood, becoming the root of chronic self-reproach. Often they are coupled with the belief that we are not entitled to the painful feelings these negative messages elicited in the first place. Parents must be helped to understand the powerful looking glass their words create. By the same token, saying no to children should not be expected to hurt their self-esteem. Setting limits authoritatively by saying no when appropriate is necessary and needs to be disentangled from the idea that negative comments hurt children, an unfortunate conflation of ideas.

It is important for counselors to understand children's actual successes and their aspirations for success in the domains of self-concept that are personally important to them (see Chapter 5). Armed with this information, counselors may be able to help reduce the discrepancy between perceived and real competence. Very often, this may involve supporting skill development to enhance performance, such as in academic subjects or social interaction. Alternatively, children, as well as older individuals, can be helped to value components of their self-concepts in which they excel, such as academics, while reducing the importance of areas where they are less successful, such as athletics. Harter's suggestion is "to spend more psychological time in those life niches where favorable self-appraisals are more common" (1999, p. 317). Remember, however, that working to reduce the importance of some components, such as behavioral conduct for an acting-out child, is not a good idea! In this case, the careful creation of a discrepancy may be what is called for.

Harter also recommends working toward a generally realistic appraisal of competencies. Bringing the self-perceptions of those who overrate their competencies more in line with external appraisers helps reduce the potential for highly inflated self-esteem. For underraters, the task is more difficult, particularly because higher order schemas, such as global self-esteem, are harder to change. Hattie (1992) believes that these kinds of self-views develop from early attachment experiences and provide durable working models of the self. One example of this might be the low global self-esteem and feelings of unworthiness of victims of severe early childhood abuse or neglect. Despite the relative intractability of such schemas, Harter argues that these self-representations may be more open to revision at critical developmental periods (e.g., transition to new school, adolescence, within intimate relationships) when the need for psychological reorganization occurs. Use of reframing strategies that encourage the person to revise beliefs about the possibility of changing her self-schema and that increase perceptions of personal control and self-efficacy may also be useful (Seligman, 1995). For older adolescents and adults, help in understanding the root causes of the negative self-schema (e.g., early abuse) may provide more cognitive control over these beliefs. Needless to say, change may be extraordinarily difficult in certain cases when the self-views are deeply negative and entrenched.

An "Inside" Job

Self-worth, particularly as linked to morality and a sense of character, is ultimately something that resides inside us. We have seen that it cannot be acquired in a social vacuum, dependent as we all are on the positive appraisals of significant others (Cooley, 1902). But just as true, it cannot be acquired by cosmetic or superficial means. Children have work to do in this area, and this "industry" is not always easy (Erikson, 1950/1963). It is unrealistic for parents and clinicians to assume that failure should be avoided at all costs, that children can be inoculated against self-doubt by unconditional love, or that being "the best" in some competitive arena (social, academic, athletic, or appearance) guarantees high self-esteem. Bednar and Petersen (1995) note that parents (and, by extension, therapists) make a critical mistake when emphasizing approval from others over approval from the self. Well-meaning adults, who are "oriented to avoiding rejection, train only for the development of the public self. The question of fostering the child's development of a private self may remain unasked and unanswered" (p. 353). Parents and teachers should be cautioned that very subtle messages can communicate the notion that pleasing others or winning others' regard is what constitutes self-worth in this world. Children should be helped to take personal responsibility for their actions and to choose internally motivated or learning goals (Pintrich, 2000) when possible. They can also be discouraged from excessive competition and overreliance on social comparison. These approaches can have positive effects on the internalization of personal standards and the fostering of a strong private self.

Moral Development: Putting Flesh on the Bone

Many programs in the past have tried to promote the development of moral reasoning using stage theories. These efforts typically included classroom presentations and discussions of moral dilemmas that students could resolve, requiring in the process some presentation of moral reasoning one level above that of the students (called "plus-one" programs). Other varieties of programs involved didactic instruction about specific character traits, one good quality at a time. Outcome research on these programs has been equivocal at best, even given their primary goal of stimulating students' level of moral reasoning (Enright, Lapsley, Harris, & Shawver, 1983). For one thing, the interventions in this category are directed toward children and adolescents as if they were homogeneous moral thinkers. Recall Piaget's notion of decalage and it becomes clear why we need to consider the variability in cognition among children. More important, these approaches focused on just one element: thinking. We are reminded again of Hartshorne and May's (1928–1930) conclusion that moral understanding does not guarantee moral behavior.

Contemporary writers have recognized the need to include affective aspects in the mix, what some are calling moral motives or moral personality, "the flesh vivifying the bare bones of cognition" (Walker & Hennig, 2004). It's difficult to conceive of morality without also considering its affective side. Developmentalists have long tied the concept of the moral self to concern for others. So perhaps, in a way that is similar to self-esteem, morality is the byproduct of prosocial behavior. Schulman (2002) defines morality as composed of three interlocking systems: (1) empathy, (2) moral affiliations or identification with moral "others," and (3) principles or standards of right and wrong. Each can be fostered in specific ways. Empathy is primarily built through security of attachments and responsive caregiving. Affiliation with moral adults is a byproduct of authoritativeness that provides a context for teaching about the reasons for rules and prohibitions. Children come to model the behavior and incorporate the reasoning of moral (just and caring) adults. Explicit teaching of principles, messages that encourage children to think about the effects of their behavior, and open discussion of moral dilemmas enhance the construction of a set of moral principles.

Damon (1995) reminds us that the development of morality is dependent on the contexts we inhabit. He notes that schooling provides an excellent opportunity to support the development of prosocial values and behavior. "Like a broad-spectrum vaccine that can block the growth of many dangerous viruses at once, a child's wholehearted engagement in schooling can stop destructive and wasteful activities before they begin to consume a child's life" (Damon, 1995, p. 195). The emphasis here, we stress, is on wholehearted engagement. Children need personal relationships with teachers who hold high intellectual, moral, and behavioral expectations in settings that are small enough to permit these relationships. They need rigorous and meaningful learning experiences that encourage diligence and depth of thinking, and they need high standards for behavior that actually hold them to account for their behavior. This is the crux of developmentally appropriate education at every level, given that most children excel when opportunities to develop competence and character are provided within a supportive environment (see Williams, Yanchar, Jenson, & Lewis, 2003, for an example of an exemplary high school program).

Finally, community organizations such as YMCA, sports leagues, and so on, composed of members who live and work in the communities they serve, have a critical part to play. The most successful ones provide a source of care and mentoring to children and require them to abide by strict rules and regulations. In this way, they provide a healthy dose of adjunct parenting by helping youth to internalize values and standards. Opportunities for children to provide meaningful service to others sharpen their sense of purpose and competence and reduce the demoralization that grows from excessive self-centeredness. Adults will provide a more powerful environment for moral development if we communicate some shared values to all our children through our words and deeds. Children learn the important messages best when homes, schools, and communities speak with one voice.

SUMMARY

Self-Concept

1. Although preschoolers can describe themselves, they have difficulty coordinating the different aspects of themselves. Also, they do not accommodate the opposition of some traits, such as "nice" and "mean," and they usually see themselves in an overly positive light. By middle childhood, the Me–self is becoming a more organized structure, although children still tend to emphasize the positive. Gradually, more traitlike concepts of self emerge, social comparison begins building on perspective-taking skills, and self-esteem tends to decline a bit.

2. During middle childhood and beyond, the self-concept can be divided into multiple domains, such as academic and nonacademic, and each of these can be further differentiated. A global sense of self and self-esteem may coexist with these more differentiated assessments of self. Appearance is particularly associated with overall self-esteem, especially for girls.

3. Global self-esteem depends on competence in areas of importance to the individual, as William James suggested. In evaluating their own competencies, children may use concrete standards (e.g., making a team), but they are also influenced by social processes, as suggested by Cooley. They internalize the assessments of others, and they engage in social comparison, evaluating their own abilities and accomplishments against those of others who resemble them in some important way. They tend to be motivated by a self-enhancing bias, sometimes making downward social comparisons when their self-esteem is at stake. Children's self-appraisals come more and more into congruence with others' appraisals as they get older.

4. There is a small but stable gender difference in self-esteem favoring males in late childhood and early adolescence, but little evidence of a self-esteem slide for girls. Level of voice is one predictor of self-esteem, but girls' and boys' levels of voice do not appear to differ at adolescence.

5. Older views that marginalized groups would have lower self-esteem than mainstream groups due to the internalization of discriminatory appraisals are not supported by current research. African Americans, for example, have a slight self-esteem advantage over White Americans. In general, strong racial or ethnic identity correlates positively with level of global self-esteem, although findings vary from group to group and from individual to individual.

The Moral Self

6. The meaning of morality varies across individuals, groups, and cultures, but generally includes fundamental principles necessary to successful functioning of society: concern for others, a sense of justice and fairness, trustworthiness or honesty, and self-control.

7. Emotions, cognitions, and behaviors are all part of morality, and are not always well coordinated.

8. In Freud's psychoanalytic theory, conscience emerges between ages 3 and 5, when children identify with the same-sex parent. In the process, children internalize the same-sex parent's values and rules, forming a superego. Much evidence is inconsistent with this view. For example, moral emotions and prosocial behavior begin as early as toddlerhood.

9. Piaget and Kohlberg propose cognitive theories, arguing that moral development is influenced by developmental changes in logical thinking and emerges in a series of stages. Although there is some clear support for these views, there are inconsistent findings. For example, Piaget assumed that preschoolers treat all rules as inviolable, determined by authorities. But even 3-year-olds judge violations of moral rules, such as rules about stealing, more seriously than violations of conventional rules, such as how one should dress.

10. Altruism may be motivated in many ways. Emotional reactions, such as empathy and sympathy, are important motivators. Even toddlers show signs that empathy can propel prosocial action such as sharing or comforting, but such emotions are much more effective motivators after the preschool years, as perspective-taking ability improves.

11. Needs-based reasoning can also affect prosocial behavior and shows predictable developments with age. It also tends to be more advanced in popular children with good social skills, especially boys. Also, younger children whose moral reasoning is needs oriented are not as likely as older children to engage in prosocial behavior unless they also experience prosocial emotions. For older children whose reasoning is needs oriented, the presence of such emotions is not so important.

12. Personality characteristics also affect tendencies toward prosocial behavior—characteristics such as sociability, social competence, positive self-concept, assertiveness, and effortful self-control.

13. Parents who use an authoritative parenting style with high levels of warmth and demandingness seem to promote prosocial behavior. Also, when parents have strong prosocial values their children are likely to follow suit. Providing children with opportunities to practice prosocial behavior increases further prosocial behavior, referred to as the "foot in the door effect."

14. Antisocial behavior can develop along several different pathways. The early-starter pathway becomes increasingly more serious over time. The adolescent-onset pathway is less likely to have long-lasting consequences. Early oppositional behaviors often recede by age 8 or so; it is when they continue into elementary school that they predict later delinquent behavior.

15. Internal risk factors for long-term antisocial behavior include difficult temperaments, attention deficits, impulsivity, high activity level, and weakness in verbal skill and problem-solving ability. Environmental risk factors include low socioeconomic status, physical abuse, authoritarian parenting, and a tendency for parents to reinforce aggressive behavior by withdrawing demands. Dodge also describes the idiosyncratic ways in which antisocial children process social information, a social-cognitive process that helps establish a trajectory of increasing antisocial feelings and behavior.

CASE STUDY

Kevin Miller, a White fifth-grade student at Greentree Elementary School, is in the principal's office with his parents. Mr. Dolan, the school principal, has just informed Mr. and Mrs. Miller that Kevin's fifth-grade trip privilege will be revoked because of an accumulation of disciplinary offenses. Kevin's behavior in fifth grade has become progressively more disruptive. This time, he has managed to create enough problems for his teachers to prevent his participation in the end-of-the-year event, which was planned as a reward for the students' effort and achievement.

Kevin is a very intelligent and physically attractive youngster with particular interests and abilities in sports and computer games. In second grade, he was identified as a candidate for the school's gifted student program, yet he invests little energy in schoolwork. He tells his teachers that he finds the assignments boring and can find no reason to involve himself in the learning process. He does little studying, but he manages to get by with a C+ average. In class, he talks to other students when he should be working, makes disrespectful comments to his teachers, and basically tries to get away with doing what he pleases most of the time.

Kevin relishes his position of power in the group. Many students in the class look up to Kevin because of his engaging bravado. They like him because he is often funny and provides a diversion from class work. Other students find him a nuisance who distracts the teachers from their instruction. Students know that if they work with Kevin on a group project, they may have a good time, but it will come with a price: getting in trouble with their teachers.

Kevin's parents have a long history of conferencing with the school principal and counselor. Over the years, problems have increased from some concerns about his attention span in the early grades to more serious issues. In fourth grade, Kevin was caught cheating on a test proctored by a substitute teacher. Kevin claimed that he was falsely accused because the teacher "didn't like him." At the beginning of fifth grade, Kevin responded to his English teacher, who was trying to get him to focus on a classroom writing assignment, with a profane comment. When confronted about his behavior, Kevin was convinced that he did not do anything seriously wrong. His explanation was that he was joking, and he suggested that the adults should "lighten up."

Kevin's parents believe it is their job to stand up for their only son and support him, even though they are unhappy about his frequent problems at school. The Millers describe their son as "lively and creative" and "smarter than they are" in some areas, such as computer literacy. Encouraged by the school counselor, they initiated private counseling for Kevin at the end of fourth grade. Kevin has seen his counselor sporadically for almost a year. Both parents believe that Kevin is a good boy whose irrepressible spirit and intellect get him into trouble with those who misunderstand him.

Faced with this new consequence, Kevin is quite upset. He was looking forward to the class trip and believes that the punishment is extreme. The Millers understand the principal's

reasoning, but they also disagree with the punishment. They indicate that they will request a meeting with the superintendent to have the decision changed. They express the view that most kids behave like Kevin sometimes. From their perspective, Kevin should be allowed to express himself and to have the autonomy to make choices about what he does. They emphasize his persistence and interest in activities that engage his attention. They come close to faulting Kevin's teachers for failing to motivate him.

The district superintendent, after considering the case, decides that depriving Kevin of the trip would jeopardize any relationship teachers would be able to develop with him in the future. Kevin's consequence is changed to an in-school suspension; he is allowed to participate in the class trip.

Discussion Questions

1. What are the issues involved in Kevin's case? What assessment can you make of his moral development and his self-concept?
2. If you were his counselor, what would you recommend to promote healthy development?

JOURNAL QUESTIONS

1. Give an example of a moral principle you learned as a child. How and when did you learn it? Provide an example from your own experience of an inconsistency between your level of moral reasoning and your behavior.
2. If you can remember struggling with some subject or concept in school, describe the impact of that experience on your sense of competence and industry. How have you resolved this struggle?

3. Rate your level of self-esteem on a scale of 1 (low) to 10 (high) in the following areas: academic, physical appearance, social (friendship relationships), athletic, and career success. Now rate each on a scale of 1 (not important) to 10 (very important) in terms of their significance to you. Where are the biggest discrepancies? How do these discrepancies affect your overall self-esteem?
4. How did your peers contribute to your understanding of yourself? Explain.

KEY TERMS

academic self-concept	immanent justice	prosocial behavior or altruism	adolescent-onset or late-starter model
nonacademic self-concept	autonomous stage	empathy	antisocial personality disorder
social comparison	preconventional morality	sympathy	oppositional defiant disorder (ODD)
self-enhancing bias	conventional morality	needs-based reasoning	conduct disorder (CD)
"downward" social comparisons	postconventional morality	hedonistic	coercive family interaction
self-esteem slide	moral rules	needs oriented	social information-processing
conscience	conventional rules	effortful control	hostile attributional bias
identification	personal rules	antisocial behavior	
premoral stage	morality of justice	early-starter model	
heteronomous stage	morality of caring		

Now go to our Companion Website to assess your understanding of chapter content with Multiple Choice Questions, apply comprehension in Essay Questions, and broaden your knowledge of development with related Web Links.

CHAPTER 8

Gender and Peer Relationships: Middle Childhood Through Early Adolescence

It's recess time for the third graders at Columbus Elementary. Four girls take turns jumping rope, while other small clusters of girls are playing hopscotch or sitting and talking. One pair whispers conspiratorially, occasionally giggling and glancing up at the girls playing jump rope. One girl skips across the grass alone and then sits on a swing, watching three friends play a climbing game on the modern jungle gym. The game has something to do with the plot of a TV show they saw the night before. A crew of boys is playing a variant of tag, in which whoever is "it" must not only catch someone else (who will then become "it") but must also dodge the assaults of players who risk being caught to race past and punch the boy who is "it" in the back or arms. A boy watching on the sidelines suddenly jumps into the tag game, punching the player who is "it." The others gather round, shoving and yelling at the intruder. When he says "I can play if I want to," one boy shouts more loudly than the rest, "Let him play, but he's gotta be it." In the remaining 10 minutes of recess, the intruder catches three different boys, but the captives are forcibly freed by their compatriots, and the intruder never escapes being "it" despite his bitter protests. Moments before the recess ends, he stomps off in a rage, shouting epithets at the others.

As the third graders move off the playground, recess begins for the higher grades. Soon a group of sixth graders, seven boys and one girl, is playing basketball on the paved court; another larger group, all boys, is playing soccer on a grassy field. Most of the sixth-grade girls are standing around in circles, talking.

We could watch a large assembly of elementary school children on any playground—the roof of a private Manhattan school; the small, fenced yard of a Chicago public school; or, as in this example, the ample playing fields, paved courts, and wood-chipped, well-equipped play area of a sprawling school in an affluent Seattle suburb. Despite the constraints of the setting, some key elements of the children's behavior would be strikingly similar. Most of the girls would be playing or talking in clusters of two or three, separately from the boys. The boys would be playing in larger groups, and often their play would consist of some mostly good-natured rough-housing. Some children would probably be alone. They might stand apart, or they might push their way into a group where they are not welcome and then find themselves in conflict with others. Occasionally, a child of one sex might play comfortably with a group of the opposite sex, but generally she or he will be a quiet, peripheral member of the group. More often than not, this child will be a girl. Sometimes, groups of boys will interfere with the play of a cluster of girls, most often to chase them or to upset their game. The girls might chase the boys back, always with their girlfriends along for support.

These patterns will be familiar to anyone who has ever participated in, or observed, a children's recess. In this chapter, we will examine two major features of child development that contribute to these patterns. The first is sex role development in childhood and early adolescence, including the formation of a gender identity and the acquisition of gender-related behaviors. (We will discuss the emergence of sexual orientation in Chapter 9.) The second is the formation and influence of peer relations in the lives of children and young adolescents, including both the degree to which children are able to establish satisfying relationships with their peers and the degree and kind of influence that peer groups wield. Sex role development and peer relations have traditionally been separate disciplines in the developmental sciences, and to some degree we will discuss them separately here. But, as you will see, it is becoming more and more clear not only that peer interactions differ as a function of gender but that peer processes may be very important in shaping gendered behavior.

For counselors and other helpers, understanding the processes of sex role development can be a key element in providing valid supports to children and adults as they struggle with identity issues, self-acceptance, and self-esteem. Many coping difficulties, both externalizing and internalizing problems, are more typical of either one gender or the other in our society, or they have different features and implications depending on the sex of the client.

It has also become increasingly obvious that a major function of counselors, especially those who work with children and adolescents, is to identify and intervene with individuals whose peer relationships are distorted. Many developments—including perspective taking, as we have already seen, and sex role development, as we will see in this chapter—are now recognized to be at least partly a function of peer group interaction. Victims, bullies, and social isolates in the world of childhood are at risk for long-term social problems. Among the more spectacular examples are the child perpetrators of major community catastrophies, such as those at Columbine High School in 1998, whose actions appear to have been at least partly a function of peer relations gone awry (Greenfield & Juvonen, 1999).

SEX ROLE DEVELOPMENT

Descriptions of sex-related phenomena, such as gender-typed behavior or sexual orientation, can elicit strong feelings and can have significant political, religious, or personal implications. One focus of some of these feelings has been the denotation of words such as *sex* and *gender*. Some authors argue that the term *sex* should be reserved for biologically determined processes and that *gender* should be used for any socially influenced characteristics. Yet, we found this formula difficult to apply because biological and environmental causes play interactive roles in all of human development (see Chapter 2). Other authors argue that *sex* should be used when the reference is based on objective characteristics of males versus females (e.g., "members of both sexes were included in the study"), whereas *gender* should be used when making references based on judgments or inferences about males and females (e.g., "the feminine gender role includes being responsible for meal preparation"; Deaux, 1993). Yet, whether references are objectively based or a function of judgment or inference is not easily determined either. For example, in our culture we dichotomize sex, recognizing only the male and female categories, but some cultures recognize other categories as well, and some people in our own culture believe that we should see gender as existing more on a continuum than as two clearly separate categories (Fausto-Sterling, 2000). Therefore, inference and judgment influence even what are considered objective criteria for the categorization of individuals as male or female (or other).

Frankly, we found all of the criteria that have been proposed for differentiating use of the terms *sex* and *gender* too difficult to apply consistently. What we have done instead is to treat the terms as interchangeable, except where one word is used in a uniform, conventional way through much of the literature, as in the phrase *gender identity.*

Let's now take a look at the development of cognitive, social, and behavioral phenomena related to one's sex. The first part of our discussion of sex role development deals with the development of gender identity. The second part centers on gender differences in behavior. We will consider some of the processes that might account for these phenomena, and later we will examine how a helping professional could use this information to benefit his clients.

Gender Identity

Augustina was the youngest girl in a family of nine children. Her parents had emigrated from Italy to the United States before she was born in 1913. When she was an elderly woman, one of Augustina's memories of herself as a young child was that she had firmly believed she would be a man when she grew up. She remembered that sometime in her preschool years she was aware of being a girl, but she was excited about the prospect of becoming like her oldest brothers, whom she saw as confident, swaggering, well-dressed young men to whom her mother deferred and who could stand toe to toe with her imposing father. (In the cultural tradition of her family, men were more privileged and powerful than women.) She could also remember a feeling of bitter disappointment that hung with her for many months after she realized, sometime later, that she was destined to remain female and that she would inevitably become a woman.

Augustina's early gender identity, her awareness of her own gender assignment and understanding of its meaning, illustrates some elements in the progress of gender identity for young children, although fortunately most kids do not associate negative feelings with the process but seem to wholeheartedly accept their status. The first step in the process is learning to categorize oneself as male or female. By late in their 1st year, babies seem to be able to make perceptual distinctions between the sexes. They can distinguish pictures of men from pictures of women (Leinbach & Fagot, 1993), they can distinguish the voices of men from those of women (even when the voices are matched for pitch; Miller, 1983), and they even seem to recognize that male voices go with male faces and female voices with female faces (Poulin-Dubois, Serbin, Kenyon, & Derbyshire, 1994).

Children show some skill at labeling males and females and at understanding labels such as "mommy" and "daddy" (for woman and man) or "girl" and "boy" by early in their 3rd year (e.g., Huston, 1983; Leinbach & Fagot, 1986, 1993). At age 2, they do not usually know the label for themselves, but soon after, by age 2½ to 3, most children can label themselves correctly and identify others who fit into the same category as they do themselves (see Maccoby, 1998).

As Augustina's experience illustrates, however, knowing your gender category today may not mean that you understand that it will stay that way forever. A second step in the process of identity formation is understanding gender stability, that over time, one's gender category stays the same: Boys grow into men, girls grow into women. A third step appears to be recognizing that gender category membership is permanent, that it could never change, even if one's behavior or appearance were changed to resemble the other gender. This is called gender constancy (see Slaby & Frey, 1975). Most children seem to have gender stability by 3 to 4 years old—a girl knows she was a girl yesterday and expects to be one again tomorrow. But even older preschoolers may not understand gender constancy. For this, children must realize that even if major surface changes were made—in hairstyle, dress, and behavior—the sex of the individual would not also change.

Controversy swirls around the question of when gender constancy develops. In some studies, preschoolers who are shown pictures of, say, a boy dressed up like a girl, with a long-haired wig and a dress, often express the belief that the boy has changed into a girl (e.g., DeLisi & Gallagher, 1991; Kohlberg, 1966). In other studies, even some 3-year-olds seem to have a pretty clear sense of gender constancy (e.g., Bem, 1989; Johnson & Ames, 1994; Leonard & Archer, 1989; Martin & Little, 1990). But it is safe to say that until about the time of school entry, a child's understanding of this concept can be fragile, and he can show uncertainty about the permanence of gender categories. By school age, children know their gender and they understand that it is permanent. But there are many other dimensions to gender identity that continue to evolve, like the child's comfort with his gender, as you will see in Box 8.1.

What influences affect the formation of a gender identity? How do children come to make gender a part of their self-concept? Like every other important behavioral development, many factors appear to contribute: social, cognitive, and biological.

THE ROLE OF SOCIAL PROCESSES IN GENDER IDENTITY

When babies are born, adults assign them to gender categories based on their genital characteristics. From the first, young children hear themselves described as male or female. They are told, "You're a big girl to help Daddy like that," "Mommy loves her sweet boy," or "You don't want to

Box 8.1 | *The Many Dimensions of Gender Identity: Beyond Gender Constancy*

Sebastian is a boy and he knows it. He understands that this gender category is essentially immutable. But at age 6, his gender identity is only beginning to develop. As he gets older, his self-knowledge will grow in many ways, as we saw in Chapter 7. This growth in self-awareness will come partly from his own active social comparisons and partly from the input and feedback about himself that he receives from others. In this process, Sebastian's sense of himself as a member of the "boy" category will differentiate. He will identify and evaluate his gender-typical behavior in many arenas, for example, "Do my interests match those of other boys?" or "Is my demeanor in the company of other boys typical?" Besides developing a more detailed and complex sense of himself as a boy, he will integrate much of this information into more general considerations of his gender typicality, such as, "Overall, am I a good fit with my gender category?" (Egan & Perry, 2001).

In several studies involving hundreds of third to eighth graders, Perry and colleagues (Carver, Yunger, & Perry, 2003; Egan & Perry, 2001; Yunger et al., 2004) have looked closely at how these more differentiated and integrated aspects of gender identity emerge in the preadolescent years. They describe three important dimensions of gender identity: felt gender compatibility or typicality, contentedness with gender assignment, and felt pressure for sex-typing. They have found clear connections among these dimensions of kids' gender identity and psychosocial adjustment over time, such as peer acceptance, internalizing problems, and feelings of global self-worth.

To measure children's self-perceptions on dimensions of gender identity, researchers met with children individually and read them a set of statements, asking the children to rate how true the statements are of them. To assess Sebastian's felt gender compatibility, for example, one of the statements he would have rated is as follows:

"Some boys don't feel they are a good example of being a boy,	BUT	Other boys do feel they are a good example of being a boy."
Very true for me	Sort of true for me	Sort of true for me	Very true for me
☐	☐	☐	☐

To measure his contentedness with his gender assignment, Sebastian would rate statements like "Some boys wish it'd be okay for them to do some of the things that usually only girls do BUT other boys never wish it would be okay for them to do some of the things that only girls do." A statement about felt pressure for sex-typing would be "Some boys think their parents would be upset if they wanted to learn an activity that only girls usually do BUT other boys don't think their parents would be upset if they wanted to learn an activity that only girls usually do" (Egan & Perry, 2001).

Other measures focused on children's interest in stereotypical male (e.g., "using tools to make things") and female (e.g., "baking") activities and traits, their "intergroup bias" (whether and how strongly they valued their own gender over the other), their global self-esteem, and their perception of their own social competence. Peer perceptions of the participants were also sought. Classmates completed a sociometric assessment, indicating which children they liked the most and which they liked the least. In one study, peers indicated whether statements representing internalizing problems (e.g., "He says bad things about himself") or externalizing problems (e.g., "She hits and pushes others around") were true of participants.

The researchers found wide variation among children in how they perceived their own gender compatibility or typicality, how satisfied they were with their gender, and how much pressure they felt to conform to gender stereotypes. Generally speaking, how typical kids felt and how content they were with their gender was associated with their gender-typical activities and traits, but the correlations were only modest. Yunger and colleagues (2004) point out that "each child is believed to employ a unique calculus to estimate his or her gender typicality" (p. 579). The characteristics one child weighs as important may not necessarily be as important to another child. Children are influenced by their culture and experience but they ultimately construct their own meanings for gender categories.

Longitudinally, there was some tendency for kids to increase in felt gender typicality over time; boys also showed a tendency to increase in gender contentedness, although girls did not. Girls at all ages felt less typical and less content with their gender than boys did, but they also reported less pressure to conform than boys. For both boys and girls, the connections between gender identity and social adjustment were largely the same. Youngsters who reported feeling that they were not very typical of their gender had lower self-esteem than kids who felt more compatible with their gender. Perhaps children with low felt gender typicality fear rejection by peers or others, or they might just feel inadequate and out of step. Such feelings seem warranted: Children who felt less typical both considered themselves less socially competent and were less well liked by peers than youngsters who felt more typical.

We might expect that children who are dissatisfied with their gender assignment would be especially prone to social adjustment problems, such as depression or low self-esteem. Children at the extreme end of gender discontent—those who are diagnosed with "gender identity disorder"—are often quite unhappy (e.g., Cohen-Kettenis, Owen, Kaijser, Bradley, & Zucker, 2003). But in the Perry studies, whether dissatisfaction with gender assignment was problematic depended in large part on whether or not children felt pressured by others (adults or children) to conform. In one study, children who scored low on gender contentment also tended to have internalizing problems, like self-deprecating behavior and social anxiety, but only if they felt that they were under pressure by others to conform to gender stereotypes (Yunger et al., 2004). In another study, such children were more likely to feel low self-esteem, but again, only if they felt social pressure to conform (Egan & Perry, 2001).

Some theorists have argued that when acceptance depends on fitting gender stereotypes, children are likely to limit the range of activities they explore and the talents that they choose to develop (e.g., Bem, 1981). As a result, children who feel strong pressure to conform have less opportunity to develop in ways that are maximally satisfying—that fit their preferences and inclinations—and they tend to be unhappy, anxious, and discontented with themselves. Although the research by Perry and colleagues supports this position to some extent, it also makes clear that felt pressure for gender

conformity interacts with other aspects of gender identity in complex ways. High felt pressure is most problematic for children who feel like they do not fit in, either because they perceive their talents and interests to cross gender boundaries or because they are not as comfortable with their gender assignment as other children. Children who feel themselves to be atypical are likely to have problems with self-esteem even when they do *not* feel much pressure from others to conform.

Egan and Perry (2001) argue that "children's adjustment is optimized when they (a) are secure in their conceptions of themselves as typical members of their sex yet (b) feel free to explore cross-sex options when they so desire" (p. 459). They recommend that parents and educators help children to feel safe pursuing activities that may include those that are not gender typical, but at the same time remain cognizant of children's needs to feel like they are "typical and adequate members of their own gender."

be a mean girl who makes her friend cry!" Children are literally surrounded by verbal reminders of their assigned gender. It's not surprising, then, that between 2 and 3, at the same time that they are learning other labels for themselves such as "naughty" or "nice" (see Chapter 5), children have learned their own gender label.

Research with gender atypical children suggests that social assignment to a gender category can influence gender identity. Gender-atypical children have either ambiguous genitalia or genitalia that are inconsistent with their sex chromosomes. In one example, biologically male children, with one X and one Y chromosome, have suffered surgical damage to their genitals during infancy, sometimes as a result of a botched circumcision. Faced with this difficult situation, some parents have raised these children as girls from infancy onward. In one recently reported example, a boy was reassigned by his family as a "girl" at age 7 months (Bradley, Oliver, Chernick, & Zucker, 1998). Physicians provided treatments with female hormones at puberty so that female secondary sexual characteristics would develop, such as enlarged breasts. At the most recent follow-up, in early adulthood, the young woman still accepted her female identity and was comfortable with her female role. (Note that the results in this case do not necessarily indicate that such a solution will be the right one in all cases. See the discussion below of another boy whose penis was ablated in infancy, and the very different outcome he experienced.)

Another gender-atypical problem is a condition called congenital adrenal hyperplasia (CAH), in which biological females with two X chromosomes are exposed to high levels of androgens (male hormones) during prenatal and postnatal development. The overproduction of androgens by their own adrenal glands is caused by a defective gene. The upshot is that although CAH females usually have the internal organs of a girl, their external genitalia may be masculinized. They may, for example, have an enlarged clitoris that looks like a penis, and they have sometimes been misidentified at birth as boys. When these girls are properly diagnosed, a set of medical interventions can minimize the overproduction of androgens postnatally, and the genitalia can be surgically altered to resemble those of a girl. But John Money and his colleagues, who have done extensive studies of children with CAH, report that if the diagnosis is not made before the age of 2½ to 3, a child's gender identity can be very difficult to alter, and physicians have often advised parents to continue raising their child as a boy (which requires intervention at puberty to provide further masculinizing hormones) (Erhardt & Baker, 1974; Money & Dalery, 1977; Money & Erhardt, 1972).

When CAH females are raised as boys, their gender identity is inconsistent with their biological sex, and yet they can accept their gender assignment. Of course, their social assignment to the status of male may not be the only factor that supports their acceptance of a male identity. Their exposure to androgens appears to have a masculinizing effect on their behavior as well as on their genitalia, and this biologically generated difference in behavior may make a male identity a comfortable "fit" for some CAH females. Indeed, as you will see shortly, research with gender-atypical children demonstrates that nature and nurture operate in tandem with regard to the development of gender identity.

THE ROLE OF COGNITION IN GENDER IDENTITY

Forming a concept of oneself as either a boy or a girl is a cognitive task. Some theorists have argued that one's gender identity changes partly as a function of general developments in cognitive ability, especially logical thinking (e.g., Kohlberg, 1966). As we have seen, when children first categorize themselves as boys or girls, they may have done little more than learn a label. Their understanding of the implications of that label is limited. Gradually, they begin to recognize that there is stability to their category membership and, finally, that their category membership is constant, based on underlying properties that do not change when superficial perceptual characteristics alter. In a sense, gender is something that is conserved (at least under normal circumstances), much like number is conserved when candies in a pile are made to look different by spreading them out in a row. We have seen (Chapter 3) that a full understanding of number conservation typically is achieved between 5 and 7 years and seems to be based on the development of logical thinking. Gender constancy may also be dependent on the logical thinking skills that emerge as children reach middle childhood.

Although developments in logical thinking may be important, there are other cognitive factors that can influence the progress of gender identity, such as being given accurate information about how gender is decided. As we pointed out earlier, adults assign babies to a gender category based on their genitalia. But unless young children are explicitly taught about the importance of genitals to gender assignment, they are likely to be unaware of the typical genital differences between the sexes. References to gender categorization are pervasive in our society, and they are a large part of children's daily experiences. Not only do children frequently hear themselves being categorized, but many references to other people contain gender labels, such as "This man will help us find the toy department." However, most of these references are not based on observation of people's genitals. They depend on people's other physical attributes, such as size and shape, and on more superficial characteristics, such as clothing and hairstyle. It's not really surprising, then, that young children are sometimes oblivious to the genital basis for gender assignment or that they might initially assume that gender categories are determined by superficial properties.

Researcher Sandra Bem (1989) tells the story of her son, Jeremy, who was informed about genital differences between boys and girls and about the importance of genitalia in gender assignment. One day, he chose to go off to nursery school wearing barrettes in his hair. When another little boy repeatedly insisted that Jeremy must be a girl because he was wearing barrettes, Jeremy just as vehemently insisted that he was a boy, because "wearing barrettes doesn't matter; being a boy means having a penis and testicles." Jeremy was even provoked enough at one point to pull down his pants to demonstrate. The other boy was not impressed. He said, "Everybody has a penis; only girls wear barrettes."

A study by Bem (1989) illustrates that when children do have knowledge of the genital basis of gender assignment, as Jeremy did, they are fortified with information that may help them to avoid some confusion about gender constancy. She presented 3- to 5-year-olds with two large photographs of nude toddlers. One was a boy (Gaw), and one a girl (Khwan; see Figure 8.1). Bem gave the pictured toddlers Thai names so that most North American youngsters would be unfamiliar with the names and would not associate them with gender. Children were asked to say whether a pictured toddler was a boy or a girl, and then were asked to explain how they knew. If no genital information was offered, the researcher probed by asking questions such as "Can you point to anything about Gaw's body that makes Gaw a boy?" Nearly half of the children showed no awareness of the relevance of genitalia for specifying sex. The children who did know about genitals also seemed to have a better grasp of gender constancy. When they were shown pictures of Gaw or Khwan with cross-gendered clothes or hairstyles, they asserted that their genders had not changed.

It appears, then, that when adults provide appropriate scaffolding, giving children accurate information about how gender is assigned, children's understanding of their own gender identity is more advanced.

FIGURE 8.1

Photographs Used to Measure Gender Constancy in Bem's (1989) Study

Source: Bem, S. L. (1989). Genital knowledge and gender constancy in preschool children. *Child Development, 60*, pp. 653, 654. Reprinted by permission of Blackwell Publishers, Inc.

THE ROLE OF BIOLOGY IN GENDER IDENTITY

If children are assigned to a gender based on their genitalia and if genitals are usually a product of underlying biological processes (such as the functioning of XX or XY chromosome pairs; see Chapter 2), then biology plays at least an indirect role in gender identity. But does biology have any other influence, beyond affecting the genitalia? That has proven a difficult question to answer, but there are some indicators that "feeling like a male" or "feeling like a female" may to some degree be related to factors other than social assignment to a gender category, and these factors could be biological.

Again, research on gender-atypical individuals provides some clues. Consider the case of a biological male, one of identical twins, who suffered surgical damage to his penis in infancy (Diamond & Sigmundson, 1997; Money & Tucker, 1975). As with the child we described earlier (Bradley et al., 1998), the parents raised this twin as a girl. Yet by age 10, unlike the child described by Bradley and colleagues, the girl twin was expressing dissatisfaction with her female gender assignment. By age 14, she had taken a stand: She refused hormone treatments that feminized her appearance. Male hormone treatments were begun, and surgical reconstruction of the penis was undertaken. By the time he was 25, the former girl was a married man.

The case of the identical twin is no more than suggestive that biology can outdo social influences in affecting gender identity. By puberty, this child had a somewhat masculinized appearance, despite the female hormones she had been getting. Because of her appearance, she experienced substantial hazing from her peers, a social factor that could have been important in creating her gender uncertainty and distress. Further, we cannot say how effective her own family had been in accepting her status as a girl and thus how unambiguous her socialization experiences had been. However, cases such as these raise the possibility that biology can exert an influence on how "male" or "female" one feels, or at least on how comfortable one is with a particular gender assignment. We should note that the results of this case appear to be quite different from the one reported earlier (Bradley et al., 1998).

Children sometimes undergo gender reassignment at birth because of rare disorders that cause malformations of genitalia. Large-scale studies of such children have produced conflicting results. In some, social reassignment of XY males to female identities, or of XX females to male identities, seems to work well (see Zucker, 1999, for a review). In more recent studies, many children have been reported to reject reassignment by the time they reach adolescence (Reiner & Gearhart, 2004), suggesting that socialization may not be as powerful as it was once thought to be in the development of gender identity.

Gender and Behavior

Many of us believe that males and females have at least some different behavioral tendencies, and some people believe that there are major differences in the distribution of personality traits between the sexes. Such beliefs about sex differences are called gender stereotypes. Researchers have found evidence for some of the differences that people believe in, but other stereotypes seem to be based on expectations that have no basis in fact. In this section, we will first take a look at some of the sex differences that have been found, especially in children. Then, we'll consider some of the theoretical explanations that have been proposed for sex differences. That is, when they actually exist, how do they develop?

SEX DIFFERENCES IN BEHAVIOR, PERSONALITY, AND PREFERENCE

In 1974, Maccoby and Jacklin did a careful review of the scientific literature on sex differences. They surprised most observers by concluding that there were only four behaviors, skills, or tendencies that clearly differed for males and females: physical aggression, language skills, math skills, and spatial skills. Even in these domains, some behaviors differed across the life span (e.g., aggression) and others only during certain developmental periods, such as after puberty (e.g., certain math skills). Since 1974, researchers have acquired a new analytic tool for assessing the effects of variables such as sex. It's called meta-analysis, in which the results from a large number of studies on the same question—such as "Are there sex differences in physical aggression?"—can be combined to produce an average estimate of the difference in a population (Glass, 1976).

The results of many meta-analyses are now available, and the list of "real" sex differences has lengthened. (See Table 8.1.) In addition, our knowledge of sex differences is now more fine tuned. With regard to math, for example, we know that boys tend to do better than girls in problem solving after puberty but that girls tend to do better than boys on computations in elementary school and early adolescence (Hyde, Fennema, & Lamon, 1990). We also have been collecting data for long enough, and in enough circumstances, that we know that these differences can

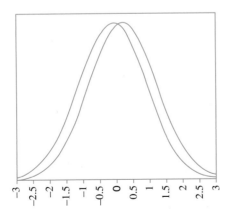

Depending on the characteristic, either boys or girls might have the higher average scores.

FIGURE 8.2

Typical Pattern of Differences for Characteristics that Show a Sex Difference

Source: Maccoby, E. E. (1998). *The two sexes: Growing up apart, coming together,* Figure 6, p. 80: Based on Eagley, 1995: *American Psychologist,* 50: pp. 145–158. Reprinted by permission of Harvard University Press.

TABLE 8.1   A Sampling of Gender Differences

Trait or Quality	More Typical of	Time of Onset
Developmental vulnerability (learning disabilities, illness, accidents, etc.)	Boys	Prebirth
Activity level	Boys	Infant
Happy, excited mood	Boys	Infant/toddler
Risk taking	Boys	Infant/toddler
Physical aggression	Boys	Toddler
Competitive play	Boys	Preschool
Controlling "egoistic" discourse style	Boys	Preschool
Dominance seeking; clear group hierarchy	Boys	Preschool
Spatial skill: mental rotation	Boys	Middle childhood
Antisocial aggressive disorders	Boys	Middle childhood
Satisfaction with one's gender assignment	Boys	Middle childhood
Math problem solving	Boys	After puberty
Homosexuality, bisexuality	Boys	Adolescence
Preference for gender-typed toys	Both	Toddler
Preference for same-gender playmates	Both	Toddler
Quiet calm mood	Girls	Infant
Language onset (vocabulary)	Girls	Toddler
Collaborative discourse style	Girls	Preschool
Verbal achievement (spelling, language tests)	Girls	Middle childhood
Emotional expressiveness	Girls	Middle childhood
Relational aggression (refusing friendship, exclusion from group)	Girls	Middle childhood
Depression	Girls	Adolescence
Social sensitivity	Girls	Adulthood

Key: Prebirth–Conception to birth; Infant–0 to 1 year; Toddler–1 to 3 years; Preschool–3 to 6 years; Middle childhood–6 to puberty; Adolescence–Puberty to 18; Adulthood–18 onward

Sources: From *The Two Sexes: Growing Up Apart, Coming Together*, by E. E. Maccoby, 1998, Cambridge, MA: Harvard University Press; "Gender Development," by D. N. Ruble and C. L. Martin, in *Handbook of Child Psychology: Vol. 3. Social, Emotional, and Personality Development* (5th ed., pp. 933–1016), by W. Damon (Series Ed.) and N. Eisenberg (Vol. Ed.), 1998, New York: Wiley; *Social and Personality Development*, by D. R. Shaffer, 2000, Belmont, CA: Wadsworth/Thomson.

change historically, and they can vary from one situation to another. For example, historical change has affected math skills, such that differences between boys and girls are smaller now than they were three or four decades ago (e.g., Feingold, 1988). An example of situational variation has been found for children's tendency to be adult oriented, that is, to want to have adults nearby. When both boys and girls are present, girls are more adult oriented than boys. But when girls are with girls, they are no more adult oriented than boys are with boys (Greeno, 1989).

It is just as interesting to note the differences that have *not* been found as those that have. Among the common sex stereotypes, for example, are that females are more sociable, more dependent, and more prosocial than males and that males are more competent at analytical tasks. Although occasional studies have reported findings that are consistent with these expectations, in most studies such differences are not found. Similarly, arguments that males and females differ in moral reasoning have received a great deal of popular and scientific attention in recent years. As we mentioned in Chapter 7, Gilligan (e.g., 1977, 1982) proposed that whereas males are more likely to focus on issues of justice or fairness in their moral reasoning, females are more concerned with issues of interpersonal responsibility and compassion. But the evidence indicates that children show no differences in their tendencies to focus on such issues (Garrod & Beal, 1993) and that both men and women raise both kinds of issues when they solve moral problems or judge moral maturity (e.g., Walker & Pitts, 1998). Occasionally, adolescent and adult females have been found to raise more concerns about people's needs than adolescent or adult males in addressing real-life dilemmas, but people of both genders raise such concerns quite frequently (Walker, 1984, 1995; Wark & Krebs, 1996).

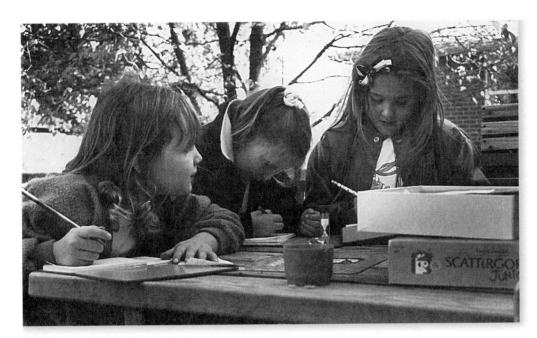

As children mature, they spend increasingly greater amounts of time in sex-segregated peer groups.

When sex differences are consistently found, they usually turn out to be small in size. Figure 8.2 illustrates the considerable overlap between males and females on those traits that show some sex difference. Some researchers have argued strongly that gender differences are too small to be important in development, especially considering that the average difference between genders is much smaller than the range of differences within each gender (Thorne, 1994).

However, average individual differences between the sexes may not be the important story in gender role development. More and more, developmentalists are recognizing that although boys and girls do not behave much differently in laboratory measures of personality or on individual abilities, they do spend their time differently. Specifically, girls spend their time interacting primarily with girls, and boys spend their time mostly with boys. In settings where there are both males and females of similar ages available, such as schools and playgrounds, and where there is freedom to choose one's companions, this sex segregation process begins by about 2½ for girls and by about 3 for boys (e.g., La Freniere, Strayer, & Gauthier, 1984), and it increases with age (Maccoby & Jacklin, 1987). Sex segregation characterizes children around the world, in both industrialized and nonindustrialized societies (e.g., Omark, Omark, & Edelman, 1973; Whiting and Edwards, 1988). When children are about 4, the time they spend with same-sex peers is triple the time they spend with other-sex peers (Fabes, Martin, & Hanish, 2003). By the time children are 6, they spend 11 times more time with same-sex peers! During elementary school, sex segregation intensifies, and it begins to ease off only after puberty, when, drawn together by sexual interest, children begin to participate more readily in mixed-gender activities. During middle childhood, mixed-gender interactions, called borderwork, tend to be quite limited (Maccoby & Jacklin, 1987; Thorne, 1986, 1994). In fact, there seem to be unwritten "rules" that govern when it is acceptable for boys and girls to engage in mixed-gender interactions. Allen Sroufe and his colleagues (Sroufe, Bennett, Englund, Urban, & Shulman, 1993) observed 10- and 11-year-olds at a summer camp, for example, and identified a set of six rules that seemed to determine when children would cross the boundaries of their single-sex groups (see Table 8.2).

When children segregate by gender, other behaviors also tend to diverge. For example, suppose that Carissa and Duane, both 6 years old, are equally active when they play alone on the playground. They climb on the jungle gym with about average vigor for children their age, and they are more inclined to skip and jog from place to place than either to walk or to run full tilt. When Carissa plays with her girlfriends, her activity level stays about the same. But when Duane plays with a group of boys, he is notably more active than when he plays alone. He moves more vigorously on the jungle gym or runs with greater intensity. "Boys are stimulated to high levels of activity by other boys" (Maccoby, 1998).

TABLE 8.2   Rules Governing Mixed-Gender Interaction, or "Borderwork"

Rule:	The contact is accidental.
Example:	You're not looking where you are going and you bump into someone.
Rule:	The contact is incidental.
Example:	You go to get some lemonade and wait while two children of the other gender get some. (There should be no conversation.)
Rule:	The contact is in the guise of some clear and necessary purpose.
Example:	You may say, "Pass the lemonade," to persons of the other gender at the next table. No interest in them is expressed.
Rule:	An adult compels you to have contact.
Example:	"Go get that map from X and Y and bring it to me."
Rule:	You are accompanied by someone of your own gender.
Example:	Two girls may talk to two boys, though physical closeness with your own partner must be maintained and intimacy with the others is disallowed.
Rule:	The interaction or contact is accompanied by disavowal.
Example:	You say someone is ugly or hurl some other insult or (more commonly for boys) push or throw something at them as you pass by.

Source: Sroufe, L. A., Bonnett, C., Englund, M., & Shulman (1993). The significance of gender. *Child Development, 64,* p. 456. Reprinted by permission of Blackwell Publishers, Inc.

Children do somewhat different things in their same-sex groups. Perhaps most notable is that boys' play in groups is more physical and more aggressive than girls' play. (This is true in all primate species, across cultures, and from the earliest ages that youngsters play together; Ruble & Martin, 1998). When Carissa and her friends ride the wheeled vehicles in the play yard of their after-school child care center, they ride around carefully to avoid hitting each other. But when Duane and his friends are in the drivers' seats, their favorite thing to do is ram into each other—the harder the better (e.g., S. Dunn & Morgan, 1987; Fabes, Martin, & Hanish, 2003).

Good-natured physical roughness is called **rough and tumble play,** an almost exclusive property of boys' play with boys. Maccoby (1998) indicates that most boys are not consistently aggressive across situations. That is, physical aggressiveness is not so much a personality trait that you see when a child is in any situation—with adults, girls, or boys—although it can be for some children. More typically, it emerges when boys are with boys. Thus, it becomes an important defining feature of boys' social groups, which differ in specific ways from girls' social groups. Boys often use rough and tumble play to help establish dominance hierarchies within their groups, with more dominant boys less likely to back down and less often aggressed against. Generally, boys play in larger groups than do girls, who are more likely to play in twos and threes, and the boys' groups are more clearly structured hierarchically. Although girls' groups usually have their more and less dominant members, the rankings are not very stable, and leadership does not depend on toughness as much as on other leadership qualities, such as social skill (Maccoby, 1998; Martin & Fabes, 2001).

Girls' and boys' groups differ on other dimensions as well. Boys compete with each other more than girls do. As preschoolers they compete for resources, such as attractive toys, and in middle childhood they compete in structured games. Girls' interactions tend to be more cooperative and to involve much more turn taking. These characteristics of gendered groups are integrally related to the kinds of activities that bring boys and girls together. In particular, boys seem to spend time with other boys who have shared interests, especially starting in middle childhood, and they are more likely than girls to be interested in sports and games and in adventure. For example, when boys pretend, their play tends to involve heroic or warlike themes (e.g., Flannery & Watson, 1993).

Girls often seem to get together just to be together, and their choice of companions is based more on personality (Erwin, 1985). On the whole, they tend to have broader interests than boys, and they are more interested in boys' activities than boys are in girls' activities. But they do have stronger tendencies than boys to like play that enacts family or school experiences, and increasingly from preschool onward, girls' pretend play themes have to do with adornment and beauty—being models or brides, doing glamorous or romantic things (Maccoby, 1998).

As you can see, girls' groups and boys' groups have different cultures to which the members, regardless of their individual characteristics, must adapt. A good example of this difference is the degree to which they use *collaborative* versus *domineering* discourse techniques (Leaper & Smith, 2004). In **collaborative or affiliative speech**, more often used in girls' groups, children's responses are keyed to what someone else has said, expressing agreement, making further suggestions, often in the form of a question rather than declarative or imperative sentences, which seems to soften the suggestion. For example, Carissa might say to a friend as they plan a game, "You want to be the mommy. Why don't we both be the mommy sometimes?" In **domineering or power assertive speech**, more typical of boys' groups, commands and restrictions are common, as when Duane says, "Don't move that block; build the road there!" It is important to note that both boys and girls will use both kinds of discourse. It is the predominance of one type over the other that differs between their groups (e.g., Sachs, 1987). On the whole, girls' discourse strategies are more "conflict mitigating" and boys strategies are more "egoistic"—threatening, demanding, interrupting, or ignoring of another's remarks (Maccoby, 1998).

Where do sex differences in behavior come from? There are theories that emphasize the importance of biology, of cognitive processes, and of socialization pressures. Clearly, all three, as always, are important. As you will see, some theorists are emphasizing the interaction of the three as children spend time in same-gender peer groups. It seems that gender segregation in childhood, perhaps the most pervasive sex difference, may be both an outcome of some sex differences and a source of others.

THE ROLE OF BIOLOGY IN GENERATING SEX DIFFERENCES

We know that genetic differences between males and females normally play a role in the differential development of reproductive organs. For a male, who has an X and a Y chromosome, a gene on the Y chromosome influences the gonads to develop into testes (see Chapter 2). Without that gene, the gonads develop into ovaries. Testes then produce masculinizing hormones (mostly androgens), which influence the development of the remaining male genitalia. Without the quantities of androgens that testes produce, other female parts gradually develop. Do masculinizing hormones also affect the developing nervous system, thus influencing postnatal behavior? In animals, there is evidence that prenatal hormones do affect neural structures (e.g., Arnold & Gorski, 1984), and in both animals and humans, there appear to be effects on early behavior. For example, male rats whose exposure to prenatal androgens is delayed not only show a slight demasculinization of their genitalia but they also show more feminized play behaviors as pups (e.g., Ward, 1992; Ward & Stehm, 1991).

In humans, girls with CAH who are overexposed to prenatal (and sometimes postnatal) androgens have been found to exhibit more **tomboyism**—playing with boys and preferring boys' toys and activities—than non-CAH girls (e.g., Berenbaum & Bailey, 2003; Berenbaum & Hines, 1992; Berenbaum & Snyder, 1995; Erhardt, Epstein, & Money, 1968). Findings such as these are open to several interpretations. For one, parents of girls with CAH may have doubts about their daughters' sexual identity that could affect their daughters' behavior; for another, these girls have many unusual experiences, such as genital surgeries and ongoing medical treatments, that could affect their behavioral development; and so on (see Collaer & Hines, 1995). However, the somewhat masculinized behaviors of CAH girls may also indicate a role for prenatal (or postnatal) hormones in some of the typical behavioral differences found between boys and girls. A somewhat more convincing demonstration of a role for prenatal androgens in the masculinizing of girls' behavior comes from a large study of normally developing children. At 3 years old, girls were rated as more masculine in their activities if their mothers had had higher than average amounts of testosterone (an androgen) in their blood during pregnancy (Hines et al., 2002).

At puberty, hormonal changes and hormonal differences between boys and girls may cause some behavioral differences that emerge at about that time. For example, although depressive symptoms increase for both girls and boys after puberty, they increase more for girls; boys show more increases in aggressive, delinquent behaviors than girls (see Table 8.1 and Chapter 9). Could these differences in problem behavior be linked to hormones? It is a sensible question to ask, and some connections have been identified. For example, there is a link between boys' androgen levels and their aggressiveness (Buchanan, Eccles, & Becker, 1992). But one difficulty in interpreting such connections is that whereas androgens may increase aggressiveness, one's experiences, such as family conflict, may change hormone levels (e.g., Steinberg, 1988). In particular, for males, aggression and dominance seeking can increase testosterone, an androgen (see Cacioppo & Berntson, 1992). So whether hormone levels cause or result from behavior and experience during and after puberty is not clear.

Research on brain structures and functioning has sometimes supported the idea that brain differences may underlie some gender differences, but many of the findings are controversial. Among the differences for which there is some evidence is greater lateralization in males than in females, that is, greater differentiation in the functioning of the two hemispheres of the brain, with language functions more clearly governed by the left hemisphere in males (Bryden, 1988; Halpern, 1992). Even in children as young as 16 months, patterns of brain activation appear to be more lateralized for word comprehension in boys than in girls (as measured by functional magnetic resonance imaging, or fMRI; Molfese, 1990). If females are less lateralized, using more of both hemispheres for language functions, it could account for the female advantage in language. But this, and other brain differences, if they exist, could as easily be the result of different experiences. That is, when behavioral differences develop, they may cause differences in brain function rather than being the result of such differences. Given what we have learned about brain development (see Chapter 3), it seems likely that the causal links work both ways.

THE ROLE OF COGNITION IN GENERATING SEX DIFFERENCES

When Ben was 5 years old, he loved to sit with his mother early in the morning while she dressed for work. He especially enjoyed watching her comb her hair and tie it back with a ribbon. One day he asked if he could have a ribbon in his own hair. His mother, who tried to encourage nonsexist ideas in her children, tied a ribbon in Ben's hair, and he spent some happy moments admiring himself in the mirror. But soon he grew still, staring at his image, and he finally asked, "Do boys wear ribbons in their hair?" to which his mother responded, "Not usually." Ben grasped the ribbon and tore it off his head, pulling strands of hair along with it. Then, bursting into tears, he ran from the room. Despite his mother's neutrality, Ben was angry and humiliated that he had done a "girl" thing. Several cognitive theories of gender differences have been proposed to explain behaviors such as Ben's. We will examine them next.

Cognitive-Developmental Theories.   Cognitive-developmental theorists such as Kohlberg (1966) have argued that when children acquire an understanding of the constancy of gender identity, partly as a function of advances in their logical thinking skills, they are intrinsically motivated to learn all they can about what it means to be male or female, and they are eager to behave in gender-appropriate ways. In other words, children actively seek to make their behavior consistent with their gender identity, whether or not they experience social pressure to do so. The anecdote about Ben seems to illustrate the power of such a cognitively based motivational system. There is also research evidence to support a cognitive basis for at least some of children's gendered behaviors, although contrary to Kohlberg's notion, a full understanding of gender constancy does not seem to be required. Rather, establishing basic gender identity (i.e., learning one's own gender category) seems to be sufficient to foster a drive to learn about gendered behavior and a tendency to make gender-typical choices (e.g., Weinraub et al., 1984). Once gender stability is established, children are increasingly likely to make gender-based choices over what may be more attractive choices, as Ben did (e.g., Frey & Ruble, 1992).

Cognitive-developmental theories also suggest that when children achieve gender constancy, their thinking about gender differences should become more "flexible" and less stereotyped. They now understand that superficial characteristics can change without changing one's underlying gender category. Therefore, children should be able to see that sex role stereotypes, such as girls wearing dresses and boys wearing pants, are social conventions, not moral imperatives or requirements for maintaining one's gender identity. Indeed, children's thinking about gender does tend to become more flexible in middle childhood, as you will see in a later section (Ruble & Martin, 1998). There is some evidence that in early adolescence kids become somewhat more rigid in their thinking about what's permissible for people of different genders (Huston, 1983; Ruble & Martin, 1998). The gender intensification hypothesis suggests that one way young teens cope with the demands of establishing an adult identity is to fall back on stereotyped notions of masculinity or femininity (Hill & Lynch, 1983; see also Chapter 9 on the development of identity in adolescence).

Gender Schema Theories.   Cognitive theorists in the information processing tradition emphasize the role of gender schemas in influencing the behavior of children and adults (Bem, 1981; Markus, Crane, Bernstein, & Siladi, 1982). A gender schema is a network of expectations and beliefs about male and female characteristics. Schemas affect what we pay attention to, what we interpret, and what we remember about events. So, for example, if elementary school children hear stories or see pictures of men or women engaged in cross-sex behaviors—such as a woman doing carpentry work—they are likely to remember the pictures later in ways more consistent with their gender schemas. In this example, they might later remember that they heard about, or saw, a man working as a carpenter (e.g., Liben & Signorella, 1980, 1993; Welch-Ross & Schmidt, 1996).

These theories posit that the gender schema children have for their own sex affects what behaviors they choose to learn about and what behaviors they choose for themselves, but the theories do not account for the exact mechanisms by which schemas are constructed. Social experiences and available role models presumably affect sex differences by affecting what children know or believe about what is gender appropriate. But, according to cognitive theorists, it is the schemas, not the social experiences directly, that motivate children to adopt sex-typed behavior. Research on schema theory has provided mixed support (Fagot, 1985; Fagot & Leinbach, 1989). Specifically, linkages between cognitive schemas and actual behavior have not been well established.

Children's Knowledge of Gender Stereotypes.   In general, cognitive theorists assume that the acquisition of knowledge about sex stereotypes influences the feminization and masculinization of children's behavior, regardless of whether others reward or otherwise pressure children to adopt gender-typed behavior. From this perspective, it is important to learn what children know about sex stereotypes and when they know it if we want to understand the development of sex differences.

Two-year-olds show little awareness of gender stereotypes. For example, Gelman, Taylor, and Nguyen (2004) recorded parent–child discussions of pictures depicting children and adults engaged in various activities. In the following exchange between a 2-year-old girl and her mother about a picture of a child playing with a toy truck, the little girl attributes ability not to gender categories but to individuals:

MOTHER:	Who can play with toy trucks?
MOTHER:	Hm?
CHILD:	Um, you.
	(Later . . .)
MOTHER:	Yeah, well who else?
CHILD:	Maybe Daddy.
MOTHER:	Daddy, yeah.
CHILD:	Maybe John.
MOTHER:	Yeah. (*Source:* Gelman et al., 2004, pp. 103–104)

But by age 3, most children know something about gender-related preferences for toys and activities, and 4- to 6-year-olds have gendered expectations about people and their behaviors. In fact, 4-year-olds tend to be quite "sexist," regardless of whether or not their parents explicitly encourage such stereotyping. Contrast the above exchange with this dialogue from the same study between a 4-year-old boy and his mother about a picture of a male dancer:

MOTHER:	Who can be a ballet dancer?
CHILD:	I don't know.
CHILD:	Why is that a boy?
MOTHER:	Well, can a boy be a ballet dancer?

CHILD:	No.
MOTHER:	Why not?
CHILD:	(sighs)
MOTHER:	I've seen boy ballet dancers.
CHILD:	I don't think so. (*Source:* Gelman et al., 2004, p. 106)

By school entry, about age 5 or 6, knowledge of gendered activities and occupations is very extensive (Liben, Bigler, & Krogh, 2002; Signorella, Bigler, & Liben, 1993). In middle childhood, children become more aware of psychological stereotypes, such as expecting boys to be more competent, and they begin to expect that a person with one gender-typical trait or behavior will have others as well. By age 10, children are aware of differences in the ways males and females are evaluated in their culture. In particular, they recognize that females and many female-typical behaviors are devalued (Intons-Peterson, 1988). Of course, such awareness may help explain why females show a greater susceptibility to depression beginning in early adolescence than males do.

Although knowledge of stereotypes increases dramatically in middle childhood, awareness that people vary in the degree to which they fit their gendered categories also grows. The following example of an exchange between a 6-year-old and her mother illustrates the child's incipient (if grudging) understanding that gender assignment does not necessarily dictate traits, abilities, or preferences:

MOTHER:	Does Cynthia ever play with trucks?
CHILD:	Sometimes.
CHILD:	Girl trucks.
MOTHER:	What are girl trucks?
CHILD:	Pink ones.
MOTHER:	Does Cynthia have pink trucks?
CHILD:	Yeah.
MOTHER:	Really?
CHILD:	(nods "yes")
CHILD:	Well she has pink cars but not pink trucks.
MOTHER:	So she drives the cars while you and Brian drive the trucks?
CHILD:	Yup. (*Source:* Gelman et al., 2004, p. 105)

However, knowledge of stereotypes does not necessarily lead to conduct in keeping with those stereotypes. Similarly, individuals may vary in their behavior (both consistent with and inconsistent with stereotypes) depending upon context (Bandura, 1986). For example, female officers in the armed services may behave in stereotypically masculine ways while on duty but may act in more stereotypically feminine ways outside work. A young boy may play house with his sister at home but never do so with other boys at school.

Research also indicates that factors other than gender knowledge affect some sex differences. For example, cognitive theories explain children's preferences for same-sex playmates as a function of the human tendency to value members of one's own in-group over members of an out-group. Once children identify themselves as male or female, they should quickly begin the gender segregation process. But even though boys tend to learn their own gender category a bit earlier than girls do, girls show same-sex playmate preferences earlier than boys do. As Maccoby (1998) suggested, knowledge of one's own gender identity may be a necessary but not a sufficient condition for gender segregation. In the next section, we will examine some of the social influences that may directly affect the development of sex differences, including children's preferences for same-sex playmates.

THE ROLE OF PARENTING PROCESSES IN GENERATING SEX DIFFERENCES

A number of theories, in many different traditions, have argued that parenting practices have a special role to play in the development of sex differences.

Freud's Psychoanalytic Theory.   One of the oldest social influence theories of sex role development is Freud's psychoanalytic theory (e.g., 1935/1960; see also Chapter 1). Freud argued that at about age 3, children begin to have vague sexual needs. These needs create a family triangle that plays out somewhat differently for boys versus girls. Boys are buffeted by a tempest of motives and emotions called an Oedipus complex. First, they direct their sexual urges toward their mothers because they are most strongly attached to their mothers as primary caretakers. Then, this desire for the mother, to usurp her time, to be physically close to her, puts a boy in competition with his father for her affections. The boy fears that his more powerful father will retaliate with a physical punishment that fits the crime—castration. Finally, the boy is so terrified by the prospect of his father's retaliation that he redirects his energy into pleasing his father by identifying with him. This identification process involves both imitation and internalization. Identification explains why boys adopt sex-typed behaviors: They are acting like their fathers. It also explains how boys form a superego, a kind of conscience: They internalize their fathers' values (see Chapter 7).

In Freud's theory, girls go through a similar process called the Electra complex. They direct their initial sexual desires toward their fathers, even though they too are more strongly attached to their mothers. That is because they experience penis envy, a desire to have what they naively assume is the greater genital pleasure that must come with having the external genitalia of a male. Then they find themselves in competition with their mothers, although their fear of their mothers' displeasure is not so great as a boy's because they assume that somehow they have already been castrated. They do not understand that their genitalia are simply more internal than are a boy's. Eventually, they identify with their mothers to make peace, although because they do not fear castration, they do not identify as closely with their mothers as boys do with their fathers. Thus, girls too become gender typed in their behavior and form a superego. However, neither process is as intense for a girl as it is for a boy. This was Freud's way of explaining why women are "morally inferior" to men, a belief that was endemic to the time and place in which Freud himself was enculturated.

Although many aspects of Freud's tale of sexual desire, competition, and fear in young children have become deeply embedded in our culture, efforts to validate the theory have been unsuccessful. For example, one prediction we can make from Freud's theory is that traditional family structure—mother as primary caregiver, father as her sexual partner and a strong presence in the home—should be necessary for children to experience normal sex role development. Yet, sex role development is not impeded in children who come from single-parent homes, nor even in children who come from homes where both parents are of one sex (e.g., Bailey, Bobrow, Wolfe, & Mikach, 1995; Golombok & Tasker, 1996; Patterson, 1992).

There is also little evidence that children model themselves after a single identification figure. Rather, research indicates that children will model themselves after others whom they perceive to be like themselves (e.g., same gender; Bussey & Bandura, 1984), as the cognitive theorists predict, and whom they perceive as competent. It also helps if the model is not scary or punitive, but rather is perceived as nurturant (Bandura, 1977; see also Ruble & Martin, 1998).

Social Learning Theories.   Social learning theorists argue that many parents and other adults influence children's sex-typed behaviors, both by modeling such behaviors and by differential treatment of boys and girls that teaches them to behave in sex-appropriate ways.

What evidence is there that adults actually do behave differently toward children based on gender? First, we should note that in many ways, boys and girls are not treated differently. Meta-analyses indicate no differences in how much parents interact with their sons and daughters, in how much parents encourage them to achieve, in how much parents encourage help-seeking, in how much warmth or responsiveness parents show, or in how effectively parents communicate or reason with them (e.g., Lytton & Romney, 1991).

However, there are some important differences in parental behaviors. Mothers talk more, use more supportive speech, and talk more about emotions with their daughters (e.g., Dunn, Bretherton, & Munn, 1987; Leaper, Anderson, & Sanders, 1998). Many parents place more pressure on preschool boys than girls not to cry or express feelings (Block, 1978). There are other parental differences as well, with fathers more likely than mothers to have different expectations of their sons than their daughters (Siegel, 1987). They are more likely to be disapproving of cross-sex behavior in their sons than in their daughters, more likely to roughhouse with their sons, and more likely to be negative or confrontational with them (Maccoby, 1998). Indeed, Katz and Walsh (1991) suggest that children come to see men as "the custodians of gender-role norms" (p. 349). In Western societies, boys typically experience stronger pressure to conform to gender-stereotypic behavior than do girls because the sanctions when boys deviate from such norms are more severe than they are for girls (Sandnabba & Alhberg, 1999).

Other differences in adult socialization practices with boys versus girls may be particularly important in laying the groundwork for later sex differences in psychopathology. Keenan and Shaw (1997) reviewed a number of findings that are consistent with such a conclusion. They report that preschool girls, in contrast to boys, are more often reinforced by their parents for compliant behavior and more often ignored for attempts to direct interaction in free-play situations (Kerig, Cowan, & Cowan, 1993). Parents also socialize children to deal with conflict in different ways. Girls are more frequently encouraged to yield to peers in conflict situations, for example, by giving up a desired toy (Ross, Tesla, Kenyon, & Lollis, 1990). Girls are also taught, to a greater degree than boys, to take others' perspectives and feelings into account in situations involving conflict (Smetana, 1989). Preschool teachers have sometimes been found to react more negatively to girls than to boys for high levels of activity, including activity levels during play, and more positively to girls than to boys for dependency behaviors (Fagot, 1984). In sum, these authors conclude that there is evidence to suggest that early socialization experiences help channel the development of internalizing behaviors in girls and externalizing behaviors in boys.

To what extent are adults' behaviors causes of sex differences in children, as social learning theorists would argue, and to what extent are they responses to already existing sex differences? As we have seen so many times, the causal processes here seem to be reciprocal. For example, parents make more attempts to "down-regulate" boys' emotional responses in the preschool years (Block, 1978), but boys are also slower to develop self-regulatory skills than are girls. It seems likely that parents are influenced in part by the fact that boys have more impulsive emotional outbursts and in part by their desire to teach boys not to display weakness (Maccoby, 1998). Another example is that parents talk more to their daughters than to their sons. This may influence girls' language development, but girls' vocabulary growth begins earlier than boys', and toddler girls are more talkative than toddler boys, which may help influence parents' behavior as well (Leaper & Smith, 2004).

THE ROLE OF PEER INTERACTIONS IN GENERATING SEX DIFFERENCES

We have already emphasized how intensive the sex segregation process is, beginning as early as 2½, and becoming by middle childhood the most extreme sex difference that there is: Girls spend much of their unstructured time with girls, boys with boys. As we have seen, gender segregation may be influenced by cognitive processes, such that when children become aware of their gender identity, they value members of the same in-group more than members of the out-group. Some preexisting sex differences, influenced by either biology or parenting or both, may also make same-gender companions more appealing. In particular, Maccoby (1990, 1998) has suggested that girls tend to be wary of boys' rough play and to turn away from it. If so, initial differences in children's play styles are then magnified in same-gender peer groups.

> Here is a plausible scenario: Individual boys, each prenatally sensitized (or primed by parents) to respond positively to overtures for rough, arousing play, will choose each other as playmates. . . . And girls, individually sensitized by their parents to others' feelings, or in a state of greater readiness to receive socialization inputs of this kind from their parents, will use (their) attributes to build a new and distinctively female type of interaction with their playmates . . . the whole is greater than the sum of its parts . . . merging individual children . . . into a group, will produce a new form of interaction that is different from what they have experienced with their parents. (Maccoby, 1998, pp. 296–297)

The important point is that within their gendered peer groups children develop interaction styles that are more differentiated than either biology or parenting would predict. In a recent study, Martin and Fabes (2001) observed 3- to 5-year-olds' play-partner choices over a 6-month period. They found that "sex segregation was pervasive" among their 61 study participants. Over

80% of the children had clear same-sex play-partner preferences, even though teachers encouraged gender equity, and the stability of these preferences increased over the 6 months of the study. The results also demonstrated that same-sex peers seem to have a socializing influence on children, just as Maccoby suggests. Stereotyped sex differences, such as activity level differences, "developed or increased over time." Most interesting was that there was a social dosage effect: Children who spent more time in same-gender groups showed greater increases in gender-related behaviors even after only a few months.

In adolescence, when boys and girls begin to build cross-gender groups and relationships, their different interaction styles can create difficulties. For example, in studies of mixed-sex problem-solving groups, young women can be at a disadvantage. They tend to express agreement with others more often than young men do, consistent with their gendered discourse style, but unlike their experience in all-female peer groups, they may never get their chance to speak because males do less turn taking and are more domineering. Overall, they tend to have less influence on the outcome (Carli, 1990). Similarly, in heterosexual dyads, males do not offer as much support to their partners as females do for the expression of feelings. As you might expect, males seem less well prepared for the mutuality of intimate relationships, perhaps because of the discourse style they acquire in their larger, less intimate childhood groups (Leaper, 1994b).

Gilligan (e.g., 1993) and Pipher (1994) describe females as "losing their voice" when they reach adolescence because they feel pressure to adapt themselves to what others want them to be. As we saw in Chapter 7, there is little evidence that girls' level of voice is compromised in this sense at adolescence (Harter et al., 1998). Perhaps, instead, the more cooperative discourse style of females, in the face of the more egoistic male style, makes girls and women less powerful agents when interacting with males than when they are interacting with other females.

A MULTIDIMENSIONAL THEORY OF SEX DIFFERENCES IN BEHAVIOR

As we have seen, several different explanations for gender differences in behavior have some empirical support, but all of them have some important limitations as well. Clearly what is needed is a multidimensional theory that takes into account multiple causal influences and that specifies how these influences transact to produce gender differences. A social-cognitive theory proposed by Bussey and Bandura (1999) takes a more complex approach to gender differences than the causal explanations we have considered so far. Bussey and Bandura specify three categories of variables that interact reciprocally to help shape the development of gender role, including gender differences in behavior. These factors include personal influences (cognitive conceptions of gender, affective and biological features of the person), behavioral influences (learning of and execution of activities that are gender linked), and environmental influences (family, peer, and societal). All these influences interact reciprocally to mold the motivational and self-regulatory structures that determine behavior. For example, family and societal influences contribute to children's knowledge base about gender and gender-linked competencies by serving as models and by providing rewards or sanctions for gender-appropriate or inappropriate behavior. In addition, both proximal and distal social forces help shape children's patterns of expectations about how genders behave, their beliefs about how these behaviors will be evaluated by others, and their constructions about their own competence to enact the behaviors in gender-appropriate ways.

Although Bussey and Bandura (1999) specify that affective and biological features of the person are important, in their more detailed analyses of how various causes interact in gender role development they tend to emphasize social (especially parental) and cognitive factors. They suggest that at least initially adult sanctions and direct teaching contribute most to the production of behaviors that are considered gender appropriate. As you have seen, research attests to the important role that children's early socialization experiences play in the development of gender-linked behavior. Clearly, there are differences across cultures in the specifics of gender-appropriate behavior, but most cultures do place restrictions on what the genders should and should not do. Yet these behaviors are not shaped just by patterns of external contingencies. Children grow increasingly more adept at monitoring and evaluating themselves according to personal standards and according to the circumstances of the contexts in which they find themselves. Self-regulatory functions become progressively more internalized and direct childrens' behavior in ways that maximize self-satisfaction and minimize self-censure (Bandura, 1986). Children learn

Children construct internalized standards for appropriate gender-linked behavior partly based upon adult models and sanctions.

to anticipate the consequences of their actions and can thus predict the responses their behaviors will elicit from others. These emerging capacities for self-monitoring and prediction are linked to the development of internalized standards for performance, largely based upon how others in the social world have responded to the behavior, the models that have been observed, and what has been taught directly. Gender-linked behavior is thus maintained by ongoing social influences operating through psychological mechanisms such as motivation, expectancy for success, and self-efficacy. These internal mechanisms have been constructed in the process of interacting with a world in which gender is a highly salient social category.

Bussey and Bandura (1999) provide an attempt to take into account some of the complexity of interacting causal processes in gender role development, but much more work is needed to construct a theory that includes all the influences that we have seen to be important. Future theorists, for example, need to integrate the recent findings on peers' power to affect the development of gendered behavior. In the next section, we will take a broader look at the whole arena of peer relationships and the place of peers in the lives of children.

PEER RELATIONSHIPS

In 1958, the Primary Mental Health Project, a program for early identification of at-risk students, was initiated in the first grades of several schools in Monroe County, New York. Data from social work interviews with mothers, classroom observations, teacher reports, other school records, and psychological evaluations such as intelligence, personality, and achievement tests were compiled for each of the children in the hope of identifying variables that would predict later adjustment difficulties. Based upon these multiple measures, children were given either a "red" or "non-red" tag. Red-tagged first graders were those whose behavior, educational achievement, and social-emotional functioning reflected moderate to severe maladaptation. Out of the total of three academic-year samples (1958–1959, 1959–1960, and 1960–1961), approximately one third of the youngsters received red tags (Cowen et al., 1963).

In a separate and fortunate development, the Medical Center of the University of Rochester initiated a county psychiatric registry concurrent with the school-based project. This registry provided an ongoing, longitudinal record of most persons in the county who were diagnosed with mental health problems and who had received treatment. These two unrelated sources of information made it possible to track the histories of the children in the Primary Mental Health Project 11 to 13 years later by means of registry entries (Cowen, Petersen, Babigian, Izzo, & Trost, 1973).

As they moved into early adulthood, individuals who had been red-tagged as children showed up in the registry in disproportionate numbers. They represented more than two out of every three individuals on the list of those needing psychiatric care. You already know from reading the previous chapters that there is evidence for continuity of behavioral and emotional problems over time, so this is not too surprising. What is intriguing about this story, however, is what predicted these later problems best. In other words, what kinds of measures separated youth who ended up in the registry from their agemates who did not? If researchers had known the answer to this question, they might have been able to identify and treat children before more serious problems surfaced.

Remember that the researchers administered intelligence, personality, and achievement tests, obtained behavior rating scale data, amassed grade and attendance information, and interviewed parents. They also asked the children themselves to nominate their peers for various hypothetical roles, half positive (e.g., the lead character) and half negative (e.g., the villain) in a "Class Play" exercise (Bower, 1960). Researchers found through retrospective comparison that individuals on the county registry performed slightly less well than their agemates on most assessment measures, but not significantly so. There was, however, one important exception: The extent to which children were nominated by their grade school peers for negative roles in the class play significantly predicted later membership in the registry. Children far and away outpredicted the adults in recognizing those children destined for later psychological problems. What did these children know?

As we have seen in our discussion of sex role development, peers are a significant force in the lives of children. The story of how effectively grade school children's feelings predicted their peers' later mental health outcomes introduces us to the fascinating world of the peer group, its dynamics in childhood and adolescence, and its relevance to later outcomes. In particular, it implies that peer relationships in childhood are significant predictors of later mental health and social adjustment.

The Peer Group, Social Competence, and Social Skills

What makes for good peer relationships? To answer this question, we need to understand something about the nature of peer groups and the distinctions researchers make between social competence and particular social skills. The study of the peer group may be distinguished from the study of simple social interactions or even the study of friendship relationships in ways that are familiar to counselors, given their special training. Group counseling, for example, differs from individual counseling not only because there are more people involved in the process but also because the interrelationships and dynamics become much more complex.

> Groups are more than mere aggregates of relationships; through emergent properties such as norms or shared cultural conventions, groups help define the type and range of relationships and interactions that are likely or permissible. Further, groups have properties and processes, such as hierarchical organization and cohesiveness, that are not relevant to descriptions of children's experiences at lower levels of social complexity. (Rubin, Bukowski, & Parker, 1998, p. 623)

Social competence, a criterion for peer group acceptance, is a broad construct that is not restricted to one set of prescribed behaviors. Affective responses, such as empathy and valuing of relationships, and cognitive processes, such as perspective taking (see Chapter 5) and ability to make mature moral judgments (see Chapter 7), play a part in the repertoire of the socially adept individual. It is impossible to assess the social competence of a child without considering his skill in relating to others at every relationship level. Social but "nonfriend" interactions, as well as friendship relationships, are embedded within the larger peer group structure, each influencing and influenced by the other levels of social exchange. Remember, then, that a child's success or lack of success within his peer group is not independent of basic interaction skills or the kinds of friendship skills we discussed in Chapter 6.

Good social skills are important contributors to socially competent behavior at every level of interaction. They may be defined as discrete, observable behaviors such as making eye contact, using appropriate language, asking appropriate questions, and so forth that promote effective social interaction and that are part of the broader construct of social competence. Social skills training approaches grew out of the recognition that students who have peer group problems lack certain essential social skills or behave in ways that are counterproductive to smooth social exchange. Consequently, modeling, coaching, and reinforcement processes are used to teach students how to interact more adaptively in very basic ways.

Both correlational and experimental studies of social skills training programs lend modest support to their usefulness in improving peer acceptance (see Ladd & Asher, 1985; Ladd & Mize, 1983; Michelson, Sugai, Wood, & Kazdin, 1983). One possible reason for their limited effects is the unidirectional approach typically employed in these interventions. In other words, treatment often assumes that the socially troubled individual owns the problem. There is evidence, however, that if children are disliked, peers also process information about them in biased ways. For example, children interpret negative acts as intentionally malicious when committed by disliked children but not when committed by popular children (Dodge, Pettit, McClaskey, & Brown, 1986). Bierman (1986) found that greater success could be achieved by combining social skills training for individual children with attempts to enhance the cooperative nature of these children's peer groups. Thus, addressing the context within which the socially unskilled child functions, along with the transactional nature of his social interactions, allows for more lasting improvements. Social competence, including particular social skills, helps children experience success in friendship relationships. The same holds for children's success in the larger peer context.

Peer groups are complicated webs of social relationships, including friendship dyads, cliques, and crowds. These complex social networks emerge and take on great significance for children as early as middle childhood (Hallinan, 1979). In contrast, the social worlds of preschoolers and early elementary school children are less intricately constructed. By middle childhood, voluntary social or friendship groups of three to nine members, called cliques, become more common, although they are still rather informal. At this age the group's structure is flexible, and member turnover is common. The importance of cliques reaches a peak in early adolescence, followed by a general decline in importance over the course of high school (called degrouping; see Shrum & Cheek, 1987). Crowds are larger, reputation-based groups, composed of numerous cliques, that become more important in midadolescence (Dunphy, 1963). The significance of both cliques and crowds for adolescent development will be discussed in Chapter 10.

The peer group serves many important functions for children and adolescents. It provides opportunities for practice in communication, conflict resolution, joint goal setting, cooperative learning, and shared decision making. Important interpersonal goals—such as the development of empathy, tolerance for others, and a sense of belonging—are met within groups of peers. Skills acquired in activities such as team sports may provide training for certain competitive aspects of adult work roles (Lever, 1978). The peer group is like a real-world laboratory where the skills of living with and getting along with others are tried out and improved.

Zarbatany, Hartmann, and Rankin (1990) explored the function of competitive activities (sports, physical games) and noncompetitive activities (talking on telephone, watching TV) within peer groups of early adolescents. These authors found that the two kinds of activities were important for facilitating different aspects of socioemotional development and social competence. Whereas participation in competitive activities provided opportunities for self-understanding by defining personal strengths and weaknesses, participation in noncompetitive activities enhanced a sense of acceptance and belonging in relationship to others.

Analysis of the World of Peers

Sarah is a sixth grader who attends middle school in a midsized school district. The school is a mix of White, Black, and Asian youngsters whose families live and work in the surrounding communities. Some parents work in the new technology industry developing on the outskirts of the town center. Others are employed in the one manufacturing plant that still operates downtown.

Sarah is a talented member of her school's track team and sings in the concert choir. She is active in her school's student council as well. She has a few close friends whom she has known since early elementary school. Sarah is the one whom they depend on if they need some advice or help. She loves to spend time with her friends, talking on the phone and going to movies.

Recently, Sarah's social life has become more important to her than ever. She spends a great deal of time in consultation with her friends, discussing what to wear and planning social activities. She pays a little less attention to her schoolwork now that she has so many other things to think about in her life. However, she still manages to maintain a B+ average. What can we say about Sarah and her place on the social map of middle school?

The attempt to answer this question presents us with an interesting challenge. We have noted the complexity of peer group structures, so you may have already guessed that there are several levels of analysis. In general, researchers have approached this question from two complementary yet distinct perspectives: analysis of the individual group member's characteristics within the peer group network and analysis of the different groups within the universe of peer groups. The first approach would help us understand Sarah's status within her peer group and would typically depend upon sociometric assessment. The second approach would help us understand the number and nature of the peer groups in Sarah's school and would depend on more ethnographic means of analysis.

Measurement of Individuals Within the Peer Group

SOCIOMETRY

Before we can understand the kinds of categories that describe children's status within peer groups, we need to appreciate the means by which these differences were first identified. Sociometry, the classic way of assessing social competence, had its origins in the work of Moreno (1934), who used children's nomination of their peers to evaluate peer status. Moreno viewed group processes as a mixture of positive forces (attractions), negative forces (repulsions), and indifference (absence of attraction or repulsion). He proposed that the interpersonal relationships within a group could be mapped out on the basis of knowing these social forces. Since this introduction by Moreno, sociometric techniques have diversified and have been applied in a variety of ways. McConnell and Odom (1986) offer the general definition of sociometric measures as "tests in which children make preferential responses to statements about peers in their social group" (p. 217), resulting in a score that defines a child's social status.

Typically, children might be asked to select the classmate or classmates he would most like to play with, work with, or sit next to in class. Although many varieties of analysis have been used in sociometric studies, such as weighting the nominations, the most straightforward approach is to count the number of positive nominations or mentions a child receives. This number, then, reflects the child's social preference score. Sociometric techniques are most useful when they also include negative nominations, or children's mention of peers with whom they do not want to work or play. Researchers have found that children who are rejected by peers cannot be identified without the inclusion of negative nominations (Hartup, Glazer, & Charlesworth, 1967). Social preference scores may range from highly positive to highly negative.

A second score, called social impact, is computed by adding up the total number of nominations, both positive and negative. This measure indicates the degree to which the child gets noticed within his group.

SOCIOMETRIC CATEGORIES

Based on their scores on the dimensions of social impact and social preference, children can be classified into a variety of sociometric categories. Contemporary researchers most often use the methodology and categories identified by Coie and his associates (Coie, Dodge, & Coppotelli, 1982), which include five subgroups: popular, average, neglected, rejected, and controversial. Popular children receive many positive nominations and few negative nominations from their peers (high preference, high impact). Generally, they are well-liked members of the group and have relatively high visibility among their peers. Remember, however, that the term *popular* refers to a specific sociometric category and has a slightly more forgiving meaning than does the contemporary use of the term. In other words, a student does not have to be the captain of the football team to achieve popular status!

Average children are those who receive an average number of positive and negative nominations (near the mean for the group on preference and impact). *Neglected* children are those who receive few nominations, either positive or negative. This latter group is characterized by its low level of social impact. Students who fall into the *rejected* category receive many negative and few positive nominations. They are typically disliked (low preference) but have generally high visibility (high impact). The final category, called *controversial*, identifies a relatively small group of students who receive many positive and many negative nominations (high impact, average preference). They have been named controversial because they share many of the characteristics of both popular and rejected youngsters. They are seen by some peers as disruptive but as class leaders by others. These categories are presented graphically in Figure 8.3.

Individual Characteristics Related to Sociometric Status

What are the children in these categories like? Although it is tempting to think of each group as homogeneous in personality and behavior and thus clearly separable from the others, this kind of simplicity does not fit well with the facts. For example, all rejected children do not behave in aggressive ways. Nor do aggressive rejected children always behave aggressively. Popular children, despite their good qualities, are not perfect. They may also experience peer-related problems from time to time.

In this section, we will describe general identifying characteristics of the groups, with greatest emphasis on popular, rejected, and neglected categories, the three groups most frequently studied. The controversial category has been more difficult to examine because of its much smaller size and lack of measurement stability. Remember that the categories suggest general tendencies to behave or to process social information in certain ways much, but not all, of the time.

POPULAR

Popular children are notable for their use of perspective-taking skills. Upon entering a group, these children can adopt the group's frame of reference and join in without calling undue attention

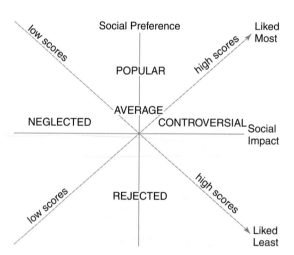

The relationships between positive and negative social choice measures, the dimensions of social preference and social impact, and five types of social status.

FIGURE 8.3

Dimensions and Types of Social Statuses

Source: Coie, J. D., Dodge, K. A., & Coppotelli, H. (182). Dimensions and types of social status: A cross-age perspective. *Developmental Psychology, 18*, 557–570. Copyright © 1982 by the American Psychological Association. Adapted with permission.

to themselves or to their own needs (Putallaz & Wasserman, 1990). They can be assertive, but they are not deliberately antagonistic or disruptive to others (Dodge, Schlundt, Schocken, & Delugach, 1983). In this, they demonstrate high levels of self-regulation and self-control. Popular children also manifest greater cognitive and social problem-solving ability than do children from other groups. Black and Hazan (1990) studied the language patterns of popular preschool children and found them to be particularly adept at communicating clearly with others and following others' conversations. Positive correlations have also been found between popular status and perceived social self-concept (Harter, 1981) and self-efficacy (Ladd & Price, 1981).

In general, popular students tend to be prosocial, cooperative, intelligent, and capable of working well with others. They are likely to enjoy close, dyadic relationships with friends, although the domains of popularity and friendship are not necessarily overlapping. In other words, popularity is not a prerequisite for friendship. Sociometrically average and neglected groups also develop friendships. Peer acceptance and friendship make separate contributions to children's overall adjustment. For example, loneliness in adolescence is more closely associated with lack of friendships than with low peer acceptance (Bukowski & Hoza, 1989).

Certain other attributes, such as physical attractiveness (Langlois & Stephan, 1981) and scholastic competence (Coie & Krehbiehl, 1984), are also associated with popular status. If you think about Sarah, the sixth grader from our earlier example, you might conclude her sociometric status to be popular.

REJECTED

The children who are rejected by their peers have received a great deal of research attention. Rejected children are the least socially skilled of all the groups and also the most heterogeneous category. Originally, researchers took the position that aggression was the primary attribute of children in this social group. In fact, being aggressive is still the most commonly cited behavior associated with being rejected by peers (Rubin, Bukowski, & Parker, 1998). However, it soon

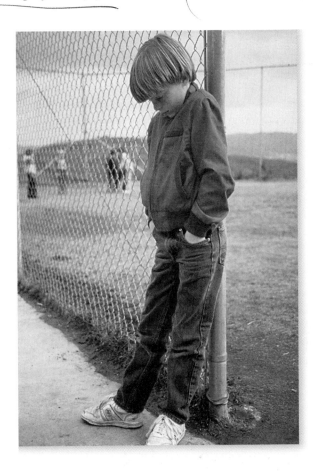

Both highly aggressive and highly withdrawn children can face rejection by peers. Efforts to enhance peer acceptance may be more effective when they address both rejected children and their peer groups as a whole.

became clear that children can be rejected not only because they aggress against their peers (**rejected-aggressive** group) but also because they withdraw from them (**rejected-withdrawn** group).

The characteristics of rejected children contrast sharply with those of the popular group. Instead of modulating negativity, as is the case with popular children, rejected-aggressive youngsters demonstrate high levels of instrumental aggression, verbal negativity, and disruptiveness. You might wonder whether these children are rejected because they are aggressive or act aggressively because they have been rejected. Several longitudinal studies demonstrate a causal link between aggression and subsequent rejection. This evidence is different from most sociometric research findings because it helps to explain what causes a child to be rejected. Over a period of several days, Dodge (1983) observed the interactions of small groups of children who initially did not know each other. After each play session, children were asked to complete a sociometric measure for their group. As the experiment progressed, some children began to take on popular status, whereas others were rejected. As in other studies of this type (Coie & Kupersmidt, 1983; Kupersmidt, Burchinal, & Patterson, 1995), aggression was the characteristic that best predicted rejection by the other children when all other differences were controlled.

In addition to aggression, rejected youngsters are more likely to demonstrate lower levels of perspective taking, self-control, and positive social interaction skills. Particular deficits in information processing, marked by perceptions of hostile intent or hostile attribution bias (see Chapter 7), are significant features of their social cognition. Once rejected, these youngsters are prevented from engaging in the very kinds of social interactions that might help them develop more positive social skills. If you remember Jason, our example from Chapter 7, you might imagine him fitting into the rejected category. Controversial children also demonstrate high levels of aggressive behavior, but they possess correspondingly positive attributes, such as greater sociability and cognitive ability, which buffer their abrasive characteristics and may make them attractive to their peers.

As we indicated earlier, however, aggression is not characteristic of all rejected children. Even though estimates indicate that approximately 50% are aggressive (Bierman, 1986), another 10% to 20% are extremely withdrawn (Parkhurst & Asher, 1992). Interestingly, social withdrawal begins to elicit the disapproval of peers in middle to late childhood. Whereas isolation in early childhood is not nearly so stigmatizing (Younger, Gentile, & Burgess, 1993), presumably because it is not very important at this age, extreme social withdrawal in middle to late childhood is perceived as deviant and may provoke rejection by the group (Hymel & Rubin, 1985).

Rejected-withdrawn children are more socially anxious than other groups and likely to behave in socially inappropriate ways. Poor perspective-taking skills and general social ineptness may lead these youngsters to behave in ways that are considered odd, infantile, unpredictable, or potentially embarrassing to peers. Consequently, popular peers may ostracize them, just as they ostracize their more aggressive counterparts, for failing to fit in. Both rejected-aggressive and rejected-withdrawn children do have social networks, but their social groups are smaller and are characterized by lower levels of social interaction. Overall, it is important for clinicians to recognize that rejected children are a heterogenous group.

NEGLECTED

Neglected children can be distinguished from children in the average group primarily because they have somewhat lower levels of peer interaction. In their meta-analysis of peer relations studies, Newcomb, Bukowski, and Pattee (1993) reported some differences between neglected and average groups. Sociometrically neglected children are less aggressive than average children, are less likely to be highly visible within the peer group, and show less sociability, but they are perceived by their peers as relatively likeable. These authors conclude that neglected children are simply not choosing to participate very actively within their group of peers. Children in the neglected group are similar to those in the average group in their ability to have friendships. Therefore, even though this group has certain sociometrically distinctive characteristics, neglected children are similar to average children in many respects. Being neglected, as distinct from being in the rejected-withdrawn subgroup, which also incurs high levels of peer neglect, does not seem to be associated with developmental problems (Rubin, Bukowski, & Parker, 1998).

AVERAGE

Average children, as you might have guessed, receive an average number of nominations. They are at neither extreme on the impact or preference dimensions. They show lower levels of social competence than popular children and less aggression than rejected-aggressive youngsters. As with the neglected group, no problematic outcomes are associated with this sociometric category.

Gender and Cultural Differences

Differences between boys and girls across sociometric classifications have received relatively little research attention. Those studies that have addressed gender differences report that as children get older, particularly as they approach adolescence, greater intolerance of gender-inconsistent behavior is expressed for males than for females. Boys are more likely to be rejected for behaving in feminine ways, whereas girls who behave in masculine ways are more likely to be accepted by their peers (Berndt & Heller, 1986).

Only limited information exists on racial and ethnic differences in peer group classifications. Khatri (1995) reported that children defined as popular across a wide variety of cultures are likely to demonstrate sociability, helpfulness, and low levels of disruptive aggression. Interestingly, a certain level of social withdrawal, indexed by cautiousness, self-restraint, and shyness, was considered a feature of popular children in China (Chen, Rubin, & Li, 1995). Similarly, when Yoshida, Kojo, and Kaku (1982) asked Japanese elementary school children to evaluate a hypothetical peer's comments on his or her athletic performance, they found that children viewed the more self-effacing child as more competent, truthful, and likeable when compared to the more self-enhancing one. These results suggest that there are some culture-specific differences in behavior, communication, and self-presentational styles preferred in group interactions and in the attributes that constitute popularity across cultures.

Other culturally based differences may give rise to divergent conflict resolution styles among peers. Increasingly, children come to peer group settings from home cultures that differ in what is considered appropriate or valued. Some of these differences may be explained by the specific orientations espoused by diverse groups. Although the frequently mentioned distinction between independence-oriented versus interdependence-oriented cultures can affect the ways peers interact, approach tasks, and solve problems, broad-based differences along this dimension have not been observed. Greenfield and Suzuki (1998) note the following in their review of cultural differences in peer settings:

> It is too simplistic to say that children from collectivist cultures are, on the average, more cooperative than children from individualistic cultures. Instead, children from more collectivistic cultures are more cooperative with in-groups and more competitive with out-groups. Second, the cross-cultural differences are far from absolute. For example, children from more individualistic environments will cooperate when competition is dysfunctional and there are strong cues for cooperating, such as a group reward. (p. 1090)

In other words, in social competence, within-group variability may be greater than between-group variability.

Stability of Categories and Outcomes

Once classified, do children maintain their status in the peer group throughout childhood and adolescence? Many researchers have studied the long-term stability of these sociometric classifications (Asher & Dodge, 1986; Newcomb & Bukowski, 1984) and have found that the most extreme categories (popular and rejected) are also the most stable, at least over short periods. Both neglected and controversial status categories show instability even in the short term. Those studies that have looked at the long-term stability of sociometric classifications have produced mixed results. In general, the impact of peer group classification is moderately stable, particularly for the broad-band dimensions of acceptance and rejection, with the category of peer rejection being the most stable of all. Denham and Holt (1993) propose that this stability stems from children's early experience with each other. Once a child's reputation has been formed on the basis of early social interaction, his reputation endures despite evidence to the contrary.

What are the long-term outcomes for children who belong to these different categories? Recently, a number of prospective or follow-up studies have used early peer group designations to predict later performance on various measures of adjustment, much like that of the Rochester Registry. The broad-based categories of early acceptance and rejection have been studied most frequently and provide the most consistent results.

Not surprisingly, peer acceptance has been associated with myriad positive outcomes, both psychologically and academically. The outcomes change dramatically, however, for rejected-aggressive children, who often have poorer academic records, are more likely to repeat grades, are absent more frequently, are at greater risk of dropping out, and report more criminal behavior and drug use (see Coie, Terry, Lenox, & Lochman, 1995; Ladd & Burgess, 1999; Parker & Asher, 1987; Wentzel & Asher, 1995). The strongest linkages, by far, have been found between early aggression and peer rejection on one hand, and later externalizing problems on the other hand (the "early starter model" of antisocial development described in Chapter 7).

Researchers have also investigated outcomes for rejected-withdrawn youngsters and have found more limited evidence for later internalizing problems such as depression, loneliness, and psychological overcontrol (see Hoza, Molina, Bukowski, & Sippola, 1995; Rubin, Chen, McDougall, Bowker, & McKinnon, 1995). A recent prospective study by Ladd and Burgess (1999) followed three groups of children from kindergarten through second grade: aggressive, withdrawn, and those with a comorbid profile of aggression and withdrawal. Consistent with predictions from developmental psychopathology, the children with multiple risks were predisposed to the most severe and enduring outcomes. The children who exhibited aggression and withdrawal in kindergarten were the most likely of all the groups to have troubled relationships with teachers and peers in second grade, to report more loneliness and dissatisfaction, and to express greater feelings of victimization.

Measurement of the Peer Group: Another Level of Analysis

Let us turn our attention to peer groups, the cliques and crowds we referred to earlier. These are networks of like-minded individuals who become associated with a specific set of norms, dress, and behaviors, like "jocks" or "brains." When we examine peer processes from this angle, we do not focus on the accepted or rejected status of particular children. It is certainly possible to be a popular member of a group of jocks as well as a popular brain. These peer groups appear to develop more significance in late childhood to early adolescence for the reasons specified in previous sections of this chapter. Moreover, adolescents may be better able to recognize and describe their peer groups effectively because they become increasingly proficient in thinking abstractly about categories as a function of their cognitive development.

Brown (1990) noted that the term *peer group* has been used rather loosely in the past, often applied to the whole spectrum of peer relationships, from dyadic friendships to membership in large crowds. This lack of clarity compromises our understanding of the role that each type of relationship plays in development. We use the terms *peer group* and *clique* somewhat interchangeably here, consistent with the view that these units are small enough to allow for regular interaction among members and to serve as the center of most peer-related interaction. Crowds, as we noted earlier, are larger collectives, composed of multiple cliques, which serve as social categories for students rather than as actual friendship groups. You might think of crowds as actual peer "cultures" that represent approaches to behavior, attitudes, and values. In Chapter 10, we will take a closer look at crowds. As we noted already, crowds are a more potent force in the lives of middle and late adolescents than for elementary school and early adolescent children.

Peer group analysis at the level of cliques and crowds can be done in various ways. In general, identification of peer groups or cliques requires students to specify who "hangs around" with whom in their classroom. Based upon this information, maps of the social structure of classrooms or schools can be drawn using sophisticated methodologies such as social network analysis (Cairns, Gariepy, & Kindermann, 1990) or composite social-cognitive mapping (Kindermann, 1993).

Why Do Cliques Form?

Perhaps you are wondering why cliques surface in middle childhood and take on such significance in the first place. Common terms such as *in-group, clique, pecking order*, and even more pedantic ones like *status hierarchy* make many adults uncomfortable, particularly when these terms are applied to children. This is so because these descriptors imply a set of winners and losers in the game of social relationships. Adults often prefer to believe that children are less critical and more tolerant of each other than these descriptors suggest. But like it or not, there is strong evidence for the existence of stable status groups among children and adolescents.

What motivates the development of distinct cliques? Two major forces are at work: first, the need to establish an identity, and second, the need for acceptance (approval) and belonging. As we shall see in Chapter 10, peers play a central role in the process of identity or self-development. The search for the self rests largely on comparing oneself to and distinguishing oneself from others by means of social comparison processes (see Chapter 6). One's own identity becomes more distinct to the degree that it can be contrasted to that of another. Children who tend to dress, act, or otherwise express themselves in similar ways gravitate to each other. Together, they form a type of social group that provides some identity to its own members and a basis of comparison to, and for, others. A group's identity is based on shared activities, values, clothes, and behaviors (see Fiske & Taylor, 1991, for a review). Recognizing and understanding group characteristics helps early adolescents construct a map of the social world and provides them with a knowledge base about human differences.

Individuals' needs for acceptance and belonging also help explain the significance of the peer group. Children as well as adults want to be liked by their associates and will typically engage in the kinds of behaviors that result in their friends' praise or approval (Hartup, 1983). In addition to this kind of external social reinforcement, youngsters are also motivated by more internal goals. Berndt and Keefe (1996) point out that children and adolescents are intrinsically motivated to identify with their friends in behavior, dress, and academic achievement, but because they get satisfaction from emulating their friends' characteristics and being part of a group, not because they fear retribution if they fail to conform.

Peer Groups' Influence on Behavior

Our understanding of peer group processes must accommodate the power of both their beneficial as well as their potentially harmful aspects. As a helper, you have undoubtedly read about peer pressure. If you are also the parent of a middle- or high-school-aged child, you may have lost some sleep over it. Adults frequently blame early to late adolescent behavior and misbehavior on peer pressure, a notion that almost always has a negative connotation. They may imagine that children and adolescents are forced to conform to peer group standards to avoid humiliation or punishment. No one disagrees that peers become increasingly more influential as children mature. However, studies also show that the influence of peers is primarily indirect rather than overtly coercive (Berndt, Miller, & Park, 1989). Furthermore, peers can motivate students to engage in beneficial as well as risky behaviors, such as avoidance of drugs (Steinberg, 1996).

Of course, not all peer group effects are totally benign. The peer group delimits the range of opportunities by its very nature as a group with norms and roles. Within any peer culture, the range of acceptable activities is circumscribed. For example, the peer group determines who may be included as a member, how leisure time is spent, and how the members should dress and behave. In some cases, peer group members may use both indirect (e.g., teasing) and direct (e.g., confrontation) means to promote adherence to these group norms (Eder & Sanford, 1986). Unfortunately, the norms for certain groups may support deviant, antisocial behavior.

Many interventions that address typical developmental problems make the implicit assumption that peer pressure is a cause of most early to late adolescent difficulties. Many of these intervention models are built upon "resistance" training, which attempts to prepare children to do battle with dangerous peers. But is this the way it really works? And do these assumptions make sense?

It may be possible to shed some light on this issue and to improve interventions, as well, by reviewing a few principles of peer group dynamics. First, peer groups or cliques are generally homogeneous. There is a well-documented tendency for peer groups to exhibit **homophily**, or a degree of similarity among members on behavioral or attitudinal attributes of importance. This is why you can often identify the members of a group by the way they dress or on the basis of what they do after school. Second, groups are formed based upon processes of **influence** and **selection** (Cohen, 1977; Kandel, 1978). Basically, *influence* refers to the fact that the peer group can cause an individual to conform to the norms of the group. For example, if a youngster is part of a peer group that disparages getting good grades, the child presumably reduces his investment in doing homework in order to be accepted by the group. Researchers have found that the influence of the group is not usually a result of coercive pressure, however. Instead, normative social processes, like positive reinforcement, observational learning, and in some cases discussion and information exchange seem to be important. "The idea of a group of friends putting pressure on a single child to do whatever they want the child to do is a myth" (Berndt & Murphy, 2002, p. 283).

Less attention has been paid to the complementary process, called *selection*, in which individuals choose to affiliate with others who share similar behaviors or attributes. For example, youngsters who are highly motivated academically are drawn to peers who are similar in this respect. This process is consistent with behavioral genetics theories of niche picking. You may recall from Chapter 2 that as children mature, they become more able to select the environments that suit them, perhaps influenced by their genetically based predispositions (Scarr & McCartney, 1983).

Contrary to conventional wisdom, which emphasizes the importance of peer influence, many recent studies have found that selection processes are at least as important in the formation of peer groups. For example, Kindermann (1993) investigated how fourth- and fifth-grade students' peer groups affected their academic motivation. He found evidence for an initial selection process, with students selecting a peer context early in the school year that reflected their unique level of motivation. Interestingly, membership in the high- or low-motivation peer groups predicted academic achievement at the end of the year, suggesting that some complementary peer influence processes were at work throughout the year to maintain the levels of motivation.

Ennett and Bauman (1994) looked at this issue as it relates to teenage cigarette smoking. Once again, they found support for both selection and influence processes. Adolescents were drawn to cliques where smoking was the norm if they smoked or viewed smoking as desirable (selection). But it was also the case that nonsmokers in smoking cliques were more likely to begin smoking than were nonsmokers in nonsmoking cliques (influence).

What is important to remember is that both processes contribute to peer group formation and maintenance. Overemphasis on peer influence processes may compromise our understanding of other dynamics, such as motivation to affiliate with similar individuals. Once established, peer groups constitute important social contexts for young people that reinforce certain ways of thinking and behaving. Obviously, peer groups differ in the degree to which they provide a healthy developmental context for children and adolescents, yet their impact can be profound regardless of their benefit or harm. Paxton and her associates (Paxton, Schutz, Weitheim, & Muir, 1999) studied female cliques that varied in their levels of concern about body image and eating. Those girls who showed higher levels of eating-related disorders also inhabited more negative social environments, which appeared to amplify their distorted ideas about body image.

As children mature into adolescents, much more of their time is spent in the company of their peers. The body of research on peer relationships teaches us that we would do well to consider the peer network in our conceptualization of problems and in the structuring of our interventions. A recent study speaks clearly to this final point. Reasoning that some positive modification in environment could alter the course of development for at-risk students, Mahoney (2000) studied the trajectories of 695 boys and girls from elementary school to young adulthood. He specifically focused on the role that participation in extracurricular activities in school played in ameliorating the difficulties of those participants who were most at risk. Not too surprisingly, most of the students who participated in extracurricular activities (1 or more years of involvement in 6th through 10th grades) graduated from high school and did not become involved in criminal activity as young adults. This result was most obvious for students in the highest risk category.

What was surprising, however, was that this benefit was limited to those high-risk students whose peer groups also participated in the activity. There was no appreciable gain from participation unless the youngster's peer group shared in the activity. Participation in positive, highly

Children's resilience is enhanced when they participate in beneficial activities along with other members of their peer group.

organized, and supervised activities enriched the adjustment of the whole group, reinforcing more socially adaptive behavior for everyone. It may be that raising the index of positive adaptation for the whole group attracts more adaptive members (selection) while providing a context that promotes healthier activity (influence).

APPLICATIONS

As children mature, they are exposed to influences from many contexts, and the relative power of these influences shifts with development. Friendships, peer groups, and other extrafamilial settings such as school play increasingly important roles.

Focusing on children's relationships with their peers has become a major clinical objective, given what we now understand about their importance. First of all, functioning well within a peer group is one of the most significant accomplishments in children's lives (Sullivan, 1965). Good peer relationships operate as a powerful protective factor, providing children and adolescents with experiences of friendship, opportunities for problem solving, and enhancement of perspective taking and empathy. The opportunity to feel validated by others in your age group, who share many of your ideas and feelings, contributes to a sense of self-worth, relatedness, and security (Sullivan, 1953). Second, problematic peer relationships are risks because they elicit or maintain maladaptive behavior and deprive youngsters of the kinds of protective effects mentioned above. Peer group problems figure prominently in developmental models of antisocial behavior (the early starter pattern). As you recall from Chapter 7, accumulated evidence supports links between early childhood characteristics, such as difficult temperament or poor emotion regulation, and family factors, such as

poverty, poor parenting skills, or insecurity of attachment, and the development of coercive family interaction patterns. These, in turn, fuel social information-processing deficits that set the stage for aggression toward peers and problems with teachers once children enter school. Lack of academic success and chronic peer rejection reduce motivation for school work and promote positive identification with aggressive and deviant groups. Conduct disorder, possibly continuing as adult antisocial behavior, can be the final outcome of this developmental trajectory. Fortunately, not all children with these high-risk profiles demonstrate adult aggressive outcomes; approximately half show no disorders in adulthood (Cairns & Cairns, 2000). Yet we are well advised to take peer problems seriously because they figure so prominently in the histories of children with conduct disorders, which are the most frequent referral problems in outpatient clinics (McMahon, Greenberg, CPPRG, 1995).

Assess Carefully

Clinicians should keep in mind that there is more than one route to peer rejection. Understanding rejection profiles can help us tailor our interventions to be most effective. Bierman (2004) describes four constellations of social behaviors that contribute to rejection: aggressive/disruptive (fighting, stubbornness, threatening, lying, meanness); inattentive/immature (disruptive, irresponsible, dependent, poorly organized), low levels of prosocial behavior (uncooperative, temperamental, bossy, humorless); and socially anxious/avoidant (solitary, withdrawn, nervous, cries easily). It is possible for aggressive children to be rather well liked if, for example, their aggression (dominance and competitiveness) is balanced by strengths in areas like athletics and sense of humor. Rejection is more likely when aggression comes in the form of being a "sore loser" or a "hothead." Meanness without provocation, inability to regulate negative affect, deliberate disruption of peer group activity, and low rates of cooperative behavior are danger signals. Peer and teacher ratings of behaviors or direct observation in naturalistic settings are useful for assessment because aggressive children do not always report feelings of distress and may overestimate their own popularity.

Rejected withdrawn children typically do not show aggression. These children annoy others by their strange or immature behavior, social awkwardness, and failure to "get" the rules governing social conventions. Because these are the children who are most likely to be victimized, self-reports of their own distress, loneliness, or social anxieties provide the most reliable estimate of problems. Some overlap in symptoms can exist in peer-problem profiles. Some victims can also be aggressive, for example, the "provocative" as opposed to "passive" victims described by Olweus (1993). These children retaliate aggressively to the taunts and teasing of their peers who are aggravated by their obnoxiousness. Careful observation and evaluation are required to understand the dynamics of each of these social categories for treatment purposes.

Skills Are Not Enough

Rejected children have obvious deficits in what are popularly called social skills. Historically, the clinical approach to peer problems was based on a behavioral-psychoeducational model, focusing on manipulating the antecedent conditions and consequences of discrete behaviors, such as reinforcing children to make eye contact or approach a peer group. Evidence has demonstrated that these prescriptive teaching approaches fell far short of their mark. The focus on isolated skills does not generalize to naturalistic settings (Gresham, 1981) and does not appreciably alter the quality of peer relationships for rejected children (Asher, Markell, & Hymel, 1981). Given advances in developmental knowledge, emphasis has turned to promotion of social competence, a more broad-based concept that involves the "capacity to coordinate adaptive responses flexibly to various interpersonal demands, and to organize social behavior in different social contexts in a manner beneficial to oneself and consistent with social conventions and morals" (Bierman, 2004, p. 141). The key is that children need to learn to regulate their social behavior in contexts that are constantly changing.

Thus, social interaction process skills might be construed as the overarching goal, even though one might also teach component skills when appropriate. Of note here is that many of the concepts we have been discussing such as social information processing, emotion regulation, perspective taking, empathy, and so forth play an enormous role in the pursuit of satisfying peer relationships. So, if teaching single skills is not advised and advancing social competence is preferred, what can counselors do to help?

Include the Peer Group

Interventions are most successful when they take into account the transactional nature of these problems, considering what elicits the difficulty and what sustains it. For example, one of the reasons behavioral skill-based approaches are not successful is because these interventions fail to change the target child's level of peer acceptance, even when the child's actual level of prosocial behavior has increased (Dodge, Coie, Pettit, & Price, 1990). Children acquire reputations in their social groups, generally pointing in either the "good" direction if the child is well liked and socially adept or in the "bad" direction if the child seems socially unskilled. Remember that children tend to see things concretely, in black and white terms, and that they will perceive new information selectively so that their schemas remain consistent. Interactions with the target child after a schema for that child has been constructed are marked by attention to evidence that confirms the disliked child's antisocial characteristics (called confirmation bias; Gurwitz & Dodge, 1977) and discounting of evidence that indicates a departure from his antisocial role. Because these social forces operate to maintain homeostasis, they are quite resistant to change.

Efforts to enhance social competence should target not only the peer-rejected child but also the child's peer group. Peers can be encouraged to initiate more positive interactions with a rejected child through cooperative activities. They may also be taught to clearly communicate that they will not tolerate aggression. The goal should be to create "niches of opportunity" (Bierman, 2004, p. 44) wherein the disliked child can behave more prosocially to modify the peer group's stereotypical schema.

Bierman and Furman (1984) found that combining cooperative activities with other social competence interventions had more lasting effects than cooperative activities alone. Olweus's Bullying Prevention Program (Olweus & Limber, 2002) also takes a comprehensive approach. This program approaches bullying as a problem that resides in the whole system, not just within the bully or victim. Consequently, this universal intervention targets all individuals in a school through classroom meetings and activities that focus on effects of bullying, parent meetings, teacher training, and outcome assessment. It is very important for helpers to offer well-researched universal programs in schools, given that

70% to 80% of children needing mental health treatment get their only services there (Burns et al., 1995).

Treat the System

Perhaps the most important clinical consideration that follows from recent research in the peer relations field is that interventions need to be directed to multiple targets simultaneously. One exemplary model based on the principles of prevention science is Fast Track, a 10-year, broad-based program that integrates both universal (school-based PATHS curriculum for all children) and targeted (parent groups, child social skills training, academic tutoring, and home visitations for high-risk children and their families) interventions. Interventions are theoretically driven by the developmental early starter model of conduct disorder and designed to conform to the principles of prevention science. To assess the effectiveness of this program, participating schools have been randomly assigned to intervention and control conditions for purposes of outcome assessment. Early assessments (after the first 3 years) have indicated that treated children are significantly less aggressive, disruptive, and noncompliant than controls (CPPRG, 2002).

The backbone of the technique used with children in this program is described as social competence coaching (Bierman, Greenberg, & CPPRG, 1996). A few guidelines for effective coaching programs (from Bierman, 2004) can be useful for counselors:

1. The content of interventions should include important research-based domains of social competence that offer children a variety of behaviors that can be flexibly applied to many different social situations. These domains include: social participation (how to join peers and feel comfortable in peer contexts, etc.), emotional understanding (how to identify and express feelings, etc.), prosocial behavior (how to interact cooperatively), self-control (how to cope effectively with frustration, etc.), communication skills (listening and speaking appropriately, etc.), fair-play skills (being a good sport, etc.), and social problem-solving skills (similar to the steps of the problem-solving models discussed in Chapter 6).

2. These skill domains should be taught by incorporating each of the following four steps: (a) presenting skills through modeling, discussion, giving examples and nonexamples; (b) allowing children to practice skills using role-plays or other structured exercises; (c) providing feedback on children's performance by means of discussions, self-evaluations, and so on; and (4) fostering generalizations of skills to the real world of peer relationships. For this last goal, the more the actual peer group is involved in activities, the better one is able to create niches of opportunity for the child with social problems.

3. Create a positive environment so that changes can be practiced and sustained. The warmth and reinforcing qualities of the counselor or coach help reduce anxiety, motivate participation, and increase group cooperation.

Gender and Risk

What, if any, are the special needs and problems of children that attach to gender? Certain clinical syndromes are more frequently reported among boys, including ADHD and learning disorders. One's risk for internalizing disorders in adolescence is clearly increased by being female as are risks for eating disorders and sexual abuse (American Psychiatric Association, 2000). Externalizing disorders are more often reported in boys, except for adolescent conduct disorder (Johnston & Ohan, 1999). However, some have suggested that we may have failed to recognize the distinct trajectory of girls' aggression that emerges by late childhood (Crick & Grotpeter, 1995). Girls tend to display a pattern of nonconfrontational, relational aggression (social ostracism, spreading rumors, alienation of others) along with direct confrontational approaches. In contrast, boys escalate their use of direct confrontational aggression at adolescence as the peer group's demands for masculine behavior increase. The fact that boys' aggression has been more visible should not diminish the importance of girls' antisocial behavior for treatment and prevention because of its links to later anxiety and depression (Robins, 1986).

The forms that problem trajectories take are also influenced by gender-role expectations. If girls' expression of emotions is tolerated, even encouraged, then boys' emotional expression is actively discouraged. You have learned that behaviors considered appropriate according to gender are more restrictive for boys than for girls and that parents often reinforce different behaviors for their sons and daughters.

Some authors, who provide clinical insights into the particular challenges faced by boys, argue that the "boy code" that is enforced in the masculine socialization process works like a gender straitjacket. Just as some girls' voices may be suppressed in certain contexts, they argue that some boys also go unheard (see Box 8.2). The boycode requires learning that feelings of fear, weakness, and vulnerability should be suppressed to appear brave and powerful. Although we may be primed to notice symptoms of depression in girls because they fit our conceptions of what depressed behavior looks like, we may miss the cues in boys. Adults need to avoid shaming boys for expressions of vulnerability and to provide them with the time and safety they need to open up. We should not take boys' stoicism as a given.

Evidence from many studies that have examined gender differences in behavior demonstrates that for most characteristics there is actually very little gender difference. Therefore, we need to remember that girls and boys have many similar qualities and needs. Feelings, either good or bad, should not be off-limits because one happens to be a boy or a girl. Counselors

Box 8.2　*Meeting the Special Needs of Boys*

Pollack (1998) and Kindlon and Thompson (1990) make the case that boys need support if they are to preserve their emotional lives in a culture that undermines and constrains the expression of emotion among males. Too often, the only messages boys hear are those that advise them to be strong, competitive, and unemotional. These authors emphasize that this state of affairs is supported by multiple systems, from peer groups to adults, that do not take kindly to expressions of male vulnerability. In fact, boys are well schooled from their very early years in a "boy code" (Pollack, 1998) that prizes courage, activity, and strength, and devalues sensitivity and empathy. Sometime the code prescribes that boys engage in bullying or be "silent witnesses to acts of cruelty to others" (Kindlon & Thompson, 1990, p. 82). In relation to adults, highly active and rambunctious boys are often more likely than girls to receive harsh punishment. As we have seen, harsh punishment is related to increases in aggression and reductions in empathy. The collective consequence of these gendered experiences can be the numbing of emotional awareness and its guarded expression.

These authors advocate that parents, teachers, and helpers who are concerned about boys' development need to support the full range of boys' emotional expression by building upon their special strengths. One way is to capitalize on boys' task orientation by encouraging good problem solving. Another way is to respect their preference for activity by providing appropriate opportunities to exhibit strength and skill. Advocating a more oblique approach to the expression of emotion, Kindlon and Thompson (1990) suggest using indirect questions with boys that presuppose underlying emotional complexity, such as "I know you were disappointed about not getting a part in the play last year. Do you want to take the risk and try out again?" (p. 241) rather than "What do you want to do?" Above all, adults need to avoid harsh and shaming punishment, combat the culture of bullying, and model that it is acceptable for men to be both caring and strong. Thus, boys will be given permission to be strong and caring as well.

Boys may feel especially ill at ease in the culture of psychotherapy where emotional expression is often *de rigueur*. For counselors who work with young male clients, Kiselica (2003) offers some practical guidelines for making psychotherapy "male-friendly." Several of his suggestions are listed below.

- Be flexible about where to meet and how long to hold sessions.
- Display magazines or other reading material in your office that is of interest to boys, such as sports magazines.
- Avoid face-to-face seating arrangements in favor of a side-by-side setup; offer a snack to the boy before starting the counseling session.
- Become acquainted with contemporary teenage slang or be honest enough to ask what the words mean if you are not familiar with the vocabulary.
- Pay attention to the boy's cues regarding pacing the session; be mindful of the boy's comfort level with respect to sensitive topics.
- Avoid asking too many questions; take the heat off from time to time by focusing on more practical problems like making a team or finding a job.
- Support autonomy strivings and motivation to continue therapy by scheduling appointments directly with the male client, if possible.
- Use appropriate humor and self-disclosure to facilitate engagement.

Sources: Adapted from Kindlon & Thompson (1999); Kiselica (2003); Pollack (1998).

can help by examining their own schemas or constructions about what it means to be male and female. That way, we will not selectively attend to information that fits our schema while we discount other important information. For healthy development, both genders need safe spaces in which to exercise their power and to express their vulnerabilities.

SUMMARY

Sex Role Development

1. The first step is learning to label oneself as male or female by about age 2½. Next comes gender stability, by 3 or 4 years, which means realizing that gender doesn't fluctuate over time. Finally comes gender constancy, realizing that gender cannot change. This may not emerge until 6 or 7, although there is controversy on this issue.

2. Social processes, involving active teaching by others, influence learning one's gender identity. Gender-atypical children, whose genitalia are either ambiguous or inconsistent with their biological sex, often acquire the identity that is socially assigned even if it is inconsistent with their biological sex.

3. Cognitive development may also influence the acquisition of gender identity. For example, logical thinking

may help a child understand gender constancy. Also, being given accurate information about what is and isn't important for gender assignment is helpful.

4. Biological sex may also influence children's gender identity, even when social input is inconsistent with biology. Some gender-atypical individuals have eventually rejected their assigned identity, apparently feeling more comfortable adopting an identity that is consistent with their biology.

5. Meta-analyses of many different behaviors, personality characteristics, and preferences have identified some that usually vary between males and females. Certain characteristics are found across the life span, whereas others typify specific developmental periods. Some have changed historically, such as differences in math problem solving. The average differences are usually quite small.

6. Perhaps more important than the small sex differences in laboratory measures of behavior, is that boys and girls spend their time differently: boys more often with boys, and girls with girls. Gender segregation begins as early as 2½ for girls and 3 for boys and increases with age. In their segregated groups, girls and boys behave differently. For example, boys are more active and engage in more aggressive play when they are with boys than with girls or adults. Girls' play and talk is more cooperative or collaborative, whereas boys' play and talk is more competitive and domineering.

7. Where do sex differences come from? Biology seems to play a role in some traits. For example, girls exposed prenatally to male hormones have stronger male play preferences in childhood than normal girls.

8. Cognitive developmental theories argue that children are motivated to acquire gender-appropriate behavior once they identify themselves as male or female. Gender schema theories also hypothesize that children choose to act in ways that are consistent with their gender schemas, that is, their networks of expectations and beliefs about male and female characteristics.

9. Parenting processes are also thought to contribute to gendered behavior. Freud's psychoanalytic theory posits that preschoolers identify with the same-sex parent in an effort to resolve the Oedipus complex (in boys) or the Electra complex (in girls). Identification involves imitation, so girls begin to act like their mothers, and boys begin to act like their fathers. There is little evidence to support this theory. Social learning theorists assume that parents play a more direct role, teaching children to adopt gendered behaviors through the use of rewards and punishments. There are some differences in the ways parents treat girls and boys, and there are differences in the kinds of pressures they place. But there are many similarities as well.

10. Peers appear to play a role in engendering sex-typed behavior. Children spend a great deal of time in their sex-segregated peer groups, and in these groups some preexisting sex differences appear to be magnified. Recent research indicates that the more time preschoolers spend in gendered groups, the more sex-typed their behavior becomes (the social dosage effect).

11. Clearly what is needed to explain sex role development is a multidimensional theory that considers all the contributing elements: biology, cognitive processes, and parent and peer socialization pressures.

Peer Relationships

12. In a longitudinal study of children at risk for later mental health problems, one early risk factor stood out as highly predictive of later problems: peer rejection.

13. Evaluating social competence involves examining social skills at every level of social interaction, both within friendships and outside them. Interventions designed to improve specific children's social skills have moderate success, but they might have more success if both the disliked child and the children with whom the target child interacts were included.

14. Peer groups include dyads, cliques, and crowds. The clique and crowd structures begin to emerge in middle childhood and are crystallized in early adolescence. They play a role in the development of self-understanding, and they provide a sense of acceptance and belonging.

15. In sociometry, children's status among their peers is measured. Children in a class are asked to select which children they would most, or least, like to interact with in different contexts. Each child can be categorized on the basis of a social preference score (number of positive less negative nominations) and a social impact score (total nominations, positive and negative).

16. Popular children have high social preference and social impact scores. They have many social skills, tend to be attractive, and are cognitively competent as well.

17. Rejected children may be either aggressive or withdrawn, and neither group demonstrates the positive social skills of the popular children. They have low social preference scores but high social impact scores.

18. Neglected children have especially low social impact scores but are not perceived negatively by their peers. They may choose not to participate centrally in group activities.

19. Controversial children have some of the qualities of popular children and some of the qualities of rejected children. They are seen by some as leaders and by others as disruptive.

20. Average children score in the average range on both social preference and social impact. They have less social competence than popular children, more than rejected or neglected children.

21. Preferred qualities in peers seem to differ somewhat across genders and cultures. For example, boys, especially as they approach adolescence, are more likely to be rejected for cross-gendered behavior than girls. In China, shy children are more likely to be popular than in Western cultures.

22. Popular and rejected categories show the most stability over time and have fairly predictable long-term consequences: positive for popular children, negative for rejected children. The strongest links are found between rejected-aggressive status in childhood and later externalizing problems.

23. Cliques play a role in identity development. Kids with similar characteristics form groups that provide some identity and a basis for social comparison. Cliques also serve needs for acceptance and belonging.

24. Peer groups are formed and maintained both through influence and through selection processes. Influence is largely indirect (e.g., teasing) rather than directly coercive (e.g., confrontation) and can cause an individual to conform. Selection refers to the fact that individuals choose to affiliate with others like themselves.

CASE STUDY

Hyun-Ki's family emigrated from Korea 3 years ago and now lives in a large city on the West Coast. His parents moved to this location because they had relatives living in the same city, and they wanted the economic and educational opportunities that they believed the United States could afford their family. Both parents immediately found work in their relatives' small business.

The family lives in a modest home in a working-class neighborhood. The daughters, 16-year-old Sun and 17-year-old Cho, attend the local public high school, and they are diligent, academically advanced students. Hyun-Ki, a fifth grader, is the youngest child. He is quiet and socially reserved. He is also physically slight for his age, shorter than most of the boys and all the girls in his grade. His heavily accented English is somewhat difficult to understand, and he is sensitive about his speech. Consequently, he does not often volunteer to answer questions in class.

Although there are many ethnic groups represented among the students in his class, Hyun-Ki seems to get the brunt of the teasing, even from other Asian American students. When he enters the classroom, students snicker and deride him. "Look what he has on today!" they call out. They make fun of his speech and his reserved ways. When he walks down the hallway to his locker, he is aware of the disparaging looks he gets from some groups of students. Hyun-Ki has a Korean friend whom he sees every Sunday at church. The two boys enjoy spending time together after the service. Hyun-Ki and his friend share an interest in nature and biking. Hyun-Ki wishes he had a friend like this in his own classroom.

Mrs. Marshall, Hyun-Ki's teacher, has assigned a class project that is to be done by small groups of students. Peter, a boy in Hyun-Ki's group, is an outgoing and popular student who is considered one of the class leaders. He has called Hyun-Ki on the phone several times to discuss the project and is always friendly and pleasant toward him. In school, however, it is a different story. Peter is often part of the group of students who make fun of Hyun-Ki when they pass him in the hall. Hyun-Ki cannot understand why Peter is so nice to him on the phone and so mean to him at school.

Mrs. Marshall observes that Hyun-Ki is not participating very actively in the cooperative group assignment. From the teacher's perspective, Hyun-Ki is "too quiet" and has not contributed sufficiently to get a passing grade for the project. She also notes Hyun-Ki's reluctance to participate in the regular class discussions. She fears that Hyun-Ki's educational needs are not being met in her classroom. Hoping to intervene on the boy's behalf, Mrs. Marshall refers Hyun-Ki to the school's child-study team, whose role is to evaluate the special needs of students in the school.

Discussion Questions

1. How does your knowledge of the topics of sex role development and peer group processes contribute to your understanding of Hyun-Ki's situation?

2. How could you help Hyun-Ki's parents and teachers understand the situation? How would you suggest they help him?

3. What prevention efforts would you like to see initiated in this school?

JOURNAL QUESTIONS

1. Gender-role training can be a straitjacket for both girls and boys. Reflect on the gender messages you received as a child and adolescent. Which ones were particularly restrictive? How did these messages affect the decisions you made in your life? Do you think gender-based messages have changed for more recent cohorts of children and adolescents?

2. Identify a gender-related issue that you are personally struggling with at the present time. How are you dealing with it? What resources would be helpful for you in dealing with it?

3. How would you assess your own peer status as an elementary school student? As a middle or junior high school student? As a high school student? What was the

most difficult thing you experienced as a child or adolescent in relation to your peers? What could have made the situation better?

4. Give a personal example of an experience you had with "peer pressure" or peer influence. Has the nature of peer pressure changed?

KEY TERMS

gender identity
gender stability
gender constancy
gender atypical
congenital adrenal
    hyperplasia (CAH)
gender stereotypes
meta-analysis
borderwork
rough and tumble play
collaborative or affiliative
    speech

domineering or power
    assertive speech
tomboyism
gender intensification
    hypothesis
gender schema
Oedipus complex
Electra complex
penis envy
social dosage effect
social competence
social skills

dyads
cliques
crowds
degrouping
sociometry
social preference
social impact
popular
average
neglected
rejected
controversial

rejected-aggressive
rejected-withdrawn
homophily
influence
selection
confirmation bias

Now go to our Companion Website to assess your understanding of chapter content with Multiple Choice Questions, apply comprehension in Essay Questions, and broaden your knowledge of development with related Web Links.

CHAPTER 9

Physical, Cognitive, and Identity Development in Adolescence

> I could not prove the Years had feet—
> Yet confident they run
> Am I, from symptoms that are past
> And Series that are done—
> I find my feet have further goals—
> I smile upon the Aims
> That felt so ample—Yesterday—
> Today's—have vaster claims—
> I do not doubt the self I was—
> Was competent to me—
> But something awkward in the fit
> Proves that—outgrown—I see—

EMILY DICKINSON (1862)

From Shakespeare's Romeo and Juliet to Salinger's Holden Caulfield to Margaret, the teenager in Judy Blume's novel who poignantly asked, "Are you there, God?" we have enjoyed many memorable literary examples of adolescents' coming of age. In many cultures and throughout many different historical periods, adolescence has evoked a certain fascination. We endow it with meaning and celebrate it as the time when innocent, dependent children are transformed into young adults. However, one reason this life stage is so interesting is that, in reality, it defies easy description. What are the tasks of adolescence, and are they completed by a certain chronological age? Are these tasks the same for all adolescents, or are there some that are culture or gender specific? Is adolescence a period of storm and stress or a relatively smooth transition? Should adolescents rebel against convention to define their uniqueness, or is rebellion a sign of maladjustment? Is legal adult status a real indicator of adulthood, or should we look to other indicators of cognitive and emotional maturity? These are some of the topics we will discuss in the next two chapters.

Because of its child-to-adult metamorphosis, writers have long recognized the centrality of identity development to the adolescent period. Erik Erikson (1950/1963, 1968) is possibly best remembered for his writing on the topic of identity. Sometimes, however, his emphasis on the shaping of identity in adolescence, which has been the popular interpretation of Erikson's work, inadvertently suggests that there is no real sense of identity beforehand.

As we consider this important task of adolescence, we should note that Erikson himself was careful to emphasize the epigenetic nature of human development. The human being, like any other growing organism, has a "ground plan" (1968, p. 92) composed of parts that unfold or come into ascendancy at certain times, to eventually become a coherent whole. Success at each new developmental task requires qualities and skills acquired from the work of prior life stages and depends upon relative mastery of earlier tasks as a basis for moving ahead. Thus, far from being divorced from the child's earlier sense of self and self-in-relationship, adolescent identity is a synthesis of earlier elements with new, more cognitively and emotionally mature aspects of the self-system. Erikson makes this point succinctly in the following statement:

> A lasting ego identity, we have said, cannot begin to exist without the trust of the first oral stage; it cannot be completed without a promise of fulfillment which from the dominant image of adulthood reaches down into the baby's beginnings and which, by the tangible evidence of social health, creates at every step of childhood and adolescence, an accruing sense of ego strength. (1950/1963, p. 246)

Let us begin our look at the adolescent period with an exploration of the physical and cognitive changes that mark this time of life. Building on the growth and maturation of these systems, we will then consider how they support the process of adolescent identity development.

PHYSICAL DEVELOPMENT

When we think of physical development and the adolescent years, we are likely to think first of the sometimes startling changes associated with puberty. We will examine these changes first, and then we will take a brief look at other physiological developments, primarily in the brain, that characterize the adolescent period.

Puberty: The Adolescent Metamorphosis

Rebecca recently had her 13th birthday. Her Aunt Cathy, who has just returned from a year abroad, hardly recognizes her. When she saw her last, Rebecca was a cute, pug-nosed pygmy with a sunny disposition and an easy laugh. Now she is 3 or 4 inches taller. But her rapid growth is not what surprises her aunt; it is the qualitative change in both her appearance and her manner. Her slim, child's body is softening and changing shape. Her breasts are emerging, her hips spreading. And her face is, well, a little weird. Suddenly she has a big nose and a pimply complexion. Although she seems genuinely happy to see her aunt, within the first hour of her reunion with the family she begins interjecting sarcastic remarks into the conversation, and she petulantly rolls her eyes at comments made by other members of her family. Little of what is said escapes her biting criticism. When her mildly exasperated mother gently suggests that she should spend some time studying for tomorrow's test, she suddenly seems near tears, whining, "I always have more to do than anyone else!"

Clearly, Rebecca has entered the land of puberty and has begun her trek across the divide from childhood to adulthood. Strictly speaking, puberty is a process of sexual maturation. When it is complete, boys and girls are fertile: Males can impregnate females, and females can conceive. But as most of us can recall, puberty is related to a wide range of emotional, behavioral, and social changes as well.

A Glandular Awakening

The process begins when the pituitary gland, located at the base of the brain, is stimulated by the maturing hypothalamus to produce hormones. These hormones stimulate other endocrine glands to increase their hormone production. These glands include the gonads—testes in males, ovaries in females—that now increase their production of both masculinizing hormones (androgens, such as testosterone) and feminizing hormones (estrogen). Interestingly, both kinds of hormones (as well as progesterone, which is involved in the reproductive cycle) are produced in males and in females, but they are produced in different ratios, so that increases in androgen production are much higher in boys than in girls, whereas estrogen production increases much more in girls. In combination with other hormones circulating in the blood, they cause a series of changes in children's bodies that promote the maturing of both primary sexual characteristics (those directly involved in reproduction, such as the genitalia) and secondary sexual characteristics (physical traits not directly involved in reproduction but indicative of sex, such as enlarged breasts in females and deeper voices in males). Early, outward signs of puberty are usually the appearance of pubic hair in both sexes, the growth of the scrotum and testes in boys, and the budding of breasts in girls. Menarche in girls (first menstruation) and spermarche in boys (first ejaculation) usually occur near the end of the process and are often treated as important social markers of sexual maturation. But fertility—ovulation in girls and adequate sperm production in boys—may not be achieved for a year or more after these outward manifestations of maturity (Chumlea, 1982; Tanner, 1962, 1990; see Figure 9.1).

The timing of puberty appears to be affected by genetic factors: Identical twins usually begin and end the process within 2 to 3 months of each other, and mothers' and daughters' ages at menarche are correlated (Brooks-Gunn, 1991; Golub, 1992; Mustanski, Viken, Kaprio, Pulkkinen, & Rose, 2004). But environmental factors are clearly important as well. For example, improvements in nutrition and health care are linked to a downward shift in the average age of menarche in the last century and a half. Today, the average age is just under 13 years, whereas in 1850 it was approximately 3 years later (Chumlea, 1982; Faust, 1983). This trend seems to have flattened out in recent years (Coleman & Coleman, 2002). Body fat affects the timing of puberty in both girls and boys, such that higher ratios of fat are associated with earlier onsets. Children whose body fat is unusually low, such as those who are malnourished or who are heavily involved in athletics, are likely to begin puberty later than other children (Brooks-Gunn, 1991; Malina, 1983).

One intriguing association between environment and timing of puberty is that the onset of puberty tends to be earlier in families where there is substantial conflict or other significant sources of stress (Ellis, 2004; Graber, Brooks-Gunn, & Warren, 1995). This conclusion derives from studies of adolescents around the world. For example, Polish boys and girls living in crowded urban conditions begin puberty earlier than those living in rural areas (Hulanicka, 1999). Puberty is accelerated for Finnish boys and girls reared in father-absent homes as

FIGURE 9.1

Typical Sequences of Pubertal Change in Males and Females

Sources: Adapted from *Adolescence and emerging adulthood: A cultural approach* by Arnett, J. J., 2001, and *Adolescence* by Atwater, E., 1996. Reprinted by permission of Pearson Education. Inc., Upper Saddle River, NJ.

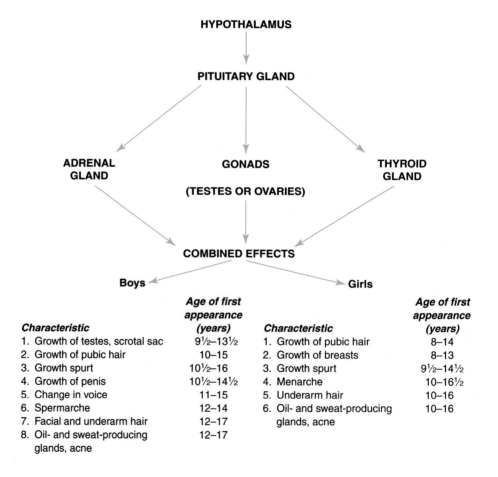

Boys		Girls	
Characteristic	*Age of first appearance (years)*	*Characteristic*	*Age of first appearance (years)*
1. Growth of testes, scrotal sac	9½–13½	1. Growth of pubic hair	8–14
2. Growth of pubic hair	10–15	2. Growth of breasts	8–13
3. Growth spurt	10½–16	3. Growth spurt	9½–14½
4. Growth of penis	10½–14½	4. Menarche	10–16½
5. Change in voice	11–15	5. Underarm hair	10–16
6. Spermarche	12–14	6. Oil- and sweat-producing glands, acne	10–16
7. Facial and underarm hair	12–17		
8. Oil- and sweat-producing glands, acne	12–17		

compared to other children (Mustanski et al., 2004). New Zealand girls from divorced families start menstruating earlier than girls whose parents are married (Moffitt, Caspi, Belsky, & Silva, 1992). There could be multiple reasons for the correlations between family stress and puberty, but one is likely to be that stress affects hormone production.

THE GROWTH SPURT

Puberty corresponds with the **adolescent growth spurt**, a rapid increase in size accompanied by changes in the shape and proportions of the body. Over about a 4-year span, the average increase in height is about 10 inches for both boys and girls; boys gain about 42 pounds on average and girls about 38 pounds. Different parts of the body grow at different times. Facial features like the nose and ears usually grow before the skull does, accounting in part for Rebecca's strange appearance. It is likely that when her head growth catches up with her features, she will no longer seem to have a big nose. Hands, feet, and limbs usually grow before the torso, which can create awkwardness and adds to the odd look. There can even be asymmetries in growth between the two sides of the body, with one breast or one testicle growing before the other (Hofmann, 1997; Tanner, 1970, 1990).

Some aspects of the growth process play out differently for girls and boys. For girls, the growth spurt begins and ends about 2 years earlier than for boys. Besides other obvious differences, such as increased breast size and greater pelvic spread in girls and broader shoulders in boys, there are gender differences in internal growth. The size of the heart and lungs increases more in boys, for example, who also develop thicker bones and more muscle tissue than girls. Many of these changes contribute to average differences in physical strength and endurance between the sexes. Adolescent and adult males are typically stronger than females of the same general size. Thus, the adolescent growth spurt increases both internal and external **sexual dimorphism**, physical differences between the sexes (Chumlea, 1982; Malina, 1990).

BEHAVIORAL CHANGES WITH PUBERTY

Part of what surprised her aunt about Rebecca was how moody she had become. Parents whose children have gone through puberty often warn parents of younger children to "Enjoy them while they're young; you don't know what you're in for!" Parents of adolescents often assume that hormones are the underlying cause when their adolescents seem difficult, making comments such as "Her hormones are raging!" Adolescent moodiness—extreme and rapid swings in emotional tone—is indeed notorious. But how extreme is it, really? And how much of it can be attributed directly to the underlying hormonal changes of puberty?

Moodiness is part of a broader set of behavioral tendencies in teens that also includes conflict with parents, negative affect, and risky behavior, such as violating norms and recklessness (Arnett, 1999). G. Stanley Hall, an early developmental researcher, referred to the full complement of difficult behaviors as the "storm and stress" of adolescence (Hall, 1904). Although there is considerable variability in the degree to which adolescents experience storm and stress, with many teens showing few signs of it, a review of research on differences between adolescents and other age groups indicates that teens do indeed experience greater average storm and stress than either younger children or adults (Arnett, 1999). We will look more closely at some features of adolescent storm and stress in the next chapter. Let's consider here adolescent moodiness and negative affect.

Larson and Richards (1994) used a technique called the **experience sampling method** to gauge adolescents' moods. Participants in their study wore beepers throughout their waking hours. When they were beeped, they made notes about what they were doing, thinking, and feeling at that moment. In the course of a day, adolescents reported more mood disruptions, more feelings of self-consciousness and embarrassment, more extremes of emotion, and less happiness than younger children or adults. In addition, their emotional reactions to the very same events tended to be more intense than those of other age groups.

Petersen and her colleagues (Petersen et al., 1993) reviewed studies of **depressed mood**, defined as a subclinical level of depression, and found that about one third of teens experience depressed mood at any given time. Although clinical depression does not appear to be higher in

"Storm and stress" in adolescence, including moodiness, negativity, and intense reactions, can be a trial for parents.

samples of adolescents than in the general population, rates of clinical depression do increase at adolescence compared to childhood. As we have noted before, both depressed mood and clinical depression occur more often in females than in males, beginning in adolescence.

Moodiness does seem to be more characteristic of adolescents than of other age groups. Do hormones make it happen? As always, when we examine causes for behavior and for developmental changes in behavior, a multidimensional model seems to best fit the available data. Increases in hormone levels early in puberty are linked to increases in the sensitivity of sensory systems (Buchanan et al., 1992), perhaps contributing to correlated increases in negative mood (Brooks-Gunn & Warren, 1989) and in young adolescents' volatility (Buchanan et al., 1992). But hormonal changes are more likely to be predictive of mood if they are combined with negative life events, such as parental divorce or academic problems. In other words, risk factors potentiate each other.

Arnett (1999) provides an interesting example of the potential interaction of biological and social causes of mood disruption in teens. Delayed phase preference is a shift in sleep patterns that has been associated with hormonal changes at puberty. Adolescents are more comfortable staying up later in the evening and sleeping later in the morning than younger children (Carskadon, Vieria, & Acebo, 1993). Arnett asks whether requiring adolescents to start school earlier in the morning than younger children, a common practice in many school districts, might contribute to sleep deprivation in teens and by so doing, contribute to emotional volatility.

Moodiness seems to be strongly associated with changes in peer relationships, parent expectations, and self-concept that often accompany sexual maturation. In the next two sections, we will consider how some of these social and psychological repercussions of puberty function to affect mood. First, we'll examine how differently puberty seems to affect mood depending on whether its onset is early or late. Second, we will take a closer look at the gender difference in depressive symptoms that emerges in adolescence and consider how the different social experiences of girls and boys might contribute.

Early Versus Late Maturation. For girls, early sexual maturation is generally associated with greater storm and stress, including moodiness, than late sexual maturation (Blyth et al., 1981; Petersen, 1988; Simmons, Blyth, & McKinney, 1983). Thus, even though early and late maturers are subject to the same hormonal influences once puberty begins, early maturers seem to be more affected. The reasons must depend on factors other than hormones. Partly because most girls begin puberty before most boys, an especially early maturing girl is bigger than most of the other children her age. She is also heavier and so is more likely than other girls to be unhappy with her body in a culture such as ours, which prizes slimness in females. Early sexual maturation (e.g., breast development) may make her a target for teasing or innuendo from peers. Also, being physically mature can be a source of outright rejection by less mature girls (Petersen, 1988). Parents of early-maturing girls tend to worry about their daughters being at risk for sexual experiences that they are not ready to handle, and they may limit their daughters' independence in ways that are grating. Parents' concerns may not be exaggerated: Early-maturing girls tend to have more behavior problems than other girls, especially if they become involved with older boys (Caspi, Lynam, Moffitt, & Silva, 1993; Ge, Conger, & Elder, 1996).

Early maturation in boys is a different story. Early-maturing boys seem to be less moody and less likely to exhibit depressed mood than later maturing boys. In fact, it is late-maturing boys who seem more affected by storm and stress. Being larger and stronger than other boys gives early-maturing boys an edge in socially approved male activities, such as athletics, whereas late-maturing boys are at a distinct disadvantage in the same activities. Generally, early-maturing boys are more confident than late-maturing boys, more popular, and more likely to be leaders among their peers. Late-maturing boys are more likely than other boys to be socially awkward, insecure, and variable in mood (Simmons & Blyth, 1987; Simmons et al., 1983).

Clearly, the storm and stress that accompany the onset of puberty can vary dramatically depending on contextual factors. Overall, these findings suggest that the volatility and negativity of adolescents are largely related to the number of stressors with which they must cope.

Girls' Versus Boys' Susceptibility to Depression. Why should adolescent girls be more susceptible to depression? It is possible that sex differences in circulating hormones directly contribute. But most developmentalists argue that sex differences in social experience are likely to play a large role in the mix of causes. Remember that both boys and girls are more subject to depressive moods in adolescence than in the preadolescent period and that each gender experiences increased stress of various kinds (see Chapter 8). But on the whole, it may be that girls face more challenges to their self-esteem and more problems in living in early adolescence than boys do (Petersen, Sarigiani, & Kennedy, 1991). That is, girls must deal with more stressors simultaneously. In comparison to their male counterparts, females report experiencing more stressors from early adolescence onward (Compas, Howell, Phares, Williams, & Giunta, 1989; Wichstrom, 1999). Here are a few:

1. As we saw in the last chapter, by age 11 children are aware that the female gender role is less valued than the male role. They believe that there are greater restrictions on behavior for females and that there is gender-based discrimination (Intons-Peterson, 1988). As they integrate these beliefs into their self-concept, girls may begin to feel less worthwhile than boys, or at least less appreciated. Many studies have found a decline in self-esteem in girls after age 9, whereas boys' self-esteem tends to stabilize (Ruble & Martin, 1998).

2. Although both boys and girls are concerned about body image (their concept of, and attitude toward, their physical appearance), girls also worry more than boys about appearance and weight after puberty (e.g., Barker & Galambos, 2003; Jones, 2004; Smolak, Levine, & Thompson, 2001).

3. Girls more often have lower expectations of success than boys (Ruble, Gruelich, Pomerantz, & Gochberg, 1993).

4. Girls may be more stressed by the burgeoning of their sexuality and their sexual desirability. The traditional double standard, by which female sexual behavior is judged more harshly than male sexual behavior, has clearly diminished over the last half century, as the rates and acceptability of premarital sex have increased among teens of both sexes (Astin, Korn, Sax, & Mahoney, 1994). Yet, American college students still consider girls who have multiple sexual partners to be more immoral than boys who do

(Crawford, 2003; Robinson, Ziss, Ganza, Katz, & Robinson, 1991), and among adolescents who have intercourse, girls are more likely to judge themselves to be bad or unlovable than boys are to judge themselves negatively (Graber, Brooks-Gunn, & Galen, 1999). Thus, even though girls' acceptance of and experience with sexuality is increasing rapidly, they are still more subject to ambiguous messages about the acceptability of sex and seem to be more uncertain about what is appropriate for them in a world of shifting values. In addition, the physical and social consequences of sexual activity are greater for girls: They are still the ones who get pregnant.

5. After puberty, girls and boys start interacting more in mixed-sex groups and in heterosexual dyads. In these contexts, the differences in their discourse styles may create more stress for girls. You'll recall from Chapter 8 that girls acquire a more cooperative discourse style and boys a more domineering style during childhood. One result is that when adolescent girls socialize with boys, they are less likely to influence the outcome of a discussion (see Maccoby, 1990). Also, in heterosexual pairs boys do not offer as much support to their partners as girls do (Leaper, 1994b). As a consequence, these relationships may be less affirming and satisfying for girls than for boys (e.g., Pipher, 1994).

6. Because puberty comes earlier for girls, they are more likely than boys to simultaneously face both the changes of puberty and the difficult transition to secondary school (i.e., junior high or middle school; Petersen, Kennedy, & Sullivan, 1991; see Chapter 10 for a discussion of this transition).

Girls may be more subject to depression than boys not only because they face more challenges but because they often adopt a coping style, **rumination**, that increases the risk of depression (Nolen-Hoeksema & Girgus, 1994; Petersen et al., 1993). Rumination (Morrow & Nolen-Hoeksema, 1990) or self-focused attention (Ingram, Cruet, Johnson, & Wisnicki, 1988) may be defined as a stable, emotion-focused coping style that involves responding to problems by directing attention internally toward negative feelings and thoughts. Ruminating about problems includes both cognitive (self-focused cognitions) and affective (increased emotional reactivity) elements. Ruminative strategies may include isolating oneself to dwell on a problem, writing in a diary about how sad one feels, or talking repetitively about a negative experience with the purpose of gaining increased personal insight. In general, however, ruminative focusing on problems while in a depressed mood may actually make the depression worse.

Experimental studies have found that this type of heightened self-focus increases the duration and intensity of depressive episodes, particularly in adolescent and adult females (Greenberg & Pyszczynski, 1986; Ingram et al., 1988; Morrow & Nolen-Hoeksema, 1990), who are much more likely to exhibit this style of coping than are males (Butler & Nolen-Hoeksema, 1994). Adolescents and adults who ruminate are more likely to experience depression than those who use **distraction** (Nolen-Hoeksema et al., 1993; Spasjevic & Alloy, 2001). Distraction as a coping style involves deliberate focusing on neutral or pleasant thoughts or engaging in activities that divert attention in more positive directions. Distraction can attenuate depressive episodes (Nolen-Hoeksema et al., 1993).

To qualify as a gender-linked preexisting risk factor, gender differences in rumination and distraction must be shown to exist prior to adolescence, before the rise in levels of depression. A study of the coping styles of fourth- and fifth-grade children revealed that girls are more likely than boys to endorse ruminative coping choices when confronted with academic, family, and peer stressors, even though at these ages girls and boys show no differences in rates of depression (Broderick, 1998). Similar to Nolen-Hoeksema's (1987) finding that older males are more likely to dampen their stress-related negative affect, boys in this study were somewhat more likely to choose distracting or avoidant ways to handle problems than girls were. Girls, on the other hand, were prone to amplifying negative affect by providing responses to stressful situations that were both very negative ("I felt like I was going to die") and persistent ("I'd be in a bad mood all day"). Thus, it appears that when girls at puberty begin to face increased stress, they, more than boys, are more likely to bring to the task a coping style that puts them at greater risk of experiencing depression (Broderick & Korteland, 2004).

However, gender role also influences how children and early adolescents cope with problems. A ruminative coping style is most pronounced among girls and some boys whose gender roles are stereotypically feminine. These individuals identify themselves as relatively passive and nondominant and are less likely to cope by using active problem solving or distraction. Having a ruminative coping style, or being uncomfortable with or incapable of psychological distraction, may be a particularly heavy burden for feminine-identified boys, for whom such behavior is clearly contrary to the peer group's expectations for appropriate masculine behavior (Broderick & Korteland, 2002).

THE EMERGENCE OF SEXUALITY AND SEXUAL PREFERENCE

Sexual pleasure is a part of human functioning even in early childhood. Preschoolers and school-aged children may fondle their own genitals for the pleasure of it, and many engage in sex play with others. "Playing doctor," for example, has been known to involve disrobing or fondling the genitals of other children (see Shaffer, 1994). However, the strength and urgency of the adult sex drive, emerging as a function of puberty, is a new experience to young adolescents. They are more sensitive to, and interested in, sexually relevant stimuli than younger children. As we have noted, despite having spent most of childhood spontaneously segregating into single-gender groups, young adolescents begin to seek out opportunities to socialize in mixed-gender groups (Maccoby, 1998).

Faced with their increased sexual interest, most adolescents begin to explore their sexuality. Figure 9.2 represents the percentages of the male and female population who engage in masturbation, which begins on average between 11 and 12 years. Table 9.1 presents a typical sequence of sexual experiences during adolescence, and Table 9.2 indicates gender and ethnic differences among American adolescents in the age of first intercourse. It should be noted that as many as 50% of young adolescents also have sexual experiences with members of the same sex, primarily displaying and touching genitals, and engaging in mutual masturbation. These activities seem to be partly a function of opportunity, because young adolescents still spend more of their time with same-sex than opposite-sex peers. For most youngsters, these sexual contacts are not indicators of a homosexual orientation (Bell, Weinberg, & Hammersmith, 1981; Ellis, Burke, & Ames, 1987; Leitenberg, Greenwald, & Tarran, 1989; Masters, Johnson, & Kolodny, 1988).

Clearly, sexual maturation is a key determiner of sexual behavior, but just as clearly, many other factors come into play. Adolescents are often moved to engage in sexual behavior out of curiosity or because of pressure to have sex from partners or peer group (e.g., Atwater, 1996; Rodgers & Rowe, 1993). Parents, by monitoring their children's behavior and by expressing their values, have more influence on the sexual behavior of early adolescents than of late adolescents (Treboux & Busch-Rossnagel, 1991). Myriad other influences—from social class and ethnicity to religious background, geographic setting (urban versus rural), popular culture (as portrayed in

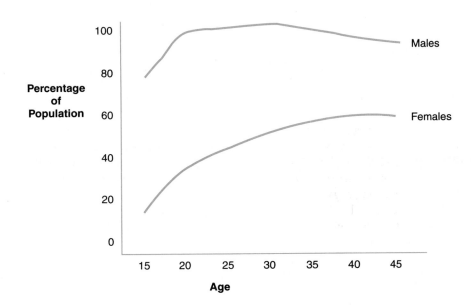

FIGURE 9.2

Age Differences in Percentage of Males and Females Who Masturbate

Source: Adapted from *Adolescence* by Atwater, E., 1996. Reprinted by permission of Pearson Education, Inc., Upper Saddle River, NJ.

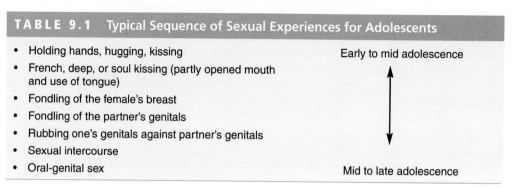

TABLE 9.1   Typical Sequence of Sexual Experiences for Adolescents

- Holding hands, hugging, kissing
- French, deep, or soul kissing (partly opened mouth and use of tongue)
- Fondling of the female's breast
- Fondling of the partner's genitals
- Rubbing one's genitals against partner's genitals
- Sexual intercourse
- Oral-genital sex

Early to mid adolescence

Mid to late adolescence

Source: Adolescence by Atwater, E., 1996. Reprinted by permission of Pearson Education, Inc., Upper Saddle River, NJ.

movies, music, teen magazines, and Internet sites), and the quality of sex education in schools—play a part in when and whether adolescents become sexually active (e.g., Crump et al., 1999; Day, 1992; Murry, 1992).

A central feature of sexual development in adolescence is the emergence of sexual orientation, referring to a preference for sexual partners of one's own sex (homosexuality) or the opposite sex (heterosexuality) or both (bisexuality). A large majority of adolescents eventually identify themselves as heterosexual. In a national survey of 18- to 59-year-olds who were assured of anonymity, only about 3% of males and 1 to 2% of females identified themselves as homosexual or bisexual (Dunlap, 1994), although some studies have found the rates to be somewhat higher (e.g., Bell et al., 1981; see also LeVay, 1996).

TABLE 9.2   Gender, Race, and Average Age of First Intercourse

Ethnicity and Race	Men	Women
African American	14.3	16.8
Caucasian	16.3	17.4
Latino[a]	15.4	17.8
Mexican-American	16.3	17.6

[a]Excludes Mexican Americans.

Source: Adolescence by Atwater, E., 1996. Reprinted by permission of Pearson Education, Inc., Upper Saddle River, NJ.

Our understanding of how sexual orientation develops is quite limited. Many theories that postulate environmental causes are clearly wrong. The most famous of these is Freud's account of the Oedipal and Electra complexes (e.g., Freud, 1935/1960). As you will recall from Chapter 8, Freud proposed in his psychoanalytic theory that 3- to 5-year-olds compete with the same-sex parent for the attentions of the opposite-sex parent. To avoid the punitive consequences of such competition, boys eventually identify with their fathers and girls with mothers, imitating the behaviors and internalizing the values of that parent. According to Freud, this identification process explains why most children eventually adopt a heterosexual orientation. It is just one more way in which the child becomes like the same-sex parent. Homosexuality or bisexuality results when something goes wrong with the identification process: The Oedipal or Electra complex cannot unfold in the usual way because there is only one parent in the home, or the same-sex parent is too weak or shows little interest in the child, or the opposite-sex parent lacks the nurturing to be attractive or is too dominant.

Freud's theory of identification is not supported by the evidence. Adults who are homosexual or bisexual are not more likely than heterosexuals to come from one-parent homes or to have weak fathers or dominant mothers (Bell et al., 1981; LeVay, 1996). Another environmental theory, the seduction hypothesis, is also wrong. In this view, children or adolescents are seduced into homosexuality by homosexual pedophiles. Yet, survey research indicates that homosexuals often feel inklings of their sexual orientation long before their first sexual experience, and they are no more likely to have had early sexual experiences with predatory adults than are heterosexuals (Bell et al., 1981). These and other theories of parental influence on sexual orientation simply do not work. Even modeling by adults does not seem to affect children's sexual preference. Studies of children raised by homosexual partners indicate that they are no more likely to become homosexual themselves than children raised by heterosexuals (e.g., Bailey et al., 1995; Golombok & Tasker, 1996; Patterson, 1992). It is also interesting to note that children raised by homosexual parents are no more likely to be sexually abused than other children and that their social-emotional adjustment, including relationships with peers, is comparable as well (Golombok et al., 2003; Patterson, 1992).

There is better evidence for biological influences on sexual orientation. First, prenatal hormones seem likely to play a role. Exposure to masculinizing hormones can affect the sexual orientation of human females. Girls who are exposed to high levels of prenatal androgens (congenital adrenal hyperplasia, or CAH; see Chapter 8) are often found to have a greater frequency of homosexual experiences and fantasies than their non-CAH female relatives (see Collaer & Hines, 1995). For males, delayed exposure to masculinizing hormones during prenatal development has been found to affect sexual behavior in several nonhuman mammalian species. For example, when a male rat fetus is prenatally stressed, effectively delaying its exposure to androgens, the rat in adulthood will show higher frequencies of female sexual posturing and lower frequencies of male sexual behaviors, such as mounting, than nonprenatally stressed males (see Chapter 8; Ward, 1992). Whether human males are similarly affected by delayed prenatal exposure to androgens is not yet established, but the generality of the finding among nonhuman mammals makes such a hypothesis plausible.

Heredity seems to have an influence on the development of sexual orientation. When one identical twin is homosexual, the other twin has about a 50% chance of also being homosexual, a much higher concordance rate than we find between less closely related family members (Bailey & Pillard, 1991; Bailey, Pillard, Neale, & Agyei, 1993). But clearly, sexual orientation cannot be just a function of heredity, or the concordance rates between identical twins would be much higher.

As with most other behavioral phenomena, it seems likely that environmental and hereditary factors interact in complex ways to produce sexual orientation. What the environmental factors might be, however, is not clear. D. J. Bem (1996) has proposed an intriguing alternative to theories that focus on parents or other adults as the primary source of environmental influence. He argues that sexual orientation is strongly affected by peer interactions. In Bem's view, the role of biology is to predispose children to prefer sex-typical activities (and same-sex playmates) or sex-atypical activities (and opposite-sex playmates). "These preferences lead children to feel different from opposite—or same-sex—peers, to perceive them as dissimilar, unfamiliar, and exotic. . . . [Eventually,] the exotic becomes erotic" (p. 320). In other words, Bem proposes that spending one's childhood with same-sex peers enhances the tendency to perceive members of the opposite sex as mysterious and interesting and contributes to heterosexuality. In this view, if a child spends most of her time in the company of opposite-sex peers, so that same-sex peers are intriguing, this promotes the development of homosexuality.

Bem's theory is provocative but is highly speculative and as yet untested. There are some existing data that are consistent with Bem's ideas. For example, children with gender identity disorder (GID), who have early preferences for the toys, clothing, and activities of the opposite sex and who show some identity problems (such as wishing to be the other sex), also prefer to spend their time with opposite-sex peers in middle childhood. According to Bem's theory, their preference for opposite-sex playmates should eventually result in a homosexual orientation, a preference for same-sex partners who are less familiar. Indeed, in one sample, 75% of boys with GID became homosexual or bisexual adults (Green, 1987). Thus, young GID boys often do grow up to be gay. Spending their time with opposite-sex peers in childhood could be a causal step in the process, as Bem claims. There are certainly other ways to explain the sexual orientation of GID boys, but these findings are at least compatible with Bem's theory, which provides another outlook on a possible role for the environment in the development of sexual orientation.

Regardless of how biology and environment transact in the determination of sexual preference, it should be noted that most homosexuals, like most heterosexuals, feel that their sexual orientation is not something they have chosen but that it is a part of what they are "naturally" (e.g., Money, 1988). Even so, there are some people who change sexual preference to become homosexuals in the course of their adult lives, and for these people personal choice often seems to play a greater role than for others (see Baumrind, 1995; Kitzinger & Wilkinson, 1995; Savin-Williams, 1998).

The Changing Brain

Whereas researchers once believed that brain development is largely complete by the onset of puberty (Siegler, 1998), studies using new technologies, such as magnetic resonance imaging (MRI), are beginning to reveal that many parts of the brain continue to change throughout adolescence. You may recall that in infancy the brain grows through a process of synaptogenesis, an increase in the number of synapses (connections) between neurons. By age 2, a pruning process has begun: Many of these synapses disappear. Pruning seems to be a response to experience, such that synapses that are used are maintained, but synapses that are not used wither (see Chapter 3; Greenough & Black, 1992). Pruning was once thought to be finished by the onset of puberty, but the latest research on brain development indicates otherwise. It now appears that in many parts of the cortex, puberty is correlated with a "growth spurt" in synaptogenesis, followed by a long reprise of the pruning process that lasts, for some parts of the brain, into early adulthood.

Several cortical areas participate in this growth process during adolescence. Current evidence implicates the frontal lobes, which play a role in organization, planning, self-control, judgment, and the regulation of emotion; the parietal lobes, which are involved in integrating information; the temporal lobes, serving language functions and contributing to emotion regulation; and the corpus callosum, the network of fibers connecting the left and right sides of the cortex, aiding in information integration and other higher functions, such as consciousness (e.g., Casey, Giedd, & Thomas, 2000; Sowell et al., 2001; Spear, 2000; Thompson et al., 2000). Interestingly, when younger teens are shown pictures of faces expressing fear, they exhibit more electrical activity in subcortical structures (such as the amygdala) than in cortical structures, whereas older adolescents and adults show substantial activity in the frontal lobes (Killgore, Oki, & Yurgelun-Todd, 2001). It is tempting to conclude that immaturity of the frontal lobes is partly responsible for extremes in emotional reactivity in early adolescence and that maturing of the frontal lobes helps older teens achieve better cognitive control over their emotions. It also seems likely that the availability of new synapses in cortical regions contributes to adolescents' increased ability to think logically about abstract contents (see the discussion of cognitive development in adolescence, below).

Another growth process previously thought to end by puberty is myelination, the sheathing of axons in a white, fatty substance called myelin, which insulates these neuronal projections and makes transmission of electrical impulses possible. As we noted in Chapter 6, there is now evidence that myelination continues in adolescence, at least in some locations (e.g., Paus et al., 1999). Ongoing myelination allows faster information processing during the teen years. Synaptogenesis, pruning, and myelination are thought to contribute to increased voluntary control of attention, more effective integration of information, and maturing of other executive functions (Gogtay et al., 2004; Luna et al., 2004; see Box 9.1).

Hormonal changes at puberty are considered important for triggering and moderating many of the brain changes we have described. Hormones can affect structural changes in the brain by influencing the onset or offset of genes. By doing so they alter protein synthesis, which is important for the growth and pruning of neurons, the production of neurotransmitters, and other neuromaturational processes. For example, among the changes that pubertal hormones initiate is a slow decrease in serotonin levels and increases in both dopamine levels and some enzymes that metabolize neurotransmitters. These and other changes may cause a heightened sensitivity to stress during adolescence (Walker, 2002).

Compared to other stages of the life span, the changes in hormone levels that occur during adolescence are the most rapid (Fadalti, Petraglia, Luisi, Bernardi, Casarosa et al., 1999). In addition to increases in pubertal sex hormones, greater activation of the HPA axis has also been demonstrated. As you recall from Chapter 2, cortisol is one product of HPA activation and is one of the major hormones associated with the body's stress response. Recent longitudinal studies have found that levels of cortisol rise gradually through middle childhood and increase rapidly around age 13 (Walker & Bollini, 2002). Studies of adults have consistently linked increases in HPA reactivity, as

Box 9.1 | *The Limits of Guilt in Adolescence*

Steven Drizin, a defense attorney who works with juvenile clients, provides the following case description:

> In November 1999, a Michigan jury convicted thirteen year old Nathaniel Abraham of second degree murder in the shooting death of Ronnie Greene, a crime committed when Abraham was only eleven years old. Under Michigan law, Judge Eugene Moore could have sentenced Nathaniel as a juvenile, as an adult, or given him a blended sentence that treated Nathaniel initially as a juvenile and then later as an adult if he failed to rehabilitate himself with services provided in the juvenile system. Judge Moore gave the boy the break of his life, sentencing Abraham as a juvenile and sparing him a sentence of between 8 and 25 years in prison. But the boy, who fidgeted and doodled during the judge's twenty-minute speech, didn't appreciate the judge's generosity. Reportedly, he turned to his attorney after the judge had concluded, and asked, 'What happened?' (Drizin, 2003, p. 8)

Drizin suggests that Nathaniel's response to his trial illustrates an important reason for treating juvenile offenders differently from adults: They are not necessarily fully capable of understanding the proceedings of a trial, participating in their own defense, or of making the many decisions that are required of an adult defendant.

The first juvenile justice system was established in Illinois in 1899. Within 25 years, in every part of the United States there were two systems of justice for individuals charged with crimes, one for adults and the other for juveniles (usually defined as those under the age of 18). The juvenile system emphasizes rehabilitation rather than punishment, and it reflects that focus even in the terminology that is used: "*petition* instead of *indictment*, *respondent* instead of *defendant*, and *disposition* instead of *sentencing*" (Trivits & Repucci, 2002, p. 694). The emphasis on rehabilitation is based on the belief that juvenile offenders are immature, not fully formed, and so can be reshaped or reformed. Further, the state's role is a parental one, to provide the right environment for future development.

But by the 1990s, "a legislative tsunami was washing over the United States" (Wilcox, 2003, p. 12). In one state after another, laws were altered to allow juveniles, especially adolescents, to be tried in adult criminal court, facing the same penalties that adults would face. A sense that predatory teens with well-established and irremediable character flaws were victimizing citizens and getting off too lightly in the juvenile justice system seemed to prevail. This "tough on crime" attitude overwhelmed the reasoning that had inspired a different approach to juveniles a century before. Yet an appreciation for that reasoning is nonetheless reflected in some recent Supreme Court decisions. For example, in limiting the death penalty to individuals whose crimes were committed after their 16th birthday, the United

States Supreme Court in 1998 acknowledged that teenagers, in comparison to adults, are likely to be less experienced, less intelligent, less educated, less able to evaluate the consequences of their actions, and more motivated by the emotion of the moment or by peer pressure (Steinberg & Scott, 2003). Implied in this assessment is the belief that inspired the juvenile justice system: that at least until the age of 16, youngsters are not fully developed. Their misconduct is not necessarily a reflection of a well-established character but may be more affected by transient factors, and their future trajectory is malleable.

Based in part on research provided by developmental scientists, a 2005 U.S. Supreme Court decision prohibited the use of capital punishment for individuals who commit crimes when they are younger than age 18. Research findings on cognitive functioning, on brain development, on identity development, and on social interactive processes, like peer relations, has the potential to inform the way the justice system treats minors who commit less serious offenses as well. This research can be brought to bear on two critical questions. First, are teens as fully culpable as adults when committing the same crimes? And second, are adolescents competent to participate in the adult justice system?

Adolescent Culpability

Even when an individual is found guilty of a crime, her guilt can be mitigated under the law. "Mitigation places the culpability of a guilty actor somewhere on a continuum of criminal culpability and, by extension, a continuum of punishment" (Steinberg & Scott, 2003, p. 1010). Mitigation does not mean excusing the crime. The perpetrator is held responsible, but she is considered less than fully blameworthy. If by virtue of being an adolescent a guilty party's culpability were mitigated, then the punishments that would be appropriate would be altered as well. Indeed, interventions aimed at rehabilitation rather than punishment might be the wisest course.

Steinberg and Scott (2003) indicate that there are roughly three sources of mitigation in adult criminal law. The first is diminished capacity, which could be due to mental illness, emotional distress, intellectual impairment, or "susceptibility to influence or domination" (p. 1011). The second, compelling circumstances, occurs when an individual faces such pressure that even an ordinary, reasonable person could be expected to give in, such as acting in the face of extreme need or under threat of injury. The third source of mitigation is when the crime represents uncharacteristic behavior on the part of the perpetrator, as in the case of a first offense or when the crime is "aberrant in light of the defendant's established character traits and respect for the law's values" (p. 1011).

Are teens as fully culpable as adults? Steinberg and Scott (2003) argue that if we look at the developmental evidence, adolescents should be considered less culpable on the basis of all three sources of mitigation. First, their cognitive and psychosocial development is likely to affect their choices in ways not characteristic of adults. In essence, their decision making tends to be immature (or we could say impaired) in comparison to adults', suggesting *diminished capacity*. Reasoning ability improves throughout adolescence into adulthood (see text in this chapter and in Chapter 11). By midadolescence, many youngsters do well on tests of formal logic if they are given hypothetical problems that have logical solutions under conditions of low emotional arousal (like the scientific problem solving described in this chapter). But as you will see in Chapter 11, teens do not perform as well as young adults on the more ambiguous problems of real life, especially when they are emotionally invested in an issue (Blanchard-Fields, 1986). In addition, teens' decisions in real-life situations may be influenced by their psychosocial immaturity and lack of experience. As you will see in Chapter 10, adolescents are particularly susceptible to peer influence, they are high risk takers, and their self-control is not fully developed. Their capacity or tendency to think about future consequences is beginning to develop but is quite limited. Teens heavily weigh short-term gains in their decision making and tend to discount long-term considerations (e.g., Halpern-Felsher & Cauffman, 2001). When they are asked to imagine themselves or their circumstances in the future, teens use a much shorter time frame than adults do (e.g., Nurmi, 1991).

Adolescent characteristics that suggest diminished capacity from a legal standpoint appear to be linked to immature, and changing, neurological processes. The teenage brain shows gradual maturing of precisely those regions that affect long-term planning, judgment, decision making, regulation of emotion, impulse control, and the evaluation of risk and reward (see text). Change in these areas continues throughout adolescence and into young adulthood.

Not only could adolescents be considered less culpable than adults on the basis of diminished capacity, but they are also more vulnerable to *compelling circumstances*. As Steinberg and Scott (2003) argue, "ordinary adolescents may respond adversely to external pressures that adults are able to resist" (p. 1014). For many of the reasons already indicated, they may be more easily provoked to aggressive responses by perceived threats. Their emotional lability and intensity seems to make many situations more stressful for adolescents than for adults (see text). Also, their need for peer support and approval makes them especially susceptible to peer influence, whether in the form of direct pressure or as a result of the adolescent's own concern for fitting in.

Finally, adolescents' criminal actions may well qualify as *uncharacteristic behaviors* on the grounds that a teen's character and identity is relatively unformed. Identity formation is a major developmental task in adolescence (see text) and can involve assessment and reassessment of every aspect of the developing self, including the moral self. Teens who are immersed in this process often experiment with (or "try on") behaviors that are potentially dangerous, like drug use or antisocial acts, but for most adolescents this delinquent activity is relatively short-lived. It is referred to as "adolescence limited" behavior (see Chapter 10).

One arena in which this adolescence limited behavior has been observed is the perpetration of sex offenses. Trivits and Repucci (2002) examined recidivism rates across a wide range of studies of adolescents and adults convicted of sex crimes, such as rape, child molesting, and exhibitionism. On the whole, adolescents' recidivism rates over many years ranged from about 8% to 12% and were substantially lower than those of adult offenders, which ranged from about 20% to 40%. As Trivits and Repucci point out, sexual offenses may tend to have very different etiologies in adolescents as compared to adults, and patterns of sexual behaviors are likely to be less established among adolescents. Sexual misconduct in teens may often represent the kind of experimentation described earlier, associated with the fact that the adolescent's identity and character is very much a "work in progress."

Adolescent Competence to Stand Trial

The same characteristics that may mitigate adolescents' culpability raise questions about their competence to be processed in the system of justice designed for adults. In this system, a criminal defendant must be competent to stand trial, meaning that she must be able to assist her counsel in preparing her defense, understand the court proceedings well enough to participate, and be capable of making decisions about her rights, like whether or not to waive a jury trial or to accept a plea bargain. Fortunately, a research consortium, the MacArthur Research Network on Adolescent Development and Juvenile Justice, is undertaking studies that are designed to assess the degree to which teens have these capabilities. In one recent study (reported in Grisso et al., 2003, and in Steinberg et al., 2003), 1,000 juveniles (ages 11 to 17) and 500 young adults (ages 18 to 24) participated. Half of the participants were either in juvenile detention centers or adult jails, and the other half were drawn from the community (and matched for socioeconomic status, ethnicity, and so on). Each of them completed two measures. One was designed to assess competence to stand trial, including factors such as "understanding" (e.g., comprehension of courtroom procedures) and "reasoning" (e.g., recognition of information relevant to a legal defense). The other measure was designed to identify the kinds of choices that might be characteristic of the different age groups with regard to legal decisions. Participants heard stories about individuals charged with crimes and were asked to make decisions for them (e.g., about how to respond to police interrogation, whether to disclose information during consultation with an attorney, and how to respond to a plea agreement that would involve a guilty plea and testifying against other defendants).

The results support the conclusion that juveniles from 11 to 15 are significantly less competent than young adults to stand trial, whereas 16- to 17-year-olds are not significantly different from young adults. Substantially more young teens showed impairments in understanding or reasoning about court-related matters in comparison to young adults. Only age and intelligence were significant predictors of competence—neither gender, ethnicity, current status as an offender, nor socioeconomic status was important.

A similar pattern was obtained on the measures of decision making. Younger teens, ages 11 through 15, were significantly more likely to make decisions based on what authorities dictated. "Thus, compared with older adolescents and young adults, adolescents aged 15 and younger are more likely to recommend confessing to the police rather than remaining silent and accepting a plea bargain offered by a prosecutor rather than going to trial" (Steinberg et al., 2003, p. 10). The researchers looked at what considerations were involved in making these decisions and found that compared to older adolescents and adults, younger juveniles often failed to identify or to adequately evaluate risks or to take into account the long-range, as opposed to short-term, consequences of their choices.

In general, the results support Drizin's (2003) judgment that juvenile offenders, at least those under the age of 16, are substantially less likely than adults to have the ability to function adequately in the adult justice system.

measured by cortisol increases, with unipolar and bipolar disorders, schizophrenia, and PTSD (Muller, Holsboer, & Keck, 2002; Post, 2002; Walker & Diforio, 1997). Some evidence suggests a similar pattern for adolescent disorders, notably depression (Birmaher & Heydl, 2001; Goodyear, Park, Netherton, & Herbert, 2001). Although all the mechanisms are not completely understood, some researchers believe that this normally heightened HPA reactivity sets the stage for increased vulnerability in adolescents who are at risk for psychiatric disorders. In other words, the surge in hormones may not just be a temporary blip during adolescence, leveling off and returning to some baseline at the end of puberty. Hormonal changes appear to have the capacity to organize the developing brain, by contributing to increases in stress-sensitivity and by activating genes involved in both normal and abnormal development (Walker, Sabuwalla, & Huot, 2004).

In sum, a new wave of brain research indicates that puberty ushers in more than the sexual maturation process. Puberty is coordinated with growth in the highest regions of the brain. The full implications of this growth are far from clear, but one may be that the adolescent period in humans substantially increases our cognitive potential, perhaps dramatically enhancing our capacity for the acquisition and integration of information. Another implication is that adolescence is a sensitive period for emotional development (Walker et al., 2004).

COGNITIVE DEVELOPMENT

When were you first introduced to the mysteries of algebra? When we asked a class of college sophomores that question, a few thought they might have been given a taste of algebra as early as sixth grade (at age 11 or 12). But the majority said it was between seventh and ninth grades (that is, between ages 12 and 15). The National Council of Teachers of Mathematics (2000a, 2000b) recommends introducing the more concrete elements of algebra in Grades 5 through 8, as a generalization of arithmetic with some precursors to that as early as Grade 3. But the Council suggests that the more abstract concepts are better introduced in Grades 9 through 12.

Why do curriculum planners wait so long to introduce even the most basic aspects of algebra? Simple equations solving for x can be solved using basic mathematical operations such as adding, subtracting, multiplying, and dividing. In a culture known for its desire to do things faster and better, often pushing children along as quickly as possible, why do we wait until fifth or sixth grade to teach them to solve even simple equations? The answer seems to be, "because it does not work if we begin earlier." We make no faster progress if we introduce algebra in second grade than if we wait until later. The juggernaut seems to be that even the simplest algebraic equation involves the use of a symbol for the unknown, the x. You may recall your first algebra teacher defining those letters that appear in equations as "symbols for unknown numbers," representing "any possible number." When we ask children to use those letters to substitute for unknown numbers, we are asking them to reason logically about an abstraction, something that cannot be represented in concrete terms. The *x* can be defined or exemplified only in words or other symbols. There is no concrete example of "an unknown number."

In middle childhood, the period Jean Piaget referred to as the stage of concrete operational thought, children clearly can reason logically. They have the capacity to hold several pieces of information in mind at one time and to discover the relations among them. But, as we saw in Chapter 6, they seem to reason most effectively if the information they are working with can be represented readily in the concrete, real world, or at least if parallels can be found in the real world. In early adolescence, we begin to see this limitation of middle childhood recede. More and more, youngsters seem able to leave the ground of reality and to spin a logical tale with abstract contents, contents such as probabilities, hypothetical possibilities, and statements that are contrary to one's belief or even to fact.

Formal Operational Thought

Suppose you have two canisters of hard candy (see Figure 9.3). Your favorite flavor is lemon, the yellow candies. You know the first canister has one green candy and two yellow ones. The second canister has five green and five yellow candies. To get a candy, you must shake one out of a canister, sight unseen. Which canister should you shake to be most certain of getting a yellow candy?

You are faced here with a probability problem. With the first canister, you would get a yellow candy 2 out of 3 times, or 67% of the time. With the second canister, you would get a yellow candy 5 out of 10 times, or 50% of the time. These odds make the first canister your best choice.

An 8-year-old would probably choose to take her chances with the second canister, arguing that it contains more yellow candies. But the absolute number of candies is not important in this case. Rather, the important features to compare are the relative proportions of yellow candies in each canister, which determine the probability of getting a yellow candy. The proportion of yellow candies is an abstraction, one that is difficult for an 8-year-old to reason about when faced with the concrete reality of a larger number of yellow candies in the second canister (see Piaget & Inhelder, 1951/1976).

Even as an adult, you may not have known which canister to choose. Perhaps you got confused about how to calculate the probabilities; perhaps you were momentarily distracted by the concrete reality that is convincing to the 8-year-old—there are more yellow in the second canister. But now that you have run through this kind of problem and seen how it works, you are likely to see the importance of the more abstract concepts—the proportion of yellow candies in each canister—as opposed to the actual numbers of candies. Given another problem like this one, you have a good chance of figuring it out correctly. An 8-year-old, however, would not be likely to attack the next problem any differently, even with explanation and training. The 8-year-old's difficulty is not just inexperience with the probability concept; it is a failure to understand and reason effectively about an abstraction.

FIGURE 9.3

From Which Canister Are You More Likely to Get a Yellow Candy?

Y = Yellow Candies
G = Green Candies

The problem of the yellow candy illustrates several characteristics of formal operational thought, the kind of thinking that Piaget and his colleague, Barbel Inhelder, identified as beginning at about 11 or 12 years (e.g., Inhelder & Piaget, 1955/1958). First, formal thought rises above particular contents and focuses on relationships that govern those contents—that is, on abstractions. In the candy example, the proportion of yellow to green candies, not the number of yellow candies, in each canister is what you had to reason about. Second, formal reasoning involves coordinating multiple relationships. In the candy example, the successful problem solver must discover the relationship between the two proportions, which are themselves relationships. Third, formal thought can be difficult even for adults. We all find logical thinking to be easier when the information we must contend with is more concrete. As a result, even adolescents and adults who are capable of formal thought do not always use it effectively (e.g., J. A. Gray, 1990). It helps if we have experience and training in solving a particular kind of problem (e.g., Overton, 1990) or if we have familiarity with the subject matter (the domain of knowledge; e.g., Kuhn, Schauble, & Garcia-Mila, 1992; Schauble, 1996), just as we saw with younger children in Chapter 6. Across a number of studies using a variety of tests of formal operational thinking, researchers report that about 30% of young adolescents (about 13 years old) show a tendency to apply formal reasoning in some situations, and about 60% of older adolescents or young adults (college students) do so (see Cowan, 1978, for a summary of early work on this issue; see Kuhn, 1989, and J. A. Gray, 1990, for more recent findings).

As we have seen before, changes in cognitive ability usually occur gradually, not in startling stagelike shifts. The development of formal reasoning is no different, so that we sometimes see glimmerings of formal thought in middle childhood. The kinds of problem-solving strategies that children use at ages 9 or 10 are likely to seem more elaborate than at ages 6 or 7, and they may even involve operating on relatively abstract contents (e.g., Kuhn, Garcia-Mila, Zohar, & Andersen, 1995). But formal thinking is more likely to emerge in adolescence.

Educators have long recognized that more can be expected of adolescents, so that, as with algebra, more abstract subject matter is likely to be introduced to the curriculum after about age 12. In science classes, where younger students may be given laboratory assignments that consist of simple demonstrations, adolescents are often expected to generate and test hypotheses with thorough rigor (see below). In literature, teachers require students to begin to analyze works of fiction at multiple levels, going beyond the sequence of events that creates the story and looking for ironic, satiric, and metaphoric themes. These themes are abstractions, relationships among words on a different plane from the literal meaning. Some of us remember pining for the simpler, easier days when a story was just a story!

The capacity for formal thought can influence many aspects of adolescent life, from the approaches teens take to academic tasks to their views of religion and politics, their self-evaluation, and their relationships with parents and peers. In the following sections, we will look at some examples of these wide-ranging implications.

Scientific Problem Solving

Suppose a high school physics teacher posed the following problem to her class: A pendulum is a swinging object at the end of a length of string. The important characteristics of a pendulum are the weight of the object, the length of the string, the force of the push that starts the swing, and the height of the dropping point. Some pendulums swing faster than others. *Your job is to figure out whether the length of the string makes any difference in the rate at which the pendulum swings.*

To solve this problem effectively, a student would need to understand the "control of variables strategy" (CVS). She would need to change the hypothesized cause of rate of swing—the length of the string—without letting any other important variable change simultaneously. Then, if a pendulum's rate of swing changed (which it would), the only possible explanation for that change would be the change in length, and she could conclude that length of the string changes the rate of swing. CVS is the essence of experimental procedure. A potential cause is changed, whereas all other potential causes (or variables) are controlled (held constant). Some elementary-school-aged children figure out CVS on their own when given problems like this one; most do not. But those who don't discover it themselves can be successfully trained to see its value and to use it consistently (Klahr & Nigam, 2004).

As teens acquire formal operational thinking skills, the science curriculum makes more demands for careful, abstract thought, such as requiring students to systematically generate and test hypotheses.

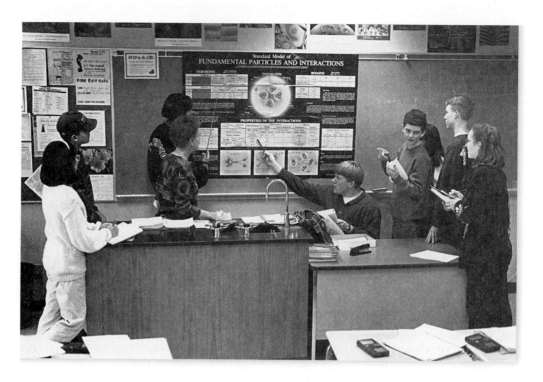

But if we change the problem, as follows, it becomes much more difficult, and most children do not do well on it until adolescence, either spontaneously or with training: A pendulum is a swinging object at the end of a length of string. The important characteristics of a pendulum are the weight of the object, the length of the string, the force of the push that starts the swing, and the height of the dropping point. Some pendulums swing faster than others. *Your job is to figure out why some pendulums swing faster than others* (problem adapted from Inhelder & Piaget, 1955/1958).

Consider how some high school students respond. One student makes a good start. She approaches the problem like this: "I think it could be any of the four characteristics that is important. First, I will try changing the weight of the object; then I'll change the length of the string; then I'll vary the force of the push; then I'll try changing the dropping point." The student makes a change in the weight with no effect on rate of swing. Then she changes the length of the string. Voila! The rate of swing changes. She stops her assessments and announces that she has found the solution: length of the string.

Another student approaches the task by changing more than one characteristic at a time. When she changes weight and length together, the rate of swing changes. She concludes that the rate of swing is a result of the combined effects of weight and length.

A third student tests each of the four characteristics and, of course, finds that changing the length affects rate of swing. But she continues her assessment, combining changes in pairs of characteristics: weight plus length, weight plus force of push, weight plus height of dropping point, and so on. Even though each pairing that includes a change of length affects the rate of swing, she continues her tests. She moves on to combine changes in weight plus length plus force of push, then weight plus length plus height of dropping point, and so on until she has tested every combination of three changes, and finally tests a combination of changes in all four characteristics at once. Only combinations in which length of string is changed affect rate of swing—no other combinations make a difference. Finally, she reports her conclusion: Length of string alone is the determining factor.

Only the third student has solved the problem using combinatorial logic, a type of formal operational thought. She has generated every possible hypothesis. Then, she has tested each hypothesis by holding constant all the factors that are not posited to contribute to the rate of swing by that hypothesis, so that by systematic examination of the results of all the tests she can eliminate all but the hypotheses that must be correct.

The first and second students provide two examples of concrete operational thinking. There is a degree of systematicity to their generation of hypotheses, but not a complete generation of all possibilities. Their conclusions are also too closely tied to concrete outcomes. When the "length of string hypothesis" works for the first student, she stops her testing, even though it remains possible that other characteristics could be involved or that some combination of characteristics could negate the effects of changing the string length. When the combination of weight and length works for the second student, she ends her investigation, drawing the false conclusion that the combination is important.

Adolescents who approach scientific problems by considering every possibility and then carefully testing each one are using formal operational reasoning. The pattern of results among all the tests is what drives the conclusions, not any particular concrete observation.

In effective scientific problem solving, we see another characteristic of people who use formal operational thought. They can generate and think about possibilities. What is real is just one of a full set of possibilities. These possibilities can be generated only in the realm of thought—they are abstractions, not dependent on observations.

As we noted in Chapter 6, even adults often fail to treat their own theories as just one in a set of possibilities. Even for individuals capable of formal thought, scientific reasoning often runs aground on the shoals of belief, so that evidence is distorted or ignored instead of carefully analyzed for overriding patterns. In other words, our motives and emotional commitments can sidetrack our logical reasoning (e.g., Kuhn, 1989; Kuhn, Amsel, & O'Loughlin, 1988). It appears that those of us who overcome these common difficulties have learned to logically analyze our own thought processes (Kuhn, 1989; Moshman, 1998). When we have favorite theories (e.g., strong beliefs about the value of capital punishment or ideas about the best approach to educating the gifted), we must take our own thinking about those theories as the subject of our formal reasoning, and we must monitor our own thought processes as we evaluate evidence, to ensure that we are maintaining logical consistency. As you will see, skill at such self-monitoring clearly advances in adolescence. However, the stronger our emotional commitment to an idea, the harder it is to engage in such self-evaluation effectively and the less likely we are to do it (e.g., Kuhn, 1989). Counselors often struggle to help clients see problematic situations in logical, objective ways to facilitate good decision making.

Constructing Ideals

Adolescents who are capable of generating possibilities, without regard for present reality, have acquired a powerful new cognitive tool that can be used to construct ideals: logically organized possible systems. As Cowan (1978) puts it, such individuals are "adept at generating ideas about the world as it could be" (p. 291). They might mentally construct an ideal political system, or religion, or school. They might also construct an ideal self, teacher, parent, or friend. Any of these ideal systems will make the real, imperfect forms seem shabby and inadequate by comparison. For some adolescents, this new capacity for constructing ideals leads to a zeal for reform. It may also contribute to a skeptical attitude toward childhood religious beliefs or toward parental politics and values (Cowan, 1978; Piaget, 1964/1968). A family belief system can become for the adolescent just one of many possibilities. Thus, the capacity to entertain possibilities and to construct ideals appears to contribute to a critical attitude, and to a skepticism about the justifications that others often give for the status quo. Rebecca's critical attitude in conversation with her family may be linked to her ability to construct ideals and her impatience with anything real that does not measure up.

The "cure" for a critical attitude is experience (Cowan, 1978; Piaget, 1964/1968). Ideals, by definition, are not real. They are perfect possibilities. But real systems and people are never perfect. Adolescent idealists are not familiar yet with the enormous complexity of putting ideas into action and with the actual limitations of the concrete world. Until they gain more experience of the difficulties, they are likely to be critical, even unforgiving. In essence, the adolescent's failure to understand the real limits of her ideas is a form of egocentrism. Interestingly, this seems to apply to her judgments not only of others but also of herself. The increase in depression in adolescence may in part be affected by a tendency to be discouraged by one's own imperfections: The real self never quite measures up to the ideal. An interesting feature of this new, self-critical attitude is that it is self-generated. Even when an adolescent's appearance or behavior does compare favorably to the standards that others hold, she may judge herself to be inadequate, based on her idealized version of the self. Such misplaced self-criticism can be very frustrating to adults who deal with adolescents, and it can play a role in some serious disorders, such as anorexia (Vandereycken & Van Deth, 1994).

Advances in Metacognitive Skill: Thinking About Thought

In middle childhood, children gain some metacognitive skill, that is, some understanding of their own cognitive processes. They get better and better, for example, at assessing when they have studied a list of words enough to remember them on a test (e.g., Flavell, Friedrichs, & Hoyt, 1970). But planful, organized thinking about one's own thought processes involves logical thinking about an abstraction—thought. The capacity for formal operational thinking seems to give this process a strong boost. Adolescents are much more likely than children to "be introspective in an analytic mode, to think critically about themselves and about the way that they think and behave" (Cowan, 1978, p. 289).

On the positive side, improved metacognitive skill seems to benefit scientific thinking, making it possible for some teens to evaluate their theories or beliefs objectively, in the light of evidence, as we noted above (Kuhn, 1989). Such skill also contributes to more careful planning and evaluation of one's activities. For example, once Rebecca sits down to study for her exam, she may test herself to determine what she has learned so far, evaluate the study strategies she has been using for their effectiveness, and allocate her study time planfully, spending the most time on the information she knows least well (e.g., Flavell et al., 1993).

On the more negative side, the self-evaluation and self-monitoring that come with improved metacognitive skill may also contribute to other forms of egocentrism that seem to emerge at adolescence. Elkind (1967), elaborating on some of Piaget's (1964/1968) ideas about adolescence, describes the young teen as intensely self-focused. In a sense, her new capacity for introspection, for evaluating her own mental processes, contributes to an inward focus that is distorting. Although she understands that others have minds of their own and that they have their own concerns, her own fascination with herself, enhanced by the compelling and unpredictable physical changes she is undergoing, leads her to mistakenly assume that others are as intrigued by and concerned about her as she is. Elkind calls this assumption the adolescent's imaginary audience. Because she is so sure that others are as interested in her as she is, she feels extremely self-conscious, acutely aware of her looks and her behavior in the presence of others.

Another feature of the adolescent's self-focus is a distorted view of her own importance. Elkind calls this assumption the personal fable. Adolescents often seem to feel that their experiences and concerns are unique. The personal fable may also include fantasies of having a special destiny, an important role to play in the lives of others or on the world stage. A feeling of being invulnerable, even immortal, called the invincibility fable, can be a part of this fantasy, perhaps contributing to increases in risk taking at adolescence. Adolescents may reason, for example, that others who drive drunk may get hurt in auto accidents or that others who have unprotected sex may get pregnant, but they don't believe that they themselves would suffer these consequences.

The notions of imaginary audience and personal fable are useful, but researchers have raised a number of questions about where they originate and when they recede. Elkind (1967) characterized these egocentric developments as a product of formal operational skill, and he suggested that they diminish in later adolescence as a function of interpersonal experience. Sharing ideas and feelings with others, especially peers, helps an adolescent do a better job of perspective taking and helps her to recognize that others are focused on themselves and that her experiences are not unique.

Studies indicate that adolescents' self-focused thought is not as closely associated with the emergence of formal operational skills as Elkind suggested (e.g., Lapsley, FitzGerald, Rice, & Jackson, 1989). Lapsley (1993; Lapsley & Murphy, 1985) argues that the social realities of adolescence—the need to separate from parents, to form an adult identity—are at least as important in explaining the egocentrism of the adolescent. He contends that the imaginary audience may

An adolescent's intense self-focus may contribute to a sense of uniqueness or invulnerability, called the invincibility fable.

be an expression of intense anxiety associated with individuation and that the personal fable may be a useful fantasy for reducing some of that anxiety (see Blos, 1962, for a theoretical discussion of the separation-individuation process).

Whatever the cause or causes of adolescent egocentrism, recent research suggests that it is not a phenomenon that belongs exclusively to teens. Several studies have found that elements of the imaginary audience (extreme self-consciousness) and of the personal fable (a sense of invulnerability) continue at least into early adulthood, sometimes not showing much decline even then (e.g., Frankenberger, 2000; Quadrel, Fischhoff, & Davis, 1993). There is little disagreement that these egocentric tendencies begin in adolescence; it may be, however, that some of us are stuck with them far beyond our teen years.

The recent work on adolescent egocentrism reminds us that even if cognitive change contributes to these processes, the adolescent's cognitive abilities do not operate in a vacuum. They are among the many causal elements in a multidimensional mix. Adolescence brings a remarkable confluence of change into a child's life: change in thinking skills, biochemical and brain functioning, physical shape and size, peer and parental expectations, and educational structures and requirements. In addition, adult responsibility lurks just around the corner. In the next section, we return to the issue of how the child's self-concept evolves, in the midst of all this change, into an adult identity.

IDENTITY DEVELOPMENT

Some Basic Considerations

Identity, or **ego identity** as Erikson first called it, is a concept that is difficult to define. It incorporates and expands on all the dimensions of self-knowledge that have been discussed in previous chapters. Furthermore, it serves as the foundation for the behavioral, affective, and cognitive commitments to career, relationships, and political and religious belief systems that will be made in adulthood. Erikson himself seemed annoyed by others' attempts to reduce the concept of identity to a flat, mental picture of the self. He described himself as registering

> a certain impatience with the faddish equation, *never suggested by me*, of the term identity with the question "Who am I?". . . The pertinent question, if it can be put into the first person at all, would be "What do I want to make of myself, and what do I have to work with?" (1968, p. 314)

Note the dynamic, future-oriented quality implied in his statement, which integrates past accomplishments with new directions.

Erikson labeled the process of identity formation in adolescence a "crisis" of "identity versus identity confusion." But his view of the process is more accurately characterized as a specific challenge or task that asserts itself at a particular point in development (see Chapter 1). Erikson himself cautioned against thinking of life stages in terms of either-or propositions. In the case of identity, individuals make choices and have experiences that take them closer to or further away from a meaningful sense of self until one kind of resolution (e.g., identity achievement) predominates over the other (e.g., identity confusion, also called "diffusion"). Some authors suggest that using the term *identity exploration* instead of *identity crisis* for this stage is more appropriate (Marcia, Waterman, Matteson, Archer, & Orlofsky, 1993). Exploration reflects the prolonged effort involved in the discovery process, whereas crisis implies a short-term and possibly traumatic event.

Before we consider the way identity is conceptualized in most research studies, it is important to mention two aspects of Erikson's theory of identity that have generated some discussion: the stability of identity over time and its individualistic emphasis. First, the formation of an identity in adolescence, which is the subject of this section, is not the end of the story. Anyone who has counseled both adolescents and adults will recognize that growth and change of self-representations take place throughout the life span. What makes this particular period of the life cycle remarkable are the impressive strides young people make during the years of adolescence and young adulthood in developing the essential core of how they will be as adults.

All of our life stories are subject to revision by time, place, and circumstance. However, a core sense of self that "fits," to use the words of the poet at the beginning of this chapter, becomes clearer as the years unfold. Erikson (1968) captures the tension between continuity and change by writing that "ego identity could be said to be characterized by the actually attained but *forever to-be-revised* [italics added] sense of the reality of the Self within social reality" (p. 211).

Second, Erikson's identity theory has been criticized by some for being focused on the realization of the autonomous self at the expense of the collectivist self (Gilligan, 1982; Josselson, 1988). Erikson's theory has also been faulted for its "eurocentric" focus, which "assumes the necessity of individuation operationalized at its extreme" (Root, 1999, p. 69). It is true that classic developmental theories originally incorporated a masculine perspective, as we shall discuss in a later section on gender. However, the idea that identity formation requires valuing extreme individual autonomy may erroneously arise from the very nature of what constitutes identity, namely, the "I-ness" of the construct.

Consider these examples. You might be the type of person who tends to be competitive, who values personal ambition, and who single-mindedly pursues certain goals. Or you might be one who is more highly invested in membership in your social network, who works at being a good partner or friend, and whose values are based less on competition and more on meeting the goals of the whole group. Either way, you possess an identity! What has been overlooked in the individualistic–collectivist discussion is Erikson's primary contribution to theorizing about personality—namely, his emphasis on the power of social contexts to shape development. His writing clearly supports the importance of the cultural milieu as formative to personality development. His view is thus quite consistent with the contemporary notion that those values held in highest regard within one's cultural context strongly affect the nature of one's self-representations, worldviews, and commitments (e.g., Markus & Kitayama, 1991).

Adolescent Identity Development

So much has been written about adolescent identity development over the years that it is indeed a formidable task to summarize this wealth of theoretical and empirical knowledge. The most comprehensive empirical exploration of Erikson's theory is provided by James Marcia and his associates (1966, 1989, 1993), who developed a categorical system for labeling the dimensions or patterns that emerge in the identity development process. We will examine this body of work by focusing on the following questions: What are the categories of identity development? How are these categories assessed? Is there a universal sequence of change? Is the developmental trajectory always the same, or does it vary for different groups?

Identity Status

Individuals at adolescence and beyond may be characterized as belonging to one of four identity status categories: diffusion, moratorium, foreclosure, or achievement. These categories borrow from Erikson's conceptualization of identity development as a task involving exploration of various possible positions in the world and ultimately making mature commitments to certain ones, such as religion, career, political affiliation, and sexual orientation. Therefore, each status category can be defined by the presence or absence of exploration and commitment. Some of the names are similar to those used by Erikson in his writings. However, even though Erikson called the negative outcome associated with failure to achieve identity "identity diffusion," he did not develop the four identity status categories. Marcia and other researchers constructed these categories in their efforts to operationalize aspects of Erikson's ideas.

Let us consider each of the statuses and examine what they mean. *Diffusion* is the state that often characterizes young adolescents as they embark on the identity development process. In this state, they lack both exploration and commitment. Persons in the diffused category are not actively involved in exploring possible life choices, nor have they made any firm commitments to them. Although this state of affairs is fairly common in early adolescence, diffusion (or confusion) can be highly problematic later on in young adulthood. Persons whose identity is diffused may not trust their ability to find and commit to a meaningful path in life, or they might deny their need to do so. They may lack a sense of optimism about the future and, "many a sick or desperate late adolescent, if faced with continuing conflict, would rather be nobody or somebody totally bad, or, indeed, dead" (Erikson, 1968, p. 176). Alternatively, they may situate themselves within a highly controlling environment that dictates the conditions of their behavior and the nature of their views such as joining a gang.

Individuals in *moratorium* also display a lack of commitment, but they are distinguished from the identity diffused by virtue of their exploration. In other words, these adolescents and young adults are straining toward the future, looking for what they might make of themselves. They may demonstrate frequent shifts in goals and changes in behavior, along with the anxiety and exhilaration that accompany active experimentation. Consequently, these exploratory periods may look like "crises" to the observer. Erikson (1950/1963) defined *moratorium* as the essence of the adolescent mind and in so doing, helped make sense of the transitory, inconsistent, and often incomprehensible nature of many adolescent behaviors. The prize to be gained from this adolescent and early adult trial and error is an identity that has been personally constructed. Constructed identity is not based upon a predetermined set of expectations, but represents either a personal redefinition of childhood and early adolescent goals and values or perhaps something very different from them. In moratorium, the future may be perceived as difficult, exciting, or even anxiety producing, but it can be shaped by one's own decision making.

Foreclosure, the third status, describes a category of individuals who make commitments with little or no exploration of alternatives. This status, along with diffusion, may also characterize young people entering adolescence who incorporate the values and goals of significant others, such as their parents, without reflection. Their commitments are, by definition, premature, preordained by family obligation or constrained by circumstance. A very early marriage or settling very early on a career might be examples of this. These kinds of decisions are not always problematic, but they can be. The identity attained by those who are foreclosed is called a conferred identity, rather than a constructed one. Foreclosure's perspective on the future involves meeting the expectations of a "prearranged set of ideals, occupational plans, and interpersonal forms" (Marcia, 1993, p. 8). These individuals proceed into the future with the goals and values of early adolescence relatively intact and experience fewer difficulties along the way.

Identity achievement, the fourth of Marcia's categories, comprises individuals whose development has been marked by exploration and commitment to certain alternatives. They have decided on a game plan, so to speak, which may be revised as needed. Their identity has been constructed by their own efforts to shape and transform their earlier selves. In theory, at least, they have reached a valued end point. Studies have generally shown positive correlations between identity achievement and psychological well-being (Meeus, Iedema, Helsen, & Vollebergh, 1999). But is identity, once achieved, really the end of the story? We will discuss this issue in a later section.

PERSONAL AND COGNITIVE CHARACTERISTICS OF EACH IDENTITY STATUS

Researchers have found that personality tends to vary across identity categories. Those in the achieved category have a more internal locus of control as compared to diffused individuals, who are the most external (Dellas & Jernigan, 1987). Anxiety seems to be lowest for foreclosed groups, whereas it is relatively high among diffused groups and highest among those in moratorium (Marcia, 1967; Sterling & Van Horn, 1989). Foreclosed individuals report the highest levels of authoritarianism, conformity, and obedience to authority; those in moratorium report the lowest levels (Marcia et al., 1993; Podd, 1972). Autonomy is highest among achieved males and females and foreclosed women, but it is lowest in diffused males and females and foreclosed men (Schenkel & Marcia, 1972; Waterman, 1993).

In a study of the role of adolescent egocentrism in identity formation, O'Connor (1995) found that more egocentrism is associated with more exploration and, ultimately, with a greater likelihood of identity achievement, especially in males. Degree of exploration is also associated with more early childhood exposure to creative, technical, and cultural activities provided by parents, as demonstrated by Schmitt-Rodermund and Vondracek (1999). Providing children with early exploratory experiences was positively related to a broader range of interests in adolescence, more exploration in these areas, and later identity achievement.

Assessment of Identity Domains

To study identity development, it must be translated into something that can be measured. Erikson viewed occupation and ideology, both political and religious, as expressions of one's identity. Marcia (1964) constructed a standardized, semistructured Ego Identity Interview designed to assess these three domains of identity: vocational choice, religious beliefs, and political ideology, using samples of male college students. When his samples were expanded to include women, the domains of work–family conflict (Marcia & Friedman, 1970) and attitudes toward premarital intercourse (Schenkel & Marcia, 1972) were added to the interview schedule. Waterman (1993) distinguishes between the core dimensions that are covered in the majority of studies using the Ego Identity Interview and those that are only occasionally included. Core domains are vocational choice, religious beliefs, political ideology, gender-role attitudes, and beliefs about sexual expression. Supplemental domains include hobbies, friendships, dating relationships, role of spouse, role of parent, experiences at school, and issues of work–family balance. The interview format consists of general questions such as "Should one believe in God or not?" "What type of work would you like to do?" and "What do you see as the advantages and disadvantages of being single versus being married?" followed up by more specific probes. (See Marcia et al., 1993, for the complete interview.)

As you reflect on this approach, you may be reminded of the construct of self-concept, which was discussed in Chapters 5 and 7. The construction of ego identity in adolescence and beyond builds on or incorporates many of the components of self-concept developed earlier, such as social, academic, and physical self-concept. Identity may be construed as an overarching construct, with each domain representing a more specific aspect. Just as individuals vary in their level of self-esteem across domains, individuals will also show variation in the nature of their identity formation and in the timing of developmental progress. Thus, a person might be foreclosed in the area of religious identity but be in moratorium in the area of vocational choice.

Developmental Sequence in Identity Formation

Based upon the previous discussion, you may think the four statuses have the look of a linear, developmental stage model. Frequently, these statuses are interpreted to be synonymous with stages, and, in fact, Marcia (1967) originally proposed that each resided on a continuum, from diffusion to foreclosure to moratorium to achievement, with achievement representing the desirable end state. More recent research has prompted a rethinking of this perspective. Even though achieved and diffused statuses retain their ultimate significance as positive and negative outcomes, there are no compelling theoretical reasons to position foreclosure and moratorium adjacent to each other on the continuum. In addition, most of the studies done on the topic of identity development have used the categories to classify individuals rather than to follow their developmental progress (Meeus, 1996).

Those studies that have tried to find evidence for a universal, step-by-step sequence of identity development have largely come up short because there are many possible ways to move from category to category over time. The theoretical trajectory advanced in early work using Marcia's categories fails to describe other relatively common pathways. Think of a foreclosed individual who unexpectedly encounters a life event that forces her to rethink her commitments. Plunged back into moratorium, she can move into either achievement or diffusion. Another individual, who has become an identity achiever, may reenter moratorium if the goals she once chose no longer fit. Stephen, Fraser, and Marcia (1992) call the frequently observed cycles of movement from identity achievement to moratorium "MAMA" cycles (moratorium-achievement-moratorium-achievement). The pattern is not as neat as was originally anticipated.

So, are we to assume that the status categories merely provide a descriptive model for all possible states of identity development, or is there also evidence for some common developmental trajectory? In general, longitudinal studies of movement across statuses, or of "progressive developmental shifts" (Waterman, 1993), have been supportive of some developmental trends in identity formation.

Meeus and colleagues (1999), who worked with Dutch adolescents, developed a classificatory system based upon Marcia's, with two main distinctions. First, exploration and commitment are separately measured in Meeus's research to provide a more powerful way to demonstrate developmental trends. Second, his classification scheme is based on an individual's current identity development activity without reference to past behavior. For example, diffusion and moratorium categories are similar to Marcia's because the former reflects current disinterest in identity seeking and the latter reflects intense engagement in it. Foreclosure, on the other hand, has been renamed closed commitment because it signifies a high level of present commitment with low levels of coexisting exploration. Achieving commitment is used instead of achievement because it connotes a dynamic linkage between high levels of commitment and high levels of exploration. Meeus and colleagues explain the differences in approach this way:

> For Marcia, exploration is mainly important in the choice of a commitment, after which it is disregarded, whereas the new statuses are based on the idea that adolescents constantly reconsider their commitments. It is also hypothesized that not only do the commitments become stronger during the course of adolescence, but so too does the exploration of the commitments. A more solid identity structure arises, which is also more carefully considered. (p. 433)

Based on their review of the identity development literature as well as the results of their own large-scale longitudinal studies, the conclusions provided by Meeus and his colleagues (1999) reinforce Waterman's (1993) finding of progressive developmental trends across categories. The number of achievements increases over time, whereas foreclosures decrease and diffusions decrease or remain the same. The number of moratoriums does not systematically increase or decrease over time. Thus, the categories defined by Marcia do have some directional, developmental significance. Generally, identity development proceeds toward achievement as a goal, with much of the movement accounted for by increases in achievement and decreases in foreclosure. These authors note, however, that a substantial percentage of adolescents remain in one of the other categories in some or all domains. Interestingly, these findings also indicate that individuals in both the achievement category and the foreclosed category experience high levels of psychological well-being. Contrary to earlier theoretical perspectives, this suggests that foreclosure may be an adaptive end point for some individuals.

Identity Crisis: Truth or Fiction?

Research such as this indicates that moratorium should be considered a transitional state that has some elements of an identity crisis. Consider the following situation. If you are in diffusion or foreclosure, you might encounter situations, people, or new information that produce a state of disequilibrium. This exposure causes you to rethink old values and adopt new ideas, albeit after some anxiety and reflection. The physical, cognitive, and emotional changes that accompany adolescence, in addition to the more diversified experiences afforded by larger school settings, provide sufficient disruptions of old patterns to jump-start this process for most adolescents.

Consistent with the notion of constructed and conferred identities, Meeus and his associates (1999) found that individuals tended toward foreclosure in areas over which they had little control (e.g., school or work), which these authors called closed identity domains. They speculate that in these domains, adolescents "do not find it so useful to reflect intensively on their commitments because they can assert very little influence on them" (p. 456). Crises in more open identity domains, such as those involving personal relationships, were found to be shorter, under more personal control, and more likely to result in achieving commitments.

What influences the outcome of a crisis? Waterman (1993) lists a number of factors that support a positive resolution: successful accomplishment of earlier psychosocial tasks, availability of positive role models with achieved identities, and support for exploration of alternatives. Waterman (1993) and Marcia (1980) report that most of the work of identity development, as measured by transitions into and out of status categories, takes place during early adulthood. This is particularly true for students who attend colleges or universities, settings that facilitate exploratory processes. The results of Meeus's (1996) longitudinal study, however, indicate that the high school years are also a time of active identity formation. He found as many, or more, progressive developmental shifts during this period as in early adulthood.

Identity Development and Diverse Groups

Do individuals differ in their identity development processes because they are members of certain groups? In recent years, there has been intense clinical and research interest in the specific identity development patterns of groups differing in gender, race, ethnicity, and sexual orientation. This body of work developed as an offshoot of more classic identity research for a number of reasons. First, there has been general interest in understanding the differences that exist among groups of people. Demographic trends that project a growing multicultural citizenry and social movements that emphasize gay, lesbian, and women's rights, as well as pride in one's ethnic heritage, have sparked increased attention to these issues.

Second, there is a growing concern that traditional theories are insufficient to explain development because they are biased in favor of single-culture or single-gender models. Feminist writers (Archer, 1992; Enns, 1992; Miller, 1991), for example, point out the need to examine women's identity development separately from men's because of their belief that female and male developmental experiences are fundamentally different. Critical of traditional, monocultural approaches, counselors and other clinicians have also called for recognition and integration of diverse perspectives into practitioner training and therapeutic practice because of the relevance of gender, race, and sexual orientation to personal well-being and to client–counselor interaction (Sue, Arrendondo, & McDavis, 1992).

One of the ways that the message of diversity has been promulgated has been through a burgeoning array of identity development theories that are based on group differences. Developmental schemes have been proposed for identity formation of Blacks (Cross, 1971), Hispanics (Bernal & Knight, 1993), Asian Americans (Sue, Mack, & Sue, 1998), Whites (Helms, 1990), womanists (Parks, Carter, & Gushue, 1996), and lesbians and gays (Cass, 1979). An example of the proliferation of theories can be observed in Eliason's (1996) summary review. She describes 11 different theories of "coming out" or identity development for lesbian, bisexual, and gay individuals published in the social science literature. Similarly, Helms (1990) describes 11 models of Black identity development.

Clearly, scholarly work in this area is long overdue. The effects of race, culture, class, and gender on development are highly significant. To their credit, these identity theories broaden our perspective and encourage a more inclusive look at developmental processes. Yet, how can the practitioner make sense of the plethora of theories? Imagine you are counseling a client who is a 19-year-old lesbian of mixed Jamaican White heritage. Which of the theories will help you understand her best? Given the diverse names, numbers, and definitions of stages proposed in these theories of identity development, it is easy to imagine clinicians feeling overwhelmed by the complexity and possibly discouraged about their ability to understand the world from their clients' perspectives. In this section, we will try to examine some of the general issues that pertain to the literature on gendered and racial or ethnic identity development and search for some commonalities.

FEMALE IDENTITY THEORIES

Recent criticism of Erikson's developmental theory has centered on its emphasizing separateness or autonomy, a salient feature of masculine personality, as the desired goal of identity development (Marcia, 1980). Failure to give equal emphasis to the desirability of connectedness to healthy personality development has been viewed as a suppression of women's "voice" (Gilligan, 1982; Josselson, 1973). Consequently, researchers have searched for gender differences in the identity formation process, investigating, for example, whether women's identity development proceeds via a different trajectory than the one traversed by men. Douvan and Adelson (1966) challenged Erikson's view by suggesting that women's successful identity formation depended upon prior resolution of intimacy issues, whereas men's successful resolution of intimacy issues depended first upon achieving identity. Note that in this formulation, the actual developmental progression is assumed to differ by gender, so that the sequence of stages and not simply the salient dimensions of identity are transposed.

How well has Erikson's theory fared when applied to women? Two main questions challenge researchers in this area. First, are certain identity domains differentially important to men versus women? Second, does Erikson's sequence of stages apply to males and females equally well? There is some support for the importance of interpersonal domains for women's identity development (Archer, 1992; Josselson, 1988; Kroger, 1983) and for the fact that relational issues may be more important for women's development than for men's (Meeus & Dekovic, 1995). Meeus and Dekovic, reporting on a cross-sectional study of 3,000 Dutch adolescents, found that girls were much more involved than boys in relationship-related activities (exploration) and experienced more personal satisfaction from them (commitment).

Findings such as these, however, do not imply that other domains, such as vocation and religion, are unimportant for women. Nor should they suggest that relational issues are unimportant for men. In fact, Matteson (1993) summarized the large number of studies in this area and found inconsistent gender differences or no differences, depending upon the methodology employed. Similarly, Archer and Waterman (1988) found no differences between genders in levels of self-actualization, internal locus of control, social interdependence, or moral reasoning,

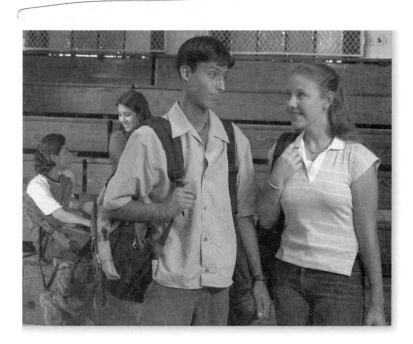

Are relationship-related issues a more important part of the self-definition process for girls than for boys?

suggesting more similarity than difference in identity development and individuation for males and females. It might be useful to interpret the results this way: When studies do identify differences in aspects of self-definition that are more important to one gender or another, it is more likely but not inevitable that women will assign interpersonal, communal aspects of themselves a higher priority.

The question of whether the actual pathways are different for males and females is also complicated. Erikson's proposal that a secure identity must be achieved before realizing intimacy has not been fully supported by research on either gender. As we have noted in earlier chapters, a secure sense of self and the ability to relate closely to others are very closely intertwined. The nature and sequence of the linkages await future, more careful studies for their unraveling. At this point, growth in both autonomy and connection appear to be important to the development of males and females alike. Furthermore, whereas some girls may differ from some boys in their developmental routes, there is no evidence that different trajectories are characteristic of most or all girls versus boys.

It is likely that the achievement of identity and intimacy progress in tandem, with each gender's expression of the outcome looking somewhat different. Cramer (1999) observed that for males and females who have achieved identity, both genders have high levels of self-esteem, adequacy, and assertiveness. But males and females express these aspects of their personalities in different ways. Males are more likely to assert their adequacy in autonomous ways, whereas females more often do so within the context of social relationships. Overall, Waterman (1993) summarized recent findings by stating that the genders showed more similarities than differences in processes of identity formation but that the content of their identity choices might differ.

RACIAL AND ETHNIC IDENTITY THEORIES

Distinct theoretical models have also been proposed to explain identity development in different racial and ethnic groups. Researchers have used multiple definitions of "ethnicity" in the studies done on this topic. For our purposes, we will use the term to signify one's sense of belonging to a group and one's beliefs or attitudes concerning group membership (Tajfel, 1981). Despite differences among particular groups, theories of racial or ethnic identity development have certain themes in common. Most describe an initial stage, not unlike diffusion, during which ethnic identity is either unrecognized or considered unimportant. Cross (1994) suggests that this stage may be accompanied by a preference for the dominant culture, although this is not the case for everyone. It may simply be that race or ethnicity is not yet a highly salient feature of one's self-concept. For example, having Mexican heritage may be less important to a young Mexican girl than the fact that she is smart in school, has lots of friends, and is the best soccer player on her team.

In most theories, this period is followed by a moratorium-like stage, typically triggered by some experience that thrusts the importance of one's race or ethnicity to the forefront. This stage is characterized by ambivalence or conflict, as the individual explores and comes to terms with her race or ethnicity. For many young adolescents, it is a time when the racism or cultural oppression that exists in society takes on personal significance. Here is how author Beverly Daniel Tatum (1997) explains the struggle that her 10-year-old son will likely experience:

> When David meets new adults, they don't say, "Gee, you're Black for your age!" If you are saying to yourself, of course they don't, think again. Imagine David, at fifteen, six-foot-two, wearing the adolescent attire of the day, passing adults he doesn't know on the sidewalk. Do the women hold their purses a little tighter, maybe even cross the street to avoid him? Does he hear the sound of the automatic door locks on the cars as he passes by? Is he being followed around by the security guards at the local mall? As he stops in town with his new bicycle, does a police officer hassle him, asking where he got it, implying that it might be stolen? Do strangers assume he plays basketball? Each of these experiences conveys a racial message. At ten, race is not yet salient for David, because it is not yet salient for society. But it will be. (p. 54)

In a looking-glass society that sorts people on the basis of race, ethnicity, and appearance and then reflects back to them the measure of their worth, early adolescence is a time when many youngsters such as David, who are members of minority or marginalized groups, confront the negative stereotypes and discriminatory practices of others head on. Theories suggest that some adolescents may immerse themselves in their racial or cultural groups or even actively reject the dominant culture during this period.

In most theoretical formulations, the highest stage is achieved when the individual, having learned more about her group, affirms her identity as a member (commitment). Phinney (1990) asserts that the resolution is twofold: (1) reconciling the differences that exist between the ethnic minority group and the dominant group, and (2) coming to terms with the lower status of one's group within the larger society. She also states, however, that this achievement does not necessarily need to coexist with a high level of involvement in one's own cultural group. The overall pattern of stages is similar to formulations of homosexual identity development as well.

ISSUES IN THE STUDY OF RACIAL OR ETHNIC AND HOMOSEXUAL IDENTITY DEVELOPMENT

Remember the question posed about the true nature of Marcia's categories: Do they represent real stage transitions or do they simply classify groups of people? We can respond that evidence is sufficient to demonstrate a directional, developmental trend toward achievement and away from diffusion, despite the fact that individual trajectories may not follow the same course or sequence in detail. The research that supports this description has been longitudinal in design.

At the present time, most writing in the area of gender, racial or ethnic, and homosexual identity development is theoretical rather than empirical, and those research studies that have been done are primarily cross-sectional in nature. Cross-sectional data do not adequately elucidate the processes underlying development. Consequently, the unique stagewise progressions proposed in many ethnic, racial, and homosexual identity theories have not yet been established as distinct developmental pathways.

Other methodological problems in the existing body of research have been noted as well. Phinney (1990), a respected researcher in the field of ethnic development, puts it this way:

> In published studies of ethnic identity, researchers have generally focused on single groups and have used widely discrepant definitions and measures of ethnic identity, which make generalizations and comparisons across studies difficult and ambiguous. The findings are often inconclusive or contradictory. (p. 2)

As we noted earlier, even terms such as *race, ethnicity*, and *culture* are often used by different authors to signify different things, adding to the confusion.

Assuming that members of a race or ethnic group are homogeneous on variables such as ethnic identity is another problem. In a study of Latino/Latina adolescents living in the United States, Umana-Taylor and Fine (2001) found evidence for heterogeneity of ethnic identification among Colombian, Guatemalan, Honduran, Mexican, Nicaraguan, Puerto Rican, and Salvadoran participants. These authors concluded that grouping individuals from these Latino/Latina cultures into one collective ethnic group masked some real differences. The authors suggest the need to consider generational status, immigration history, and nationality to refine our understanding of ethnic identity.

Is whiteness a racial characteristic or a social-cultural one? Whatever stance you take on this issue, it is generally a good idea for people to consider the place of their own race, culture, and ethnicity in their self-definition. For members of the dominant White culture, race is often a nonissue in conceptualizations of identity, and many writers have pointed out that Whites are largely unaware of themselves in racial terms. In other words, White people fail to recognize how their being White (i.e., the "in-group") in a society stratified on the basis of race influences their attitudes and behaviors toward themselves and toward members of other racial groups (i.e., the "out-groups"; see Helms, 1990). This myopic and possibly unintentional perspective comes at a price, these authors conclude, because it perpetuates one's point of view as the "real" one, serves as a filter for all information that is race related, and has the effect of maintaining White dominance or privilege. Essentially, it is a failure of perspective taking, with serious consequences for the broader society.

It seems reasonable to interpret the issues of race and ethnicity as content domains that figure prominently in the identities of group members, somewhat like vocation, ideology, and relationship domains. Fully understanding identity construction in adolescence requires uncovering the factors that influence how young people view themselves vis-a-vis these domains. (See Box 9.2.) Phinney (2000) noted that for members of ethnic minorities, identity development is more complex than it is for persons in the dominant culture because they have to confront and integrate more aspects of themselves. However, as with gender, the underlying developmental processes of identity formation, such as exploration and commitment, are the same.

Box 9.2 | *Choosing an Identity: The Case of Multiracial Youth*

Carlos was born in California. His mother is part Filipino and part Mexican. His father is White. In ninth grade, he filled out a questionnaire that asked him to "Select the major ethnic group that best describes you." Carlos picked "White." How did he make his choice?

That was the question that Melissa Herman (2004) addressed as she examined questionnaire data from nearly 9,000 adolescents surveyed in California and Wisconsin schools in the 1980s. Students were asked to "select the one major ethnic group that best describes you" with the choices being Black, Native American, White, Asian, Hispanic, and Pacific Islander. Students were also asked to select the ethnic background(s) of their parents, and in this case they were given the opportunity to select more than one answer. From the data they provided on their parents, Herman was able to identify nearly 1,500 kids with multiracial or multiethnic backgrounds.

Americans are frequently asked to identify race or ethnicity on questionnaires, from political surveys to SAT exams, and in many of these situations they are not given the choice of identifying themselves in more than one way. Herman looked for what factors seem to influence the choices that young people make when forced to choose. The questionnaire they completed also probed the teens' views of themselves and their ethnicity with questions on global self-esteem, on perceived importance of ethnic background for self-definition, on overall feelings about their ethnic background (from strongly negative to strongly positive), and on perceived ethnic discrimination (e.g., "How often are teachers unfair or negative to you because of your ethnic background?"). In addition, data were collected from other sources. The respondents' yearbook pictures were coded for apparent race by a group of independent observers. Demographic information like socioeconomic status was assessed by looking at parents' education level and at U.S. Census Bureau information on average income in a census tract.

Herman also looked at context variables. Did one or both parents reside with the adolescent? If just one, which one? What ethnic group characterized the adolescents' friends? What was the ethnic makeup of the student's neighborhood and school?

Herman categorized students as either monoracial or biracial, using a complex formula to determine biracial status if they reported more than two racial backgrounds for their parents. Biracial minority White adolescents, especially those whose minority category was "Black," were more likely to identify with their minority category than to identify as White, a finding reported by other researchers as well (e.g., Quintana, 1999). All groups felt positively about their ethnic background, and biracial adolescents' feelings were about the same as monoracials'. For example, monoracial Asians and biracial Asian Whites reported similar feelings about their ethnicity, although both were somewhat less positive than most other groups. Interestingly, although both monoracial non-Whites and biracial kids reported experiencing ethnic discrimination, they also had self-esteem scores that were comparable to those of Whites who reported experiencing little or no discrimination. In fact, monoracial Blacks had somewhat higher self-esteem scores than Whites, although monoracial Asians had somewhat lower scores.

How did students decide what racial identity to report? As we saw already, the majority of biracial adolescents identified with their minority category. Those biracial teens who identified as "White" were more likely than others to look White to observers or to live with a White parent. There were some effects of larger contexts as well, mostly for Hispanic White biracials. For these kids, living in a more affluent or White neighborhood predicted identifying as White. Ironically though, attending a largely White high school predicted identifying as Hispanic. Perhaps for some teens, under some conditions, being in the minority highlights their distinctiveness and makes a non-White category identification more likely. There were other findings that were specific to certain biracial groups. For example, Native American White biracials, even those who looked White to observers, almost never identified as being White.

Biracial adolescents' perceptions of the importance of ethnicity issues in their lives were among the strongest predictors of their identity choices. First, if a minority White biracial teen reported experiencing a good deal of ethnic discrimination, she was more likely to identify as non-White. Second, if she felt that ethnicity was an important aspect of her identity, she was also more likely to identify as non-White. Similarly, Quintana (1999) reported that for college students, sensitivity to ethnicity issues was a key factor in deciding their ethnic identity. Most of her respondents identified as non-White, they said, because they felt it was "the right thing to do." They cited reasons such as the history of oppression of non-White groups or their loyalty to a non-White parent (who was likely to be the parent with whom they had most contact). It is not clear from these data whether focus on ethnicity causes adolescents to adopt a minority identity or the reverse. More than likely, it is a bidirectional process, such that kids who are sensitive to ethnicity issues (e.g., who experience or have concern about racial discrimination) are prone to adopt a minority status, and kids who adopt a minority status are more likely to confront and be sensitized to issues like discrimination. In contrast, Whites do not usually perceive racial status to be an important aspect of their own identities (see text), and they tend not to recognize the privilege it conveys. Herman found this to be true of both White monoracials and of biracials who identified as White in her study.

APPLICATIONS

The explorations of adolescent cognition and identity development have been fruitful areas of scholarship. Literature in these areas not only provides us with a general developmental framework for understanding intellectual and identity development processes but also expands our knowledge of how individual differences are shaped by particular biological and social forces. Some general principles from this body of research offer practical implications for dealing with adolescents and their families at this stage of the life span.

Growing Pains

Psychologically, all adolescents need room to grow and safe places to test their newly emerging selves. Using knowledge of the processes of exploration and commitment as a framework, counselors can start the assessment process by considering how the particular adolescent before them is going about meeting her needs for autonomy, relatedness, and competence. The ways in which adolescents try to meet each of these needs will look very different at age 14 than they did at age 8. Some teenage behaviors seem strange and annoying, but they might not be dangerous. Helping parents and others sort this out can be very helpful. In other cases when alternatives may be lacking, teenagers might try to meet their fundamental needs in ways that are potentially harmful. Helping adolescents find healthy and developmentally appropriate routes for expressing independence, for feeling part of a social group, and for experiencing satisfaction in accomplishment provides a sound basis for helping. Based upon the material presented in this chapter, counselors should also keep in mind that the teenage years are a time of active exploration. Striving to make early college decisions or committing to a career path while in high school may be developmentally inappropriate goals for many adolescents who lack the life experience necessary to make personally meaningful choices. Although teenagers who make these decisions may appear mature to observers and may establish themselves as role models for their peers, their behavior may actually reflect a pseudo-maturity that is more akin to premature foreclosure in certain domains, such as vocational identity.

As we have seen, a certain amount of egocentrism appears to go with the adolescent territory. It is often quite a bit easier for parents and other adults to respond authoritatively, with love and limits, to children when they are young. Something in the nature of their open dependence makes adults feel needed, valued, and important. The task often gets harder during the teenage years, at least in cultures and families that value independence and opportunities for personal expression. Being an adult authority figure in an adolescent's life may entail some hard times, when love and patience are put to the test. Sometimes adolescents' self-absorption seems impenetrable. In what may mirror adolescents' own sense of separateness, adults also can feel isolated.

Watching teenagers struggle with the problems of adolescence is painful, particularly when they behave egocentrically, when they are emotionally volatile, when they act as if they do not want or need our help, or when they actively rebel against the limits we have set. In some especially difficult situations, teenagers have managed to convince the adults around them that they are their equals and that they are entitled to wield much of the power. Some adults are inclined to avoid the grueling job of limit setter and enforcer because they may feel worn down, may have their own personal struggles to contend with, or may simply not know what to do. Sometimes parents take their cues, despite their better judgment, from other teenagers' more permissive families. Adults who are responsible for adolescents need to be committed to authoritative practices for the long haul. Despite their protestations, the last thing adolescents need is for parents, teachers, or counselors to disengage from them or abdicate their authoritative role (see Chapter 10). In particular, research has shown that involved and vigilant parenting has been critically important in protecting poor African American youth from potentially dangerous outcomes like delinquency (Brody et al., 2001).

Navigating Special Challenges

For adolescents from socially stigmatized or other disadvantaged groups, the process of resolving the challenge posed by Erikson (1968), "What do I want to make of myself, and what do I have to work with?" may be more complicated than for others. The constricted opportunity experienced by some adolescents because of societal discrimination, cultural intolerance, poverty, or lack of support can make the identity domains of relationships, school, and work "closed" domains, accommodating little positive exploration. Prevention and/or intervention in this situation might depend upon opening up opportunities for exploration as well as supporting commitments.

Given the salience of racial and ethnic group membership for minority individuals, the emergent identity development process in adolescence, and the benefits that attach to a healthy sense of self-worth in general, culturally sensitive efforts have been advanced that combine goals of fostering pride in one's group affiliation with meeting developmental challenges adaptively. Some of these efforts blend storytelling or narrative therapy with social-learning theory principles such as modeling and reinforcement. Costantino, Malgady, and Rogler (1994) developed narrative role-modeling therapy as a way to help Hispanic older children and early adolescents (ages 9 to 11) take pride in their heritage and learn to overcome obstacles using techniques of story construction and role-play. The group treatment consists of three phases: (1) group members create a story using a card from the picture set of the Tell-Me-a-Story (TEMAS) test (Costantino, Malgady, & Rogler, 1986) portraying multiracial Hispanic characters; (2) group members share their own personal experiences with problems depicted in the constructed stories while the therapist reinforces adaptive responses; and (3) group members role-play the story which is videotaped and later discussed. In one study, results of this treatment showed reductions in conduct problems for the treatment group but these effects were strongest for the younger participants. Interventions intended for older participants (ages 12 to 14) aimed at enhancing pride in ethnic identity by highlighting stories of cultural heroes and heroines had mixed success (Malgady, Rogler, & Costantino, 1990). These researchers hypothesized that age and family context mediated outcomes for early adolescents. For example, even though female adolescents who lived with both parents felt "more Puerto Rican" after the intervention, their self-esteem decreased, possibly due to the idealized heroism of the role models compared to their own parents. As adolescents, they could construct ideals and were more able to use them to make social comparisons. In contrast, both males and females from single-parent homes reported higher self-esteem following the program. These results underscore the need for more context-specific and gender-specific research in culture-sensitive interventions as well as careful clinical judgment when selecting treatments.

An example of a culturally sensitive program that supports adolescent identity development more broadly is the Strong African American Families Program (SAAF; Brody et al., 2004). This prevention program, designed for rural African American mothers and their 11-year-old children, is based on strengthening parent and youth protective factors. Of primary interest here is that adaptive racial socialization is considered a protective factor based on evidence that minority children who receive explicit information about the nature of racial prejudice, adaptive ways of dealing with discrimination, and the clear message that they can be successful despite

this reality have better academic success and more positive expectations about the future (Hughes & Chen, 1999).

Presumably, these active socialization practices assist adolescents in managing their personal encounters with racism and help reduce internalization of negative messages as their sense of personal identity matures. One trial of the 7-week program included seven separate meetings for mothers and adolescents (Brody et al., 2004). Parent sessions covered topics about involved parenting, racial socialization, and communication about sexuality and alcohol use. Youth sessions covered such topics as following family rules, setting goals for the future, adaptive ways of handling racism, and resistance strategies for alcohol and drugs. Joint parent–child sessions were also held once a week. Outcome assessment revealed increased goal-directed future orientation and more negative attitudes about drug and alcohol use for youth participants and improved communication skills for parent participants 7 months after program completion.

Programs such as this demonstrate a more layered approach to the developmental challenges facing adolescents in their search for identity, teaching them skills for meeting life's challenges and mobilizing important family support systems concurrently. Although not an explicit focus of these interventions, schools also have a part to play. Helms (2003) suggests that educators foster appreciation of students' cultures by infusing culture-specific information into academic work and group discussions. She advises professionals to model empathy for their students, to notice the ways that cultural differences play out in schools and affect student achievement, and to advocate for policies that promote healthy development for all.

Stages: Pros and Cons

As we have noted, most identity development theories contain elements of exploration and commitment. But, as Savin-Williams and Diamond (1999) note in regard to "coming-out" models of gay, lesbian and bisexual identity, "with few exceptions, their empirical base is extraordinarily weak, in large part because they are top-down models and few researchers have been willing to investigate the methodological complexities of assessing these models" (p. 247). Counselors should be wary of rigid adherence to a single developmental pathway. Real life is rarely as orderly as the stage theories might suggest.

However, the goal of many of these theoretical frameworks is to promote sensitivity to the unique needs and particular challenges faced by members of specific groups. Even though external behaviors or outcomes may differ for different groups, underlying developmental processes are similar. For gay, lesbian, and bisexual adolescents, two central identity development processes, sexual questioning and disclosure to others, have been identified by Savin-Williams and Diamond (1999). These bear some resemblance to exploration and commitment. Individuals' paths through the processes of self-questioning and self-labeling, however, are extremely diverse, related to their gender, complicated by minority group membership, influenced by family acceptance or rejection, and without any one necessarily correct end point. These authors advise clinicians to be sensitive to the fact that lesbian, gay, and bisexual youth are struggling to come to terms with their own sexual orientation often *before* they understand what the issue really is. At first, conflicts might be expressed as feeling "different." This feeling can exist in the context of societal condemnation or actual threats and rejection, a state of affairs that exacerbates the sense of isolation. For some, the struggle can seriously undermine positive identity development and put them at risk for depression and even suicide (Garafolo, Wolf, Wissow, Woods, & Goodman, 1999).

As is the case with other identity domains, the timing and nature of sexual identity development is quite varied. Although more young people today begin to self-disclose shortly after puberty and to identify as gay, lesbian, or bisexual by the end of the adolescent period, others don't self-identify until late adolescence (Savin-Williams & Diamond, 1999). Contrary to what has been the conventional wisdom, the majority of gender-minority youth experience same-sex as well as other-sex attractions in the process of coming out (Garafolo et al., 1999). Consequently, clinicians should provide youth with support, information, and a safe place to explore their concerns without imposing any sexual identity on them prematurely. Putting youth in touch with agencies or support groups may be helpful in providing both a sense of belonging and the recognition that others have shared their struggles. Finally, counselors should not forget that these youth are more than just the sum of their sexual identity. Positive development requires attention to the full range of adolescent experiences, including promoting positive peer and family relationships, successful academic performance, and vocational development (Diamond & Savin-Williams, 2003).

Sexuality in Adolescence

National surveys reflect what adults probably already know: Teenagers are engaging in sexual activity. Fortunately, there is some good news in this area. The rates of teen pregnancy are down (from 85.7 per 1,000 women ages 15 to 19 in 1999 to 83.6 in 2000; Guttmacher Institute, 2004). Rates of 9th- through 12th-grade students who report having sexual intercourse are holding steady (46.7% in 2003 compared to 45.6% in 2001), and for those students reporting sexual activity in the past 3 months, use of condoms has increased (63% in 2003 compared to 57.9% in 2001). However, the number of youth who report first sexual intercourse before age 13 is ticking upward (from 6.6% in 2001 to 7.4% in 2003; Youth Risk Behavior Surveillance System, 2004). Teens are also still at high risk for sexually transmitted diseases (STDs) because they are likely to have multiple sexual partners, to have older sexual partners, and to engage in unprotected sex (CDC, 2003). More than half of new HIV infections occur in young people ages 15 to 24 years old.

And, increasingly, this disease has a "female face." Thirteen- to-19-year-old females worldwide account for a staggering 57% of new HIV infections and 48% of all new AIDS cases (CDC, 2002; UNAIDS, 2004).

So despite some declines, these reports indicate that young people are engaging in sexual practices in greater numbers and at earlier ages than generations before them (Nahom et al., 2001). Yet most adolescents do not have accurate information about the risks associated with these practices. This may not be too surprising, given adolescents' egocentrism and their sense of invulnerability. A recent study published by the Washington, DC Urban Institute discovered that most teenagers did not believe that oral or anal sex was "real" sex. Thus, kids concluded, it was safe and had the added benefit of preserving girls' virginity (see Gaiter, 2001). Fewer than one quarter of teenagers ages 16 to 24 indicate that they have any knowledge at all about HIV/AIDS, according to an MTV survey of 4,140 U.S., Asian, European, and Latin American youth. Approximately one third of the group believed that only drug users who shared needles could get it; 16% believed that only homosexuals contracted the disease. This ignorance exists within a climate of adult reluctance to discuss sexuality and exaggerated and, some say, degrading sexual saturation in movies, music, TV, and Internet, all of which bombard media-savvy teenagers (Brown, Steele, & Walsh-Childers, 2002).

Caring adults need to address this situation with a combination of information, vigilance, empathy, awareness, and authority. Counselors can establish a trusting, nonpunitive relationship that fosters sharing of information and reduces the anxiety involved in disclosing personal information. With respect to younger adolescents who are particularly dependent upon the support of adults, counselors must work to include a family member or other guardian in treatment. Given the earlier onset of puberty today, experts recommend that efforts to educate about health and sexuality begin at earlier ages, before or at pubertal onset both for boys and for girls (Susman, Dorn, & Schiefelbein, 2003).

More research is needed to identify the most effective ways to reduce risky sexual behavior. In general, education about health promotion and disease prevention is an important component. Some research demonstrates that abstinence-only programs are ineffective in delaying sexual activity, pregnancy, and STDs compared to comprehensive sex education that incorporates discussion of the benefits of abstinence with information about contraception (Starkman & Rajani, 2002). Schools that offer on-site clinic services and health counseling to students have lower rates of pregnancy when compared with schools without these services (Zabin, Hirsch, Smith, Streett, & Hardy, 1986).

Education, important as it is, appears to be less effective than the combination of education and appropriate counseling. St. Lawrence and associates (1995) report that youth enrolled in a cognitive-behavioral treatment program that trained them in refusal skills, problem solving, knowledge of contraceptive choices, and coping had lower rates of risky sexual activity than youth given education alone. Based upon their work with HIV prevention in adults, Schreibmen and Freidland (2003) suggest that clinicians should incorporate prevention-focused information in each counseling session when dealing with clients at risk. Their advice might be useful to adapt to at-risk adolescents as well. Counselors' focus on prevention need not take the form of didactic messages but rather should be the basis for discussing practical steps toward risk reduction. Because topics of sexuality (or other risky behaviors, for that matter) may be difficult to broach, clinicians may use scripted phrases to introduce these issues sensitively. These are a series of questions that can draw clients into the conversation while minimizing discomfort. For example,

> "Now that we've finished discussing your medications, I'd like to ask you some questions about your sex and drug behaviors. What behaviors are you involved in now? Would you feel comfortable discussing them? Can you think of anything you might like to change about these behaviors? . . . How important is reducing risk behavior to you (on a scale of 1 to 10) and how confident are you that you can do this (on a scale of 1 to 10)?" (p. 1174)

The Path Ahead

Some adolescents manage to make the transition to young adulthood in ways that evidence only mild or sporadic periods of upset, whereas others appear to be on a long roller-coaster ride. The temperament and capacities of the adolescent, the contributions of earlier experience, and the fit between the individual and the spheres that influence her will uniquely affect the adolescent experience. Despite the widely different ways that adolescents engage in the process of exploration, Erikson (1968) believed that the reward for the search was the achievement of "fidelity," or something to hold on to:

> The evidence in young lives of the search for something and somebody to be true to can be seen in a variety of pursuits more or less sanctioned by society. It is often hidden in a bewildering combination of shifting devotion and sudden perversity, sometimes more devotedly perverse, sometimes more perversely devoted. Yet in all youth's seeming shiftiness, a seeking after some durability in change can be detected, whether in the accuracy of scientific and technical method or in the sincerity of obedience; in the veracity of historical and fictional accounts or the fairness of the rules of the game, in the authenticity of artistic production, and the high fidelity of reproduction, or in the genuineness of convictions and the reliability of commitments. This search is easily misunderstood, and often it is only dimly perceived by the individual himself, because youth, always set to grasp both diversity in principle and principle in diversity, must often test extremes before settling on a considered course. These extremes, particularly in times of ideological confusion and widespread marginality of identity, may include not only rebellious but also deviant, delinquent, and self-destructive tendencies. However, all this can be in the nature of a moratorium, a period of delay in which to test the rock-bottom of some truth before committing the powers of body and mind to a segment of the existing (or a coming) order. (pp. 235–236)

As Josselson (1994) points out, this search is fundamentally a dialogue that the adolescent does not engage in alone. The success of adolescents' search for fidelity depends upon the community's fidelity to adolescents as they search.

SUMMARY

Physical Development

1. Puberty begins when the pituitary gland produces hormones that stimulate hormone production in the gonads. These and other circulating hormones promote the maturing of both primary and secondary sexual characteristics. The timing of puberty is affected both by genes and by environmental factors such as nutrition.
2. The adolescent growth spurt parallels puberty and includes large increases in height and weight. Different parts of the body grow at different times, such as the arms and legs before the torso. Gender differences in growth increase both internal and external sexual dimorphism.
3. The storm and stress of adolescence includes characteristics such as increased conflict with parents, moodiness, negative affect, and risky behavior. Moodiness and negative affect, including depressed mood, are affected by increases in hormones, but only if they are combined with negative life events. In girls, early maturation usually means greater storm and stress; in boys, later maturation is more problematic. Generally, storm and stress seems to depend on the number of stressors children are experiencing.
4. At adolescence, girls are more susceptible to depressed mood than boys are, apparently because of differences in stress and methods of coping with stress. Among the stressors girls experience more than boys are the devaluing of the female role; worries about appearance and weight; fewer expectations of success; the double standard regarding sexuality; the use of a cooperative discourse that makes them less influential in mixed-sex groups; and earlier puberty, which means that girls are more likely to be making school transitions and coping

with the onset of puberty simultaneously. Girls are also more likely than boys to deal with stress using a ruminative coping style, which increases the risk of depression relative to the distracting style, which is more characteristic of boys.

5. Sexual activity and exploration, both with the opposite sex and with the same sex, increases at puberty. Sexual maturation is primarily responsible, but familial, social, and cultural factors are also important.

6. Sexual orientation becomes manifest in adolescence, with up to 97% of males and more than 98% of females becoming heterosexual. The development of sexual orientation is not well understood. Many traditional environmental theories, such as Freud's theory of identification and the seduction hypothesis, are not supported by evidence. Even modeling is not a viable explanation: Children parented by homosexuals are no more likely than other children to become homosexual. There is some evidence for a strong biological contribution to sexual orientation, through prenatal hormones and heredity. Environment appears to play some role, but the nature of that role is unclear. Bem has proposed that peer processes may be important.

7. Brain growth continues during adolescence, involving synaptogenesis, pruning, and continued myelination. Several areas of the cortex and the corpus callosum are involved in this development.

Cognitive Development

8. At Piaget's fourth stage in the development of logical thinking, 11- or 12-year-olds begin to be able to think logically about abstract contents, discovering relationships among relationships. Formal thought is difficult even for adults and is easier to apply in domains of knowledge with which we have some expertise.

9. When a formal operational thinker approaches scientific problems, she generates and considers every possible solution, then tests each one. The pattern of results among all the tests determines the conclusions. Generating and evaluating possibilities is a hallmark of formal operational thought.

10. With formal operations comes the ability to construct ideals, such as ideal political systems or ideal people. Young adolescents do not understand, however, that the real always falls short of the ideal. This failure to understand the limits of her ideas is a form of adolescent egocentrism, and it contributes to a critical attitude toward anything that is less than perfect, including the self.

11. Other aspects of adolescent egocentrism are derived from a distorting inward focus, which is partially a function of an improved capacity to think about one's own thinking. Self-focus may be a function of other factors as well, such as the need to form an adult identity. The imaginary audience and personal fable of adolescents are thought to be results.

Identity Development

12. Erikson's notion of an adolescent identity crisis is better characterized as an identity exploration, a search for answers to questions such as "What do I want to make of myself, and what do I have to work with?" Identity attainment does not imply that no further change occurs; identity is always to some degree in revision. Identity is also a product of the cultural contexts that shape development.

13. Marcia described four identity status categories. Diffusion characterizes adolescents who lack both exploration and commitment. Moratorium describes adolescents who are actively exploring but have made no commitments. Adolescents in foreclosure have not experienced exploration but have made commitments. Achievement comprises individuals whose development has involved exploration and has reached commitment. Each identity status is associated with certain personal and cognitive characteristics.

14. Assessment of identity status usually involves a semi-structured interview procedure in which status within several domains is assessed. For example, Marcia's original Ego Identity Interview assessed status in vocational choice, religious beliefs, and political ideology.

15. There is no fixed sequence of identity statuses, but longitudinal research has found some developmental trends. The number of achievements increases over time, foreclosures decrease, and diffusions decrease or remain the same. The number of moratoriums does not increase or decrease.

16. Both the high school and college years are times of active identity development. Successful accomplishment seems to rest partly on successful accomplishment of earlier psychosocial tasks, availability of positive role-models, and support for exploration.

17. There is a proliferation of theories to describe identity development in many diverse groups. Research on gender differences has produced inconsistent results: Some studies find gender differences, some do not. When differences are found, women, as a group, are more likely to assign interpersonal, communal aspects of themselves a higher priority. Suggestions that women achieve intimacy before identity are not supported by research. Growth in both autonomy and connection are important for both males and females, and for both, achievements in identity and intimacy issues seem to progress in tandem.

18. Achievement of ethnic identity has been described in different ways for many different groups, but most theories have some sequential aspects in common. Initially, race or ethnicity is not a salient feature of self-concept or one's search for identity. Then a moratoriumlike period occurs, when the individual experiences some ambivalence or conflict that makes her ethnicity a personal matter, and she begins to explore its meaning (exploration). The highest stage is achieved when an individual affirms her identity

as a group member (commitment). Identity development in homosexuals has been described in a similar way.

19. As yet, little longitudinal research is available to support these theories. At present, it seems reasonable to see race and ethnicity as content domains that figure prominently in the identities of group members, making identity development for minorities more complex than for majority group members.

CASE STUDY

Dean is a White 16-year-old. He is a sophomore at George Washington Carver High School. He lives with his father and his stepmother in a semirural community in the South. His father and mother divorced when Dean was 8 years old, and both parents remarried shortly after the breakup. Dean's mother moved to another state, and, although she calls him from time to time, the two have little contact. Dean gets along well with his father and stepmother. He is also a good "older brother" to his 5-year-old stepbrother, Jesse.

Dean's father owns and operates an auto-repair shop in town. His wife works part time, managing the accounts for the business. She is also an active contributor to many community projects in her neighborhood. She regularly works as a parent volunteer in the elementary school library and is a member of her church's executive council. Both parents try hard to make a good life for their children.

Dean has always been a somewhat lackluster student. His grades fell precipitously during third grade, when his parents divorced. However, things stabilized for Dean over the next few years, and he has been able to maintain a C average. Neither Dean nor his father take his less-than-stellar grades too seriously. In middle school, his father encouraged him to try out for football. He played for a few seasons but dropped out in high school. Dean has a few close friends who like him for his easygoing nature and his sense of humor. Dean's father has told him many times that he can work in the family business after graduation. At his father's urging, Dean is pursuing a course of study in automobile repair at the regional vo-tech school.

Now in his sophomore year, Dean's circle of friends includes mostly other vo-tech students. He doesn't see many of his former friends, who are taking college preparatory courses. Kids in his class are beginning to drive, enabling them to go to places on weekends that had formerly been off-limits. He knows many kids who are having sex and drinking at parties. He has been friendly with several girls over the years, but these relationships have been casual and platonic. Dean wishes he would meet someone with whom he could talk about his feelings and share his thoughts.

Although he is already quite accustomed to the lewd conversations and sexual jokes that circulate around the locker room, he participates only halfheartedly in the banter. He has listened for years to friends who brag about their sexual exploits. He wonders with increasing frequency why he is not attracted to the same things that seem so important to his friends. The thought that he might be gay has crossed his mind, largely because of the scathing comments made by his peers about boys who show no interest in girls. This terrifies him, and he usually manages to distract himself by reasoning that he will develop sexual feeling "when the right girl comes along."

As time passes, however, he becomes more and more morose. His attention is diverted even more from his classwork. He finds it more difficult to be around the kids at school. Dean starts to drink heavily and is arrested for driving under the influence of alcohol. He is sentenced to a 6-week drug education program and is assigned community service. His parents are disappointed in him because of this incident, but they believe he has learned his lesson and will not repeat his mistake. Dean's father believes that his son will be fine as soon as he finds a girlfriend to "turn him around."

Discussion Questions

1. What are the issues facing Dean at this point in his development?
2. Enumerate the risks and the protective factors that are present in his life.
3. How would you, as his counselor, assess Dean's situation? What approaches could you take with this adolescent?

JOURNAL QUESTIONS

1. Recount an example of the imaginary audience or the personal fable from your own adolescence. How can this knowledge help you in counseling young people?
2. Were you an early, an on-time, or a late-maturing adolescent? What impact did your physical development have on your adjustment and your peer group relationships?
3. Remember back to the time when you were 18 or 19. Using Marcia's identity categories, assess your own status in the following domains: relationships, career, religious or political ideology, ethnicity, and sexual orientation.

KEY TERMS

puberty
gonads
testes
ovaries
androgens
testosterone
estrogen
progesterone
primary sexual
    characteristics
secondary sexual
    characteristics
menarche

spermarche
adolescent growth spurt
sexual dimorphism
experience sampling
    method
depressed mood
delayed phase preference
body image
double standard
rumination
distraction
sexual orientation
homosexuality

heterosexuality
bisexuality
seduction hypothesis
gender identity
    disorder (GID)
mitigation
diminished capacity
compelling circumstances
uncharacteristic behavior
formal operational thought
ideals
imaginary audience
personal fable

invincibility fable
ego identity
diffusion
moratorium
foreclosure
achievement
constructed identity
conferred identity
Ego Identity Interview
closed commitment
achieving commitment
closed identity domains
open identity domains

Now go to our Companion Website to assess your understanding of chapter content with Multiple Choice Questions, apply comprehension in Essay Questions, and broaden your knowledge of development with related Web Links.

10

The Social World of Adolescence

The search for identity is considered the primary developmental task of the adolescent period. In this chapter, you will find that the outcome of an adolescent's search is very much affected by the social world. Peers play a critical role, and so do parents, schools, and neighborhoods. All are in turn influenced by the cultural and historical context in which the adolescent's identity is formed. Counselors and therapists who support adolescents through their explorations and struggles must consider the impact of these multiple, interdependent factors. As we have seen repeatedly, no single factor or influence fully explains any developmental outcome. In this chapter, we present a model of the mechanism for social identity development and explore research on the influence of peers, parents, schools, leisure, work, and culture on that process. We conclude with a discussion of implications for professionals who work with adolescents.

Let's begin with an example: As a balmy October turned into a frigid November, 12-year-old Tamara's mother repeatedly suggested to her daughter that they go shopping to replace Tamara's outgrown winter jacket. Tamara refused. She said she wasn't sure what sort of jacket she wanted, admitting that it depended on what the other girls in her class would be wearing. The popular girls had not yet worn jackets to school, despite the cold. They, too, were waiting and watching! Finally, in mid-December, one popular girl in the seventh-grade class capitulated to her mother's demands and made a jacket choice. Tamara and her classmates at last knew what to wear.

Parents and teachers are often perplexed, even dismayed, by the importance of peers to the adolescent. Why would an otherwise sensible young person become so dependent upon the actions and choices of others, and what role do parents and other concerned adults play in an adolescent's life when peers become so important?

Dependence upon peers is a normal and important developmental process for the young adolescent. As you will see, the search for identity (see Chapter 9) that characterizes the adolescent period takes place largely within the world of peers. The adolescent period roughly begins at puberty, although in today's world many of the processes discussed in this chapter are beginning to affect the lives of children even before the onset of puberty.

FRAMEWORKLESSNESS AND AUTONOMY: A MODEL OF ADOLESCENT SOCIAL IDENTITY

Many theorists have noted that one's identity develops within the context of interpersonal interactions (e.g., Cooley, 1902; Mead, 1934; see also Chapter 7). Erikson (1968) argued that peers are particularly important in the construction of identity at adolescence. Seltzer (1982) expanded upon Erikson's ideas, specifying how and why the peer group plays such a central role. To understand fully the function of peers, let's look again at what happens when a child enters adolescence. The body changes in appearance, adult sexual needs emerge, hormonal shifts may heighten irritability, the capacity to reflect on the future and on the self expands bringing its own

Think about your own experiences as a young adolescent. Can you relate to the sense of frameworklessness?

brand of egocentrism, maturity demands increase, and so on. These profound changes produce a state of instability and anxiety unique to adolescence, which Seltzer calls frameworklessness.

> The adolescent is at sea. Previous boundaries and guideposts are no longer functional. In earlier developmental periods, expansion and growth exist within a context of familiar motion and exercise. The adolescent condition is different, however. The adolescent is possessed of new physical and intellectual capabilities that are both mystical and mystifying. . . . The allure of the adult world calls, and is strong, even as the safety of childhood is close and still beckons. Yet neither fits; the one is outgrown, the other not yet encompassable. (1982, p. 59)

The adolescent's passage to adulthood is in some ways parallel to the infant's passage to childhood status. To exercise their developing skills and to explore the beckoning world, infants must give up the security of the caregiver's continual presence and care. Most attachment theorists believe that toddlers manage the stress of this separation by referring to their working model of the other, a kind of mental representation of the caregiver, which provides feelings of security and makes independent exploration possible. For adolescents, the task of establishing adult independence requires separating from caregivers on a new plane, a process called the "second" individuation (Blos, 1975). Adolescents rework their views of their parents, deidealize them, and loosen, somewhat, their emotional dependency (Steinberg & Belsky, 1991). Thus, the mental representation or concept of the parent becomes more peripheral to the adolescent's self-system. However, a teenager's increasing individuation and sense of autonomy does not come without a price. As adolescents experience a loss in feelings of security, their sense of frameworklessness increases.

The Peer Arena

Paradoxically, as adolescents seek autonomy from their parents, they become more dependent on their peers. Steinberg and Silverberg (1986) asked children ages 10 to 16 questions about their relationships with parents and agemates. Children between fifth and eighth grades showed a marked increase in agreement on items assessing emotional autonomy, such as "There are some things about me that my parents don't know" and "There are things that I would do differently from my mother and father when I become a parent." Yet, when the students in this study were asked "What would you really do?" if a friend suggested either some antisocial act such as cheating or some neutral act such as joining a club, they showed a marked decrease between the fifth and ninth grades in their ability to resist peer influence. Roughly between the ages of 11 and 16 it appears that children transfer at least some of their emotional dependency from their parents to their peers. Figure 10.1 illustrates the different trajectories of adolescents' feelings of autonomy from parents versus peers.

Why do peers become so important? Seltzer (1982) proposes that it is because adolescents share in common the unique state of frameworklessness. She describes nine basic characteristics that define this age group in contemporary society. Among them are similar chronological age and educational status and shared coping with feelings of aloneness and the loss of past certainties. Research demonstrates that people under stress tend to affiliate with others perceived as having similar experiences (Schacter, 1959), so that adolescents' shared sense of instability makes the peer group a likely target of affiliation. The sometimes difficult movement toward identity can, at least in part, be shared.

Peers are thus a source of support. But Seltzer (1982) argues also that the peer group becomes both the site and the raw material for constructing an identity. There are twin processes at work: The first is social comparison. As we saw in Chapter 7, younger school-aged children evaluate themselves in comparison to others. In later chapters we will find that adults continue to use social comparison as a means of self-assessment and self-refinement. But for adolescents, the lack of identity makes this process intense and all consuming.

Second is a process of **attribute substitution**, which involves both imitation and identification. Adolescents need to borrow and "try on" various behaviors and attributes that they observe in others because the state of frameworklessness leaves them without clearly defined ways of behaving and thinking. Peers become an important resource for such borrowing. A formerly quiet boy might imitate the wisecracking style of a friend, a girl may explore the mysteries of Buddhism espoused by a classmate, or a mediocre student might work for hours on a special project, mimicking the approach of a more successful peer. The borrowing goes beyond imitation to partial identification with friends, so that if a boy's friend has a special talent for hockey, the boy might appropriate a sense of accomplishment as a hockey player from his association with the friend. This appropriation of "stand-in elements" provides relief for the adolescent from the anxiety of being without a stable sense of self. The twin processes of social comparison and imitation constitute a type of experimentation that is necessary for mature identity construction. At first, the trying-on process is rapid, intense, and undifferentiated, but toward later adolescence, some features actually become more stable elements that will form the foundation of the young adult's identity. Ideally, the goal of all this effort is the development or construction of a fundamental sense of what fits for the particular adolescent.

In summary, Seltzer (1982) argues that peers in large part provide the arena for identity formation. She also describes the Eriksonian ideal of unrestricted sampling of various "identities" as a normative process, but in reality what adolescents are able to do may be more circumscribed. As we will see in the next section, the structure of the peer culture may constrain the opportunity to try on some characteristics and behaviors.

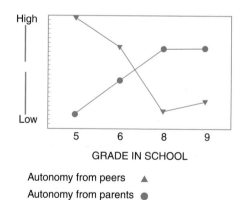

FIGURE 10.1

Parents, Peers, and Adolescent Feelings of Autonomy

Source: Steinberg, L., & Silverberg, S. B. (1986). The vicissitudes of autonomy in early adolescence. *Child Development, 57,* 847. Adapted by permission of Blackwell Publishers, Inc.

THE STRUCTURE OF THE PEER NETWORK

As we saw in Chapter 8, by early adolescence a typical youngster is part of a complicated network of peer relationships. He interacts with close friends in dyads, hangs out with a small group or clique, and belongs to a crowd. Brown (1990) defined adolescent crowds as large "reputation-based collectives of similarly stereotyped individuals who may or may not spend much time together" (p. 177). Once a member, a teen's sampling of elements of behavior will be limited to some degree by the crowd to which the teen belongs. Few would be surprised to find that adolescents are strongly influenced by their closest friends. What is striking about the recent data on peer affiliation is how powerful crowd membership seems to be.

Support for the impact of crowds on adolescent behavior is provided in a large scale study by Steinberg and his associates (e.g., Lamborn, Mounts, Steinberg, & Dornbusch, 1991; Mounts & Steinberg, 1995; Steinberg, 1996; Steinberg, Fegley, & Dornbusch, 1993; Steinberg, Lamborn, Darling, Mounts, & Dornbusch, 1994; Steinberg, Lamborn, Dornbusch, & Darling, 1992). More than 20,000 adolescents and their families from nine public high schools in Wisconsin and northern California were studied. Students came from ethnically and socioeconomically diverse communities (more than 40% were ethnic minorities) and from a variety of family structures (intact, divorced, and remarried). Student data were collected over a 3-year period from 9th through 12th grades. Teens answered questions about their emotional adjustment, academic achievement, and behavior, the parenting practices of their families, and their peer associations.

Just as other researchers have found (see Chapter 8), from these data Steinberg (1996) identified three levels of peer association, which can be described as concentric circles. One or two best friends, with whom adolescents spend most of their free time, comprise the innermost circle. A larger clique of about 6 to 10 members forms a less intimate second circle, composed of friends who eat lunch or go to class together. The clique's boundaries are somewhat permeable, and the membership may fluctuate. Finally, the third circle is the adolescent's crowd. What crowd members share is not necessarily friendship, but similar interests, attitudes, behaviors, and appearance. Crowds tend to be large, and they reflect the individual's social status.

In typical American high schools, one finds a characteristic crowd structure (Barber, Eccles, & Stone, 2001; Steinberg, 1996). Roughly 20% of students belong to popularity-conscious crowds ("populars" and "jocks"), who are moderately achievement oriented and may engage in some illicit behavior, such as drug use. About 20% belong to "alienated" crowds ("druggies" or "burnouts"), who are even less invested in academic success and who may be involved in heavy drug use and delinquent behavior. "Average" crowds, comprising about 30% of students, are not openly hostile to academics but, like the populars, are only moderately concerned about grades. Some crowds are defined primarily by ethnicity (roughly 10% to 15% depending on the school), and academic achievement differences exist among these ethnically defined crowds. Less than 5% of high schoolers belong to crowds characterized by high academic achievement. These students are unlikely to use drugs and may form strong ties with teachers.

How teens find a niche among the available crowds is not well understood (Brown, 1990). Steinberg (1996) suggests three determining factors: children's personalities and interests as they enter adolescence; the types of crowds available; and the ways that parents attempt to manage their children's peer relationships. We'll take a close look at parents' role in children's crowd membership later in this chapter.

How are adolescents influenced by their crowds? As we noted in Chapter 8, adults frequently attribute the behavior of adolescents to "peer pressure," what we have called the influence of peers, which implies that the individual teenager might conform to others' demands despite his or her better judgment. What Seltzer's (1982) theory suggests, and what research findings support, however, is that adolescents operate according to the principles of group dynamics that govern any social group—namely, they choose to participate in shared norms, roles, and expectations, a process called selection. In other words, teens are willing members of their crowds, influenced by and influencing others. As Seltzer puts it, they are motivated to borrow from others, and they serve as models from whom others borrow.

Steinberg (1996) provides a specific example of the crowd's effects on academic achievement. Recall from the data on teens' distribution among their high school crowds that a relatively small percentage are committed to academic excellence (i.e., are A students). Membership in the largest, most appealing, and preferred crowds (populars, jocks, and average) prescribes more modest academic achievement. Most students in these crowds, representing about 50% of high schoolers, earn Bs on average.

Could it be that these data simply indicate that students who begin with only moderate academic commitments and abilities gravitate toward groups of similar individuals? Several longitudinal studies (e.g., Eccles & Barber, 1999; Steinberg, 1996) suggest otherwise. For example, after tracking students for 3 years who began with similar academic records and behavior profiles, Steinberg (1996) found that students' crowd affiliation was highly correlated with their later grades and delinquent activities. So, crowd membership made a unique contribution to these outcomes over and above early developmental characteristics.

THE ROLE OF PARENTS

Given that peers become so important to young adolescents, what is the role of adults, especially parents, in adolescents' lives? A brief history of perspectives on adolescent development may be useful here. Early psychoanalytic writers described this period as one of conflict between parents and their teens that is sparked by the reemergence of latent sexual impulses as the child reaches puberty (Freud, 1958). The classic interpretation is that the young adolescent's emotional attachments become sexualized and need to be redirected to agemates. In this view, the child's press for autonomy creates conflict with the parents but is seen as normal and necessary. Neopsychoanalytic views have become more moderate over time (e.g., Blos, 1975), but still assume that the child's cognitive and affective detachment from parents is to be expected in the service of autonomy. Erikson's (1968) view of adolescence as a "normative crisis" supports this as a time of potential upheaval. The early psychoanalytic tradition framed the typical parent–adolescent relationship as a struggle, with teens trying to pull away from parents to the point of rebellion. Prescriptions for appropriate parental behavior often focused on the child's legitimate need to break away and the parents' responsibility to "let go" and allow their adolescents to "be themselves." Parents were advised to back off because teens must be free to explore with their peers to consolidate their identity.

In the 1970s and beyond, studies of adolescence contradicted earlier constructions based on psychoanalytic thought. They indicated that major transformations do occur in family relations as

Parents who are invested in their adolescents' well-being balance acceptance with appropriate limit-setting and monitoring.

children pass through adolescence but that becoming more independent and personally responsible is not necessarily accompanied by emotional detachment from parents (e.g., Hill & Holmbeck, 1986). Offer (1969) reported that roughly two thirds of teens experienced adolescence as a tranquil period or at least experienced only minor conflicts with parents. Montemayor (1983) reported that in typical families, teens and their parents argued on average twice a week, hardly a matter of great concern. A recent meta-analysis indicates that conflicts with parents occur most frequently in early adolescence. By middle adolescence, they begin to decline in frequency but tend to increase in intensity (Laursen, Coy, & Collins, 1998). Both adolescents and parents view some aspects of parental control to be quite legitimate. Parents can exercise authority over *moral* issues (like stealing and justice) or even issues governed by *conventional* rules (such as table manners), especially when conventional rules have prudential consequences (having to do with an individual's health or safety; e.g., Smetana, 1995; Smetana & Gaines, 1999). It's when parents impose rules on what their teens perceive as *personal* issues (like what you can say to a friend in an email, how you wear your hair, or what music you listen to) that conflicts are most likely to arise (e.g., Smetana & Daddis, 2002). For teens, gaining control over this personal domain is a way of establishing autonomy and therefore is an important identity issue.

Observers began to argue that if disagreements with parents center on relatively mundane issues like music and hairstyles, perhaps the storminess of relations between parents and adolescents has been overstated (Rutter, 1995). Parenting prescriptions began to include the implicit advice, "Don't worry, things will work out fine." As you might guess, things are not so simple.

Arnett (2000), for example, raises a word of caution. He suggests that conflicts over relatively minor matters are nonetheless stressful for both parents and children. He further warns that the "mundane" matters that adolescents argue with their parents about may not be as trivial as they seem. Rather, they

> often concern issues such as when adolescents should begin dating and whom they should date, where they should be allowed to go, and how late they should stay out. All of these issues can serve as proxies for arguments over more serious issues such as substance use, automobile driving safety, and sex. (p. 320)

In other words, some of the behaviors that adolescents categorize as "personal," their parents probably see as "prudential/conventional" because the behaviors have potentially serious consequences for a teen's future (see Hasebe, Nucci, & Nucci, 2004; Smetana & Daddis, 2002).

Yet the notion that parents should "let go" and that they should "not worry" seem to have permeated contemporary American culture. Paradoxically, warning signals that adolescents today face greater pressures and dangers than they have in the past are sounding in both the scientific and popular press. The Carnegie Council on Adolescent Development in 1996 described the risks facing young adolescents: "Altogether, nearly half of American adolescents are at high or moderate risk of seriously damaging their life chances. The damage may be near term and vivid, or it may be delayed, like a time bomb set in youth" (p. 2). Increasing risks were identified in physical health, in mental health, and in academic preparedness for children ages 10 to 14. Prevalence indicators from the 1980s and '90s revealed rising rates of death by firearms; more child abuse and victimization; greater use of drugs, alcohol, and cigarettes; higher suicide rates; decreasing age of first intercourse and thus increasing risk of early pregnancy and sexually transmitted diseases, including HIV/AIDS; and lower academic achievement, among other worrisome changes. Even though some of these trends have recently leveled off or been reversed, we still feel a combination of helplessness and desensitization when we read statistics such as these. How can we reconcile our assumptions of what young people need, and what adolescence should be like, with the realities of today? More specifically, how should we parent, how should we educate, how should we counsel and consult to meet the needs of contemporary adolescents?

Research on the family as one supportive context for adolescent development has been growing rapidly. Its theoretical framework rests upon Baumrind's (e.g., 1971, 1978, 1991) studies of parenting styles, in which, you will recall from Chapter 5, she identified two important dimensions of parental behavior, each of which is predictive of a particular constellation of child characteristics. First is parental warmth or responsiveness. Responsive parents seem to encourage their children's self-acceptance, confidence, and assertiveness by being warm, involved, and accepting of their children's needs and feelings. They take their children's feelings and expressed needs seriously and are willing to explain their own actions, particularly when they impose limits on the child. The second dimension is parental control or demandingness. Demanding parents apparently foster self-discipline and achievement by making maturity demands on their children. They make and enforce rules, provide consistent supervision or **parental monitoring**, and confront their children when their behavior does not measure up. According to a large body of research by Baumrind and others, the most effective parenting style, authoritative parenting, combines high responsiveness and high demandingness. It is as if the key to parenting effectiveness is to blend the listening skills and empathy of a well-trained counselor with the firmness of a watchful vice-principal for discipline.

As we noted in Chapter 5, treating responsiveness and demandingness as two distinct dimensions, three other categories of parenting style can be derived. Besides authoritative, there are authoritarian, permissive (also called **indulgent**), and neglecting (also called uninvolved or **dismissive**) styles (Maccoby & Martin, 1983). Authoritarian parents are low on responsiveness but high on demandingness. Permissive parents are high on responsiveness but low on demandingness, and neglecting or dismissive parents are essentially disengaged, scoring low on both dimensions. Before you read Box 10.1 on how authoritative parenting of adolescents "looks in action," consider the evidence that it can positively influence teen behavior and well-being. Baumrind (e.g., 1991) assessed the behavior of parents and their young adolescents and found that "authoritative parents put out exceptional effort . . . and their adolescents were exceptionally competent (mature, prosocial, high internal locus of control, low internalizing and externalizing problem behavior, low substance use)" (1993, p. 1308). In the large-scale study of 14- to 18-year-olds by Steinberg and his colleagues, parenting style was linked to four aspects of teens' adjustment: psychosocial development, school achievement, internalized distress, and problem behavior. The children of authoritative parents scored best on the majority of these indicators, and those of neglectful parents scored worst (Lamborn et al., 1991). After 1 year, the adolescents' adjustment status was reassessed. Parenting style was predictive of patterns of change over the year. For example, adolescents from authoritative homes showed increases in self-reliance, whereas other adolescents showed little change or, if they had neglectful parents, actually declined somewhat (Steinberg et al., 1994).

In general, research on parenting styles from as early as the 1940s (e.g., Baldwin, 1948) has produced results that are consistent with the large-scale studies of today, supporting the notion that both responsiveness and demandingness are beneficial. Overall, responsiveness seems more closely tied to adolescents' self-confidence and social competence, and demandingness is more closely associated with "good" behavior and self-control. Recent work indicates that it can be useful to consider responsiveness as comprising separable factors: **acceptance** is being affectionate, praising the child, being involved in the child's life, and accepting the child's strengths and limitations, showing concern for the child's needs, and it is correlated with children's self-esteem and social adjustment. **Democracy** is the degree to which parents encourage children's psychological autonomy by soliciting their opinions or encouraging self-expression, and it is most closely linked to children's self-reliance, self-confidence, willingness to work hard, and general competence (Steinberg, 1990, 1996). Whether we construe there to be two or three primary dimensions of parenting style, few would deny that the parenting characteristics they comprise are highly desirable. But, relatively speaking, how powerful a role can such parental behaviors actually play by adolescence, when the influence of peers has been found to be so great?

An important key to answering this question is to recall, again, that multiple determinants interact to affect outcomes at every developmental stage. Let's reconsider, for example, school achievement in the teen years. When authoritative parents involve themselves in their adolescents' schooling by attending school programs, helping with course selection, and monitoring student progress, their children are more likely to achieve (Gutman, Sameroff, & Eccles, 2002; Mounts & Steinberg, 1995; Steinberg, Lamborn, Dornbusch et al., 1992). However, as we have seen, an adolescent's crowd affiliation also impacts school achievement. Steinberg (1996) found that teens who began with similar academic records showed change over time in school performance consistent with their crowd membership, indicating the importance of peer influence despite parental efforts. But parents can affect crowd membership. First, characteristic behaviors of the child are probably important in determining crowd membership, and a child's behaviors are associated

Box 10.1 | *Authoritative Parenting with Adolescents*

Is authoritative parenting for real or some magician's trick? How can a parent, especially the parent of a savvy teenager, be warm, responsive, respectful, and democratic on one hand but firm, controlling, and watchful on the other?

Imagine that 14-year-old Risa bursts into the house on a Friday after school, literally jumping for joy at a party invitation she has just received. It's from Katy, one of the most popular girls in school, and being at the party will automatically define Risa as one of the popular elite. Risa prattles on about who will be there, and what to wear, and "Oh my god! I've got to start getting ready *now*!" Dad is working at home this afternoon, so he's the P.I.C.—parent in charge. First, he listens with interest and expresses understanding. It is not that difficult in this case. Risa is given to emotional extremes, but when the extreme is ecstasy, Dad has little trouble smiling, nodding, and reflecting ("This party is really something special!") compassionately. But before Risa bolts for the shower, Dad begins to ask questions about who, where, when, and under what circumstances. Risa's joyful prattle turns to impatient disdain: "It doesn't matter, and I don't have time to answer all these questions." Dad continues to try to reflect without being deflected. "I know you're busy, but the answers are very important to me. So let's just take a minute." Risa really does not know the answers, so Dad points out that he can find out more when he calls Katy's parents. "No! You can't! These kids don't even want to know I have parents. If you call I'll be completely humiliated!" Here is the challenge to the authoritative parent: balancing the child's feelings and concerns with the critical monitoring responsibility. Risa's dad stands firm: She is not permitted to attend parties where responsible adults are not present, and the only way to be sure is to speak directly to Katy's parents. Without belittling Risa's concerns, Dad insists on the phone call. He explains, as he has before, why unsupervised parties are not acceptable, and then invites Risa to help problem solve. "I know this is awkward, Risa. Let's try to think of ways to make this go smoothly for everyone. For example, I could call and thank Katy's parents for having the party at their house, and offer to bring over a case of soda." But Risa's idea of reasonable is not consistent with her father's. She has an inkling that the party is not going to be supervised, and in any case she does not want to risk the popular crowd seeing her as a "baby." She attacks her father as "old-fashioned," "overprotective," and "stupid," alternately raging and whining.

At this point, it is difficult for parents to repeat explanations calmly and to hold firm. Sometimes they give up, or lose all patience. Personal assaults from the teenager complicate the parents' role: These attacks are hurtful and demeaning, and they too need to be addressed. In this case, Dad manages to respond, "I know you're upset, but your attacking me hurts my feelings, and it's not going to change my mind. Let's stick to the subject of the party." At another point, he takes a timeout for 5 minutes to cool down. Rarely do conflicts like these feel happily resolved in the immediate situation. In this case, Risa finally tells her father not to bother to call because she will not go to the party—she will call and make an excuse. She then sulks in her room all night. Both her mother and her father talk to her about it again, giving her an opportunity to vent, to discuss again the pros and cons of the rule about unsupervised parties, and to consider ways of promoting her relationships with her friends, such as having a party herself. Their restrictions on her social life never stop grating on Risa, but her parents hold firm.

These confrontations can be frightening for the most confident parents. On a different occasion, Risa might just walk out rather than sulk in her room. Parents are dependent not only on the quality of the mutual caring that has been established with a child up to the teen years but also on the support that is available in the child's circle of friends. If her friends' parents routinely allow unsupervised parties, Risa's parents are soon going to feel besieged and may have limited success in helping Risa navigate her adolescence safely. On the other hand, if her friends' parents have similar values and are also authoritative, then the impact of her parents' authoritative style will be enhanced: Her psychosocial competence, including her self-esteem and self-reliance, will be benefited, and her chances of delinquency, drug abuse, and psychological distress will be reduced (Fletcher, Darling, Steinberg, & Dornbusch, 1995).

---

with parenting style. Steinberg (1996) describes parenting as "launching" children on a trajectory through adolescence. That launching may directly influence what crowd a teenager joins. Mounts and Steinberg (1995) found that specific parenting practices, such as monitoring and encouraging achievement, were correlated with children's choice of more academically oriented peers. Walker-Barnes and Mason (2001) found that urban parents who show high levels of monitoring and involvement have kids who tend to steer clear of joining delinquent groups or gangs.

But the availability of crowds is also important. If, for example, all crowds value high academic achievement, or if none do, the child's trajectory with regard to school performance will be much less affected by authoritative parents who value academic excellence than if there is a diversity of crowds. Here is a clue to other ways in which parenting style may influence behavior. Steinberg proposes that authoritative parents, who are heavily involved in their children's lives, may do things to help structure the child's peer group options and thus indirectly affect achievement by affecting the accessibility of peers. Does the local high school have few, if any, academically oriented students? Parents may arrange for their children to go elsewhere; they might move, or put their children in private schools, or choose to home school. It is not uncommon for parents who live in dangerous environments to send their children to live for brief periods with relatives. Such behavior, of course, depends on income and on the availability of such options, but it also depends on parental involvement. Authoritative parents are invested parents, often making personal sacrifices to maintain their commitment to their view of good parenting (Greenberger & Goldberg, 1989).

Parents, Peers, and Ethnicity

The complex interplay of parenting style with peer influences stands out in bold relief when we look at teens in different ethnic groups in the United States. Several researchers have found that for minority youngsters, authoritative parenting is not as strongly associated with positive outcomes as it is for White teens (e.g., Baumrind, 1972; Chao, 2001; Dornbusch, Ritter, Leiderman, Roberts, & Fraleigh, 1987; Walker-Barnes & Mason, 2001). (See also Chapter 5 for a discussion of ethnicity and parenting styles.) Steinberg, Dornbusch, and Brown (1992) found ethnic differences in their large survey of adolescents, particularly in the likelihood of academic success: Authoritative parenting was not as good a predictor of academic success for teens from Asian American, African American, and Hispanic families as it was for White teens. However, Steinberg, Dornbusch, et al. (1992) found some fundamental similarities across all ethnic groups. First, not surprisingly, hard work is linked to academic success regardless of ethnicity; students who put in the most time on homework, for example, are the best school performers. Second, teens across all ethnic groups were equally likely to believe that getting a good education pays off. But the researchers also found some surprising differences in beliefs about the negative consequences of not getting a good education. Asian American students were most likely to believe that poor academic preparation could limit their job options later, whereas African American and Hispanic youngsters were the most optimistic, that is, the least likely to believe that poor academic preparation would hurt their job prospects.

These differences in belief systems were reflected in the degree to which various ethnic peer groups supported academic achievement: Asian crowds were usually highly supportive, whereas African American and Hispanic crowds were not. Unlike White students, minority students often have little choice of which crowd to join; they typically are relegated to one or a few crowds defined primarily by ethnicity. Thus, regardless of their parents' support for academics or parenting style, Asian American youngsters might join a crowd that supports academics, whereas African American and Hispanic teens might be part of a crowd that does not. Steinberg, Dornbusch, et al. (1992) found that for all ethnic groups, the most successful students were those whose parents and peers supported academics. When peers were at odds with parents, the crowd's support, or lack of it, for homework and hard work was the better predictor of a student's day-to-day school behaviors. Thus, even though Asian American parents in this study were among the least likely to be authoritative or to be actively involved in their children's schooling, their children tended to be academically successful. As Steinberg (1996) noted, even Asian students of disengaged parents are often "saved from academic failure" by their friends' support of academics (p. 157). Yet African American youngsters with authoritative parents often face giving up their academic aspirations to keep their friends because the crowds they join not only fail to support school effort but may even criticize it as an attempt to "act White" (Fordham & Ogbu, 1986). Indeed, at a very vulnerable age many Black adolescents are forced to choose low academic standards, greatly limiting their future opportunities, or be ostracized.

The complex interactions between parenting and peer influences can also be seen in the arena of high-risk and deviant behavior. Again, an authoritative approach is the best protection a parent can provide. Lamborn, Dornbusch, and Steinberg (1996) found, for example, that children from permissive or disengaged families were most likely to experiment with alcohol and marijuana, and children from authoritative homes were least likely to do so. But they also found that the peer group had more influence than the parents on whether experimentation would lead to regular use. For example, even the most vulnerable youngsters, those who had experimented with drugs and whose parents were disengaged, were unlikely to become regular users if their peers were not.

As with school achievement, ethnicity and social class are among the predictors of drug use and deviant behavior in America, so that authoritative parenting is less effective for some teens than for others. But interestingly, several recent studies suggest that even among minority teens from poor neighborhoods, one component of authoritative parenting can be a strong force against deviant behavior and drug use: high levels of parental demandingness or control. Parents who closely monitor their children have teens who engage less often in delinquent behavior. These are parents who manage to keep track of their children and to place limits on where they spend their time after school and at night. These parents know with whom their children spend their time and what they spend their time doing. In one large, longitudinal study of rural preadolescent and adolescent children, one quarter of the sample was American Indian. About 4 years after the study began, a casino opened on the Indian reservation. Income supplements were paid to every Indian family thereafter, moving 14% of the Indian families out of poverty. Researchers found that for the children in these families (the "ex-poor"), there was a significant decline in conduct disorder and oppositional defiant disorders over 4 years. Statistical evaluation of a number of variables suggested that a key mediator of the children's behavioral change in the ex-poor families was that parents' time to supervise and monitor their children increased after the change in income (Costello, Compton, Keeler, and Angold, 2003).

Even when parents are not particularly warm or democratic, that is, when they are more authoritarian than authoritative, high levels of monitoring, especially for minority teens, has often been found to help protect youngsters from high-risk behavior (e.g., Fletcher, Steinberg, & Williams-Wheeler, 2004; Gorman-Smith, Tolan, Zelli, & Huesmann, 1996; Lamborn et al., 1996; Lansford et al., 2004; Smith & Krohn, 1995; Walker-Barnes & Mason, 2001). Why are levels of parental monitoring and control so strongly associated with reduced levels of delinquent behavior among Black and other minority teens, even when parents appear to be authoritarian rather than authoritative in their style? As we indicated in Chapter 5, how children construe, or interpret, parenting behaviors may have an influence on how they respond to them. In some ethnic groups, under some environmental circumstances, parents who require absolute obedience to authority without question may be seen by children as operating out of love and concern. For example, if a family lives in a low-income neighborhood where the real dangers of risky behavior may be all too obvious to youngsters, an authoritarian style might be read by a child in just such a way. Interestingly, recent research on Black and White neighborhoods in the United States indicates that Black communities may be more dangerous places for children than White communities even when they are middle class. When Sampson, Morenoff, and Earls (1999) compared middle-class Black versus White communities, they found them to be quite similar internally. But the neighborhoods bordering Black and White communities could be quite different. For White middle-class families the surrounding neighborhoods were often affluent and reasonably safe; but Black middle-class enclaves were more likely to be surrounded by low-income and dangerous neighborhoods. Thus, Black parents, regardless of social class, may more often than White parents perceive a need to monitor and control their children closely to keep them safe. Their children, in turn, may perceive even heavy-handed control as an indicator of affection.

THE ROLE OF SCHOOL

As we have seen, the adolescent experience is strongly influenced by parents and peers. In addition, school plays a major part in the psychosocial, intellectual, and vocational development of adolescents. Teachers, curricula, school activities, and school culture all provide raw material that contributes to the adolescent's growing sense of self and increasing base of knowledge and skill.

Much has been written about the problems with American schools (National Center for Educational Statistics, 2002; National Commission on Excellence in Education, 1983), and it is beyond the scope and purpose of this chapter to articulate all the aspects of the debate about American educational reform. It is important to note, however, that educational institutions have been increasingly challenged to make changes that support the developmental needs of adolescents (Carnegie Council on Adolescent Development, 1996). This movement derives both from the recognition that many contemporary adolescents face a host of social and academic problems

Large schools tend to be more impersonal and reduce adolescents' opportunities to be mentored by nurturing adults.

that threaten their well-being (National Center for Educational Statistics, 1998) and from the increasing body of evidence that demonstrates a stage-environment mismatch between adolescents and their schools (Eccles et al., 1993).

Many researchers and theorists have noted a decline in academic orientation and motivation starting in the early adolescent years that for some individuals continues throughout high school or culminates in "dropping out" (Harter, 1981; Parsons & Ruble, 1977; Simmons & Blyth, 1987). Instructional practices such as whole-group lectures (Feldlaufer, Midgley, & Eccles, 1988), ability grouping (Oakes, Quartz, Gong, Guiton, & Lipton, 1993), and competitive rather than cooperative activities and assessment (Ward et al., 1982) all occur more frequently in middle and junior high schools than in the elementary grades. These practices have been linked to low levels of student motivation and heightened social comparison. For example, just as adolescents become exquisitely sensitive to their place in the peer scene, school-based evaluative policies such as "tracked" academic classes may make differences in ability more noticeable to the adolescent's peers and teachers, leading to decreased status for some (Eccles, Midgley, & Adler, 1984). Compared with elementary schools, middle or junior high schools place a heavier emphasis on discipline and teacher control and provide relatively fewer opportunities for student decision making (Brophy & Evertson, 1976; Midgley, Feldlaufer, & Eccles, 1988). In contrast to this traditional model, longitudinal research by Wentzel (1997) documents the benefits associated with a more personal system of middle and secondary schooling. She found that students who perceived their teachers as caring and supportive were more likely than were students of less nurturant teachers to show greater academic effort and to express more prosocial goals. Interestingly, when students described teachers "who cared," they named characteristics that were quite similar to those of authoritative parents.

The large size of most middle and secondary schools is another factor that detracts from personal, mentoring relationships between students and available adults. Ravitch (1983) writes that the trade-off for bigger, more "efficient" schools means "impersonality, bureaucratization, diminished contact between faculty and students, formalization of relationships among colleagues, a weakening of the bonds of community" (p. 327). Although large school size, per se, has not been correlated with reductions in standardized test scores (Rutter, Maughan, Mortimore, Ouston, & Smith, 1979), smaller schools have been shown to promote prosocial behavior among teenagers (Barker & Gump, 1964) and more community activism among their adult graduates (Lindsay, 1984). Calls for smaller counselor-to-student ratios in secondary schools reflect the fact that critical goals such as curriculum choice and career planning are dependent upon personal knowledge of the student and a trusting relationship (Herr, 1989). Elkind (1984) asserts that the adolescent's identity formation is enhanced by being surrounded by a relatively small group of adults who know the student well and who, over time, are able to support the movement toward responsible autonomy.

The timing and types of transitions involved in the passage from primary to middle to secondary school are also important. These transitions represent turning points that involve a redefinition of social status (e.g., from middle school "top dog" to senior high "bottom dog," Entwisle, 1990) and the experience of several simultaneous stressors. Simmons and Blyth (1987) present evidence for "cumulative stress" theory in a study of the effects of different transition patterns on academic achievement and self-esteem. Investigating the school-related outcomes of students who followed a K–8, 9–12 transition model and those who followed a K–6, 7–9, 10–12 model, the researchers found more negative outcomes related to the latter plan. They interpreted these findings as resulting from an interaction between the stresses of puberty (see Chapter 9) and the cumulative stresses inherent in multiple school changes. For students who might be already at risk, the cost of these educational practices could be extremely high. Feldlaufer et al. (1988) found low levels of perceived teacher support were particularly harmful for low-achieving students who enter a less supportive classroom after a school transition.

But providing an emotionally supportive academic climate for young adolescents is not all that is needed to ensure their educational progress. Evidence from a study of 23 middle schools demonstrated that the combination of demanding teachers and rigorous curricula was strongly related to increased student achievement in mathematics, whereas warm teacher–student relations and communal classroom organization were not (Phillips, 1997). Perhaps we need to remember that both elements, responsiveness and demandingness, make important contributions to success in schools as well as in homes. In another study of middle school students, Wentzel (2002) found that teachers' high expectations for their students was most predictive of students' achievement and motivation to learn. But in addition, negative feedback or criticism from teachers, even in combination with high expectations, was found to be most clearly associated with diminished motivation and poor achievement. This finding applied to all students in her sample, regardless of gender, race, or ethnicity. She points out that "by creating a context free of harsh criticism *and* [italics added] one in which students are expected to do their best, teachers might be better able to convey information clearly and efficiently, encourage student engagement, and focus students' attention on academic tasks" (p. 298).

Finally, the level of involvement by parents in the schooling of adolescents also influences achievement outcomes. Despite scientific and government support of parental involvement as a critical ingredient in school success (e.g., U.S. Department of Education, 1990) particularly for poor and minority children (Comer, 1988), the idea of parents becoming involved in the academic life of the adolescent has been met with serious resistance. Consistent with the "hands-off" philosophy described earlier, many adults tend to leave the business of education to teachers or to the adolescents themselves. Involvement declines sharply at the middle and high school levels (Steinberg, 1996; Stevenson & Stigler, 1992). Steinberg has indicated that approximately one third of the students in his study said their parents were uninformed about their school performance, and another one sixth said that their parents did not care. More than 40% of participants said their parents did not attend any school function or activity. This parental unresponsiveness seems closely tied to the child's age and possibly to parental beliefs about an adolescent's right to autonomy. Broderick and Mastrilli (1997) found that parents and teachers viewed various dimensions of involvement (for example, monitoring homework and use of time, helping at school, attending meetings and conferences, plus serving as a partner with the school in decision making) as appropriately decreasing once the child has made the transition out of the elementary grades.

LEISURE AND WORK

Outside school, leisure activities occupy much of an adolescent's time. Leisure activities can promote skill mastery, such as sports participation, hobbies, and artistic pursuits, or they may be more purely recreational, such as playing video games, watching TV, daydreaming, or hanging out with friends (Fine, Mortimer, & Roberts, 1990). Young people who are involved in extracurricular activities sponsored by their schools and other community organizations—athletics, social service organizations, school newspaper staff, student government, band, and so on—are more likely to be academic achievers and to have other desirable qualities than students who are not involved in sponsored activities (Barber et al., 2001; Carnegie Council on Adolescent Development, 1996; Eccles & Barber, 1999; Steinberg, 1996). Although there are general benefits to extracurricular participation, it is becoming clear that the kind of benefit varies somewhat by activity and that not all the outcomes are positive. One longitudinal study followed over 1,000 Michigan young people for 14 years, beginning when they were in the 6th grade and keeping track of, among other things, their extracurricular involvements (Barber et al., 2001; Eccles & Barber, 1999). High school participation in either prosocial activities or sports was associated with long-term educational achievements (e.g., going to college). But although kids who participated in prosocial activities were unlikely to use alcohol or other drugs in high school, those who participated in sports were more likely than most other teens to use alcohol in high school. Both personal qualities and peer influences appeared to play a role in shaping these outcomes.

Today's adolescents spend a lot of time doing work for pay. Are there benefits to these early jobs for teens? It seems reasonable to propose some developmental advantages. Having adult responsibilities might help adolescents feel independent and grown up, enhancing self-esteem. Searching for work and being employed might provide training that is hard to come by in any other way, such as learning how to find a job, learning one's own job preferences, and clarifying one's work values (Mortimer, Harley, & Aronson, 1999). Parents often assume that working will help adolescents to learn to manage their money and their time. Mortimer et al. (1999) report that teens who work generally endorse many of these presumed benefits, seeing their jobs as helping them to be more responsible, to manage their time and their money, to establish a work ethic, and to learn social skills. Adolescents also list some negative outcomes, primarily feeling fatigued and having less time for homework and leisure activities, but on balance they see their work in a positive light.

Do adolescents who work need to work—to save for college or even to help ease financial burdens at home? During the Great Depression, economic hardship did send adolescents into the workplace, and working was apparently linked to more responsible use of money and a more "adult" orientation (Elder, 1974). But the culture has changed dramatically since then. Whereas in 1940 only about 3% of 16-year-olds still in school were employed, by 1980 the government estimated that more than 40% were working. Of course, relatively more youngsters complete high school today than in 1940, so that today's students may be more representative of the general population, but there is evidence of a substantial shift in students' priorities as well. Large surveys that depend on students' self-reports rather than government data indicate that in fact about 65% of today's teens are gainfully employed (Fine et al., 1990). Middle-class teens are more likely to be employed than those from lower socioeconomic groups, and their money is unlikely to be saved or contributed to family expenses. Rather, working teens more frequently spend their money on materialistic pursuits: wardrobes, entertainment, drugs, and alcohol (e.g., Steinberg & Cauffman, 1995; Steinberg et al., 1993).

Cultural change has also affected the kinds of jobs adolescents acquire. In 1940, many teens worked on farms or in manufacturing, in jobs where they were supervised by adults (frequently adults who were family members or were known to their families), and they often received some training that was directly relevant to the jobs they would have after high school. Today, teens are much more likely to work in retail establishments, including restaurants, and to be under the direct supervision of other young people rather than adults. It appears that the work teens do today is often less educational than in 1940 and may have less long-term career value (Aronson, Mortimer, Zierman, & Hacker, 1996).

Although adolescents themselves seem enthusiastic about the value of their part-time work, researchers report that there can be some serious side effects. Note that negative consequences are substantially related to hours of employment—the more hours, the more problematic the effects in most cases. The most troublesome finding is that long hours of employment (especially 20 or more hours per week) are associated with increases in problem behaviors like theft (e.g., giving away store products to friends), school misconduct, and alcohol and drug use, including cigarette smoking (e.g., Mihalic & Elliot, 1997; Mortimer et al., 1999; Steinberg & Cauffman, 1995). The effects of work on schooling and school involvement are mixed. Several large-scale studies have found no effects on students' grades but negative effects on total educational attainment: Years of schooling tend to be reduced for students who invest long hours in their jobs. Other studies have found negative correlations between working and grades even for relatively few hours of work (Largie, Field, Hernandez-Reif, Sanders, & Diego, 2001). Steinberg et al. (1993) point out that negative associations between schooling and work appear to be bidirectional—for example, teens with less school involvement are more likely to seek jobs, and once they are working substantial hours, teens become even less involved in school. In a review of the literature, Mortimer et al. (1999) conclude that benefits from high school employment, like feelings of self-efficacy and self-esteem, are most likely when work hours are short and the quality of the work experience is good. Quality includes opportunities to learn new skills, to use one's skills, to discuss work tasks with supervisors, to be helpful to others, and to have relative freedom from stressors like time pressure, work overload, and responsibility for aspects of the work that are outside the adolescent's control.

The research on adolescent employment helps illustrate the power of historical and social context to influence the well-being of adolescents. Many of the students who seek part-time work today would not have done so in the first half of this century. The urge to earn is apparently spawned largely by teenagers' wanting the material goods and pleasures so prominently advertised and modeled in today's print media, movies, and television, as we will discuss in the next section. Ironically, the temporary affluence teens experience as a result of working in low-level, part-time jobs actually may, for some, help diminish their chances of pursuing high-paying, education-dependent careers later in their lives (Steinberg & Cauffman, 1995).

MEDIA AND THE CONSUMER CULTURE

Development is affected by the dynamic interaction between the individual and various other forces that extend beyond the friendship circle, the family, and the school. Peer networks, families, and schools operate, as Bronfenbrenner (1979) pointed out (see Chapter 1), within an even larger context called the exosystem, or the level of the culture. The culture's values, laws, politics, customs, and so on directly and indirectly contribute elements and experiences that the adolescent uses to construct a map of the world. Clearly, this influence process is reciprocal and multidirectional. For example, changes in the workplace because of economic forces may put excess demands on parents already suffering from a time deficit. Because they cannot be available to supervise, these parents may then adopt practices that encourage relatively high levels of independent behavior from their adolescents. The economic market may move in to provide goods and services, such as structured tutoring or television programming attractive to teens, to fill their time. Teen preferences and interests then influence the advertising and marketing of goods. (See Hewlett, 1991, or Hochschild, 1997, for a discussion of workplace effects on children.) Recent large scale studies of children up to age 6 as well as older children and adolescents from 8 to 18 indicate increasing use of electronic media. For example, one third of all 6-years-olds in America have a television in their bedrooms, and children ages 6 and under spend approximately two hours a day watching either videos, television, or a computer screen (Kaiser Family Foundation, 2003). Among 8- to 18-year-olds, total electronic media use a day has reached 6 hours and 21 minutes (Kaiser Family Foundation, 2005).

It is important for mental health professionals to concern themselves with the effects of cultural forces on adolescent development if they are to take a position that promotes healthy growth and functioning. Jessor (1993) noted that the distal effects of the larger cultural context are rarely taken into consideration when studying development, although "understanding contextual change is as important as understanding individual change" (p. 120). Perhaps the major question to be addressed is: How adolescent-friendly is the society we live in? If family, peers, and teachers are fellow players in the unfolding drama of adolescent identity formation, the culture with its values and broader institutions provides the stage upon which that drama is acted out.

Many writers from diverse fields of study have noted a general loss of community and a focus on individualism and material success evident in American culture at this point in its history (Barber, 1992; Bellah, Madsen, Sullivan, Swidler, & Tipton, 1985; Hewlett & West, 1998;

Lasch, 1991). In their discussion of a culture they call "poisonous," Hewlett and West describe punitive economic forces that undermine family stability and negative media forces that shape attitudes and beliefs. Few adults would deny that the exposure to the realities of the adult world that teens have today has been ratcheted up several levels compared to even recent generations. For example, media exposure to violent, sexualized, and commercial messages occurs at a more intense level and starts at earlier ages.

But how does this kind of media exposure affect children and adolescents and how much of a threat is it? The link between viewing televised violence and behaving aggressively for certain individuals has been well researched and is generally accepted (see Comstock & Scharrer, 1999). Modeling processes (see Chapter 1) are presumed to account for much of this relationship. Recent interest in the role of media (TV, movies, music, and Internet exposure) as a socializer of values expands upon social learning principles to include constructivist conceptions of how individuals make sense of their environments. In other words, people use what they perceive as raw material from which to construct ideas, beliefs, and guiding principles.

One area of particular concern for adolescents is the learning of sexual messages and attitudes. Studies using correlational methods have found relationships between frequent viewing of televised portrayals of sexuality with more distorted cognitions, more liberal attitudes about sex, and more tolerance for sexual harassment (Strouse, Goodwin, & Roscoe, 1994). Frequent consumption of sexualized media has also been linked to increased sexual behavior—that is, more sexual partners and earlier sexual initiation than for individuals without such media exposure (Brown et al., 2002). This may have something to do with the perception that "everybody's doing it." Researchers have found that people's expectations or constructions about what is normative influence what they choose to do. Adolescents who believe that teens in general have frequent sexual experiences engage in riskier and more frequent sexual activity themselves (Whitaker & Miller, 2000).

A recent study by Ward (2002) employed both correlational and experimental methods to study whether television's messages influenced attitudes about sexuality in a multiethnic sample of older adolescents. This study confirmed that the three beliefs investigated in this study—that men are driven by sex, that women are sex objects, and that dating is a recreational sport—were very strongly related to heavy TV viewing and to personal involvement with TV. High personal involvement was measured by individuals' goals for TV (entertainment and a way to learn about the world), discussions about TV shows with others, and identification with TV characters, among other things. Outcomes of the experimental part of the study revealed that females more strongly endorsed the stereotypical beliefs after viewing sexual TV clips than did women who saw nonsexual episodes.

Like it or not, teens assimilate views of acceptable behavior from many sources, including TV, movies, popular music, and the Internet.

Interestingly, this pattern was not the same for males. Males' agreement with the three stereotypes was already much higher than women's, so it may not have been realistic to expect this experimental manipulation to generate higher rates of agreement. Another possibility is that males' attitudes might be differentially influenced by exposure to other types of media, such as music videos.

Certainly not all media use is associated with negative outcomes. Yet it is important to consider the impact of repeated exposure to the violent, sexual, and materialistic images in much of the media adolescents consume. Media messages can provide elements for the construction of identity via the processes we have described in this chapter. Moreover, media images serve as standards for social comparison, molding expectations for normative behavior and amplifying values that may be at odds with those of families and communities. As the report from the Carnegie Council of Adolescent Development (1996) points out, adolescents are careening down the information superhighway, and electronic conduits (TV, videos, cable, computers, movies, and popular music) "have become strong competitors to the traditional societal institutions in shaping young people's attitudes and values" (p. 41).

How do contemporary cultural conditions interact with the adolescent's struggle for autonomy and self-definition? In the next section, we will explore some answers to this question.

RISKY BEHAVIOR AND SOCIAL DEVIANCE

Dane and Andy are talking about drinking to an author who is interviewing them for a book about teenage life. "Another way to get beer is just to go to find a kegger somewhere," Andy says. Dane laughs and says, "Pound it down and get out of there. Go drive around." They realize they've just admitted to drinking and driving. Dane says, "I strongly believe against it, but there are some instances when you just can't help it. And we've done it enough so . . ." Andy adds, "Yes, we're good at it and we know the limit. Driving's kinda habitual anyway. We really don't pay attention to it. We're as responsible as we can be, I guess." Dane admits, "Not really." When asked by the interviewer whether their parents know about this, Dane replies, "My parents are pretty mellow; they're real trusting and stuff. I like my parents pretty well. They're pretty supportive, whatever I do, but they're pretty oblivious to teenage life. Like they say, We can always tell; you can't get away with this stuff. And I'm thinking to myself, I've been drinking and smoking for like three years now, so you guys just don't have a clue" (adapted from Pratt and Pryor, 1995).

Are the behaviors Dane and Andy describe normal or deviant? Are they part of a passing phase or predictive of future problems? Should we crack down on these behaviors or look the other way? These questions pose real problems, not only for parents and clinicians but also for social policy makers in fields such as education and criminal justice. These behaviors epitomize a paradox at this stage of development, for rebellion against adult norms, expressed through experimentation with deviant behaviors, has always been part of the adolescent experience and is, in fact, statistically normative (Barnes, Welte, & Dintcheff, 1992; Jessor et al., 1991).

Risky behaviors are behaviors that constitute a departure from socially accepted norms or behaviors that pose a threat to the well-being of individuals or groups. Various writers have used different terms to refer to these behaviors, including *reckless, problem, deviant, antisocial,* and *delinquent.* Here we use the adjectives somewhat interchangeably, although risky and reckless connote slightly more benign behaviors than do deviant, antisocial, or delinquent. Even so, separating these activities into bad and not-so-bad is tricky because, as we shall see, they all pose potential dangers. They vary on a continuum of severity and, when severe, tend to appear in clusters in the lives of teenagers at risk. Some examples of these problem behaviors include drinking and other drug use, smoking, truancy, sexual behavior, high-speed driving, drunk driving, vandalism, and other kinds of delinquency. Society considers some of these behaviors to be not only reckless but illegal as well. Consequently, statistics show that fully four fifths of adolescent males have experienced some police contact for minor infractions during their teenage years (Farrington, 1989). Although most crime statistics indicate that males are disproportionately involved in these offenses, recent evidence points to increasing delinquency among girls (Henggeler, Schoenwald, Borduin, Rowland, & Cunningham, 1998). Risky behaviors escalate sharply during adolescence, peaking around age 17 and then dropping off in early adulthood for most individuals (Moffitt, 1993a). Figure 10.2, for example, shows the drop in speeding while driving after the teen years. Not all adolescents experiment with reckless behavior, but a high percentage do. Thus, the proportion of adolescents who engage in some variety of reckless or deviant behavior is higher than for groups at any other stage of the life span.

It is hard to get a handle on the actual amount of risky behavior enacted by adolescents. Even though incidence rates of violent crime, including juvenile incidence rates, have fallen since the mid-1990s (U.S. Bureau of Justice Statistics, 2000), the problems associated with risky behavior among teenagers have not disappeared. Consider that approximately two thirds of the 12 million estimated cases of sexually transmitted diseases in the United States each year involve adolescents and young adults (Boyer, Shafer, & Tschann, 1997). Although the proportion of teens who were sexually active did not change between 1991 and 2003, condom use increased during this period (Centers for Disease Control, 2004), perhaps contributing to a decline in teen pregnancies at the end of the 1990s. However, the number of babies born to teen mothers in the United States is still the highest of all developed countries. Great Britain, whose teenage birth rate is next highest, has only about half the teenage birth rate of the United States (Annie E. Casey Foundation, 1998).

In 1997, approximately 30% of children in 4th through 6th grades reported being offered drugs, representing an increase of 47% from 1993 to 1997 (Partnership for a Drug-Free America, 1998). When a national sample of adolescents was surveyed in the early 1990s about binge drinking (drinking at least five drinks in a row), 28% of high school seniors and 40% of 20- to 21-year-olds admitted they had binged on alcohol at least once during the previous 2-week period (Johnston, O'Malley, & Bachman, 1994). Results of the same survey in 2000 revealed that 30% of twelfth graders, 26.2% of tenth graders, and 14.1% of eighth graders reported binge drinking in the 2 weeks prior to the survey. In addition, twelfth-graders' perceptions of the risks of drinking one or two alcoholic drinks decreased from 1999 to 2000. From 2000 to 2003 the situation improved somewhat: There were some declines in drinking for eighth, tenth, and twelfth graders, and teens' awareness of the risks of alcohol use had increased. Still, nearly half of twelfth graders indicated they had consumed alcohol within the last month and over 21% reported having smoked marijuana (Johnston, O'Malley, & Bachman, 2003). Furthermore, a significant increase in the use of painkillers (vicodin and oxycontin) was reported among 8 to 12th graders between 2002 and 2004 (Johnston, O'Malley, & Bachman, 2004).

Sometimes, clinicians choose to treat the reckless or deviant behaviors of adolescents as separable conditions. When this approach is used, interventions get targeted to specific problems, such

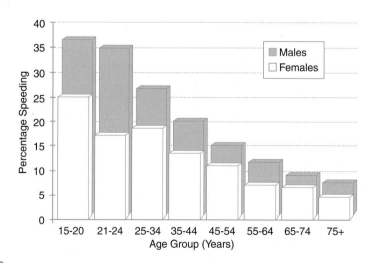

FIGURE 10.2

Percentage of Drivers Who Were Speeding in Fatal Crashes in 1996, by Age and Sex.

Source: From U.S. Department of Transportation (1996, Fig. 4) as cited in Nell, V. (2002). Why young men drive dangerously: Implications for injury prevention. *Current Directions in Psychological Science, 11,* 75–79.

as drug use or unsafe sexual practices or drunk driving. However, most problem behaviors come in packages. They frequently coexist on a spectrum of less harmful to dysfunctional. Consider Brianna, a high school sophomore who drinks alcohol at parties, but never to excess, and smokes cigarettes with her friends. She has tried pot now and again, but she thinks she does not want to try anything stronger until she gets older. She is an average student, has a sociable personality, and has stabilizing family and peer supports. Despite this, Brianna and her best friend recently were arrested for shoplifting in the local mall. The girls explained that they did this "on a dare."

Shauna is a 9th grader who has had academic and behavioral problems since elementary school. Her headstrong, impulsive, and aggressive characteristics have always put her at odds with people in authority. Her boyfriend is part of a gang that steals beer and cigarettes, later selling them to buy harder drugs. The lure of her boyfriend and his lifestyle is stronger than her single mother can overcome. Shauna is now pregnant and will soon drop out of high school. Although there are some similar features in both girls' risky behavior, namely, the easy availability of alcohol and drugs, freedom to spend time with peers who may influence risk taking, and the ubiquitous adolescent urge to experiment, there are also some important differences. Consequently, the level of intervention used to address Brianna's problem behaviors would probably be less effective with Shauna (see Box 1.3 in Chapter 1 on prevention issues).

Moffitt (1993a) makes a valuable contribution to understanding these differences by distinguishing between two major developmental trajectories of adolescent antisocial behavior: life-course-persistent and adolescence-limited. These developmental patterns are also called early-starter and adolescent-onset trajectories. (See Chapter 7 for descriptions.) The life-course-persistent pattern begins in early childhood and continues throughout life. In general, this pattern is associated with early conduct problems, aggressiveness, and academic difficulties, as typified by Shauna. For this particular package of problems, early intervention for children and families is most effective. In contrast, adolescence-limited antisocial behavior, such as Brianna's, develops in adolescence and usually ends shortly thereafter. The prognosis for the latter kind of pathway is generally more favorable.

Is adolescence-limited antisocial behavior the same as reckless behavior in adolescence? The answer may be a matter of degree. Certainly, some teenagers go to more extreme lengths, have more accumulated risk factors and fewer protective ones in their lives, and thus suffer more from the consequences of their behavior than others. But the paradox we introduced earlier seems to apply here. Behaviors traditionally considered deviant are increasingly becoming part of the experimental repertoire of teens who are considered well adjusted. Hersch (1998) closely followed the activities of adolescents in a suburban high school for several years. She got to know the students well, becoming an "insider" in the world of adolescents, and was able to document the escalation of dangerous pursuits as a normal part of contemporary adolescent life. "Behaviors once at the fringe of adolescent rebelliousness have not only permeated the mainstream culture of high school but are seeping into the fabric of middle school" (p. 156). As Jessica, an eighth-grade student interviewed by Hersch said, "This [smoking, using drugs, having sex] is *what you are supposed to do* [italics added]. . . . It's our teenage phase. You are only a kid once" (p. 156). Clinicians who work on the front lines, in middle and high schools or in practices that include adolescents, deal with these problems and attitudes every day. Let us try to examine why reckless behavior is such a part of the adolescent phase in the first place, and then we will consider its benefits and costs to young people.

Setting the Stage for Risk Taking

Arnett (1992) proposes that reckless behavior is a typical feature of adolescence and provides three main reasons why. First, adolescents tend to score higher than other age groups on a dimension called sensation seeking, which is defined as "the need for varied, novel, and complex sensation and experiences and the willingness to take physical and social risk for the sake of these experiences" (Zuckerman, 1979, p. 10). Sensation seeking is related to certain physiological processes, including brain arousal and hormone and neurotransmitter levels (Zuckerman, 1994). All the physiological processes implicated in high levels of sensation seeking are more active in increasing or intensifying stimulation during the period of adolescence than at other periods of life. Second, as we have learned, cognitive limitations such as egocentrism support the fiction that risky behavior is exciting but not potentially catastrophic. Arnett implicates adolescents' weaknesses in reasoning about probability, a kind of formal operational thinking familiar to students of statistics, as particularly important here.

Drawing upon Piaget's ideas, Arnett points out that

> in every judgement of probability, there is a reference, implicit or explicit, to a system of distributions or frequencies. Adolescents' perceptions of these systems are skewed by their desire for sensation and by the personal fable that convinces them of their immunity from disaster. . . . But even if an adolescent were exceptionally proficient at estimating probabilities, on a given occasion, the likelihood of disaster resulting from drunk driving, or sex without contraception, or illegal drug use, or delinquency/crime is, in fact, statistically small—even when applied to others, and seen through the lens of sensation seeking and egocentrism, the perceived probability fades even further. (p. 350)

Finally, Arnett implicates peer influences in maintaining risky behavior. Peers provide not only role models for deviancy but a kind of **collective egocentrism**. Shauna might reason, for example, that if her boyfriend and his friends aren't worried about getting caught in some illegal scheme, then neither should she worry. Each adolescent's illusion of invincibility strengthens that of the other members of the peer group.

Are these reasons the only explanations for teenage risk taking? Or could reckless behavior possibly serve some beneficial purpose? Chronic, life-course-persistent antisocial behavior exacts an enormous cost from the individual involved, from his family, and from society in general. So it is hard to imagine any redeeming features to this condition. The impact of adolescent-limited antisocial behavior, however, is less clear-cut. In one view, recklessness in adolescents, especially in males, once had a strong fitness value. Nell (2002), for example, argues that in the evolutionary history of the human species, young males who were willing to risk their own safety to fight for territory and for dominance won the most desirable mates. The legacy of this evolutionary history is that, even today, adolescent boys are biochemically prepared to take risks and to engage in aggressive behavior. Another view is that adolescent limited antisocial behavior is adaptive because it promotes individuation and self-determination. Goldstein (1990), for example, suggests that risky behavior is instrumental in relieving the **maturity gap** that afflicts adolescents who are caught in a time warp between physical and social maturity. To possess the symbolic trappings of adult status (sexual intimacy, material possessions, autonomy, and respect from parents), adolescents mimic the behavior of more advanced, and often more antisocial, peers, borrowing those elements that elicit respect from others and that affirm personal independence.

Maggs, Almeida, and Galambos (1995) found that increasing levels of engagement in risk-taking behavior across adolescence (disobeying parents, school misconduct, substance abuse, antisocial behavior) were associated with decreased levels of positive self-concept but with increased levels of peer acceptance. In a longitudinal study of youth from preschool through age 18, Shedler and Block (1990) found that adolescents defined as drug "experimenters," as compared with drug users and drug abstainers, had healthier psychological profiles (characterized by flexibility, openness to new experiences, less overcontrol yet less impulsivity) than the other two groups. Wilson (1996) noted that some socially deviant behaviors of disadvantaged inner-city youth represent situationally adaptive means of coping with ghetto life.

Engaging in risk-taking behavior thus represents a paradox that has both positive (status-provision) and negative (social-deviance) aspects. Arnett (1992) theorizes that reckless behavior is a fact of life in cultures with **broad** as opposed to **narrow socialization** practices. Societies with broad socializing practices permit and encourage high levels of individual freedom of expression, have fewer social constraints, expect less community responsibility, and thus tolerate a wider variety of socially deviant behaviors. Cultures with narrow socialization practices, more characteristic of nonindustrialized cultures, exert more control over the expression of behaviors that violate social standards and expect more conformity from young members of the society.

So is reckless behavior among adolescents the price we must pay for living in a society that encourages freedom of expression? What kinds of trade-offs should we be willing to tolerate? Even though adolescent-limited antisocial patterns usually attenuate sometime in early adulthood, when more conventional roles of employee, spouse, or parent are assumed, we should not conclude that this pattern poses no risk at all. To be sure, Moffitt (1993a) notes that risky behavior, while enhancing peer involvement, may also ensnare adolescents in situations that can ultimately prove quite harmful, such as fostering drug dependence or depressing academic achievement.

Society's Role in Adolescent Problem Behavior: Then and Now

Let's reflect again about the continuum of narrow to broad socialization. At which point along the continuum would you place contemporary U.S. culture? Although there are certainly regional and ethnic variations, it is likely that you identify contemporary socializing practices as quite broad. Adolescents, and even younger children, seem to have a lot more freedom now than they have had in the past. However, we can also consider this question from a slightly different perspective, focusing not just on freedom but on support. How much support does our contemporary culture provide for young people? How is level of support related to engagement in risky behavior? Has our collective level of responsibility changed in any way from that of the past decades, or is this idea just a nostalgic myth?

Siegel and Scovill (2000) provide a comprehensive look at the approach U.S. society has taken toward young people from the 1920s onward. In the 1920s, society viewed deviant adolescent behavior—as much a problem then as it is now—as an expression of youthful energies gone awry. In addition, social deviancy was considered an alternative pathway that some teenagers used to meet normal developmental goals, such as autonomy and relatedness, when more socially conventional means were unavailable to them. Consequently, it was generally believed that society as a whole was responsible for providing more productive outlets for adolescent energies. Many institutions and organizations were established to encourage teenagers to participate in socially constructive activities, to provide them with structured adult contact, and to facilitate prosocial interactions among youth themselves. Some examples of these organizations, most initiated before the 1920s, include Boy and Girl Scouts, Campfire Girls, Pioneer Youth of America, 4-H Clubs, Junior Achievement, Kiwanis, Order of the Rainbow for Girls, and Optimist International Boys' Work Council. Institutions dedicated to special interests, such as the National Recreation Association, the Girls' Service League of America, and the Sportmanship Brotherhood, as well as religiously affiliated groups such as the YMCA, the YWCA, the Knights of King Arthur, and the Ladies of Avalon, were also established. All were united in their purpose of providing guidance and character-building activities for youth.

Today, Siegel and Scovill (2000) point out, many of these age-appropriate community support systems have disappeared or have more limited scope. Consequently, the social envelope, which in the past strengthened families and schools and provided a safety net for youth who lacked family support or good educational opportunities, is weak or even absent. Many academic and recreational opportunities, often available free of charge to past generations of children and adolescents as part of their neighborhoods or communities, now come with a price tag. What has happened to cause this shift in attitudes and priorities?

Society's view of the cause of adolescent problem behaviors undoubtedly shapes its attitudes toward responsibility, prevention, and treatment. Contemporary society leans toward perceiving the source of deviancy as something within the individual adolescent rather than within society at large.

> While problem behavior was largely "socialized" through the 1960's, it has become "medicalized" in the 1990's. In an age in which we have been led to believe that there is a "magic scientific bullet" for nearly all physiological and social problems, we have "medicalized" problem behavior. An unspoken corollary of the "intrapsychic" view is that if the locus of the problem is in the adolescent, then parents and society are off the hook. The genetic or biological perspective provides that out: "There's nothing we could do; our child was born a delinquent." (Siegel & Scovill, 2000, p. 781)

No one should interpret these comments as suggesting that we return to either–or, nature–nurture thinking. As we have seen repeatedly, temperamental influences on behavior are strong, and they contribute significantly to developmental outcomes. What these authors recommend is a serious examination of the personal needs and rationalizations we adults use in interpreting adolescent problem behavior. If, as a society, we emphasize adolescent self-sufficiency and sophistication and deemphasize adolescent needs for adult time, guidance, and connection, then we do them, and us, a great disservice.

Parents, teachers, and other responsible adults who wish to limit adolescents' exposure to antisocial models or who wish to restrict their teens' experimentation are in a position of having to do battle with the culture. In many domains, the best judgment of responsible adults is at odds with information coming from the macrosystem. African American parents, for example, who recognize and support the value of academic achievement, report that music and movies that are made to appeal to their youngsters often explicitly disparage their values (Steinberg, 1996). Sometimes this battle can seem overwhelming. Steinberg estimates from his and other survey research that about 25% of American parents across all ethnic groups are disengaging from the struggle. He aptly describes them as follows:

> [They have] "checked out" of child-rearing. They have disengaged from responsibilities of parental discipline—they do not know how their child is doing in school, have no idea who their child's friends are, and are not aware of how their child spends his or her free time—but they have also disengaged from being accepting and supportive as well. They rarely spend time in activities with their child, and seldom just talk with their adolescent about the day's events. (p. 118)

As we have noted, adolescents whose parents are neglectful experience poorer social and academic outcomes than adolescents from authoritative families.

As Elkind (1994) has suggested, and as we noted earlier, the conceptualization of adolescents typical of the 1950s, '60s, and '70s was that they should be "let go" to experiment and allowed to "be themselves." However, this idea developed within a culture that provided teenagers with a protective "adult envelope" that usually prevented their doing too much harm to themselves. In contemporary society, adolescence is not perceived as an adult apprenticeship but rather as an early pseudo-adulthood. Elkind believes that actively encouraging adolescent experimentation or, at least, looking the other way does not fit with postmodern realities.

With societal attitudes that place the burden of responsibility on the individual adolescent, with more mothers and fathers working longer hours, with larger classrooms and reductions in funding for recreational activities, and with fewer "old heads" around to listen and offer guidance, teens may come to depend more and more on their peers for support and information about life. In the colonized or segregated space Taffel (2001) dubs "Planet Youth," adolescent mimicry of risky behaviors may increasingly become the norm.

APPLICATIONS

Adolescence is the life stage characterized by the highest overall level of risk taking. Some risk taking is a healthy expression of autonomy in the service of identity development. Some risky pathways lead in less adaptive directions. Helping professionals who work with adolescents spend a good deal of their time attempting to encourage healthy behaviors and to discourage or reduce harmful ones. Clearly, there is no shortage of work in this area given the cultural possibilities for exploration in potentially dangerous areas like drugs, alcohol, sexuality, violence, and truancy that are open to younger and younger generations. What is the best way to make headway with adolescents given their natural proclivity to take risks? First, we need to recognize that adults can't prevent all risky behaviors. But assuming the attitude that "they'll grow out of it" can be ill-advised as well, given the convergence of research on the power of cumulative risk to affect later outcomes (Grant & Dawson, 1997; Robins & Pryzbeck, 1985). With regard to adolescent well-being, we introduce some ideas that draw upon developmental knowledge at the level of individual counseling, family and peer systems, and broadbased prevention. Approaches like these will not eliminate all risky behavior, but they can reduce it or help youth engage in it less impulsively.

The Personal Meaning of Risk

It would be easy if adolescents bought the argument that risky behaviors should be avoided. Some adolescents are inclined to do so, but many others seem impervious to adult logic. Those in the latter group might be more likely to show up in a counselor's office. Although we have discussed many of the theories about why adolescents take risks in general, it is important from a counseling perspective to consider the personal motivation that drives a young person and, in so doing, to uncover the personal meaning of risky behavior for that individual. Counselors know how important empathy is for the success of therapeutic relationships. It is good to be mindful that, at its core, real empathy incorporates perspective taking. In work with adolescents, adults cannot assume that mature perspective-taking skills are on-line or that adolescent perspectives will necessarily resonate with their own adult points of view. Consequently, until we become aware of our own perspective and differentiate it from that of our adolescent clients, attempts to reason with youth across this "great divide" can be ineffective.

In individual counseling, a good place for the therapist to start might be with the questions "How does this young person perceive the risky behavior? What purpose does it serve?" Although not yet fully developed as an intervention strategy, Selman and Adalbjarnardottir (2000) describe a method for understanding adolescents' reasoning about risky behaviors that is based on social perspective taking. In their study, a developmental lens was applied to themes that emerged from extensive interviews with Icelandic adolescents about their alcohol use. The interview questions used in this study included two semistructured protocols, the Risky Business Interview (Levitt & Selman, 1993) and the Relationship Interview (Schultz, 1993), both comprised of open- and closed-ended prompts. The use of these instruments underscores the central connection between risky behavior and the world of peer relationships in adolescence.

In this research study, verbal responses of adolescent participants were coded to produce highly nuanced portraits of social perspective taking, meaning making, and relationships. Some have noted that this level of analysis may be too time consuming for clinicians to use on a regular basis (Nangle, Hecker, Grover & Smith, 2003). However, a few general implications can be adapted for clinical purposes to help us better understand adolescent thinking and behavior.

Recall that perspective taking develops in stagelike shifts from unilateral/noninclusive awareness of multiple perspectives to contextualized/highly inclusive awareness. The coordination of multiple perspectives gradually improves with time and experience. The theory posits that adolescents are likely to make more risky choices, especially in social contexts, when they lack the ability to coordinate their own perspectives with those of parents and other significant adults. Coordination of perspectives on risk actually involves the reciprocal interplay of three related competencies: (1) the adolescent's level of general knowledge about risks and their place in social interactions, (2) the variety of risk-management strategies that are available to the adolescent, and (3) the adolescent's level of awareness about the personal meaning of risky behavior. The last of these skills, personal meaning, is considered the "linchpin between understanding of factual knowledge and actual behavior—and between adolescents' perspectives on risk and relationship. Even individuals with sophisticated levels of understanding and a full repertoire of high-level social strategies are vulnerable to addictive influences of alcohol—especially if genetically disposed—if they do not have a mature perspective on what drinking means to them personally" (p. 62).

Consider the example (adapted from the study results) of an adolescent who believes that adults prohibit alcohol because they don't want kids to drink, that kids should just go ahead and drink anyway to have fun with their friends, and that drinking makes kids "cool." Here we see a unilateral, undifferentiated perspective demonstrated in rule-based thinking (adults try to control people and drinking is cool) and in one-way, nonmutual problem solving (just do what you want to do). Another adolescent with more highly developed perspective-taking skills might say that adults don't want kids to drink because kids might not be able to handle alcohol, that kids should go out with friends but stick to their own decision not to drink if they have to drive, and that drinking makes social situations easier so it might be hard to stop. Here the notion of intent to protect children, the costs as well as benefits of alcohol, and the possibility of more reciprocity in problem solving are apparent.

The authors hold that more mature functioning depends upon adolescents' ability to allow aspects of others' perspectives, even if these perspectives complicate the issue, into the thinking process. In other words, both the advantages and meaning of risk must be weighed simultaneously against the possibility of harm to oneself and to important relationships. This presents a difficult cognitive challenge for adolescents who, when confronted with such dilemmas, begin to wade into the muddy waters of ill-defined problems (see Chapter 11). Recall that formal operational skills, which are marked by increased capacity to reason about abstract ideas simultaneously and to engage in introspection, are still developing throughout the adolescent period. In general, the younger the adolescent, the less well-developed are these skills.

Interventions that provide factual information in isolation address only one part of the equation. Interventions that focus on changing behaviors may not work either if the adolescent does not "see" the point of changing behavior and thus become motivated to do so. Information and risk management skills need to be tied to personally meaningful real-world social contexts where costs and benefits of risk taking are acknowledged to coexist.

What are some specific ways to help adolescents become more reflective about their behaviors in the peer arena? Using the interviewing methods employed in this research as a springboard, therapists can start a dialogue with adolescent clients that focuses on coordinating their subjective points of view with the realities of alcohol (or other risks) and the wishes of adults who are important to them. The kinds of questions included in the interviews focus on perspective-taking deficits and are intended to move the adolescent toward more differentiated perspectives (see Table 10.1).

Counselors might apply these questions to the individual's actual risky behavior or employ videotaped or narrative vignettes as the basis for discussion. In addition to the questions in the table, other probes can help clinicians assess the maturity of adolescents' differentiation of feelings: "If you feel happy about drinking with your friends but you don't like it when your parents get angry about it, how do you feel overall? Can

TABLE 10.1   The Risky Business Interview: Psychosocial Components, Issues, and Key Questions

Psychosocial Components	Issues	Key Questions
Understanding of the risk (here "drinking")	Initial (past) experiment	Why do you think someone your age starts to drink beer or other alcoholic drinks?
	Current purposes	Why do people your age like to drink these days?
	Further consequences	What can happen to people your age if they continue to drink? Is it more difficult for some people to stop drinking than others? Why?
Interpersonal strategies (from hypothetical dilemmas with parents[a] and peers[b])	Definition of the problem	What is the problem in this dilemma?
	Alternative strategies	What are some ways they can solve these problems?
	Best strategy	What is the best way to solve this problem?
	Evaluation	How would they know the problem is solved?
Personal meaning of the risk	Past motivation for experimenting	When you first began drinking, why did you decide to give it a try?
	Present attitude	What are the reasons for your drinking *now*?
	Further orientation	Do you think at some time you might decide to change your drinking habit? If you decided to stop drinking, do you think you could stick to that decision if you wanted to? How do you know?

[a]Gunnar/Gudrun goes to a party one weekend evening and comes home late and drunk. His/her dad is waiting for him/her when he/she comes home and is very angry. He tells Gunnar/Gudrun that he/she is to be grounded for a month. Gunnar/Gudrun feels this is too severe a penalty and that he/she is old enough to decide for himself/herself whether he/she drinks or not. How can Gunnar/Gudrun deal with his/her father?
[b]See text for the dilemma between Jon and Dori.

Source: Selman, R. L. & Adalbjarnardottir, S. (2000). A developmental method to analyze the personal meaning adolescents make of risk and relationship: The case of "drinking." *Applied Developmental Science, 4(1)*, 47–65. Copyright 2000 by Lawrence Erlbaum, Inc.

you have mixed feelings? How can feelings be mixed?" Others assess levels of self-reflection: "Can a person fool himself into thinking that he doesn't care about getting into trouble?" and "Is there a difference between fooling yourself and fooling another person? What is it?" (Questions are from Selman, 1979).

The goal is to introduce some dissonance into the discussion to promote reflection and increase motivation to consider alternative ways of handling risks. The ultimate goal is more careful decision making. In practice, this approach blends developmental knowledge with an approach similar to motivational interviewing (Miller & Rollnick, 1991). Considering that many adolescents would be appropriately classified in the precontemplative stage (Prochaska & DiClemente, 1982) with regard to the risks they take, introducing some doubt in the context of a warm and supportive counseling relationship might help them gain new perspective and assist them in managing the inevitable risks of adolescence.

The Power of Parents and Peers

In general, advocating for authoritative parenting and providing the information and support parents need to get the job done can have wonderfully beneficial effects on adolescents.

Steinberg (1996) asserts that the high rates of parental disengagement in the United States amount to a public health problem that must be remedied by means of parent-education programs in communities and schools and through public-service programming. Encouragement and support should be given to adults who are trying to maintain connections with their adolescents, especially for teenagers at risk.

Steinberg (1994) found that parents of adolescents go through their own perilous transition and that 40% of them experience strong feelings of powerlessness, rejection, and personal regrets when their children become adolescents. Whereas sharing stories of problem behaviors is rather common among parents of younger children, parents of adolescents are often uncomfortable doing so (Sandmaier, 1996). Therefore, in addition to reconnecting adolescents to their families, mental health specialists need to reconnect adults to each other. Parent support or discussion groups, "safe-house" programs, and more informal "phone-tree" arrangements allow parents to communicate with each other. Taffel (1996) suggests that groups of parents develop common guidelines for their adolescents' social lives, related to concerns such as curfews, parties, and supervisory responsibility.

Ways to encourage parental involvement in education should also be strongly promoted. Many parents who have had unpleasant school experiences themselves resist dealing with school personnel despite their concern for their children. Sometimes schools present formidable obstacles, either real or perceived, to parents who wish to obtain help or information. Mental health practitioners can facilitate communication by advocating for parents, by explaining policy and procedures, and by working to develop good relationships with school personnel. Steinberg (1996) found that the most effective parental involvement strategy was to "work the system" on behalf of the student (for example, contacting the school when there is a problem, meeting with teachers or counselors, etc.). When school personnel encourage and facilitate this kind of participation instead of viewing it as an intrusion, it can be very helpful to the adolescents they serve. For difficult teens who are failing in school, coordinating both systems (home and school) creates a powerfully watchful force that signals caring and demandingness. Some schools have created confidential hotlines to allow students to get their friends help if needed. Other implications drawn from the literature include supporting a wide variety of extracurricular activities that provide positive outlets for teens and limiting the number of hours spent in paid employment.

Efforts to change peer networks directly appear less realistic. Peer groups by their very nature represent adolescent attempts to establish independent social networks and to provide a supportive structure that is an alternative to parent and family (Eckert, 1989). Peer society is influenced by so many factors (individual personalities, availability of types, social context, ethnicity, media, and so forth) that single proximal interventions are likely to be difficult. Consequently, calls for changes in the broader societal context and in the more immediate family and school environment are thought to be the best way to exert influence on the chemistry of the peer groups formed. For example, in the matter of achievement, Steinberg (1996) strongly advocates refocusing the American discussion away from the problems of schools to the problem of changing adolescents' and parents' minds (or the collective culture's mind) about what is really important—schooling—and about what is less important: socializing, organized sports, paid employment, and so on.

This is not to suggest that counselors should necessarily leave peer groups alone. Indeed, the school counselor is in a unique position to provide information and a forum for discussion about important topics through developmental guidance programs. Other strategies, such as peer mediation and peer counseling, are useful approaches for teens because they capitalize on the adolescent's dependence upon peers.

Some research indicates that teens of all ethnic groups prefer not to seek help about personal problems from school professionals such as teachers and counselors but prefer to turn to their peers for advice about personal, educational and vocational concerns (Branwhite, 2000; Mau, 1995). As a way to engage adolescents, Taffel (1996) suggests including peers in the guidance process. In counseling sessions, constructing a genogram of the "second family," or the teen's peer group, can be a technique that allows the therapist to gain some entry into this system. Sometimes, he suggests, peers can be brought into the therapy process.

Pipher (1996), a family therapist who has written about the problems today's adolescents face, has taken therapists to task about the myopic focus of many traditional therapeutic practices. She notes that counseling theories, like the great therapists who developed them, are embedded in historical time and place. Ideas such as intrapsychic causes of distress and even the "dysfunctional family," if emphasized in counseling and diagnosis to the exclusion of culture, history, economics, and politics, ignore critical dimensions affecting adolescents and do a disservice to their already stressed families. She has argued that communities as well as families raise the nation's children and that therapists can do more harm than good by misdiagnosing problems and giving simplistic answers to complicated situations without according due consideration to the effects of the culture. She pointedly notes:

> In the past when therapists saw troubled teenagers, they could generally assume that the parents had problems. That's because most teenagers were fine. Troubled teens were an exception and required some explaining. Today most teenagers are not fine. At one time we helped kids differentiate from enmeshed families. Now we need to help families differentiate from the culture. (p. 34)

Pipher (1996) advocates for "protecting" family time by deliberately limiting the encroachment of work and media entertainment and creating family rituals and celebrations to strengthen positive connections. Hewlett and West (1998) have called for a national initiative similar to the American Association of Retired Persons (AARP), called a Parents' Bill of Rights, which would guarantee family-friendly policies such as parenting leave, economic security, help with housing, responsible media, year-round educational programs, and quality schools, to name a few.

It Takes a Village

Because successful negotiation of the adolescent period depends upon the interaction of a number of variables—biology or genetics, social environment, perceptions, personality and behavior, individual counseling may only temporarily address problems unless the more systemic roots of the difficulties are also addressed (Cairns & Cairns, 1994). The fact that so many influential systems touch on adolescents' lives and that some systems, such as the peer network, can be resistant to adult intrusion makes it critical to use a wide-angle lens when evaluating and treating teenagers. Figure 10.3 illustrates the transactional nature of the multiple systems that affect development.

One way to put the pieces together comes from the work of prevention researchers who have stressed the need to view successful adolescent development as a function of interrelated risk and protective factors (Jessor, 1993). This two-pronged

FIGURE 10.3

Illustration of Embedded Systems at Multiple Levels. Dashed Lines Represent Interactions Between Systems or Individuals Within Different Systems.

From Masten, A. S. Commentary: Developmental Psychopathology as a Unifying Context for Mental Health and Education Models, Research, and Practice in Schools. Copyright 2003 by the National Association of School Psychologists, Bethesda, MD. Reprinted with permission of the publisher.

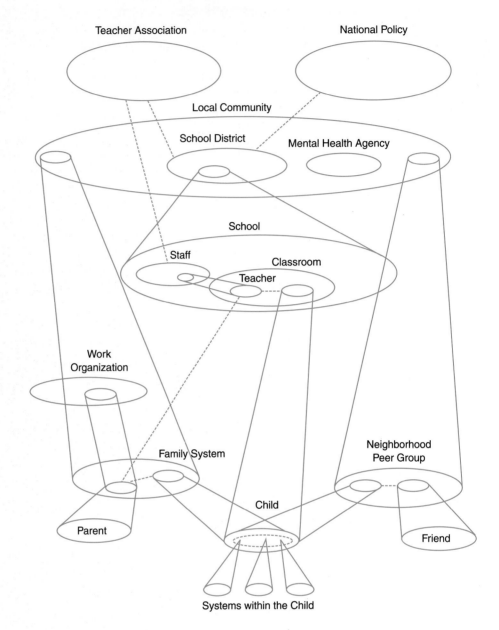

approach, building resilience while addressing risk, is central to the traditions of counseling (Van Hesteren & Ivey, 1990). In the past, many problem-reduction interventions (e.g., for drinking, drug use, smoking, etc.) were fear-based attempts to reduce these behaviors by providing information alone. Blum (2003) describes several characteristics of ineffective risk-reduction interventions. They include interventions that use scare tactics, are of short-term duration, that only provide factual information, that primarily target self-esteem, and that segregate at-risk students for special treatment. Some implications we can draw from these findings include the ineffectiveness of "talking at" adolescents, the futility of quick solutions, the importance of developmentally sensitive interventions, and the necessity of broad-based contextualized support.

Recently, we have witnessed an increased interest in supporting positive youth development. In general, these efforts recognize the importance of providing resources at all levels of the system. The Search Institute, for example, has identified useful lists of personal, family, and community assets that can serve as benchmarks for healthy adolescent development (Benson, 1997). Although positive youth development has been described in a variety of ways, some essential elements exist: the presence of caring adults and mentors on a regular basis, schools that build academic competence and offer vocational preparation, an atmosphere of hope, encouragement of positive values, and high but achievable expectations (Lerner, Fisher & Weinberg, 2000). Clearly, professionals and nonprofessionals alike need to join forces to create the kinds of communities that offer these opportunities for everyone.

The Midwestern Prevention Project (Pentz, Mihalic, & Grotpeter, 2002) is a good example of a comprehensive, theoretically driven program that was developed to reduce or prevent adolescent use of gateway drugs. The program introduces 5 components in sequence every 6 months to 1 year over a 5-year period. The first component is the school-based

TABLE 10.2 Risk Taking in Adolescence: Examples, Functions, Damaging and Healthy Practices

Examples of Antisocial or Problem Behaviors	Possible Functions of Behavior (i.e., Outcomes Teens May Be Seeking)	Developmental Task	Developmentally Damaging Practices	Developmentally Healthy Alternatives
Skipping school, disobeying teachers	Expression of frustration with inability to succeed in school setting	Competence	Large schools, high student to teacher ratios in classrooms, ability grouping	Provide individualized programs where youth with a wide range of skills can be successful
Engaging in pseudoadult behaviors such as drinking, drug use, and early sexual activity	Means of coping with anxiety, frustration, and fear of inadequacy—seeking to be recognized as competent, capable, respected through mimicry of pseudoadult peers	Transition to adulthood	Lack of connectedness with adults created by lack of parental presence at home, few opportunities to develop relationships with adults at school or in the community, little one-on-one time with adults	Teach alternative methods for coping with stress, presence of adult role models, opportunities to learn career skills, involvement in mentoring or apprenticeship programs
"Teenage behaviors" (e.g., outrageous clothing, music, use of profanity), violation of minor rules such as curfew, status offenses	Means of making a personal statement (how I'm different, important, angry, etc.) seeking to be recognized as an individual of worth, capable of making a unique contribution	Identity, autonomy, individuation	Targeting of teens as consumer group by media, lack of opportunities for teens to make a positive contribution to family and society	Allow teens to participate in rule making; allow teens to participate in decision making; increase the types of contributions teens can make to society; increase variety of socially sanctioned clubs at school
Joining a gang, involvement with delinquent peers	Means of meeting the need to belong (I want to be part of something)	Intimacy, relationship building	Lack of opportunities to meet and interact with prosocial peers, coercive family interactions	Teach relationship enhancement skills, conversations skills, empathy skills; provide alternative niches or ecologies with prosocial peers and adults
"Acting out" (e.g., causing trouble at school, getting into fights, making threats, theft, running away)	To be heard or understood; to bring attention to perceived inequity of treatment	Identity, competence, industry	Failure to listen to teens, not allowing teens to participate in rule and decision making, doing things "to" teens rather than "with" them	Provide strong adult role models who listen to teens; teach youth to identify and express anger and other emotions (rational self-talk); teach negotiation skills; include teens in decision making
Smoking, having sex, drinking, status offenses	Way of asserting/affirming the transition from childhood to adulthood—seeking to be recognized as a person with an opinion that counts; attempting to establish a role for oneself	Transition to adulthood	Double standard of behavior for adults and teens	Create more formalized markers to acknowledge transitions; recognize the cost to children/adolescents when adults fail to "walk the way they talk"
Speeding, riding on the hoods of cars, "sensation seeking" (Zuckerman, 1979)	Way to avoid boredom and seek excitement—seeking a way to not feel put down, ignored or unimportant	Competence	Few community centers, clubs, or other environments where adult-monitored youth activities are provided	Develop exciting, adult-monitored activities for adolescents (e.g., midnight basketball)
Playing "chicken" with yourself and others, shoplifting, vandalism	Means of testing personal limits and status—seeking competence, finding something to be "in charge of"	Identity	Few opportunities for teens to succeed and to learn adult skills (e.g., career skills, communication skills) or to make a contribution to society	Create environments where adolescents can gain confidence and excel in something; broaden the scope of what defines success for adolescents beyond academics and sports
Violent behavior, law violations, conduct disorder	Expression of opposition to or outrage at adult authority—seeking control and power over disruptive/unsafe environment	Trust vs. mistrust, safety needs	Failure to protect children from poverty, child abuse, neglect, mistreatment, physiological disadvantages	Early childhood intervention has been most successful here; prognosis in adolescence is poor

Source: Siegel, A. W., and Scovill, L. C. (2000). Problem behavior: The double symptom of adolescence. *Development and Psychopathology, 12,* 787–788. Reprinted with the permission of Cambridge University Press.

program, begun during the transition to high school (either Grades 6 or 7). School interventions include interactive classroom lessons that provide drug resistance training, initiation of peer counseling, and schoolwide efforts to make nonuse of drugs the social norm. During the 2nd year, parents are included in the program through parent education groups and opportunities for participation in leadership and mentoring activities. Community, religious, and political leaders are brought on board in years 3 through 5 to develop resources, plan, and implement initiatives that support adolescent health in the community as a whole. Mass media outlets (print, TV, and radio) are used throughout the entire 5-year period to introduce the program, promote the prevention message, and spotlight program successes. Overall, follow-up studies show significant reductions in use of cigarettes, marijuana, and, to a lesser extent, alcohol for those involved in the project (Pentz et al., 2002). Multisystemic Therapy (MST; Henggeler et al., 1998) is another effective prevention program that targets multiple levels of the system (family, peers, schools, and neighborhoods) to reduce antisocial behavior in at-risk populations.

To transform the social world of adolescents into a healthier place will take team effort. Neither families nor schools, two of our major socializing institutions, can do this alone. A few general guidelines from Siegel and Scovill (2000) summarize and reemphasize important points.

1. Take the social context seriously. Don't rely on intrapsychic interpretations alone when identifying or assessing problems. Adolescents do not engineer all their problems, despite how appealing that argument might appear.

2. Consider adolescent problem behavior as a means to an end. Table 10.2 provides some suggestions to help clinicians understand the functions that problem behaviors serve.

3. Construct healthy and attractive alternatives to help adolescents meet their developmental needs, including social as well as educational alternatives. Not all adolescents fit into the traditional academic mold for success, yet they want success and they are worthy of it.

SUMMARY

Frameworklessness and Autonomy: Seltzer's Model of Adolescent Social Identity

1. The profound physical, cognitive, and social changes that accompany entry into adolescence create a state of instability and anxiety Seltzer called frameworklessness. Establishing adult independence requires separating from caregivers on a psychological level, with the concept of the parent becoming more peripheral to the adolescent's self-system, accompanied by a loss in feelings of security. Simultaneously, teens increase their affiliation with and dependency on peers, others who share their state of frameworklessness.

2. Peers are a source of support, of social comparison, and of attribute substitution or imitation and identification. Adolescents borrow from their peers' ways of behaving and thinking, providing some relief from the anxiety of being without a stable sense of self. Thus, peers provide an arena for identity formation.

The Structure of the Peer Network

3. Most adolescents have one or two best friends, who are part of a clique of individuals who tend to do things together. Larger groups composed of many cliques comprise crowds, whose members may not be friends but share interests, attitudes, behaviors, and appearance.

4. Most American high schools are characterized by fairly similar crowd structures, consisting of populars and jocks, some alienated groups such as druggies, an average crowd, and an academically high-achieving group. Crowd membership is likely to be determined by the child's personality and interests entering adolescence, the types of crowds available, and parents' attempts to manage peer relationships.

5. Crowds influence their members, but they are also freely selected by their members, who choose to participate in shared norms, roles, and expectations.

The Role of Parents

6. Parents have often been advised to let go—that conflicts with adolescents and adolescent rebellion is normal and not something to worry about. But more recent research has focused on whether certain kinds of parenting at adolescence may be more predictive of positive outcomes and have found that both warmth (responsiveness) and control (demandingness, close monitoring) are as important with adolescents as they are with younger children. This kind of authoritative parenting is associated with, among other things, higher achievement, self-confidence, self-esteem, social adjustment, and self-control.

7. But crowd affiliations are also powerful in adolescence and can mitigate parent influences. The complex relationships among peers and parenting are evident across

different ethnic groups and social classes. For example, Asian American teens tend to belong to ethnically defined crowds that usually value high achievement. Even if parents are not involved in their children's schooling, these teens are likely to be high achievers because of their crowd affiliation. Conversely, some Black teens are also members of ethnically defined crowds, and these crowds sometimes disparage school achievement as trying to act White. Even though parents are often quite supportive of school achievement, Black teens may sacrifice high grades, or hide them, to be true to their crowd.

The Role of School

8. Declines in academic orientation and motivation are noted in early adolescence and may be associated with shifting school structures and processes as children enter middle school or junior high school. Larger classes and schools, whole-group lecture, and heavy emphasis on competition are among these practices. Timing of the shift from elementary to secondary schools is also important: Later shifts are less stressful than earlier ones. Also, parental involvement declines sharply at secondary school levels, despite evidence that it remains just as important for teens' achievement as for younger children's.

Leisure and Work

9. When teens are involved in school- or community-sponsored out-of-school activities, they tend to be higher achievers and to have other desirable qualities. Many teens work for pay, but spending substantial hours working is associated with lower school achievement, less involvement in school activities, more drug and alcohol use, and more delinquency.

Media and the Consumer Culture

10. Adolescents, their peers, families, and schools are affected by the larger culture, and vice versa. Present culture may not be very "adolescent friendly" due to loss of community and a focus on individualism and material success. Negative media forces seem to shape attitudes and beliefs. Teens are increasingly exposed to violence, sex, and commercial messages through the media, affecting what they view as normative and acceptable behavior. Thus, media messages often compete with other, more traditional messages from families and schools, and research demonstrates that media messages do influence teens' beliefs and behaviors.

Risky Behavior and Social Deviance

11. Risky behavior increases sharply during adolescence, peaking at about age 17, and rates of risky behavior have increased over the last one or two decades. Life-course-persistent antisocial behavior begins in childhood and continues throughout life, whereas adolescent-limited antisocial behavior develops in adolescence and usually ends shortly thereafter. Risky behavior, ranging from mild to severe, may be characteristic of adolescents for several reasons: the need for sensation seeking; egocentric beliefs about one's own invulnerability; modeling of deviant behavior by peers; and the exacerbation of illusions of invulnerability by the collective egocentrism of groups of peers.

12. Risky behavior may also provide some advantages in the teen years, making it, in some cases, adaptive. It can sometimes serve as an indicator of individuation and self-determination and as a source of peer acceptance. Thus, risk taking has both positive and negative aspects. It may be inevitable in cultures with "broad" socialization practices, which encourage high levels of individual freedom.

13. Although the United States provides high levels of freedom to adolescents, it may not provide adequate supports to ensure that risk taking is within reasonable limits. In the 1920s, concerns about adolescent risk taking fostered a sense of community responsibility to provide adequate supervision and healthy outlets for young people, and a number of youth-oriented institutions sprang up offering free services to teens. Today such community support systems are often in short supply, and costly when they are available. The current approach seems to be based on a reconceptualization of the issue. Risky behavior is seen as a problem of the individual rather than a problem of society as it was seen in the 1920s.

CASE STUDY

Mark Spencer is a White 16-year-old sophomore at a suburban public school. He lives with his mother, father, and older brother in a middle-class community. Mark has attended the local public schools since kindergarten, and until 8th grade he was an above-average student who frequently made honor roll. Mark's father Doug commutes to his job at an insurance company and in recent years has increased his hours at the office as his company has downsized and shifted responsibilities to remaining employees. His mother Joanne works as a secretary at a local real estate agency. Mark's brother Dave is a senior who is also an above-average student and who has been very active in intermural sports, especially soccer and baseball.

During middle school, Mark had a strong interest in scouting and was particularly involved in camping and developing survival skills. Several of Mark's friends in the scout troop left scouting in the 7th grade and began spending more time hanging out with girlfriends and playing sports. Mark continued scouting until 8th grade, but teasing from his friends became unbearable, and he finally gave up. Mark was shy with girls and not particularly interested in sports, so he was left with little in common with his middle school friends. At the same time, his grades began to slip.

When Mark's parents expressed concern about his poor grades, he told them that his teachers were jerks and his classes were boring. Although Doug and Joanne tried to encourage him to study more and to continue scouting or to try sports, Mark would generally react angrily, and his parents would back off to not upset him further. By 9th grade he was spending more and more time alone, playing video games and watching television in his room. When Mark turned 16, he begged for a car, and his parents agreed. Because they were so busy, Doug and Joanne felt it would be helpful to give Mark more independence, and they hoped it would increase his social acceptance. Mark was one of the first students in the sophomore class to turn 16, and he found that his old friends' interest in him was piqued when he began driving his new car to school.

Mark began to hang out with his old friends, and began smoking, drinking, and experimenting with drugs. His grades slipped further, although with almost no effort he was able to maintain a C average. Once again his parents became concerned about his grades, particularly because college loomed. They even threatened to remove the television from his room, but, as usual, they backed down when confronted by his anger. Doug and Joanne were also loath to rock the boat when Mark finally seemed to be enjoying his social life. He was no longer moping around the house, watching TV, and worrying his parents.

When Mark asked to be allowed to drive his friends to a concert in a nearby city, with plans to spend the weekend at the home of a friend's uncle, his parents disagreed about how to handle his request. Joanne was afraid of giving him so much freedom and worried about the safety of the group. Doug, remembering how restrictive his own parents were, argued that "you're only young once" and that "you have to hope that what you've taught them up to now will stick, because that's all you can do. At 16, kids are really on their own."

The weekend trip was a disaster. After the concert, the group partied at the uncle's home, without adult supervision. Neighbors called the police about the noise. Parents were notified after the police found evidence of underage drinking. Mark persuaded his parents that he did not know the uncle would be away and that he had no control over his friends' drinking. Doug and Joanne gave Mark the benefit of the doubt, but a month later, Joanne found a bottle of vodka hidden in Mark's room. Both parents realized that they needed to seek help.

Discussion Questions

1. Consider the developmental path that Mark has followed. Describe the elements that have been influential in shaping this adolescent's experience.
2. Describe and comment on the parenting style used by Doug and Joanne. Evaluate the parents' approach to Mark throughout his early adolescence and suggest ways they might have responded differently.
3. What role could the school have played in modifying the course of Mark's development?
4. What specific suggestions for treatment might you make for Mark and his family?

JOURNAL QUESTIONS

1. Compare and contrast the social world of adolescents today with that of your own adolescence. What similarities and differences do you find?
2. Think of a middle school, junior high school, or high school with which you are familiar. If you could change the school (academically, structurally, or otherwise), what changes would you make, and why?
3. Identify one action step that you could take to improve the lives of adolescents with whom you are in contact.

KEY TERMS

frameworklessness	dismissive parenting	life-course-persistent antisocial pattern	collective egocentrism
attribute substitution	acceptance factor	adolescence-limited antisocial pattern	maturity gap
prudential consequences	democracy factor		broad socialization
parental monitoring	risky behaviors	sensation seeking	narrow socialization
indulgent parenting	binge drinking		

11

Physical and Cognitive Development in Young Adulthood

Javier, a 19-year-old, is a 2nd-year college student. He enjoys many privileges that could be construed as "adult." He drives a car, votes in elections, and owns a credit card. He shares an apartment near his college campus with two other undergraduates. He drinks alcohol with his friends at parties (albeit illegally) and has regular sexual relations with his girlfriend of 10 months. The couple split up once and subsequently reunited. During the separation, Javier dated another young woman. At this point, Javier and his girlfriend have no plans to marry. He wanted to get a job immediately after high school, but job opportunities in the trade he aspired to went to more experienced workers. He decided to give higher education a try. Javier has little idea of what his ultimate career path will be. Javier's father, who is divorced from Javier's mother, pays for his tuition and housing costs. He has taken out loans to help finance his son's education. Javier's mother provides him with an allowance for food. He works part time for low wages at a clothing store in a local mall, which helps him pay for clothes and entertainment. Javier is very responsible at work, but he is an unenthusiastic college student. His study habits lean toward procrastinating and then trying to make up for lost time by staying up all night to finish assignments by their deadlines. When Javier broke his wrist playing sports, his mother had to take a few days off from her job to accompany him to doctor's visits. Her health insurance covered most of the bills. Yet, despite their financial support, Javier's parents have no legal right to see Javier's college grades.

Is Javier an adult? Scholars are likely to disagree about the answer to this question. Most would agree that the onset of adolescence is marked by the changes of puberty. But there are no easily observed physical changes that signal entry into adulthood. Instead, adulthood is a social construction. One or more culturally determined criteria usually must be met before one's maturity is established (Hogan & Astone, 1986), and the criteria vary depending on the observer and the culture.

In the past, sociologists have emphasized the achievement and timing of marker events as criteria for adulthood. These have included completing formal education, entering the adult workforce, leaving the family home, getting married, and becoming parents. Around the middle of the last century, a large proportion of the American population achieved these marker events between the ages of 18 and 24 (Rindfuss, 1991). However, if we evaluate our hypothetical student, Javier, according to these traditional marker events, he would not be an adult despite being in the right age range.

From a sociological perspective, it seems to take longer to grow up today than it did at earlier points in history for many reasons. Some of these include the demand for a highly educated workforce and the increased cost of this education (Jacobs & Stoner-Eby, 1998), the difficulties inherent in earning enough to support children and in achieving stable employment (Halperin, 1998b), and the frequency of early, nonmarital sexual activity and the availability of contraception (Warner et al., 1998). All have had profound effects on the timing of life events. On one hand then, attainment of some traditional measures of adulthood has been considerably delayed. For example, the median age for marriage in 1950 was about 20 for women and 23 for men. By

1993, the median age for marriage had risen to about 25 for women and 27 for men (Arnett & Taber, 1994). On the other hand, other indicators of adulthood, such as the onset of sexual activity, occur much earlier than they did in the past.

Such shifts in the timing of marker events appear to have delayed the onset of adulthood, especially in Western societies, where these shifts have most often occurred. However, even in more traditional, nonindustrialized cultures, the transition to adulthood can be a slow process. For example, after completing the puberty rites that induct boys into the adult ranks of some societies, young males in about 25% of cultures pass through a period of **youth** (Schlegel & Barry, 1991). In these societies, males are seen as needing a period of time to prepare for marriage. Serving as warriors during the transition period, for example, allows boys an opportunity to develop skills and to accumulate the material goods needed to afford a family. Girls enjoy a similar period of youth in 20% of cultures. Thus, even in many non-Western societies, the movement to full adult status takes time.

In cultures such as that of the United States, the pathways to adulthood are remarkable in their variability, so that specifying when adulthood has been achieved is difficult. Recently, Arnett (1997, 2000, 2002; Arnett & Taber, 1994) explored a new way of conceptualizing adulthood. In addition to examining the timing of marker events, he considered individuals' own conceptions about what makes them adults. The reasoning goes like this: If one's own judgment of adult status were based on criteria other than marker events, we might find more consistency in criteria across cultures or even within the same culture over a certain period. Arnett (2000) asked young people in the United States to rate the importance of criteria in several areas (such as cognitive, behavioral, emotional, biological, and legal criteria, role transitions, and responsibilities) as definitions of adult status. He also asked participants whether they felt they had reached adulthood. A majority of respondents in their late teens and early twenties answered both "yes and no." Perhaps Javier would say something similar. As you can see in Figure 11.1, the proportion of young people in Arnett's study who judged themselves to be adults gradually increased with age, with a clear majority of participants in their late 20s and early 30s doing so.

Can this delay in identifying oneself as an adult be attributed to the timing of role transitions? Apparently not. Chronological age and role transitions such as marriage and parenthood, on their own, were not considered significant markers. Arnett's respondents indicated that the

In past decades, adult status was conferred through the achievement of marker events, such as marriage and parenthood.

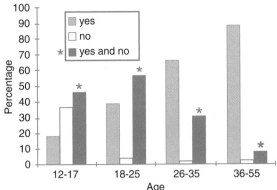

FIGURE 11.1

"Do You Feel That You Have Reached Adulthood?"

Source: Arnett, J. (2000). Emerging adulthood: A theory of development from the late teens through the twenties. *American Psychologist, 55,* 472. Copyright © 2000 by the American Psychological Association. Reprinted with permission.

two most important qualifications for adulthood are first, accepting responsibility for the consequences of one's actions and second, making independent decisions. Becoming financially independent, a traditional marker event, was third. Consequently, the subjective sense of being an adult may be more important than accomplishment and timing of discrete tasks. There is consensus among many researchers that a broad psychological shift toward increasing independence and autonomy characterizes the subjective experience of what it means to be an adult, at least for members of the American majority culture (Greene & Wheatley, 1992; Scheer, Unger, & Brown, 1994). Moreover, achieving a sense of autonomy is among the identity-related tasks described in Chapter 9. Because the shift to feeling autonomous is a lengthy process for many, Arnett (2000) advocates that the time period roughly between ages 18 and 25 be considered a distinct stage of life called emerging adulthood.

We should note that emerging adulthood is made possible by the kind of economic development that characterizes industrialized, Western cultures. If the labor of young people is not urgently needed for the economic well-being of their families, and if many occupations require extended years of education, then work is postponed, marriage and childbearing are likely to be delayed, and self-exploration can continue. Recently, Arnett (2002) has argued that increasing globalization is spreading the experience of this new stage from Western societies to other parts of the world. *Globalization* is "a process by which cultures influence one another and become more alike through trade, immigration, and the exchange of information and ideas" (p. 774), a process that has shifted into high gear with advances in telecommunications and transportation. In developing countries, young people increasingly move from rural communities to urban centers as they pursue expanding economic opportunities. More occupational and lifestyle options are available, and self-development tends to continue well past the teen years. "For young people in developing countries, emerging adulthood exists only for the wealthier segment of society . . . however, as globalization proceeds . . . the emerging adulthood now normative in the middle class is likely to increase as the middle class expands" (p. 781).

Whereas Arnett (2000) found that American respondents to his questionnaire emphasized individualistic criteria in defining adulthood, we should note that they also acknowledged the importance of emotional support. As you will see in the next chapter, strong relationships with others are important in and of themselves and can provide a bulwark for the development of personal autonomy. Encouragement and tolerance for independent action and belief, however, may continue to be greater for young people in the American majority culture than for those in non-Western societies, such as China (Yang, 1988), or in some diverse communities in the United States. Even so, a study of African Americans found that males' perceptions of adulthood resonated with findings from White majority samples. Hunter and Davis (1992) report that Black males defined manhood individualistically, characterized by personal responsibility and self-determination, so the cultural differences were not great. Furstenburg (2000) calls for more research on young people that crosses lines of gender, ethnicity, and social class. Citing the hazards of segregating our research samples into different categories, he concludes that we are left with the impression that "the issues, practices, and identities of youth in different social locations are highly dissimilar, a proposition that calls for further investigation" (p. 900). Much more research is needed to understand both the universals and uniqueness of the transition to young adulthood.

In this and the next chapter we will examine some of the key characteristics of life after adolescence, primarily for young people in the United States. We will refer to the period from about 18 to 30 as young adulthood, although we acknowledge Arnett's (2000) argument that many 18- to 25-year-olds are better described as "emerging adults." The early years of young adulthood are often an extended period of transition involving exploration of potential adult identities.

In this chapter, we begin by examining the physical characteristics of young adults and then move on to consider the cognitive changes that are likely in this period of life. In Chapter 12, we will explore the complexities of forming intimate, enduring adult attachments, maintaining or revamping family relationships, and making vocational commitments. That is, we will look at some of the myriad processes involved in taking one's place as a contributing member of an adult community.

PHYSICAL DEVELOPMENT IN YOUNG ADULTHOOD

Reaching Peak Physical Status

By age 18 to 20, most people have reached their full physical growth. Sometime between 18 and 30, all our biological systems reach peak potential. For example, we can see, hear, taste, and smell as well as we ever will; our skin is as firm and resilient as it can be; the potential strength of muscle and bone is as great as we will ever experience; and our immune systems provide us with the most effective protection we will ever have from diseases ranging from the common cold to cancer. Not all physical capacities reach their peak simultaneously. Visual acuity, for example, reaches a maximum level at about age 20, with little decline for most people until about age 40. But auditory acuity appears to peak before age 20 and may show some declines soon after (Saxon & Etten, 1987; Whitbourne, 1996).

There are certainly individual differences among us in the achievement of peak physical status—for example, some people reach their full height by age 15, whereas others may not finish growing until age 18 or 20. There are also substantial differences among different physical skills in the timing of peak performance. Schulz and Curnow (1988) examined athletic performance records for "superathletes" in a wide variety of sports. On one hand, they found that maximal performance for most sports is reached within the young adult period; on the other hand, they found that the average age of greatest skill (e.g., winning an Olympic gold medal in track or achieving a Number 1 world ranking in tennis) is different from one sport to another, and sometimes depends on which particular skill is examined within a given sport. For example, the average age at which Olympic swimmers win gold medals is 19; professional golfers typically do not achieve a Number 1 ranking until they are moving out of the young adult period, at about age 34. For a professional baseball player, the average age for "most stolen bases" is 23, but the mean age for "peak batting average" is 28 and for "hitting the most doubles" is 32! (See Table 11.1.)

The differences in age of peak performance suggest that the relative importance of practice, training, knowledge, experience, and biological capacity varies from one skill to another. Skills that are based on muscle strength, flexibility, and speed of movement and response tend to peak early. Abilities that are heavily dependent on control, arm–hand steadiness, precision, and stamina tend to peak later. Overall, the greater the importance of cognitive factors in performance, factors such as strategy knowledge and use, the later a skill will top out (Schulz & Curnow, 1988).

An interesting finding from the research on superathletes is that physical development progresses at different rates for the two sexes. Men reach their peak of performance in many skills approximately 1 year later than women do (see Table 11.1). No simple explanation is available for the gender differences, but in some instances they appear to be based on earlier skeletal–muscular maturation in women. In other cases, they may depend on the fact that the smaller, more streamlined bodies of young adolescent females confer some speed advantages, as in long-distance swimming.

Superathletes are those whose performance of a skill seems to match their full potential. Most of the rest of us are not concerned about achieving maximal skill, but we usually are motivated to maintain our physical capacities at high levels—including not only performance skills, but also sensory abilities, good health, and youthful appearance—during and beyond the early adult

TABLE 11.1	Age of Peak Performance for Some Athletic Skills	
Age	**Men**	**Women**
17		swimming
18		
19	swimming	
20		
21		
22		running short distance
23	running short distance	jumping
24	jumping	running medium distance
	running medium distance	tennis
	tennis	
25		
26		
27	running long distance	running long distance
28	baseball	
29		
30		
31	golf	golf
32		
33		
34		

Source: Schulz, R., & Curnow, C. (1988). Peak performance and age among superathletes: Track and field, swimming, baseball, tennis, and golf. *Journal of Gerontology: Psychological Sciences, 43*, p. 119. Copyright © The Gerontological Society of America. Reproduced by permission of the publisher.

period. Clearly, biology plays a role here. For example, regardless of activity level, muscular strength begins to decline somewhat by about age 30. But research supports the importance of lifestyle in this process. There are good habits that help maintain peak or near-peak functioning and appearance, and there are bad habits that can erode functioning (e.g., see Whitbourne, 1996). For example, regular exercise can help both younger and older adults maintain muscle and bone strength and keeps the cardiovascular and respiratory systems functioning well. Smoking, poor diet, and a sedentary lifestyle accelerate loss of peak cardiovascular and respiratory functioning and loss of muscle and bone. Smoking or any excessive drug or alcohol use can diminish functioning in a variety of physiological systems. For example, smoking contributes to more rapid wrinkling of the skin, and alcohol causes damage to the nervous system, the liver, and the urinary tract.

"Eating right" is part of a healthy lifestyle. It means having regularly spaced meals (including breakfast) that are low in fat and that sample a range of food groups, allowing a proper balance of nutrients. Failure to eat right contributes to obesity, to depressed mood, and to many aspects of physical decline. Longitudinal studies that have followed participants for 40 to 50 years have made clear that people who fail to follow healthy lifestyles in their young adult years suffer from poorer health later and that they are less satisfied with their lives in late adulthood when compared to people who do adopt healthy habits in young adulthood (e.g., Belloc & Breslow, 1972; Mussen, Honzik, & Eichorn, 1982).

None of this information is likely to be new to you. Many Americans, including young adults, are aware of the benefits of a healthy lifestyle and of the liabilities that bad living habits pose. Do they heed what they know? We learned in Chapter 10 that adolescents often act in reckless ways that compromise their health and wellness. Often young adults are not much better. Consider their alcohol use. As we have seen, nearly half of college students report that they drink heavily, often binge drinking (i.e., having at least five drinks at a time), and many indicate that their drinking has caused them problems, such as having unplanned or unprotected sex, getting hurt, or causing property damage (Johnson et al., 1994; Presley, Meilman, & Lyerla, 1995). Studies of adolescents and young adults indicate that the ongoing development of memory and learning abilities may be inhibited in binge drinkers (Ballie, 2001). In a longitudinal study of 33,000 people, Bachman (1997) found that problem drinking and drug use shifts during the young adult period. These problems begin to decline by the mid-20s. This study also indicates that being in college is a contributing factor to substance abuse in the United States, because college students drink more alcohol and smoke more marijuana than same-age peers who have never attended college. Attending college appears to have negative health effects in general. In another survey, over 20,000 college students completed a questionnaire in the fall of their 1st year of college and again 1 year later (Keup & Stolzenberg, 2004). Over the course of that year, they reported substantial declines in their emotional well-being, in their physical health, and in their health habits (e.g., reduced levels of exercise).

The unhealthy, underregulated lifestyles of many young adults are probably an outgrowth of multiple factors: poor application of problem-solving skills to practical problems (see the next section on cognitive development); a continuing sense of invulnerability that began in the adolescent years, which may be exacerbated by the fact that young adults can bounce back from physical stress far more readily than they will in later years; and the stresses of leaving home and facing the social and academic demands of college or the workplace—all steps that create new challenges to one's identity.

The Changing Brain

Study of developmental, age-related changes in the brain has been given a boost in recent years by the emergence of new technologies that allow the mapping of brain tissue and activity without the use of invasive procedures such as surgery. Much of the newer developmental work has focused on infancy and childhood (see Chapter 3), but some researchers have begun to examine systematic brain changes in adolescence and adulthood (e.g., Sowell et al., 2003; Thompson et al., 2000). As we saw in Chapter 9, it is now clear that major brain developments continue in adolescence and into early adulthood, to the surprise of many researchers. Measures of brain growth (utilizing magnetic resonance imaging, or MRI, procedures) indicate that a resurgent growth of synapses (synaptogenesis) occurs around puberty in some parts of the brain, followed by a long period of pruning, which continues into the adult years. Such changes may mean an expanded capacity for cognitive advancement.

Hudspeth and Pribram (1992) measured brain activity in children and adults up to 21 years old (using electroencephalography, or EEG, technologies), and they were astonished to find accelerated maturing of electrical activity in the frontal cortex of the 17- to 21-year-olds. Pribram (1997) argues that such acceleration could mean that early adulthood is especially important for the advanced development of frontal lobe functions, such as the ability to organize and reorganize attention, to plan, and to exercise control over one's behavior and emotions. He suggests that the typical timing of a college education may be ideally suited to what he assumes is the heightened flexibility and plasticity of the frontal cortex in young adulthood. A great deal more research needs to be done to determine the degree to which accelerated brain growth is related to the acquisition of cognitive skills and to evaluate the direction of effects. To what extent are observed brain changes the cause, as opposed to the outcome, of learning and learning opportunities? Clearly, new technologies are making this an exciting time in the study of adult brain development.

COGNITIVE DEVELOPMENT IN YOUNG ADULTHOOD

Each year, millions of young people participate in a rite of passage that marks their entry into young adulthood, the transition to college. Although not all adolescents go on to higher education, statistics indicate the numbers continue to increase. A century ago, fewer than 5% of young adults attended college in the United States; today, over 60% do (Arnett, 2000). So, at least for a sizable subset of American youth, the college experience represents a major influence on their cognitive and social development.

We can all picture the scenes: students piling out of cars driven by their anxious parents, descending upon dorms at the beginning of the semester, bustling across campus as fall's first colors begin to tint the foliage, eagerly anticipating the educational challenges that await them in their classes, gathered late into the night, talking and laughing with their newfound community of peers, relishing the heady freedom of young adulthood.

If these images remind you of far too many movies you have seen, it may be because they have been overly romanticized, due in equal parts to advertising and to nostalgia. Below the attractive exterior these images suggest lies a core set of developmental challenges that await individuals at this time of life. For the most part, these tasks involve continuing the hard work of carving out an identity, now all the more pressing because of one's status as an "adult." Moreover, most of the work takes place outside the protected environments of home and high school, even though continuing attachments to family remain important, as we shall see in the next chapter.

In this section, we will examine the changes in cognitive functioning that appear to characterize many young adults. Most of the research on young adult development has been done on college students and focuses on the kinds of change that one can expect to find among people with the opportunity to continue their education beyond high school, delaying many other adult responsibilities. As we noted earlier, over half of young Americans fall into this category. We know very little about cognitive change in those individuals who move directly from adolescence into the world of work. In the next chapter, we examine some of the special issues that may apply to this segment of our young people.

Unquestionably, early adulthood is a time of great learning. Whether in college or on the job, young people are faced with being the "novices," the "unknowledgeable," or the "inexperienced" when they enter the world of adults, and they spend a great deal of time building their knowledge base and becoming more expert in particular domains of knowledge, such as computer science or philosophy or mechanics. Not surprisingly, at the end of 4 years of college, students perform better on tests of general knowledge than they do as entering students, and the majority judge themselves to be "much stronger" than they were as 1st-year students in knowledge of a particular field (Astin, 1993). Comparable change measures are not available for young people who enter the workforce after high school, but it seems reasonable to assume that after 4 years on the job, some of which may be in job training programs, at least their knowledge of a particular field would have increased.

On the whole, longitudinal research on intellectual change across the life span indicates that many skills (such as spatial orientation abilities and inductive reasoning skills) improve throughout young adulthood, with measures of knowledge acquisition or breadth, such as understanding of verbal meanings, showing the most improvement in this time frame (e.g., Schaie, 1994). As long as opportunities to learn exist, the acquisition of knowledge seems to proceed rapidly during early adulthood. In later chapters, we will look in more detail at the typical progress of specific intellectual abilities throughout adulthood.

Logical Thinking: Is There Qualitative Change?

Is growth of knowledge and skill the only kind of cognitive change that we can expect to find in early adulthood? Or, as in childhood, does the nature of one's thinking and problem solving change as well? Piaget's analysis of structural shifts in children's logical thinking skills ends with the description of formal operational thought in the adolescent years (see Chapter 9). Formal operational thinking allows us to think logically about abstract contents. We can discover and understand the implications of relationships among pieces of information that may themselves be abstract relationships—such as proportions, for example. But many theorists have speculated that more advanced forms of rational thought are possible and emerge sometime in adulthood.

Several schemes, many borrowing heavily from Piaget's seminal work, attempt to describe the cognitive shifts that might occur in the adult years. Among these theories are those that propose a stage of adult cognitive thought that has variously been called postformal or fifth-stage thinking, implying an extension of Piaget's sequence of stages (e.g., Arlin, 1984; Basseches, 1984; Commons & Richards, 1984; Sinnott, 1984, 1998). Some of these theories actually elaborate a number of substages in the movement from formal operations to postformal thought. Two of these—Perry's (1970/1999) and Kitchener's (Kitchener & King, 1981; Kitchener, King, Wood, & Davison, 1989)—we describe in detail in later sections to illustrate the possible processes of change in young adulthood.

In all these theories, a fifth stage of logical thought is said to evolve as people begin to recognize that logical solutions to problems can come out differently depending on the perspective of the problem solver. In postformal thinking, the problem solver is said to coordinate contradictory formal operational approaches to the same problem. Each approach is logically consistent and leads to a necessary conclusion, and each can be valid. The postformal thinker both can understand the logic of each of the contradictory perspectives and can integrate the perspectives into a larger whole. Although she will likely make a commitment to one of these for her purposes, she recognizes that more than one can be valid. Thus, postformal thought incorporates formal thinking and goes beyond it. The assumption is that one could not be a postformal thinker without going through Piaget's four stages of thought development.

As you can see, postformal stage theorists have incorporated some features of the Piagetian framework, including stage sequences, into their theories. They assume that there are qualitatively different structural organizations of thought and its contents at each stage. They also have a constructivist focus. That is, they assume that what one knows and understands about the world is partly a function of the way one's thought is, or can be structured. Yet gradual reorganizations of thought are possible as one confronts and accommodates her thinking to stimuli that cannot be fully assimilated into her current ways of thinking.

Some theorists disagree with the concept of a fifth stage of cognitive development. They often argue that the formal operational system of thinking is powerful enough to address any kind of logical problem. They are more inclined to see qualitative differences in adult problem solving and logical thinking not so much as an indication of a stage beyond formal operations but as a sign that the kinds of problems adults must solve are different from those that children are usually trained and tested on. As a result, adults must adapt their existing problem-solving skills to the new kinds of problems they face in adulthood (e.g., Chandler & Boutilier, 1992; Labouvie-Vief, 1984; Schaie, 1977–1978). Part of what people may learn as they confront adult problems and responsibilities is the limits of their own problem-solving abilities. That is, they may grow in metacognitive understanding, recognizing that in some circumstances logical thinking will lead to a clear solution but that in other circumstances they must make decisions based in part on values, needs, and goals (e.g., Chandler, Boyes, & Ball, 1990; Kuhn et al., 1995; Moshman, 1998).

In sum, theorists disagree about whether adult problem solving represents a fifth stage in the development of logical thinking or is a reflection of the fact that life presents adults with new problems. In the latter view, adults do not achieve a new rational system but learn to recognize the limits of their existing problem-solving systems and to evolve new strategies for applying them. Despite some disagreements, nearly all theorists agree that problem solving takes on a different look and feel in adulthood. In the following sections, we will summarize a few theoretical descriptions of adult logical thinking, and we will examine some of the research demonstrating that indeed, something changes as people face life's grown-up challenges.

Schaie's View of Adults Adjusting to Environmental Pressures

Schaie's (1977–1978; Schaie & Willis, 2000) theory emphasizes the importance of new roles, needs, and responsibilities in determining adult intellectual functioning. Schaie does not argue for postformal thought but for shifts in cognitive functioning, or in the use of knowledge and skills, that are straightforward adaptations to the new demands that adults face at different times of life. According to Schaie, we can think of the child and adolescent years as a time when the individual is sheltered from much of life's responsibilities. Schaie calls this the acquisition stage of cognitive development, when youngsters can learn a skill or a body of knowledge regardless of whether it has any practical goal or social implications. Practical problems and goal setting are monitored by parents and others who take on the responsibility for making decisions that will affect the child's life course. The child has the luxury of learning for learning's sake or problem solving just to sharpen her logical thinking skills. Many of the problems she confronts in this phase are those with preestablished answers.

In young adulthood the protections of childhood rapidly recede and the individual is faced with taking responsibility for her own decisions. The problems she must solve—such as how to maintain good health, what career path to choose, whom to vote for, or whether to marry—usually do not have preestablished answers. Many theorists have described these kinds of problems as

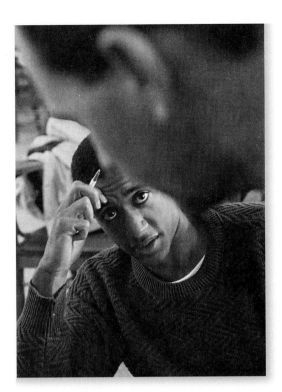

ill-defined or ill-structured. Not only do they have no preestablished answers, but the "right" answer may be different depending on circumstances and on the perspective of the problem solver. Further, when we solve such problems we often do not have access to all the information that might be helpful.

Young adults are in the achieving stage of cognitive development, when an individual must apply her intellectual skills to the achievement of long-term goals, carefully attending to the consequences of the problem-solving process. Schaie assumes not that additional thinking skills are emerging beyond formal operational abilities but that previously acquired skills are being sharpened and honed on very different kinds of problems, such that the solution to one problem must be considered and adjusted relative to other life problems and goals. For example, an adult who is contemplating a divorce must contend with a number of issues: her future happiness, her economic status, and the well-being of her children, just to name a few.

According to Schaie, each new stage of adult life brings new kinds of problems, with different skills more likely to play an important role in one stage than in another. In middle adulthood, the responsible stage, ill-defined problems are still the norm, but problem solving must take into account not only one's own personal needs and goals but also those of others in one's life who have become one's responsibility: spouse, children, coworkers, members of the community. Schaie suggests that the greater impact of one's problem solutions leads adults to become more flexible in their thinking and to expand their knowledge and expertise and use those qualities more widely than before. For people who take on executive functions at work and in the community, the extended impact of one's problem solving is even greater than for others, and the responsible stage becomes the executive stage, requiring that one focus heavily on learning about complex relationships, multiple perspectives, commitment, and conflict resolution. Such individuals must sharpen skills in integrating and hierarchically organizing such relationships.

People's responsibilities usually narrow in early old age as their children grow up and retirement becomes an option. This is the reorganizational stage, when flexibility in problem solving is needed to create a satisfying, meaningful environment for the rest of life, but the focus tends to narrow again to a changed set of personal goals and needs. Practical concerns, such as planning and managing one's finances without an income from work, require applying one's knowledge in new ways.

As people move further into their elder years, called the reintegrative stage, they need less and less to acquire new domains of knowledge or to figure out new ways of applying what they know, and many are motivated to conserve physical and psychological energy. Schaie suggests that elderly people are often unwilling to waste time on tasks that are meaningless to them, and their cognitive efforts are aimed more and more at solving immediate, practical problems that seem critically important to their daily functioning.

A legacy-leaving stage may also characterize people whose minds are sound but whose frailty signals that their lives are ending. Such people often work on establishing a written or oral account of their lives or of the history of their families to pass on to others. Consider Jean, who used her considerable organizational ability to construct a detailed genealogy to pass along to her only son. The activity gave her a sense of satisfaction, purpose, and meaning. Clearly, these goals require substantial use of long-term memory and narrative skill, more than problem-solving skills, but as Schaie points out, such accounts do require decision making, or the use of judgment, about what is important and what is not.

This discussion of Schaie's theory has involved describing cognitive functions beyond early adulthood. We will return to the later stages in Chapters 13 and 14. For now, Schaie's depiction of cognitive functioning as heavily affected by the environmental pressures people face at different times of life should help set the stage for understanding other theories of young adult cognition. Most theories emphasize that advancements or changes in problem solving are embedded in the new experiences faced during adulthood.

Schaie's description of environmental pressures clearly is focused on typical middle-class experiences in Western cultures. He would probably be the first to acknowledge that adults in other cultures, or in some North American cultural groups, might show different shifts in the polishing or use of cognitive skills through life, depending on the unique demands that their environments impose. Arnett and Taber (1994) point out, for example, that in Amish communities within the United States, the importance of mutual responsibility and interdependence is emphasized from childhood through all phases of adulthood. A sense of duty and of the need to sacrifice on behalf of others is central to everyone's life within the culture. Thus, these obligations should be expected to affect cognitive functioning in important ways well before middle adulthood, which is when Schaie considers them to become influential. Keep in mind as you read the following accounts of postformal thought that they are almost entirely based on observations of members of the majority culture in Western societies and that it remains to be seen whether these conceptions adequately characterize adult cognitive development in other cultures.

Postformal Thought

Many theorists argue that the realities of adult experience actually lead to new forms of thought (e.g., Arlin, 1984; Basseches, 1984; Commons & Richards, 1984; Sinnott, 1984, 1998). In many views, the full flower of postformal thinking may not be realized until middle adulthood or even later, but the experiences of young adulthood contribute to the reconstruction of logical thinking. As we saw with formal operations, not all individuals will necessarily reach postformal operations. If they do, we can expect them to "skip in and out" of this type of thinking (Sinnott, 1998).

Sinnott (1984, 1998) captures many of the features of postformal thinking described by others. For Sinnott, the essence of postformal thought is that it is relativistic: "[S]everal truth systems exist describing the reality of the same event, and they appear to be logically equivalent" (1998, p. 25). The knower recognizes both the consistencies and the contradictions among the multiple systems of truth, or systems of formal operations, and depending on her goals and concerns, in many situations she will make a subjective commitment to one; in other situations, she may seek a compromise solution that integrates some of each perspective, but will not lose sight of the inherent contradictions.

For example, advanced study of a science often reveals that more than one theoretical system can account for much of the data, although perhaps not all of it. Let's use Sinnott's example from mathematics to begin our demonstration:

> The knower may be aware that both Euclidean and non-Euclidean geometries exist and that each has contradictory things to say about parallel lines. In Euclidean geometry parallel lines never

come together; in non-Euclidean geometry, parallel lines eventually converge. These are two logically contradictory truth systems that are logically consistent within themselves and logically equivalent to one another. A mathematician bent on knowing reality must decide at a given point which system he or she intends to use, and must make a commitment to that system, working within it, knowing all along that the other system is equally valid, though perhaps not equally valid in this particular context. (Sinnott, 1998, p. 25)

In the behavioral sciences and the helping professions, we are quite familiar with the phenomenon of competing truth systems. For example, a counselor may be aware of multiple theories to account for snake phobias. One might be biologically based, another based on assumptions about the symbolic meaning of snakes in a person's life, and another a behavioral theory arguing that irrational fears are classically conditioned. Suppose she understands the logic of each theory and knows that each is supported by a set of evidence. Yet, in a therapeutic situation, she must make a commitment to one of these systems of "truth" for the purposes of developing a therapeutic plan that will achieve relief for her client as quickly as possible. As Sinnott argues, for her purposes that system then becomes her "true description of the world," but if she remains aware of the inherent contradictions among the different systems and realizes that each has some claim on being true, her thinking has postformal characteristics. Truth is relative, but one truth system may be more valid than another, depending on our goals. This example illustrates that descriptions of postformal thinking have parallels in the descriptions of "reflective practice" presented in Chapter 1.

Sinnott's characterization of postformal thought is consistent with what Chandler (1987; Chandler et al., 1990) calls postrational skepticism, in which we abandon

> the empty quest for absolute knowledge in favor of what amounts to a search for arguably good reasons for choosing one belief or course of action over another . . . an endorsement of the possibility and practicality of making rational commitments in the face of the clear knowledge that other defensible alternatives to one's views continue to exist. (Chandler et al., 1990, p. 380)

Interestingly, Chandler and his colleagues disagree that postskeptical rationalism actually represents thinking that is more advanced than formal operational thought. They are more inclined to see it as a result of self-reflection, a growing metacognitive awareness that is the product of "an ongoing effort to reflect upon the status of the general knowing process" (p. 380) and to understand its strengths and its limits.

Whether or not relativistic thinking is truly postformal is perhaps less important than when and under what circumstances it emerges. Let's consider in greater detail two descriptions of cognitive change in the college years and the research in which they are grounded. In each of these theories, the final accomplishment is relativistic reasoning like that described by Sinnott. But each draws on data from studies of young adults to specify in detail how thinking might be restructured and why it is, especially for college students. They each describe a series of stages that we might consider substages in the progression from early formal operational thought to a postformal kind of thinking.

PERRY'S THEORY OF INTELLECTUAL AND ETHICAL DEVELOPMENT IN THE COLLEGE YEARS

William Perry's (1970/1999) theory focuses on the cognitive and moral development of college students. Perry was a professor of education at Harvard and founder of the Harvard Bureau of Study Council, a counseling and tutoring center. Using many of Piaget's ideas, Perry proposed a stage-based theory that depicts the typical intellectual and ethical transitions experienced by students in higher education settings, from absolute adherence to authority to beliefs founded on personal commitment. Perry's theory examines the changes that occur over time in the structure of young adults' knowledge, or, put another way, the changes in their expectations and assumptions about the world.

Perry's original study involved hundreds of volunteer Harvard and Radcliffe students from 1954 through 1963. The theory was constructed from extensive interviews of students as they moved through their college years. In general, interview questions were open ended, such as "Why don't you start with whatever stands out for you about the year?" (1970/1999, p. 21), allowing students maximum freedom to talk about their experiences. Initially, Perry considered

Emerging adults may find the challenges of new academic and social responsibilities difficult to cope with, without the familiar supports of home and family.

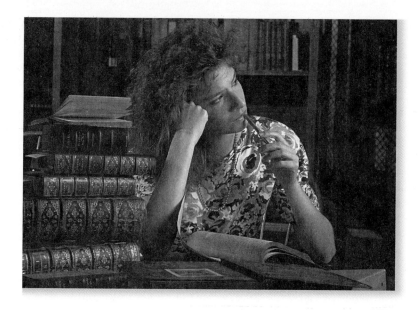

the differences in students' thinking or worldviews to be a function of their personality differences. It was only after careful reflection on many transcriptions that Perry and his team of raters began to consider the possibility of a developmental sequence. He states, "We gradually came to feel that we could detect behind the individuality of the reports a common sequence of challenges to which each student addressed himself in his own particular way" (p. 8). Athough Perry acknowledged that specific forms of knowing do vary across domains of knowledge (as we saw in our examinations of cognitive development in childhood), he believed it was possible to identify a dominant position or overarching form of thought for a given individual at a given time.

Perry constructed a sequence of nine "positions," or stages, ranging from extreme dualistic thinking to high levels of personally committed beliefs. What happens in between is the stuff of intellectual growth during the college years. Few students, if any, enter college at the first position, and few leave having achieved the ninth position. Like Piaget's theory, Perry's is a theory of continual movement and transition. Students "rest" for a time at each of the positions, but the dynamic clearly moves forward. From his perspective, the experience of a liberal arts college education accelerates the growth process, particularly in a society that values pluralism, because students are invariably confronted with diversity of thought, values, and beliefs.

To understand Perry's ideas, let's consider each of the positions and the three alternatives to growth. (See Table 11.2 for a summary.)

Position 1: Strict Dualism. Strict dualism is really a downward extrapolation of higher stages, given that virtually no one enters college at this level. Strict dualistic thinking implies a rigid adherence to authoritarian views, a childlike division between in-group (the group that includes me, my family, and authorities that have the "right" idea) and out-group (the group who are "wrong" or have no legitimate authority). Individuals in this stage simply never think to question their belief that authority embodies rightness. Because most adolescents have struggled with parents over autonomy issues and have experienced peers and teachers who, at the very least, have exposed them to various viewpoints, it is unlikely that many students would enter college with this extremely simplistic view of the world.

Position 2: Multiplicity (Prelegitimate). Multiplicity (prelegitimate) is characterized by the student's first encounters with multiplicity, that is, multiple ideas, answers to life's questions, or points of view. Students now find themselves face-to-face with uncertainty when exposed to a mass of theories, social experiences, and information. Their confusion is exacerbated because they lack the structure to accommodate the sheer volume of ideas. Despite their confusion, however, individuals at this stage maintain the belief that some "authority" possesses the ultimate truth or right answers. It is just up to the individual to find it. It is not uncommon, according to Perry, for students to sort through and organize confusing or contradictory

TABLE 11.2   Moving Toward Postformal Thought: Descriptions by Perry and Kitchener

Perry From Dualism to Relativism	Kitchener Emergence of Reflective Judgment
Dualism	
Position 1: Strict Dualism There is right vs. wrong; authorities know the truth.	**Stage 1** Knowing is limited to single concrete instances.
	Stage 2 Two categories for knowing: right answers and wrong answers.
Position 2: Multiplicity (Prelegitimate) Multiple ideas exist; some authority knows what's right.	**Stage 3** Knowledge is uncertain in some areas and certain in others.
Position 3: Multiplicity (Subordinate) or Early Multiplicity Multiple perspectives are real and legitimate.	**Stage 4** Given that knowledge in unknown in some cases, knowledge is assumed to be uncertain in general.
Position 4: Late Multiplicity A) *Oppositional Solution:* Either "authority is right" or "no one is right." B) *Relative Subordinate Solution:* Some opinions are more legitimate (better supported); outside guidance may be needed to learn how to evaluate and to reach this conclusion.	**Stage 5** Knowledge is uncertain and must be understood within a context; can be justified by arguments within those contexts.
Relativism	
Position 5: Contextual Relativism Respectful of differing opinions, but belief that ideas can be evaluated based on evidence.	**Stage 6** Knowledge is uncertain; constructed by comparing and coordinating evidence and opinions.
Position 6: Commitment Foreseen Preference for a worldview begins to emerge despite awareness of legitimacy of other views.	**Stage 7** Knowledge develops probabilistically through inquiry that generalizes across domains.
Positions 7, 8, and 9: Commitment and Resolve (see Text) "Flowering" of commitment; resolve to continue reflecting.	

Sources: Adapted from Kitchener, Lynch, Fischer, & Wood, 1993; Perry, 1970/1999.

information by creating mental dichotomies. For example, they may distinguish between "factual" courses, such as those in the sciences, and "vague" courses, such as those in the humanities. Students who pursue fields that are relatively clear-cut, at least at the early stages of study, may experience confusion when they later have to confront the multiplicity inherent in advanced levels of study. (Remember our examples of multiple truth systems in advanced sciences.) As one student in Perry's study complained about an instructor,

> "He takes all sort of stuff that, that isn't directly connected with what he's talking about . . . so you get just a sort of huge amorphous mass of junk thrown at you which doesn't really mean much until you actually have some sort of foundation in what the man is talking about." (1970/1999, p. 97)

Position 3: Multiplicity (Subordinate), or Early Multiplicity. In the stage of multiplicity (subordinate), the individual grudgingly acknowledges the reality and legitimacy of multiple perspectives. For example, it becomes more difficult to deny that reasonable people can differ in their perspectives on life, and people who hold different views are not so easily dismissed as being wrong. Some of the students' beliefs in a just world (Lerner, 1980), beliefs that the world is fair and that people in it get what they deserve, are now reevaluated. Students realize that working hard on assignments or putting many hours into studying does not necessarily guarantee wished-for results. They may observe other students doing far less work than they do themselves and getting better grades. They may be distressed by their inability to understand "what the professors want." They are nudged toward the sometimes painful realization that even their professors and other authority figures around them don't have all the answers. They may also be distressed by the fact that their teachers continue to evaluate them, despite not having the "right" answers themselves.

Position 4: Late Multiplicity. Late multiplicity was the modal position of Harvard and Radcliffe students in the original study in the latter part of their first year. Perry's research identified two possible epistemologies or adaptations to the problem of multiplicity at this point in development. In effect, students at this stage now fully realize that even experts differ among themselves in regard to what is true. Students handle the realization in one of two ways. One response, identified as oppositional, is characterized by legitimizing multiplicity as one pole of a new kind of dualism. The right–wrong dualism of Position 1 moves to one end of a new continuum, with multiplicity on the other end. Individuals taking this view of the world succeed in maintaining a dualistic either–or structure in their thinking. In other words, either "authority is right" or "all opinions are equally right." One student in Perry's study captured the essence of this position when commenting to the interviewer about his English course: "I mean if you read them [critics], that's the great thing about a book like *Moby Dick*. Nobody understands it" (1970/1999, p. 108). The viewpoint that nobody possesses the truth, thus rendering all people's opinions equally valid, can provoke students to irritation when they believe their work or the content of their ideas has been evaluated unfairly.

The second alternative, called relative subordinate, is less oppositional. Students with this perspective begin to understand that some opinions are more legitimate than others, presaging the relativism of Position 5. The value of a perspective is now understood to be related to the supporting arguments and evidence for the position. However, the consideration of alternative points of view is still done primarily under the guidance of authority. A Perry interviewee reported that his first set of grades in a literature course were mediocre because he could not understand the kinds of thinking required.

> "Finally I came to realize, about the middle of the second term, that they were trying to get you to look at something in a complex *way* and to try to weigh more factors than one, and talk about things in a concrete manner. That is, with words that have some meaning and some relevance to the material you were studying." (1970/1999, p. 112)

Often students receive explicit guidance in helping them weigh opinions or compare and contrast ideas. Instruction such as this fosters the kind of metacognition—awareness of how rational arguments are constructed and weighed—that is the foundation of later relativistic thinking.

Position 5: Contextual Relativism. The move to Position 5, contextual relativism, represents a major achievement in intellectual development. The first four positions are variants of a basic dualistic structure. The later positions represent a qualitatively different way of looking at the world. Kneflekamp (1999) reports on a common misunderstanding of Perry's theory, which confuses the "anything goes" quality of late multiplicity with the concept of relativism. He recalls what Perry himself used to say: "Relativism means *relative to what—to something—it implies comparison, criteria, and judgment!* [italics added]" (pp. xix–xx). The individual can no longer accept the fiction that everyone's ideas are as good as everyone else's. Although she respects the rights of others to hold diverse views, the student at this stage possesses sufficient detachment to "stand back" on her own and consider ideas and values more objectively than before. In a very real way, the student develops the habit of thinking that relies on some standard of evidence that is appropriate to the domain in question. Students' new analytic abilities allow them to appreciate the merits of diverse perspectives and to find convincing elements in multiple points of view. Thinking relativistically, or thinking about knowledge in context, becomes more habitual.

Authority figures are seen more as colleagues than they were before, as people grappling with the same conflicts that beset students, only with more experience in dealing with those conflicts. They are figures no longer to be opposed but to be respected, as this 3rd-year college student from the study illustrates:

> "I think when I was younger, when people in general are young, there's so many problems that they feel they don't have to face, and that's why they're indifferent to them. Either it's something that somebody else—the hierarchy, like the family—worries about, or it's something in the future that isn't any problem yet. And then you, when you mature you begin facing these problems for yourself, and looking at them, and then the family just becomes a help to people . . . with more, with a lot of experience. To help you, and not to take the brunt of the problem or something that's *your* worry." (Perry, 1970/1999, p. 138)

Position 5 also represents a watershed stage for religious belief, the point of demarcation between belief and the possibility of faith. No longer can an individual's religious belief rest on blind adherence to authority. Real faith, Perry purports, has been tested and affirmed in the context of a relativistic world. This implies that those who hold viewpoints other than one's own may be wrong, but no more wrong than oneself, given that the student now rejects the idea of absolute truth. With some effort, individuals come to respect and tolerate those who hold different viewpoints even while they struggle to clarify their own beliefs.

Position 6: Commitment Foreseen or Anticipation of Commitment. With commitment foreseen, we hear echoes of Erikson's discussion of identity development (see Chapter 9). Thinking at this stage incorporates a measure of moral courage, as the individual begins to affirm what it is she believes in, all the while knowing that reason will never provide absolute proof that her ideas or perspectives are right or better than others. Commitments to a set of beliefs, to a field of study or career, to relationships, and so forth, like the constructed commitments we discussed in Chapter 9, can take place "after detachment, doubt, and awareness of alternatives have made the experience of choice a possibility" (Perry, 1970/1999, p. 151). This way of thinking incorporates not only respect for diverse ideas and understanding of their rationales but also emerging, personally chosen, preferences for worldviews. One student captures this element of Position 6:

> "It seems to me that so much of what I've been forced to do here, this taking of two sides at once, just suspends my judgment. There is a value in it, in seeing any perspective, or any one particular facet of, of a problem. But there's also a value in, in being able to articulate one side more than another." (p. 157)

One notices a general trend in thinking toward personal meaning making or reflective thinking.

Positions 7, 8, and 9. Perry discusses Positions 7 (initial commitment), 8 (multiple commitments), and 9 (resolve) together. Taken together, they suggest a flowering of the commitments anticipated in Positions 5 and 6. Changes in thinking are more qualitative than structural. According to Perry, 75% of students in the study had a level of commitment at Positions 7 or 8 at graduation. Despite its place at the end of the line, Position 9 does not imply a static resolution of existential conflict. On the contrary, it characterizes a state of courageous resolve to continue the work of reflecting on one's commitments throughout adulthood.

Perry also accounted for individuals who refrain from taking the intellectual challenge necessary for growth through these stages. Fall-back positions include temporizing, retreat, and escape. Temporizing refers to delaying movement to the next stage. Escape characterizes a movement back to relativism when the demands of commitment prove too taxing. Retreat occurs when individuals revert to dualistic thinking in times of stress in order to seek the intellectual security of absolute right or wrong, a position that is unavailable at the level of committed relativism.

Although Perry's theory has been extremely popular, particularly among student personnel professionals, it has some limitations. The first five positions of the theory emphasize intellectual development; the last four pertain to moral and identity development. Thus, Perry's scheme incorporates several abstract constructs such as identity, ego development, and cognitive development simultaneously, making it difficult for researchers to agree on definitions and measurement. Some have noted that the lack of uniformity in assessment of stages prevents researchers from making valid comparisons of their findings across studies. Consequently, there is a paucity of recent empirical data on the linkages between Perry's theory and general cognitive processes in adulthood.

Some efforts have been made to address the issue of assessment. Several instruments and questionnaires have been developed to identify stages of reasoning that are less time consuming to administer than the interview method used in Perry's original work (see Baxter-Magolda & Porterfield, 1985; Moore, 1982; Taylor, 1983). Suggestions for informal assessment of cognitive development for use by residence life professionals have also been proposed (see Stonewater & Stonewater, 1983).

There is some research using Perry's framework to explore the connection between students' beliefs about knowledge and their approach to learning. For example, Ryan (1984) found that relativists were more successful in their college classes because they tended to use more constructivist approaches to studying course material. They paid attention to context, constructed meaningful interpretations of textual information, and summarized main ideas. Dualists, on the contrary, were more likely to focus on memorization of factual information. These differences were significant even when the effects of scholastic aptitude were eliminated statistically.

Using slightly different conceptual frameworks, other researchers have demonstrated that effective problem solving is related to relativistic thinking (Schommer, Crouse, & Rhodes, 1992) and that relativistic thinkers are more likely than dualistic thinkers to provide legitimate evidence to support their thinking and problem solving (Kuhn, 1992). Wilkinson and Maxwell (1991) found support for the relationship between college students' epistemological style (dualistic, multiplistic, or relativistic) and their approach to problem-solving tasks. Dualists took a rather narrow view of the tasks, breaking them down into unrelated, discrete parts and ignoring some important aspects. Relativists were more likely to consider the whole problem, processing and taking into cognitive account all of its components before attempting a solution.

Gilligan (1977) applied Perry's description of the development of relativistic thinking to an analysis of Kohlberg's scoring of young people's responses to moral dilemmas. She discussed a phenomenon called "late adolescent regression," wherein about one third of Kohlberg's samples actually regressed to lower levels on his scoring criteria. Gilligan argued that this "regression" actually indicates a more contextualized, relativistic stance in response to moral dilemmas, representing a more inclusive form of principled reasoning. As such, so-called regressions should more reasonably be considered advances. Kohlberg's original scoring system has since been revised.

KITCHENER'S MODEL OF THE DEVELOPMENT OF REFLECTIVE JUDGMENT

As we noted earlier, and as counselors know all too well, many problems of adulthood are ill-defined. An ill-defined problem has neither one acceptable solution nor one agreed-upon way to solve it (Kitchener, 1983). Should a talented athlete stay in college or accept an attractive job offer? Should a young woman pursue a high-powered career that will leave little room in her life for marriage and child rearing? How can a young adult deal with the pressures of academic and social life? Moreover, how do counselors deal with the messy issues that come to them on a daily basis?

Kitchener and her associates (Kitchener & King, 1981; Kitchener et al., 1989) have proposed a seven-stage theory outlining the development of reflective judgment, how people analyze elements of a problem and justify their problem solving (see Table 11.2). They presented individuals with a standard set of ill-structured problems from the social and physical sciences and questioned them about the reasoning they used in coming to conclusions about the problems. Like Perry, these researchers found a predictable, sequential progression that moved from a belief in the existence of absolute, fixed certainty to a kind of contextual relativism.

For Kitchener, different stages of thinking can be differentiated on the basis of three dimensions: certainty of knowledge, processes used to acquire knowledge, and the kind of evidence used to justify one's judgments. As you can see from Table 11.2, the early stages (1 through 3) are characterized by a belief in the existence of certainties and the use of personal justification ("This is just the way it is") or reliance on authorities for guidance. Individuals in the early stages also tend to use personal observation as evidence of the rightness of their judgments. Individuals in the middle stages (4 and 5), similar to Perry's multiplists, perceive knowledge as uncertain. They believe in the supremacy of personal opinion and tend to make judgments based upon idiosyncratic kinds of reasoning. Those in the later stages (5 through 7) resemble Perry's contextual relativists in that they tend to make judgments based upon a set of rules or logic in combination with personal reflection. For example, one reflective judgment problem concerned whether certain chemicals in foods, such as preservatives, are good or bad for us. The following is a prototypic example of a Stage 5 response to such a problem:

> "I am on the side that chemicals in food cause cancer, but we can never know without a doubt. There is evidence on both sides of the issue. On the one hand there is evidence relating certain chemicals to cancer, and on the other hand there is evidence that certain chemicals in foods prevent

things like food poisoning. People look at the evidence differently because of their own perspective, so what they conclude is relative to their perspective." (Kitchener et al., 1993, p. 896)

Some research demonstrates that reflective judgment is related to level of education (Dunkle, Schraw, & Bendixen, 1993; Kitchener & King, 1981) as well as to the kind of training one has received (Lehman, Lempert, & Nisbett, 1988). Graduate students, for example, reason at higher levels than do college undergraduates, and graduate students in psychology, a discipline that emphasizes statistical reasoning, show higher levels of proficiency on such tasks than do graduate students in chemistry, medicine, or law. Specific kinds of training or support appear to improve skills in reasoning and judgment. In one study, individuals from middle through graduate school were provided with prototypic statements like the one quoted above, with each statement modeling successively higher levels of reflective judgment, and then they were asked to explain the reasoning in the prototypic statement. The results indicated that after such modeling and practice, participants' own levels of reasoning on such problems had advanced.

Another study illustrates that reflective judgment in social and personal issues tends to lag behind problem solving in domains that do not relate to one's own personal concerns (Blanchard-Fields, 1986). In this study, participants ranging in age from 14 to 46 were presented with two accounts of each of three events. One event that had little personal relevance for most people was an account of war (the Livia task) by two opposing parties (see Kuhn, Pennington, & Leadbeater, 1982, for a full description of the task). The remaining two events were characterized as "the visit to the grandparents" and "the pregnancy," and both events were rated by participants as emotionally involving. In the first of these, a teenage boy and his parent each present a story about a time when the boy was required to accompany his parents on a visit to his grandparents. The two stories are inconsistent in emotional tone and in many details. (See Box 11.1 for the full text of the competing accounts.) In the second emotionally involving event, a woman and a man each take a different stance on the woman's pregnancy, she favoring an abortion, he against an abortion. For each of the three events, study participants were asked to explain what the conflict was about and what happened. They also responded to probe questions such as "Who was at fault?" and "Could both accounts be right?" The participants' understanding and analysis of the events were scored based on six levels of reasoning, combining features of Perry's (1970/1999) and Kitchener and King's (1981) levels of cognitive maturity. Performance on the Livia task was better at earlier ages than performance on the more emotionally involving tasks. Performance continued to improve on all tasks from adolescence to young adulthood and from young adulthood to middle adulthood.

The following are examples of performance for these three age groups on the emotionally involving "visit to the grandparents" event (from Blanchard-Fields, 1986).

Level 2. This was the average level of response for adolescents on the two emotionally involving events. It is close to an absolutist conception of reality.

> "There's a lot more said by John of what they did and they had an argument and the parents did not say it like—how he talked, and that he wanted to be treated like an adult. It seems more right because I don't like the parent's talk." (Blanchard-Fields, 1986, p. 327)

Level 3. This level was about average for young adults in this sample. They recognized that different perspectives appear valid, but they tended to cling to the possibility that there may be an absolute truth, even in such ill-defined situations.

> "Yes [they could both be right]. I think you'd have to have a third person not involved emotionally with either party. They'd be able to write without feeling, the facts, just what happened." (Blanchard-Fields, 1986, p. 327)

Note that "just what happened" suggests one correct interpretation of events.

Level 4. This level was about average for middle-aged adults. They were not biased toward one side or the other, and the idea that more than one truth might exist was intimated, but there was still a strong sense that one can identify an essential similarity or truth despite the different perspectives.

Box 11.1 | *A Visit to the Grandparents*

Blanchard-Fields (1986, p. 333) presented adolescents and adults with three tasks, each consisting of two discrepant accounts of the same event. Participants were interviewed to assess their reasoning about the events (see the text). The following are the two accounts for the task called "A Visit to the Grandparents."

Adolescent's Perspective

I'd been planning on spending the whole weekend with my friends. Friday, in school, we'd made plans to go to the video game arcade and the school carnival. We were all looking forward to a lot of fun. Saturday morning my parents surprised me by telling me that we were going to visit my grandparents that day. They reminded me that they'd planned this a long time ago. But how am I supposed to remember those things? So, we ended up in one of those big arguments with the typical results; I gave in and went with them. The worst part was when they lectured me on why it was my duty to go without ever once looking at my side of it. When we finally got to my grandparents, I had to do everything they wanted to do. I had to answer silly questions about school, play their games, and see their old slides and movies. It eventually blew up in an argument between me and my parents over the legal age for drinking.

Even though I was being as polite as I could, it was boring. I felt forced into everything. I just can't wait until I am free and out on my own. I was really angry with them. So, on the way home I told them that I wanted to be treated more like an adult; that I wanted more respect from them and I wanted them to take my plans seriously. They seemed to agree with this and decided that I was now old enough to make my own decisions.

Parent's Perspective

Two months had gone by since we had visited the grandparents. We try to visit them at least once a month, but everyone gets so busy that a month slips away very quickly. This time, we planned the visit far enough in advance so that everyone would come. When we tried to get John ready to go with us on Saturday morning, he put up a battle. After all, he hadn't seen his grandparents for a long time. They are getting old and won't be around much longer. We tried reasoning with John, stressing the importance of family unity and obligation as well as consideration of others. Certainly, in the future, he would regret not spending more time with his grandparents after they've gone. Although John was reluctant to go, he finally came with us and actually seemed to really enjoy himself. Since he seemed to be having a good time, we were surprised by how angry he became when we all got into a discussion about the legal age of drinking.

Even though he was reluctant to go with us at first, he seemed to have a good time, to enjoy the family closeness. He showed respect for his grandparents and seemed to understand how good it made them feel to see him. What this means to us is that he's old enough now to enjoy being with adults more and to learn from them. On the way home we agreed that John should take a more active part in discussions about family matters.

"I think the accounts, as far as the actual events, are pretty much the same. The important differences are in the presentation . . . the important differences are in their perceptions of what was going on. The actual 'this happened' are the same, but the interpretation of it is different." (Blanchard-Fields, 1986, p. 328)

Level 6. Perhaps you will recognize this relativistic view as one that helping professionals are trained to assume in highly personal matters. There is no hint here that one experience of the event was more valid than the other.

"They'd have to be able to really share [to resolve this conflict] . . . this way with each other, and even deeper, in terms of getting into some of their fears and some of their angers. They have to be able to accept it in each other, and maybe, they can resolve the conflict, only if they can accept feelings in each other." (Blanchard-Fields, 1986, p. 328)

Only a few participants, all of them middle-aged, responded at such an advanced relativistic level in this study. As Kuhn et al. (1995) point out, "topics in the social sphere both engage people and challenge them. They are easy to think about *but hard to think well about*" (p. 120, italics added). In Box 11.2 we consider some of the mistakes in problem solving that researchers have found to be quite common, even among adults. You will notice that these tend to occur in situations that can be very personally involving, so they have particular relevance to helping professionals.

Box 11.2 | *Counselor Beware: Decision-Making Pitfalls*

Our ability to think our way logically through problems improves and expands throughout childhood and adolescence. As this chapter indicates, problem-solving skill continues to improve in adulthood as well, especially for ill-defined problems. We have also seen in this chapter that using our logical abilities effectively to make decisions can be especially difficult when we deal with social or emotional issues that have personal relevance. Among the many kinds of logical fallacies that commonly ensnare adults are some that may be especially problematic for helping professionals and their clients.

Suppose you want to encourage a client to consider beginning an exercise program. You are concerned that her sedentary lifestyle is contributing both to her depression and to other health problems. When you introduce the idea, however, she counters, "That won't help. I have a neighbor who has run twenty miles a week for all the years I've known her, but she had to be hospitalized last year because she was suicidal." The logical error that your client is making is sometimes called "the person who" fallacy. She is refuting a well-documented finding, like the correlation between regular exercise and well-being (both physical and emotional), by calling on knowledge of a person who is an exception. Especially when dealing with psychological and social issues, matters in which most of us have great personal interest, "people tend to forget the fundamental principle that knowledge does not have to be certain to be useful—that even though individual cases cannot be predicted, the ability to accurately forecast group trends is often very informative. The prediction of outcomes based on group characteristics is often called aggregate or actuarial prediction" (Stanovich, 1998, p. 149). So, for any individual, a prediction about the effectiveness of a treatment is more likely to be accurate if we base that prediction on general findings for people with that individual's characteristics than if we base it on one or a few other individuals whom we have known or observed.

Like many logical mistakes, "the person who" fallacy involves failing to step back and consider how well the evidence supports one's theory. Your hypothetical client has a theory that exercise will not relieve her depressive symptoms, perhaps motivated in part by her distaste for exercise. She is aware of one instance in which the prediction of her theory appears to have been correct. She fails to recognize that a single case is an inadequate test of a treatment's effectiveness. One outcome can be influenced by a myriad of factors, many of them unknown. Also, your client completely ignores the evidence *against* her theory: Proportionally, more people experience long-term emotional benefits from exercise than not. In other words, probabilistically, regular exercise has a good chance of helping.

Part of the reason that "the person who" fallacy occurs is because of the vividness effect. When we are trying to make decisions, some salient or vivid facts are likely to attract our attention regardless of their actual value as evidence. Even when other facts are available the *vividness* of personal experience or of the personal testimony of other individuals can be greater than that of any other information that we might access. Wilson and Brekke (1994) documented the strength of the vividness effect in a study of consumer behavior. Participants in the study were told they would be given free condoms and that they could choose between two brands. They were also given access to two kinds of information about the condoms to help them choose a brand: One was an extensive analysis of survey data on the performance of condoms from a *Consumer Reports* magazine and the other was a pair of student testimonials. Objectively, the data from the *Consumer Reports* analysis were more useful in this case, but most participants asked for the testimonials as well, and when the testimonials were in conflict with the survey research, about one third of the participants were swayed by the testimonials. Thus, even in a situation where *both* carefully collected group data *and* individual testimony were readily available, the vividness of the less appropriate individual testimony was hard for many participants to resist.

The insidiousness of vividness effects is especially problematic when testimonials are one's source of evidence for the effectiveness of a treatment. When your client's Cousin George swears that his son was relieved of his depression by "Dr. Olivino's oil immersion therapy," the appeal of Cousin George's testimonial may be irresistible to your client, especially when she observes for herself that George's son does indeed appear to be doing quite well. Unfortunately, people can be found to offer testimonials for any therapy or treatment that has ever been offered. One reason for the ready availability of testimonials is, of course, the placebo effect. People sometimes improve over time, no matter what the medical or psychological intervention. The actual effectiveness of a treatment can only be determined in careful studies in which some participants are given the treatment and some are given a dummy, or placebo, version of the treatment. Typically in such studies, a substantial percentage of participants given the placebo control will improve, and typically they are convinced that their "treatment" is responsible. Clearly, the actual effectiveness of a treatment approach cannot be determined by testimonials. The only useful indicator of the effectiveness of a treatment is whether or not treatment participants are benefited more than placebo controls.

Counselors, too, often find the vividness effect hard to resist. For example, our own experience with individual cases often looms larger in our decision making about probable treatment outcomes than the actuarial evidence that is available to us from controlled studies of a treatment's effectiveness.

How can we protect ourselves and our clients from making poor decisions based on "the person who" fallacy and the vividness effect? Increased metacognitive awareness—that is, awareness of one's own thinking—seems to be the key. For example, educating clients to see that personal experience or the testimony of others can be limited in its generality, despite its vividness, can help them resist the appeal of such evidence. More generally, we can encourage clients to understand the decision-making process itself. When we try to decide whether a treatment should be pursued, we are actually evaluating the *theory* that a particular treatment alternative will cause improvement. Our task is to specify all the possible theories (treatment options) and to evaluate the evidence for each. When people have a favorite theory, they often do not realize that it is just a theory. As Kuhn (1991) points out, they think *with* their theory, not *about* their theory. In other words, the theory guides their thought and what they pay attention to instead of being an object of thought and evaluation. So, for example, if your client believes that

Dr. Olivino's oil immersion therapy works, she will pay more attention to examples that support her theory and may either fail to look for, or will ignore, counterevidence.

Helping clients make better decisions, then, will include encouraging them to recognize that they are working with a theory not a fact. A theory must be justified by evidence, and *all* the available evidence, both pro and con, should be considered. In addition, alternative theories (treatment options) and the evidence for them should be considered. Testimonials or personal experiences are not likely to become less vivid in this process. But when our clients are armed with knowledge about the shortcomings of such data, they may become more cautious about using them as evidence.

(*Sources*: Kuhn, 1991; Stanovich, 1998.)

APPLICATIONS

On the cusp of adulthood, individuals in their late teens and 20s confront a number of new developmental milestones. The serious tasks of consolidating an identity, solidifying a career path, and realizing the capacity for intimacy (Erikson, 1968; Keniston, 1971) are both challenging and time consuming. One competency required for each of these tasks is the ability to make decisions and choices given a wide array of possible alternatives. Counselors are frequently called upon to help clients make decisions, and, to some, this is the quintessential role of the counselor. Decision-making (Krumboltz, 1966; Stewart, Winborn, Johnson, Burks, & Engelkes, 1978) and problem-solving (D'Zurilla, 1986; Egan, 1975) models are widely used among clinicians to help people with personal and career-related issues.

Such models have in common a series of general steps, including (1) defining the problem, (2) setting realistic goals, (3) developing a variety of possible solutions, (4) assessing the costs and benefits of each alternative solution, (5) selecting and implementing one alternative, and (6) reviewing the effectiveness of the solution after implementation (Nezu, Nezu, & Lombardo, 2003). On its face, this strategy appears to incorporate some aspects of postformal thinking, specifically the relativistic, pro-and-con nature of solutions to fuzzy problems, for it is rare to find solutions to difficult problems that don't have potential disadvantages as well as advantages. But it can also suggest to more dualistic thinkers that problems are "well defined" and have correct solutions, if only someone can figure them out. Although most counselors understand that any solution or decision incorporates some good and some bad, their clients may not.

Given what we know about the importance of belief systems, the counselor might be remiss if she did not consider the client's epistemology, or her beliefs about the nature of knowledge, when working on decision making—or other problems, for that matter. In other words, seeing a dilemma through the client's eyes requires an appreciation of the way she views truth, knowledge, and meaning in life.

If a client tends to see the world in absolute terms, she might be confused as to why alternatives are even being considered! Twenty-year-old Hannah recently moved into her boyfriend Mike's apartment near the college campus where both are students. She is upset that Mike wants to spend so much time with his friends, playing basketball and going to bars. Hannah resents the fact that he doesn't spend his free time with her, and, to make matters worse, she believes drinking alcohol is morally wrong. Because the tension between the two is so great, Hannah consults a counselor for advice about how to change Mike's behavior. Hannah becomes indignant when the counselor asks her to consider the advantages of allowing Mike to socialize with his friends and to reflect on her role in the relationship problems. "Mike is the one with the problem," Hannah states emphatically. "I came here to find out how to get him to stop drinking and to spend time with me." Hannah will become frustrated if the counselor presses her to adopt a relativistic stance too quickly, and she may seek out another "authority." She will probably not return to this counselor.

Level of epistemological thinking also influences academic success. Research has demonstrated that students who believe that learning should be quick, that prolonged concentration is a waste of time, and that memorization of concrete facts is sufficient for learning demonstrate poor performance on mastery tests despite reporting high levels of confidence in their ability (Schommer, 1990). Students who perform better on mastery tests are more likely to disagree with the view that knowledge is certain and that single, simple answers are most reflective of reality (Schommer, 1993). Skills in reflective thinking are also correlated with greater understanding of multicultural issues (King & Howard-Hamilton, 1999).

In general, relativistic thinking is considered to be more sophisticated because most problems in life involve uncertainty as well as some measure of uncontrollability. Expectations that complex problems should have clear-cut solutions can complicate the problem-solving process by increasing individuals' anxiety when simple answers prove inadequate

(D'Zurilla, 1988). The ability to generate solutions, assess advantages and disadvantages of each, and then integrate aspects of several solutions into one presumes a level of epistemic knowledge that has come to terms with the ambiguity of real-world problems. Yet as Perry and others have demonstrated, this skill develops gradually; it does not necessarily come with a high school diploma. Counselors who are knowledgeable about cognitive development can help clients resolve specific problems and help them acquire more general skills in decision making, such as knowing when and where a strategy is effective.

Stonewater and Stonewater (1984) have proposed a problem-solving model based on Perry's theory that balances a bit of challenge (to introduce disequilibrium) with support and engagement by the counselor. They suggest that individuals who are closer to the dualistic end of the continuum need more carefully controlled exposure to diverse ways of thinking and can benefit from the provision of adequate structure as a framework for incorporating new ideas. For example, students who find the process of career selection overwhelming may be aided by a very specific set of activities that guide them through the exploration process. Students who are at the stages of dualism or early multiplicity may find that knowing what questions to ask or what criteria to investigate allows them to engage in the confusing career decision-making process with a supportive road map. In a process very consistent with Piaget's ideas, individuals will not be able to accommodate new ways of thinking if the complexity of the information is too great and the support is not sufficient. Likewise, individuals will not be motivated to accommodate at all if the challenge is minimal and support is overdone.

King (2002) offers specific suggestions for teachers and others who work with emerging adults. Several of these ideas can be useful in promoting reflective thinking about academic and psychoeducational content. First, demonstrate respect for young adults' thinking, keeping in mind that they are most likely to open up to new ways of reflection in a supportive atmosphere. Second, provide opportunities for young adults to gather information about an issue evaluate the quality of that information, and draw conclusions based upon that data. Third, teach young adults to explicitly examine the epistemological assumptions they use in making decisions about ill-defined problems.

The theories of cognitive development described in this chapter make another important contribution to the practicing clinician. They help us understand that certain kinds of thinking, sometimes labeled "irrational," may not be attributes of a dysfunctional personality style but rather the manifestation of a developmental stage. Construing clients' thinking and judgments from this perspective allows us to be more forgiving of their idiosyncrasies and more supportive about their potential for growth and change. Sometimes, clients with fairly rigid belief systems may not have been exposed to the kinds of contexts that encourage them to examine beliefs carefully or consider alternative explanations. Or clients who hold less mature perspectives may be retreating from the confusion of too many ideas and too little support. Here the counselor has a good opportunity to assess the person's thinking and provide a balance of support and challenge that facilitates progress from a dualistic, polarized belief system to one that is more cognitively complex (Sanford, 1962).

Putting Things Off

The road to adulthood is marked by a point when individuals are no longer bound by the externally controlled routines of home and school. This freedom can be exhilarating, but many are set adrift by the lack of structure. Feeling unsafe and frameworkless once again, many young people search for the certainty of "right" answers and struggle with the challenge of organizing large blocks of unstructured time to work on tasks that may have no clear-cut boundaries. In the past, they could rely on authoritative sources to provide guidelines and directions. Now, the need to become more self-reliant increases dramatically.

One problem that arises frequently at this point in the life span is procrastination. This problem has the power to derail, even if temporarily, emerging adults' potential success in academic and work environments. Procrastination is a multidimensional construct, having motivational, behavioral, cognitive, and personality components and may be the end product of diverse pathways. Those who investigate procrastination as a dispositional, traitlike characteristic (Paunonen & Ashton, 2001; Schouwenburg, 2004) report that procrastinators share low levels of trait conscientiousness (see the section on personality in Chapter 13), rendering this group more likely to be disorganized, poor at planning, and lacking the self-regulation needed to accomplish things in a timely way. Several subtypes have been identified within the general population of procrastinators. Those with low levels of conscientiousness and high levels of neuroticism tend to be fearful, anxiety-prone, and perfectionistic. These perfectionistic procrastinators abide by the "procrastinator's code" (Burka & Yuen, 1983), that specific cognitive tendency to equate failure in one area to a generalized sense of failure in all aspects of the self. An unrealistic set of perfectionistic standards and irrational beliefs, namely that failure is a fate worse than death, may fuel their avoidant behavior.

Those whose combination of personality traits include low conscientiousness, low neuroticism, and high extraversion are more likely to procrastinate without the worry. These individuals also avoid tasks they consider unpleasant and prefer to engage in more satisfying pursuits but do not do so because they are averse to failure. Some have also identified a "rebellious" type of procrastinator who resists authority and asserts independence through procrastination. In counseling situations, care should be taken not to try to fit everyone who procrastinates into one of these "types" nor to assume that patterns of dilatory behavior in certain contexts necessarily reveal the nature of that person's personality. Most of us have avoided aversive tasks at one time or another and sometimes we may procrastinate in one setting (academic) but not in another (job). We suggest, as well, that there are developmental reasons for the ubiquity of procrastination at this stage of the lifespan. The landscape of emerging adulthood can be perceived by some as a frontier with open-ended possibilities and many high-stakes choices. The skills of decision making and self-management are honed in the identity development process which proceeds concurrently with entry into college, military service, or the world of work. Procrastination may be the manifestation of confusion or lack of certainty about how to proceed. Although this is a growing area of research, we still need more evidence to sort out information about the nature of procrastination and ways to intervene to reduce it.

Behavioral approaches such as instruction in time management and organizational skills are very popular (Tuckman, Abry, & Smith, 2002). These techniques can be useful in helping students learn to segment tasks into manageable components, develop timelines and benchmarks for task completion, and provide themselves with regular feedback about performance. Other approaches blend behavioral elements with specific components that address underlying psychological needs. For example, van Essen, van den Heuvell, and Ossebaard (2004) developed a self-management course that facilitated self-reflection about personal reasons for procrastination as the basis for change. Rational Emotive Behavior Therapy (REBT) principles were incorporated to address the irrational beliefs that supported procrastination. These authors reported that the program was effective in enhancing self-efficacy and reducing procrastination. For perfectionistic procrastinators, counselors may find stress-management interventions such as guided relaxation training and systematic desensitization procedures helpful adjunctive therapies (Flett, Hewitt, Davis, & Sherry, 2004).

Painful Passages

In some cases, the role transitions involved in moving out of the home into the larger world of adult responsibilities can be so great that they lead to depression. Recent research shows that the incidence of depression is increasing worldwide, and its age of onset is decreasing, such that younger cohorts now stand a higher chance than did older generations of developing depression during their lifetimes (Cross-National Collaborative Group, 1992). As we have seen, females suffer disproportionately, with incidence rates of subclinical syndromes and more serious disorders approximately twice as high as those for men from midadolescence through late adulthood (Compas, Ey, & Grant, 1993). Before puberty, boys' rates of depressive symptoms and disorders are equal to or higher than those of prepubescent girls (Nolen-Hoeksema, Girgus, & Seligman, 1992). Both genders suffer from **bipolar disorder** in equal numbers, an exception to the sex-based trends found in **unipolar disorders** (American Psychiatric Association, 2000). Depression has no single, clearly identifiable cause. Early life experiences, genetic predispositions, hormonal changes in puberty, cognitive and motivational processes such as attributional and coping style, number and intensity of stressors, and

the presence or absence of protective factors like social support all have influential parts to play (Rutter, 1986).

Although not all emerging adults experience depression or even depressive symptoms, the challenges that are part of the developmental work of constructing an adult identity can take their toll on mental health. The separation and losses involved in the predictable life transitions and changes in interpersonal relationships that occur at this stage are stressful and can make already vulnerable individuals more vulnerable. Emerging adulthood typically involves a major separation from home—physically, psychologically, or both. For some, the combination of leaving family and friends, disruptions in romantic attachments, stresses of academic or work responsibilities, and the day-to-day challenges of caring for oneself may seem overwhelming. A stark reminder is the fact that the highest prevalence rate for depression across the entire life span occurs during the ages of 15 to 24 (Blazer, Kessler, McGonagle, & Schwartz, 1994).

Fortunately, there are effective treatments for depression, including pharmacological, cognitive-behavioral (CBT), and interpersonal (IPT) therapies. All three have demonstrated efficacy in reducing symptoms in adolescents and adults (Garber, 2000). The foundations of interpersonal therapy may have particular relevance for development, insofar as the struggles involved in normal life transitions are one of the factors assumed to cause the disorder. Interpersonal therapy (Klerman, Weissman, Rounsaville, & Chevron, 1984; Weissman, Makowitz, & Klerman, 2000) assumes that depression is affected by and affects interpersonal relationships, and aspects of the depressed person's social network are of primary importance in understanding and treating the disorder.

The theoretical foundations of the interpersonal approach derive from the work of Sullivan (1953) and Meyer (1957), among others, who emphasized the *here and now* social contexts of the depressed individual over causes of depression that were intrapsychic and rooted in the distant past. Although IPT does not dismiss the cognitive processes that support depression, irrational, distorted thinking is not the primary focus of treatment.

The causes of depression are presumed to be four broadly defined interpersonal situations: grief, role disputes (conflicts with significant others), life changes or role transitions, and significant interpersonal deficits. Using a time-limited approach (roughly up to 20 sessions) and functioning as a supportive ally, the therapist assesses symptoms, connects depression to one of the four major problematic areas, and assigns the client a "sick role" (Parsons, 1951). Assigning a sick role legitimizes the client's needs for support from others who may be included in the therapeutic process, temporarily frees the client from unmanageable responsibility, and allows the person to focus on recovery during the restricted period of therapy. During the intermediate stage of therapy, the therapist takes a moderately directive role and helps clients make real changes in relationships and renegotiate their roles in interpersonal contexts. In the case of difficult role transitions, such as the transition to adulthood, clients are helped to mourn the old "adolescent" role by reviewing what was good and bad about it, clarify feelings about the new role, and explore opportunities that the new role offers. When anxieties about one's ability to manage the new life stage successfully surface, expectations about what "being an adult" might be are discussed and readjusted if necessary. Sources of social support are identified and recruited and incentives for taking on new developmental challenges are created. The final stage of therapy acknowledges termination as a loss but also focuses on sustaining the gains made in therapy in the post-therapy social environment. Some techniques used in IPT include those common to supportive psychotherapies: questioning, clarification, support of emotional expression, behavior change strategies, and development of a strong therapeutic alliance. IPT has also been adapted for use with younger depressed adolescents (Mufson, Moreau, Weissman, & Klerman, 1993).

A key point in the interpersonal conceptualization of depression is its transactional emphasis. Unfortunately, it has been repeatedly demonstrated that depressed people suffer more frequent rejection from others than do nondepressed counterparts (Segrin & Abramson, 1994) and thus need to exert more effort and display more skill to overcome this social tendency. However, the life events that may have precipitated depression in vulnerable individuals in the first place, such as a move to a new school, reduction in contact with family and friends, and increased maturity demands, can produce symptoms (chronic fatigue, poor concentration, indecisiveness, sad mood, anhedonia, etc.) that make engaging in positive social interactions an enormous effort (Coyne, 1999). The vicious cycle is obvious. Regardless of theoretical bent, it is important for counselors to pay serious attention to the environmental contexts that sustain depression. As Coyne warns, "depressed individuals' statements about themselves and their relationships get interpreted as enduring cognitive structures, a sociotropic trait, or working model of relationships, and these *reified entities* are then given causal priority over any interpersonal processes" (1999, p. 368). Even though IPT is an individual approach to counseling, the usefulness of including significant others in some manner in treatment should be emphasized. More research is needed to help us understand how to intervene in these interpersonal processes more directly.

Growth and Change in Professionals' Epistemology

Don't be alarmed if you recognize that some aspects of your own thinking might seem dualistic or authority oriented. Perry noted that new learning in any discipline can evolve in a similar stagelike way. Table 11.3 presents Stoltenberg and Delworth's (1987) model of stages in counselor development.

TABLE 11.3   Client Conceptualizations at Stages of Counselor Development

Level 1

Self- and Other-Awareness—Emotional and cognitive self-focus. *Indications:* Diagnoses/conceptualizations will be "canned" or stereotypical, trying to fit clients into categories. Incomplete treatment plans will focus on specific skills or interventions, often quite similar across clients. Treatment plans may not reflect diagnoses.

Motivation—High, with strong desire to learn to become effective diagnostician and therapist. *Indications:* Willing student, will seek out additional information from books, colleagues, and other sources.

Autonomy—Dependent. *Indications:* Relies on supervisor for diagnoses and treatment plans. Locus of evaluation rests with supervisor.

Level 2

Self- and Other-Awareness—Emotional and cognitive focus on the client. *Indications:* Realizes treatment plan is necessary and logical extension of diagnosis. May resist "labeling" client into diagnostic classifications. Treatment plans may prove difficult due to lack of objectivity. May reflect various orientations yet lacks integration.

Motivation—Fluctuates depending upon clarity regarding various clients. *Indications:* May be pessimistic, overly optimistic or confident at times.

Autonomy—Dependency-autonomy conflict. *Indications:* May depend upon supervisor for diagnoses and treatment plans for difficult clients, may avoid or resist supervisor suggestions concerning others. Confident with some less-confusing clients. More resistance to perceived unreasonable demands of supervisor, threats to tenuous independence and therapeutic self-esteem.

Level 3

Self- and Other-Awareness—Emotional and cognitive awareness of client and self. *Indications:* Able to "pull back" affectively and cognitively, monitor own reactions to client. The client's perspective and a more objective evaluation will be reflected in conceptualizations. Treatment plans will flow from diagnoses, taking into account client and environmental characteristics. Reflects therapist's own therapeutic orientation.

Motivation—Consistently high, based upon greater understanding of personality-learning theory and self. *Indications:* Not as susceptible to permission or undue optimism. Diagnoses and treatment plans consistently thought through and integrated.

Autonomy—Independent functioning. *Indications:* Seeks consultation when necessary. Open to alternative conceptualizations and treatment approaches but retains responsibility for decisions. Makes appropriate referrals.

Source: Stoltenberg, C. D., and Delworth, U. (1987). *Supervising counselors and therapists: A developmental approach.* Copyright © 1987 by Jossey-Bass. This material is used by permission of John Wiley & Sons, Inc.

As you can see, Level 1 counselors operate somewhat like dualists. They tend to be dependent upon supervisors to tell them the "right" way to conceptualize cases. Level 1 counselors try to fit clients into categories and often rely on canned strategies. In general, they also tend to attribute too much pathology to their clients because of their own anxiety level. Level 2 counselors vacillate between dependence on supervisors and personal autonomy. Because they have more experience with difficult cases, they may be less optimistic about the possibilities for change in certain circumstances. As with multiplists, exposure to competing theories of human behavior and therapy undermines confidence in the validity of each. Counselors at this level are more skillful yet also more confused about their own efficacy. At Level 3, helping professionals are more independent and also more tolerant of divergent opinions. They come to accept the ambiguity that is inherent in the helping process. They are creative problem solvers and more objective in their assessment of their clients. In the fluid way they utilize the discipline's knowledge base to adjust to the needs of the client, these counselors truly embody the characteristics of reflective practice.

SUMMARY

1. Specifying exactly when an individual reaches adulthood is surprisingly complex. Sociologists look to marker events, such as completing one's education, entering the workforce, leaving the family home, and so on. Young adults themselves tend to emphasize accepting responsibility for their own behavior and making independent decisions. In today's society, the period from about 18 to 25 may be described as a time of emerging adulthood.

Physical Development in Young Adulthood

2. Between 18 and 30, all biological systems reach peak potential. There are individual differences in when people reach peak potential, and there are differences among different systems and skills in the timing of peak status. For different skills, these differences reflect differences in the relative importance of practice, training, knowledge, experience, and biological capacity. Males and females also peak at different times.

3. Lifestyle affects the achievement and maintenance of peak or near-peak functioning. Healthy lifestyles include getting regular exercise, eating a healthy diet, and avoiding bad habits such as smoking and drug use. Bad habits in young adulthood are reflected in poorer health later in adulthood, yet many young adults have unhealthy, underregulated lifestyles, probably as a result of poor application of problem-solving skills, continued feelings of invulnerability, the fact that young adults "bounce back" quickly from physical stress, and the many stresses they face.

4. The pruning of synapses continues in young adulthood. The frontal lobes continue to mature, perhaps playing an important role in the young adult's advancing abilities in organization, attention, planning, and self-regulation.

Cognitive Development in Young Adulthood

5. Young adulthood is a time of great learning. We have clear data on the growth of knowledge in the college population (roughly 60% of young adults today), but it seems likely that rapid growth of knowledge characterizes all young adults as they gain training and experience in their vocations and avocations.

6. Logical thinking also appears to change beginning in young adulthood. Theorists and researchers disagree as to the nature of the change. Some propose that a more advanced kind of thinking, postformal or fifth-stage thinking, emerges. Others argue that the formal operational abilities of the adolescent period represent the most advanced form of thinking for humans but that adults learn to apply this kind of thinking to the more ill-defined or ill-structured problems that adults face. As part of this process, they may also gain better understanding of the limits of their own problem-solving abilities. That is, they may grow in metacognitive understanding.

7. Schaie argues against a new kind of adult thinking. Rather, he argues that at different times of adult life people face different kinds of problems, and different skills are brought to bear on those problems. He describes seven stages in adults' intellectual functioning, with each new stage a result of shifts in the challenges people face.

8. Theorists who argue that there is a stage of postformal thought suggest that it may not reach full development until middle adulthood, but its emergence begins in young adulthood. Most theorists, such as Sinnott, describe postformal thought as relativistic. The same reality can be described within several different truth systems, all of which are valid from one perspective or within some context. The postformal thinker recognizes the validity of different truth systems. She may make a subjective commitment to one in some situations or seek a compromise in other situations. Sinnott's description of postformal thought is similar to what Chandler called postrational skepticism, although Chandler disagrees that this kind of thinking is more advanced than formal operational thought.

9. Perry's stage theory of intellectual and ethical development in the college years describes a sequence of steps in the movement from more absolutist or dualistic thinking

(there is one right answer, other answers are wrong) to relativistic thinking (there is more than one correct way to view the same issue). In addition to Perry's own longitudinal interview study, a number of researchers have provided some evidence for aspects of Perry's theory. For example, students' beliefs about knowledge have been found to relate to their approach to learning, as Perry's theory predicts.

10. Kitchener provides a seven-stage theory of the development of relativistic thinking, calling it reflective judgment. Research in which subjects are given ill-defined problems indicates that in the early stages of adult thinking, individuals believe in the existence of certainties. In the middle stages, people perceive knowledge as uncertain. In the later stages, they base their judgments on a set of rules or logic in combination with personal reflection. Essentially, they are relativistic.

11. Some research indicates that reflective judgment is related to level of education and to the specific kind of training people have received. Graduate students in psychology, for example, tend to show more proficiency than graduate students in other disciplines. Evidence also indicates that people are benefited by modeling of forms of thinking more advanced than their own.

CASE STUDY

Angela, a young Black woman, comes from a close-knit and very religious family who have always taken great pride in her accomplishments. Despite some minor rebelliousness during high school, Angela maintains close ties to her family and considers her parents and younger sister to be her best friends. A solid student all through school and a leader in her church's youth ministry, Angela knew for a long time that she wanted to go to college to be a teacher. Angela's father attended community college for 2 years, and her mother graduated from high school. Both parents were delighted when Angela became the first member of the family to pursue a baccalaureate degree.

Now in her 1st year at a state university in the South, she is getting used to college and to life in a dormitory. She enjoys the freedom and the challenge of college but is also experiencing some problems getting along with other students. Her roommate, a young White woman named Jen, poses a particular dilemma for her. It bothers Angela that Jen never goes to church, never prays, frequently spends the night at her boyfriend's apartment, and is an outspoken agnostic. Jen makes various comments about what she has learned in her religion and philosophy classes that trouble Angela, who firmly believes that Jen lacks a proper moral center. Angela has tried to convince Jen about the importance of belief in God and the consequences of her disbelief, but to no avail. Because it is important to Angela to maintain her beliefs, she starts to avoid being in the room when Jen is there and considers finding a new roommate.

During the spring semester, Angela develops a serious infection that confines her to bed and makes her unable to attend classes or to care for herself. She is both surprised and pleased when Jen comes to her assistance. Jen runs errands for her, brings her meals, and does her laundry. Even Jen's boyfriend pitches in to help Angela make up her missed assignments. She is touched by their generosity and confused about how this goodness can coexist with a nonreligious perspective on life. These are the kind of people she had thought were immoral. When the time comes to plan for next year's housing arrangement, Angela is uncertain. Her friends in the ministry counsel her to find a more appropriate roommate. Yet Angela cannot reconcile Jen's kindness toward her with what she believes to be an immoral lifestyle. This disjunction causes her great distress. She decides to seek out a counselor in the University Counseling Center to help her with her decision.

Discussion Questions

1. Discuss Angela's level of development according to the various theories presented in the chapter.
2. How would you respond to her problem as a counselor in a university setting? How would you take her cognitive development into account?

JOURNAL QUESTIONS

1. Give examples of your own thinking at one or more points in your life that reflected dualism, multiplicity, and relativism.
2. In what respect and in what areas have you achieved the stage of committed relativism? Discuss this process from your personal experience.
3. Describe your transition to college. What aspects of this adjustment were particularly difficult for you? If you were a counselor working with similar problems, how would you approach them?

KEY TERMS

marker events
youth
emerging adulthood
globalization
young adulthood
postformal or fifth-stage
   thinking
acquisition stage
ill-defined or ill-structured
   problems

achieving stage
responsible stage
executive stage
reorganizational stage
reintegrative stage
legacy-leaving stage
relativistic thought
postrational skepticism
strict dualism
multiplicity (prelegitimate)

multiplicity (subordinate)
just world
late multiplicity
oppositional
relative subordinate
contextual relativism
commitment foreseen
initial commitment
multiple commitments
resolve

temporizing
retreat
escape
reflective judgment
"the person who" fallacy
actuarial prediction
vividness effect
placebo effect
bipolar disorder
unipolar disorder

Now go to our Companion Website to assess your understanding of chapter content with Multiple Choice Questions, apply comprehension in Essay Questions, and broaden your knowledge of development with related Web Links.

Socioemotional and Vocational Development in Young Adulthood

What is required for a happy, well-adjusted adult life? Sigmund Freud's response to a similar question was simple: "Lieben und arbeiten"— "To love and to work" (Erikson, 1950/1963). For Freud, both love and work are powerful methods by which we "strive to gain happiness and keep suffering away" (1930/1989, p. 732). Love, he felt, may bring us closer to the goal of happiness than anything else we do. The disadvantage of love, of course, is that "we are never so defenseless . . . never so helplessly unhappy as when we have lost our loved object or its love" (p. 733). Work, from Freud's perspective, not only helps justify our existence in society, providing the worker with a "secure place . . . in the human community," but it also can be a source of special satisfaction if it is "freely chosen—if, that is . . . it makes possible the use of existing inclinations" (p. 732).

For Erikson (e.g., 1950/1963), both intimacy (love) and generativity (work) are arenas for expressing and developing the self, dominating the concerns of adults in their young and middle years. True intimacy and generativity require achieving an adult identity and are part of its further enrichment and evolution. "Intimacy is a quality of interpersonal relating through which partners share personal thoughts, feelings, and other important aspects of themselves with each other" (McAdams, 2000, p. 118). True intimacy is marked by openness, affection, and trust. Generativity is a motive or need that can be filled through one's vocation or avocations, through child rearing, or through community service. It includes productivity and creativity (Erikson, 1950/1963). Generativity is also a trait that people can be described as having when they are contributing members of society. "It is about generating: creating and producing things, people, and outcomes that are aimed at benefiting, in some sense, the next generation, and even the next" (McAdams, Hart, & Maruna, 1998). For most adults, achieving generativity is central to their belief in the meaningfulness of their lives. Erikson considered young adults to be especially driven by needs for intimacy, middle adults by needs for generativity. Modern research suggests that both are powerful influences on behavior throughout adulthood, although intimacy needs may predominate early and generativity needs later.

More recent conceptions of how adults achieve happiness or mental health or "wellness" are quite consistent with the importance that Freud and Erikson placed on love and work. Close relationships with lovers, friends, and family, as well as the opportunity to make productive use of one's time and talents, figure prominently in nearly all modern theorizing about what people need to be happy and well-adjusted (e.g., Ryan & Deci, 2000). From a developmental perspective, then, the period of young adulthood should be a time when identity issues are resolved sufficiently to allow a person to make significant progress on two major tasks: The first is establishing and strengthening bonds with people who will accompany him on his life journey, and the second is becoming a productive worker.

"LIEBEN"—TO LOVE

Making connections with others in adulthood—establishing intimacy with a mate, making friends, reworking family ties—has been studied from many perspectives. One promising developmental approach examines the impact of attachment style, which is assumed to have its roots in infancy and childhood, on the formation of adult relationships.

Adult Attachment Theory

Attachment theory has enjoyed a prominent place in the child development literature since the groundbreaking work of John Bowlby and Mary Ainsworth (see Chapter 4). Following an explosion of studies on childhood attachment, researchers began to train their sights on attachment theorists' suggestion that early bonds with caregivers could have a bearing on relationship building throughout the life span (Ainsworth, 1989; Bowlby, 1980). Today, attachment theory provides a useful framework for conceptualizing adult intimacy. The abundance of research in this area makes it the most empirically grounded theory available for explaining the formation and nature of close interpersonal relationships throughout adulthood.

As we saw in Chapter 4, the process of attaching to a caregiver in infancy is considered species-typical. According to Bowlby (1969/1982, 1973, 1980), the attachment bonds of infancy serve survival needs. Infant behaviors, such as distress at separation, ensure proximity to the caregiver, who acts as a secure base for exploration, a safe haven in case of threat, and a preferred provider of emotional warmth and affect regulation.

How the attachment process unfolds is a function of the caregiving relationship. Depending on the caregiver's sensitivity and responsiveness, an infant becomes securely or insecurely attached to that caregiver. To the extent possible, he adapts his behavior to the caregiver's style to get his needs met, and he begins to internalize a working model of how relationships operate.

Despite diminishing demands for physical caretaking as individuals age, adults continue to need the emotional and practical support of significant others. As we have noted, Erikson (1950/1963) identified the achievement of intimacy as the central task of early adulthood. In his view, even though adults are much more independent than children, they still need to establish and maintain intimate connections to people who will provide them with love and care. Although you may never have thought of your adult relationships with significant others, including your bonds to your parents, as attachment relationships, many researchers believe that they are precisely that. Let us look more closely at the various manifestations of attachments in adulthood and consider a framework for organizing the existing research.

Research Traditions in Adult Attachment

Attachment theory has been used to understand relationships as divergent as those between parents and their adult children (Scharf, Mayseless, & Kivenson-Baron, 2004; Vivona, 2000) and those between romantic partners (Simpson & Rholes, 1998b). It provides a conceptual framework for individual differences in people's responses to bereavement and loss (Rando, 1993), to stress (Mikulincer & Florian, 1998), and to the processing of information about relationships (Mikulincer, 1997). And, as you will see below, attachment theory predicts intergenerational transmission of attachment classifications (van IJzendoorn, 1995). Among clinicians, attachment theory has been used as a framework for explaining conflict resolution in interpersonal relationships (Creasey & Hesson-McInnis, 2001), family dysfunction (Byng-Hall, 1995), and psychopathology (Brennan & Shaver, 1998; Dozier, Stovall, & Albus, 1999), and it provides a basis for therapeutic interventions (Dozier & Tyrell, 1998).

One way to make sense of the multitude of studies on adult attachment is to identify which kind of attachment relationship is being explored. Simpson and Rholes (1998b) offer a useful organizational framework that distinguishes between two major research traditions. First, there is a body of work that examines the outcomes of a person's attachment to his primary caregiver in infancy, once the person becomes an adult. This has been referred to as the **nuclear family tradition**. Research in this area seeks to understand the degree to which one's earliest attachments to primary caregivers may endure throughout life and how they might affect the quality of the caregiving provided to one's own children. A parallel line of research, called the **peer/romantic partner tradition**, focuses on the peer attachments of adults. Questions about how early attachments impact the quality of romantic and friendship relationships in adulthood form the core of inquiry from this angle. The two bodies of work share conceptual linkages, to be sure. However, they differ in their methodologies and even in their terminology, and they "tend to speak past each other" (Bartholomew and Shaver, 1998, p. 27).

It is sometimes assumed that findings from both traditions should converge into a coherent picture of an adult's attachment status. This has been a difficult goal to achieve, primarily because different domains are studied, different methodologies are used, and different typologies are employed. Despite these problems, there is some correlation between the different kinds of attachment findings in adulthood. As Bartholomew and Shaver (1998) note:

> When we step back from the details of specific measures and measure-specific findings, the results produced by attachment researchers are all compatible with the possibility that various forms of adult attachment arise from a continuous but branching tree of attachment experiences, beginning in infancy and developing throughout the life course. (p. 42)

We will continue our discussion of adult attachment by focusing on each approach in turn. First, we will consider how the nuclear family tradition contributes to our understanding of adult caregiving. Then we will present an overview of significant contributions from the peer/romantic partner tradition.

THE NUCLEAR FAMILY TRADITION: THE PAST AS PROLOGUE

Does the nature of your attachment to your caregiver predict your behavior in adulthood, influencing the quality of attachment you will form with your own children? This is the intriguing question that is at the heart of the nuclear family line of research. We briefly examined this issue in Chapter 4. Now we'll take a closer look.

You may recall that the primary instrument used to measure the attachment representations of adults vis-à-vis their early caregivers is the Adult Attachment Interview (AAI) developed by Main and Goldwyn (1984). It is composed of a series of 18 open-ended questions with follow-up prompts that are transcribed verbatim by a trained interviewer. The questions concern memories of relationships with mother and father, recollections of stressful events such as separations, loss, harsh discipline, or abuse, interpretations of parental behaviors, and evaluation of the effects of these early events on the interviewee's later development.

Main and her colleagues (see Hesse, 1996) hypothesized that the primary task for the interviewee is to resurrect emotionally loaded memories of early childhood experiences while simultaneously presenting them in a coherent fashion to an interviewer. Because the questions deal with very complicated, personal, and often intense issues in a person's early history, they may never have been articulated by the individual prior to this interview experience. The rapidity of questioning, combined with the nature of the items and the interview setting, are thought to elicit material often heretofore unconscious, yet highly descriptive of the adult's state of mind regarding early attachments to primary caregivers. The assumption is that by adulthood, security has become a characteristic of the individual. Representations of different relationships—like relationships with mother versus father—tend to coalesce, and a single working model of attachment can be tapped (Furman & Simon, 2004).

Interviews are scored according to Grice's (1975) criteria for coherent discourse: truthfulness as supported by evidence, succinctness, relevance to the topic, clarity, and organization of responses. Additional scoring criteria include the coder's assessment of the interviewee's early attachment quality as well as an assessment of the language used in the interview (e.g., angry, passive, derogating). Four qualitatively different classifications, or attachment styles, are then assigned to adults based upon their verbatim transcripts. These are secure or insecure (which includes three subcategories: dismissing, preoccupied, and unresolved) categories. Different classifications of insecurity are thought to reflect the different strategies and rules of information processing that the person has developed to manage the anxiety of early relationship failure, loss, or trauma. Let us examine each of these categories in turn (see Cassidy & Shaver, 1999, for more detail).

Autonomous (secure) adults provide a transcript that is coherent and collaborative. They answer questions with enough detail to provide sufficient evidence without giving excessive information. For example, incidents of caregiver insensitivity are described matter-of-factly, without embellishment or defensiveness. Secure adults also demonstrate the ability to integrate and monitor their thinking, summarize answers, and return the conversation to the interviewer. They seem to be less egocentric in their presentation than insecure individuals, and they demonstrate good perspective-taking skills. Secure individuals acknowledge the importance of attachment-related experiences in their development. Their memories of the parenting they received match up with the specific instances they present to the interviewer as illustrations. The emotions they express, both verbally and facially, are consistent with the content of their remarks (e.g., Roisman, Tsai, & Chiang, 2004).

Can adults be classified as secure if they have had less than favorable experiences as a child? Some individuals do come from circumstances of early adversity but describe their painful backgrounds truthfully and believably, while acknowledging the stressors their own parents faced. This ability to reflect on a difficult past realistically, yet with a certain level of generosity toward parents, results in a special classification called **earned secure**. Such adults appear to have come to terms with less than optimal early experiences, quite possibly with the help of a secure spouse or partner. Individuals in both secure categories typically have children who are securely attached to them (see Chapter 4 for a detailed discussion of children's attachment categories).

Dismissing (insecure) individuals provide transcripts that are characterized by markedly low levels of detail and coherence. They are likely to describe parents as very positive or idealized; however, they do not support their evaluations with any specific evidence. Whatever details they do offer may contradict their generally favorable presentation of parental behavior. Dismissive respondents tend to minimize or avoid discussion of attachment-related issues and downplay the importance of close relationships. When discussing nonemotional topics, dismissing individuals generate coherent and comprehensive records and can talk at some length. Responses to attachment themes, in contrast, lack elaboration. Failure to remember is often cited as a reason for the impoverished answers. Adults classified as dismissive tend to have children who are in the avoidant attachment category.

The dismissive style has been linked to early experiences of rejection or other trauma and the development of repressive personality styles. Do these individuals simply hide their distress, or have they managed to actually suppress their attachment needs? Some evidence using an information-processing approach indicates that these individuals, over time, function with the goal of avoiding emotional thoughts and other reminders of unpleasant emotional experiences, such as parental unavailability (Fraley, Davis, & Shaver, 1998). This motivated avoidance may lead to less cognitive elaboration of attachment themes and reduction of behaviors that would encourage intimacy, such as sharing intimate conversation, mutual gazing, cuddling, and so on.

However, it is unlikely that the system has been deactivated completely. Dozier and Kobak (1992) provide interesting evidence that dismissive individuals do react strongly to emotional issues. These researchers interviewed college students using the AAI while measuring their rates of skin conductance. Dismissive subjects, although outwardly appearing unfazed during questioning, had significantly elevated levels of skin conductance, as compared to baseline levels, when asked questions about the emotional availability of their parents and the effects of early attachments on their self-development. Roisman et al. (2004) replicated these results cross-culturally, studying European Americans, Chinese Americans, and Chinese nationals who were students at a midwestern American university. This physiological phenomenon suggests that dismissive interviewees are effortfully engaged in diversionary tactics (either idealizing parents or restricting memory) to deal with the anxiety generated by the topics. Thus, the early attachment system may never be fully deactivated, but rather just kept at bay. The attachment system responds to emotionally provocative issues when they cannot be avoided.

Individuals in a third group, classified as **preoccupied** (insecure), typically violate the rule of collaboration on the AAI interview. These individuals provide very long, incoherent, egocentric responses that shift from topic to topic. They perform in ways that suggest they are overwhelmed by the emotional memories elicited by the interview questions and are sidetracked from the task of responding succinctly. Such speakers often sound angry, sad, or fearful, as if they have never resolved the painful problems of their childhood. Parents may be remembered as intrusive or egocentric. Their transcripts paint a picture of substantial enmeshment or preoccupation with parents, registered by angry, accusatory language or by conflicted descriptions that connote ambivalence and confusion about early relationships. Both their facial expressions and self-reported emotions during the AAI are often inconsistent with the childhood memories they describe. For example, distressed facial expression might be combined with their description of a positive experience (e.g., Roisman et al., 2004). Linguistic features of their transcripts include run-on sentences, idiosyncratic uses of words, and juxtaposition of past and present tense, as though early problems continue to persist in the present. The children of preoccupied adults often have anxious-ambivalent attachments.

Individuals in the fourth category, called unresolved (insecure), produce transcripts characterized by marked lapses in logical thinking, particularly when these individuals discuss loss or other traumatic memories. One example of a lapse in reasoning might be an interviewee's mention of a deceased parent as still living. Hesse and Main (1999) have suggested that these abrupt shifts may be related to temporary changes in consciousness, possibly due to the arousal of unintegrated fear. Individuals in this category may also receive a secondary classification of dismissive or preoccupied. The children of unresolved individuals show a higher frequency of disorganized attachment patterns than other children.

A fifth category, cannot classify, is used when protocols do not meet the criteria for other categories. Only a very small number of cases fall into this classification. Data on AAI classifications and psychopathology demonstrate that psychiatric disorders are clearly associated with insecure status and that, in particular, unresolved status is the clearest predictor of emotional disturbance (Dozier et al., 1999).

A number of longitudinal studies have now provided evidence that an infant's attachment behavior, as measured by the strange situation test, reliably predicts the same individual's secure or insecure responses on the AAI in adolescence or adulthood (Beckwith, Cohen, & Hamilton, 1999; Hamilton, 2000; Waters, Merrick, Treboux, Crowell, & Albersheim, 2000). As we saw in Chapter 4, however, a child's attachment status can become either more or less secure if he has either positive or negative experiences with close relationships after the infant–toddler period. Longitudinal studies in which participants have reached adolescence or young adulthood are finding that people can either "earn" security, as we have already noted, by experiencing later supportive relationships or can develop insecure representations of attachment if they experience negative life events after early childhood. Adults who were secure as children can later demonstrate insecure states of mind because of intervening, highly stressful events such as parental loss, divorce, abuse, illness, or psychiatric disorder. Such findings suggest that deviations from the predicted pathway are most likely explained by lawful rather than random discontinuity (Weinfield, Sroufe, & Egeland, 2000).

IN SEARCH OF THE WORKING MODEL

Perhaps you are wondering if the attachment representation categories that are derived from adults' AAI performances could simply be measures of general linguistic style. If so, then interviews would have no particular relevance to attachment, and their predictive value for children's attachment characteristics might be coincidental. Crowell et al. (1996) investigated whether the different linguistic features used to make AAI classifications characterize individuals on other measures of discourse. Using the Employment Experience Interview, he examined a group of adults who had been assigned AAI classifications. The Employment Experience Interview had the same structure as the AAI and was coded using the same criteria. Note that the only difference between the two was in the nature of the questions: about job skills or early attachment relationships. Results showed differences among the transcripts (e.g., vague vs. clear discourse). However, the interesting finding was that respondents' classifications were different on each measure. In other words, an adult who might be judged "secure" on the employment interview could be "insecure" on the AAI. The researchers concluded that there is something unique about the attachment questions. They appear to provide a window into a person's state of mind concerning interpersonal representations.

The power of attachment theory rests upon the concept of the inner working model. The AAI was designed to tap an adult's representation of attachments to primary caregivers. The assumption is that the individual's narrative reflects partly unconscious representations. Results are not considered to be a direct measure of an individual's attachment to any one person, but rather are an indicator of the individual's state of mind regarding attachment-related issues. Like an algorithm for our close interpersonal associations, the working model is thought to provide rules for processing information about relationships and for behaving in relationships.

Researchers agree that the working model of relationships that one has as an adult cannot simply be a carbon copy of the one that was formed with the primary caregiver in infancy. It is a cognitive structure or schema that must evolve with time and experience, becoming more elaborate, incorporating new elements into the original version in dynamic, qualitatively transformed ways. Like all cognitive schemas, our working models of relationships help us understand, predict, and act on information that is only fragmentary (Kempson, 1988). The obvious advantage is that they allow us to process information and to respond quickly. The downside is that we may fail to accommodate real differences in present relationships, and we may behave in these relationships in ways that are adapted to quite different circumstances.

For example, consider Sheila, whose mother was depressed and dependent. As a youngster, Sheila felt that her mother's needs always came before her own. Because even the simplest task was a chore for her mother, Sheila began taking on the care of the household and her younger siblings in order to spare her mother. Sheila grew increasingly competent as a caretaker, which, in turn, caused her mother to depend upon her even more. As a young adult, Sheila has difficulty getting close to people. She bristles when any friend or romantic partner, in an attempt to get close to her emotionally, talks about a personal problem. She quickly changes the subject of conversation. Sheila's relationships in adulthood appear to be affected by the legacy of her earlier attachments. She exaggerates other people's reliance on her and fears she will be overcome by their needs, despite any real evidence for this.

Because this is a relatively new area of research, several important questions are yet unanswered. In particular, no one fully understands how the working model of infant–caregiver attachment gets transformed into a working model of attachments in adulthood. Main (1999) suggests that the multiple attachments formed in childhood coalesce into a "classifiable state of mind with respect to attachment in adulthood and that whatever this particular state of mind, it is predictive of a concordant and 'classifiable' form of caregiving" (p. 863). In this description, Main uses the phrase "state of mind with regard to attachment" instead of "working model" because she wants to avoid the oversimplified assumption that adult states of mind are always derivative of early experiences with parents in straightforward, linear ways. Main notes that insecure children often have multiple, contradictory models of attachment that are harder to integrate than those of secure children, who tend to have more unified models.

As we have seen, adults' attachment representations predict the quality of their attachments to their children (see Chapter 4). This link suggests that attachment representation is a determinant of parental caregiving behavior. Does attachment representation also affect the way that adults interact with other adults? If the working model, in fact, functions like an algorithm for close relationships, individual differences in attachment representations should also affect adults' ability to relate to others in romantic and friendship relationships. This is the subject of our next section.

The Peer/Romantic Relationship Tradition

Any reader of romance novels can testify that the topic of adult love relationships has considerable appeal. In the research community as well, quite a bit of time and energy has been devoted to understanding the formation and development of adult pair-bonds. Researchers have examined specific issues such as mate selection, relationship satisfaction, conflict resolution, relationship dissolution, and so on and have produced a wealth of findings in each of these areas. Studies have also been done that show consistent individual differences in adults' approaches to romantic relationships, sometimes called "love styles" (Lee, 1973). Similarly, there are theories about the elements of love, such as Sternberg's (1986) passion, intimacy, and commitment, and the ways they function in relationship formation. Passion refers to erotic attraction or feelings of being in love. Intimacy includes elements of love that promote connection and closeness, whereas commitment refers to making a decision to sustain a relationship with a loved one. We will discuss these elements further in the next chapter.

An early investigation by Shaver and Hazan (1988) contributed significantly to the growing body of knowledge on adult relationships by anchoring the fledgling field within the conceptual framework of attachment theory. These researchers tried to integrate the disparate threads of data into a comprehensive theory of relationships. Today, research conceptualizing adult pair-bonds as attachments represents the second influential offshoot of attachment theory.

FEATURES OF ADULT PAIR-BONDS

Do adult pair-bonds qualify as bona fide attachment relationships? Although there are some dissenting opinions (e.g., McAdams, 2000), many researchers answer yes (see Hazan and Zeifman, 1999). Consider Bowlby's definition of a behavioral system as a set of behaviors that serve the same function or goal. Human beings are equipped with multiple behavioral systems, meeting multiple goals, which interact in coordinated ways. In early childhood, attachment behavior—which includes proximity maintenance, separation distress, and treatment of the caregiver as both a safe haven and a secure base—is the most important behavioral system because it serves the ultimate goal of survival. When security is felt, other behavioral systems, such as exploration, can be activated. When security is threatened, the attachment system is triggered, and proximity-seeking behaviors increase.

In adulthood, as in childhood, particular behavioral systems are organized to meet specific needs. Attachment (based on the need for felt security) is just one of the adult behavioral systems serving psychosocial needs, which also include caregiving, sexual mating, and exploration. Because of their structure and function, pair-bonds in adults provide an effective way to integrate three of the basic systems: caregiving, attachment (felt security), and sexual mating (Shaver, Hazan, & Bradshaw, 1988). The support provided by the secure base of an attachment relationship also enhances exploration in adults, just as it does in children. Hazan and Zeifman (1999) conclude that adult attachments generally enhance reproductive success (or promotion of the species) as well as provide for the psychological and physical well-being of partners.

Infant–caregiver bonds and adult pair-bonds are notably similar in the kinds of physical contact they involve, such as mutual gazing, kissing, cuddling, and so on, and in the goals they serve (support, emotional closeness, etc.). Adult attachments, however, do differ from childhood attachments in the following three ways. First, the attachments adults have with adults are structured more symmetrically than are parent–child bonds. Both partners mutually provide and receive caregiving, whereas the parent is the unilateral source of caregiving for the child. Second, adults rely more than children do on "felt security" rather than on the actual physical presence of the attachment figure (Sroufe & Waters, 1977). Longer periods of separation can be tolerated by adolescents and adults because they understand that attachment figures will be dependable and available when they need contact. Third, adult attachments typically involve a sexual partner or peer rather than a parent figure.

THE PROCESS OF RELATIONSHIP FORMATION IN ADULTHOOD

How does the attachment system of early childhood become transformed into the attachments of adulthood? Hazan and Zeifman (1999) chart the progress of attachments by tracing the behaviors that serve the goals of the system. In infancy, as we have stated, all four functions of the attachment system (proximity maintenance, separation distress, secure base, safe haven) depend upon the presence of an attachment figure, and infant behavior toward the caregiver clearly is adapted to meet these goals. As children get older, behaviors toward peers appear to serve some attachment functions as well. For example, children transfer some proximity-seeking behaviors to peers by early childhood. Children begin to spend more time with agemates and seek them out as preferred playmates (Gottman, 1983). By early adolescence, needs for intimacy and support are often met within the peer group (e.g., Steinberg & Silverberg, 1986), suggesting that

Adult pair-bonds meet multiple needs, such as attachment needs (especially the need for security) the need for caregiving or nurture, and sexual needs.

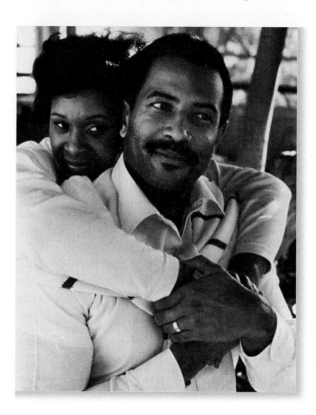

needs for a safe haven in times of distress are directed to peers as well as parents (see Chapter 10). By late adolescence and early adulthood, romantic partners may satisfy all the needs of the attachment system.

To provide support for this theory, Hazan and Zeifman (1999) asked children and adolescents from 6 to 17 years old a number of questions that tapped attachment needs. Researchers asked the participants whom they preferred to spend time with (proximity maintenance), whom they turned to if they were feeling bad (safe haven), whom they disliked being separated from (separation distress), and whom they could always count on when they needed help (secure base). Results of this study supported shifts away from parents to peers, apparently preparing the way for adult attachment behaviors. The great majority of respondents sought proximity to peers instead of parents at all ages. Between the ages of 8 and 14, participants' responses indicated a shift toward use of peers for safe haven as well. Most children and adolescents identified parents as their secure base and the source of their separation distress. However, among those older participants who had established romantic relationships, all four attachment needs were met in the context of their pair-bonds. See Figure 12.1 for a model of the attachment transfer process across age.

INDIVIDUAL DIFFERENCES IN ADULT ATTACHMENTS

The preceding discussion describes what might be considered normative processes involved in the development of adult attachments. Remember, however, that individuals differ in their states of mind regarding attachment experiences. Do these different "states of mind" predict different approaches to peer or romantic relationships in adulthood? To shed light on this question, we must recall that each tradition of attachment research has its own way of looking at these issues. Even though researchers start from the same premise, namely that adults' attachment styles will resemble Ainsworth's infant attachment typology, the typical measures used are different from those of the nuclear family tradition. Adult romantic relationship research began with self-report or questionnaire measures that were presumed to tap conscious, rather than unconscious, expectations about relationships. The sheer volume of work done in the area of measurement

DEVELOPMENTAL PHASE	TARGET OF ATTACHMENT BEHAVIORS	
	Parents	Peers
Infancy	proximity maintenance safe haven secure base	
Early Childhood	safe haven secure base	proximity maintenance
Late Childhood/ Early Adolescence	secure base	proximity maintenance safe haven
Adulthood		proximity maintenance safe haven secure base

FIGURE 12.1

Age Changes in Attachment and Close Relationships

Source: Hazan, C. & Shaver, R. (1994). Attachment as an organizational framework for research on close relationships. *Psychological Inquiry, 5,* pp. 1–22. Reprinted by permission of Lawrence Erlbaum Associates.

prevents a comprehensive discussion of this topic in this chapter. However, we will present an introduction to certain key issues and describe some important instruments. The interested reader is referred to Simpson and Rholes (1998b) for a more thorough presentation.

The first influential measure of adult romantic attachment, developed by Hazan and Shaver (1987), asked adults to identify which of three statements (see Table 12.1) best captured their approach to and beliefs about romantic relationships. Descriptive statements represented avoidant, ambivalent, and secure classifications. As measurement was refined and attempts to integrate the fields of nuclear family and adult peer attachments increased, researchers recognized that the category called "avoidant" from Hazan and Shaver's instrument did not correspond to the "dismissing" category of the AAI. The avoidant person clearly acknowledged anxiety about getting too close to another, whereas the dismissive individual reported no subjective distress.

TABLE 12.1   Three Attachment Prototypes in Peer/Romantic Tradition

Avoidant. I am somewhat uncomfortable being close to others; I find it difficult to trust them completely, difficult to allow myself to depend on them. I am nervous when anyone gets too close, and often, love partners want me to be more intimate than I feel comfortable being.

Anxious–ambivalent. I find that others are reluctant to get as close as I would like. I often worry that my partner doesn't really love me or won't want to stay with me. I want to get very close to my partner, and this sometimes scares people away.

Secure. I find it relatively easy to get close to others and am comfortable depending on them. I don't often worry about being abandoned or about someone getting too close to me.

Source: Hazan, C. & Shaver, P. R. (1987). Romantic love conceptualized as an attachment process. *Journal of Personality and Social Psychology, 52,* 515. Copyright © 1987 by the American Psychological Association. Reprinted with permission.

Faced with the needs to include both aspects of avoidance, Bartholomew (1991) proposed a new conceptual framework consisting of four categories across two dimensions. Figure 12.2 illustrates her typology. She and her colleagues (Bartholomew and Horowitz, 1991) operationalized Bowlby's (1973) view that working models of the self and of others are interrelated. People are thought to develop expectations about how reliably their significant others will behave in close relationships, as well as expectations about how worthy or unworthy they are of care and support. Four categories of attachment orientation are defined by crossing the working model of self with the working model of others.

RE 12.2

Bartholomew's Typology: A Four Category Model of Adult Attachment Categories

Source: Bartholomew, K. & Shaver, P. (1998). Methods of assessing adult attachment: Do they converge? In J. A. Simpson & W. S. Rholes (Eds.), *Attachment theory and close relationships* (pp. 25–45). New York: Guilford Press.

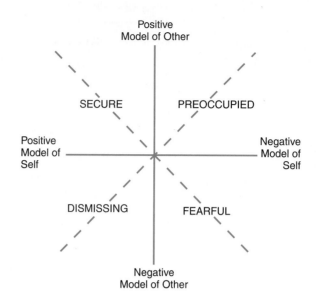

In Bartholomew's typology, **secure** individuals have internalized a positive sense of themselves along with positive models of others. In general, they expect others to be available and supportive of their needs in close relationships. They are comfortable with emotional closeness but are also reasonably autonomous. Individuals classified as **preoccupied** hold positive models of others but negative models of themselves. Others are viewed as not valuing the preoccupied person as much as he values them. Preoccupied attachment is marked by emotional demandingness, anxiety about gaining acceptance from others, fear of and hypervigilance to cues of rejection, and excessive preoccupation with relationships.

The **avoidant** category is subdivided into two, based on reports of felt distress. **Dismissing** individuals are characterized by a positive model of the self but a negative model of the other. Denying the need for close relationships permits these adults to maintain a sense of superiority while devaluing the importance of others to their well-being. Self-sufficiency is preferred, and anxiety about attachment relationships is inhibited. A **fearful** attachment is the product of negative models of both self and others. For individuals with this style, attachments are desirable but seen as out of reach. Their desire for close relationships with others is thwarted by fear of rejection, and ultimately they withdraw. A high level of distress surrounds attachment themes.

Several researchers have pointed out that use of categories such as the ones we have just described is intuitively understandable and attractive but poses a number of problems. There is a danger of failing to recognize that individual differences often exist on a continuum, reflecting the degree to which a certain tendency is exhibited (e.g., high to low levels of anxiety), as opposed to differences in kind (highly anxious vs. not anxious). Therefore, measurements that place people in quadrants will undoubtedly mask the continuity that actually exists along the underlying dimensions. Fraley and Waller (1998) also caution that this kind of categorization actually underestimates the real continuity of attachment patterns from childhood to adulthood and diminishes the strength of associations between attachment research from the parental and romantic traditions. They suggest that attachment status should not be construed as a typology with three or four classifications just because it is convenient. Brennan and colleagues (Brennan, Clark, & Shaver, 1998) expand on these points by demonstrating that most attachment scales are really measuring two continuous dimensions: avoidance and anxiety. The benefit of this dimensional perspective may be that it allows clinicians to think of individuals as operating within a range of possible behaviors. Specific attachment patterns should be viewed as tendencies to perceive and act in certain ways but not as guarantees that individuals will always operate according to type. So clinicians should avoid "typecasting" clients on the basis of attachment categories that are fixed and orthogonal, a practice that can distort clinical judgment by acting as a cognitive bias or stereotype. It may be more helpful to keep in mind that the most basic issues involved in relationships concern a person's level of anxiety about social interaction and his level of approach or avoidance. The prototypical classifications may best represent individuals with very pronounced characteristics at the extremes of the anxiety-avoidance dimensions. It is probably more accurate to think of people having particular attachment styles rather than classifications, which is a less forgiving term. It may also be helpful to keep in mind that there is wide variability in behavioral expression of anxiety and of approach-avoidance in relationships.

RESEARCH ON YOUNG ADULT DYADIC RELATIONSHIPS

Research in the peer/romantic tradition has uncovered a number of interesting aspects of dyadic relationship patterns that are related to attachment style. The focus of most of this work has been the exploration of how individual differences in attachment orientations play out in areas of social interaction. Let us take a brief look at some of the results of these investigations in areas of concern to young adults: partner selection, satisfaction with and stability of relationships, and communication and conflict resolution styles. When appropriate, we will also consider how gender differences mediate these relationships.

Partner Selection. Attachment theory offers an intuitively reasonable framework for understanding why partners choose one another. First, secure individuals, who neither avoid intimacy nor are desperately in search of it, should be more likely to seek out balanced partners like themselves. Research indicates that secure individuals tend to be paired more often with other secure rather than insecure partners (Senchak & Leonard, 1992).

Insecure individuals, according to attachment theory, should also be likely to select partners who confirm their expectations or working models of close relationships. Avoidant partners, who are fearful or dismissing of intimacy, expect partners to cling and overwhelm them with their demandingness. Anxious partners, who crave closeness, may expect rejection and believe that their needs for intimacy will go unmet. Thus, a certain synergy might propel an avoidant individual to pair with an anxious one, fulfilling expectations of both partners.

Several studies have documented the fact that avoidant-avoidant and anxious-anxious pairings are rare. In Kirkpatrick and Davis's (1994) study of 354 heterosexual couples, not a single couple showed either of the above patterns. From the perspective of attachment theory, such

Mate selection may be influenced by one's adult attachment status: Secure individuals are likely to be paired with other secure individuals.

symmetrical matches would not make sense because they do not fit the expectations predicted from working models. What is far more likely is the complementary pairing of avoidant with anxious mates, and several studies have found a preponderance of anxious-ambivalent matches among insecure individuals (Collins & Read, 1990; Kirkpatrick and Davis, 1994; Pietromonaco & Carnelley, 1994; Simpson, 1990).

At this point, although the findings match the predictions of attachment theory, it is unclear whether romantic partners actually enter relationships with these complementary attachment styles or whether something in the nature of the relationship alters the attachment style. As you will see in Box 12.1, attachment styles can change with experience in a romantic relationship, but the probability of change is not large. Although distribution of attachment classification is independent of gender, gender-related stereotypes might be one possible contributor to changes in relationship quality over time. It may be, for example, that once a relationship is established, traditional masculine stereotypes encouraging emotional distance or traditional feminine ones encouraging preoccupation exacerbate preexisting patterns.

Intimacy, Satisfaction, and Stability of Relationships. Does attachment style affect a person's capacity for intimacy—the degree of emotional closeness and mutual acceptance that individuals can find in relationships? Scharf et al. (2004) used the AAI to determine the attachment style of young Israeli men (about age 18) a year before they began 3 years of mandatory military service. The researchers also measured the quality of participants' relationships with their parents. After their military service was complete, the young men were asked about the intimacy of their relationships with parents, friends, and romantic partners. They answered questions about emotional closeness, relationship satisfaction, and feelings of commitment. Parents also answered questions about their sons' relationships and relationship capacity. Men who were rated as secure in the first assessment were more likely than other men to have good relationships with their parents and to show improvements in those relationships over the 4 years of the study. Secure attachment style also predicted a greater capacity for intimacy in their friendships and romantic partnerships. Interestingly, dismissive individuals tended to distance themselves from parents over time, especially if they experienced substantial stress during their military service.

When researchers actually study romantic partners they find similar results. Simpson (1990) assessed 144 dating couples, examining participants' levels of trust, commitment, interdependence, and emotional expression as a function of their attachment style. Attachment was measured using a 13-item scale developed by Hazan and Shaver (1987). Six months after the initial data collection, Simpson contacted each of the couples to inquire about the status of their relationship.

Results showed that different relationship experiences were associated with three attachment patterns. Secure individuals experienced more positive and less negative emotion in relationships than those who were insecure. They also reported more trust, commitment, and interdependence, as attachment theory would predict. Highly avoidant individuals were less interdependent and less committed to their partners than secure individuals; highly anxious people were more likely to report that their relationships lacked trust. In one interesting gender difference, Simpson found that avoidant males experienced the lowest levels of distress when their relationships ended, but no differences in breakup distress were found for categories of women. Perhaps this is due to the commonly held perception that women are primarily responsible for maintenance of personal relationships and are held accountable for their success. Evidence from this study and others (Collins and Read, 1990) also indicates that the attachment status of one partner influences the relationship satisfaction of the other. Both male and female partners reported being less satisfied in relationships when males were avoidant and when females were preoccupied or anxious.

Kirkpatrick and Davis (1994) also studied relationship satisfaction and stability over a 3-year period. Security of partners in this study was associated with greater satisfaction with the relationship. As we have seen, the lowest level of satisfaction was reported by couples composed of avoidant men and anxious women. Interestingly, however, when these researchers measured stability at the 3-year follow-up, avoidant-anxious matches were as stable as the more satisfied secure couples. Couples made up of anxious men and avoidant women were more likely than others to

Box 12.1 | The Benefits of Love: Stability and Change in Adult Attachment Styles

A child's attachment status can change if the caregiving environment changes. We saw in Chapter 4, for example, that major disruptions of family life, such as parents' divorce or loss of employment, can impact the quality of care a child receives and alter the security of the child's attachment. Is an adult's attachment style open to revision? If so, it seems likely that such change would happen primarily in the context of major relationship shifts—after marriage, or with parenting, or because of the dissolution of an intimate partnership. Crowell, Treboux, and Waters (2002) studied stability and change in young adults' attachment representations after they were married, expecting that although stability might be the rule, the intimacy and intensity of marital relationships could be especially conducive to positive change for some individuals.

One hundred fifty-seven couples, averaging about 24 years old, were recruited for the study when they sought marriage licenses in one county of New York State. None were previously married and none had children. They had already been together for an average of 51 months, although most (about 67%) were still living separately, usually with their parents. These young men and women were tested 3 months before and 18 months after their weddings. At each assessment they were given an attachment classification based on an Adult Attachment Interview (AAI). In addition, participants completed a "Family Behavior Survey," answering questions about amount of happiness, discord, and aggression in their relationship. Finally, each partner participated in a "Current Relationship Interview." In these interviews, participants were required to use adjectives to characterize their own and their partners' behaviors, and they had to provide examples that supported those descriptions. They also talked about what factors were important aspects of, and influences on, their relationships, and about qualities of their interaction in different circumstances, such as when one partner was sick or upset. From these interviews, the researchers assigned each participant a relationship rating. A relationship, like an attachment status, could be classified as "secure," "dismissing," "preoccupied," or "unresolved." Individuals whose relationships were secure, for example, were likely to report examples of shared comfort and support, saw their partnership as an opportunity for both partners to grow, and spoke coherently about the importance of attachment elements, like emotional closeness. In dismissive relationships, individuals tended to express support for their partners only conditionally, that is, only for concerns that they regarded as important. They also talked more about the material or personal goals they had for their relationship (e.g., we'll be buying a house together) than they did on factors like their emotional bond. In preoccupied relationships, partners spoke of feeling anxious about their partners' expressed concerns and about the relationship, sometimes manifesting that anxiety as anger or confusion.

As expected, for the majority of participants (78%), attachment status remained stable through the marriage transition. This was especially true of those who began with a secure attachment. The relationships formed by secure partners were also more secure. As we would expect from other studies (see text), the partnerships of secure individuals were more intimate from the beginning, and they had fewer difficulties, like arguments or verbal aggression, during the first 18 months of marriage. According to attachment theory, a working model of attachment *should* be fairly stable by adulthood, representing a characteristic state of mind in relationship contexts that affects the behavior of the individual and that in turn affects the responses of the relationship partner. As we have seen, these mental and behavioral patterns begin in infancy, evolve through childhood and adolescence, and become more entrenched with time. As a result, we should not only expect stability in the attachment status of the typical adult, but we should also find that his relationships tend to reflect his attachment style.

However, the idea of a "working model" is that it *can* be influenced by new input. If a new relationship provides truly different interactive experiences from those that have come before, then change is possible (Bowlby, 1988). Crowell et al. (2002) found that nearly all secure individuals remained secure at the end of the study, but over 20% of individuals who were insecure at the beginning of the study were secure by the second assessment. Those who changed were more likely to have been classified as preoccupied than dismissive at the beginning of the study. It may be that because dismissive individuals tend to avoid intimacy, they are less likely to experience the kinds of support that can transform one's expectations of relationships. The "became secure" participants were no more likely than the "stable insecure" participants to be paired with a secure partner, suggesting that "a committed, devoted, but insecure partner can be as effective as a secure partner in fostering growth and change, and may even be relatively tolerant and supportive of a partner's secure-base 'missteps'" (p. 476). The telling difference between the became secure and the stable insecure groups was that the became secure group had more positive relationships, even before the wedding. They were more intimate, happy, and passionate, and there was somewhat less discord than in the relationships of the stable insecure participants. The became secure group also tended to have more education and to have lived away from parents prior to marriage. "This suggests that experiences and opportunity in such settings (e.g., exposure to new ideas, new people, and new relationships), as well as physical and psychological distance from parents, facilitate the reconceptualization of childhood attachment relationships" (p. 476). If we think of the parent–child relationship as a child's "first love," it does indeed seem that love can be sweeter the second time around.

break up over the course of the study. Once again, the authors speculated that this result had something to do with women being the stereotypical tenders of relationships. Avoidant women may be less skilled at accommodating, or less motivated to accommodate, the needs of the more dependent partner. Anxious women, overly concerned with possibilities of abandonment, might be more willing to do what it takes to maintain a relationship with an avoidant partner, hence accounting for the high level of stability in these relationships.

Communication Style and Conflict Resolution. Consider for a moment a problem that you experienced at some time in one of your close relationships. Now reflect on how you dealt with that problem. Was your response typical of the way you usually deal with relationship problems? You undoubtedly know, by virtue of your training, that when faced with a relationship's inevitable glitches, it is a good idea to be open, nondefensive, reasonably assertive, and yet flexible enough to compromise. Keeping a clear head so that problem solving can be effective is another requirement. Easier said than done, you're probably thinking! Why is it often so hard to do this well?

One reason is that conflict and communication in close relationships frequently have one or more subtexts: love, loss, trust, and abandonment, to name a few. In short, conflicts are stressful, they elicit emotions, and, perhaps, they can trigger the patterns of emotion regulation learned in the earliest of attachment relationships. Many studies have documented the advantages of attachment security for interpersonal communication (Keelan, Dion, & Dion, 1998; Mikulincer & Arad, 1999). Secure individuals display more reciprocity and flexibility in communication. Greater self-disclosure characterizes the communication of secure and anxious groups as compared to avoidant ones. Several studies also document the advantages of having a secure orientation when it comes to solving problems (Pistole, 1989). In general, secure individuals are more apt to compromise in ways that are mutually beneficial. Avoidant individuals tend to be more uncompromising, whereas anxious individuals tend to give in.

What actually happens when a couple has to deal with conflict in the relationship? According to attachment theory, the conflict produces stress, which activates the attachment system, makes the working models more accessible and influences how affect gets regulated. Simpson, Rholes, and Phillips (1996) asked 123 heterosexual couples, who had been dating from 6 months to 2 years, to discuss problems in their relationships. Participants were videotaped, and their interactions were rated by observers. Secure individuals were less defensive than insecure ones and held the most favorable views of their partners after discussing a major problem. Avoidant participants kept the greatest emotional distance in the discussion. Presumably uncomfortable with the expression of emotion, they appeared to minimize personal involvement. By the same token, they did not display evidence of anger, distress, or less positive views of their partners. Avoidant men provided less warmth and supportiveness to their partners, consistent with theoretical predictions. In contrast, avoidant women did not display this pattern in this study. The strength of society's mandate that women be relationship caretakers might, in certain circumstances, override avoidant dispositions. But this is not the case in every close relationship. In at least one other study, both men and women with avoidant styles were less likely to give emotional support to close friends (Phillips, Simpson, Lanigan, & Rholes, 1995).

Ambivalent partners in the study by Simpson and colleagues (1996) reacted with the most negative emotion to the discussion of problems, displaying high levels of stress and anxiety during the interaction. They also reported feeling more hostility and anger toward their partners after the session. Ambivalent couples report more disruptions and more shifts in satisfaction in general when compared to other types (Tidwell, Reis, & Shaver, 1996). Consistent with attachment theory, these individuals expect their partners to fail at meeting their needs in stressful situations. Rholes and his colleagues (Rholes, Simpson, & Stevens, 1998) explain the phenomenon in this way:

> Conflict elicits a cascade of unpleasant feelings in ambivalent persons, and it should raise doubts about the quality and viability of their current partner and relationship. Moreover, if fears of abandonment become salient, ambivalent partners ought to derogate the partner and relationship to minimize or "prepare for" potential loss. Persons who are not ambivalent, in contrast, may not experience conflict as aversive, but as an occasion in which open communication and the joint, constructive sharing of feelings can occur. (pp. 181–182)

In general, attachment theory serves as a useful template for conceptualizing the universal human needs served by close, interpersonal relationships as well as the systematic differences individuals display in their personal associations. Clinicians are already very familiar with the notion that certain qualities of family relationships experienced early in life tend to get repeated in later relationships. Although not derivative of attachment theory per se, psychoanalytic and some family therapy approaches such as Bowen's (1978) advise clients to examine the nature of conflicted childhood relationships within one's family of origin in an effort to achieve insight and gain the freedom to make more adaptive relationship choices in the present.

"ARBEITEN"—TO WORK

For most young adults, the launching of a vocational life is as important a developmental task as the process of forming or reforming attachments. What are the key elements in a successful launch? A large body of theory and research has addressed this question. The theories share in common a general notion that career success and satisfaction depend heavily on matching the characteristics of an individual and the demands of a job. If this notion is correct, then self-knowledge is a critical element in career decision making. Thus, not only is establishing an occupational role an important part of identity or self-concept development, it is also an emergent property of that process. The stronger our sense of who we are as we become adults, the more likely we are to make good career choices. Two classic theories of career development will illustrate.

Some Theories of the Career Development Process

HOLLAND'S THEORY OF PERSONALITY–ENVIRONMENT TYPES

Holland (e.g., 1966, 1985) suggests that by early adulthood each individual has a modal personal orientation: a typical and preferred style or approach to dealing with social and environmental tasks. Holland proposed that most people can be categorized as having one of six modal orientations (described in Table 12.2), which can be seen as part of the individual's personality. According to Holland, a job or career typically makes demands on an individual that are compatible with one or more of these interactive types. That is, a job can be construed as creating an environment within which a certain personal orientation will lead to both success and happiness. For example, one of the personal orientation types is "social." A social type is likely to be sociable, friendly, cooperative, kind, tactful, and understanding and is often a good match to occupations that involve working with others to educate, to cure, or to enlighten them—such as counseling or social work. A contrasting type is the "enterprising" individual. He too is likely to be sociable, but more domineering, energetic, ambitious, talkative, and attention getting. He is also likely to be more effective in vocational tasks that involve maneuvering others to achieve goals, such as reaching a certain level of sales, or more efficiently delivering services as a salesperson, for instance, or an executive. Thus, each type of modal personal orientation, such as social or enterprising, is also a type of vocational environment. Usually, neither individuals nor environments fall neatly into only one "type." Holland and his colleagues have developed coding systems for rating both individuals and environments. In these systems, three-letter codes indicate the most characteristic style for the individual (e.g., Holland, Viernstein, Kuo, Karweit, & Blum, 1970) or the environment (e.g., Gottfredson, Holland, & Ogawa, 1982), as well as the second and third most characteristic styles. So, for example, a person (or environment) might be coded RIS, meaning primarily realistic (R), secondarily investigative (I), and finally social (S). (See Table 12.2 for some characteristics of these types for individuals.)

Studies spanning several decades have corroborated the notion that a good fit between modal orientation (also called personal style) and job characteristics is correlated with job satisfaction, performance, and stability, as well as feelings of personal well-being (e.g., Kieffer, Schinka, & Curtiss, 2004; Tyler, 1961; see Spokane, Meir, & Catalano, 2000, for a recent review). For example, Gottfredson and Holland (1990) studied young adult bank tellers for 4 months after they were first hired. Congruence between an individual's personal style and job

TABLE 12.2	Some Characteristics of Holland's Personality Types	
Realistic	**Investigative**	**Artistic**
Conforming	Analytical	Complicated
Dogmatic	Cautious	Disorderly
Genuine	Complex	Emotional
Hardheaded	Critical	Expressive
Inflexible	Curious	Idealistic
Materialistic	Independent	Imaginative
Natural	Intellectual	Impractical
Normal	Introverted	Impulsive
Persistent	Pessimistic	Independent
Practical	Precise	Introspective
Realistic	Radical	Intuitive
Reserved	Rational	Nonconforming
Robust	Reserved	Open
Self-effacing	Retiring	Original
Uninsightful	Unassuming	Sensitive
Social	**Enterprising**	**Conventional**
Agreeable	Acquisitive	Careful
Cooperative	Adventurous	Conforming
Empathic	Ambitious	Conscientious
Friendly	Assertive	Dogmatic
Generous	Domineering	Efficient
Helpful	Energetic	Inflexible
Idealistic	Enthusiastic	Inhibited
Kind	Excitement seeking	Methodical
Patient	Exhibitionistic	Obedient
Persuasive	Extroverted	Orderly
Responsible	Forceful	Persistent
Sociable	Optimistic	Practical
Tactful	Resourceful	Thorough
Understanding	Self-confident	Thrifty
Warm	Sociable	Unimaginative

type was clearly correlated with job satisfaction. In two studies of school teachers, Meir (1989) examined several kinds of congruence or fit: between personal style and job type, between personal style and outside activities (avocations), and between the individual's particular skills and opportunities to use those skills on the job. All three kinds of congruence appeared to contribute to the participants' reported feelings of well-being. A person's happiness seems to be closely linked to the fit between his personality characteristics and both his work, as Holland predicted, and his leisure pursuits. It appears that creating a good match in one arena can help compensate for a lack of congruence in another (see also Tinsley, Hinson, Tinsley, & Holt, 1993).

SUPER'S DEVELOPMENTAL APPROACH

Super (e.g., 1972, 1984, 1990) agrees with Holland's notion that a satisfying work life is most likely when an individual's personal characteristics are well matched to the demands of a job. His theorizing about career development, however, focuses less on specifying personal style or job types and more on describing the developmental processes that determine both the emergence of one's vocational self-concept and the multiple factors that influence job choices through the life span. Vocational self-concept is part of one's total identity. It includes ideas about which qualities of the self would (or would not) provide a match to the requirements of an occupation (Super, 1984). Vocational self-concept is a function of two things: first, a person's view of his personal or psychological characteristics, and second, how he assesses his life circumstances, such as the limits or opportunities created by economic conditions; by his socioeconomic status; by his family, friendship network, and community; and so on.

Super described a series of typical life stages in the development of vocational self-concept and experience, beginning in childhood. In the growth stage (up to age 14 or so), children are developing many elements of identity that will have a bearing on vocational self-concept, including ideas about their interests, attitudes, skills, and needs. In the exploratory stage, which includes adolescence and young adulthood up to about age 24, vocational self-concept is tentatively narrowed down, but often career choices are not finalized. General vocational goals are formulated in the earlier part of this stage (crystallization), gradually leading to the identification of more specific vocational preferences (specification) and finally to the completion of education along with entry into full-time employment (implementation). In the establishment stage, from about 25 to 44, work experiences provide the laboratory within which the matching of vocational self-concept and job settings is tried out, sometimes reevaluated, sometimes confirmed, and eventually stabilized (stabilization). From about 45 to 64, in the maintenance stage, an individual makes ongoing adjustments to improve his work situation, often achieving more advanced status and seniority (consolidation). If not, this can also be a time of increasing frustration with work. Finally, in the decline stage, right before and after 65 for most people, the career winds down, with retirement planning and actual retirement taking precedence over career advancement and consolidation. Note that although these are typical life stages, at least partially verified by longitudinal research (e.g., Super & Overstreet, 1960), an individual can go through additional sequences of crystallization, specification, implementation, and stabilization when life circumstances change. These "mini-cycles" of reevaluation can be initiated by any number of events: disappointment with a career choice, job loss, changes in family life, and so on. Note the similarity to MAMA cycles in identity development described in Chapter 9.

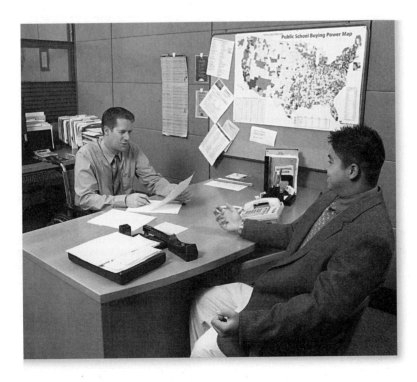

Classic career development theories emphasize the importance of fitting personal characteristics to the demands of the job. Self-knowledge is seen as critical to making the right career choices.

Perhaps Super's most important insight is his recognition that career development is a continuing process. It serves as both a source of and an outgrowth of an individual's overall personal growth. For Super, a career is

> the life course of a person encountering a series of developmental tasks and attempting to handle them in such a way as to become the kind of person he or she wants to become. With a changing self and changing situations, the matching process is never really completed. (1990, pp. 225–226)

Research indicates that many aspects of a job beyond compatibility with one's interests and talents influence how rewarding it is. Quality of supervision, participation in decision making, interaction with others on the job, geographic location, personal health, pay, and a number of other factors are also correlated with job satisfaction (e.g., Decker & Borgen, 1993; Herr & Cramer, 1992; Perry-Jenkins et al., 2000; Rhoades & Eisenberger, 2002). However, theories and research such as Holland's and Super's make the powerful suggestion that even when all these other factors are acceptable, a person's work responsibilities can be incompatible with his or her personality characteristics. Under these circumstances, although a hard-working individual could succeed in meeting his responsibilities, real satisfaction and the opportunity to truly excel are likely to elude him. We will have more to say about personality characteristics in Chapter 13.

The interdependence of career and self-development is an important focus of some current career counseling approaches. McAuliffe (1993), for example, describes a developmentally oriented career counseling system that has an Eriksonian flavor. He argues that a central role of the counselor is to help clients address the following key question: "Who am I becoming and how shall I express this emerging self?" He points out that many clients may begin counseling with a different, but less helpful, way of conceptualizing their career issues. Some, for example, may be asking themselves, "What does my community, my family, my ethnic or religious group expect of me?" That is, they frame the issue such that their career, and their self-definition, is embedded in interpersonal relationships, not authored from within. Perhaps for this group, career identity represents a closed, rather than a constructed, facet of their identity (see Chapter 9). Other clients, especially those facing some career threat, such as downsizing, may begin with the question, "How do I maintain the current form I am in?" With this conceptual framework the self is embedded in what the person has always done, so that new career paths, expressing other needs or dimensions of the self, are not imaginable. The task for counselors may be to facilitate the development of a new, personally constructed sense of self as worker.

For many clients, then, career counseling may need to begin with help in reframing the way one construes the self. In McAuliffe's words,

> it is the counselor's challenge to assist clients in their transformations of meaning making. . . . For example, for the young adult college student whose seemingly simple dilemma is to choose between pursuing a parent-approved pre-medical track or to consider the internal voice that draws her to the social sciences, counseling would operate on two levels: one to weigh the pros and cons of various fields of study and the other to support and challenge the person so that the tacit assumptions about "who's in charge" become conscious, so that the dissonant voice that implicitly calls the person to author his or her own career can be considered. (1993, pp. 25–26)

The Realities of Career Development in Young Adulthood

For young adults launching a work life, many variables influence the speed and form of that process. Consider the prospects of two 18-year-olds, Akil and Jarod, who have just graduated from high school. Akil comes from a middle-class family. His parents take great pride in being the first ones in their own families to have graduated from college and to provide their children with a comfortable middle-class life. They expect their children to attend college and to select careers that will help them maintain or even improve upon their socioeconomic status. They have several children to educate, but they are quite savvy about how to finance a college education, having put themselves through college, and they are convinced that college is a necessity for career success. Akil sees college as a necessary step on his way to a professional career, although his future plans are not specific. He expects his college experience to help him figure out what profession to enter.

The expectations that Jarod and his family have are quite different. Jarod's mother earns low wages working for a janitorial service, and she often puts in overtime to help make ends meet. Neither she nor Jarod's father (from whom she is estranged) completed high school, and both are quite proud that Jarod has. However, they have never even considered the possibility of college for Jarod. As they see it, he has completed his education and should now be able to earn a living. His mother expects him to find his own apartment to relieve the crowding in her small place. Jarod himself is quite unsure of what he can do in the world of work. He is simply hoping to find a job, any job, one that will give him a start, providing an opportunity to learn a skill and to find a niche.

Even if these two young men happen to have similar interests and personalities, their careers are likely to follow very different trajectories, largely because of the differences in their socioeconomic class, their families' views of education, and the opportunities that they perceive to be available to them. In the following sections, we will consider what the typical course of career development is for individuals like Akil and Jarod. We will specifically examine the characteristics of the process when young people move on to college from high school and when they do not. We will also consider the impact of other major factors on one's early career experiences, factors such as immediate environment, social class, race, and gender.

THE COLLEGE STUDENT

Young adults entering college have many hopes and expectations for the college years. Some of their concerns are incidental to the educational setting and are focused on either maintaining or establishing social networks or finding intimate relationships—the pursuit of "lieben." But many of their hopes are relevant to "arbeiten," their vocational lives. Some 1st-year students expect the college years to be a time of self-development, when they will "construct a philosophy of life" and become more clear about the course their adult lives might take. For most, very practical, work-related issues are among their highest priorities. The majority of students entering college indicate that "to get a better job" and "to make more money" are important reasons why they chose to go to college. Figure 12.3 also illustrates that more recent cohorts of college students are even more likely to emphasize these kinds of practical career concerns than students did 20 or 30 years ago (American Council on Education, 1999; Astin, 1993; Myers, 2000).

The first vocationally relevant decision that students make is the choice of a major. Those students who are career oriented tend to decide on an occupation first and then select a major, whereas students more focused on self-development tend to select a major first and then consider possible occupational choices (Goodson, 1978). A majority of students change their majors at least once during college, although the changes they make are usually among related disciplines (Herr & Cramer, 1992). There are substantial cohort differences regarding which majors and occupations are more popular with students. For example, Astin (1993) compared two large samples of college students who entered college 17 years apart: the first in 1968 and the second in 1985. Members of the 1985 cohort were more likely to want careers in business, law, or medicine and less likely to choose teaching or scientific research than members of the 1968 sample.

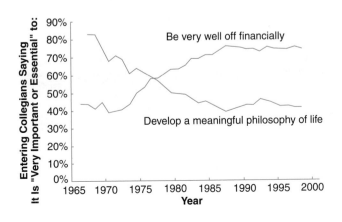

FIGURE 12.3

What College Students Consider Important Reasons for Attending College

Myers, D. G. (2000). The funds, friends, and faith of happy people. *American Psychologist, 55*, 56–67. Copyright © 2000 by the American Psychological Association. Reprinted with permission.

Surveys of more recent cohorts indicate that the most popular majors in the 1990s were business, psychology, engineering, education, English literature, and accounting (Murray, 1996). By 2004, first year college students were showing record high interest in majors related to the biological sciences and health careers such as nursing (Higher Education Research Institute, 2004).

We have seen that theorists such as Holland and Super argue that career choices often are, and should be, based on one's personal characteristics. What other factors, besides self-concept or personal style, might influence the choice of a major in college, and ultimately the choice of a career? First, variations over time in the relative popularity of a major indicate that social and economic changes over time influence choice of major. This might include economic upturns and downturns, change in the kinds of goods and services that are in demand, shifts in population size and composition, advances in technology, and developments in political and legal philosophy, such as in the area of civil rights law.

For example, some of the most interesting changes in majors and occupational choices across recent decades are gender specific and appear to reflect political and social trends in our beliefs about the role of women in society. The Higher Education Research Institute at UCLA reports that the proportion of women majoring in traditionally male-dominated fields, such as the biological sciences, the physical sciences, engineering, prelaw, premed, and business, increased dramatically in the last three decades of the twentieth century, as hiring patterns in related fields became less gender biased than they once were (Dey & Hurtado, 1999).

In addition to the influence of social, civil, and economic change, other more stable factors appear to play a role. As the stories of Akil and Jarod indicate, socioeconomic status (SES) is important in shaping the expectations of young people, heavily influencing the educational choices that they make and the jobs to which they aspire. Research indicates that other family and environmental factors, such as race and ethnicity, also affect the choice of whether or not to go to college. Individuals from minority and low SES groups are less likely than other groups to make the college choice. If an individual enrolls in college, are a student's career aspirations affected by such variables? Some indicators suggest that the answer is yes. To illustrate, the probability of retention, staying in college long enough to graduate, is related to SES (National

Reflecting social and political change over recent decades, women often choose occupations traditionally occupied by men.

Center for Education Statistics, 1998). The influence of SES on retention is probably multifaceted. Lower SES students often are not as well prepared academically for the demands of college as higher SES students, although it should be noted that the majority of students who drop out of college are doing adequate work. Lower SES students also have more problems paying for college, and they may experience less support from family and friends to remain in college than higher SES students do (e.g., Ryland, Riordan, & Brack, 1994). Being of minority status is also linked to lower rates of retention. African American students are at particular risk for dropping out, a problem that may be partially a result of the stress of dealing with minority status, such as feeling unwelcome in predominantly White institutions (Newman & Newman, 1999; Sailes, 1993; Zea, Reisen, Beil, & Caplan, 1997).

Do factors such as SES affect one's choice of a college major? There is indirect evidence that they can. For example, students attending private universities are more likely to choose premed majors than students attending public 4-year colleges, and students at public institutions are more likely to choose school teaching as a career than students at private universities (Astin, 1993). Given that SES has some influence on the choice of private versus public educational facilities, it appears that SES may contribute to these differences.

Other characteristics of the college environment also seem to influence choice of major or career (see Astin, 1993). For example, students are more likely to select college teaching as a career if they attend smaller colleges that provide high levels of student–faculty interaction, opportunities for independent research, and written evaluations of students' work. African American students are more likely to choose premed if they attend a traditionally Black college than if they do not. Membership in a fraternity or sorority is linked to greater tendencies to select business or prelaw as a major. Of course, whether one attends a small college or a Black college, or joins a sorority or fraternity, is probably influenced by preexisting characteristics of the student. For example, extroverts appear to be more attracted to Greek life on campus than introverts (e.g., Sher, Bartholow, & Nanda, 2001). Therefore, it is difficult to say whether such features of college life have a causal influence on students' major or career choices or whether students who favor such environments also tend to prefer certain fields of study. It seems likely that the causal connections work both ways.

One role that the college experience seems to play in choosing a major and ultimately a career is that it provides opportunities to try out different choices with relatively little cost. Some students enter college aspiring to be lawyers or physicians or engineers, for example, only to find that the prelaw, premed, or engineering coursework is not suitable to their interests or abilities. Such majors often lose enrollment as students move through their college years. Other majors tend to draw increasing numbers over the college years. Education and business majors are among these. Interestingly, some of the more academically challenging fields also increase their draw somewhat after students get a taste of college, fields like scientific research and college teaching (see Astin, 1993).

Since one's choice of a college major is associated with college success as well as career choice, career counseling in college should begin with advisement on choice of a major. Unfortunately, leaving this task to relatively untrained faculty advisors seems to be insufficient for helping students to make good choices. Herr and Cramer (1992), in their text on career guidance throughout the life span, argue that career guidance professionals at the college level should provide students with assistance in selecting a major. In pursuit of this and other career goals, even 1st-year students should have help available in self-assessment and self-analysis, as well as in decision making.

It is clear that a college education plays a critical role in occupational opportunity. One's highest educational degree is the single most important predictor of level of job entry, and level of job entry weighs more heavily than IQ or job skill in predicting career advancement. But the value of a college education goes beyond its contribution to career development. For example, being a college graduate means a greater likelihood of being healthy or of having a successful marriage. Some of the effects of higher education are probably due to the income opportunities it creates and so are career linked; others may be related to the development of critical thinking skills and flexibility in problem solving that it seems to foster (Pascarella, Bohr, Nora, & Terenzini, 1995; Pascarella & Terenzini, 1991).

THE FORGOTTEN HALF

The "forgotten half" was the name given by the William T. Grant Foundation Commission on Work, Family, and Citizenship (1988) to 18- to 24-year-olds who do not go to college. These were just under half of the total young adult population in the United States in 1988. They were described as

> the young people who build our homes, drive our buses, repair our automobiles, fix our televisions, maintain and serve our offices, schools and hospitals, and keep the production lines of our mills and factories moving. To a great extent, they determine how well the American family, economy and democracy function. They are also the thousands of young men and women who aspire to work productively but never quite "make it" to that kind of employment. For these members of the Forgotten Half, their lives as adults start in the economic limbo of unemployment, part-time jobs, and poverty wages. Many of them never break free. (1988, as cited in Halperin, 1998a, cover)

Ten years later, the American Youth Policy Forum sponsored a follow-up report on the "forgotten half" (Halperin, 1998a). The good news was that the high school dropout rate had declined since the original report, and the numbers of high school graduates entering 2- or 4-year colleges had increased, so that the proportion of young adults with no postsecondary training had dropped several percentage points. The bad news, however, was that the real income of young adults in the United States had declined, and the most serious losses were experienced by those with the least education. Further, poverty rates had increased for those at every educational level except college graduates (see Figure 12.4). "In the 1990's, the wide income gaps correlated with formal educational attainment continued to widen" (Halperin, 1998b, p. 13). Unfortunately, more recent reports from the American Youth Policy Forum suggest that of the high school graduates who begin college today, fewer than half complete a degree and a third never move on to their sophomore year (Pennington, 2003).

Interestingly, the basic attitudes of young adults toward work and family do not differ regardless of whether they go to college. Young people usually rank good pay and opportunities for advancement as highly desirable features of a job. They also want their work to make a meaningful contribution to society. As for their social aspirations, young people of all backgrounds generally consider having a good marriage and having children to be important life goals for them (e.g., Hill & Yeung, 1999).

Despite the broad similarities in the goals of college and noncollege youth in the United States, the chances of achieving these goals are substantially reduced for the latter group. As we have already seen, education is a key predictor of employment success, career advancement, and general success in life, so that when a young person chooses to end education with high school, he places limits on his options and opportunities. "Until the last few decades, young people without an education beyond high school were often able to find family-sustaining work in service industries or manufacturing operations. Today, they face lives of grinding economic struggle virtually shut out from jobs that will allow them to build assets and support children of their

FIGURE 12.4

Percentage of Young Families Living in Poverty

Source: Halperin, S. (1998). Today's forgotten half: Still losing ground. In S. Halperin (Ed.), *The forgotten half revisited: American youth and young families, 1988–2008,* p. 8. Washington, D.C.: American Youth Policy Forum. Reprinted by permission.

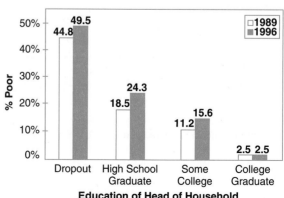

own" (Pennington, 2003, p. 60). A number of other factors also affect the degree to which a young person's goals are likely to be achieved. These factors include socioeconomic status, as was the case with Jarod. Even when young people fail to attend college, coming from a family of relatively high socioeconomic status provides opportunities and advantages that youth from lower SES families usually do not have. Another important factor is race, which can have profound impact on the probability of employment across all education levels (see Figure 12.5). Finally, a variety of "behavioral obstacles," including having a child early or out of wedlock and engaging in criminal behavior, are important determiners of whether or not young adults will make significant strides toward meeting their goals. Among noncollege youth, those most at risk of slipping into poverty, for example, are Blacks with criminal records who come from low-income families (e.g., Halperin, 1998b; Hill & Yeung, 1999). As we have discussed earlier, these outcomes may be the result of histories of accumulating and interlocking risks.

Although many factors can contribute to a slide into poverty, adequate educational preparation is clearly the most effective avenue to avoiding poverty and to achieving the typical goals that young people have for work and family. But both the 1988 and 1998 reports on the forgotten half argue that the difficulties faced by noncollege youth in America are partly a function of a disorganized and inadequate system for training adolescents and young adults for the kinds of skilled employment that are personally rewarding and that can provide an adequate income to support a family. It is often difficult for young people even to obtain information on how to prepare themselves for particular jobs and occupations. Recommendations for improving the lot of noncollege youth begin with ideas for improving basic skill training in public schools, including the teaching of such traditional academic skills as reading, writing, math, and speaking abilities, as well as thinking skills, self-management, and social skills. The particular concern is to improve the quality of secondary education for students who go through general or vocational (noncollege preparatory) tracks in high school. These programs are often criticized for having watered-down, boring curricula (Bailey & Morest, 1998).

Next, reports on the forgotten half encourage providing high school students with better access to extensive vocational counseling and with opportunities for work-based learning. They also suggest increasing the participation of employers in providing training and apprenticeship programs, using the community college system to create expanded opportunities for technical training, and creating community-based resources to provide young adults with information about pathways into specific occupations (Bailey & Morest, 1998; Pennington, 2003).

For some young adults, special training programs designed for economically disadvantaged participants who face multiple risks can be quite effective. The American Youth Policy Forum

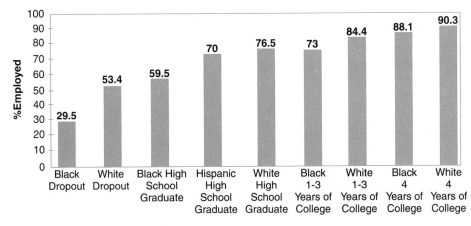

FIGURE 12.5

1996 Employment Percentages of Out-of-School 16- to 24-Year-Olds by Race and Education

Source: Halperin, S. (1998). Today's forgotten half: Still losing ground. In S. Halperin (Ed.), *The forgotten half revisited: American youth and young families, 1988–2008*, p. 14. Washington, D.C.: American Youth Policy Forum. Reprinted by permission.

(Partee, 2003) evaluated a large number of programs launched in the United States over the last several decades. The most successful of these have helped young men and women move on to postsecondary education or to quality employment opportunities, simultaneously supporting the young adults they serve and reaping economic and social benefits for their communities. For example, Job Corp, a public–private partnership administered by the U.S. Department of Labor, returns about $2.00 to society for every $1.00 invested. Private programs like Strive, operated in New York City's Harlem, have helped at-risk young adults sustain employment over multiple years. Like other effective interventions (see Box 1.2 in Chapter 1), these programs tend to have certain characteristics in common, such as implementation quality (e.g., sufficient and sustained resources, strong leadership, and professional staff development); caring and knowledgeable teachers, counselors, and mentors; high standards and expectations; and a holistic approach, meaning that they address multiple needs (e.g., providing child care and transportation, life skills and assertiveness training, individualized attention, and so on).

Many researchers note that there is a particularly sinister trend that affects the forgotten half. Arrest and imprisonment for minor crimes (e.g., drug possession) have increased in recent decades, in particular for males in minority groups. The number of young men incarcerated in federal and state prisons more than doubled between 1986 and 1995 (Halperin, 1998b; see also Table 12.3). The rate of incarceration for both White and minority women is low in comparison, but it has also increased dramatically in recent years (Harrison & Beck, 2004).

> For some segments of society, crime control policy . . . has regressed to the point that imprisonment is the major governmental intervention in the transition to young adulthood. . . . This means that segments of the population are cut off from voting, employment, and community organizations. This disenfranchisement will further contribute to increased unemployment and undermine family life. (Laub, 1999)

Given that friendships, family ties, and a sense of belonging in a community play a significant role in a young adult's hope for the future and chances for upward mobility, school- and community-based vocational training and counseling seem like a much better alternative than jail for many adolescent and young adult delinquents.

WOMEN VERSUS MEN

Traditionally, gender has been a significant factor in career development. In 1957, Super found that a variety of career patterns characterized adults in the mid-20th century in the United States. For men, the "conventional career pattern" included a period or periods of "trial work," that is, trying out possible jobs and then launching into a stable career. The conventional career pattern for women, however, involved entry into work as a stopgap after high school or college. Once married, women tended to shift to full-time homemaking. Even in 1957, there were other patterns for both men and women that were common enough not to be considered atypical, but most of the alternative patterns also displayed gender differences. For example, women sometimes

TABLE 12.3   Young Men, Ages 18 to 24, Incarcerated in Federal, State, and Local Prisons in 1986 and 1995

Year	Total Population of Young Men	Number in Prisons & Jails	Percent in Prisons & Jails
1986	13,502,061	177,952	1.3
1995	12,904,674	359,419	2.8
Change: 1986 to 1995	−594,387	+181,467	+1.5

Source: Adapted from Halperin, S. (1998). Today's forgotten half: Still losing ground. In S. Halperin (Ed.), *The forgotten half revisited: American youth and young families, 1998–2008* (pp. 1–26). Washington, D.C.: American Youth Policy Forum.

followed the "double-track career pattern," first establishing a career and then adding a second career as homemaker. Or they might show the "interrupted career pattern," first establishing a career, then marrying and becoming a full-time homemaker, and then shifting back to a career when home responsibilities were less pressing. Interestingly, none of the patterns Super characterized as typical of men included double-track or any kind of interruption based on family or homemaking concerns.

How important is gender in career development today? As we have already seen, there have certainly been substantial changes relevant to gender in our culture since 1950. These changes have grown out of the civil rights movement, the women's rights movement in particular, and are also linked to technological changes such as the availability of reliable contraceptives and an increase in the use of machines to do heavy labor. Many work-related gender differences have diminished, and some have even disappeared or reversed. For example, women now enter college in larger numbers than men do, whereas up until about 1980, men outnumbered women (U.S. Bureau of the Census, 1999). As we have already noted, women now often choose majors in college that traditionally were the preserve of men, such as premed and business. Women currently earn 40% of the graduate degrees granted, and many of these are in traditionally "masculine" fields such as dentistry and law (Dey & Hurtado, 1999). Women constitute approximately half of the employed labor force (Bond, Thompson, Galinsky, & Prottas, 2002), and in 2002, women filled about 46% of executive, administrative, and managerial positions in the United States, more than doubling their representation in these kinds of jobs in 30 years (U.S. Bureau of Labor Statistics, 2003).

But gender differences in career development have by no means disappeared. Women are still more likely than men to select majors in education and the social sciences and to express stronger interests in helping people and in artistic activities. In fact, vocational interests are affected much more by gender than by other individual differences, such as race or ethnicity (e.g., Fouad, 2004). Some careers are still overwhelmingly pursued by one gender, such as secretarial work (by women) and firefighting (by men; e.g., Burgess & Borgida, 1997; Scozarro & Subich, 1990). Although men and women use most of the same criteria to evaluate potential careers (they try to match their interests, and they carefully consider professional advancement and income opportunities), women are more likely than men to consider relationships with people (opportunity for and kinds of) as an important factor in selecting a career (e.g., Gati, Osipow, & Givon, 1995). These differences are influenced at least in part by gender-role beliefs. Both men and women anticipate that marriage and parenting will be important to their lives, for example, but men give greater priority to their role as breadwinner in the family, and women give greater priority to their role as caregiver (e.g., Gati et al., 1995; Vermeulen & Minor, 1998).

Different role expectations are nowhere more evident than in the typical patterns of career development. There have been several noteworthy changes in career patterns for women, and to some extent for men, but these changes continue to reflect the tendency for women to focus more than men on family and childrearing concerns at every stage of career planning. For example, despite the fact that both men and women have the right to take parental or family leaves in some companies in the United States (a right that is mandated by law in many European countries), it is quite rare for a man to exercise that right. The most dramatic change in women's career patterns since the 1950s has been the great increase in women's choice of a double-track pattern. To illustrate the enormity of the change, in 1950, most mothers of children under age 6 were full-time homemakers (88%). In 2002, over 62% mothers of preschoolers were employed, and the percentage of employed mothers continues to rise (e.g., U.S. Bureau of Labor Statistics, 2003; White & Rogers, 2000). Figure 12.6 illustrates that full-time employment (as compared to part-time) has increased dramatically for women in the last four decades. This trend is partly a result of women moving into occupations that tend to require full-time, year-round employment.

Mothers who work are described as having two careers because they typically take more responsibility for child care and daily household tasks than fathers who work, although there is an increasing tendency for men to share somewhat more equitably in homemaking responsibilities and to make job-related decisions that take into account their parenting role (e.g., Bond et al., 2002). Men have also become more likely to take their wives' careers into account in making other job-related decisions, such as whether to relocate (e.g., Gill & Haurin, 1998).

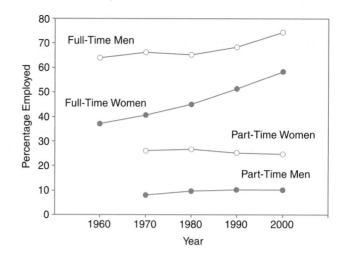

Despite some improvements, old habits do die hard. Women in general are still overrepresented in lower level positions, make less money than men, and have less power to make decisions at work than their male counterparts (Stockard & Johnson, 1992; U.S. Bureau of Labor Statistics, 2003). Organizational structures, possibly constructed and maintained to build in certain privileges for select groups, are slow to change. Research has demonstrated that women in male-dominated occupations are not viewed as favorably as men, despite comparable skills. Their work is evaluated more negatively than men's, and they face more exclusion from the kinds of informal networks and social activities that often pave the way for advancement in the workplace (see Alban-Metcalfe & West, 1991; Eagly & Johannesen-Schmidt, 2001; Pfost & Fiore, 1990). Clearly, both traditional gender roles and the realities of secular change are influencing career patterns for both women and men. We will revisit the issue of dual careers and parenting in the next chapter.

Work and the Development of Self-Concept

As we have now seen, theorists in the arena of career development see an individual's vocational self-concept as critical for the evolution of a successful, satisfying career. Both Holland and Super specify the importance of self-knowledge in career development: accurate assessment of one's own style, interests, and characteristics. Super also emphasizes that one's vocational self both emerges from his broader sense of identity and contributes to it. Thus, it seems that self-concept is a central force behind career development and is, in turn, a product of it. These ideas have formed the backbone of many career counseling approaches. In the following sections, we will consider how feelings and attitudes toward the self as a worker develop. What do these aspects of identity contribute to work and its role in the life of an adult and vice versa? We begin by recapping Erik Erikson's ideas about how work and self-concept are related in development.

ERIKSON'S THEORY OF IDENTITY DEVELOPMENT

In Erikson's (1950/1963) view of the developing self-concept, children begin to formulate a sense of themselves as workers when they first confront serious work. In both nonindustrial and industrial societies around the world, children are expected to begin to work by the time they are 5 or 6 years old. In nonindustrial societies, they work alongside adults, caring for younger children, doing household tasks, helping with farm animals, working in the fields, or hunting. They are expected both to contribute to the productive efforts of the community and to learn the skills they will need as full-fledged adults. In most industrial societies today, children's work begins in school, where they are expected to achieve competence in basic skills, such as reading and arithmetic, that will serve them in nearly any adult work they might take on. Erikson argued that these early work experiences can provide a child with a feeling of **industry**, which is both a belief in his ability to master the skills and tools needed to be productive and a sense of "the pleasure of work completion by steady attention and persevering diligence" (p. 259). Feelings of industry help the child to be "an eager and absorbed unit of a productive situation" (p. 259). The child can, unfortunately, also slip into feeling inadequate and inferior if he cannot seem to master the skills that are required of him and begins to be discouraged about how effective he can be in contributing to productive work efforts. Feelings of inferiority can also begin at this point if social barriers, such as those experienced by the poor, limit a child's opportunities to try out challenging work, provide substandard educational opportunities, or lead him to question his abilities.

Thus, for Erikson, the elementary school years are a crucial time for establishing a strong sense of industry. In adolescence, teens work on fashioning an adult identity, which includes developing a sense of direction for their vocational lives. This process continues, as we have seen, well into young adulthood. Identity formation is influenced by the attitudes toward self that evolved in childhood. We can expect that young people who bring to this process a strong sense of industry will find the task of vocational self-development less cumbersome than those who are plagued by self-doubt.

As you know, Erikson theorized that in adulthood the process of self-concept development continues. Individuals with a sense of who they are and what they can do are motivated to use their lives and their skills to leave a legacy for the next generation. Erikson called this a need for generativity and hypothesized that generativity motives have a strong influence on one's work life as adults move into middle age. Concepts akin to what Erikson called "industry" and "generativity" have been the focus of intensive study in several different research traditions. In the following sections, we will take a closer look at some findings on the importance of these two aspects of self-concept for young adults.

The Importance of Industry. Erikson's ideas about one's sense of industry are similar to what Bandura and his colleagues have called self-efficacy beliefs, meaning beliefs about our ability to exercise control over events that affect our lives (see Bandura, 1989, for a summary). A positive, optimistic sense of personal efficacy, like a feeling of industry, motivates a person to work hard at a task and to persevere even in the face of obstacles. There is evidence that high levels of achievement usually depend upon "an optimistic sense of personal efficacy" (Bandura, 1989, p. 1176; Cervone & Peake, 1986; Taylor & Brown, 1988).

Closely related to Bandura's work on self-efficacy is research by Dweck and her colleagues who have studied mastery orientation and the helpless pattern in school children and in college-aged adults (see Dweck, 1999, for a summary). These are two different orientations to failure. Individuals with a mastery orientation move forward optimistically even when they fail, assuming that they can succeed with further effort. They seem to construe failure as a challenge rather than as an obstacle. Individuals with a helpless pattern, however, often begin to denigrate their abilities when they encounter failure and typically stop applying themselves or trying to improve their performance. Dweck emphasizes the importance of one's theories of intelligence or ability in influencing how one deals with failure. She has found that mastery-oriented people are likely to be incremental theorists, seeing intelligence as a dynamic and malleable quality that can be increased by hard work and instruction. People who show a helpless pattern are more often entity theorists, who see intelligence or ability as a fixed, concrete thing: "You can only have a certain amount of it, so you'd better show that it's enough and you'd better hide it if it isn't" (p. 20).

When individuals with different orientations to failure move out of work environments where they have been successful into more challenging situations where they encounter more experiences of failure, they show different degrees of progress and different emotional reactions. Mastery-oriented people dig in and try harder and by that very effort make success more likely in the future. Helpless people tend to turn away from the new challenges. They seek tasks where they feel more certain they can succeed, settle for mediocre performance, or give up altogether. They also tend to feel more stress and shame when they find the new work they are faced with difficult. This pattern has been observed in children moving out of elementary school, where teachers often protect children from failure, into the more impersonal and competitive environment of a junior high school (Henderson & Dweck, 1992; Sorich & Dweck, 1996). It has also been found with young adults as they move through challenging college programs (Grant & Dweck, 2003; Robins & Pals, 1998). In both kinds of transitions, individuals with entity theories of ability performed less well than those with incremental theories, and they found their experiences in the new situations more emotionally distressing. This was true despite the fact that both groups entered the new environments with equally good credentials.

Findings like these might have particular significance for the patterns of career development observed among women and some minority groups. Gender differences in the choice of a career in male-dominated fields have been linked to lower self-efficacy in women, especially women who perceive themselves as highly feminine. Whereas women in general tend to have lower self-efficacy beliefs for "masculine" occupations requiring quantitative or leadership skills, males have about the same sense of efficacy for both masculine and "feminine" career options (Betz & Hackett, 1981; Betz & Schifano, 2000).

As we noted earlier, African American college students are more likely than White students to drop out of college. We also saw that when African American students attend Black colleges, they are more likely to pursue some particularly challenging majors, such as premed, than when they attend predominantly White colleges. Aronson and Fried (1998) posited that African American students are burdened by the stereotype that Blacks are less intelligent than Whites. Being in school with White students may have a tendency to evoke this stereotype and may make some Black students more susceptible to a helpless pattern, interfering with their achievement. Aronson and Fried devised a training program for undergraduates that they hoped would reduce **stereotype threat**, the fear that a stereotype might be true or that one will be judged by that stereotype (see Steele, 1997). The researchers hoped to foster a mastery orientation and thereby help improve achievements. Through film and lecture, citing scientific research, they instructed both Black and White undergraduates at Stanford University on the processes by which intelligence can actually be cultivated and changed. The training emphasized that when people take on new tasks and learn new skills there is neuronal growth so that they literally become smarter. To make sure that students had consolidated the information, participants were required to explain the incremental view of intelligence in letters to elementary school children. By the end of the school year, African American students who had been taught the incremental theory showed significant increases in achievement, reflected in their grade point averages. These students also were enjoying school more and felt more academically oriented than African American students in a control group, who had not been part of the incremental theory training.

There is evidence that many interacting variables in one's development affect the feelings of industry or positive self-efficacy or mastery orientation that people carry into adulthood. Such variables ultimately influence the likelihood of long-term achievement. These variables include parenting styles (e.g., Lamborn et al., 1991), teacher expectations (e.g., Rosenthal & Jacobson, 1968), stimulation and opportunities for personal challenge in one's home environment (e.g., Van Doorninck, Caldwell, Wright, & Frankenberg, 1981), security of attachments (e.g., Jacobsen & Hofmann, 1997), and, as we have just seen, gender and cultural stereotypes.

The Importance of Generativity.   How important are generativity needs in career development? As we have seen, Erikson described generativity as most influential in middle adulthood, but some recent work indicates that young adults are also influenced by generativity as they plan and launch their work lives.

Stewart and Vandewater (1998) examined two broad features of **generativity**—**desire** and **accomplishment**—and found that the desire for generativity is quite strong even in early adulthood and actually declines through middle and late adulthood. Desire was defined as expression of generativity goals, such as caring for future generations ("I'm concerned about the planet"), wanting to produce something of lasting value ("I want to write a major piece of non-fiction"), and being concerned about being needed ("It's nice to discover that my kids still come to me for advice and help"). In two cohorts of women who were studied longitudinally, such desires were strong through early adulthood, peaking in the early 30s, and then declining. Generative accomplishment peaked later, in middle adulthood. The authors propose that "healthy early adulthood includes the formulation of generativity goals or desires, while healthy midlife includes the subjective experience of the capacity to be generative as well as the beginning of a sense of satisfaction in generative accomplishment" (p. 94). Stewart and Vandewater's results seem consistent with the finding, noted earlier, that even right after high school, young adults from all walks of life are likely to say that they would like their work to make a meaningful contribution (Hill & Yeung, 1999). We will look again at generativity issues in the next chapter, as we consider the development of adults in midlife.

APPLICATIONS

The search for intimacy in adulthood demonstrates the continuing human need for social connectedness. The deepest aspects of a person's emotional life as an adult are often expressed within the confines of pair-bonds. The importance of these associations is evidenced by the fact that the most common referral problems for counselors are those involving interpersonal relationships (Veroff, Kulka, & Douvan, 1981). As we have seen, early attachment experiences can act as templates for the intimate relationships of adulthood. In particular, they may influence our willingness to rely on others to meet our needs for intimacy and to help us manage stress (approach). They can also affect how trusting we are that others will meet these needs (anxiety). These representations are intimately linked to how we view ourselves. Attachment theory provides a dynamic theoretical framework to explain the simultaneous pulls for intimacy and autonomy that can make interpersonal behaviors seem puzzling and contradictory. As the poet David Whyte puts it, "We are strange, difficult creatures who long for both freedom and belonging at the same time, and often run a mile when the real thing appears" (2001, p. 234).

Attachment in Counseling Contexts

The major theoretical tenets of attachment theory can be applied to individual, marital, and family therapies in some of the following ways.

1. For helpers who assume an attachment perspective, the therapeutic bond is the primary mechanism of change. The therapist functions as the secure base, provides the client with appropriate responsiveness and availability, and offers opportunities to explore models of self and others. Traditional views of therapy have long held that early attachment patterns carry over into therapeutic relationships (transference) and that therapy provides a chance for a corrective experience (Alexander & French, 1946). The way to revise insecure internal models, according to Bowlby (1988), is through the power of another, more secure and more responsive, base.

2. Therapeutic issues that are most applicable to an attachment-based approach include, but are not necessarily limited to, loss, separation, feelings of connectedness to others, and response to stress. Problems in close interpersonal relationships—particularly pair-bonds—are viewed as recapitulations of early childhood problems. When clients are capable of insight, some connection between childhood patterns and adult attachment relationships might be appropriate. Clients can be helped to understand that their ideas of self and others might not conform to the reality of their present circumstances. In general, this involves helping clients articulate their feelings about current interpersonal encounters or conflicts, explore how they handle such situations, and draw connections between prior experiences in close relationships and present patterns of relating.

3. One central task for the therapist is to make attachment-based interpretations of how the client behaves in relationships. "The qualities Ainsworth called for—sensitivity in perceiving the patient's signals and the capacity to interpret them correctly and react to them appropriately and promptly—are just as necessary in the therapeutic situation and are just as helpful there as they are in the creation of attachment between mother and child" (Brisch, 1999, p. 79).

   Remember that attachment is a flexible construct; many different behaviors can signal similar intent. Bowlby noted that when people feel threatened by loss of or separation from the secure base, the attachment system is activated and responds in protest (see Chapter 15). If protest behaviors prove ineffective in restoring connection, despair and detachment may follow. We have seen in earlier chapters what these behaviors look like in children. In adult partners whose attachment systems are activated due to conflict, protest can include crying, pleading, controlling, nagging, or seeking reassurance. Despair behaviors might include detachment, withdrawal from the partner, or anhedonia. These behaviors have been frequently reported in depressed individuals with respect to their partners (Anderson, Beach, & Kaslow, 1999; Coyne, 1976). Interpreting behaviors as expressions of attachment needs shifts the ownership for marital or family problems away from only one member of the system.

   A principal task in therapy involves appraising what the verbal or nonverbal behaviors communicate about the felt security or insecurity of partners vis-a-vis each other. Emotionally distressed individuals or couples, viewed from this perspective, may be chronically "on alert," never quite sure that their bids for connection will be read accurately by intimate others, expecting rejection, and prepared to respond to threats of rejection by escalating demands or defensive withdrawal. Their real need for emotional closeness is hard to see when their bids for intimacy are accompanied by irritable, critical, or dismissive acts that are sometimes incorrectly interpreted by their counselors as resistance or regression.

4. Individuals can be helped to understand how their attachment needs are provoked and what their responses to provocation are. Although not an attachment-based therapy per se, Greenberg's (2002) emotion-focused therapy provides a framework for working with the deep emotions at the heart of human relationships. In this model, the counselor acts as an "emotion coach" who guides clients to greater awareness and acceptance of their true feelings, helps them access their primary feelings, encourages them to listen to healthy feelings, and facilitates the transformation of less healthy ones. This approach can be useful for individuals as well as couples whose emotions are dysregulated or who are trapped in repetitive cycles of unresolved or unexpressed sadness or anger. In a manner that draws on many attachment-related concepts, the therapist provides a safe place in which clients can disclose "soft" attachment-related feelings of vulnerability, fear, loneliness, or grief through use of skills like reflective listening, use of "I" statements, non-blaming, and other structured activities (see Greenberg, 2002). The goal is to help clients use the wisdom of their emotions to achieve greater empathy for themselves and others, to improve emotion regulation skills, and, ultimately, to achieve greater intimacy with others.

5. The therapist has to be mindful of his own level of closeness and distance so as not to activate avoidance or dependency inadvertently (Brisch, 1999). With anxious clients, therapists need to monitor arrangements to avoid starting late, postponing sessions, or taking frequent vacations, or avoid other situations that trigger the client's needs for care. These events can be easily interpreted as rejection. For the avoidant client, too much emotional closeness may trigger anxiety as well and prompt premature termination.

6. Attachment behaviors are about exploration as well as connection. Healthy independence, assuming the presence of a secure base, should be a goal of therapy. It might be appropriate, therefore, for therapists to interpret their clients' need for a break in therapy or their desire for some choice in the counseling arrangements as a signal of healthy exploration rather than as indicating rejection of the therapy or therapist.

Attachment Applied to Couples and Families

One example of a therapy that applies attachment theory directly and that shares links with interpersonal therapy (see Chapter 11) is attachment-based family therapy (ABFT; Diamond, 1998; Diamond, Siqueland, & Diamond, 2003), a model typically used for families with adolescent children. According to ABFT, the major components of therapy are (1) alliance building, (2) reattribution, (3) teaching effective parenting, and (4) reattachment. Alliance building involves creating a relationship that provides a safe place for the therapeutic work and a source of ongoing support for family members. The target of alliance building, typically the relationship between therapist and client in individual counseling, is the relationship among family members. The therapist does, however, build personal alliances with parents and their adolescent to ensure a safe haven for expression of emotions and to provide the empathy needed for parents and children to feel heard and understood. "Alliance with the therapist is best understood as a transitional relationship that helps individual family members to uncover or learn about new parts of themselves" (Diamond & Diamond, 2002, p. 51). The task of reattribution involves helping family members conceptualize their conflicts in more positive ways. Questions take an attachment perspective by orienting clients' attention to a family member's need for connection. For example, asking parents "When your child feels so bad that she acts out, what is getting in the way of you being a resource for her?" (Diamond et al., 2003) makes the connection between negative emotion and problematic behavior explicit and evokes parents' motivation to help rather than blame. Effective parenting education may be part of the therapy if appropriate. Finally, the task of reattachment is accomplished by supporting communication and conflict resolution skills. The ultimate goals are to repair attachment relationships, strengthen emotional connections, and support family members' ability to recognize and acknowledge each other's needs for closeness and autonomy.

Caveats

Obviously, clinicians should avoid overdiagnosing attachment-related problems because there is such wide individual and cultural variation within the range of normal functioning. Some people's relationships appear distant or enmeshed to observers, but they may be perfectly satisfactory to the couple involved. Clinicians should also resist viewing attachment style as a monolithic, traitlike characteristic that resides within a person. Working models of self and relationship are always shaped in context. Even though there has been a surge of interest in attachment-related issues in adulthood, many more questions remain to be answered by researchers (Colin, 1996). Caution is advised as well in regard to "attachment" therapies that try to rebuild attachments by resorting to high levels of confrontation and restraint to break down defenses. These therapies, typically used with children, may involve coercive holding or "rebirthing" techniques. In some cases, such coercive techniques have proved very harmful to clients (Shermer, 2003).

The Counselor's Working Model

If counselors keep these reservations in mind, attachment theory can also help them understand the meaning in their own patterns of interaction, conflict resolution, and stress management. Dozier, Cue, and Barnett (1994) found that the therapists' level of attachment security was related to counter-transference processes. In other words, secure therapists were more likely to respond empathically to the dependency needs of their dismissing or avoidant clients. They were able to see the needs hidden beneath a detached or a rejecting exterior, whereas insecure therapists were more likely to be driven away by the negativity. Secure therapists were also better able to manage clients with ambivalent attachment styles. They were less likely to get trapped into "taking care of" these clients by responding to their obvious needs rather than attending to the more important, underlying ones.

Are working models open to revision? Bowlby believed that working models can change in more positive directions, and recent research supports this (see Box 12.1). The question that needs much more empirical support concerns how this is accomplished. Bowlby (1988) viewed good therapy somewhat like good parenting. He theorized that in a relationship with an emotionally available therapist, a person is able to reflect on the past, lower defenses, engage in perspective taking, know the experience of "felt security," and, together, co-construct a revision of the internal working model. Lopez and Brennan (2000) make a similar point by suggesting that counseling offers clients a context in which to learn ways of minimizing the negative consequences of insecure attachments (hyperactivation or deactivation) and to find ways of coping more effectively. Although more evidence is needed, some data indicate that attempts to improve social self-efficacy and perspective taking can mediate improvements in working model representations (Corcoran & Mallinckrodt, 2000).

If working models can be changed, it is probably a slow process. Revising representational models happens by engaging in a curative, therapeutic attachment that takes time, patience, and dedication. Slade (1999) draws our attention to the limitation of certain kinds of short-term, problem-centered therapies that are not well suited to reworking fundamental models of social and emotional relationships.

The Importance of Work

Finding a place in the world of work is another important challenge at this time of life. Historically, the counseling profession has contributed significantly to the theory and practice of career development. A central tenet of this field is that finding a career is more than a simple choice. This task, like so many others, is a process that requires self-understanding and the ability to use self-knowledge to make informed decisions. Kegan (1982) believed that vocational development is a function of people's levels of self-awareness and the kinds of meaning they attribute to themselves as workers. His theoretical ideas have some things in common with Perry's scheme, which was described in Chapter 11.

According to Kegan, adolescent vocational aspirations are heavily influenced by family and peers. From their foreclosed position, adolescents often construe their early career aspirations as the "right" choice. When confronted with confusing or contradictory feedback about their skills or when given opportunities to pursue other career paths, they may cope by becoming even more rigidly entrenched in the pursuit of their original career goals. They mistake the form of the career (such as medical school) with the underlying functions it serves (such as prestige and service). In other words, vocational identity is construed as a position rather than as an aspect of one's self. Individuals at this stage may resist revising a career goal, even when personal experience or feedback from others challenges its suitability. With maturity, individuals can reflect on this dissonance, integrate the contradictions, and reach a new level of self-understanding and acceptance. They can also identify career goals that are a better fit with their underlying dispositions and goals. Counseling can be particularly helpful for those who need guidance in self-exploration and who may need to reconstruct new meanings about career (McAuliffe, 1993).

Building Self-Efficacy

One important component of success in life and work is the set of beliefs a person has about his ability to be successful. Self-efficacy is a construct that is meaningful in many different domains of development, as we have seen. It has rather recently been integrated into a model of career decision making (Social Cognitive Career Theory, SCCT; Lent, Brown, & Hackett, 1996) that is based on Bandura's (1977, 1997) self-efficacy theory. In this approach, client beliefs about how successful they will be in certain roles and work settings are given a prominent position in the career decision-making process. Our sense of self-efficacy shapes our best guess about whether some outcome is likely to be successful or not and, thus, influences the level of exploration we are willing to undertake in regard to pursuing that outcome. Self-efficacy level also influences our willingness to sustain effort in achieving desired outcomes and to learn the skills that might be needed for successful accomplishment of some goal. One's sense of self-efficacy is shaped by past experiences with success and failure as well as opportunities to try things out. These opportunities can be constrained by social class, gender, age, race, disability, the quality of educational experience, or family and peer influences.

Counselors can be both tutors and coaches in this process, scaffolding the development of a personal sense of efficacy in regard to many of life's important challenges. Because self-efficacy beliefs influence functioning in a whole host of ways, from making decisions (What major shall I select?) to behavioral performance (Shall I ask this person for a date? Or my boss for a raise?), it is a useful target for clinical intervention. Bussey and Bandura (1999) describe four major ways to instill a strong sense of self-efficacy.

1. Construct and try out graded mastery experiences that are tailored to the individual's level of ability and that maximize the chances of success. To do this effectively, counselors need to listen to clients explain why they try

or don't try certain activities and what they think are their roadblocks to success. In relation to career counseling, Betz (2004) suggests asking clients what they would choose to do if they could do "anything," what skills they need to improve their career opportunities, and what they feel is standing in their way of improving their skills. These kinds of questions can reveal something about how clients view their own capabilities and limitations and thus provide a guide for selecting specific corrective experiences.

2. Discuss or provide models who demonstrate success in an area of difficulty for the client. Successful models encourage individuals to believe in their own capacity for success and provide skills and know-how to the motivated observer.

3. A third way to enhance self-efficacy is to apply social persuasion. This might be done by challenging erroneous beliefs about lack of ability, making attributions for failure to lack of effort (incremental) rather than lack of ability (fixed), and providing support as well as realistic, helpful suggestions for improvement.

4. Finally, attempt to reduce coexisting factors that lower self-efficacy, such as stress, depression, or features of the environment, like restricted opportunity structure, whenever possible. By means of these processes, clients revise versions of their expectancies, which can lead to changes in behavior.

"As they (clients) continue to accumulate more and more of such success experiences, processing this information within the therapy session helps them realign their anticipatory thoughts and feelings with an appropriate self-evaluation of the outcome of their response. Eventually, a new behavior pattern, together with a greater sense of self-efficacy, begins to emerge" (Goldfried, 1995, p. 113).

Adjusting to the World of Work

Finding productive work enhances our lives, but choosing a career is only one step in the career development process. People also need to adjust to the demands of the workplace. Hershenson's (1996) contextual model proposes that work adjustment is most likely to occur if the ongoing characteristics of the individual (work values, skills, goals, habits, etc.) mesh with the day-to-day demands of the job (behavioral expectations, skill requirements, available rewards and opportunities). For example, an organizational position that is highly structured and requires adherence to routine may be unsatisfying to an individual with high needs for autonomy and little motivation to work in a corporate culture. Helping clients consider the person–environment dimensions of a career can promote more successful adjustment.

Of course, not all problems in the workplace are amenable to change. Finding the ideal fit, although a desirable goal, is not always realistic. The workplace is harsh and unsatisfying for many people due to job-related threats to health, lack of job security, lack of control over tasks performed, and pressure to increase productivity with limited time and resources (Jones, 1996). In his description of the current state of work in the United States, Reich (2000) points to several significant changes that have had profound effects on workers: the end of steady, dependable work, the obsolescence of loyalty between employers and employees, the ever-widening inequality of wages, and the shrinking time factor. "In 1999, the average middle-income married couple with children worked a combined 3,918 hours—about seven weeks more *than a decade before* [italics added]" (pp. 111–112).

Work stresses can have adverse effects on workers and their families, especially on their dependent children. Jones suggests that counselors help clients consider workplace safety and stability issues when contemplating career choices. In a departure from more traditional ways of viewing career development, he suggests that counselors avoid portraying job success as the primary means of achieving self-esteem. For many people, work may never be particularly meaningful or personally satisfying. The stresses of the contemporary working world should also be factored in when clients come to counseling for other problems, such as problems in relationships or difficulties with children. He also suggests that counselors take an advocacy position on issues related to work, such as government or company policies that support high-quality child care. Given the importance of love and work in adults' lives, understanding and supporting successful adjustment in these two areas is a worthy task for clinicians.

SUMMARY

1. Freud characterized love (*lieben*) and work (*arbeiten*) as the means by which adults strive for happiness. Erikson described intimacy—closeness to another that is marked by trust, openness, and affection—as the goal of young adulthood, and generativity—creating, producing, and contributing to the human community—as the goal of middle adulthood. Recent conceptions of mental health or "wellness" also emphasize both having close relationships and feeling competent and productive as essential ingredients for happiness.

"Lieben"—To Love

2. Attachment theory provides one framework for conceptualizing adult intimacy. It suggests that early bonds with caregivers could have a bearing on relationship building

in adulthood and that intimate adult relationships provide some of the same benefits as infant–adult relationships: a secure base, safe haven, and emotional warmth.

3. Two traditions or lines of inquiry characterize adult attachment research: the nuclear family tradition, exploring how early attachments might affect the quality of caregiving that an adult gives his own children, and the peer/romantic partner tradition, which focuses on the peer attachments of adults.

4. The Adult Attachment Interview (AAI) consists of questions about early memories of relationships with parents. Autonomous (secure) adults provide a coherent, collaborative narrative, acknowledging the importance of attachment-related experiences in their development. Individuals described as earned secure appear to have come to terms with painful backgrounds. They reflect on their past realistically, acknowledging their parents' perspective. Autonomous adults tend to have securely attached children.

5. Dismissing (insecure) adults describe parents positively but provide either no evidence or contradictory evidence. Generally, they downplay the importance of early relationships. Their children tend to form avoidant attachments.

6. Preoccupied (insecure) individuals provide long, incoherent, egocentric monologues. They seem overwhelmed by the interview questions and are often angry, sad, or fearful. They seem preoccupied with parents, who are remembered as intrusive or egocentric. Their children often have anxious-ambivalent attachments.

7. Unresolved individuals produce narratives with notable lapses in logical thinking. Their children have a tendency to show disorganized attachment patterns. Insecure adults are the most likely to be emotionally disturbed.

8. Longitudinal studies find that an individual's infant attachment status (as measured by the strange situation test) predicts his adult AAI attachment status, although intervening events can shift that status from secure to insecure or vice versa.

9. AAI narratives are different from other interview narratives with the same interviewees, suggesting that the AAI specifically reflects a person's state of mind regarding interpersonal representations. This working model of attachments is assumed to be a schema that has evolved with time and experience and that serves as a guide for understanding, predicting, and acting.

10. Adult pair-bonds integrate three basic behavioral systems: caregiving, attachment, and sexual mating. The attachment system involves proximity seeking and separation distress and serves safe haven and secure base functions. Attachment functions gradually transfer from parents to peers and, eventually, to romantic partners. Proximity seeking begins to shift as early as the preschool years. Between 8 and 14 years, peers also provide safe haven. Eventually attachments to romantic partners involve proximity seeking and separation distress, and they also serve safe haven and secure base functions.

11. The measurement procedures and typologies in the peer/romantic relationship tradition have been different from those in the nuclear family tradition. Several typologies have been proposed, and in the most recent work it is suggested that people may be better characterized as differing along two continuous dimensions, one having to do with their degree of anxiety about close relationships and the other with their approach-avoidance tendencies.

12. Partner selection can be predicted to some degree by the attachment characteristics of the partners. Secure individuals tend to pair with secure partners; anxious and avoidant individuals tend to pair up; but anxious-anxious pairs or avoidant-avoidant pairs are uncommon. Whether individuals actually enter relationships with these characteristics or tend to evolve these styles within their relationships has not been determined.

13. Partnerships between secure individuals seem to involve more positive and less negative emotions than other pairings. Male avoidant individuals show less distress during breakups than other males, but females of all attachment types show similar levels of distress. Ambivalent partners are most stressed by conflict within a relationship.

"Arbeiten"—To Work

14. In Holland's theory of career development, people are categorized as having one of six modal personal orientations, part of their personality. Jobs or careers make demands that are compatible with one or more of these orientations. A good fit between modal orientation and job characteristics benefits job satisfaction and feelings of well-being.

15. In Super's theory, the focus is on the development of a vocational self-concept, part of one's total identity. He describes five stages in its development, from the growth stage in early childhood through the decline stage in people of retirement age. Super emphasizes that career development is a continuing, lifelong process. Many career counseling approaches emphasize the important relationship between career and self-development, with self-discovery an important ingredient in career satisfaction.

16. College students' first vocationally relevant decision is choice of a major. Whereas personal characteristics and interests influence the choice, so do cultural changes (e.g., economic shifts) and cohort characteristics. Ethnic and socioeconomic differences appear to influence not only who attends college but also the likelihood of college retention and career choices. Career counseling in college should begin with advisement on choice of a major.

17. For the forgotten half, those who do not attend college, the chances of achieving career goals shared by all young adults (e.g., good pay, opportunities for advancement, opportunities to make a meaningful contribution to society) are substantially reduced. As with college students, factors such as socioeconomic status and ethnicity affect these chances as well.

18. Career opportunities for noncollege young people could be improved if there were more systematic and effective resources for them, such as basic skill training in public schools, extensive vocational counseling, and opportunities for work-based learning. Some well-designed training interventions for high-risk groups have been successful, such as the Job Corp program.

19. Traditionally, women with careers have followed different career paths from men. Substantial changes have occurred, such as women outnumbering men in college. But there are still gender differences: Some careers are still highly gendered, and women are still more likely to consider the impact of career choices on their relationship opportunities, although men are increasingly attending to such concerns as well.

20. Self-concept and self-understanding are central features of many theories of career development. How do basic feelings and attitudes toward the self as a worker develop? Erikson describes a sense of industry, belief in one's ability to work productively and expectation of satisfaction from work, as beginning in middle childhood, when children have their first work experiences. Generativity becomes important in adulthood, as people become motivated to leave a legacy for the next generation.

21. Bandura has studied self-efficacy beliefs, beliefs in one's own ability to affect events, as motivating people to work hard and persevere even in the face of failure. Such beliefs are correlated with high levels of achievement.

22. Mastery orientation is similar to self-efficacy and to a sense of industry. Mastery-oriented individuals move forward even when they fail, apparently because they are incremental theorists, believing that hard work and instruction can affect ability. Conversely, people who show a helplessness pattern, who give up when they fail, tend to be entity theorists, seeing ability as fixed.

23. Differences in self-efficacy beliefs, or mastery orientation, may have significant effects on minority groups and women. Stereotype threat, the fear that an inferiority stereotype might be true, can influence achievement. In some research, stereotype threat has been reduced and achievement improved when individuals have received intensive training on the scientific evidence for the malleability of intelligence and ability.

CASE STUDY

Tayib, who is 29 years old, works as a paralegal in a public defender's office. His parents came to the United States from India before he was born. Tayib's extended family in India were highly educated people, and his parents encouraged him to get a good education as well. Although he considered going to law school, Tayib never felt confident enough to pursue this goal. In his current place of employment, many coworkers rely on his conscientiousness. He feels that others, including his superiors, often take advantage of him by giving him the most difficult cases to sort out and the shortest deadlines for getting them done. He was recently passed over for a promotion by his boss, who decided to fill the higher level post by hiring someone from outside the department. He feels unsatisfied in his position, but he thinks that his chances for advancement may be best if he remains in civil service. His parents encourage him to find a position with more prestige and a better income.

Tayib has been dating Rachael, a 27-year-old White woman with a young son, for the past 6 months. Rachael works as a public relations executive in one of the corporate offices in the city. Rachael and her son, Luke, share an apartment with one of Rachael's girlfriends. This has been her living arrangement since the breakup of her relationship with Luke's father Kevin 3 years ago. The couple were never married, a factor that led to strained relationships with her own mother and father.

Tayib and Rachael are both interested in finding someone with whom they can have a serious relationship. Lately, however, their relationship has not been going as smoothly as it did in the beginning. As Luke's 4th birthday approached, Rachael wanted to plan a celebration for him. Tayib had already taken Luke and Rachael to an amusement park as a birthday present for the youngster. Rachael decided to have a special birthday dinner for Luke and invited her parents and Tayib. Tayib, in the midst of an important project at work, declined the invitation.

Rachael feels totally rejected by his refusal to attend the dinner. She cannot understand why she and Luke mean so little to Tayib. She believes that she does everything she possibly can in order to keep Tayib interested in her. She prepares meals for him, works on her appearance, listens to him talk about problems at work, calls him to let him know she cares about him, and tries to accommodate her schedule to his. She wonders now if she will ever find someone who wants to make a commitment to her. Tayib can't understand why Rachael is so upset about the dinner. Since she is a working woman with a child to support, he feels that she should understand how important it is to have and keep a job. Tayib begins to wonder if she really understands what is important to him. Although the two do not discuss this incident directly, they both feel tension growing in the relationship.

Discussion Questions

1. What are the issues involved in this case?
2. From an attachment perspective, what inferences can you draw about the relationship styles of Tayib and Rachael?
3. What are the challenges each person faces at this point in his or her development? As a counselor, how would you help them cope with these challenges?

JOURNAL QUESTIONS

1. Write a brief relationship autobiography describing how you behaved, thought, and felt about one significant relationship. How would you describe your own attachment style?
2. Describe how you solve conflicts in your closest relationship. How do you deal with stress in this relationship?

Explain how these patterns relate to what you experienced in your family of origin.
3. How has your own career history changed since you held your first job? What were the influences (both internal and external) on your career trajectory? How would you evaluate your sense of self-efficacy regarding your career?

KEY TERMS

intimacy	passion	exploratory stage	industry
generativity	intimacy	crystallization	self-efficacy beliefs
nuclear family tradition	commitment	specification	mastery orientation
peer/romantic partner	secure	implementation	the helpless pattern
tradition	preoccupied	establishment stage	incremental theorists
autonomous	avoidant	stabilization	entity theorists
earned secure	dismissing	maintenance stage	stereotype threat
dismissing	fearful	consolidation	generativity desire
preoccupied	modal personal orientation	decline stage	generativity
unresolved	vocational self-concept	retention	accomplishment
cannot classify	growth stage	forgotten half	

Now go to our Companion Website to assess your understanding of chapter content with Multiple Choice Questions, apply comprehension in Essay Questions, and broaden your knowledge of development with related Web Links.

CHAPTER 13

Middle Adulthood: Cognitive, Personality, and Social Development

What is the nature of development at midlife? This is a perplexing question because adult lives are complex and multifaceted. Adults seek out jobs, select them, and sometimes ascend to positions of responsibility in their fields of work. Adults also change employment voluntarily to work in other settings or in other careers. Some adults lose their jobs and may experience unemployment or underemployment. Some work at multiple jobs. Adults take on leadership, executive, or mentoring roles in their communities. Adults move from one location to another, historically now more than ever before. They marry, cohabitate, divorce, date, and often go on to marry again. Some adults have children and grandchildren; others are childless. Adults may have responsibilities for the care of their own aging parents. Those who are parents or stepparents have to deal with the ever-changing developmental needs of their children. Adults are also affected by the close relationships they share with partners or friends. They may experience financial difficulties. They may sustain illness themselves or experience the illness or loss of loved ones. Some adults experience catastrophic events, such as wars, accidents, or natural disasters. Many more deal with chronic adversities such as discrimination of one sort or another, mental problems such as depression, or simply the gradual physical changes involved in the aging process. Moreover, many of these events occur simultaneously.

The complexity of people's experience and functioning is what is most striking about middle adulthood. How are we to make sense of all the variables operating in adult lives? Is there some coherent scheme that helpers can use to understand development in the adult years? In Chapter 1, we examined some of the many theoretical approaches that explain developmental processes, including stage models, such as Erikson's or Piaget's, and incremental models, such as learning and information processing accounts. As we have seen throughout this book, these approaches to development can be quite helpful in understanding some aspects of psychological functioning, but modern theorists are more and more turning to multidimensional models, which are focused on the complexity of interrelated causal processes in development. Recall in Bronfenbrenner's multidimensional model, for example, the description of proximal processes in development—reciprocal interactions between an "active, evolving biopsychological human organism and the persons, objects, and symbols in its immediate environment" (Bronfenbrenner & Morris, 1998, p. 996). These proximal processes are modified by more distal processes, some within the organism, such as genes, and some outside the organism, such as the family, the workplace, the community, the broader economic and political context, and other aspects of the culture.

As we saw in Chapter 1, multidimensional theories of adult development, called life span developmental theories or models, address all the fundamental questions of development, such as the role of heredity versus environment in adulthood and the extent to which adult characteristics are continuous with previous traits and propensities versus how much genuine change there is in adult behavior. Life span developmental models (e.g., Baltes et al., 1998) make one fundamental assumption in addressing such questions—that from birth to death, adaptation continues. The development of psychological functioning does not end or become fixed when adulthood is reached but goes on until death. The reciprocal interaction of many biological and environmental factors forms an ever-changing "architecture" or scaffolding that supports the development of behavioral and mental functioning (e.g., Baltes, 1997). Thus, middle adulthood is not some kind of holding pattern before the slide into death. An adult's cognitive and socioemotional functioning continues to evolve through her 30s, 40s, 50s, and beyond.

LIFE SPAN DEVELOPMENTAL THEORY

Historically, developmental study in North America focused on children and adolescents. With some rare exceptions, such as Erikson's stage theory, adulthood was given short shrift in most theory and research. Yet in some parts of Europe, such as Germany and Belgium, interest in development over the whole life span was the scientific norm. Baltes et al. (1998) speculate that when developmental psychology became a specialty in the United States around 1900, the strong influence of Darwinian theories, which describe growth as a process of maturation, may have helped establish childhood as the primary focus of attention. In contrast, in German-speaking countries, important essays on development began to emerge in the 18th and 19th centuries, before there was much biological science. Early developmental writings were rooted more in philosophy and the humanities, with a special emphasis on concerns about how to optimize human functioning. Thus, there was no special impetus to limit the discussion of development to descriptions of the childhood period.

Around the middle of the 20th century, some American developmentalists began to shift their attention from the growth that characterizes childhood to the declines of aging, and developmental psychology was soon represented by two somewhat independent groups, the child developmentalists and the gerontologists. Even today, textbooks often reflect this disjunction. Chapters on middle adulthood discuss career motivation, stress, marriage, family roles, sexuality, and leisure time, which are all important issues for adults. But there is often a notable absence of an overarching framework for understanding how middle adult life is linked to the childhood years, on one hand, and to old age, on the other.

Life span developmental theory provides such an organizational framework. It can be construed as a kind of macrotheory under whose umbrella all the processes of ontogeny, or the development of organisms, fall into place. This orientation offers a clear benefit to those in the helping professions. First, it provides a way of organizing developmental processes across the life cycle. Think of the multiplicity of challenges and possibilities in adult life, some of which we mentioned at the beginning of this chapter. Rather than viewing them as disconnected parts of a life story, counselors can interpret the choices people make and the ways they adapt as reflecting some degree of lawful continuity. Second, life span developmental theory emphasizes the importance of learning about successful or effective development. Thus, this perspective fits well with therapeutic or psychoeducational goals. Let's now consider some of the elements of life span developmental theory.

Gains and Losses in Development: The Changing Architecture of Biology and Culture

At any point in development, a person brings to proximal processes—the interactive interface with the environment—a set of dispositions and resources (existing abilities, knowledge, skills, and so on; Bronfenbrenner & Morris, 1998). These are influenced by biological and physical levels of functioning, including the genes, and by the many levels of the environment. You may recall that Baltes describes this web of interacting organismic and environmental influences as the architecture of biology and culture. He argues that for children, the biological processes that support development have a long evolutionary history. Natural selection through many generations has created a biological trajectory that tends to optimize development in most typical environments, allowing most individuals to grow up and become fully functioning adults who can contribute to the success of the species by reproducing. Of course, basic cultural supports—adequate parenting, nutrition, education, protection from environmental hazards, and so on—are fundamental for the success of this process as well.

As individuals move through adulthood, the biological supports for life weaken because the reproductive process is complete, and the selection pressure that the need for reproductive success creates for a species is no longer operative. Thus, biological dysfunctions are more likely. "Evolution and biology are not good friends of old age" (Baltes, 1997, p. 368). During middle adulthood (defined here as ages 30 to 55), people begin to depend more and more on cultural supports for adequate functioning. Indeed, "old age" exists primarily because of modern culture. Advances in economics, nutrition, general knowledge, technology, and medicine have compensated for the weakening of the biological supports for life. As a result, from 1900 to 1995, the average life span increased in Western societies from about 45 years to around 75 years!

Viewing development as a life span process makes clear that development or change in functioning with age involves both gains and losses for the individual. Gains are most obvious early in life, losses are more obvious later. But once we are sensitized to the fact that development involves both, we begin to notice that gains and losses characterize change throughout life. Thus, children, not just adults, experience some losses in the normal course of development. One familiar illustration is characteristic of language development. As an infant, you were capable of hearing and producing all of the kinds of sound distinctions that are used across all human languages. But as you learned your native language, you became less adept at discriminating and producing sounds that were not part of that language. If you were introduced to a second language after the preschool years, you probably had trouble producing sounds that were not part of your native tongue, and so you probably speak the second language with a "foreign accent." Another example, suggested by Baltes (1997), is that as adolescents strive for personal autonomy, their relationships with their parents are often strained, as we have seen. The intimacy of the parent–child relationship is diminished for both partners as the adolescent struggles to achieve an adult identity.

Of course, loss is more obvious to us in adulthood as biological declines occur. We saw in Chapter 11, for example, that our biological systems, like our sensory abilities and our immune functions, all reach peak potential between ages 18 and 30. Many of these systems begin to decline soon after (see below). But the increase in losses through adulthood should not mask the fact that the gains also continue. For example, in Chapter 11 we discussed the gains in postformal thinking that seem to characterize some people as they move into middle adulthood. Other examples of gains will become clear throughout this chapter. However, the relative balance of gains and losses clearly shifts across the life span, until eventually losses outstrip gains for most people in old age (see Figure 13.1). Given this increase in relative losses, how does development proceed in adulthood?

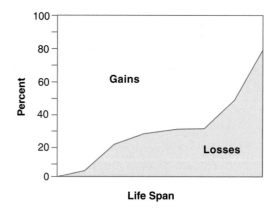

FIGURE 13.1

The Shifting Relationship Between Gains and Losses Across the Life Span

Source: Baltes, P. B. (1997). On the incomplete architecture of human ontology: Selection, optimization, and compensation as foundation of developmental theory. *American Psychologist, 52,* 366–380. Copyright © 1997 by the American Psychological Association. Reprinted with permission.

Development as Growth, Maintenance, and Regulation of Loss

Life span developmental theory defines development as a process of adapting to the constant flux of influences on our lives (see Baltes, 1997; Baltes et al., 1998). One kind of adaptation is growth. We grow when we add new characteristics, understandings, skills, and so on to our behavioral repertoire. So, for example, an adult might grow by becoming more expert at some task at work, or she might acquire a more balanced and thus empathic perspective on her relationship with her parents. Another kind of adaptive functioning is maintenance or resilience, finding ways to continue functioning at the same level in the face of challenges or restoring our functioning after suffering some loss. For example, an adult might maintain the concept of herself as a poet despite repeated rejections of her work by persistently revising and resubmitting her work until eventually a piece is published. Or despite the death of a partner, she might eventually reestablish intimacy in her life by returning to social circulation and finding a new partner. A third kind of adaptation is regulation of loss. Like maintenance, this form of adaptation involves reorganizing the way we behave. But unlike maintenance, regulation of loss involves adjusting our expectations and accepting a lower level of functioning. Suppose that a woman who prides herself on her ability to remember names, faces, and telephone numbers suffers a reduction in learning ability as she ages. She adapts by using strategies that include writing down essential information that she previously would have recalled. She accepts that she will never have the breadth of information available to her that she had before, but by using her new strategies she ensures that she will remember what is really necessary.

According to life span developmental theory, all three adaptive processes—growth, maintenance, and regulation of loss—are part of development from infancy through old age. What changes is the relative probability of each. Growth is much more characteristic of children than it is of the elderly, and regulation of loss is much more characteristic of the elderly (see Figure 13.2). The middle adult years appear to be a time when the balance is shifting among the three adaptive processes. It is important to recognize that all three processes occur across the life span. Children experience the need to compensate for loss through maintenance or regulation, and adults of all ages experience growth. However, knowing the relative proportions of each, given a client's stage of life, may provide clinicians with a frame for understanding presenting problems.

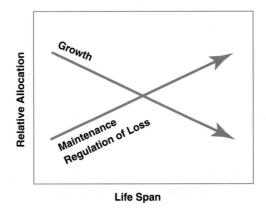

FIGURE 13.2

The Relative Increase in Maintenance and Regulation of Loss and the Relative Decrease in Growth as Adaptive Processes Across the Life Span

Source: Baltes, P. B. (1997). On the incomplete architecture of human ontology: Selection, optimization, and compensation as foundation of developmental theory. *American Psychologist, 52*, 366–380. Copyright © 1997 by the American Psychological Association. Reprinted with permission.

Defining Successful Development at Any Age

What counts as successful development? Life span theorists typically describe it as "the relative maximization of gains and the minimization of losses" (Baltes, 1997, p. 367; see also Brandstadter & Wentura, 1995). The adaptation processes we have just described are the means by which successful development is achieved. These processes are made possible both by the physical and psychological resources that individuals bring to the task of adaptation and by the biological and cultural scaffolding that is available. As we have seen, as adulthood proceeds, the more cultural scaffolding there is, the more likely the individual will be able to adapt well.

Consider the nature of developmental success at different times in the life of Emma, now a 91-year-old woman. Emma never married or had children, which she experienced as a loss. In her young adulthood, she compensated for her childlessness by dedicating her considerable talents to teaching poor urban children in public schools. In middle adulthood, she became an administrator, developing innovative programs for young children and mentoring teachers in the public school system. In her early old age, the physical demands of a daily work schedule became too great, so she retired, thereby losing her power to influence the lives of young children in the public schools. But she managed the loss, maintaining her view of herself as a child advocate, by serving on the governing boards of nonprofit organizations that provide services for children. Now, Emma suffers from a number of biological losses—near blindness, breathing problems, and general frailty—and she has confined her living space to her small apartment. A good deal of her functioning involves regulating her biological losses by living a quiet, sedentary life in her small space and depending on some outside help, which she has the means to pay for as a result of careful financial planning. But she also continues to grow: She has learned to use a computer, and she has begun to write for her own enjoyment. She also maintains her contacts with friends through email.

At each stage of her life, Emma found ways to manage losses through maintenance or regulation and to continue to grow. The balance of losses and gains in her life has now clearly shifted so that much of her adaptive energy is dedicated to managing losses. With the help of technological supports, such as the computer, Emma has minimized the overwhelming losses of her late life and has continued to maximize her gains, to the extent possible. She provides an example of successful development even in old age.

Our description of successful development will sound familiar to most helpers because it is clearly continuous with what we think of as healthy coping. The life span developmental view

Growth, maintenance, and regulation of loss are part of human adaptation, but their relative proportions change at different points of the life cycle.

helps us see that healthy coping evolves and changes throughout life. What is adaptive coping at one stage of life may be less adaptive at another. In the following sections, we will consider some relatively stable influences on adult life as well as the sources of change. As we look at these influences, we will begin to identify what resources the mature individual brings to the task of development and which of these resources might most effectively contribute to success.

INFLUENCES ON ADULT DEVELOPMENT: SOURCES OF STABILITY

A popular series of films produced by the British Broadcasting Company (BBC) documents the lives of several men and women at 7-year intervals, from the time they were 7 years old to age 42. The more recently filmed documentaries, which include scenes from earlier films, illuminate the thread of stability that runs through these individual lives. For example, Nick, who at age 7 expressed the desire "to find out all about the moon," is a full professor teaching science at age 42. Sue, who was a vibrant, independent youngster, is now a fun-loving, independent divorced woman. Is this kind of continuity typical of people in general? What are the sources of relative stability in development from childhood through adulthood? Many personality researchers, buoyed by the results of longitudinal studies (e.g., Conley, 1985; Costa & McCrae, 1988; Finn, 1986; Shiner, Masten, & Roberts, 2003), have expressed renewed confidence in the stability of personality across the life span. However, how one defines personality will make a critical difference in one's perception of personality as stable or changing. Those who espouse personality continuity generally construe personality as a set of traits that may be likened to the temperament characteristics of infants (see Chapter 4). The theory of McCrae and Costa (1999), for example, specifically assumes that traits are biologically based, inherent tendencies that are not influenced by environment.

What are these traits that appear to be so stable? In the 1980s, researchers recognized that the hundreds of words used to express aspects of human personality (called trait adjectives) could be reliably boiled down to five. The **Big 5**, as they are called, represent the most basic dimensions of personality: **neuroticism** (N), **extraversion** (E), **openness** (O), **agreeableness** (A), and **conscientiousness** (C). Table 13.1 provides additional detail on these dimensions. Cross-sectional studies of personality traits as measured by questionnaires find evidence of striking similarity across age groups in the degree to which they are characterized by each of these traits, even when different instruments are used. Costa and McCrae (1994) interpret their large body of evidence on the temporal stability of the Big 5 to suggest that personality traits are stable after age 30, although there continues to be some increase in trait consistency even into the fifth decade (McCrae & Costa, 2003; Roberts & DelVecchio, 2000). Before age 30, certain shifts are noted in large cross-sectional samples and among samples from different cultural groups.

TABLE 13.1 The Big 5 Personality Traits	
Trait	**Synonyms**
Neuroticism	Tense, touchy, self-pitying, unstable, anxious, worrying
Extraversion	Outgoing, active, assertive, energetic, talkative, enthusiastic
Agreeableness	Warm, sympathetic, generous, forgiving, kind, affectionate
Conscientiousness	Organized, planful, reliable, responsible, careful, efficient
Openness to experience	Creative, artistic, curious, insightful, original, wide-ranging interests

Source: McCrae, R. R., & John, O. T. (1992). An introduction to the five-factor model and its applications. *Journal of Personality, 60,* 175–215.

For example, college-aged students score higher on neuroticism, extraversion, and openness to experience than older adults, and somewhat lower on agreeableness and conscientiousness. This profile reverses in individuals approaching age 30, who show slight increases in A and C and slight decreases in N, E, and O as compared to younger groups. Less change in basic traits is found after that time (McCrae & Costa, 1990).

Longitudinal and cross-cultural studies have found similar patterns. For example, Watson and Walker (1996) found that negative affect (similar to neuroticism) declined after college, and Mortimer, Finch, and Kumka (1982) found a reduction in reported sociability, similar to extraversion, in their subjects as they moved through their 20s. In addition, some studies have also noted increases in self-control and achievement (similar to C) among participants as they approached middle age (Helson & Klohnen, 1998).

In an impressive cross-sectional study of adults across five different cultures, McCrae et al. (1999) found highly consistent trends among German, Italian, Portuguese, Croatian, and Korean groups. Despite their differing historical experiences and cultural contexts, older individuals across cultures were slightly higher in agreeableness and conscientiousness and somewhat lower in extraversion and openness to experience than younger adults. The authors suggest that these trends are universal, maturity-dependent, and unrelated to environment. In other words, "persons grow and change, but they do so on the foundation of enduring dispositions" (Costa & McCrae, 1994, p. 36).

The Link to Temperament

Where do these adult traits come from? As we noted, some researchers have looked for links between childhood temperament characteristics and adult personality dispositions because both are construed to have some basis in biology. Rothbart and her colleagues (Rothbart, Ahadi, & Evans, 2000) call adult personality an outcome of temperament because it arises from constitutionally based differences in systems such as reactivity (excitability, responsivity) and self-regulation (modulation of activity). A growing literature in the field of developmental psychobiology provides evidence for brain-mediated systems of positive approach, fear, irritability or anger, effortful control, and reactive orienting (Rothbart, Derryberry, & Posner, 1994). As children develop and experience age-related changes, their temperamental characteristics become increasingly more differentiated and integrated into more mature self-systems. So, for example, early manifestations of positive approach, such as smiling and laughing, may be translated into more mature forms, such as social extraversion. When Rothbart and her associates (2000) correlated young adults' temperaments with their Big 5 personality traits, they found evidence for relationships between extraversion and positive approach, between effortful attention and conscientiousness, between irritability or anger and neuroticism, and between orienting sensitivity and openness to experience. Additional cross-cultural support is provided by McCrae and his colleagues (2000) who found modest correlations between the temperamental characteristics of German, British, Turkish, Czech, and Spanish samples with their adult personality traits.

But what if we looked at individual development over time? Would early temperamental patterns reliably predict adult personality? Caspi (2000) investigated the continuity of temperament in a cohort of New Zealanders from age 3 to age 21. The sample for this study consisted of all children born in Dunedin, New Zealand, between April 1972 and March 1973. Temperamental characteristics were assessed at various points by means of parent report, clinical examiner ratings, and self-report. Data on home environment, school, employment, and social history were also gathered. The assessment measures reflected the typologies, developed by Chess and Thomas, that were available in 1972 (see Chess & Thomas, 1987): undercontrolled or difficult (impulsive, restless, negative), inhibited or slow-to-warm-up (introverted, fearful), and well-adjusted or easy (see Chapter 4).

Results paint a picture of moderate personality stability over time. At age 21, the 10% of children identified at age 3 as undercontrolled were more likely than other groups to be aggressive, sensation-seeking, impulsive, and prone to troubles with the law. They also tended to experience higher levels of interpersonal conflict in family and romantic relationships. Even if the surface features of behavior changed over time, these undercontrolled children were more likely to grow up to be adults whose behavior reflected a similar lack of control and problematic adjustment. The inhibited children (8% of the sample) at 21 were more likely than the other participants to have suffered from depression. As adults, they were more shy, fearful, and nonassertive and less connected to sources of social support.

Several possible explanations might account for trait stability over time. First, genes probably play a role in stability of personality. McCue, Bacon, and Lykken (1993) found that of the roughly 50% consistency in twins' personality traits measured over 10 years, about 80% of that similarity could be attributed to genetics. Remember, however, that we do not inherit trait patterns per se, but rather chemical templates that regulate the building of the nervous system. As multidimensional models of development predict, personality features are also shaped by contextual circumstances. In other words, the transactional interplay between individual and context is what sculpts personality (Buss, 1987).

Viewed from this perspective, personality or trait consistency will be highest if other variables, in addition to biology, provide support or scaffolding for that consistency. For example, the individual's environment should remain consistent. Helson and Roberts's (1994) study of 81 women from Mills College from ages 21 to 52 is illustrative here. Those women whose level of ego development showed no change or whose level of ego development even slightly decreased over the years of the study were the least likely to have experienced disruptive experiences or high levels of responsibility. They seemed to have found comfortable niches for themselves that required little accommodation or change. Personality could remain fairly consistent over time, because these women appeared to have selected environments that suited their personalities in the first place (proactive transactions). Or they may have behaved in ways that communicated their reluctance to change, thus eliciting compliance from others (evocative transactions).

Yet another possible explanation for continuity is that certain kinds of personality styles show more consistency than others. Clausen (1993), for example, suggested that planful competence, a trait found in people who are highly dependable and self-reliant, tends to be consistent across adulthood. Generally, people who possess resilient characteristics tend to be more stable and consistent throughout life. Perhaps any strong, "achieved" identity operates as a cognitive schema or organizer that interprets information and situations in ways that promote consistency with one's personality or reputation (Vandewater, Ostrove, & Stewart, 1997).

INFLUENCES ON ADULT DEVELOPMENT: SOURCES OF CHANGE

Although personality characteristics can be a relatively stable set of influences on the adult's development, there are many changes to which an adult must adapt. Some of these are strongly age determined or age graded, such as physical changes that come more or less inevitably with time. Other changes in our life experience are more a function of historical circumstance and are called history-graded changes. These include events that we share with our whole cohort, like living through the Great Depression or the Vietnam War. Finally, there are changes that apply specifically to our own lives. These are nonnormative changes, often accidents of fate, like being in a train wreck or winning the lottery.

Age-Graded Changes

We will consider three kinds of age-graded changes. The first two are the physical and cognitive changes that have been documented as a function of aging in adulthood. The last concerns shifts in the relative importance of various life tasks that seem to occur with age. These shifts in life tasks, described by theorists such as Erik Erikson and Daniel Levinson, are generally thought to be a product of one's psychological response to reaching adulthood and facing the typical burdens and challenges that life presents to all of us. All three kinds of change represent challenges to our adaptive functioning as we get older.

PHYSICAL CHANGES IN ADULTHOOD

Bodily changes may be the most obvious ones in adult life. By about age 30, as people enter middle adulthood, there begins a shift from **adolescing**, or growing up, to **senescing**, or "growing down" (Levinson, 1986). Although there are physical declines that most people are aware of fairly early in this process, such as some skin wrinkling or hair loss, most declines are much more subtle, such as a decrease in the effectiveness of immune processes or in cardiovascular functioning. For the most part, people continue to feel that they are at peak or near peak levels of physical functioning until they are 40 or older. In their 40s and 50s, most people become more aware of physical losses. In the United States, the majority of middle adults enjoy good health, but this period is one in which many individuals, especially those in lower socioeconomic groups, begin to deal with chronic illnesses and other health problems that can limit their activities. In the 40s, 7% of adults have some kind of disability; by the early 60s, 30% do (Lachman, 2004).

Most sensory systems decline in sensitivity or acuity, although there is considerable variation among the systems and among individuals (see Whitbourne, 2002). Developmental changes in some systems have proven more difficult to study effectively than others. The experience of pain, for example, is caused by the stimulation of free nerve endings in damaged tissue. Some studies indicate that pain detection diminishes with age, and others indicate that pain sensitivity increases with age! The aging of the visual and auditory systems is probably best understood. Visual acuity is maintained at near peak levels until about age 40 and then starts to wane. Individuals who never before wore glasses or contact lenses are likely to need them now, and those who required some visual correction in the past begin to experience more frequent prescription changes, or they now need bifocals or trifocals. Middle adults also begin to notice that they need more light to see well than their younger friends, and they may begin to notice that it takes longer to adapt to lighting changes than it used to. They are most likely to be bothered when there is a sudden change in lighting: coming out of a dark movie theater into daylight or encountering the headlights of an oncoming car on a dark road. Changes in the neurons of the retina, as well as changes in the cornea and lens of the eye, all contribute to these growing problems.

Similar declines in hearing or auditory sensitivity begin in the 30s. Sensitivity to high-frequency (high-pitched) sounds declines earlier and more rapidly, and the losses are usually greater in men than in women. Note that women's voices are therefore more difficult to hear in the later years than are men's, so that men are more likely to have difficulty hearing women than vice versa. There is much individual variation in the degree and kind of hearing loss, but most individuals find their lives somewhat affected by the end of middle age (Whitbourne, 2002).

Among the functional systems that show developmental changes sometime in middle adulthood is the reproductive system (Whitbourne, 2002). As with the sensory systems, noticeable changes tend to begin in the 40s and 50s. The menstrual cycle usually begins to shorten and becomes somewhat more erratic by the time a woman is in her late 30s. The female **climacteric**, the gradual reduction of reproductive ability, ending in **menopause**, the cessation of menstruation, usually begins in the 40s and continues for at least 10 years. The climacteric is largely a function of a reduction in circulating **estradiol**, a form of the primary female hormone, **estrogen**, produced by the ovaries. Having less estradiol eventually influences many other changes: the thinning and coarsening of pubic hair, the thinning and wrinkling of the labia, and changes in vaginal chemistry that can cause dryness and a greater likelihood of vaginal infections. Women commonly experience other physical symptoms as well, such as fatigue, headaches, insomnia, nightsweats, and hot flashes—"sudden, internal sensations of intense heat accompanied by sweating on the face, neck, and chest" (Whitbourne, 2002, pp. 155–156). One reason for such symptoms is that lowered estrogen triggers the release of other hormones and these have widespread effects on the body, such as altering its temperature control mechanisms. Despite these changes, and despite a general slowing of sexual response times, sexual functioning and sexual pleasure seem to be affected very little for most women (Avis, Stellato, Crawford, Johannes, & Longcope, 2000), as long as one key ingredient remains—the availability of sexual partners (see Kellett, 2000, for a review). Many researchers have found only small declines, if any, in the frequency of female sexual activity in middle age (see Table 13.2).

TABLE 13.2 Frequency of Sexual Activity by Age and Gender

	M	F	M	F	M	F	M	F	M	F
Age	18–26		27–38		39–50		51–64		65+	
N	254	268	353	380	282	295	227	230	212	221
>1/wk	53%	46%	60%	49%	54%	39%	63%	32%	53%	41%
"rarely"	13%	17%	9%	12%	8%	21%	8%	21%	11%	22%

Source: Kellett, J. M. Older adult sexuality, In L. T. Szuchman & F. Muscarella (Eds.), *Psychological perspectives on human sexuality* (p. 357). Copyright © 2000 John Wiley & Sons, Inc. This material is used by permission of John Wiley & Sons. Inc.

For men in the middle years, changes in the production of testosterone, the primary male hormone, are not as dramatic. Some controversy has existed over whether testosterone production declines at all in healthy men, but longitudinal studies in recent years confirm that small average declines do occur, starting as early as the 20s (see Whitbourne, 2002, for a review). Men with health problems, such as cardiovascular disease and overweight, are likely to show a larger drop in testosterone. Lower testosterone levels are thought to contribute to some aspects of physical aging in men, such as loss of muscle mass and bone density. Some erectile dysfunction is also experienced by about 50% of men between 40 and 70 years old, but this seems to be more related to changes in the circulatory system than to hormones. Healthy men remain fertile through old age, even though reproductive structures like the testes, seminal vesicles, and prostate gland do undergo some changes (e.g., Plas, Berger, Hermann, & Pfluger, 2000). These changes have little effect on sperm production, but they result in reduced amounts of seminal fluid by the 40s and 50s and a steady decline in the volume and force of ejaculations. Yet, as with women, whereas sexual response times begin to increase in middle age, sexual functioning and sexual pleasure can be maintained (see Table 13.2). For a man with an available sexual partner, how sexually active he will be in his older years is closely correlated with how strong his sex drive was in his younger years (see Kellett, 2000). For both men and women, understanding that sexual activity need not be derailed by the normal changes in sexual function that come with age (e.g., slower responses, erectile changes, vaginal dryness, and so on) can be key to maintaining a satisfying sex life.

In today's popular culture, personal worth is linked to physical beauty, defined in part as a youthful, fit appearance. In such a climate, the most problematic physical changes of middle adulthood for some people can be the wrinkling and sagging of the skin and an increase in body fat (e.g., Katchadourian, 1987). Weight gain is not inevitable in middle adulthood, but rather is directly linked to overeating, poor nutrition, or inadequate exercise. Unfortunately, the typical habits of many Americans do result in their gaining weight throughout middle adulthood, mostly around the waist and hips. Among the factors contributing to the wrinkling and sagging process are changes in the layers of the skin. For example, elastin, a substance in the cells of the dermis, or middle layer of skin, allows the skin to stretch and contract as we move. After age 30, elastin gradually becomes more brittle, reducing skin elasticity. Areas of the body containing fat, such as the arms, legs, torso, and breasts, usually begin to sag by the 40s and 50s (Whitbourne, 2002).

COGNITIVE CHANGES IN ADULTHOOD

Age-graded changes in cognitive functioning are experienced throughout adulthood. An enormous research literature exists on adult cognitive change. We humans, including developmental researchers, seem to worry a great deal about what kinds of intellectual declines we can expect as we get older and how we might avoid them. Early findings, from cross-sectional studies, tended to be a bit discouraging, producing data such as those in Figure 13.3a, reported by Schaie (1994). In such studies, most intellectual skills appear to decline fairly steadily after age 25. But in cross-sectional studies, different ages are represented by people from different cohorts.

a.

a. An illustration of *cross-sectional* findings for six intellectual abilities. Note that it appears that most skills decline throughout adulthood. An interesting exception are numerical abilities, which appear to increase through the mid-forties. Longitudinal data, however, make it clear that the increases really represent cohort effects. Younger cohorts (more recent generations) have poorer math skills than older cohorts.

b.

b. An illustration of *longitudinal* findings for the same six intellectual abilities. Now you can see that people's numerical skills are best, on average, in early adulthood. However, most skills are maintained or improved until after age 60.

FIGURE 13.3

Cross-Sectional and Longitudinal Findings for Six Intellectual Abilities

Source: Schaie, K. W. The course of adult intellectual development. *American Psychologist, 49,* 307. Copyright © 1994 by the American Psychological Association. Reprinted with permission.

For example, in Schaie's cross-sectional data (collected in 1991), the 81-year-old cohort was born in 1910 and the 25-year-old cohort was born in 1966. Many factors could contribute to what appear to be age effects because different cohorts are not just different in age. They have also grown up in different eras, such that they may have experienced very different educational, economic, and cultural opportunities. Older cohorts, for example, have on average fewer years of postelementary school education than younger cohorts. Their test results may reflect these cohort differences rather than the typical changes in cognitive function that come with age.

A better way to assess cognitive change across the life span is to conduct prospective or longitudinal research, that is, studies that reassess the same individuals periodically as they get older. Figure 13.3b illustrates longitudinal data on the progress of six ability factors, also reported by Schaie (1994). These findings suggest a very different and more complex picture of intellectual change in adulthood. Although some abilities begin to decline early, most cognitive capacities seem to show improvements with age and show only small average declines after ages 55 to 60 (Schaie, 1994).

One way to make sense of the mixed pattern of improvement and decline through adulthood is to categorize cognitive skills with regard to how heavily they depend on two kinds of underlying intellectual resources. One resource is called **fluid intelligence** by some (e.g., Horn & Cattell, 1966) and is called the **mechanics** of intelligence by others (e.g., Baltes et al., 1998). These terms refer to basic operational characteristics that seem to directly reflect how well the "hardware" of the nervous system is working. Fluid, or mechanical, functions include such things as processing speed and inhibitory mechanisms. They are the most likely kinds of intellectual processes to show declines sometime in middle adulthood. For example, information processing speed may begin to slow down as early as age 30 and declines fairly rapidly after age 40, so that we are slower to take in information as we get older and slower to respond to it (e.g., Kail & Salthouse, 1994). Inhibitory mechanisms show decrements by about age 40, so that in some tasks, older adults are more easily distracted by irrelevant stimulation than younger adults (Hasher & Zacks, 1988; Zacks & Hasher, 1994).

Another intellectual resource is called **crystallized intelligence** (e.g., Horn & Cattell, 1966) or the **pragmatics** of intelligence (e.g., Baltes et al., 1998). It is the compilation of skills and information we have acquired in the course of our lives. Crystallized intelligence, or pragmatics, is a little like the pile of software programs that most of us accumulate for our computers. Our knowledge of language, of how to do a job or to play an instrument, the strategies we have learned for memorizing information or solving problems—all forms of declarative and procedural knowledge (see Chapter 6)—are included. Crystallized intelligence is less likely than fluid intelligence to show declines with age and, for some individuals, can increase even into old age. For most people in middle adulthood, and for most abilities, declining fluid resources are usually balanced or outweighed by continuing steady increases in crystallized resources (Baltes et al., 1998). It is only after about age 60 that losses in fluid intelligence may be great enough to contribute to overall declines in intellectual functioning.

Changing memory abilities provide a good illustration of the interactive influences of mechanics and pragmatics in overall functioning. Some forms of memory show losses in middle and late adulthood, and some do not. Working memory, for example, seems most disrupted by age. You'll remember from Chapter 6 that working memory stores information that we are thinking about or working with at the present moment. This is the part of the information processing system with which we solve problems, make inferences, or transfer information to long-term storage. Working memory has a limited capacity, so that only a restricted number of information units can be retained there at one time, and usually only for 15 to 30 seconds, unless we actually keep working with it—that is, unless we make an effort to pay attention to the information. To put it a different way, working memory is the active, attentive part of the mind, where we solve problems and learn new information. In late middle adulthood, working memory capacity seems to decline. Fewer pieces of information can be attended to at one time, and either problem solving or learning or both can be somewhat affected as a result. For example, imagine a situation in which you look up and dial a 10-digit phone number, and then you immediately attempt to redial the number. Suppose that at age 30, you could remember about 6 of the digits when you redialed. At age 50, given the same kind of memory task, you would probably remember only 5 of the digits. Clearly, what we are describing here are not catastrophic losses. The modest change is more a nuisance factor than anything else. Most people, by about age 50, notice that they have a little more difficulty than they used to recalling the name of a new acquaintance or solving a complex problem that requires attending to several pieces of information at once. Declines in fluid intelligence seem to make the difference. Slower processing speed may make it harder to keep as many pieces of information in mind simultaneously as we once could or make it difficult to work our way through to the end of a problem before some of the information that we need has disappeared from short-term storage (Salthouse, 1996). Reduced inhibitory control might also be important. For example, we might experience at times "a kind of 'mental clutter' in which extraneous thoughts and plans can interfere with, and possibly crowd out, goal-relevant thoughts and plans" (Zacks, Hasher, & Li, 2000, p. 297).

The decline of working memory affects problem solving most when either the information that is relevant to the solution or the problem-solving situation is new. But when middle adults are solving familiar, everyday problems or problems in areas of their own expertise, the crystallized resources at their disposal often help them to be more effective than younger adults (e.g., Willis, 1996).

Although the limitations of working memory make it more difficult to get new information into long-term memory, we nonetheless do continue to learn in middle and late adulthood, storing new information from our experiences despite our reduced efficiency. Thus, both younger and older adults add new information to episodic memory—memory for personal experiences—but younger subjects typically learn more with greater ease (e.g., Zelinski, Gilewski, & Schaie, 1993).

To put it differently, we are somewhat less likely, as we get older, to remember specific daily experiences, such as where we parked the car this morning. However, information already learned appears to be maintained as well as in our younger years. In fact, an older person's semantic memory, her store of factual information, seems to have a richer network of interrelationships as a result of her greater experience, allowing her to retrieve information through many more routes than a younger person can (e.g., Laver & Burke, 1993; MacKay & Abrams, 1996). As Whitbourne (1996), suggested, you might be well advised to choose an older partner the next time you play a memory game like Trivial Pursuit!

Charness and Bosman (1990) provide an interesting example of the differential effects of age changes in fluid and crystallized intelligence on performance in adulthood. They describe two kinds of chess competitions. In tournament chess, participants make their moves quickly, after deliberating for about three minutes. In correspondence chess, the participants can have three days to make a move. Clearly, tournament chess makes greater demands on processing speed, whereas correspondence chess seems to draw much more completely on one's knowledge and experience. Not surprisingly, then, top performers win their first world championship in tournament chess at much younger ages, about age 30 on average, than they do in correspondence chess, where the average first-time champion is 46! It is not unusual for middle-aged chess devotees to adapt to declines in fluid intelligence by shifting their focus from tournament chess to correspondence chess as they get older.

In Chapter 15 we will look more closely at cognitive changes in late adulthood, focusing especially on how older adults compensate for losses in fluid intelligence and on the debate over the growth of wisdom.

LIFE-TASK OR LIFE-COURSE CHANGES IN ADULTHOOD

People experience another kind of age-graded change as they move through adulthood. Life-course changes, brought on by shifts in the life tasks that seem most important to us at different times of our lives, have been described by many different theorists. Although each of these theorists tends to emphasize somewhat different aspects of the life experience, you will see commonalities in their observations as we briefly summarize a sampling of these descriptions.

You may recall that Schaie (1977–1978; Schaie & Willis, 2000; see also Chapter 11) proposed a series of stages in adult life, each of which requires the development of new ways to apply and use one's intellectual resources. These changes are directly related to shifts in family roles and in the life tasks that we face as we grow older. In the achieving stage of young adulthood, the individual must learn to use logical thinking skills to plan the achievement of long-term goals. In the responsible stage of middle adulthood, one must learn to use her problem-solving skills not only to achieve her own goals but also to help coordinate her needs with those of others for whom she is responsible at home, at work, and in the community. In the reorganizational stage of one's elder years, one's focus narrows again to reaching personal, practical, day-to-day goals as an adult devotes her thinking skills to managing her losses. Finally, in late adulthood, people move into the reintegrative stage, when their goals are primarily to conserve energy, and perhaps into a legacy-leaving stage, when they use their cognitive resources to help them leave behind a written or oral account of their experience or wisdom.

Schaie emphasizes the shifting allocation of intellectual skills across adulthood, as people confront different kinds of problems related to their age and stage of life. Most other theorists emphasize changes in personality. They do not focus on personality traits, which, as we have seen, are relatively stable in middle adulthood and beyond, but rather they describe structural changes in self-concept and in self-expression.

Perhaps the best-known theory of life-course changes in self-concept is Erik Erikson's, by now quite familiar to you. Erikson (e.g., 1950/1963) describes three stages in self-development in adulthood, based on the kinds of life tasks that become most important to people as they find themselves fully matured and facing the fact that this is the one life that they have to live. Very briefly, in young adulthood, intimacy (versus isolation) is one's quest; finding a way to validate and expand her own sense of self by committing to a shared life with others. In middle adulthood, generativity (versus stagnation) becomes most important, giving one's own life purpose by producing and building for the next generation, through work, community service, or child rearing. By old age, establishing ego integrity (vs. despair) becomes life's task. Ideally, a process of life review helps the elderly adult to develop a sense that her own life is "something that had to be," that she has lived a life that has order, meaning, and dignity (see Chapter 1, especially Table 1.1).

Erikson argued that different concerns reach ascendancy in different age periods. Vaillant (1977; Vaillant & Koury, 1994) suggested that two more adult life stages should be added to Erikson's scheme, reflecting that forming deep bonds, becoming productive, and finding meaning in one's life are recurring themes throughout adulthood. In one's mid-20s, career consolidation (vs. self-absorption) is a key focus of self-development. In this phase of life, in addition to ongoing intimacy concerns, making a commitment to work that brings personal satisfaction, regardless of its other rewards, rather than just having a job, becomes important. The most positive development for this period is that such a commitment emerges as an important part of one's identity.

Vaillant also described a stage that comes near the end of Erikson's generativity stage, in late middle adulthood. This he called the keeper of meaning (vs. rigidity) stage, when the adult expands her generative concerns beyond just making a productive contribution, in order to actually preserve something that is part of the culture. In this sense, adults seek ways to establish the meaningfulness of the work or contributions they have made. For example, Tien, a woman who worked as an aid at her children's day care center, might move on after her own children are grown to join a child care advocacy group in her community, hoping to ensure that future generations of children in her region will have access to the high-quality child care she was able to provide her own children.

As we saw in Chapter 12, research indicates that both intimacy and generativity are central to the lives of young adults. Later in this chapter we will discuss research on how these concerns tend to play out in the arenas of marriage, family life, parenting, and work during the middle years of adulthood.

Several other theorists have proposed stages in adult personality development that repeat many of the themes that we see in Erikson's work. They all emphasize that people have fundamental concerns or needs that shift in importance from one adult stage to another. We will briefly describe Levinson's theory here; some additional theories (e.g., Gould, 1978; Loevinger, 1976) are included in schematic comparison in Table 13.3.

TABLE 13.3 Adult Life Stages: Some Theories of Self-Development

Approximate Age Period	Erikson	Vaillant	Loevinger	Gould
Adolescence	Identity (vs. Identity Diffusion)	(like Erikson)	Conscientious—Conformist	Separating from parents: becoming independent
Young Adulthood	Intimacy (vs. Isolation)	(like Erikson)	Individualistic	"Nobody's baby": becoming a competent, self-maintaining adult
Middle Adulthood (Early)	Generativity (vs. Stagnation)	Generativity—Career consolidation (vs. Self-Absorption); producing	Autonomous	Opening up: exploring inner consciousness, coming to deeper understanding of self and needs
Middle Adulthood (Late)		Generativity—Keeper of Meaning (vs. Rigidity); giving, mentoring		Midlife: finding the courage and resourcefulness to act on deeper feelings; awareness of pressure of time
Late Adulthood	Ego Integration (vs. Despair)		Integrated	Beyond midlife: establishing true autonomy; becoming inner-directed rather than governed by roles; "I own myself"

In Levinson's account (e.g., Levinson, 1986; Levinson & Levinson, 1996; Levinson, Darrow, Klein, Levinson, & McKee, 1978), a person's life has structure at any given time. One's **life struc-ture** is a pattern of relationships between the self and the external world, such as relationships to one's "spouse, lover, family, occupation, religion, leisure, and so on" (Levinson, 1986). There may be many components to the life structure, but Levinson found that at any one time there are usually only one or two really significant, defining components for the self, usually marriage-family and/or occupational components. Levinson identified three major adult stages, or eras: early, middle, and late adulthood. Each of these eras begins with a 5-year transitional period and is marked by a smaller mid-era transition, when the life structure's effectiveness for serving the person's goals is reexamined and may be altered.

Whereas Erikson and Vaillant suggest that certain life tasks occur in relatively predictable sequence (e.g., first intimacy needs are greater, then generativity needs), Levinson (1986) argues that life events unfold in many ways depending on a particular individual's life circumstances, gender, and culture and that specific concerns are not necessarily more important in one era than in another. What is predictable, he argues, is the sequence of age periods for building and chang-ing first one life structure and then another. The experience of life changes from one era to the next. Put a different way, what is inevitable in adulthood is that a person will establish and then revise her life structure at particular times as she ages. Figure 13.4 presents the age and sequence of the eras Levinson describes and his view of the general character of the life structure changes in each era.

In sum, many theorists have identified life-course changes affecting self-concept or self-expression during adulthood. There is by no means complete agreement among these theorists on the character of these changes. For example, following Jung (1963), Levinson (e.g., 1986) and Gould (1978) describe the midlife transition as an often tumultuous time, a period of major upheaval and self-evaluation, not unlike adolescence. You may have heard it referred to as a "midlife crisis." Their research, consisting of longitudinal interview studies of relatively small and somewhat selective samples of adults, tends to support these claims (e.g., Gould, 1978; Levinson et al., 1978; Levinson & Levinson, 1996). But in much larger interview and questionnaire stud-ies, many researchers have found little evidence of widespread midlife distress, although they have found indications of shifting concerns at midlife (e.g., Almeida & Horn, 2004; McCrae & Costa, 1990; Vaillant, 1977; Whitbourne, 1996). Crisis-level distress seems most likely to occur as a function of major life events, like financial problems or job loss, which can happen at any

FIGURE 13.4

Levinson's Conception of the Early and Middle Adult Eras and Transitions

Source: From *The Seasons of a Man's Life* by Daniel Levinson, copyright © 1978 by Daniel J. Levinson. Used by permission of Alfred A. Knopf, a division of Random House, Inc.

time. Individuals who score high on the personality trait of neuroticism are particularly likely to suffer acute distress (see Lachman, 2004).

Regardless of such disagreements, there is some similarity among the theoretical descriptions of adult life-course changes. The available empirical work supports the general idea of such change. Despite the enormous variation in the immediate details of adult lives—from culture to culture, from cohort to cohort, from family to family, and from individual to individual—there appear to be some life changes that are widely experienced. These changes lead each of us to reformulate, or at least reevaluate, our selves and our lives periodically. Much more research is needed to establish the specifics of these changes and whom they do and do not affect.

For counselors, awareness of potential stage changes can help enrich our understanding of clients. For example, suppose a woman at 45 comes to a counselor looking for help with marital problems she has tolerated for 20 years. We might be inclined to wonder, why now, and, how likely is it that change can be effected after so many years of entrenched behavior patterns? The answers to both questions may be partly a function of life stage. Many theorists see the 40s as a time when reassessment of one's life structure is very likely and when willingness to act on the basis of one's individual propensities, rather than strictly in adherence with social expectations, increases (see Table 13.3). Vaillant (1977) suggests that generativity needs are likely to reorganize, so that direct caregiving to one's spouse or children is less likely to meet one's needs than opportunities to seek broader meaning in one's life by finding ways to preserve the culture. Thus, not only is it a likely time for this woman to reassess her life, but it may also be a time when she will be open to trying new ways of meeting her needs.

History-Graded Changes

The historical events that affect our whole cohort are another source of change in adult lives. People are partly a product of the historical context in which they develop. Imagine that you were a young adult parent trying to support your children during the years of the Great Depression. You would take a job wherever you found one, no matter how difficult the work, and you would probably be grateful for it. What effect might years of deprivation and struggle have on your tendency toward conscientiousness? Or think about moving through early adulthood during the social upheavals and sexual revolution of the 1960s. Do you think this experience might have some effect on your openness to experience? History-graded events, also called cohort effects, provide a context for development and also influence it directly (e.g., Rogler, 2002).

The year of your birth marks your entry into a cohort of peers who accompany you through age-graded developmental changes (toddlerhood, puberty, and so on) within the context of a specific set of historical events (wars, technological shifts, etc.). The effect of history is particularly linked to a person's age and stage of life (such as coming of age in a time of war, when you could be drafted into military service). In addition to age-graded and history-graded changes, we also progress through stages of the family life cycle as child, parent, grandparent, and so on. Researchers who take a life-course perspective remind us that development is influenced by the intersection of chronological age (life time), family-related roles (family time), and membership in a birth cohort (historical time; Elder, 1994). If society experiences an economic recession that results in a lengthy period of corporate downsizing, a young father who has just completed a training program in computer repair might see his chances of getting a well-paying job shrink. He may have to wait to buy a first house, ultimately limiting the lifetime equity he can accrue. Because his family must continue to reside in a low-cost apartment, his preschool son might also be affected because of missed educational opportunities that would have been available with a move to a more advantaged school district. Note that despite the important implications of the economic downturn for this young parent's life, his own grandparents, who are retired and receiving a fixed pension, would not be much affected.

Twenge (2000) provides a recent example of how sociocultural and historical context influences the personality development of cohorts of individuals. She reviewed published reports of child and adolescent anxiety from 1952 to 1993 to see if levels had changed over these years. Her distressing finding showed that the average child in America during the 1980s scored higher on

What do you think might be the nonnormative and cohort effects of the events of September 11, 2001 on your life?

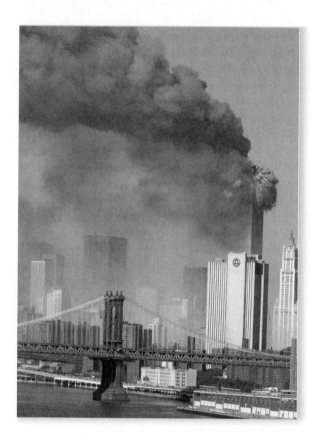

anxiety than child psychiatric patients from the 1950s. Further analysis allowed her to demonstrate that these increases were associated with the breakdown of social connections and with increases in physical and psychological threats. Economic recessions were not related to the increase in anxiety. Twenge's results imply that recent cohorts are living in a world that is less favorable to their positive development than the world in which their own parents grew up. A context that provides for fewer or weaker social bonds at the same time that threats are expanding heightens the sense of vulnerability for these young people, who are truly growing up in an "age of anxiety."

Nonnormative Changes

Just as history-graded changes can significantly affect the development of a whole cohort, individual lives are also changed by unexpected events. These events are called nonnormative events, "bolt from the blue" experiences that we don't anticipate, yet that can have powerful developmental effects. Crises such as traumatic illnesses, accidents, imprisonment, the untimely death of a loved one, or even positive events such as winning a lottery can be considered nonnormative. They create new sets of circumstances for people, and these have the potential to alter developmental trajectories (Datan & Ginsburg, 1975).

Imagine a woman at age 45 who has worked hard as a parent and homemaker and looks forward to seeing each of her children move into adult independence. A car accident suddenly leaves her 19-year-old son a quadraplegic. The financial resources she and her husband had carefully saved for their retirement and their children's college years are soon gone, and the mother's dreams of opening a small craft shop are dashed. She is a somewhat introverted woman, but the special needs of her son create circumstances that move her to take initiative with lawyers, insurance companies, and government agencies. Literally, her personality and the whole course of her life begin to move in a new direction. So middle age, like the "ages" before it, is both continuous and changing. Stable personality traits are influenced by age, life stage, history, and unplanned events as people continue to adapt to life.

KEY DEVELOPMENTAL TASKS OF MIDLIFE: THE CONTINUING PURSUIT OF INTIMACY AND GENERATIVITY

In middle adulthood, as in young adulthood, loving relationships and productive, meaningful work continue to be critical elements in the construction of a satisfying life. As you know, Erikson saw intimacy, broadly defined as sharing oneself with another, as a more prominent concern in young adulthood and generativity, defined as the need to create and produce, as a more central focus of middle adulthood. However, it is clear from available research that although the relative balance between these two concerns may shift (see Chapter 12), both remain important in middle adulthood and beyond. In the following sections we will further explore intimacy issues by examining how marital relationships form, develop, and sometimes fail during adulthood. We will continue our discussion of generativity by considering the parental role from the adult's perspective, and we will touch on other generativity issues in the middle years, having to do with work and community.

Intimacy: Marriage and Other Primary Relationships

One of the most valuable adaptations we humans can make is to establish and maintain close interpersonal relationships. In adulthood, close ties take on a variety of forms, and the number and diversity of forms is increasing. Marriage has provided the traditional structure within which such relationships exist. Approximately 52% of the U.S. population were married, according to 2000 census data, a figure down from 60% in 1980. One quarter of all households in the United States were single-person households. Cohabitation was also on the rise. Although there has been a steep rise in the number of people living alone or as unmarried partners, this condition might be temporary for some. According to 1990 data, only 8.4% of men and 7.1% of women have never wed by the time they reach age 45 to 54. Thus, estimates of the marriage rate for people over their lifetimes predict that approximately 90% of the population will have been married at least one time.

The definition of "family" has indeed become more inclusive in the 21st century and refers to more than the traditional nuclear family with its own biological children. Particularly since the social changes initiated in the 1960s, people have felt freer to meet their needs for intimacy and connection in a variety of ways. Extended, multigenerational families, adoptive and foster families, same-sex unions, remarried or blended families, single-parent families, and "families" composed of several people living together without legal ties are all examples of new trends in family formation. Some individuals will be part of several different kinds of families as they progress through their lives.

Clearly, psychological wellness does not depend upon any one specific relationship configuration. Kaslow (2001) encourages clinicians to expand their definition of family and to work toward ways of promoting optimal functioning for each of these forms. Yet despite greater social acceptance of alternative family styles, researchers have discovered that good marriages or primary relationships confer a number of physical and psychological benefits that other states may not provide (Horwitz & White, 1998; Ross, 1995). For example, married people report generally higher levels of happiness than unmarried people. They have lower rates of mental illness, drug and alcohol abuse, and physical illness than their unmarried counterparts. They report higher levels of sexual and emotional satisfaction (Waite & Joyner, 2001). Research has even documented that married partners tend to live longer (Freidman et al., 1995)! Perhaps the day-to-day economic and social support that accrues to married couples over the years helps to account for some of these effects. Married couples may also receive more social approval and less social rejection than individuals in other situations, although tolerance for alternative family arrangements is growing. The economic benefits that come with marital status in U.S. culture, including those that provide retirement income for surviving spouses, probably make a major contribution to the increased happiness and even health of married people over time. In one study, single mothers who were the sole support for their children for a period of ten years or more during their lifetimes were 55% more likely to live in poverty at ages 65–75, regardless of their current marital status (Johnson & Favreault, 2004). Thus, marriage appears to serve as an economic protective factor, given the structure of the current laws and benefit systems in this country. More research is needed to understand whether the same benefits are conferred by alternative relationship forms as well.

Although we use marriage as the prototypical vehicle to illustrate the development of intimacy over the adult life span, we acknowledge that this is not the only road, nor even the best one, for many people. We do not underestimate the importance of friendships nor devalue single status in adulthood. However, as you have seen, demographics show that the majority of people will marry or participate in some kind of committed relationship, such as between gay and lesbian couples, for at least some period of time in their lives. In some Latin American cultures, there is a historical acceptance of long-term consensual unions (Landale & Fennelly, 1992) even though couples are not formally wed. After divorce, rates of remarriage are still very high. Approximately 80% remarry within 3 years after divorce (Glick & Lin, 1986). Even though the traditional marital and family life cycle may not be the best descriptive fit for everyone, there are aspects of its stages that can help us understand many kinds of close adult relationships. The nature of intimate relationships, inside or outside marriage, is defined by mutual sharing of joys and sorrows, reaching compromises and working out problems, and developing a sense of "we-ness."

THE FAMILY LIFE CYCLE

Marriages (and other primary relationships) change as partners age and the demands of family life ebb and flow. The family life cycle, a normative, stagelike sequence of traditional family development in intact marriages, has been described in several ways. Figure 13.5 shows a well-known early example proposed by Duvall (1971) that depicts a historically traditional breakdown of time. Duvall emphasized the time spent in each of the stages of family life as partners become parents, rear and launch their children, become "empty-nesters," and subsequently face old age. Carter and McGoldrick (1999) developed a similar model that incorporates the tasks that accompany each stage (see Table 13.4). In the next section, we borrow from this latter model to highlight some important transitions and challenges facing families. Then we take a closer look at marriage itself and address theories of marital satisfaction and dysfunction.

1. Married Couples (without children).
2. Childbearing Families (Oldest child, birth – 30 months).
3. Families with Preschool Children (Oldest child 30 months – 6 years).
4. Families with Schoolchildren (Oldest child 6 – 13 years).
5. Families with Teenagers (Oldest child 13 – 20 years).
6. Families as Launching Centers (First child gone to last child leaving home).
7. Middle-aged Parents (Empty nest to retirement).
8. Aging Family Members (Retirement to death of both spouses).

FIGURE 13.5

The Family Life Cycle: Approximate Number of Years Spent in Each Stage for Families with Children

Source: Duvall, E. M. *Family development* (4th ed.) (p. 121). Published by Allyn and Bacon, Boston, MA. Copyright © 1971 by Pearson Education. Reprinted by permission of the publisher.

TABLE 13.4 Family Life Cycle Stages, Transitions, and Tasks

Family Life Cycle Stage	Emotional Process of Transition: Key Principles	Second-Order Changes in Family Status Required to Proceed Developmentally
Leaving home: single young adults	Accepting emotional and financial responsibility for self	a. Differentiation of self in relation to family of origin b. Development of intimate peer relationships c. Establishment of self in respect to work and financial independence
The joining of families through marriage: the new couple	Commitment to new system	a. Formation of marital system b. Realignment of relationships with extended families and friends to include spouse
Families with young children	Accepting new members into the system	a. Adjusting marital system to make space for children b. Joining in child rearing, financial and household tasks c. Realignment of relationships with extended family to include parenting and grandparenting roles
Families with adolescents	Increasing flexibility of family boundaries to permit children's independence and grandparents' frailties	a. Shifting of parent/child relationships to permit adolescent to move into and out of system b. Refocus on midlife marital and career issues c. Beginning shift toward caring for older generation
Launching children and moving on	Accepting a multitude of exits from and entries into the family system	a. Renegotiation of marital system as a dyad b. Development of adult-to-adult relationships between grown children and their parents c. Realignment of relationships to include in-laws and grandchildren d. Dealing with disabilities and death of parents (grandparents)
Families in later life	Accepting the shifting generational roles	a. Maintaining own and/or couple functioning and interests in face of physiological decline: exploration of new familial and social role options b. Support for more central role of middle generation c. Making room in the system for the wisdom and experience of the elderly, supporting the older generation without overfunctioning for them d. Dealing with loss of spouse, siblings, and other peers and preparation for death

Source: From Carter & McGoldrick, *Expanded family life cycle: Individual family and social perspectives*, 3/e. Published by Allyn and Bacon, Boston, MA. Copyright © 1999 by Pearson Education. Reprinted by permission of the publisher.

STAGES OF THE FAMILY LIFE CYCLE

Finding a mate is a task that typically involves a relatively lengthy period of experimentation, given that people in the United States marry at later ages than they did in previous generations. Mate selection has been compared to a "filtering process" by which people go through the step-by-step elimination of ineligible candidates until they settle on a partner (Janda & Klenke-Hamel, 1980). According to this theory, people initially select potential dates on the basis of physical attractiveness and personality characteristics from a pool of available, eligible candidates. Further sorting or filtering out follows on the basis of homogomy, or similarity to oneself in religion, SES, race, education, and so on, as well as on personality compatibility (Diamond, 1986). A trial period, such as an engagement or a period of cohabitation, represents the final step in the decision-making or filtering process.

If homogamy and compatibility are the actual standards for mate selection, what about love? In the United States, most people believe that love is the most important consideration when choosing a mate. You might be surprised to learn that this belief is not universal. People from other cultures consider other factors to be more important. Males in South Africa, for example, consider a mate's maturity and ability to keep house as more significant than love in choosing a partner. Chinese women value emotional stability and the desire for a family as important criteria for mate selection (see Buss, 1989).

Sternberg's (1986) view of love, composed of the three elements of passion, intimacy, and commitment, which were introduced in Chapter 12, may help us understand these differences. The romantic ideal of love portrayed in many movies and songs embodies the element of passion. This is the aspect of love most closely associated with sexuality and romance. Love that includes passion without intimacy or commitment is called infatuation. Intimacy refers to feelings of attachment or emotional closeness. It characterizes one's willingness to trust another, to value her support, and to care about her well-being. (Note that Sternberg defines "intimacy" differently from Erikson, who defines it more broadly.) According to Sternberg, when intimacy is present in a relationship without the other elements, a state of liking exists, which is similar to friendship.

The third element, commitment, is present when partners agree to love each other or make a commitment to sustain that love. Maintaining a commitment without intimacy or passion results in the state of "empty love." Sternberg proposed that any of the three elements can be either present or absent in a relationship, accounting for eight different kinds of love (see Table 13.5). He has expanded on these ideas by suggesting that people hold implicit narratives for love or "love stories," which direct their choice of a mate and the course of their relationships (Beall & Sternberg, 1995; Sternberg, 1998). Sternberg posits that those who have matching scripts, or similar implicit narratives, stand the best chance of having a compatible relationship. Each script emphasizes certain elements, such as emotional maturity or the commitment factor, as more important than others, and "love scripts" are heavily influenced by cultural values. In contemporary U.S. culture, elements of romance and sexual passion are typically central to the definition of love and are considered very important for relationship satisfaction and mate selection. These authors conclude that love is a social construction and that we are strongly influenced by the conceptions of love that are taught by our culture.

Once the members of a couple make a commitment to each other, they begin to develop a new marital or relationship system that is a creative synthesis of the couple's original family systems. Marriages, then, are more than the joining of two individuals. The couple must develop a sense of we-ness that is not so rigid that it isolates them from their original family systems nor so weak that it dissolves under pressure from them.

With time, the couple may become parents, creating a new rung on the generational ladder and reaching a new stage in the family life cycle. Caretaking responsibilities then must be integrated into the marital relationship, and each partner needs to adjust to the new parental role. As children move through the adolescent period, the family needs to adapt to children's increasing demands for independence. They must learn how to provide the stability and flexibility that characterize authoritative parenting for adolescents.

Next, a couple must deal with the transition of launching their children and renegotiating the marital relationship. Adult children need to balance the attachments they have with parents

TABLE 13.5 Sternberg's Eight Kinds of Love			
	Elements*		
Kinds of Love	**Intimacy**	**Passion**	**Decision/Commitment**
Nonlove	−	−	−
Liking	+	−	−
Infatuation	−	+	−
Empty Love	−	−	+
Romantic Love	+	+	−
Companionate Love	+	−	+
Fatuous Love	−	+	+
Consummate Love	+	+	+

*Element present (+) or absent (−)

Source: Sternberg, R. J. A triangular theory of love. *Psychological Review, 93*, 123. Copyright © 1986 by the American Psychological Association. Adapted with permission.

with those they form outside the family. Parents need to strive for acceptance of their adult children's extrafamilial attachments as well as of their careers and other personal choices. Overall, all generations need to work toward two goals: tolerance of independence and maintenance of connections. Among families in later life, the transitions involved in grandparenthood, loss of spouse, and physical decline produce further challenges that must be dealt with flexibly.

MARRIAGE AND ITS DISCONTENTS

Recall that the great majority of individuals marry at least once during their lifetimes. Clearly, many of these unions do not last "till death do us part." People still divorce in record numbers despite a modest decline in the divorce rate since 1979. According to U.S. statistics (Krieder & Fields, 2002; U.S. Bureau of the Census, 1997) about 50% of first marriages and 60% of remarriages end in divorce. These rates do not account for the number of unions that break up without benefit of legal divorce, considering that the average cost of divorce is $15,000 and the average length of time it takes to finalize is 1 year.

Women typically experience a 45% drop in standard of living following a divorce. Each year approximately one million children witness the dissolution of their parents' marriages and subsequently often share in their mothers' reduced circumstances. Yet divorce wreaks more than financial hardship for children. Researchers have documented increased emotional and behavioral problems, such as underachievement, antisocial behavior, and depression (Amato, 1993; McLanahan & Sandefur, 1994; Parke & Buriel, 1998) in children and adolescents after divorce. One longitudinal study of children of divorce found enduring problems with establishing intimacy 25 years after the divorce of the participants' parents (Wallerstein, Lewis, & Blakeslee, 2000). Given that divorce is sometimes the best or the only alternative to a troubled marriage and that not every child of divorce suffers dire consequences, we should nonetheless consider how to help prevent what is so often a powerfully negative event in people's lives.

WHAT MAKES A MARRIAGE FAIL?

Consider two final statistics from the 1997 census data: Only 4.2% of all divorces were attributed to financial problems, whereas 80% were attributed to irreconcilable differences (U.S. Bureau of the Census, 1998). What makes a difference irreconcilable? How do some people manage to reconcile their conflicts whereas others do not? Are the differences due to the nature of the conflicts or to something about the individuals themselves? These are some of the questions that marital and family researchers have attempted to answer. Increasingly, researchers have relied upon longitudinal studies to describe the course of marriage and to help them identify predictors of distress and divorce as they develop over time. On a more fine-grained level, they have also explored the nature of distressed and nondistressed couples' interaction so that therapeutic recommendations can be made. We will focus on some important research findings in both of these areas to give clinicians a framework for understanding the life of a marriage, the behaviors that lead to successful outcomes, and the behaviors that may foreshadow divorce.

Research done in the 1970s indicated consistent U-shaped patterns for quality of marriage. Couples' satisfaction declined shortly after the marriage, reached a low point when children were adolescents, and recovered initial levels of satisfaction when children were launched (Burr, 1970; Rollins & Feldman, 1970). The problem with this portrayal is that these early studies were cross-sectional rather than longitudinal. The high level of satisfaction reported by long-married couples could have been due to the fact that these marriages were happy enough to have survived, long after less satisfied unions had dissolved. Vaillant and Vaillant (1993) collected assessments of marital satisfaction both prospectively (in a longitudinal study) and retrospectively (in which couples reported what they could remember of their marriages over the past 40 years). Results were different depending on how the data were collected. Although retrospective accounts resembled the U-shaped curve found in previous research, prospective ratings showed gradual declines in satisfaction over the entire course of the marriage for both partners, with somewhat greater declines in women's ratings. It appears that fluctuations in the family life cycle did not predict changes in marital satisfaction but were an artifact of the cross-sectional design.

If life cycle changes do not influence satisfaction, then what does? And why, at least for some, does marital satisfaction persistently decline? Let us consider three contemporary hypotheses about marital success and breakdown for some possible answers. Imagine three hypothetical newlywed couples, the Grays, the Whites, and the Greens. Mr. and Mrs. Gray are very much in love. Even when they are in the presence of other people, they behave as if they see only each other. They are highly affectionate and romantic, and their courtship was a whirlwind of exciting events. The Grays believe that they are one another's soul mates, possessing few, if any, negative characteristics. They have no doubts about the happiness that awaits them in marriage.

The Whites are also an affectionate couple. Their view of each other, however, is not quite as rosy as that of the Grays. Their engagement period was a long one because both husband and wife worked to save up enough money to buy a house. Shortly after the wedding, Mrs. White noticed that her husband was becoming less willing to part with any of his income for furniture or other items for the house that she considered important. This has already become a source of tension in the marriage.

The Greens met each other through a dating service that they employed because each was having difficulty meeting eligible romantic partners. Mrs. Green was very insecure in social situations and worried constantly that she would never find a husband. Mr. Green did not want to get married so soon, but he consented because he was afraid that he might lose his chance. Their courtship was a rocky one from the start.

As you read about each of these couples, did you think one or more of them would be more likely to divorce than another? If so, why? Your answers might illustrate popular hypotheses about why marriages succeed or fail. Those who espouse the **disillusionment model** might choose the hypothetical Grays as the couple most likely to experience marital breakdown. This view posits that overly romantic idealizations of marriage and blissfully optimistic views of one's partner set people up for eventual disappointment. Such fantasies cannot coexist for long with the reality of married life (Miller, 1997; Waller, 1938). The rise in divorce rates and incidence of cohabitation might be partially attributable to the fact that young adults today have high expectations for marriage. Barich and Bielby (1996) reported that contemporary young adults had higher expectations than their 1960s counterparts that marriage would satisfy their needs for emotional security, personality development, and companionship. Disappointment in these areas might be seen as a reason to abandon the relationship.

However, another possibility is that the Grays are not especially likely candidates for divorce because they will work hard to maintain their favorable beliefs about each other, despite the inevitable challenges of marriage. Their positive illusions are supportive of the relationship; thus they may be reluctant to abandon them to face reality. This perspective is called the **maintenance hypothesis** (Karney & Bradbury, 1997; Murray, Holmes, & Griffin, 1996).

Perhaps you thought that the Whites were the most likely couple to divorce because of the growing tension in the marriage. Another perspective on marital breakdown, built on **social exchange and behavioral theories**, proposes that increasing problems and mounting conflicts gradually escalate to overwhelm the originally positive perceptions spouses held for each other. Over time, couples who experience chronic conflict and who fail to negotiate it adequately may "fall out of love" with each other once they perceive that the costs of the relationship outweigh its benefits. In truth, no marriage escapes conflict. Approximately half of all divorces occur within the first 7 years of marriage (Cherlin, 1981), suggesting that satisfaction makes its steepest slide during the early period. At this point in development, couples must adjust to each other, work out routines for household tasks, pool resources, and if they have children, take care of them. Several studies have implicated the transition to parenthood as the culprit in the loss of marital satisfaction. For example, Belsky and his colleagues found that many new parents experience a sharp drop in positive interactions and a dramatic increase in conflict following the birth of the first child (Belsky & Kelly, 1994; Belsky, Spanier, & Rovine, 1983). But even couples who remain childless report similar declines in satisfaction. Several prospective studies of young couples' marriages have found much higher rates of divorce among childless couples than among those with children (Cowan & Cowan, 1992; Shapiro, Gottman, & Carrere, 2000). Thus, the existence of conflict in a marriage is simply not a good predictor of its prognosis, but the way couples handle it may be, as we will see later on.

Finally, let's consider the Greens. You may have predicted this couple's marital demise because they seem to bring more personal problems into the marriage in the first place.

Intrapersonal models, which draw on theories of attachment or personality, emphasize the contribution of one's personal history or temperament to the success or failure of relationships. In some studies, intrapersonal variables like a person's tendency to make positive or negative attributions about her partner and her expectations about the future of the relationship have been found to affect relationship quality over time (e.g., McNulty & Karney, 2004). Intrapersonal traits are also important. One particularly robust finding from many investigations of marriages is that neuroticism is moderately related to lower levels of marital satisfaction and higher levels of relationship dissolution (Karney & Bradbury, 1995; Kelly & Conley, 1987; Kurdek, 1993). Also, people who have higher levels of negative affect tend to view life as more stressful (Marco & Suls, 1993). These individuals may be more easily overwhelmed by the conflicts that are inherent in family life and, therefore, more prone to marital distress.

In an empirical test of this hypothesis, Karney and Bradbury (1997) measured the level of marital satisfaction of 60 newlywed couples at 6-month intervals over a period of 4 years. A measure of neuroticism was obtained for each participant at each of the first two data collections. Questions examined things such as tendency to worry and moodiness. Measures of initial satisfaction and observations of problem-solving interactions were also collected.

The researchers found that marital satisfaction declined, on average, for all participants over the 4 years, replicating many earlier findings. However, the drop in satisfaction was several times greater for couples who divorced than for those who remained together. Spouses' levels of neuroticism, a presumably stable variable, were related primarily to how satisfied they were at the beginning of the marriage and less so to rates of change in satisfaction. The way couples solved problems was also strongly related to the rates of decline in satisfaction. In this case, both intrapersonal and interpersonal variables made independent contributions to the health of the relationship but in different ways and at different points in time.

KEEPING LOVE ALIVE

Although the models we have described all may contribute something to our understanding of marriage, each by itself is inadequate to explain its complexity. The marital trajectory seems to be affected by intrapersonal (traits, expectations), interpersonal (problem-solving skills), situational (life stresses, environmental conditions), and developmental (transitions, role change) factors. A comprehensive, multidimensional theory of marriage or other committed relationships has yet to be developed. Nevertheless, we can learn a great deal from the research that has been done, particularly during the last decade, to help us improve the relationships of our clients.

Research an marital communication styles has helped clinicians understand more about the elements of successful relationships.

Some of the most therapist-friendly information comes from the "love-lab" of John Gottman, who has a unique approach to the study of marital dynamics. Gottman and his colleagues have spent years observing and videotaping couples interacting with each other to understand, from the inside out, what makes marriages work or fail. Gottman (1993, 1999) has used this descriptive approach as a step toward building a theory of marital stability and dissolution that can be closely tied to clinical application.

Three fundamental ideas are important in understanding Gottman's research. First, he conceptualizes marriage or any primary relationship as a new system that represents a synthesis of the preexisting elements of each partner's personal history and temperament. Second, he draws upon systems theory to describe marriage as a relational system that seeks a stable or **homeostatic steady state** (von Bertalanffy, 1968). This steady state is maintained over time by the couple's unique balance of positive and negative elements in areas of interactive behavior, perception, and physiology. Behavior refers here to a couple's interactions and accompanying affect; perception refers to self-perceptions and attributions directed to partners; and physiology refers to the autonomic, endocrine, and immune system functioning of the partners. Third, he premises his approach on research done in the last few decades, which consistently documents a ratio of high negative to low positive behaviors in distressed/divorcing couples as opposed to nondistressed/stable couples.

Thinking about a marital relationship as a ratio of positive and negative factors is somewhat like considering the relationship to have a typical kind of "weather," for example, sunny, calm, cloudy, stormy, and so forth. The marital climate or stable steady state is made up of uninfluenced (intrapersonal elements like neuroticism) and influenced (couple's interaction) elements. From a systems perspective, a marital union tends toward stability in its positivity to negativity ratio over time. Obviously, contextual features and crises also play a part in the nature of relationships, but these factors are not emphasized because they are less predictable.

Gottman and his colleagues developed ways to measure levels of positivity and negativity in couples' behavioral interactions, in their perceptions of each other, and in their physiological states, such as arousal or calmness, using observational coding systems, measures of physiological responding, and questionnaire and interview data. Over several extensive longitudinal studies, they set out to predict which couples would divorce and which would remain together. Moreover, they sought to determine whether particular elements were associated with marital breakup or success (see Gottman, 1994; Gottman & Levenson, 2000).

In general, making this kind of marital "weather report" has surprising predictive ability. Assessments done at the beginning of a marriage, including those made from videotapes of the first 3 minutes of a newlywed marital conflict discussion, predicted later outcomes with a high degree of accuracy (Carrere & Gottman, 1999; Carrere, Buehlman, Gottman, Coan, & Ruckstuhl, 2000; Gottman & Levenson, 2000). What turns out to predict marital dissolution best? A high level of **negative affect reciprocity** is a distinguishing feature. This construct refers to the likelihood that negative emotions in one partner will follow from the other partner's negativity. You may think of it as the likelihood that partners will bring out the worst in each other. This is accomplished through the combined influences of information processing biases (e.g., seeing the other's qualities as negative), heightened physiological arousal (e.g., interpreting arousal as anger), negative behavioral interactions (e.g., being critical and defensive), and failing to respond to a partner's bids for attention.

But a number of fine points bear mentioning. As it turns out, conflict and angry feelings are part of all intimate relationships, so simply trying to avoid conflict won't help. Furthermore, not all negative affect is equally deleterious to relationships. Anger can play a constructive function when it is a justifiable reaction to a partner's behavior or reflects airing of grievances (Gottman, 1994). The trick is to distinguish between functional and dysfunctional types of negativity. Other researchers have drawn similar distinctions (e.g., Markman, Stanley, & Blumberg, 1994), but, for the sake of simplicity, we will present Gottman's definitions here.

The four kinds of negativity that do the most damage to relationships and that are highly predictive of divorce are criticism, defensiveness, contempt, and stonewalling (see Table 13.6). The presence of these "**four horsemen of the apocalypse**," particularly contempt, can be very destructive. But suppose you recognize some of these elements in your own close relationship? Does this forecast an inevitable breakup? You may be somewhat relieved to know that Gottman

TABLE 13.6 "Four Horsemen of the Apocalypse"

1. *Criticism:*
   A statement that implies that the partner has some global deficit that is an enduring feature of personality: "You always . . . ; You never . . . "

2. *Defensiveness:*
   A statement that serves to defend against the criticism and that implies denying any responsibility for the problem: "Who me? . . . I do not!"

3. *Contempt:*
   A statement or nonverbal behavior that serves to put down the partner while elevating the speaker to a higher level (such as insulting, using hostile humor, or mocking the partner).

4. *Stonewalling:*
   Withdrawal of a partner from verbal interaction, leaving, or nonverbal behaviors that communicate impassiveness (looking away, looking bored).

Source: Based on Gottman, J. M. (1999). *The marriage clinic: A scientifically-based marital therapy.* New York: Norton.

found criticism, defensiveness, and stonewalling even in happy marriages. In couples headed toward divorce, however, these three behaviors were more frequent, contempt was also present, and there was much less positive affect in the relationship overall. Most important, the distressed couples he observed were not skilled in repairing the relationship after conflict occurred. Instead, prolonged periods of unrelieved distress, accompanied by heightened physiological arousal, fueled negative perceptions of the partner, overwhelmed spouses' positive feelings for each other, and led to a state of isolation and loneliness. Over time, if negativity surpassed positivity, it contributed to the derailment of the relationship.

With the accumulation of stresses and losses that we all experience in adulthood, it makes sense that good coping skills would be an essential component of personal and interpersonal wellness. Therefore, a critical part of marriage maintenance (and probably that of any close relationship) is the capacity to repair the frayed relationship after conflict. Gottman observed that the particular type of conflict style that couples demonstrated did not matter as much as the amount of overall positivity in the relationship (humor, interest, affection, and validation) and the couples' ability to soothe hurt or angry feelings. Some couples tended to avoid conflict, others embraced it with gusto, whereas some discussed their differences with the validating ("I hear what you are saying . . .") style of counselors. Surprisingly, all three types could be very happily married if the steady state ratios of positivity to negativity in their relationships were 5 to 1. In other words, if a marital climate has substantially more periods of sun than rain, the chances of long-term success are pretty good.

Generativity: Making a Mark at Midlife

Establishing generativity is the primary developmental task of middle adulthood according to Erikson (1950/1963). Generativity has been described as having several components (e.g., McAdams et al., 1998; Stewart & Vandewater, 1998). As we saw in Chapter 12, two primary components are desire and accomplishment (Stewart & Vandewater). Desire refers to wanting to be creative, productive, or giving, and accomplishment means actually feeling that you are creative, productive, or giving. Generative desire is more characteristic of young adults, but generative accomplishment is more typical of middle adults.

THE EXPERIENCE OF CHILD REARING

For many people, raising children is a significant part of adult life. Parents experience more stress than nonparents, but they usually view their parenting role as a generative process (Marks, Bumpass, & Jun, 2003). The nature and quality of the parenting experience, including the parent's feelings of generativity, change substantially as both children and parents grow older.

Each major period or stage of a child's life creates new challenges for a parent, challenges that the parent is more or less prepared to face depending on her age and stage of life, her

A core feature of generativity is taking care of or showing concern for the next generation.

personality and coping skills, her socioeconomic status, and the available support systems. For example, the gratifications of parenthood and marriage are usually greater for older rather than younger first-time parents. Older parents tend to have a more fully developed self-concept and greater self-esteem, are more advanced in their careers, have more money, and are more likely to find balancing work and family responsibilities easier to negotiate. Older fathers tend to spend more time caring for their children than younger fathers, a factor that not only increases satisfaction with parenting but also improves satisfaction for both partners (Belsky & Hsieh, 1998; Belsky & Rovine, 1990; Levy-Schiff, 1994).

Not surprisingly, very young first-time parents (under 20) are at greater risk than other groups to find that the stress of parenting outweighs its satisfactions. They typically complete fewer years of education than older parents and have lower incomes, they are more likely to divorce than other groups, and their children are more likely to experience developmental problems (e.g., Furstenberg, Brooks-Gunn, & Chase-Lansdale, 1987). The satisfactions of parenting, like all other developmental outcomes, are a function of many interacting risk and protective factors.

The normative experience of parents as they move through each stage of parenting is that the challenges bring both intense new stresses and delightful new pleasures (Kach & McGee, 1982; Levy-Schiff, 1994; Levy-Shiff, Goldshmidt, & Har-Even, 1991; Miller & Sollie, 1980; Ventura, 1987). For example, in the newborn period, first-time parents often feel distressed and overwhelmed (Kach & McGee, 1982; Ventura, 1987). Caring for an infant is far more demanding than most people expect it to be. Distress is linked to insufficient sleep, money worries, anxieties about the baby's dependency and vulnerability, feelings of uncertainty about one's caretaking skill, difficulty balancing the needs of self, partner, and baby, and disillusionment with the "yucky" side of infant care (such as mounds of laundry, endless spit-up, and baffling crying fits just when it's time for the parents to eat dinner). Simultaneously, however, most parents of newborns report feeling like they have now truly grown up, that their lives have new purpose and meaning, and that they have a strong sense of shared joy.

The parent of the toddler or preschooler must begin to discipline a child who is still very dependent but who is skilled enough to need continuous supervision. Because a toddler is a proficient climber, for example, a parent can no longer put her in a crib to keep her safe while the parent takes a quick shower or talks on the phone. Parents begin to have conflicts with their children as disciplinary efforts are resisted by a child who has little capacity to take the parent's perspective. Also, partners often find themselves in conflict about their children as they negotiate disciplinary styles, time commitments, and divisions of labor. And parents feel physically exhausted as they try to keep up with energetic, active youngsters who have little self-control. Although many parents experience this period as especially stressful, there are new pleasures as well (Crnic & Booth, 1991; Crnic & Greenberg, 1990). Children begin to talk, to participate in organized activities, and to do things on their own, such as feeding themselves. Their temperaments are blossoming into personalities, and a new little self becomes part of the family system. Most parents experience these developments as intriguing and as a source of pride, despite the heavy dose of frustration that these advances can bring.

As children move into middle childhood, the family waters are often somewhat becalmed. If there is a honeymoon period between parents and children, this is it. The child's thinking is more logical, she has a growing capacity to take another's perspective, and she can in many situations keep herself safe, so that supervision can be reduced. At the same time, the child does not yet feel much ambivalence about her dependence on her parents, and parents still enjoy the role of preferred companion. There are plenty of challenges in this period, of course. Outside factors—such as peers, teachers, and the media—are increasingly influential. Helping children learn to interpret and negotiate the outside world and to deal with the stress it creates can be difficult (e.g., Compas, Banez, Malcarne, & Worsham, 1991).

Parenting usually becomes more demanding and difficult when children reach adolescence. The child's push for independence, parental worries about the child's risk taking and sexual maturity, and the child's often critical and rejecting attitudes are tough to bear, even when parents are well versed in the needs of adolescents. Many parents reach their 40s and 50s when their children are adolescents, so that they are beginning to confront their own physical aging and perhaps engage in a "midlife review" at the same time. Silverberg and Steinberg (1990) report that adolescent development and parental distress about midlife are interacting factors. For example, parents whose teens are actively dating and involved in mixed-sex activities are more likely to express midlife concerns and to feel less satisfaction with their lives than parents whose teens are not yet dating.

The **launching period**, when emerging adults begin to move away and become more self-sufficient, brings some new challenges. On the whole, by the time adult children are in their 20s parents begin to feel the benefits of fewer parental responsibilities, and their relationships with their children improve (e.g., Fingerman, 2003). We often hear about how sad parents are, especially mothers, when their young adult children depart, leaving an "empty nest." Lewis and Lin (1996) report that although parents often anticipate that the transition will be difficult for them, only about 25% feel very unhappy. Also, fathers usually experience more distress than mothers. They seem to struggle more with the concept of their adult children becoming autonomous, which modifies their role as decision maker and changes the structure of the family (e.g., Lewis & Lin, 1996). Mothers, who typically do more of the day-to-day child rearing, are more struck by the relief they experience from those duties. Their greater involvement may also lead them to prepare more and to do more planning for the next phase of their lives. There is, however, a strong link between both mothers' and fathers' feelings of well-being and generativity, on one hand, and their children's functioning, on the other. If adult children are seen as personally and socially well-adjusted, parents are likely to experience greater self-acceptance, purpose in life, and feelings of mastery (e.g., Ryff, Lee, Essex, & Schmutte, 1994).

The typical parent is exiting middle age when her children are entering it. Parents whose children are over 30 may find the quality of their relationships changing further, such that they now tend to relate to their children more as equals. Adult children often begin to identify with their parents, appreciating more profoundly what an adult's life is like than they ever could before (Fingerman, 1996, 1997). However, the relationship is still not egalitarian. Assistance and support, such as financial help, are still more likely to be provided by the older generation to the younger one.

As adults move through middle age, they sometimes find themselves in the role of **kinkeeper**, the person in an extended family who helps the generations maintain contact with one another (e.g., Haraven & Adams, 1996). They may also take on new family responsibilities involving care of an ailing parent or another elderly relative. Most adults in the United States enter midlife with one or both parents living, but by the end of midlife 77% have lost both parents and many have participated in some way in their parents' terminal care (Lachman, 2004).

Women are much more likely to play these roles than men in most cultures, although many men take on some kinkeeping or caregiving responsibilities. These tasks can be particularly challenging if they coincide with the adolescence of one's children. People who carry these double responsibilities are described as being in the sandwich generation (e.g., Hamill & Goldberg, 1997; Zal, 1992). Many factors affect how stressful this position is, such as the coping style of the sandwiched individual, educational and cultural factors, and the availability of other family help, especially the support of the partner. As with the challenges of parenting, kinkeeping and elder care often bring emotional rewards as well, such as feelings of mastery and meaningfulness (e.g., Martire, Stephens, & Townsend, 1998).

WORK AND COMMUNITY INVOLVEMENT

Our careers begin in young adulthood, but it is in the middle adult years that people usually feel they are becoming expert in their work. The full fruits of a career are likely to be experienced in this stage of life, and for many, identity is heavily affected by work (Sterns & Huyck, 2001). Incomes for both men and women tend to reach their peak between ages 45 and 54 (U.S. Bureau of the Census, 1997). Top levels of management and professional advancement are most likely to characterize people in this age period as well. Work intensity and time invested in work usually increase in the first half of middle adulthood and then begin to taper off, as many people begin to strike a balance between time spent working and time spent with family and friends and in community service. This shift seems to be motivated for some people by increased confidence in their productivity and their value in the workplace, allowing them to invest more energy and effort into other aspects of their lives. For others, the shift may be motivated by a sense that their work will not bring them the satisfactions they may have once expected or dreamed about (e.g., Levinson, 1986).

This temporal pattern, of course, varies considerably across individuals, and tends to be linked somewhat to gender. Women who continue to work after having children generally give more priority to child rearing over career responsibilities (e.g., Gati et al., 1995; Vermeulen & Minor, 1998). Men are less likely to do so, although fathers are more likely to modify the intensity of their work effort if both parents work than if the father is the sole breadwinner. Dual-earner couples now represent the most typical arrangement in the American middle class, a substantial change since the 1950s and 1960s (Barnett & Hyde, 2001). With this change has come a shift in role structures, with men becoming more active, involved parents and taking on more household responsibilities, although women still shoulder more of these burdens (Bond et al., 2002). There is some evidence that for more recent cohorts of parents—those born in the 1950s and 1960s— self-esteem goes up for fathers who adjust their work schedules to accommodate family needs, even though they are likely to worry about negative effects on their careers. Conversely, for mothers from these cohorts self-esteem tends to decline if they cut back on employment to take care of family responsibilities; older cohorts of men show a similar tendency (Carr, 2002). Note the impact of historical context on the interplay of social roles and psychological functioning!

Regardless of cohort, researchers have found that participating in multiple roles (active parent, spouse, worker, caregiver to aging parents, and so on) makes middle adulthood hectic but can contribute to life satisfaction, to mental health, and to better relationships (see Barnett & Hyde, 2001). For example, the degree to which both parents modify their work time and share child care and household duties is a significant factor in determining marital satisfaction and feelings of spousal commitment, especially for women (e.g., Feeney, Peterson, & Noller, 1994; Hyde, DeLamater, & Durik, 2001; Schafer & Keith, 1980).

One of the benefits of participating in multiple roles is role buffering: If one role is a source of psychological stress or failure experiences, success and satisfaction in another role may compensate (Barnett & Hyde, 2001). For example, when women interrupt their careers to take on full-time parenting, they may in midlife restart their careers or start new ones, especially after their children reach adolescence. For them, the intensity of work involvement may be greater than it would otherwise be at this stage of their lives, and it can be out of phase with their husbands' work involvement, because they are at an earlier point in career development. Yet, the opportunity to be productive in another setting seems to provide a buffer against some of the stresses involved in parenting an adolescent (e.g., Larson & Richards, 1994).

Money and promotion are the external markers of achievement for middle adults, but a sense of generative accomplishment appears to be more dependent on how creative and productive we feel. The latter experiences are in turn related to how challenging the work is and to the level of interest and expertise that we bring to the work (see Csikszentmihalyi, 1999; Myers, 1993; Ryan & Deci, 2000). McAdams (1985; Mansfield & McAdams, 1996) explains generativity as constituting both **agency** and **communion**. Agency "involves generating, creating, and producing things, ideas, people, events, and so on as powerful extensions or expressions of the self [italics added]" (Mansfield & McAdams, 1996, p. 721). Agentic generativity, then, depends on self-knowledge, a sense of identity, and the opportunity to work on tasks that match our interests, values, and skills, all key features of successful career planning, as we saw in Chapter 12. Generativity also involves communion, expressed "in the adult's desire to care for the next generation, even to the point of sacrificing his or her own well-being for the good of those who will follow" (pp. 721–722). Behaviors involving giving, offering, and contributing are aspects of communion. Research indicates that adults who are identified by others as "generative" do tend to combine both agency and communion in the concerns that they express and in their occupational and community behaviors (Mansfield & McAdams, 1996). Read Box 13.1 for a perspective on how agency and communion affect leadership.

Box 13.1 | *Men, Women, and Leadership*

In high school, Regina loved math and science, and as a 1st-year college student she signed up to be a chemistry major. Regina liked her courses, but she also loved to party, and hours in the lab, along with grinding competition with premed students in organic chemistry, were not much fun. She began to feel that she was floundering—how could she combine her sociability with her sharp, analytic intellectual style to carve out a future? To satisfy distribution requirements she signed up for an economics course her second semester, and the rest is history. Regina was a very successful economics major, and by the time she was a senior was being wooed by several major banking institutions for their management training programs. It was the early 1970s in corporate America, and recruitment of at least some women for executive management tracks was beginning to be "politically correct." But a foot in the door is only that. What did it take for Regina to become one of the top ranking banking executives in the U.S. by the time she was 50?

Traditional research on gender and leadership seemed to indicate that women and men have different "leadership styles." This research often involved bringing together strangers to accomplish some goal and assigning one participant as leader. Under these conditions, gender seems to make a big difference: Men are more "task oriented," focusing on doing whatever will get the job done, whereas women tend to be more "interpersonal," putting more time and effort into the quality of the social interaction. But in a meta-analysis of leadership style research, Eagly and Johnson (1990) found that when actual managers who occupy the same organizational positions are compared, both women and men are characterized by task-oriented, not interpersonal, styles. They did find one sex difference in leadership style, however. Women were more likely to be democratic, whereas men were more likely to be autocratic.

Social role theory, like that of Eagly and her colleagues, paints a complex picture of what contributes to leadership development and success for women and men in today's world. When an individual fills a role, like a leadership role, the role itself influences their behavior. But their occupational role is only one of many social roles they are fulfilling. Another important one is their gender role, which is comprised of a set of expectancies, or "shared beliefs that apply to individuals on the basis of their socially identified sex" (Eagly & Johannesen-Schmidt, 2001, p. 783). Understanding leadership behavior and its effectiveness, for men or women, requires understanding how the demands of these various roles are met within the particular organizational context.

As we saw in Chapter 8, expectancies or stereotypes about gender differences may or may not actually be real, and even when they are substantiated by empirical measures (e.g., males on average are more physically aggressive than females), average sex differences in behavior or traits tend to be small. The range of differences among individuals of the same sex is much greater than the average differences between sexes. But social role theorists argue that the importance of sex differences is not just a function of their real size but of the impact they have on people's expectations of their own and others' behavior.

Two aspects of gender roles that are important in the discussion of leadership are *agency*, which is more strongly ascribed to men, and *communion*, which is seen as more characteristic of women. As you have seen in the discussion of generativity, *agency* is a kind of powerful "get things done" expression of self. It can be captured by descriptors like *assertive, ambitious, dominant, controlling, forceful, independent*, and *confident. Communion* involves expression of concern for others. Descriptors like *affectionate, helpful, sensitive to others, sympathetic*, and *nurturing* apply.

Social role theory predicts that how a woman or a man will behave in a managerial or other leadership position is largely constrained by the nature of the position. They do not discount the influence of individual characteristics, like personality traits, but they emphasize that regardless of the individual filling the role, certain task requirements must be met, such as supervising the work of others, planning, gathering information, and disseminating it. These responsibilities require agentic behavior, and managers tend to behave agentically regardless of gender, as the meta-analysis by Eagly and Johnson illustrates. People also adjust their agentic behavior depending on whether they are interacting with subordinates or with a boss. Moskowitz, Suh, and Desaulniers (1994) used an experience sampling method to monitor managers' interpersonal behavior at work for 20 days. The same individuals were highly agentic with their subordinates, but less agentic with their superiors. It seems clear that managerial status predicts agentic behavior. But in the Moskowitz et al. study, the same participants' communal behavior was affected by their gender role, not by their managerial status: Women behaved more communally than men, especially with other women.

It appears, then, that women and men may tend to display different leadership styles, not with regard to whether they are task oriented or agentic, but with regard to how they treat people in the process. In other words, although their agentic behavior is constrained by their managerial role, their communal behavior is constrained by their own or others' expectations with regard to gender. Eagly and her colleagues propose that an important reason for this gender difference is that when women are leaders, there is an incongruity in role expectations that does not hold for men. *Agency* is important for leadership and is also expected of men. Therefore, people are likely to accept a domineering, even autocratic, management approach from men. Women must be agentic as leaders because the role requires it, but agency is incongruent with the female gender role and may tend to be perceived negatively by others as a result. In other words, many people may feel ambivalent about yielding power to women. Therefore, for many leadership positions, women will be more successful if they exercise their authority with special attention to at least some communal aspects of the process. They may have to be more democratic, inviting others to participate more in decision making, whereas men may have more freedom to be authoritarian if they choose. Fortunately, women are more likely than men to have developed skill using a collaborative, negotiating style as we saw in Chapter 8.

Research supports this analysis. Eagly, Makhijani, and Klonsky (1992) did a meta-analysis of studies in which participants rated others' leadership skill. In all of these studies, the behaviors of men and women leaders had been equated by the researchers. Participants gave significantly lower ratings to women who behaved autocratically than to men. Eagly and Johannesen-Schmidt (2001) report on an international study of managerial style. They assessed the behaviors and effectiveness of 2,874 female and 6,126 male managers, looking at ratings by subordinates, peers, superiors, and by the managers themselves. The most effective managers of either gender were characterized by the same leadership behaviors: acknowledging good performance by followers (giving performance-based rewards), developing and mentoring their followers, attending to followers' individual needs, and inspiring their followers' optimism and excitement about the future as well as their respect and pride in their leader. Women managers outscored men on all of these behaviors, especially the most communal of them (e.g., attending to the individual needs of their followers). The least effective managers were those who focused on their followers' mistakes, procrastinated in solving problems, and were absent or uninvolved at critical times. These were not common behaviors for any of these managers, but they were more common for men than for women.

Why were women leaders more effective than men? Eagly and Johannesen-Schmidt offer two explanations. First, women probably have to meet a higher standard to be successful managers. "Men may have greater leeway to remain in leadership roles, despite poor performance" (2001, p. 793). Second, the behaviors that are especially effective for leaders—for example, individualized consideration, rewarding positive performance—"may involve being attentive, considerate, and nurturing" (p. 793) communal behaviors that women may be more likely to engage in because of gender role expectations.

McAdams and his colleagues have developed a variety of measures of generativity. For example, on a 20-item questionnaire respondents rate the degree to which statements are true of them, such as, "I have a responsibility to improve the neighborhood in which I live" (McAdams & de St. Aubin, 1992). In a measure of generative goals, respondents are asked to describe 10 "personal strivings," and the responses are coded for "generative imagery" (McAdams, de St. Aubin, & Logan, 1993). Using these techniques, people who rate high on generativity are found to be more likely to use authoritative, child-centered parenting styles; are more actively involved in political, religious, and social reform activities; and report higher levels of self-esteem and happiness than people who score low on generativity (see McAdams & Bowman, 2001, for a review).

One of the more interesting differences between midlife adults who score high versus low on generativity measures is in the kind of narrative they produce when asked to tell their life stories. McAdams (e.g., 1993) argues that the narratives we construct about our lives are reconstructions that are based on the real events in our lives but that they also indicate our characteristic ways of making sense of things. They contribute to and reflect our identities and our sense of well-being. Generative adults, for example, tend to tell life stories with "redemption" themes (McAdams & Bowman, 2001). That is, even though the individual may describe many serious difficulties, her story often progresses from describing an emotionally negative event or bad scene to an emotionally positive or good outcome. Conversely, adults low on generativity tend to include more "contamination" sequences in their life stories. These are descriptions that go from good or positive experiences to negative outcomes.

Generative adults also are more likely to describe themselves as "sensitized to others' suffering at an early age" and as "guided by a clear and compelling ideology that remains relatively stable over time" (McAdams & Bowman, 2001, p. 14). Overall, there is a progressive structure to the generative adult's life story that suggests a reasonably coherent sense of a self who is moving in a positive direction and who feels able and willing to make a difference. In particular, such individuals seem to be able to move on despite sometimes serious setbacks. People low in generativity by midlife, however, seem to be stuck, "unable to grow." McAdams and Bowman (2001) describe one woman who, at 41, is still setting goals that are markedly like those she set as a young woman—"to graduate from high school" and to be "better able to take care of myself." She tells the interviewer that she is "desperately seeking" herself. Unfortunately, her persistent expectation that what appears to be good will turn out bad—reflected in the many contamination sequences she includes in her life story narrative—seems to make her quest overwhelming.

Generativity seems to be foreshadowed in the personality characteristics that emerge in adolescence and young adulthood. Petersen and Steward (1996) found that individuals who as adolescents already had strong power and achievement needs, combined with strong needs for affiliation, were most likely to demonstrate generativity when they reached middle adulthood. The Big 5 personality traits can play a role as well. For example, de St. Aubin and McAdams (1995) found that higher scores on extraversion (which is somewhat agentic) and agreeableness (which is strongly communal) were moderately correlated with generativity in a sample of adults. Finally, as we pointed out above, identity development contributes to generativity. For example, self-knowledge can help a person make choices, such as choices of career and community activities, that provide a good match to her skills and interests, so that she can maintain her intrinsic motivation to produce and create.

APPLICATIONS

The middle years are a challenging period of life. Adults have to contend with jobs, children, partners, and themselves, as well as the unexpected crises that occur. They bring very different experiences and dreams into adulthood. It is impossible to establish a life-stage trajectory that could take into account all this diversity with any level of precision. However, there do seem to be powerful themes, such as the quest for intimacy and generativity that characterize most adult lives.

We have seen that many theorists (e.g., Erikson, 1950/1963; Levinson, 1986; Vaillant, 1977) have attempted to specify these themes and their typical progress, though they all seem to recognize that we cannot expect every life story to unfold in some inevitable sequence of events or experiences. These same theorists have also described psychological requirements for healthy functioning as people move through adulthood. One consistent message that these authors communicate in various ways is this: Adults have to grow up. Growing up is not always easy and often not much fun, particularly in an age and in a society that heavily invests in the notion of personal satisfaction, youth, and freedom of choice. However, the very nature of the life cycle makes certain changes inevitable, and once those changes are accepted, they can be the source of great personal satisfaction and pride.

Adult Commitments

For most married people and other intimate partners, both joyous and painful experiences make up the fabric of close relationships and both wax and wane over the course of the life span. Some of these changes are predictable: when a new baby arrives, when children become adolescents, when adult children marry, when parents age and die, when partners experience age-related declines or the onset of illness. Some changes are due to unpredictable events: the loss of a job or the demands of a new one, an unexpected illness, a relocation, a war or economic recession.

Counselors who work with couples can find it helpful to identify the sources of stress as coming from nonnormative or normative causes. Couples in crisis, for example, may be reeling from an unexpected and rather obvious stressor that has taken its toll on the relationship. On the other hand, changes involved in predictable life events, such as steadily accumulating time demands or eroding incomes of working families with children, can affect the quality of relationships just as significantly and may not be quite as obvious to the people involved. Furthermore, changes that come with daily give and take, such as increased realization of a partner's flaws and idiosyncracies combined with greater awareness of personal needs and preferences, can set the stage for relationship conflict.

Clinicians often report that couples come to counseling after their relationships have reached a state of meltdown. Partners can become trapped in destructive patterns of relating that create persistent distress (Weiss & Hayman, 1990). In the demand–withdraw pattern, for example, one partner withdraws to escape the demands of the other and, as a result, demands escalate and withdrawal is reinforced. Various methodologies have been employed to address couple difficulties, including behavioral approaches to improving communication and problem-solving skills, cognitive techniques for changing negative thoughts, affective or emotion-focused methods for teaching partners to own and express feelings more effectively, and intrapsychic models that relate present problems to early attachment histories. At this point, both behavioral marital therapy (BMT; Jacobson & Addis, 1993) and emotionally focused couples therapy (EFT; Johnson, Hunsley, Greenberg, & Schindler, 1999) have demonstrated empirical support. Insight-oriented couples therapy (IOCT; Snyder & Wills, 1989), which fosters awareness of the nature of relationship problems and promotes positive interaction, has also demonstrated long-term effectiveness in helping distressed couples (Snyder, Wills, & Grady-Fletcher, 1991).

A few common themes have emerged from this growing body of research to guide counselors who work in this area. Simply stated, relationships tend to flourish when the psychological atmosphere is positive and they tend to deteriorate when it becomes negative. Because stress and disagreements are an inevitable part of all long-term relationships, successful therapies appear to blend skills of conflict management with those of positive relationship enhancement. This is the theme of Gottman's approach to marital therapy. He has made the interesting observation, based upon his studies of marital interaction, that the content of couples' problem discussions remains remarkably stable over time. Fully 69% of the time, couples' arguments are about a problem that has existed in the relationship for a long time (Gottman, 1999). These "perpetual problems," which have to do with partners' personalities, may be expressed in the partners' different behavioral

styles or ways of approaching issues such as money, sex, or in-laws. As we have learned, there is evidence for continuity in many temperamental characteristics, and they constitute relatively stable features of individuals' behavior and cognition throughout their life span. Based on his work, Gottman (1999) suggests that therapists "encourage couples to think of these relationship problems as inevitable, much the way we learn to deal with chronic physical ailments as we get older. The chronic back pain, the trick knee and tennis elbow or irritable bowel do not go away, but we learn to have a dialogue with these problems. We keep trying to make things a little better all the time, but we learn to live with these problems and manage our world so as to minimize them. . . . So it is in all relationships" (p. 57).

The target of therapist intervention will undoubtedly depend upon the nature of the problem as well as therapist orientation. However, most couple therapists, regardless of orientation, know to set clear limits on hostile and aggressive displays in therapy sessions to guard against further erosion of the partnership. Gottman (1994) translates findings from a large set of research studies into several core strategies that clinicians can teach clients in order to foster relational well being.

1. *Calm down.*   Emotions such as anger are highly arousing and can escalate into a cascade of negative feelings that shut down real communication. Gottman (1994) describes in precise detail how these escalating emotions affect interaction.

   From the data gathered in our lab, we've seen how quickly discussions fall apart as soon as one spouse's heart rate begins to soar. Because physical responses are such an accurate barometer of your ability to communicate at a particular moment, tracking your arousal level during intense conversation will help keep your discussions on track as well. (p. 176).

   This requires that each person be aware of his or her own physiological and emotional reactions. We will have more to say about this in Chapter 14. However, we see this as a two-step process in actual practice: becoming aware of one's reactivity and taking steps toward regulating it effectively. Awareness can be fostered by helping clients learn to take their pulse rate as a measure of physiological arousal, to learn to ask for and take time-outs, and to engage in relaxation activities in order to return to baseline levels of arousal, a process that takes an average of 20 minutes after becoming aroused. Gottman notes that this is a particularly important step for males who typically get physiologically "flooded" with emotion more quickly than women and who take longer to return to baseline (Levenson & Gottman, 1985).

2. *Speak nondefensively.*   The emphasis on improving communication has a long-established history in marital therapy and in relationship education (Halford, Markman, Kline, & Stanley, 2003). The goal of such interventions is generally to help couples express their feelings and

disagreements in ways the other can understand. What is critical here appears to be reducing the tendency to come out swinging when conflicts arise. Called "harsh startups" by Gottman and Silver (1999), a conversation about a problem that starts with criticism, contempt, or sarcasm is likely to become an argument that deteriorates quickly. This speedy buildup of emotional negativity results in feelings of being flooded and can lead one or both partners to protect themselves by stonewalling. Taking a "softer" approach when addressing potentially difficult issues can reduce defensive responding and maintain a more positive state.

3. *Validate.*   Among the Zulu, a person is traditionally greeted with a word that is roughly translated to mean "I see you." The response to this greeting is "I am here." Notice the direction of this interchange: Until you see me, I am not here. We are psychologically "here" because we are seen and known by intimate others, much in the way Cooley describes the looking-glass phenomenon. In the intimate world of close relationships, individuals do not need so much for their partners to solve their problems as for their partners to see and validate what they're going through.

Counselors are often called upon to help couples work on empathy-building, particularly when their attachment relationship is weakened due to neglect, injury, or prolonged conflict. Sometimes old wounds reemerge in the present and need to be readdressed. Success in relationships often depends upon "the wounded partner being able to express deep hurts and losses and the other partner staying emotionally engaged and actively responding to these emotions with compassion and comfort" (Johnson, 2003, p. 373). Browning's (1998) empathy-expansion procedure helps partners address a long-standing relationship hurt though a specific process facilitated by the therapist. Through a sequence of steps, the counselor coaches one partner to recognize and apologize for the injury that has been causing the impasse. The goal is to enhance empathic responding and to give the aggrieved partner real validation for his or her pain. Clearly, this is most appropriate for couples who are motivated to put past hurts behind them and who are willing to "do whatever it takes" to mend the relationship.

4. *Overlearning.*   In the spirit of the graded mastery experiences described in Chapter 12, small successes in important areas can reap rewards in increased motivation. Applied to relationships, practicing behaviors of self-soothing, nondefensive listening and validating fosters good emotion regulation, increases the level of positivity in the relationship and, over time, becomes more automatic. These overlearned responses can be especially useful when conflicts arise.

5. *Pay attention to the little things.*   A final recommendation reflects the importance of cultivating positive affect in daily interactions. In one study, the use of humor,

affection, and playfulness in addition to noticing and responding to partners' bids for attention in the course of daily life were strongly associated with better conflict resolution and greater marital satisfaction overall (Driver & Gottman, 2004). In particular, a husband's playfulness and enthusiasm were related to his wife's willingness to be more affectionate when the couple did experience a conflict. It appears that relationship satisfaction is not only related to how conflicts are resolved but also to the quality of the emotional connection constructed bit by bit though the mundane interchanges that fill couples' lives. These authors suggest that this aspect of a relationship might be amenable to therapeutic intervention. "Building positive affect during everyday life may be easier to influence than directly changing positive affect during conflict. For example, it may be easier to teach a couple to use enthusiastic responses in daily moments then to ask them to use affection during an argument" (p. 312).

Out of Work

The experience of nonnormative events can affect well-being and, in some cases, permanently alter one's life course. Job loss represents a particular challenge to the normative expectations that most adults hold about their lives: to provide for themselves and their loved ones consistently and independently. When workers lose their jobs, a singular expression of their generative capacity is compromised. A recent longitudinal study of more than 24,000 German respondents over 15 years found that for people who experienced episodes of unemployment, their lives were never quite the same (Lucas, Clark, Georgellis, & Diener, 2004). Workers experienced a decline in overall life satisfaction following job loss and a trending upward toward pre-unemployment levels of satisfaction after reemployment. Nevertheless, their sense of life satisfaction did not return to baseline, even many years after being reemployed.

The connection between job loss and mental and physical health problems is quite strong (Kessler, Turner, & House, 1989). Although financial strain is the most significant reason for depression following job loss, Price, Choi, and Vinokur (2002) have shown that the effects on physical and mental health are mediated by the erosion of a sense of personal control that accompanies the reduction of financial resources. Furthermore, these elements operate transactionally. As the authors indicate, "while job loss and financial strain may influence depression, depression, in turn, may reduce access to opportunities to reduce financial strain through reemployment. Thus, chains of adversity are clearly complex and may contain spirals of disadvantage that reduce the life chances of vulnerable individuals still further" (2002, p. 310). The ripples extend to children, as well, who suffer from more behavioral and academic problems when their parents are under financial strain (Conger, Ge, Elder, Lorenz, & Simons, 1994).

Counselors who work with people experiencing job loss need to take into account such psychological consequences, namely increased stress, anxiety, feelings of hopelessness, as well as physical problems that may arise, as they help clients deal with this stressful event. Sometimes, individuals might try to cope through behaviors like excessive use of drugs or alcohol. Although the ultimate goal of counseling may be to find new employment, it is important to remember that the clients' confidence may be badly bruised and in need of shoring up. This might help explain why some clients do not pursue reemployment in active ways like sending out resumes or going on job interviews. It may be their way of avoiding further damage to self-esteem (Price, 1992).

Prevention programs offer some demonstrated success in curtailing the downward spiral of disadvantage following job loss. Participants in the JOBS project, developed by researchers at the Michigan Prevention Research Center, showed more success in finding reemployment, demonstrated fewer symptoms of depression, and reflected better overall adjustment than nonparticipants at a 2-year follow up (Vinokur, Price & Schul, 1995; Vinokur, Schul, Vuori, & Price, 2000). This program is delivered to small groups of 12 to 18 participants who meet for five 4-hour counseling sessions. There are three main elements to the program: (1) building skills for the job search, such as improving resume writing, learning to "think like" the employer, networking and contacting potential employers; (2) increasing participants' sense of self-efficacy through graded exposure exercises, role-modeling, and reinforcement of effective behavior; and (3) inoculating participants against setbacks that they might encounter in the job search process by identifying possible barriers while practicing the skills needed to overcome the obstacles (Price & Vinokur, 1995).

Off-Time

Adulthood is a time when individuals may have to contend with the realization that events or accomplishments that they once wished for have not been achieved. Individuals of all ages may feel distressed by a sense that they did not meet their developmental goals or expectations "on-time." Feeling "off-time," as it relates to such things as getting married, having children, reaching career goals, or other normative achievements, reflects the fact that we all have a set of age-related expectations for the appropriate timing of major life events. This phenomenon is called the social clock. Clinicians should be sensitive to this particular source of distress in the lives of their clients to help them cope more effectively. Certainly clinicians can support client strivings to find outlets for generative needs that might be met in flexible ways. Even the strains of caring for children or older relatives can be reframed as valuable contributions. For clients without such responsibilities, other outlets might be explored.

Becoming generative can be viewed as a way of growing up, by taking and accepting responsibility for oneself and for dependents, by forgiving past generations for what they may have done, and by working to leave a legacy. As we have learned, flexibility and adaptability in the face of life's demands support this process. One developmental task involves the shift in expectations that may occur gradually over this time from adolescent idealism to mature acceptance of reality (Gould, 1978).

Adulthood means getting far enough outside oneself to do as Margaret Mead urged:

"to cherish the life of the world," that is, to connect with life itself rather than just with oneself, to overcome the narcissism of our youth and make give-and-take connections from which we can feel the pain and pleasure of others rather than crouching selfishly and alone in our own protective skins. . . . The maturing function of psychotherapy is to get people past a narcissistic state where they notice only what other people do and how it makes them feel, and move them into a mature state where they notice what they do and how it makes other people feel (p. 257).

SUMMARY

Life Span Developmental Theory

1. The complexity of adult development makes it clear that multidimensional models are needed to adequately understand the processes of change. Life span developmental models focus on both hereditary and environmental influences and on the continuities and changes that characterize adults. They emphasize that adaptation continues from birth to death.
2. Baltes describes the architecture of biology and culture, a web of interacting organismic and environmental influences on development. During childhood, he argues, optimal development is strongly supported by the processes of natural selection, such that most people reach adulthood and can contribute to the success of the species by reproducing. But biological supports weaken by middle adulthood, as selection pressures decline. Thus, from middle adulthood on, more cultural supports are required to ensure optimal development.
3. Throughout the life span, change involves both gains and losses, but the relative balance of gains and losses shifts as people move toward old age. Adaptation throughout life involves growth, maintenance or resilience,

and the regulation of loss, but growth is more common in childhood, whereas regulation of loss is more common in old age. Successful development, or healthy coping, at any age is the relative maximization of gains and the minimization of losses, but coping changes as people age.

Influences on Adult Development: Sources of Stability

4. The Big 5 personality traits—neuroticism, extraversion, openness, agreeableness, and conscientiousness—are relatively stable after approximately age 30, according to cross-sectional, longitudinal, and cross-cultural research.

5. Adult personality traits are somewhat correlated with temperament in childhood. Although heredity is implicated in the development and stability of traits, a relatively stable environment is probably equally important.

Influences on Adult Development: Sources of Change

6. Age-graded change refers to change that comes as a function of time. Some predictable physical changes in adulthood include declines in sensory ability and in reproductive ability (much more for women than for men). Appearance changes as skin wrinkles and sags, and weight gain is common though not inevitable.

7. Cognitive changes with age are best studied with longitudinal methods. A mixed pattern of improvement and decline occurs, related to differences in fluid intelligence (mechanics) versus crystallized intelligence (pragmatics). Fluid or mechanical processes, such as processing speed and inhibitory mechanisms, begin to show declines in middle adulthood. Crystallized resources, including all forms of declarative and procedural knowledge, are not as likely to decline, and for many people they increase throughout middle and even old age. Only after about age 60 do losses in fluid intelligence somewhat outweigh crystallized gains for the average individual.

8. The relative losses and gains are illustrated by memory effects. The capacity of working memory declines with age, which can affect problem solving negatively, as fewer pieces of information can be held in mind simultaneously. Semantic memory, however, continues to expand with age, as we learn more and more information, and often older adults solve problems better than younger ones because they are more likely to have expertise they can bring to the task.

9. Life-task or life-course changes are age-graded changes in the tasks and responsibilities that confront us or seem important as we age. Theorists such as Schaie, Erikson, Vaillant, Levinson, Jung, Gould, and so on have all described stages or phases in life-task change. Despite the significant differences in the lives of individuals,

there do seem to be relatively predictable sequences of change in our concerns as we move through adulthood.

10. History-graded changes affect the development of a whole cohort. A life-course perspective emphasizes that development is influenced by chronological age, family-related roles, and membership in a birth cohort. Thus, the same historical events can have different effects on members of different cohorts. Recent cohorts of children are experiencing a time of increased breakdown in social connections. Apparently as a result, they experience more anxiety than older cohorts did as children.

11. Nonnormative changes refer to unexpected events, such as an accident or untimely death of a loved one, that can alter developmental trajectories.

Key Developmental Tasks of Midlife: The Continuing Pursuit of Intimacy and Generativity

12. Adults involved in a primary relationship such as marriage are generally happier than single adults. Other relationships, such as friendships, are also important sources of life satisfaction. Critical features of such relationships involve sharing, working out problems, and developing a sense of we-ness.

13. The family life cycle begins with mate selection, a kind of filtering process based largely on homogamy and compatibility. Love is also seen as important in our culture. Sternberg described three elements: passion, intimacy, and decision/commitment. Once a commitment is established, a blending of family systems is involved, not just a joining of individuals. Other stages in the more typical family life cycle include becoming parents and then the transition of launching and renegotiating the marital relationship.

14. Sixty percent of marriages end in divorce in the United States, often creating financial hardship for the wife and emotional and behavioral difficulties for children. For many people, marital satisfaction persistently declines over the life of a marriage. Theories about the causes of marital harmony and discord include the disillusionment model (when romantic notions are dashed, marriages fail), the maintenance hypothesis (romantic couples work to maintain their illusions and therefore their marriage), and the social exchange and behavioral theories (marriages fail when problems and conflict escalate to become overwhelming because of inadequate strategies for coping with conflict). Intrapersonal models draw on attachment theory and notions about temperament to explain marital success or failure.

15. Studies of marital dynamics (e.g., Gottman) suggest that marriages are successful or satisfying to the extent that positive factors outweigh negative factors, including interactive behaviors, perceptions, and physiology

(e.g., endocrine functioning). High levels of negative affect reciprocity (likelihood that negativity in one partner will be followed by negativity from the other) is especially predictive of marital dissolution. What are termed the four horsemen of the apocalypse are especially problematic: criticism, defensiveness, contempt, and stonewalling.

Generativity: Making a Mark at Midlife

16. Each period of a child's life presents new challenges to parents. A parent's age, SES, personality and coping skills, and support systems all contribute to how satisfying parenting is (e.g., older parents generally find parenting more rewarding than younger parents).

17. Most parents find their task both stressful and rewarding. Infants are far more difficult to care for than most people expect, but they also bring joy to most parents. Toddlers, combining new skills with poor self-control or understanding, need very close supervision, so they are time and energy consuming. As their unique "selfhood" begins to blossom, they also become more interesting. In middle childhood, parenting is usually much easier as children become logical thinkers but are still relatively unambivalent about their dependence on their parents. Adolescent children are usually experienced as more demanding and difficult as they push for independence, take more risks, and de-idealize their parents. The launching period usually is experienced as positive, as parents have fewer responsibilities and their children become more self-sufficient. Parents of middle adults relate to their children more as equals, although assistance and support still tends to flow more from parent to child.

18. Sometimes middle-aged adults find themselves with dual caregiving responsibilities—parents to their children and caretaker for their aging parents. This sandwiched position can be very stressful, depending on factors such as the availability of other sources of support.

19. In middle age, people generally feel they have reached the peak of their career in terms of expertise, income, and advancement. Work intensity and time invested increase in the first half of middle adulthood and taper off thereafter, with most people increasing time spent with friends and family. This pattern can vary dramatically across individuals and is linked to gender. A rise in dual-career couples in recent decades is linked to increases in men's involvement in family roles. Middle adults usually function in many roles, which can increase stress but also allows for role buffering.

20. A sense of generative accomplishment depends on how creative and productive adults feel. Two kinds of generativity have been described: agency (creating, producing) and communion (wishing to care for the next generation). People who score high on measures of generativity report higher levels of self-esteem and happiness than others. A coherent sense of a self moving in a positive direction seems to characterize people who score high on generativity.

CASE STUDY

Lupe is a 45-year-old Mexican American woman. She has two adult children, a son and a daughter, as well as one granddaughter. She lives in a small apartment near her mother, now in her late 60s. Lupe visits her mother several times a week to check on her health and her emotional state. Although she is relatively self-sufficient, Lupe's mother expects this kind of attention from her daughter. Lupe has always been very responsible and concerned about the well-being of her family members. Even though this takes a lot of her time, she faithfully attends to her mother's needs without complaint.

When Lupe's children were young, she and her children's father lived together. He left the family after a few years, however, because he found the stress of family life to be overwhelming. In particular, he felt that he could not make enough money to support two children. Although he and Lupe were never legally married, she considered them to be a "married" couple. Single now for 16 years, she feels that she would like to meet someone with whom she could share her life. This is a new feeling for Lupe. Until recently, she was too distracted with the problems of raising her children to think about herself.

Now she feels that she only has a limited amount of time left to pursue some of her own wishes. She can envision herself, like her mother, old and alone, and that prospect disturbs her. She has started to attend social functions at her church and has accepted some social invitations from members of the congregation. Lupe feels comfortable with this approach, because she is very close to the members of her parish community.

Lupe's life has recently become more complicated. Her daughter, Lucia, and her 2-year-old granddaughter, Eva, have moved in with her. Lucia and her boyfriend, Tomas, were living together and were planning to marry. Their relationship deteriorated after the baby's birth, and the couple fought frequently. Lucia accused Tomas of spending too much of his paycheck on frivolous things. Tomas, in response, withdrew even further, spent more time with his friends, and continued to spend money as he pleased. Lucia finally took the baby and threatened not to come back.

In addition to this, Lupe was injured on her job as a practical nurse in a large hospital. She was trying to prevent a patient from falling and hurt her back in the process. She will need to receive physical therapy, which means she will be out of work for a few months. Her physician, noticing her depressed mood, referred her to a counselor at the local mental health clinic.

Discussion Questions

1. What are the developmental stresses (age-related) and contextual stresses (nonnormative) in Lupe's life at the present time? Consider her age, family role, and cultural context.

2. What are Lupe's sources of strength? What aspects of her cognitive functioning and her personality might support her resilience in the face of difficulties?

3. What is the potential impact of Lucia's return on her mother? On Eva? On Tomas?

4. What advice might you give to Lupe? To Lucia and Tomas?

JOURNAL QUESTIONS

1. If you can, ask your parent or a member of your family to describe you using the Big 5 personality traits. Which of your personality traits have remained stable over time? Which have changed?

2. Do you think people normally go through a midlife crisis? Why or why not?

3. Think of a married (or otherwise committed) couple you know well. What are the major challenges of their marriage? What are the benefits? What style of relating best characterizes the couple?

4. What are the normative and nonnormative challenges you are facing now? How are you coping with each? What other coping strategies could you try?

KEY TERMS

life span developmental theories or models
ontogeny
growth
maintenance or resilience
regulation of loss
Big 5
neuroticism
extraversion
openness
agreeableness
conscientiousness
age-graded changes
history-graded changes

nonnormative changes
adolescing
senescing
climacteric
menopause
estradiol
estrogen
testosterone
elastin
fluid intelligence (mechanics)
crystallized intelligence (pragmatics)
ego integrity (vs. despair)

career consolidation (vs. self-absorption)
keeper of meaning (vs. rigidity)
life structure
cohort effects
life-course perspective
family life cycle
homogomy
compatibility
disillusionment model
maintenance hypothesis
social exchange and behavior theories

intrapersonal models
homeostatic steady state
negative affect reciprocity
"four horsemen of the apocalypse"
launching period
kinkeeper
sandwich generation
role buffering
agency
communion
social role theory
social clock

Now go to our Companion Website to assess your understanding of chapter content with Multiple Choice Questions, apply comprehension in Essay Questions, and broaden your knowledge of development with related Web Links.

CHAPTER 14

Living Well: Stress, Coping, and Life Satisfaction in Adulthood

Although young adults often feel as though life is still "about to happen," during middle adulthood people see themselves as having "grown up." Their lives have all the trappings of adults in their culture. For Americans this is likely to mean they are married or have a life partner, have children, are owners or leasers of major possessions like a car or a house, and have substantial commitments to their work, place of worship, or other community organizations.

So how does it feel to be all grown up? Are most people satisfied with their lives? What does it take to be happy as an adult? Western philosophers have debated the ingredients of "the good life" since the days of the ancient Hebrews and Greeks. Religious traditions throughout the world each take a stand on what constitutes "right living," and what leads to true happiness, either in this life or the next. For helping professionals, the question of what constitutes well-being is at the heart of their work. Although ameliorating psychopathology is an important clinical focus, it is subsumed by the broader goal of promoting well-being, happiness, and the fulfillment of human potential (see Chapter 1).

Midlife is often the time when adults take stock of their lives

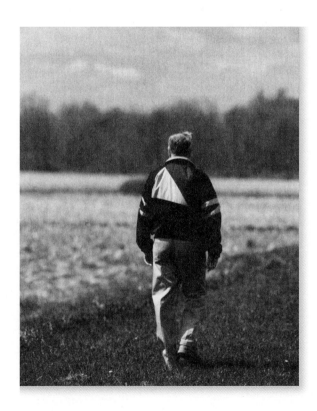

Empirical investigations of subjective well-being, an individual's experience of overall life satisfaction, satisfaction with particular domains of life (such as work), or frequency of positive mood (as well as relative infrequency of negative mood), is one approach to understanding what constitutes a well-lived life (e.g., Deiner, 2000). Measures usually involve asking people to rate their lives or their feelings about their lives (or specific aspects of their lives) on a continuum, say from "very happy" to "very unhappy," or to rate statements like "In most ways my life is ideal," on a scale from "very true" to "not at all true" (Compton, 2005). See Box 14.1 for a look at another research method. A rapidly growing body of studies has led to some surprising revelations about what is really important for people to sustain a sense of well-being as they negotiate the complex and frequently stressful and conflicting realities of adulthood.

| Box 14.1 | *What Makes People Happy?* |

In most cases, the constructs of life satisfaction and subjective well-being are studied by asking respondents to complete questionnaires. For example, participants might be asked to respond on a scale of 1 to 10 to questions like "I believe that I make enough money" or "I am getting what I want out of my life." Such survey results can be very enlightening, but they cannot answer some of the most interesting questions about people's lived experience in a real-time context. For that data, researchers can utilize the technique called the experience-sampling method (ESM). (See Chapter 9.) Typically, those who use this methodology give participants beepers that are programmed to beep at various points during the day. The beep alerts participants to record what they are doing and how they are feeling at that moment. This strategy is a good way to observe lives as they unfold. However, it can be expensive and intrusive to participants. Furthermore, events are recorded as discrete snapshots instead of a continuous picture of time use or a reflection of the ebb and flow of well-being across situations.

Recently, Kahneman and his associates (Kahneman, Krueger, Schkade, Schwartz, & Stone, 2004) developed an alternative approach called the day reconstruction method (DRM), which combines elements of experience sampling with elicitation of memories of affective experience. One major difference is that DRM does not require beepers or present-moment reporting of experience. Instead, participants are asked to recall the previous day and to construct a running account or diary that describes the day's events. The instructions direct participants to "think of your day as a continuous series of scenes or episodes in a film. Give each episode a brief name that will help you remember it (for example 'commuting to work', or 'at lunch with B . . .')" (p. 1778). After the day's "scenes" are remembered and described, participants respond to more structured questions about each one, including how they felt while each was happening. Indices of positive affect (happy, friendly, enjoying myself) and negative affect (frustrated, depressed, hassled, angry, worried, criticized) are gathered. The result is a chronology of daily events linked to subjective ratings of positive or negative feeling.

This method was used to gather information about the life satisfaction of a sample of 909 racially diverse, middle-class women. The average age of participants was 38 years. Results demonstrate that this method can access information that other methods generally cannot. For example, most surveys of life satisfaction report that people believe their children to be a source of great happiness. In this study, the activity of *taking care of children* ranked close to the bottom of enjoyable activities. Only working, housework, and commuting had lower positive ratings. The authors suggest that this finding may be due to the fact that DRM taps experience instead of the kind of global beliefs that are assessed in traditional life satisfaction surveys. Respondents may feel less constrained by socially appropriate or "belief-based generic judgments" (p. 1777) such as the valuing of children. With this method, they report on the reality of their lived experience. Activities that were associated with the most positive affect were intimate relations, socializing, and relaxing. This methodology reveals how enjoyable people's lives are on a day-to-day basis instead of global estimates of life satisfaction.

Similar to other research reported in this chapter, the life circumstances of these women, such as income, religion, and education, made only modest contributions to the affective quality of their daily lives. What did matter? Things that made for a happy day were related to their personality and mental health (like absence of depression) and, notably, the quality of their sleep! The authors found very large differences in women's enjoyment of home-related activities as a function of good or poor sleep, which had a surprisingly powerful impact on the quality of their satisfaction and enjoyment of life overall. In the work arena, job pressure exerted a similarly large effect. Although factors like job security and the presence of adequate benefits were important predictors of job satisfaction, they did not influence women's daily enjoyment at work. What made for a happier workday was less pressure to work quickly and more opportunities to talk with coworkers. Overall, life satisfaction, based upon results of this study, was determined by the difference in net negative and net positive affect. Consequently, this study suggests that it may be the little things in our day-to-day lives that can make us happy.

LIFE SATISFACTION: WHAT IS A WELL-LIVED LIFE?

Worldly Goods and Well-Being

First, let's consider the importance of money. Although we would probably all concede some truth to the dictum "money can't buy happiness," research indicates that most of us *believe* that even a little more income would improve our lives and make us happier (Myers, 2000). Yet, on the whole, happiness and wealth are only weakly correlated, and people whose incomes increase over time do not experience more happiness than people whose incomes fail to increase (Diener, Sandvik, Seidlitz, & Diener, 1993). It is true that the poor are not as happy as the rich. But people with adequate though modest incomes report nearly the same levels of life satisfaction as the wealthiest individuals, both within and between cultures and subcultures (see Table 14.1). Even people who have a sudden economic windfall, like those who win a lottery, "typically only gain a temporary jolt of joy from their winnings" (Myers, 2000, p. 61).

TABLE 14.1 Life Satisfaction for Various Groups

Group	Rating
Forbes magazine's "richest Americans"	5.8
Pennsylvania Amish	5.8
Inughuit (Inuit people in northern Greenland)	5.8
African Maasai	5.7
Swedish probability sample	5.6
International college-student sample (47 nations in 2000)	4.9
Illinois Amish	4.9
Calcutta slum dwellers	4.6
Fresno, California, homeless	2.9
Calcutta pavement dwellers (homeless)	2.9

Note: Respondents indicated their agreement with the statement "You are satisfied with your life" using a scale from 1 (complete disagreement) to 7 (complete agreement); 4 is a neutral rating.

Source: Diener, E., & Seligman, M. E. P. (2004). Beyond money: Toward an economy of well-being. *Psychological Science in the Public Interest, 5,* 1–31. Reprinted by permission of Blackwell Publishing.

Pursuing wealth may not bring the life satisfaction that many people expect.

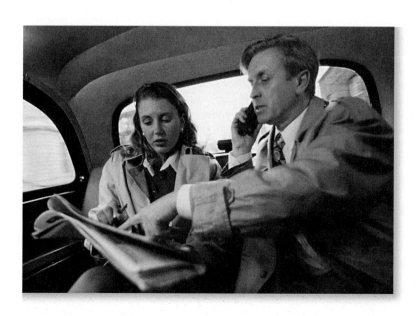

Like individuals, the well-being of national populations is affected by wealth only up to the point that a nation is no longer "poor." Once per capita income reaches about $10,000, measures of happiness or life satisfaction are about the same among societies that differ substantially in wealth (Diener & Seligman, 2004). For Americans, per capita income and standard of living rose steadily from the mid 1950s through the late 1990s, yet the percentage of people who claimed to be very happy remained level or declined slightly (see Figure 14.1). At the same time, rates of depression and other pathologies soared. Myers (2000) calls this inverse ratio of affluence to pathology "the American paradox." The materialistic goals that motivate many Americans (and Europeans and Japanese, to name a few other national groups for whom we have data) certainly do not bring happiness, and they seem to have toxic side effects.

This paradox may have many sources; we will mention a few. First, it may be linked to what is described as the "hedonic treadmill" (Brickman & Campbell, 1971). When people are driven to strive for material gain, they are often quickly habituated to each new level of wealth and thus can't be satisfied (Kasser & Ryan, 1996). Pittman (1985) argued that "Wealth is addictive. It enticingly offers happiness, but it cannot provide satisfaction, so those who attain some of it keep thinking more of it will provide satisfaction" (p. 470). Ironically, the more an individual strives for further material gain, the less attention he is likely to give to other pursuits that are more strongly linked to satisfaction, like having supportive social relationships.

Second, the lifestyle that affluence makes possible may reduce some of the forces that ordinarily help create supportive relationships (Luthar, 2003). For example, people who can buy services from the marketplace, such as child care and elder care, are less likely to turn to family, friends, and neighbors for those kinds of support (Putnam, 2000). Further, people living in affluent societies rarely need to rely on others for physical support in "tough times," such as help with food, clothing, and shelter, and so opportunities for friends and neighbors to demonstrate "genuine friendship" by making sacrifices for one another are minimal. Absent such opportunities, it may be more difficult for people to feel that others in their lives can be relied upon (Tooby & Cosmides, 1996).

Third, having material resources allows people to make choices and to control much of their lives. But the more control people have the more likely they are to expect to be able to create a "perfect" life (Schwartz, 2000). Of course, perfection is impossible to achieve, but when it is not, people blame themselves, creating fertile ground for depression. Oddly enough, because materialistic cultures foster the belief that material gain brings happiness, when affluent people do become depressed they often feel confused and guilty, making it difficult to reach out to friends and share their distress (Wolfe & Fodor, 1996).

These analyses suggest that whereas material gain is not a major source of well-being, supportive relationships might be. In what follows we will explore several factors that are positively correlated with well-being, including social relationships. We'll begin with the characteristics of the individual himself.

FIGURE 14.1

Economic Growth and Happiness

Source: Myers, D. G. (2000). The funds, friends, and faith of happy people. *American Psychologist, 55,* 56–67. Copyright © 2000 by The American Psychological Association. Reprinted with permission.

Personality and Well-Being

Could personality be more important than exterior conditions for explaining life satisfaction? Personality traits like extraversion and neuroticism *are* strongly correlated with subjective well-being measures, much more so than external factors like wealth (see Diener, Oishi, & Lucas, 2003). Extraverts, who tend to focus interest on things outside the self, are happier than introverts, who focus more attention on their own interior experience. Not surprisingly, neuroticism, which includes tendencies to be self-conscious, anxious, hostile and impulsive, is negatively correlated with happiness. Personality probably influences well-being for many reasons. One is that personality traits affect what information people pay attention to and remember. Information that is congruent with an individual's personality is more likely to be fully processed. So, for example, extraverts process rewarding stimuli for longer periods than introverts (Derryberry & Reed, 1994). In addition, people who approach situations differently may construe the same life events in different ways (Lyubomirsky, 2001).

Relationships and Well-Being

As we saw in Chapter 12, many theorists, like Freud and Erikson, have emphasized the importance of "love" for happiness. Evidence strongly supports this view. Regardless of personality characteristics, social relationships appear to be essential ingredients of well-being. Both extraverts and introverts report more pleasant emotions in social situations (Pavot, Diener, & Fujita, 1990). *Receiving* social support is clearly linked to better coping with life's stresses, as you will see later in this chapter, but having opportunities to *give* social support is also a key ingredient in happiness. Life is more stressful for people who have limited opportunities to be a source of support to others or who experience limited success in their efforts to do so (Brown, Nesse, Vinokur, & Smith, 2003; Herzberg et al., 1998).

A wide variety of converging evidence links the quality and quantity of social relationships with life satisfaction in adulthood. In a study of "very happy people," Diener and Seligman (2002) found that *all* of their happiest respondents had "excellent" social relationships. In a survey of 800 college graduates, those who valued material success and prestige more than close friends and a close marriage were twice as likely to describe themselves as unhappy in comparison to people who valued relationships more strongly (Perkins, 1991). People with more friends also experience greater happiness than people with fewer friends (Hintikka, Koskela, Kontula, Koskela, & Viinamaeki, 2000). Women with at least one confidant are less susceptible to depression than women with no confidants (Antonucci, Lansford, & Akiyama, 2001), and Hammen (e.g., 1996) suggests that without strong, positive interpersonal bonds, both men and women are particularly vulnerable to depression.

Marriages (and comparable long-term intimate partnerships) are a major source of companionship in Western societies. In surveys that include tens of thousands of people from the

Life satisfaction in adulthood is strongly correlated with good social relationships.

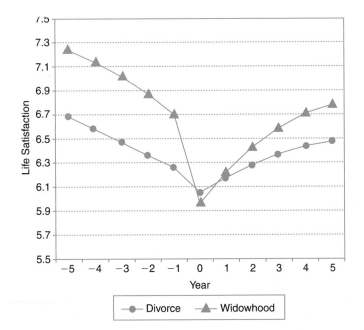

FIGURE 14.2

Life Satisfaction Before and After Divorce or Death of a Spouse

Source: Diener, E., & Seligman, M. E. P. (2004). Beyond money: Toward an economy of well-being. *Psychological Science in the Public Interest, 5*, 1–31. Reprinted by permission of Blackwell Publishing.

United States and many other countries, married women and men report more happiness than unmarried people (e.g., Mastekaasa, 1994). Being married is also associated with a lower risk of depression (Myers, 2000).

Do social relationships cause happiness, or are happy people more likely to be involved in social relationships? There is evidence that it works both ways. People who are more secure, who have more positive attitudes and better social skills are more likely to successfully make friends, develop confidants, and create long-term partnerships, as we have seen in our earlier discussions of friendship (e.g., Chapter 6) and marriage (e.g., Chapters 12 and 13). But when we study life satisfaction within individuals over time, we find that social relationships do affect people's happiness as well. The same people are happier when they are with others than when they are by themselves. For example, Kahneman and colleagues tracked women's affective states during 15 daily activities—like exercising, resting, commuting, and so on—and found that emotions were more positive when people were with others than when they were alone (Kahneman et al., 2004; see Box 14.1). People whose closest relationships end, as with divorce or death of a partner, may show precipitous declines in well-being. Their life satisfaction recovers only slowly and not usually to the same level as before the loss (e.g., Diener & Seligman, 2004; see also Figure 14.2).

Work, Achievement, Generativity, and Well-Being

As theorists like Freud and Erikson proposed, work experience and the general sense of oneself as a competent worker are also important predictors of happiness. Feeling that one is making competent progress toward challenging goals, both in work and in nonwork settings, is correlated with well-being (see Ryan & Deci, 2003). Similarly, scores on measures of generativity are predictors of well-being (e.g., Ackerman, Zuroff, & Moskowitz, 2000). As we have seen, generativity is a sense that one's skills and efforts are creatively or productively contributing to the world—to family, coworkers, community, or future generations.

Work experiences in general are often associated with subjective well-being. In the study by Kahneman et al. (2004) comparing affective states during daily tasks, people generally reported positive emotions at work, although not as positive as during sex or socializing after work! As we saw in Chapter 12, *congruence* between personality characteristics and the skills and qualities required by a job is part of what makes work satisfying. But there are also many characteristics of the workplace itself that contribute to happiness. Opportunities for personal control, the variety of tasks, the support of the supervisor, interpersonal contact, good pay and fringe benefits, respect and status, and so on can all influence the degree of satisfaction people derive from work (Warr, 1999).

Universal Needs and Values and Well-Being

In sum, material success, beyond a basic level, is not what constitutes the good life for adults. Personality characteristics that support an "other" rather than a "self" orientation do seem to help promote happiness. Good social relationships are particularly important, and productive work opportunities support life satisfaction as well. What can we deduce from this overview of factors that either do or do not promote well-being?

One approach to understanding and integrating these and other findings on well-being is to propose that what really counts is living a life that meets our most fundamental and universal needs. Extrapolating from the insights of philosophers through the ages, the views of personality theorists from many different traditions, and the available research, modern theorists propose that there are basic psychological needs, and meeting these needs is the source of well-being. Waterman (1993), for example, argued that people need to express their "true self." If their activities are congruent with their own deeply held values and are fully engaged, then people can achieve a state of "personal expressiveness," meaning that they feel intensely alive and authentic. Waterman devised measures of personal expressiveness and found that they correlated highly with traditional measures of subjective well-being. But subjective well-being, with its emphasis on happiness and positive emotion (what has also been called hedonic well-being) was not exactly the same as the kind of feeling that Waterman called personal expressiveness. The latter has been called eudaemonic well-being, and describes feeling a sense of purpose, growth, and mastery.

In a similar vein, Ryff and her colleagues (e.g., Ryff & Keyes, 1995) differentiated psychological well-being from subjective well-being, defining it as "the striving for the realization of one's true potential" (Ryff, 1995, p. 100). They list six fundamental elements of psychological well-being: autonomy, personal growth, self-acceptance, life purpose, mastery, and positive relatedess. Questionnaire measures of these six aspects of experience are highly correlated with measures of positive affect in which individuals are asked to describe how intensely they usually experience 20 different positive feeling states (e.g., interested, excited, strong, etc.; Urry, et al., 2004).

In what is called self-determination theory, Ryan and Deci (2000) have also argued that self-realization is at the core of well-being. They suggest that life satisfaction is derived from the fulfillment of fundamental psychological needs for autonomy (feeling that one's behaviors are self-endorsed), competence (expressing one's talents and skills), and relatedness (opportunities to feel cared for and valued by others). These psychological needs, like hunger and other basic physiological needs, are energizing. Their relative salience and the ways in which they are satisfied can be different across the life span and in different cultures. But there is cross-cultural evidence that satisfaction of these needs supports feelings of well-being in general (e.g., Deci et al., 2001; Ryan et al., 1999). It is not difficult to see how research on subjective well-being can be interpreted as consistent with this view. For example, a wide range of studies indicate that focusing on, investing in, and acting within social relationships predicts well-being, findings that support the existence of a universal need for relatedness. Also, the fact that feelings of well-being are linked to opportunities to express one's skills and personality traits in one's work could be support for the importance of both autonomy (involvement in intrinsically motivated activity) and competence needs. In Chapter 15, we will define these needs more fully and examine specifically how these needs are met as elderly people face the increasing challenges of aging.

The Importance of Meaning

Many observers of human nature have proposed that the well-lived life is one that is grounded in the conviction that life has meaning. Park and Folkman (1997) define *meaning* as simply the perception of significance, and they propose that the need to find meaning may be intrinsic to human beings. They differentiate between "global meaning," a sense of what the universe and human existence is about, or what is universally true, and a sense of "situational meaning," finding a purpose for one's own life. Generally, they see the second as heavily dependent on the first.

Baumeister (1991) argues that we humans have a need to understand our lives, to see them as making sense, and he proposes four reasons why people seek meaning. First, they feel a need for their lives to have a purpose, which basically is synonymous with having goals. Such goals help people place their current actions in context, providing a connection between past, present, and future. In other words, they help us see our lives as coherent and making sense. Second, when people have a sense of meaning in their lives, they feel like they have control, that what they do is consistent with a purpose they endorse, perhaps helping them meet what Ryan and Deci (2000) describe as the need for autonomy. Third, a sense of meaning helps people define what actions are legitimate and what actions are not. In this way, people can justify their actions and construct or identify values, morals, and ethics to help guide their behavior. Fourth, a sense of meaning helps people value themselves, fostering self-worth. Baumeister also suggests that becoming part of a social group both can help people feel valued and valuable and can enhance their sense of meaning.

As we have seen, despite the growth of wealth in the United States and other affluent nations in the last several decades, depression and other mental health problems have been on the rise (Diener & Seligman, 2004). Perhaps one of the reasons that increased wealth is not substantially correlated with well-being is that it is often linked to the valuing of materialistic goals, the pursuit of material goods, status, and financial advancement over other life goals. When materialism substitutes for a philosophy of life that provides a deeper sense of meaning and purpose, it may block the development of true satisfaction with life.

Some of the reasons for seeking meaning that Baumeister proposes are associated with the basic self-actualization needs or values that Ryan and Deci and others have specified, such as needs for autonomy and relatedness. In fact, one way to construe self-realization is that it means to find your true meaning or value—where you fit into a larger whole. Because religious traditions are in large part institutionalized meaning systems, they can help people establish global meaning, which in turn can support the creation of situational meaning. In Box 14.2, we review some scientific work on the role of spiritual and religious experience in adult life.

Box 14.2 | *Spirituality, Religion, and Well-Being*

Personality theorists have sometimes argued that spirituality is built into the human psyche. Carl G. Jung in particular felt that religion and spirituality are expressions of an innate need "to find meaning in life, to create a sense of wholeness or completeness, and to connect with something larger than the individual self" (Compton, 2005, p. 210). Modern researchers make a distinction between spirituality and religion (or religiosity). A person can have a spiritual side or spiritual strivings without practicing a particular religion, although the two are closely allied for many people (Hill et al., 2000). Both are concerned with "a search for the sacred" (Zinnbauer, Pargament, & Scott, 1999), which means attempting to identify, articulate, or move toward an understanding or association with a divine being, or divine object, or some kind of ultimate reality or truth (Hill et al., 2000). Religion also involves affiliation with "a covenant faith community" that has prescriptive and revelatory teachings and may include rituals, all of which are intended to support the search for the sacred and to encourage morality (Dollahite, 1998). Religion also may serve nonsacred goals, like creating a social identity (Hill et al., 2000). The empirical study of spirituality and religion is beginning to paint a picture of the role that both play in adults' everyday psychological functioning.

Religiosity and Well-Being

Both Eastern and Western religions and philosophies prescribe regulation of negative or destructive emotions, like anger and envy. Some religious movements (e.g., charismatic movements) also emphasize cultivating strong positive emotions, but others foster moderation of all emotional reactions (Emmons & Paloutzian, 2003). In traditional Buddhist teachings, for example, the ultimate emotional (albeit transient) state is nirvana, a realization of truth and an experience of pure happiness, compassion, and serenity that is also the complete absence of negative emotions, such as anxiety, envy, and anger (Compton, 2005). The practice of meditation is prescribed as one element in achieving such serene states. As reported in the text, Davidson and his colleagues (2003) have found that areas of the brain associated with positive mood show increased activity during meditation. They have also found that the most experienced practitioners, such as Tibetan monks, show the most extreme shifts toward patterns associated with positive emotions.

Many less striking studies have demonstrated that adherence to religious practices by people of many different faiths is moderately correlated with measures of subjective well-being. For example, widowed women who worship regularly report more joy in their lives than those who do not (e.g., Siegel & Kuykendall, 1990). Indeed, after many kinds of negative life experiences—divorce, unemployment, death of a child, and so on—religious people seem to recover more happiness more quickly than the nonreligious (e.g., Ellison, 1991). These benefits are more likely to accrue to people who are active religious participants (attending services, praying, meditating) than to those who describe themselves as pro-religious but are not active practitioners (e.g., George, Larson, Koenig, & McCullough, 2000). In survey assessments of spiritual commitment (e.g., asking whether people agree with statements like "My religious faith is the most important influence in my life," or "I feel very close to God"), those who score highest are also more likely than those who score lowest to rate themselves as "very happy" (Myers, 2000). Studies linking religiosity to subjective well-being have found rather small but significant correlations between the two. Therefore, religious practice seems to have a modest, albeit positive influence on well-being.

However, when researchers assess psychological well-being, focusing on people's feelings of mastery, growth, and purpose rather than on subjective well-being (that is, measures of happiness or positive mood), there is a stronger relationship between religiosity and well-being (Poloma & Pendleton, 1990). This connection is thought to be mediated by the fact that spirituality and religion support people's efforts to find meaning in life and may help them construct a sense of how their own lives fit into a larger plan or system. Counselors need to be aware of the importance of religious and spiritual issues in their clients' lives and work respectfully with these concerns (see Zinnbauer & Pargament, 2000).

Sorting Out the Benefits of Religiosity

Researchers have suggested that religion and spirituality may benefit well-being for many reasons. We have already mentioned the role that religion can play in helping people find meaning in their lives. Another important factor may be that religious communities provide their members with social support, a critical ingredient in well-being (Myers, 2000). The role of religion in fostering hope and optimism may also be important. Seligman (2002) describes a survey of religious congregations in which level of hope was the best predictor of feelings of well-being.

It should be noted that religions, like all human institutions, have their dark side. For example, although some religious doctrines and practices foster positive feelings, such as hope and compassion, others foster negative emotions and attitudes, such as guilt and fear of retribution. Another example is that some religious doctrines and beliefs encourage a distrust or intolerance of others, especially outgroup members, or promote retribution or revenge against those who are construed as evil or guilty (Chatters, 2000). Freud, having seen the dark side, assumed that religion must be "corrosive to happiness" (Myers, 2000, p. 63). Indeed, current evidence suggests that only positive elements of religious doctrine are correlated with well-being (Pargament, Smith, Koenig, & Perez, 1998).

Spirituality, Religion, and Personality

One question that researchers have asked is whether there is a link between spirituality or religiosity and personality. Do personality characteristics, like the Big 5 (see Chapter 13), affect the degree to which people are drawn to spiritual exploration or religious involvement? One meta-analysis found that across a large number of studies, high agreeableness and conscientiousness were associated with religiousness (Saraglou, 2002). One interesting set of studies by Piedmont and colleagues suggests that there may even be a sixth personality trait that specifically relates to spirituality or "spiritual transcendence," which can be defined as the ability to view life from a perspective that transcends space and time and to achieve a sense of fundamental unity with nature. These investigators consulted theological experts from many different Eastern and Western faith traditions to develop an assessment of spiritual transcendence that seemed to be common to all faiths. They then developed the "spiritual transcendence scale" that required individuals to rate how true spiritually based statements are of them, statements such as "I find inner strength and/or peace from my prayers or meditations" and "I feel that on a higher level all of us share a common bond." Piedmont has found that adults' scores on spiritual transcendence improve prediction of important characteristics like interpersonal style above and beyond their scores on the Big 5 personality traits (e.g., Piedmont, 1999; Piedmont & Leach, 2002).

Developmental Shifts in Spirituality and Faith

In what ways does the understanding and experience of spirituality change across the life span? Fowler (1981) interviewed over 350 individuals, ranging in age from 3 to 84 years, exploring their past and "life-shaping experiences," their values and commitments, and their religious thoughts and feelings. From these interviews, he derived a description of six stages in the development of faith. His definition of *faith* is "our way of finding coherence in and giving meaning to the multiple forces and relations that make up our lives" (p. 4). Faith and religion are not synonymous in his view. People with no religious commitments still develop faith, construed as "an orientation of the total person, giving purpose and goal to one's hopes and strivings, thoughts and actions" (p. 14). He acknowledges that because his interviewees were all reared in Judeo-Christian traditions, it remains to be seen what elements of his descriptions represent universal features of faith development and which are specific to Western culture. As always with stage theories, the ages are approximate and there is substantial variability, with some individuals moving more slowly than others, and many not progressing past the first few stages. Fowler found only one person who had achieved Stage 6. Note that the most advanced middle-aged adults in this model can be expected to move through Stages 4 and 5, beginning to understand the inherent inconsistencies in any spiritual perspective and how profoundly unknowable ultimate truth is. As you will see in Chapter 15, Fowler's description of these stages is consistent with features of a definition of *wisdom*.

Stage 1 (0 to 6 years): Intuitive-Projective

At these ages children are intuitive, egocentric, and not logical. Their understandings of sex, death, and taboo begin, and they may be overwhelmed by a sense of danger with regard to doing what's wrong versus right.

Stage 2 (7 to 12 years): Mythic-Literal

At these ages children can narrate a life story of sorts. They tend to repeat what they have been taught by parents and other close adults about truths and beliefs, which then serve as their morals and rules. They still literally see God as a father, and they see distinct categories of right and wrong.

Stage 3 (13 to 20 years): Synthetic-Conventional

By adolescence, the individual is constructing a life story. A "they" beyond the family is ascribed the authority to dictate values and beliefs, so faith remains conformist at this stage. Beliefs are not yet understood to be abstractions, and when others have different beliefs, they are judged to be wrong.

Stage 4 (21 to 30 years): Individuative-Reflective

Authority is shifting from the "they" to the self. People can recognize inconsistencies and conflicts in the beliefs and morals they have been taught, and they can think critically about them. People take responsibility for making commitments to a worldview, lifestyle, beliefs, and attitudes. They see those commitments as individual, belonging to self.

Stage 5 (31 to 60 years): Conjunctive

In early midlife, some individuals begin to see both sides of a problem at once and are able to resolve the conflicts in their beliefs using dialectical (postformal) thinking. The individual begins to appreciate the unknowable—what must be the unfathomable complexity of ultimate truth.

Stage 6 (over 60): Universalizing

Transcending specific belief systems, perceiving a universal community, this individual actively makes "real and tangible . . . the imperatives of absolute love and justice," unfettered by concerns about self. People at this stage live with "felt participation in a power that unifies and transforms the world."

STRESS, COPING, AND WELL-BEING IN MIDLIFE

In Chapter 13 you saw that nonnormative events are often the source of traumatic loss regardless of when they occur during the life span. The normative changes associated with growing older produce more predictable losses. Even when adults are healthy and self-sufficient, the physical changes of midlife and late life "raise concerns and lamentations about the woes of getting older" (Whitbourne, 2001, as cited in Lachman, 2004).

Clearly, the capacity to adapt to stress and challenge is critical to survival at every stage of the life span. In many ways throughout this text, we have emphasized the important goal of fostering resilience in children, adolescents, and adults and the promotion of effective coping regardless of one's age or stage in life. As you recall from Chapter 13, resilience refers to the presence of healthy coping and adaptation *in spite of* challenges and risks, or in the words of Ryff and Singer, "the capacity to flourish under fire" (2003, p. 15). To understand and foster resilience, we must consider the nature of the risks and protective factors that mark each individual's life and attend to the ways that these might change as a function of age.

Midlife brings its own set of challenges, not the least of which is the recognition of "time left to live," slowly accumulating losses related to getting older, and often great demands in the areas of the family and workplace. Some research suggests that stress is higher among young and middle-aged adults than it is for older adults (Chiriboga, 1997). As we will discuss in Chapter 15, older adults are often more skilled at managing their emotions and sustaining joy. But it may also be that the life space midlife adults occupy is filled with more conflicting pulls on time and attention than it is for older individuals. In the middle years, adults are frequently in positions of increased responsibility and authority at work; they may have obligations to children and grandchildren; they

People in midlife frequently find themselves responsible for meeting the needs of family members from older and younger generations at the same time.

may also take on the physical, emotional, or financial care of aging parents, situations that can increase risk load. These circumstances are a defining characteristic of the sandwich generation, namely that group of individuals described in Chapter 13 who have caregiving responsibilities for generations both younger and older than themselves.

Who, then, are the resilient people? Questions about who thrives and why they do so defy easy answers. True to the principles of multifinality and equifinality (see Chapter 1), eventual life outcomes are dependent upon a whole array of variables that interact in complicated ways. What we are learning, however, is that pathways to adult disorder and well-being are not random but have their roots in the experiences of childhood and each succeeding stage. And, as with earlier parts of the lifespan, there are multiple pathways to well-being as well as to disorder.

The Wisconsin Longitudinal Study (Singer & Ryff, 1999), one of the most comprehensive studies of adult development, offers a look at the lives of adults who graduated from Wisconsin High Schools in 1957. This study of 10,317 men and women provides extensive information about participants' education, IQ, employment, marriage/family status, experience of stressful life events, accomplishments, goals, social support, and history of depression gathered over three data collections in 1957, 1975, and 1992/1993. Such a rich body of information offers many windows into adult development.

One subgroup that was studied intensively was the group of resilient women. *Resilient women* were defined as those who had experienced depression sometime during their lives but who had subsequently regained a high level of well-being (Singer, Ryff, Carr, & Magee, 1998). Aggregating the life stories of this group, the authors identified four pathways to wellness following the experience of adversity. Their life stories reflected a diversity of experiences in the following major areas: educational level of parents; alcoholism in the home as a child; marriage or cohabitation with an alcoholic as an adult; being a single parent; upward or downward mobility at work; and comparisons with parents and siblings with regard to education, finances, and occupation.

One group of resilient women had more cumulative advantages than the other groups, namely, educated parents, family financial stability, stable marriages, and so on. These women, however, did experience stressful life events, like the death of a parent or the onset of chronic illness, that presumably were related to their depression. A second group experienced more childhood adversity, including growing up in a family where there were problems with alcoholism.

Women in this group also experienced similar losses and illness in adulthood. A third group was advantaged in childhood but experienced important setbacks in adulthood, like involuntary unemployment or divorce. The fourth group had lives that incorporated mixtures of advantages and disadvantages throughout early childhood and adulthood. What this work most clearly illustrates is the presence of multiple pathways to resilience. All four groups of women had at least one experience with depression, yet found their way out of it to reclaim a sense of well-being. Although not directly assessed in this sample, the ways in which these women perceived their difficulties and their capacity to master them might have played a role in their resilient outcomes.

Certain elements were identified as protective factors that seemed to buffer the adversity that occurred in other domains. Some of these were childhood advantages, like educated parents, no problems with alcohol either in the family of origin or within marriage, and not having to raise children alone. Other advantages included social attachments (like close confidants, friends, spouses, church or civic groups), relatively stable or upward mobility in employment with only one involuntary job loss, and positive social comparisons with parents and siblings with regard to economic and educational achievement. Clearly, all of these women faced stressful circumstances and suffered because of them. But their ability to flourish despite adversity raises intriguing questions about the nature of stress and coping over the life span.

The stressful circumstances of middle age are frequently a taxing set of demands related to managing family and work in the context of diminishing resources, such as time and energy. When circumstances exist that buffer the effects of competing role demands, such as good social support and adequate income, these demands may be perceived as less stressful. However, when the demands are too great given available resources, role strain (Goode, 1960) can occur, taking a toll on health and well-being. Perrone and Worthington (2001) found that having more resources, including income and social support, was associated with greater marital satisfaction among their sample of dual-income couples and presumably compensated for some of their work strains. Some others have demonstrated that multiple roles can be beneficial when they buffer the negative effects of one role with the protective function of a more satisfying one. Rozario, Morrow-Howell, and Hinterlong (2004) found that older caregivers with multiple productive roles reported more positive health outcomes compared to those without such roles.

Social support, as found in marriage or other close relationships, can be a potent protective factor in managing stress and promoting health. In a sample of middle-aged rural adults, Wickrama and associates found that unsupportive or distressed marital relationships were linked to early onset of hypertension for both husbands and wives. Problematic relationships with children contributed independently to the early onset of hypertension for mothers, but not for fathers. Husbands' satisfaction with employment, particularly the opportunity for advancement in the workplace, was negatively related to early onset of hypertension (Wickrama et al., 2001). These results suggest that chronic exposure to stressors in relationships can have direct negative effects on health and that these effects may be further exacerbated by gender-salient roles and expectations.

Stress: A Review

The nature and effect of stress on individuals is important to review because of its clear impact on emotional and physical health. Some have argued that the term *stress* is vague and open to many interpretations (Kemeny, 2003); consequently we adopt the recommended term *stressors*. Stressors have been divided into two varieties: life events (Holmes & Rahe, 1967) which are discrete, often traumatic, events that have a clear onset (like a death or accident) and daily hassles (Lazarus & Folkman, 1984), which are chronic, problematic situations (like day-to-day care of a sick relative or chronic illness). Research has suggested that chronic daily stress is very important in the development of psychological (Compas, Davis, Forsythe, & Wagner, 1987) as well as physical symptoms (Selye, 1980). McEwen (1998) refers to the cumulative physical effects of chronic stress hormones on the body as allostatic load. For example, the stress of keeping a job while caring for a sick child or older relative may cause a person to go without sleep for a prolonged period of time. As a result the caregiver might succumb to illness herself due, in large part, to physical exhaustion. In some cases, stressors aggregate in people's lives, often subsequent to a traumatic event, and with this accumulation, their power multiplies (Garmezy, 1993). Caregivers like the one just described can lose a job, thus causing them to forfeit access to health care coverage and enough income to maintain a house or an automobile. Such cycles of disadvantage can exert a powerful impact on the lives of children as well as adults and have been consistently linked to the onset of physical and mental health problems (Turner & Lloyd, 1995).

A phenomenon that has been useful in explaining the effects of cumulative stressors on vulnerability is called kindling-behavioral sensitization (Post, 1985; Post, Weiss, Smith, Rosen, & Frye, 1995). This psychological model has been useful in conceptualizing mechanisms involved in drug tolerance, epilepsy, and affective disorders (Goddard, McIntyre, & Leech, 1969). Kindling-sensitization describes a process of progressive illness severity or illness incidence that results from gradual increases in sensitivity to stressful triggers. Consider how this model is applied to affective disorders. An initial episode of depression is triggered by stressful life events (Dohrenwend & Dohrenwend, 1974), which leaves residual neurological changes in the individual's brain (neurotransmitters, receptors, etc.) rendering him more reactive to stressors. Following this experience of "sensitization," subsequent episodes of depression can occur spontaneously or with very little external provocation (Kendler, Thornton & Gardner, 2001).

Hlastala and her colleagues (2000) investigated whether this model explained the progression of episodes of bipolar disorder over the life span. The number of previous bipolar episodes per se did not predict later episodes of disorder. However, increasing age was related to increasing incidents of bipolar illness. As people got older, their episodes were preceded by relatively less external stress. This suggests that some specific aspects of the aging process, possibly medical or biological factors, may interact with stressors in a way that heightens vulnerability. Mroczek and Almeida (2004) report a similar finding showing that older adults reported heightened stress reactivity, consistent with kindling, when compared to younger groups. "A lifetime of frequent activation of the neural pathways associated with negative affect may bring about such sensitization" (p. 371). Even if people report more life satisfaction as they age, they may still be more affected by stressors.

Diatheses and Stress

Many contemporary models that address the development of problems posit a diathesis-stress transaction. Diatheses are premorbid conditions or predispositions that render individuals vulnerable to some disorder under certain circumstances. Individual vulnerability or diatheses may be genetically based (e.g., inherited traits) or acquired through learning (as in the case of self-defeating cognitions). These underlying vulnerabilities may come to light only if individuals experience a sufficient number, type, or intensity of stressful experience to trigger the manifestation of disorder. According to this model, people of all ages with multiple or severe underlying vulnerabilities require less situational stress to trigger a maladaptive outcome. This is one way to explain why only a portion of individuals who experience traumatic events go on to develop posttraumatic stress disorder (PTSD; McFarlane, 1990). Presumably, those individuals who possess sufficient levels of preexisting biological and environmental vulnerabilities reach a tipping point when traumatic stress is experienced, whereas others do not (McKeever & Huff, 2003).

Those who flourish despite challenging circumstances might enjoy the protections of biology or environment, but explanations are far from crystal clear at this point. Nonetheless, these questions are attracting the attention of many contemporary researchers who are interested in understanding what contributes to positive development. One approach has been provided by Tedeschi and Calhoun (2004) who offer evidence for a phenomenon they call posttraumatic growth. This is defined as "positive psychological change experienced as a result of the struggle with highly challenging life circumstances" (p. 1). People who evidence posttraumatic growth, following experiences like bereavement, accident, illness, and so on, are marked by demonstrable improvements in psychological functioning that exceed pretraumatic event levels. Some of these gains include an altered set of priorities about life, a greater appreciation for one's life, closer and more positive relationships with others, improved sense of life's possibilities, and heightened spirituality (Tedeschi & Calhoun, 1996). These authors provide evidence that posttraumatic growth is related to certain personality traits, notably extraversion and openness to experience, and to a lesser extent, dispositional optimism. Growth following trauma is believed to occur via the mechanism of cognitive processing, which refers to qualitative shifts in schemata about the self and the world that need to occur to accommodate the enormously traumatic event. "This process is likely to involve a powerful combination of demand for emotional relief and cognitive clarity, that is achieved through construction of higher order schemata that allow for appreciation of paradox" (Tedeschi & Calhoun, 2004, p. 15). Others have pointed out that part of this process also includes the construction of positive illusions, like the belief that trauma makes one a better person (Taylor, 1983). These cognitive distortions may protect traumatized individuals by reinforcing their sense of mastery and self-worth along with soothing the acute stress (Maercker & Zoellner, 2004). Monumental positive experiences, like the birth of a child, can also enhance growth in comparable ways and should not be discounted as a vehicle for positive development (Aldwin & Levenson, 2004).

Stressors and the Body-Mind

It is worthwhile to revisit the body's way of reacting to stressors and examine how they affect a variety of physiological systems to appreciate these processes more fully. As you may recall from Chapter 2, stressors engage the body's autonomic nervous system, activating the HPA axis, causing the release of hormones into the bloodstream, and preparing the body to respond to the perceived attack. Although this process serves us well in emergency situations or in relatively short hormonal bursts, there are costs associated with chronic activation of the system (Sapolsky, 1992). For example, during the acute phase of the body's stress response, immune system functioning is depressed.

Remember that stressors mobilize the body's energy resources to enhance certain functions (such as motor and sensory abilities, all the better to see and run away from the big, bad threat). The immune system, intended to surround and destroy attacking foreign bodies such as viruses or bacteria, requires mobilization of the body's energy to do its work as well. Our immune system operates through a process of inflammation to limit the spread of such harmful pathogens and to repair their damage.

Each of these important processes requires that the body's energy be directed to different ends (Maier, Watkins & Fleshner, 1994). During a stressful event, energy reserves need to be devoted to the immediate fight-flight response and any alternative expenditure of energy, such as that required for immune system functions, is suppressed in service of the more immediate need. If homeostasis does not resume following the acute stress-response phase, the ill effects of chronic stress result. High levels of cortisol, the body's primary stress hormone, can dysregulate immune functions and reduce the body's capacity to protect itself against disease. You may have noticed, for example, that when you are dealing with some ongoing stressor, you might be more likely to catch a cold or flu, an example of the process of immunosuppression. This occurs because cortisol inhibits the proliferation or blunts the responses of certain types of cytokines (Cohen & Williamson, 1991; Kemeny, 2003). Cytokines are small protein molecules of many different varieties that are secreted by cells of the immune system and that help to regulate its functioning. Operating somewhat like neurotransmitters, cytokines are messenger molecules that communicate instructions to other cells to respond or to inhibit a response.

Another immune system process, inflammation, is also affected when the body confronts chronic stressors. Inflammatory processes, which take their marching orders from cortisol, can be destructive to the body unless their force is regulated. Remember that these functions are temporarily suppressed when the body needs to respond to acute stressors, and then, ideally, return to baseline. The problem arises when the stressors become chronic. Chronic exposure increases cortisol production, but also desensitizes the immune cells' ability to respond to cortisol's instructions to inhibit inflammatory processes. Consequently, high concentrations of proinflammatory cytokines, which are related to maladaptive inflammation, go unchecked. Many disease conditions, such as cardiovascular disease, allergies, rheumatoid arthritis, and other autoimmune disorders, have been associated with unregulated inflammatory processes (Kemeny, 2003; Steptoe, Willemsen, Owen, Flower, & Mohamed-Ali, 2001). These immune-related effects have been demonstrated in a study of adult parents of children with pediatric cancer. This group, presumably under chronic stress, showed impairment in the capacity of their immune system to downregulate inflammatory processes in comparison to parents of healthy children (Miller, Cohen, & Ritchey, 2002).

Maier and Watkins (1998) conclude from their review of research that psychological stressors, such as traumatic environmental events, operate on the body in much the same way as infectious agents. Stressors, both psychological and physical, produce the same kinds of immune-related symptoms that we see in the body's normal infection response. These include some combination of fever, increased sleep, reduction in eating and drinking, reduced exploration and activity, reduced aggression, reduction in social interaction, cognitive alterations, increased pain sensitivity, increased HPA activity, and depressed mood. Viewed from this perspective, these authors argue that certain types of depression are associated with hyperactivation of the immune response, even though the precise direction of these effects is still unclear. The important point in this discussion is the establishment of the connection between emotional experiences and the dysregulation of body mechanisms (like immune system functioning).

> The argument is not that depression is caused by immune activation. The argument is that whatever does cause depression (e.g., negative cognitions about the self or loss of a loved one) may have access to the same neural circuitry that evolved to mediate sickness and activate that circuitry. Some of the symptoms of depression, particularly the vegetative symptoms, may then be the result of this process and represent essentially *sickness* responses. In addition, as noted earlier, the circuit is bi-directional, and the products of these activated immune cells in turn provide signals to the brain. It is conceivable that this positive feedback circuit could help to maintain depression. (Maier & Watkins, 1998, p. 98)

So it's a bit more interesting than the top-down, brain-in-charge picture of stress management that is commonly described. Recent evidence has clearly supported the existence of bidirectional communication processes between the brain and the immune systems in relation to stressors, be they psychological or physical (Pert, 1997; Sternberg, 2001). Pert, for example, discovered that opiate receptors for the body's natural opiates, called **endorphins**, are present on the surface of cells in the immune system (spleen and thymus). This discovery uncovered the connections between the brain, the immune system and emotions, linking the mind and body in new and exciting ways. As we are learning, the brain and the immune system operate together in a highly orchestrated dance that maintains homeostasis or balance within systems of the body-mind. Originally, it was thought that the brain "talked" and the immune system responded. Now researchers increasingly recognize that the brain also "listens" to the communication of the immune system which sends its chemical messengers to various parts of the nervous system, including the brain. Findings such as these have helped usher in a new field, **psychoneuroimmunology**, the study of the interactions between the central nervous system, the immune system and behavior (Cohen & Williamson, 1991).

Stress Management

Given that everyone deals with stressors in their lives, that they critically influence our health, and that many of them derive from the aging process itself, the question becomes how best to manage inevitable stressful circumstances. Do people learn to restrict their exposure to stressful experiences as they age? Or do they learn better ways of managing stress? What separates resilient individuals from those who adapt less effectively? Why is it that not all people who experience similarly stressful events suffer similar adverse consequences?

We suggest that management of stress is essentially the same thing as coping. Many typologies have been developed to explain the nature of coping and a voluminous body of research has been devoted to the question of whether coping in certain ways makes a difference in outcomes.

The highly influential model proposed by Lazarus and Folkman (1984) makes a basic distinction between efforts aimed at changing the situation (problem-focused, problem-solving) and those directed toward emotion management (emotion-focused, tension-reduction). The two-dimensional model of primary and secondary control (Rothbaum, Weisz, & Snyder, 1982; see also Chapter 15) emphasizes the role of controllability of stressors as a determinant of coping responses. The repression-sensitization model (Byrne, 1964; Krohne & Rogner, 1982) describes coping behavior as a traitlike characteristic or style of coping that has two primary manifestations. The first (sensitizing) is marked by typically heightened perception of threat and increased attention to stressful information; the second (repression) is characterized by appraisal of stressors as less threatening and/or avoidance. This conceptualization bears some resemblance to other models such as approach-avoidance (Roth & Cohen, 1986), monitoring-blunting (Miller & Green, 1984), and rumination-distraction (Nolen-Hoeksema, 1987).

At present, researchers have recognized that some of these dichotomous distinctions fail to capture the real nature of coping, which does not manifest in mutually exclusive categories. Virtually all coping needs to accommodate cognitive (decision making) as well as emotional (anxiety management) aspects. Therefore, attempts to compartmentalize coping into sets of behaviors that address problem fixing or feeling better do not acknowledge that some coping falls outside these boundaries (such as seeking social support) and that categories are not mutually exclusive (such as taking a "mental health" day that allows you to avoid an unpleasant meeting and makes you feel more relaxed at the same time). Lazarus himself (1996) stated that treating problem- and emotion-focused coping as two highly distinctive types leads to oversimplification of the nature of coping itself. These distinctions are also problematic because they do not consider the function or intention of the coping behavior. In a recent review, Skinner and her colleagues state:

> If the ways that an individual copes are assembled based on the specific stressor(s) and situational constraints, then any way of coping can be locally adaptive. For example, if a set of stressors is actually uncontrollable, it may be adaptive to give up (to conserve resources). Or if an important goal is arbitrarily blocked, it may be adaptive to attack the obstacle (to defend the goal). In this sense, given the right circumstances, every possible way of coping can be appropriate, normative or right. (Skinner, Edge, Altman, & Sherwood, 2003, p. 231)

Hobfoll (1989, 2001) presents a theory of coping with stressors that is relevant to midlife and aging because it emphasizes the centrality of loss experiences. His theory, called conservation of resources (COR) theory, posits that the primary stress trigger is loss, either through a primary loss event (bereavement, injury), transitions that involve loss (children leaving home, retirement), threats to aspects of the self (demotion, lack of acknowledgment for accomplishments), or challenges that incorporate some aspects of loss (job promotion that involves a move to a new location). Even though some of these events might have positive elements, the experience of stress, according to this theory, is the consequence of the loss component.

Researchers have demonstrated that people tend to weight resource loss as more important in their lives than resource gain (Kahneman & Tversky, 1984; Tversky & Kahneman, 1974). In other words, negative events in people's lives appear to produce more powerful physiological, emotional, and cognitive consequences than do positive events. Resource loss is a critical predictor of distress following traumatic events, such as those due to natural disasters (Freedy, Saladin, Kilpatrick, Resnick, & Saunders, 1994), as well as in more chronic, day-to-day stressful events (Siegrist, 1996). That is, "losses make us hurt more than gains make us feel good" (Schwartz, 2004).

To deal with loss in its multiplicity of forms, individuals tend to act in ways that conserve their resources. Resources may be understood as things that people value in and of themselves or things that enable people to achieve or obtain that which is important to them (Baltes, 1987; Hobfoll, 1989). Resources can include objects (material possessions like a home or car), conditions (marriage, job status), personal characteristics (self-esteem, hope), or energies (time). When stressed, people seek to minimize the cost to their net resource capacity. Individuals also seek to increase their resources during nonstressful times, to accumulate a reserve. These ideas bear some resemblance, from a behavioral perspective, to the "sickness" response of the body under attack that was previously described.

Wellness

With increasing attention to the negative effects of chronic stressors, there is a complementary, growing interest in the interrelationships among health, coping, and stress management. The emphasis these days is not on any rigid "right" or "wrong" strategy for coping, but on adaptive flexibility (Bonanno, Papa, Lalande, Westphal, & Coifman, 2004). Certain resources have been construed as particularly important to the process of healthy coping. A general sense of self-efficacy (Bandura, 1989), optimism (Schier & Carver, 1985), self-esteem (Rosenberg, 1979), personal control over important goals (Seligman, 1975), and social support (Sarason & Sarason, 1985) are among the characteristics that are associated with greater physical and emotional health and well-being.

But how does one demonstrate these qualities in the midst of stress? What if the stressor is uncontrollable, such as the onset of chronic ailments as people age? Is it just a fortunate few, blessed by temperament, who tend toward resilience? In line with COR theory, it makes sense to support the development of attributes like self-efficacy and optimistic cognitions because these qualities serve as protective factors in the face of hardship. But there is currently a strong interest in the pivotal role positive emotions play in the experience of well-being and their role in the stress management process. The encouraging news is that these qualities can be cultivated as well.

As we have emphasized, not everyone who is exposed to the same stressor will have the same response. This is due, in part, to the way people appraise threats relative to the way they appraise their capacities to deal with them. The appraisal part of coping is the target for many cognitive and behavioral interventions that are geared toward self-efficacy and that enhance a sense of mastery and personal control. But affective elements are also in play in stress management, coping, and more generally, well-being.

The Affectivity Connection

Human emotional experience can be broadly construed as positive and negative and recent conceptualizations link positive and negative emotions to separate neurological systems (Watson, Wiese, Vaidya, & Tellegen, 1999). You may recall from Chapter 4 that the emotional brain is comprised of several circuits or systems. **Negative affectivity**, or the extent to which a person experiences nervousness, fear, anger, sadness, contempt and guilt, is a part of the **behavioral-inhibition system**. This circuit is related to withdrawal and avoidance behaviors shaped through evolution to help people keep out of harm's way. **Positive affectivity**, or the extent to which a person experiences enthusiasm, alertness, joy, confidence, and determination, is part of the **behavioral facilitation system**, that system intended to allow people to respond to reinforcement and to approach and engage with the environment. Both positive and negative affectivity have trait-like as well as state-like qualities. This means that individuals' emotions may change from happy to sad based on certain events. But it also means that people tend to vary in their baseline levels of positive and negative affectivity or emotional style overall.

Studies assessing hemispheric brain activation indicate that the left prefrontal cortex (LPC) is activated during the experience of positive emotions, whereas the right prefrontal cortex (RPC) is activated during periods of negative emotion (Davidson, 2000). This prefrontal asymmetry can be measured in individuals in resting states and points to what might be thought of as temperamentally related emotional style. When researchers asked participants to watch film clips designed to elicit positive (animals at a zoo) and negative (a burn victim) emotional responses, having recorded their baseline brain activity prior to exposure to the films, they found reliable individual differences in responses that were predicted by prefrontal activity. Those with higher left frontal activity reported more positive affect in response to the positive stimuli; those with the reverse prefrontal pattern reported more fear and disgust in response to the negative stimuli. These results suggest that people are different in their tendencies to respond to emotional stimuli (Tomarken, Davidson, & Henriques, 1990).

So what does this have to do with stress and coping? As you might imagine, negative affectivity has been associated with greater reactivity to stress (Watson & Pennebaker, 1989). Research also demonstrates that the immune systems of individuals with greater left PFC activation were less compromised following a traumatic stressor (Davidson, Coe, Dolski, & Donzella, 1999). In other research, participants viewed an emotionally distressing film while hemispheric activity and hormone levels were measured. Researchers employed a procedure that allowed participants to see the film using only their right or left hemisphere. Results demonstrated that viewing the film using the right hemisphere was associated with a significantly higher release of cortisol than was left-hemisphere viewing. The authors concluded that cortisol regulation may be related to RH activation (Wittling & Pflüger, 1990). Finally, Cohen and his colleagues found that people who tended to have a positive emotional style were significantly more likely, compared to those with a negative emotional style, to be resistant to the common cold (Cohen, Doyle, Turner, Alper, & Skoner, 2003).

Does this mean that those of us with higher levels of RPC activation are doomed to a life of greater unhappiness? The good news is that emotional affectivity is not a zero sum game; in other words, positive and negative affectivity circuits are independent of each other rather than opposite ends of a continuum (Cacioppo & Gardner, 1999; Diener & Emmons, 1985). People do not express only one type of emotionality or the other but can have access to the full range of emotions. So even if we view the pattern of trait-like negative affectivity as a risk factor, emerging research suggests that we can encourage the development of positive emotions through certain practices. As Ingram and Price (2001) conclude, "Even though vulnerability is conceptualized as a trait according to some conceptualizations, vulnerability is not necessarily permanent or unalterable. Corrective experiences can occur that may attenuate the vulnerability, or, alternately, certain experiences may increase vulnerability factors" (p. 12).

What are the protections against encroaching stress sensitivity due to temperament, stressful life events, or age? In general, practicing positive emotions is being viewed increasingly as an antidote to health-compromising emotions like anger and hostility (Goleman, 2003). If we consider negative emotional style as a risk factor that is tied to increases in levels of stress hormones and depressed immune functioning, it is reasonable to conclude that practicing a positive emotional style may serve as an antidote, buffering the effects of stress. You might have thought of emotional style as a hard-wired tendency. Recent research is revolutionizing our way of thinking about emotion and providing support for the view that the brain is somewhat plastic with regard to affective style, more similar to an incremental viewpoint. Although much more research needs to be done in this area, one preliminary study of a stress reduction technique offers some tantalizing possibilities.

Because many studies have demonstrated the effectiveness of meditation and other stress reduction procedures as a way of reducing anxiety and enhancing positive mood, Davidson and his colleagues (Davidson et al., 2003) sought to investigate the effects of a stress reduction meditation course on brain and immune system functioning. A group of healthy male and female employees at a biotechnology corporation were recruited to participate in an 8-week meditation-based stress reduction program at their workplace, forming a treatment group and a wait-list control. Before beginning the program, participants' brain electrical activity was measured while they were asked to write about a series of positive and negative events in their lives. At the end of the 8 weeks, the same assessments of brain activity were performed. Participants also rated their experience of positive and negative emotions following each group session. Finally, all participants (including the wait-list group) were vaccinated with flu influenza vaccine at the end of the 8 weeks. Blood samples were obtained 3 to 5 weeks and again at 8 to 9 weeks postvaccination to assess the immune response.

Results demonstrated that meditators showed a significant increase in left prefrontal brain activity, related to the experience of positive affectivity, compared to the control group. Self-report measures reflected a significant decrease in anxiety for those in the program compared to those who did not participate. Interestingly, program participants reported significant decreases in their own experiences of negative affectivity over time, wheras control group members did not. When blood draws were examined, participants in the meditation group had significantly increased concentrations of antibodies in their blood compared to nonmeditators (see Figure 14.3). This finding suggests a greater and more rapid immune system response compared to controls. These findings are promising because they reflect that even a relatively short intervention carried out in a work setting can reduce negative affectivity and anxiety and promote health and well-being.

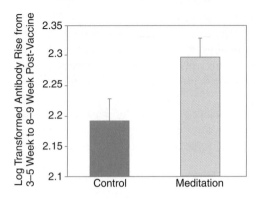

FIGURE 14.3

Differences in Immune Responses in Control and Meditation Groups

Reprinted from *Brain, Behavior, and Immunity 13*, Davidson, R. J., Coe, C. C., Dolski, I., & Donzella, B. Individual differences in prefrontal activation asymmetry predicts natural killer cell activity at rest and in response to challenge. Copyright © 1999, with permission from Elsevier.

APPLICATIONS

Threaded throughout this book is the theme of emotion regulation, that capacity that allows us to regulate levels of emotional arousal. The behaviors and capacities that constitute emotion regulation also include recognition of feelings and appropriate expression and modulation of emotional expression. In infancy and toddlerhood, attachments with caregivers channel youngsters' developing capacity to self-soothe, to tolerate frustration, and to stay for longer and longer periods of time in a regulated emotional state. In childhood and adolescence, social development is promoted by the young person's ability to delay gratification in service of peers, to control impulses that could hurt or antagonize others, and to benefit from capacities for friendship. In emerging and young adulthood, good emotion regulation is associated with better overall adjustment and satisfying communication in close relationships. Conversely, difficulties in emotion regulation have been associated with a wide variety of problems. Recall that temperamental differences in intensity of perceived emotions can make emotion regulation a particular challenge for some children.

What we have been calling "emotion regulation" typically refers to the experience of negative emotions—that is, what we do when we feel bad or when we don't get our own way. Helpers might be heartened by the growing literature indicating that emotional affectivity, both positive and negative, is not immutable and can be shaped by certain practices. All the efforts to support resiliency affirm this conclusion. As Davidson reflects about his own work, "It was the possibility of altered *traits* of consciousness that was particularly appealing to me. Altered traits implied the transformation of consciousness and personality in an enduring fashion to foster increased well-being" (2002, p. 107).

Counselors should be proud of their history of fostering wellness in various ways (see Keyes & Haidt, 2003; Walsh, 2003). The paths to well-being include the development of mastery and optimism, teaching of effective problem solving and decision making, encouragement of social competence, support for health-promoting behaviors related to diet and exercise, and advocacy for improved environmental circumstances. In this press toward well-being, however, it is important to take note of the real suffering that serious negative life events produce in the lives of those who sustain them. There are no easy therapeutic interventions that can guarantee rapid recovery or put an end to serious distress, such as simply reframing the problem or learning to perceive stressful events in different ways. Often the coping process, as in the case of recovery from addictions or traumatic assault, happens one step at a time on a day-to-day basis. Counselors clearly have much to offer their clients in this regard. But we should not forget that clients' struggles to cope with stressors and to make their own lives meaningful have a great deal to teach us as well.

Mindfulness

Within the body of techniques that address stress reduction, interventions that target stress-reactivity—the quick response that often switches on the cascade of potentially harmful biopsychological events described in this chapter—are particularly important. One promising approach is to work with the mind's own plasticity and capacity for reducing negative reactivity through present-moment and somatic awareness (Cioffe, 1991; Kabat-Zinn, 2003). Therapy of this sort provides an alternative to traditional therapies that emphasize past history, future goals, distraction, or even the restructuring of thinking. In fact, this approach deemphasizes the role of thinking and verbal analysis precisely because "the illusion of language is that one is dealing with the world through thought. In fact, one is actually structuring the world through thought" (Hayes, 2002). Varela, Thompson, and Rosch (1991) note the tendency of the mind to reside in the domain of abstraction and refer to this inclination as "the spacesuit, the padding of habits and preconceptions, the armor with which one habitually distances oneself from one's own experience" (p. 25). As we have noted, worrying about something stressful can amplify the stress. Even without the presence of stressors, our minds are constantly engaged in inner conversations that remove us from the direct experience of what is actually happening in the present moment.

The direct experience of the present, as opposed to mental reruns of past events, discursive ruminations about abstract ideas, or fantasy scenarios about future possibilities, is a very different type of mental event. Being present in the moment involves stepping out of the automatic pilot mode that characterizes much of our mental life. With practice in noticing and taking account of the present moment, it becomes possible to disengage from dominating ruminative patterns of thinking. Moreover, it becomes possible to extricate oneself from the attitude of abstraction to reconnect the mind and body. Approaches that foster somatic present-moment awareness help develop the skill of being in the "here and now" without attaching any evaluative valence to the experience. Attention available for discursive thought is deliberately reduced, whereas nonjudgmental acceptance of one's experience and also oneself is increased. Greater awareness of present-moment experience improves the capacity to respond to stressors in a more skillful and less reactive way.

Recently researchers have proposed that one of the key features of cognitive therapy—that is, metacognitively standing back from one's negative thoughts to notice their accuracy—promotes the type of psychological decentering or distancing that helps interrupt the ruminative cycle. This phenomenon, often called **mindfulness**, has been defined as "paying attention in particular way: on purpose, in the present moment, and nonjudgmentally" (Kabat-Zinn, 1994). Teasdale and colleagues (Teasdale et al., 2000; Teasdale et al., 2002) view mindfulness as the main ingredient in therapeutic change in cognitive behavioral therapy because of its capacity to short circuit negative thought cycling, to liberate us from the tyranny of the mental rules we establish for ourselves and others, and to allow for dispassionate observation of thinking.

Meditation-based mindfulness approaches are beginning to be subject to enthusiastic inquiry by those who translate Eastern traditions for modern Western readers (Goleman, 2003; Kabat-Zinn, 2005). Mindfulness-based stress reduction (MBSR), developed by Kabat-Zinn and colleagues at the University of Massachusetts Stress Reduction Clinic, is a generic program based on a psychoeducational rather than a clinical treatment model. Originally developed as a hospital-based program for stress reduction, MBSR programs have proliferated in recent years to include training for groups as diverse as students, educators, corporate employees, health care professionals, attorneys, inmates, clergy, and athletes. The course has a structured curriculum that is taught in a group format over 8 weeks and involves daily homework practice. In comparison to therapies that emphasize discussion or analysis, MBSR emphasizes practice in working with attention. A core feature of mindfulness is learning to transform stressful situations by going through them in a skillful way, not trying to avoid or eradicate them. Essentially, to be mindful is to develop skills in attention and moment-to-moment awareness. Therefore, developing the ability to take note of thoughts, feelings, and sensations increases the capacity to work skillfully with negative ones and replace automatic, habitual, and often judgmental reactions with relaxed observing and awareness.

Some of the session themes include noticing the automaticity of thinking and behavior, becoming more aware of bodily sensations, learning how to get "unstuck" from reactive patterns, enhancing stress hardiness, and so forth. The program employs various activities such as walking, sitting, and eating meditation, yoga/mindful movement, and discussion. One of the primary foundations of the program is daily home practice.

MBSR principles have been incorporated into cognitive-behavioral therapy resulting in a new treatment modality called mindfulness-based cognitive therapy (MBCT; Segal, Williams, & Teasdale, 2002). This approach was designed to reduce the risk of depressive relapse. Mindfulness approaches are also a prominent part of Linehan's (1993) dialectical behavior therapy, originally designed for individuals diagnosed with borderline personality disorder, as well as in acceptance and commitment therapy (Hayes, 2004).

MBSR outcome studies show improvements in physical and psychological functioning for individuals suffering from chronic pain (Kabat-Zinn, Lipworth, Burney, & Sellers, 1986; Randolph et al., 1999), in overall quality of life, stress reduction, and sleep quality for cancer patients (Carlson, Speca, Patel, & Goodey, 2004; Shapiro, Bootzin, Figueredo, Lopez, & Schwartz, 2003), in healing of psoriasis (Kabat-Zinn et al., 1998), in immune system functioning among HIV-positive patients (Robinson, Mathews, & Witek-Janusek, 2003), in reduction of pain, fatigue, and sleep disturbances associated with fibromyalgia (Weissbecker, et al., 2002), in symptom reduction among women with binge-eating disorder (Kristeller, Hallett, & Brendan, 1999), as well as decreases in anxiety and depression (Kabat-Zinn et al., 1992) and reduction in depressive relapse (Ma & Teasdale, 2004). A period of mindfulness meditation was shown to be more effective than distraction in reducing dysphoric mood among college students following a negative mood induction (Broderick, 2005). A recent meta-analysis (Grossman, Niemann, Schmidt & Walach, 2004) concluded that MBSR was an effective intervention for enhancing both physical and mental wellness and for improving coping with both day-to-day and more serious stressors.

Forgiveness

Part of the acceptance process must involve forgiveness of past hurts. Increasingly, forgiveness is being accorded more importance in therapeutic contexts as it is shown to contribute to physical and psychological features of well-being (McCullough & Witvliet, 2002). For example, consider this empirical study of the effects of forgiveness or lack of forgiveness on physiology. Witvliet, Ludwig and Vander Laan (2001) asked participants in this study to imagine a person who had harmed or mistreated them. Participants were then instructed to rehearse unforgiving feelings (like holding the grudge) for a brief period of time while physiological measurements were made. They were next instructed to practice forgiving responses (like empathizing with the offender by trying to take an alternative perspective on the offense) while the same assessments were taken. Blood pressure, facial tension, cardiovascular reactivity, arterial pressure and sympathetic nervous system arousal as measured by skin conductivity were all significantly higher in the unforgiving condition. Participants reported more negative mood (angry, sad, aroused, etc.) while being unforgiving. Furthermore, negative physiological effects of the period of "holding a grudge" as measured by cardiovascular and sympathetic nervous system indicators persisted into the subsequent stage of the experiment. This finding suggests that the physiological systems activated in the unforgiving state may "resist recovery (p. 122)", contribute to overall stress, and have implications for overall health.

Forgiveness does not involve excusing hurtful behavior, necessarily reconciling with the offender, suppressing one's pain or forgetting the offense. Rather, it involves a shift in thoughts, feelings and behaviors in relation to offenders in a more positive direction (McCollough, Pargament & Thoresen, 2000). It generally involves a long and gradual process of transforming the tendency to seek revenge and to let go of enmity. As Kornfield puts it, "Forgiveness means giving up all hope of a better past" (2002, p. 25).

Forgiveness therapy (Enright & Fitzgibbons, 2000) proposes a series of stages that map the process of forgiveness in a therapeutic setting. The first phase, uncovering, is spent in a thorough examination of the traumatic injury or event. Recognizing and confronting anger or shame, readjusting an old view of a "just world," and coming to terms with the injury are parts of this process. In phase two, the decision phase, injured clients face up to the realization that carrying the burden of rage or seeking revenge may be an unskillful resolution. Here the therapist attempts to motivate clients to see the benefits of forgiveness to physical and emotional well-being. Perhaps for the first time, forgiveness is seen as a possibility. In the work phase, clients might be asked to write about whom it is they wish to forgive. Reframing questions posed by the therapist, such as "What was it like for the offender when he or she was growing up?" encourage perspective taking and empathy, which may plant the seeds of compassion. The authors caution that compassion aids in the healing process but must unfold in its own time, so

therapists should not rush this process. Clients may also be asked to write about the impact that acceptance and forgiveness might have on their lives. In the last phase, called deepening, clients continue to construct a narrative to account for the painful experience, which allows the episode to become integrated into a meaningful life story. Sometimes, sharing one's story with others or working to help others who have been similarly hurt provides a therapeutic resolution.

Self-Compassion

Looking ahead toward the last of Erikson's psychosocial tasks, we see that everyone needs to come to terms with his or her own life story, regardless of the paths their lives have taken. "Coming to terms" may include forgiving ourselves for real or imagined offenses as well as forgiving those who might have hurt us. The fact that people are developmentally more inclined to take stock in midlife (Erikson, 1968) does not mean that reflection is nonexistent at other points in the life span. However, the salience of this theme in the "second half of life" (Jung, 1963) suggests that self-acceptance is truly a life's work. The world's great religions have all adopted some version of the "golden rule," to love both one's neighbor and oneself. The great philosophical traditions have also championed the values of love for all humanity. But what does it really mean to love oneself? Clearly, this advice has merit not only on theological or philosophical grounds. Self-acceptance offers many advantages for personal happiness, adjustment, and physical health. Empathy for others also makes relationships less confrontational and more satisfying. Perhaps those in the helping professions need to be particularly mindful of their own needs for self-care because they so often share in the emotional experiences of others.

A meditation practice, akin to those described earlier, can be useful to enhance positive affectivity by cultivating lovingkindness. *Lovingkindness* may be defined as an attitude that extends care and empathy toward self and others (Goleman, 2003). This should not be mistaken for some transient sentimental state. Rather it is the basis for a broad-based altruism and a strong positive regard for others. The lovingkindness exercise is essentially a way to practice benevolence directed first toward oneself and then toward friends, neutral acquaintances, and finally enemies. Often people find it easier to be compassionate toward others than toward themselves; indeed, practicing self-acceptance at an affective level may seem strange to many of us in the West.

Disrespect for ourselves and disregard for our basic physical, social, and emotional needs underlies many self-destructive behaviors that take their toll on health and happiness. To cultivate this attitude of compassion in this way, the person first concentrates his attention, repeats inwardly a set of phrases "May I be happy; May I be peaceful; May I be healthy and strong" and so forth, as he generates the emotions of compassion. Recent research using neuroimaging techniques has shown that such practice produces long-lasting alterations in brain function in areas related to development of positive affective states (Lutz, Greischan, Rawlings, Ricard, & Davidson, 2004). Positive practices like these, that help us manage stress and regulate mood, are beneficial for clients and helpers alike. One broad implication we can draw from work in this area is that well-being is not just the "absence" of disorder, experienced only some of the time by a fortunate few. Instead, it involves the deliberate cultivation of those elements that make life worthwhile.

SUMMARY

Life Satisfaction: What Is a Well-Lived Life?

1. Subjective well-being, an individual's overall satisfaction with life and general happiness, is usually measured using questionnaires or interviews asking people to rate their lives or their feelings about their lives on a continuum, say from "very happy" to "very unhappy."
2. The well-being of individuals and of national populations is correlated with wealth only weakly. People who are poor report less well-being than those who are not, but after a certain basic level of income is attained, greater wealth is not strongly associated with greater happiness.
3. The American paradox, which characterizes many wealthy nations, is that as income and standard of living have increased steadily in recent decades, so have emotional problems such as depression. There may be several reasons, among which are that pursuit of material gain may put many people on a hedonic treadmill. Because they expect more money to make them happier, when it doesn't they feel compelled to further pursue material gain. Also, the lifestyles made possible by affluence tend to reduce the need for support from others, limiting opportunities for others to demonstrate genuine friendship. Finally, having wealth means having control. When that control can't create a "perfect" life, people may blame themselves, fostering depression.
4. Some personality characteristics, like extraversion and neuroticism, are strongly correlated with subjective well-being measures.
5. Social relationships appear to be essential to well-being. Giving and receiving social support are both important. People who are happy have better social relationships, but social relationships also play a causal role in creating happiness. Having friends, confidants, and marriage partners are all linked to well-being.
6. Work also is linked to happiness. People who feel generative report more well-being. Well-being is also associated with making progress toward goals and having opportunities to exercise skills.
7. People may have universal psychological needs that must be met to feel satisfied with life. Among those that have been suggested are needs for autonomy, competence, and relatedness. When such needs are met, people are thought to experience psychological well-being (also called eudaemonic well-being) which is distinguished from subjective well-being (also called hedonic well-being).

Although the two kinds of well-being are closely correlated, psychological well-being specifically involves feeling a sense of purpose, growth, and mastery.

8. Many theorists propose that having a sense that one's life has meaning (situational meaning) that is linked to the meaning or purpose of the universe and of human kind (universal meaning) is an important ingredient in well-being.

Stress, Coping, and Well-Being in Midlife

9. Many stressors affect people at midlife including awareness of limited time left to live, accumulated losses related to aging, and increased responsibilities and obligations in the family and at work that can cause role strain. What determines resilience in this stage of life? Among the protective factors identified in one large-scale study of adults were childhood factors (e.g., educated parents), social attachments (e.g., confidants and spouses), stable employment, and positive social comparisons with parents and siblings.
10. Two kinds of stressors are life events, which are discrete events, and daily hassles, which are more chronic. The cumulative effects of chronic stressors on the body is called allostatic load. People can experience gradually increasing sensitivity to stressful triggers, called kindling-behavioral sensitization.
11. Diathesis-stress models suggest that some individuals have specific vulnerabilities (diatheses) to a disorder under the right stress conditions. This would explain, for example, why only some people develop posttraumatic stress disorder after experiencing traumatic events.
12. Some people experience posttraumatic growth, positive psychological change after struggling with difficult circumstances. Personality traits like extraversion and openness are linked to this kind of change.
13. In response to stress, the body mobilizes energy to enhance functions that would support fight or flight, such as motor and sensory abilities. In response to disease, the immune system also mobilizes energy to fight pathogens. The two systems direct energy to different ends; when under stress, the body inhibits functions that support the immune system, causing immunosuppression.
14. The new field of psychoneuroimmunology, the study of interactions between the central nervous system, the immune system and behavior, indicates that the brain influences the immune system, and the immune system

also influences the brain, playing a role, for example, in depression.

15. Management of stress, or coping, has often been conceptualized as constituting binary approaches, such as problem-focused versus emotion-focused coping. But instead of mutually exclusive categories of coping behavior, there may be many ways of coping that work differently depending on the situation. At midlife, stress may be largely a function of loss. To deal with loss, people act in ways to conserve or rebuild their resources.

16. Among the ways of conserving or rebuilding resources is to cultivate a sense of self-efficacy, mastery, and control.

Cultivation of positive affectivity, and reduction of negative affectivity, is also beneficial. The left prefrontal cortex is activated during the experience of positive emotions, and the right prefrontal cortex is activated during periods of negative emotion. More negative affectivity is associated with greater reactivity to stress. Immune responses are less compromised during stress when positive emotions are increased. Increasingly, practicing a positive emotional style is seen as an antidote to health-compromising emotions like anger and hostility. A study of meditation, for example, which increases positive feelings and left prefrontal cortex activation, found that it improves immune system response as well.

CASE STUDY

David is a 52-year-old White male who has spent the last 24 years in the human resource field. Most recently, he held the position of supervisor in the billing department of a mid-sized hospital in a rural state. He worked hard to obtain a master's degree while on the job at the hospital and always had high aspirations for himself professionally. David has three children from his first marriage which ended in divorce. His first wife Anne, who is 52, works as a preschool teacher in another part of the state. Their children's ages are 17, 20, and 22. Both older children started to attend college but may have to drop out temporarily due to financial difficulties. David feels that it is his responsibility to support his children's education, and he has been paying as much of their tuition as he can afford. David and his second wife live in a new, but modest home in a community on the outskirts of the state capital close to David's job. David's second wife, Sandy, has twin 15-year-old boys. One of the twins has a serious learning disability and needs extra tutoring and a great deal of parent support to keep up academically. Sandy works part time in a department store to be home to help her sons.

Recently, the hospital system that employs David merged with a large network of medical providers to cut costs and use resources more efficiently. David's job at the hospital is becoming more complicated, requiring more and more processing of information that involves advanced computer technology. At a recent professional meeting, David learned from others in his network that many jobs were being cut and many tasks redistributed to the employees that remained. David feels that this has already happened in his workplace.

He has noted a dramatic increase in the amount of paperwork required and a distinct decrease in the time allotted to meet deadlines. His supervisory responsibilities have expanded to include workers from another unit that merged with his own in a major departmental realignment. David's direct supervisor will be retiring soon, and David will be a candidate for that position. He knows that this promotion would mean more income, but it would also mean even more work responsibility. David now spends his weekends going to the office to catch up on tasks. He is not as available as he once was to spend time with his children and this has caused some problems in his relationship with his wife.

David has recently begun to suffer from significant pain in his lower back that he believes might have resulted from a minor traffic accident. The pain keeps him from sleeping well and has contributed to his feeling more "on edge" during the day. David's physician prescribes two medications to help him sleep better and reduce anxiety. David has begun to use alcohol when he comes home at night to "calm himself down" as well.

Discussion Questions

1. Identify the risks and protective factors that are present in David's life story. What information, not presented here, would be helpful to know if you were to make a more comprehensive list of risks and protections?

2. How do you conceptualize David's situation and what treatment approach would you take if he were to come to you for counseling?

JOURNAL QUESTIONS

1. What is your stereotypic view of midlife? Does it or does it not conform to what you have read in this chapter? Explain how your thinking about midlife might have changed.

2. What is your view of a well-lived life? What are your priorities? How do you plan to realize your goals?

3. What does spirituality mean to you? What does "faith" mean to you? Are they the same?

4. What do you imagine will be the way you will deal with the expected and unplanned stressors of your own midlife period?

KEY TERMS

subjective well-being
experience-sampling
   method (ESM)
day reconstruction
   method (DRM)
hedonic well-being
eudaemonic well-being
psychological well-being
self-determination theory

autonomy
competence
relatedness
role strain
life events
daily hassles
allostatic load
kindling-behavioral
   sensitization

diathesis-stress
diatheses
posttraumatic stress
   disorder (PTSD)
posttraumatic growth
cytokines
immunosuppression
endorphins
psychoneuroimmunology

negative affectivity
behavioral-inhibition
   system
positive affectivity
behavioral facilitation
   system
mindfulness

Now go to our Companion Website to assess your understanding of chapter content with Multiple Choice Questions, apply comprehension in Essay Questions, and broaden your knowledge of development with related Web Links.

CHAPTER 15

Gains and Losses in Late Adulthood

In Chapter 13, we described successful development as "the relative maximization of gains and the minimization of losses" (Baltes, 1997, p. 367). In life span developmental theory, we are developing successfully when we are able to grow (acquiring new abilities or skills), when we can maintain our previous capacities, perhaps restoring them if they are temporarily lost, or when we find ways to regulate losses by accepting them and reorganizing the ways that we function. As people move into old age, in their 60s and 70s, or into old-old age, in their 80s and 90s, both gains and losses continue, but losses may considerably outweigh gains. "Even in young people's lives, not everything goes well. Old age is a genuinely difficult situation with lots of sadness and frustration. Many things do not go well" (Pipher, 1999, p. 26). How can the elderly effectively manage the ever-increasing losses they experience? For example, can their developmental trajectory be a positive one when they experience multiple health problems or find themselves in chronic pain? An important focus of this chapter will be to identify the means by which elderly adults manage their lives and the extent to which they can grow, maintain themselves, and regulate their losses.

Clearly, different people manage their late-life losses with varying degrees of success. But you may be surprised to learn that for a majority of us, successful development is what we can expect for much of our old age. At age 81, Helen still maintains her job in a bookstore. As one of the oldest siblings in a large working-class family, she learned early to value hard work and has always been active and productive. Her job provides her with opportunities to maintain her skills as well as the chance to learn new ones, such as the new computerized system her company uses to inventory material. Helen is fortunate in that her health is good, aside from some problems with arthritis that slow down her movement. She recognizes that she must regulate her activity now more than before, reducing extraneous activities so she can be well rested and prepared for work, thus optimizing her performance there. She is an avid crossword puzzle fan, her recipe for staying mentally active. When she noticed herself becoming more forgetful, she compensated by writing notes to herself and establishing and following set routines. She travels and volunteers less these days, compared to what she did years ago when her husband was alive. Now she chooses to spend more time with her family and has eliminated activities she considers unnecessary. She knows what she can do and what gives her a sense of satisfaction. Helen's adaptation is a good example of how a person can cope successfully with the challenges of aging.

The process of healthy adaptation to increasing loss can be thought of as effective coping. For this reason, investigators often look at mental health and life satisfaction to gauge the degree to which elderly people are successfully developing. The findings are heartening: "The inherent paradox of aging . . . [is] . . . that despite loss and physical decline, adults enjoy good mental health and positive life satisfaction well into old age" (Carstensen & Charles, 1998).

In what follows, we will first review the nature of the losses and challenges that typically confront people in old age. Then we will look at the ways in which the elderly cope with these challenges, paying special attention to the processes that seem most important for the lifelong experience of psychological well-being.

AGING WELL

Challenge and Loss in Late Adulthood

PHYSICAL CHANGE

We saw in Chapter 13 that a gradual decline from peak functioning is characteristic of most physiological systems beginning as early as age 30. By late adulthood, the losses are usually noticeable and have required some adjustment in expectations or lifestyle. A lifelong runner who still entered marathons at age 62 remarked, "At 30, my goal was to win. At 50, I celebrated every race that I finished. Today, I'm delighted to be at the starting line."

Maintaining good health becomes more challenging with age, as the immune system becomes progressively less effective in staving off cancer and infections and as the cardiovascular, respiratory, and organ systems function less adequately. Chronic illness and the need for more vigilant health maintenance therefore increase dramatically with age. Age shifts in the leading causes of death illustrate these changing health concerns. In the United States, accidents are the leading cause of death in adults up to age 45. But at 45, heart disease and cancer take over as the leading causes of death (U.S. Bureau of the Census, 1993, 1998). People of any age can suffer from acute or chronic illnesses, such as cancer, heart problems, diabetes, and so on. But the risk of these illnesses climbs dramatically and steadily in our later years (U.S. Department of Health and Human Services, 1998).

Among the continuing declines of old age are two that are common and often especially debilitating. First are increasing sensory deficits (see Chapter 13). Changes in the visual system can be particularly important for one daily activity: driving. A number of aging changes make driving more difficult, including loss of visual acuity, loss of sensitivity to movement in the periphery, increased recovery time after exposure to glare, and reduced night vision. However, these changes do not contribute significantly to accident rates until people reach their mid-70s, when driving fatalities climb to the same level as that for 17-year-olds (Whitbourne, 2002).

A second important decline in older adults is the onset of pain, stiffness, and swelling of joints and surrounding tissues that we call arthritis. After 65, about half of women and about 40% of men experience the most common form, osteoarthritis, which involves the thinning, fraying, and cracking of cartilage at the ends of bones. Ordinarily, this cartilage helps protect our joints from the friction of bone to bone contact. As cartilage degenerates and other joint changes occur, such as the growth of bony spurs and modifications in connective tissues, joints may stiffen and swell. The upshot is often pain and reduced movement. Being overweight or

Attention to health maintenance is an important aspect of successful coping in late adulthood.

overusing a particular joint (for example, the knees in sports such as running and tennis) can contribute to susceptibility, but ordinary degeneration with age is part of the problem. Osteoarthritis can range from being a painful nuisance to being a source of major disability, affecting the performance of simple tasks, such as opening a jar or walking, as well as more complex skills such as playing the piano or swinging a golf club (Whitbourne, 2002).

COGNITIVE CHANGE

We have already seen that cognitive decline begins in middle adulthood, with gradual decrements in fluid intelligence, or in other words, in the mechanics of intellectual functioning. Processing speed slows and inhibitory functions decline with age. In middle adulthood, such declines may limit the efficiency of working memory operations, such as learning and problem solving, but these effects seem to be balanced by the maintenance or advancement of crystallized intelligence or pragmatics, so that, for example, semantic memory is enriched with age.

But what happens when people move into their 60s—or into their 90s? Does crystallized intelligence begin to decline along with continuing losses in fluid intelligence? Longitudinal studies suggest that crystallized intelligence, as represented by measures of verbal ability and factual knowledge, for example, does not show average declines until about age 74, and the declines are modest thereafter (Schaie, 1996). Good health is a very important factor in these trends. It appears that the bulk of the average decline in the later decades is attributable to sensory and health problems (Backman, Small, Wahlin, & Larsson, 2000). Many old individuals show no declines, and some who have maintained good health actually continue to improve on crystallized intelligence measures. For example, in one longitudinal study of 70- to 100-year-olds vocabulary knowledge increased until age 90 and showed only slow declines thereafter (Singer, Verhaeghen, Ghisletta, Lindenberger, & Baltes, 2003).

Dementia. The importance of health to cognitive functioning in the elderly is revealed in research on **dementia** and on a phenomenon called **terminal drop**, or **terminal decline**. When cognitive functioning is so severely impaired that it affects our ability to relate to others and to manage our own daily activities, we are suffering from dementia. Many of us have seen the ravages of dementia in a relative or friend, and we worry that extreme memory loss and disorientation are the inevitable consequences of aging. But they are not. Normal aging does not lead to dementia, although the frequency of illnesses and conditions that cause dementia does increase with age. Among these, for example, are cardiovascular problems that limit the oxygen supply to the brain for some period of time. These include **cerebrovascular accidents**, or **strokes**, in which an artery serving the brain is either clogged or bursts. A single stroke can lead to acute onset of dementia; more typically, many minor strokes (**multi-infarct dementia**) can gradually do sufficient damage to cause dementia (see de la Torre, 1997).

Many diseases that affect the brain may eventually lead to dementia. The most common of these is **Alzheimer's disease (AD)**. Its prevalence increases with age such that it affects about 1% of 65-year-olds in the United States and about 20 to 25% of 85-year-olds (see Zarit & Zarit, 1998). There appear to be different forms of AD with different onsets and courses. Early-onset AD strikes 40- to 50-year-olds, ends in death after about 5 years, and clearly has a genetic contribution. Several forms of later-onset AD have been identified, some in which genetic contributions are clearly involved, and some in which the environment may play a greater role. Later-onset AD tends to take longer to run its course. In all forms of AD, extensive brain changes, often identified on autopsy, including the formation of **plaques**, clumps of insoluble protein that are damaging to neurons, and **tangles**, twisted filaments of another protein, which may interfere with communication between neurons and even cause cell death (see Dickson, 1997).

AD is diagnosed primarily by its clinical characteristics and by excluding other possible causes of dementia. In its early stages, it looks like absentmindedness: forgetting where you recently put something or forgetting something that happened in the last few days or the last few hours. More general confusion may follow, especially noticeable in the use of language. Common problems are rambling speech and word substitutions, such as saying "window" when the right word would be "door." People at this stage may be quite distressed by their memory loss,

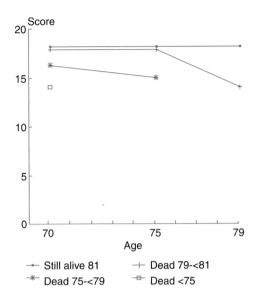

FIGURE 15.1

The Relationship Between Survival and Scores on an Intelligence Test of Verbal Meaning in a Longitudinal Study

Source: Figure from "Aging, behavior, and terminal decline" by S. Berg in *Handbook of the psychology of aging.* Fourth Edition, edited by James E. Birrens, et al., copyright 1996, Elsevier Science (USA), reproduced by permission of the publisher.

perhaps even paranoid if they frequently cannot remember what they have done or where they've put things, and they also assume that others are responsible. A relative of one of the authors, for example, would insist that people had entered her apartment and had turned on her TV when she wasn't looking. Others may become hostile in their frustration and confusion. In later stages, memory and language problems get worse, disorientation is extreme, and physical coordination is affected. Eventually, Alzheimer's patients, often mute and bedridden, need full-time care and supervision, and death is the outcome (see Whitbourne, 2002).

AD and other forms of dementia are not characteristic of the majority of elderly, although there is some suspicion that the formation of plaques and tangles may occur to some extent in all of us. Some environments seem to enhance or reduce AD rates. For example, lifelong education and intellectual stimulation seem to decrease the risk (Snowdon, 1997).

Terminal drop, or terminal decline, is just what it sounds like. As adults approach the end of their lives, between 6 months and 5 years prior to death, they may show a substantial decline in intellectual functioning as indicated by scores on intelligence tests (e.g., Berg, 1987; Lieberman, 1965). Figure 15.1 illustrates this finding from one set of longitudinal data. Terminal drop apparently reflects the individual's declining health status, which leads to "lessened ability to cope adequately with environmental demands because of lowered ability to integrate stimuli" (Berg, 1996, p. 326). Interestingly, people often seem to be able to detect in themselves whatever changes in health status are predictive of death. A number of studies have found that when older adults self-rate their health as "poor," they are much more likely to die within the next few years than when they rate their health as "excellent" (e.g., Idler & Kasl, 1991; Wolinsky & Johnson, 1992). Apparently, people often realize when they are going into decline (Berg, 1996).

Autobiographical Memory. One cognitive function that has particular significance for one's sense of self as well as for social interactions throughout the life span is called autobiographical memory. This is the remembered self, "representations of who we have been at various points in the past" (Fitzgerald, 1999, p. 143). It draws from several long-term memory systems (see Chapter 6 for an introduction to these systems). When we recall specific experiences in our lives we are calling on episodic memory; when we remember that we know some fact we're using our semantic memory; and when we remember how to do something we depend on our procedural memory. Autobiographical memory has often been treated as synonymous with episodic memory, which is a very important part of it, but our self-recollections are not episodic alone.

Autobiographical memory is important in many ways. It provides us with a "sense of identity in narrative form" (Fitzgerald, 1999, p. 143). It also is a source of information about social interactions that have worked and that have not worked for us in the past. Finally, when we draw on autobiographical memory to tell stories about ourselves to others, it helps us reveal and share ourselves, get closer to others, create impressions, even teach lessons (Fitzgerald, 1999; Hyman & Faries, 1992).

One stereotype that people often have about the aged is that they remember more about their early lives than about what has happened to them recently. Studies of autobiographical memory indicate that this belief is only partially true. Elderly people actually do remember their more recent experiences better than earlier experiences, although the stories that they tell about themselves are often well-rehearsed experiences from the distant past.

There are two very salient characteristics of self-memories for adults of all ages. One is recency: The strength of a memory declines the more time has passed since the memory was formed. That is, we are more likely to remember something that has happened to us recently than something that happened in the more distant past. For example, one way to study autobiographical memory is to say a word, like "dog," and ask a person to report a specific experience in his life that the word calls to mind. Regardless of the age of the respondent, half of all such cue-prompted memories will be from the most recent 12 months of his life. Eighty percent are from the most recent decade. "The remembered self is largely a now-self, not a distant-self," even for old people (Fitzgerald, 1999, p. 159).

This may sound a bit confusing, given that adults learn new information less efficiently with age. As we saw in Chapter 13, information in working memory is not as easily transferred to long-term memory at later ages. However, older people nonetheless do continue to learn, and newer memories are more readily retrieved than older memories.

However, a second salient feature of self-memories is a phenomenon that is ignominiously called "the bump." Regardless of age, adults' cue-prompted memories of the self from the young adult period (from about ages 18 to 22) are slightly but reliably overproduced. That is, more memories are produced from this era than we would predict on the basis of recency (see Figure 15.2). If we explore autobiographical memory in a different way, by asking adults to tell us about their flashbulb memories, nearly all of what they tell us comes from the bump era (e.g., Fitzgerald, 1988). Flashbulb memories in these studies are defined as recollections that are especially vivid and personally relevant. It appears that when people talk about memories that are intense and important to them, they draw very heavily on experiences from young adulthood, even in their old age. If we ask people to tell stories that they would include in a book about themselves, again, a disproportionate number of the narratives come from the bump era (Fitzgerald, 1992). Similar results come from studies in which people are asked to name the most memorable books they have read (Larsen, 2000), the songs they find most desirable to listen to (Holbrook & Schindler, 1989), or the films that help describe their era (Schulster, 1996). That is, the elderly

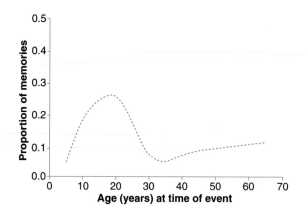

FIGURE 15.2

Proportion of Reported Flashbulb Memories (Vivid and Personally Important) by Age at Time of Event for Older Adults

Source: Figure adapted from "Autobiographical memory and social cognition. Development of the remembered self-adulthood" by J. M. Fitzgerald in *Social cognition and aging*, edited by Thomas M. Hess, copyright 1999, Elsevier Science (USA), reproduced by permission of the publisher.

refer more often to items from their young adulthood than from any other time of their lives. Fitzgerald (1999) argues that the strength of the bump phenomenon for people's most important memories and preferences reveals the significance of late adolescence and young adulthood as a period of intense self-development. However, the recency effect in cue-prompted memory research makes it very clear that people continue to add to their self-stories throughout their adulthood and that healthy older people have their recent past available to them despite some declines in learning efficiency.

STEREOTYPES AND AGE DISCRIMINATION

Among the challenges that elderly people face are stereotyped attitudes and responses from others based on age category rather than on actual characteristics. An *age stereotype* can be defined as a set of widely held beliefs about the characteristics of older people. These knowledge structures or schemas can lead to relatively uniform treatment of older people regardless of their own individual characteristics and are thought to account for certain discriminatory or demeaning practices, such as mandatory retirement and patronizing talk (Hummert, 1999).

Research on the content of old-age schemas in Western cultures has identified seven common stereotypes. Four of these are negative, such as "severely impaired" or "shrew/curmudgeon," but three are more positive, such as "perfect grandparent" (Hummert, Garstka, Shaner, & Strahm, 1994). A description of each is provided in Table 15.1. Facial features associated with aging play a significant role in activating these stereotypes. The older people look, the more likely they are to be described in ways that fit a negative stereotype. In one study, participants were asked to match the photographs of people perceived to be in their 60s, 70s, or 80s with trait sets describing either positive or negative stereotypes (Hummert, Garstka, & Shaner, 1997). The older the appearance of the person in the picture, the more likely participants were to match the picture with a negative stereotype. Sex of the pictured person played a role as well. For example, pictures of unsmiling women were more likely to be matched with a negative stereotype than pictures of unsmiling men.

Because of age stereotypes, the very same behavior in younger versus older individuals is perceived differently. For example, the seriousness and the causes of a memory failure, such as forgetting the name of a new acquaintance, tend to be perceived quite differently depending on whether the failure is ascribed to a 30-year-old or to a 70-year-old. When younger adults forget, the cause is more likely to be seen as transient and external, such as "that's a hard thing to remember." When older people forget, the cause is more likely to be seen as something stable and internal, such as having a poor memory (see Erber & Prager, 1999, for a review of this work).

TABLE 15.1 Traits Associated with Stereotypes of Older Adults

Stereotype	Traits
Negative	
Severely impaired	Slow-thinking, incompetent, feeble, inarticulate, incoherent, senile
Despondent	Depressed, sad, hopeless, afraid, neglected, lonely
Shrew/curmudgeon	Complaining, ill-tempered, demanding, stubborn, bitter, prejudiced
Recluse	Quiet, timid, naive
Positive	
Golden ager	Active, capable, sociable, independent, happy, interesting
Perfect grandparent	Loving, supportive, understanding, wise, generous, kind
John Wayne conservative	Patriotic, conservative, determined, proud, religious, nostalgic

Source: From "A social cognitive perspective on age stereotypes" by M. L. Hummert in *Social cognition and aging*, edited by Thomas M. Hess, copyright 1999, Elsevier Science (USA), reproduced by permission of the publisher.

When age stereotypes are triggered, the quality of social interactions can be affected. For example, people, including clinicians, often use "patronizing talk" when speaking with an elderly person. This kind of conversation has many characteristics: simplified vocabulary and sentence structure, slower pace, careful articulation, an overly familiar or overbearing tone, and disapproving, controlling, or superficial content (e.g., Hummert & Ryan, 1996; Hummert, Shaner, Garstka, & Henry, 1998). Hummert (1999) has argued that such talk is probably grounded in stereotypic ideas about declining memory and hearing abilities in the aged.

It appears, then, that aging brings with it stereotypic reactions and expectations from others, which seem likely to interfere with satisfying social interactions. Researchers have found that when older individuals perceive themselves as the target of age discrimination, their sense of well-being is negatively affected (Gartska, Schmitt, Branscombe, & Hummert, 2004).

Some research also indicates that the conversational styles of older people often include features that may cue stereotypes. For example, older people are sometimes prone to making "painful self-disclosures" to relative strangers about illnesses, loss of a loved one, and other personal problems (e.g., Coupland, Coupland, Giles, Henwood, & Wiemann, 1988). For the elderly, self-disclosures may serve self-presentational goals, such as indicating resilience, but for younger listeners they tend to strengthen stereotypes of the elderly as weak or lonely. Thus, misinterpretations of some characteristic behaviors of older adults probably contribute to stereotypic responses from others (Hummert, 1999).

THE SHRINKING SOCIAL CONVOY

Aging brings with it the more and more frequent experience of social loss. Friends, partners, and relatives may die or suffer from debilitating disorders such as Alzheimer's disease. In one study of 85-year-olds, 59% of the men and 42% of the women had lost a friend to death in the past year (Johnson & Troll, 1994). But illness and death are not the only sources of social loss. When people retire they lose daily contact with their colleagues at work. If the elderly person is constrained by limited finances or health problems, opportunities to visit others or to be part of club or other social activities may be reduced. Adult children may move to geographically distant locations. The elderly may leave behind neighbors and shopkeepers of long acquaintance if they move from a larger home to an apartment, an adult community, or an assisted-living facility. The shrinking of the social network and the pain of bereavement are problems that increase in late adulthood (Rook, 2000).

In Chapter 10, we noted that adolescents are largely segregated into age-bound communities that share language, interests, and a dress code, among other things. Mary Pipher (1999) proposes that the physical, cognitive, and social changes of late life segregate older people as well, in ways that are important for helpers to understand. As we have noted, older people often live in circumstances that separate them from their families and their communities, often because poor health makes independent living impossible. Although these arrangements may provide the benefit of day-to-day care and companionship, they may also prevent older people from interacting with members of younger generations and deprive them of opportunities for service to others. Thus, some of their own developmental needs may be going unmet. "The old look for their existential place. They ask, 'How did my life matter? Was my time well spent? What did I mean to others?' " (p. 15). Social segregation creates islands of culture that discourage intergenerational bonding and may make older people feel less valued and useful to others.

The elderly are restricted in other, less obvious ways. Older individuals' use of language (e.g., "depression" meaning a period of economic downturn rather than a mental health problem) positions them within a cultural group or cohort that is separated from younger generations. Many elderly people also feel segregated from society because it simply moves too fast. Pipher (1999) recalls the adjustments she needed to make when interviewing her older clients:

> I learned to let the phone ring fifteen times. I learned to wait at doors five minutes after I rang the bell. I had to slow down to work with the old. Their conversation is less linear, and there are pauses and repetitions. Points are made via stories; memories lead to more memories. . . . When I walked the old I walked slowly and held hands at intersections or when sidewalks were slick. . . . Because their bones break more easily, the old are afraid of falling . . . a broken hip can mean the end of independent living. (p. 27)

In the next section, we will consider how older adults face these and many of the other losses and challenges that we have described. Later in this chapter, we will take a special look at bereavement across the life span, with particular attention to how the elderly cope with the deaths of those close to them and with their own dying process.

Maintaining Well-Being in the Face of Loss: Successful Aging

How do aging adults adapt to, or cope with, the increasing losses they face? Baltes and Baltes (e.g., Baltes, 1987; Baltes & Baltes, 1990; Baltes et al., 1998) suggest that three processes are key to successful development at any age, and especially in the later years. The first is **selection**. This is a process of narrowing our goals and limiting the domains in which we expend effort. It is not difficult to see that selection is important at any time in the life cycle. For example, at 20, Len selected a career, limiting the possible directions his life could take but also enabling him to achieve high levels of expertise and productivity by focusing his training and practice on career-related skills. At 62, Len selected family life instead of career. Because he felt his stamina waning somewhat, and despite the many satisfactions he still gained from his work, he decided to retire earlier than originally planned so that he could give more energy to developing relationships with his young grandchildren.

The second process is **optimization**, finding ways to enhance the achievement of remaining goals or finding environments that are enhancing. Len, for example, traded in his sporty two-door coupe for a larger sedan so that he could take the grandchildren on excursions to movies or museums. He also moved from a small apartment in the city to a place in the suburbs, closer to his children and having amenities such as a yard where he could amuse his grandchildren.

The final process that contributes to successful development is **compensation**. When a loss of some kind prevents the use of one means to an end, we can compensate by finding another means. For example, by age 74, as Len's eyesight began to fail, chauffeuring his grandchildren was no longer possible. He now entertains the youngest ones at his home most of the time, planning special events such as "video marathons" and backyard camping "trips."

Baltes provides the following real-life example of successful development in old age:

> When the concert pianist Arthur Rubinstein, as an 80-year-old, was asked in a television interview how he managed to maintain such a high level of expert piano playing, he hinted at the coordination of three strategies. First, Rubinstein said that he played fewer pieces (selection); second, he indicated that he now practiced these pieces more often (optimization); and third, he said that to counteract his loss in mechanical speed he now used a kind of impression management such as introducing slower play before fast segments, so to make the latter appear faster (compensation). (Baltes et al., 1998, p. 1055)

The three combined processes of successful development are called **selective optimization with compensation** (e.g., Baltes & Baltes, 1990; Marsiskei, Lang, Baltes, & Baltes, 1995). Other theorists have described adaptation processes in similar ways and have also attempted to specify the kinds of motivations that might drive such processes. As we saw in Chapter 14, Ryan and Deci (2000) proposed in what's called self-determination theory that people are motivated by needs for *autonomy, competence,* and *relatedness.* These basic psychological needs are said to motivate our adaptation efforts at any age (e.g., Ryan & Deci, 2000; Ryan & LaGuardia, 2000). Autonomy is defined as being in control of oneself, that is, feeling that one's behavior is congruent with one's "true self," meaning that it is intrinsically motivated. What is especially pertinent here to understanding old age is that autonomy is not the same thing as independence. A person can be dependent on others for much of her care, as a result of poor health or disability, for example, but can still feel autonomous if she has set the goals. Several studies of nursing home residents, who are clearly dependent on others for physical care, indicate that residents' vitality, life satisfaction, and psychological adjustment are linked to the extent to which the policies of the home are respectful of the residents' rights to choose their religious practices, daily activities, and approaches to self-care (e.g., Kasser & Ryan, 1999; Vallerand & O'Connor, 1989).

A second basic need, according to self-determination theory, is for competence, defined as "feeling effective in one's interactions with the social environment and experiencing opportunities to exercise and express one's capacities" (Ryan & LaGuardia, 2000, p. 150). The feeling of competence comes with finding ways of achieving goals that are self-endorsed. Meeting goals set by others, then, will not satisfy this need. Apparently, feelings of competence depend more on whether one's personally identified goals of the moment are being effectively managed than on whether a person can do all or more than he ever was capable of doing.

Consider Bernard, a retired social studies teacher, who spent his early and middle adulthood working in a small rural town. Always a scholar of history and economics, he was able to share his expertise in these areas with generations of high school students. He is now retired and lives in another part of the country. Although he no longer teaches, he has found other outlets for his energies. He expresses his interest in athletics and his commitment to good health in a daily game of golf, although his experience with heart disease and a recent stroke caused him to reduce his exercise regimen for a period of time while he recovered. Bernard also puts his expertise about the stock market, a subject he taught in high school, to good use: He invests wisely and plans to help support his grandchildren's higher education. He also keeps well informed about the state of current affairs, serving as a resource for his family on matters of history. At 82, Bernard has coped well with his losses and physical limitations by identifying and working toward those self-endorsed goals that are meaningful to him.

Finally, relatedness is considered a basic need. People need to feel that they are important to others, valued enough to be sensitively and responsively cared for, from infancy onward. In this view, even though social interactions may change greatly over the life span, the processes that create feelings of well-being and security in the earliest attachments do not change with age (Ryan & LaGuardia, 2000). Some research on widowhood seems consistent with this idea. For married adults, relatedness needs have been found to be met in large part by spouses, who serve as supportive confidants and companions (e.g., Connidis & Davies, 1992). Widowed adults are more likely to adjust effectively to their loss if close relatives, especially children, are available to meet their relatedness needs. Friends, including new friends, can eventually meet these needs, but in the initial phases of widowhood there is added value in the care provided by children, perhaps because the newly widowed person feels her relatedness needs so sharply undercut, and her significance in the lives of her children is more certain (see Rook & Schuster, 1996; Stylianos & Vachon, 1993).

The degree to which basic needs for autonomy, competence, and relatedness are met substantially determines a person's sense of well-being and life satisfaction, according to self-determination theory (e.g., Ryan & Deci, 2000). Several theorists argue that whatever challenges we face in meeting our needs, there are two broad types of strategies that people use to control their destinies. Heckhausen (e.g., Heckhausen, 1999; Schultz & Heckhausen, 1996) refers to primary and secondary control strategies. When our control efforts are attempts to affect the immediate environment beyond ourselves, we are exerting **primary control**. The growth of competencies of all kinds serves primary control functions and contributes to feelings of mastery and self-esteem. When we choose to develop some competencies and not others (that is, when we engage in selection, such as choosing a career) we are using a primary control strategy. When new retirees freely choose and plan their retirements, they are using primary control strategies (see Box 15.1).

From the perspective of self-determination theory, exercising primary control could serve autonomy, competence, and/or relatedness needs. **Secondary control** generally refers to our attempts to change ourselves. We are using secondary control strategies when, for example, we change our aspirations and goals because we cannot do everything we used to do or when we deny or minimize the importance of our needs after failing to achieve some end.

> Both primary and secondary control may involve cognition and action, although primary control is almost always characterized in terms of behavior engaging the external world, whereas secondary control is predominantly characterized in terms of cognitive processes localized within the individual. (Schultz & Heckhausen, 1996, p. 708)

Box 15.1 | *Navigating the Transition to Retirement*

Beverly, a counseling psychologist and community activist, began to think about her retirement in earnest when she was 57 years old, after a bout with cancer. She recuperated well and her prognosis was good, but the sudden confrontation with ill health helped her to see that she might not always be able to work. Until then, she had vaguely assumed she would work until she dropped. Indeed, at first, she couldn't imagine her life without the challenge of a full schedule of diverse clients and community speaking engagements. But her illness led her to examine her goals for the future more carefully. She decided that in time she would like to reduce her work commitments to have time for other interests. She had always wanted to explore her artistic talent, and when her long-time partner retired, they both hoped to have more time and energy to pursue the activities they enjoyed together, especially international travel. By the age of 65, Beverly felt she was ready to make the change. She stopped taking new clients and reduced her speaking engagements to one or fewer a month. She began thinking of herself as a retiree.

Most modern adults, both men and women, have been part of the workforce for 30 or more years by the time they retire. How do they navigate the sometimes dramatic transition from being a worker to being a retiree?

Not everyone who can retire chooses to do so. And when people retire (defined by *Webster's* dictionary as "withdrawal from one's position or occupation") the strategies people devise for making the shift are quite diverse. Nancy Schlossberg, a retired counselor herself, identified multiple paths from an interview study of 100 retirees. Some were "continuers" who continued to use their work skills part time or in different settings. Beverly is a continuer; she maintains a small client roster and continues her community activities at a reduced level. "Involved spectators" keep a hand in their previous work but adopt some new role. Schlossberg herself is an example of this category. A former counseling professor, she has become an author and consultant who applies her counseling knowledge to developing guidelines for retirees. "Adventurers" leave behind their old work skills and develop new talents or skills, sometimes taking on a new job. "Easy gliders" try to keep their time unscheduled. They seem especially comfortable with the flexibility they have without work or other regular commitments. "Searchers" in Schlossberg's study have not yet found a path that works for them, but see themselves in a trial-and-error phase. "Retreaters" seem to give up on finding a satisfactory lifestyle and become depressed (Dittman, 2004; Schlossberg, 2004).

Some of the diversity in Schlossberg's findings may reflect not only different pathways of retirement but also different stages. Atchley (1976) argued that adjustment to retirement follows a typical progression for many people. Stage 1, honeymoon, is a time when people focus on the pleasures of being free from the constraints of old schedules, dress codes, and other work demands. In Stage 2, disenchantment occurs when people begin to experience an emotional "letdown" as they face the day-to-day realities of retirement, such as separation from work colleagues, uncertainties about how to feel competent and in control, a sense of diminished generativity and meaningfulness, new tensions that may arise with one's partner, financial concerns, and perhaps, boredom. Stage 3, reorientation, can be a time of active trial and error. The retiree seeks solutions for the problems that retirement presents and tries strategies for building a satisfactory life. In Stage 4, stability is achieved. The retiree finds a functional path that seems to work. Life span theorists would say that *selective optimization with compensation* is achieved. Finally, Stage 5 is termination, the end-of-life transition, when the individual's health declines and she becomes dependent on others for her care.

Research suggests that Atchley's stage descriptions do capture some predictable phases of retirement for many individuals. But there are substantial individual differences in the experience as well. In addition, there may be several cycles of reorientation and stability, with the same individual renegotiating her retirement strategy several times as her life continues to change with the death of a partner, shifting health status, financial changes, and so on. The longer we live, the more cycles we are likely to experience.

In a recent longitudinal study of retirees, Reitzes and Mutran (2004) found general support for the idea that retirement is a dynamic, and to some degree, stagelike process. Satisfaction was high after 6 months (honeymoon), but had declined after a year (disenchantment) and had increased again after 2 years (reorientation and stability). They also identified a number of factors that impact how well people adjust to the retirement transition both in the honeymoon stage and thereafter. They assessed 800 men and women who were between the ages of 58 and 64 and who were employed full time (at least 35 hours per week) as the study began. The participants represented a random sample of people in this age range living in the Raleigh–Durham–Chapel Hill, North Carolina metropolitan area, so the sample was diverse with respect to race and socioeconomic status. The participants completed an initial screening, and they were tracked with follow-up phone calls until they retired. About 600 of the original sample had retired within 5 years. Those who were willing to continue the study were reassessed at 6 months, 1 year, and 2 years postretirement.

In addition to providing information on income, pension eligibility, health status, marital status, and so on, at every assessment period the participants completed a questionnaire designed to measure their attitudes toward retirement. At the preretirement assessment, they also completed measures of their self-esteem, the social roles they filled in their current lives (e.g., parent, spouse, widow/widower, divorcee, etc.), and their "friend identity," which captured how they viewed themselves in the friend role. The participant rated herself as a friend on a five-point scale, from (1) passive to (5) active, from (1) anxious to (5) confident, and from (1) unsuccessful to (5) successful. The researchers also collected information on the participants' retirement experience, like how much retirement planning the participants had done preretirement, what reasons they had for retirement, whether they continued working in any capacity during retirement, and so on.

Reitzes and Mutran found little difference between men and women or among different socioeconomic groups with regard to the basic ingredients of a successful retirement. Several factors at preretirement were strong predictors of positive attitudes toward retirement both early in retirement and later: pension eligibility, high self-esteem, and a positive friend identity. Not surprisingly, pension eligibility allows a degree of financial security that reduces some of the stress of the shift to retirement. As Reitzes and Mutran suggest, individuals with a strong sense of self-worth and who feel confident about their relationships with friends probably are better able to organize and structure new opportunities with confidence. High self-esteem helps people be optimistic that they will be successful in new activities and pursuits. A positive friend identity would seem to be especially valuable when release from work constraints provides more time for interactions with friends.

Some other factors were very helpful for ensuring a happy honeymoon phase: being in control of the decision to retire (that is, doing so voluntarily), and approaching retirement with a plan of action. People who felt that they had no choice but to retire, because of the conditions of their employment or because of ill health, were not as happy as others in the 1st year of retirement. The same was true for people who had not carefully considered what they would do in retirement. These individuals were less satisfied at the start, but with time their situations tended to improve, and they were often doing as well as other retirees after 2 years.

One retiree provides a good example of some of these factors at work, and of the typical stages that many retirees experience. Jack just plunged into retirement optimistically with no plan but his usual belief that he could "handle it." For a while he enjoyed finishing some carpentry projects he had never had time for and some travel. But he was deep into disillusionment within a few months. He missed the opportunity to interact with colleagues and he missed the status he had achieved in his work life. With some help from a counselor, he identified the problems and mapped out some alternative solutions. He chose to begin consulting on a part-time basis (often voluntarily for nonprofit organizations), which brought him in touch with a wider range of people and helped him feel generative. At 72, Jack still enjoys good health, and after 4 years of retirement he believes that this is the best time of his life.

When primary control efforts fail or we suffer losses that we cannot overcome, secondary controls are likely to become important. Schultz and Heckhausen indicate that our repertoire of both primary and secondary control strategies will increase with age until late midlife but that the sheer weight of late-life declines will make primary control decline as well, so that people are likely to use more secondary control strategies in old age. Heckhausen (1997) found, for example, that adults in their 60s demonstrated more flexibility in adjusting their goals than adults in their 20s. When young, middle-aged, and elderly adults were asked to state their five most important goals and plans for the next 5 years, there was a clear shift in aspirations across age (Heckhausen, 1997). Elderly people had fewer aspirations regarding work, finances, and family and more aspirations related to health, community, and leisure pursuits than young adults. Heckhausen argues that these shifts reflect the fact that older people generally have less primary control potential over work, finances, and family. They therefore shift their goals in a compensatory way to those over which they may be able to take some primary control. This appears to be exactly the kind of coping that helped Bernard, the retired teacher we described earlier, continue to meet his needs for competence as he became older.

On the whole, how well do people in old age adapt to the challenges of late life? As we suggested earlier in this chapter, quite well! Ryff and Keyes (1995) analyzed measures of six dimensions of well-being from interviews with 1,108 adults. The responses of young (25 to 29), middle-aged (30 to 64), and old (65 or over) adults were compared, and several measures were found to increase over age. Old adults scored higher on a measure of positive relationships than both younger groups. They scored as well as the middle-aged and higher than the young adults on measures of environmental mastery and autonomy, and they scored as well as both younger groups on self-acceptance. Older adults did score lower than the younger groups on two dimensions of well-being: purpose in life and personal growth. Perhaps as a person leaves behind the arenas in which generativity is most directly expressed—work, parenting, and community service—opportunities to feel useful or to grow seem diminished. This conclusion is consistent with findings that elderly women who continue to care for a disabled adult child report a much greater sense of purpose in life than elderly women who do not have such responsibilities (Kling, Seltzer, & Ryff, 1997). Generativity issues aside, it does appear that, overall, aging and a sense of well-being are often quite compatible and that some aspects of well-being actually improve in old age. Note, however, that longitudinal data are needed to be sure that some of these effects are not attributable to cohort differences.

Are there any specific behavioral characteristics of elderly people that might benefit their general well-being? To put it differently, are there any particular advantages to being old? Let's consider some candidates.

THE ROLE OF WISDOM

Wisdom has been defined as "expertise in the fundamental pragmatics of life" (Baltes et al., 1998, p. 1970). We have seen that the practical problems that adults must face do not necessarily have one right answer. These kinds of problems are described as ill-defined or ill-structured. We saw in Chapter 11 that as young adults gain experience with the complexities of real-life problems, the adolescent expectation that logical, absolute right answers always exist may give way to a more relativistic perspective, acknowledging that there are multiple, contextually embedded truth systems (e.g., Perry, 1970/1999). Some theorists argue that such relativistic thinking represents a new, qualitatively more advanced form of logical thinking, called postformal thought. Other theorists regard more relativistic thinking as a function of reflection and experience, perhaps benefited by advancing metacognitive understanding of the limits of one's own thought processes. In the latter view, relativistic thought does not represent a qualitatively different level of functioning, but the outcome of accumulating knowledge. From either perspective, the result for some, not all, adults, is the achievement of wisdom, which represents "a truly superior level of knowledge, judgment, and advice" addressing "important and difficult questions . . . about the conduct and meaning of life" (Baltes & Staudinger, 2000, p. 123).

Sternberg (2001) describes wise people as both creative and intelligent: "They are perhaps most effective and sought after in positions of leadership because they are likely to balance the need for change (or shaping of the environment) with the need for stability (or adaptation to the environment)" (p. 362). Being able to change, finding new, but effective, solutions to problems, is the creative element; being able to adapt well to existing environments, serving as an agent who will preserve what is valuable, is the intelligent component.

Is wisdom associated with particular behaviors or emotional responses? Recent research suggests that it is. For example, Kunzmann and Baltes (2003) found that individuals scoring high on wisdom tend to prefer cooperative conflict management, as opposed to say, dominant strategies. They also score high on involvement with others, yet at the same time tend to moderate their emotional reactivity more than other people. They also seem more committed than others to pursuits that have the goal of enhancing the growth and potential of both themselves and other people.

Is wisdom more likely in old age? If it were, it might greatly benefit the older person's ability to manage the problems of decline and loss that aging can bring. In a program of research on wisdom by Staudinger, Baltes, and their colleagues, participants are told about people experiencing difficult real-life problems and are asked to describe and explain what the fictional people should do. One example of such a real-life problem, along with a response that received a low score for wisdom and one that received a high score, is presented in Table 15.2. Scores for wisdom were based on raters' judgments of how rich the respondent's factual and procedural knowledge seemed to be, whether the response took into account the developmental context, the degree to which the response reflected a relativistic view and a recognition of uncertainty, as well as attempts to manage uncertainty (e.g., Staudinger & Baltes, 1996).

Findings from studies using this technique indicate that wisdom, as defined by Staudinger and Baltes (1996), does seem to require experience and thus is somewhat enhanced by age. The years from 15 to 25 appear to be very important for wisdom acquisition (Pasupathi, Staudinger, & Baltes, 1999, 2001), but after 25, the proportion of people whose wisdom scores are above average does not change substantially. After 75, fewer people continue to function at above-average

For some elderly people, wisdom may be a special asset in managing the problems of life.

levels on measures of wisdom (Baltes & Staudinger, 2000). Studies using somewhat different methods have found a tendency for wisdom to increase well into middle adulthood (e.g., Blanchard-Fields, 1986) but also to decline thereafter (e.g., Labouvie-Vief, Chiodo, Goguen, Diehl, & Orwoll, 1995). There is some indication, though, that very high scores on wisdom are more likely in older than younger people. Baltes and Staudinger (2000) therefore predict that if there were a "world record" for wisdom, it would be likely that someone over 60 would hold it. Thus, for some elderly people at least, wisdom may well be a special asset in the management of their problems.

One interesting finding from the wisdom research is that in addition to age, training and experience in occupations that involve managing and reviewing life's problems seem to promote

---

TABLE 15.2   Wisdom Problem and Abbreviated Responses

Wisdom Problem

A 15-year-old girl wants to get married right away. What should one/she consider and do?

Low Wisdom-Related Score

A 15-year-old girl wants to get married? No, no way, marrying at age 15 would be utterly wrong. One has to tell the girl that marriage is not possible. (After further probing) It would be irresponsible to support such an idea. No, this is just a crazy idea.

High Wisdom-Related Score

Well, on the surface, this seems like an easy problem. On average, marriage for 15-year-old girls is not a good thing. But there are situations where the average case does not fit. Perhaps in this instance, special life circumstances are involved, such that the girl has a terminal illness. Or the girl has just lost her parents. And also, this girl may live in another culture or historical period. Perhaps she was raised with a value system different from ours. In addition, one has to think about adequate ways of talking with the girl and to consider her emotional state.

Source: Baltes, P. B., & Staudinger, O. M. (2000). Wisdom: A metaheuristic (pragmatic) to orchestrate mind and virtue toward excellence. *American Psychologist, 55*, 122–136. Copyright © 2000 by the American Psychological Association. Adapted with permission.

wisdom. Clinical psychologists, for example, receive higher wisdom scores than people with similar levels of education who are in fields that do not focus on "the fundamental pragmatics of life" (e.g., Smith, Staudinger, & Baltes, 1994). Clinical training itself seems to be important, because even when analyses controlled for the contribution of intelligence and personality differences across professions, clinicians had a wisdom advantage (e.g., Staudinger, Maciel, Smith, & Baltes, 1998).

THE SELECTIVE OPTIMIZATION OF SOCIAL-EMOTIONAL EXPERIENCE

Despite the declines and losses we described earlier in this chapter, there is one domain of experience that often shows significant growth in the second half of life. The socioemotional domain seems to be enhanced and better regulated with age. One reason is that older adults become more selective about the social relationships in which they invest their time. We saw earlier that the social convoy shrinks as we get older, sometimes as a function of the death of loved ones but also because opportunities for casual contacts are reduced. However, recent research indicates that the shrinking of the social convoy is not just a function of involuntary changes. Instead, the elderly tend to selectively invest in fewer social relationships, keeping or replacing close, deeply satisfying relationships and eliminating more peripheral ties (Carstensen, 1998; Carstensen & Charles, 1998). Figure 15.3 demonstrates that in one study the number of very close social partners stayed about the same for people ranging in age from 69 to 104, but the numbers of less close social partners dropped dramatically (Lang & Carstensen, 1994).

Laura Carstensen and her colleagues explain this socioemotional selectivity as a function of people's expectations that the time remaining in their lives is limited (e.g., Carstensen, 1998; Carstensen & Charles, 1998). In both Western and Eastern cultures, they have found that people of any age will become more selective about whom they spend time with if they perceive their remaining time in life to be constrained (e.g., Fredrickson & Carstensen, 1990; Fung, Carstensen, & Lutz, 1999).

Because older people (and others who expect their lives to end soon) pay more attention to their feelings, their emotional experiences are more enhanced and complex (Carstensen, 1998). For example, for older adults, emotional characteristics play a greater role than for younger adults in how they categorize potential social partners (Frederickson & Carstensen, 1990). Older adults also remember relatively more emotional information from descriptions of people than younger adults do (Carstensen & Turk-Charles, 1994).

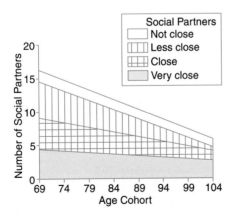

FIGURE 15.3

Numbers of Very Close Social Partners are Maintained Across Old Age, Whereas More Peripheral Partners Are Reduced in Number

Source: Lang, F. R. & Carstensen, L. L. (1994). Close emotional relationships in late life: Further support for proactive aging in the social domain. *Psychology and Aging, 9,* 315–324. Copyright © 1994 by the American Psychological Association. Reprinted with permission.

Positive emotional experience is maintained in old age, negative emotional experience is reduced, and the complexity of emotional experience is increased. In an experience-sampling study, participants from 18 to 94 years old wore pagers for a week (Carstensen, Pasupathi, & Mayr, 1998). They were asked to check off the emotion or emotions they were experiencing when they were randomly paged throughout the week. Older adults reported positive emotions as often as younger adults, but they reported significantly fewer negative emotions. They also experienced more mixed emotions. For example, while spending time with an old friend, poignancy might be added to the positive feelings experienced.

Other evidence for a decline in negative emotional experience with age comes from memory studies. First, older adults are more likely to remember positive experiences than negative ones. In one study, researchers showed participants pictures with positive, negative, and neutral content. The older adult participants were more likely to remember the positive pictures than the negative ones, even though they paid equal attention to all of the pictures. Young adults showed no difference in the recollection of positive and negative pictures (Charles, Mather, & Carstensen, 2003). Second, when older adults remember emotionally arousing events, they have a weaker reaction to the negative events. Labouvie-Vief, Lumky, Jain, and Heinze (2003) measured the cardiac responses of people from ages 15 through 88, while the participants thought about emotion arousing experiences in their lives. Older adults showed less heart rate reactivity than younger adults, especially for negative emotions like anger and fear. The researchers also found some interesting gender differences. The most reactive group were the younger women and the greatest decline in reactivity with age was shown by women.

Finally, emotion regulation seems to improve in later years. In the experience-sampling study described earlier, negative emotional states ended more quickly for older participants, but positive states lasted just as long as they did for the younger participants. In a variety of cultures, older adults describe themselves as having greater control over their emotions than younger adults do (Gross et al., 1997). In direct observations of conflict management between spouses, older couples were more skillful than long-married middle-aged couples at interspersing positive, affectionate statements with negative ones and keeping negative expressions to a minimum (e.g., Levenson, Carstensen, & Gottman, 1993, 1994). It appears that older people may be wise in the ways they deal with emotions: Don't dwell on sorrow, and make happiness last.

Interestingly, these socioemotional growth patterns occur simultaneously with the tendency for some depressive characteristics to increase in old age. Overall rates of diagnosed mood disorders, including major depression, are lowest in elderly samples (see Figure 15.4), but self-reported depressive symptoms increase from middle adulthood into very old age (Gatz, 2000).

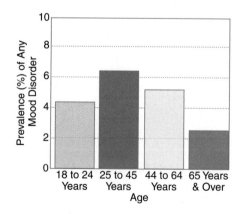

FIGURE 15.4

Prevalence of Diagnosed Mood Disorders, Including Major Depression, over Age

Source: Regier, D. A., Boyd, J. H., Burke, J. D., Rae, D. S., Myers, J. K., Kramer, M., Robins, L. N., George, L. K., Karro, M., & Locke, B. Z. (1988). One month prevalence of mental disorders in the United States. *Archives of General Psychiatry, 45,* 977–986. Reprinted by permission of the American Medical Association.

These depressive symptoms, however, are different from those that younger people are most likely to report, perhaps reflecting the greater emotion regulation of older adults. The elderly are more likely to experience loss of interest and hopelessness rather than self-deprecation or dysphoric mood (Gatz, 2000; Joiner, 2000). Depressive symptoms in old age are also heavily linked to health status. In relatively healthy community samples, depressive symptoms occur in about 15% of the elderly. But 33% of older hospitalized patients and 40% of nursing home residents report depressive symptoms (Blazer, 1994). Fortunately, despite the intractability of many health problems in old age, research on the effectiveness of treatment for depressive symptoms has been encouraging. As with younger clients, elderly people, including nursing home residents, respond positively to a variety of psychotherapeutic interventions, including cognitive, behavioral (e.g., Rybarczyk et al., 1992), and brief psychodynamic, interpersonal, and life-review therapies (Scogin & McElreath, 1994).

EXPERIENCING LOSS

Death and Dying

In the expectable rhythm of life, most people begin to take the prospect of their own mortality more seriously during middle adulthood. Illness, the deaths of parents, spouses, siblings, or friends, the experience of watching adult children struggle with problems, and many other bumps in the road grow more frequent, and they signal what has already been lost. At some point, we begin to think of time not as unlimited "time to live" but as "time left to live." In old age, the reality of death and loss are inescapable. Even though advances in medicine have extended life and greatly improved its quality for many people, all of us face the certainty of death. And though death can occur at any point in the life cycle, the proportion of individuals who die in late adulthood is much greater than at any other time. Currently, close to 80% of the U.S. population live beyond age 65. Of this group, more than 75% will struggle with heart disease, cancer, stroke, lung disease, or dementia during their last 12 months of life (Lynn, 2000). Despite these statistics, elderly individuals report less anxiety about death and are more realistic about its inevitability than are middle-aged adults (Gesser, Wong, & Reker, 1988).

Clinicians will undoubtedly come face to face with the emotionally challenging issues of death and dying in their work. They may be called on to support children who experience a parent's death, relatives or friends of a suicide victim, families struggling to cope with the aftermath of a fatal accident, or individuals facing their own deaths from illnesses such as cancer or HIV/AIDS. Or they may work with the elderly, for whom the prospect of death ever more insistently intrudes into daily life. Death in later life is generally expected. The experience of death for younger persons can be particularly traumatic. Although the older person and his family may have time to prepare themselves for the separation, death at earlier ages defies the natural order. Even though we present the issues of death and dying in the context of later life, many of the issues involved in dying and bereavement are similar across the life span. First we will consider the issues involved in dying. Then we will look at the psychological work of bereavement.

FACING DEATH

Dame Cicely Saunders, founder of the modern hospice movement, recounted a dying patient's words to her: "I thought it so strange. Nobody wants to look at me" (Ewens & Herrington, 1983, p. 5). This remark captures many elements that describe the experience of dying: general reluctance to address the topic of death openly, anxiety about death that informs this reluctance, guilt that emanates from the lack of openness, and the loneliness and isolation of the dying person. If death is a part of every human life, why do many of us avoid discussing it? Death clearly represents unknown territory, and it is difficult to comprehend a more painful or stressful life event than the prospect of dying or of losing a loved one. According to some existential therapists, fear of death is the ultimate source of anxiety and the foundation of most depression and alienation

TABLE 15.3 Core Principles for End-of-Life Care

1. Respecting the dignity of both patients and caregivers;
2. Being sensitive and respectful of the patient's and family's wishes;
3. Using the most appropriate measures that are consistent with patient choices;
4. Encompassing alleviation of pain and other physical symptoms;
5. Assessing and managing psychological, social, and spiritual/religious problems;
6. Offering continuity (the patient should be able to continue to be cared for, if so desired, by his/her primary care and specialist providers);
7. Providing access to any therapy that may realistically be expected to improve the patient's quality of life, including alternative and nontraditional treatments;
8. Providing access to palliative care and hospice care;
9. Respecting the right to refuse treatment;
10. Respecting the physician's professional right to discontinue some treatments when appropriate, with consideration for both patient and family preferences;
11. Promoting clinical evidence–based research on providing care at end-of-life.

Source: Cassel, C. K. and Foley, K. M. *Principles for care of patients at the end of life*, p. 2. © 1999 Milbank Memorial Fund. Used by permission.

(May, 1979; Yalom, 1980). Some people have also pointed out that the advances of modern medicine, despite their obvious benefits, have encouraged us to think of dying in some of the same ways we conceptualize treatable illnesses (Kane, 1996).

Fortunately, much progress has been made in understanding death and dying relatively recently. Modern U.S. culture is very gradually moving away from one that denies or sanitizes death to one that supports death with dignity. Courageous pioneers such as Elizabeth Kubler-Ross (1969) have directed our collective attention to the issues facing the dying and the bereaved and, in doing so, have shed much-needed light on their needs and concerns. Faced with a growing population of elderly and prompted by advances in research, the field of medicine has taken steps toward more compassionate care of the dying. An emerging consensus among medical specialties regarding end-of-life care is reflected in the development of a set of core principles for providers (see Table 15.3). These eleven principles list the responsibilities of end-of-life caregivers to patients and their patients' families or support systems. Societies such as the American Medical Association and the Joint Commission on the Accreditation of Healthcare Organizations, to name a few, have adopted these principles (Cassel & Foley, 1999). In general, the principles support more humanistic approaches to end-of-life care, including better pain management, continuity of care, and attention to the psychological dimensions of death and dying. These principles are reflected at the practical level in state initiatives such as Oregon's policies to improve end-of-life care (Wyden, 2000).

WHAT IS A GOOD DEATH?

Most people hope for a good death, but what does that really mean? As the poet Robert Frost observed, "Hope does not lie in a way out, but in a way through." You might imagine that dying quickly without unnecessary suffering or dying at home surrounded by loved ones would provide good ways through this final passage. But preferences may be different for different people. Steinhauser and her colleagues (Steinhauser et al., 2000) investigated the relative importance of factors that signify a good death in a survey of 2,000 seriously ill patients, physicians, recently bereaved family members, and other care providers. There was general agreement among all respondents that certain attributes were highly important. These included elements of symptom management and care (freedom from pain and anxiety, freedom from shortness of breath, being touched, and kept clean), certain practical details (having financial affairs in order, knowing what to expect about one's condition), and patient–professional relationship quality (having caring, trustworthy providers who listen). In addition, specific psychological attributes (maintaining dignity, not dying alone, having the opportunity to resolve unfinished business and say good-bye) were also rated highly by all respondents.

But some differences among respondents were noted as well. In contrast to physicians, patients felt that it was very important for them to remain mentally aware, to have made funeral arrangements, and to feel a sense of completion about their life. African American patients were more likely than their White counterparts to want all available life-sustaining treatments. The entire patient group expressed concern about being burdensome to their families. Somewhat surprisingly, they also viewed being able to help others as an important contribution to their end-of-life quality, suggesting the significance of generativity across the life span. Though many people assume that patients prefer to die at home, this was not the overwhelming preference of this sample. Physicians and clinicians need to take cultural preferences for end of life care into account when working with diverse groups (Searight & Gafford, 2005). In contrast to the value placed on autonomous decision making by many professionals, members of certain cultures prefer to share decision making with relatives because this is perceived as supportive. Members of Chinese, Pakistani and Hispanic communities may actively strive to protect their loved ones from knowledge of the full extent of their illness because it is deemed impolite, cruel or deleterious to health. In some Asian communities, a family's desire for extraordinary measures to preserve the life of a relative may reflect the deep reverence in which they hold their elders. In general, it is important to recognize that there are many ways to define a good death. Some of these preferences may be shaped by cultural and religious perspectives on death. It is incumbent on caregivers not to make assumptions about their clients, but to ask for and listen to individuals' needs.

Despite the importance of these individual differences, many studies have demonstrated that **palliative care** (Hanson, Danis, & Garrett, 1997; Singer, Martin, & Merrijoy, 1999) and the ability to prepare for death (Christakis, 2000; Emanuel & Emanuel, 1998) are two of the most consistently wished-for aspects of end-of-life care reported by patients and families. *Palliative care*, or comfort care, involves services provided by caregivers from several disciplines. It embodies a comprehensive approach to care that addresses pain management, emotional and spiritual care, and psychological support for caregivers and survivors (Billings, 1998).

The philosophy of care embodied in the modern **hospice movement**, which serves people suffering from terminal illness, is a good example of a palliative, patient-centered approach. Considered a hospitable respite for weary travelers in medieval times, hospice is now a place where people on another kind of journey, from life to death, can find peace and comfort. The hospice philosophy of end-of-life care says much about its philosophy of death, primarily about what the dying person needs in order to have a good death (Callanan & Kelley, 1992). Hospice emphasizes the importance of giving patients as much knowledge about their condition as possible so that they maintain some control over their care. The focus is not on curing disease but on managing symptoms and pain by means of palliative (pain-reducing) medicine. Perhaps more difficult to manage are other aspects of dying: the emotional, social, and spiritual sequelae of illness. In this approach to treatment, patients and their families are assisted in coping with the feelings of depression, anxiety, rejection, abandonment, and spiritual discomfort that may arise from the process of dying and losing a loved one.

Some studies have found that hospice patients are more satisfied with their care than conventional hospital patients (Kane, Wales, Bernstein, Leibowitz, & Kaplan, 1984) and that provision of hospice care in nursing homes improves quality of care there (Baer & Hanson, 2000; Wilson, Kovach, & Stearns, 1996). As noted earlier, there are clear worldwide trends toward improving end-of-life care by incorporating palliative care for all patients, regardless of setting (Lynn, 2000). In some areas, coalitions of hospitals, hospices, medical practices, nursing associations, long-term care facilities, social workers, and pastoral and mental health counselors have been formed to provide high-quality, comprehensive services to seriously ill individuals and their families (Mitka, 2000).

Having a good death appears to be related to the person's ability to make informed decisions about treatment, a notion congruent with what has been said about the psychological benefits of control. However, even though the importance of this kind of control has generally been acknowledged by practitioners of palliative care, studies suggest that a significant number of patients, even the most highly educated ones, still misunderstand the treatment options available to them. Silveira and her associates (Silveira, DiPiero, Gerrity, & Feudtner, 2000) examined whether knowledge about end-of-life options such as **refusal of treatment**, **physician-assisted suicide**, **active euthanasia**, and **double effect** was improved among patients who had signed **advance directives** or **living wills**, who had experienced previous illness, or who had previously cared for a dying loved one. *Refusal of treatment* refers to patients' refusal of any food, water, or medical treatment that prolongs life. *Physician-assisted suicide* involves prescribing medicine that enables patients to take their own lives. *Active euthanasia* refers to injection of a medication by someone else that causes immediate death. The *double effect* means giving medication intended to relieve pain even though there is a chance that death can result. *Advance directives* or *living wills* are statements, typically in writing, that describe a person's wishes regarding medical treatment in the event of incurable illness.

The results of the study showed that knowledge about end-of-life treatment options was generally poor. It was not improved for those who had signed advance directives or who were ill themselves. Knowledge was somewhat more accurate for those who had cared for dying loved ones. In general, caregivers often wait too long to discuss end-of-life preferences. Decisions may be made in haste, when the dying person is too ill or caregivers too distressed to make reflective choices (Gleeson & Wise, 1993). It is important, therefore, to initiate conversations about end-of-life decisions well in advance of the stresses of illness. Table 15.4 presents important legal information about end-of-life care. A sampling of questions that can be used by caregivers to initiate discussions about issues of care is presented in Table 15.5.

THE PROCESS OF DYING

In the late 1950s, Elizabeth Kubler-Ross (1969), a Swiss-born psychiatrist, began to study the ways that people who were dying faced death. At that time, the dying were largely invisible among hospital patients, and she encountered a high degree of professional resistance to her

---

TABLE 15.4   Myths and Realities About End-of-Life Care

Myth	Current Status
There must be a law authorizing the termination of life support.	Currently existing law supports the termination of life support in all 50 states for both competent patients and for those who have lost capacity if there is consensus among those who care about the patient that it would be the patient's will or in his/her best interests.
Termination of life support is murder, assisted suicide, or suicide.	Termination of life supports is considered to be freeing the patient from unwanted bodily invasion. Death is legally considered to be a result of the patient's underlying disease. The law clearly distinguishes such acts from suicide, assisted suicide, or euthanasia.
A patient must be terminally ill for life support to be stopped.	The law allows any patient to refuse any treatment that he/she does not want, in the interest of protecting bodily integrity, even if that treatment would be life sustaining and the patient is not terminally ill.
It is permissible to terminate extraordinary treatments, but not ordinary ones.	The distinction between ordinary and extraordinary treatments is not relevant as a matter of law or ethics. The patient has the right to terminate any treatment, potentially life sustaining or not.
It is permissible to withhold treatment, but once started, it must be continued.	Although many clinicians think and feel differently about these types of actions, the law and medical ethics treat the withholding and the cessation of life-sustaining treatment the same.
Stopping artificial nutrition and hydration is legally different from stopping other treatments.	In most states, artificial hydration and nutrition are considered medical treatments like any other.
Termination of life support requires going to court.	The courts generally want clinicians to make these decisions without going to court, provided there is a consensus among those who care about the patient about how to proceed.
Living wills are not legal.	Living wills have legal support in all 50 states, either through legislation or case law.

Source: Meisel, A., Snyder, L., & Quill, T. (2000). Seven legal barriers to end-of-life care: Myths, realities, and grains of truth. *Journal of the American Medical Association, 284* (p. 2496, table 1). Reprinted by permission of the American Medical Association.

TABLE 15.5	Questions for End-of-Life Decision Making
Domain	**Representative Questions**
Goals	Given the severity of your illness, what is most important for you to achieve?
	How do you think about balancing quality of life with length of life in terms of your treatment?
	What are your most important hopes?
	What are your biggest fears?
Values	What makes life most worth living for you?
	Would there be any circumstances under which you would find life not worth living?
	What do you consider your quality of life to be like now?
	Have you seen or been with someone who had a particularly good death or particularly difficult death?
Advance directives	If with future progression of your illness you are not able to speak for yourself, who would be best able to represent your views and values? (health care proxy)
	Have you given any thought to what kinds of treatment you would want (and not want) if you become unable to speak for yourself in the future? (living will)
Do-not-resuscitate order	If you were to die suddenly, that is, you stopped breathing or your heart stopped, we could try to revive you by using cardiopulmonary resuscitation (CPR). Are you familiar with CPR?
	Have you given thought as to whether you would want it? Given the severity of your illness, CPR would in all likelihood be ineffective. I would recommend that you choose not to have it, but that we continue all potentially effective treatments. What do you think?
Palliative care (pain and other symptoms)	Have you ever heard of hospice (palliative care)? What has been your experience with it?
	Tell me about your pain. Can you rate it on a 10-point scale?
	What is your breathing like when you feel at your best? How about when you are having trouble?
Palliative care ("unfinished business")	If you were to die sooner rather than later, what would be left undone?
	How is your family handling your illness? What are their reactions?
	Has religion been an important part of your life? Are there any spiritual issues you are concerned about at this point?

Source: Quill, T. E. (2000). Initiating end-of-life discussions with seriously ill patients. *Journal of the American Medical Association, 285* (p. 2506, table 3). Reprinted by permission of the American Medical Association.

work. When she asked her fellow physicians to recommend to her their dying patients so that she could talk to them, she was told that there were no dying patients in her 600-bed hospital (Ewens & Herrington, 1983). But after meeting people who realized that they were dying and after listening carefully to their stories, she described responses to death that appeared to characterize the process: denial, anger, bargaining, depression, and acceptance. Each of these responses represents a type of coping or defense mechanism for dealing with death. Perhaps it was unfortunate that she referred to these processes as "stages" and linked them together in sequence. Although Kubler-Ross herself (1974) emphasized that the stages do not always occur in order and that they can and often do occur simultaneously, the use of a stair-step approach is fraught with the kinds of problems we discussed in Chapter 1. Foremost, perhaps, is that a stage sequence can be irresistible to clinicians who are looking for fixed, clear guidelines for understanding grief.

Criticism of the model has centered on the overall lack of empirical evidence for the existence of stages (Kastenbaum, 1986; Klass, 1982) and the problems that arise when counselors and other caregivers use the stages as a road map by which to evaluate functional versus dysfunctional adjustment to death and dying (Corr, 1993). The belief among caregivers that these five responses are the only appropriate ones for the dying represents another limitation of the model as it is applied to practice. Studies of individuals who have received terminal diagnoses do provide some support for the initial manifestation of shock or disbelief as well as for the presence of greater acceptance before death (Kalish, 1985). In general, however, counselors should remember that there is much greater variation in the process than is allowed for by a strict interpretation of these stages. Perhaps the reactions can be viewed as some important ways that people cope with impending loss, but by no means is the sequence fixed nor the range of coping mechanisms exhaustive.

With these caveats in mind, let us consider each of these coping mechanisms in more detail. Denial may follow the initial shock that is associated with news of a terminal illness. At best, it temporarily protects the person from the reality of a terrifying situation. Denial is associated with feelings of numbness or disbelief and buffers the person from the full weight of the threat. Considered in this way, some measure of denial can be adaptive. It allows a person to temper the emotional impact, thus rendering it more manageable (Janoff-Bulman, 1993).

Anger is a normal reaction to separation and loss. Anger may be directed toward God ("Why me?"), toward others ("Why didn't you do something to help me?"), or toward the disease itself, which is viewed as an enemy to be battled. Often this is a very difficult response for family members to tolerate from loved ones who are dying. Resentment or hostility toward family members or caregivers who are healthy may reflect the depth of the dying person's pain. Anger can ebb and flow throughout the course of illness, depending upon the individual and the specific circumstances (Rosenblatt, Walsh, & Jackson, 1972).

The essence of bargaining is to try to postpone the inevitable by making promises, usually to a divine other. Sometimes individuals will try to delay death until some memorable event, such as an anniversary or a child's marriage, takes place. The individual may offer some prize, such as "a life dedicated to God," if the chance to live longer is granted.

Depression as a reaction to impending death is characterized by sadness and feelings of hopelessness. Kubler-Ross distinguished between reactive depression, or depression that results from loss of functioning or other problems associated with the disease process, and preparatory depression, which is related to prospective loss and separation. Acceptance is characterized by a sense of peace and relative tranquility, which suggests that the person has come to terms with his impending death. We stress, however, that this peace is relative. No one should be evaluated on how quickly or completely she accepts death. Remember, too, that these reactions, although important, do not reflect all possible ways of managing the dying process.

Bereavement

Life is death
kept at an arm's length.
Love is grief
dressed in its Sunday best.
And sadness is the tax
assessed on any happiness.

—From *St. James' Park Epistle* by Thomas Lynch

Sadness is not the sole province of the dying person. Those who suffer the loss of loved ones are themselves deeply grieved. Grief is a universal reaction to loss or separation, and, as you recall from the discussion of attachment theory, it takes a number of behavioral forms, such as active distress, protest, and searching for the lost attachment figure. Grief has been described with great poignancy from the earliest times by philosophers, poets, and religious leaders. It has been memorialized in song and codified in ritual. Grief is often so unsettling to observe that it elicits from others a desire to give comfort and solace. Many religious and secular customs have grown up around the grieving process in an attempt to help people survive the rigors of suffering and to give meaning to death. Culture also plays a role in determining how grief is expressed, for example, as an emotional versus a physical set of symptoms (Kleinman & Kleinman, 1985). Box 15.2 describes various rituals from different cultures that demonstrate some of the diversity in people's beliefs about, and experiences with, death.

Clinicians are often called upon to offer support to people who have experienced the loss of loved ones. An extensive clinical folklore has developed, primarily about the ways that grief should be expressed and the best ways to help people express it. In the 1980s, a vibrant debate commenced when researchers began to question the lack of empirical support for many of these traditionally accepted assumptions about grief. A number of inconsistencies or "myths" about

Box 15.2 | *Funeral Rituals in Different Cultures*

In virtually every culture, distinct funeral rituals have evolved that are fascinating reflections of people's beliefs about death. Social anthropologists suggest that these rituals serve to bind a culture together by expressing its "collective representations" about fundamental issues such as life, death, and spirituality (Metcalf & Huntington, 1991). To illustrate the diversity of beliefs and the many ways of demonstrating grief, we present a look at funeral practices in four cultures: the Chinese of San Francisco's Chinatown (Crowder, 1999; Hill, 1992), the Luo of Kenya (Nyamongo, 1999), traditional Jewish families (Schindler, 1996), and the San Francisco gay community (Richards, Wrubel, & Folkman, 1992–2000).

For the Chinese, a funeral signifies the important transition from family member to ancestor, that beneficent spirit who will look our for the family's well-being from the spirit world. The connection between living family members and their ancestors is so important that prior to the mid-20th century Chinese immigrants living in the United States routinely returned their dead to China to be buried next to other family members. The Chinese community in San Francisco continues to practice elaborate traditional rituals, complete with funeral processions and brass bands. Funerals draw large groups of family members and friends, and they provide an occasion to tell the world about the accomplishments of the deceased. So fundamentally important is this practice that funerals in the Chinese province of Gansu are held *before* the person dies, so that he can be present to hear about the good things he has accomplished in his lifetime (2001, N. Zhang, personal communication).

Chinese funerals in San Francisco may incorporate Christian or Buddhist elements into a ceremony that traditionally consists of five parts: the visit, the service, the procession, the burial, and the dinner. The visit, or wake, allows visitors to view the body of the deceased. Near the body are placed a portrait of the dead person, usually framed with flowers, and items of food, such as chicken, vegetables, rice, and tea, intended to sustain the soul of the person through the journey to the afterlife. Various items such as jewelry, money, and clothing are placed in the coffin for his use as well. The funeral service, usually held the day after the visit, includes prayers and a eulogy. The funeral procession consists of a hearse, the funeral cortege, and a band, which plays hymns and other traditional music. On its way to the cemetery, the procession typically stops at the deceased's home or place of business. The portrait of the dead person is then taken from the hearse and set up facing the building. The mourners bow to pay their respects and may toss "spirit money," pieces of white paper in the shape of bills that are intended to placate malevolent spirits, into the air. Some relatives and friends await the procession at the house and greet the spirit of the ancestor with offerings of food, incense, and candles. At the gravesite, members of the funeral party, males first, followed by females, toss dirt, flowers, coins, or rice into the grave. The ritual is concluded with a formal seven-course meal, because seven is the number for death. At the center of each table is a cup of white rice liquor in honor of the departed.

The Luo live in the western part of Kenya near Lake Victoria. They, like the Chinese, believe that a person who dies becomes transformed from an earthly member of the family into a spiritual one. The funeral ritual is a transformative rite of passage. Death among the Luo is marked by a funeral fire, which is kept burning for approximately one week. The body of a deceased male is prepared by the men of the same clan and lies in state for 4 days, while that of a deceased woman lies in state for 3. After the burial, animals are slaughtered at the site of the funeral fire. Their numbers and kind depend upon the socioeconomic status of the deceased. Relatives and neighbors might contribute some animals for slaughter, knowing that the same will be done for them in their time of bereavement.

During the period of mourning, the sons of the deceased keep company around the fire. Their wives stay together in the house of the deceased, avoiding any sexual contact because of their belief that sexual relations will cause the death of their own sons. The widow of a deceased man is inherited by the dead man's brother, thus transferring her care to another relative and giving him the benefit of an additional laborer.

Traditional Jewish funeral practices emphasize honoring the deceased as well as giving the bereaved time and freedom to grieve. Jewish law is very sensitive to the emotional pain experienced by grieving persons and structures rituals to provide explicit comfort for them. During the funeral service, an emotional eulogy encourages mourners to vent their feelings by crying. A similarly cathartic release is elicited during the recitation of the *Kaddish*, or ritual prayer. Flowers are not customarily given in this cultural tradition because they signify happiness, an emotion that is discordant with the painfulness of death.

Throughout the period of mourning, called *Aninut*, great care is taken to support the bereaved. Jewish law indicates that those who have experienced a loss should be exempt form normal religious obligations, such as studying the scriptures. Customs such as *Kreiah*, or the ritual tearing of garments and the breaking of a shard on the lintel of the deceased's house, provide religious sanctions for outward displays of anger and sadness during the time of mourning. The period of *Shiva*, a 7-day mourning period, is dedicated to visiting and consoling the bereaved. Providing emotional comfort and social support for the survivors is viewed as an important religious obligation that helps to move people beyond the pain of their loss to a state of acceptance. Once the official 12-month grieving period is over, the *Kaddish* prayer is recited again, and excessive outward displays of mourning are expected to cease.

A relatively new culture, that of the gay community in San Francisco, has developed its own ways of dealing with bereavement due to the unfortunate increase in HIV/AIDS related deaths. Because many members of this community die in hospice or home settings, their dying often takes the form of a vigil. Family and friends attend the dying person, keeping him as comfortable as possible while saying their good-byes. After death, rituals such as bathing and dressing the body honor the wishes of the deceased and allow the bereaved to feel connected to the loved one. Photos may be placed around the bedside, and valued objects, such as let-ters or items of religious significance, are placed near the body. Funeral services may combine elements of formal religious rites with those that signify some personal meaning. For example, planting trees in the loved one's memory, burning incense, playing music, and so forth may be incorporated into the service.

These examples, although certainly not exhaustive, emphasize the healing function of rituals, either traditional ones or those that are newly created. Whatever their type or origin, regardless of their religious or cultural underpinnings, rituals appear to draw people together in their encounter with death. They give voice to fears and to sadness, and they signify love and respect for the persons who have died.

grieving were uncovered in the process (Wortman & Silver, 1989, 2001), and researchers and clinicians have since continued this important dialogue. What follows is a discussion of some classic approaches to grief, an examination of some of the major tenets of bereavement counseling, and a brief summary of evidence from recent studies.

CLASSIC APPROACHES TO BEREAVEMENT

Freud's (1917/1957) theorizing about grief and mourning was very influential in shaping the legacy that came to be known as grief work. In simple terms, Freud believed that individuals who lose a loved one (or object) must withdraw their emotional attachments or energy (or libido) and detach (or decathect) from the lost object. Loss causes great pain, and bereaved people, Freud believed, inevitably need to struggle with the process of letting go. As manifestations of their mourning, they may lose interest in the world, prefer to isolate themselves from others, dwell on thoughts of the deceased, and suffer from depression. Gradually, the reality of loss is accepted. From Freud's perspective, successful resolution involves decathecting, or detaching emotionally, from the former relationship and reinvesting psychic energy into the formation of new attachments.

Freud presented these theoretical ideas on mourning well in advance of some important deaths that were to occur in his own personal life. The loss of his daughter at age 25 and of his grandson at age 4 affected him greatly. He wrote that his life was permanently altered by these enormous losses and that, although acute grief may subside, people "remain unconsolable and will never find a substitute" (1929/1961, p. 239). These words suggest that Freud, in his later years, recognized that one does not necessarily recover from grief nor cut the cords of old attachments. However, his earlier notion that active grieving leads to recovery is one idea that he never formally revised and one that has permeated the canon of grief counseling. Other assumptions, that successful resolution of grief necessitates detachment from lost loved ones and reinvestment in other relationships and that abnormal mourning may follow from conflicted relationships, have also influenced clinical practice.

Bowlby's (1969/1982, 1980) highly influential construction of the bereavement process, based on attachment theory, depicts his view of typical human reactions to the experience of separation from or loss of attachment figures. The theory was initially developed to describe the responses of children temporarily separated from their caregivers (see Chapter 4, Box 4.2) and was later adapted to describe permanent separation, or bereavement, in adults. Bowlby's description of various reactions to separation gave rise to popular stage conceptions of dying, such as those of Kubler-Ross (Archer, 1999).

Bowlby's description of the grieving process includes four phases. At first, the loss is met by disbelief, a phase Bowlby called shock. The grieving person may experience numbness or feelings of unreality. Emotions may be blunted, and some individuals may even appear unaffected by the loss. Others may display emotional outbursts or may experience dizziness or other physical symptoms. The sense of disbelief eventually subsides when the reality of loss sets in. A second

Funeral traditions vary dramatically across cultures, reflecting fundamental beliefs about life, death, and spirituality.

phase, protest, follows. Bereaved individuals may experience periods of obsessive yearning or searching for the lost loved one as well as bouts of restlessness or irritability.

The subsequent period, called **despair**, may be characterized by great sadness; social withdrawal; sleeping, eating, or somatic disturbances; and other symptoms of depression or emotional upset. People may experience flashbacks or intrusive memories of the deceased. They may actively seek support from others by telling and retelling the story of their loss. Yet, as with a child whose attachment figure has left him, the comfort of others cannot replace the presence of the lost loved one. Gradually, the bereaved person begins to adjust to the loss. Bowlby used the term **reorganization** to describe the last phase of grieving a permanent separation. Taking a position in opposition to Freud's, Bowlby believed that bereaved individuals do not decathect, or detach, from their lost loved ones. Instead, they discover ways to hold on to the memory of the deceased and integrate that memory into their current life and new attachments. They heal, in part, by drawing comfort from the sense of the deceased person's presence (see Fraley & Shaver, 1999).

ASSUMPTIONS ABOUT GRIEF WORK AND EMPIRICAL SUPPORT

As we have noted, a number of assumptions about bereavement, many derived from classic theories such as these, have been reexamined in the light of new evidence and cross-cultural information. One of the most prevalent myths is that people need to deal with their loss, by confronting the pain in an active way, for healing to occur. Avoiding the sadness, it is assumed, leads to later emotional problems. The tenets of *grief work* explicitly encourage bereaved individuals to confront and "work through" their feelings about loss for recovery to take place (Parkes & Weiss, 1983; Stroebe, 1992). This process, often facilitated by therapeutic intervention, might involve reflecting upon one's relationship to the deceased, expressing anger and other negative emotions related to the death, questioning and trying to construct meaning from the death, and ultimately resigning oneself to the loss. Unexpressed grief and unexamined loss, which have not been integrated into one's revised view of the world and the self, are thought to place the bereaved person's long-term physical and psychological well-being at risk. Another assumption is that the normal grieving process evolves in a sequence of stages that take a usually brief but arbitrarily determined period of time, such as 6 months to a year, to complete.

Those studies that have investigated the existence of stages in bereavement find little evidence to support the belief that people grieve in a linear, predictable fashion (van der Waal, 1989–1990;

Wortman & Silver, 1987). Although many people do report initial shock and, later, some measure of reorganization, the intervening process does not necessarily follow in a clear sequence of compartmentalized, independent reactions. There is also a great deal of confusion over how long the manifestations of grief should persist before the grief is judged "abnormal." Diagnostic criteria (see American Psychiatric Association, DSM IV-TR, 2000, p. 740) indicate that a clinician may consider a diagnosis of major depression if the depressive symptoms attendant to bereavement persist beyond two months. However, it is common for people to show grief symptoms much longer than 2 months. Several studies report gradual declines in depressive symptoms within the first 2 years after loss (Middleton, Raphael, Burnett, & Martinek, 1997; Stroebe & Stroebe, 1993), but depression may persist even longer (Martinson, Davies, & McClowry, 1991), particularly if the circumstances surrounding the death have been especially traumatic. Such findings have led to newly proposed criteria for use in the diagnosis of complicated or abnormal grief that allow for longer periods of normal grieving (see Horowitz et al., 1997).

But many other assumptions about what constitutes "normal" and "pathological" (also called chronic, unresolved, or complicated) mourning have also been questioned, and presently there is no widespread consensus about their definitions (Middleton, Raphael, Martinek, & Misso, 1993). Abnormal grief was viewed by Bowlby (1980) as grief that is either excessive and protracted or absent. At one end of the continuum is chronic grief, which, like a preoccupied attachment, is marked by persistent yearning, anxiety, and unremitting distress. This type of mourning immobilizes bereaved individuals and prevents their return to normal functioning. Absence of grieving, on the other end of the continuum, was viewed by Bowlby and others (Deutch, 1937; Parkes, 1965) as a maladaptive defense against the trauma of loss. In this response, characteristic of a highly avoidant attachment pattern, bereaved individuals suppress grief and try to exclude frightening and painful feelings from consciousness. Despite the lack of consistency in empirical support, the concept of abnormal grief has been accepted in clinical practice (Rando, 1993). It is widely assumed that people should demonstrate great distress after a loss and that failure to do so is abnormal, a condition often called the "requirement of mourning" (Wright, 1983).

In general, some recent research has failed to find support for the assumption that all people need to work through loss in the highly cathartic fashion advised by advocates of grief work to adjust successfully. Contrary to what counselors might expect, a certain amount of detachment during the grieving process predicts healthy recovery for many bereaved individuals. Bonanno and Keltner (1997; see also Bonanno & Kaltman, 1999 for a review) provide data demonstrating that minimizing expression of negative emotions can offer some benefit to the bereaved. In this study of individuals whose spouses had died, the remaining partners who manifested a high degree of emotional distress (fear, anger, disgust, and the like) at 6 months after their loss continued to report poorer outcomes after 2 years. Those individuals who had lower initial levels of distress had better health and lower levels of grief after 2 years. Similarly, in a study designed to explore the coping styles of bereaved individuals, Bonanno and his colleagues (Bonanno, Znoj, Siddique, & Horowitz, 1999) reported that some detachment or emotional dissociation was not related to the development of later adjustment problems but was, in fact, predictive of positive outcomes. Neimeyer (2000) concludes from an examination of research that the use of grief-focused interventions with individuals who are not highly distressed risks doing them harm.

Other studies of bereaved individuals (Lund et al., 1985–1986; Vachon et al., 1982), of parents whose babies died from SIDS (Wortman & Silver, 1987), and of individuals who experienced spinal cord injuries (Dinardo, 1971) showed similar results. Those individuals who demonstrated the highest levels of distress initially were also most distressed and less effective in coping with the loss up to several years later. Individuals who showed lower levels of initial distress were generally better adjusted later and were not more likely to experience delayed grief reactions. One conceptual explanation for these findings draws on the framework of individual differences in attachment representations. Specifically, adjustment to loss may be less difficult for individuals whose emotional systems can be deactivated more easily (avoidant) than for those who have difficulty suppressing emotions (ambivalent) (see Fraley & Shaver, 1999). Another hypothesis is linked to gender. For example, one study demonstrated that females gave priority to sharing feelings after a loss, while males viewed problem-solving approaches as more important (Hopmeyer & Werk, 1994). Also, extreme levels of distress might indicate longstanding difficulties in emotion regulation. Certainly, much more research is needed to understand fully the significance of individual differences in grieving.

Overall, the evidence presented above should not be interpreted to suggest that outward signs of distress are necessarily unhealthy. Either side of an either-or argument is problematic. Just as a prescription to demonstrate intense grief is not right for everyone, neither is the advice to remain stoic. What we need to understand are the mechanisms that might explain individual differences in grief reactions, in hopes of constructing a more comprehensive theory of grieving. For those who take the stoic approach, perhaps it is not simply detachment, or the temporary psychic space it provides, but also the restricted focus on loss that makes for better overall adjustment. The traditional advice of grief work, which is to confront pain head-on, may be problematic for some people because of the risk of engaging in excessive yearning or "pining" for the lost loved one. We saw earlier in this chapter that rumination, an emotion-focused style of coping, is correlated with poor adjustment. Excessive preoccupation with the deceased or obsessive dwelling on thoughts of pain and sadness may qualify as rumination.

In a longitudinal study of hundreds of bereaved individuals conducted over 18 months, Nolen-Hoeksema and Larson (1999) found that the use of rumination as a way to cope with loss was highly related to depression at each interview point. In addition, people who ruminated tended to have great difficulty finding meaning in the loss, despite the significant amount of time they spent trying to do so. These findings are consistent with the strong association between ruminative coping and depression in general (Nolen-Hoeksema, 1991).

You might wonder how a bereaved person can make sense of his loss, another assumed measure of successful grieving, if he does not engage in some rumination. Yet, is it really necessary for people to make sense of the loss to adapt successfully? Davis, Lehman, and Wortman (1997) report that not all people who struggle to make sense of deaths, accidents, illnesses, and other tragedies are able to explain these events in satisfactory ways. Many people do not try to do so, preferring to move ahead with their lives without searching for existential or philosophical meaning.

Davis and his associates (Davis, Wortman, Lehman, & Silver, 2000) reported very consistent findings from several studies that investigated the benefits of meaning-making for later adjustment. In general, individuals who were able to derive meaning from the event relatively early on were least distressed at follow-up interviews. Interestingly, those who were able to find something positive in the experience or who were able to reappraise the loss to extract some benefit from it were the best adjusted. Religious or spiritual beliefs often helped people find meaning in the loss. However, others found that loss precipitated a cascade of doubts about faith because it shattered their views of a just world. Those who did not initiate a search for meaning were also found to have relatively good adjustments. It was the group that struggled for meaning without finding it that suffered most.

Nolen-Hoeksema and Larson (1999) reported significant associations in their bereavement study between the tendency to ruminate and the inability to find meaning in the experience of loss. The highest level of distress at follow-up interviews was demonstrated by the group who struggled continually to make sense of the inexplicable. Certain contextual circumstances may make it more difficult for people to find meaning or benefits from the deaths of loved ones. Among these kinds of deaths are those that occur suddenly (Parkes & Weiss, 1983); deaths of children (Nolen-Hoeksema & Larson, 1999); deaths due to intentional, malicious causes such as homicide (Murphy, 1997); and deaths due to the negligence of others, such as those involving motor vehicle accidents (Wortman, Battle, & Lemkau, 1997). Some measure of restitution made by the perpetrators of these acts can be beneficial in reducing the bereaved families' distress and promoting resolution of grief (Davis et al., 2000).

AN INTEGRATED PERSPECTIVE ON GRIEF

As research in this area increases, more sophisticated models of grieving have been developed (Cook & Oltjenbruns, 1998; Rubin, 1981). One such model that weaves together some of the theoretical and empirical threads described above is the **dual-process model** proposed by Stroebe and Schut (1999). This conceptualization depicts an interplay of stressors and coping strategies within a flexible, oscillating framework. Specifically, the authors propose that bereaved

[handwritten margin notes: "Debunk idea that you must face the grief 'head-on'" and "American perspective"]

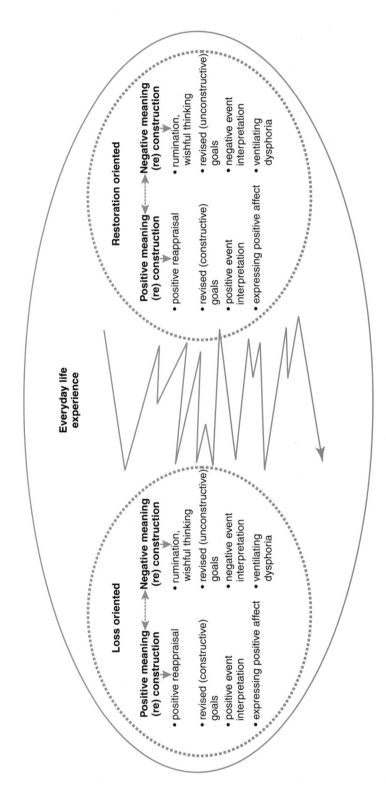

FIGURE 15.5

A Dual-Process Model of Coping with Loss: Pathways

Source: Stroebe, M. S., & Schut, H. (2001). Model of coping with bereavement: A review. In M. S. Stroebe, R. O Hansson, W. Stroebe & H. Schut (Eds.), *Handbook of bereavement research: Consequences, coping, and care* (p. 397). Used by permission of the authors.

individuals simultaneously engage in two kinds of coping mechanisms, approach and avoidance, that wax and wane over the course of grieving.

Approach tendencies are reflected in activities synonymous with grief work: confronting the painful reality of death, expressing sadness, and gradually desensitizing oneself to the reminders of loss. Approach tendencies can be tolerated for only so long. They are loss focused and can lead to rumination or excessive preoccupation and, often, great distress. According to the dual-process model, the loss-focused work of grieving is balanced by parallel activities that are restoration focused. This type of coping strategy is directed toward handling the practical tasks that need to be done to carry on with daily life. For example, a widow might experience intense periods of grief during which she focuses on memories of her life with her deceased spouse; however, she might also have dependent children who need care. Attending to their needs serves as a distraction, mitigating the periods of loss-related distress. Both loss and restoration coping strategies are part of the grieving process, and Stroebe and Schut view their dynamic oscillation as a healthy regulatory mechanism. Bereaved individuals go back and forth between emotion-focused (loss-oriented) and problem-focused (restoration-oriented) modes of coping. This approach-avoidance interplay protects bereaved individuals from the exacting extremes of unrelieved distress or rigid mental suppression. In general, there is more loss-oriented coping early in the grieving process and more restoration-oriented coping at later points. Traditional conceptions of abnormal grief can be viewed as "disturbances of oscillation" (Stroebe & Schut, 1999, p. 217), either overly loss oriented or excessively avoidant. Figure 15.5 presents a diagram of the dual-process model of coping.

APPLICATIONS

This chapter presents information about some key ways people change in later life and how they adapt to or cope with those changes. Coping has been defined as a person's "cognitive and behavioral efforts to manage (reduce, minimize, master, or tolerate) the internal and external demands of the person–environment transaction that is appraised as taxing or exceeding the resources of the person" (Folkman, Lazarus, Gruen, & DeLongis, 1986, p. 572). Adaptive coping, or managing the demands of life relatively well, is at the heart of achieving and maintaining optimal health and wellness. This is certainly true at any age, but perhaps even more so in old age, when the threat of overtaxed resources and the need to tolerate limitations becomes inevitable. Life involves gains and losses. It is naïve to assume that everyone can and will maintain a high quality of life right up to their death. But on the other hand, unnecessarily pessimistic views of old age, fueled by negative stereotypes of the elderly, restrict the ways people choose to adapt to aging and limit their sense of control over their lives. Counselors who are knowledgeable about and skilled in understanding coping mechanisms can promote healthy adaptation, regardless of client age (Ponzo, 1992). Sources of concrete information about how to cope with getting old (Skinner & Vaughan, 1983/1997), how to understand the perspective of elders (Pipher, 1999), and how to deal with dementia (Mace & Rabins, 1999) can help clinicians build their foundation of knowledge. Whitbourne (1989) summarizes the task:

> The main point that a clinician must keep foremost in mind when working with an aging client is the need to be

flexible. The aging process involves multiple physical, psychological, and social demands that can all potentially impact on the individual's ability to function. Clinicians may be called upon to perform advocacy services, environmental interventions, and interdisciplinary consultations, which they would not ordinarily regard as falling within the domain of "psychotherapy." It is only by maintaining an open approach to the multiple needs of the aged client that the clinician can hope to bring about successful change. (p. 168)

A Good Fit: Adaptations for Counselors

Myers and Harper (2004) offer useful suggestions for clinicians who work with older clients. In general, counselors who work with this population may be younger than their clients. Consequently, more time and sensitivity are required to build rapport with individuals who may be less comfortable with sharing feelings or with asking questions of "authority" figures. Younger counselors also need to be prepared to deal nondefensively with older clients who might view them as unable to understand the lived experience of old age. Lengthening the sessions in individual counseling and increasing the number of sessions for support groups or other group therapy formats is more important in reducing relapse for older clients than is the case for younger ones. Psychological treatments should be modified as well. Kennedy and Tannenbaum (2000) show how many typical counseling approaches can be accommodated to meet the

Older people often meet their need to feel competent and productive by engaging in part-time or volunteer work.

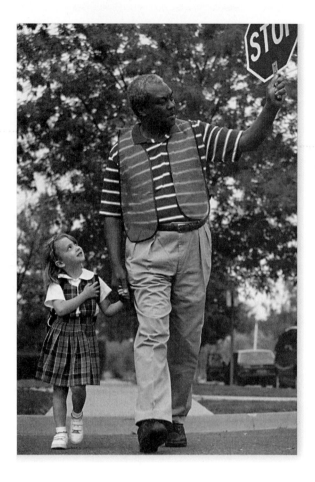

needs of older clients. These modifications have been summarized for a selection of therapies in Table 15.6.

The flexibility described by Whitbourne above should extend to the physical environment in which counseling is provided. For example, older clients may have physical limitations that affect their ability to sit for long periods or may need modifications to assessment procedures due to hearing or vision problems. Lyness (2004) advises medical and counseling professionals who work with an older population to screen routinely for depression and other mental health issues because mental health concerns can be the underlying cause of many other presenting problems.

Healthy Aging and Prevention

The amount of research on aging continues to grow, due, at least in part, to the aging of the U.S. population. The newest wave of research is focused on "successful aging," a perspective that assumes that healthy functioning and even the achievement of certain gains is possible in late life. One such initiative is actually a series of studies called the MacArthur study because of the financial support provided by the John D. and Catherine T. MacArthur Foundation (Rowe & Kahn, 1998). The fruits of 10 years of intensive investigations involving thousands of participants, millions of dollars, and

the combined expertise of biologists, neuropsychologists, sociologists, epidemiologists, geneticists, and gerontologists, among others, tell us a great deal about successful aging.

To summarize briefly, enjoying a healthy and productive old age is possible. The more physically and mentally fit older individuals are, the more likely they will age successfully. Clearly, one's lifestyle prior to old age can have a tremendous influence on the quality of later life. A healthy diet and regular exercise, including aerobics and weight training, confers a real physical advantage. Although maintaining healthy habits provides protection from disease and should, ideally, be maintained consistently, the MacArthur study revealed that positive changes in eating and exercise habits, even in old age, can help people live longer and healthier lives.

One of the most interesting findings from the study is that good physical health in old age is strongly related to mental ability and social support. Those who had higher levels of cognitive functioning and higher levels of social support prior to later life were likely to maintain their physical capacities. Continuing to learn, whether it be formal learning or the "just for fun" mental activity of crossword puzzles, provides important environmental stimulation or cognitive "exercise." Surprisingly, the kind of social support that is most important is not instrumental support (for example, providing help in cooking, cleaning, etc.), important as this is, but emotional support (for example, patient listening, cheering up, comforting touch,

TABLE 15.6 Therapeutic Adaptations for Older Clients

Type of Therapy	Examples of Target Therapeutic Outcomes	Some Adaptations for Older Clients
Brief Psychodynamic	Resolving survivor guilt; reducing negative attitudes toward self related to aging	Recognition and skillful handling of specific kinds of transference issues, such as client's view of therapist as unable to help senior citizens due to "inexperience."
Cognitive Behavioral	Changing dysfunctional thoughts; active problem solving	Understanding of older clients' learning styles; recognition of cognitive and sensory impairments that might interfere with learning; use of concrete written material and provision of ample review.
Behavioral Therapy for Depression	Improving mood through increasing positive reinforcement	Provision of methodical and concrete approaches to identify and engage in positive, mood-enhancing experiences and systematically avoid unpleasant experiences.
Interpersonal Therapy for Depression	Improving interpersonal relationships through time-limited approach to problem-solving using therapist as supportive resource	Active therapeutic stance that focuses on solving real problems within the context of old age; provision of ample social support.
Life Review or Reminiscence Therapy	Finding meaning in life at present through integration of past conflicts	Empathic listening that provides a context for a review of the past; review of memorabilia like photographs, journals, and writing exercises.
Group Therapy	Addressing multiple needs of older clients, particularly clients in institutionalized settings	Screening of participants to ensure a relatively high degree of homogeneity in cognitive and sensory functioning; provision of structured format; ample positive reinforcement of group members; timing of meeting in midmorning to early afternoon.

Source: Adapted from Kennedy, G. J., & Tanenbaum, S. (2000). Psychotherapy with older adults. *American Journal of Psychotherapy,* *54*, 386–407. Reprinted by permission of the Association for the Advancement of Psychotherapy.

etc.). Not only is it important for older people to get emotional support from others, but many successful agers say that it is important for them to give it, too.

A sense of being productive appears to be a benchmark of healthy aging as well. Healthy men and women are three times more likely than those with physical or mental health problems to be engaged in paid work or volunteer activities. However, as we have seen, even people with physical limitations often manage, with some creativity, to engage in activities that keep them in touch with the world. Productive engagement with others, in whatever form it takes, is linked to a sense of mastery or personal self-efficacy. A "can-do" attitude contributes enormously to well-being. Counselors can facilitate the development of self-efficacy by fashioning opportunities for older individuals that reflect their self-endorsed goals and that challenge their capacities without overwhelming them. Counselors also need to provide encouragement to older people to engage in these challenges, give confirming feedback for mastery, and help dispel negative stereotypes that lead to passivity and hopelessness.

When Losses Occur

What should we do to help when the losses of later life occur? Based on recent longitudinal studies, several principles appear to be important. Counselors should be aware that grief has many affective, behavioral, and physical manifestations and that there is wide variation in expressions of mourning at the level of the individual and culture. The oversimplified use of stage theories may suggest that there is one correct way to grieve and one circumscribed time frame in which to do so. One can only imagine how discouraging it must be for a bereaved person to be told that she is not grieving correctly. In our fast-paced world, it is often difficult to let people take the time they need to heal. Clinicians should not hold prescriptive rules for how long grief should last, because many people continue to grieve well beyond the limits of several months or even years.

Remember as well that the absence of overt, intense grief is not necessarily problematic. Not everyone who fails to demonstrate great distress or who does not search for meaning in a loss will suffer eventual emotional problems. Furthermore, we often expect people to "recover" from a loss by returning to an earlier level of functioning, despite evidence that this is often impossible.

Difficulties in the grief process may be considered to be an imbalance between too much expression and too little, but even this is mediated by personality, gender, culture, and beliefs. Some interventions that have traditionally been favored by bereavement counselors, such as grief work interventions, may not be useful and may actually be more distressing for individuals given to ruminative tendencies. Even support seeking, a style of coping that involves seeking help from other people, may be a source of stress unless those sought after for help are themselves compassionate and willing to listen (Nolen-Hoeksema & Larson, 1999).

Several sets of tasks have been developed that describe the responsibilities of helpers or other caregivers in times of bereavement (Rando, 1993; Worden, 1982). The following is a brief description of Worden's tasks with evidence-based recommendations derived from the bereavement coping project of Nolen-Hoeksema & Larson (1999). Keep in mind that bereaved individuals differ in their needs, so these recommendations should be considered general guidelines.

1. Bereaved individuals may need support in order to accept the reality of loss. Providing assistance with funeral arrangements and helping to prepare meals or clean up are all useful ways to be of help. It is important not to "push" the person to accept the loss but to be respectful of the individual's style of coping.

2. Helpers and other loved ones should allow bereaved persons to identify and express feelings if they want to do so. Judicious use of open-ended questions and provisional language ("Sometimes people say that they occasionally feel anxious or impatient. I wonder if you ever feel that way?" Nolen-Hoeksema & Larson, 1999, p. 182) can promote feelings of safety and acceptance.

3. Bereaved persons need to learn how to live without their lost loved ones. For example, they may need to learn restoration-focused tasks previously handled by the deceased, such as managing finances or cooking for children. The helper can scaffold the development of these skills by anticipating possible needs, helping to break them down into manageable tasks, and providing concrete assistance or information.

4. Survivors may need help in finding a place in their lives for the deceased. This may take many forms, depending upon the individual, but generally entails finding a way to maintain some emotional connection. For some people, talking about the deceased is easier and more beneficial than talking about themselves. Silverman (2000) noticed in her work with bereaved children that they were much more articulate when asked to talk about the person who died than they were when asked to talk about their own feelings about the death. She called this process "constructing a relationship to the deceased."

5. The next task for helpers requires them to be patient and allow time and a nurturing context for grieving.

6. Helpers may need to help normalize grief for the bereaved. Grieving people often report fears about "going crazy" because of symptoms such as visual or sensory hallucinations, panic attacks, and other signs of intense distress. Learning that these are common occurrences in bereavement that will go away in time is very reassuring.

7. Counselors should provide continuing support, as needed, to help survivors weather the trials of grieving and to assist them in examining the effectiveness or ineffectiveness of their coping strategies. Taking notice of strategies that are effective is an empowering exercise because it allows people to recognize that they have some choice. Strategies that are less helpful can be identified, and more useful possibilities can be suggested.

8. Finally, helpers need to identify and find other sources of support if they, for whatever reason, cannot provide for the range of needs described above.

Integrity: The Life Cycle Completed

From Erikson's (1950/1963) perspective, people struggle continuously throughout the life cycle with the "hazards of existence" (p. 274) and should not expect to reach a level of achievement in any of the stages that is completely impervious to conflict. The negative pole of each developmental task represents its counterpoint, a reminder of each stage's dynamic quality (see Chapter 1, Table 1.2). The period of old age is no exception. Facing old age and death are awesome challenges. Yet over a lifetime, the struggles of earlier stages ideally bear fruit. The resulting integrity, that sense of coherence or wholeness that comes from "acceptance of *one's own and only life cycle* [italics added]" (p. 268) is the product of strengths accumulated from each earlier period: hope, self-control, direction, love, devotion, affiliation, and care. Renunciation, the outcome of the final stage according to Erikson, is consummate generativity. It embodies acceptance of the natural order, namely that wisdom which allows us to view death as a stage of life. "Healthy children will not fear life," Erikson wrote, "if their elders have integrity enough not to fear death" (p. 269).

Erikson's view of the life span, then, is less of a straight line and more of a circle, with its final stage a gift of courage and caring for the generations that follow. In his psychosocial view of development, the quality of life from beginning to end is touched by its social intersections. As we are learning, positive relationships keep people well (Ryff & Singer, 2000); they offer long-term protective factors. Nurturing others, so necessary for survival of our species, returns on the investment at the end of life when we receive others' care. As we age, some have suggested the need to reminisce or review life events as a way of integrating the features of one's identity and achieving integrity (Butler, 1963). Part of the benefit of this process, undoubtedly, involves sharing the story with others.

We have provided throughout this book descriptions of various aspects of human functioning: attachments, social networks, cognition, identity, marriage, family ties and aging, among many others. There is much left to learn about these topics and about how that knowledge can be used to benefit individuals and societies. The research agendas of the 21st century promise to improve even further our working knowledge of the life span. With this knowledge, clinicians are in a unique position to promote positive development, to foster wellbeing, and to create conditions that support resilience in the face of life's challenges.

SUMMARY

Aging Well

1. Despite the increasing number of losses older people experience as they move into old age (60s and 70s) or into old-old age (80s and 90s), most older individuals manage to adapt to old age successfully.

2. As people age, they experience declines in many physical systems, including the immune and sensory systems. Arthritis, particularly osteoarthritis, is especially common.

3. Cognitive declines in fluid intelligence (e.g., processing speed and working memory) may be partially offset by maintenance or even advancements in crystallized intelligence (e.g., verbal ability and factual knowledge). Cognitive functioning in old age is related to overall health, and substantial declines in cognitive functioning, known as dementia, are usually due to cardiovascular accidents or disease processes such as Alzheimer's disease. Terminal drop refers to a rapid decline in intellectual functioning shortly before death.

4. Studies of autobiographical memory indicate that, contrary to stereotypic notions, older people remember their more recent experiences better than earlier experiences (recency), even though older adults learn new information less efficiently than younger adults. However, if adults are asked about flashbulb memories, especially vivid and personally relevant recollections, their reports are largely about events in their early adulthood, referred to as the bump period. That is probably why elderly people often tell stories about their early years.

5. As people age, their network of friends and family members shrinks. Social loss is exacerbated by negative stereotypes about aging that assume all elderly people share certain negative characteristics. These stereotypes can lead to discriminatory or demeaning practices that interfere with positive social interactions.

6. Three processes appear to be important for successful development in old age. Selection involves limiting activities to a few that are particularly rewarding. Optimization involves finding ways of enhancing achievement of remaining goals. Compensation involves finding new means to achieve our ends. Together these processes are called selective optimization with compensation.

7. There are other, similar ways of describing adaptation processes. In self-determination theory, three needs are said to motivate adaptation at any age: autonomy, competence, and relatedness.

8. Another description of techniques for facing challenges emphasizes two broad strategies. Primary-control strategies are attempts to affect the immediate environment and often increase feelings of mastery and self-esteem. Secondary-control strategies are attempts to change ourselves, such as changing goals. If the latter approach allows a person to then take primary control over some stressor, feelings of happiness and well-being are likely to be enhanced.

9. On the whole, older people seem to cope well with the challenges of late life. They compare positively with younger adults on some aspects of well-being, such as positive relationships and self-acceptance.

10. Does increased wisdom help the elderly to cope? Wisdom involves superior knowledge, judgment, and advice with regard to important questions about life. Research indicates that it is somewhat more likely to characterize older rather than younger adults, although wisdom seems to be as much a quality of the individual person as it is of age.

11. As people age, they pay more attention to their feelings, and their emotions are more enhanced and complex. Positive emotions are as common among the old as the young, but negative emotions occur less often. Also, emotion regulation seems to improve.

Experiencing Loss

12. Elderly people report less anxiety about death than younger people. Dying adults often must deal with others' reluctance to deal with death and may feel lonely and isolated.

13. A good death for most people includes symptom management and care (such as freedom from pain, being clean), practical details (such as knowing what to expect), a good patient–professional relationship, and certain psychological attributes (such as maintaining dignity, not dying alone). But many people have very individual needs and desires as well. For example, some people prefer to die at home, but many do not. Palliative care, such as that promoted by the hospice movement, is important to most people.

14. People who sign living wills or advance directives do not necessarily know more about their end-of-life options, although those who have recently cared for a dying patient are more aware.

15. Kubler-Ross described several reactions to dying that are called stages but that do not necessarily occur for all dying adults and do not occur in any fixed sequence: These are denial, anger, bargaining, depression, and acceptance.

16. Both Freud and Bowlby proposed influential theories of the grief process. Freud originally believed that bereaved individuals needed to withdraw from the lost loved one and reinvest emotional energy into forming new attachments. Bowlby used attachment theory concepts to describe stages of the grief process: shock, protest, despair, and reorganization. Assumptions derived from these theories have been disputed by contemporary

researchers. In particular, the existence of a stage sequence of grief reactions has not been validated. The concept of abnormal grief and the need for cathartic grief work have been called into question as well.

17. Contemporary models of grieving include diverse ways of coping with loss. The dual-process model of Stroebe and Schut incorporates both loss-focused elements and restoration-focused elements within a flexible framework.

CASE STUDY

Isabelle and her husband Victor lived together for 53 years in a small, close-knit Italian American section of a big city. Victor made a living for the family working as a forklift operator. Isabelle, a stay-at-home mother when her children were young, returned to work as a sales clerk once the youngest two children entered high school. Isabelle enjoyed her years of full-time mothering, but she also loves the social interaction and camaraderie she finds in her job. The family has four grown children, Paul, 51, Sophia, 49, and twins Lenore and Joseph, 45. Paul and his wife own and operate a small restaurant in a nearby suburb. They have two young adult children. Sophia, also married with two children, teaches in a middle school about an hour away from her parents' home. Lenore has recently remarried after a divorce. She lives with her second husband and her three children in the city. Joseph is a salesperson who has never married but who lives in another state with his longtime partner, Joanne.

At this time, the family is struggling to come to grips with Victor's recent death. After years of robust health, Victor was diagnosed with pancreatic cancer. During the last 4 months of his life, he was in and out of the hospital as his health demanded. Isabelle tried to care for him as best she could, but it was very difficult. The side effects of Victor's treatment protocol left him feeling ill and in need of constant care. The family members tried to help, but the greatest burden fell to Paul because in this family the oldest child is perceived to have the most responsibility.

As time went on and it became clear that Victor was dying, Isabelle mentioned to her children that their father had not wanted any extraordinary measures to be used to keep him alive in his final illness. Victor had never put this in writing, but Isabelle was sure of his wishes. Victor's family physician, a deeply religious man, Victor's older brother, and Joseph all strongly disagreed with this plan. They believed that every effort should be made to save Victor's life. One night, Victor lapsed into a coma and was having trouble breathing. Joseph prevailed upon his mother to allow the physician to insert a ventilator. Joseph's siblings were very upset about this turn of events, for they believed it caused their father unnecessary suffering. Victor died several days later.

Now 4 months after the death of her husband, Isabelle is grieving the loss of her spouse. She lives alone but is seriously contemplating asking her son Paul to let her move in with his family. She quit her job at the department store because she felt she was unable to concentrate well enough to perform in a satisfactory manner. She has been unable to sleep through the night, and her mind keeps returning to memories of Victor during his illness.

Relationships are strained among the children. Neither daughter speaks to Joseph or Joanne because of their disagreement about Victor's care. Joanne believes that Joseph should "move on" and concentrate on her and their life together. Lenore avoids calling her mother because she does not want to hear her repeat the same troubles over and over again. She uses her hectic schedule as a full-time mother as an excuse. Sophia is somewhat more attentive, but she is also uncomfortable listening to her mother's reminiscences. She wants to believe that her mother is still the same vibrant person she has always known, so she discounts the sadness she hears in Isabelle's voice. Paul is overwhelmed by the responsibility he feels for his family, his business, and his mother. He knows his mother is grieving, but he cannot find a way to make her feel better. For her part, Isabelle feels that she has come to the end of her life as well. She believes that she will end up like many of the other lonely widows she knows in her neighborhood.

Discussion Questions

1. What are the emotional and behavioral responses of each person to Victor's death?
2. Identify the stressors that are operating on this family. Distinguish between those that can be controlled and those that cannot be changed. Develop a list of coping strategies that might be useful in dealing with these problems.
3. As a counselor, how would you begin to work with this family? With Isabelle?

JOURNAL QUESTIONS

1. Identify someone you know whom you see as aging successfully. Write a letter to this person (to be given or not) describing how you think the person is dealing with growing old and why you admire the person.

2. What would you do if you had only 6 months to live?
3. What kind of ceremony or funeral ritual would you like to have when you die? Why would you choose this particular type of ritual?

KEY TERMS

arthritis
osteoarthritis
dementia
terminal drop (terminal decline)
cerebrovascular accidents (strokes)
multi-infarct dementia
Alzheimer's disease (AD)
plaques
tangles
autobiographical memory
recency
"the bump"

flashbulb memories
selection
optimization
compensation
selective optimization with compensation
primary control
secondary control
stages of retirement
   honeymoon
   disenchantment
   reorientation
   stability
   termination

wisdom
end-of-life care
palliative care
hospice movement
refusal of treatment
physician-assisted suicide
active euthanasia
double effect
advance directives (living wills)
denial
anger
bargaining

depression
acceptance
grief work
decathecting
shock
protest
despair
reorganization
complicated or abnormal grief
dual-process model
loss-focused grief
restoration-focused grief

Now go to our Companion Website to assess your understanding of chapter content with Multiple Choice Questions, apply comprehension in Essay Questions, and broaden your knowledge of development with related Web Links.

A Practitioner's Guide to Psychological Science

UNDERSTANDING THE SCIENTIFIC PROCESS

We have argued that information gained from scientific research on development is important for clinical practitioners to know. Yet, practitioners often do not find research findings helpful or relevant to the problems they face with their clients. What is going on here? Is scientific work of practical value or not? It can be, but only if the practitioner understands the scientific process.

Most of us are enculturated to believe that the sciences provide answers to life's conundrums, and sometimes they do. For example, at one time the causes of diseases such as tuberculosis or polio were a mystery, but biological research has now established that microorganisms are the culprits. The path that biologists followed to achieve this insight was a laborious and time-consuming one, with many wrong turns or apparent missteps. Adequate scientific answers almost always are found at the end of similarly circuitous routes. As a result, practitioners closely allied to any scientific field sometimes find that the best scientific information of today can change tomorrow. In addition, scientists may offer competing answers to the same question until enough work has been done on a phenomenon to establish one answer, or some amalgam of previous answers, as valid. It is not unusual for practitioners faced with competing scientific "answers" to begin to wonder, "What good is science?"

Let's address this question by first looking at the nature of the scientific process. Then we will examine how practitioners can effectively use science to achieve their goals.

Psychology as the Study of Human Behavior

The study of human behavior and its associated mental processes—motivations, cognitions, emotions, and so on—is a topic of great interest to most of us, and it is the subject of many disciplines besides the social sciences. Most of the humanities, such as literature, history, and philosophy, are focused primarily on human behavior. What differentiates these disciplines are the *methods* that they use to gain understanding. For example, the study of *literature* is in part the study of human behavior as seen through the eyes of great writers of fiction. Through their literary work, writers share with us their observations and beliefs about human motivation, morality, social functioning, and so on. *History* examines the unfolding of human behavior in past events, lining up the facts that can be uncovered about the actions of real people in earlier times and speculating about the connections between these actions and their underlying causes. *Philosophers* usually focus their attention on human behavior as well, but their preferred method is rational analysis. For example, a particular philosopher may take human language as her subject matter and attempt to analyze its sources and its implications for the operation of the human mind. The social sciences are like these other disciplines in their subject matter, human behavior, but they use different methods—the methods of science.

The Three Steps in Scientific Investigation

Across different scientific disciplines—psychology, biology, physics, or any other science—the subject matter changes, but the general methods are the same. Some specific techniques may vary, adapted to the particulars of the topics under scrutiny, but three broad steps are alike for all sciences: *description*, *explanation*, and *verification*.

DESCRIPTION

Description is a research step aimed at answering factual questions about a phenomenon, questions such as who, what, when, where, and with whom. Suppose we were interested in understanding the phenomenon of juvenile delinquency. We would begin our scientific exploration by seeking answers to questions such as the following: *Who* engages in juvenile delinquency? (What are the usual ages, gender, socioeconomic status, family characteristics, intellectual characteristics, academic performance, social skills, personality characteristics, and so on, of children identified as delinquent?) *What* kinds of behaviors usually characterize delinquency? (Are most delinquents truants, or nonviolent thieves, or violent murderers, or other kinds of perpetrators?) *Where* and *when* are delinquent acts most likely to occur? *With whom* are delinquents likely to associate and to commit their evil deeds?

EXPLANATION

With an arsenal of facts gained from descriptive research, we are ready to take the next step, *explanation*. At this point, we frame a *theory* or set of *hypotheses* about *how* the facts are related to each other and *why* they occur. Our other theoretical commitments are likely to influence us here. For example, we may tend to make stage assumptions, or we may be more apt to formulate incremental theories. Our theories may be broad in scope, attempting to integrate all the data we've collected, or they may be simple hypotheses, focused on particular aspects of the facts. In formulating a theory, we should meet certain criteria. First, the theory must be *comprehensive*, that is, either it must take into account all of the known facts (for a broad theory) or at least it should not be inconsistent with any of the known facts (for a more simple, focused hypothesis). Second, it must be presented with sufficient clarity that we can make *verifiable predictions* from it.

A note of caution here: It is important to recognize that by definition, a theory or hypothesis is an *inference* rather than an observed fact. Statements about causes are always inferences, because causal relationships cannot be directly observed. We can obtain evidence for them—as you will see in the next step—but we cannot actually *prove* them without a doubt.

VERIFICATION

The gathering of evidence for our theories, or *verification*, is the third step in scientific method. Verification processes provide means of judging theories *objectively*, on the basis of factual support, rather than *subjectively*, on the basis of how appealing they might be or how well they might fit our biases. At this point again, the scientist turns to research. It is not good enough for a theory to be effective at *post hoc* explanation, that is, comprehensively explaining the facts we already have. To be really convincing, a theory must generate predictions about events or behaviors that have not yet been observed. Research is designed to test those predictions. If they come true, there is evidence to support the theory. If the predictions fail to come true, there is evidence against the theory. Albert Einstein's theory of relativity revolutionized physics, posing relationships among known facts and suggesting causal processes not previously proposed. It was appealing because it helped explain some findings that had not fit with previous theories. But, like any scientific theory, Einstein's view had to pass the litmus test; could it predict events not previously observed? Despite the abstractness of his principles, the theory did succeed in generating a few predictions about concrete events that had not yet been observed, and these predictions did come true. Thus, Einstein's idea now has the status of being not just a creative explanation of known data, but a theory with supporting evidence.

Suppose, however, that we formulate a theory that sounds good, but its predictions do not come true. Or, as more often happens, some of its predictions come true, and some do not. Or, even more disconcerting, the predictions of our theory come true, but so do the predictions of a very different theory to explain the same phenomenon! This is a situation that drives many students of a science, and allied practitioners, to distraction: scientists providing more than one answer to the same question!

There is a scientific approach to resolving such dilemmas. The next step is to go back to the explanation process, taking the new data we have gained from our verification efforts to craft a new, or at least a modified theory. Then we move forward again to the verification process. Science advances in this fashion, taking the evidence (both pro and con) gathered from testing one theory to help develop a better one, then subjecting the new theory to the same rigorous tests, until eventually we have a theory that encompasses all the known facts and can generate valid predictions.

In our everyday lives, all of us sometimes operate a little like scientists. Suppose there is a phenomenon that concerns us. Perhaps a close friend begins to behave erratically, laughing or grunting inappropriately during conversations, having animated discussions with no one at all, acting irritable or becoming strangely silent. Our first step in confronting, this problem is somewhat comparable to the scientist's *description* process. We try to gather more facts about our friend's behavior from coworkers, family, and friends, and we make more observations of our own. Our second step is similar to the scientist's *explanation* process: We try to develop a coherent theory that will explain how these facts fit together and why they are happening at all. Perhaps we hypothesize a schizophrenic breakdown or the onset of a degenerative brain disorder. At this point, however, our approach to our friend's behavior will probably lose its resemblance to the scientific process. Scientists would put all action on hold, make predictions from their theories, and proceed to test the predictions in carefully designed studies (see *Testing Scientific Theories*). In our everyday lives, however, we are more likely to jump into practical application, such as urging the family to seek medical help. We rarely have the time or the resources to actually verify our theories in systematic ways. We simply act on them and hope that we've made the right guesses. Scientists advance more slowly to action, avoiding practical application until theories are strongly supported by evidence.

Helping professionals, too, use a process closely akin to scientific method if they follow the tenets of reflective practice. First, as in the scientist's description process, they gather all the information they can about a client and the client's problem. This part of reflective practice includes examining theories and information available from scientific work that might be relevant, as well as considering both standard practices for dealing with similar problems and the practitioner's own experiences. From all of this information, the practitioner formulates hypotheses about the client and about the most appropriate clinical strategy (as in the scientist's explanation process) and then "tests" these hypotheses (as in the scientist's verification process). However, for the practitioner, testing hypotheses occurs in the practice itself, so that, unlike the scientist, clinical professionals apply and adjust their hypotheses in the context of practice. In sum, scientifically generated knowledge informs clinical practice not by providing *answers* but by providing *options* for the development of hypotheses that can be tested in application and by suggesting strategies for handling problems.

TESTING THEORIES SCIENTIFICALLY

To understand how scientific research is done, particularly in the social sciences, let's consider examples of research done to test a hypothesis that was popular among developmental scientists about fifty years ago. The hypothesis was that a baby's dependency is substantially caused by parental nurturance. When parents respond to their infant's cries or give their babies attention of any kind, they are reinforcing help-seeking behavior, or "dependency." So, for example, a baby who gets a lot of attention for crying will become more of a crybaby. No one suggested that babies should be ignored, but the implications of this theory were that nonessential caregiving should be sparse if one hoped that they babies would learn to tolerate waiting and eventually learn to do things for themselves. The idea was consistent with some common ideas about appropriate baby care, such as the warning that running to a baby every time it cries will "spoil" the child.

The proposal that "nurturance causes infant dependency" is a simple theory or hypothesis. "Nurturance" is the single postulated cause, or **causal variable**, and "infant dependency" is what is said to be affected by the cause, or the **outcome variable**. Some theories are much more complex, posing more than one cause, suggesting interactions among causes, or speculating about effects on more than one outcome variable. But regardless of how complex a theory becomes, it can be verified only by testing its predictions. There are two general techniques for testing the predictions of any theory, **experiments** and **correlational studies**. These techniques can be as complex as the theories that inspire them, but no matter how complex they become they are only extensions of the basic experimental or correlational procedures that we will now describe.

Experiments

An experiment is a study in which the researcher purposely changes (or manipulates) the causal variable in order to observe or measure the effects of the manipulation on the outcome variable. In a good experiment, the researcher also takes care that nothing else systematically changes at the same time as the causal variable. This ensures that if the outcome variable does seem to be affected, only the postulated causal variable could be responsible. When a scientist succeeds in eliminating alternative explanations for the changes in the outcome variable, we say that the researcher has exercised *control* over other, possible causes.

When proposed causes of human behavior are put to experimental test, psychologists and other social scientists use certain standard procedures, adapted to the study of people. To test the hypothesis that "nurturance causes infant dependency," Rheingold (1956) conducted an experiment with babies in an orphanage who ordinarily did not get any attention beyond essential physical care. Her plan was to increase the babies' nurturance (manipulate the causal variable) and later determine whether the babies' dependency had also increased (observe/measure the outcome variable). However, Rheingold needed to be sure that no other changes in the babies' lives could account for any observed change in the babies' dependency. If Rheingold were studying inanimate objects, she might have been able to make certain that nothing else changed at the same time that she changed the causal variable. But with human infants, it was not possible to simply keep everything else from changing. In most studies with humans, researchers simply do not have that much power. For example, the babies' nurturance was increased for a 6-week period. But during this period the babies changed in age as well, a process that could not be stopped. There may also have been other, less obvious changes in the babies' experiences. For example, the orphanage could have contracted to buy baby formula from a different vendor, so that the taste and quality of the babies' food could have changed. Rheingold exercised control over all of these alternative explanations of the outcome not by preventing them from changing, but by using a **control group**.

The control group was a second group of babies from the same orphanage nursery who experienced all of the "unstoppable" changes that the first group of babies (the experimental group) experienced: they got older in the 6 weeks of the study, and if anything else in the nursery changed, such as the baby formula, it changed for them, too. However, Rheingold did not increase the amount of nurturance that the control group babies received. In the end, the babies in the experimental group, for whom nurturance was increased, showed increased dependency, just as predicted, but the babies in the control group showed no change in their dependency. Because the control group babies experienced everything that the experimental group babies experienced except for increased nurturance, *only* the increased nurturance could have been the cause of greater dependency in the experimental group babies.

Experiments with humans usually "control" causes other than the postulated causal variable by incorporating control groups to which the experimental group can be compared. The experimental group is defined as the group for which the causal variable is purposely changed. The control group is a group like the experimental group in every way except that the causal variable is not purposely changed. Chemists and other scientists who study the inanimate, physical world need not use control group procedures, but psychologists need this technique because, either for practical or for ethical reasons, they cannot necessarily prevent other possible causes from changing during the course of an experiment.

Correlational Studies

Sometimes, both in psychology and in other sciences, predictions cannot be tested using experiments. Remember, in an experiment, the researcher purposely changes the causal variable. But what if the researcher does not have the power to change the causal variable? In some sciences, such as astronomy, this is usually the case. Suppose an astronomer hypothesizes that "meteor showers cause temperature increases in the outer atmosphere of planet X" (a hypothesis invented by a textbook author who knows little about astronomy). To do an experiment, the astronomer would have to manipulate the occurrence of meteor showers (the causal variable) and then observe or measure atmospheric temperature (the outcome variable) to see whether it also changes. But astronomers cannot (at least at the present time) manipulate the occurrence of meteor showers, so such an experiment could not be done. The alternative, in such a case, is to do a *correlational study*, a technique in which both the causal variable and the outcome variable are measured or observed, and nothing is actually manipulated by the researcher. The research question is, do the two variables change together in the ways predicted by the hypothesis? In this astronomical example, the prediction is that the more intense a naturally occurring meteor shower is, the greater will be the temperature increase in planet X's atmosphere.

A correlational study can determine whether changes in the causal variable are matched by predicted changes in the outcome variable. What a correlational study *cannot* do is tell us whether the changes in the causal variable actually determined the matching changes in the outcome variable. For example, an astronomer would not know if some other variable might also have changed when the meteor shower occurred. If it did, the other variable might actually have caused the increased temperature of planet X's atmosphere. Only experiments, with proper controls, can tell us whether the postulated causal variable is the real cause. But when the predictions of a theory come true in a correlational study, it is still evidence *for* the theory that made the prediction, because the results are consistent with the theory. And, when the predictions do not come true, it is still evidence *against* the theory, because the results are inconsistent with the theory.

Correlational studies are usually done in the social sciences when experiments are either impractical or unethical. Consider again the hypothesis that "nurturance causes infant dependency." Rheingold was able to purposely change the nurturance of babies in an orphanage because they were getting very little nurturance already, and no one considered it unethical to increase their nurturance for a while. But if Rheingold had wanted to change the nurturance of babies being cared for by their own parents, it is unlikely that the parents would have considered that reasonable. Parents have their own ideas about how much nurturance their babies should get. For this reason, when Ainsworth and her colleagues (e.g., Ainsworth, Bell, & Stayton, 1972; Ainsworth, Blehar, Waters, & Wall, 1978) wanted to look at the relationship between parental nurturance and infant dependency, they did a correlational study. They asked parents only to allow them to watch the nurturing process. Over a period of many months, they observed and measured mothers' nurturance of their infants (the causal variable in this hypothesis) and also measured infants' dependency (the outcome variable in this hypothesis). The hypothesis predicts that the more nurturance that mothers give their babies, the more dependent the babies become. This would be a ***positive correlation***: the two variables would change in the same direction, either both increasing or both decreasing. Surprisingly, given Rheingold's findings, the prediction did not come true. In fact, the results were just the opposite. At 8 months old, the infants whose mothers had provided the most nurturance until then were the ones who were the most independent! So, Ainsworth and her colleagues found a ***negative correlation***: The two variables (nurturance and dependency) changed together but in *opposite* directions, so that as one increased, the other decreased. Ainsworth's correlational study provided evidence *against* the hypothesis that "nurturance causes infant dependency."

When theories are tested, contradictory findings like Rheingold's and Ainsworth's are typical. No single study, either experiment or correlational study, is ever a sufficient test of a theory. Theories become more convincing as the stockpile of supporting evidence grows. If the evidence is contradictory, it's time to go back to the drawing board and consider how to change or replace this theory in order to explain all of the new findings. As you will see in Chapter 4, the studies of nurturance and dependency just described have led most researchers to prefer a more complex explanation of their relationship, now referred to as "attachment theory."

A Special Case: Studying Age Effects

Suppose we have a theory that some behavior or skill changes with age, for example, "In adulthood, aging causes declines in intelligence." We can use only correlational studies to test hypotheses where age is the causal variable, because age is not something that a researcher can directly change or manipulate. So age is observed, and the outcome variable (such as intelligence in this hypothesis) is observed or measured. However, age can be observed in three different ways, and each method has its own advantages and disadvantages.

CROSS-SECTIONAL STUDIES

In *cross-sectional studies*, different ages are represented by different groups of people. For example, a group of 20-year-olds might represent young adults, a group of 40-year-olds might represent middle-aged adults, and a group of 70-year-olds might represent older adults. Then all the subjects would be measured for the outcome variable (such as intelligence). When age and intelligence have been examined in this way, typically intelligence scores have declined with age as our sample hypothesis predicts.

But in cross-sectional studies, what look like the effects of age could be the result of **cohort** differences. Participants in each age group belong to a *cohort*: They were born in the same historical period, and they grew up at about the same time. People in different age groups belong to different cohorts. When it appears that age is causing some change, such as a decline in intelligence, the change could be the result of other differences among the cohorts. For example, educational approaches and opportunities may have changed dramatically from the time that today's 70-year-olds were kids to the time that today's 40-year-olds were kids, and these changes in education may be the cause of their differences in measured intelligence. Age may have nothing to do with it!

LONGITUDINAL STUDIES

Some researchers study age and its effects by doing **longitudinal** research. Only one group of subjects, all the same age, participates. They are measured several times as they get older. For example, in place of the cross-sectional study we just described, we could do a longitudinal study testing the intelligence of one group of participants several times throughout their lives, starting when they were all 20 years old.

This kind of design eliminates cohort differences because only one cohort is included. In longitudinal studies of intelligence, no declines are usually found until after age 50 or 60, and many individuals show increasing scores through much of adulthood, indicating that the steady declines in intelligence often observed in cross-sectional studies are due to cohort effects (see Chapter 13).

But longitudinal studies have their own disadvantages. First, they can take so long that the original researchers are retired or dead before the studies are completed! Second, age is not the only thing that could be causing the observed changes. Cultural changes could also be a cause of what look like age changes. For example, medical care and nutrition improved dramatically after World War II. If subjects in our imaginary longitudinal study have benefitted from such improvements, they may actually enjoy greater mental alertness as older adults than they did when they were young, helping them to perform better in a testing situation even though other elements of intelligence have not actually improved and may even have declined as a function of age.

Take heart, however, because there is a way to combine the advantages of both cross-sectional and longitudinal studies that helps to isolate the effects of age.

SEQUENTIAL STUDIES

A *sequential* study is like a cross-sectional study in that more than one cohort is included, and it is like a longitudinal study in that each cohort is measured at more than one age. Suppose again that we want to know if intelligence changes with age. We might include three cohorts in our study. Let's say one cohort, born in 1930, is measured at age 60 and again at 70; the second cohort, born in 1940, is measured at ages 50 and 60; and the last cohort, born in 1950, is measured at ages 40 and 50. All subjects are measured in the years 1990 and 2000. Our study will be 10 years long, but we will have information on whether intelligence increases or decreases over each 10-year age period from age 40 to age 70. The subjects who were born first may not have intelligence scores as high as those born later, but we are examining increases or decreases with age, not absolute scores. And cultural changes will be uniform for all cohorts because they are all being measured at the same times. Cultural changes could still explain results if all groups change the same way from the first to the second testing, but if there are improvements in some cohorts and declines in others, these differences cannot be explained by cultural change and are more likely the result of age.

QUALITATIVE RESEARCH METHODS

Qualitative research methods afford the developmentalist another, less traditional way of doing research. **Qualitative research** has been defined as "any kind of research that produces findings not arrived at by means of statistical procedures or other means of quantification" (Strauss & Corbin, 1990, p. 17). This definition appears to allow for many types of methodologies and techniques and may seem somewhat ambiguous. One way to clarify the concept is to view qualitative research as a way of answering questions not readily answerable by quantitative methods. For example, qualitative studies can be aimed at providing rich descriptive information about some concept or experience that is not well understood. Rather than using tests or other assessment instruments, the qualitative researcher may choose to interview the participants, make observations, or gather life histories. Although one of the purposes of this kind of research is to build theory, the actual data are not analyzed and tested as in more traditional methods. Instead, the data are the "voices" of the participants, who are allowed to speak for themselves. The data are not categorized according to any predetermined scheme but are allowed to evolve in novel ways. Consider, for example, the question of how middle-aged men cope over time with the death of a spouse when adolescent children are still in the home. A researcher may legitimately choose to study this topic using standardized questionnaires or interviews in an effort to categorize the fathers according to various established typologies of coping behavior. In contrast, a qualitative analysis would probably involve extensive, ongoing interviews without a predetermined typology or way of categorizing the fathers and would allow a "theory" of fathers' coping styles to build over the course of the project.

Daniel Levinson's (1996) study of the stages of a woman's life represents a good example of a qualitative research project. Using methods he called biographical interviewing and biographical reconstruction, he studied 45 women in order to learn about "the nature of women's development and about specific life issues relating to friendship, work, love, marriage, motherhood, good times and bad times, the stuff life is made of" (pp. 7–8). Levinson's intensive work with these participants resulted in complex, descriptive narratives that provided a framework for a theoretical construction about women's life trajectories.

Qualitative research approaches differ from more traditional methodologies in a number of ways. First, the data, as we have indicated, consist primarily of the words and actions of participants instead of numerical scores or frequencies. Second, the design of a study may change as the study progresses and the "data" are collected and considered. Third, a qualitative researcher may appear to be less objective than the more traditional researcher and may write about the study in a narrative style. Sometimes the data are reported in the first person. Fourth, no hypothesis is used to guide the study. However, a research question identifies the topic of the project, as in "how do middle-aged men, with adolescent children, cope with the death of a spouse?" Other differences exist as well, but these are some of the primary ones. Despite these differences, qualitative and traditional (quantitative) research methods share some similar features. Both approaches can be descriptive and have theory building as their goal (see *Understanding the Scientific Process*). Most importantly, perhaps, both maintain their own rigorous standards for reliability and validity (Lincoln & Guba, 1985).

Qualitative and quantitative methods can enhance each other by approaching a problem from more than one direction. Recently, a consortium of editors of developmental psychology journals endorsed the importance of qualitative methods and encouraged researchers to use them in their research projects. The editors stated that quantitative tools alone "cannot reveal the complex processes that likely give rise to normal and abnormal behavior among different children and adolescents" (Azar, 1999, pp. 20–21).

Glossary

academic self-concept: One of two divisions of children's general self-concept, referring to sense of self as an achiever in school subjects. Can be further divided into specific school subject areas such as math, science, English, and social studies.

acceptance: A reaction to impending death that is characterized by a sense of peace and relative tranquility, suggesting that one has come to terms with the inevitable.

acceptance factor: An aspect of parental responsiveness that includes being affectionate, praising the child, being involved in the child's life, and showing concern for the child's needs. Correlated with children's self-esteem and social adjustment.

accommodation: In Piaget's theory of cognitive development, the adaptation process by which existing knowledge structures are modified somewhat when an individual is exposed to new information.

achievement: One of Marcia's four identity status categories characterizing individuals whose development has been marked by exploration and then commitment to certain alternatives. Persons in this category have constructed their identity by their own efforts to shape and transform their earlier selves.

achieving commitment: An alternative name for Marcia's "achievement" that is used by Meeus and colleagues, because it emphasizes the dynamic linkage between high levels of commitment and high levels of exploration.

achieving stage: In Schaie's theory, the stage of cognitive development when a young adult must apply her intellectual skills to the achievement of long-term goals, carefully attending to the consequences of the problem-solving process.

acquisition stage: In Schaie's theory, the time in cognitive development (during childhood and adolescence) when an individual is sheltered from the majority of life's responsibilities and can learn a skill or a body of knowledge regardless of whether it has any practical goal or social implications.

active euthanasia: Injection of a medication by someone else that causes immediate death.

active gene effects: The influence of genes on an individual's choice of environments, companions, and activities. People choose environments that are compatible with their interests, and those interests may be influenced by genes.

activity level: The intensity and quantity of movement an individual displays. One aspect of infant temperament.

actuarial prediction: Predicting an individual's outcome based on group characteristics, such as predicting how likely an individual is to suffer a heart attack based on the frequency of heart attacks in large samples of people with similar characteristics (same age, gender, socioeconomic status, etc.).

adaptation: In Piaget's theory of cognitive development, the process by which the human mind constructs its knowledge, both assimilating new information to existing knowledge structures or understandings, and accommodating those structures to create a better fit to what is new.

adolescence-limited antisocial pattern: A developmental pattern of adolescent antisocial behavior that develops in adolescence and usually ends shortly thereafter.

adolescent growth spurt: Corresponding with puberty, a rapid increase in size accompanied by changes in the shape and proportions of the body.

adolescent-onset: A developmental pathway of antisocial behavior that begins in adolescence and is not likely to result in adult criminality. Although serious, seems to be reflective of a difficult or exaggerated reaction to the adolescent period.

adolescing: The process of advancing with age, improving or growing.

adrenocorticotropic hormone (ACTH): A hormone, released into the bloodstream during the body's response to stress, which prompts the adrenal glands to release "stress hormones."

Adult Attachment Inventory (AAI): A structured interview in which adults describe their memories of the parenting they received and their evaluation of whether and how that parenting influenced their own development. Based on coding of the verbatim transcripts, adults are categorized as having one of four attachment styles: autonomous (secure), dismissing (insecure), preoccupied (insecure), and unresolved (insecure). The security of an adult's attachment style tends to be correlated with the attachment security of their own infants.

advance directives (living wills): Statements, typically in writing, that describe a person's wishes regarding treatment in the event of incurable illness.

age-graded changes: Changes to which a person must adapt that are strongly age determined, such as physical changes.

agency: In cognitive functioning, the ability to act without an external trigger or to engage in self-motivated behavior. In social-emotional functioning, a constituent of generativity that involves generating, creating, and producing things, ideas, people, events, and so on as powerful extensions of the self.

agreeableness (A): One of the Big 5 personality traits that is described using synonyms including warm, sympathetic, generous, forgiving, kind, and affectionate.

alarm phase: The first phase in the body's reaction to a stressor, during which the activity of the sympathetic nervous system and adrenal glands increases in preparation for flight or fight.

alleles: Different forms of the same gene, such as the many forms of the eye color gene.

allostatic load: Cumulative physical effects of chronic stress hormones on the body.

Alzheimer's disease (AD): A brain disease that leads to dementia. Becomes more prevalent with age. Extensive brain changes including the development of plaques and tangles lead to the common symptom characteristics of the disease including absentmindedness, confusion, language and memory problems, disorientation, and problems with physical coordination. The eventual outcome is death.

amniocentesis: A medical procedure that can be done during a woman's pregnancy, usually at about the 16th week. A small amount of amniotic fluid is extracted from the uterus with a special syringe. Cells from the fluid have the same genetic makeup as the fetus and can be used to identify chromosomal and other abnormalities in the fetus.

amniotic fluid: A watery substance that surrounds a fetus, protecting the fetus from bumps and helping it maintain a constant temperature.

amniotic sac: A membrane that surrounds the fetus and contains amniotic fluid, providing a protective buffer from outside influences.

amygdala: A brain structure that influences motivation, emotional control, fear responses, and interpretation of nonverbal, emotional expressions.

anal fixation: In Freud's personality theory, the result of an unsatisfactory experience at the anal stage that can include being withholding (of mental and emotional resources), being compulsively cautious about keeping things clean and in order, or being overly messy and disorganized.

anal personality: In Freud's personality theory, a person who has an anal fixation.

anal stage: In Freud's theory, the second of psychosexual stage, beginning in the 2nd year of life, when the anal area of the body becomes the focus of greatest pleasure. During this stage, parenting practices associated with toilet training that are either overcontrolling or overindulgent could have long-lasting effects on personality development.

androgens: Male hormones, produced in the testes, which contribute to the development of male reproductive organs and may affect some aspects of brain development.

anger: A type of coping mechanism experienced by one nearing death that is a normal reaction to separation and loss. May be directed toward God, toward others, or toward the disease itself.

antisocial behavior: Behavior characterized by the presence of aggression or the intent to harm another person. More broadly may include such acts as risky sexual activity, substance abuse, defiance, cheating, lying, and vandalism.

antisocial personality disorder: A disorder characterized by antisocial behavior, with conduct problems typically beginning in early childhood.

anxious-ambivalent: An attachment category describing babies who show a great deal of distress on separation from their mothers, and who may act angry upon reunion, alternately approaching and resisting the mother, or who may respond listlessly to her efforts to comfort. They seem preoccupied with their mothers and rarely return to exploration after a separation.

anxious arousal: A state that children are thought to experience when parents discipline them. Hoffman proposed that mild forms help a child pay attention to the parent's socialization message, but more intense arousal attracts the child's attention to other concerns, like their own fear.

applied developmental science: An emerging field that has begun to synthesize and apply the findings of developmental psychology to the solution of real-world problems.

arthritis: A debilitating disease common in the elderly that is characterized by the onset of pain, stiffness, and swelling of joints and surrounding tissues.

assimilation: In Piaget's theory of cognitive development, the process of interpreting new stimulation or information as fitting with what one already knows, sometimes distorting the new information as a result.

association area: A part of the cortex that is not a "primary" area involved in vision, hearing, sensory, or motor functions. Integrates information coming from the various primary cortical areas and appears to be important for complex cognitive functioning.

attachment theory: According to Bowlby, the infant and his primary caregiver(s) participate in an interactive system that has evolved to keep the infant safe and ensures survival. As the infant changes cognitively and emotionally, an affectional bond with the caregiver emerges in stages, with a full-fledged attachment likely by about 7 or 8 months.

Attention Deficit/Hyperactivity Disorder (ADHD): A disability marked by the following features: inattention, hyperactivity, and impulsivity.

attention-persistence: Length of uninterrupted orienting or attention to a single activity and tendency to return to a task after interruption. An aspect of infant temperament.

attribute substitution: A process involving imitation and identification in which adolescents need to borrow and "try on" various behaviors and attributes that they observe in others, because the state of frameworklessness leaves them without clearly defined ways of behaving and thinking.

authoritarian style: An interactive parenting style that combines low levels of warmth (cold emotional climate) with high levels of control or demandingness. Associated with negative emotional tone, poor social skills, and other negative outcomes in children.

authoritative style: An interactive parenting style that combines high levels of warmth (affection, sensitivity and responsivity) with moderate to high levels of control or demandingness. Associated with many positive child outcomes.

autobiographical memory: What we remember of our own history of experiences, including representations of who we have been at various points in the past. Largely synonymous with episodic memory.

autonomic functions: A set of bodily functions, such as those involving the organ systems, that are outside an individual's conscious control.

autonomous (secure): An attachment category characterizing adults who provide an AAI transcript that is coherent and collaborative. They integrate and monitor their thinking, summarize answers, return the conversation to the interviewer, demonstrate good perspective-taking skills, acknowledge the importance of attachment-related experiences in their development, and tend to have children who are securely attached.

autonomous stage: Stage of moral development described by Piaget that begins in middle childhood. Children now understand that rules are based on social agreements and can be changed.

autonomy: In Ryan and Deci's self-determination theory, one of three basic or universal needs. Being in control of oneself, or feeling that one's behavior is congruent with one's "true self," meaning that it is intrinsically motivated.

autonomy versus shame and doubt: The crisis faced in the second of Erikson's "Eight Stages of Man," in which the 1- to 3-year-old child may develop feelings of autonomy ("I can do things myself") or of shame and self-doubt, depending on whether his caregiver strikes the right balance between exercising control and being sensitive to the child's new need for independence.

autosomes: The 22 of 23 pairs of chromosomes in humans that are matched (they look and function alike).

average: A sociometric category that includes those children who receive an average number of positive and negative nominations from their peers (near the mean for the group on social preference and social impact).

avoidant: An attachment category describing babies who typically fail to cry when separated from their mothers in a strange situation test. They actively avoid or ignore her when she returns, sometimes combining proximity seeking and moving away, but mostly turning away and often appearing unemotional. In Bartholomew's typology of adult attachments, a category that is subdivided into two types (dismissing and fearful) based on the individual's reports of felt distress.

axon: A long extension, projecting from the cell body of a neuron, which is like a cable attached to a piece of electronic equipment. Electrical impulses travel from the cell body through the axon toward synapses with other neurons.

axon terminals: Structures found at the ends of axons, which contain tiny sacs of neurotransmitters.

babbling: Infant vocal sounds, usually beginning around 6 months of age, consisting of repeated consonant-vowel-consonant sequences such as "bababa" or "doodoodoo." By 9 months of age, they tend to be limited to the sounds permissible in the baby's native language.

bargaining: A reaction to impending death that serves as an attempt to postpone an inevitable death by making promises, usually to a divine other, or trying to delay death until some memorable event has taken place.

basic trust: In Erikson's theory of personality development, an infant's ability to see others as dependable and trustworthy as a result of caregiving that is timely, sensitive to the infant's needs, and consistently available.

behavioral facilitation system: Neural system that regulates approach behaviors, response to incentives, positive affect, and psychomotor activity.

behavioral inhibition: In late infancy and childhood, a tendency toward shyness, manifested as avoidance or distress in new situations. This trait is linked to high reactivity (including irritability in response to new sensory stimulation) in early infancy.

behavioral inhibition system: Neural system that regulates withdrawal and avoidance behaviors.

behavior genetics: The field of quantitative genetics that explores the extent to which behavioral differences among individuals may be related to genetic influences.

behaviorist tradition: Approaches to explaining learning in which behavioral change is seen as a function of chains of specific environmental events, such as those that occur in classical and operant conditioning.

Big 5: The five most basic dimensions of personality including neuroticism (N), extraversion (E), openness (O), agreeableness (A), and conscientiousness (C).

binge drinking: Drinking many drinks in a row.

bipolar disorder: An affective disorder that is generally characterized by episodes of mania or hypomania, sometimes alternating with episodes of depression.

bisexuality: A characteristic of individuals who have interest in sexual relations with partners of both sexes.

body image: The concept of, and attitude toward one's physical appearance.

borderwork: Interactions between boys and girls during middle childhood when there appear to be unwritten rules governing when and how the two genders will interact.

brainstem: A set of lower brain structures that include the medulla, pons, and midbrain.

broad socialization: Socialization that permits and encourages high levels of individual freedom of expression, has few social constraints, expects less community responsibility, and thus tolerates a wide variety of socially deviant behaviors.

Bronfenbrenner's bioecological model: A comprehensive developmental model proposed by Bronfenbrenner that takes into account the many levels of influence the environment can have on an individual. The interacting systems in this model are the microsystem, the mesosystem, the exosystem, and the macrosystem.

"the bump": A salient feature of self-memories. Regardless of age, adults' cue-prompted memories of the self from the young adult period (ages 18–22) are slightly but reliably overproduced.

canalization: The development of a behavior or outcome that is not really the result of learning but is a limiting or channeling of the behavior over the course of ontogenesis, such as ducks coming to respond only to the cries of their own species. Both genetic and environmental input is needed for the behavior to unfold. Once established, the behavior is unlikely to change.

cannot classify: An attachment category characterizing adults who may have psychiatric disorders and who do not fit in any of the other four attachment style categories.

career consolidation (vs. self-absorption): A life stage that Vaillant added to Erikson's sequence of stages, characterizing the mid-20s, when in addition to ongoing intimacy concerns, one becomes concerned with making a commitment to work that brings personal satisfaction, regardless of its other rewards, rather than just having a job.

carrier: Someone with a gene in his genotype that is unexpressed in his phenotype but can be passed on to offspring.

causal variable: The postulated cause of a given phenomenon.

central sulcus: A fissure in the cerebrum that is used to locate the parietal lobe, which sits behind this fissure.

centration: A characteristic of preoperational thought in which the child tends to focus on one salient feature of an experience or event at a time.

centromere: The central location where duplicate chromosomes remain joined during cell division.

cephalo-caudal: Describes the "head to tail" direction of prenatal development.

cerebellum: A brain structure located in the hindbrain that is involved in the planning, coordination, and smooth operation of complex motor activities.

cerebral cortex: The outer layer of the gray matter of the cerebrum, which is the highest and most recently evolved portion of the brain.

cerebrovascular accident (stroke): A cardiovascular problem in which an artery serving the brain is either clogged or bursts.

cerebrum: The highest brain structure, comprising two thirds of the forebrain, and coordinating most other brain activity. Involved in higher brain processes like thinking, language, decision making, and so on.

child centered: Describes caregivers who set aside their own needs (for time and convenience) to meet a child's developmental needs.

chorionic villa sampling (CVS): A medical procedure that can be done during a woman's pregnancy, usually after the 3rd week. The woman's cervix is dilated and a tiny sample of the fetus's placenta is excised. Placental cells, which have the same genetic characteristics as the fetus, are then analyzed for chromosomal and DNA abnormalities.

chromosomes: Forty-six tiny strands of DNA, found in the nucleus of each cell of the body, which are the source of biological inheritance.

chunking: The cognitive process of linking several pieces of information together into a single meaningful unit, such as remembering the digits 1, 7, 7, and 6 by thinking of the year 1776.

circuits: Series of neurons that are joined via their synaptic connections into groups and are part of larger organizations of neurons.

classical conditioning: A process by which a change in behavior takes place when a neutral event or stimulus is associated with a stimulus that causes an automatic response. As a result the neutral stimulus causes the person to make the same automatic response in the future.

climacteric: The gradual reduction of reproductive ability in women usually beginning in their late 30s when the menstrual cycle begins to shorten and become somewhat more erratic as a result of a reduction in the amount of circulating estradiol.

clinical-developmental psychology: A therapeutic approach developed by Noam, which blends developmental knowledge with clinical practice.

cliques: Voluntary social or friendship groups of three to nine members characterizing children in early to middle adolescence.

closed commitment: Meeus and colleagues' alternative name for Marcia's "foreclosure." It signifies an identity with a high level of present commitment and low levels of coexisting exploration.

closed identity domains: Areas of identity in which individuals tend toward foreclosure because they have little control over them.

coaction: The intricate pattern by which genes and environment mutually influence one another. The activity of the genes is affected by the environment of the cell that is affected by other levels of the environment including the outside world. One result is that the same complement of genes produces different outcomes in different environments. Also, the same environment can have different effects on outcomes when interacting with different genes.

code switching: Shifting from one form or style of speech to another depending on context, such as shifting from using slang with friends to using more polite forms with authority figures.

codominance: A type of relationship between two alleles of the same gene (located at matching sites on a pair of chromosomes) in which neither allele is suppressed, producing a blended outcome.

coercive family interaction: Patterson's description of how children learn to act aggressively. Aggressive children respond to parental demands by behaving aversively (whining, etc.), parents retreat, rewarding the child's noncompliance, and parents are reinforced with short-lived peace and quiet. Children are trained in the effectiveness of aggressive noncompliance and learn powerful parent-control strategies.

cohort: A group of people who were born in the same historical period and grew up at about the same time.

cohort effects: Also called history-graded events, they are events that provide a context for development and also influence it directly. The year of your birth marks your entry into a cohort of peers who accompany you through age-graded developmental changes within the context of a specific set of historical events.

collaborative/affiliative speech: A type of speech, more often used among girls, in which children's responses are keyed to what someone else has said, expressing agreement or making further suggestions, often in the form of a question rather than declarative or imperative sentences.

collective egocentrism: Peer influences on maintaining risky behavior; each adolescent's illusion of invincibility strengthens that of the other members of the peer group.

commitment: An element of love that refers to making a decision to sustain a relationship with a loved one.

commitment foreseen: Position 6 in Perry's model in which thinking incorporates not only respect for diverse ideas and understanding of their rationale, but also the individual's affirmation of what it is she believes in, all the while knowing that that reason will never provide absolute proof that her ideas or perspectives are right or better than others.

committed compliance: Describes toddlers' eager and enthusiastic willingness to go along with parental requests. Predicts measures of internalization and conscience in the later preschool period.

communion: A constituent of generativity that is expressed in the adult's desire to care for the next generation, even to the point of sacrificing her own well-being for the good of those who will follow.

compatibility: A standard for mate selection in which one chooses a potential mate based on how his personality meshes with one's own personality.

compelling circumstances: Conditions that mitigate the guilt of a criminal defendant because he or she faced such pressure when the crime was committed that even an ordinary, reasonable person could be expected to have acted in the same way, such as acting in the face of extreme need or under threat of injury.

compensation: A process that contributes to successful development. When a loss of some kind prevents the use of one means to an end, the individual finds another means.

competence: In self-determination theory, feeling effective in one's interactions with the social environment and experiencing opportunities to exercise and express one's capacities.

competence versus performance: Competence refers to the child's level of perspective-taking ability and performance refers to the child's actual use of skills for getting along with others. Adequate competence (perspective taking) is necessary but not sufficient for good performance (social functioning).

complicated or abnormal grief: A response to bereavement that is generally accompanied by other disorders such as major depression, substance abuse, or post-traumatic stress disorder that is intense and lasts for an extended period of time, greatly interfering with functioning. Abnormal grief may also be marked by a complete absence of grief and the total inability to experience grief reactions.

compulsive caregiving: Describes a behavioral pattern in which children (usually insecurely attached, avoidant children) take emotional care of their parents.

compulsive self-sufficiency: Describes a behavioral pattern in which children (usually insecurely attached, avoidant children) appear very self-possessed, perhaps related to experiences of shaming for expressions of dependency or needs for closeness.

concrete operational stage: In Piaget's theory of cognitive development, the period from about age 6 to 12 when children begin to think logically but have difficulty applying logical thought to abstract contents.

conditioned stimulus: A formerly neutral stimulus that has become associated with a stimulus that causes an automatic response, thus causing the same automatic response in the future.

conduct disorder (CD): A pattern of serious behavior problems that violate the basic rights of others, such as stealing, aggression, or property destruction. Presently, this diagnosis requires that three such behaviors be demonstrated within the past year.

conferred identity: The identity attained by those who are foreclosed (individuals who make commitments with little or no exploration of alternatives).

confirmation bias: When a child's peers have already developed schemas or constructions for him that are built on his social reputation, the interactions with the target child that follow are marked by attention to evidence that confirms the target child's characteristics.

congenital adrenal hyperplasia (CAH): A gender-atypical condition in which biological females with two X chromosomes are exposed to high levels of androgens (male hormones) during prenatal and postnatal development.

conscience: An internalized slate of standards and principles that constitutes a person's primary guide to action. May cause feelings of discomfort or distress when the violation of a rule is contemplated or carried out.

conscientiousness (C): One of the Big 5 personality traits that is described using synonyms including *organized, planful, reliable, responsible, careful,* and *efficient*.

consolidation: In Super's theory, achievement of advanced status and seniority in the workplace that often accompanies the maintenance stage.

constructed identity: The identity not based upon a predetermined set of expectations, but rather representative either of a personal redefinition of childhood and early adolescent goals and values or perhaps something very different from them.

constructivism: Rooted in theories such as Piaget's, assumes that individuals are not just passive receptors of information who acquire knowledge via external manipulations. Instead, people actively construct their knowledge by interpreting information in light of prior learning, by actively restructuring prior knowledge, or by co-constructing knowledge in interactions with others.

contextual relativism: Position 5 in Perry's model that represents a major achievement in intellectual development because the student now possesses analytic abilities that allow her to appreciate the merits of diverse perspectives and to find convincing elements in multiple points of view. Thinking relativistically, or thinking about knowledge in context, becomes more habitual.

control dimension (parental demandingness): One of two major features of parenting style. The degree to which parents impose discipline, requiring their children to curb some of their behaviors and to perform other behaviors that are suitable to their level of maturity.

control group: In experimental design, a group like the experimental group in every way except that the causal variable is not purposely changed.

controversial: A sociometric category that identifies a relatively small group of children who receive many positive and many negative nominations from peers (high social impact, average social preference).

conventional morality: Kohlberg's second stage of moral reasoning in which what is right depends on others' approval or on the need to maintain social order.

conventional rules: Social rules of conduct that vary from one culture to another and are a function of social agreement, such as rules about appropriate dress, forms of address, and table manners.

cooperative learning environments: Classrooms or other organizations that encourage children to work in pairs or in groups to solve academic problems and to improve their understanding of concepts or skills.

corpus callosum: A network of fibers that connects the right and left cerebral hemispheres of the brain. Its maturation from early childhood through adolescence contributes to coordination and integration of information and aids in the development of consciousness.

correlational studies: Often utilized when experiments are impractical or unethical, a technique in which both the causal variable and outcome variable are measured or observed, and nothing is actually manipulated by the researcher. Such studies can determine whether changes in the causal variable are matched by predicted changes in the outcome variable, but they cannot determine whether changes in the causal variable *caused* the changes in the outcome variable.

cortisol: A hormone, released during the body's response to stress, that increases blood glucose levels and suppresses the immune response.

counting all strategy: Rudimentary addition strategy of young children. For example, given the problem of adding 2 plus 3, holding up two fingers on one hand, three fingers on the other hand and counting all of them.

counting on strategy: Addition strategy of young children. For example, given the problem of adding 2 plus 3, starting at 2 and counting three more digits on from there.

critical period: A certain time frame in which some developments, such as first language learning, must take place or the opportunity is missed.

cross-sectional studies: A study design in which different ages are represented by different groups of people as opposed to one group of people over time.

crowds: Large, reputation-based groups, composed of numerous cliques, that form in early to midadolescence.

crystallization: In Super's theory, the formulation of general vocational goals in the early part of the exploratory stage.

crystallized intelligence (pragmatics): The compilation of skills and information we have acquired in the course of our lives that can be viewed as the software programs of our nervous system.

culture: Shared traditions, attitudes, values, and beliefs handed down from one generation to the next.

cytokines: Small protein molecules of many different varieties that are secreted by cells of the immune system and that help regulate its functioning.

daily hassles: Category of stressor that is chronic and cumulative in its effect.

day reconstruction method (DRM): Method of research in which participants revive memories of a previous day, describe the days' experiences, and rate affective valence of experiences.

décalages: Within-stage variations in Piaget's cognitive stage theory. Children sometimes show more advanced or less advanced functioning in one or another cognitive domain than is typical of their overall stage of development.

decathecting: Detaching emotionally from the relationship one had experienced with a loved one prior to their death and reinvesting psychic energy into the formation of new attachments.

decentration: A characteristic of concrete and formal operational thought in Piaget's cognitive theory. Attending to multiple pieces of information (or multiple aspects of a situation) at one time; a necessary ingredient in logical thinking.

declarative knowledge: Knowledge about facts (semantic information) and events (episodic information).

decline stage: In Super's theory, just before and after age 65, when one's career winds down, retirement is planned and takes precedence over career advancement and consolidation.

deferred imitation: Imitation in which children observe the actions of another on one occasion, and then imitate those actions sometime later. In order to do so, the child must be able to recall the observed actions.

degrouping: A general decline in the importance of cliques over the course of the high school years.

delayed phase preference: A shift in sleep patterns characterized by staying up later in the evening and sleeping later in the morning than younger children that has been associated with hormonal changes at puberty.

demand characteristics: Behavioral tendencies that often either encourage or discourage certain kinds of reactions from others.

dementia: Cognitive functioning that is so severely impaired that it negatively affects ability to relate to others and to manage one's own daily activities.

democracy factor: An aspect of parental responsiveness. The degree to which parents encourage children's psychological autonomy by soliciting their opinions or encouraging self-expression. Related to children's self-reliance, self-confidence, willingness to work hard, and general competence.

dendrites: Small projections which grow out from a neuron's cell body. They receive transmissions from other neurons.

denial: A type of defense mechanism for dealing with stressful events, such as approaching death, associated with feelings of numbness or disbelief that buffers the person from the full weight of the threat.

deoxyribonucleic acid (DNA): A complex organic substance that comprises chromosomes and genes.

depressed mood: A subclinical level of depression.

depression: A pattern of symptoms that include depressed mood, sadness, feelings of hopelessness, and loss of pleasure or interest in formerly pleasurable activities. In clinical usage, various subtypes of depression have been identified and all cause significant impairment in functioning.

description: The first step in the scientific method, aimed at answering factual questions about a phenomenon, such as who, what, when, where, and with whom.

despair: The third phase in the grieving process characterized by great sadness; social withdrawal; sleeping, eating, or somatic disturbances; and other symptoms of depression or emotional upset.

developmental lines: Two sources or routes of cognitive development according to Vygotsky. One is the "socio-historical" or cultural route, which involves input from other people, and the other is the "natural" route, deriving from the child's own processing of information.

developmental psychopathology: A relatively new and influential field that has applied a developmental focus to the study of abnormal behavior and dysfunction.

diathesis: Underlying predispositions to some disease or abnormal condition.

diathesis-stress: Model for the development of psychopathology that assumes a genetic predisposition (diathesis) that confers particular sensitivity to environmental risk (stress).

differential emotions theory: Izard's view that facial expressions in infants are the direct manifestation of underlying neural processes related to the emotion expressed. For example, a sad expression implies the operation of the neural circuitry associated with sadness, so that if a baby looks sad, he is sad.

difficult babies: A temperament type described by Thomas and Chess. These babies are fearful, irritable, active, display low levels of positive affect, are irregular in biological rhythms, and so on, making them more challenging to care for than other babies.

diffusion: One of Marcia's four identity status categories that often describes young adolescents as they embark on the identity development process. The individual is not actively involved in exploring possible life choices, nor has she made any firm commitments to them.

digit span tests: A test of working memory in which a series of digits are presented and the participant must repeat them in the correct order.

diminished capacity: One source of mitigation in adult criminal law. A guilty actor is considered less than fully blameworthy because of some deficiency at the time of the offense. Perhaps he was mentally ill, emotionally distressed, or intellectually impaired.

discipline: The tendency of parents to limit or demand behavior by exerting or requiring control.

disenchantment: The second stage of retirement, when people begin to experience an emotional "letdown" as they face the day-to-day realities of the change, such as separation from work colleagues, uncertainties about how to feel competent and in control, a sense of diminished generativity and meaningfulness, new tensions that may arise with one's partner, financial concerns, and perhaps, boredom.

dishabituation: After habituating to one stimulus, an infant may show reinstatement of the orienting response if the stimulus is changed. This response is dishabituation and indicates that the baby has noticed the difference between the original stimulus and the new stimulus.

disillusionment model: The view that posits that overly romantic idealizations of marriage and blissfully optimistic views of one's partner set people up for eventual disappointment.

dismissing (insecure): An attachment style characterizing adults whose AAI transcripts provide little detail and coherence. They may describe their parents positively but provide either no evidence or contradictory evidence. They downplay close relationships and tend to have children who are in the avoidant attachment category. In Bartholomew's typology, these individuals prefer self-sufficiency and maintain a sense of superiority while devaluing the importance of others to their well-being.

dismissive parenting: Also called neglecting, a parenting style that describes parents who are essentially disengaged, scoring low on both responsiveness and demandingness.

disorganized-disoriented: An attachment category describing babies who produce contradictory and even bizarre behaviors in the strange situation test, showing both an inclination to approach the mother when stressed and a tendency to avoid her when she approaches.

distal processes: Factors outside the immediate external environment, including internal forces (genes) and external forces (features of the educational system or of the broader culture), which modify the proximal processes in Bronfenbrenner's bioecological model and other multidimensional theories.

distraction: A coping style that involves deliberate focusing on neutral or pleasant thoughts or engaging activities that divert attention in more positive directions. Distraction can attenuate depressive episodes.

distress: A form of negative stress that includes the kinds of frustrations, conflicts, pressures, and negative events that people experience in their lives either intermittently or chronically.

domain of knowledge: A specific subject matter, such as mathematics or chess or history.

domain specific: Describing a level of knowledge or skill that has been achieved in one subject area but not in others, such as being able to think logically about math but not about baseball or biology.

dominant-recessive: A type of relationship between two alleles of the same gene, in which one allele is expressed whereas the other is suppressed.

domineering/power assertive speech: Discourse containing many commands and restrictions. Tends to be "egotistic," ignoring others' remarks, and often includes threats and interruptions, more typical of males than females.

double effect: Giving medication intended to relieve pain even though there is a chance that death can result.

double standard: The idea that female sexual behavior is judged more harshly than male sexual behavior.

Down syndrome (Trisomy 21): A disorder caused by an extra copy of chromosome number 21 and often characterized by mental retardation, flattened facial features, poor muscle tone, and heart problems.

"downward" social comparisons: Comparing oneself to less competent or less successful peers when one's own self-esteem is at stake. Such comparisons protect the individual from negative self-evaluations.

dual-process model: The model that proposes that bereaved individuals simultaneously engage in two kinds of coping mechanisms, approach and avoidance, that wax and wane over the course of grieving.

dyads: A social unit or "group" that consists of two people.

early-starter model: One developmental pathway to antisocial behavior. Oppositional behavior begins in early childhood, persists and diversifies over time, and becomes increasingly more serious.

earned secure: An attachment style characterizing adults who in AAI transcripts reveal experiences of early adversity, describe their painful backgrounds truthfully, acknowledge the stressors their own parents faced, and come to terms with their early experiences. Their children are usually securely attached.

easy babies: A temperament type described by Thomas and Chess. These babies are placid, not very active, show positive affect, and are regular in their rhythms, making them easier to care for than other babies.

effortful control: The inhibition of a compelling response that is "dominant" or preferred (e.g., eating dessert) to perform a response that is less compelling (e.g., complying with a diet). Plays a role in regulating or modulating emotional reactions.

ego: In Freud's personality theory, the second of three aspects of personality, which represents the rational, realistic self that seeks to meet bodily needs in sensible ways that take into account all aspects of a situation.

egocentric speech: Speech for self, a use of language typical of preschoolers that has no apparent communicative function. Piaget suggested that it serves no useful purpose, but Vygotsky argued that it is the precursor of inner speech and important for problem solving, planning, and self-control.

egocentrism: A failure to recognize one's own subjectivity. One fails to see things realistically because one is, in a sense, trapped in one's own perspective, and cannot imagine that others may have a different perspective on the same situation.

ego identity: Includes all the dimensions of self-knowledge and serves as the foundation for the behavioral, affective, and cognitive commitments to career, relationships, and political and religious belief systems that will be made in adulthood.

Ego Identity Interview: A standardized, semi-structured interview designed by Marcia to assess these core domains of identity: vocational choice, religious beliefs, and political ideology, gender-role attitudes, and beliefs about sexual expression through first asking general questions and then following up with more specific probes. Supplemental domains may include hobbies, friendships, dating relationships, role of spouse, role of parent, experiences at school, and issues of work–family balance.

ego integrity (vs. despair): In Erikson's theory, the result of life review in the elderly. Integrity is a sense that one's own life is "something that had to be," and had order, meaning, and dignity. Despair is a sense of hopelessness, that one's life has no coherence or meaning.

elaboration strategy: A memory strategy that requires finding or creating some kind of meaningful link between to-be-remembered items, such as creating a story that includes all the items.

elaborative style: A style that characterizes some adults' conversations with children about past experiences. Adults using this style engage in lengthy discussions providing lots of details, asking questions and encouraging children to provide details as well.

elastin: A substance in the cells of the dermis, or middle layer of skin, that allows the skin to stretch and contract as we move.

Electra complex: In Freud's theory, the belief that young girls direct their sexual urges toward their fathers, even though they are more strongly attached to their mothers, because they experience penis envy. Young girls find themselves in competition with their mothers, although their fear of their mothers' displeasure is not as great as a young boy's because they assume that somehow they have already been castrated. The girl will identify with her mother to make peace and, therefore, become gender typed in her behavior and form a superego.

emerging adulthood: The time period from about 18 to 25, which is characterized by the shift toward increasing independence and autonomy.

emotional intelligence: The ability to perceive emotions, to identify and understand their meaning, to integrate them with other kinds of cognition, and to manage them.

empathy: "Feeling with" another person, recognizing her emotional condition and experiencing what she is assumed to be feeling.

end-of-life care: Principles that support more humanistic approaches to aiding individuals nearing death including better pain management, continuity of care, and attention to the psychological dimensions of death and dying.

endocrine system: A system of ductless glands that secrete their hormones directly into the bloodstream. Responds to messages from the hypothalamus.

endorphins: Biochemical substances produced by the body under conditions of stress or vigorous exercise that serve to alleviate pain.

entity theorists: A theory of intelligence usually held by individuals who show a helpless pattern and who see intelligence or ability as a fixed, concrete thing.

enzymes: Proteinlike substances that facilitate chemical reactions in the body, such as those involved in metabolizing food.

epigenetic model: A type of multidimensional or systems theory that assumes that development is the result of complex interactions between genetic and environmental elements. According to this approach, the effects of developmental changes are bidirectional, influencing both the environment and the biological system.

epinephrine: Also called adrenaline, it is a substance that is both a hormone and a neurotransmitter. One place it is produced is in the adrenal glands as part of the body's response to stress. Among its effects is increased heart rate.

episodic: Description of knowledge of the events that one has experienced. This knowledge is organized around time and space.

Erikson's psychosocial stages: Erik Erikson's eight-stage model of personality that focuses on explaining attitudes and feelings toward the self and others. The first five correspond to the age periods in Freud's psychosexual stages, whereas three adult life stages suggest that personality development continues until death.

escape: Perry's characterization of the behavior of individuals who revert to relativism when the demands of commitment are too stressful.

establishment stage: In Super's theory, the final stage in the development of vocational self-concept (about 25 to 44), when work experiences provide the laboratory within which the matching of vocational self-concept and job settings is tried out, sometimes reevaluated, sometimes confirmed, and eventually stabilized.

estradiol: A form of the primary female hormone, estrogen, produced by the ovaries.

estrogen: A feminizing hormone that is produced by the ovaries in females and to a lesser extent by the testes in males.

ethnic group: People who share cultural traditions, attitudes, values, and beliefs that have been handed down through generations.

ethologists: Biologists who do careful observations of animal behavior in natural environments.

eudaemonic well-being: A term synonymous with psychological well-being.

eustress: A form of positive stress.

evocative gene effects: One kind of effect that genes can have on the environment. Genes can affect the individual's behavior which in turn can affect the reactions of others.

executive stage: In Schaie's theory, a stage that some middle adults experience who take on executive functions at work and in the community that extends beyond the responsible stage. This stage requires one to focus heavily on learning about complex relationships, multiple perspectives, commitment, and conflict resolution.

exhaustion phase: The final stage in the body's reaction to a stressor, which occurs if the struggles persists to the point that the body's resources are depleted. Depression, illness, or even death can occur after severe, prolonged stress.

exosystem: In Bronfenbrenner's bioecological model, the level of the environment that children may not directly interact with but that influences the child nonetheless.

experience-dependent: Describes neural growth that is stimulated by environmental experiences and may vary from one individual to another.

experience-expectant: Describes neural growth that requires a certain kind of environmental stimulation that is almost certain to occur in the experience of most members of a species. An example is development of the visual system that requires exposure to light in order to occur.

experience sampling method (ESM): A research technique in which participants are interrupted at random times during the day and asked to report on what they are doing, thinking, and feeling.

experiments: A technique for testing the predictions of a theory in which the researcher purposely manipulates the causal variable to observe the effects of the manipulation on the outcome variable.

explanation: The second step in the scientific method, when the researcher frames a theory or set of hypotheses about how the facts gained from descriptive research are related to each other and why they occur.

exploratory stage: In Super's theory, the second life stage in the development of vocational self-concept from about 14 to 24, in which vocational self-concept is tentatively narrowed down, but often career choices are not finalized.

externalizing problems: Problem behavior that involves engaging in inappropriate conduct, especially aggressive acts.

extraversion (E): One of the Big 5 personality traits that is described using synonyms including *outgoing, active, assertive, energetic, talkative,* and *enthusiastic.*

false belief tasks: Tasks in which one person has correct knowledge of a situation, but another person (or the same person at another time) has incorrect knowledge, or a "false belief." Used to test children's theory of mind, specifically their understanding of others' mental states.

family life cycle: A normative, stagelike sequence of traditional family developments

in intact marriages as partners become parents, rear and launch their children, become "empty nesters," and subsequently face old age.

fast mapping: The rapidity with which young children add new words to functional vocabulary after only one or two exposures.

fearful: In Bartholomew's typology of adult attachment categories, a subcategory of avoidant attachment. Describes individuals who have negative models of both self and others and who see relationships as desirable but out of reach. Their desire for close relationships with others is thwarted by fear of rejection, and ultimately they withdraw. A high level of distress surrounds attachment themes.

fearfulness or reactivity: In infants, proneness to crying or pulling away from new sensory stimuli.

fetal alcohol effects (FAE): Symptoms, usually in the form of cognitive impairments, affecting babies who do not have the physical or structural problems of fetal alcohol syndrome but who were exposed to small amounts of alcohol prenatally.

fetal alcohol syndrome (FAS): A condition found in babies who are exposed to alcohol prenatally. It is characterized by a unique facial configuration (small head, widely spaced eyes, flattened nose) as well as possible mental retardation and behavioral problems.

flashbulb memories: Recollections that are especially vivid and personally relevant because of the emotions associated with them.

fluid intelligence (mechanics): Basic operational characteristics that seem to directly reflect how well the "hardware" of the nervous system is working. Its functions include such things as processing speed and inhibitory mechanisms.

forebrain: The largest and most recently evolved portion of a mammalian brain; includes the cerebrum.

foreclosure: One of Marcia's four identity status categories that describes individuals who make commitments with little or no exploration of alternatives. They incorporate the values and goals of significant others without reflection.

forgotten half: The name given to 18- to 24-year-olds who do not go to college.

formal operational thought: In Piaget's theory of cognitive development, the kind of thinking that begins at about 11 or 12 years, that (1) rises above particular contents and focuses on relationships that govern those contents (abstractions), (2) involves coordinating multiple relationships, and (3) can be difficult even for adults.

"four horsemen of the apocalypse": The four kinds of negativity that do the most damage to relationships and that are highly predictive of divorce. They are criticism, defensiveness, contempt, and stonewalling.

fragile X syndrome: A condition caused by a gene mutation on the X chromosome. It is the heading cause of mild to moderate mental retardation.

frameworklessness: A state of instability and anxiety unique to adolescents. This state is a result of the body changing in appearance, the emergence of adult sexual needs, hormonal shifts, the expanding capacity to reflect on the future and the self, and increased maturity demands.

fraternal twins (dizygotic): Twins who develop from two separate zygotes and, like any two siblings, share about 50% of their genes.

Freud's psychosexual stages: The five developmental stages that Freud believed were initiated by changes in the id and its energy levels.

friendship skills: Behavioral skills, such as appropriate assertiveness, good communication, and conflict resolution, that maintain and enhance friendships.

friendship understanding: A child's changing knowledge of what friendship implies.

friendship valuing: Emotional attachment or investment that a child makes in a friendship.

frontal lobe: The part of the cerebrum that is situated at the top front part of each hemisphere and controls voluntary muscle movements and higher-level cognitive functions such as planning, goal setting, and decision making.

gender atypical: Individuals who have either ambiguous genitalia or genitalia that are inconsistent with their sex chromosomes.

gender constancy: Recognizing the permanency of one's gender category membership and understanding that it could never change.

gender identity: The awareness of one's own gender assignment and understanding of its meaning.

gender identity disorder (GID): A disorder seen in children who have early preferences for the toys, clothing, and activities of the opposite sex and who show some identity problems (such as wishing to be the other sex).

gender intensification hypothesis: A hypothesis that suggests that one way young teens cope with the demands of establishing an adult identity is to fall back on stereotyped notions of masculinity or femininity.

gender schema: A network of ideas and expectations of male and female beliefs about male and female characteristics that affect what we pay attention to, what we interpret, and what we remember about events.

gender stability: The understanding that over time, one's gender category stays the same: Boys grow into men, girls grow into women.

gender stereotypes: The beliefs and expectations that individuals have concerning the different behavioral tendencies and distribution of personality traits between the sexes.

gene expression: The process by which DNA information is transmitted and translated to cells.

generalization: The process by which learned behaviors may be extended to new events that are very similar to events in the original learning context.

generativity: A motive or need that can be filled through one's vocation or avocations, through child rearing, or through community service. It includes productivity and creativity. Generativity also describes people who are contributing members of society.

generativity accomplishment: A sense of satisfaction in making a meaningful contribution.

generativity desire: Expression of generativity goals, such as caring for future generations, wanting to produce something of lasting value, and being concerned about being needed.

genes: Functional units or sections of DNA that provide a blueprint or code to the cell for how to produce proteins and enzymes. Found on chromosomes, they come in matching pairs, one from each parent.

genetic counselors: People who help screen candidates for testing that would help determine the risk of genetic disorders for their offspring. Genetic counselors provide information and support to prospective parents regarding their choices about testing, childbearing, and parenting.

genital stage: The fifth and last of Freud's psychosexual stages, when the changes of puberty mean that id energy is especially invested in adult sexual impulses.

genomic imprinting: A process in which some gene alleles in the sperm or the ovum are deactivated. Imprinted gene alleles do not influence the phenotype of the offspring.

genotype: An individual's genetic endowment, including both expressed and unexpressed genes.

genotype–environment interaction: The varying ways in which the same genes express themselves depending on variations in the environment. Similar to coaction.

germ cells: Special cells located only in the ovaries of females and the testes of males which undergo a special kind of cell division, called meiosis, that produces eggs (ova) in females and sperm in males.

germline gene therapy: An experimental approach to correcting defective genes that involves altering the sperm or egg cells to pass on healthy genes to future generations.

glia: Supporting cells in the central nervous system that provide a type of scaffolding for the neurons.

globalization: The process by which, as a result of international communication, transportation, and trade, countries around the world influence one another's lifestyle, economics, and culture, so that similarities among nations increase along with interaction.

gonads: Testes in males and ovaries in females. Produce eggs (ova) in females and sperm in males. Increase their hormone production at puberty after being stimulated by hormones released from the pituitary gland in response to the maturing hypothalamus.

goodness of fit model: Thomas and Chess's view that when adults provide care that is adjusted to the temperament of an infant or child, even difficult early temperaments are unlikely to lead to later adjustment problems.

grief work: A process that explicitly encourages bereaved individuals to confront and "work through" their feelings about loss for recovery to take place.

growth: Developmental change or adaptation to the constant flux of influences on our lives that involves adding new characteristics, understandings, skills, and so on to our behavioral repertoire.

growth stage: In Super's theory, the first stage in the development of vocational self-concept lasting until about age 14. Many elements of identity develop in this stage including ideas about their interests, attitudes, skills, and needs.

guided imagery: A technique used to aid memory of an event or person. For example, a child might be asked to pretend that an event

occurred, then create a mental picture of the event and its details.

habituation: A decrease in an infant's responses to a stimulus over time, including decreased looking, decreased sucking, a return to a resting heart rate, and so on.

habituation paradigm: A research technique which takes advantage of a baby's tendency to orient to new stimulation and to habituate to repeated or old stimulation. Once an infant habituates to one stimulus a new stimulus can be presented. The baby's reorienting to the new stimulus (or failure to do so) reveals whether or not she perceives or notices the differences between the stimuli.

hedonic well-being: A term synonymous with subjective well-being.

hedonistic: Preschool-aged children's tendency to be more concerned about their own needs than those of someone else in need.

the helpless pattern: An orientation to failure in which individuals begin to denigrate their abilities when they encounter failure and typically stop applying themselves or trying to improve their performance.

hemispheric specialization: The two symmetrical halves of the cerebrum process information from and control opposite sides of the body. They also control some different higher cognitive functions, with the left hemisphere largely responsible for language and the right hemisphere largely responsible for visual-spatial skills.

heritability: The degree to which differences among individuals on a trait may be the result of their having different genes.

heteronomous stage: Stage of moral development described by Piaget characterizes children from about ages 5 through 8, when they regard rules as immutable, existing outside the self, and requiring strict adherence.

heterosexuality: A sexual preference for partners of the opposite sex.

hidden object test: A research technique invented by Piaget to assess object permanence in infants from 6 months old. An interesting object, like a small toy, is placed in front of a baby within her reach. As the baby watches, the experimenter covers the object so that it is out of sight. If the baby searches for the object under the cloth she demonstrates that she has a sense of the continued existence of absent objects.

hierarchical integration: The organization and integration of activities and skills from one stage of development into broader, more complex patterns at the next stage.

hindbrain: The part of the mammalian brain that evolved first. Includes the medulla, pons, cerebellum and reticular formation.

hippocampus: The region of the forebrain that plays a role in emotions, the ability to remember, and the ability to compare sensory information to expectations.

history-graded changes: Changes in our life experience that are a function of historical circumstance, including events that we share with our whole cohort.

homeostatic steady state: A stable state maintained over time by a couple's unique balance of positive and negative elements in areas of interactive behavior, perception, and physiology.

homogomy: A standard for mate selection in which one chooses a potential mate based on her similarity to oneself in religion, SES, race, education, and so on.

homophily: A degree of similarity among members of a peer group on behavior or attitudinal attributes of importance.

homosexuality: A sexual preference for partners of one's own sex.

honeymoon: The earliest stage of retirement, when people focus on the pleasures of being free from the constraints of old schedules, dress codes, and other work demands.

hospice movement: A patient-centered approach for people suffering from terminal illness that emphasizes the importance of giving patients as much knowledge about their condition as possible so that they maintain some control over their care and focuses not on curing disease but on managing symptoms and pain by means of palliative medicine.

hostile attributional bias: A tendency to interpret or perceive what is neutral behavior as threatening. Often characterizes aggressive individuals.

Human Genome Project: A massive effort in molecular genetics that involved thousands of scientists around the world for 13 years (ending in 2003) and successfully mapped the sequence of chemical bases comprising all human chromosomes.

Huntington's chorea: A lethal genetic disorder, usually beginning between 30 and 40 years of age, that causes the nervous system to deteriorate, leading to uncontrolled movements, increasingly disordered psychological functioning, and eventually death. Because the dominant, defective alleles causing this disorder do not have their effects until after the childbearing years, it continues to be passed from one generation to another.

hypothalamic-pituitary-adrenal (HPA) axis: The system involved in the body's physical response to stress. When a person experiences or anticipates stress, the amygdala detects the danger and informs the hypothalamus, which communicates the danger to the pituitary gland, which responds by releasing adrenocorticotropic hormone (ACTH) into the bloodstream. ACTH causes the adrenal glands to release the hormones epinephrine, norepinephrine, and cortisol, which travel back to the brain and prepare the body to resist the stressor.

hypothalamus: The brain structure that plays a role in emotions, ability to remember, and ability to compare sensory information to expectations.

"I" or self-as-subject: The part of the self that is an active agent or is the knower. The part of the self that experiences a sense of subjective self-awareness.

id: In Freud's personality theory, one of three aspects of personality. Represents the biological self and its function is to keep the individual alive. It is irrational, blindly pursuing the fulfillment of physical needs or "instincts," such as the hunger drive and the sex drive.

ideals: Imagined, logically organized, perfect systems (such as political systems or persons) that do not match reality.

identical twins (monozygotic): Twins who come from a single zygote and have exactly the same genotype.

identification: Trying to become like another person by both imitating the model's behaviors and internalizing her attitudes, standards, and values.

ill-defined or ill-structured problems: Problems faced in adulthood that lack preestablished answers. The "right" answer to an ill-defined problem may be different depending on circumstances and on the perspective of the problem solver.

imaginary audience: An individual's mistaken assumption that others are as intrigued by and concerned about him as he is. A characteristic feature of adolescents' self-focus.

immanent justice: The expectation that misbehavior will eventually be punished, even if no one knows about it, as though some higher authority is always watching.

immunosuppression: Suppressed or weakened state of the immune system.

implantation: The process by which a zygote, which has migrated down the mother's fallopian tube into the uterus, becomes attached to the uterine lining.

implementation: In Super's theory, completion of education along with entry into full-time employment that is the final step in the exploratory stage.

incremental models: Theoretical models in which change is considered steady and specific to particular behaviors or mental activities, rather than being marked by major, sweeping reorganizations that affect many behaviors at once, as in stage theories.

incremental theorists: Usually mastery-oriented people who see intelligence as a dynamic and malleable quality that can be increased by hard work and instruction.

indicated prevention: A category of prevention efforts that address individuals who show subclinical symptoms of disorders.

induction: One method parents use to enforce control of children's behavior. Involves use of explanation, giving reasons for rules and appealing to children's desires to be grown-up. The most effective way to promote the internalization of rules.

indulgent parenting: Also called permissive parenting, it is a parenting style that describes parents who are high on responsiveness but low on demandingness.

industry: In Erikson's theory, an aspect of self-concept that develops as a function of the first work experiences in childhood. A belief in one's ability to master the skills and tools needed to be productive and an expectation of pleasure in completion of challenging work.

infantile amnesia: The difficulty people experience remembering events in their lives before they were 3 or 4 years old.

inferior colliculi: Small structures in the midbrain involved in receiving sensory input from the ears.

influence: The process by which a peer group can cause an individual to conform to the norms of the group.

information processing theories: Theories that tend to liken human cognitive functioning to computer processing of information.

initial commitment: Position 7 in Perry's model that, taken together with multiple commitments (Position 8) and resolve (Position 9), suggests a flowering of the commitments anticipated in Positions 5 and 6. Changes in thinking are more qualitative than structural.

inner speech: Internal, subvocal dialogue that in Vygotsky's theory facilitates thinking.

intention: A mental state, such as a plan or a desire, that is the source of voluntary action.

interactive repair: During caregiver–infant interactions, a caregiver's effort to help the infant shift from a negative emotional state that has derailed the interaction back to a positive emotional state, mending the interaction.

intergenic DNA: The 97% of chromosomal DNA that is not made up of genes, and which is not well understood.

internalization: The process by which children adopt adults' standards and rules as their own.

internalizing problems: Problem behavior that involves negative feelings about self and other symptoms of depression.

interneuron: One of two main types of neurons in systems of neurons. These have short projections (e.g., short axons) and affect other cells relatively close to the circuit of which they are a part.

interpersonal orientation: The way an individual characteristically interacts on a social level.

intersensory integration (or intermodal perception): The notion that the senses are already somewhat related very early in infancy, perhaps at birth, and that when babies perceive an object in one way, they can construct some notion of the object's other perceptual characteristics.

intimacy: A quality of interpersonal relating through which partners share personal thoughts, feelings, and other important aspects of themselves with each other. True intimacy is marked by openness, affection, and trust.

intrapersonal models: Drawing on theories of attachment or personality, this model emphasizes the contribution of one's personal history or temperament to the success or failure of relationships.

invincibility fable: A feeling of being invulnerable, or even immortal, that can be part of an adolescent's personal fable.

irritability or negative emotionality: The infant's tendency to cry, squirm, and otherwise react with fussiness to negative or frustrating events. An aspect of infant temperament.

just world: Beliefs that the world is fair and that people in it get what they deserve.

karyotype: A display of the actual chromosomes from human body cells, photographed under a microscope and laid out in matching pairs.

keeper of meaning (vs. rigidity): A stage of life that Vaillant added to Erikson's sequence of stages, characterizing late middle adulthood when the adult expands his generative concerns beyond just making a productive contribution, to actually preserve something that is part of the culture and, in doing so, establish the meaningfulness of the work or contributions he has made.

kindling-behavioral sensitization: Phenomenon characterized by progressive illness severity or illness incidence following an initial illness episode due to increased sensitivity to stressful triggers.

kinkeeper: The person in an extended family who helps the generations maintain contact with one another.

knowledge base: An individual's mentally stored information. Adults generally have a larger base for most domains of knowledge than children do.

kwashiorkor: A condition occurring in children who suffer severe protein and calorie shortages, which is characterized by stunted growth, a protuberant belly, and extreme apathy. Although therapeutic diets can reverse some effects, cognitive impairments are likely to persist.

lactase: An enzyme necessary for digesting milk.

late multiplicity: Position 4 in Perry's model in which students fully realize that even experts differ among themselves in regard to what is true. Students handle this realization by embracing either the oppositional or relative subordinate response to late multiplicity.

latency stage: The fourth of Freud's psychosexual stages, beginning around age 5, during which the id's energy is not especially linked to any particular pleasure or body part, and the potential conflicts among the three aspects of personality are largely latent and unexpressed.

launching period: The time when emerging adults begin to move away from home and become more self-sufficient.

legacy-leaving stage: In Schaie's theory, a late life stage when the mind is sound but frailty signals that life is ending. Individuals often work on establishing a written or oral account of their lives or of the history of their families to pass on to others.

life-course-persistent antisocial pattern: A developmental pattern of adolescent antisocial behavior that begins in early childhood and continues throughout life. This pattern is generally associated with early conduct problems, aggressiveness, and academic difficulties.

life-course perspective: The view that development is influenced by the intersection of chronological age (life time), family-related (family time), and membership in a birth cohort (historical time).

life events: Category of stressor that is discrete, often traumatic, and with a clear onset.

life span development or life span developmental psychology: The study of human development from conception to death.

life span developmental theories or models: A type of multidimensional theory that emphasizes the continuity of developmental processes from birth through death. Developmental change, seen as adaptation, involves proximal interactions between the organism and the immediate context modified by more distal processes both within the individual and in the environment.

life structure: A pattern of relationships between the self and the external world, such as relationships to one's spouse, lover, family, occupation, religion, leisure, and so on.

limbic system: A collection of structures in the brain that includes the hippocampus, amygdala, septum, thalamus, and hypothalamus. These structures produce feelings such as pleasure, pain, anger, sexuality, fear, and affection. Referred to as the "emotional brain" and works in concert with other parts of the brain, such as the frontal lobes.

longitudinal: A study design in which one group of subjects is measured several times as they grow older, eliminating cohort differences.

long-term memory: An almost unlimited mental store of knowledge.

"looking-glass self": According to Cooley, a self-concept that develops from the reflected appraisals of others, primarily attachment figures.

loss-focused grief: Confronting the painful reality of death, expressing sadness, and gradually desensitizing oneself to the reminders of loss that can lead to rumination or excessive preoccupation and, often, great distress.

love withdrawal: One method parents use to enforce control of children's behavior. Involves parents withdrawing attention or affection, expressing disappointment or disillusionment with a child, turning away from a child, cutting off verbal or emotional contact, or enforcing separations. Generates high anxiety and elicits immediate compliance.

low birth weight (LBW): A newborn weight of less than 5.5 lbs, often related to premature birth. Approximately 16% of infants in the United States are born with disorders related to prematurity and LBW, the leading cause of death for neonates. Preterm/LBW infants may have chronic medical problems such as respiratory infections, delays in achievement of developmental milestones, behavioral problems, feeding problems, low IQ or learning problems.

lowest observable adverse effect level: A level of prenatal alcohol exposure at which a baby will experience some functional impairment but is not likely to sustain structural malformations.

macrosystem: In Bronfenbrenner's bioecological model, the customs and character of the larger culture that help shape the microsystems.

maintenance hypothesis: The view that couples typically work hard to maintain their favorable beliefs about each other, despite the inevitable challenges of marriage. Positive illusions support the relationship, and people are often reluctant to abandon them to face reality.

maintenance or resilience: In life span developmental theory, a kind of adaptation that involves finding ways to continue functioning at the same level in the face of challenges or to restore one's functioning after suffering some loss.

maintenance stage: In Super's theory, a stage from about 45 to 64, when an individual makes ongoing adjustments to improve her work situation, often achieving more advanced status and seniority.

making interesting sights last: Occurs when an infant's behavior accidentally produces an interesting event, the child notices the effect, and repeats the action. A precursor to intentional behavior in Piaget's view.

marker events: Events that are used as criteria for adulthood, including completing formal education, entering the adult workforce, leaving the family home, getting married, and becoming a parent.

mastery orientation: An orientation to failure in which individuals move forward optimistically, assuming that they can succeed with further effort. They seem to construe failure as a challenge rather than as an obstacle.

maturity demands: Parents' requirements that children perform behaviors that are suitable to their level of maturity.

maturity gap: A time in adolescence when physical maturity is achieved but social maturity is not. Adolescents may mimic the behavior of more advanced peers to possess the symbolic trappings of adult status (sexual intimacy, material possessions, autonomy, and respect from parents).

means-end behavior: A type of intentional behavior that characterizes infants by 8 to 12 months. Babies divert their attention from a goal, such as grasping a toy, in order to produce another action that will help achieve the goal.

mechanistic view: The perspective that individuals are passively affected by external events. They are thus highly malleable and receptive to outside intervention.

mediated learning: A central concept in Vygotsky's theory. The child's acquisition of knowledge is "mediated" in the sense that it is highly influenced by the surrounding environment and culture.

mediation: In Vygotsky's theory, the intermediary role of other people in determining the meaning of signs and symbols, like words, which in turn affect the child's thinking.

medulla: A brain structure found in the hindbrain that helps to regulate functions which are basic for survival, such as heart rate, blood pressure, and respiration.

meiosis: A special kind of cell division whereby germ cells located in the ovaries and testes divide and form four new cells, each containing only 23 chromosomes, one member of each pair.

"Me" self-concept: The known part of the self that is the object of one's own or others' observations.

memory strategies: Potentially conscious activities a person may voluntarily carry out to remember something.

menarche: A girl's first menstruation.

menopause: The cessation of menstruation that usually begins in the 40s and continues for at least 10 years.

mesosystem: In Bronfenbrenner's bioecological model, the network of microsystems that relate with and modify one another.

messenger ribonucleic acid (mRNA): The organic compound that cells synthesize by copying strands of DNA. The sequence of bases in a gene is replicated in the mRNA, and then the RNA serves as a "messenger" to the cell from the gene, guiding the cell's construction of a protein.

meta-analysis: An analytic tool for assessing the effects of variables in which data from a large number of studies on the same topic are analyzed together to determine which effects are consistent across studies and what the strength of those effects are.

metacognition: The ability to think about and understand one's own cognitive processes and their effects.

method of control: A technique that parents use to enforce control of their children's behavior. The three primary methods are power assertion, love withdrawal, and induction.

microsystem: In Bronfenbrenner's bioecological model, the immediate environment where proximal processes are played out.

midbrain: A set of brain structures that are between hindbrain and forebrain and include the superior colliculi, inferior colliculi, and the substantia nigra.

mindfulness: Intentional, non-judgmental awareness of the present moment.

mitigation: When the perpetrator of a crime is guilty and is held responsible for the crime but is considered less than fully blameworthy. Mitigation applies not only to degree of culpability but also to degree of punishment.

mitosis: A kind of cell division that produces two new cells identical to the original cell.

modal personal orientation: In Holland's theory, an aspect of personality that is a typical and preferred style or approach to dealing with social and environmental tasks. Most jobs or careers will be compatible with one of the six orientations: realistic, investigative, artistic, social, enterprising, and conventional.

modeling: See *observational learning.*

molecular genetics: The study of what genes do and how their products influence the body and behavior.

morality of caring: A focus on concern for others (as opposed to establishing justice) when making moral evaluations decisions and when evaluating decisions of others.

morality of justice: A focus on establishing justice (as opposed to concern for others) when making moral decisions and when evaluating decisions made by others.

moral rules: The standards used to address fundamental issues of justice, welfare, and rights, such as rules about stealing, hurting others, or sharing. Rules of behavior that are relatively universal as opposed to being culturally based.

moratorium: One of Marcia's four identity status categories in which individuals are actively involved in exploring possible life choices, but not having made any firm commitments to them.

multidimensional models: A class of theoretical models in which theorists consider development to be the result of the relationships among many causal components. They generally apply to all domains of development from the cognitive to the social and suggest that there are layers, or levels, of interacting causes for behavioral change: physical/molecular, biological, psychological, social, and cultural. These models may also be called transactional, relational, systems, or bioecological models.

multi-infarct dementia: A number of minor strokes that gradually do sufficient damage to cause dementia.

multiple commitments: Position 8 in Perry's model that, taken together with initial commitment (Position 7) and resolve (Position 9), suggests a flowering of the commitments anticipated in Positions 5 and 6. Changes in thinking are more qualitative than structural.

multiplicity (prelegitimate):   Position 2 in Perry's model that is characterized by the student's first encounters with multiplicity, that is, multiple ideas, multiple answers to life's questions, or multiple points of view. Individuals in this stage face confusion, yet maintain the belief that some "authority" possesses the ultimate truth or right answers.

multiplicity (subordinate):   Position 3 in Perry's model in which the individual grudgingly acknowledges the reality and legitimacy of multiple perspectives. Individuals in this stage find it more difficult to deny that reasonable people can differ in their perspectives on life, and people who hold different views are not so easily dismissed as being wrong.

mutation: A change in the chemical structure of an existing gene, sometimes occurring spontaneously and sometimes occurring due to environmental influences, such as exposure to radiation or toxic chemicals.

myelination: The phenomenon in which glial cells wrap themselves around the axons of neurons, providing an insulating sheath that facilitates the conduction of electrical impulses.

narrative: A story or event description that conveys the full sense of an experience or gets at the point of an event while taking into account what the listener needs to hear to understand.

narrative skill: The ability to tell a coherent story.

narrow socialization: Socialization more characteristic of nonindustrialized cultures that exert extensive control over the expression of behaviors that violate social standards and expect substantial conformity from young members of the society.

needs-based reasoning: Reasoning about other people's needs in which one must weigh one's own personal needs against those of others.

needs oriented: Describes the understanding that another person's need is a good reason for helping, usually characteristic of children sometime in the elementary school years.

negative affectivity: The state or trait tendency to experience nervousness, fear, anger, sadness, contempt, or guilt.

negative affect reciprocity: A tendency for negative emotions in one partner to follow from the other partner's negativity.

negative correlation: A relationship between variables in which they change together but in opposite directions, so that as one increases, the other decreases.

negative reinforcement: When a behavior is rewarded by the removal of aversive consequences. For example, if a parent insists that a child clean his room, but relents when the child has a temper tantrum, the *withdrawal* of the aversive demand is a negative reinforcement, rewarding the child's temper tantrum.

neglected: A sociometric category that includes those children who receive few nominations, either positive or negative, from their peers. Neglected children are characterized by their low level of social impact.

neglecting–uninvolved style: An interactive parenting style that combines low levels of warmth (emotional distance) and low levels of control or demandingness, so that parents invest very little time or attention in a child. Associated with many negative child outcomes.

neoPiagetians: Theorists who explain Piaget's stages or revise the stages using many information processing concepts. These theorists attempt to combine the best components of both Piagetian and information processing approaches.

nerve growth factor: A substance found within the brain that is absorbed by neurons and aids in the process of synapse production.

neural pruning: A gradual process in brain development that continues through adolescence into young adulthood in which neurons die off and many synaptic connections are selectively discarded.

neural tube: A structure that represents the first step in the development of an embryo's central nervous system. It is formed when a sheet of cells from the embryo's upper surface turns inward and curls into a tube.

neurons: The building blocks of the brain, these nerve cells are specialized for the transmission of electrical impulses.

neuroticism (N):   One of the Big 5 personality traits that is described using synonyms including *tense, touchy, self-pitying, unstable, anxious,* and *worrying.*

neurotransmitters: Chemical substances found in the nervous system which communicate messages between neurons when released. The chemical message, once picked up by the dendrites, the cell body or the axon of a neighboring neuron, is read by that cell as a message to "fire" or "stop firing."

neurulation: The prenatal formation of a neural tube that begins the development of the central nervous system.

niche picking: The process whereby children, as they grow older, are less constrained by their parents' choices and choose environments that are compatible with their interests. These environments then provide support for and probably strengthen those interests.

no observable effect level: The threshold of alcohol ingestion by a pregnant mother above which the fetus will experience some functional impairment.

nonacademic self-concept: One of two major divisions of a child's general self-concept that includes his view of self in the social, emotional, and physical domains.

nondeclarative knowledge: Knowledge that one cannot adequately put into words and might not enter awareness, including procedural knowledge, knowing how to do things.

nonnormative changes: Changes that are expected, such as the death of a family member.

nonshared environment: Different environmental input that is considered to be responsible for the degree to which two individuals differ on a given trait.

norepinephrine: Also called noradrenaline, it is one of the stress hormones released by the adrenal glands and has no effects on heart rate and other "fight or flight" responses in the body. Also functions as a neurotransmitter.

nuclear family tradition: A body of work that examines the outcomes of a person's attachment to his primary caregiver in infancy, once the person becomes an adult.

nucleus: In the brain, a cluster of cells creating a functional structure.

number conservation task: A procedure designed by Piaget to test children's understanding of number. Children must be able to recognize that the number of items in a set does not change when the appearance of the set changes; for example, when a row of buttons is spread out or bunched together.

object concept: Understanding of what an object is, including recognition that an object has properties that can stimulate all of our senses and that an object has "permanence"— it continues to exist even when we are not perceiving it.

object permanence: The fact that objects have a separate existence from the perceiver; that is, they continue to exist even when no one is perceiving them.

observational learning or modeling: Learning by imitation. Occurs when an individual repeats an act or sequence of actions that she has observed another individual (the model) performing.

occipital lobe: The part of the cerebrum, located at the back of each hemisphere, that processes visual information.

Oedipus complex: In Freud's theory, the belief that young boys direct their sexual urges toward their mothers because they are most strongly attached to their mothers as primary caretakers. This desire for the mother, to usurp her time, to be physically close to her, puts a boy in competition with his father for her affections. The boy fears that his more powerful father will retaliate with a physical punishment that fits the crime—castration. The boy is so terrified by the prospect of his father's retaliation that he redirects his energy into pleasing his father by identifying with him.

ontogeny: The development of organisms.

open identity domains: Areas, such as those involving personal relationships, in which individuals assert much control and can be successful in achieving commitment.

openness (O): One of the Big 5 personality traits that is described using synonyms including *creative, artistic, curious, insightful, original,* and *wide-ranging interests.*

operant: An accidental or random action.

operant conditioning: The process by which a person learns to produce a formerly random behavior (or operant) in response to a cue because the behavior was previously reinforced in that situation.

oppositional: In Perry's theory, a response to late multiplicity characterized by legitimizing multiplicity as one pole of a new kind of dualism and the right–wrong dualism of Position 1 (strict dualism) at the other end of the new continuum. Allows individuals to maintain a dualistic either-or structure in their thinking.

oppositional defiant disorder (ODD): A pattern of hostile, negative or defiant behaviors, such as arguing with adults, spitefulness, or throwing tantrums. Presently, this diagnosis requires that the behaviors be present for at least 6 months.

optimization: A process of finding ways to enhance the achievement of remaining goals or finding environments that are enhancing that is key to successful development.

oral fixation: In Freud's personality theory, an excessive need for oral pleasures (such as eating or talking) that results from extreme denial or excessive indulgence of them during the oral stage.

oral stage: The first of Freud's psychosexual stages, corresponding to the 1st year of life, when Freud believed that a disproportionate amount of id energy is invested in drives satisfied through the mouth.

organismic theories: A class of theories characterized by the view that human beings are active initiators of their own development.

organization strategy: A memory strategy that involves sorting items to be learned on some meaningful basis, such as grouping the names by region.

orienting response: In infants, a set of behaviors that suggest that the baby is attending to a stimulus. May include head turn toward the stimulus, looking, decreased heart rate, and increased sucking.

orthogenetic principle: The notion that as behavior becomes differentiated or elaborated, the multiple behaviors that develop also are hierarchically organized or controlled by higher levels of functioning. For example, with age the generalized distress of newborns differentiates into several different negative emotions, such as anger and sadness, the expression of which is controlled by higher brain processes.

osteoarthritis: The most common form of arthritis, which involves the thinning, fraying, and cracking of cartilage at the ends of bones.

other-directed coping behaviors: Efforts to deal with stress that appear to be aimed at changing the behaviors of others, such as when infants use facial expressions, movements, and verbalizations that seem designed to get a caregiver to respond positively in an interaction.

other-transforming: An immature interpersonal style in which an individual tries to dominate or coerce a friend into meeting his needs. Acting to change or transform the other; can involve bullying, aggression, or manipulation.

outcome variable: The variable that is said to be affected by the cause of a given phenomenon.

ovaries: Female gonads that primarily produce estrogen and progesterone, but also produce lesser amounts of androgens (such as testosterone). Site of egg (ovum) production in females.

ovum: Reproductive egg cell, containing only 23 chromosomes, produced in and released by the ovaries of females.

pair therapy: Selman's approach to treating children and adolescents with social interactive difficulties. Two individuals with equally ineffective social styles, such as a controlling child and a fearful one, meet regularly with a helper who encourages them to be effectively assertive and empathic.

palliative care: Comfort care that involves services provided by caregivers from several disciplines embodying a comprehensive approach to care that addresses pain management, emotional and spiritual care, and psychological support for caregivers and survivors.

parent centered: Describes parents whose interactions with their children are driven by parental needs rather than focusing on children's needs. Parents with this approach may make hostile attributions when children's needs are out of line with their own.

parental monitoring: Consistent parental supervision.

parenting styles: Approaches that characterize parents' typical interactions with and attitudes toward their children. Four styles have been identified, combining and crossing the positive and negative poles of two parenting dimensions—warmth and control. These styles are often predictive of child characteristics.

parietal lobe: A part of the cerebrum located between the frontal lobe (at the front of the cerebrum) and the occipital lobe (at the back of the cerebrum) and above the temporal lobe (on the side of the cerebrum) of each hemisphere. It processes somatosensory information such as touch, temperature, and pain.

passion: An element of love that refers to erotic attraction or feelings.

passive gene effects: The effects of parents' genes on the kind of environment that they create for their children. When these effects are compatible with a child's own hereditary tendencies, the child's genes are a passive source of environmental influence.

peer/romantic partner tradition: A body of work that focuses on the peer attachments of adults by questioning how early attachments impact the quality of romantic and friendship relationships in adulthood.

penis envy: According to Freud's theory, a girl's desire to have what she naively assumes is the greater genital pleasure that must come with having the external genitalia of a man.

performance: See competence vs. performance.

period of the embryo: Lasting from the 4th through the 8th week of gestation, the time that most of the body's organ systems and structures are forming.

period of the fetus: Lasting from the 9th week of gestation until birth, the time of rapid growth and further differentiation when the reproductive system forms, gains in body weight occur, and the brain and nervous system continue to develop.

period of the ovum: The first 3 weeks of pregnancy, from the time of fertilization through implantation into the uterine lining to the development of the neural tube.

permissive style: An interactive parenting style that combines moderate to high levels of warmth (positive emotional climate, sensitivity and responsivity) with low levels of control or demandingness. Associated with impulsive behavior and low levels of self-reliance in children.

personal fable: A distorted view of one's uniqueness that is a feature of adolescents' egocentrism.

personal rules: Rules about areas of functioning that individuals or families might have standards about, such as choices of friends or recreational activities or participation in family life, that are not governed by formal social rules in Western societies.

"the person who" fallacy: Refuting a well-documented finding by calling on knowledge of a person who is an exception.

perspective taking: Consideration of the viewpoints of others; putting oneself, metaphorically, in the shoes of another and seeing self and others from that alternative stance.

phallic stage: The third of Freud's psychosexual stages, lasting from age 3 to about 5, in which id energy is focused primarily in the genital region. This stage draws the greatest parental discipline, leads to feelings of guilt and the development of the superego, and can have long-lasting effects on how a child copes with postpubertal sexual needs.

phenotype: The aspect of a genetic blueprint that is actually expressed in the physical and behavioral characteristics of an individual.

phenylketonuria (PKU): A genetic disorder resulting from the absence of an important enzyme, without which the amino acid phenylalanine cannot be metabolized. Unless the victim's diet is severely restricted, phenylalanine soon accumulates in the body and causes mental retardation.

Phineas Gage matrix: Syndrome related to injury of the frontal cortex. Consists of cognitive dysfunctions (such as poor planning, inadequate decision making, inability to take another's perspective, and problems in sustaining employment) and emotional problems (such as shallow affect, lack of an enriched emotional life, lack of passion and initiative, and a diminished sense of pleasure and pain).

phonology: The sound system of a language. Includes rules for arranging the basic sounds or "phonemes" of the language.

physician-assisted suicide: The prescribing of medicine that enables patients to take their own lives.

Piaget's cognitive development: Jean Piaget's theory of the development of cognition, which outlines four childhood stages in which the capacity to think logically about both concrete and abstract concepts evolves.

placebo effect: Occurs when individuals receiving a placebo (a "dummy" version of a treatment) experience improvement in their symptoms and attribute the improvement to the placebo.

placenta: A nourishing barrier that surrounds the developing fetus, allowing nutrients from the mother's blood to pass to the fetus's blood while allowing waste to be removed by the mother's blood. Otherwise, it keeps the two circulatory systems separate.

plaques: In the brain, clumps of insoluble protein that are damaging to neurons and associated with Alzheimer's disease.

plasticity: The malleability of the human brain, its capacity to change and grow especially in response to new environmental input. Includes the capacity of neurons to shift functions to compensate for damage to other cells or because they have been transplanted to a different part of the brain.

pleasure principle: The pursuit of gratification, which motivates the id in Freud's personality theory.

polygenic: Describes traits that are affected by the products of multiple gene pairs, often located on different chromosomes, so that any one pair of gene alleles has only a limited affect on a given trait.

pons: A brain structure located in the hindbrain that is involved in the regulation of the sleep–wake cycle.

popular: A sociometric category that includes those children who receive many positive nominations and few negative nominations from their peers (have high social preference and high social impact). Popular children are generally well-liked members of the group and have relatively high visibility among their peers.

positive affect: Tendency to express happy mood states by smiling and laughing especially to social stimuli. An aspect of infant temperament.

positive affectivity: The state or trait tendency to experience enthusiasm, alertness, joy, confidence, and determination.

positive correlation: A relationship between variables in which they change in the same direction, either both increasing or both decreasing.

postconventional morality: Kohlberg's third stage of moral reasoning achieved by some adults in which what is considered right is defined not by specific rules or laws but by general processes such as democratic principles or individual rights.

postformal or fifth-stage thinking: Characteristic of a stage beyond Piaget's sequence of stages that describes the changes in logical thinking that might occur in the adult years. Characterized by the ability of the problem solver to coordinate contradictory formal operational approaches to the same problem. The postformal thinker can understand the logic of each of the contradictory perspectives and integrate the perspectives into a larger whole.

postrational skepticism: A characterization of postformal thought that suggests that the search for absolute truth gives way to a search for arguably good reasons for choosing one belief or course of action over another; an endorsement of the possibility and practicality of making rational commitments in the face of the clear knowledge that other defensible alternatives to one's views continue to exist.

posttraumatic growth: Positive psychological change experienced as a result of the struggle with highly stressful or traumatic events.

Posttraumatic Stress Disorder: An anxiety disorder that follows a traumatic event. PTSD is characterized by clinically significant symptoms such as re-experience of the traumatic event, general numbing of responsiveness to others, heightened arousal, disturbed sleep, and so forth

power assertion: One method parents use to enforce control of children's behavior. Can involve physical punishment or the threat of physical punishment, or it can involve withdrawal of privileges. Effective for the immediate control of behavior, but over the long term, children show higher levels of anger, aggressiveness and anxiety.

pragmatics: One of the aspects of language that children must learn that goes beyond learning semantics and syntax and involves using the language effectively to communicate. Includes skills such as crafting a narrative and "code switching," using different language styles in different contexts.

preconventional morality: Kohlberg's first stage of moral reasoning characterizing middle childhood in which what is right is what avoids punishment, what conforms to the dictates of authority, or what serves one's personal interests.

preferential looking paradigm: A research technique used with infants. Two visual stimuli are presented simultaneously on a split screen and babies' eye movements are recorded to assess their preferences for one stimulus over the other.

premoral stage: In Piaget's theory of moral development, characterizes preschoolers who are unconcerned about established rules or standards.

preoccupied (insecure): An attachment style classifying adults who provide transcripts in the AAI that are not collaborative and that are characterized by very long, incoherent, egocentric responses that shift from topic to topic. They indicate substantial enmeshment or preoccupation with parents, registered by angry, accusatory language or by conflicted descriptions that connote ambivalence and confusion about early relationships. Their children tend to have anxious-ambivalent attachments. In Bartholomew's typology, these individuals are emotionally demanding, anxious about gaining acceptance, fearful of rejection, and preoccupied with relationships.

preoperational egocentrism: The tendency of preschoolers to be aware only of their own perspective. Demonstrated in their expectations that others will know what they know, believe what they believe, and so on.

preoperational stage: In Piaget's theory of cognitive development, the time period from approximately ages 2 to 7 when children are capable of representational thought but appear to be prelogical in their thinking.

pre-self: An infant's early inklings of the permanence of her body, its separateness from others, and the rhythms of interpersonal connections.

prevention science: A new and evolving multidisciplinary mix of human development, psychopathology, epidemiology, education, and criminology that offers us useful guidelines for understanding what constitutes effective prevention.

primary control: Control efforts that are attempts to affect the immediate environment beyond ourselves.

primary prevention: An attempt to forestall the development of problems by promoting health and wellness in the general population through group-oriented interventions.

primary sexual characteristics: The physical traits directly involved in reproduction, such as the genitalia.

principle of equifinality: Many early developmental pathways can produce similar outcomes.

principle of multifinality: The same developmental pathways may result in a wide range of possible outcomes.

procedural knowledge: Describes the often unconscious, nondeclarative knowledge of how to do things that underlies many physical skills.

production deficiency: Failure to use a memory strategy one has knowledge of even in a situation where it is ordinarily helpful.

progeria: A fatal genetic disorder that causes rapid aging, so that by late childhood its victims are dying of "old age." Because progeria sufferers do not survive long enough to reproduce, the disease must be caused by a genetic mutation.

progesterone: A hormone involved in the reproductive cycle, especially in females.

projection neuron: One of two main types of neurons in systems of neurons. These have long projections, especially axons, that extend far away from the cell body.

prosocial behavior or altruism: Voluntarily acting in ways that seem intended to benefit someone else.

protective factors: Aspects of the organism or the environment that moderate the negative effects of risk.

proteins: The chemical building blocks of the body that are constructed when cells follow the codes provided by genes.

protest: The second phase in the grieving process where bereaved individuals may experience periods of obsessive yearning or searching for the lost loved one as well as bouts of restlessness or irritability.

proximal processes: Reciprocal interactions between a person and her immediate external environment, including other people, the physical environment, or informational sources such as books or movies. In Bronfenbrenner's biological model, all developments are a function of these processes.

proximity maintenance: One of three purposes of the attachment system. Bonds between infant and caregiver encourage and sustain physical closeness.

proximo-distal: The "near-to-far" (or inner to outer) direction of prenatal development.

prudential consequences: Negative effects on an individual's health, safety, or future as a result of an action that violates some social expectation or rule. Getting arrested or having an accident would be a prudential consequence of driving too fast.

psychological well-being: Feeling a sense of purpose, growth, and mastery, or that one is striving for realization of one's true potential.

psychoneuroimmunology: The study of the interactions between the central nervous system, the immune system and behavior.

psychosocial development: Change with age in the psychological processes of interpersonal understanding, skills, and values that affect an individual's capacity for interpersonal relationships, including friendships.

puberty: A process of sexual maturing in late childhood related to a wide range of emotional, behavioral, and social changes.

qualitative research: Any kind of research which does not use statistical procedures or quantitative methods to arrive at conclusions.

racial group: Groups of people, like Blacks, Whites, and Asians, who have historically been assumed to be genetically different, identifiable by variations in hair, skin color, bone structure, or other physiological markers. Genetic indicators of race have not been found, so that racial groups appear to be a social construction.

reactive attachment disorder (RAD): A lack of ability to form affectional bonds with other people and a pattern of markedly disturbed social relationships. RAD can result when a child receives grossly neglectful or pathological care in the early years.

reality monitoring: The ability to distinguish what is imagined from what is real.

reality principle: A focus on understanding the world and behavioral consequences that leads to sensible and self-protective behavior. In Freud's personality theory, the ego operates on this principle.

recall: Remembering information or events that are not currently available to the senses. Requires the ability to mentally represent the absent information.

recency: A salient characteristic of self-memories. The tendency to remember something that has happened to us recently better than something that happened in the more distant past.

recognition: Remembering in the sense of knowing that information currently available to the senses has been previously experienced.

reflective judgment: In Kitchener's theory of the development of problem solving, the analysis of the elements of a problem and justification of problem solutions.

reflective practice: A method used by counselors that emphasizes careful consideration of theoretical and empirical sources of knowledge, as well as one's own beliefs and assumptions, as a precursor to practice.

refusal of treatment: Patients' refusal of any food, water, or medical treatment that prolongs life.

regulation of loss: In life span developmental theory, a kind of adaptive functioning that involves reorganizing the way we behave by adjusting our expectations and accepting a lower level of functioning.

regulator genes: Genes, possibly located on the long stretches of intergenic DNA, that help determine how and when coded genes will be transcribed by the cell to guide the production of proteins.

rehearsal: A strategy for remembering that usually involves continuing to actively process to-be-remembered material, like repeating it to oneself.

reinforcement: An event that an individual experiences as pleasurable or rewarding, which increases the frequency of a behavior that occurred immediately before the pleasurable event.

reintegrative stage: In Schaie's theory, the elder years when individuals do not often need to acquire new domains of knowledge or to figure out new ways of applying what they know. Many are motivated to conserve energy (physical and psychological). Cognitive efforts are aimed at solving immediate, practical problems that seem critically important to daily functioning.

rejected: A sociometric category that includes those children who receive many negative nominations and few positive nominations from their peers. Rejected children are typically disliked (low social preference) but have generally high visibility (high social impact).

rejected-aggressive: Describes children who are rejected because they aggress against their peers.

rejected-withdrawn: Describes children who are rejected because they withdraw from their peers.

relatedness: In self-determination theory, one of three basic needs. Feeling that one is important to others and valued enough to be sensitively and responsively cared for, from infancy onward.

relational models: Another term for multidimensional models.

relative subordinate: In Perry's theory, a response to late multiplicity in which students (primarily under the guidance of authority) begin to understand that some opinions are more legitimate than others. The value of a perspective is now understood to be related to the supporting arguments and evidence for the position.

relativistic thought: The essence of postformal thought in which several truth systems exist describing the reality of the same event, and they appear to be logically equivalent.

releasers: Infant physical characteristics that elicit nurturant responses from adults, such as small body size, large eyes, and large head size relative to the total body size.

reorganization: The last phase in the grieving process in which the grieving individual discovers ways to hold on to the memory of the deceased and integrate that memory into their current life and new attachments.

reorganizational stage: In Schaie's theory, a stage of early old age, when responsibilities narrow as children grow up and retirement becomes an option. Flexibility in problem solving is needed to create a satisfying, meaningful environment for the rest of life, but the focus tends to narrow to a changed set of personal goals and needs.

reorientation: The third stage of retirement, which is a time of active trial and error. The retiree seeks solutions to the problems that retirement presents and tries strategies for building a satisfactory life.

representational thought: The capacity to think about things or events that are not currently stimulating one's senses. Utilizes mental images or symbols to "re-present" the absent experience.

representations of interactions (or RIGs): A kind of sensorimotor or procedural memory or expectation that infants form of how interactions with others are likely to proceed. These representations are based on repeated experiences and are preverbal and unconscious.

resilience (resilient): The quality that permits developmental success for some individuals despite grave setbacks, early adversity, or other risk factors. (Describes a person who has this quality.)

resistance phase: The second phase in the body's reaction to a stressor, during which the body is moderately aroused, the parasympathetic system takes over, and the body continues to resist the effects of the stressor.

resolve: Position 9 in Perry's model that, taken together with initial commitment (Position 7) and multiple commitments (Position 8), suggests a flowering of the commitments anticipated in Positions 5 and 6. Position 9, although placed at the end of the line, does not imply a static resolution of existential conflict; rather, it characterizes a state of courageous resolve to continue the work of reflecting on one's commitments throughout adulthood.

responsible stage: In Schaie's theory, the stage of cognitive development faced during middle adulthood in which ill-defined problems remain the norm, but problem solving must now take into account not only one's own personal needs and goals but also those of others in one's life who have become one's responsibility (spouse, children, coworkers, member of the community).

restoration-focused grief: A type of coping strategy directed toward handling the practical tasks that need to be done to carry on with daily life.

retention: Staying in college long enough to graduate.

reticular activating system: A set of brain structures including the reticular formation located in the brain stem that filters out some of the stimuli we perceive and alerts higher structures to "pay attention" to other stimuli.

reticular formation: A bundle of neural tissue in the brainstem that acts together with other nuclei to form the reticular activating system which affects attention to incoming stimuli.

retreat: Perry's characterization of the behavior of individuals who move back to dualistic thinking in times of stress to seek the intellectual security of absolute right and wrong.

retrieval: What we usually mean by remembering, that is, getting information out of mental storage so we can use it.

retrieval strategy: An approach to finding and recovering information stored in memory. In math, this refers to solving arithmetic problems by recovering a memorized answer (e.g., remembering that 3 plus 2 equals 5 rather than solving the problem).

reversible relationship: A kind of logical relationship in one change reverses the effects of another change (and also implies the existence of its reverse). For example, in math, subtraction is the reverse of addition.

rhythmicity: The predictability of an individual's sleep, feeding, elimination, and other biological cycles. An aspect of infant temperament.

risk factors: Aspects of the organism or the environment that compromise healthy development.

risky behaviors: Behaviors that constitute a departure from socially accepted norms or behaviors that pose a threat to the well being of individuals or groups.

role buffering: For individuals who participate in multiple roles, such as "mother," "wife," "caregiver to ailing parent," and "employee," if one role is a source of psychological stress or failure experiences, success and satisfaction in another role may compensate.

role strain: The stress or strain of meeting obligations that are associated with certain roles, e.g., caregiver.

rough and tumble play: Good-natured physical roughness that is an almost exclusive property of boys' play with boys.

rumination: A stable, emotion-focused coping style that involves responding to problems by directing attention internally toward negative feelings and thoughts. Rumination includes both cognitive (self-focused cognitions) and affective (increased emotional reactivity) elements.

safe haven: One of the three purposes of the attachment system. Bonds between infant and caregiver make the caregiver a source of comfort when distressed.

sandwich generation: Those who carry the double responsibilities of taking care of both an elderly relative and their own children.

scaffolding: In Vygotsky's theory, the process whereby more advanced thinkers or more capable members of a culture provide novice learners with a supportive temporary prop that enables the novice to learn and to reach higher levels of thinking.

scientific concepts: In Vygotsky's theory, culturally defined concepts that can provide children with a basis for organizing their thinking in line with the knowledge and skills of the culture.

script: A schematic representation of the typical features of an event and the order in which they happen.

secondary control: Control efforts that involve attempts to change ourselves.

secondary prevention: An attempt to reduce the incidence of disorders among those who are at high risk or to provide treatment to forestall the development of more serious psychopathology in cases that are already established.

secondary sexual characteristics: Physical traits not directly involved in reproduction but indicative of sex, such as enlarged breasts in females and deeper voices in males.

secure base: One of the three purposes of the attachment system. The bond between infant and caregiver provides the infant a protective resource as she develops and learns.

securely attached: An attachment category describing babies who typically show distress on separation from the mother in the strange situation test, but who greet her happily on her return, usually seeking comfort by reaching to be picked up. Once reassured they tend to return to exploring. In Bartholomew's description of adult attachment categories, describes individuals who expect others to be available and supportive of their needs in close relationships, who are comfortable with emotional closeness, but are also reasonably autonomous.

seduction hypothesis: The view that children or adolescents are seduced into homosexuality by homosexual pedophiles.

selection (as an adaptive strategy):   A process of narrowing our goals and limiting the domains in which we expend effort that is important for successful development.

selection (as a peer group process):   The process by which individuals choose to affiliate with others who share similar behaviors or attributes.

selective attention: Deployment of attention to only a chosen subset of the information available for processing in a situation. Selective attention to information that must be remembered later can be used as a memorization strategy.

selective optimization with compensation: The three combined processes of successful development according to life span development theory (selection, optimization, and compensation).

selective prevention: A category of prevention efforts that target individuals at some epidemiological risk.

self-system: A term currently used in place of the "self" because "self" seems too unidimensional. Includes multiple aspects of the self, such as self-concept, self-regulation, and self-esteem.

self-conscious emotions: Feelings such as shame, embarrassment, guilt, and pride that become available to toddlers after they develop objective self-awareness, or self-recognition, usually late in the 2nd year of life.

self-control: Ability to stop the self from performing a proscribed act or to make the self perform an act that is not appealing or attractive in itself.

self-determination theory: The theory that three basic psychological needs including autonomy, competence, and relatedness motivate our adaptation efforts at any age.

self-directed coping behaviors: Efforts to deal with stress that appear to be aimed at self comfort. In infants these behaviors include looking away from the source of distress or self-stimulating behavior, such as rocking and sucking.

self-efficacy beliefs: Beliefs about our ability to exercise control over events that affect our lives.

self-enhancing bias: The motivation to maintain moderately positive beliefs about oneself which is reflected in a tendency to make comparisons of oneself to people who are similar.

self-esteem: A person's evaluation of his or her attributes or the positive or negative valence associated with those attributes. In William James's opinion, self-esteem depends on the number of successes we enjoy relative to our aspirations.

self-esteem slide: A drop in self-esteem presumably experienced by girls at adolescence.

self-instruction (or self-monitoring):   The clinical and educational practices in which the general goal is to effect some behavior change (such as control of impulsivity or improvement in test-taking skills) by attending to, regulating, and sometimes changing cognitions.

self-organizing: Filtering incoming information through one's own existing mental constructs and influencing the environment's inputs with one's actions and reactions.

self-recognition: Awareness of self, usually manifested by the individual's display of self-directed behavior upon viewing her own reflection. For example, a child capable of self-recognition will touch a spot of rouge on her nose when she looks in a mirror rather than touching the mirror.

self-regulation: An advanced and flexible version of self-control. The ability to comply with a request, to initiate and cease activities according to situational demands, to modulate the intensity, frequency, and duration of verbal and motor acts in social and educational settings, to postpone acting upon a desired object or goal, and to generate socially approved behavior in the absence of external monitors.

self-transforming: An immature interpersonal style in which an individual gives in so as to reduce the level of tension. He changes his own behaviors or feelings in order to conform to the needs or demands of another.

semantic: Describing knowledge about factual information, rules, and concepts.

semantic system: An aspect of a language that children must learn, including the words and word parts that express meanings in that language.

senescing: The process of declining with age or "growing down."

sensation seeking: The need for varied, novel, and complex sensation and experiences and the willingness to take physical and social risk for the sake of these experiences.

sensorimotor stage: In Piaget's theory of cognitive development, the period from birth to about age 2 when infants are not yet capable of representational thought, so they are unable to form mental images or to plan their behavior. Babies have sensory experiences, organize them on the basis of inborn reflexes or patterns of motor responses, and make motor responses to them.

sensory integration dysfunction: A disorder marked by difficulties such as extreme hypersensitivity or hyposensitivity to sensations such as bright lights, loud sounds, pain, certain textures, or human touch. Usually includes motor clumsiness, balance problems, fidgeting, and poor eye–hand coordination.

sensory memory: Very brief retention of sensory experiences.

separation anxiety: Distress of an infant or young child when a primary caregiver leaves the child in someone else's care. Usually begins in the second half of the 1st year, demonstrating the infant's capacity to recall the absent caregiver, and is viewed as a sign of attachment to that caregiver.

septum: A brain structure located in the forebrain that is part of the limbic system or "emotional brain," which produces feelings such as pleasure, pain, anger, sexuality, fear, and affection.

sequential: Describes a kind of study that is like a cross-sectional study in that more than one cohort is included, but is like a longitudinal study in that each cohort is measured at more than one age.

sex chromosomes: The 23rd pair of chromosomes, which are alike in females but mismatched in males, and which determine an individual's sex.

sexual dimorphism: Both internal and external physical differences between the sexes, which increase during the adolescent growth spurt.

sexual orientation: A preference for partners of one's own sex (homosexuality), the opposite sex (heterosexuality), or both (bisexuality).

shared environment: Similar experiences, which are considered to explain similarities between twins that go beyond estimates of genetic influence.

shock: The first phase in the grieving process when the loss is met by disbelief and the grieving person may experience blunted emotions, or emotional outbursts.

sickle cell anemia: A hereditary disease caused by a recessive, defective gene allele affecting the red blood cells. These are abnormally (half-moon) shaped and not as efficient as normal, round red blood cells in carrying oxygen to the tissues. Symptoms can include breathing problems, a variety of organ dysfunctions, and often death by adolescence. Most common in individuals of African descent.

slow-to-warm-up babies: A temperament type described by Thomas and Chess. These babies are like easy babies in most ways, but they are like difficult babies in their fearfulness, showing more wariness in new situations than most other babies.

social clock: The set of age-related expectations that we all have for the appropriate timing of major life events.

social cognition: A person's mental processing (thoughts, beliefs, and so on) of information about other people and their reasoning about social relationships.

social comparison: The process whereby people observe the performance of others and use it as a basis for evaluating their own abilities and accomplishments.

social competence: A set of abilities that are important for peer group acceptance. Not one set of prescribed behaviors, but rather a range of effective responses, cognitive processes, and abilities to make mature judgments.

social constructivism: A variation of cognitive constructivism which emphasizes that knowledge is constructed within the context of social relationships with others and stresses the influence of such variables as gender, class, and culture on the development of beliefs.

social dosage effect: The more time children spend in same-gender groups the more gender-typical behaviors they exhibit.

social exchange and behavior theories: Related to marriage, views that assume satisfaction results from negotiated exchange between partners. Problems arise when costs of relationship exceed benefits.

social impact: A sociometric measure that is computed by adding the total number of nom-inations a child receives from her peers, both positive and negative, which indicates the degree to which a child gets noticed within her group.

social information-processing: Dodge's model of antisocial youth's idiosyncratic ways of processing social information, such as use of a hostile attributional bias to interpret neutral social cues.

social learning theories: Theories that focus specifically on how children acquire personality characteristics and social skills.

social preference: A sociometric measure that is computed by adding the total number of positive nominations a child receives from his peers, which indicates the degree to which a child is positively viewed by his social group.

social referencing: A baby's adjustment of its reactions to objects or events based on feedback provided by a caregiver. For example, a baby may look at a caregiver's facial expression before approaching a new toy.

social role theory: The view that the social roles an individual fills, such as parent, spouse, manager, and so on, are important influences on her behavior, and that different individuals will typically behave in similar ways when filling the same role.

socialize: To limit some behaviors of the child while demanding others, so that the child will be safe and she will learn the standards of her culture and behave in ways that are conventionally acceptable.

social skills: Discrete, observable behaviors such as making eye contact, using appropriate language, asking appropriate questions, and so forth, which promote effective social interaction and which are part of the broader construct of social competence.

sociocultural theories: Theories proposing that there are differences in how people develop in different cultures and sub-cultures. Many of these theories trace their roots to Lev Vygotsky.

socioeconomic status (SES) group: A group of people having the same social standing or power, and defined by characteristics of the adults in a household, including educational background, income, and occupational type.

sociometry: The classic way of assessing social competence and determining the kinds of categories that describe children's status within peer groups. Usually involves asking members of a social group (e.g., children in a classroom) to indicate which members of the group they prefer to spend time with (sit with, play with, etc.) and which they do not.

somatic cell therapy: An experimental approach to correcting defective genes that involves insertion of healthy genes into appropriate tissue.

specification: In Super's theory, the identification of specific vocational preferences during the middle of the exploratory stage.

sperm: Reproductive cell produced by males, which contains only 23 chromosomes.

spermarche: A boy's first ejaculation.

stability: The fourth stage of retirement, when the retiree settles into a lifestyle that is satisfactory to her.

stabilization: In Super's theory, an individual's settling on a vocational self-concept and job that completes the establishment stage.

stage: A period of time, perhaps several years, during which a person's activities (at least in one broad domain) have certain characteristics in common.

stages of retirement: For many people, adjustment to retirement follows a typical stagelike progression, from "honeymoon" to "disenchantment" to "reorientation" to "stability" to "termination."

stereotype induction: An interview strategy that involves slanting the interviewee's view of an individual, such as implying that an alleged perpetrator is a bad person to encourage children to reveal information.

stereotype threat: The fear that a stereotype might be true of oneself or that one will be judged by that stereotype.

still-face paradigm: A research technique for assessing infant coping strategies. The infant is seated facing the mother who is instructed to interact in normally pleasant and playful ways at first and then is asked to change her behavior and to be completely unresponsive or withdrawn.

storage: The acquisition knowledge or learning; maintaining information in memory.

stranger anxiety: The tendency of an infant or young child to be wary of strangers and to seek the comfort and protection of the primary caregiver when a stranger is present. May begin early in infancy but is likely to intensify at about 8 months when separation anxiety begins.

strange situation test: A measurement technique designed by Ainsworth to assess the quality of an infant's attachment to a caregiver. Infants (12 months or older) and their caregivers are brought to a room (the strange situation) where the child experiences a series of eight 3-minute episodes, each one introducing changes in the social situation, some of which are likely to be stressful, such as an episode when the mother leaves the baby with a stranger. The infant's willingness to explore the toys and his reactions to his mother and the strangers are observed.

strict dualism: Position 1 in Perry's model that implies a rigid adherence to authoritarian views and a childlike division between in-group and out-group. Individuals in this stage never think to question their belief that authority embodies rightness.

subjective well-being: An individual's experience of overall life satisfaction, including satisfaction with particular domains of life, frequency of positive mood, and relative infrequency of negative mood.

substantia nigra: One structure in the midbrain. It is involved in vision, hearing, and consciousness.

sudden infant death syndrome (SIDS): The acronym for Sudden Infant Death Syndrome, also known as crib death. Sudden death during infancy, usually while sleeping, with no known cause.

superego: In Freud's personality theory, the last of three aspects of personality, that serves as an "internalized parent" that causes one to feel guilty if his behavior deviates from parental and societal restrictions.

superior colliculi: Structures that are part of the midbrain and play a role in vision, hearing, and consciousness.

symbolic artifacts: Analogical symbols, such as pictures or maps or scale models that are both concrete objects themselves and symbols for other things. To understand a symbolic artifact, a child must mentally represent the same thing in two ways at once.

symbols: Representational indicators or stand-ins for other things, such as words serving as symbols for concepts or drawings serving as symbols of objects.

sympathy: An emotion related to empathy that involves "feeling for" another; that is, having concern for the other person, but not necessarily sharing the feelings of the other.

synapses: Connections among neurons, usually between the dendrite of one neuron and the axon of another neuron, or between the dendrites of one neuron and the cell body of a second neuron. At the synapse there is a gap between neurons which can be bridged by chemicals called neurotransmitters.

synaptic gap: The space between neurons where they "connect." In transmission of an electrical impulse from one neuron to the next, the gap is bridged by the release of chemicals called neurotransmitters from the first neuron, which then stimulate or inhibit an electrical impulse in the second neuron.

synaptic overproduction: The generation of more synapses than are needed in the process of brain growth. Those synapses that are not used are later eliminated or "pruned."

synaptogenesis: The generation of synapses or connections between neurons, usually as a result of the growth of axons and dendrites.

syntactic system or grammar: The aspect of language that specifies how to link words into meaningful sentences. A system of rules for generating and decoding sentences.

systems models: Another term for multidimensional models.

tangles: Twisted filaments of protein, which may interfere with communication between neurons and even cause cell death; they are associated with Alzheimer's disease.

temperament: Describes the usual emotional and behavioral characteristics of a given individual. For infants, includes activity level, degree of fearfulness and irritability, attention persistence, typical mood, and so on.

temporal lobe: The part of the cerebrum that is situated on the sides of each hemisphere and is responsible for auditory processing. The left temporal lobe is especially important in language processing.

temporizing: Perry's description of the what individuals are doing when they delay movement to the next stage of thought development.

teratogens: Substances or agents that can cross the placental barrier and produce fetal deformities when taken or absorbed by the mother during pregnancy.

terminal drop (terminal decline): A substantial decline in intellectual functioning that adults may show as they approach the end of their lives, between 6 months and 5 years prior to death.

termination: The fifth and final stage of retirement, which is the end-of-life transition when the individual's health declines and he becomes dependent on others for care.

tertiary prevention: An attempt to rehabilitate persons with established disorders; similar to treatment.

testes: Male gonads that primarily produce androgens (such as testosterone), but also produce lesser amounts of estrogen and progesterone. Site of sperm production in males.

testosterone: The primary masculinizing hormone or androgen produced by the testes in males and to a lesser extent by the ovaries in females.

thalamus: A part of the forebrain that relays information from sensory organs and other brain structures to appropriate sites on the cerebral cortex.

theory of mind: Degree of knowledge of the existence of mental (psychological) processes in self and other people. Includes understanding that people have thoughts, beliefs, intentions, desires, feelings, and so on, that these mental experiences may or may not reflect reality accurately, and that they may be different in other people than they are in the self. Makes possible the capacity to take the perspective of another person.

time-out: A disciplinary technique in which for a short span of time a child is required to discontinue his involvement in ongoing activities to quietly sit somewhere apart. This technique involves mild power assertion and is suitable for use with toddlers and preschoolers.

tomboyism: A trait girls exhibit when they prefer to play with boys and prefer boys' toys and activities.

tools or signs: In Vygotsky's theory anything that people use to help them think and learn such as numbering or writing systems.

transactional models: Another term for multidimensional models.

transcription: The complex chain of cellular processes that involves translating the code specified by a gene into the production of a protein. This series of biochemical events ultimately accounts for genetic expression or influence.

trinucleotide repeats: Repeated sequences of three bases that are part of the code in many normal gene alleles, such as several sequences of CGG (cytonine-guanine-guanine) in a row. The number of trinucleotide repeats sometimes spontaneously increases, constituting one type of gene mutation. Too large a number can cause a gene to function improperly or not at all.

trust versus mistrust: The crisis faced in the first of Erikson's "Eight Stages of Man," in which the responsiveness of an infant's caregiver will determine whether the baby establishes basic trust and a sense of being valuable.

uncharacteristic behavior: A condition that mitigates a criminal defendant's guilt because the crime is not typical of her, such as when it is a first offense or is not consistent with the individual's values.

unipolar disorder: A term used to indicate a clinical course marked by episodes of depression but not of mania.

universal prevention: A category of prevention efforts that are directed to the general population.

unresolved (insecure): An attachment style characterizing adults whose AAI transcripts show marked lapses in logical thinking, particularly during discussions of loss or other traumatic memories. These individuals may receive a secondary classification of dismissive or preoccupied, and often have children who show more disorganized attachment patterns than other children.

utilization deficiency: A situation in which using a memory strategy does not seem to boost memory.

verification: The third step in the scientific method, when the researcher judges a theory objectively by testing predictions about events and theories to see if they come true.

vividness effect: Occurs during decision making when some salient or vivid facts attract our attention regardless of their actual value as evidence.

vocabulary spurt: Describes the rapid growth of productive vocabulary from 50 to about 500 words in just a few months. Tends to occur between 18 and 24 months in most children.

vocational self-concept: Part of one's total identity that includes ideas about which qualities of the self would or would not provide a match to the requirements of an occupation. Includes person's view of his own characteristics and of his life circumstances, such as the limits or opportunities created by economic conditions and so on.

voicing: In phonology, vibration of the vocal cords in the production of a sound. Some consonant sounds in English are voiced (e.g., the *d* and *v* sounds) and some, which are identical to the voiced consonants in other ways, are not voiced (e.g., *t* and *f*).

warmth dimension (parental responsiveness): One of two major features of parenting style. The degree to which parents create a positive emotional climate for their children by listening to them, being involved and interested in their activities, accepting them, making positive attributions about their behavior, and being sensitive and supportive.

wisdom: Expertise in the fundamental pragmatics of life. Superior knowledge and judgment in solving problems or addressing issues that arise in the course of living and that affect the meaning and quality of life.

working memory: The part of the cognitive machinery that holds information one is actively thinking about at the moment. Also referred to as short-term memory.

working model: In Bowlby's attachment theory, an individual's mental representation of self, other, and relationships, which serves as a prototype of social functioning and affects the individual's expectations and behaviors in future relationships. A cognitive schema that begins in infancy and is refined and elaborated over time; a state-of-mind about attachment related issues.

X chromosomes: The female sex chromosomes, a matched pair of elongated chromosomes that determine that one will be a female.

X-linked recessive disorders: A class of genetic disorders that are carried on the X chromosome and are recessive, meaning that they are more likely to affect males, who do not have a matching X chromosome that might have the corresponding (and dominant) normal gene. Examples include hemophilia, baldness, color blindness, night blindness, and Duchenne's muscular dystrophy.

Y chromosome: The male sex chromosome, which pairs with an X chromosome and determines that one will be a male.

young adulthood: The time period from about 18 to 30 years that is often an extended period of transition involving exploration of potential adult identities.

youth: A period of time after completing puberty that serves as a transition into adulthood.

zone of proximal development: In Vygotsky's theory, the range of concepts and skills that a learner is to understand or perform only with support or scaffolding from someone else.

zygote: An ovum that has been fertilized by a sperm and thus contains a full complement of 46 chromosomes, half from the mother and half from the father.

Aboud, F. (1977). Interest in ethnic information: A cross-cultural developmental study. *Canadian Journal of Behavioral Science, 9*, 134–146.

Achenbach, T., & Edelbrock, C. S. (1983). *Manual for the Child Behavior Checklist and Revised Child Behavior Profile.* Burlington: University of Vermont, Department of Psychiatry.

Achenbach, T., & Howell, C. (1993). Are American children's problems getting worse? A 13-year comparison. *Journal of the American Academy of Child and Adolescent Psychiatry, 32*, 1145–1154.

Ackerman, S., Zuroff, D. C., & Moskowitz, D. S. (2000). Generativity in midlife and young adults: Links to agency, communion, and subjective well-being. *International Journal of Aging and Human Development, 50*, 17–41.

Ackil, J. K., & Zaragoza, M. S. (1995). Developmental differences in eyewitness suggestibility and memory for source. *Journal of Experimental Child Psychology, 60*, 57–83.

Acolet, D., Modi, N., Giannakoulopoulos, X., Bond, C., Clow, A., & Glover, V. (1993). Changes in plasma cortisol and catecholamine concentrations in response to massage in preterm infants. *Archives of Disease in Childhood, 70* (1, Spec.No.), F80.

Acosta, F. X., Cristo, M. H. (1981). Development of a bilingual interpreter program: An alternative model for Spanish-speaking services. *Professional Psychology: Research & Practice, 12*, 474–482.

Adams, G. R. (1983). Social competence during adolescence: Social sensitivity, locus of control, empathy, and peer popularity. *Journal of Youth and Adolescence, 12*, 203–211.

Ainsworth, M. D. S. (1967). *Infancy in Uganda: Infant care and the growth of love.* Baltimore: The Johns Hopkins University Press.

Ainsworth, M. D. S. (1989). Attachments beyond infancy. *American Psychologist, 44*, 709–716.

Ainsworth, M. D. S., Bell, S. M., & Stayton, D. J. (1972). Individual differences in the development of some attachment behaviors. *Merrill-Palmer Quarterly, 18*, 123–143.

Ainsworth, M. D. S., Blehar, M. C., Waters, E., & Wall, S. (1978). *Patterns of attachment.* Hillsdale, NJ: Erlbaum.

Alban-Metcalfe, B., & West, M. A. (1991). Women managers. In J. Firth-Cozens & M. A. West (Eds.), *Women at work: Psychological and organizational perspectives* (pp. 154–171). Milton Keynes, England: Open University Press.

Aldwin, C. M. & Levenson, M. R. (2004). Posttraumatic growth: A developmental perspective. *Psychological Inquiry, 15*, 19–22.

Alexander, F., & French, T. M. (1946). *Psychoanalytic therapy.* New York: Rolande.

Allgood-Merten, B., Lewinsohn, P. M., & Hops, R. (1990). Sex differences and adolescent depression. *Journal of Abnormal Psychology, 99*, 55–63.

Almeida, D. M., & Horn, M. C. (2004). Is daily life more stressful during middle adulthood? In O. G. Brim, C. D. Ryff, & R. C. Kessler (Eds.), *How healthy are we? A national study of well-being at midlife* (pp. 425–451). Chicago: University of Chicago Press.

Als, H. (1986). A syntactive model of neonatal behavioral organization: Framework for the assessment of neurobehavioral development in the premature infant and for support of infants and parents in the neonatal intensive care environment. *Physical and Occupational Therapy in Pediatrics, 6*, 3–53.

Als, H., & Gillkerson, I. (1997). The neurobehavioral development of the preterm infant. In A. Fanaroff & R. Martin (Eds.), *Neonatal-perinatal medicine* (6th ed., pp. 964–987). St. Louis: Mosby.

Amato, P. R. (1993). Children's adjustment to divorce: Theories, hypotheses, and empirical support. *Journal of Marriage and the Family, 55*, 23–38.

American Academy of Pediatrics. (1997). Breastfeeding and the use of human milk. *Pediatrics, 100*, 1035–1039.

American Academy of Pediatrics, American Public Health Association, and National Resource Center for Health and Safety in Child Care. (2002). *Caring for our children: National health and safety performance standards: Guidelines for out-of-home child care* (2nd ed.). Elf Grove Village, IL: American Academy of Pediatrics.

American Council on Education. (1999). *The American freshman: National norms for Fall 1999.* Los Angeles: Higher Education Research Institute, UCLA.

American Psychiatric Association. (2000). *Diagnostic and statistical manual of mental disorders* (4th ed.) Washington, DC: Author.

American Psychological Association's Board of Educational Affairs. (1995). *Learner-centered psychological principles: A framework for school redesign and reform.* Washington, DC: American Psychological Association.

American Speech-Language-Hearing Association. (1997–2004). *How does your child hear and talk?* Rockville, MD: Author. Retrieved October 30, 2004, from http://www.asha.org/public/speech/development/child_hear_talk.html

Anand, B. K., & Brobeck, J. R. (1951). Hypothalamic control of food intake in rats and cats. *Yale Journal of Biology and Medicine, 24*, 123–140.

Anderson, E. (1994, May). The code of the streets. *Atlantic Monthly, 273*(5), 81–94.

Anderson, J. R. (1980). *Cognitive psychology and its implications.* San Francisco: Freeman.

Anderson, J. R. (1993). Problem solving and learning. *American Psychologist, 48*, 35–44.

Anderson, P., Beach, S. R. H., & Kaslow, N. J. (1999). Marital discord and depression: The potential of attachment theory to guide integrative clinical intervention. In T. Joiner & J. C. Coyne (Eds.), *The interactional nature of depression* (pp. 271–297). Washington, DC: American Psychological Association.

Anderson, R. N., & Smith, B. L. (2003). Deaths: Leading causes for 2001. *CDC National Vital Statistics Report, 54*(9).

Andreasen, N. C., Arndt, S., Swayze, V., Cizadlo, T., Flaum, M., O'Leary, et al. (1994). Thalamic abnormalities in schizophrenia visualized through magnetic resonance image averaging. *Science, 266*, 294–298.

Angoff, W. H. (1988). The nature-nurture debate, aptitudes, and group differences. *American Psychologist, 43*, 713–720.

Annie E. Casey Foundation. (1998). *When teens have sex. Issues and trends: A Kids Count Special Report.* Baltimore: Author.

Antell, S. E., & Keating, D. P. (1983). Perception of numerical invariance in neonates. *Child Development, 54*, 695–701.

Antonucci, T. C., Lansford, J. E., & Akiyama, H. (2001). Impact of positive and negative aspects of marital relationships and friendships on well-being of older adults. *Applied Developmental Science, 5*, 68–75.

Archer, J. (1994). Testosterone and aggression: A theoretical review. *Journal of Offender Rehabilitation, 21*, 2–39.

Archer, J. (1999). *The nature of grief: The evolution and psychology of reactions to loss.* London: Routledge.

Archer, S. L. (1992). A feminist's approach to identity research. In G. R. Adams, R. Montmayor, & T. P. Gullotta (Eds.), *Advances in adolescent development: Vol. 4. Adolescent identity formation* (pp. 25–49). Newbury Park, CA: Sage.

Archer, S. L., & Waterman, A. S. (1988). Psychological individualism: Gender differences or gender neutrality? *Human Development, 31*, 65–81.

Arlin, P. K. (1984). Adolescent and adult thought: A structural interpretation. In M. L. Commons, F. A. Richards, & C. Armon (Eds.), *Beyond formal operations* (pp. 258–271). New York: Praeger.

Arnett, J. J. (1992). Reckless behavior in adolescence: A developmental perspective. *Developmental Review, 12*, 339–373.

Arnett, J. J. (1997). Young people's conceptions of the transition to adulthood. *Youth and Society, 29*, 1–23.

Arnett, J. J. (1999). Adolescent storm and stress, reconsidered. *American Psychologist, 54*, 317–326.

Arnett, J. J. (2000). Emerging adulthood: A theory of development from the late teens through the twenties. *American Psychologist, 55*, 469–480.

Arnett, J. J. (2002). The psychology of globalization. *American Psychologist, 57*, 774–783.

Arnett, J. J., & Taber, S. (1994). Adolescence terminable and interminable: When does adolescence end? *Journal of Youth and Adolescence, 23*, 517–523.

Arnold, A. P., & Gorski, R. A. (1984). Gonadal steroid induction of structural sex differences in the central nervous system. *Annual Review of Neuroscience, 7*, 413–442.

Arnold, L. E., Chuang, S., Davies, M., Abikoff, H.B., Conners, C. K., Elliott, G. R., et al. (2004). Nine months of multicomponent behavioral treatment for ADHD and effectiveness of MTS fading procedures. *Journal of Abnormal Child Psychology, 32*, 39–51.

Aronson, J., & Fried, C. (1998). *Reducing stereotype threat and boosting academic achievement of African Americans: The role of conceptions of intelligence.* Unpublished manuscript.

Aronson, P. J., Mortimer, J. T., Zierman, C., & Hacker, M. (1996). Generational differences in early work experiences and evaluations. In J. T. Mortimer & M. D. Finch (Eds.), *Adolescents, work, and family: An intergenerational developmental analysis* (pp. 25–62). Newbury Park, CA: Sage.

Asher, S. R., & Dodge, K. A. (1986). Identifying children who are rejected by their peers. *Developmental Psychology, 22*, 444–449.

Asher, S. R., Markell, R. A., & Hymel, S. (1981). Identifying children at risk in peer relations: A critique of the rate-of-interaction approach to assessment. *Child Development, 52*, 1239–1245.

Astin, A. W. (1993). *What matters in college?: Four critical years revisited.* San Francisco: Jossey-Bass.

Astin, A. W., Korn, W. S., Sax, L. J., & Mahoney, K. M. (1994). *The American freshman: National norms for Fall 1994.* Los Angeles: Higher Education Research Institute, UCLA.

Atchley, R. C. (1976). *The sociology of retirement.* New York: Wiley.

Atwater, E. (1996). *Adolescence.* Upper Saddle River, NJ: Prentice Hall.

Avis, N. E., Stellato, R., Crawford, S., Johannes, C., & Longcope, C. (2000). Is there an association between menopause status and sexual functioning? *Menopause, 7*, 297–309.

Axline, V. (1947). *Play therapy: The inner dynamics of childhood.* New York: Houghton Mifflin.

Azar, B. (1999, February). Consortium of editors pushes for shift in child research methods. *APA Monitor, 30*, 20–21.

Azmitia, M. (1996). Peer interactive minds. In P. B. Baltes & U. M. Staudinger (Eds.), *Interactive minds.* Cambridge, England: Cambridge University Press.

Azmitia, M., & Hesser, J. (1993). Why siblings are important agents of cognitive development: A comparison of siblings and peers. *Child Development, 64*, 430–444.

Bachman, J. (1997). *Smoking, drinking, and drug use in young adulthood: The impact of new freedoms and responsibilities.* Mahwah, NJ: Erlbaum.

Backman, L., Small, B. J., Wahlin, A., & Larsson, M. (2000). Cognitive functioning in very old age. In F. I. M. Craik & T. A. Salthouse (Eds.), *The handbook of aging and cognition* (pp. 499–558). Hillsdale, NJ: Erlbaum.

Baer, W. M., & Hanson, L. C. (2000). Families' perceptions of the added value of hospice in the nursing home. *Journal of the American Geriatric Society, 48*, 879–882.

Bahrick, L. E., & Pickens, J. N. (1995). Infant memory for object motion across a period of three months: Implications for a four-phase attention function. *Journal of Experimental Child Psychology, 59*, 343–371.

Bailey, J. M., Bobrow, D., Wolfe, M., & Mikach, S. (1995). Sexual orientation of adult sons of gay fathers. *Developmental Psychology, 31*, 124–129.

Bailey, J. M., & Pillard, R. C. (1991). A genetic study of male sexual orientation. *Archives of General Psychiatry, 48*, 1089–1096.

Bailey, J. M., Pillard, R. C., Neale, M. C., & Agyei, Y. (1993). Heritable factors influence sexual orientation in women. *Archives of General Psychiatry, 50*, 217–223.

Bailey, T., & Morest, V. S. (1998). Preparing youth for employment. In S. Halperin (Ed.), *The forgotten half revisited: American youth and young families, 1988–2008* (pp. 115–136). Washington, DC: American Youth Policy Forum.

Baillargeon, R. (1987). Object permanence in 3½- and 4½-month-old infants. *Developmental Psychology, 23*, 655–664.

Bakermans-Kranenburg, M. J., van IJzendoorn, M. H., & Juffer, F. (2003). Less is more: Meta-analyses of sensitivity and attachment interventions in early childhood. *Psychological Bulletin, 129*, 195–215.

Baker-Ward, L., Ornstein, P. A., & Holden, D. J. (1984). The expression of memorization in early childhood. *Journal of Experimental Child Psychology, 37*, 555–575.

Baldwin, A. L. (1948). Socialization and the parent–child relationship. *Child Development, 19*, 127–136.

Ballie, R. (2001). Teen drinking more dangerous than previously thought. *Monitor on Psychology, 32*, 12.

Baltes, M. M., & Baltes, P. B. (1990). *The psychology of control and aging.* Hillsdale, NJ: Erlbaum.

Baltes, P. B. (1987). Theoretical propositions of life-span developmental psychology: On the dynamics between growth and decline. *Developmental Psychology, 23*, 611–626.

Baltes, P. B. (1997). On the incomplete architecture of human ontogeny: Selection, optimization, and compensation as foundation of developmental theory. *American Psychologist, 52*, 366–380.

Baltes, P. B., Lindenberger, U., & Staudinger, U. M. (1998). Life-span theory in developmental psychology. In W. Damon (Series Ed.) & R. M. Lerner (Vol. Ed.), *Handbook of child psychology: Vol. 1. Theoretical models of human development* (5th ed., pp. 1029–1143). New York: Wiley.

Baltes, P. B., & Staudinger, U. M. (2000). Wisdom: A metaheuristic (pragmatic) to orchestrate mind and virtue toward excellence. *American Psychologist, 55*, 122–136.

Bamshad, M. J., & Olson, S. E. (2003). Does race exist? *Scientific American, 289*, 78–85.

Bandura, A. (1974). Behavior theory and the models of man. *American Psychologist, 29*, 859–869.

Bandura, A. (1977). *Social learning theory.* Upper Saddle River, NJ: Prentice Hall.

Bandura, A. (1986). *Social foundations of thought and action: A social cognitive theory.* Upper Saddle River, NJ: Prentice Hall.

Bandura, A. (1989). Human agency in social cognitive theory. *American Psychologist, 44*, 1175–1184.

Bandura, A. (1990). Conclusion: Reflections on nonability determinants of competence. In R. J. Sternberg & J. Kolligian, Jr. (Eds.), *Competence considered* (pp. 316–352). New Haven, CT: Yale University Press.

Bandura, A. (1997). *Self-efficacy: The exercise of control.* New York: Freeman.

Bandura, A. (1999). Social cognitive theory of personality. In L. Pervin & O. John (Eds.), *Handbook of personality* (2nd ed., pp. 154–196). New York: Guilford Press.

Banks, W. C. (1976). White preference in blacks: A paradigm in search of a phenomenon. *Psychological Bulletin, 83*, 1179–1186.

Banyai, I. (1995). *Zoom.* New York: Viking Press.

Barber, B. L., Eccles, J. S., & Stone, M. R. (2001). Whatever happened to the jock, the brain, and the princess? Young adult pathways linked to adolescent activity involvement and social identity. *Journal of Adolescent Research, 16*, 429–455.

Barber, B. R. (1992). *An aristocracy of everyone: The politics of education and the future of America.* New York: Oxford University Press.

Barich, R. R., & Bielby, D. D. (1996). Rethinking marriage: Change and stability in expectations. *Journal of Family Issues, 17*, 505–525.

Barker, E. T., & Galambos, N. L. (2003). Body dissatisfaction of adolescent girls and boys: Risk and resource factors. *Journal of Early Adolescence, 23*, 141–165.

Barker, R. G., & Gump, P. V. (1964). *Big school, small school: High school size and student behavior.* Stanford, CA: Stanford University Press.

Barkley, R. A. (1997). Behavioral inhibition, sustained attention, and executive function: Constructing a unified theory of ADHD. *Psychological Bulletin, 121*, 65–94.

Barnes, G. M., Welte, J. W., & Dintcheff, B. (1992). Alcohol misuse among college students and other young adults: Findings from a general population study in New York State. *International Journal of the Addictions, 27*, 917–934.

Barnett, R. C., & Hyde, J. S. (2001). Women, men, work, and family. *American Psychologist, 56*, 781–796.

Barr, D. (1997). Friendship and belonging. In R. L. Selman, C. L. Watts, & L. H. Schultz (Eds.), *Fostering friendship: Pair therapy for treatment and prevention* (pp. 19–30). New York: Aldine de Gruyer.

Barrett, E. E., Radke-Yarrow, M., & Klein, R. E. (1983). Chronic malnutrition and child behavior: Effects of early caloric supplementation on social and emotional functioning at school age. In S. Chess & A. Thomas (Eds.), *Annual progress in child psychology and child development* (pp. 489–492). New York: Brunner/Mazel.

Bartholomew, K., & Horowitz, L. (1991). Attachment styles among young adults: A test of the four category model. *Journal of Personality and Social Psychology, 61*, 226–244.

Bartholomew, K., & Shaver, P. R. (1998). Methods of assessing adult attachment: Do they converge? In J. A. Simpson & W. S. Rholes (Eds.), *Attachment theory and close relationships* (pp. 25–45). New York: Guilford Press.

Basseches, M. (1984). *Dialectical thinking and adult development.* Norwood, NJ: Ablex.

Bates, J. E., Maslin, C. A., & Frankel, K. A. (1995). Attachment security, mother-child interaction, and temperament as predictors of behavior-problem ratings at age three years. *Monographs of the Society for Research in Child Development, 50*, 167–193.

Bauer, P. J., & Mandler, J. M. (1989). One thing follows another: Effects of temporal structure on 1- to 2-year-olds' recall of events. *Developmental Psychology, 25*, 197–206.

Bauer, P. J., & Mandler, J. M. (1990). Remembering what happened next: Very young children's recall of event sequences. In R. Fivush & J. A. Hudson (Eds.), *Knowing and remembering in young children.* Cambridge, England: Cambridge University Press.

Baumeister, R. F. (1991). *Meanings of life.* New York: Guilford Press.

Baumeister, R. F., & Boden, J. M. (1994). Shrinking the self. In T. M. Brinthaupt & R. P. Lipka (Eds.), *Changing the self: Philosophies, techniques, and experiences.* Albany: State University of New York Press.

Baumrind, D. (1971). Current patterns of parental authority. *Development Psychology Monographs, 4*(1, Pt. 2), 1–103.

Baumrind, D. (1972). An exploratory study of socialization effects on Black children: Some Black/White comparisons. *Child Development, 43*, 261–267.

Baumrind, D. (1978). Parental disciplinary patterns and social competence in children. *Youth and Society, 9*, 239–276.

Baumrind, D. (1989). Rearing competent children. In W. Damon (Ed.), *Child development today and tomorrow* (pp. 349–378). San Francisco: Jossey-Bass.

Baumrind, D. (1991). Parenting styles and adolescent development. In J. Brooks, R. Lerner, & A. C. Petersen (Eds.), *The encyclopedia of adolescence* (pp. 758–772). New York: Garland.

Baumrind, D. (1993). The average expectable environment is not good enough: A response to Scarr. *Child Development, 64*, 1299–1317.

Baumrind, D. (1995). Commentary on sexual orientation: Research and social policy implications. *Developmental Psychology, 31*, 130–136.

Baumrind, D. (1997). Necessary distinctions. *Psychological Inquiry, 8*, 176–229.

Baumrind, D. (2001). *Does causally relevant research support a blanket injunction against the use of spanking?* Paper presented at the annual meeting of the American Psychological Association, San Francisco.

Baxter-Magolda, M., & Porterfield, W. D. (1985). A new approach to assessing intellectual development on the Perry Scheme. *Journal of College Student Personnel, 21*, 46–58.

Beall, A. E., & Sternberg, R. J. (1995). The social construction of love. *Journal of Social and Personal Relationships, 12*, 417–438.

Bear, G. G., & Rys, G. S. (1994). Moral reasoning, classroom behavior, and sociometric status among elementary school children. *Developmental Psychology, 30*, 633–638.

Beck, A. T. (1963). *Depression: Causes and treatment.* Philadelphia: University of Pennsylvania Press.

Beckwith, L., Cohen, S. E., & Hamilton, C. E. (1999). Maternal sensitivity during infancy and subsequent life events relate to attachment representations at early adulthood. *Developmental Psychology, 35*, 693–700.

Bednar, R. L., & Petersen, S. R. (1995). *Self-esteem: Paradoxes and innovations in clinical theory and practice* (2nd ed.). Washington, DC: American Psychological Association.

Beeghly, M., & Cicchetti, D. (1994). Child maltreatment, attachment, and the self-system: Emergence of an internal state lexicon in toddlers at high social risk. *Development and Psychopathology, 6*, 5–30.

Beelman, A., Pfingsten, U., & Losel, F. (1994). Effects of training social competence in children: A meta-analysis of recent evaluation studies. *Journal of Clinical Child Psychology, 23*, 260–271.

Beilin, H. (1999). Understanding the photographic image. *Journal of Applied Developmental Psychology, 20,* 1–30.

Bell, A., Weinberg, M., & Hammersmith, S. (1981). *Sexual preference: Its development in men and women.* Bloomington: Indiana University Press.

Bell, R. Q., & Chapman, M. (1986). Child effects in studies using experimental or brief longitudinal approaches to socialization. *Developmental Psychology, 22,* 595–603.

Bell, R. Q., & Harper, L. V. (Eds.). (1977). *Child effects on adults.* Hillsdale, NJ: Erlbaum.

Bell, T. W. (1971). Stimulus control of parent or caretaker behavior by offspring. *Developmental Psychology, 4,* 63–72.

Bellah, R. N., Madsen, R., Sullivan, W. M., Swidler, A., & Tipton, S. M. (1985). *Habits of the heart: Individualism and commitment in American life.* New York: Harper & Row.

Belloc, N. B., & Breslow, L. (1972). Relationships of physical health status and health practices. *Preventive Medicine, 1,* 409–421.

Belsky, J. (2001). Emanuel Miller lecture: Developmental risks (still) associated with early child care. *Journal of Clinical Psychology and Psychiatry, 42,* 845–859.

Belsky, J., Garduque, L., & Hrncir, E. (1984). Assessing performance, competence, and executive capacity in infant play: Relations to home environment and security of attachment. *Developmental Psychology, 20,* 406–417.

Belsky, J., Gilstrap, B., & Rovine, M. (1984). The Pennsylvania infant and family development project: I. Stability and change in mother-infant and father-infant interaction in a family setting at one, three, and nine months. *Child Development, 55,* 692–705.

Belsky, J., & Hsieh, K. H. (1998). Patterns of marital change during the early years: Parent personality, coparenting, and division-of-labor correlates. *Journal of Family Psychology, 12,* 511–528.

Belsky, J., & Kelly, J. (1994). *The transition to parenthood: How a first child changes a marriage. Why some couples grow closer and some grow apart.* New York: Dell.

Belsky, J., & Rovine, M. (1988). Nonmaternal care in the first year of life and the security of infant-parent attachment. *Child Development, 59,* 157–167.

Belsky, J., & Rovine, M. (1990). Patterns of marital change across the transition to parenthood: Pregnancy to three years postpartum. *Journal of Marriage and the Family, 52,* 5–19.

Belsky, J., Spanier, G., & Rovine, M. (1983). Stability and change in a marriage across the transition to parenthood. *Journal of Marriage and the Family, 45,* 567–577.

Belsky, J., Spritz, B., & Crnic, K. (1996). Infant attachment security and affective-cognitive information processing at age 3. *Psychological Science, 7,* 111–114.

Belsky, J., & Volling, B. L. (1987). Mothering, fathering, and marital interaction in the family triad during infancy: Exploring family systems' processes. In P. W. Berman & F. A. Pedersen (Eds.), *Men's transitions to parenthood: Longitudinal studies of early family experience* (pp. 37–63). Hillsdale, NJ: Erlbaum.

Bem, D. J. (1996). Exotic becomes erotic: A developmental theory of sexual orientation. *Psychological Review, 103,* 320–335.

Bem, S. L. (1981). Gender schema theory: A cognitive account of sex typing. *Psychological Review, 88,* 354–364.

Bem, S. L. (1989). Genital knowledge and gender constancy in preschool children. *Child Development, 60,* 649–662.

Bendersky, M., & Lewis, M. (1998). Arousal modulation in cocaine-exposed infants. *Developmental Psychology, 43,* 555–564.

Benes, F. M. (1994). Developmental changes in stress adaptation in relation to psychopathology. *Development and Psychopathology, 6,* 723–739.

Bennett, R. L., Hampel, H. L., Mandell, J. B., & Marks, J. H. (2003). Genetic counselors: Translating genomic science into clinical practice. *Journal of Clinical Investigation, 112*(9), 1274–1279.

Bennett, R. L., Pettersen, B. J., Niendorf, K. B., & Anderson, R. R. (2003). Developing standard recommendations (guidelines) for genetic counseling practice: A process of the National Society of Genetic Counselors. *Journal of Genetic Counseling, 12*(4), 287–295.

Bennett, R. L., Steinhaus, K. A., Uhrich, S. B., O'Sullivan, C. K., Resta, R. G., Doyle, D. L., et al. (1995). Recommendation for standardized human pedigree nomenclature. *American Journal of Human Genetics, 56,* 745–752.

Benninga, J. S., & Wynne, E. A. (1998, February). Keeping in character. A time-tested solution. *Phi Delta Kappan, 79,* 439–445, 448.

Benson, P. (1997). *All kids are our kids.* San Francisco: Jossey-Bass.

Berenbaum, S. A., & Bailey, J. M. (2003). Effects of gender identity of prenatal androgens and genital appearance: Evidence from girls with congenital adrenal hyperplasia. *Journal of Clinical Endocrinology and Metabolism, 88,* 1102–1106.

Berenbaum, S. A., & Hines, M. (1992). Early androgens are related to childhood sex-typed toy preferences. *Psychological Science, 3,* 203–206.

Berenbaum, S. A., & Snyder, E. (1995). Early hormonal influences on childhood sex-typed activity and playmate preferences: Implications for the development of sexual orientation. *Developmental Psychology, 31,* 31–42.

Berg, S. (1987). Intelligence and terminal decline. In G. L. Maddox & E. W. Busse (Eds.), *Aging: The universal experience* (pp. 414–415). New York: Springer.

Berg, S. (1996). Aging, behavior, and terminal decline. In J. E. Birren, K. W. Schaie (Series Eds.), R. P. Abeles, M. Gatz, & T. A. Salthouse (Vol. Eds.), *Handbook of the psychology of aging* (4th ed., pp. 323–337). San Diego, CA: Academic Press.

Berk, L. E., & Spuhl, S. (1995). Maternal interaction, private speech, and task performance in preschool children. *Early Childhood Research Quarterly, 10,* 145–169.

Berkowitz, M., & Gibbs, J. C. (1983). Measuring the developmental features of moral discussion. *Merrill-Palmer Quarterly, 29,* 399–410.

Bernal, M. E., & Knight, G. P. (1993). *Ethnic identity: Formation and transmission among Hispanics and other minorities.* Albany: State University of New York Press.

Berndt, Thomas J. (1982). The features and effects of friendship in early adolescence. *Child Development, 53,* 1447–1460.

Berndt, T. J., & Heller, K. A. (1986). Gender stereotypes and social inferences: A developmental study. *Journal of Personality and Social Psychology, 50,* 889–898.

Berndt, T. J., & Keefe, K. (1996). Friends' influence on social adjustment. In J. Juvonen & K. R. Wentzel (Eds.), *Social motivation: Understanding children's school adjustment.* New York: Cambridge University Press.

Berndt, T. J., Miller, K. A., & Park, K. (1989). Adolescents' perceptions of friends' and parents' influence on aspects of school adjustment. *Journal of Early Adolescence, 9,* 419–435.

Berndt, T. J., & Murphy, L. M. (2002). Influences of friends and friendships: Myths, truths, and research recommendations. *Advances in Child Development and Behavior, 30,* 275–310.

Berninger, V. W., & Hart, T. M. (1992). A developmental neuropsychological perspective for reading and writing acquisition. *Educational Psychologist, 27,* pp. 415–434.

Bernstein, A. C., & Cowan, P. A. (1975). Children's concepts of how people get babies. *Child Development, 46,* 77–91.

Betz, N. E. (2004). Contributions of self-efficacy to career counseling: A personal perspective. *Career Development Quarterly, 52*(4), 340–353.

Betz, N. E., & Hackett, G. (1981). The relationship of career-related self-efficacy expectations to perceived career options in college women and men. *Journal of Counseling Psychology, 28,* 399–410.

Betz, N. E., & Schifano, R. S. (2000). Evaluation of an intervention to increase realistic self-efficacy and interests in college women. *Journal of Vocational Behavior, 56,* 35–52.

Beuf, A. H. (1977). *Red children in White America.* University Park: Pennsylvania State University Press.

Bidell, T. R., & Fischer, K. W. (1997). Between nature and nurture: The role of human agency in the epigenesis of intelligence. In R. J. Sternberg & E. L. Grigorenko (Eds.), *Intelligence, heredity, and environment* (pp. 193–242). New York: Cambridge University Press.

Bierman, K. (1986). Process of change during social skills training with preadolescents and its relation to treatment outcomes. *Child Development, 55,* 151–162.

Bierman, K. L. (2004). *Peer rejection: Developmental processes and intervention strategies.* New York: Guilford Press.

Bierman, K. L., & Furman, W. (1984). The effects of social skills training and peer involvement on the social adjustment of preadolescents. *Child Development, 55,* 151–162.

Bierman, K. L., Greenberg, M. T., & the Conduct Problems Prevention Research Group. (1996). Social skills training in the Fast Track Program. In R. D. Peters & J. McMahon (Eds.), *Preventing childhood disorders, substance abuse, and delinquency* (pp. 65–89). Thousand Oaks, CA: Sage.

Bigler, R. S., & Liben, L. S. (1992). Cognitive mechanisms in children's gender stereotyping: Theoretical and educational implications of a cognitive-based intervention. *Child Development, 63,* 1351–1363.

Billings, J. A. (1998). What is palliative care? *Journal of Palliative Medicine, 1,* 73–81.

Birditt, K. S., & Fingerman, K. L. (2003). Age and gender differences in adults' descriptions of emotional reactions to interpersonal problems. *Journal of Gerontology, 58,* 237–245.

Birmaher, B., & Heydl, P. (2003). Biological studies in depressed children and adolescents. *International Journal of Neuropsychopharmacology, 4,* 149–157.

Black, B., & Hazan, N. (1990). Social status and patterns of communication in acquainted and unacquainted preschool children. *Developmental Psychology, 26,* 379–387.

Blackman, J. A. (2002). Early intervention: A global perspective. *Infants and Young Children, 15,* 11–19.

Blanchard-Fields, F. (1986). Reasoning on social dilemmas varying in emotional salience: An adult developmental perspective. *Psychology and Aging, 1,* 325–333.

Blazer, D. G. (1994). Epidemiology of late life depression. In L. S. Schneider, C. F. Reynolds III, B. D. Lebowitz, & A. J. Friedhoff (Eds.), *Diagnosis and treatment of depression in late life* (pp. 9–19). Washington, DC: American Psychiatric Press.

Blazer, D. G., Kessler, R. C., McGonagle, K. A., & Schwartz, M. S. (1994). The prevalence and distribution of major depression in a national community sample: The national comorbidity survey. *American Journal of Psychiatry, 151,* 979–986.

Blewitt, P. (1989). Category hierarchies: Levels of knowledge and skill. *Genetic Epistemologist, 17,* 21–30.

Blewitt, P. (1994). Understanding categorical hierarchies: The earliest levels of skill. *Child Development, 65*, 1279–1298.

Block, J. H. (1978). Another look at sex differentiation in the socialization behaviors of mothers and fathers. In J. Sherman & F. L. Denmark (Eds.), *The psychology of women: Future directions of research* (pp. 29–87). New York: Psychological Dimensions.

Bloom, L. (1998). Language acquisition in its developmental context. In W. Damon (Series Ed.), D. Kuhn, & R. S. Siegler (Vol. Eds.), *Handbook of child psychology: Vol. 2. Cognition, perception, and language* (5th ed., pp. 309–370). New York: Wiley.

Blos, P. (1962). *On adolescence: A psychoanalytic interpretation.* New York: Free Press.

Blos, P. (1975). The second individuation process of adolescence. In A. Esman (Ed.), *The psychology of adolescence* (pp. 156–176). New York: International Universities Press.

Blum, R. W. (2003). Positive youth development: A strategy for improving adolescent health. In I. B. Weiner (Series Ed.), F. Jacobs, D. Wertlieb, & R. M. Lerner (Vol. Eds.), *Handbook of applied developmental science: Vol. 2. Enhancing the life chances of youth and families* (pp. 237–252). Thousand Oaks, CA: Sage.

Blyth, D. A., Simmons, R. G., Bulcroft, R., Felt, D., VanCleave, E. F., & Bush, D. M. (1981). The effects of physical development on self-image and satisfaction with body-image for early adolescent males. In R. G. Simmons (Ed.), *Research in Community and Mental Health, 2*, 43–73.

Bodenhorn, N., & Lawson, G. (2003). Genetic counseling: Implications for community counselors. *Journal of Counseling and Development, 81*, 497–501.

Boland, A. M., Haden, C. A., & Ornstein, P. A. (2003). Boosting children's memory by training mothers in the use of an elaborative conversational style as events unfold. *Journal of Cognition and Development, 4*, 39–64.

Bolger, K. E., & Patterson, C. J. (2001, April). Developmental pathways from child maltreatment to peer rejection. *Child Development, 72*(2), 549–568.

Bolger, K. E., & Patterson, C. J. (2003). Sequelae of child maltreatment: Vulnerability and resilience. In S. S. Luthar (Ed.), *Resilience and vulnerability: Adaptation in the context of childhood adversities* (pp. 156–181). Cambridge, England: Cambridge University Press.

Bolotin, S. (1999, February 14). The disciples of discipline. *The New York Times Magazine,* 32–77.

Bonanno, G. A., & Kaltman, S. (1999). Toward an integrative perspective on bereavement. *Psychological Bulletin, 125*, 760–776.

Bonanno, G. A., & Keltner, D. (1997). Facial expression of emotion and the course of conjugal bereavement. *Journal of Abnormal Psychology, 106*, 126–137.

Bonanno, G. A., Papa, A., Lalande, K., Westphal, M., & Coifman, K. (2004). The importance of being flexible: The ability to both enhance and suppress emotional expression predicts long-term adjustment. *Psychological Science, 15*, 482–487.

Bonanno, G. A., Znoj, H., Siddique, H. I., & Horowitz, M. J. (1999). Verbal-autonomic dissociation and adaptation to midlife conjugal loss: A follow-up at 25 months. *Cognitive Therapy and Research, 23*, 605–624.

Bond, J. T., Thompson, C., Galinsky, E., & Prottas, D. (2002). *Highlights of the national study of the changing workforce.* New York: Families and Work Institute.

Boom, J., Brugman, D., van der Heijden, P. G. M. (2001). Hierarchical structure of moral stages assessed by a sorting task. *Child Development, 72*, 535–548.

Bornstein, M. H., & Sigman, M. D. (1986). Continuity in mental development from infancy. *Child Development, 57*, 251–274.

Borod, J. C., Koff, E., & Buck, R. (1986). The neuropsychology of facial expression: Data from normal and brain-damaged adults. In P. Blanck, R. Buck, & R. Rosenthal (Eds.), *Nonverbal communication in the clinical context.* University Park: Pennsylvania State University Press.

Bouchard, T. J., Lykken, D. T., McGue, M., Segal, N. L., & Tellegen, A. (1990). Sources of human psychological differences: The Minnesota study of twins reared apart. *Science, 250*, 223–228.

Bowen, M. (1978). *Family therapy in clinical practice.* New York: Jason Aronson.

Bower, E. M. (1960). *Early identification of emotionally handicapped children in school.* Springfield, IL: Charles C. Thomas.

Bowlby, J. (1969/1982). *Attachment and loss: Vol. 1. Attachment.* New York: Basic Books.

Bowlby, J. (1973). *Attachment and loss: Vol. 2. Separation.* New York: Basic Books.

Bowlby, J. (1980). *Attachment and loss: Vol. 3. Loss: Sadness and depression.* New York: Basic Books.

Bowlby, J. (1988). *A secure base: Parent-child attachment and healthy human development.* New York: Basic Books.

Boyer, C. B., Shafer, M., & Tschann, J. M. (1997). Evaluation of a knowledge and cognitive-behavioral skill-building intervention to prevent STDs and HIV infection in high school students. *Adolescence, 32*, 25–42.

Bradley, R. H., & Corwyn, R. F. (2002). Socioeconomic status and child development. *Annual Review of Psychology, 53*, 371–399.

Bradley, S. J., Oliver, G. D., Chernick, A. B., & Zucker, K. J. (1998). Experiment of nurture: Ablatio penis at 2 months, sex reassignment at 7 months, and psychosexual follow-up in young adulthood. *Pediatrics, 102*, 132–133.

Brainerd, C. J. (1996). Piaget: A centennial celebration. *Psychological Science, 7*, 191–195.

Brandstadter, J., & Wentura, D. (1995). Adjustment to shifting possibility frontiers in later life: Complementary adaptive modes. In R. A. Dixon & L. Backman (Eds.), *Psychological compensation: Managing losses and promoting gains* (pp. 83–106). Hillsdale, NJ: Erlbaum.

Branwhite, T. (2000). *Helping adolescents in school.* Westport, CT: Praeger.

Brazelton, T. B. (1986). Issues for working parents. *American Journal of Orthopsychiatry, 56*, 14–25.

Brazelton, T. B., & Greenspan, S. I. (2000). *The irreducible needs of children: What every child must have to grow, learn, and flourish.* Cambridge, MA: Perseus.

Brazelton, T. B., Koslowski, B., & Main, M. (1974). The origins of reciprocity: The early mother-infant interaction. In M. Lewis & L. A. Rosenblum (Eds.), *The effect of the infant on its caregiver* (pp. 49–76). New York: Wiley-Interscience.

Brennan, K. A., Clark, C. L., & Shaver, P. R. (1998). Self-report measurement of adult attachment: An integrative interview. In J. A. Simpson & W. S. Rholes (Eds.), *Attachment theory and close relationships* (pp. 46–76). New York: Guilford Press.

Brennan, K. A., & Shaver, P. R. (1998). Attachment styles and personality disorders: Their connections to each other and to parental divorce, parental death, and perceptions of parental caregiving. *Journal of Personality, 66*, 835–878.

Brennan, P., Hammen, C., Andersen, M., Bor, W., Najman, J., & Williams, G. (2000). Chronicity, severity, and timing of maternal depressive symptoms: Relationships with child outcomes at age five. *Developmental Psychology, 36*, 759–766.

Brestan, E. V., & Eyberg, S. M. (1998). Effective psychosocial treatment of conduct-disordered children and adolescents: 29 years, 82 studies, and 5275 kids. *Journal of Clinical Child Psychology, 27*, 180–189.

Brickman, P. D., & Campbell, D. T. (1971). Hedonic relativism and planning the good society. In M. H. Appley (Ed.). *Adaptation level theory: A symposium* (pp. 287–304). New York. Academic Press.

Brisch, K. H. (1999). *Treating attachment disorders: From theory to therapy.* New York: Guilford Press.

Broderick, P. C. (1998). Early adolescent differences in the use of ruminative and distracting coping styles. *Journal of Early Adolescence, 18*, 173–191.

Broderick, P. C. (2005, in press). Mindfulness and coping with dysphoric mood: Contrasts with rumination and distraction. *Cognitive Therapy and Research.*

Broderick, P. C., & Korteland, C. (2002). Coping style and depression in early adolescence: Relationships to gender, gender role, and implicit beliefs. *Sex Roles: A Journal of Research.*

Broderick, P. C., & Korteland, C. (2004). A prospective study of rumination and depression in early adolescence. *Clinical Child Psychology and Psychiatry, 9*, 383–394.

Broderick, P. C., & Mastrilli, T. (1997). Attitudes concerning parental involvement: Parent and teacher perspectives. *Pennsylvania Educational Leadership, 16*, 30–36.

Brody, G. H., Ge, X., Conger, R., Gibbons, F. X., Murry, V. M., Gerrard, M., et al. (2001). The influence of neighborhood disadvantage, collective socialization, and parenting on African American children's affiliation with deviant peers. *Child Development, 72*, 1231–1246.

Brody, G. H., Murry, V. M., Gerrard, M., Gibbons, F. X., Molgaard, V., McNair, L., et al. (2004). The Strong African American Families Program: Translating research into prevention programming. *Child Development, 75*, 900–917.

Broidy, L. M., Nagin, D. S., Tremblay, R. E., Bates, J. E., Brame, B., Dodge, K. A., et al. (2003). Developmental trajectories of childhood disruptive behaviors and adolescent delinquency: A six-site, cross-national study. *Developmental Psychology, 39*, 222–245.

Bronfenbrenner, U. (1979). *The ecology of human development: Experiments by nature and by design.* Cambridge, MA: Harvard University Press.

Bronfenbrenner, U., & Ceci, S. J. (1994). Nature-nurture reconceptualized in developmental perspective: A bioecological model. *Psychological Review, 101*, 568–586.

Bronfenbrenner, U., & Morris, P. A. (1998). The ecology of developmental processes. In W. Damon (Series Ed.) & R. M. Lerner (Vol. Ed.), *Handbook of child psychology: Vol. 1. Theoretical models of human development* (5th ed., pp. 993–1028). New York: Wiley.

Brooks-Gunn, J. (1991). Maturational timing variations in adolescent girls, antecedents of. In R. M. Lerner, A. C. Petersen, & J. Brooks-Gunn (Eds.), *Encyclopedia of adolescence* (Vol. 2). New York: Garland.

Brooks-Gunn, J., Han, W., & Waldfogel, J. (2002). Maternal employment and child cognitive outcomes in the first three years of life: The NICHD study of early child care. *Child Development, 73*, 1052–1072.

Brooks-Gunn, J., & Warren, M. P. (1989). Biological and social contributions to negative affect in young adolescent girls. *Child Development, 60*, 40–55.

Brooten, D., Youngblut, J. M., Brown, L., Finkler, S. A., Neff, D. F., & Madigan, E. (2001). A randomized trial of nurse specialist home care for women with high-risk pregnancies: Outcome and costs. *American Journal of Managed Care, 7*, 793–803.

Brophy, J. E., & Evertson, C. M. (1976). *Learning from teaching: A developmental perspective.* Boston: Allyn & Bacon.

Brown, B. B. (1990). Peer groups and peer cultures. In S. S. Feldman & G. R. Elliott (Eds.), *At the threshold: The developing adolescent* (pp. 171–196). Cambridge, MA: Harvard University Press.

Brown, J., Steele, J., & Walsh-Childers, K. (2002). *Sexual teens, sexual media: Investigating media's influence on adolescent sexuality.* Hillsdale, NJ: Erlbaum.

Brown, L. Y., & Brown, S. A. (2004). Alanine tracts: The expanding story of human illness and trinucleotide repeats. *Trends in Genetics, 20,* 51–59.

Brown, L., & Gilligan, C. (1992). *Meeting at the crossroads: Women's psychology and girls' development.* Cambridge, MA: Harvard University Press.

Brown, R. (1973). *A first language: The early stages.* Cambridge MA: Harvard University Press.

Brown, R., & Hanlon, C. (1970). Derivational complexity and order of acquisition. In J. R. Hayes (Ed.), *Cognition and the development of language* (pp. 11–53). New York: Wiley.

Brown, S. L., Nesse, N. M., Vinokur, A., & Smith, D. M. (2003). Providing social support may be more beneficial than receiving it: Results from a prospective study of mortality. *Psychological Science, 14,* 320–327.

Browning, S. W. (1998). The empathy expansion procedure: A method of assisting couples in healing from traumatic incidents. In L. L. Hecker & S. A. Deacon (Eds.), *The therapist's notebook: Homework, handouts, and activities for use in psychotherapy.* New York: Haworth Press.

Brunner, H. G., Nelen, M., Breakefield, X. O., Ropers, H. H., & van Oost, B. A. (1993). Abnormal behavior associated with a point mutation in the structural gene for monoamine oxidase A. *Science, 262,* 578–580.

Bryden, M. P. (1988). Does laterality make any difference? Thoughts on the relation between cerebral asymmetry and reading. In D. L. Molfese & S. J. Segalowitz (Eds.), *Brain lateralization in children: Developmental implications* (pp. 509–525). New York: Guilford Press.

Brynner, J. M., O'Malley, P. M., & Bachman, J. C. (1981). Self-esteem and delinquency revisited. *Journal of Youth and Adolescence, 10,* 407–441.

Buchanan, C. M., Eccles, J. S., & Becker, J. B. (1992). Are adolescents the victims of raging hormones? Evidence for activational effects of hormones on moods and behavior at adolescence. *Psychological Bulletin, 111,* 62–107.

Bukowski, W. M., & Hoza, B. (1989). Popularity and friendship: Issues in theory, measurement, and outcome. In T. J. Berndt & G. Ladd (Eds.), *Peer relations in child development* (pp. 15–45). New York: Wiley.

Burgess, D., & Borgida, E. (1997). Sexual harassment: An experimental test of sex-role spillover theory. *Personality and Social Psychology Bulletin, 23,* 63–75.

Burka, J. B., & Yuen, L. M. (1983). *Procrastination: Why you do it, what to do about it.* Reading, MA: Addison-Wesley.

Burns, B. J., Costello, E. J., Angold, A., Erkanli, A., Stangl, D., & Tweed, D. L. (1995). Children's mental health service use across service sectors. *Health Affairs, 14,* 147–159.

Burns, B. J., Hoagwood, K., & Mrazek, P. J. (1999). Effective treatments for mental disorders in children and adolescents. *Clinical Child and Family Psychology Review, 2,* 199–254.

Burr, W. R. (1970). Satisfaction with various aspects of marriage over the life cycle: A random middle class sample. *Journal of Marriage and the Family, 32,* 29–37.

Buss, D. M. (1987). Selection, evocation and manipulation. *Journal of Personality and Social Psychology, 53,* 1214–1221.

Buss, D. M. (1989). Sex differences in human mate preferences: Evolutionary hypotheses tested in 37 cultures. *Behavioral and Brain Sciences, 12,* 1–49.

Bussey, K., & Bandura, A. (1984). Influence of gender constancy and social power on sex-linked modeling. *Journal of Personality and Social Psychology, 47,* 1292–1302.

Bussey, K., & Bandura, A. (1999). A social cognitive theory of gender development and differentiation. *Psychological Bulletin, 106,* 676–713.

Butler, L. D., & Nolen-Hoeksema, S. (1994). Gender differences in response to depressed mood in a college sample. *Sex Roles, 30,* 331–346.

Butler, R. N. (1963). The life review: An interpretation of reminiscence in the aged. *Psychiatry, 26,* 65–76.

Byng-Hall, J. (1995). *Rewriting family scripts: Improvisation and systems change.* New York: Guilford Press.

Byrne, B. M., & Shavelson, R. J. (1996). On the structure of social self-concept for pre-, early- and late adolescents: A test of the Shavelson, Hubner, and Stanton (1976) model. *Journal of Personality and Social Psychology, 70,* 599–613.

Byrne, D. (1964). Repression-sensitization as a dimension of personality. In B. A. Maher (Ed.), *Progress in experimental personality research* (pp. 169–220). New York: Academic Press.

Cacioppo, J. T., & Berntson, G. G. (1992). Social psychological contributions to the decade of the brain: Doctrine of multilevel analysis. *American Psychologist, 47,* 1019–1028.

Cacioppo, J. T., & Gardner, W. L. (1999). Emotion. *Annual Review of Psychology, 50,* 191–214.

Cairns, R. B., & Cairns, B. D. (1994). *Lifelines and risks: Pathways of youth in our time.* New York: Cambridge University Press.

Cairns, R. B., & Cairns, B. D. (2000). The natural history and developmental functions of aggression. In A. J. Sameroff, M. Lewis, & S. M. Miller (Eds.), *Handbook of developmental psychopathology* (2nd ed., pp. 403–429). New York: Kluwer Academic/Plenum Press.

Cairns, R. B., Gariepy, J. L., & Kindermann, T. A. (1990). *Identifying social clusters in natural settings.* Unpublished manuscript, University of North Carolina at Chapel Hill, Social Development Laboratory.

Callanan, M., & Kelley, P. (1992). *Final gifts: Understanding the special awareness, needs and communications of the dying.* New York: Bantam Books.

Cameron, C. A., & Wang, M. (1999). Frog, where are you? Children's narrative expression over the telephone. *Discourse Processes, 28,* 217–236.

Campbell, F. A., Pungello, E. P., Miller-Johnson, S., Burchinal, M., & Ramey, C. T. (2001). The development of cognitive and academic abilities: Growth curves from an early childhood educational experiment. *Developmental Psychology, 37,* 231–242.

Campbell, J. D. (1990). Self-esteem and clarity of the self-concept. *Journal of Personality and Social Psychology, 59,* 538–549.

Campbell, J. D., & Lavallee, L. F. (1993). Who am I? The role of self-concept confusion in understanding the behavior of people with low self-esteem. In R. F. Baumeister (Ed.), *Self-esteem: The puzzle of low self-regard* (pp. 3–20). New York: Plenum Press.

Campbell, S. B. (1987). Parent-referred problem 3-year-olds: Developmental changes in symptoms. *Journal of Child Psychology and Psychiatry, 28,* 835–845.

Campos, J., Barrett, K., Lamb, M., Goldsmith, H., & Sternberg, C. (1983). Socioemotional development. In P. H. Mussen (Ed.), *Handbook of child psychology: Vol. 2. Infancy and developmental psychology* (pp. 783–915). New York: Wiley.

Campos, J. J., Campos, R. G., & Barrett, K. C. (1989). Emergent themes in the study of emotional development and emotion regulation. *Developmental Psychology, 25,* 394–402.

Canobi, K. H., Reeve, R. A., & Pattison, P. E. (1998). The role of conceptual understanding in children's addition problem solving. *Developmental Psychology, 34,* 882–891.

Cantor, J., & Wilson, B. J. (1998). Helping children cope with frightening media presentations. *Current Psychology: Research & Reviews, 7,* 58–75.

Carli, L. L. (1990). Gender, language, and influence. *Journal of Personality and Social Psychology, 59,* 941–951.

Carlson, J., & Lewis, J. (1993). Motivation: Building students' feelings of confidence and self-worth. In J. Carlson & J. Lewis (Eds.), *Counseling the adolescent: Individual, family and school interventions* (2nd ed., pp. 249–270). Denver, CO: Love.

Carlson, L. E., Speca, M., Patel, K. D., Goodey, E. (2004). Mindfulness-based stress reduction in relation to quality of life, mood, symptoms of stress and levels of cortisol, dehydroepiandrosterone sulfate (DHEAS) and melatonin in breast and prostate cancer outpatients. *Psychoneuroendocrinology, 29,* 448–474.

Carnegie Council on Adolescent Development. (1996). *Great transitions: Preparing adolescents for a new century.* New York: Carnegie Corporation of New York.

Carr, D. (2002). The psychological consequences of work-family trade-offs for three cohorts of men and women. *Social Psychology Quarterly, 65,* 103–124.

Carrere, S., Buehlman, K. T., Gottman, J. M., Coan, J. A., & Ruckstuhl, L. (2000). Predicting marital stability in divorced and newlywed couples. *Journal of Family Psychology, 14,* 42–58.

Carrere, S., & Gottman, J. M. (1999). Predicting divorce among newlyweds from the first three minutes of a marital conflict discussion. *Family Process, 38,* 293–301.

Carskadon, M., Vieria, C., & Acebo, C. (1993). Association between puberty and delayed phase preference. *Sleep, 16,* 258–262.

Carstensen, L. L. (1998). A life-span approach to social motivation. In J. Heckhausen & C. S. Dweck (Eds.), *Motivation and self-regulation across the life span* (pp. 341–364). Cambridge, England: Cambridge University Press.

Carstensen, L. L., & Charles, S. T. (1998). Emotion in the second half of life. *Current Directions in Psychological Science, 7,* 144–149.

Carstensen, L. L., Pasupathi, M., & Mayr, U. (1998). *Emotion experience in the daily lives of older and younger adults.* Unpublished manuscript.

Carstensen, L. L., & Turk-Charles, S. (1994). The salience of emotion across the adult life span. *Psychology and Aging, 9,* 259–264.

Carter, B., & McGoldrick, M. (Eds.). (1999). *The expanded family life cycle: Individual, family and social perspectives* (3rd ed.). Boston: Allyn & Bacon.

Cartwright, D. (1950). Emotional dimensions of group life. In M. L. Reymert (Ed.), *Feelings and emotions* (pp. 437–447). New York: McGraw-Hill.

Carver, P. R., Yunger, J. L., & Perry, D. G. (2003). Gender identity and adjustment in middle childhood. *Sex Roles, 49,* 95–109.

Case, R. (1985). *Intellectual development: Birth to adulthood.* New York: Academic Press.

Case, R. (1991). Stages in the development of the young child's first sense of self. *Developmental Review, 11,* 210–230.

Case, R. (1992). *The mind's staircase: Exploring the conceptual underpinnings of children's thought and knowledge.* Hillsdale, NJ: Erlbaum.

Casey, B. J., Giedd, J. N., & Thomas, K. M. (2000). Structural and functional brain development and its relation to cognitive development. *Biological Psychology, 54,* 241–257.

Caspi, A. (2000). The child is father of the man: Personality continuities from childhood to adulthood. *Journal of Personality and Social Psychology, 78,* 158–172.

Caspi, A., Lynam, D., Moffitt, T. E., & Silva, P. A. (1993). Unraveling girls' delinquency: Biological, dispositional, and contextual contributions to adolescent misbehavior. *Developmental Psychology, 29,* 19–30.

Caspi, A., McClay, J., Moffitt, T. E., Mill, J., Martin, J., Craig, I. W., et al. (2002). Role of genotype in the cycle of violence in maltreated children. *Science, 297,* 851–855.

Cass, V. (1979). Homosexual identity formation: A theoretical model. *Journal of Homosexuality, 4,* 143–167.

Cassel, C. K., & Foley, K. M. (1999). *Principles for care of patients at the end of life: An emerging consensus among the specialities of medicine.* New York: Millbank Memorial Fund.

Cassidy, J., & Berlin, L. J. (1994). The insecure/ambivalent pattern of attachment: Theory and research. *Child Development, 65,* 971–991.

Cassidy, J., & Shaver, P. R. (Eds.). (1999). *Handbook of attachment: Theory, research, and clinical applications.* New York: Guilford Press.

Ceci, S. J., & Bruck, M. (1998). Children's testimony: Applied and basic issues. In W. Damon (Series Ed.), I. E. Sigel, & K. A. Renninger (Vol. Eds.), *Handbook of child psychology: Vol. 4. Child psychology in practice* (5th ed., pp. 713–774). New York: Wiley.

Ceci, S. J., Bruck, M., & Battin, D. B. (2000). The suggestibility of children's testimony. In D. F. Bjorklund (Ed.), *False-memory creation in children and adults: Theory, research, and implications* (pp. 169–201). Mahwah, NJ: Erlbaum.

Ceci, S. J., & Liker, J. (1986). A day at the races: A study of IQ, expertise, and cognitive complexity. *Journal of Experimental Psychology: General, 115,* 255–266.

Ceci, S. J., Loftus, E. W., Leichtman, M., & Bruck, M. (1994). The role of source misattributions in the creation of false beliefs among preschoolers. *International Journal of Clinical and Experimental Hypnosis, 62,* 304–320.

Ceci, S. J., Rosenblum, T., de Bruyn, E., & Lee, D. Y. (1997). A bio-ecological model of intellectual development: Moving beyond h-sup-2. In R. J. Sternberg & E. L. Grigorenko (Eds.), *Intelligence, heredity, and environment* (pp. 303–322). New York: Cambridge University Press.

Centers for Disease Control (2004). *YRBSS: Youth Risk Behavior Surveillance System.* www.cdc.gov/yrbss.

Centers for Disease Control and Prevention. (1998). *Youth risk surveillance: United States, 1997.* Washington, DC: U.S. Department of Health and Human Services.

Centers for Disease Control and Prevention. (2002). *HIV/AIDS surveillance report, 2001.* Atlanta, GA: Author, National Center for HIV, STD and TB Prevention, Division of HIV/AIDS Prevention. Available from http://www.cdc.gov/hiv/stats/hasr1302.htm

Centers for Disease Control and Prevention. (2003). *Sexually transmitted disease surveillance report, 2002.* Atlanta, GA: Author, National Center for HIV, STD and TB Prevention, Division of Sexually Transmitted Diseases. Available from http://www.cdc.gov/nchstp/dstd/Stats_Trends/Stats_and_Trends.htm

Cervone, D., & Peake, P. K. (1986). Anchoring, efficacy, and action: The influence of judgmental heuristics on self-efficacy judgments and behavior. *Journal of Personality and Social Psychology, 50,* 492–501.

Chalmers, J. B., & Townsend, M. A. (1990). The effects of training in social perspective taking on socially maladjusted girls. *Child Development, 61,* 178–179.

Champion, L. A., Goodall, G. M., & Rutter, M. (1995). Behavioural problems in childhood and stressors in early adult life: A 20-year follow-up of London school children. *Psychological Medicine, 25,* 231–246.

Chandler, M. J. (1973). Egocentrism and antisocial behavior: The assessment and training of social and perspective-taking skills. *Developmental Psychology, 9,* 326–332.

Chandler, M. J. (1987). The Othello effect: Essay on the emergence and eclipse of skeptical doubt. *Human Development, 30,* 137–139.

Chandler, M. J., & Boutilier, R. G. (1992). The development of dynamic system reasoning. *Human Development, 35,* 129–137.

Chandler, M. J., Boyes, M., & Ball, L. (1990). Relativism and stations of epistemic doubt. *Journal of Experimental Child Psychology, 50,* 370–395.

Chao, R. K. (2001). Extending research on the consequences of parenting style for Chinese Americans and European Americans. *Child Development, 72,* 1832–1843.

Character Education Partnership. (1995). *Eleven principles of effective character education.* Washington, DC: Author.

Charles, S. T., Mather, M., & Carstensen, L. L. (2003). Aging and emotional memory: The forgettable nature of negative images for older adults. *Journal of Experimental Psychology: General, 132,* 310–234.

Charness, N., & Bosman, E. A. (1990). Expertise and aging: Life in the lab. In T. H. Hess (Ed.), *Aging and cognition: Knowledge organization and utilization* (pp. 343–385). Amsterdam: Elsevier.

Charney, D. S., Nestler, E. J., & Bunney, B. S. (1999). *Neurobiology of mental illness.* New York: Oxford University Press.

Chase, W. G., & Simon, H. A. (1973). Perception in chess. *Cognitive Psychology, 4,* 55–81.

Chase-Lansdale, P. L., & Brooks-Gunn, J. (1994). Correlates of adolescent pregnancy and parenthood. In C. B. Fisher & R. M. Lerner (Eds.), *Applied developmental psychology* (pp. 207–236). New York: McGraw-Hill.

Chatters, L. M. (2000). Religion and health: Public health research and practice. *Annual Review of Public Health, 21,* 335–367.

Chen, X., Rubin, K. H., & Li, Z. (1995). Social functioning and adjustment in Chinese children: A longitudinal study. *Developmental Psychology, 31,* 531–539.

Cherlin, A. (1981). *Marriage, divorce, remarriage.* Cambridge, MA: Harvard University Press.

Chess, S., & Hassibi, M. (1978). *Principles and practice of child psychiatry.* New York: Plenum Press.

Chess, S., & Thomas, A. (1987). *Origins and evolution of behavior: From infancy to early adult life.* Cambridge, MA: Harvard University Press.

Chi, M. T. H. (1978). Knowledge structures and memory development. In R. S. Siegler (Ed.), *Children's thinking: What develops?* Hillsdale, NJ: Erlbaum.

Chi, M. T. H., Hutchinson, J. E., & Robin, A. F. (1989). How inferences about novel domain-related concepts can be constrained by structured knowledge. *Merrill-Palmer Quarterly, 35,* 27–62.

Chi, M. T. H., & Koeske, R. D. (1983). Network representation of a child's dinosaur knowledge. *Developmental Psychology, 19,* 29–39.

Chiriboga, D. A. (1997). Crisis, challenge, and stability in the middle years. In M. E. Lachman & J. B. James (Eds.), *Multiple paths of midlife development* (pp. 293–322). Chicago: University of Chicago Press.

Chisholm, K. (1998). A three-year follow-up of attachment and indiscriminate friendliness in children adopted from Romanian orphanges. *Child Development, 69,* 1092–1106.

Chomsky, N. (1968). *Language and mind.* New York: Harcourt Brace World.

Christakis, N. (2000). *Death foretold: Prophecy and prognosis in medical care.* Chicago: University of Chicago Press.

Chrousos, G. P., & Gold, P. W. (1999). The inhibited child "syndrome": Thoughts on its potential pathogenesis and sequelae. In L. A. Schmidt & J. Schulkin (Eds.), *Extreme fear, shyness, and social phobia: Origins, biological mechanisms, and clinical outcomes* (pp. 193–200). New York: Oxford University Press.

Chumlea, W. C. (1982). Physical growth in adolescence. In B. J. Wolman (Ed.), *Handbook of developmental psychology* (pp. 471–485). Upper Saddle River, NJ: Prentice Hall.

Cicchetti, D. (1989). How research on child maltreatment has informed the study of child maltreatment: Perspectives from developmental psychopathology. In D. Cicchetti & V. Carlson (Eds.), *Child maltreatment: Theory and research on the causes and consequences of child abuse and neglect* (pp. 377–431). New York: Cambridge University Press.

Cicchetti, D., & Toth, S. L. (Eds.). (1994). *Rochester Symposium on Developmental Psychopathology: Vol. 5. Disorders and dysfunctions of the self* (pp. 79–148). Rochester, NY: University of Rochester Press.

Cicchetti, D., Toth, S. L., & Lynch, M. (1995). Bowlby's dream comes full circle: The application of attachment theory to risk and psychopathology. *Advances in Clinical Child Psychology, 17,* 1–75.

Cicchetti, D., Toth, S. L., & Maughan, A. (2000). An ecological-transactional model of child maltreatment. In A. J. Sameroff, M. Lewis, & S. M. Miller (Eds.), *Handbook of developmental psychopathology* (2nd ed., pp. 689–722). New York: Kluwer Academic/Plenum.

Cierpal, M. A., & McCarty, R. (1987). Hypertension in SHR rats: Contribution of maternal environment. *American Journal of Physiology, 253,* 980–984.

Cioffe, D. (1991). Beyond attentional strategies: A cognitive-perceptual model of somatic interpretations. *Psychological Bulletin, 109,* 25–39.

Clark, M. L. (1982). Racial group concept and self-esteem in black children. *Journal of Black Psychology, 8,* 75–88.

Clark, R., Hyde, J. S., Essex, J. J., & Klein, M. H. (1997). Length of maternity leave and quality of mother-infant interactions. *Child Development, 68,* 364–383.

Clarke-Stewart, K. A. (1989). Infant day care: Maligned or malignant? *American Psychologist, 44,* 266–273.

Clausen, J. A. (1993). *American lives: Looking back at the children of the Great Depression.* New York: Free Press.

Cohen, D., & Strayer, J. (1996). Empathy in conduct disordered and comparison youth. *Developmental Psychology, 32,* 988–998.

Cohen, J. M. (1977). Sources of peer group homogeneity. *Sociology of Education, 50,* 227–241.

Cohen, S., Doyle, W. J., Turner, R. B., Alper, C. M., Skoner, D. P. (2003). Emotional style and susceptibility to the common cold. *Psychosomatic Medicine, 65,* 652–657.

Cohen, S., & Williamson, G. M. (1991). Stress and infectious diseases in humans. *Psychological Bulletin, 109,* 5–24.

Cohen-Kettenis, P. T., Owen, A., Kaijser, V. G., Bradley, S. J., & Zucker, K. J. (2003). Demographic characteristics, social competence, and behavior problems in children with gender identity disorder: A cross-national, cross-clinic comparative analysis. *Journal of Abnormal Child Psychology, 32,* 41–53.

Coie, J., Terry, R., Lenox, K., & Lochman, J. (1995). Childhood peer rejection and aggression as predictors of stable patterns of adolescent disorder. *Development & Psychopathology, 7,* 697–713.

Coie, J. D., & Dodge, K. A. (1998). Aggression and antisocial behavior. In W. Damon (Ed.) & N. Eisenberg (Vol. Ed.), *Handbook of child psychology: Vol. 3. Social, emotional, and personality development* (5th ed., pp. 779–862). New York: Wiley.

Coie, J. D., Dodge, K. A., & Coppotelli, H. (1982). Dimensions and types of social status: A cross-age perspective. *Developmental Psychology, 18,* 557–570.

Coie, J. D., Dodge, K. A., & Kupersmidt, J. B. (1990). Peer group behavior and social status. In S. R. Asher & J. D. Coie (Eds.), *Peer rejection in childhood* (pp. 17–59). Cambridge, England: Cambridge University Press.

Coie, J. D., & Krehbiehl, G. (1984). Effects of academic tutoring on the social status of low-achieving, socially rejected children. *Child Development, 55,* 1465–1478.

Coie, J. D., & Kupersmidt, J. (1983). A behavioral analysis of emerging social status in boys' groups. *Child Development, 54,* 1400–1416.

Coie, J. D., Watt, N. F., West, S. G., Hawkins, J. D., Asamow, J. R., Markman, H. J., et al. (1993). The science of prevention: A conceptual framework and some directions for a national research program. *American Psychologist, 48,* 1013–1022.

Colapinto, John (1999). *As nature made him: The boy who was raised as a girl.* New York: HarperCollins.

Colby, A., & Damon, W. (1992). *Some do care: Contemporary lives of moral commitment.* New York: Free Press.

Colby, A., & Kohlberg, L. (1987). *The measurement of moral judgment: Vol. 1. Theoretical foundations and research validation; Vol. 2. Standard issue scoring manual.* New York: Cambridge University Press.

Colby, A., Kohlberg, L., Gibbs, J., & Lieberman, M. (1983). A longitudinal study of moral judgment. *Monographs of the Society for Research in Child Development, 48*(1–2, Serial No. 200).

Cole, D. A., Maxwell, S. E., & Martin, J. M. (1997). Reflected self-appraisals: Strength and structure of the relation of teacher, peer, and parent ratings to children's self-perceived competencies. *Journal of Educational Psychology, 89,* 55–70.

Cole, M. (1998). *Cultural psychology: A once and future discipline.* Cambridge, MA: Belknap.

Cole, M., & Wertsch, J. V. (1996). Beyond the individual-social antinomy in discussions of Piaget and Vygotsky. *Human Development, 39,* 250–256.

Cole, P. M., Barrett, K. C., & Zahn-Waxler, C. (1992). Emotion displays in two-year-olds during mishaps. *Child Development, 63,* 314–324.

Coleman, L., & Coleman, U. J. (2002). The measurement of puberty: A review. *Journal of Adolescence, 25,* 535.

Coles, R. (1970). *Erik H. Erikson: The growth of his work.* Boston: Little, Brown.

Colin, V. L. (1996). *Human attachment.* New York: McGraw-Hill.

Collaer, M. L., & Hines, M. (1995). Human behavioral sex differences: A role for gonadal hormones during early development? *Psychological Bulletin, 118,* 55–107.

Collins, N. L., & Read, S. J. (1990). Adult attachment, working models, and relationship quality in dating couples. *Journal of Personality and Social Psychology, 58,* 644–663.

Collins, W. A., Maccoby, E. E., Steinberg, L., Hetherington, E. M., & Bornstein, M. H. (2000). Contemporary research on parenting: The case for nature and nature. *American Psychologist, 55,* 218–232.

Comer, J. P. (1988). Educating poor minority children. *Scientific American, 5,* 42–48.

Commons, M. L., & Richards, F. A. (1984). A general model of stage theory. In M. L. Commons, F. A. Richards, & C. Armon (Eds.), *Beyond formal operations: Late adolescent and adult cognitive development* (pp. 120–140). New York: Praeger.

Compas, B. E., Banez, G. A., Malcarne, V., & Worsham, N. (1991). Perceived control and coping with stress: A developmental perspective. *Journal of Social Issues, 47,* 23–43.

Compas, B. E., Davis, G. E., Forsythe, C. J., & Wagner, B. M. (1987). Assessment of major and daily stressful events during adolescence: The Adolescent Perceived Events Scale. *Journal of Consulting and Clinical Psychology, 55,* 534–541.

Compas, B. E., Ey, S., & Grant, K. E. (1993). Taxonomy, assessment, and diagnosis of depression during adolescence. *Psychological Bulletin, 114,* 323–344.

Compas, B. E., Howell, D. C., Phares, V., Williams, R. A., & Giunta, C. (1989). Risk factors for emotional/behavioral problems in young adolescents: A prospective analysis of adolescent and parental stress and symptoms. *Journal of Consulting and Clinical Psychology, 57,* 732–740.

Compton, W. C. (2005). *Introduction to positive psychology.* Belmont, CA: Thomson/Wadsworth.

Comstock, G., & Scharrer, E. (1999). *Television: What's on, who's watching, and what it means.* San Diego, CA: Academic Press.

Condon, W. S., & Sander, L. W. (1974). Synchrony demonstrated between movements of the neonate and adult speech. *Child Development, 45,* 1191–1193.

Conduct Problems Prevention Research Group. (1999). Initial impact of the Fast Track Prevention Trial for conduct problems: II. Classroom effects. *Journal of Consulting and Clinical Psychology, 67,* 648–657.

Conduct Problems Prevention Research Group. (2002). Evaluation of the first 3 years of the Fast Track Prevention Trial with children at high risk for adolescent conduct problems. *Journal of Abnormal Child Psychology, 30,* 19–35.

Conger, R. D., Ge, X., Elder, G., Lorenz, F., & Simons, R. (1994). Economic stress, coercive family process, and developmental problems in adolescents. *Child Development, 65,* 541–561.

Conley, D., & Bennett, N. (2002). Comment: Outcomes in young adulthood for very low birth-weight infants. *New England Journal of Medicine, 347,* 141–143.

Conley, J. J. (1985). Longitudinal study of personality traits: A multitrait-multimethod-multioccasion analysis. *Journal of Personality and Social Psychology, 49,* 1266–1282.

Connidis, I. A., & Davies, L. (1992). Confidants and companions: Choices in later life. *Journal of Gerontology: Social Sciences, 47,* S115–S122.

Cook, A. S., & Oltjenbruns, K. A. (1998). The bereaved family. In A. S. Cook & K. A. Oltjenbruns (Eds.), *Dying and grieving: Life span and family perspectives* (pp. 91–115). Fort Worth, TX: Harcourt, Brace.

Cooley, C. H. (1902). *Human nature and the social order.* New York: Scribner's.

Coon, H., Carey, G., Corley, R., & Fulker, D. W. (1992). Identifying children in Colorado Adoption Project at risk for conduct disorder. *Journal of the American Academy of Child and Adolescent Psychiatry, 31,* 503–511.

Corcoran, K. O., & Mallinckrodt, B. (2000). Adult attachment, self-efficacy, perspective-taking, and conflict resolution. *Journal of Counseling and Development, 78,* 473–483.

Corr, C. A. (1993). Coping with dying: Lessons that we should and should not learn from the work of Elizabeth Kubler-Ross. *Death Studies, 17,* 69–83.

Cost, Quality, and Child Care Outcomes Study Team. (1995). *Cost, quality and child outcomes in child care centers, public report.* Denver: University of Colorado, Center for Research in Economics and Social Policy.

Costa, P. T., & McCrae, R. R. (1988). Personality in adulthood: A six-year longitudinal study of self-reports and spouse ratings on the NEO Personality Inventory. *Journal of Personality and Social Psychology, 54,* 853–863.

Costa, P. T., & McCrae, R. R. (1994). Set like plaster? Evidence for the stability of adult personality. In T. F. Heatherton & J. L. Weinberger (Eds.), *Can personality change?* (pp. 21–40). Washington, DC: American Psychological Association.

Costantino, G., Malgady, R. G., & Rogler, L. H. (1986). *The TEMAS thematic perception test: Technical manual.* Los Angeles: Western Psychological Association.

Costantino, G., Malgady, R. G., & Rogler, L. H. (1994). Storytelling-through-pictures: Culturally sensitive psychotherapy for Hispanic children and adolescents. *Journal of Clinical Child Psychology, 23,* 13–20.

Costello, E. J., Compton, S. N., Keeler, G., & Angold, A. (2003). Relationships between poverty and psychopathology: A natural experiment. *Journal of the American Medical Association, 290,* 2023–2063.

Coupland, N., Coupland, J., Giles, H., Henwood, K., & Wiemann, J. (1988). Elderly self-disclosure: Interactional and intergroup issues. *Language and Communication, 8,* 109–133.

Cowan, C. P., & Cowan, P. A. (1992). *When partners become parents.* New York: Basic Books.

Cowan, P. A. (1978). *Piaget with feeling: Cognitive, social and emotional dimensions.* New York: Holt, Rinehart & Winston.

Cowan, W. M. (1979). The development of the brain. In R. R. Llinas (Ed.), *The workings of the brain: Development, memory, and perception.* New York: Freeman.

Cowen, E. L., Hightower, A. D., Pedro-Carroll, J. L., Work, W. C., Wyman, P. A., & Haffey, W. G. (1996). *School-based prevention for children at risk: The Primary Mental Health Project.* Washington, DC: American Psychological Association.

Cowen, E. L., Izzo, L. D., Miles, H., Telschow, E. F., Trost, M. A., & Zax, M. A. (1963). A mental health program in the school setting: Description and evaluation. *Journal of Psychology, 56,* 307–356.

Cowen, E. L., Petersen, A., Babigian, H., Izzo, L. D., & Trost, M. A. (1973). Long-term follow-up of early detected vulnerable children. *Journal of Consulting and Clinical Psychology, 41,* 438–446.

Coyne, J. C. (1976). Depression and the response of others. *Journal of Abnormal Psychology, 85,* 186–193.

Coyne, J. C. (1999). Thinking interactionally about depression: A radical restatement. In T. Joiner & J. C. Coyne (Eds.), *The interactional nature of depression* (pp. 365–392). Washington, DC: American Psychological Association.

Crago, M., & Crago, H. (1983). *Prelude to literacy: A preschool child's encounter with picture and story.* Carbondale: Southern Illinois University Press.

Crain, W. (1992). *Theories of development: Concepts and applications.* Upper Saddle River, NJ: Prentice Hall.

Cramer, P. (1999). Development of identity: Gender makes a difference. *Journal of Research in Personality, 34,* 42–72.

Crane, D. A., & Tisak, M. (1995). Mixed-domain events: The influence of moral and conventional components on the development of social reasoning. *Early Education and Development, 6,* 169–180.

Crawford, M. (2003). Sexual double standards: A review and methodological critique of two decades of research. *Journal of Sex Research, 40,* 13–26.

Creasey, G., & Hesson-McInnis, M. (2001). Affective responses, cognitive appraisals, and conflict tactics in late adolescent romantic relationships: Associations with attachment orientations. *Journal of Counseling Psychology, 48,* 85–96.

Crews, D. (1994). Animal sexuality. *Scientific American, 270,* 108–114.

Crick, N. R., & Dodge, K. A. (1994). A review and reformation of social information processing mechanisms in children's social adjustment. *Psychological Bulletin, 115,* 74–101.

Crick, N. R., & Grotpeter, J. K. (1995). Relational aggression, gender, and social-psychological adjustment. *Child Development, 66,* 710–722.

Crittendon, P. M. (1994). Peering into the black box: An exploratory treatise on the development of self in young children. In D. Cicchetti & S. L. Toth (Eds.), *Rochester Symposium on Developmental Psychopathology: Vol. 5. Disorders and dysfunctions of the self* (pp. 79–148). Rochester, NY: University of Rochester Press.

Crittendon, P. M. (1997). Patterns of attachment and sexual behavior: Risk of dysfunction versus opportunity for creative integration. In L. Atkinson & K. J. Zucker (Eds.), *Attachment and psychopathology* (pp. 47–93). New York: Guilford Press.

Crittendon, P. M., & DiLalla, D. L. (1988). Compulsive compliance: The development of an inhibitory coping strategy in infancy. *Journal of Abnormal Child Psychology, 16,* 585–599.

Crnic, K. A., & Booth, C. L. (1991). Mothers' and fathers' perceptions of daily hassles of parenting across early childhood. *Journal of Marriage and the Family, 53,* 1042–1050.

Crnic, K. A., & Greenberg, M. T. (1990). Minor parenting stresses with young children. *Child Development, 61,* 1628–1637.

Crockenberg, S. C. (2003). Rescuing the baby from the bathwater: How gender and temperament (may) influence how child care affects child development. *Child Development, 74,* 1034–1038.

Crockenberg, S., & Litman, C. (1991). Effects of maternal employment on maternal and two-year-old child behavior. *Child Development, 62,* 930–953.

Crocker, J., & Major, B. (1989). Social stigma and self-esteem: The self-protective properties of stigma. *Psychological Review, 96,* 608–630.

Crocker, J., & Park, L. E. (2004). The costly pursuit of self-esteem. *Psychological Bulletin, 130*(3), 392–414.

Cross-National Collaborative Group. (1992). The changing rate of major depression: Cross-national comparisons. *Journal of the American Medical Association, 268,* 3098–3105.

Cross, W. E. (1971). The Negro to Black conversion experience. *Black World, 20,* 13–17.

Cross, W. E. (1994). Nigrescence theory: Historical and explanatory notes. *Journal of Vocational Behavior, 44,* 119–123.

Crowder, L. S. (1999). Mortuary practices in San Francisco Chinatown. *Chinese America, History & Perspectives,* pp. 33–47.

Crowell, J. A., Treboux, D., & Waters, E. (2002). Stability of attachment representations: The transition to marriage. *Developmental Psychology, 38,* 467–479.

Crowell, J. A., Waters, E., Treboux, D., O'Connor, E., Colon-Downs, C., Feider, O., et al. (1996). Discriminant validity of the Adult Attachment Interview. *Child Development, 67,* 2584–2599.

Crowley, K., & Siegler, R. S. (1993). Flexible strategy use in young children's tic-tac-toe. *Cognitive Science, 17,* 531–561.

Crump, A. D., Haynie, D. L., Aarons, S. J., Adair, E., Woodward, K., & Simons-Morton, B. G. (1999). Pregnancy among urban African-American teens: Ambivalence about prevention. *American Journal of Health Behavior, 23,* 32–42.

Csikszentmihalyi, M. (1999). If we are so rich, why aren't we happy? *American Psychologist, 54,* 821–827.

Csikszentmihalyi, M., & Larson, R. (1984). *Being adolescent.* New York: Basic Books.

Cultice, J. C., Somerville, S. C., & Wellman, H. M. (1983). Preschooler's memory monitoring: Feeling-of-knowing judgements. *Child Development, 54,* 1480–1486.

Cunningham, A. E., Stanovich, K. E., & West, R. F. (1994). Literacy environment and the development of children's cognitive skills. In E. Assink (Ed.), *Literacy acquisition and social context.* Wheatsheaf, NY: Harvester.

Daley, S. (1991, January 9). Little girls lose their self-esteem on way to adolescence, study finds. *The New York Times,* p. B6.

Damasio, A. R. (1994). *Descartes' error: Emotion, reason, and the human brain.* New York: Grosset/Putnam.

Damon, W. (1983). *Social and personality development.* New York: Norton.

Damon, W. (1988). *The moral child: Nurturing children's natural moral growth.* New York: Free Press.

Damon, W. (1996). *Greater expectations: Overcoming the culture of indulgence in America's homes and schools.* New York: Free Press.

Damon, W., & Hart, D. (1988). *Self-understanding in childhood and adolescence.* New York: Cambridge University Press.

Damon, W., & Hart, D. (1992). Self-understanding and its role in social and moral development. In M. H. Bornstein & M. E. Lamb (Eds.), *Developmental psychology: An advanced textbook* (3rd ed., pp. 421–464). Hillsdale, NJ: Erlbaum.

Darling, N., & Steinberg, L. (1993). Parenting style as context: An integrative model. *Psychological Bulletin, 113,* 487–496.

Datan, N., & Ginsberg, L. H. (Eds.). (1975). *Life-span developmental psychology: Normative life crises.* New York: Academic Press.

Davidson, P., Turiel, E., & Black, A. (1983). The effect of stimulus familiarity on the use of criteria and justifications in children's social reasoning. *British Journal of Developmental Psychology, 1,* 49–65.

Davidson, R. J. (2000). Affective style, psychopathology, and resilience: Brain mechanisms and plasticity. *American Psychologist, 55,* 1193–1214.

Davidson, R. J. (2002). Toward a biology of positive affect and compassion. In R. J. Davidson & A. Harrington (Eds.), *Visions of compassion: Western scientists and Tibetan Buddhists examine human nature* (pp. 107–130). NY: Oxford University Press.

Davidson, R. J., Coe, C. C., Dolski, I., & Donzella, B. (1999). Individual differences in prefrontal activation asymmetry predicts natural killer cell activity at rest and in response to challenge. *Brain, Behavior, and Immunity, 13,* 93–108.

Davidson, R. J., Kabat-Zinn, J., Schumacher, J., Rosenkranz, M., Muller, D., Santorelli, S. F., et al. (2003). Alterations in brain and immune function produced by mindfulness meditation. *Psychosomatic Medicine, 65,* 564–570.

Davis, C. (1852). *Lecture on the duties and relations of parents, teachers, and pupils as connected with education.* Delivered at the First Session of the Teachers' Institute at the Normal School at Ypsilanti, MI. Free Press Book and Job Office.

Davis, C. G., Lehman, D. R., & Wortman, C. B. (1997). *Finding meaning in loss and trauma: Making sense of the literature.* Unpublished manuscript, University of Michigan.

Davis, C. G., Wortman, C. B., Lehman, D. R., & Silver, R. C. (2000). Searching for meaning in loss: Are clinical assumptions correct? *Death Studies, 24,* 497–540.

Davis, J. (1997). *Mapping the mind: The secrets of the human brain and how it works.* Secaucus, NJ: Birch Lane Press.

Dawson, G., Frey, K., Panagiotides, H., Yamada, E., Hessl, D., & Osterling, J. (1999). Infants of depressed mothers exhibit atypical frontal electrical brain activity during interactions with mother and with a familiar, non-depressed adult. *Child Development, 70,* 1058–1066.

Dawson, G., Hessl, D., & Frey, K (1994). Social influences on early developing biological and behavioral systems related to risk for affective disorder. *Development and Psychopathology, 6,* 759–779.

Day, R. D. (1992). The transition to first intercourse among racially and culturally diverse youth. *Journal of Marriage and the Family, 54,* 749–762.

DeAngelis, T. (1997). Chromosomes contain clues on schizophrenia. *APA Monitor, 28,* 26.

Deater-Deckard, K., & Dodge, K. A. (1997). Externalizing behavior problems and discipline revisited: Nonlinear effects and variation by culture, context, and gender. *Psychological Inquiry, 8,* 161–175.

Deater-Deckard, K., Dodge, K. A., Bates, J. E., & Pettit, G. S. (1996). Physical discipline among African American and European American mothers: Links to children's externalizing behaviors. *Developmental Psychology, 32,* 1065–1072.

Deaux, K. (1993). Commentary: Sorry, wrong number: A reply to Gentile's call. Sex or gender? [Special section]. *Psychological Science, 4,* 125–126.

DeCasper, A. J., & Fifer, W. P. (1980). Of human bonding: Newborns prefer their mothers' voices. *Science, 208,* 1174–1176.

DeCasper, A. J., Lecanuet, J., Busnel, M., Granier-Deferre, C., & Maugeais, R. (1994). Fetal reactions to recurrent maternal speech. *Infant Behavior and Development, 17,* 159–164.

DeCasper, A. J., & Prescott, P. A. (1984). Human newborns' perception of male voices: Preference, discrimination, and reinforcing value. *Developmental Psychobiology, 17,* 481–491.

DeCasper, A. J., & Spence, M. J. (1986). Newborns prefer a familiar story over an unfamiliar one. *Infant Behavior and Development, 9,* 133–150.

de Castro, B. O., Veerman, J. W., Koops, W., Bosche, J. D., & Monshouwer, H. J. (2002). Hostile attribution, intent, and aggressive behavior: A meta-analysis. *Child Development, 73,* 916–934.

DeCatanzaro, D. A. (1999). *Motivation and emotion: Evolutionary, physiological, developmental, and social perspectives.* Upper Saddle River, NJ: Prentice Hall.

Deci, E. L., Ryan, R. M., Gagne, M., Leone, D.R., Usunov, J., & Kornazheva, B. P. (2001). Need satisfaction, motivation, and well-being in work organizations of a former Eastern Bloc country: A cross-cultural study of self-determination. *Personality and Social Psychology Bulletin, 27,* 930–942.

Decker, P. J., & Borgen, F. H. (1993). Dimensions of work appraisal: Stress, strain, coping, job satisfaction, and negative affectivity. *Journal of Counseling Psychology, 40,* 470–478.

Deiner, E. (2000). Subjective well-being: The science of happiness, and a proposal for a national index. *American Psychologist, 55,* 34–43.

Deiner, E., Oishi, S., & Lucas, R. E. Personality, culture, and subjective well-being: Emotional and cognitive evaluations of life. *Annual Review of Psychology, 54,* 403–425.

de la Torre, J. C. (1997). Cerebrovascular changes in the aging brain. In P. S. Timiras, E. E. Bittar (Series Eds.), M. P. Mattson, & J. W. Geddes (Guest Eds.), *Advances in cell aging and gerontology* (Vol. 2, pp. 77–107). Greenwich, CT: JAI Press.

DeLisi, R., & Gallagher, A. M. (1991). Understanding of gender stability and constancy in Argentinean children. *Merrill-Palmer Quarterly, 37,* 483–502.

Dellas, M., & Jernigan, L. P. (1987). Affective personality characteristics associated with undergraduate ego identity formation. *Journal of Adolescent Research, 3,* 306–324.

DeLoache, J. S. (1987). Rapid change in the symbolic functioning of very young children. *Science, 238,* 1556–1557.

DeLoache, J. S. (1999, April). *Becoming symbol minded.* Paper presented at the biennial meetings of the Society for Research in Child Development, Albuquerque, NM.

DeLoache, J. S., Miller, K. F., & Pierroutsakos, S. L. (1998). Reasoning and problem solving. In W. Damon (Series Ed.), D. Kuhn, & R. S. Siegler (Vol. Eds.), *Handbook of child psychology: Vol. 2. Cognition, perception, and language* (5th ed., pp. 801–850). New York: Wiley.

DeLoache, J. S., Miller, K. F., & Rosengren, K. (1997). The credible shrinking room: Very young children's performance in symbolic and non-symbolic tasks. *Psychological Science, 8,* 308–313.

Dempster, F. N. (1981). Memory span: Sources of individual and developmental differences. *Psychological Bulletin, 89,* 63–100.

Denham, S. A., & Holt, R. W. (1993). Preschoolers' likability as cause or consequence of their social behavior. *Developmental Psychology, 29,* 271–275.

Derryberry, D., & Reed, M. A. (1994). Temperament and attention: Orienting toward and away from positive and negative signals. *Journal of Personality and Social Psychology, 66,* 1128–1139.

de St. Aubin, E., & McAdams, D. P. (1995). The relations of generative concern and generative action to personality traits, satisfaction/happiness with life, and ego development. *Journal of Adult Development, 2,* 99–112.

Dettling, A. C., Gunnar, M. R., & Donzella, B. (1999). Cortisol levels of young children in full-day child care centers: Relations with age and temperament. *Psychoneuroendocrinology, 24,* 519–536.

Dettling, A. C., Parker, S., Lane, S. K., Sebanc, A. M., & Gunnar, M. R. (2000). Quality of care and temperament determine whether cortisol levels rise over the day for children in full-day childcare. *Psychoneuroendocrinology, 25,* 819–836.

Deutch, H. (1937). Absence of grief. *Psychoanalytic Quarterly, 6,* 12–22.

Developmental Studies Center. (1996). *Child development project.* Oakland, CA: Author.

Dewey, J. (1933/1998). *How we think: A restatement of the relation of reflective thinking to the educative process.* Boston: Houghton Mifflin.

de Wolf, M. S., & van IJzendoorn, M. H. (1997). Sensitivity and attachment: A meta-analysis on parental antecedents of infant attachment. *Child Development, 68,* 571–591.

Dey, E. L., & Hurtado, S. (1999). Students, colleges, and society: Considering the interconnections. In P. G. Altbach, R. O. Berndahl, & P. J. Gumport (Eds.), *American higher education in the twenty-first century: Social, political, and economic challenges* (pp. 298–322). Baltimore: Johns Hopkins University Press.

Diamond, A. (2000). Close interrelation of motor development and cognitive development and of the cerebellum and prefrontal cortex. *Child Development, 71,* 44–56.

Diamond, G. S. (1998, August). *Anatomy of a family-based model for treating adolescent depression.* Paper presented at the American Psychological Association Convention, San Francisco.

Diamond, G. S., & Diamond, G. M. (2002). Studying a matrix of change mechanisms: An agenda for family-based process research. In H. A. Liddle, D. A. Santisteban, R. F. Levant, & J. H. Bray (Eds.), *Family psychology: Science-based interventions* (pp. 41–66). Washington, DC: American Psychological Association.

Diamond, G., Siqueland, L., & Diamond, G. M. (2003). Attachment-based family therapy for depressed adolescents: Programmatic treatment

development. *Clinical Child and Family Psychology Review, 6*(2), 107–127.

Diamond, J. (1986). I want a girl, just like the girl . . . *Discover, 7,* 65–68.

Diamond, L. M. (1998). Development of sexual orientation among adolescent and young adult women. *Developmental Psychology, 34,* 1085–1095.

Diamond, L. M. & Savin-Williams, R. C. (2003). Gender and sexual identity. In I. B. Weiner (Series Ed.), R. M. Lerner, F. Jacobs, & D. Wertlieb (Vol. Eds.), *Handbook of applied developmental science: Vol. 1. Applying developmental science for youth and families: Historical and theoretical foundations* (pp. 101–121). Thousand Oaks, CA: Sage.

Diamond, M., & Sigmundson, K. (1997). Sex reassignment at birth: Long-term review and clinical implications. *Archives of Pediatric Adolescent Medicine, 151,* 298–304.

Dick, D. M., & Rose, R. J. (2002). Behavior genetics: What's new? What's next? *Current Directions in Psychological Science, 11,* 70–74.

Dickinson, E. (1960). *The complete works of Emily Dickinson.* Little Brown Publishers.

Dickson, D. W. (1997). Structural changes in the aged brain. In P. S. Timiras, E. E. Bittar (Series Eds.), M. P. Mattson, & J. W. Geddes (Guest Eds.), *Advances in cell aging and gerontology* (Vol. 2, pp. 51–76). Greenwich, CT: JAI Press.

Diener, E., & Emmons, R. A. (1985). The independence of positive and negative affect. *Journal of Personality and Social Psychology, 47,* 71–75.

Diener, E., Sandvik, E., Seidlitz, L., & Diener, M. (1993). The relationship between income and subjective well-being: Relative or absolute? *Social Indicators Research, 28,* 195–223.

Diener, E., & Seligman, M. E. P. (2002). Very happy people. *Psychological Science, 13,* 80–83.

Diener, E., & Seligman, M. E. P. (2004). Beyond money: Toward an economy of well-being. *Psychological Science in the Public Interest, 5,* 1–31.

Dinardo, Q. (1971). *Psychological adjustment to spinal cord injury.* Unpublished doctoral dissertation, University of Houston, Houston, TX.

Dion, K. K., Berscheid, E., & Walster, E. (1972). What is beautiful is good. *Journal of Personality and Social Psychology, 24,* 285–290.

Dittman, M. (2004). A new face to retirement. *Monitor on Psychology, 35,* 78–79.

Dix, T. (1991). The affective organization of parenting: Adaptive and maladaptive processes. *Psychological Bulletin, 110,* 3–25.

Dix, T., Gershoff, E. T., Maunier, L. N., & Miller, P. C. (2004). The affective structure of supportive parenting: Depressive symptoms, immediate emotions, and child-oriented motivation. *Developmental Psychology, 40,* 1212–1227.

Dixon, J. A., & Moore, C. F. (1990). The development of perspective taking: Understanding differences in information and weighting. *Child Development, 61,* 1502–1513.

Dodge, K. A. (1983). Behavioral antecedents of peer social status. *Child Development, 54,* 1386–1399.

Dodge, K. A., Bates, J. E., & Petit, G. S. (1990). Mechanisms in the cycle of violence. *Science, 250,* 1678–1683.

Dodge, K. A., Coie, J. D., Pettit, G. S., & Price, J. M. (1990). Peer status and aggression in boys' groups: Developmental and contextual analyses. *Child Development, 61,* 1289–1309.

Dodge, K. A., Pettit, J. M., McClaskey, C. L., & Brown, M. M. (1986). Social competence in children. *Monographs of the Society for Research in Child Development, 51,* 1–80.

Dodge, K. A., Schlundt, D. G., Schocken, I., & Delugach, J. D. (1983). Social competence and children's social status: The role of peer group entry strategies. *Merrill-Palmer Quarterly, 29,* 309–336.

Dohrenwend, B. S., & Dohrenwend, B. P. (1974). Overview and prospects for research on stressful

life events. In B. S. Dohrenwend & B. P. Dohrenwend (Eds.), *Stressful life events: Their nature and effects* (pp. 313–331). New York: Wiley.

Dollahite, D. C. (1998). Fathering, faith, and spirituality. *Journal of Men's Studies, 7,* 3–15.

Donovan, W. L., Leavitt, L. A., & Walsh, R. (1990). Maternal self-efficacy: Illusory control and its effect on susceptibility to learned helplessness. *Child Development, 61,* 1638–1647.

Dornbusch, S. M., Ritter, P. L., Leiderman, P. H., Roberts, D. F., & Fraleigh, M. J. (1987). The relation of parenting style to adolescent school performance. *Child Development, 58,* 1244–1257.

Douvan, E., & Adelson, J. (1966). *The adolescent experience.* New York: Wiley.

Dozier, M., Cue, K., & Barnett, L. (1994). Clinicians as caregivers: Role of attachment organization in treatment. *Journal of Consulting and Clinical Psychology, 62,* 793–800.

Dozier, M., & Kobak, R. R. (1992). Psychophysiology in attachment interviews: Converging evidence for deactivating strategies. *Child Development, 63,* 1473–1480.

Dozier, M., Stovall, K. C., & Albus, K. E. (1999). Attachment and psychopathology in adulthood. In J. Cassidy & P. R. Shaver (Eds.), *Handbook of attachment: Theory, research, and clinical applications* (pp. 497–519). New York: Guilford Press.

Dozier, M., & Tyrell, C. (1998). The role of attachment in therapeutic relationships. In J. A. Simpson & W. S. Rholes (Eds.), *Attachment theory and close relationships* (pp. 221–248). New York: Guilford Press.

Driver, J. L., & Gottman, J. M. (2004). Daily marital interactions and positive affect during marital conflict among newlywed couples. *Family Process, 43,* 301–304.

Drizin, S. A. (2003). Research on juvenile competency: A defender's perspective. *Social Policy Report, 17*(4), 8–9.

Dryfoos, J. G. (1990). *Adolescents at risk: Prevalence and prevention.* New York: Oxford University Press.

Dryfoos, J. G. (1997). The prevalence of problem behaviors: Implications for programs. In R. P. Weissberg, T. P. Gullotta, R. L. Hampton, B. A. Ryan, & G. R. Adams (Eds.), *Enhancing children's wellness* (Vol. 8, pp. 17–46). Thousand Oaks, CA: Sage.

Dunkle, M. F., Schraw, G., & Bendixen, L. (1993, April). *The relationship between epistemological beliefs, causal attributions, and reflective judgement.* Paper presented at the Annual Meeting of the American Educational Research Association, Atlanta, GA.

Dunlap, D. W. (1994, October 18). Gay survey raises a new question. *The New York Times,* p. B8.

Dunn, J., Bretherton, I., & Munn, P. (1987). Conversations about feeling states between mothers and their young children. *Developmental Psychology, 23,* 132–139.

Dunn, S., & Morgan, V. (1987). Nursery and infant school play patterns: Sex-related differences. *British Educational Research Journal, 13,* 271–281.

Dunphy, D. C. (1963). The social structure of urban adolescent peer groups. *Sociometry, 26,* 230–246.

DuPont, R. L. (1997). *The selfish brain: Learning from addiction.* Washington, DC: American Psychiatric Press.

Duran, R. T., & Gauvain, M. (1993). The role of age versus expertise in peer collaboration during joint planning. *Journal of Experimental Child Psychology, 55,* 227–242.

Duvall, E. M. (1971). *Family Development* (4th ed.). Philadelphia: J. B. Lippincott.

Dweck, C. S. (1999). *Self-theories: Their role in motivation, personality, and development.* Philadelphia: Taylor & Francis.

D'Zurilla, T. J. (1986). *Problem-solving therapy: A social competence approach to clinical intervention.* New York: Springer.

D'Zurilla, T. J. (1988). Problem-solving therapies. In K. S. Dobson (Ed.), *Handbook of cognitive-behavioral therapies* (pp. 85–135). New York: Guilford Press.

Eagly, A. H., & Johannesen-Schmidt, M. C. (2001). The leadership styles of women and men. *Journal of Social Issues, 57,* 781–797.

Eagly, A. H., & Johnson, B. T. (1990). Gender and leadership style: A meta-analysis. *Psychological Bulletin, 108,* 233–256.

Eagly, A. H., Makhijani, M. G., & Klonsky, B. G. (1992). Gender and the evaluation of leaders: A meta-analysis. *Psychological Bulletin, 117,* 125–145.

Easterbrooks, M. A., & Goldberg, W. A. (1990). Security of toddler-parent attachment: Relation to children's sociopersonality functioning during kindergarten. In M. T. Greenberg, D. Cicchetti, & E. M. Cumings (Eds.), *Attachment in the preschool years* (pp. 221–244). Chicago: University of Chicago Press.

Eaton, W. O., & Enns, L. R. (1986). Sex differences in human motor activity level. *Psychological Bulletin, 100,* 19–28.

Eccles, J., Midgley, C., & Adler, T. (1984). Grade-related changes in the school environment: Effects on achievement motivation. In J. J. Nicholls (Ed.), *Advances in motivation and achievement* (Vol. 3, pp. 283–331). Greenwich, CT: JAI Press.

Eccles, J. S., & Barber, B. L. (1999). Student council, volunteering, basketball, or marching band: What kind of extracurricular involvement matters? *Journal of Adolescent Research, 14,* 10–43.

Eccles, J. S., Midgley, C., Wigfield, A., Buchanan, C. M., Reuman, D., Flanagan, C., et al. (1993). Development during adolescence: The impact of stage-environment fit on young adolescents' experiences in schools and in families. *American Psychologist, 48,* 90–101.

Eckert, P. (1989). *Jocks and burnouts: Social categories and identity in the high school.* New York: Teachers College Press.

Eder, D., & Sanford, S. (1986). The development and maintenance of interactional norms among early adolescents. *Sociological Studies of Child Development, 1,* 283–300.

Egan, G. (1975). *The skilled helper: A model for systemic helping and interpersonal relating.* Monterey, CA: Brooks/Cole.

Egan, S. K., & Perry, D. G. (2001). Gender identity: A multidimensional analysis with implications for psychosocial adjustment. *Developmental Psychology, 37,* 451–463.

Eisenberg, N., Cialdini, R., McCreath, H., & Shell, R. (1987). Consistency-based compliance: When and why do children become vulnerable? *Journal of Personality and Social Psychology, 52,* 1174–1181.

Eisenberg, N., & Fabes, R. A. (1992). Emotion, regulation, and the development of social competence. In M. S. Clark (Ed.), *Review of personality and social psychology* (Vol. 12, pp. 34–61). Newbury Park, CA: Sage.

Eisenberg, N., & Fabes, R. A. (1998). Prosocial development. In W. Damon (Ed.) & N. Eisenberg (Vol. Ed.), *Handbook of child psychology: Vol. 3. Social, emotional, and personality development* (5th ed., pp. 701–778). New York: Wiley.

Eisenberg, N., Fabes, R. A., Karbon, M., Murphy, B. C., Wosinski, M., Polazzi, L., et al. (1996). The relations of children's dispositional prosocial behavior to emotionality, regulation, and social functioning. *Child Development, 67,* 974–992.

Eisenberg, N., Lennon, R., & Roth, K. (1983). Prosocial development: A longitudinal study. *Developmental Psychology, 19,* 846–855.

Eisenberg, N., Pasternack, J. F., Cameron, E., & Tryon, K. (1984). The relation of quality and mode of prosocial behavior to moral cognitions

and social style. *Child Development, 155,* 1479–1485.

Eisenberg, N., Shell, R., Pasternack, J., Lennon, R., Beller, R., & Mathy, R. M. (1987). Prosocial development in middle childhood: A longitudinal study. *Developmental Psychology, 24,* 712–718.

Eisenberg, N., Zhou, Q., & Koller, S. (2001). Brazilian adolescents' prosocial moral judgment and behavior: Relations to sympathy, perspective taking, gender-role orientation, and demographic characteristics. *Child Development, 72,* 518–534.

Ekman, P. (1992). Are there basic emotions? *Psychological Review, 99,* 550–553.

Ekman, P. (1994). Strong evidence for universals in facial expression: A reply to Russell's mistaken critique. *Psychological Bulletin, 115,* 268–276.

Ekman, P., & Friesen, W. V. (1969). The repertoire of nonverbal behavior: Categories, origins, uses, and coding. *Semiotica, 1,* 49–98.

Ekman, P., & Friesen, W. V. (1971). Constants across cultures in the face and emotion. *Journal of Personality and Social Psychology, 17,* 124–129.

Ekman, P., & Oster, H. (1979). Facial expression of emotion. *Annual Review of Psychology, 30,* 527–554.

Elder, G. (1974). *Children of the Great Depression.* Chicago: University of Chicago Press.

Elder, G. H., Jr. (1994). Time, human agency, and social change: Perspectives on the life course. *Social Psychology Quarterly, 57,* 4–15.

Eliason, M. J. (1996). Identity formation for lesbian, bisexual and gay persons: Beyond a "minoritizing" view. *Journal of Homosexuality, 30,* 31–58.

Elkind, D. (1967). Egocentrism in adolescence. *Child Development, 38,* 1025–1031.

Elkind, D. (1968, May 26). Giant in the nursery—Jean Piaget. *The New York Times Magazine.*

Elkind, D. (1981). *Children and adolescents.* New York: Oxford University Press.

Elkind, D. (1984). *All grown up and no place to go: Teenagers in crisis.* Reading, MA: Addison-Wesley.

Elkind, D. (1994). *Ties that stress: The new family imbalance.* Cambridge, MA: Harvard University Press.

Ellis, B. J. (2004). Timing of pubertal maturation in girls: An integrated life history approach. *Phychological Bulletin, 130,* 920–958.

Ellis, L., Burke, D., & Ames, M. A. (1987). Sexual orientation as a continuous variable: A comparison between the sexes. *Archives of Sexual Behavior, 16,* 523–529.

Ellis, S., Klahr, D., & Siegler, R. S. (1993, March). *Effects of feedback and collaboration on changes in children's use of mathematical rules.* Paper presented at the meeting of the Society for Research in Child Development, New Orleans, LA.

Ellis, S., & Rogoff, B. (1986). Problem solving inchildren's management of instruction. In E. Mueller & C. Cooper (Eds.), *Process and outcome in peer relationships* (pp. 301–325). Orlando, FL: Academic.

Ellison, C. G., (1991). Religious involvement and subjective well-being. *Journal of Health and Social Behavior, 32,* 80–99.

Emanuel, E., & Emanuel, L. (1998). The promise of a good death. *The Lancet, 251,* 21–29.

Emde, R. N., Biringen, Z., Clyman, R. B., & Oppenheim, D. (1991). The moral self of infancy: Affective core and procedural knowledge. *Developmental Review, 11,* 251–270.

Emde, R. N., & Buchsbaum, H. (1990). "Didn't you hear my mommy?" Autonomy with connectedness in moral self-emergence. In D. Cicchetti & M. Beeghly (Eds.), *The self in transition: Infancy to adulthood* (pp. 35–60). Chicago: University of Chicago Press.

Emde, R. N., Johnson, W., & Easterbrooks, M. (1987). The do's and don'ts of early moral development: Psychoanalytic tradition and current research. In J. Kagan & S. Lamb (Eds.),

The emergence of morality in young children (pp. 245–276). Chicago: University of Chicago Press.

Emmons, R. A., & Paloutzian, R. F. (2003). The psychology of religion. *Annual Review of Psychology, 54,* 377–402.

Ennett, S. T., & Bauman, K. E. (1994). The contribution of influence and selection to adolescent peer group homogeneity: The case of adolescent cigarette smoking. *Journal of Personality and Social Psychology, 67,* 653–663.

Enns, C. Z. (1992). Toward integrating feminist psychotherapy and feminist philosophy. *Professional Psychology: Research and Practice, 23,* 453–466.

Enright, D. R., Lapsley, D. K., Harris, D. J., & Shawver, D. J. (1983). Moral development interventions in early adolescence. *Theory into Practice, 22,* 134–145.

Enright, R. D., & Fitzgibbons, R. P. (2002). *Helping clients forgive: An empirical guide for resolving anger and restoring hope.* Washington, DC: American Psychological Association.

Entwisle, D. R. (1990). Schools and the adolescent. In S. S. Feldman & G. R. Elliott (Eds.), *At the threshold: The developing adolescent* (pp. 197–224). Cambridge, MA: Harvard University Press.

Erber, J. T., & Prager, I. G. (1999). Age and memory: Perceptions of forgetful young and older adults. In T. M. Hess & F. Blanchard-Fields (Eds.), *Social cognition and aging* (pp. 197–217). San Diego, CA: Academic Press.

Erhardt, A. A., & Baker, S. W. (1974). Fetal androgens, human central nervous system, differentiation, and behavior sex differences. In R. C. Friedman, R. M. Richart, & R. L. Van de Wiele (Eds.), *Sex differences in behavior* (pp. 33–51). New York: Wiley.

Erhardt, A. A., Epstein, R., & Money, J. (1968). Fetal androgens and female gender identity in the early-treated adrenogenital syndrome. *Johns Hopkins Medical Journal, 122,* 160–167.

Erickson, M. F., Sroufe, L. A., & Egeland, B. (1985). The relationship between quality of attachment and behavior problems in preschool in a high-risk sample. In I. Bretherton & E. Waters (Eds.), Growing points of attachment theory and research. *Monographs of the Society for Research in Child Development, 50* (Serial No. 209), 147–166.

Erikson, E. (1975). The problem of ego identity. In A. H. Asman (Ed.), *The psychology of adolescence: Essential readings* (pp. 318–346). New York: International Universities Press.

Erikson, E. H. (1950/1963). Childhood and society (2nd ed.). New York: Norton.

Erikson, E. H. (1968). *Identity, youth, and crisis.* New York: Norton.

Erwin, P. (1985). Similarity of attitudes and constructs in children's friendships. *Journal of Experimental Child Psychology, 40,* 470–485.

Etzioni, A. (1998, February). How not to discuss character education. *Phi Delta Kappan, 79,* 446–448.

Evans, G. W. (2004). The environment of childhood poverty. *American Psychologist, 59,* 77–92.

Ewens, J., & Herrington, P. (1983). *Hospice.* Santa Fe, NM: Bear & Co.

Eysenck, H. J., & Schoenthaler, S. J. (1997). Raising IQ level by vitamin and mineral supplementation. In R. J. Steinberg & E. Grigorenko (Eds.), *Intelligence, heredity, and environment* (pp. 362–393). Cambridge, England: Cambridge University Press.

Ezzo, G., & Bucknam, R. (1995). *On becoming babywise: Vol. 2: Parenting your pretoddler.* Sisters, OR: Multnomah Books.

Ezzo, G., & Bucknam, R. (1999). *On becoming childwise: Parenting your child from three to seven years.* Sisters, OR: Multnomah Books.

Fabes, R. A., Martin, C. L., & Hanish, L. D. (2003). Young children's play qualities in same-, other-, and mixed-sex peer groups. *Child Development, 74,* 921–932.

Fagan, J. F. (1990). The paired-comparison paradigm and infant intelligence. In A. Diamond (Ed.), The developmental and neural bases of higher cognitive functions. *Annals of the New York Academy of Sciences, 608,* 337–364.

Fagot, B. I. (1984). The consequences of problem behavior in toddler children. *Journal of Abnormal Child Psychology, 12,* 385–397.

Fagot, B. I. (1985). Changes in thinking about early sex-role development. *Developmental Review, 5,* 83–98.

Fagot, B. I., & Leinbach, M. D. (1989). The young child's gender schema: Environmental input, internal organization. *Child Development, 60,* 663–672.

Farrington, D. P. (1989). Self-reported and official offending from adolescence to adulthood. In M. W. Klein (Ed.), *Cross-national research in self-reported crime and delinquency.* Boston: Kluwer Academic.

Fataldi, M., Petraglia, F., Luisi, S., Bernardi, F., Casarosa, F., Ferrari, F., Luisi, M., Saggese, G., Genazzani, A. R., & Bernasconi, S. (1999). Changes of serum allopregnanolone levels in the first 2 years of life and during pubertal development. *Pediatric Research, 46,* 323–327.

Faust, M. S. (1983). Alternative constructions of adolescence and growth. In J. Brooks-Gunn & A. C. Petersen (Eds.), *Girls at puberty: Biological, psychological, and social perspectives* (pp. 105–125). New York: Plenum Press.

Fausto-Sterling, A. (2000). *Sexing the body: Gender politics and the construction of sexuality.* New York: Basic Books.

Feagans, L., & Farran, D. C. (1981). How demonstrated comprehension can get muddled in production. *Developmental Psychology, 17,* 718–727.

Feeney, J., Peterson, C., & Noller, P. (1994). Equity and marital satisfaction over the family life cycle. *Personality Relationships, 1,* 83–99.

Feingold, A. (1988). Cognitive gender differences are disappearing. *American Psychologist, 43,* 95–103.

Feinman, S., & Entwhistle, D. R. (1976). Children's ability to recognize other children's faces. *Child Development, 47,* 506–510.

Feldlaufer, H., Midgley, C., & Eccles, J. S. (1988). Student, teacher, and observer perceptions of the classroom environment before and after the transition to junior high school. *Journal of Early Adolescence, 8,* 133–156.

Feldman, J., & Kazdin, A. E. (1995). Parent management training for oppositional and conduct problem children. *The Clinical Psychologist, 48*(4), 3–5.

Fenson, L., Dale, P. S., Reznick, J. S., Bates, E., Thal, D. J., Pethick, S. J. (1994). Variability in early communicative development. *Monographs of the Society for Research in Child Development, 59*(5, Serial No. 242).

Feschbach, N. D., & Feschbach, S. (1982). Empathy training and the regulation of aggression: Potentialities and limitations. *Academic Psychology Bulletin, 4,* 399–413.

Festinger, L. (1954). A theory of social comparison. *Human Relations, 7,* 117–140.

Field, T. (1989). Maternal depression effects on infant interaction and attachment behavior. In D. Cicchetti (Ed.), *Rochester Symposium on Developmental Psychology: Vol. 1. The emergence of a discipline* (pp. 139–163). Rochester, NY: University of Rochester Press.

Field, T., Fox, N., Pickens, J., & Nawrocki, T. (1995). Relative right frontal activation in 3- to 6-month-old infants of depressed mothers. *Developmental Psychology, 31,* 358–363.

Field, T., Hernandez-Reif, M., & Freedman, J. (2004). Stimulation programs for preterm infants. *SRCD Social Policy Report, 18*(1), 1–19.

Field, T., Scafidi, F., & Schanberg, S. (1987). Massage of preterm infants to improve growth and development. *Pediatric Nursing, 13,* 385–387.

Field, T., Schanberg, S. M., Scafidi, F., Bauer, C. R., Vega-Lahr, N., Garcia, R., et al. (1986). Tactile/kinesthetic stimulation effects on preterm neonates. *Pediatrics, 77,* 654–658.

Field, T. M., Healy, B., Goldstein, S., Perry, S., Bendell, D., Schnanberg, S., et al. (1988). Infants of depressed mothers show "depressed" behavior even with nondepressed adults. *Child Development, 59,* 1569–1579.

Finch, A. J., Nelson, W. M., & Ott, E. S. (1993). *Cognitive-behavioral procedures with children and adolescents.* Boston: Allyn & Bacon.

Fine, G. A., Mortimer, J. T., & Roberts, D. F. (1990). Leisure, work, and the mass media. In S. S. Feldman & G. R. Elliott (Eds.), *At the threshold: The developing adolescent* (pp. 225–253). Cambridge, MA: Harvard University Press.

Fingerman, K. L. (1996). Sources of tension in the aging mother and adult daughter relationship. *Psychology and Aging, 11,* 591–606.

Fingerman, K. L. (1997). Being more than a daughter: Middle-aged women's conceptions of their mothers. *Journal of Women and Aging, 9,* 55–72.

Fingerman, K. L. (2003). *Mothers and their adult daughters: Mixed emotions, enduring bonds.* Amherst, NY: Prometheus Books.

Finn, S. E. (1986). Stability of personality self-ratings over 30 years: Evidence for an age-cohort interaction. *Journal of Personality and Social Psychology, 50,* 813–818.

Fischer, K. (1987). Relations between brain and cognitive development. *Child Development, 58,* 623–632.

Fischer, K. W. (1980). A theory of cognitive development: The control and construction of hierarchies of skills. *Psychological Review, 87,* 477–531.

Fischer, K. W., Hand, H. H., Watson, M. W., Van Parys, M., & Tucker, J. (1984). Putting the child into socialization: The development of social categories in preschool children. In L. Katz (Ed.), *Current topics in early childhood education* (Vol. 5, pp. 27–72). Norwood, NJ: Ablex.

Fisher, C. B., & Lerner, R. M. (1994). *Applied developmental psychology.* New York: McGraw-Hill.

Fiske, S. T., & Taylor, S. E. (1991). *Social cognition* (2nd ed.). New York: McGraw-Hill.

Fitzgerald, J. M. (1988). Vivid memories and the reminiscence phenomenon: The role of a self narrative. *Human Development, 31,* 261–273.

Fitzgerald, J. M. (1992). Autobiographical memory and conceptualizations of the self. In M. A. Conway, D. C. Rubin, H. Spinnler, & W. A. Wagenaar (Eds.), *Theoretical perspectives on autobiographical memory* (pp. 99–114). Boston: Kluwer Academic Press.

Fitzgerald, J. M. (1999). Autobiographical memory and social cognition: Development of the remembered self in adulthood. In T. M. Hess & F. Blanchard-Fields (Eds.), *Social cognition and aging* (pp. 145–171). San Diego, CA: Academic Press.

Fivush, R., & Vesuveda, A. (2002). Remembering to relate socioemotional correlates of mother-child reminiscing. *Journal of Cognition and Development, 3,* 73–90.

Flannery, K. A., & Watson, M. W. (1993). Are individual differences in fantasy play related to peer acceptance levels? *Journal of Genetic Psychology, 154,* 407–416.

Flavell, J. H. (1963). *The developmental psychology of Jean Piaget.* New York: Van Nostrand.

Flavell, J. H., Botkin, P., Fry, C. L., Wright, J. & Jarvis, P. (1968). *The development of role-taking and communication skills in children.* New York: Wiley.

Flavell, J. H., Friedrichs, A. G., & Hoyt, J. D. (1970). Developmental changes in memorization processes. *Cognitive Psychology, 1,* 324–340.

Flavell, J. H., & Miller, P. H. (1998). Social cognition. In W. Damon (Series Ed.), D. Kuhn, & R. S. Siegler (Vol. Eds.), *Handbook of child psychology: Vol. 2. Cognition, perception, and language* (5th ed., pp. 851–898). New York: Wiley.

Flavell, J. H., Miller, P. H., & Miller, S. A. (1993). *Cognitive development* (3rd ed) Upper Saddle River, NJ: Prentice Hall.

Flavell, J. H., Mumme, D. L., Green, F. L., & Flavell, E. R. (1992). Young children's understanding of different types of beliefs. *Child Development, 63,* 960–977.

Flavell, J. II., Flavell, E. R., & Green, F. L. (1987). Young children's knowledge about the apparent-real and pretend-real distinctions. *Developmental Psychology, 23,* 816–822.

Fleming, A. S., Ruble, D. L., Flett, G. L., & Schaul, D. L. (1988). Postpartum adjustment in first-time mothers: Relations between mood, maternal attitudes, and mother-infant interactions. *Developmental Psychology, 24,* 71–81.

Fletcher, A. C., Darling, N. E., Steinberg, L., & Dornbusch, S. M. (1995). The company they keep: Relationships of adolescents' adjustment and behavior to their friends' perceptions of authoritative parenting in the social network. *Developmental Psychology, 31,* 300–310.

Fletcher, A. C., Steinberg, L., & Williams-Wheeler, M. (2004). Parental influences on adolescent problem behavior: Revisiting Stattin and Kerr. *Child Development 75,* 781–796.

Flett, G. L., Hewitt, P. L., Davis, R. A., & Sherry, S. B. (2004). Description and counseling of the perfectionistic procrastinator. In H. C. Schouwenburg, C. H. Lay, T. A. Pychyl, & J. R. Ferrari (Eds.), *Counseling the procrastinator in academic settings* (pp. 181–194). Washington, DC: American Psychological Association.

Foley, M. A., Harris, J., & Hermann, S. (1994). Developmental comparison of the ability to discriminate between memories for symbolic play enactment. *Developmental Psychology, 30,* 206–217.

Folkman, S., Lazarus, R. S., Gruen, R. J., & DeLongis, A. (1986). Appraisal, coping, health status, and psychological symptoms. *Journal of Personality and Social Psychology, 50,* 571–579.

Fordham, S., & Ogbu, J. U. (1986). Black students' school success: Coping with the burden of "acting white." *Urban Review, 18,* 176–206.

Fouad, N. A. (2004). Cross-cultural differences in vocational interests: Between-groups differences on the strong interest inventory. *Journal of Counseling Psychology, 49,* 283–289.

Fowler, J. W. (1981). *Stages of faith: The psychology of human development and the quest for meaning.* San Francisco: Harper & Row.

Fox, N. A., Kimmerly, N. L., & Schafer, W. D. (1991). Attachment to mother/attachment to father: A meta-analysis. *Child Development, 62,* 210–225.

Fraley, R. C., Davis, K. E., & Shaver, P. R. (1998). Dismissing-avoidance and the defensive organization of emotion, cognition, and behavior. In J. A. Simpson & W. S. Rholes (Eds.), *Attachment theory and close relationships* (pp. 249–279). New York: Guilford Press.

Fraley, R. C., & Shaver, P. R. (1999). Loss and bereavement: Attachment theory and recent controversies concerning "grief work" and the nature of detachment. In J. Cassidy & P. R. Shaver (Eds.), *Handbook of attachment: Theory, research and clinical applications* (pp. 735–759). New York: Guilford Press.

Fraley, R. C., & Waller, N. G. (1998). Adult attachment patterns: A test of the typological model. In J. A. Simpson & W. S. Rholes (Eds.), *Attachment theory and close relationships* (pp. 77–114). New York: Guilford Press.

Frankenberger, K. D. (2000). Adolescent egocentrism: A comparison among adolescents and adults. *Journal of Adolescence, 23,* 343–347.

Fredrickson, B. L., & Carstensen, L. L. (1990). Choosing social partners: How old age and anticipated endings make us more selective. *Psychology and Aging, 5,* 335–347.

Freedy, J. R., Saladin, M. E., Kilpatrick, D. G., Resnick, H. S., & Saunders, B. E. (1994). Understanding acute psychological distress following natural disaster. *Journal of Traumatic Stress, 7,* 257–273.

Freud, A. (1958). Child observation and prediction of development. *The Psychoanalytic Study of the Child, 13,* 92–116.

Freud, S. (1905/1989). Three essays on the theory of sexuality. In P. Gay (Ed.), *The Freud reader.* New York: Norton.

Freud, S. (1917/1957). Mourning and melancholia. In J. Strachey (Ed.), *Standard edition of the complete works of Sigmund Freud.* London: Hogarth Press.

Freud, S. (1929/1961). To Ludwig Binswanger [Letter]. In E. L. Freud (Ed.), *Letters of Sigmund Freud 1873–1939* (T. & J. Stern, Trans.). London: Hogarth Press.

Freud, S. (1930/1989). Civilization and its discontents. In P. Gay (Ed.), *The Freud reader* (pp. 722–772). New York: Norton.

Freud, S. (1935/1960). *A general introduction to psychoanalysis.* New York: Washington Square Press.

Freud, S. (1949/1969). *An outline of psychoanalysis.* New York: Norton.

Freud, S. (1956). *Delusion and dream: An interpretation in the light of psychoanalysis of Gravida, a novel, by Wilhelm Jensen.* Boston: Beacon Press.

Frey, K. S., & Ruble, D. N. (1992). Gender constancy and the "cost" of sex-typed behavior: A test of the conflict hypothesis. *Developmental Psychology, 28,* 714–721.

Friedman, H. S., Tucker, J. S., Schwartz, J. E., Tomlinson-Keasey, C., Martin, L. R., Wingard, D. L., et al. (1995). Psychosocial and behavioral predictors of longevity: The aging and death of the "Termites." *American Psychologist, 50,* 69–78.

Fullard, W., & Reiling, A. M. (1976). An investigation of Lorenz's "babyness." *Child Development, 47,* 1191–1193.

Fung, H., Carstensen, L. L., & Lutz, A. (1999). The role of time perspective in age differences in social preferences. *Psychology and Aging, 14,* 595–604.

Furman, W., & Simon, V. A. (2004). Concordance in attachment states of mind and styles with respect to fathers and mothers. *Developmental Psychology, 40,* 1239–1247.

Furstenberg, F. E. (2000). The socialization of adolescence and youth in the 1990's: A critical commentary. *Journal of Marriage and the Family, 62,* 896–911.

Furstenberg, F. F., Brooks-Gunn, J., & Chase-Lansdale, L. (1987). *Adolescent mothers in later life.* New York: Cambridge University Press.

Furstenberg, F. F., Brooks-Gunn, J., & Chase-Lansdale, L. (1989). Teenaged pregnancy and childbearing. *American Psychologist, 44,* 313–320.

Fuson, K. C., & Kwon, Y. (1992). Effects on children's addition and subtraction of the system of number words and other cultural tools. In J. Bideauc, C. Meljac, & J. P. Fischer (Eds.), *Pathways to number: Children's developing numerical abilities* (pp. 283–306). Hillsdale, NJ: Erlbaum.

Gaiter, J. M. (2001). Let's talk about sex and health. *Essence, 32,* 214.

Garafolo, R., Wolf, R. C., Wissow, L. S., Woods, E. R., & Goodman, E. (1999). Sexual orientation and risk of suicide attempts among a representative sample of youth. *Archives of Pediatrics and Adolescent Medicine, 153,* 487–493.

Garbarino, J. (1999). *Lost boys: Why our sons turn violent and how we can save them.* New York: Free Press.

Garber, J. (2000). Development and depression. In A. J. Sameroff, M. Lewis, & S. M. Miller (Eds.), *Handbook of developmental psychopathology* (2nd ed., pp. 467–490). New York: Kluwer Academic/Plenum Press.

Garcia, J. L. (1995). Freud's psychosexual stage conception: A developmental metaphor for counselors. *Journal of Counseling and Development, 73,* 498–502.

Gardner, H. (1983). *Frames of mind: The theory of multiple intelligences.* New York: Basic Books.

Gardner, H. (1991). *The unschooled mind: How children think, how schools should teach.* New York: Basic Books.

Garmezy, N., & Masten, A. (1994). Chronic adversities. In M. Rutter, L. Hersov, & E. Taylor (Eds.), *Child and adolescent psychiatry* (3rd ed., pp. 191–208). Oxford, England: Blackwell.

Garmezy, N. U. (1993). Vulnerability and resilience. In D. C. Funder, R. D. Parke, & C. Tomlinson-Keasey (Eds.), *Studying lives through time: Personality and development* (pp. 377–398). Washington, DC: American Psychological Association.

Garrod, A., & Beal, C. (1993). Voices of care and justice in children's responses to fable dilemmas. In A. Garrod (Ed.), *Approaches to moral development: New research and emerging themes* (pp. 59–71). New York: Teachers College Press.

Gartska, T. A., Schmitt, M. T., Branscombe, N. R., & Hummert, M. L. (2004). How young and older adults differ in their responses to perceived age discrimination. *Psychology and Aging, 19,* 326–335.

Gati, I., Osipow, S. H., & Givon, M. (1995). Gender differences in career decision making: The content and structure of preferences. *Journal of Counseling Psychology, 42,* 204–216.

Gatz, M. (2000). Variations on depression in later life. In S. H. Qualls & N. Abeles (Eds.), *Psychology and the aging revolution: How we adapt to longer life* (pp. 239–254). Washington, DC: American Psychological Association.

Gauvain, M. (1992). Social influences on the development of planning in advance and during action. *International Journal of Behavioral Development, 15,* 377–398.

Gauvain, M. (2001). *The social context of cognitive development.* New York: Guilford Press.

Gauvain, M., & Rogoff, B. (1989). Collaborative problem solving and children's planning skills. *Developmental Psychology, 25,* 139–151.

Ge, X., Conger, R. D., & Elder, G. H., Jr. (1996). Coming of age too early: Pubertal influences on girls' vulnerability to psychological distress. *Child Development, 67,* 3386–3400.

Gelehrter, T. D., & Collins, F. S. (1990). *Principles of medical genetics.* Baltimore: Williams & Wilkins.

Gelman, R. (1982). Basic numerical abilities. In R. J. Sternberg (Ed.), *Advances in the psychology of human intelligence* (Vol. 1). Hillsdale, NJ: Erlbaum.

Gelman, R., & Gallistel, C. R. (1978). *The child's understanding of number.* Cambridge, MA: Harvard University Press.

Gelman, R., & Williams, E. M. (1998). Enabling constraints for cognitive development and learning: Domain specificity and epigenesis. In W. Damon (Series Ed.), D. Kuhn, & R. S. Siegler (Vol. Eds.), *Handbook of child psychology: Vol. 2. Cognition, perception, and language* (5th ed., pp. 575–630). New York: Wiley.

Gelman, S. A., Taylor, M. G., & Nguyen, S. P. (2004). Mother-child conversations about gender. *Monographs of the Society for Research in Child Development, 69* (Serial No. 275), vii–127.

George, L. K., Larson, D. B., Koenig, H. G., & McCullough, M. E. (2000). Spirituality and health: What we know, what we need to know. *Journal of Social and Clinical Psychology, 19,* 102–119.

Gergen, K. J. (1971). *The concept of self.* New York: Holt, Rinehart and Winston.

Gershoff, E. T. (2002). Corporal punishment by parents and associated child behavior and experiences: A meta-analytic and theoretical review. *Psychological Bulletin, 128,* 539–579.

Gerth, H., & Mills, C. W. (1953). *Character and social structure: The psychology of social institutions.* New York: Harcourt, Brace.

Geschwind, N. (1990). Specializations of the human brain. In R. R. Llinas (Ed.), *The workings of the brain: Development, memory, and perception* (pp. 105–120). New York: Freeman.

Gesser, G., Wong, P. T., & Reker, G. T. (1988). Death attitudes across the life span: The development and validation of the Death Attitude Profile (DAP). *Omega: Journal of Death and Dying, 18,* 113–128.

Gewirtz, J. L., & Boyd, E. F. (1977). Does maternal responding imply reduced infant crying? A critique of the 1972 Bell and Ainsworth report. *Child Development, 48,* 1200–1207.

Gibbs, J. (1987). Social processes in delinquency: The need to facilitate empathy as well as sociomoral reasoning. In W. Kurtines & J. Gewirtz (Eds.), *Moral development through social interaction.* New York: Wiley.

Gill, H. L., & Haurin, D. R. (1998). Wherever he may go: How wives affect their husband's career decisions. *Social Science Research, 29,* 264–279.

Gilligan, C. (1977). In a different voice: Women's conceptions of self and of morality. *Harvard Educational Review, 47,* 481–517.

Gilligan, C. (1982). *In a different voice.* Cambridge, MA: Harvard University Press.

Gilligan, C. (1993). Adolescent development reconsidered. In A. Garrod (Ed.), *Approaches to moral development: New research and emerging themes.* New York: Teachers College Press.

Gilligan, C., & Attanucci, J. (1988). Two moral orientations: Gender differences and similarities. *Merrill-Palmer Quarterly, 23,* 77–104.

Gilstrap, L. L. (2004). A missing link in suggestibility research: What is known about the behavior of field interviewers in unstructured interviews with young children? *Journal of Experimental Psychology: Applied, 10,* 13–24.

Ginsburg, H. P. (1989). *Children's arithmetic: How they learn it and how you teach it* (2nd ed.). Austin, TX: Pro-Ed.

Ginsburg, H. P., Klein, A., & Starkey, P. (1998). The development of children's mathematical thinking: Connecting research with practice. In W. Damon (Series Ed.), I. E. Sigel, & K. A. Renninger (Vol. Eds.), *Handbook of child psychology: Vol. 4. Child psychology in practice* (5th ed., pp. 401–478). New York: Wiley.

Glanzer, P. L. (1998, February). The character to seek justice: Showing fairness to diverse visions of character education. *Phi Delta Kappan,* pp. 434–438, 448.

Glass, G. (1976). Primary, secondary and meta-analysis of research. *Educational Research, 5,* 3–8.

Gleeson, K., & Wise, S. (1993). The do-not-resuscitate order. Still too late. *Archives of Internal Medicine, 153,* 1999–2003.

Glick, P. C., & Lin, S. (1986). Recent changes in divorce and remarriage. *Journal of Marriage and the Family, 48,* 737–747.

Goddard, L. S., McIntyre, D. C., & Leech, C. K. (1969). A permanent change in brain function resulting from daily electrical stimulation. *Experimental Neurology, 25,* 295–330.

Gogtay, N., Giedd, J. N., Lusk, L., Hayashi, K. M., Greenstein, D., Vaituzis, A. C., et al. (2004). Dynamic mapping of human cortical development during childhood through early adulthood. *Proceedings of the National Academy of Science, 101,* 8174–8179.

Goldfried, M. R. (1995). *From cognitive-behavior therapy to psychotherapy integration.* New York: Springer.

Goldstein, A. P. (1990). *Delinquents on delinquency.* Champaign, IL: Research Press.

Goldstein, A. P. (1992, May 4). *School violence: Its community context and potential solutions*. Testimony presented to the Subcommittee on Elementary, Secondary, and Vocational Education of the Committee on Education and Labor of the United States House of Representatives.

Goleman, D. (1995). *Emotional intelligence*. New York: Bantam Books.

Goleman, D. (1998). *Working with emotional intelligence*. New York: Bantam Books.

Goleman, D. (2003). *Destructive emotions: How can we overcome them?* New York: Bantam Books.

Golinkoff, R. M. (1983). The preverbal negotiation of failed messages: Insights into the transition period. In R. M. Golinkoff (Ed.), *The transition from prelinguistic to linguistic communication*. Hillsdale, NJ: Erlbaum.

Golombok, S., Perry, B., Burston, A., Murray, C., Mooney-Somers, J., Stevens, M., et al. (2003). Children with lesbian parents: A community study. *Developmental Psychology, 29*, 20–33.

Golombok, S., & Tasker, F. (1996). Do parents influence the sexual orientation of their children? Findings from a longitudinal study of lesbian families. *Developmental Psychology, 32*, 3–11.

Golub, S. (1992). *Periods: From menarche to menopause*. Newbury Park, CA: Sage.

Gondolf, E. W. (1985). *Men who batter*. Holmes Beach, FL: Learning Publications.

Goode, W. J. (1960). A theory of role strain. *American Sociological Review, 25*, 483–496.

Goodman, G. S., & Clarke-Stewart, A. (1991). Suggestibility in children's testimony: Implications for child sexual abuse investigations. In J. L. Doris (Ed.), *The suggestibility of children's recollections* (pp. 92–105). Washington, DC: American Psychological Association.

Goodson, W. D. (1978). Which do college students choose first—their major or their occupation? *Vocational Guidance Quarterly, 30*, 230–235.

Goodstein, R., & Ponterotto, J. G. (1997). Racial and ethnic identity: Their relationship to and their contribution to self-esteem. *Journal of Black Psychology, 23*, 275–292.

Goodyear, I. M., Park, R., Netherton, C. M., & Herbert, J. (2001). Possible role of cortisol and dehydroepiandrosterone in human development and psychopathology. *British Journal of Psychiatry, 179*, 243–249.

Goossens, F. A., & Van IJzendoorn, M. H. (1990). Quality of infants; attachments to professional caregivers: Relation to infant-parent attachment and day-care characteristics. *Child Development, 61*, 832–837.

Gopnik, A., & Astington, J. W. (1988). Children's understanding of representational change and its relation to the understanding of false belief and the appearance-reality distinction. *Child Development, 59*, 26–37.

Gordon, B., Ornstein, P. A., Clubb, P. A., Nida, R. E., & Baker-Ward, L. E. (1991). *Visiting the pediatrician: Long-term retention and forgetting*. Paper presented at the annual meeting of the Psychonomic Society, San Francisco.

Gordon, E. W., & Lemons, M. P. (1997). An interactionist perspective on the genesis of intelligence. In R. J. Steinberg & E. Grigorenko (Eds.), *Intelligence, heredity, and environment* (pp. 323–342). Cambridge, England: Cambridge University Press.

Gorman-Smith, D., Tolan, P. H., Zelli, A., & Huesmann, L. R. (1996). The relation of family functioning to violence among inner city youths. *Journal of Family Psychology, 10*, 115–129.

Gottfredson, D. C., Fink, C. M., Skroban, S., Gottfredson, G. D., & Weissberg, R. P. (1997). Making prevention work. In R. P. Weissberg, T. P. Gullotta, R. L. Hampton, B. A. Ryan, & G. R. Adams (Eds.), *Healthy children 2010: Establishing preventive services* (pp. 219–252). Thousand Oaks, CA: Sage.

Gottfredson, G. D., & Holland, J. L. (1990). A longitudinal test of the influence of congruence: Job satisfaction, competency utilization, and counterproductive behavior. *Journal of Counseling Psychology, 37*, 389–398.

Gottfredson, G. D., Holland, J. L., & Ogawa, D. K. (1982). *Dictionary of Holland occupational codes*. Palo Alto, CA: Consulting Psychologists Press.

Gottlieb, G. (1970). Conceptions of prenatal development. In L. R. Aronson, E. Tobach, D. S. Lehrman, & J. S. Rosenblatt (Eds.), *Development and evolution of behavior* (pp. 111–137). San Francisco: Freeman.

Gottlieb, G. (1991). Experiential canalization of behavioral development: Theory. *Developmental Psychology, 27*, 4–13.

Gottlieb, G. (1992). *Individual development and evolution: The genesis of novel behavior*. New York: Oxford University Press.

Gottlieb, G. (2003). Probabilistic epigenesis of development. In J. Valsiner & K. J. Connolly (Eds.), *Handbook of developmental psychology* (pp. 3–17). London: Sage.

Gottman, J. (1994). *Why marriages succeed or fail . . . And how you can make yours last*. New York: Simon & Schuster.

Gottman, J. M. (1983). How children become friends. *Monographs of the Society for Research in Child Development, 48* (3, Serial No. 201).

Gottman, J. M. (1993). A theory of marital dissolution and stability. *Journal of Family psychology, 7*, 57–75.

Gottman, J. M. (1994). *What predicts divorce?* Hillsdale, NJ: Erlbaum.

Gottman, J. M. (1999). *The marriage clinic: A scientifically-based marital therapy*. New York: Norton.

Gottman, J. M., & Levenson, R. W. (2000). The timing of divorce: Predicting when a couple will divorce over a 14-year period. *Journal of Marriage and the Family, 62*, 737–745.

Gottman, J., & Silver, N. (1999). *The seven principles for making marriages work*. New York: Three Rivers Press.

Gould, R. L. (1978). *Transformations: Growth and change in adult life*. New York: Simon & Schuster.

Graber, J. A., Brooks-Gunn, J., & Galen, B. R. (1999). Betwixt and between: Sexuality in the context of adolescent transitions. In R. Jessor (Ed.), *New perspectives on adolescent risk behavior* (pp. 270–318). New York: Cambridge University Press.

Graber, J. A., Brooks-Gunn, J., & Warren, M. P. (1995). The antecedents of menarcheal age: Heredity, family environment, and stressful life events. *Child Development, 66*, 346–359.

Grammer, K. (1993). 5-a-androst-16en-3a-on: A male pheromone? *Ethology and Sociobiology, 14*, 201–207.

Grant, B. F., & Dawson, D. (1997). Age of onset of alcohol use and its association with DSM-IV alcohol use and dependence: Results from the National Longitudinal Alcohol Epidemiological Survey. *Journal of Substance Abuse, 9*, 103–111.

Grant, H., & Dweck, C. S. (2003). Clarifying achievement goals and their impact. *Journal of Personality and Social Psychology, 85*, 541–553.

Gray, J. A. (1990). Brain systems that mediate both emotion and cognition. *Cognition and Emotion, 4*, 270–288.

Gray, W. M. (1990). Formal operation thought. In W. F. Overton (Ed.), *Reasoning, necessity, and logic: Developmental perspectives* (pp. 227–254). Hillsdale, NJ: Erlbaum.

Gray-Little, B., & Hafdahl, A. R. (2000). Factors influencing racial comparisons of self-esteem: A quantitative review. *Psychological Bulletin, 126*, 26–54.

Green, R. (1987). *The "sissy boy syndrome" and the development of homosexuality*. New Haven, CT: Yale University Press.

Greenberg, J., & Pyszczynski, T. (1986). Persistent high self-focus after a failure and low self-focus after success: The depressive self-focusing style. *Journal of Personality and Social Psychology, 55*, 1039–1044.

Greenberg, L. S. (2002). *Emotion-focused therapy: Coaching clients to work through their feelings*. Washington, DC: American Psychological Association.

Greenberg, L. S., & Safran, J. D. (1989). Emotion in psychotherapy. *American Psychologist, 44*, 19–29.

Greenberg, M. T., & Kusche, C. (1998). Preventive intervention for school-age deaf children. *Journal of Deaf Studies and Deaf Education, 3*, 49–63.

Greenberg, M. T., & Kusche, C. (2002). Promoting alternative thinking strategies (PATHS). In D. S. Elliot (Series Ed.) & S. F. Mihalic (Contributing Ed.), *Blueprints for violence prevention: Book Ten*. Boulder: University of Colorado, Center for the Study and Prevention of Violence.

Greenberg, M. T., & Speltz, M. L. (1988). Attachment and the ontogeny of conduct problems. In J. Belsky & T. Nezworski (Eds.), *Clinical implications of attachment* (pp. 177–218). Hillsdale, NJ: Erlbaum.

Greenberger, E., & Goldberg, W. (1989). Work, parenting, and the socialization of children. *Developmental Psychology, 25*, 22–35.

Greene, A. L., & Wheatley, S. M. (1992). "I've got a lot to do and I don't think I'll have the time": Gender differences in late adolescents' narratives of the future. *Journal of Youth and Adolescence, 21*, 667–685.

Greenfield, P. M. (1994). Independence and interdependence as developmental scripts: Implications for theory, research, and practice. In P. M. Greenfield & R. R. Cocking (Eds.), *Cross-cultural roots of minority child development* (pp. 1–40). Hillsdale, NJ: Erlbaum.

Greenfield, P. M., & Juvonen, J. (1999, July/August). A developmental look at Columbine. *APA Monitor*.

Greenfield, P. M., & Suzuki, L. K. (1998). Culture and human development: Implications for parenting, education, pediatrics, and mental health. In W. Damon (Series Ed.), I. E. Sigel, & K. A. Renninger (Vol. Eds.), *Handbook of child psychology: Vol. 4. Child psychology in practice* (5th ed., pp. 1059–1109). New York: Wiley.

Greeno, K. (1989). *Gender differences in children's proximity to adults* (Doctoral dissertation, Stanford University).

Greenough, W. T., & Black, J. E. (1992). Induction of brain structure by experience: Substrates for cognitive development. In M. R. Gunnar & C. A. Nelson (Eds.), *Minnesota Symposium on Child Psychology: Vol. 24. Developmental behavioral neuroscience* (pp. 155–200). Hillsdale, NJ: Erlbaum.

Greenspan, S. I. (2003). Child care research: A clinical perspective. *Child Development, 74*, 1064–1068.

Greenspan, S. I., & Weider, S. (1997). An integrated developmental approach to interventions for young children with severe difficulties in relating and communicating. *Zero to Three, 17*(5), 279–306.

Greenspan, S. L. (1981). *The clinical interview of the child*. New York: McGraw-Hill.

Greenspan, S., & Weider, S. (1999). A functional developmental approach to autism spectrum disorders. *Journal of Association for Persons with Severe Handicaps, 24*, 147–161.

Gresham, F. M. (1981). Social skills training with handicapped children: A review. *Review of Educational Research, 51*, 139–176.

Grice, P. (1975). Logic and conversation. In P. Cole & J. L. Moran (Eds.), *Syntax and semantics: Vol. 3. Speech acts* (pp. 41–58). New York: Academic Press.

Grisso, T., Steinberg, L., Woolard, J., Cauffman, E., Scott, E., Graham, S., et al. (2003). Juveniles' competence to stand trial: A comparison of adolescents' and adults' capacities as trial defendants. *Law and Human Behavior, 27,* 333–363.

Gross, J. J., Carstensen, L. L., Pasupathi, M., Tsai, J. L., Gottestam, K., & Hsu, A. Y. C. (1997). Emotion and aging: Changes in experience, expression, and control. *Psychology and Aging, 12,* 590–599.

Grossman, P., Niemann, L., Schmidt, S., & Walach, H. (2004). Mindfulness-based stress reduction and health benefits. *Journal of Psychosomatic Research, 57,* 35–43.

Grossmann, K. E., Grossmann, K., Huber, F., & Wartner, U. (1981). German children's behavior towards their mothers at 12 months and their fathers at 18 months in Ainsworth's strange situation. *International Journal of Behavioral Development, 4,* 157–181.

Gunnar, M. R., & Cheatham, C. L. (2003). Brain and behavior interface: Stress and the developing brain. *Infant Mental Health Journal, 24,* 195–211.

Gurwitz, S. B., & Dodge, K. A. (1977). Effects of confirmations and disconfirmations on stereotype-based attributions. *Journal of Personality and Social Psychology, 35,* 495–500.

Guterman, J. T. (1994). A social constructionist position for mental health counseling. *Journal of Mental Health Counseling, 16,* 226–244.

Gutman, L. M., Sameroff, A. J., & Eccles, J. S. (2002). The academic achievement of African-American students during early adolescence: An examination of multiple risk, promotive, and protective factors. *American Journal of Community Psychology, 30,* 367–399.

Guttmacher Institute. (2004). *U.S. Teenage Pregnancy Statistics Overall Trends.* New York: Author.

Haden, C. A., Ornstein, P. A., Eckerman, C. O., & Didow, S. M. (2001). Mother-child conversational interactions as events unfold: Linkages to subsequent remembering. *Child Development, 72,* 1016–1031.

Haith, M. M., & Benson, J. B. (1998). Infant cognition. In W. Damon (Series Ed.), D. Kuhn, & R. S. Siegler (Vol. Eds.), *Handbook of child psychology: Vol. 2. Cognition, perception, and language* (5th ed., pp. 199–254). New York: Wiley.

Haley, J. (1976). *Problem-solving therapy.* San Francisco: Jossey-Bass.

Halford, G. S. (1993). *Children's understanding: The development of mental models.* Hillsdale, NJ: Erlbaum.

Halford, W. K., Markman, H. J., Kline, G. H., & Stanley, S. M. (2003). Best practice in couple relationship education. *Journal of Marital and Family Therapy, 29,* 385–406.

Hall, G. S. (1904). *Adolescence: Its psychology and its relation to physiology, anthropology, sociology, sex, crime, religion, and education* (Vols. 1 & 2). Upper Saddle River, NJ: Prentice Hall.

Hall, T. M., Kaduson, H. G., & Schaefer, C. E. (2002). Fifteen effective play therapy techniques. *Professional Psychology: Research and Practice, 33,* 515–522.

Hallinan, M. T. (1979). Structural effects on children's friendships and cliques. *Social Psychology Quarterly, 42,* 43–54.

Halperin, S. (1998b). Today's forgotten half: Still losing ground. In S. Halperin (Ed.), *The forgotten half revisited: American youth and young families, 1988–2008* (pp. 1–26). Washington, DC: American Youth Policy Forum.

Halperin, S. (Ed.). (1998a). *The forgotten half revisited: American youth and young families, 1988–2008.* Washington, DC: American Youth Policy Forum.

Halpern, D. F. (1992). *Sex differences in cognitive abilities* (2nd ed.). Hillsdale, NJ: Erlbaum.

Halpern-Felsher, B., & Cauffman, E. (2001). Costs and benefits of a decision: Decision-making competence in adolescents and adults. *Journal of Applied Developmental Psychology, 22,* 257–273.

Hamer, D., & Copeland, P. (1998). *Living with our genes: Why they matter more than you think.* New York: Doubleday.

Hamill, S. B., & Goldberg, W. A. (1997). Between adolescents and aging grandparents: Midlife concerns of adults in the sandwich generation. *Journal of Adult Development, 4,* 135–147.

Hamilton, C. E. (2000). Continuity and discontinuity of attachment from infancy through adolescence. *Child Development, 71,* 690–694.

Hamilton, J. E. (1993, June). Smart ways to use time-out. *Parents Magazine,* 110–112.

Hammen, C. (1996). Stress, families, and the risk for depression. In C. Mundt, M. J. Goldstein, K. Hahlweg, & P. Fiedler (Eds.), *Interpersonal factors in the origin and course of affective disorders* (pp. 101–112). London: Gaskell-Royal College of Psychiatrists.

Hammen, C. (2003). Risk and protective factors for children of depressed parents. In S. S. Luthar (Ed.), *Resilience and vulnerability: Adaptation in the context of childhood adversities* (pp. 50–75). Cambridge, England: Cambridge University Press.

Hanson, L., Danis, M., & Garrett, J. (1997). What is wrong with end-of-life care? Opinions of bereaved family members. *Journal of the American Geriatric Society, 45,* 1339–1344.

Haraven, T. K., & Adams, K. (1996). The generation in the middle: Cohort comparisons in assistance to aging parents in an American community. In T. K. Haraven (Ed.), *Aging and generational relations: Life course and cross-cultural perspectives* (pp. 3–29). New York: Aldine de Gruyter.

Harris, J. R. (1998). *The nurture assumption: Why children turn out the way they do.* New York: Touchstone.

Harris, P. L. (1983). What children know about situations that provoke emotions. In M. Lewis & C. Saarni (Eds.), *The socialization of affect* (pp. 117–130). New York: Plenum Press.

Harrison, P. M., & Beck, A. J. (2004, November). Prisoners in 2003. *Bureau of Justice Statistics Bulletin.* Washington, DC: United States Department of Justice.

Hart, B., & Risley, T. R. (1992). American parenting of language-learning children: Persisting difference in family-child interactions observed in natural home environment. *Developmental Psychology, 28,* 1096–1105.

Hart, B., & Risley, T. R. (1999). *Meaningful differences in the everyday experience of young American children.* Baltimore: Brookes.

Hart, N. (1993). Famine, maternal nutrition and infant mortality: A re-examination of Dutch hunger winter. *Population Studies, 47,* 27–46.

Harter, S. (1981). A new self-report scale of intrinsic versus extrinsic orientation in the classroom: Motivational and informational components. *Developmental Psychology, 17,* 300–312.

Harter, S. (1985). *The self-perception profile for children.* Unpublished manual, University of Denver, CO.

Harter, S. (1988a). Developmental and dynamic changes in the nature of the self concept: Implications for child psychotherapy. In S. R. Shirk (Ed.), *Cognitive development and child psychotherapy,* (pp. 119–160). New York: Plenum Press.

Harter, S. (1988b). *The self-perception profile for adolescents.* Unpublished manual, University of Denver, CO.

Harter, S. (1990). Causes, correlates, and the functional role of global self-worth: A life-span perspective. In R. Sternberg & J. Kolligian, Jr. (Eds.), *Competence considered* (pp. 67–98). New Haven, CT: Yale University Press.

Harter, S. (1993). Causes and consequences of low self-esteem in children and adolescents. In R. F. Baumeister (Ed.), *Self-esteem: The puzzle of low self-regard* (pp. 3–20). New York: Plenum Press.

Harter, S. (1998). The development of self-representations. In W. Damon (Ed.) & N. Eisenberg (Vol. Ed.), *Handbook of child psychology: Vol. 3. Social, emotional, and personality development* (5th ed., pp. 553–618). New York: Wiley.

Harter, S. (1999). *The construction of the self: A developmental perspective.* New York: Guilford Press.

Harter, S., & Pike, R. (1984). The pictorial scale of perceived competence and social acceptance for young children. *Child Development, 55,* 1969–1982.

Harter, S., Waters, P. L., Whitesell, N. R., & Kastelic, D. (1998). Level of voice among female and male high school students: Relational context, support, and gender orientation. *Developmental Psychology, 34,* 892–901.

Hartshorne, H., & May, M. A. (1928–1930). *Studies in the nature of character* (Vols. 1–3). New York: Macmillan.

Hartup, W. W. (1983). Peer relations. In P. H. Mussen (Series Ed.) & E. M. Hetherington (Vol. Ed.), *Handbook of child psychology: Vol. 4. Socialization, personality and social development* (pp. 103–196). New York: Wiley.

Hartup, W. W., Glazer, J., & Charlesworth, R. (1967). Peer reinforcement and sociometric status. *Child Development, 38,* 1017–1024.

Harwood, R. L., Schoelmerich, A., Schulze, P. A., & Gonzalez, Z. (1999). Cultural differences in maternal beliefs and behaviors: A study of middle-class Anglo and Puerto Rican mother-infant pairs in four everyday situations. *Child Development, 70,* 1005–1016.

Hasebe, Y., Nucci, L., & Nucci, M. S. (2004). Parental control of the personal domain and adolescent symptoms of psychopathology: A cross-national study in the United States and Japan. *Child Development, 75,* 815–828.

Hasher, L., & Zacks, R. T. (1988). Working memory, comprehension, and aging: A review and a new view. *The Psychology of Learning and Motivations, 22,* 193–225.

Hastings, P. D., & Grusec, J. E. (1998). Parenting goals as organizers of responses to parent-child disagreement. *Developmental Psychology, 34,* 465–479.

Hatano, G. (1994). Introduction: Conceptual change—Japanese perspectives. *Human Development, 37,* 189–197.

Hatfield, E., & Sprecher, S. (1986). Measuring passionate love in intimate relationships. *Journal of Adolescence, 9,* 383–410.

Hattie, J. (1992). *Self-concept.* New York: Erlbaum.

Hauser, S. T. (1999). Understanding resilient outcomes: Adolescent lives across time and generations. *Journal of Research on Adolescence, 9,* 1–24.

Hawkins, J. (1987, April). *Collaboration and dissent.* Paper presented at the meetings of the Society for Research in Child Development, Baltimore.

Hayes, C. D. (Ed.). (1987). *Risking the future: Adolescent sexuality, pregnancy, and childbearing* (Vol. 1). Washington, DC: National Academy Press.

Hayes, D. S., & Birnbaum, D. W. (1980). Preschooler's retention of televised events: Is a picture worth a thousand words? *Developmental Psychology, 16,* 410–416.

Hayes, R. L. (1994). The legacy of Lawrence Kohlberg: Implications for counseling and human development. *Journal of Counseling and Development, 72,* 498–502.

Hayes, S. C. (2002). Acceptance, mindfulness and science. *Clinical Psychology: Science and Practice, 9,* 101–106.

Hayes, S. C. (2004). Acceptance and commitment therapy and the new behavior therapies: Mindfulness, acceptance and relationship. In S. C. Hayes, V. M. Follette, & M. M. Linehan (Eds.), *Mindfulness and acceptance: Expanding the cognitive-behavioral tradition* (pp. 1–29). New York: Guilford Press.

Hazan, C., & Shaver, P. (1987). Romantic love conceptualized as an attachment process. *Journal of Personality and Social Psychology, 52,* 511–524.

Hazan, C., & Shaver, P. R. (1994). Attachment as an organizational framework for research on close relationships. *Psychological Inquiry, 5,* 1–22.

Hazan, C., & Zeifman, D. (1999). Pair bonds as attachments. In J. Cassidy & P. R. Shaver (Eds.), *Handbook of attachment: Theory, research, and clinical applications* (pp. 336–377). New York: Guilford Press.

Heath, A. C., Bucholz, K. K., Madden, P. A. F., Dinwiddie, S. H., Slutske, W. S., Bierut, L. J., et al. (1997). Genetic and environmental contributions to alcohol dependence risk in a national twin sample: Consistency of findings in women and men. *Psychological Medicine, 27,* 1381–1396.

Heckhausen, J. (1997). Developmental regulation across adulthood: Primary and secondary control of age-related challenges. *American Psychologist, 33,* 176–187.

Heckhausen, J. (1999). *Developmental regulation in adulthood: Age-normative and sociostructural constraints as adaptive challenges.* New York: Cambridge University Press.

Helms, J. E. (1990). An overview of Black racial identity theory. In J. E. Helms (Ed.), *Black and White racial identity: Theory, research and practice* (pp. 9–32). New York: Greenwood Press.

Helms, J. E. (2003). Racial identity in the social environment. In P. B. Pedersen & J. Carey (Eds.), *Multicultural counseling in schools: A practical handbook* (2nd ed., pp. 44–58). Boston: Allyn & Bacon.

Helmuth, L. (2001). Brain calls dibs on many genes. *Science, 291,* 1188.

Helson, R., & Klohnen, E. C. (1998). Affective coloring of personality from young adulthood to midlife. *Personality and Social Psychology Bulletin, 24,* 241–252.

Helson, R., & Roberts, B. W. (1994). Ego development and personality change in adulthood. *Journal of Personality and Social Psychology, 66,* 911–920.

Henderson, V., & Dweck, C. S. (1992). Achievement and motivation in adolescence: A new model and data. In S. Feldman & G. Elliott (Eds.), *At the threshold: The developing adolescent.* Cambridge, MA: Harvard University Press.

Henggler, S. W., Schoenwald, S. K., Borduin, C. M., Rowland, M. D., & Cunningham, P. B. (1998). *Multisystemic treatment of antisocial behavior in children and adolescents.* New York: Guilford Press.

Herman, M. (2004). Forced to choose: Some determinants of racial identification in multiracial adolescents. *Child Development, 75,* 730–748.

Herold, E., Goodwin, M., & Lero, D. (1979). Self-esteem, locus of control, and adolescent contraception. *Journal of Psychology, 101,* 83–88.

Herr, E. L. (1989). *Counseling in a dynamic society: Opportunities and challenges.* Alexandria, VA: American Counseling Association.

Herr, E. L., & Cramer, S. H. (1992). *Career guidance and counseling through the life span: Systematic approaches* (4th ed.). New York: HarperCollins.

Hersch, P. (1998). *A tribe apart: A journey into the heart of American adolescence.* New York: Fawcett Columbine.

Herschenson, D. B. (1996). Work adjustment: A neglected area in career counseling. *Journal of Counseling and Development, 74,* 442–446.

Hertenstein, M. J. (2002). Touch: Its communicative functions in infancy. *Human Development, 45,* 70–94.

Herzberg, D. S., Hammen, C., Burge, D., Daley, S. E., Davila, J., & Lindberg, N. (1998). Social competence as a predictor of chronic

interpersonal stress. *Personal Relationships, 5,* 207–218.

Hesse, E. (1996). Discourse, memory, and the Adult Attachment Interview: A note with emphasis on the emerging cannot classify category. *Infant Mental Health Journal, 17,* 4–11.

Hesse, E., & Main, M. (1999). Frightened behavior in traumatizing but non-maltreating parents: Previously unexamined risk factor for offspring. In D. Diamond & S. J. Blatt (Eds.), *Psychoanalytic theory and attachment research I: Theoretical considerations. Psychoanalytic Inquiry, 19.*

Hetherington, E. M. (1998). Relevant issues in developmental science. *American Psychologist, 53,* 93–94.

Hetherington, E. M., Reiss, D., & Plomin, R. (Eds.). (1994). *Separate social worlds of siblings.* Hillsdale, NJ: Erlbaum.

Hewlett, S. A. (1991). *When the bough breaks: The cost of neglecting our children.* New York: Basic Books.

Hewlett, S. A., & West, C. (1998). *The war against parents: What we can do for America's beleaguered moms and dads.* Boston: Houghton Mifflin.

Higgins, E. T. (1991). Development of self-regulatory and self-evaluative processes: Costs, benefits, and tradeoffs. In M. R. Gunnar & L. A. Sroufe (Eds.), *Minnesota Symposium on Child Development: Vol. 23. Self processes and development* (pp. 125–166). Hillsdale, NJ: Erlbaum.

Higher Education Research Institute (HERI) (2004). *The American Freshman: National Norms for Fall 2004.* www.gseis.uda.edu/heri/findings.html

Hill, A. M. (1992). Chinese funerals and Chinese ethnicity in Chiang Mai, Thailand. *Ethnology, 31,* 315–330.

Hill, J. P., & Lynch, M. E. (1983). The intensification of gender-related role expectations during early adolescence. In J. Brooks-Gunn & A. C. Petersen (Eds.), *Girls at puberty: Biological and psychosocial perspectives* (pp. 201–228). New York: Plenum Press.

Hill, M. S., & Yeung, W. J. (1999). How has the changing structure of opportunities affected transitions to adulthood? In A. Booth, A. C. Crouter, & M. J. Shanahan (Eds.), *Transitions to adulthood in a changing economy: No work, no family, no future?* (pp. 3–39). Westport, CT: Praeger.

Hill, N. E., Bush, K. R., & Roosa, M. W. (2003). Parenting and family socialization strategies and children's mental health: Low-income Mexican-American and Euro-American mothers and children. *Child Development, 74,* 189–204.

Hill, P. C., Pargament, K. I., Wood, R. W., Jr., McCullough, M. E., Swyers, J. P., Larson, D., et al. (2000). Conceptualizing religion and spirituality: Points of commonality, points of departure. *Journal of Theory in Social Behavior, 30,* 51–77.

Hines, M., Golombok, S., Rust, J., Johnston, K. J., Golding, J., & Avon Longitudinal Study of Parents and Children Study Team. (2002). Testosterone during pregnancy and gender role behavior of preschool children: A longitudinal, population study. *Child Development, 73,* 1678–1687.

Hinshaw, S. P. (1987). On the distinction between attentional deficits/hyperactivity and conduct problems/aggression in child psychopathology. *Psychological Bulletin, 101,* 443–463.

Hintikka, J., Koskela, T., Kontula, O., Koskela, K., & Viinamaeki, H. (2000). Men, women and friends: Are there differences in relation to mental well-being? *Quality of Life Research, 9,* 841–845.

Hlastala, S. A., Frank, E., Kowalski, J., Sherrill, J. T., Tu, X. M., Anderson, B., et al. (2000). Stressful life events, bipolar disorder, and the "Kindling Model." *Journal of Abnormal Psychology, 109,* 777–786.

Hobfoll, S. E. (1989). Conservation of resources: A new attempt at conceptualizing stress. *American Psychologist, 44*(3), 513–524.

Hobfoll, S. E. (2001). The influence of culture, community, and the nested-self in the stress process: Advancing conservation of resources theory. *Applied Psychology: An International Review, 50*(3), 337–421.

Hochschild, A. R. (1997). *The time bind: When work becomes home and home becomes work.* New York: Metropolitan Books.

Hoffman, M. L. (1970). Moral development. In P. H. Mussen (Ed.), M. M. Haith, & J. J. Campos (Vol. Eds.), *Handbook of child psychology: Vol. 2. Infancy and developmental psychobiology* (pp. 261–354). New York: Wiley.

Hoffman, M. L. (1975). Altruistic behavior and the parent-child relationship. *Journal of Personality and Social Psychology, 31,* 937–943.

Hoffman, M. L. (1982). Development of prosocial motivation: Empathy and guilt. In N. Eisenberg (Ed.), *The development of prosocial behavior* (pp. 281–313). New York: Academic Press.

Hoffman, M. L. (1983). Affective and cognitive processes in moral internalization. In E. T. Higgins, D. Ruble, & W. Hartup (Eds.), *Social cognition and social development: A sociocultural perspective* (pp. 236–274). New York: Cambridge University Press.

Hofmann, A. D. (1997). Adolescent growth and development. In A. D. Hofmann & D. E. Greydanus (Eds.), *Adolescent medicine* (3rd ed.). Stamford, CT: Appleton and Lange.

Hogan, D. P., & Astone, N. M. (1986). The transition to adulthood. *American Sociological Review, 12,* 109–130.

Holbrook, M., & Schindler, R. M. (1989). Some exploratory findings on the development of musical taste. *Journal of Consumer Research, 16,* 119–124.

Holland, J. L. (1966). *The psychology of vocational choice.* Waltham, MA: Blaisdell.

Holland, J. L. (1985). *Making vocational choices. A theory of vocational personalities and work environments* (2nd ed.). Upper Saddle River, NJ: Prentice Hall.

Holland, J. L., Viernstein, M. C., Kuo, H. M., Karweit, N. L., & Blum, S. D. (1970). *A psychological classification of occupations* (Report No. 90). Baltimore: Johns Hopkins University, Center for the Study of Social Organization of Schools.

Holmes, T. H., & Rahe, R. H. (1967). The Social Readjustment Rating Scale. *Journal of Psychosomatic Research, 11,* 213–218.

Homer, B. D., Brockmeier, J., Kamawar, D., & Olson, D. R. (2001). Between realism and nominalism: Learning to think about names and words. *Genetic, Social, and General Psychology Monographs, 127,* 5–25.

Hopmeyer, E., & Werk, A. (1994). A comparative study of family bereavement groups. *Death Studies, 18,* 243–256.

Horn, J. L., & Cattell, R. B. (1966). Refinement and test of the theory of fluid and crystallized intelligence. *Journal of Educational Psychology, 57,* 253–270.

Horney, K. (1950). *Neurosis and human growth.* New York: Norton.

Horowitz, M. J., Siegel, B., Holen, A., Bonanno, G. A., Milbrath, C., & Stinson, C. H. (1997). Diagnostic criteria for complicated grief disorder. *American Journal of Psychiatry, 154,* 904–910.

Horwitz, A. B., & White, H. R. (1998). The relationship of cohabitation and mental health: A study of a young adult cohort. *Journal of Marriage and the Family, 60,* 505–514.

Hoshman, L. T., & Polkinghorne, D. E. (1992). Redefining the science-practice relationship and professional training. *American Psychologist, 47,* 55–66.

Howes, C., & Olenick, M. (1986). Family and child care influences on toddler's compliance. *Child Development, 57,* 202–216.

Hoza, B., Molina, B. S., Bukowski, W. M., & Sippola, L. K. (1995). Peer variables as predictors of later childhood adjustment. *Development and Psychopathology, 7,* 787–802.

Hudspeth, W. J., & Pribram, K. H. (1992). Psychophysiological indices of cognitive maturation. *International Journal of Psychophysiology, 12,* 19–29.

Hughes, C., & Dunn, J. (1998). Understanding mind and emotion: Longitudinal associations with mental-state talk between young friends. *Developmental Psychology, 34,* 1026–1037.

Hughes, D., & Chen, L. A. (1999). The nature of parents' race-related communications to children: A developmental perspective. In L. Bolter & C. S. Tamis-LeMonda (Eds.), *Child psychology: A handbook of contemporary issues* (pp. 467–490). Philadelphia: Psychology Press.

Hughes, J. N., Cavell, T. A., & Grossman, P. B. (1997). A positive view of self: Risk or protection for aggressive children? *Development and Psychopathology, 9,* 75–94.

Hulanicka, B. (1999). Acceleration of menarcheal age of girls from dysfunctional families. *Journal of Reproductive and Infant Psychology, 17,* 119–132.

Human Genome Program, U.S. Department of Energy. (2003). *Genomics and its impact on science and society: A 2003 primer.* Washington, DC: U.S. Department of Energy.

Hummert, M. L. (1999). A social cognitive perspective on age stereotypes. In T. M. Hess & F. Blanchard-Fields (Eds.), *Social cognition and aging* (pp. 176–196). San Diego, CA: Academic Press.

Hummert, M. L., Garstka, T. A., & Shaner, J. L. (1997). Stereotyping of older adults: The role of target facial cues and perceiver characteristics. *Psychology and Aging, 12,* 107–114.

Hummert, M. L., Garstka, T. A., Shaner, J. L., & Strahm, S. (1994). Stereotypes of the elderly held by young, middle-aged, and elderly adults. *Journal of Gerontology: Psychological Sciences, 49,* P240–P249.

Hummert, M. L., & Ryan, E. B. (1996). Toward understanding variations in patronizing talk addressed to older adults: Psycholinguistic features of care and control. *International Journal of Psycholinguistics, 12,* 149–169.

Hummert, M. L., Shaner, J. L., Garstka, T. A., & Henry, C. (1998). Communication with older adults: The influence of age stereotypes, context, and communicator age. *Human Communication Research, 25,* 124–151.

Hunter, A. G., & Davis, J. E. (1992). Constructing gender: An exploration of Afro-American men's conceptualization of manhood. *American Sociological Review, 12,* 109–130.

Huston, A. C. (1983). Sex-typing. In P. H. Mussen (Series Ed.) & E. M. Hetherington (Vol. Ed.), *Handbook of child psychology: Vol. 4. Socialization, personality and social development* (pp. 388–467). New York: Wiley.

Huttenlocher, J., & Smiley, P. (1990). Emerging notions of persons. In N. L. Stein, B. Leventhal, & T. Trabasso (Eds.), *Psychological and biological approaches to emotion* (pp. 283–295). Chicago: University of Chicago.

Huttenlocher, P. (1994). Synaptogenesis, synapse elimination, and neural plasticity in human cerebral cortex. In C. A. Nelson (Ed.), *Minnesota Symposium on Child Psychology: Vol. 27. Threats to optimal development: Integrating biological, psychological, and social risk factors* (pp. 35–54). Hillsdale, NJ: Erlbaum.

Hyde, J. S. (1984). How large are gender differences in aggression? A developmental meta-analysis. *Developmental Psychology, 20,* 722–736.

Hyde, J. S., DeLamater, J. D., & Durik, A. M. (2001). Sexuality and the dual-earner couple: Part II. Beyond the baby years. *Journal of Sex Research, 38,* 10–23.

Hyde, J. S., Fennema, E., & Lamon, S. J. (1990). Gender differences in mathematics performance: A meta-analysis. *Psychological Bulletin, 107,* 139–155.

Hyman, I. E., & Faries, J. M. (1992). The function of autobiographical memory. In M. A. Conway, D. C. Rubin, H. Spinnler, & W. A. Wagenaar (Eds.), *Theoretical perspectives on autobiographical memory* (pp. 207–221). Boston: Kluwer Academic Press.

Hymel, S., & Rubin, K. H. (1985). Children with peer relationship and social skills problems: Conceptual, methodological, and developmental issues. In G. J. Whitehurst (Ed.), *Annals of child development* (Vol. 2, pp. 254–297). Greenwich, CT: JAI Press.

Idler, E. L., & Kasl, S. (1991). Health perceptions and survival: Do global evaluations of health status really predict mortality? *Journal of Gerontology: Social Sciences, 46,* S55–S65.

Ingram, R. E., Cruet, D., Johnson, B., & Wisnicki, K. (1988). Self-focused attention, gender, gender-role, and vulnerability to negative affect. *Journal of Personality and Social Psychology, 55,* 1039–1044.

Ingram, R. E., & Price, J. M. (2001). *Vulnerability to psychopathology: Risk across the lifespan.* New York: Guilford Press.

Inhelder, B., & Piaget, J. (1955/1958). *The growth of logical thinking from childhood to adolescence.* New York: Basic Books.

Inhelder, B., & Piaget, P. (1964). *The early growth of logic in the child.* New York: Harper & Row.

Institute of Medicine. (1994). *Reducing risks for mental disorders: Frontiers for preventive intervention research.* Washington, DC: National Academy Press.

International Human Genome Sequencing Consortium. (2004). Finishing the euchromatic sequence of the human genome. *Nature, 431,* 931–945.

Intons-Peterson, M. J. (1988). *Gender concepts of Swedish and American youth.* Hillsdale, NJ: Erlbaum.

Ivey, A. E. (1986). *Developmental therapy: Theory into practice.* San Francisco: Jossey-Bass.

Ivey, A. E., & Ivey, M. B. (1998). Reframing DSM-IV: Positive strategies from developmental counseling and therapy. *Journal of Counseling and Development, 76,* 334–350.

Ivey, A. E., & Ivey, M. B. (1999). Toward a developmental diagnostic and statistical manual: The vitality of a contextualist framework. *Journal of Counseling and Development, 77,* 484–490.

Izard, C. (1991). *The psychology of emotion.* New York: Plenum Press.

Izard, C. E. (1979). *The maximally discriminative facial movement coding system (Max).* Newark: University of Delaware, Information Technologies and University Media Services.

Izard, C. E. (1991). *The psychology of emotions.* New York: Plenum Press.

Izard, C. E. (1992). Basic emotions, relations among emotions, and emotion-cognition relations. *Psychological Review, 99,* 561–565.

Izard, C. E., Dougherty, L. M., & Hembree, E. A. (1983). *A system for identifying affect expression by holistic judgments (Affex).* Newark: University of Delaware, Computer Network Services and University Media Services.

Izard, C. E., & Malatesta, C. Z. (1987). Perspectives on emotional development I: Differential emotions theory of early emotional development. In J. D. Osofsky (Ed.), *Handbook of infant development* (2nd ed., pp. 494–554). New York: Wiley.

Jacobs, J. A., & Stoner-Eby, S. (1998). Adult enrollment in higher education and cumulative educational attainment, 1970–1990. *The Annals of the Academy of Political and Social Science, 559,* 91–108.

Jacobs, J. E., Lanza, S., Osgood, D. W., Eccles, J. A., & Wigfield, A. (2002). Changes in children's self-competence and values: Gender and domain differences across grades one through twelve. *Child Development, 73,* 509–527.

Jacobsen, T., & Hofmann, V. (1997). Children's attachment representations: Longitudinal relations to school behavior and academic competency in middle childhood and adolescence. *Developmental Psychology, 33,* 703–710.

Jacobson, N. S., & Addis, M. E. (1993). Research on couples and couple therapy: What do we know? Where are we going? *Journal of Consulting and Clinical Psychology, 61,* 547–557.

Jahromi, L. B., Putnam, S. P., & Stifter, C. A. (2004). Maternal regulation of infant reactivity from 2 to 6 months. *Developmental Psychology, 40,* 477–487.

James, W. (1890). *Principles of psychology.* Chicago: Encyclopedia Britannica.

Janda, L. H., & Klenke-Hamel, K. E. (1980). *Human sexuality.* New York: Van Nostrand.

Janoff-Bulman, R. (1993). *Shattered assumptions: Toward a new psychology of trauma.* New York: Free Press.

Janowsky, J. S., & Carper, R. (1996). Is there a neural basis for cognitive transitions in school age children? In A. J. Sameroff & M. M. Haith (Eds.), *The five to seven shift: The age of reason and responsibility* (pp. 33–60). Chicago: University of Chicago Press.

Jensen, P. S., & Hoagwood, K. (1997). The book of names: DSM-IV in context. *Development and Psychopathology, 9,* 231–249.

Jessor, R. (1993). Successful adolescent development among youth in high-risk settings. *American Psychologist, 48,* 117–126.

Jessor, R., Donovan, J. E., & Costa, F. M. (1991). *Beyond adolescence: Problem behavior and young adult development.* New York: Cambridge University Press.

Jessor, R., Van Den Bos, J., Vanderryn, J., Costa, F. M., & Turbin, M. S. (1995). Protective factors in adolescent problem behavior: Moderator effects and developmental change. *Developmental Psychology, 31,* 923–933.

Johnson, A., & Ames, E. (1994). The influence of gender labelling on preschoolers' gender constancy judgements. *British Journal of Developmental Psychology, 12,* 241–249.

Johnson, C. A., Pentz, M. A., Weber, M. D., Dwyer, J. H., Baer, N., MacKinnon, D. R., et al. (1990). Relative effectiveness of comprehensive community programming for drug abuse prevention with high-risk and low-risk adolescents. *Journal of Consulting and Clinical Psychology, 58,* 447–456.

Johnson, C. L., & Troll, L. (1994). Constraints and facilitators to friendships in late late life. *The Gerontologist, 34,* 79–87.

Johnson, L. D., O'Malley, P. M., & Bachman, J. G. (1994). *National survey results on drug use from the Monitoring the Future Study: 1975–1993.* Rockville, MD: National Institute on Drug Abuse.

Johnson, M. H. (1998). The neural basis of cognitive development. In W. Daman (Series Ed.), D. Kuhn, & R. S. Siegler (Vol. 2, Eds.), *Handbook of child psychology: Vol. 2 Cognition, perception, and language.* (5th ed., pp. 1–49). New York: Wiley.

Johnson, R. W., & Favreault, M. M. (2004). Economic status in later life among women who raised children outside of marriage. *Journals of Gerontology: Series B: Psychological Sciences & Social Sciences, 59,* 315–323.

Johnson, S. M. (2003). The revolution in couple therapy: A practitioner-scientist perspective. *Journal of Marital and Family Therapy, 29,* 365–384.

Johnson, S. M., Hunsley, J., Greenberg, L., & Schindler, D. (1999). Emotionally-focused couples therapy: Status and challenges. *Clinical Psychology: Science and Practice, 6,* 67–79.

Johnson, T. H. (1960). *The complete poems of Emily Dickinson.* Boston: Little, Brown.

Johnston, C., & Ohan, J. L. (1999). Externalizing disorders. In W. K. Silverman & T. H. Ollendick (Eds.), *Developmental issues in the clinical treatment of children,* (pp. 279–294). Needham Heights, MA: Allyn & Bacon.

Johnston, L. D., O'Malley, P. M., & Bachman, J. G. (2004). *The monitoring the future national survey results on adolescent drug use. Overview of key findings, 2003.* Bethesada, MD: National Institute on Drug Abuse.

Joiner, T. E., Jr. (2000). Depression: Current developments and controversies. In S. H. Qualls & N. Abeles (Eds.), *Psychology and the aging revolution: How we adapt to longer life* (pp. 223–237). Washington, DC: American Psychological Association.

Jones, D. C. (2004). Body image among adolescent girls and boys: A longitudinal study. *Developmental Psychology, 40,* 823–835.

Jones, L. K. (1996). A harsh and challenging world of work: Implications for counselors. *Journal of Counseling and Development, 74,* 453–459.

Jordan, N. C., Huttenlocher, J., & Levine, S. C. (1994). Assessing early arithmetic abilities: Effects of verbal and nonverbal response types on the calculation performance of middle- and low-income children. *Learning and Individual Differences, 6,* 413–432.

Josselson, R. L. (1973). Psychodynamic aspects of identity formation in college women. *Journal of Youth and Adolescence, 2,* 3–15.

Josselson, R. L. (1988). *Finding herself: Pathways of identity development in women.* New York: Jossey-Bass.

Josselson, R. L. (1994). The theory of identity development and the question of intervention: An introduction. In S. Archer (Ed.), *Interventions for adolescent identity development* (pp. 12–25). Thousand Oaks, CA: Sage.

Judd, C. M., Park, B., Ryan, C. S., Bauer, M., & Kraus, S. (1995). Stereotypes and ethnocentrism: Diverging interethnic perceptions of African American and White American youth. *Journal of Personality and Social Psychology, 69,* 460–481.

Jung, C. G. (1928). *Two essays on analytical psychology.* New York: Dodd, Mead.

Jung, C. G. (1963). *Memories, dreams, reflections.* New York: Random House.

Kabat-Zinn, J. (1994). *Wherever you go, there you are.* New York: Hyperion.

Kabat-Zinn, J. (2003). Mindfulness-based interventions in context: Past, present and future. *Clinical Psychology: Science and Practice, 10,* 144–156.

Kabat-Zinn, J. (2005). *Coming to our senses: Healing ourselves and the world through mindfulness.* New York: Hyperion.

Kabat-Zinn, J., Lipworth, L., Burney, R., & Sellers, W. (1986). Four-year follow-up of a meditation-based stress reduction program for the self-regulation of chronic pain: Treatment outcomes and compliance. *Clinical Journal of Pain, 2,* 159–173.

Kabat-Zinn, J., Massion, A. O., Kristeller, J., Peterson, L. G., Fletcher, K., Pbert, L., Linderking, W., & Santorelli, S. F. (1992). Effectiveness of a meditation-based stress reduction program in the treatment of anxiety disorders. *American Journal of Psychiatry, 149,* 936–943.

Kabat-Zinn, J., Wheeler, E., Light, T., Skillings, A., Scharf, M., Cropley, T. G., et al. (1998). Influence of a mindfulness-based stress reduction intervention on rates of skin clearing in patients with moderate to severe psoriasis undergoing phototherapy (UVB) and photochemotherapy (PUVA). *Psychosomatic Medicine, 60,* 625–632.

Kach, J. A., & McGee, P. E. (1982). Adjustment of early parenthood. *Journal of Family Issues, 3,* 375–388.

Kagan, J. (1981). *The second year: The emergence of self-awareness.* Cambridge, MA: Harvard University Press.

Kagan, J. (1984). *The nature of the child.* New York: Basic Books.

Kagan, J. (1994). Yesterday's premises: Tomorrow's promises. In R. D. Parke, R. A. Ornstein, J. J. Rieser, & C. Sahn-Waxler (Eds.), *A century of developmental psychology* (pp. 551–568). Washington, DC: American Psychological Association.

Kagan, J. (1997). Temperament and the reactions to unfamiliarity. *Child Development, 68,* 139–143.

Kagan, J. (1998). Biology and the child. In W. Damon (Series Ed.) & N. Eisenberg (Vol. Ed.), *Handbook of child psychology: Vol. 3. Social, emotional, and personality development* (5th ed., pp. 177–236).

Kagan, J. (2002). *Surprise, uncertainty, and mental structures.* Cambridge, MA: Harvard University Press.

Kagan, J., Arcus, D., Snidman, N., & Rimm, S. E. (1995). Assymmetry of forehead temperature and cardiac activity. *Neuropsychology, 9,* 1–5.

Kagan, J., Arcus, D., Snidman, N., Yufeng, W., Hendler, J., & Greene, S. (1994). Reactivity in infants: A cross-national comparison. *Developmental Psychology, 30,* 342–345.

Kagan, J., Kearsley, R., & Zelazo, P. (1978). *Infancy: Its place in human development.* Cambridge, MA: Harvard University Press.

Kahneman, D., Krueger, A. B., Schkade, D., Schwarz, N., & Stone, A. (2004). A survey method for characterizing daily life experience: The day reconstruction method. *Science, 306,* 1776–1781.

Kahneman, D., & Tversky, A. (1984). Choices, values and frames. *American Psychologist, 39,* 341–350.

Kail, R. (1991). Developmental changes in speed of processing during childhood and adolescence. *Psychological Bulletin, 109,* 490–501.

Kail, R. (1993). Processing time decreases globally at an exponential rate during childhood and adolescence. *Journal of Experimental Child Psychology, 56,* 254–265.

Kail, R., & Salthouse, T. (1994). Processing speed as a mental capacity. *Acta Psychologica, 86,* 199–225.

Kaiser Family Foundation (2003). *Zero to Six: Electronic media in the lives of infants toddlers and preschoolers.* Washington, DC: Author.

Kaiser Family Foundation (2005). Executive Summary: *Generation M: Media in the lives of 8–18 year-olds.* Washington, DC: Author.

Kalish, R. A. (1985). The social context of death and dying. In R. H. Binstock & E. Shanas (Eds.), *Handbook of aging and the social sciences* (2nd ed., pp. 147–170). New York: Van Nostrand Reinhold.

Kamii, C. (1986). Place value: An explanation of its difficulty and educational implications for the primary grades. *Journal of Research in Childhood Education, 1,* 75–86.

Kamii, M. (1990). Why Big Bird can't teach calculus: The case of place value and cognitive development in the middle years. In N. Lauter-Klatell (Ed.), *Readings in child development.* (pp. 101–104, 170). Mountain View, CA: Mayfield.

Kandel, D. B. (1978). Homophily, selection, and socialization in adolescent friendships. *American Journal of Sociology, 84,* 427–436.

Kane, R. S. (1996). The defeat of aging versus the importance of death. *Journal of the American Geriatric Society, 44,* 321–325.

Kane, R., Wales, J., Bernstein, L., Leibowitz, A., & Kaplan, S. (1984). A randomized controlled trial of hospice care. *The Lancet, 302,* 890–894.

Kaplan, H. B. (1980). *Deviant behavior in defense of self.* New York: Academic Press.

Karen, R. (1998). *Becoming attached: First relationships and how they shape our capacity to love.* New York: Oxford University Press.

Karmiloff-Smith, A. (1992). *Beyond modularity: A developmental perspective on cognitive science.* Cambridge, MA: MIT Press.

Karmiloff-Smith, A. (2000). Why babies' brains are not Swiss army knives. In H. Rose & S. Rose (Eds.), *Alas, poor Darwin* (pp. 173–187). New York: Harmony Books.

Karney, B. R., & Bradbury, T. N. (1995). The longitudinal course of marital quality and stability: A review of theory, method, and research. *Psychological Bulletin, 118,* 3–34.

Karney, B. R., & Bradbury, T. N. (1997). Neuroticism, marital interaction, and the trajectory of marital satisfaction. *Journal of Personality and Social Psychology, 72,* 1075–1092.

Kaslow, F. W. (2001). Families and family psychology at the millennium. *American Psychologist, 56,* 37–46.

Kasser, T., & Ryan, R. M. (1996). Further examining the American dream: Differential correlates of intrinsic and extrinsic goals. *Personality and Social Psychology Bulletin, 22,* 280–287.

Kasser, T., & Ryan, R. M. (1999). The relation of psychological needs for autonomy and relatedness to vitality, well-being, mortality in a nursing home. *Journal of Applied Social Psychology, 29,* 935–954.

Kastenbaum, R. (1986). *Death, society, and human experience* (3rd ed.). Columbus, OH: Merrill.

Katchadourian, H. A. (1987). *Fifty: Midlife in perspective.* New York: Freeman.

Katz, L. C., & Shatz, C. J. (1996). Synaptic activity and the construction of cortical circuits. *Science, 274,* 1133–1138.

Katz, P. A., & Walsh, V. (1991). Developmental aspects of gender role flexibility and traditionality in middle childhood and adolescence. *Child Development, 30,* 272–282.

Katz, P., & Zalk, S. (1974). Doll preferences: An index of racial attitudes? *Journal of Educational Psychology, 66,* 663–668.

Kazdin, A. E. (1991). Effectiveness of psychotherapy with children and adolescents. *Journal of Consulting and Clinical Psychology, 59(6),* 785–798.

Kazdin, A. E. (2003). Psychotherapy for children and adolescents. *Annual Review of Psychology, 54,* 273–276.

Keelan, J. P. R., Dion, K. K., & Dion, K. L. (1998). Attachment style and relationship satisfaction: Test of a self-disclosure explanation. *Canadian Journal of Behavioural Science, 30,* 24–35.

Keenan, K., & Shaw, D. (1997). Developmental and social influences on young girls' early problem behavior. *Psychological Bulletin, 121,* 95–113.

Kegan, R. (1982). *The evolving self.* Cambridge, MA: Harvard University Press.

Kellett, J. M. (2000). Older adult sexuality. In L. T. Szuchman & F. Muscarella (Eds.), *Psychological perspectives on human sexuality* (pp. 355–379). New York: Wiley.

Kelly, E. L., & Conley, J. J. (1987). Personality and compatibility: An analysis of marital stability and marital satisfaction. *Journal of Personality and Social Psychology, 52,* 27–40.

Kemeny, M. E. (2003). The psychobiology of stress. *Current Directions in Psychological Science, 12,* 124–129.

Kempermann, G., & Gage, F. H. (1999). New nerve cells for the adult brain. *Scientific American, 280,* 48–53.

Kempson, R. M. (1988). Mental representations: *The interface between language and reality.* Cambridge, MA: Cambridge University Press.

Kendall, P. C. (1991). *Child and adolescent therapy.* New York: Guilford Press.

Kendall, P. C. (1993). Cognitive-behavioral therapies with youth: Guiding theory, current status, and emerging developments. *Journal of Consulting and Clinical Psychology, 61,* 235–247.

Kendler, K. S., Thornton, L. M., & Gardner, C. O. (2001). Genetic risk, number of previous depressive episodes, and stressful life events in predicting onset of major depression. *American Journal of Psychiatry, 158,* 582–586.

Kendall, P. C., & Wilcox, L. E. (1980). Cognitive-behavioral treatment for impulsivity: Concrete versus conceptual training in non-self-controlled problem children. *Journal of Consulting and Clinical Psychology, 48,* 80–91.

Keniston, K. (1971). *Youth in dissent: The rise of a new opposition.* New York: Harcourt Brace Jovanovich.

Kennedy, G. J., & Tanenbaum, S. (2000). Psychotherapy with older adults. *American Journal of Psychotherapy, 54,* 386–407.

Kerig, P. K., Cowan, P. A., & Cowan, C. P. (1993). Marital quality and gender differences in parent–child interaction. *Developmental Psychology, 29,* 931–939.

Kernberg, O. (1976). *Object relations theory and clinical psychoanalysis.* New York: Aronson.

Kessler, R. C., Turner, J. B., & House, J. S. (1989). Unemployment, reemployment, and emotional functioning in a community sample. *American Sociological Review, 54,* 648–657.

Keup, J. R., & Stolzenberg, E. B. (2004). *The 2003 Your First College Year (YFCY) survey: Exploring the academic and personal experiences of first-year students.* Los Angeles: National Resource Center for The First-Year Experience & Students in Transition & Higher Education Research Institute at UCLA.

Keyes, C. L. M., & Haidt, J. (2003). *Flourishing: Positive psychology and the well-lived life.* Washington, DC: American Psychological Association.

Khatri, P. (1995, March). *Behavioral and academic correlates of sociometric status among rural Indian children.* Paper presented at the biennial meeting of the Society for Research in Child Development, Indianapolis, IN.

Kieffer, K. M., Schinka, J. A., & Curtiss, G. (2004). Person-environment congruence and personality domains in the prediction of job performance and work quality. *Journal of Counseling Psychology, 51,* 168–177.

Kikuchi, J. (1988, Fall). Rhode Island develops successful intervention program for adolescents. *National Coalition Against Sexual Assault Newsletter.*

Killgore, W. D. S., Oki, M., & Yurgelun-Todd, D. A. (2001). Sex-specific developmental changes in amygdala responses to affective faces. *Neuroreport: For Rapid Communication of Neuroscience Research, 12,* 427–433.

Kilmartin, C. T. (1994). *The masculine self.* New York: Macmillan.

Kindermann, T. A. (1993). Natural peer groups as contexts for individual development: The case of children's motivation in school. *Developmental Psychology, 29,* 970–977.

Kindlon, D., & Thompson, M. (1990). *Raising Cain: Protecting the emotional life of boys.* New York: Ballantine Books.

King, P. M. (2000). Learning to make reflective judgments. *New Directions for Teaching and Learning, 82,* 15–26.

King, P. M., & Howard-Hamilton, M. F. (1999). *Becoming a multiculturally competent student affairs professional.* Final report submitted to the National Association of Student Personal Association, 1999. [http://www.naspa.org]

Kirkpatrick, L. A., & Davis, K. E. (1994). Attachment style, gender, and relationship stability: A longitudinal analysis. *Journal of Personality and Social Psychology, 66,* 502–512.

Kirschner, D. (1992). Understanding adoptees who kill: Dissociation, patricide, and the psychodynamics of adoption. *International Journal of Offender Therapy and Comparative Criminology, 36,* 323–333.

Kiselica, M. S. (2003). Transforming psychotherapy in order to succeed with adolescent boys: Male-friendly practices. *Journal of Clinical Psychology, 59,* 1225–1236.

Kitchener, K. S. (1983). Cognition, metacognition, and epistemic cognition: A three-level model of cognitive processing. *Human Development, 4,* 222–232.

Kitchener, K. S., & King, P. M. (1981). Reflective judgment: Concepts of justification and their relationship to age and education. *Journal of Applied Developmental Psychology, 2,* 89–116.

Kitchener, K. S., King, P. M., Wood, P. K., & Davison, M. L. (1989). Sequentiality and consistency in the development of reflective judgment: A six-year longitudinal study. *Journal of Applied Developmental Psychology, 10,* 73–95.

Kitchener, K. S., Lynch, C. L., Fischer, K. W., & Wood, P. K. (1993). Developmental range of reflective judgment: The effect of contextual support and practice on developmental stage. *Developmental Psychology, 29,* 893–906.

Kitzinger, C., & Wilkinson, S. (1995). Transitions from heterosexuality to lesbianism: The discursive production of lesbian identities. *Developmental Psychology, 31,* 95–104.

Klahr, D., & Nigam, M. (2004). The equivalence of learning paths in early science instruction: Effects of direct instruction and discovery learning. *Psychological Science, 15,* 661–667.

Klass, D. (1982). Elisabeth Kubler-Ross and the tradition of the private sphere: An analysis of symbols. *Omega, 16,* 241–261.

Klein, A., & Starkey, P. (1995). *Preparing for the transition to school mathematics: The Head Start Family Math project.* Paper presented at the meeting of the Society for Research in Child Development, Indianapolis, IN.

Klein, M. (1921–1945). *Contributions to psychoanalysis.* London: Hogarth.

Kleinman, A., & Kleinman, J. (1985). Somatization: The interconnections in Chinese society among culture, depressive experiences, and the meanings of pain. In A. Kleinman & B. Good (Eds.), *Culture and depression: Studies in the anthropology and cross-cultural psychiatry of affect and disorder* (pp. 429–490). Berkeley: University of California Press.

Klerman, G. L., Weissman, M. M., Rounsaville, B. J., & Chevron, E. S. (1984). *Interpersonal psychotherapy for depression.* New York: Basic Books.

Kling, K. C., Hyde, J. S., Showers, C. J., & Buswell, B. N. (1999). Gender differences in self-esteem: A meta-analysis. *Psychological Bulletin, 125,* 470–500.

Kling, K. C., Seltzer, M. M., & Ryff, C. D. (1997). Distinctive late-life challenges: Implications for coping and well-being. *Psychology and Aging, 12,* 288–295.

Klinnert, M. (1984). The regulation of infant behavior by maternal facial expression. *Infant Behavior and Development, 7,* 447–465.

Knafo, A., Iervolino, A. C., & Plomin, R. (2005). Masculine girls and feminine boys: Genetic and environmental contributions to atypical gender development in early childhood. *Journal of Personality and Social Psychology, 88,* 400–412.

Kneflekamp, L. L. (1999). Introduction. In W. G. Perry, *Forms of ethical development in the college years: A scheme* (p. xix). San Francisco: Jossey-Bass.

Kochanska, G. (1993). Toward a synthesis of parental socialization and child temperament in early development of conscience. *Child Development, 64,* 325–347.

Kochanska, G. (1995). Children's temperament, mothers' discipline, and security of attachment: Multiple pathways to emerging internalization. *Child Development, 66,* 597–615.

Kochanska, G. (1998). Mother-child relationship, child fearfulness, and emerging attachment: A short-term longitudinal study. *Developmental Psychology, 34,* 480–490.

Kochanska, G., Aksan, N., & Koenig, A. L. (1995). A longitudinal study of the roots of preschoolers' conscience: Committed compliance and emerging internalization. *Child Development, 66,* 1752–1769.

Kochanska, G., Casey, R. J., & Fukumoto, A. (1995). Toddlers' sensitivity to standard violations. *Child Development, 66,* 643–656.

Kochanska, G., & Murray, K. T. (2000). Mother-child mutually responsive orientation and conscience development: From toddler to early school age. *Child Development, 71,* 417–431.

Kochanska, G., Tjebkes, T. L., & Forman, D. R. (1998). Children's emerging regulation of conduct: Restraint, compliance, and internalization from infancy to the second year. *Child Development, 69,* 1378–1389.

Kohlberg, L. (1966). Moral education in the school. *School Review, 74,* 1–30.

Kohlberg, L. (1976). Moral stages and moralization: The cognitive developmental approach. In T. Lickona (Ed.), *Moral development and behavior: Theory, research and social issues* (pp. 31–53). New York: Holt, Rinehart and Winston.

Kohlberg, L. (1984). *Essays on moral development: The psychology of moral development.* San Francisco: Harper & Row.

Kohlberg, L. A. (1966). A cognitive-developmental analysis of children's sex role concepts and attitudes. In E. E. Maccoby (Ed.), *The development of sex differences* (pp. 82–173). Stanford, CA: Stanford University Press.

Kohn, A. (1997, February). How not to teach values: A critical look at character education. *Phi Delta Kappan,* pp. 428–439.

Kolb, B., Gibb, R., & Robinson, T. E. (2003). Brain plasticity and behavior. *Current Directions in Psychological Science, 12,* 1–5.

Kondo-Ikemura, K. (2001). Insufficient evidence. *American Psychologist, 56,* 825–826.

Konner, M. J., & Worthman, C. (1980). Nursing frequency, gonadal function and birth-spacing among !Kung hunters and gatherers. *Science, 207,* 788–791.

Kopp, C. B. (1982). Antecedents of self-regulation: A developmental perspective. *Developmental Psychology, 18,* 199–214.

Kopp, C. B., & Wyer, N. (1994). Self-regulation in normal and atypical development. In D. Cicchetti & S. L. Toth (Eds.), *Rochester Symposium on Developmental Psychopathology: Vol. 5. Disorders and dysfunctions of the self* (pp. 31–56). Rochester, NY: University of Rochester Press.

Kornfield, J. (2002). *The art of forgiveness, lovingkindness, and peace.* New York: Bantam Books.

Kotch, J. B., Blakely, C. H., Brown, S. S., & Wong, F. Y. (Eds.). (1992). *A pound of prevention: The case for universal maternity care in the US.* Washington, DC: American Public Health Association.

Kreutzer, M. A., Leonard, C., & Flavell, J. H. (1975). An interview study of children's knowledge about memory. *Monographs of the Society for Research in Child Development, 40* (Serial No. 159).

Krieder, R. M., & Fields, J. M. (2002). Number, timing and durations of marriages and divorces: 1996. *U.S. Census Bureau Current Population Reports, February 2002.* 18.

Kristeller, J., Hallett, L., & Brendan, C. (1999). An exploratory study of a meditation-based intervention for binge eating disorder. *Journal of Health Psychology, 4,* 357–363.

Kroger, J. (1983). A developmental study of identity formation among late adolescent and adult women. *Psychological Documents, 13* (Ms. No. 2537).

Krohne, H. W., & Rogner, J. (1982). Repression-sensitization as a central construct in coping research. In J. G. Schulterbrandt & A. Raskin (Eds.), *Depression in childhood: Diagnosis, treatment, and conceptual models* (pp. 1–25). New York: Raven.

Kruger, A. C. (1992). The effect of peer and adult-child transductive discussions on moral reasoning. *Merrill-Palmer Quarterly, 38,* 191–211.

Kruger, A. C., & Tomasello, M. (1986). Transactive discussions with peers and adults. *Developmental Psychology, 22,* 681–685.

Krumboltz, J. D. (1966). Behavioral goals for counseling. *Journal of Counseling Psychology, 13,* 153–159.

Kubler-Ross, E. (1969). *On death and dying.* New York: Macmillan.

Kubler-Ross, E. (1974). *Questions and answers on death and dying.* New York: Macmillan.

Kuczynski, L. (1984). Socialization goals and mother-child interaction: Strategies for long-term and short-term compliance. *Developmental Psychology, 20,* 1061–1073.

Kuhl, P. K., Williams, K. A., Lacerda, F., Stevens, K. N., & Lindblom, B. (1992). Linguistic experience alters phonetic perception in infants by 6 months of age. *Science, 255,* 606–608.

Kuhn, D. (1989). Children and adults as intuitive scientists. *Psychological Review, 96,* 674–689.

Kuhn, D. (1991). *The skills of argument.* Cambridge, England: Cambridge University Press.

Kuhn, D. (1992). Thinking as argument. *Harvard Educational Review, 62,* 155–178.

Kuhn, D. (2000a). Does memory development belong on an endangered topic list? *Child Development, 71,* 21–25.

Kuhn, D. (2000b). Metacognitive development. *Current Directions in Psychological Science, 9,* 178–181.

Kuhn, D., Amsel, E., & O'Loughlin, M. (1988). *The development of scientific reasoning skills.* New York: Academic Press.

Kuhn, D., Garcia-Mila, M., Zohar, A., & Andersen, C. (1995). Strategies of knowledge acquisition. *Monographs of the Society for Research in Child Development, 60* (Serial No. 245).

Kuhn, D., Pennington, N., & Leadbeater, B. (1982). Adult thinking in developmental perspective. In P. B. Baltes & O. Brim (Eds.), *Life span development and behavior* (pp. 157–195). New York: Academic Press.

Kuhn, D., Schauble, L., & Garcia-Mila, M. (1992). Cross-domain development of scientific reasoning. *Cognition and Instruction, 9,* 285–327.

Kunzmann, U., & Baltes, P. B. (2003). Wisdom-related knowledge: Affective, motivational, and interpersonal correlates. *Personality and Social Psychology Bulletin, 29,* 1104–1119.

Kupersmidt, J. B., Burchinal, M., & Patterson, C. J. (1995). Developmental patterns of childhood peer relations as predictors of externalizing problems in adolescence. *Child Development, 61,* 1350–1362.

Kurdek, L. A. (1993). Predicting marital dissolution: A 5-year prospective longitudinal study of newlywed couples. *Journal of Personality and Social Psychology, 64,* 221–242.

Kurtz, B. E., Carr, M., Borkowski, J. G., Schneider, W., & Rellinger, E. (1990). Strategy instruction and attributional beliefs in West Germany and the United States: Do teachers foster metacognitive development? *Contemporary Educational Psychology, 15,* 268–283.

Labouvie-Vief, G. (1984). Logic and self regulation from youth to maturity: A model. In M. L. Commons, F. A. Richards, & C. Armon (Eds.), *Beyond formal operations: Late adolescent and adult cognitive development* (pp. 158–179). New York: Praeger.

Labouvie-Vief, G., Chiodo, L. M., Goguen, L. A., Diehl, M., & Orwoll, L. (1995). Representations of self across the life span. *Psychology and Aging, 10,* 404–415.

Labouvie-Vief, G., Lumley, M. A., Jain, E., & Heinze, H. (2003). Age and gender differences in cardiac reactivity and subjective emotion responses to emotional autobiographical memories. *Emotion, 3,* 115–126.

Lacasa, P., & Villuendas, D. (1990). Adult-child and peer relationship: Action, representation,

and learning process. *Learning and Instruction, 2,* 75–93.

Lachman, M. E. (2004). Development in midlife. *Annual Review of Psychology, 55,* 305–331.

Ladd, G. W., & Asher, S. R. (1985). Social skills training and children's peer relations. In L. L'Abate & M. Milan (Eds.), *Handbook of social skills training and research* (pp. 219–244). New York: Wiley.

Ladd, G. W., & Burgess, K. B. (1999). Charting the relationship trajectories of aggressive, withdrawn, and aggressive/withdrawn children during early grade school. *Child Development, 70,* 910–929.

Ladd, G. W., & Ladd, B. K. (1998). Parenting behaviors and parent-child relationships: Correlates of peer victimization in kindergarten? *Developmental Psychology, 34,* 1450–1458.

Ladd, G. W., & Mize, J. (1983). A cognitive-social learning model of social skills training. *Psychological Review, 90,* 127–157.

La Freniere, P., Strayer, F. F., and Gauthier, R. (1984). The emergence of same-sex affiliative preferences among preschool peers: A developmental/ethological perspective. *Child Development, 55,* 1958–1965.

Lahey, B. B., McBurnett, K., Loeber, R. (2000). Are attention-deficit/hyperactivity disorder and oppositional defiant disorder developmental precursors to conduct disorder? In A. J. Sameroff, M. Lewis, & S. M. Miller (Eds.), *Handbook of developmental psychopathology* (2nd ed., pp.431–446). New York: Kluwer Academic/Plenum.

Lahey, B., Loeber, R., Quay, H. C., Frick, P. J., & Grimm, J. (1992). Oppositional defiant and conduct disorders: Issues to be resolved for DSM-IV. *Journal of the American Academy of Child and Adolescent Psychiatry, 31,* 539–546.

Laible, D. J. (2004). Mother-child discourse surrounding a child's past behavior at 30 months: Links to emotional understanding and early conscience development at 36 months. *Merrill-Palmer Quarterly, 30,* 159–180.

Laible, D. J., & Thompson, R. A. (1998). Attachment and emotional understanding in preschool children. *Developmental Psychology, 34,* 1038–1045.

Laible, D. J., & Thompson, R. A. (2002). Mother-child Lessons in emotion, morality, and relationships. *Child Development, 73,* 1187–1203.

Lamb, M. E., & Sternberg, K. J. (1990). Do we really know how day care affects children? *Journal of Applied Developmental Psychology, 11,* 352–379.

Lambert, M. J., Bergin, A. E. (1994), The effectiveness of psychotherapy. In A. E. Bergin & S. L. Garfield (Eds.), *Handbook of psychotherapy and behavior change* (4th ed., pp. 143–189). New York: Wiley.

Lamborn, S. D., Dornbusch, S. M., & Steinberg, L. (1996). Ethnicity and community context as moderators of the relations between family decision making and adolescent adjustment. *Child Development, 67,* 283–301.

Lamborn, S. D., Mounts, N. S., Steinberg, L., & Dornbusch, S. M. (1991). Patterns of competence and adjustment among adolescents from authoritative, authoritarian, indulgent, and neglectful families. *Child Development, 62,* 1049–1065.

Landale, N. S., & Fennelly, K. (1992). Informal unions among mainland Puerto Ricans: Cohabitation or an alternative to legal marriage? *Journal of Marriage and the Family, 54,* 269–280.

Landreth, G. L. (2002a). *Play therapy: The art of the relationship* (2nd ed.). New York: Brunner-Routledge.

Landreth, G. L. (2002b). Therapeutic limits in the play therapy relationship. *Professional Psychology: Research and Practice, 33,* 529–522.

Lang, F. R., & Carstensen, L. L. (1994). Close emotional relationships in late life: Further support for proactive aging in the social domain. *Psychology and Aging, 9,* 315–324.

Langlois, J. H., Ritter, J. M., Casey, R. J., & Savin, D. B. (1995). Infant attractiveness predicts maternal behaviors and attitudes. *Developmental Psychology, 31,* 164–172.

Langlois, J. H., & Stephan, C. W. (1981). Beauty and the beast: The role of physical attraction in peer relationships and social behavior. In S. S. Brehm, S. M. Kassin, & S. X. Gibbans (Eds.), *Developmental social psychology: Theory and research* (pp. 152–168). New York: Oxford University Press.

Lansford, J. E., Deater-Deckard, K., Dodge, K. A., Bates, J. E., & Pettit, G. S. (2004). Ethnic differences in the link between physical discipline and later adolescent externalizing behaviors. *Journal of Child Psychology and Psychiatry, 45,* 801–812.

Lapsley, D. K. (1993). Toward an integrated theory of adolescent ego development: The "new look" at adolescent egocentrism. *American Journal of Orthopsychiatry, 63,* 562–571.

Lapsley, D. K., FitzGerald, D. P., Rice, K. G., & Jackson, S. (1989). Separation-individuation and the "new look" at the imaginary audience and personal fable: A test of an integrative model. *Journal of Adolescent Research, 4,* 483–505.

Lapsley, D. K., & Murphy, M. N. (1985). Another look at the theoretical assumptions of adolescent egocentrism. *Developmental Review, 5,* 201–217.

Largie, S., Field, T., Hernandez-Reif, M., Sanders, C. E., & Diego, M. (2001). Employment during adolescence is associated with depression, inferior relationships, lower grades, and smoking. *Adolescence, 36,* 395–401.

Larrieu, J. A., & Mussen, P. (1986). Some personality and motivational correlates of children's prosocial behavior. *Journal of Genetic Psychology, 147,* 529–542.

Larsen, S. F. (2000). Memorable books: Recall of reading in its personal context. In M. S. MacNealey & R. Kreuz (Eds.), *Empirical approaches to literature and aesthetics: Advances in discourse processes* (Vol. 52, pp. 583–599). Norwood, NJ: Ablex.

Larson, R., & Richards, M. H. (1994). *Divergent realities: The emotional lives of mothers, fathers, and adolescents.* New York: Basic Books.

Lasch, C. (1991). *The true and only heaven: Progress and its critics.* New York: Norton.

Laub, J. H. (1999). Alterations in the opportunity structure: A criminological perspective. In A. Booth, A. C. Crouter, & M. J. Shanahan (Eds.), *Transitions to adulthood in a changing economy: No work, no family, no future?* (pp. 48–55). Westport, CT: Praeger.

Laursen, B. M., Coy, K. C., & Collins, W. A. (1998). Reconsidering changes in parent-child conflict across adolescence: A meta-analysis. *Child Development, 69,* 817–832.

Laver, G. D., & Burke, D. M. (1993). Why do semantic priming effects increase in old age? A meta-analysis. *Psychology and Aging, 8,* 34–43.

Lay, K. L., Waters, E., & Parke, K. A. (1989). Maternal responsiveness and child compliance: The role of mood as a mediator. *Child Development, 60,* 1405–1411.

Lazarus, R. S. (1996). The role of coping in the emotions and how coping changes over the life course. In C. Malatesta-Magni & S. H. McFadden (Eds.), *Handbook of emotion, adult development, and aging* (pp. 289–306). New York: Academic Press.

Lazarus, R. S., & Folkman, S. (1984). *Stress, appraisal, and coping.* New York: Springer.

Leaper, C. (1994). Exploring the correlates and consequences of gender segregation: Social relationships in childhood, adolescence, and adulthood. In B. Damon (Series Ed.) & C. Leaper

(Vol. Ed.), *New directions for child development: The development of gender relationships*. San Francisco: Jossey-Bass.

Leaper, C., Anderson, K. J., & Sanders, P. (1998). Moderators of gender effects on parents' talk to their children. *Developmental Psychology, 34,* 3–27.

Leaper, C., & Smith, T. E. (2004). A meta-analytic review of gender variations in children's language use: Talkativeness, affiliative speech, and assertive speech. *Developmental Psychology, 40,* 993–1027.

L'Ecuyer, R. (1992). An experimental-developmental framework and methodology to study the transformations of the self-concept from infancy to old age. In T. M. Brinthaupt & R. P. Lipka (Eds.), *The self: Definitional and methodological issues* (pp. 96–136). Albany: Albany State University of New York Press.

Lederman, R. P. (1996). Relationship of anxiety, stress, and psychosocial development to reproductive health. *Behavioral Medicine, 21,* 101–112.

LeDoux, J. (1996). *The emotional brain: The mysterious underpinnings of emotional life.* New York: Simon & Schuster.

LeDoux, J. E. (1995). Emotion: Clues from the brain. *Annual Review of Psychology, 46,* 209–236.

Lee, J. A. (1973). *The colors of love: An exploration of the ways of loving.* Don Mills, Ontario, Canada: New Press.

Lehman, D. R., Lempert, R. O., & Nisbett, R. E. (1988). The effects of graduate training on reasoning. *American Psychologist, 43,* 431–442.

Leibowitz, S. F., Hammer, N. J., & Chang, K. (1981). Hypothalamic paraventricular nucleus lesions produce overeating and obesity in the rat. *Physiology and Behavior, 27,* 1031–1040.

Leichtman, M. D., & Ceci, S. J. (1995). The effects of stereotypes and suggestions on preschoolers' reports. *Developmental Psychology, 31,* 568–578.

Leinbach, M. D., & Fagot, B. I. (1986). Acquisition of gender labeling: A test for toddlers. *Sex Roles, 15,* 655–666.

Leinbach, M. D., & Fagot, B. I. (1993). Categorical habituation to male and female faces: Gender schematic processing in infancy. *Infant Behavior and Development, 16,* 317–332.

Leitenberg, H., Greenwald, E., & Tarran, M. J. (1989). The relation between sexual activity among children during preadolescence and in early adolescence and sexual behavior and sexual adjustment in young adulthood. *Archives of Sexual Behavior, 18,* 299–313.

Leming, J. S. (1986). Kohlbergian programs in moral education: A practical review and assessment. In S. Modgil & C. Modgil (Eds.), *Lawrence Kohlberg: Consensus and controversy* (pp. 245–262, 275–276). Philadelphia: Falmer Press.

Leming, J. S. (1997). Whither goes character education? Objectives, pedagogy, and research in education programs. *Journal of Education, 179,* 11–34.

Lent, R. W., Brown, S. D., & Hackett, G. (1996). Career development from a social cognitive perspective. In D. Brown, L. Brooks, & Associates (Eds.), *Career choice and development* (3rd ed., pp. 373–421). San Francisco: Jossey-Bass.

Leonard, S. P., & Archer, J. (1989). A naturalistic investigation of gender constancy in three- and four-year-old children. *British Journal of Developmental Psychology, 7,* 341–346.

Lepore, S. J., & Sesco, B. (1994). Distorting children's reports and interpretations of events through suggestion. *Applied Psychology, 79,* 108–120.

Lerner, M. J. (1980). *The belief in a just world: A fundamental delusion.* New York: Plenum Press.

Lerner, R. M. (1996). Relative plasticity, integration, temporality, and diversity in human development: A developmental contextual perspective about

theory, process, and method. *Developmental Psychology, 32,* 781–786.

Lerner, R. M. (1998). Theories of human development: Contemporary perspectives. In W. Damon (Series Ed.) & R. M. Lerner (Vol. Ed.), *Handbook of child psychology: Vol. 1. Theoretical models of human development* (5th ed., pp. 1–24). New York: Wiley.

Lerner, R. M., Fisher, C. B., & Weinberg, R. A. (2000). Toward a science for and of the people: Promoting civil society through the application of developmental science. *Child Development, 71,* 11–20.

Lester, B. M., Freier, K., & LaGasse, L. (1995). Prenatal cocaine exposure and child outcome: What do we really know? In M. Lewis & M. Bendersky (Eds.), *Mothers, babies, and cocaine: The role of toxins in development* (pp. 19–39). Hillsdale, NJ: Erlbaum.

LeVay, S. (1991). A difference in hypothalamic structure between heterosexual and homosexual men. *Science, 253,* 1034–1037.

LeVay, S. (1996). *Queer Science: The use and abuse of research into homosexuality.* Cambridge, MA: MIT Press.

Levenson, R. W., Carstensen, L. L., & Gottman, J. M. (1993). Long-term marriage: Age, gender, and satisfaction. *Psychology and Aging, 8,* 301–313.

Levenson, R. W., Carstensen, L. L., & Gottman, J. M. (1994). Marital interaction in old and middle-age long-term marriages: Physiology, affect, and their interrelations. *Journal of Personality and Social Psychology, 67,* 56–68.

Levenson, R. W., & Gottman, J. M. (1985). Physiological and affective predictors of change in relationship satisfaction. *Journal of Personality and Social Psychology, 49,* 85–94.

Lever, J. (1978). Sex differences in the complexity of children's play and games. *American Sociological Review, 43,* 471–483.

Levin, J., & McDevitt, J. (1993). *Hate crimes: The rising tide of bigotry.* New York: Plenum Press.

Levine, S. (1969). Infantile stimulation: A perspective. In A. Ambrose (Ed.), *Stimulation in early infancy* (pp. 3–19). New York: Academic Press.

Levinson, D. J. (1986). A conception of adult development. *American Psychologist, 41,* 3–13.

Levinson, D. J., Darrow, C. N., Klein, E. B., Levinson, M. H., & McKee, B. (1978). *The seasons of a man's life.* New York: Knopf.

Levinson, D. J., & Levinson, J. D. (1996). *The seasons of a woman's life.* New York: Knopf.

Levitt, M. Z., & Selman, R. L. (1993). *A manual for the assessment and coding of personal meaning.* Unpublished manuscript, Harvard University, Cambridge, MA.

Levy, S. R., Stoessner, S. J., & Dweck, C. S. (1998). Stereotype formation and endorsement: The role of implicit theories. *Journal of Personality and Social Psychology, 74,* 1421–1436.

Levy-Shiff, R. (1994). Individual and contextual correlates of marital change across the transition to parenthood. *Developmental Psychology, 30,* 591–601.

Levy-Shiff, R., Goldshmidt, I., & Har-Even, D. (1991). Transition to parenthood in adoptive families. *Developmental Psychology, 27,* 131–140.

Lewis, M. (1993). The emergence of human emotions. In M. Lewis & J. Haviland (Eds.), *Handbook of emotions* (pp. 563–573). New York: Guilford Press.

Lewis, M. (1994). Myself and me. In S. T. Parker, R. W. Mitchell, & M. L. Boccia (Eds.), *Self-awareness in animals and humans: Developmental perspectives* (pp. 20–34). New York: Cambridge University Press.

Lewis, M. (1997). *Altering fate: Why the past does not predict the future.* New York: Guilford Press.

Lewis, M. (2000). Toward a development of psychopathology: Models, definitions, and prediction. In J. Sameroff, M. Lewis, &

S. M. Miller (Eds.), *Handbook of developmental psychopathology* (2nd ed., pp. 3–22). New York: Kluwer Academic/Plenum Press.

Lewis, M., & Brooks-Gunn, J. (1979). *Social cognition and the acquisition of the self.* New York: Plenum Press.

Lewis, M., & Michalson, L. (1983). *Children's emotions and moods: Developmental theory and measurement.* New York: Plenum Press.

Lewis, R. A., & Lin, L. W. (1996). Adults and their midlife parents. In N. Vanzetti & S. Duck (Eds.), *A lifetime of relationships* (pp. 364–382). Pacific Grove, CA: Brooks/Cole.

Lewkowicz, D. J., & Turkewitz, G. (1980). Cross-modal equivalence in early infancy: Auditory-visual intensity matching. *Developmental Psychology, 16,* 597–607.

Lewkowicz, D. J., & Turkewitz, G. (1981). Intersensory interaction in newborns: Modification of visual preferences following exposure to sound. *Child Development, 52,* 827–832.

Liben, L. S., Bigler, R. S., & Krogh, H. R. (2002). Language at work: Children's gendered interpretations of occupational titles. *Child Development, 73,* 810–828.

Liben, L. S., & Signorella, M. L. (1980). Gender-related schemata and constructive memory in children. *Child Development, 57,* 11–18.

Liben, L. S., & Signorella, M. L. (1993). Gender-schematic processing in children: The role of initial interpretations of stimuli. *Developmental Psychology, 29,* 141–149.

Lickona, T. (1998, February). A more complex analysis is needed. *Phi Delta Kappan, 79,* 449–454.

Lieberman, M. A. (1965). Psychological correlates of impending death: Some preliminary observations. *Journal of Gerontology, 20,* 181–190.

Light, P., Littleton, K., Messer, D., & Joiner, R. (1994). Social and communicative processes in computer based problem solving. *European Journal of Psychology of Education, 9,* 93–109.

Lincoln, Y. S., & Guba, E. G. (1985). *Naturalistic inquiry.* Beverly Hills, CA: Sage.

Lindsay, P. (1984). High school size, participation in activities, and young adult social participation: Some enduring effects of schooling. *Educational Evaluation and Policy Analysis, 6,* 73–83.

Linehan, M. (1993). *Skills training manual for treating borderline personality disorder.* New York: Guilford Press.

Locke, J. L. (1993). *The child's path to spoken language.* Cambridge, MA: Harvard University Press.

Lodge, J., Tripp, G., & Harte, D. K. (2000). Think-aloud, thought-listing, and video-mediated recall procedures in the assessment of children's self-talk. *Cognitive Therapy and Research, 24,(4),* 399–418.

Loeber, R., Wung, P., Keenan, K., Giroux, B., Stouthamer-Loeber, M., van Kammen, W. B., et al. (1993). Developmental pathways in disruptive child behavior. *Development and Psychopathology, 5,* 103–133.

Loevinger, J. (1976). *Ego development: Conception and theory.* San Francisco: Jossey-Bass.

Loftus, E. F. (1979). *Eyewitness testimony.* Cambridge, MA: Harvard University Press.

Lomax, E. M. R., Kagan, J., & Rosenkrantz, B. G. (1978). *Science and patterns of child care.* San Francisco: Freeman.

Looft, W. R. (1972). Egocentrism and social interaction across the lifespan. *Psychological Bulletin, 78,* 73–92.

Lopez, F. G., & Brennan, K. A. (2000). Dynamic processes underlying adult attachment organization: Toward an attachment theoretical perspective on the healthy and effective self. *Journal of Counseling Psychology, 47,* 283–300.

Lucas, R. E., Clark, A. E., Georgellis, Y., & Diener, E. (2004). Unemployment alters the set point for life satisfaction. *Psychological Science: Research, Theory, and Application in Psychology and Related Sciences, 15,* (1), 8–13.

Luna, B., Garver, K. E., Urban, T. A., Lazar, N. A., & Sweeney, J. A. (2004). Maturation of cognitive processes from late childhood to adulthood. *Child Development, 75,* 1357–1372.

Lund, D. A., Dimond, M. F., Caserta, M. S., Johnson, R. J., Poulton, J. L., & Connelly, J. R. (1985–1986). Identifying elderly with coping difficulties after two years of bereavement. *Omega, 16,* 213–224.

Luthar, S. (2003). The culture of affluence: Psychological costs of material wealth. *Child Development, 74,* 1581–1983.

Lutz, A., Greischar, L. L., Rawlings, N. B., Ricard, M., & Davidson, R. J. (2004). Long-term meditators self-induce high-amplitude gamma synchrony during mental practice. *Proceedings of the National Academy of Sciences, 101,* 16369–16373.

Lyddon, W. J. (1990). First- and second-order change: Implications for rationalist and constructivist cognitive therapies. *Journal of Counseling and Development, 69,* 122–127.

Lyddon, W. J. (1995). Forms and facts of constructivism. In R. A. Neimeyer & M. J. Neimeyer (Eds.), *Constructivism in psychotherapy* (pp. 69–92). Washington, DC: American Psychological Association.

Lyness, J. M. (2004). Treatment of depressive conditions in later life: Real-world light for dark (or dim) tunnels. *Journal of the American Medical Association, 291,* 1626–1628.

Lynn, J. (2000). Learning to care for people with chronic illness facing the end of life. *Journal of the American Medical Association, 284,* 2508–2513.

Lyons, M., True, W. R., Eisen, S. A., Goldberg, J., Meyer, J. M., Faraone, S. V., et al. (1995). Differential heritability of adult and juvenile antisocial traits. *Archives of General Psychiatry, 52,* 906–915.

Lyons-Ruth, K., Connell, D. B., Grunebaum, H. U., & Botein, S. (1990). Infants at social risk: Maternal depression and family support services as mediators of infant development and security of attachment. *Child Development, 61,* 85–98.

Lyons-Ruth, K., Repacholi, B., McLeod, S., & Silva, E. (1991). Disorganized attachment behavior in infancy: Short-term stability, maternal and infant correlates, and risk-related subtypes. *Development and Psychopathology, 3,* 377–396.

Lytton, H. (1990). Child and parent effects in boys' conduct disorder: A reinterpretation. *Developmental Psychology, 26,* 683–697.

Lytton, H., & Romney, D. M. (1991). Parents' differential socialization of boys and girls: A meta-analysis. *Psychological Bulletin, 109,* 267–296.

Lyubomirsky, S. (2001). Why are some people happier than others? The role of cognitive and motivational processes in well-being. *American Psychologist, 56,* 239–249.

Ma, H., & Teasdale, J. (2004) Mindfulness-based cognitive therapy for depression: Replication and exploration of differential relapse prevention effects. *Journal of Consulting and Clinical Psychology, 72,* 31–40.

Maccoby, E. E. (1990). Gender and relationships: A developmental account. *American Psychologist, 45,* 513–520.

Maccoby, E. E. (1998). *The two sexes: Growing up apart, coming together.* Cambridge, MA: Harvard University Press.

Maccoby, E. E., & Jacklin, C. N. (1974). *The psychology of sex differences.* Stanford, CA: Stanford University Press.

Maccoby, E. E., & Jacklin, C. N. (1987). Gender segregation in childhood. In H. Reese (Ed.), *Advances in child behavior and development* (pp. 239–288). New York: Academic Press.

Maccoby, E. E., & Martin, J. A. (1983). Socialization in the context of the family: Parent-child interaction. In P. H. Mussen (Series Ed.) & E. M. Hetherington (Vol. Ed.), *Handbook of child psychology: Vol. 4. Socialization, personality and social development* (4th ed., pp. 1–101). New York: Wiley.

MacDonald, K. B., & Parke, R. D. (1986). Parent-child physical play: The effects of sex and age of children and parents. *Sex Roles, 15,* 367–379.

Mace, N. L., & Rabins, P. V. (1999). *The 36-hour-day: A family guide to caring for persons with Alzheimers Disease, related dementing illnessess, and memory of later in life.* Baltimore, MD: The Johns Hopkins University Press.

MacKay, D. G., & Abrams, L. (1996). Language, memory, and aging: Distributed deficits and the structure of new-versus-old connections. In J. E. Birren, K. W. Schaie (Series Eds.), R. P. Abeles, M. Gatz, & T. A. Salthouse (Vol. Eds.), *Handbook of the psychology of aging* (4th ed., pp. 287–307). San Diego, CA: Academic Press.

MacLean, P. D. (1952). Some psychiatric implications of the physiological studies on the frontotemporal portion of the limbic system. *Electroencephalography and Clinical Neurophysiology, 4,* 407–418.

MacLean, P. D. (1970). The triune brain, emotion, and scientific basis. In F. O. Schmidt (Ed.), *The neurosciences: Second study program* (pp. 336–349). New York: Rockefeller University Press.

Maercker, A., & Zoellner, T. (2004). The Janus-face of self-perceived growth: Toward a two component-model of posttraumatic growth. *Psychological Inquiry, 15,* 41–48.

Maggs, J. L., Almeida, D. M., & Galambos, N. L. (1995). Risky business: The paradoxical meaning of problem behavior for young adolescents. *Journal of Early Adolescence, 15,* 344–362.

Mahler, M. S., Pine, F., & Bergman, A. (1975). *The psychological birth of the human infant: Symbiosis and individuation.* New York: Basic Books.

Mahoney, J. L. (2000). School extracurricular activity participation as a moderator in the development of antisocial patterns. *Child Development, 71,* 502–516.

Mahoney, M. J. (1993). Introduction to special section: Theoretical development in the cognitive psychotherapies. *Journal of Consulting and Clinical Psychology, 61,* 187–193.

Mahoney, M. J. (Ed.). (1995). *Cognitive and constructive psychotherapies.* New York: Springer.

Maier, S. F., & Watkins, L. R. (1998). Cytokines for psychologists: Implications of bi-directional immune-to-brain communication for understanding behavior, mood, and cognition. *Psychological Review, 105,* 83–107.

Maier, S. F., Watkins, L. R., & Fleshner, M. (1994). Psychoneuroimmunology: The interface between behavior, brain and immunity. *American Psychologist, 49,* 1004–1017.

Main, M. (1996). Overview of the field of attachment. *Journal of Consulting and Clinical Psychology, 64,* 237–243.

Main, M. (1999). Epilogue: Attachment theory: Eighteen points with suggestions for future studies. In J. Cassidy & P. R. Shaver (Eds.), *Handbook of attachment: Theory, research, and clinical applications* (pp. 845–887). New York: Guilford Press.

Main, M., & George, C. (1985). Responses of abused and disadvantaged toddlers to distress in agemates: A study in the day care setting. *Developmental Psychology, 21,* 407–412.

Main, M., & Goldwyn, R. (1984). Predicting rejection of her infant from mother's representation of her own experience: Implications for the abused-abusing intergenerational cycle. *International Journal of Child Abuse and Neglect, 8,* 203–217.

Main, M., & Goldwyn, R. (1985–1994). *Adult attachment classification system.* Unpublished manuscript, University of California at Berkeley.

Main, M., & Hesse, E. (1990). Parents' unresolved traumatic experiences are related to infant disorganized attachment status: Is frightened and/or frightening parental behavior the linking mechanism? In M. Greenberg, D. Cicchetti, & E. M. Cummings (Eds.), *Attachment in the preschool years* (pp. 161–182). Chicago: University of Chicago Press.

Main, M., Kaplan, N., & Cassidy, J. (1985). Security in infancy, childhood, and adulthood: A move to the level of representation. In I. Bretherton & E. Waters (Eds.), Growing points of attachment theory and research. *Monographs of the Society for Research in Child Development, 50* (Serial No. 209), 55–104.

Main, M., & Soloman, J. (1990). Procedures for identifying infants as disorganized/ disoriented during the Ainsworth strange situation. In M. Greenberg, D. Cicchetti, & E. M. Cummings (Eds.), *Attachment in the preschool years: Theory, research, and intervention* (pp. 121–160). Chicago: University of Chicago Press.

Malgady, R. G., Rogler, L. H., & Costantino, G. (1990). Hero/heroine modeling for Puerto Rican adolescents: A preventive mental health intervention. *Journal of Consulting and Clinical Psychology, 58,* 469–474.

Malina, R. M. (1983). Menarche in athletes: A synthesis and hypothesis. *Annals of Human Biology, 10,* 1–24.

Malina, R. M. (1990). Physical growth and performance during the transitional years (9–16). In R. Montemayer, G. R. Adams, & T. P. Gullotta (Eds.), *From childhood to adolescence: A transitional period?* (pp. 41–62). Newbury Park, CA: Sage.

Mandler, J. M. (2004). *The foundations of mind: Origins of conceptual thought.* New York: Oxford University Press.

Mangelsdorf, S., Gunnar, M., Kestenbaum, R., Lang, S., & Andreas, D. (1990). Infant proneness-to-distress temperament, maternal personality, and mother-infant attachment: Associations and goodness of fit. *Child Development, 61,* 820–831.

Mansfield, E. D., & McAdams, D. P. (1996). Generativity and themes of agency and communion in adult autobiography. *Personality and Social Psychology Bulletin, 22,* 721–731.

Marcia, J. E. (1964). *Determination and construct validity of ego identity status.* Unpublished doctoral dissertation, University of California at Davis.

Marcia, J. E. (1966). Development and validation of ego identity status. *Journal of Personality and Social Psychology, 3,* 551–558.

Marcia, J. E. (1967). Ego identity status: Relationship to change in self-esteem, "general maladjustment," and authoritarianism. *Journal of Personality, 35,* 118–133.

Marcia, J. E. (1980). Identity in adolescence. In J. Adelson (Ed.), *Handbook of adolescent psychology* (pp. 159–187). New York: Wiley.

Marcia, J. E. (1989). Identity and intervention. *Journal of Intervention, 12,* 401–410.

Marcia, J. E. (1993). The status of the statuses: Research review. In J. E. Marcia, A. S. Waterman, D. R. Matteson, S. L. Archer, & J. L. Orlofsky (Eds.), *Ego identity: A handbook for psychosocial research* (pp. 22–41). New York: Springer-Verlag.

Marcia, J. E., & Friedman, M. L. (1970). Ego identity status in college women. *Journal of Personality, 38,* 249–263.

Marcia, J. E., Waterman, A. S., Matteson, D. R., Archer, S. L., & Orlofsky, J. L. (1993). *Ego identity: A handbook for psychosocial research.* New York: Springer-Verlag.

Marco, C. A., & Suls, J. (1993). Daily stress and the trajectory of mood: Spillover, response assimilation contrast, and negative affectivity. *Journal of Personality and Social Psychology, 64,* 1053–1063.

Marcus, R. F. (1975). The child as elicitor of parental sanctions for independent and dependent behavior: A simulation of parent-child interaction. *Developmental Psychology, 11,* 443–452.

Marcus, R. F. (1976). The effects of children's emotional and instrumental dependent behavior on parental response. *Journal of Psychology, 92,* 57–63.

Markman, H. J., Stanley, S., & Blumberg, S. L. (1994). *Fighting for your marriage: Positive steps for preventing divorce and preserving a lasting love.* San Francisco: Jossey-Bass.

Marks, N. F., Bumpass, L. L., & Jun, H. (2003). Family roles and well-being during the middle life course. O. G. Brim, C. D. Ryff, & R. Kessler, (Eds.), *How healthy are we: A national study of well-being in midlife* (pp. 514–549). Chicago: University of Chicago Press.

Markus, H. (1977). Self-schemata and processing information about the self. *Journal of Personality and Social Psychology, 35,* 63–78.

Markus, H., Crane, M., Bernstein, S., & Siladi, M. (1982). Self-schemas and gender. *Journal of Personality and Social Psychology, 42,* 38–50.

Markus, H., & Kitayama, S. (1991a). Culture and the self: Implications for cognition, emotion, and motivation. *Psychological Review, 98,* 224–253.

Markus, H., & Kitayama, S. (1991b). Culture and the self: Implications for cognition, emotion, and motivation. *Psychological Review, 41,* 954–969.

Markus, H., & Nurius, P. (1986). Possible selves. *American Psychologist, 41,* 954–969.

Marsh, H. W. (1990). The structure of academic self-concept: The Marsh/Shavelson model. *Journal of Educational Psychology, 82,* 623–636.

Marsh, H. W. (1994). Using the National Longitudinal Study of 1988 to evaluate theoretical models of self-concept: The Self-Description Questionnaire. *Journal of Educational Psychology, 86,* 107–116.

Marsh, H. W., & Hattie, J. (1996). Theoretical perspectives on the structure of the self-concept. In B. A. Bracken (Ed.), *Handbook of self-concept* (pp. 38–90). New York: Wiley.

Marsh, H. W., & Roche, L. A. (1996). Structure of artistic self-concepts for performing arts and non-performing arts students in a performing arts high school: "Setting the stage" with multigroup confirmatory factor analysis. *Journal of Educational Psychology, 88,* 461–477.

Marsh, H. W., & Shavelson, R. (1985). Self-concept: Its multifaceted, hierarchical structure. *Educational Psychologist, 20,* 107–123.

Marsiskei, M., Lang, F. R., Baltes, M. M., & Baltes, P. B. (1995). Selective optimization with compensation: Life-span perspectives on successful human development. In R. A. Dixon & L. Backman (Eds.), *Compensation for psychological defects and declines: Managing losses and promoting gains* (pp. 35–79). Hillsdale, NJ: Erlbaum.

Martel, J. G. (1974). *Smashed potatoes: A kid's-eye view of the kitchen.* Boston: Houghton Mifflin.

Martin, C. L., & Fabes, R. A. (2001). The stability and consequences of young children's same-sex peer interactions. *Developmental Psychology, 37,* 431–446.

Martin, C. L., & Little, J. K. (1990). The relation of gender understanding to children's sex-typed preferences and gender stereotypes. *Child Development, 61,* 1427–1439.

Martinson, I. M., Davies, B., & McClowry, S. (1991). Parental depression following death of a child. *Death Studies, 15,* 259–267.

Martire, L. M., Stephens, M. A. P., & Townsend, A. L. (1998). Emotional support and well-being of midlife women: Role-specific mastery as a mediational mechanism. *Psychology and Aging, 13,* 196–404.

Marx, K., & Engels, F. (1972). The German ideology. In R. C. Tucker (Ed.), *The Marx-Engels reader.* New York: Norton. (Original work published 1846)

Masangkay, Z. S., McCluskey, K. A., McIntyre, C. W., Sims-Knight, J., Vaughn, B. E., & Flavell, J. H. (1974). The early development of inferences about the visual percepts of others. *Child Development, 45,* 237–246.

Maslow, A. H. (1954). *Motivation and personality.* New York: Harper & Row.

Mastekaasa, A. (1994). Marital status, distresss, and well-being: An international comparison. *Journal of Comparative Family Studies, 25,* 183–206.

Masten, A. S. (2003). Commentary: Developmental psychopathology as a unifying context for mental health and education models, research, and practice in schools. *School Psychology Review, 32,* 169–173. (Figure is #1 on page 170: *Illustration of embedded systems*).

Masters, W. H., Johnson, V. E., & Kolodny, R. C. (1988). *Human sexuality* (3rd ed.). Boston: Little, Brown.

Matteson, D. R. (1993). Differences within and between genders: A challenge to the theory. In J. E. Marcia, A. S. Waterman, D. R. Matteson, S. L. Archer, & J. L. Orlofsky (Eds.), *Ego identity: A handbook for psychosocial research* (pp. 69–110). New York: Springer-Verlag.

Mattson, S. N., Riley, E. P., Gramling, L., Delis, D. C., & Jones, K. L. (1998). Neuropsychological comparison of alcohol-exposed children with or without physical features of fetal-alcohol syndrome. *Neuropsychology, 12,* 146–153.

Mau, W. (1995). Educational planning and academic achievement of middle school students: A racial and cultural comparison. *Journal of Counseling and Development, 73,* 518–526.

May, R. (1979). *Psychology and the human dilemma.* New York: Norton.

Mayer, J. D., & Cobb, C. D. (2000). Educational policy on emotional intelligence. Does it make sense? *Educational Psychology Review, 12,* 163–183.

McAdams, D. P. (1985). *Power, intimacy, and the life story: Personalogical inquiries into identity.* New York: Guilford Press.

McAdams, D. P. (1993). *The stories we live by: Personal myths and the making of the self.* New York: Morrow.

McAdams, D. P. (2000). Attachment, intimacy, and generativity. *Psychological Inquiry, 11,* 117–120.

McAdams, D. P., & Bowman, P. J. (2001). Narrating life's turning points: Redemption and contamination. In D. P. McAdams, R. Josselson, & A. Lieblich (Eds.), *Turns in the road: Narrative studies of lives in transition* (pp. 3–34). Washington, DC: American Psychological Association.

McAdams, D. P., & de St. Aubin, E. (1992). A theory of generativity and its assessment through self-report, behavioral acts, and narrative themes in autobiography. *Journal of Personality and Social Psychology, 62,* 1003–1015.

McAdams, D. P., de St. Aubin, E., & Logan, R. L. (1993). Generativity among young, midlife, and older adults. *Psychology and Aging, 8,* 221–230.

McAdams, D. P., Hart, H. M., & Maruna, S. (1998). The anatomy of generativity. In D. P. McAdams & E. de St. Aubin (Eds.), *Generativity and adult development: How and why we care for the next generation* (pp. 7–44). Washington, DC: American Psychological Association.

McAuliffe, G. J. (1993). Constructive development and career transition: Implications for counseling. *Journal of Counseling and Development, 72,* 23–28.

McBride, S. L., & DiCero, K. (1990). Separation: Maternal and child perspectives. In N. Lauter-Klatell (Ed.), *Readings in child development.* Mountain View, CA: Mayfield.

McClellan, B. E. (1992). *Schools and the shaping of character: Moral education in America, 1607–present.* Bloomington, IN: ERIC Clearinghouse for Social Studies/Social Science Education and the Social Studies Development Center.

McConnell, S. R., & Odom, S. L. (1986). Sociometrics: Peer-referenced measures and the assessment of social competence. In P. S. Strain, M. J. Guralnick, & H. M. Walker (Eds.), *Children's social behavior: Development, assessment, and modification* (pp. 215–284). New York: Academic Press.

McCrae, R., & Costa, P. T. (Eds.). (2003). *Personality in adulthood: A five-factor theory perspective* (2nd ed.). New York: Guilford Press.

McCrae, R. R., & Costa, P. T. (1990). *Personality in adulthood.* New York: Guilford Press.

McCrae, R. R., & Costa, P. T. (1999). A five-factor theory of personality. In L. Pervin & O. P. John (Eds.), *Handbook of personality* (2nd ed., pp. 139–153). New York: Guilford Press.

McCrae, R. R., Costa, P. T., Ostendorf, F., Angleitner, A., Hrebickova, M., Avia, J., et al. (2000). Nature over nurture: Temperament, personality and life span development. *Journal of Personality and Social Psychology, 78,* 173–186.

McCrae, R. R., Costa, P. T., Pedroso de Lima, M., Simoes, A., Ostendorf, F., Angleitner, A., et al. (1999). Age differences in personality across the adult life span: Parallels in five cultures. *Developmental Psychology, 35,* 466–477.

McCrae, R. R., & John, O. T. (1992). An introduction to the five-factor model and its applications. *Journal of Personality, 60,* 175–215.

McCue, M., Bacon, S., & Lykken, D. T. (1993). Personality stability and change in early adulthood: A behavioral genetic analysis. *Developmental Psychology, 29,* 96–109.

McCullough, M. E., Pargament, K. I., & Thoresen, C. T. (Eds.). (2002). *Forgiveness: Theory, research and practice.* New York: Guilford Press.

McCullough, M. E., & Witvliet, C. V. (2002). The psychology of forgiveness. In C. R. Snyder & S. J. Lopez (Eds.), *Handbook of positive psychology* (pp. 446–458). New York: Oxford University Press.

McEwen, B. (1998) Protective and damaging effects of stress mediators. *New England Journal of Medicine, 338,* 171–179.

McEwen, B. S., & Sapolsky, R. M. (1995). Stress and cognitive function. *Current Opinion in Neurobiology, 5,* 205–216.

McFarlane, A. C. (1990). Vulnerability to posttraumatic stress disorder. In M. E. Wolf & A. D. Mosnaim (Eds.), *Posttraumatic stress disorder: Etiology, phenomenology, and treatment* (pp. 2–20). Washington, DC: American Psychiatric Press.

McGuigan, F., & Salmon, K. (2004). The time to talk: The influence of the timing of adult-child talk on children's event memory. *Child Development, 75,* 669–686.

McKeever, V. M., & Huff, M. E. (2003). A diathesis-stress model of posttraumatic stress disorder: Ecological, biological, and residual stress pathways. *Review of General Psychology, 7,* 237–250.

McLanahan, S. S., & Sandefur, G. (1994). *Growing up with a single parent: What hurts, what helps.* Cambridge, MA: Harvard University Press.

McLane, J. B. (1987). Interaction, context, and the zone of proximal development. In M. Hickmann (Ed.), *Social and functional approaches to language and thought* (pp. 267–285). Orlando, FL: Academic Press.

McLoyd, V. C. (1990). The impact of economic hardship on black families and children: Psychological distress, parenting, and socioemotional development. *Child Development, 61,* 311–436.

McLoyd, V. C., & Smith, J. (2002). Physical discipline and behavior problems in African American, European American, and Hispanic children: Emotional support as a moderator. *Journal of Marriage and the Family, 64,* 40–54.

McMahon, J. R., Greenberg, M. T., & the Conduct Problems Prevention Research Group. (1995). The Fast Track Program: A developmentally focused intervention for children with conduct problems. *Clinician's Research Digest* (Suppl. Bulletin 13), 1–2.

McNulty, J. K., & Karney, B. R. (2004). Positive expectations in the early years of marriage: Should couples expect the best or brace for the worst? *Journal of Personality and Social Psychology, 86,* 729–743.

Mead, G. H. (1934). *Mind, self, and society.* Chicago: University of Chicago Press.

Means, M., & Voss, J. (1985). Star wars: A developmental study of expert and novice knowledge structures. *Memory and Language, 24,* 746–757.

Meeus, W. (1996). Studies on identity development in adolescence: An overview of research and some new data. *Journal of Youth and Adolescence, 25,* 569–597.

Meeus, W., & Dekovic, M. (1995). Identity development, parental and peer support in adolescence: Results of a national Dutch study. *Adolescence, 30,* 931–944.

Meeus, W., Iedema, J., Helsen, M., & Vollebergh, W. (1999). Patterns of adolescent identity development: Review of literature and longitudinal analysis. *Developmental Review, 19,* 419–461.

Meichenbaum, D. (1986). Cognitive behavior modification. In F. Kanfer & A. Goldstein (Eds.), *Helping people change: A textbook of methods* (3rd ed., pp. 346–380). New York: Pergamon.

Meichenbaum, D. H., & Goodman, J. (1971). Training impulsive children to talk to themselves: A means for self-control. *Journal of Abnormal Psychology, 77,* 115–126.

Meir, E. I. (1989). Integrative elaboration of the congruence theory. *Journal of Vocational Behavior, 35,* 219–230.

Meisel, A., Snyder, L., & Quill, T. (2000). Seven legal barriers to end-of-life care: Myths, realities, and grains of truth. *Journal of the American Medical Association, 284,* 2495–2501.

Meltzoff, A. N. (1988). Infant imitation and memory: Nine-month-old infants in immediate and deferred tests. *Child Development, 59,* 217–225.

Meltzoff, A. N. (1990). Foundations for developing a concept of self: The role of imitation in relating self to other and the value of social mirroring, social modeling, and self practice in infancy. In D. Cicchetti & M. Beeghly (Eds.), *The self in transition: Infancy to childhood* (pp. 139–164). Chicago: University of Chicago Press.

Meltzoff, A. N., & Borton, R. W. (1979). Intermodal matching by human neonates. *Nature, 282,* 403–404.

Meltzoff, A. N., & Moore, M. K. (1977). Imitation of facial and manual gestures by human neonates. *Science, 198,* 75–78.

Mennella, J. A., Jagnow, C. P., & Beauchamp, G. K. (2001). Prenatal and postnatal flavor learning by human infants. *Pediatrics, 107,* E88.

Mennella, J. A., Johnson, A., & Beauchamp, G. K. (1995). Garlic ingestion by pregnant women alters the odor of amniotic fluid. *Chemical Senses, 20,* 207–209.

Merewood, A. (1991, April). Sperm under seige. *Health,* 53–57, 76–77.

Metcalf, P., & Huntington, R. (1991). *Celebrations of death: The anthology of mortuary ritual* (2nd ed.). New York: Cambridge University Press.

Meyer, A. (1957). *Psychobiology: A science of man.* Springfield, IL: Charles C. Thomas.

Meyer, E. E., Chrousos, G. P., & Gold, P. (2001). Major depression and the stress system: A life-span perspective. *Development and Psychopathology, 13,* 565–580.

Michel, G. F., & Moore, C. L. (1995). *Developmental psychobiology: An interdisciplinary science.* Cambridge, MA: MIT Press.

Michelson, L., Sugai, D., Wood, R., & Kazdin, A. E. (1983). *Social skills assessment and training with children: An empirical handbook.* New York: Plenum Press.

Middleton, W., Raphael, B., Burnett, P., & Martinek, N. (1997). Psychological distress and bereavement. *Journal of Nervous and Mental Diseases, 185,* 447–453.

Middleton, W., Raphael, B., Martinek, N., & Misso, V. (1993). Pathological grief reactions. In M. Stroebe, W. Stroebe, & R. O. Hansson (Eds.), *Handbook of bereavement: Theory, research and intervention* (pp. 44–61). New York: Cambridge University Press.

Midgley, C., Fedlaufer, H., & Eccles, J. S. (1988). The transition to junior high school: Beliefs of pre- and post-transition teachers. *Journal of Youth and Adolescence, 17,* 543–562.

Mihalic, S. W., & Elliot, D. (1997). Short- and long-term consequences of adolescent work. *Youth and Society, 28,* 464–498.

Mikulincer, M. (1997). Adult attachment style and information processing: Individual differences in curiosity and cognitive closure. *Journal of Personality and Social Psychology, 72,* 1217–1230.

Mikulincer, M., & Arad, D. (1999). Attachment working models and cognitive openness in close relationships: A test of chronic and temporary accessibility effects. *Journal of Personality and Social Psychology, 77,* 710–725.

Mikulincer, M., & Florian, V. (1996). Emotional reactions to interpersonal losses over the lifespan: An attachment theory perspective. In C. Magai & S. H. McFadden (Eds.), *Handbook of emotion, adult development and aging* (pp. 269–285). San Diego, CA: Academic Press.

Mikulincer, M., & Florian, V. (1998). The relationship between adult attachment styles and emotional and cognitive reactions to stressful events. In J. A. Simpson & W. S. Rholes (Eds.), *Attachment theory and close relationships* (pp. 143–165). New York: Guilford Press.

Miller, A. (1981). *The drama of the gifted child.* New York: Basic Books.

Miller, B. C., & Sollie, D. L. (1980). Normal stresses during the transition to parenthood. *Family Relations, 29,* 459–465.

Miller, D. L. (1983). Developmental changes in male/female voice classification by infants. *Infant Behavior and Development, 6,* 313–330.

Miller, G. E., Cohen, S., & Ritchey, A. K. (2002). Chronic psychological stress and the regulation of pro-inflammatory cytokines: A glucocorticoid-resistance model. *Health Psychology, 21,* 531–541.

Miller, J. B. (1991). The development of women's sense of self. In J. V. Jordan, A. G. Kaplan, J. B. Miller, I. P. Stiver, & J. L. Surrey (Eds.), *Women's growth in connection* (pp. 11–26). New York: Guilford Press.

Miller, K. F., & Stigler, J. W. (1987). Counting in Chinese: Cultural variation in a basic cognitive skill. *Cognitive Development, 2,* 279–305.

Miller, P. A., & Eisenberg, N. (1988). The relation of empathy to aggression and externalizing/antisocial behavior. *Psychological Bulletin, 103,* 324–344.

Miller, P. A., Eisenberg, N., Fabes, R. A., & Shell, R. (1996). Relations of moral reasoning and vicarious emotion to young children's prosocial behavior toward peers and adults. *Developmental Psychology, 32,* 210–219.

Miller, P. H. (1994). Individual differences in children's strategic behavior: Utilization deficiencies. *Learning and Individual Differences, 6,* 285–307.

Miller, R. S. (1997). We always hurt the ones we love: Aversive interactions in close relationships. In R. M. Kowalski (Ed.), *Aversive interpersonal behaviors* (pp. 11–29). New York: Plenum Press.

Miller, S. M., & Green, M. L. (1984). Coping with stress and frustration: Origins, nature, and development. In M. Lewis & C. Saarni (Eds.), *The socialization of emotions* (pp. 263–314). New York: Plenum Press.

Miller, W. R., & Rollnick, S. (1991). *Motivational interviewing: Preparing people to change addictive behavior.* New York: Guilford Press.

Mitka, M. (2000). Suggestions for help when the end is near. *Journal of the American Medical Association, 284,* 2441–2444.

Miura, I. T., Okamoto, Y., Kim, C. C., Steere, M., & Fayol, M. (1993). First graders' cognitive representation of number and understanding of place value: Cross-national comparisons—France, Japan, Korea, Sweden, and the United States. *Journal of Educational Psychology, 85,* 24–30.

Moffitt, T. E. (1993a). Adolescence-limited and life-course persistent antisocial behavior: A developmental taxonomy. *Psychological Bulletin, 100,* 674–701.

Moffitt, T. E. (1993b). The neuropsychology of conduct disorder. *Development and Psychopathology, 5,* 135–151.

Moffitt, T. E., Caspi, A., Belsky, J., & Silva, P. A. (1992). Childhood experience and the onset of menarche. *Child Development, 63,* 47–53.

Moffitt, T. E., & Lynam, D. R. (1994). The neuropsychology of conduct disorder and delinquency: Implications for understanding antisocial behavior. In D. C. Fowles, P. Sutker, & S. H. Goodman (Eds.), *Progress in experimental personality and psychopathology research* (pp. 233–262). New York: Springer-Verlag.

Molfese, D. (1990). Auditory evoked responses recorded from 16-month-old human infants to words they did and did not know. *Brain and Language, 38,* 345–363.

Money, J. (1988). *Gay, straight, and in-between: The sexology of erotic orientation.* New York: Oxford University Press.

Money, J., & Dalery, J. (1977). Hyperadrenocortical 46, XX hermaphroditism with penile urethra: Psychological studies in seven cases, three reared as boys, four as girls. In P. A. Lee, L. P. Plotnick, A. A. Kowarski, & C. J. Migeon (Eds.), *Congenital adrenal hyperplasia* (pp. 433–446). Baltimore: University Park Press.

Money, J., & Ehrhardt, A. (1972). *Man and woman, boy and girl.* Baltimore: Johns Hopkins University Press.

Money, J., & Tucker, P. (1975). *Sexual signatures: On being a man or a woman.* Boston: Little, Brown.

Montemayor, R. (1983). Parents and adolescents in conflict: All families some of the time and some families all of the time. *Journal of Early Adolescence, 3,* 83–103.

Moore, K. J. & Patterson, G. R. (2003). Parent training. In W. O'Donohue, J. E. Fisher & S. C. Hayes (Eds.) *Cognitive behavior therapy: Applying empirically supported techniques on your practice* (pp. 280–287). Hoboken, N. J.: John Wiley & Sons.

Moore, W. (1982). *The Measure of Intellectual Development: A brief review.* Baltimore: University of Maryland Center for Application of Developmental Instruction.

Morell, V. (1993). The puzzle of the triple repeats. *Science, 260,* 1422–1423.

Morelli, G. A., Rogoff, B., Oppenheim, D., & Goldsmith, D. (1992). Cultural variations in infants' sleeping arrangements. Questions of independence. *Developmental Psychology, 28,* 604–613.

Moreno, J. L. (1934). *Who shall survive? A new approach to the problem of human interrelations.* Washington, DC: Nervous and Mental Disease Publishing Co.

Morgane, P. J., Austin-LaFrance, R., Bronzino, J., Tonkiss, J., Diaz-Cintra, S., Cintra, L., et al. (1993). Prenatal malnutrition and development of the brain. *Neuroscience and Biobehavioral Reviews, 17,* 91–128.

Morrison, F. J., Holmes, D. L., & Haith, M. M. (1974). A developmental study of the effects of familiarity on short-term visual memory. *Journal of Experimental Child Psychology, 18,* 412–425.

Morrow, J., & Nolen-Hoeksema, S. (1990). Effects of responses to depression on the remediation of depressive affect. *Journal of Personality and Social Psychology, 58,* 519–527.

Mortimer, J. T., Finch, M. D., & Kumka, D. (1982). Persistence and change in development: The multidimensional self-concept. In P. B. Baltes & O. G. Brim, Jr. (Eds.), *Life-span development and behavior* (Vol. 4, pp. 264–315). New York: Academic Press.

Mortimer, J. T., Harley, C., & Aronson, P. J. (1999). How do prior experiences in the workplace set the stage for transitions to adulthood? In A. Booth, A. C. Crouter, & M. J. Shanahan (Eds.), *Transitions to adulthood in a changing economy: No work, no family, no future?* New York: Praeger.

Mosher, R. L. (1995). Educational and psychological applications of theories of human development: A brief overview. *Journal of Education, 177,* 1–15.

Moshman, D. (1982). Exogenous, endogenous, and dialectical constructivism. *Developmental Review, 2,* 371–384.

Moshman, D. (1998). Cognitive development beyond childhood. In W. Damon (Series Ed.), D. Kuhn & R. S. Siegler (Vol. Eds.), *Handbook of child psychology: Vol. 2. Cognition, perception, and language* (5th ed., pp. 947–978). New York: Wiley.

Moskowitz, D. W., Suh, E. J., & Desaulniers, J. (1994). Situational influences on gender differences in agency and communion. *Journal of Personality and Social Psychology, 66,* 753–761.

Mounts, N. S., & Steinberg, L. (1995). An ecological analysis of peer influence on adolescent grade point average and drug use. *Developmental Psychology, 31,* 915–922.

Moyer-Mileur, L., Brubstetter, V., McNaught, T., Gill, G., & Chan, G. (2000). Daily physical activity programs increases bone mineralization and growth in very low birth weight infants. *Pediatrics, 106,* 1088–1092.

Mroczek, D. K., & Almeida, D. M. (2004). The effect of daily stress, personality, and age on daily negative affect. *Journal of Personality, 72,* 355–378.

Mufson, L., Moreau, D., Weissman, M. M., & Klerman, G. L. (1993). *Interpersonal psychotherapy for depressed adolescents.* New York: Guilford Press.

Muller, M., Holsboer, F., & Keck, M. E. (2002). Genetic modification of corticosteroid receptor signaling: Novel insights into pathophysiology and treatment strategies of human affective disorders. *Neuropeptides, 36,* 117–131.

Murphy, D. M. (1985). Fears in preschool-age children. *Child Care Quarterly, 14,* 171–189.

Murphy, S. A. (1997). A bereavement intervention for parents following the sudden, violent deaths of their 12–28-year-old children: Descriptions and applications to clinical practice. *Canadian Journal of Nursing Research, 29,* 51–72.

Murray, B. (1996, February). Psychology remains top college major. *APA Monitor,* p. 1.

Murray, S. L., Holmes, J. G., & Griffin, D. W. (1996). The benefits of positive illusions: Idealization and the construction of satisfaction in close relationships. *Journal of Personality and Social Psychology, 70,* 79–98.

Murry, V. M. (1992). Sexual career paths of Black adolescent females. *Journal of Adolescent Research, 7,* 4–27.

Mussen, P. H., Honzik, M., & Eichorn, D. (1982). Early adult antecedents of life satisfaction at age 70. *Journal of Gerontology, 37,* 316–322.

Mustanski, B. S., Viken, R. J., Kaprio, J., Pulkkinen, L., & Rose, R. J. (2004). Genetic and environmental influences on pubertal development: Longitudinal data from Finnish twins at ages 11 and 14. *Developmental Psychology, 40,* 1188–1198.

Myers, D. G. (1993). *The pursuit of happiness.* New York: Avon.

Myers, D. G. (2000). The funds, friends, and faith of happy people. *American Psychologist, 55,* 56–57.

Myers, J. E., & Harper, M. C. (2004). Evidence-based effective practices with older adults. *Journal of Counseling and Development, 82,* 207–218.

Nahom, D., Wells, E., Gillmore, M. R., Hoppe, M., Morrison, D. M., Archibald, M., et al. (2001). Differences by gender and sexual experience in adolescent sexual behavior: Implications for education and HIV prevention. *Journal of School Health, 71,* 153–159.

Nangle, D. W., Hecker, J. E., Grover, R. L., & Smith, M. G. (2003). Perspective-taking and adolescent sex offenders: From developmental theory to clinical practice. *Cognitive and Behavioral Practice, 10,* 73–84.

Nathanielz, P. W. (1992). *Life before birth: The challenges of fetal development.* New York: Freeman.

National Campaign to Prevent Teen Pregnancy. (1999). Teenpregnancy.org. Retrieved April 5, 2002, from http://www.teenpregnancy.org

National Center for Education Statistics. (1998). *America's children: Key national indicators of well-being.* Washington, DC: U.S. Department of Education.

National Center for Education Statistics. (2002). *The condition of education, 2002.* Washington, DC: U.S. Department of Education.

National Commission on Excellence in Education. (1983). *A nation at risk: The imperative for educational reform.* Washington, DC: U.S. Government Printing Office.

National Council on the Teaching of Mathematics. (2000a). *Principles and standards for school mathematics: Grades 5-8: Standard 9-Algebra.* Available from http://www.standards.nctm.org/previous/currevstds/5-8s9.htm

National Council on the Teaching of Mathematics. (2000b). *Principles and standards for school mathematics: Grades 9-12: Standard 5-Algebra.* Available from http://www.standards.nctm.org/previous/currevstds/9-12s5.htm

National Institute of Child Health and Human Development, Early Child Care Research Network. (2000). Characteristics and quality of child care for toddlers and preschoolers. *Applied Developmental Science, 4,* 116–135.

National Institute of Child Health and Human Development, Early Child Care Research Network. (2003a). Does amount of time spent in child care predict socioemotional adjustment during the transition to kindergarten? *Child Development, 74,* 976–1005.

National Institute of child Health and Human Development, Early Child Care Research Network. (2003b). Social functioning in first grade: Associations with earlier home care and child care predictors and with current classroom experiences. *Child Development, 74,* 1639–1662.

National Institute of Child Health and Human Development, Early Child Care Research Network. (1997). The effects of infant child care on infant-mother attachment security: Results of the NICHD study of early child care. *Child Development, 68,* 860–879.

National Institute of Child Health and Human Development, Early Child Care Research Network. (1998). Early child care and self-control, compliance, and problem behavior at twenty-four and thirty-six months. *Child Development, 69,* 1145–1170.

National Institute of Child Health and Human Development, Early Child Care Research Network. (1999). Chronicity of maternal depressive symptoms, maternal sensitivity, and child functioning at 36 months. *Developmental Psychology, 35,* 1297–1310.

Neimeyer, R. A. (2000). Searching for the meaning of meaning: Grief therapy and the process of reconstruction. *Death Studies, 24,* 541–558.

Neisser, U. (1967). *Cognitive psychology.* New York: Appleton-Century-Crofts.

Neisser, U. (1993). *The perceived self: Ecological and interpersonal sources of self-knowledge.* New York: Cambridge University Press.

Nell, V. (2002). Why young men drive dangerously: Implications for injury prevention. *Current Directions in Psychological Science, 11,* 75–79.

Nelson, K. (1993a). Events, narratives, memory: What develops? In C. A. Nelson (Ed.), *Minnesota Symposium on Child Psychology: Vol. 26. Memory and affect* (pp. 1–24). Hillsdale, NJ: Erlbaum.

Nelson, K. (1993b). The psychological and social origins of autobiographical memory. *Psychological Science, 4,* 7–14.

Nelson, K. (1996). Memory development from 4 to 7 years. In A. J. Sameroff & M. M. Haith (Eds.), *The 5 to 7 shift* (pp. 141–160). Chicago: University of Chicago Press.

Nelson, M. L., & Neufelt, S. A. (1998). The pedagogy of counseling: A critical examination. *Counselor Education and Supervision, 38,* 70–88.

Nelson, S. A. (1980). Factors influencing young children's use of motives and outcomes as moral criteria. *Child Development, 51,* 823–829.

Newcomb, A. F., & Bukowski, W. M. (1984). A longitudinal study of the utility of social preference and social impact sociometric classification schemes. *Child Development, 55,* 1434–1447.

Newcomb, A. F., Bukowski, W. M., & Pattee, L. (1993). Children's peer relations: A meta-analytic review of popular, rejected, neglected, and average sociometric status. *Psychological Bulletin, 113,* 99–128.

Newman, P. R., & Newman, B. M. (1999). What does it take to have a positive impact on minority students' college retention? *Adolescence, 34,* 483–492.

Nezu, A. M., Nezu, C. M., & Lombardo, E. (2003). Problem-solving therapy. In W. O'Donohue, J. E. Fisher, & S. C. Hayes (Eds.), *Cognitive behavior therapy: Applying empirically supported techniques in your practice* (pp. 301–307). Hoboken, NY: Wiley.

Nix, R. L., Pinderhughes, E. E., Dodge, K. A., Bates, J. E., Pettit, G. S., & McFayden-Ketchum, S. A. (1999). The relation between mothers' hostile attribution tendencies and children's externalizing behavior problems: The mediating role of mothers' harsh discipline practices. *Child Development, 70,* 896–909.

Noam, G. G. (1992). Development as the aim of clinical intervention. *Development and Psychopathology, 4,* 679–696.

Noam, G. G. (1998). Clinical-developmental psychology: Toward developmentally differentiated interventions. In W. Damon (Series Ed.), I. E. Sigel & K. A. Renninger (Vol. Eds.), Handbook of child psychology: Vol. 4. *Child psychology in practice* (5th ed., pp. 585–634). New York: Wiley.

Noam, G. G., & Fischer, K. W. (Eds.). (1996). *Development and vulnerability in close relationships.* Mahwah, NJ: Erlbaum.

Nolen-Hoeksema, S. (1987). Sex differences in unipolar depression: Evidence and theory. *Psychological Bulletin, 101,* 259–282.

Nolen-Hoeksema, S. (1991). Responses to depression and their effects on the duration of depressive episodes. *Journal of Abnormal Psychology, 100,* 569–582.

Nolen-Hoeksema, S., & Girgus, J. S. (1994). The emergence of gender differences in depression during adolescence. *Psychological Bulletin, 115,* 424–443.

Nolen-Hoeksema, S., & Larson, J. (1999). *Coping with loss.* Mahwah, NJ: Erlbaum.

Nolen-Hoeksema, S., Morrow, J., & Fredrickson, B. L. (1993). Response styles and the duration of episodes of depressed moods. *Journal of Abnormal Psychology, 102,* 20–28.

Northcutt, R. G., & Kaas, J. H. (1995). The emergence and evolution of mammalian neocortex. *Trends in Neuroscience, 18,* 373–379.

Nurmi, J. (1991). How do adolescents see their future? A review of the development of future orientation and planning. *Developmental Review, 11*, 1–59.

Nyamongo, I. K. (1999). Burying the dead, culture, and economics: An assessment of two Kenyan cases. *International Social Science Journal, 51*, 255–262.

Oakes, J., Quartz, K. H., Gong, J., Guiton, G., & Lipton, M. (1993). Creating middle schools: Technical, normative, and political considerations. *The Elementary School Journal, 93*, 461–480.

O'Connor, B. P. (1995). Identity development and perceived parental behavior as sources of adolescent egocentrism. *Journal of Youth and Adolescence, 24*, 204–227.

O'Connor, K. J., & Braverman, L. M. (1997). *Play therapy theory and practice: A comparative presentation.* New York: Wiley.

O'Connor, T. G., Deater-Deckard, K., Fulker, D., Rutter, M., & Plomin, R. (1998). Genetic-environment correlations in later childhood and early adolescence: Antisocial behavioral problems and coercive parenting. *Developmental Psychology, 34*, 970–981.

O'Connor, T. G., Heron, J., Golding, J., Glover, V., & the ALSPAC Study Team. (2003). Maternal antenatal anxiety and behavioural/emotional problems in children: A test of a programming hypothesis. *Journal of Child Psychology and Psychiatry, 44*, 1025–1036.

Offer, D. (1969). *The psychological world of the teenager.* New York: Basic Books.

O'Leary, D. D. M. (1989). Do cortical areas emerge from a protocortex? *Trends in Neuroscience, 12*, 400–406.

O'Leary, D. D. M., & Stanfield, B. B. (1989). Selective elimination of axons extended by developing cortical neurons is dependent on regional locale: Experiments utilizing fetal cortical transplants. *Journal of Neuroscience, 9*, 2230–2246.

Oliner, S. P., & Oliner, P. M. (1988). *The altruistic personality: Rescuers of Jews in Nazi Europe.* New York: Free Press.

Olweus, D. (1993). Victimization by peers: Antecedents and long-term consequences. In K. H. Rubin & J. B. Asendorf (Eds.), *Social withdrawal, inhibition, and shyness* (pp. 315–341). Hillsdale, NJ.: Erlbaum.

Olweus, D., & Limber, S. (2002). *Blueprints for violence prevention: Bullying prevention program.* Boulder: University for the Study and Prevention of Violence, University of Colorado at Boulder.

Omark, D. R., Omark, M., and Edelman, M. (1973). Formation of dominance hierarchies in young children. In T. R. Williams (Ed.), *Psychological anthropology.* The Hague, Netherlands: Mouton.

Ontai, L. L., & Thompson, R. A. (2002). Patterns of attachment and maternal discourse effects on children's emotion understanding from 3 to 5 years of age. *Social Development, 12*, 657–675.

Orcutt, H. (1874). *The parent's manual or home and school training.* Boston: Thompson, Brown.

Ornstein, P. (1994). *School girls: Young women, self-esteem, and the confidence gap.* New York: Anchor Books, Doubleday.

Ornstein, R., & Thompson, R. F. (1984). *The amazing brain.* Boston: Houghton Mifflin.

Ortony, A., & Turner, T. T. (1992). Basic emotions: Can conflicting criteria converge? *Psychological Bulletin, 99*, 566–571.

Osherson, D. N., & Markman, E. M. (1975). Language and the ability to evaluate contradictions and tautologies. *Cognition, 2*, 213–226.

Osofsky, H. J., & Osofsky, J. D. (2001). Violent and aggressive behaviors in youth: A mental health and prevention perspective. *Psychiatry: Interpersonal & Biological Processes, 64*, 285–295.

Overton, W. F. (1990). Competence and procedures: Constraints on the development of logical reasoning. In W. F. Overton (Ed.), *Reasoning, necessity, and logic: Developmental perspectives* (pp. 1–32). Hillsdale, NJ: Erlbaum.

Overton, W. F. (1998). Developmental psychology: Philosophy, concepts, and methodology. In W. Damon (Series Ed.) & R. M. Lerner (Vol. Ed.), *Handbook of child psychology: Vol. 1. Theoretical models of human development* (5th ed., pp. 107–188). New York: Wiley.

Oyserman, D., Coon, H. M., & Kemmelmeier, M. (2002). Rethinking individualism and collectivism: Evaluation of theoretical assumptions and meta-analyses. *Psychological Bulletin, 128*, 3–72.

Pandley, U. B., Phadke, S. R., & Mittal, B. (2004). Molecular diagnosis and genetic counseling for fragile X mental retardation. *Neurology India, 52*, 36–43.

Panksepp, J. (1982). Toward a general psychobiological theory of emotions. *The Behavioral and Brain Sciences, 5*, 407–467.

Panksepp, J. (1992). A critical role for "affective neuroscience" in resolving what is basic about basic emotions. *Psychological Review, 99*, 554–560.

Panksepp, J., Herman, B., Conner, R., Bishop, P., & Scott, J. P. (1978). The biology of social attachments: Opiates alleviate separation distress. *Biological Psychiatry, 13*, 607–618.

Papez, J. W. (1937). A proposed mechanism of emotion. *Archives of Neurology and Psychiatry, 79*, 217–224.

Pargament, K. I., Smith, B. W., Koenig, H. G., & Perez, L. M. (1998). Patterns of positive and negative religious coping with major life stressors. *Journal for the Scientific Study of Religion, 37*, 710–724.

Paris, S. G., Newman, R. S., & McVey, K. A. (1982). Learning the functional significance of mnemonic actions: A microgenetic study of strategy acquisition. *Journal of Experimental Child Psychology, 34*, 490–509.

Park, C. L., & Folkman, S. (1997). Meaning in the context of stress and coping. *Review of General Psychology, 1*, 115–144.

Parke, R. D., & Buriel, R. (1998). Socialization in the family: Ethnic and ethological perspectives. In W. Damon (Series Ed.) & N. Eisenberg (Vol. Ed.), *Handbook of child psychology: Vol. 3. Social, emotional, and personality development* (5th ed., pp. 463–552). New York: Wiley.

Parker, J. (1995). Age differences in source monitoring of performed and imagined actions on immediate and delayed tests. *Journal of Experimental Child Psychology, 60*, 84–101.

Parker, J. G., & Asher, S. R. (1987). Peer relations and later personal adjustment: Are low-accepted children at risk? *Psychological Bulletin, 102*, 357–389.

Parkes, C. M. (1965). Bereavement and mental illness. *British Journal of Medical Psychology, 38*, 388–397.

Parkes, C. M., & Weiss, R. S. (1983). *Recovery from bereavement.* New York: Basic Books.

Parks, E. E., Carter, R. T., & Gushue, G. V. (1996). At the crossroads: Racial and womanist identity development in Black and White women. *Journal of Counseling and Development, 74*, 624–631.

Parkurst, J. T., & Asher, S. R. (1992). Peer rejection in middle school: Subgroup differences in behavior, loneliness, and interpersonal concerns. *Developmental Psychology, 28*, 231–241.

Parsons, J. E., & Ruble, D. N. (1977). The development of achievement-related expectancies. *Child Development, 48*, 1975–1979.

Parsons, T. (1951). Illness and the role of the physician: A sociological perspective. *American Journal of Orthopsychiatry, 21*, 452–460.

Partee, G. L. (2003). *Preparing youth for employment: Principles and characteristics of five leading United States youth development programs.* Washington, DC: American Youth Policy Forum.

Partnership for a Drug-Free America. (1998). *The boomer-rang: Baby boomers seriously underestimate the presence of drugs in their children's lives.* Retrieved March 28, 2002, from http://www.drugfreeamerica.org

Pascarella, E., & Terenzini, P. (1991). *How college affects students: Findings and insights from twenty years of research.* New York: Wiley.

Pascarella, E., Bohr, L., Nora, A., & Terenzini, P. (1995). Cognitive effects of 2-year and 4-year colleges: New evidence. *Educational Evaluation and Policy Analysis, 17*, 83–96.

Pasupathi, M., Staudinger, U. M., & Baltes, P. B. (1999). *The emergence of wisdom-related knowledge and judgment during adolescence.* Berlin: Max Planck Institute for Human Development.

Pasupathi, M., Staudinger, U. M., & Baltes, P. B. (2001). Seeds of wisdom: Adolescents' knowledge and judgment about difficult problems. *Developmental Psychology, 37*, 351–369.

Patterson, C. J. (1992). Children of lesbian and gay parents. *Child Development, 63*, 1025–1042.

Patterson, G. R. (1982). *Coercive family process.* Eugene, OR: Castalia Press.

Patterson, G. R., Chamberlain, P., & Reid, J. B. (1982). A comparative evaluation of parent training procedures. *Behavior Therapy, 13*, 638–651.

Paunonen, S. V., & Ashton, M. C. (2001b). Big Five predictors of academic achievement. *Journal of Research in Personality, 35*, 78–90.

Paus, T., Zijdenbos, A., Worsley, K., Collins, D. L., Blumenthal, J., Giedd, J. N., et al. (1999). Structural maturation of neural pathways in children and adolescents: In vivo study. *Science, 283*, 1908–1911.

Pavot, W., Diener, E., & Fujita, F. (1990). Extraversion and happiness. *Personality and Individual Differences, 11*, 1299–1306.

Paxton, S. J., Schutz, H. K., Weitheim, E. H., & Muir, S. L. (1999). Friendship clique and peer influences on body image concerns, dietary restraint, extreme weight-loss behaviors, and binge-eating in adolescent girls. *Journal of Abnormal Psychology, 108*, 255–266.

Pecheux, M. G., & Labrell, F. (1994). Parent-infant interactions and early cognitive development. In A. Vyt, H. Bloch, & M. H. Bornstein (Eds.), *Early child development in the French tradition: Contributions from current research.* Hillsdale, NJ: Erlbaum.

Peery, J. C. (1979). Popular, amiable, isolated, rejected: A reconceptualization of sociometric status in preschool children. *Child Development, 50*, 1231–1234.

Pennington, H. (2003). Building one system for youth development and opportunity. In A. Lewis (Ed.), *Shaping the future of American youth: Youth policy in the 21st century* (pp. 59–68). Washington DC: American Youth Policy Forum.

Pentz, M. A., Mihalic, S. F., & Grotpeter, J. K. (2002). *Blueprints for violence prevention: Book One. The Midwestern Prevention Project.* Boulder, CO: Center for the Study and Prevention of Violence.

Pentz, M. A., Trebow, E. A., Hansen, W. B., MacKinnon, D. P., Dwyer, J. H., Johnson, C. A., et al. (1990). Effects of program implementation on adolescent drug use behavior: The Midwestern Prevention Project (MPP). *Evaluation Review, 14*, 264–289.

Perkins, H. W. (1991). Religious commitment, Yuppie values, and well-being in post-collegiate life. *Review of Religious Research, 32*, 244–251.

Perrone, K. M., & Worthington, E. L. (2001). Factors influencing ratings of marital quality by individuals within dual-career marriages: A conceptual model. *Journal of Counseling Psychology, 48*, 3–9.

Perry, W. G. (1970/1999). *Forms of ethical and intellectual development in the college years: A scheme.* San Francisco: Jossey-Bass.

Perry-Jenkins, M., Repetti, R. L., & Crouter, A. C. (2000). Work and family in the 1990s. *Journal of Marriage and the Family, 62*, 981–998.

Pert, C. B. (1997). *Molecules of emotion: The science behind mind-body medicine*. New York: Simon & Schuster.

Petersen, A. C. (1988). Adolescent development. *Annual Review of Psychology, 39*, 583–608.

Petersen, A. C., Compas, B. E., Brooks-Gunn, J., Stemmler, M., Ey, S., & Grant, K. E. (1993). Depression in adolescence. *American Psychologist, 48*, 155–168.

Petersen, A. C., Kennedy, R. E., & Sullivan, P. (1991). Coping with adolescence. In M. E. Colten & S. Gore (Eds.), *Adolescent stress: Causes and consequences* (pp. 93–110). New York: Aldine de Gruyter.

Petersen, A. C., Sarigiani, P. A., & Kennedy, R. E. (1991). Adolescent depression: Why more girls? *Journal of Youth and Adolescence, 10*, 247–271.

Petersen, B. E., & Steward, A. J. (1996). Antecedents and contexts of generativity motivation at midlife. *Psychology and Aging, 11*, 21–33.

Peterson, C., Maier, S., & Seligman, M. (1993). *Learned helplessness*. New York: Oxford University Press.

Pettit, F., Fegan, M., & Howie, P. (1990, September). *Interviewer effects on children's testimony*. Paper presented at the International Congress on Child Abuse and Neglect, Hamburg, Germany.

Pfeiffer, S. (2001). Emotional intelligence: Popular but elusive construct. *Roeper Review, 23*, 138–142.

Pfost, K. S., & Fiore, M. (1990). Pursuit of nontraditional occupations: Fear of success or fear of not being chosen? *Sex Roles, 23*, 15–24.

Philips, D., Simpson, J. A., Lanigan, L., & Rholes, S. W. (1995). *Providing social support: A study of adult attachment styles*. Paper presented at the joint meeting of the European Association of Social Psychology and the Society of Experimental Social Psychology, Washington, DC.

Phillips, M. (1997). What makes schools effective? A comparison of the relationships of communitarian climate and academic achievement and attendance during middle school. *American Educational Research Journal, 34*, 633–662.

Phinney, J. S. (1990). Ethnic identity in adolescents and adults: Review of research. *Psychological Bulletin, 108*, 499–514.

Phinney, J. S. (2000). Identity formation across cultures: The interaction of personal, societal, and historical change. *Human Development, 43*, 27–31.

Piaget, J. (1926). *The language and thought of the child*. New York: Harcourt, Brace.

Piaget, J. (1928). *Judgment and reasoning in the child*. New York: Harcourt, Brace.

Piaget, J. (1932/1965). *The moral judgment of the child*. New York: Free Press.

Piaget, J. (1951). *Play, dreams, and imitation in childhood*. London: Kegan Paul, Trench, & Trubner.

Piaget, J. (1952). *The origins of intelligence in children*. New York: International Universities Press.

Piaget, J. (1954). *The construction of reality in the child*. New York: Basic Books.

Piaget, J. (1962). *Play, dreams, and imitation in childhood*. New York: Norton.

Piaget, J. (1964/1968). *Six psychological studies*. New York: Random House.

Piaget, J. (1970). *Science of education and the psychology of the child*. New York: Orion Press.

Piaget, J. (1975/1985). *The equilibration of cognitive structures*. Chicago: University of Chicago Press.

Piaget, J. (1977). *The development of thought. Equilibration of cognitive structures*. New York: Viking Press.

Piaget, J., & Inhelder, B. (1951/1976). *The origin of the idea of chance in children*. New York: Norton.

Piaget, J., & Inhelder, B. (1956). *The child's conception of space*. New York: Norton.

Piaget, J., & Inhelder, B. (1973). *Memory and intelligence*. New York: Basic Books.

Piedmont, R. L. (1999). Does spirituality represent the sixth factor of personality? Spiritual transcendence and the five-factor model. *Journal of Personality, 67*, 985--1014.

Piedmont, R. L., & Leach, M. M. (2002). Cross-cultural generalizability of the spiritual transcendence scale in India: Spirituality as a universal aspect of human experience. *American Behavioral Scientist, 45*, 1888–1901.

Pietromonaco, P. R., & Carnelley, K. B. (1994). Gender and working models of attachment: Consequences for self and romantic relationships. *Personal Relationships, 1*, 63–82.

Pinker, S. (1994). *The language instinct*. New York: Morrow.

Pintrich, P. R. (2000). Multiple goals, multiple pathways: The role of goal orientation in learning and achievement. *Journal of Educational Psychology, 92*, 544–555.

Pipher, M. (1994). *Reviving Ophelia: Saving the selves of adolescent girls*. New York: Ballantine Books.

Pipher, M. (1996). *The shelter of each other: Rebuilding our families*. New York: Ballantine Books.

Pipher, M. (1999). *Another country: Navigating the emotional terrain of our elders*. New York: Riverhead Books.

Pistole, M. C. (1989). Attachment in adult romantic relationships: Style of conflict resolution and relationship satisfaction. *Journal of Social and Personal Relationships, 6*, 505–510.

Pittman, F. (1998). *Grow up! How taking responsibility can make you a happy adult*. New York: St. Martin's Press.

Pittman, F. S. (1985). Children of the rich. *Family Process, 24*, 461–472.

Plas, E., Berger, P., Hermann, M., & Pfluger, H. (2000). Effects of aging on male fertility? *Experimental Gerontology, 35*, 543–551.

Plomin, R. (1986). *Development, genetics, and psychology*. Hillsdale, NJ: Erlbaum.

Plomin, R., Corley, R., DeFries, J. C., & Fulker, D. W. (1990). Individual differences in television viewing in early childhood: Nature as well as nurture. *Psychological Science, 1*, 371–377.

Plomin, R., DeFries, J., Craig, I. W., & McGuffin, P. (2003). *Behavioral genetics in the postgenomic era*. Washington, DC: American Psychological Association.

Plomin, R., Fulker, D. W., Corley, R., & DeFries, J. C. (1997). Nature, nurture, and cognitive development from 1 to 16 years: A parent-offspring adoption study. *Psychological Science, 8*, 442–447.

Plomin, R., Owen, M. J., & McGuffin, P. (1994). The genetic basis of complex human behaviors. *Science, 264*, 1733–1739.

Plomin, R., & Rutter, M. (1998). Child development, molecular genetics, and what to do with genetics once they are found. *Child Development, 69*, 1223–1242.

Podd, M. H. (1972). Ego identity status and morality: The relationship between two developmental constructs. *Developmental Psychology, 6*, 497–507.

Pollack, W. (1998). *Real boys: Rescuing our sons from the myths of boyhood*. New York: Henry Holt.

Pollitt, E., Golub, D., Gorman, K., Grantham-McGregor, S., Levitsky, D., Schurch, B., et al. (1996). A reconceptualization of the effects of undernutrition on children's psychological, psychosocial, and behavioral development (Social Policy Report, Vol. 10, No. 5). Ann Arbor, MI: Society for Research in Child Development.

Pollitt, E., Gorman, K. S., Engle, P. L., Martorell, R., & Rivera, J. (1993). Early supplementary feeding and cognition. *Monographs of the Society for Research in Child Development, 58* (Serial No. 235).

Poloma, M. M., & Pendleton, B. F. (1990). Religious domains and general well-being. *Social Indicators Research, 22*, 255–276.

Ponzo, Z. (1992). Promoting successful aging: Problems, opportunities, and counseling guidelines. *Journal of Counseling and Development, 71*, 210–213.

Posada, G., Carbonell, O. A., Aolzate, G., & Plata, S. J. (2004). Through Colombian lenses: Ethnographic and conventional analyses of maternal care and their associations with secure base behavior. *Developmental Psychology, 40*, 508–518.

Post, R. M. (1985). Stress sensitization, kindling, and conditioning. *Behavioral and Brain Sciences, 8*, 372–373.

Post, R. M., Leverich, G. S., Xing, G., & Weiss, S. R. B. (2001). Developmental vulnerabilities to the onset and course of bipolar disorder. *Development & Psychopathology, 13*, 581–598.

Post, R. M., Weiss, S. R., Smith, M., Rosen, J., & Frye, M. (1995). Stress, conditioning, and the temporal aspects of affective disorders. *Annals of the New York Academy of Sciences, 771*, 677–696.

Poulin-Dubois, D., Serbin, L. A., Kenyon, B., & Derbyshire, A. (1994). Infants' intermodal knowledge about gender. *Developmental Psychology, 30*, 436–442.

Powell, G. J. (1985). Self-concepts among African-Americans in racially isolated minority schools: Some regional differences. *Journal of the American Academy of Child Psychiatry, 24*, 142–149.

Pratt, J., & Pryor, K. (1995). *For real: The uncensored truth about America's teenagers*. New York: Hyperion.

Presley, C. A., Meilman, P., & Lyerla, R. (1995). *Alcohol and drugs on American college campuses*. Carbondale: Southern Illinois University Press.

Pribram, K. H. (1997). The work in working memory: Implications for development. In N. A. Krasnegor, G. R. Lyon, & P. S. Goldman-Rakic (Eds.), *Development of the prefrontal cortex: Evolution, neurobiology, and behavior* (pp. 359–378). Baltimore: Brookes.

Price, J. M., & Dodge, K. A. (1989). Peers' contributions to children's social maladjustment: Description and intervention. In T. J. Berndt & G. W. Ladd (Eds.) *Peer relationships in child development* (pp. 341–370). New York: Wiley and Sons.

Price, R. H. (1992). Psychosocial impact of job loss on individuals and families. *Current Directions in Psychological Science, 1*, 9–11.

Price, R. H., Choi, J. N., & Vinokur, A. D. (2002). Links in the chain of adversity following job loss: How financial strain and loss of personal control lead to depression, impaired functioning and poor health. *Journal of Occupational Health Psychology, 7*, 302–312.

Price, R. H., & Vinokur, A. D. (1995). Supporting career transitions in time of organizational downsizing: The Michigan JOBS Program. In M. London (Ed.), *Employees, careers, and job creation: Developing growth-oriented human resource strategies and programs* (pp. 191–209). San Francisco: Jossey-Bass.

Prochaska, J. O., & DiClementi, C. C. (1982). Transtheoretical therapy: Toward a more integrated model of change. *Psychotherapy: Theory, research and practice, 19*, 276–288.

Putallaz, M. (1983). Predicting children's sociometric status from their behavior. *Child Development, 54*, 1417–1426.

Putallaz, M., & Wasserman, A. (1990). Children's entry behaviors. In S. P. Asher & J. D. Coie (Eds.), *Peer rejection in childhood*. New York: Cambridge University Press.

Putnam, R. D. (2000). *Bowling alone: The collapse and revival of American community*. New York: Simon & Schuster.

Pyszczynski, T., Greenberg, J., & LaPrelle, J. (1985). Social comparison after success and failure: Biased search for information consistent with a self-servicing conclusion. *Journal of Experimental Social Psychology, 21*, 129–138.

Quadrel, M. J., Fischhoff, B., & Davis, W. (1993). Adolescent (in) vulnerability. *American Psychologist, 48*, 102–116.

Quill, T. E. (2000). Initiating end-of-life discussions with seriously ill patients. *Journal of the American Medical Association, 285*, 2502–2507.

Quintana, E. D. (1999). Racial and ethnic identity development in biracial people. *Dissertation Abstracts International: Section B. The Physical Sciences & Engineering, 60* (3-B), 1313.

Quinton, D., Pickles, A., Maughan, B., & Rutter, M. (1993). Partners, peers, and pathways: Assortative pairing and continuities in conduct disorder. *Development and Psychopathology, 5*, 763–783.

Rakic, P. (1988). Specification of cerebral cortical areas. *Science, 241*, 170–176.

Ramsey, P. G., & Myers, L. C. (1990). Young children's responses to racial differences: Relations among cognitive, affective, and behavioral dimensions. *Journal of Applied Developmental Psychology, 11*, 49–67.

Rando, T. A. (1993). *Treatment of complicated mourning.* Champaign, IL: Research Press.

Randolph, P. D., Caldera, Y. M., Tacone, A. M. et al. (1999). The long-term combined effects of medical treatment and a mindfulness-based behavioral program for the multidisciplinary management of chronic pain in West Texas. *Pain Digest, 9*, 103–112.

Raths, L., Harmin, M., & Simon, S. (1966). *Values and teaching.* Columbus, OH: Merrill.

Ravitch, D. (1983). *The troubled crusade: American education, 1945–1980.* New York: Basic Books.

Reese, E. (2002). Social factors in the development of autobiographical memory: The state of the art. *Social Development, 11*, 124–142.

Reese, E., & Fivush, R. (1993). Parental styles of talking about the past. *Developmental Psychology, 29*, 596–606.

Reich, R. B. (2000). *The future of success.* New York: Knopf.

Reid, J. B., Patterson, G. R., & Snyder, J. J. (2002). *Antisocial behavior in children and adolescents: A developmental analysis and the Oregon model for intervention.* Washington, DC: American Psychological Association.

Reik, W., & Walter, J. (2001). Genomic imprinting: Parental influence on the genome. *Nature Reviews Genetics, 2*, 21–32.

Reiner, W. G., & Gearhart, J. P. (2004). Discordant sexual identity in some genetic males with cloacal exstrophy assigned to female sex at birth. *The New England Journal of Medicine, 350*, 333–341.

Reisman, J. E. (1987). Touch, motion, and proprioception. In P. Salapatek & L. Cohen (Eds.), *Handbook of infant perception: Vol. 1. From sensation to perception* (pp. 265–304). Orlando, FL: Academic Press.

Reiss, D., & Neiderhiser, J. M. (2000). The interplay of genetic influences and social processes in developmental theory: Specific mechanisms are coming into view. *Development and Psychopathology, 12*, 357–372.

Reiss, D., Neiderhiser, J. M., Hetherington, E. M., & Plomin, R. (2000). *The relationship code: Deciphering genetic and social influences on adolescent development.* Cambridge, MA: Harvard University Press.

Reitzes, D. C., & Mutran, E. J. (2004). The transition to retirement: Stages and factors that influence retirement adjustment. *International Journal of Aging and Human Development, 59*, 63–84.

Renner, M. J., & Rosenzweig, M. R. (1987). *Enriched and impoverished environments.* New York: Springer.

Reynolds, A. J., & Suh-Ruu, O. (2003). Promoting resilience through early childhood intervention. In S. S. Luthar (Ed.), *Resilience and vulnerability: Adaptation in the context of childhood adversities* (pp. 436–462). Cambridge, England: Cambridge University Press.

Rheingold, H. L. (1956). The modification of social responsiveness in institutional babies. *Monographs of the Society for Research in Child Development, 21* (2, Serial No. 63).

Rhoades, L., & Eisenberger, R. (2002). Perceived organizational support: A review of the literature. *Journal of Applied Psychology, 87*, 698–714.

Rholes, W. S., Simpson, J. A., & Stevens, J. G. (1998). Attachment orientations, social support, and conflict resolution in close relationships. In J. A. Simpson & W. S. Rholes (Eds.), *Attachment theory and close relationships* (pp. 166–188). New York: Guilford Press.

Richards, T. A., Wrubel, J., & Folkman, S. (1999–2000). Death rites in the San Francisco gay community: Cultural developments of the AIDS epidemic. *Omega, 40*, 335–350.

Rindfuss, R. R. (1991). The young adult years: Diversity, structural change, and fertility. *Demography, 28*, 493–512.

Roberts, B. W., & DelVecchio, W. F. (2000). The rank-order consistency of personality traits from childhood to old age: A quantitative review of longitudinal studies. *Psychological Bulletin, 126*, 3–25.

Roberts, T., & Kraft, R. (1987). Reading comprehension performance and laterality: Evidence for concurrent validity of dichotic, haptic, and EEG laterality measures. *Neuropsychologia, 25*, 817–828.

Roberts, W., & Strayer, J. (1996). Empathy, emotional expressiveness, and prosocial behavior. *Child Development, 67*, 449–470.

Robertson, J., & Robertson, J. (1989). *Separation and the very young.* London: Free Association Books.

Robins, L., & Pryzbeck, T. (1985). Age of onset of drug use as a factor in drug and other disorders. In C. R. Jones & R. J. Battjes (Eds.), *Etiology of drug abuse: Implications for prevention* (pp.178–192). Washington, DC: U.S. Government Printing Office.

Robins, L. N. (1978). Sturdy childhood predictors of adult antisocial behavior: Replications from longitudinal studies. *Psychological Medicine, 8*, 611–622.

Robins, L. N. (1986). The consequences of conduct disorder in girls. In D. Olweus, J. Block, & M. Radke-Yarrow (Eds.), *The development of antisocial and prosocial behavior: Research, theories, and issues* (pp. 358–414). Orlando, FL: Academic Press.

Robins, R. W., & Pals, J. (1998). *Implicit self-theories of ability in the academic domain: A test of Dweck's model.* Unpublished manuscript.

Robinson, F. P., Mathews, H. L., & Witek-Janusek, L. (2003). Psycho-endocrine-immune response to mindfulness-based stress reduction in individuals infected with the human immunodeficiency virus: A quasi-experimental study. *Journal of Alternative and Complementary Medicine, 9*, 683–694.

Robinson, I., Ziss, K., Ganza, B., Katz, S., & Robinson, E. (1991). Twenty years of sexual revolution, 1965–1985: An update. *Journal of Marriage and the Family, 53*, 216–220.

Robinson, J. L., Zahn-Waxler, C., & Emde, R. N. (1994). Patterns of development in early empathic behavior: Environmental and child constitutional influences. *Social Development, 3*, 125–145.

Rodgers, J., & Rowe, D. (1993). Social contagion and adolescent sexual behavior: A developmental EMOSA model. *Psychological Review, 100*, 479–510.

Rogan, W. J., & Gladen, B. C. (1993). Breast-feeding and cognitive development. *Early Human Development, 31*, 181–193.

Rogers, C. R. (1951). *Client-centered therapy.* Boston: Houghton Mifflin.

Rogler, L. H. (2002). Historical generations and psychology: The case of the Great Depression

and World War II. *American Psychologist, 57*, 1013–1023.

Rogoff, B. (1998). In W. Damon (Series Ed.), D. Kuhn & R. S. Siegler (Vol. Eds.), *Handbook of child psychology: Vol. 2. Cognition, perception, and language* (5th ed., pp. 679–744). New York: Wiley.

Rogoff, B. (2003). *The cultural nature of human development.* New York: Oxford University Press.

Rogoff, B., & Gauvain, M. (1986). A method for the analysis of patterns illustrated with data on mother-child instructional interaction. In J. Valsiner (Ed.), *The individual subject and scientific psychology* (pp. 261–290). New York: Plenum Press.

Roisman, G. I., Tsai, J. L., & Chiang K-H. S. (2004). The emotional integration of childhood experience: Physiological, facial expressive, and self-reported emotional response during the adult attachment interview. *Developmental Psychology, 40*, 776–789.

Rolf, J., Masten, A., Cicchetti, D., Neuchterlein, K., & Weintraub, S. (Eds.). (1990). *Risk and protective factors in the development of psychopathology.* New York: Cambridge University Press.

Rollins, B. C., & Feldman, H. (1970). Marital satisfaction over the family life cycle. *Journal of Marriage and the Family, 32*, 20–28.

Rook, K. S. (2000). The evolution of social relationships in later adulthood. In S. H. Qualls & N. Abeles (Eds.), *Psychology and the aging revolution: How we adapt to longer life* (pp. 173–191). Washington, DC: American Psychological Association.

Rook, K. S., & Schuster, T. L. (1996). Compensatory processes in the social networks of older adults. In G. Pierce, B. R. Sarason, & I. G. Sarason (Eds.), *The handbook of social support and family relationships* (pp. 219–248). New York: Plenum Press.

Root, M. P. P. (1999). The biracial baby boom: Understanding ecological constructions of racial identity in the 21st century. In R. H. Sheets & E. R. Hollins (Eds.), *Racial and ethnic identity in school practices* (pp. 67–89). Mahwah, NJ: Erlbaum.

Rose, R. J. (2002). How do adolescents select their friends? A behavior-genetic perspective. In A. Caspi & L. Pulkkinen (Eds.), *Paths to successful development* (pp. 106–125). Cambridge, England: Cambridge University Press.

Rosemond, J. K. (1991). *Parent power: A common sense approach to parenting in the 90's and beyond.* Kansas City, MO: Andrews McMeel.

Rosenberg, M. (1979). *Conceiving the self.* New York: Basic Books.

Rosenblatt, P. C., Walsh, R., & Jackson, D. A. (1972). Coping with anger and aggression in mourning. *Omega, 3*, 271–284.

Rosenthal, R., & Jacobson, L. (1968). *Pygmalion in the classroom.* New York: Henry Holt.

Ross, C. E. (1995). Reconceptualizing marital status as a continuum of social attachment. *Journal of Marriage and the Family, 57*, 129–140.

Ross, H., Tesla, C., Kenyon, B., & Lollis, S. (1990). Maternal intervention in toddler peer conflict: The socialization of principles of justice. *Developmental Psychology, 26*, 994–1003.

Roth, S., & Cohen, L. J. (1986). Approach, avoidance, and coping with stress. *American Psychologist, 41*, 813–819.

Rothbart, M. K., Ahadi, S. A., & Evans, D. E. (2000). Temperament and personality: Origins and outcomes. *Journal of Personality and Social Psychology, 78*, 122–135.

Rothbart, M. K., & Bates, J. E. (1998). Temperament. In W. Damon (Series Ed.) & N. Eisenberg (Vol. Ed.), *Handbook of child psychology: Vol. 3. Social, emotional, and personality development* (5th ed., pp. 105–176).

Rothbart, M. K., Derryberry, D., & Posner, M. I. (1994). A psychobiological approach to the development of temperament. In J. E. Bates & T. D. Wachs (Eds.), *Temperament: Individual differences at the interface of biology and behavior* (pp. 83–116). Washington, DC: American Psychological Association.

Rothbaum, F., Weisz, J., Pott, M., Miyake, K., & Morelli, G. (2000). Attachment and culture: Security in the United States and Japan. *American Psychologist, 55,* 1093–1104.

Rothbaum, F., Weisz, J. R., & Snyder, S. (1982). Changing the world and changing the self: A two process model of perceived control. *Journal of Personality and Social Psychology, 42,* 5–37.

Rourke, B. P., & Conway, J. (1997). Disabilities of arithmetic and mathematical reasoning: Perspectives from neurology and neuropsychology. *Journal of Learning Disabilities, 30,* 34–46.

Rovee-Collier, C. K. (1990). The "memory system" of prelinguistic infants. In A. Diamond (Ed.), *The development and neural bases of higher cognitive functions.* New York: New York Academy of Sciences.

Rowe, J. W., & Kahn, R. L. (1998). *Successful aging.* New York: Pantheon Books.

Rozario, P. A., Morrow-Howell, N., & Hinterlong, J. E. (2004). Role enhancement or role strain: Assessing the impact of multiple productive roles on older caregiver well-being. *Research on Aging, 26,* 413–428.

Rubin, K. H., Bukowski, W., & Parker, J. G. (1998). Peer interactions, relationships, and groups. In W. Damon (Series Ed.) & N. Eisenberg (Vol. Ed.), *Handbook of child psychology: Vol. 3. Social, emotional, and personality development* (5th ed., pp. 619–700). New York: Wiley.

Rubin, K. H., Chen, J. S., McDougall, P., Bowker, A., & McKinnon, J. (1995). The Waterloo Longitudinal Project: Predicting internalizing and externalizing problems in adolescence. *Development and Psychopathology, 7,* 751–764.

Rubin, K. H., & Coplan, R. J. (1992). Peer relationships in childhood. In M. H. Bornstein & M. E. Lamb (Eds.), *Developmental psychology: An advanced textbook* (3rd ed., pp. 519–578). Hillsdale, NJ: Erlbaum.

Rubin, K. H., Hastings, P., Chen, X., Stewart, S., & McNichol, K. (1998). Intrapersonal and maternal correlates of aggression, conflict, and externalizing problems in toddlers. *Child Development, 69,* 1614–1629.

Rubin, S. (1981). A two-track model of bereavement: Theory and application in research. *American Journal of Orthopsychiatry, 51,* 101–109.

Ruble, D. N., Gruelich, F., Pomerantz, E. M., & Gochberg, G. (1993). The role of gender-related processes in the development of sex differences in self-evaluation and depression. *Journal of Affective Disorders, 29,* 97–128.

Ruble, D. N., & Martin, C. L. (1998). Gender development. In W. Damon (Series Ed.) & N. Eisenberg (Vol. Ed.), *Handbook of child psychology: Vol. 3. Social, emotional, and personality development* (5th ed., pp. 933–1016). New York: Wiley.

Ruffman, T., Slade, L., & Crowe, E. (2002). The relation between children's and mother's mental state language and theory-of-mind understanding. *Child Development, 73,* 734–751.

Rush, D., Stein, Z., & Susser, M. (Eds.). (1980). *Diet in pregnancy: A randomized controlled trial of nutritional supplements.* New York: Liss.

Rutter, M. (1986). The developmental pathology of depression: Issues and perspectives. In M. Rutter, C. E. Izard, & P. B. Read (Eds.), *Depression in young people: Developmental and clinical perspectives* (pp. 3–30). New York: Guilford Press.

Rutter, M. (1997). Nature-nurture integration: The example of antisocial behavior. *American Psychologist, 52,* 390–398.

Rutter, M., Maughan, B., Mortimore, P., Ouston, J., & Smith, A. (1979). *Fifteen thousand hours: Secondary schools and their effects on children.* Cambridge, MA: Harvard University Press.

Rutter, M., O'Connor, T. G., & the English and Romanian Adoptees Study Team. (2004). Are there biological programming effects for psychological development? Findings from a study of Romanian adoptees. *Developmental Psychology, 40,* 81–94.

Rutter, V. (1995, January/February). Adolescence: Whose hell is it? *Psychology Today,* pp. 54–60, 62, 64, 66, 68.

Ryan, M. P. (1984). Monitoring text comprehension: Individual differences in epistemological standards. *Journal of Educational Psychology, 76,* 248–258.

Ryan, R. M., Chirkov, V. I., Little, T. D., Sheldon, K. M., Timoshina, E., & Deci, E. L. (1999). The American Dream in Russia: Extrinsic aspirations and well-being in two cultures. *Personality and Social Psychology Bulletin, 25,* 1509–1524.

Ryan, R. M., & Deci, E. L. (2000). Self-determination theory and the facilitation of intrinsic motivation, social development, and well-being. *American Psychologist, 55,* 68–78.

Ryan, R. M., & Deci, E. L. (2003). On happiness and human potentials: A review of research on hedonic and eudaimonic well-being. *Annual Review of Psychology, 52,* 141–166.

Ryan, R. M., & LaGuardia, J. G. (2000). What is being optimized?: Self-determination theory and basic psychological needs. In S. H. Qualls & N. Abeles (Eds.), *Psychology and the aging revolution: How we adapt to longer life* (pp. 145–172). Washington, DC: American Psychological Association.

Rybarczyk, B., Gallagher-Thompson, D., Rodman, J., Zeiss, A., Gantz, F. E., & Yesavage, J. (1992). Applying cognitive-behavioral psychotherapy to the chronically ill elderly: Treatment issues and case illustration. *International Psychogeriatrics, 4,* 127–140.

Ryff, C. D., & Keyes, C. L. M. (1995). The structure of psychological well-being revisited. *Journal of Personality and Social Psychology, 69,* 719–727.

Ryff, C. D., Lee, Y. H., Essex, M. J., & Schmutte, P. S. (1994). My children and me: Mid-life evaluations of grown children and of self. *Psychology and Aging, 9,* 195–205.

Ryff, C. D., & Singer, B. (2000). Interpersonal flourishing: A positive health agenda for the new millennium. *Personality and Social Psychology Review, 4,* 30–44.

Ryff, C. D., & Singer, B. (2003). Flourishing under fire: Resilience as a prototype of challenged thriving. In C. L. M. Keyes & J. Haidt (Eds.), *Flourishing: Positive psychology and the life well-lived* (pp. 15–36). Washington, DC: American Psychological Association.

Ryland, E. B., Riordan, R. J., & Brack, G. (1994). Selected characteristics of high-risk students and their enrollment persistence. *Journal of College Student Development, 35,* 54–58.

Sachs, J. (1987). Preschool boys' and girls' language use in pretend play. In S. U. Phillips, S. Steele, & C. Tanz (Eds.), *Language, gender, and sex in comparative perspective* (pp. 178–188). Cambridge, England: Cambridge University Press.

Sadker, M. P., & Sadker, D. M. (1991). *Teachers, schools, and society* (2nd ed). New York: Random House.

Sadler, J. Z., & Hulgus, Y. F. (1994). Enriching the psychosocial context of a multiaxial nosology. In J. Z. Sadler, O. P. Wiggins, & M. A. Schwartz (Eds.), *Philosophical perspectives on psychiatric diagnostic classification* (pp. 261–278). Baltimore: Johns Hopkins University Press.

Sagi, A., Koren-Karie, N., Gini, M., Ziv, Y., & Joels, T. (2002). Shedding light on the effects of various types and quality of early child care on infant-mother attachment relationship: The Haifa study of early child care. *Child Development, 73,* 1166–1186.

Sagi, A., Koren-Karie, N., Gini, Y. Z., & Tirtsa, J. (2002). Shedding further light on the effects of various types and quality of early child care on infant-mother attachment relationship: The Haifa study of early child care. *Child Development, 73,* 1166–1186.

Sagi, A., Lamb, M. E., Lewkowicz, K. S., Shoham, R., Dvir, R., & Estes, D. (1985). Security of infant-mother, -father, and -metapelet attachments among kibbutz-reared Israeli children. In I. Bretherton & E. Waters (Eds.), Growing points of attachment theory and research. *Monographs of the Society for Research in Child Development, 50* (Serial No. 209), 257–275.

Sagi, A., van IJzendoorn, M. H., Aviezer, O., Donnell, F., Koren-Karie, N., Joels, T., et al. (1995). Attachments in a multiple-caregiver and multiple-infant environment: The case of the Israeli kibbutzim. In E. Waters, B. E. Vaughn, G. Posada, & K. Kondo-Ikemura (Eds.), Caregiving, cultural and cognitive perspectives on secure-base behavior and working models: New growing points in attachment theory and research. *Monographs of the Society for Research in Child Development, 60* (Serial No. 244), 71–91.

Sailes, G. A. (1993). An investigation of Black student attrition at a large, predominantly White, midwestern university. *Western Journal of Black Studies, 17,* 179–182.

Salovey, P., & Mayer, J. D. (1990). Emotional intelligence. *Imagination, Cognition, and Personality, 9,* 185–211.

Salthouse, T. A. (1996). The processing-speed theory of adult age differences in cognition. *Psychological Review, 103,* 403–428.

Sameroff, A. (1989). General systems and the regulation of development. In M. Gunner & E. Thelen (Eds.), *Systems and development.* Hillsdale, NJ: Erlbaum.

Sameroff, A., & Chandler, M. J. (1975). Reproductive risk and the continuum of caretaking casualty. In F. D. Horowitz, M. Hetherington, S. Scarr-Salapatek, & G. Siegel (Eds.), *Review of child development research* (Vol. 4, pp. 187–244). Chicago: University of Chicago Press.

Sameroff, A. J. (2000). Dialectical processes in developmental psychopathology. In A. J. Sameroff, M. Lewis, & S. M. Miller (Eds.), *Handbook of developmental psychopathology* (2nd ed., pp. 23–40). New York: Kluwer Academic/Plenum Press.

Sameroff, A. J., Gutman, L. M., & Peck, S. C. (2003). Adaptation among youth facing multiple risks: Prospective research findings. In S. S. Luthar (Ed.), *Resilience and vulnerability: Adaptation in the context of childhood adversities* (pp. 364–391). Cambridge, England: Cambridge University Press.

Sampson, R. J., Morenoff, J. D., & Earls, F. (1999). Beyond social capital: Spatial dynamics of collective efficacy for children. *American Sociological Review, 64,* 633–660.

Sandmaier, M. (1996, May/June). More than love. *Family Therapy Networker,* pp. 21–33.

Sandnabba, N. K., & Alhberg, C. (1999). Parents' attitudes and expectations about children's cross-gender behavior. *Sex Roles, 40,* 249–264.

Sanford, N. (1962). *The American college: A psychological and social interpretation of higher learning.* New York: Wiley.

Sapolski, R. M. (1992). *Stress: The aging brain and the mechanisms of neuron death.* Cambridge, MA: MIT Press.

Saraglou, V. (2002). Religion and the five factors of personality: A meta-analytic review. *Personality and Individual Differences, 32,* 15–25.

Sarason, I. G., & Sarason, B. R. (1985). *Social support: Theory, research, and applications.* Boston: Martinus Nijhoff.

Sattler, J. M., & Ryan, J. J. (1998). *Assessment of children* (3rd ed.). San Diego, CA: Sattler.

Savin-Williams, R. C. (1998). *And then I became gay: Young men's stories.* New York: Routledge.

Savin-Williams, R. C., & Diamond, L. M. (1999). Sexual orientation. In W. K. Silverman & T. H. Ollendick (Eds.), *Developmental issues in the clinical treatment of children* (pp. 241–258). Boston: Allyn & Bacon.

Saxe, G. B. (1991). *Culture and cognitive development: Studies in mathematical understanding.* Hillsdale, NJ: Erlbaum.

Saxe, G. B., Guberman, S. R., & Gearhart, M. (1987). Social processes in early number development. *Monographs of the Society for Research in Child Development, 52* (Serial No. 216).

Saxon, S. V., & Etten, M. J. (1987). *Physical change and aging: A guide for the helping professions.* New York: Tiresias Press.

Scafidi, F., Field, T., & Schanberg, S.M.(1993). Factors that predict which preterm infants benefit most from massage therapy. *Journal of Developmental and Behavioral Pediatrics, 14,* 176–180.

Scarr, S. (1992). Developmental theories for the 1990's: Development and individual differences. *Child Development, 63,* 1–19.

Scarr, S. (1993). Biological and cultural diversity: The legacy of Darwin for development. *Child Development, 64,* 1333–1353.

Scarr, S. (1997). Behavior-genetic and socialization theories of intelligence: Truce and reconciliation. In R. J. Sternberg & E. L. Girgorenko (Eds.), *Intelligence, heredity, and environment* (pp. 3–41). Cambridge, England: Cambridge University Press.

Scarr, S. (1998). American child care today. *American Psychologist, 53,* 95–108.

Scarr, S., & McCartney, K. (1983). How people make their own environments: A theory of genotype-environment effects. *Child Development, 54,* 424–435.

Schacter, S. (1959). *The psychology of affiliation.* Stanford, CA: Stanford University Press.

Schacter, S., & Singer, J. E. (1962). Cognitive, social, and physiological determinants of emotional state. *Psychological Review, 69,* 379–399.

Schafer, R. B., & Keith, P. M. (1980). Equity and depression among married couples. *Social Psychology Quarterly, 43,* 430–435.

Schaffer, H. R., & Emerson, P. E. (1964). The development of social attachments in infancy. *Monographs of the Society for Research in Child Development, 29*(3, Serial No. 94).

Schaie, K. W. (1977–1978). Toward a stage theory of adult cognitive development. *Journal of Aging and Human Development, 8,* 129–139.

Schaie, K. W. (1994). The course of adult intellectual development. *American Psychologist, 49,* 304–313.

Schaie, K. W. (1996). *Intellectual development in adulthood: The Seattle Longitudinal Study.* New York: Cambridge University Press.

Schaie, K. W., & Willis, S. L. (2000). A stage theory model of adult cognitive development revisited. In R. L. Rubinstein, M. Moss, & M. H. Kleban (Eds.), *The many dimensions of aging* (pp. 175–193). New York: Springer.

Scharf, M., Mayseless, O, & Kivenson-Baron, I. (2004). Adolescents' attachment representations and developmental tasks in emerging adulthood. *Developmental Psychology, 40,* 430–440.

Schauble, L. (1991). Belief revision in children: The role of prior knowledge and strategies for generating evidence. *Journal of Experimental Child Psychology, 49,* 31–57.

Schauble, L. (1996). The development of scientific reasoning in knowledge-rich contexts. *Developmental Psychology, 32,* 102–119.

Scheer, S. D., Unger, D. G., & Brown, M. (1994, February). *Adolescents becoming adults: Attributes for adulthood.* Poster presented at the biennial meeting of the Society for Research on Adolescence, San Diego, CA.

Schenkel, S., & Marcia, J. E. (1972). Attitudes toward premarital intercourse in determining ego identity status in college women. *Journal of Personality, 3,* 472–482.

Schermer, M. (2003). Death by theory. *Scientific American, 290*(6), 48.

Schier, M. F., & Carver, C. S. (1985). Optimism, coping and health: Assessment and implications of generalized outcome expectancies. *Health Psychology, 4,* 219–247.

Schindler, R. (1996). Mourning and bereavement among Jewish religious families: A time for reflection and recovery. *Omega, 33,* 121–129.

Schlegel, A., & Barry, H. III. (1991). *Adolescence: An anthropological inquiry.* New York: Free Press.

Schlossberg, N. (2004). *Retire smart, retire happy: Finding your true path in life.* Washington, DC: American Psychological Association.

Schmitt-Rodermund, E., & Vondracek, F. W. (1999). Breadth of interests, exploration, and identity development in adolescence. *Journal of Vocational Behavior, 55,* 298–317.

Schneider, W. (1993). Acquiring expertise: Determinant of exceptional performance. In K. A. Heller, F. J. Monks, & A. H. Passow (Eds.), *International handbook of research and development of giftedness and talent.* Oxford, England: Pergamon Press.

Schneider, W., & Bjorklund, B. F. (1998). Memory. In W. Damon (Series Ed.,) D. Kuhn & R. S. Siegler (Vol. Eds.), *Handbook of child psychology: Vol. 2. Cognition, perception, and language* (5th ed., pp. 467–522). New York: Wiley.

Schneider, W., & Pressley, M. (1997). *Memory development between 2 and 20* (2nd ed.). New York: Springer.

Schneider-Rosen, K., Braunwald, K. G., Carlson, V., & Cicchetti, D. (1985). Current perspectives in attachment theory: Illustration from the study of maltreated infants. In I. Bretherton & E. Waters (Eds.), Growing points of attachment theory and research. *Monographs of the Society for Research in Child Development, 50*(Serial No. 209), 194–210.

Schneider-Rosen, K., & Cicchetti, D. (1984). The relationship between affect and cognition in maltreated infants: Quality of attachment and visual self-recognition. *Child Development, 55,* 648–658.

Schneider-Rosen, K., & Cicchetti, D. (1991). Early self-knowledge and emotional development: Visual self-recognition and affective reactions to mirror self-image in maltreated and non-maltreated toddlers. *Developmental Psychology, 27,* 481–488.

Schoenthaler, S., Doraz, W., & Wakefield, J. (1986). The impact of a low food additive and sucrose diet on academic performance in 803 New York City public schools. *The International Journal of Biosocial Research, 7,* 189–195.

Schommer, M. A. (1990). Effects of beliefs about the nature of knowledge on comprehension. *Journal of Educational Psychology, 82,* 498–504.

Schommer, M. (1993). Epistemological development and academic performance among secondary students. *Journal of Educational Psychology, 85,* 1–6.

Schommer, M., Crouse, A., & Rhodes, N. (1992). Epistemological beliefs and mathematical text comprehension: Believing it is simple does not make it so. *Journal of Educational Psychology, 84,* 435–443.

Schon, D. (1987). *Educating the reflective practitioner: Toward a new design for teaching and learning in the professions.* San Francisco: Jossey-Bass.

Schore, A. N. (1994). *Affect regulation and the origin of the self: The neurobiology of affective development.* Hillsdale, NJ: Erlbaum.

Schouwenburg, H. C. (2004). Procrastination in academic settings: General introduction. In H. C. Schouwenburg, C. H. Lay, T. A. Pychyl, & J. R. Ferrari (Eds.), *Counseling the procrastinator in academic settings* (pp. 3–17). Washington, DC: American Psychological Association.

Schraw, G., & Moshman, D. (1995). Metacognitive theories. *Educational Psychology Review, 7,* 351–371.

Schreibman, T., & Friedland, G. (2003). Human immunodeficiency virus infection prevention: Strategies for clinicians. *Clinical Infectious Diseases, 36,* 1171–1176.

Schubert, J. B., Bradley-Johnson, S., & Nuttal, J. (1980). Mother-infant communication and maternal employment. *Child Development, 51,* 246–249.

Schulman, M. (2002). How we become moral: The sources of moral motivation. In C. R. Snyder & S. J. Lopez (Eds), *Handbook of positive psychology* (pp. 499–512). New York: Oxford University Press.

Schulster, J. R. (1996). In my era: Evidence for the perception of a special period of the past. *Memory, 4,* 145–158.

Schultz, L. H. (1993). *Close peer relationship interview scoring manual.* Unpublished manual, Harvard University, Cambridge, MA.

Schultz, L. H., Barr, D. J., & Selman, R. L. (2000). *The value of a developmental approach to evaluating character education programs: An outcome study of facing history and ourselves.* Manuscript submitted for publication.

Schultz, R., & Heckhausen, R. (1996). The life span model of successful aging. *American Psychologist, 51,* 702–713.

Schulz, R., & Curnow, C. (1988). Peak performance and age among superathletes: Track and field, swimming, baseball, tennis, and golf. *Journal of Gerontology, 43,* 113–120.

Schwartz, B. (2000). Self-determination: The tyranny of freedom. *American Psychologist, 55,* 79–88.

Schwartz, B. (2004). The tyranny of choice. *Scientific American, 290,* 70–76.

Schwartz, R. M., & Garamoni, G. L. (1989). Cognitive balance and psychopathology: Evaluation of an information processing model of positive and negative states of mind. *Clinical Psychology Review, 9*(3), 271–294.

Scogin, F., & McElreath, L. (1994). Efficacy of psychosocial treatments for geriatric depression: A quantitative review. *Journal of Consulting and Clinical Psychology, 62,* 69–74.

Scott, C. G., Murray, G. C., Mertens, C., & Dustin, E. R. (1996). Student self-esteem and the school system: Perceptions and implications. *Journal of Educational Research, 89,* 286–293.

Scozarro, P. P., & Subich, L. M. (1990). Gender and occupational sex-type differences in job outcome factor perceptions. *Journal of Vocational Behavior, 36,* 109–119.

Searight, H. R., & Gafford, J. (2005). Cultural diversity at the end of life: Issues and guidelines for family physicians. *American Family Physician, 71,* 515–522.

Sears, R., Maccoby, E., & Levin, H. (1957). *Patterns of child rearing.* Evanston, IL: Row, Peterson.

Segal, Z. V., Williams, J. M. G., & Teasdale, J. D. (2002). *Mindfulness-based cognitive therapy for depression: A new approach to preventing relapse.* New York: Guilford Press.

Segrin, C., & Abramson, L. (1994). Negative reactions to depressed behaviors: A communications theory analysis. *Journal of Abnormal Psychology, 103*(4), 655–668.

Seifer, R. (2003). Young children with mentally ill parents: Resilient developmental systems. In S. S. Luthar (Ed.), *Resilience and vulnerability: Adaptation in the context of childhood adversities* (pp. 364–391). Cambridge, England: Cambridge University Press.

Seligman, M.E.P. (1975). *Helplessness: On depression, development, and death.* San Francisco: Freeman.

Seligman, M. E. P. (1993). *What you can change and what you can't.* New York: Ballantine Books.

Seligman, M. E. P. (1995). *The optimistic child.* Boston: Houghton Mifflin.

Seligman, M. E. P. (2002). *Authentic happiness.* New York: Free Press.

Selman, R. L. (1980). *The growth of interpersonal understanding: Developmental and clinical analysis.* Orlando, FL: Academic Press.

Selman, R. L., & Adalbjarnardottir, S. (2000). A developmental method to analyze the personal meaning adolescents make of risk and relationship: The case of "drinking." *Applied Developmental Science, 4*(1), 47–65.

Selman, R. L., Jaquette, D., & Bruss-Saunders, E. (1979). *Assessing interpersonal understanding: An interview an dscoring manual in five parts constructed by the Harvard-Judge Baker Social Reasoning Project.* Unpublished manuscript, Harvard University, Cambridge, MA.

Selman, R. L., Levitt, M. Z., & Schultz, L. H. (1997a) The friendship framework: Tools for the assessment of psychosocial development. In R. L. Selman, C. L. Watts & L. H. Schultz (Eds.), *Fostering friendship: Pair therapy for treatment and prevention* (pp. 31–52). New York: Aldine de Gruyer.

Selman, R. L., & Schultz, L. H. (1990). Making a friend in youth: Developmental theory and pair therapy. Chicago: University of Chicago Press.

Selman, R. L., Watts, C. L., & Schultz, L. H. (Eds.). (1997b). *Fostering friendship: Pair therapy for treatment and prevention.* New York: Aldine de Gruyer.

Seltzer, V. C. (1982). *Adolescent social development: Dynamic functional interaction.* Lexington, MA: Heath.

Selye, H. (1980). The stress concept today. In I. L. Kutash, L. B. Schlesinger, & Associates (Eds.), *Handbook on stress and anxiety* (pp. 127–143). San Francisco: Jossey-Bass.

Senchak, M., & Leonard, K. E. (1992). Attachment styles and marital adjustment among newlywed couples. *Journal of Personality and Social Psychology, 9,* 51–64.

Senchal, M., & LeFevre, J. (2002). Parental involvement in the development of children's reading skill: A five-year longitudinal study. *Child Development, 73,* 445–460.

Serbin, L. A., & Karp, J. (2004). The intergeneration transfer of psychosocial risk mediators of vulnerability and resilience. *Annual Review of Psychology, 55,* 333–363.

Shaffer, D. R. (1994). *Social and personality development* (3rd ed.). Pacific Grove, CA: Brooks/Cole.

Shaffer, D. R. (2000). *Social and personality development.* Belmont, CA: Wadsworth/Thomson.

Shapiro, A. F., Gottman, J. M., & Carrere, S. (2000). The baby and the marriage: Identifying factors that buffer against decline in marital satisfaction after the first baby arrives. *Journal of Family Psychology, 14,* 59–70.

Shapiro, S. L., Bootzin, R. R., Figueredo, A. J., Lopez, A. M., & Schwartz, G. E. (2003). The efficacy of mindfulness-based stress reduction in the treatment of sleep disturbance in women with breast cancer: An exploratory study. *Journal of Psychosomatic Research, 54,* 85–91.

Shavelson, R. J., Hubner, J. J., & Stanton, G. C. (1976). Validation of construct interpretations. *Review of Educational Research, 46,* 407–441.

Shaver, P. R., & Hazan, C. (1988). A biased overview of the study of love. *Journal of Personal and Social Relationships, 5,* 473–501.

Shaver, P. R., Hazan, C., & Bradshaw, D. (1988). Love as attachment: The integration of three behavioral systems. In R. J. Sternberg & M. L. Barnes (Eds.), *The psychology of love* (pp. 68–99). New Haven, CT: Yale University Press.

Shedler, J., & Block, J. (1990). Adolescent drug use and psychological health: A longitudinal inquiry. *American Psychologist, 45,* 612–630.

Sher, K. J., Bartholow, B. D., & Nanda, S. (2001). Short- and long-term effects of fraternity and sorority membership on heavy drinking: A social norms perspective. *Psychology of Addictive Behaviors, 15,* 42–51.

Shettles, L. B. (1961). Conception and birth ratios. *Obstetrics and Gynecology, 18,* 122–130.

Shiloh, S. (1996). Genetic counseling: A developing area of interest for psychologists. *Professional Psychology: Research and Practice, 27,* 475–486.

Shiner, R. L., Masten, A. S., & Roberts, J. M. (2003). Childhood personality foreshadows adult personality and life outcomes two decades later. *Journal of Personality, 71,* 1145–1170.

Shirk, S. R. (1988). *Cognitive development and child psychotherapy.* New York: Plenum Press.

Shrum, W., & Cheek, N. H. (1987). Social structure during the school years: Onset of the degrouping process. *American Sociological Review, 52,* 218–223.

Shure, M. B., & Spivak, G. (1988). Interpersonal cognitive problem-solving. In R. H. Price, E. L. Cowen, R. P .Lorion, & J. Ramos-McKay (Eds.), *Fourteen ounces of prevention: A casebook for practitioners* (pp. 69–82). Washington, DC: American Psychological Association.

Siegel, A. W., & Scovill, L. C. (2000). Problem behavior: The double symptom of adolescence. *Development and Psychopathology, 12,* 763–793.

Siegel, J. M., & Kuykendall, D. H. (1990). Loss, widowhood, and psychological distress among the elderly. *Journal of Consulting and Clinical Psychology, 58,* 519–524.

Siegel, M. (1987). Are sons and daughters treated more differently by fathers than mothers? *Developmental Review, 7,* 183–209.

Siegel, M., & Peterson, C. C. (1998). Preschoolers' understanding of lies and innocent and negligent mistakes. *Developmental Psychology, 34,* 332–341.

Siegler, R. S. (1987). Strategy choices in subtraction. In J. A. Sloboda & D. Rogers (Eds.), *Cognitive processes in mathematics* (pp. 81–106). Oxford: Clarendon.

Siegler, R. S. (1996). *Emerging minds: The process of change in children's thinking.* New York: Oxford University Press.

Siegler, R. S. (1998). *Children's thinking* (3rd ed.). Upper Saddle River, NJ: Prentice Hall.

Siegler, R. S., & Shrager, J. (1984). Strategy choices in addition and subtraction: How do children know what to do? In C. Sophian (Ed.), *The origins of cognitive skills.* Hillsdale, NJ: Erlbaum.

Siegrist, J. (1996). Adverse health effects of high-effort/low-reward conditions. *Journal of Occupational Health Psychology, 1,* 27–41.

Signorella, M. L., Bigler, R. S., & Liben, L. S. (1993). Developmental differences in children's gender schemata about others: A meta-analytic review. *Developmental Review, 13,* 147–183.

Signorella, M. L., & Liben, L. S. (1984). Recall and reconstruction of gender-related pictures: Effects of attitude, task difficulty, and age. *Child Development, 55,* 393–405.

Silberg, J., Meyer, J., Pickles, A., Simonoff, E., Eaves, L., Hewitt, J., et al. (1996). Heterogeneity among juvenile antisocial behaviors: Findings from the Virginia Twin Study of Adolescent Behavioural Development. In G. R. Bock & J. A. Goode (Eds.), *Genetics of criminal and antisocial behaviour* (pp. 76–86). Chichester, England: Wiley.

Silveira, M., DiPiero, A., Gerrity, M. S., & Feudtner, C. (2000). Patients' knowledge of options at the end of life. *Journal of the American Medical Association, 284,* 2483–2488.

Silverberg, S. B., & Steinberg, L. (1990). Psychological well-being of parents with early adolescent children. *Developmental Psychology, 26,* 658–666.

Silverman, P. (2000). Research, clinical practice, and the human experience: Putting the pieces together. *Death Studies, 24,* 469–478.

Simmons, R. G., & Blyth, D. A. (1987). *Moving into adolescence: The impact of pubertal change and school context.* Hawthorne, NY: Aldine de Gruyter.

Simmons, R. G., Blyth, D. A., & McKinney, K. L. (1983). The social and psychological effects of puberty on white females. In J. Brooks-Gunn & A. C. Petersen (Eds.), *Girls at puberty: Biological and psychological perspectives* (pp. 229–272). New York: Plenum Press.

Simpson, J. A. (1990). Influence of attachment styles on romantic relationships. *Journal of Personality and Social Psychology, 59,* 971–980.

Simpson, J. A., & Rholes, W. S. (1998a). Attachment in adulthood. In J. A. Simpson & W. S. Rholes (Eds.), *Attachment theory and close relationships* (pp. 3–21). New York: Guilford Press.

Simpson, J. A., & Rholes, W. S. (1998b). *Attachment theory and close relationships.* New York: Guilford Press.

Simpson, J. A., Rholes, W. S., & Phillips, D. (1996). Conflict in close relationships: An attachment perspective. *Journal of Personality and Social Psychology, 71,* 899–914.

Singer, B., & Ryff, C. D. (1999) Hierarchies of life stories and associated health risks. In N. E. Adler, B. S. McEwen, & M. Marmot (Eds.), *Socioeconomic status and health in industrialized nations: Social, psychological, and biological pathways* (pp. 96–115). New York: New York Academy of Sciences, 896.

Singer, B., Ryff, C. D., Carr, D., & Magee, W. J. (1998). Life histories and mental health: A person-centered strategy. In A. Raferty (Ed.), *Sociological methodology* (pp. 1–51). Washington, DC: American Sociological Association.

Singer, P., Martin, D., & Merrijoy, K. (1999). Quality of end-of-life care. *Journal of the American Medical Association, 281,* 163–168.

Singer, T., Verhaeghen, P., Ghisletta, P., Lindenberger, U., & Baltes, P. B. (2003). The fate of cognition in very old age: Six-year longitudinal findings in the Berlin Aging Study (BASE). *Psychology and Aging, 18,* 318–331.

Sinnott, J. D. (1984). Postformal reasoning: The relativistic stage. In M. L. Commons, F. A. Richards, & C. Armon (Eds.), *Beyond formal operations: Late adolescent and adult cognitive development* (pp. 298–325). New York: Praeger.

Sinnott, J. D. (1998). *The development of logic in adulthood: Postformal thought and its applications.* New York: Plenum Press.

Skinner, B. F., & Vaughan, M. E. (1983/1997). *Enjoy old age: A practical guide.* New York: Norton.

Skinner, E. A., Edge, K., Altman, J., & Sherwood, H. (2003). Searching for the structure of coping: A review and critique of category systems for classifying ways of coping. *Psychological Bulletin, 129,* 216–269.

Skogan, W. G. (1989). Social change and the future of violent crime. In T. R. Gurr (Ed.), *Violence in America: Vol. 1. The history of crime.* Newbury Park, CA: Sage.

Slaby, R. G., & Frey, K. S. (1975). Development of gender constancy and selective attention to same-sex models. *Child Development, 52,* 849–856.

Slade, A. (1999). Attachment theory and research: Implications for the theory and practice of individual psychotherapy with adults. In J. Cassidy & P. R. Shaver (Eds.), *Handbook of attachment: Theory, research, and clinical applications* (pp. 575–594). New York: Guilford Press.

Slavin, R. E. (1995). *Cooperative learning: Theory, research, and practice* (2nd ed.). Boston: Allyn & Bacon.

Slomkowski, C., & Dunn, J. (1996). Young children's understanding of other people's beliefs and feelings and their connected communication with friends. *Developmental Psychology, 32,* 442–447.

Smetana, J. G. (1988). Adolescents' and parents' conceptions of parental authority. *Child Development, 59,* 321–335.

Smetana, J. G. (1989). Toddlers' social interactions in the context of moral and conventional transgressions in the home. *Developmental Psychology, 25,* 499–508.

Smetana, J. G. (1995). Parenting styles and conceptions of parental authority during adolescence. *Child Development, 66,* 299–316.

Smetana, J. G., & Asquith, P. (1994). Adolescents' and parents' conceptions of parental authority and adolescent autonomy. *Child Development, 65,* 1147–1162.

Smetana, J. G., & Braeges, J. L. (1990). The development of toddler's moral and conventional judgments. *Merrill-Palmer Quarterly, 36,* 329–346.

Smetana, J. G., & Daddis, C. (2002). Domain-specific antecedents of parental psychological control and monitoring: The role of parenting beliefs and practices. *Child Development, 73,* 563–580.

Smetana, J. G., & Gaines, C. (1999). Adolescent-parent conflict in middle class African American families. *Child Development, 70,* 1447–1463.

Smetana, J. G., Schlagman, N., & Adams, P. W. (1993). Preschool children's judgements about hypothetical and actual transgressions. *Child Development, 64,* 204–214.

Smith, C., & Krohn, M. D. (1955). Delinquency and family life among male adolescents: The role of ethnicity. *Journal of Youth and Adolescence, 24,* 69–93.

Smith C. A., Haynes, K. N., Lazarus, R. S., & Pope, L. K. (1993). In search of the "hot" cognitions: Attributions, appraisals, and their relation to emotion. *Journal of Personality and Social Psychology, 65,* 916–929.

Smith, C. L. (1979). Children's understanding of natural language hierarchies. *Journal of Experimental Child Psychology, 27,* 437–458.

Smith, J., Staudinger, U. M., & Baltes, P. B. (1994). Occupational settings facilitating wisdom-related knowledge: The sample case of clinical psychologists. *Journal of Counseling and Clinical Psychology, 62,* 989–999.

Smith, K. R. (2002). Gene transfer in higher animals: Theoretical considerations and key concepts. *Journal of Biotechnology, 99,* 1–22.

Smith, K. R. (2003). Gene therapy: Theoretical and bioethical concepts. *Archives of Medical Research, 34,* 247–268.

Smith, R. E., & Smoll, F. L. (1990). Self-esteem and children's enhancement to youth coaching behaviors: A field study of self-enhancement processes. *Developmental Psychology, 26,* 987–993.

Smolak, L., Levine, M. P., & Thompson, J. K. (2001). The use of the Sociocultural Attitudes Towards Appearance Questionnnaire with middle school boys and girls. *International Journal of Eating Disorders, 29,* 216–223.

Snowdon, D. A. (1997). Aging and Alzheimer's disease: Lessons from the Nun Study. *Gerontologist, 37,* 150–156.

Snyder, D., & Wills, R. (1989). Behavioral versus insight-oriented marital therapy: Effects on individual and interspousal functioning. *Journal of Consulting and Clinical Psychology, 57,* 39–46.

Snyder, D. K., Wills, R. M., & Grady-Fletcher, A. (1991). Long-term effectiveness of behavioral versus insight-oriented marital therapy: A four-year follow-up study. *Journal of Consulting and Clinical Psychology, 59,* 138–144.

Snyder, J. J., & Patterson, G. R. (1995). Individual differences in social aggression: A test of a reinforcement model of socialization info-processing mechanisms in children's social adjustment. *Behavior Therapy, 26,* 371–391.

Socha, T. J., & Socha, D. M. (1994). Children's task-group communication. In L. R. Frey (Ed.), *Group communication in context: Studies of natural groups* (pp. 227–246). Hillsdale, NJ: Erlbaum.

Sonderegger, T. B. (Ed.). (1992). *Perinatal substance abuse: Research findings and clinical implications.* Baltimore: Johns Hopkins University Press.

Sorich, L., & Dweck, C. S. (1996). Mastery-oriented thinking. In C. R. Snyder (Ed.), *Coping.* New York: Oxford University Press.

Sowell, E. R., Delis, D., Stiles, J., & Jernigan, T. L. (2001). Improved memory functioning and frontal lobe maturation between childhood and adolescence: A structural MRI study. *Journal of the International Neuropsychological Society, 7,* 312–322.

Sowell, E. R., Peterson, B. S., Thompson, P. M., Welcome, S. E., Hendkenius, A. L. & Toga, A. W. (2003). Mapping cortical change across the human life span. *Natural Neuroscience, 6,* 309–315.

Sowell, E. R., Thompson, P. M., & Toga, A. W. (2004). Mapping changes in the human cortex throughout the span of life. *The Neuroscientist, 10,* 372–392.

Spangler, G., & Grossmann, K. E. (1993). Biobehavioral organization in securely and insecurely attached infants. *Child Development, 64,* 1439–1450.

Spasojevic, J., & Alloy, L. B. (2001). Rumination as a common mechanism relating depressive risk factors to depression. *Emotion, 1,* 25–37.

Spaulding, J., & Balch, P. (1983). A brief history of primary prevention in the twentieth century: 1908 to 1980. *American Journal of Community Psychology, 11,* 59–80.

Spear, L. P. (2000). Neurobehavioral changes in adolescence. *Current Directions in Psychological Science, 9,* 111–114.

Spencer, M. B. (1982). Preschool children's social cognition and cultural cognition: A cognitive developmental interpretation of race dissonance findings. *Journal of Psychology, 112,* 275–286.

Spencer, M. B., & Markstrom-Adams, C. (1990). Identity processes among racial and ethnic minority children in America. *Child Development, 61,* 290–310.

Spenser, J. T. (1970). *The effects of systematic and token reinforcement on the modification of racial and color-concept attitudes in preschool-age children.* Unpublished master's thesis, University of Kansas.

Sperry, R. W. (1964). The great cerebral commissure. *Scientific American, 201,* 42–52.

Spokane, A. R., Meir, E. I., & Catalano, M. (2000). Person-environment congruence and Holland's theory: A review and reconsideration. *Journal of Vocational Behavior, 57,* 137–187.

Sroufe, L. A. (1989). Pathways to adaptation and maladaptation: Psychopathology as developmental deviation: The roots of maladaptation and competence. In D. Cicchetti (Ed.), *Rochester Symposium on Developmental Psychopathology: Vol. 1. The emergence of a discipline* (pp. 13–40). Hillsdale, NJ: Erlbaum.

Sroufe, L. A. (1996). *Emotional development: The organization of emotional life in the early years.* New York: Cambridge University Press.

Sroufe, L. A. (1997). Psychopathology as an outcome of development. *Development and Psychopathology, 9,* 251–268.

Sroufe, L. A., Bennett, C., Englund, M., Urban, J., and Shulman, S. (1993). The significance of gender boundaries in preadolescence: Contemporary correlates and antecedents of boundary violation and maintenance. *Child Development, 64,* 455–466.

Sroufe, L. A., Fox, N. E., & Pancake, V. R. (1983). Attachment and dependency in developmental perspective. *Child Development, 54,* 1615–1627.

Sroufe, L. A., & Waters, E. (1977). Attachment as an organizational construct. *Child Development, 48,* 1184–1199.

Stanhope, L., Bell, R. Q., & Parker-Cohen, N. Y. (1987). Temperament and helping behavior in preschool children. *Developmental Psychology, 23,* 347–353.

Stanovich, K. E. (1998). *How to think straight about psychology.* New York: Addison-Wesley/Longman.

Starkman, N., & Rajani, N. (2002). The case for comprehensive sex education. *AIDS Patient Care and STDs, 16*(7), 313–318.

Staudinger, U. M., & Baltes, P. B. (1996). Interactive minds: A facilitative setting for wisdom-related performance? *Journal of Personality and Social Psychology, 71,* 746–762.

Staudinger, U. M., Maciel, A. G., Smith, J., & Baltes, P. B. (1998). What predicts wisdom-related performance? A first look at personality, intelligence, and facilitative experiential contexts. *European Journal of Personality, 12,* 1–17.

Steele, C. (1997). A threat in the air: How stereotypes shape intellectual identity and performance. *American Psychologist, 52,* 613–629.

Steenbarger, B. N. (1991). All the world is not a stage: Emerging contextualist themes in counseling and development. *Journal of Counseling and Development, 70,* 288–296.

Stein, Z., Susser, M., Saenger, G., & Marolla, F. (1975). *Famine and human development: The Dutch hunger winter of 1944/45.* New York: Oxford University Press.

Steinberg, L. (1988). Reciprocal relation between parent-child distance and pubertal maturation. *Developmental Psychology, 24,* 122–128.

Steinberg, L. (1990). Interdependency in the family: Autonomy, conflict, and harmony. In S. Feldman & G. Elliot (Eds.), *At the threshold: The developing adolescent* (pp. 255–276). Cambridge, MA: Harvard University Press.

Steinberg, L. (1994). *Crossing paths: How your child's adolescence triggers your own crisis.* New York: Simon & Schuster.

Steinberg, L. (1996). *Beyond the classroom: Why school reform has failed and what parents need to do.* New York: Simon & Schuster.

Steinberg, L., & Avenevoli, S. (2000). The role of context in the development of psychopathology: A conceptual framework and some speculative propositions. *Child Development, 71,* 66–74.

Steinberg, L., & Belsky, J. (1991). *Infancy, childhood, and adolescence: Development in context.* New York: McGraw-Hill.

Steinberg, L., & Cauffman, E. (1995). The impact of employment on adolescent development. In R. Vasta (Ed.), *Annals of child development* (Vol. 11, pp. 131–166). London: Kingsley.

Steinberg, L., Dornbusch, S. M., & Brown, B. B. (1992). Ethnic differences in adolescent achievement: An ecological perspective. *American Psychologist, 47,* 723–729.

Steinberg, L., Fegley, S., & Dornbusch, S. M. (1993). The negative impact of part-time work on adolescent adjustment: Evidence from a longitudinal study. *Developmental Psychology, 29,* 171–180.

Steinberg, L., Grisso, T., Woolard, J., Cauffman, E., Scott, E., Graham, S., et al. (2003). Juveniles' competence to stand trial as adults. *Social Policy Report, 17*(4), 3–7, 11, 13–15.

Steinberg, L., Lamborn, S. D., Darling, N., Mounts, N. S., & Dornbusch, S. M. (1994). Overtime changes in adjustment and competence among adolescents from authoritative, authoritarian, indulgent and neglectful families. *Child Development, 65,* 754–770.

Steinberg, L., Lamborn, S. D., Dornbusch, S. M., & Darling, N. (1992). Impact of parenting practices on adolescent achievement: Authoritative parenting, school involvement and encouragement to succeed. *Child Development, 63,* 1266–1281.

Steinberg, L., & Scott, E. S. (2003). Less guilty by reason of adolescence: Developmental immaturity, diminished responsibility, and the juvenile death penalty. *American Psychologist, 58,* 1009–1018.

Steinberg, L., & Silverberg, S. B. (1986). The vicissitudes of autonomy in early adolescence. *Child Development, 57,* 841–851.

Steinhauser, K. E., Christakis, N. A., Clipp, E. C., McNeilly, M., McIntyre, L., & Tulsky, J. A. (2000). Factors considered important at the end of life by patients, family, physicians, and other care providers. *Journal of the American Medical Association, 284,* 2476–2482.

Stephen, J., Fraser, E., & Marcia, J. E. (1992). Moratorium-achievement (MAMA) cycles in lifespan identity development: Value orientations and reasoning system. *Journal of Adolescence, 15,* 283–300.

Steptoe, A., Willemsen, G., Owen, N., Flower, L., & Mohamed-Ali, V. (2001). Acute mental stress elicits delayed increases in circulating inflammatory cytokine levels. *Clinical Science, 101,* 185–192.

Sterling, C. M., & Van Horn, K. R. (1989). Identity and death anxiety. *Adolescence, 24,* 321–326.

Stern, D. (1985). *The interpersonal world of the infant.* New York: Basic Books.

Sternberg, E. M. (2001). *The balance within: The science connecting health and emotions.* New York: Freeman.

Sternberg, R. J. (1985). *Beyond IQ: A triarchic theory of human intelligence.* New York: Cambridge University Press.

Sternberg, R. J. (1986). A triangular theory of love. *Psychological Review, 93,* 119–135.

Sternberg, R. J. (1998). *Love is a story.* New York: Oxford University Press.

Sternberg, R. J. (2001). What is the common thread of creativity: Its dialectical relation to intelligence and wisdom. *American Psychologist, 56,* 360–362.

Sternberg, R. J. (2004). Culture and intelligence. *American Psychologist, 59,* 325–338.

Sternberg, R. J., & Grigorenko, E. L. (1999). *Our labeled children.* Reading, MA: Perseus Books.

Sterns, H. L., & Huyck, M. H. (2001). The role of work in midlife. In M. E. Lachman (Ed.), *Handbook of midlife development* (pp. 447–486). New York: Wiley.

Stevens-Long, J. (1973). The effect of behavioral context on some aspects of adult disciplinary practice and affect. *Child Development, 44,* 476–484.

Stevenson, H. W., Chen, C., & Lee, S. (1993). Mathematics achievement of Chinese, Japanese, and American children: Ten years later. *Science, 159,* 53–59.

Stevenson, H. W., & Stigler, J. W. (1992). *The learning gap: Why our schools are failing and what we can learn from Chinese and Japanese education.* New York: Simon & Schuster.

Stevenson-Hinde, J., & Marshall, P. J. (1999). Behavioral inhibition, heart period, and respiratory sinus arrhythmia: An attachment perspective. *Child Development, 70,* 805–816.

Stewart, A. J., & Vandewater, E. A. (1998). The course of generativity. In D. P. McAdams & E. de St. Aubin (Eds.), *Generativity and adult development: How and why we care for the next generation* (pp. 45–74). Washington, DC: American Psychological Association.

Stewart, N., Winborn, B., Johnson, R., Burks, H., & Engelkes, J. (1978). *Systematic counseling.* Upper Saddle River, NJ: Prentice Hall.

Stipek, D., Recchia, A., & McClintic, S. (1992). Self-evaluation in young children. *Monographs of the Society for Research in Child Development, 57*(1, Serial No. 226).

Stipek, D. J., Gralinski, J. H., & Kopp, C. B. (1990). Self-concept development in the toddler years. *Developmental Psychology, 26,* 972–977.

St. Lawrence, J. S., Brasfield, T. L., Jefferson, K. W., Alleyne, E., O'Bannon, R. E., & Shirley, A. (1995). Cognitive behavioral interventions to reduce African-American adolescents risk for HIV infection. *Journal of Consulting and Clinical Psychology, 63*(1), 154–157.

Stockard, J., & Johnson, M. M. (1992). *Sex and gender in society.* Upper Saddle River, NJ: Prentice Hall.

Stoltenberg, C. D., & Delworth, U. (1987). *Supervising counselors and therapists: A developmental approach.* San Francisco: Jossey-Bass.

Stonewater, B. B., & Stonewater, J. K. (1983). Developmental clues: An aid for the practitioner. *NASPA Journal, 21,* 52–59.

Stonewater, B. B., & Stonewater, J. K. (1984). Teaching problem-solving: Implications from cognitive development research. *AAHE Bulletin, 36,* 7–10. Washington, DC: American Association for Higher Education.

Strachan, T., & Read, A. P. (2000). *Human molecular genetics* (2nd ed.). New York: Wiley.

Strassberg, Z., Pettit, K. A., Gregory, S., & Bates, J. E. (1994). Spanking in the home and children's subsequent aggression toward their peers. *Development and Psychopathology, 6,* 445–462.

Stratton, K., Howe, C., & Battaglia, F. (1996). *Fetal alcohol syndrome: Diagnosis, epidemiology, prevention, and treatment.* Washington, DC: National Academy Press.

Straus, M. A., & Gelles, R. J. (1990). *Physical violence in American families: Risk factors and adaptation to violence in 841 families.* New Brunswick, NJ: Transaction Books.

Straus, M. A., & Yodanis, C. L. (1996). Corporal punishment in adolescence and physical assault on spouses in later life: What accounts for the link? *Journal of Marriage and the Family, 58,* 825–841.

Straus, M. A., Sugarman, D. B., Giles-Sims, J. (1997). Spanking by parents and subsequent antisocial behavior of children. *Archives of Pediatric and Adolescent Medicine, 151,* 761–767.

Strauss, A., & Corbin, J. (1990). *Basics of qualitative research: Grounded theory, procedures, and techniques.* Newbury Park, CA: Sage.

Streissguth, A. P., & Dehaene, P. (1993). Fetal alcohol syndrome in twins of alcoholic mothers: Concordance of diagnosis and IQ. *American Journal of Medical Genetics, 47,* 857–861.

Strickberger, M. W. (1985). *Genetics* (3rd ed.). New York: Macmillan.

Stroebe, M. (1992). Coping with bereavement: A review of the grief work hypothesis. *Omega, 26,* 19–42.

Stroebe, M., & Schut, H. (1999). The dual process model of coping with bereavement: Rationale and description. *Death Studies, 23,* 197–224.

Stroebe, M., & Stroebe, W. (1993). Determinants of adjustment to bereavement among younger widows and widowers. In M. Stroebe, W. Stroebe, & R. O. Hansson (Eds.), *Handbook of bereavement: Theory, research, and intervention* (pp. 208–226). New York: Cambridge University Press.

Stroebe, M. S., & Schut, H. (2001). Models of coping with bereavement: A review. In M. S. Stroebe, R. O. Hansson, W. Stroebe, & H. Schut (Eds.), *Handbook of bereavement research: Consequences, coping, and care* (pp. 375–403). Washington, DC: American Psychological Association.

Strouse, J., Goodwin, M. P., & Roscoe, B. (1994). Correlates of attitudes toward sexual harassment among early adolescents. *Sex Roles, 31,* 559–577.

Strupp, H. H. (1988). What is therapeutic change? *Journal of Cognitive Psychotherapy, 2,* 75–82.

Stylianos, S. K., & Vachon, M. L. S. (1993). The role of social support in bereavement. In M. S. Stroebe, W. Stroebe, & R. O. Hansson (Eds.), *Handbook of bereavement: Theory, research, and intervention* (pp. 397–410). New York: Cambridge University Press.

Suda, W., & Fouts, G. (1980). Effects of peer presence on helping in introverted children. *Child Development, 51,* 1272–1275.

Sue, D., Mack, W. S., & Sue, D. W. (1998). Ethnic identity. In L. C. Lee & N. W. S. Zane (Eds.), *Handbook of Asian American psychology* (pp. 289–323). Thousand Oaks, CA: Sage.

Sue, D. W., Arrendondo, P., & McDavis, R. J. (1992). Multicultural counseling competencies and standards: A call to the profession. *Journal of Counseling and Development, 70,* 477–486.

Suess, G. J., Grossmann, K. E., & Sroufe, L. A. (1992). Effects of infant attachment to mother and father on quality of adaptation in preschool: From dyadic to individual organization of self. *International Journal of Behavioral Development, 15,* 43–65.

Sullivan, H. S. (1953). *Conceptions of modern psychiatry.* New York: Norton.

Sullivan, H. S. (1953). *The interpersonal theory of psychiatry.* New York: Norton.

Sullivan, H. S. (1965). *Personal psychopathology.* New York: Norton.

Suls, J. M., & Miller, R. L. (1977). *Social comparison processes: Theoretical and empirical perspectives.* Washington, DC: Hemisphere.

Super, D. E. (1957). *The psychology of careers.* New York: Harper & Row.

Super, D. E. (1972). Vocational development theory: Persons, positions, and processes. In J. M. Whiteley & A. Resnikoff (Eds.), *Perspectives on vocational development* (pp. 13–33). Washington, DC: American Personnel and Guidance Association.

Super, D. E. (1984). Career and life development. In D. Brown & L. Brooks (Eds.), *Career choice and development* (pp. 192–234). San Francisco: Jossey-Bass.

Super, D. E. (1990). A life-span, life-space approach to career development. In D. Brown & I. Brooks (Eds.), *Career choice and development: Applying contemporary theories to practice* (pp. 197–261). San Francisco: Jossey-Bass.

Super, D. E., & Overstreet, P. L. (1960). *The vocational maturity of ninth-grade boys.* New York: Teachers College, Columbia University.

Susman, E. J., Dorn, L. D., & Schiefelbein, V. L. (2003). Puberty, sexuality and health. In I. B. Weiner (Series Ed.), R. M. Lerner, M. A. Easterbrook, & J. Mistry (Vol. Eds.), *Handbook of psychology: Vol. 6. Developmental psychology* (pp. 295–324). Hoboken, NJ: Wiley.

Szechter, L. E., & Liben, L. S. (2004). Parental guidance in preschoolers' understanding of spatial-graphic representations. *Child Development, 75,* 869–885.

Taffel, R. (1996, May/June). The second family. *Family Therapy Networker,* 36–45.

Taffel, R. (2001). *The second family: How adolescent power is challenging the American family.* New York: St. Martin's Press.

Tajfel, H. (1981). *Human groups and social categories.* Cambridge, England: Cambridge University Press.

Takahashi, K. (1986). Examining the strange-situation procedure with Japanese mothers and 12-month-old infants. *Developmental Psychology, 22,* 265–270.

Takahashi, K. (1990). Are the key assumptions of the "Strange Situation" procedure universal? A view from Japanese research. *Human Development, 33,* 223–230.

Tanner, J. M. (1962). *Growth at adolescence.* Oxford, England: Blackwell Scientific Publications.

Tanner, J. M. (1970). Physical growth. In P. H. Mussen (Ed.), *Carmichael's manual of child psychology* (3rd ed., Vol. 2, pp. 77–156). New York: Wiley.

Tanner, J. M. (1990). *Fetus into man: Physical growth from conception to maturity* (2nd ed.). Cambridge, MA: Harvard University Press.

Tatum, B. D. (1997). *"Why are all the Black kids sitting together in the cafeteria?" and other conversations about race.* New York: Basic Books.

Tavris, C. (1998). A grain of salt: Some annotations to "Lessons of the new genetics." *Family Therapy Networker, 42,* 109.

Taylor, M. B. (1983). The development of the Measure of Epistemological Reflection. *Dissertation Abstracts International, 44,* 1065A (University Microfilms No. DA83–18, 441).

Taylor, S. E. (1983). Adjustment to threatening events: A theory of cognitive adaptation. *American Psychologist, 38,* 1161–1173.

Taylor, S. E., & Brown, J. D. (1988). Illusion and well-being: A social-psychological perspective on mental health. *Psychological Bulletin, 103,* 193–210.

Teasdale, J. D., Moore, R. G., Hayhurst, H., Pope, M., Williams, J. M., & Segal, Z. V. (2002). Metacognitive awareness and prevention of relapse in depression: Empirical evidence. *Journal of Consulting and Clinical Psychology, 70,* 272–287.

Teasdale, J. D., Segal, Z. V., Williams, J. M., Ridgeway, V. A., Soulsby, J. M., & Lau, M. A. (2000). Prevention of relapse/recurrence in major depression by mindfulness-based cognitive therapy. *Journal of Consulting and Clinical Psychology, 68,* 615–623.

Teasley, S. D. (1995). The role of talk in children's peer collaborations. *Developmental Psychology, 31,* 207–220.

Tedeschi, R. G., & Calhoun, L. G. (1996). The posttraumatic growth inventory: Measuring the positive legacy of trauma. *Journal of Traumatic Stress, 9,* 455–471.

Tedeschi, R. G., & Calhoun, L. G. (2004). Posttraumatic growth: Conceptual foundations and empirical evidence. *Psychological Inquiry, 15,* 1–18.

Tessler, M., & Nelson, K. (1994). Making memories: The influence of joint encoding on later recall by young children. *Consciousness and Cognition, 3,* 307–326.

Tesson, G., Lewko, J. H., & Bigelow, B. J. (1987). The social rules that children use in their interpersonal relations. *Contributions of Human Development, 18,* 36–57.

Teti, D. M., & Gelfand, D. M. (1991). Behavioral competence among mothers of infants in the first year: The mediational role of maternal self-efficacy. *Child Development, 62,* 918–929.

Tharp, R. G., & Gallimore, R. (1988). *Rousing minds to life: Teaching, learning, and schooling in social context.* New York: Cambridge University Press.

The Risky Business Interview Selman, R. J. & Adalbjarnottir, S. (2000). A developmental method to analyze the personal meaning adolescents make of risk and relationship: The case of drinking. *Applied Developmental Science, 4,* page 52. (Table 1)

Thelen, E., & Smith, L. B. (1998). Dynamic systems theories. In W. Damon (Series Ed.) & R. M. Lerner (Vol. Ed.), *Handbook of child psychology: Vol. 1. Theoretical models of human development* (5th ed., pp. 563–634). New York: Wiley.

Thomas, A., & Chess, S. (1977). *Temperament and development.* New York: Brunner/Mazel.

Thompson, P. M., Giedd, J. N., Woods, R. P., MacDonald, D., Evans, A. C., & Toga, A. W. (2000). Growth patterns in the developing brain detected by using continuum mechanical tensor maps. *Nature, 404,* 190–193.

Thompson, R. A. (1998). Early sociopersonality development. In W. Damon (Series Ed.) & N. Eisenberg (Vol. Ed.), *Handbook of child psychology: Vol. 3. Social, emotional, and personality development* (5th ed., pp. 25–104). New York: Wiley.

Thompson, R. A., Laible, D. J., & Ontai, L. L. (2003). Early understandings of emotion, morality, and self: Developing a working model. In R. V. Kail (Ed.), *Advances in child development and behavior* (Vol. 31, pp. 137–171). San Diego, CA: Academic Press.

Thompson, R. A., & Leger, D. W. (1999). From squalls to calls: The cry as a developing socio-emotional signal. In B. Lester, J. Newman, & F. Pedersen (Eds.), *Biological and social aspects of infant crying.* New York: Plenum Press.

Thorne, B. (1986). Girls and boys together, but mostly apart: Gender arrangements in elementary schools. In W. W. Jartup and Z. Rubin (Ed.), *Relationships and development.* Hillsdale, NJ: Erlbaum.

Thorne, B. (1994). *Gender play: Girls and boys in school.* New Brunswick, NJ: Rutgers University Press.

Tidwell, M. O., Reis, H. T., & Shaver, P. R. (1996). Attachment, attractiveness, and social interaction: A diary study. *Journal of Personality and Social Psychology, 71,* 729–745.

Tinsley, H. E. A., Hinson, J. A., Tinsley, D. J., & Holt, M. S. (1993). Attributes of leisure and work experiences. *Journal of Counseling Psychology, 40,* 447–455.

Tisak, M. S. (1993). Preschool children's judgments of moral and personal events involving physical harm and property damage. *Merrill-Palmer Quarterly, 39,* 375–390.

Tobler, N. S. (1992). Drug prevention programs can work: Research findings. *Journal of Addictive Diseases, 11,* 1–28.

Toma, C. (1991a, April). *Speech genre of school in U.S. and Japan.* Paper presented at the meeting of the American Education Research Association, Chicago.

Toma, C. (1991b, October). *Explicit use of others' voices for constructing arguments in Japanese classroom discourse: An analysis of the use of reported speech.* Paper presented at the Boston University Conference on Language Development, Boston.

Tomarken, A. J., Davidson, R. J., & Henriques, J. B. (1990). Resting frontal activation asymmetry predicts emotional reactivity to film clips. *Journal of Personality and Social Psychology, 59,* 791–801.

Tomlin, A. M., & Viehweg, S. A. (2003). Infant mental health: Making a difference. *Professional Psychology: Research and Practice, 34,* 617–625.

Tomlinson-Keasey, C., & Keasey, C. B. (1974). The mediating role of cognitive development in moral judgment. *Child Development, 45,* 291–298.

Tooby, J., & Cosmides, L. (1996). Friendship and the banker's paradox: Other pathways to the evolution of adaptations for altruism. In W. G. Runciman, J. M. Smith, & R. I. M. Dunbar (Eds.), Evolution of social behavior patterns in primates and man: A joint discussion meeting of the Royal Society and the British Academy. Proceedings of the British Academy, 88, 119–143.

Tout, de Haan, Campbell, & Gunnar (1998). Social behavior correlates of cortisol activity in child care: Gender differences and time-of-day effects. *Child Development, 69,* 1247–1262.

Townsend, J. W., Klein, R. E., Irwin, M. H., Owens, W., Yarbrough, C., & Engle, P. L. (1982). Nutrition and preschool mental development. In D. A. Wagner & H. W. Stevenson (Eds.), *Cross-cultural perspectives on child development.* San Francisco: Freeman.

Treboux, D. A., & Busch-Rossnagel, N. A. (1991). Sexual behavior, sexual attitudes, and contraceptive use, age differences in adolescence. In R. M. Lerner, A. C. Petersen, & J. Brooks-Gunn (Eds.), *Encyclopedia of adolescence* (Vol. 2). New York: Garland.

Trivits, L. C., & Repucci, N. D. (2002). Application of Megan's law to juveniles. *American Psychologist, 57,* 690–704.

Tronick, E. (1989). Emotions and emotional communication in infants. *American Psychologist, 44,* 112–119.

Tronick, E. Z., Als, H., & Brazelton, T. B. (1980). Monadic phase: A structural descriptive analysis of the infant-mother face to face interaction. *Merrill-Palmer Quarterly, 26,* 3–24.

Troseth, G. L., & DeLoache, J. S. (1996, April). *The medium can obscure the message: Understanding the relation between video and reality.* Poster presented at the biennial meeting of the International Conference on Infant Studies, Providence, RI.

Tucker, D. M. (1986). Neural control of emotional communication. In P. Blanck, R. Buck, & R. Rosenthal (Eds.), *Nonverbal communication in the clinical context.* University Park: Pennsylvania State University Press.

Tuckman, B. W., Abry, D. A., & Smith, D. R. (2002). *Learning and motivational strategies: Your guide to success.* Upper Saddle River, NJ: Prentice Hall.

Turiel, E. (1978). Social regulation and domains of social concepts. In W. Damon (Ed.), *Social cognition: New directions for child development* (pp. 45–74). San Francisco: Jossey-Bass.

Turiel, E. (1998). The development of morality. In W. Damon (Series Ed.) & N. Eisenberg (Vol. Ed.), *Handbook of child psychology: Vol. 3. Social, emotional, and personality development* (5th ed., pp. 863–932). New York: Wiley.

Turkheimer, E., Haley, A., Waldron, M., D'Onofrio, B., & Gottesman, I. I. (2003). Socioeconomic status modifies heritability of IQ in young children. *Psychological Science, 14,* 623–628.

Turner, F. J. (1986). *Social work treatment: Interlocking theoretical approaches* (3rd ed.). New York: Free Press.

Turner, R. J., & Lloyd, D. A. (1995). Lifetime traumas and mental health: The significance of cumulative adversity. *Journal of Health and Social Behavior, 36,* 360–376.

Tversky, A., & Kahneman, D. (1974). Judgment under uncertainty: heuristics and biases. *Science, 185,* 1124–1131.

Tversky, A., & Kahneman, D. (1981). The framing of decisions and the psychology of choice. *Science, 24,* 453–458.

Twenge, J. M. (2000). The age of anxiety? The birth cohort change in anxiety and neuroticism, 1952–1993. *Journal of Personality & Social Psychology, 79,* 1007–1021.

Tyler, L. E. (1961). Research explorations in the realm of choice. *Journal of Counseling Psychology, 8,* 195–201.

Uba, L., & Huang, K. (1999). *Psychology.* New York: Longman.

Uccelli, P., Hemphill, L., Pan, B. A., & Snow, C. E. (1999). Telling two kinds of stories: Sources of narrative skill. In L. Batter & C. S. Tamis-LeMonda (Eds.), *Child psychology: A handbook of contemporary issues* (pp. 215–233). Philadelphia: Psychology Press.

Umana-Taylor, A., & Fine, M. A. (2001). Methodological implications of grouping Latino adolescents into one collective ethnic group. *Hispanic Journal of Behavioral Sciences, 23,* 347–362.

UNAIDS. (2004). *Report on the global AIDS epidemic.* UNAIDS: Joint United Nations Programme on HIV/AIDS. Geneva, Switzerland. Retrieved from http://www.unaids.org/bangkok2004/GAR2004_pdf/GAR2004_Execsumm_en.pdf

United Nation International Children's Emergency Fund. (1995). *The state of the world's children, 1995.* New York: United Nations.

Urry, H. L., Nitschke, J. B., Dolski, I., Jackson, D. C., Dalton, K. M., Mueller, C. J., et al. (2004). Making a life worth living: Neural correlates of well-being. *Psychological Science, 15,* 367–372.

U.S. Bureau of Justice Statistics. (2000). *Violent crime rate trends.* Washington, DC: Author.

U.S. Bureau of Labor Statistics (2003). *Women at work: A visual essay.* Washington, DC: United States Department of Labor.

U.S. Bureau of the Census. (1993). *Statistical abstract of the United States: 1993* (113th ed.). Washington, DC: U.S. Government Printing Office.

U.S. Bureau of the Census. (1997). Current Population Reports, P60–200, *Money income in the United States: 1997* (with separate data on valuation of noncash benefits). Washington, DC: U.S. Government Printing Office.

U.S. Bureau of the Census. (1998). *Statistical abstract of the United States: 1998* (118th ed.). Washington, DC: U.S. Government Printing Office.

U.S. Bureau of the Census. (1999). *Statistical abstract of the United States: 1999*. Washington, DC: U.S. Government Printing Office.

U.S. Department of Education. (1990). *National goals for education*. Washington, DC: U.S. Government Printing Office.

U.S. Department of Health and Human Services. (1998). Health, *United States 1997* (DHHS Publication No. PHS 90–1232). Washington, DC: U.S. Government Printing Office.

U.S. Department of Labor Statistics (2003). Women at work: A visual essay. Washington, DC: U.S. Dept. of Labor (Figures 3 and 4).

U.S. Department of Transportation. (1996). Traffic Safety CD-ROM, 1975–1994 (BTS-CD-10)). Washington, DC: Bureau of Transportation Statistics.

U.S. Dept. of Transportation (1996). Traffic Safety CD-ROM, 1975–1994. (BTS-CD-10). Washington, DC: Bureau of Transportation Statistics. (Figure 4).

Vachon, M. L., Rogers, J., Lyall, W. A., Lancee, W. J., Sheldon, A. R., & Freeman, S. J. J. (1982). Predictors and correlates of adaptation to conjugal bereavement. *American Journal of Psychiatry, 139*, 998–1002.

Vaillant, C. O., & Vaillant, G. E. (1993). Is the U-curve of marital satisfaction an illusion? A 40-year study of marriage. *Journal of Marriage and the Family, 55*, 230–239.

Vaillant, G. E. (1977). *Adaptation to life*. Boston: Little, Brown.

Vaillant, G. E. (1993). *The wisdom of the ego*. Cambridge, MA: Harvard University Press.

Vaillant, G. E., & Koury, S. H. (1994). Late midlife development. In G. H. Pollock & S. I. Greenspan (Eds.), *The course of life*. Madison, CT: International Universities Press.

Valenzuela, M. (1997). Maternal sensitivity in a developing society: The context of urban poverty and infant chronic undernutrition. *Developmental Psychology, 33*, 845–855.

Valiente, D., Eisenberg, N., Fabes, R. A., Shepard, S. A., Cumberland, A., & Losoya, S. H. (2004). Prediction of chidlren's empathy-related responding from their effortful control and parents' expressivity. *Developmental Psychology, 40*, 911–926.

Vallerand, R. J., & O'Conner, B. P. (1989). Motivation in the elderly: A theoretical framework and some promising findings. *Canadian Psychology, 30*, 538–550.

Valsiner, J., & Connolly, K. J. (2003). The nature of development: The continuing dialogue of processes and outcomes. In J. Valsiner & K. J. Connolly (Eds.), *Handbook of developmental psychology* (pp. ix–xvii). London: Sage.

van den Boom, D. C. (1994). The influence of temperament and mothering on attachment and exploration: An experimental manipulation of sensitive responsiveness among lower-class mothers with irritable infants. *Child Development, 65*, 1457–1477.

Vandereycken, W., & Van Deth, R. (1994). *From fasting saints to anorexic girls: The history of self-starvation*. New York: New York University Press.

van der Veer, R. (1996). Vygotsky and Piaget: A collective monologue. *Human Development, 39*, 237–242.

van der Veer, R., & Valsiner, J. (1994). *The Vygotsky reader*. Cambridge, MA: Blackwell.

van der Waal, J. (1989–1990). The aftermath of suicide: A review of empirical evidence. *Omega, 20*, 149–171.

Vandewater, E. A., Ostrove, J. M., & Stewart, A. J. (1997). Predicting women's well-being in midlife: The importance of personality development and social role involvements. *Journal of Personality and Social Psychology, 72*, 1147–1160.

van Doorninck, W. J., Caldwell, B. M., Wright, C., & Frankenberg, W. K. (1981). The relationship between twelve-month home stimulation and school achievement. *Child Development, 52*, 1080–1083.

van Essen, T., van den Heuvell, S., & Ossebaard, M. (2004). A student course on self-management for procrastinators. In H. C. Schouwenburg, C. Lay, T. Pychyl, & J. R. Ferrari (Eds.), *Counseling the procrastinator in academic settings* (pp. 59–73). Washington, DC: American Psychological Association.

van Geert, P. (1998). A dynamic systems model of basic developmental mechanisms: Piaget, Vygotsky and beyond. *Psychological Review, 105*, 634–677.

van Geert, P. (2003). Dynamic systems approaches and modeling of developmental processes. In J. Valsiner & K. J. Connolly (Eds.), *Handbook of developmental psychology* (pp. 640–672). London: Sage.

Van Hesteren, F., & Ivey, A. E. (1990). Counseling and development: Toward a new identity for a profession in transition. *Journal of Counseling and Development, 68*, 524–528.

van IJzendoorn, M. H. (1993). The association between adult attachment representations and infant attachment, parental responsiveness, and clinical status: A meta-analysis on the predictive validity of the Adult Attachment Interview. *Psychological Bulletin, 113*, 404–410.

van IJzendoorn, M. H. (1995). Adult attachment representations, parental responsiveness, and infant attachment: A meta-analysis on the predictive validity of the Adult Attachment Interview. *Psychological Bulletin, 117*, 387–403.

van IJzendoorn, M. H., & Bakermans-Kranenburg, M. J. (1997). Intergenerational transmission of attachment: A move to the contextual level. In L. Atkinson & K. Zucker (Eds.), *Attachment and psychopathology*. New York: Guilford Press.

van IJzendorn, M. H., & Sagi, A. (1999). Cross-cultural patterns of attachment. In J. Cassidy & P. R. Shaver (Eds.), *Handbook of attachment* (pp. 713–734). New York: Guilford Press.

Varela, F. J., Thompson, E., & Rosch, E. (1991). *The embodied mind: Cognitive science and human experience*. Cambridge, MA: MIT Press.

Vasquez, C. & Javier, R. A. (1991). The problem with interpreters: Communicating with Spanish-speaking patients. *Hospital and Community Psychiatry, 42*, 163–165.

Vaughn, B. E., Egeland, B., Sroufe, L. A., & Waters, E. (1979). Individual differences in infant-mother attachment at twelve and eighteen months: Stability and change in families under stress. *Child Development, 50*, 971–975.

Ventura, J. N. (1987). The stresses of parenthood reexamined. *Family Relations, 36*, 26–29.

Vereijken, C., Riksen-Walraven, J., & Kondo-Ikemura, K. (1997). Maternal sensitivity and infant attachment security in Japan: A longitudinal study. *International Journal of Behavioral Development, 21*, 35–49.

Vermeulen, M. E., & Minor, C. W. (1998). Context of career decisions: Women reared in a rural community. *The Career Development Quarterly, 46*, 230–245.

Veroff, J., Kulka, R. A., & Douvan, E. (1981). *Mental health in America: Patterns of help-seeking from 1957 to 1976*. New York: Basic Books.

Vinokur, A. D., Price, R. H., & Schul, Y. (1995). Impact of the JOBS intervention on unemployed workers varying in risk for depression. *American Journal of Community Psychology, 23*, 39–74.

Vinokur, A. D., Schul, Y., Vuori, J., & Price, R. H. (2000). Two years after a job loss: Long-term impact of the JOBS program on reemployment and mental health. *Journal of Occupational Health Psychology, 5*, 32–47.

Vispoel, W. P. (1995). Self-concept in the arts: An extension of the Shavelson, Hubner, and Stanton (1976) model. *Educational and Psychological Measurement, 53*, 1023–1033.

Vivona, J. M. (2000). Parental attachment style of late adolescents: Qualities of attachment relationships and consequences for adjustment. *Journal of Counseling Psychology, 47*, 316–329.

von Bertalanffy, L. (1968). *General systems theory: Foundations, development, applications*. New York: Brazilles.

Vosniadou, S., & Brewer, W. F. (1992). Mental models of the earth: A study of conceptual change in childhood. *Cognitive Psychology, 24*, 535–585.

Vygotsky, L. S. (1934). *Thought and language*. Cambridge, MA: MIT Press.

Vygotsky, L. S. (1978). *Mind and society*. Cambridge, MA: MIT Press.

Vygotsky, L. S. (1981). Development of higher mental functions. In J. V. Wertsch (Ed.), *The concept of activity in sovletic psychology* (pp. 144–188) Armonk, NY: Sharpe. (Originally published in 1931).

Vygotsky, L. S., & Luria, A. R. (1930). The function and fate of egocentric speech. In J. M. Cattell (Ed.), *Ninth international congress of psychology*. Proceedings and papers (pp. 464–465). Princeton, NJ: Psychological Review Company.

Wahlsten, D. (2003). Genetics and the development of brain and behavior. In J. Valsiner & K. J. Connolly (Eds.), *Handbook of developmental psychology* (pp.18–47). London: Sage.

Wahlstein, D., & Gottlieb, G. (1997). The invalid separation of effects of nature and nurture: Lessons from animal experimentation. In R. J. Sternberg & E. L. Grigorenko (Eds.), *Intelligence, heredity, and environment* (pp. 303–322). New York: Cambridge University Press.

Waite, L. J., & Joyner, K. (2001). Emotional satisfaction and physical pleasure in sexual unions: Time horizon, sexual behavior, and sexual exclusivity. *Journal of Marriage and the Family, 63*, 247–264.

Walker, E. F. (2002). Adolescent neurodevelopment and psychopathology. *Current Directions in Psychological Science, 11*, 24–28.

Walker, E., & Bollini, A. M. (2002). Pubertal neurodevelopment and the emergence of psychotic symptoms. *Schizophrenia Research, 54*, 17–23.

Walker, E., & Deforio, D. (1997). Schizophrenia: A neural diathesis-stress model. *Psychological Review, 104*, 667–685.

Walker, E., Sabuwalla, Z., & Huot, R. (2004). Pubertal maturation, stress sensitivity, and psychopathology. *Development & Psychopathology, 16*, 807–824.

Walker, L. J. (1980). Cognitive and perspective-taking prerequisites for moral development. *Child Development, 51*, 131–139.

Walker, L. J. (1984). Sex differences in the development of moral reasoning: A critical review. *Child Development, 55*, 677–691.

Walker, L. J. (1995). Sexism in Kohlberg's moral psychology? In W. M. Kurtines & J. L. Gewirtz (Eds.), *Moral development: An introduction* (pp. 83–107). Boston: Allyn & Bacon.

Walker, L. J., & Hennig, K. H. (2004). Differing conceptions of moral exemplarity: Just, brave, and caring . *Journal of Personality and Social Psychology, 86*(4), 629–647.

Walker, L. J., & Pitts, R. C. (1998). Naturalistic conceptions of moral maturity. *Developmental Psychology, 34*, 403–419.

Walker, L. J., & Taylor, J. H. (1991). Family interactions and the development of moral reasoning. *Child Development, 62*, 264–283.

Walker-Barnes, C. J., & Mason, C. A. (2001). Ethnic differences in the effect of parenting on gang involvement and gang delinquency: A longitudinal, hierarchical linear modeling perspective. *Child Development, 72*, 1814–1831.

Wallace, I., & McCarton, C. (1997). Neurodevelopmental outcomes of the premature, small-for-gestational infant through age 6. *Clinical Obsterics and Gynecology, 40,* 843–852.

Waller, W. (1938). *The family: A dynamic interpretation.* New York: Cordon.

Wallerstein, J. S., Lewis, J. M., & Blakeslee, S. (2000). *The unexpected legacy of divorce: A 25-year landmark study.* New York: Hyperion.

Walsh, W. B. (Ed.). (2003). *Counseling psychology and optimal human functioning.* Mahwah, NJ: Erlbaum.

Ward, B. A., Mergendoller, J. R., Tikunoff, W. J., Rounds, T. S., Dadey, G. J., & Mitman, A. L. (1982). *Junior high school transition study: Executive summary.* San Francisco: Far West Laboratory.

Ward, I. L. (1992). Sexual behavior: The product of perinatal hormonal and prepuberal social factors. In A. A. Gerall, H. Moltz, & I. L. Ward (Eds.), *Handbook of behavioral neurobiology: Vol. 11. Sexual differentiation* (pp. 157–180). New York: Plenum Press.

Ward, I. L., & Stehm, K. E. (1991). Prenatal stress feminizes juvenile play patterns in male rats. *Physiology and Behavior, 50,* 601–605.

Ward, L. M. (2002). Does television exposure affect emerging adults' attitudes and assumptions about sexual relationships? Correlational and experimental confirmation. *Journal of Youth and Adolescence, 31,* 1–15.

Wark, G. R., & Krebs, D. L. (1996). Gender and dilemma differences in real-life moral judgments. *Developmental Psychology, 32,* 220–230.

Warner, C. W., Santelli, J. S., Everett, S. A., Kann, L., Collins, J. L., Cassell, C., et al. (1998). Sexual behavior among U.S. high school students, 1990–1995. *Family Planning Perspectives, 30,* 170–172, 200.

Warr, P. (1999). Well-being and the workplace. In D. Kahneman, E. Diener, & N. Schwarz (Eds.), *Well-being: The foundations of hedonic psychology* (pp. 392–412). New York: Russell Sage Foundation.

Watamura, S. E., Donzella, B., Alwin, J., & Gunnar M. R. (2003). Morening-to-afternoon increases in cortisol concentrations for infants and toddlers at child care: Age differences and behavioral correlates. *Child Development, 74,* 1006–1020.

Waterman, A. (1993). Two conceptions of happiness: Contrasts of personal expressiveness (eudaimonia) and hedonic enjoyment. *Journal of Personality and Social Psychology, 64,* 678–691.

Waterman, A. S. (1993). Developmental perspectives on identity formation. In J. E. Marcia, A. S. Waterman, D. R. Matteson, S. L. Archer, & J. L. Orlofsky (Eds.), *Ego identity: A handbook for psychosocial research* (pp. 42–68). New York: Springer-Verlag.

Waters, E., & Deane, K. E. (1985). Defining and assessing individual differences in attachment relationships: Q-methodology and the organization of behavior in infancy and early childhood. In I. Bretherton & E. Waters (Eds.), Growing points of attachment theory and research. *Monographs of the Society for Research in Child Development, 50,* (Serial No. 209), 41–65.

Waters, E., Merrick, S., Treboux, D., Crowell, J., & Albersheim, L. (2000). Attachment security in infancy and early adulthood: A twenty-year longitudinal study. *Child Development, 71,* 684–689.

Watson, D., & Pennebaker, J. W. (1989). Health complaints, stress, and distress: Exploring the central role of negative affectivity. *Psychological Review, 96,* 234–254.

Watson, D., & Walker, L. M. (1996). The long-term stability and predictive validity of trait measures of affect. *Journal of Personality and Social Psychology, 70,* 567–577.

Watson, D., Wiese, D., Vaidya, J. & Tellegen, A. (1999). The two general activation systems of affect: Structural findings, evolutionary considerations, and psychobiological evidence. *Journal of Personality and Social Psychology, 76,* 820–838.

Watts, C. L., Nakkula, M. J., & Barr, D. (1997). Person-in-pairs, pairs-in-program: Pair therapy in different institutional contexts. In R. J. Selman, C. L. Watts, & L. H. Schultz (Eds.), *Fostering friendship: Pair therapy for treatment and prevention* (pp. 167–184). New York: Aldine de Gruyter.

Weinfield, N. S., Sroufe, L. A., & Egeland, B. (2000). Attachment from infancy to early adulthood in a high-risk sample: Continuity, discontinuity and their correlates. *Child Development, 71,* 695–702.

Weinraub, M., Clemens, L. P., Sockloff, A., Ethridge, R., Gracely, E., & Myers, B. (1984). The development of sex role stereotypes in the third year: Relationships to gender labeling, gender identity, sex-typed toy preferences, and family characteristics. *Child Development, 55,* 1493–1503.

Weiss, R. L., & Hayman, R. E. (1990). Observation of marital distress. In F. D. Findham & T. N. Bradlary (Eds.), *The psychology of marriage* (pp. 87–117). New York: Guilford Press.

Weissbecker, I., Salmon, P., Studts, J. L., Floyd, A. R., Dedert, E. A., & Sephton, S. E. (2002). Mindfulness-based stress reduction and sense of coherence among women with fibromyalgia. *Journal of Clinical Psychology in Medical Settings, 9,* 297–307.

Weissberg, R. P., Caplan, M. Z., & Bennetto, L. (1988). *The Yale-New Haven Middle School Social Problem Solving (SPS) Program.* New Haven, CT: Yale University.

Weissberg, R. P., Kumpfer, K. L., & Seligman, M. E. P. (2003). Prevention that works for children and youth: An introduction. *American Psychologist, 58,* 425–432.

Weissman, M. M., Markowitz, J. C., Klerman, G. L. (2000). *Comprehensive guide to interpersonal psychotherapy.* New York: Basic Books.

Weizman, Z. O., & Snow, C. E. (2001). Lexical input as related to children's vocabulary acquisition: Effects of sophisticated exposure and support for meaning. *Developmental Psychology, 37,* 265–279.

Welch-Ross, M. K., & Schmidt, E. R. (1996). Gender-schema development and children's constructive story memory: Evidence for a developmental model. *Child Development, 67,* 820–835.

Wellman, H. M. (1990). *The child's theory of mind.* Cambridge, MA: MIT Press.

Wellman, H. M., Cross, D., & Watson, J. (2001). Meta-analysis of theory of mind development: The truth about false belief. *Child Development, 72,* 655–684.

Wentzel, K. (2002). Are effective teachers like good parents? Teaching styles and student adjustment in early adolescence. *Child Development, 73,* 287–301.

Wentzel, K. R. (1997). Student motivation in middle school: The role of perceived pedagogical caring. *Journal of Educational Psychology, 89,* 411–419.

Wentzel, K. R., & Asher, S. R. (1995). The academic lives of neglected, rejected, popular, and controversial children. *Child Development, 66,* 754–763.

Werner, H. (1948/1973). *The comparative psychology of mental development.* New York: International Universities Press.

Wertsch, J. V. (1991). *Voices of the mind: A sociocultural approach to mediated action.* Cambridge, MA: Harvard University Press.

Wheedon, A., Scafidi, F., Field, T., Ironson, G., Valdeon, C., & Bandstra, E. (1993). Massage effects on cocaine-exposed preterm neonates. *Journal of Developmental and Behavioral Pediatrics, 14,* 318–322.

Whitaker, D., & Miller, K. (2000). Parent-adolescent discussions about sex and condoms: Impact on peer influences of sexual risk behavior. *Journal of Adolescent Research, 15,* 251–273.

Whitbourne, S. K. (1989). Psychological treatment of the aging individual. *Journal of Integrative and Eclectic Psychotherapy, 8,* 161–173.

Whitbourne, S. K. (1996). *The aging individual: Physical and psychological perspectives.* New York: Springer.

Whitbourne, S. K. (2002). *The aging individual: Physical and psychological perspectives* (2nd ed.). New York: Springer.

White, L., & Rogers, S. J. (2000). *Economic circumstances and family outcomes: A review of the 90s* (Working Paper No. 00-02). University Park: Pennsylvania State University Press.

Whiteley, J. M. (Ed.). (1984). Counseling psychology: A historical perspective. *The Counseling Psychologist, 12,* 1–26.

Whiting, B. B., & Edwards, C. P. (1988). *Children of different worlds: The formation of social behavior.* Cambridge, MA: Harvard University Press.

Whyte, D. (2001). *Crossing the unknown sea: Work as a pilgrimage of identity.* New York: Riverhead Books.

Wichstrom, L. (1999). The emergence of gender differences in depressed mood during adolescence: The role of intensified gender socialization. *Developmental Psychology, 35,* 232–245.

Wickrama, K. A. S., Lorenz, F. O., Wallace, L. E., Peiris, L., Conger, R. D., & Elder, G. H. (2001). Family influence on physical health during the middle years: The case of onset of hypertension. *Journal of Marriage and the Family, 63,* 527–539.

Wiesel, T. N., & Hubel, D. H. (1965). Comparison of the effects of unilateral and bilateral eye closure on cortical response in kittens. *Journal of Neurophysiology, 26,* 1029–1040.

Wilcox, B. L. (2003). Developmental research and the formulation and evaluation of legal policy. *Social Policy Report, 17*(4), 12.

Wilkinson, W. K., & Maxwell, S. (1991). The influence of college students' epistemological style on selected problem-solving processes. *Research in Higher Education, 32,* 333–350.

Willatts, P. (1989). Development of problem-solving in infancy. In A. Slater & G. Bremner (Eds.), *Infant development.* Hove, England: Erlbaum.

William T. Grant Foundation Commission on Work, Family, and Citizenship. (1988). *The forgotten half: Noncollege-bound youth in America.* New York: William T. Grant Foundation.

Williams, C. D. (1933). A nutritional disease of childhood associated with a maize diet. *Archives of Disease in Childhood, 8,* 423–433.

Williams, D. D., Yanchar, S. C., Jenson, L. C., & Lewis, C. (2003). Character education in a public high school: A multi-year inquiry into Unified Studies. *Journal of Moral Education, 32,* 3–33.

Willis, S. L. (1996). Everyday problem solving. In J. E. Birren, K. W. Schaie (Series Eds.), R. P. Abeles, M. Gatz, & T. A. Salthouse (Vol. Eds.), *Handbook of the psychology of aging* (4th ed., pp. 287–307). San Diego, CA: Academic Press.

Wilson, J. G. (1973). *Environment and birth defects.* New York: Academic Press.

Wilson, S. A., Kovach, C. R., & Stearns, S. A. (1996). Hospice concepts in the care for end-stage dementia. *Geriatric Nursing, 17,* 6–10.

Wilson, T. D., & Brekke, N. (1994). Mental contamination and mental correction: Unwanted influences on judgments and evaluations. *Psychological Bulletin, 116,* 117–142.

Wilson, W. J. (1996). *When work disappears: The world of the new urban poor.* New York: Random House.

Wimmer, H., & Perner, J. (1983). Beliefs about beliefs: Representation and constraining function of wrong beliefs in young children's understanding of deception. *Cognition, 13,* 103–128.

Winnicott, D. W. (1965). *The maturational processes and the facilitating environment.* New York: International Universities Press.

Wittling, W., & Pflüger, M. (1990). Neuroendocrine hemisphere asymmetries: Salivary cortisol secretion during lateralized viewing of emotion-related and neutral films. *Brain and Cognition 14,* 243–265.

Witvliet, C. V., Ludwig, T. E., & Vander Laan, K. L. (2001). Granting forgiveness or harboring grudges: Implications for emotion, physiology, and health. *Psychological Science, 12,* 117–123.

Wolfe, J. L., & Fodor, I. G. (1996). The poverty of privilege: Therapy with women of the "upper classes." *Women and Therapy, 18,* 73–89.

Wolinsky, F. D., & Johnson, R. D. (1992). Perceived health status and mortality among older men and women. *Journal of Gerontology: Social Sciences, 47,* S304–S312.

Wood, D., Bruner, J. A., & Ross, G. (1976). The role of tutoring in problem solving. *Journal of Child Psychology and Psychiatry, 17,* 89–100.

Woodward, A. L. (1998). Infants selectively encode the goal object of an actor's reach. *Cognition, 69,* 1–34.

Worden, J. W. (1982). *Grief counseling and grief therapy: A handbook for the mental health practitioner.* New York: Springer.

Wortman, C. B., Battle, E. S., & Lemkau, J. P. (1997). Coming to terms with sudden, traumatic death of a spouse or child. In R. C. Davis & A. J. Lurigio (Eds.), *Victims of crime* (pp. 108–133). Thousand Oaks, CA: Sage.

Wortman, C. B., & Silver, R. C. (1987). Coping with irrevocable loss. In G. R. Vanden Bos & B. K. Bryant (Eds.), *Cataclysms, crises, and catastrophes: Psychology in action* (pp. 189–235). Washington, DC: American Psychological Association.

Wortman, C. B., & Silver, R. C. (1989). The myths of coping with loss. *Journal of Consulting and Clinical Psychology, 57,* 349–357.

Wortman, C. B., & Silver, R. C. (2001). The myths of coping with loss revisited. In M. S. Stroebe, R. O. Hansson, W. Stroebe, & H. Schut (Eds.), *Handbook of bereavement research: Consequences, coping, and care* (pp. 405–429). Washington, DC: American Psychological Association.

Wrenn, C. G. (1962). *The counselor in a changing world.* Washington, DC: American Personnel and Guidance Association.

Wright, B. A. (1983). *Physical disability: A psychosocial approach.* New York: Harper & Row.

Wyden, R. (2000). Steps to improve the quality of life for people who are dying. *Psychology, Public Policy, and Law, 6,* 575–581.

Yager, S., Johnson, R. T., Johnson, D. W., & Snider, B. (1986). The impact of group processing on achievement in cooperative learning groups. *Journal of Social Psychology, 126,* 389–397.

Yalom, I. (1980). *Existential psychotherapy.* New York: Basic Books.

Yang, K. S. (1988). Will societal modernization eventually eliminate cross-cultural psychological

differences? In M. H. Bond (Ed.), *The cross-cultural challenge to social psychology* (pp. 67–85). Newbury Park, CA: Sage.

Yates, M., & Youniss, J. (1996). A developmental perspective on community service in adolescence. *Social Development, 5,* 85–111.

Yatkin, U. S., & McClaren, D. S. (1970). The behavioral development of infants recovering from severe malnutrition. *Journal of Mental Deficiency Research, 14,* 25–32.

Yoon, J., Yoon, C., Lim, H., Huang, Q., Kang, Y., Pryn, K., et al. (1999). Control of autoimmune diabetes in NOD mice by GAD expression or suppression in Beta cells. *Science, 284,* 1183.

Yoshida, T., Kojo, K., & Kaku, H. (1982). A study on the development of self-presentation in children. *Japanese Journal of Educational Psychology, 30,* 120–127.

Yoshinaga, K., & Mori, T. (Eds.). (1989). *Development of preimplantation embryos and their environment.* New York: Wiley-Liss.

Youngblade, L. M., & Belsky, J. (1992). Parent-child antecedents of 5-year-olds' close friendships: A longitudinal analysis. *Developmental Psychology, 28,* 700–713.

Younger, A. J., Gentile, C., & Burgess, K. (1993). Children's perceptions of withdrawal: Changes across age. In K. H. Rubin & J. Asendorpf (Eds.), *Social withdrawal, inhibition, and shyness in childhood* (pp. 215–236). Hillsdale, NJ: Erlbaum.

Youth Risk Behavior Surveillance System, Centers for Disease Control and Prevention, (2004) *Youth Online: Comprehensive Results.* Retrieved from http://apps.nccd.cdc.gov/yrbss/ CategoryQuestions.asp?Cat=4&desc= Sexual%20Behaviors

Yunger, J. L., Carver, P. R., & Perry, D. G. (2004). Does gender identity influence children's psychological well-being? *Developmental Psychology, 40,* 572–582.

Zabin, L. S., Hirsch, M. B., Smith, E. A., Streett, R., & Hardy, J. B. (1986). Evaluation of a pregnancy prevention program for urban teenagers. *Family Planning Perspectives, 18*(3), 119–126.

Zacks, R. T., & Hasher, L. (1994). Directed ignoring: Inhibitory regulation of working memory. In D. Dagenbach & T. H. Carr (Eds.), *Inhibitory mechanisms in attention, memory, and language* (pp. 241–264). San Diego, CA: Academic Press.

Zacks, R. T., Hasher, L., & Li, K. Z. H. (2000). Human memory. In F. I. M. Craik & T. A. Salthouse (Eds.), *The handbook of aging and cognition* (2nd ed., pp. 293–357). Mahwah, NJ: Erlbaum.

Zagar, R., Arbit, J., Sylvies, R., & Busch, K. G. (1991). Homicidal adolescents: A replication. *Psychological Reports, 67,* 1235–1242.

Zahn-Waxler, C., Cole, P. M., Welsh, J. D., & Fox, N. A. (1995). Psychophysiological correlates of empathy and prosocial behaviors in preschool children with problem behaviors. *Development and Psychopathology, 7,* 27–48.

Zahn-Waxler, C., Iannotti, R. J., Cummings, E. M., & Denham, S. (1990). Antecedents of problem behaviors in children of depressed mothers. *Development and Psychopathology, 2,* 349–366.

Zahn-Waxler, C., & Kochanska, G. (1990). The origins of guilt. In R. Thompson (Ed.), *The 36th Annual Nebraska Symposium on Motivation: Socioemotional development* (pp. 183–258). Lincoln: University of Nebraska Press.

Zahn-Waxler, C., & Radke-Yarrow, M. (1982). The development of altruism: Alternative research strategies. In N. Eisenberg (Ed.), *The Development of prosocial behavior* (pp. 109–137). New York: Academic Press.

Zahn-Waxler, C.; Radke-Yarrow, M., Wagner, E., & Chapman, M. (1992). Development of concern for others. *Developmental Psychology, 28,* 126–136.

Zahn-Waxler, C., Robinson, J., & Emde, R. N. (1992). The development of empathy in twins. *Developmental Psychology, 28,* 1038–1047.

Zal, H. M. (1992). *The sandwich generation: Caught between growing children and aging parents.* New York: Insight Books/Plenum Press.

Zarbatany, L., Hartmann, D. P., & Rankin, D. B. (1990). The psychological functions of preadolescent peer activities. *Child Development, 61,* 1067–1080.

Zarit, S. H., & Zarit, J. M. (1998). *Mental disorders in older adults: Fundamentals of assessment and treatment.* New York: Guilford Press.

Zaslow, M. J., & Hayes, C. D. (1986). Sex differences in children's responses to psychosocial stress: Toward a cross-context analysis. In M. E. Lamb, A. L. Brown, & B. Rogoff (Eds.), *Advances in developmental psychology* (Vol. 4). Hillside, NJ: Erlbaum.

Zea, M. C., Reisen, C. A., Beil, C., & Caplan, R. D. (1997). Predicting intention to remain in college among ethnic minority and nonminority students. *Journal of Social Psychology, 137,* 149–160.

Zeanah, C. H., & Zeanah, P. D. (2001). Towards a definition of infant mental health. *Zero to three, 22,* 13–20.

Zelazo, P. D., Helwig, C. C., & Lau, A. (1996). Intention, act, and outcome in behavioral prediction and moral judgment. *Child Development, 67,* 2478–2492.

Zelinski, E. M., Gilewski, M., & Schaie, K. W. (1993). Individual differences in cross-sectional and 3-year longitudinal memory performance across the adult life span. *Psychology and Aging, 8,* 176–186.

Zinnbauer, B. J., Pargament, K. I. (2000). Working with the sacred: Four approaches to religious and spiritual issues in counseling. *Journal of Counseling and Development, 78,* 162–171.

Zinnbauer, B. J., Pargament, K. I., & Scott, A. B. (1999). The emerging meanings of religiousness and spirituality: Problems and prospects. *Journal of Personality, 67,* 889–920.

Zucker, K. J. (1999). Intersexuality and gender identity differentiation. *Annual Review of Sex Research, 10,* 1–69.

Zuckerman, M. (1979). *Sensation seeking: Beyond the optimal level of arousal.* Hillsdale, NJ: Erlbaum.

Zuckerman, M. (1994). *Behavioral expressions and bisocial bases of sensation seeking.* Cambridge, England: Cambridge University Press.